A SELECT LIBRARY

OF THE

NICENE AND POST-NICENE FATHERS

OF

THE CHRISTIAN CHURCH

EDITED BY

PHILIP SCHAFF, D.D., LL.D.,

PROFESSOR IN THE UNION THEOLOGICAL SEMINARY, NEW YORK,

IN CONNECTION WITH A NUMBER OF PATRISTIC SCHOLARS OF EUROPE AND AMERICA.

VOLUME IV

ST. AUGUSTIN:

THE WRITINGS AGAINST THE MANICHÆANS

AND

AGAINST THE DONATISTS

WM. B. EERDMANS PUBLISHING COMPANY

GRAND RAPIDS **1956** **MICHIGAN**

PHOTOLITHOPRINTED BY CUSHING - MALLOY, INC.
ANN ARBOR, MICHIGAN, UNITED STATES OF AMERICA
1956

EDITOR'S PREFACE.

This fourth volume of St. Augustin's Works contains his polemical writings in vindication of the Catholic Church against the heresy of the Manichæans, and the schism of the Donatists. The former are contained in Tom. II. and VIII., the latter in Tom. IX., of the Benedictine edition.

Like the preceding volumes, this also is more than a reprint of older translations, and contains important additions not previously published.

I.—SEVEN WRITINGS AGAINST THE MANICHÆAN HERESY. Four of these were translated by the Rev. RICHARD STOTHERT, of Bombay, for Dr. Dods' edition, published by T. & T. Clark, Edinburgh, 1872, and revised by Dr. ALBERT H. NEWMAN, of Toronto, for the American edition. The other three treatises are translated, I believe for the first time, by Dr. Newman for this edition. (See Contents.)

The Edinburgh translation, especially of the first two treatises, is sufficiently faithful and idiomatic, and needed very little alteration by the American editor, who compared it sentence by sentence with the Latin original, and made changes only where they seemed necessary.

This part of the volume is also enriched by an introductory essay of Dr. NEWMAN, which embodies the literature and the results of the most recent as well as the earlier researches concerning that anti-Christian heresy.

II.—THE WRITINGS AGAINST THE DONATISTS. These were well translated by the Rev. J. R. King, of Oxford, and are slightly revised by Dr. HARTRANFT, of Hartford, after a careful comparison with the Latin.

The literary introduction of Dr. Hartranft, in connection with the translator's historical preface, will place the reader in the situation of the controversy between the Catholic Church and the Donatists at the time of St. Augustin.

In both sections the treatises are arranged in chronological order.

The fifth volume will contain the writings of St. Augustin against the Pelagians and Semi-Pelagians. It is in the hands of the printer and will be published in October.

PHILIP SCHAFF.

NEW YORK, June, 1887.

CONTENTS.

WRITINGS

IN CONNECTION WITH THE

MANICHÆAN CONTROVERSY.

TRANSLATED BY THE

REV. RICHARD STOTHERT, M.A.,

BOMBAY;

AND

ALBERT H. NEWMAN, D.D., L.L.D.

PROFESSOR OF CHURCH HISTORY AND COMPARATIVE RELIGION, IN TORONTO
BAPTIST (THEOLOGICAL) COLLEGE, TORONTO, CANADA.

INTRODUCTORY ESSAY ON

THE MANICHÆAN HERESY,

By Albert H. Newman, D.D., LL.D.

CHAPTER I.—LITERATURE.

I. Sources.

The following bibliography of Manichæism is taken from Schaff's *History of the Christian Church*, vol. II. pp. 498–500 (new edition). Additions are indicated by brackets.

1. Oriental Sources: The most important, though of comparatively late date.

(a) Mohammedan (Arabic): *Kitâb al Fihrist.* A history of Arabic literature to 987, by an Arab of Bagdad, usually called Ibn Abi Jakub an-Nadîm; brought to light by Flügel, and published after his death by Rödiger and Müller, in 2 vols. Leipz. 1871–'72. Book IX. section first, treats of Manichæism. Flügel's translation, see below. Kessler calls the Fihrist a "*Fündstätte allerersten Ranges.*" Next to it comes the relation of the Mohammedan philosopher, Al-Shahrastani (d. 1153), in his *History of Religious Parties and Philosophical Sects*, Ed. Cureton, Lond. 1842, 2 vols. (I. 188–192); German translation by Haarbrücker, Halle, 1851. On other Mohammedan sources, see Kessler in Herzog,[2] IX., 225 sq.

(b) Persian Sources: relating to the life of Mani, the Shâhnâmeh (the King's Book) of Firdausi; ed. by Jul. Mohl, Paris, 1866 (V. 472–475). See Kessler, *ibid.* 225.

[Albiruni's *Chronology of Ancient Nations*, tr. by E. Sachau, and published by the Oriental Translation Fund, Lond. 1879. Albîrunî lived 973–1048, and is said to have possessed vast literary resources no longer available to us. His work seems to be based on early Manichæan sources, and strikingly confirms the narrative preserved by the *Fihrist.* See also articles by West and Thomas in *Journal of the Asiatic Society*, 1868, 1870, 1871.]

(c) Christian Sources: In Arabic, the Alexandrian Patriarch Eutychius (d. 916). *Annales*, ed. Pococke, Oxon. 1628; Barhebræus (d. 1286), in his *Historia Dynastiarum*, ed. Pococke. In Syriac: Ephraem Syrus (d. 393), in various writings. Esnig or Esnik, an Armenian bishop of the 5th Century, who wrote against Marcion and Mani (German translation from the Armenian by C. Fr. Neumann, in Illgen's *Zeitschrift für die Hist. Theologie*, 1834, pp. 77–78).

2. Greek Sources: [Alexander of Lycopolis: *The Tenets of the Manichæans* (first published by Combefis, with a Latin version, in the *Auctararium Novissimum*, *Bibl. S. S. Patrum;* again by Gallandi, in his *Bibl. Patrum*, vol. IV. p. 73 sq. An English translation by Rev. James B. H. Hawkins, M.A., appeared in Clark's *Ante-Nicene Library*, Vol. XIV. p. 236 sq.; Am. ed. vol. VI. p. 237 sq. Alexander represents himself as a convert from Paganism to Manichæism, and from Manichæism to Orthodoxy. He claims to have learned Man-

ichæism from those who were intimately associated with Mani himself, and is, therefore, one of the earliest witnesses.[1]] EUSEBIUS (*H. E.* VII. 31, a brief account). EPIPHANIUS (*Haer.* 66). CYRIL OF JERUSALEM (*Catech.* VI. 20 sq.). TITUS OF BOSTRA (*πρὸσ Μανιχαίουσ*, ed P. de Lagarde, 1859). PHOTIUS: *Adv. Manichæos* (Cod. 179, *Biblioth.*). JOHN OF DAMASCUS: *De Haeres.* and *Dial.* [PETRUS SICULUS, *Hist. Manichæorum.*]

3. Latin Sources: ARCHELAUS (Bishop of Cascar in Mesopotamia, d. about 278): *Acta Disputationis cum Manete Hæresiarcha ;* first written in Syriac, and so far belonging to the Oriental Christian Sources (Comp. Jerome, *de Vir. Ill.* 72), but extant only in a Latin translation, which seems to have been made from the Greek, edited by ZACAGNI (Rome, 1698), and ROUTH (in *Reliquiæ Sacræ*, vol. V. 3–206); Eng. transl. in Clark's *Ante-Nicene Library* (vol. XX. 272–419). [Am. ed. vol. VI. p. 173 sq.]. These Acts purport to contain the report of a disputation between Archelaus and Mani before a large assembly, which was in full sympathy with the orthodox bishop, but (as Beausobre first proved), they are in form a fiction from the first quarter of the fourth century (about 320), by a Syrian ecclesiastic (probably of Edessa), yet based upon Manichæan documents, and containing much information about Manichæan doctrines. They consist of various pieces, and were the chief source of information to the West. Mani is represented (ch. 12), as appearing in a many-colored cloak and trousers, with a sturdy staff of ebony, a Babylonian book under his left arm, and with a mien of an old Persian master. In his defense he quotes freely from the N. T. At the end, he makes his escape to Persia (ch. 55). Comp. H. v. ZITTWITZ: *Die Acta Archelai et Manetis untersucht,* in Kahnis' *Zeitschrift für d. Hist. Theol.* 1873, No. IV. OBLASINSKI: *Acta Disput. Arch.*, etc. Lips. 1874 (inaugural dissert.). AD. HARNACK: *Die Acta Archelai und das Diatessaron Tatians*, in *Texte und Untersuchungen zur Gesch. der altchristl. Lit.* vol. I. Heft 3 (1883), p. 137–153. Harnack tries to prove that the Gospel variations of Archelaus are taken from Tatian's Diatessaron.

ST. AUGUSTIN (d. 430, the chief Latin authority next to the translation of Archelaus). [Besides the treatises published in Clark's series, *Contra Fortunatum quendam Manichæorum Presbyterum Disput. I. et II.*, *Contra Adimantum Manichæi discipulum*, *Contra Secundinum Manichæum*, *De Natura Boni*, *De duabus Animabus*, *De Utilitate Credendi*, *De Haeres.* XLVI. Of these, *De duabus Animabus*, *Contra Fortunatum*, and *De Natura Boni* are added in the present edition, and *De Utilitate Credendi* has been included among Augustin's shorter theological treatises in vol. III. of the present series. In the *Confessions* and the *Letters*, moreover, the Manichæans figure prominently. The treatises included in the present series may be said to fairly represent Augustin's manner of dealing with Manichæism. The Anti-Manichæan writings are found chiefly in vol. VIII. of the Benedictine edition, and in volumes I. and XI. of the Migne reprint. Augustin's personal connection with the sect extending over a period of nine years, and his consummate ability in dealing with this form of error, together with the fact that he quotes largely from Manichæan literature, render his works the highest authority for Manichæism as it existed in the West at the close of the fifth century.] Comp. also the Acts of Councils against the Manichæans from the fourth century onwards, in Mansi and Hefele [and Hardouin].

II. MODERN WORKS.

ISAAC DE BEAUSOBRE (b. 1659 in France, pastor of the French church in Berlin, d. 1738): *Histoire Crit. de Manichée et du Manichéisme*, Amst. 1634 and '39, 2 vols. 4to. Part of the first volume is historical, the second doctrinal. Very full and scholarly. He intended to write a third volume on the later Manichæans. F. CHR. BAUR: *Das Manichäische Religionssystem nach den Quellen neu untersucht und entwickelt*, Tüb. 1831 (500 pages). A compre-

[1] Baur discredits this claim on internal grounds (*Das Manich. Religionssystem*, p. 7).

hensive, philosophical and critical view. He calls the Manich. system a "*glühend prächtiges Natur-und Weltgedicht.*" [An able critique of Baur's work by Schneckenburger appeared in the "*Theol. Studien u. Kritiken,*" 1833, p. 875 sq. Schneckenburger strives to make it appear that Baur unduly minifies the Christian element in Manichæism. Later researches have tended to confirm Baur's main position. The Oriental sources employed by Flügel and Kessler have thrown much light upon the character of primitive Manichæism, and have enabled us to determine more precisely than Beausobre and Baur were able to do the constituent elements of Mani's system. A. v. WEGNERN: *Manichæorum Indulgentiæ*, Lips. 1827. Wegnern points out the resemblance between the Manichæan system, in accordance with which the "hearers" participate in the merits of the "elect" without subjecting themselves to the rigorous asceticism practiced by the latter, and the later doctrine and practice of indulgences in the Roman Catholic church] TRECHSEL: *Ueber Kanon, Kritik und Exegese der Manichäer*, Bern, 1832. D. CHWOLSON: *Die Ssabier und der Ssabismus*, Petersb. 1856, 2 vols. G. FLUGEL: *Mani, seine Lehre und seine Scriften. Aus dem Fihrist des Abî Jakub an-Nadîm* (987), Leipz. 1862. Text, translation and commentary, 440 pages. [Of the highest value, the principal document on which the work is based being, probably, the most authentic exposition of primitive Manichæan doctrine.] K. KESSLER: *Untersuchungen zur Genesis des Manich. Rel. Systems*, Leipz. 1876. By the same: *Mânî oder Beiträge zur Kenntniss der Religionsmischung im Semitismus*, Leipz. 1887. See also his thorough article, *Mânî und die Manichær*, in "Herzog," new ed. vol. IX. 223–259 (abridged in Schaff's "Encyclop." II. 1396–1398). [Kessler has done more than any other writer to establish the relation between the Manichæans and the earlier Oriental sects, and between these and the old Babylonian religion. The author of this introduction wishes to express his deep obligation to Kessler. The article on the "*Mandäer*" in "Herzog," by the same author, is valuable in this connection, though his attempt to exclude all historical connection between this Babylonian Gnostic sect and Palestine can hardly be pronounced a success. J. B. MOZLEY: *Ruling Ideas in Early Ages;* lecture on "The Manichæans and the Jewish Fathers," with special reference to Augustin's method of dealing with the cavils of the Manichæans.] G. T. STOKES: *Manes* and *Manichæans*, in "Smith and Wace," III. 792–801. A. HARNACK: *Manichæism*, in 9th ed. of the "Encycl. Britannica," vol. XV. (1883), 481–487. [Also in German, as a *Beigabe* to his *Lehrbuch d. Dogmengeschichte*, vol. I. p. 681 sq. Harnack follows Kessler in all essential particulars. Of Kessler's article in "Herzog" he says: "This article contains the best that we possess on Manichæism." In this we concur. W. CUNNINGHAM: *S. Austin and his Place in the History of Christian Thought*, Hulsean Lectures, 1885, p. 45–72, and *passim*, Lond. 1886. This treatise is of considerable value, especially as it regards the philosophical attitude of Augustin towards Manichæism.] The accounts of Mosheim, Lardner, Schröckh, Walch, Neander, Gieseler [and Wolf].

CHAPTER II.—PHILOSOPHICAL BASIS, AND ANTECEDENTS OF MANICHÆISM.

"About 500 years before the commencement of the Christian era," writes Professor Monier Williams,[1] "a great stir seems to have taken place in Indo-Aryan, as in Grecian minds, and indeed in thinking minds everywhere throughout the then civilized world. Thus when Buddha arose in India, Greece had her thinkers in Pythagoras, Persia in Zoroaster, and China in Confucius. Men began to ask themselves earnestly such questions as—What am I? Whence have I come? Whither am I going? How can I explain my consciousness of personal existence? What is the relationship between my material and immaterial nature? What is the world in which I find myself? did a wise, good and all-powerful Being create it out of nothing? or did it evolve out of an eternal germ? or did it come together by

[1] *Indian Wisdom*, 3rd ed. (1876), p. 49.

the combination of eternal atoms? If created by a Being of infinite wisdom, how can I account for the inequality of condition in it—good and evil, happiness and misery. Has the Creator form or is he formless? Has he any qualities or none?"

It is true that such questions pressed themselves with special importunity upon the thinkers of the age mentioned, but we should be far astray if we should think for a moment that now for the first time they suggested themselves and demanded solution. The fact is that the earliest literary records of the human race bear evidence of high thinking on the fundamental problems of God, man, and the world, and the relations of these to each other. Recent scholars have brought to light facts of the utmost interest with reference to the pre-Babylonian (Accadian) religion. A rude nature-worship, with a pantheistic basis, but assuming a polytheistic form, seems to have prevailed in Mesopotamia from a very early period. "Spirit everywhere dispersed produced all the phenomena of nature, and directed and animated all created beings. They caused evil and good, guided the movements of the celestial bodies, brought back the seasons in their order, made the wind to blow and the rain to fall, and produced by their influence atmospheric phenomena both beneficial and destructive; they also rendered the earth fertile, and caused plants to germinate and to bear fruit, presided over the births and preserved the lives of living beings, and yet at the same time sent death and disease. There were spirits of this kind everywhere, in the starry heavens, in the earth, and in the intermediate region of the atmosphere; each element was full of them, earth, air, fire and water; and nothing could exist without them . . . As evil is everywhere present in nature side by side with good, plagues with favorable influences, death with life, destruction with fruitfulness; an idea of dualism as decided as in the religion of Zoroaster pervaded the conceptions of the supernatural world formed by the Accadian magicians, the evil beings of which they feared more than they valued the powers of good. There were essentially good spirits, and others equally bad. These opposing troops constituted a vast dualism, which embraced the whole universe and kept up a perpetual struggle in all parts of the creation."[1] This primitive Turanian quasi-dualism (it was not dualism in the strictest sense of the term) was not entirely obliterated by the Cushite and Semitic civilizations and cults that successively overlaid it. So firmly rooted had this early mode of viewing the world become that it materially influenced the religions of the invaders rather than suffered extermination. In the Babylonian religion of the Semitic period the dualistic element was manifest chiefly in the magical rites of the Chaldean priests who long continued to use Accadian as their sacred language. "Upon this dualistic conception rested the whole edifice of sacred magic, of magic regarded as a holy and legitimate intercourse established by rites of divine origin, between man and the supernatural beings surrounding him on all sides. Placed unhappily in the midst of this perpetual struggle between the good and bad spirits, man felt himself attacked by them at every moment; his fate depended upon them. . . . He needed then some aid against the attacks of the bad spirits, against the plagues and diseases which they sent upon him. This help he hoped to find in incantations, in mysterious and powerful words, the secret of which was known only to the priests of magic, in their prescribed rites and their talismans. . . . The Chaldeans had such a great idea of the power and efficacy of their formulæ, rites and amulets, that they came to regard them as required to fortify the good spirits themselves in their combat with the demons, and as able to give them help by providing them with invincible weapons which should ensure success."[2] A large number of magical texts have been preserved and deciphered, and among them "the 'favorable *Alad*,' the 'favorable *Lamma*,' and the 'favorable *Utuq*,' are very frequently opposed . . to the 'evil *Alad*,' the 'evil *Lamma*,' the 'evil *Utuq*.'"[3] It would be interesting to give in detail the results of the researches of George Smith, Lenor-

[1] Lenormant, *Chaldean Magic* (1877), p. 144-145. [2] *Ibid.* p. 146-147. [3] *Ibid.* p. 148.

mant, A. H. Sayce, E. Schrader, Friedrich Delitzsch and others, with reference to the elaborate mythological and cosmological systems of the Babylonians. Some of the features thereof will be brought out further on by way of comparison with the Manichæan mythology and cosmology. Suffice it to say that the dualistic element is everywhere manifest, though not in so consistent and definite a form as in Zoroastrianism, to say nothing of Manichæism.

The Medo-Persian invasion brought into Babylonia the Zoroastrian system, already modified, no doubt, by the Elamitic (Cushite) cult. Yet the old Babylonian religion was too firmly rooted to be supplanted, even by the religion of such conquerors as Darius and Cyrus. Modifications, however, it undoubtedly underwent. The dualism inherent in the system became more definite. The influence of the Jews in Mesopotamia upon the ancient population cannot have been inconsiderable, especially as many of the former, including probably most of the captives of the Northern tribes, were absorbed by the latter. As a result of this blending of old Babylonian, Persian, and Hebrew blood, traditions, and religious ideas, there was developed in Mesopotomia a type of religious thought that furnished a philosophical basis and a mythological and cosmological garnishing for the Manichæan system. Dualism, therefore, arising from efforts of the unaided human mind to account for the natural phenomena that appear beneficent and malignant, partly of old Babylonian origin and partly of Persian, but essentially modified by Hebrew influence more or less pure, furnished to Mani the foundation of his system. We shall attempt at a later stage of the discussion to determine more accurately the relations of Manichæism to the various systems with which correctly or incorrectly it has been associated. Suffice it to say, at present, that no new problem presented itself to Mani, and that he furnished no essentially new solution of the problems that had occupied the attention of his countrymen for more than 2500 years. Before proceeding to institute a comparison between Manichæism and the various systems of religious thought to which it stands related, it will be advantageous to have before us an exposition of the Manichæan system itself, based upon the most authentic sources.

CHAPTER III.—THE MANICHÆAN SYSTEM.

Earlier writers on Manichæism have, for the most part, made the *Acta Disp. Archelai et Manetis* and the anti-Manichæan writings of Augustin the basis of their representations. For later Manichæism in the West, Augustin is beyond question the highest authority, and the various polemical treatises which he put forth exhibit the system under almost every imaginable aspect. The "Acts of the Disputation of Archelaus and Manes," while it certainly rests upon a somewhat extensive and accurative knowledge of early Manichæism, is partially discredited by its generally admitted spuriousness—spuriousness in the sense that it is not a genuine record of a real debate. It is highly probable that debates of this kind occurred between Mani and various Christian leaders in the East, and so Mani may at one time or other have given utterance to most of the statements that are attributed to him in this writing; or these statements may have been derived, for substance, from his numerous treatises, and have been artfully adapted to the purposes of the writer of the "Acts." It is certain that most of the representations are correct. But we can no longer rely upon it as an authentic first-hand authority. Since Flügel published the treatise from the *Fihrist* entitled "The Doctrines of the Manichæans, by Muhammad ben Ishâk," with a German translation and learned annotations, it has been admitted that this treatise must be made the basis for all future representations of Manichæism. Kessler, while he has had access to many other Oriental documents bearing upon the subject, agrees with Flügel in giving the first place to this writing. On this exposition of the doctrines of the Manichæans, therefore, as expounded by Flügel and Kessler, we must chiefly rely. The highly poetical mythological form which Mani gave to his speculations renders it exceedingly difficult to arrive at assured results with reference to fundamental principles. If we attempt to state in a plain matter-of-fact way just what Mani taught we are in constant danger of misrepresenting him. In fact one of the favorite methods employed against Mani's doctrines by the writer of the "Acts of the Disputation," etc., as well as by Augustin and others, was to reduce Mani's poetical fancies to plain language and thus to show their absurdity. The considerations which have led experts like Flügel and Kessler to put so high an estimate upon this document, and the discussions as to the original language in which the sources of the document were written, are beyond the scope of this essay. Suffice it to say, that so far as we are able to form a judgment on the matter, the reasons for ascribing antiquity and authenticity to the representation of Manichæism contained in the document are decisive.

1. *Mani's Life.* According to the *Fihrist,* Mani's father, a Persian by race, resided at Coche on the Tigris, about forty miles north of Babylon. Afterwards he removed into Babylonia and settled at Modein, where he frequented an idol-temple like the rest of the people. He next became associated with a party named Mugtasila (Baptizers), probably identical with or closely related to the Mandæans and Sabeans, both of which parties made much of ceremonial bathings. Mani, who was born after the removal to Babylonia, is related to have been the recipient of angelic visitations at the age of twelve. Even at this time he was forewarned that he must leave the religion of his father at the age of twenty-four. At the appointed time the angel At-Taum appeared again and announced to him his mission. "Hail, Mani, from me and the Lord, who has sent me to thee and chosen thee for his mission. But he commands thee to invite men to thy doctrine and to proclaim the glad tidings of truth that comes from him, and to bestow thereon all thy zeal." Mani entered upon his work, according to Flügel's careful computation, April 1, 238, or, according to calculations based on another statement, in 252. Mani maintained that he was the Paraclete promised by Jesus. He is said, in this document, to have derived his teaching from the Magi and the Christians, and the characters in which he wrote his books, from the Syriac and the Persian. After travelling in many lands for forty years and disseminating his doctrines in India, China, and Turkestan, he succeeded in impressing his views upon Fîrûz, brother of King Sapor, who had intended to put him to death. Sapor became warmly attached to Mani and granted toleration to his followers. Afterwards, according to some accounts, Mani was imprisoned by Sapor and liberated by his successor Hormizd. He is said to have been crucified by order of King Bahraîm I. (276–'7), and his skin stuffed with straw is said to have been suspended at the city gate. Eusebius (H. E. VII. 31) describes Mani as "a barbarian in life, both in speech and conduct, who attempted to form himself into a Christ, and then also proclaimed himself to be the very Paraclete and the Holy Spirit. Then, as if he had been Christ, he selected twelve disciples, the partners of his new religion, and after patching together false and ungodly doctrines collected from a thousand heresies long since extinct, he swept them off like a deadly poison from Persia, upon this part of the world." The account given in the *Acta Archel.* (written probably about 330–'40), is far more detailed than that of the *Fihrist* and differs widely therefrom. It contains much that is highly improbable. Mani is represented as having for his predecessors one Scythianus, an Egyptian heretic of Apostolic times, and Terebinthus, who went with him to Palestine and after the death of Scythianus removed to Babylonia. The writings of Terebinthus or Scythianus came into the possession of a certain widow, who purchased Mani when seven years of age (then named Cubricus) and made him heir of her property and books. He changed his name to Mani (Manes), and, having become imbued with the teachings of the books, began at about sixty years of age to promulgate their teachings, choosing three disciples, Thomas, Addas and Hermas, to whom he entrusted the writings mentioned above, along with some of his own. Up to this time he knew little of Christianity, but having been imprisoned by the king

for failure in a promised cure of the king's son, he studied the Christian Scriptures and derived therefrom the idea of the Paraclete, which he henceforth applied to himself. After his escape the famous dialogue with Archelaus and that with Diodorus occurred. Returning to Arabion he was arrested, carried to Persia, flayed alive, and his skin stuffed and suspended as above. Some additional facts from an Oriental source used by Beausobre have more or less verisimilitude. According to this, Mani was born of Magian parents about 240 A.D. He became skilled in music, mathematics, geography, astronomy, painting, medicine, and in the Scriptures. The account of his ascendancy over Sapor and his subsequent martyrdom is substantially the same as that of the *Fihrist*. Albîrunî's work (see bibliography preceding) confirms the account given by the *Fihrist*. The conversion of Sapor to Manichæism (in A.D. 261) is said to be confirmed by Sassanian inscriptions (see *Journal of Asiat. Soc.* 1868, p. 310–'41, and ibid. p. 376, and 1871 p. 416).

The *Fihrist's* account contains a long list of the works of Mani, which is supplemented by other Oriental and Western notices. The list is interesting as showing the wide range of Mani's literary activity, or at least of the literature that was afterwards connected with his name.

2. *Mani's System*. As the life of Mani has been the subject of diversified and contradictory representations, so also have his doctrines. Here, too, we must make the account given by the *Fihrist* fundamental. It will be convenient to treat the subject under the following heads: Theology, Cosmogony, Anthropology, Soteriology, Cultus, Eschatology, and Ethics.

(1.) *Theology*. Mani taught *dualism* in the most unqualified sense. Zoroastrianism is commonly characterized as dualistic, yet it is so in no such sense as is Manichæism. According to the *Fihrist*, "Mani teaches: Two subsistences form the beginning of the world, the one light the other darkness; the two are separated from each other. The light is the first most glorious being, limited by no number, God himself, the King of the Paradise of Light. He has five members: meekness, knowledge, understanding, mystery, insight; and five other spiritual members: love, faith, truth, nobleness, and wisdom. He maintained furthermore that the God of light, with these his attributes, is without beginning, but with him two equally eternal things likewise exist, the one the atmosphere, the other the earth. Mani adds: and the members of the atmosphere are five [the first series of divine attributes mentioned above are enumerated]; and the members of the earth are five [the second series]. The other being is the darkness, and his members are five: cloud, burning, hot wind, poison, and darkness. Mani teaches: that the light subsistence borders immediately on the dark subsistence, without a dividing wall between them; the light touches with its (lowest) side the darkness, while upwards to the right and left it is unbounded. Even so the darkness is endless downwards and to the right and left."

This represents Mani's view of the eternally existent *status quo*, before the conflict began, and the endless state after the conflict ceases. What does Mani mean, when he enumerates two series of five attributes each as members of God, and straightway postulates the coeternity of atmosphere and earth and divides these self-same attributes between the latter? Doubtless Mani's theology was fundamentally pantheistic, *i.e.*, pantheistic within the limits of each member of the dualism. The God of Light himself is apparently conceived of as transcending thought. Atmosphere and Earth (not the atmosphere and earth that we know, but ideal atmosphere and earth) are the æons derived immediately from the Ineffable One and coëternal with him. The ten attributes are æons which all belong primarily to the Supreme Being and secondarily to the two great æons, half to each. The question may arise, and has been often discussed, whether Mani meant to identify God (the Prince of Light) with the Kingdom of Light? His language, in this treatise, is wavering. He seems to struggle against such a representation, yet without complete success.

What do the other sources teach with reference to the absoluteness of the dualism and with reference to the identification of the Prince of Light with the Kingdom of Light? According to the *Acts of the Disputation of Archelaus and Manes*,[1] Manes "worships two deities, unoriginated, self-existent, eternal, opposed the one to the other. Of them he represents the one as good, and the other as evil, and assigned the name of *Light* to the former, and that of *Darkness* to the latter." Again, Manes is represented as saying: "I hold that there are two natures, one good and another evil; and that the one which is good dwells in a certain part proper to it, but that the evil one is this world as well as all things in it, which are placed there like objects imprisoned in the portion of the wicked one" (1 John 5, 19). According to Alexander of Lycopolis,[2] Mani laid down two principles, God and matter (*Hyle*). God he called good, and matter he affirmed to be evil. But God excelled more in good than matter in evil." Alexander goes on to show how Mani used the word *Hyle*, comparing the Manichæan with the Platonic teaching. Statements of substantially the same purport might be multiplied. As regards the identification of God (the King of Light) with the Kingdom of Light, and of Satan (the King of Darkness) with the Kingdom of Darkness, the sensuous poetical way in which Mani expressed his doctrines may leave us in doubt. The probability is, however, that he did pantheistically identify each element of the dualism with his Kingdom. He personifies the Kingdom of Light and the Kingdom of Darkness, and peoples these Kingdoms with fanciful beings, which are to be regarded as personified attributes of the principles of darkness and light.

A word on the Manichæan conception of matter or *Hyle* may not be out of place in this connection. It would seem that the Manichæans practically identified *Hyle* or matter with the Kingdom of Darkness. At any rate *Hyle* is unoriginated and belongs wholly to this Kingdom.

(2.) *Cosmogony.* So much for the Manichæan idea of the Kingdom of Light and the Kingdom of Darkness before the great conflict that resulted in the present order of things. Why did not they remain separate? Let us learn from the *Fihrist's* narrative: "Mani teaches further: Out of this dark earth [the Kingdom of Darkness] arose Satan, not that he was in himself eternal from the beginning, yet were his substances in his elements unoriginated. These substances now united themselves out of his elements and went forth as Satan, his head as the head of a lion, his body as the body of a dragon, his wings as the wings of a bird, his tail as the tail of a great fish, and his four feet as the feet of creeping animals. When this Satan under the name Iblis, the (temporally considered) eternal (primeval), had arisen out of the darkness, he devoured and consumed everything, spread destruction right and left, and plunged into the deep, in all these movements bringing down from above desolation and annihilation. Then he strove for the height, and descried the beams of light; but they were opposed to him. When he saw later how exalted these were, he was terrified, shrivelled up, and merged himself in his elements. Hereupon he strove anew with such violence after the height, that the land of light descried the doings of Satan and how he was bent upon murder and destruction. After they had been apprised thereof, the world of Insight learned of it, then the world of Knowledge, then the world of Mystery, then the world of Understanding, then the world of Meekness. When at last, he further teaches, the King of the Paradise of Light had also learned of it, he thought how he might suppress Satan, and, Mani adds, those hosts of his would have been mighty enough to overpower Satan. Yet he desired to do this by means of his own might. Accordingly, he produced by means of the spirit of his right hand [*i.e.*, the Gentle Breeze], his five worlds, and his twelve elements, a creature, and this is the (temporally considered) Eternal Man

1 *Ante-Nicene Library*, Am. ed. vol. vi. pp. 182 and 188. 2 *Ibid.* p. 241.

[Primordial Man], and summoned him to do battle with the Darkness. But Primordial Man, Mani adds, armed himself with the five races [natures], and these are the five gods, the Gentle Breeze, the Wind, the Light, the Water and the Fire. Of them he made his armor, and the first that he put on was the Gentle Breeze. He then covered the Gentle Breeze with the burning Light as with a mantle. He drew over the Light Water filled with atoms, and covered himself with the blowing Wind. Hereupon he took the Fire as a shield and as a lance in his hand, and precipitated himself suddenly out of Paradise until he reached the border of the region that is contiguous to the battle-field. The Primordial Devil also took his five races [natures]: Smoke, Burning, Darkness, Hot Wind and Cloud; armed himself with them; made of them a shield for himself; and went to meet Primordial Man. After they had fought for a long time the Primordial Devil vanquished the Primordial Man, devoured some of his light, and surrounded him at the same time with his races and elements. Then the King of the Paradise of Light sent other gods, freed him, and vanquished the Darkness. But he who was sent by the King of Light to rescue Primordial Man is called the Friend of the Light. This one made a precipitate descent, and Primordial Man was freed from the hellish substances, along with that which he had snatched from the spirit of Darkness and which had adhered to him. When, therefore, Mani proceeds, Joyfulness and the Spirit of Life drew near to the border, they looked down into the abyss of this deep hell and saw Primordial Man and the angels [*i.e.*, the races or natures with which he was armed], how Iblis, the Proud Oppressors, and the Dark Life surrounded them. And the Spirit of Life, says Mani, called Primordial Man with a loud voice as quick as lightning and Primordial Man became another god. When the Primordial Devil had ensnared Primordial Man in the battle, Mani further teaches, the five parts of the Light were mingled with the five parts of the Darkness."

Let us see if we can get at the meaning of this great cosmological poem as far as we have gone. The thing to be accounted for is the mixture of good and evil. The complete separation of the eternally existent Kingdoms of Light and Darkness has been posited. How now are we to account for the mixture of light and darkness, of good and evil, in the present order of things? Mani would account for it by supposing that a conflict had occurred between an insufficiently equipped representative of the King of Light and the fully equipped ruler of the Kingdom of Darkness. His view of the vastly superior power of the King of Light would not allow him to suppose that the King of Light fully equipped had personally contended with the King of Darkness, and suffered the loss and contamination of his elements. Yet he only clumsily obviates this difficulty; for Primordial Man is produced and equipped by the King of Light for the very purpose of combating the King of Darkness, and Mani saves the King of Light from personal contamination only by impugning his judgment.

We have now reached the point where, as a result of the conflict, good and evil are blended. We must beware of supposing that Mani meant to ascribe any kind of materiality to the members of the Kingdom of Light. The Kingdom of Light, on the contrary, he regarded as purely spiritual; the Kingdom of Darkness as material. We have now the conditions for the creation of the present order of things, including man. How does Mani picture the process and the results of this mixing of the elements?

"The smoke (or vapor) was mingled with the gentle breeze (zephyr), and the present atmosphere resulted. So that whatever of agreeableness and power to quicken the soul and animal life is found in it [resultant air], is from the zephyr, and whatever of destructiveness and noisomeness is found in it, proceeds from the smoke. The burning was mingled with the fire; therefore whatever of conflagration, destruction and ruin is found, is from the burning, but whatever of brightness and illumination is in it [the resultant fire], springs from the fire. The light mingled itself with the darkness; therefore in dense bodies as gold, silver and the like, whatever of brightness, beauty, purity and other useful qualities occurs, is from the light, and whatever of tarnish, impurity, density and hardness occurs, springs from the darkness. The hot wind was mingled with the wind; whatever now is useful and agreeable in this [resultant wind] springs from the wind, and whatever of uneasiness, hurtfulness and deleterious property is found in it [resultant wind] is from the hot wind. Finally, the mist was mingled with the water, so that what is found in this [resultant water] of clearness, sweetness, and soul-satisfying property, is from the water; whatever, on the contrary, of overwhelming, suffocating, and destroying power, of heaviness, and corruption, is found in it, springs from the mist."

But we must from this point abbreviate the somewhat prolix account. Primordial Man, after the blending of the elements, ascended on high accompanied by "one of the angels of this intermingling;" in other words, snatching away a part of the imprisoned elements of the Kingdom of Light.

The next step is the creation of the present world, which Mani ascribes to the King of the World of Light, the object being to provide for the escape of the imprisoned elements of Light. Through an angel he constructed ten heavens and eight earths, an angel being appointed to hold heavens and earths in their places. A description of the stairways, doors, and halls of the heavens is given in the *Fihrist's* narrative. The stairways lead to the "height of heaven." The air was used as a medium for connecting heaven and earth. A pit was formed to be the receptacle of darkness from which the light should be liberated. The sun and the moon were created to be the receptacles of the light that should be liberated from the darkness, the sun for light that has been mingled with "hot devils," the moon for that which had been mingled with "cold devils." The moon is represented as collecting light during the first half-month, and during the second pouring it into the sun. When the sun and moon have liberated all the light they are able, there will be a fire kindled on the earth which will burn for 1468 years, when there will be no light left. The King of Darkness and his hosts will thereupon withdraw into the pit prepared for them.

(3.) *Anthropology*. So much for the liberation of the imprisoned light, which, according to Mani, was the sole object of creation. As yet we have heard nothing of the creation of living creatures. What place do man, the lower animals, and plants sustain in the Manichæan economy? We are to keep constantly in mind that Primordial Man was not Adam, but a divine æon, and that he ascended into the heights immediately after the blending of parts of his armor with darkness. The creation of earthly man was an altogether different affair. We must give the account of man's creation in Mani's own words, as preserved by the *Fihrist:* "Hereupon one of those Arch-fiends and [one] of the Stars, and Overmastering Violence, Avarice, Lust, and Sin, copulated, and from their copulation sprang the first man, who is Adam, two Arch-fiends, a male and a female, directing the process. A second copulation followed and from this sprang the beautiful woman who is Eve."

Man, therefore, unlike the world, is the creature of demons, the aim of the demons being to imprison in man, through the propagation of the race, as much as possible of the light, and so to hinder the separating process by the sun and the moon. Avarice is represented as having secretly seized some of the divine light and imprisoned it in man. The part played by the Star in the production of man is somewhat obscure in the narrative, yet the Star could hardly have been regarded as wholly evil. Probably the Star was thought of as a detached portion of the light that had not entered into the sun or the moon. "When, therefore, the five Angels saw what had taken place, they besought the Messenger of Joyful Knowledge, the Mother of Life, Primordial Man and the Spirit of Life, to send some one to liberate and save man, to reveal to him knowledge and righteousness, and to free him from the power of the devils. They sent, accordingly, Jesus, whom a god accompanied. These seized the two Arch-fiends, imprisoned them and freed the two creatures (Adam and Eve.)"

Jesus warned Adam of Eve's violent importunity, and Adam obeyed his injunction not to go near her. One of the Arch-fiends, however, begat with her a son named Cain, who in turn begat Abel of his mother, and afterwards two maidens Worldly-wise and Daughter-of-Avarice. Cain took the first to wife and gave the other to Abel. An angel having begotten of Worldly-wise two beautiful daughters (Raufarjâd and Barfarjâd), Abel accused Cain of the act. Cain enraged by the false accusation slew Abel and took Worldly-wise to wife. So far Adam had kept himself pure, but Eve was instructed by a demon in the art of enchanting, and she was enabled to excite his lust and to entrap him. By Adam she bore a beautiful son, whom the demon urged Eve to destroy. Adam stole the child away and brought it up on cow's milk and fruit. This son was named Seth (*Schatil*). Adam once more yielded to Eve's fascinations, but through Seth's exhortations was induced to flee "eastward to the light and the wisdom of God." Adam, Seth, Raufarjâd, Barfarjâd, and Worldly-wise died and went to Paradise; while Eve, Cain, and Daughter-of-Avarice went into Hell. This fantastic perversion of the Biblical narrative of the creation and fall of man has many parallels in Rabbinic literature, and doubtless Mani first became acquainted with the narrative in a corrupted form. The teaching, however, of this mythologizing evidently is that the indulgence of the flesh and the begetting of children furnish the chief obstacle to the separation of light from darkness. Adam is represented as striving to escape from the allurements of Eve, but Eve is aided by demonic craft in overcoming him. Yet Adam does not become enslaved to lust, and so at last is saved. Eve, lustful from the beginning, is lost along with those of like disposition.

(4.) *Soteriology*. Such was, apparently, Mani's conception of the creation of man, and of the attempts to liberate the light that was in him. What were his practical teachings to men of his time as to the means of escape from the Kingdom of Darkness into the Kingdom of Light? What view did Mani take of the historical Jesus? The Jesus who warned Adam against the seductions of Eve was evidently not the Jesus of the New Testament. According to the narrative of the *Fihrist*, Mani "maintained that Jesus is a devil." Such a statement occurs nowhere else, so far as we are aware, in the literature of Manichæism. The sources, however, are unanimous in ascribing to Mani a completely docetical view of the person of Christ. In using this blasphemous language, he probably referred to the representations of Jesus as God manifest in the flesh, which he regarded as Jewish and abominable. The New Testament narratives Mani [or at least his followers] regarded as interpolated in the interest of Judaism. Later Manichæans, under the influence of Marcionism (and orthodoxy) gave to Jesus a far more prominent place in the economy of man's salvation than did mani himself.

How then is man to be saved according to Mani? It is by rigorous asceticism, and by the practice of certain ceremonial observances. Mani does not rise above the plane of ordinary heathenism in his plan of salvation. "It is incumbent upon him who will enter into the religion that he prove himself, and that if he sees that he is able to subdue lust and avarice, to leave off the eating of all kinds of flesh, the drinking of wine, and connubial intercourse, and to withhold himself from what is injurious in water, fire, magic and hypocrisy, he may enter into the religion; but if not let him abstain from entering. But if he loves religion, yet is not able to repress sensuality and avarice, yet he may make himself serviceable for the maintenance of religion and of the Truthful [*i.e.* the 'Elect'], and may meet (offset) his corrupt deeds through the use of opportunities where he wholly gives himself up to activity, righteousness, zealous watchfulness, prayer and pious humiliation; for this suffices him in this transitory world and in the future eternal world, and his form in the last day will be the second form, of which, God willing, we shall treat further below."

The doctrine of indulgences of which the germs appeared in the Catholic church even before the time of Mani, is here seen fully developed. What the Greek and Latin sources call the *Elect* or *Perfect* and the *Hearers*, are undoubtedly indicated here by those who are able to devote themselves to rigidly ascetical living, and those who, without such qualifications, are willing to exert themselves fully on behalf of the cause. These latter evidently become partakers of the merits of those who carry out the ascetical regulations. That this is primitive Manichæan doctrine is abundantly proved by the general agreement of ancient writers of all classes. It is noteworthy that nothing Christian appears among the conditions of Manichæan discipleship. It is not faith in Christ, but the ability to follow a particular kind of outward life that confers standing in the Manichæan society.

(5.) *Cultus*. Let us next look at the precepts of Mani to the initiated: "Mani imposed upon his disciples commandments, namely, ten commandments, and to these are attached three seals, and fasts of seven days in each month. The commandments are: Faith in the four most glorious essences: God, his Light, his Power, and his Wisdom. But God, whose name is glorious, is the King of the Paradise of Light; his Light is the sun and the moon, his Power the five angels: Gentle Breeze, Wind, Light, Water and Fire; and his Wisdom the Sacred Religion. This embraces five ideas: that of teachers, the sons of Meekness; that of those enlightened by the Sun, sons of Knowledge; that of the presbyters, sons of Reason; that of the Truthful, sons of Mystery; that of Hearers, sons of Insight. The ten commandments are: Abandoning of prayer to idols, of lies, avarice, murder, adultery, theft, of the teaching of jugglery and magic, of duplicity of mind, which betrays doubt on religion, of drowsiness and inertness in business; and the commandment of four or seven prayers. In prayer one is to stand upright, rub himself with flowing water or with something else, and turn while standing to the great light (the Sun), then prostrate himself and in this position pray: Blessed be our Leader, the Paraclete, the Ambassador of the Light, blessed be his angels, the Guardians, and highly praised be his resplendent hosts. . . . In the second prostration let him say: Thou highly praised, O thou enlightening one, Mani, our Leader, thou root of enlightenment, stem of honorableness, thou great tree who art altogether the means of salvation. In the third prostration let him say: I fall down and praise with pure heart and upright tongue the great God, the Father of Light, and their element, highly praised, Blessed One, thou and thy whole glory and thy blessed world, which thou hast called into being. For he praises thee who praises thy Host, thy Righteous Ones, thy Word, thy Glory, and thy Good Pleasure, because thou art the God who is wholly truth, life and righteousness. In the fourth prostration let him say: I praise and fall down before all the gods, all the enlightening angels, before all Light and all Hosts, who are from the great God. In the fifth prostration let him say: I fall down and praise the great Host and the enlightening Gods, who with their wisdom assail the Darkness, drive it out and triumph over it. In the sixth prostration let him say: I fall down and praise the Father of Glory, the Exalted One, the Enlightening One, who has come forth from the two sciences (see note in Flügel p. 310), and so on to the twelfth prostration. * * The first prayer is accomplished at mid-day, the second between this hour and sunset; then follows the prayer at eventide, after sunset, and hereupon the prayer in the first quarter of the night, three hours after sunset.

"As regards fasting, when the sun is in *Sagittarius*, and the moon has its full light, fasting is to take place for two days without interruption, also when the new moon begins to appear; likewise when the moon first becomes visible again after the sun has entered into the sign of *Capricorn;* then when the new moon begins to appear, the sun stands in *Aquarius* and from the moon eight days have flowed, a fast of thirty days occurs, broken, however, daily at sunset. The common Manichæans celebrate Sunday, the consecrated ones (the 'Elect') Monday."

Here we have a somewhat detailed account of the cultus of the early Manichæans. The forms of invocation do not differ materially from those of the Zoroastrians, of the early Indians, of the Babylonians, and of the Egyptians. There is not the slightest evidence of Christian influence. The times of worship and of fasting are determined by the sun and the moon, and practically these are the principal objects of worship. It is certain that Mani himself was regarded by his followers as the most perfect revealer of God that had ever appeared among men, and, according to this account, he taught his followers to worship him. We cannot fail to see in this Manichæan cult the old Oriental pantheism modified by a dualism, of which the most fully developed form was the Persian, but which, as we have seen, was by no means confined to Zoroastrianism.

(6.) *Eschatology*. We must conclude our exposition of the doctrines of the Manichæans by quoting from the *Fihrist* Mani's teachings on eschatology.

"When death approaches a Truthful One ('Elect'), teaches Mani, Primordial Man sends a Light-God in the form of a guiding Wise One, and with him three gods, and along with these the water-vessel, clothing, head-gear, crown, and garland of light. With them comes the maiden, like the soul of this Truthful One. There appears to him also the devil of avarice and lust, along with other devils. As soon as the Truthful Man sees these he calls the goddess who has assumed the form of the Wise One and the three other gods to his help, and they draw near him. As soon as the devils are aware of their presence they turn and flee. The former, however, take this Truthful One, clothe him with the crown, the garland and the robe, put the water-vessel in his hand and mount with him upon the pillars of promise to the sphere of the moon, to Primordial Man, and to Nahnaha, the Mother of the Living, to the position in which he was at first in the Paradise of Light. But his body remains lying as before in order that the sun, the moon, and the gods of Light may withdraw from it the powers, *i.e.*, the water, the fire and the gentle breeze, and he rises to the sun and becomes a god. But the rest of his body, which is wholly darkness, is cast into hell."

In the case of Manichæans of the lower order, described above, the same divine personages appear at his summons. "They free him also from devils, but he ceases not to be like a man in the world, who in his dreams sees frightful forms and sinks into filth and mire. In this condition he remains, until his light and his spirit are liberated and he has attained to the place of union with the Truthful, and after a long period of wandering to and fro puts on their garments."

To the sinful man, on the other hand, the divine personages appear, not to free him from the devils that are tormenting him, but rather to "overwhelm him with reproaches, to remind him of his deeds, and strikingly to convince him that he has renounced help for himself, from the side of the Truthful. Then wanders he round about in the world, unceasingly chased by torments, until this order of things ceases, and along with the world he is cast into hell."

There is nothing original about the eschatology of Mani, and scarcely anything Christian. We see in it a fully developed doctrine of purgatory, somewhat like the Platonic, and still more like that of the later Catholic church. Salvation consists simply in the liberation of the light from the darkness. In the case of the Elect this takes place immediately after death; in the case of adherents who have not practiced the prescribed forms of asceticism, it takes place only after considerable torment. In the case of the ordinary sensual man, there is no deliverance. Doubtless Mani would have held that in his case, too, whatever particles of light may have been involved in his animal structure are liberated from the dead body.

(7.) *Ethics.* As regards ceremonies we find little that enlightens us in the *Fihrist's* account. Water (that is, water apart from the deleterious elements that have become blended with it) was regarded by Mani as one of the divine elements. The ablutions in running water mentioned above in connection with the prayers may have sustained some relation to baptism, but can hardly be ascribed to Christian influence. The connection of the Manichæans with the Mandæans, who made much of ceremonial bathing, will be considered below. It is certain that Mani's father was connected with a baptizing party, *viz.*, the Mugtasilah. According to the *Fihrist* Mani was the author of an Epistle on Baptism. The question whether Mani and his followers practised water-baptism or not is by no means an easy one to solve. The passage cited by Giesseler from Augustin to prove that the "Elect" were initiated by baptism is inconclusive. Augustin acknowledges that God and the Manichæans themselves alone know what takes place in the secret meetings of the "Elect." Whatever ceremonies they performed, whether baptism or the Lord's supper, or some other, were matters of profound secrecy, and so we need not wonder at the lack of definite information. From a passage quoted by Augustin in his report of a discussion with Felix the Manichæan, we should certainly infer that both ordinances were practised in some form by the Manichæans of the West. But Augustin himself says that Manichæans deny the saving efficacy of baptism, maintain that it is superfluous, do not require it of those whom they win to their views, etc. It is certain, therefore, that if they practised baptism and the Lord's supper at all, they attached to it a meaning radically different from that of Augustin. It is possible that a ceremonial anointing with oil took the place of baptism. (BAUR, p. 277 sq.). Augustin mentions a disgusting ceremony in which human semen was partaken of by the Elect in order to deliver the imprisoned light contained therein (*De Haeres*. 46), and he calls this ceremony a sort of Eucharist. But his confessed ignorance of the doings of the "Elect" discredits in some measure this accusation.

The *Fihrist* gives us no definite information about the three *signacula.* The seals (not signs) of the mouth, the hand (or hands), and of the bosom. In these are contained symbolically the Manichæan moral system. In the book *Sadder* (HYDE, p. 492) we read: "It is taught [by the Manichæans] to abstain from every sin, to eliminate every sin from hand, and tongue and thought." Augustin explains the *signacula* more fully and represents the Manichæans as attaching great importance to them: "When I name the mouth, I mean all the senses that are in the head; when I name the hand I mean every operation; when I name the bosom I mean every seminal lust."

It is confidently believed that the foregoing account of the Manichæan system, based upon the Arabic narratives preserved by the *Fihrist*, supplemented by the principal Eastern and Western sources, contains the essential facts with reference to this strange system of religious thought. Our next task will to be to ascertain, as precisely as possible, the relations that Manichæism sustained to the various religious systems with which it has commonly been associated.

CHAPTER IV.—RELATION OF MANICHÆISM TO ZOROASTRIANISM.

The very close connection of these two systems has commonly been presupposed, and is undeniable. In fact Manichæism has frequently been represented as Zoroastrian dualism, slightly modified by contact with Christianity and other systems. No one could possibly gain even a superficial view of the two systems without being strongly impressed with their points of resemblance. A closer examination, however, will reveal points of antagonism just as striking, and will enable us to account for the fact that Mani was put to death by a zealous Zoroastrian ruler on account of his recognized hostility to the state religion. The leading features of the Manichæan system are already before us. Instead of quoting at length from the Zend-Avesta, which is now happily accessible in an excellent English translation, we may for the sake of brevity quote Tiele's description of Zoroastrian dualism as a basis of comparison:[1]

"Parsism is decidedly dualistic, not in the sense of accepting two hostile deities, for it recognizes no worship of evil beings, and teaches the adoration only of Ahura Mazda and the spirits subject to him; but in the sense of placing in hostility to each other two sharply divided kingdoms, that of light, of truth, and of purity, and that of darkness, of falsehood, and of impurity. This division is carried through the whole creation, organic and inorganic, material and spiritual. Above, in the highest sphere, is the domain of the undisputed sovereignty of the All-wise God; beneath, in the lowest abyss, the kingdom of his mighty adversary; midway between the two lies this world, the theatre of the contest. . . . . This dualism further dominates the cosmogony, the cultus, and the entire view of the moral order of the world held by the Mazda worshippers. Not only does Anro-Maînyus (Ahriman) spoil by his counter-creations all the good creations of Ahura-Mazda (Ormuzd), but by slaying the protoplasts of man and beast, he brings death into the world, seduces the first pair to sin, and also brings forth noxious animals and plants. Man finds himself, in consequence, surrounded on all sides by the works of the spirits of darkness and by his hosts. It is the object of worship to secure the pious against their influence."

Let us bring in review some of the points of resemblance between the two systems. Both are in a sense *dualistic*. In both the kingdoms of Light and Darkness are set over against each other in the sharpest antagonism. In both we have similar emanations from these kingdoms (or kings). Yet, while in the Manichæan system the dualism is absolute and eternal, in the later Zoroastrian system (as in the Jewish and Christian doctrine of Satan), Ahriman (Satan) if not merely a fallen creature[2] of Ormuzd (the good and supreme God) was at least an immeasurably inferior being. The supreme control of the universe, to which it owes its perfect order, was ascribed by Zoroastrianism to Ormuzd. The struggle between good and evil, beneficent and malevolent, was due to the opposition of the mighty, but not almighty, Ahriman. Whatever form of Mazdeism (Zoroastrianism) we take for purposes of comparison, we are safe in saying that the Manichæan dualism was by far the more absolute.

In both systems each side of the dualism is represented by a series (or rather several series) of *personified principles*. These agree in the two systems in some particulars. Yet the variations are quite as noticeable as the agreements. There is much in common between the Manichæan and the Zoroastrian delineations of the fearful conflict between the Kingdom of Light and the Kingdom of Darkness, yet the beginning of the conflict is quite differently conceived of in the two systems. In Manichæism the creation is accounted for by the conflict in which Primordial Man was beaten by the powers of Darkness and suffered the mixing of his elements with the elements of darkness. The actual world was made by the good God, or rather by his subordinates, as a means of liberating the imprisoned light.

---

[1] *Outlines of the Hist. of Religion* (1877), p. 173. Cf. J. Darmsteter, *Introduction to the Zend-Avesta*, p. xliii., xliv., lvi., lxxii., lxxiv. sq.; and his article in the *Contemporary Review* (Oct. 1879), on "*The Supreme God in the Indo-European Mythology.*"

[2] This is confidently asserted by Kessler (Art. Mani in *Herzog's RE*. 2d ed. vol. IX. p. 258), and after him by Harnack, *Encyclopædia Britannica*, art. Manichæism. On the other hand, Lenormant (*Anc. Hist.* II. p. 30), says: "Ahriman had been eternal in the past, he had no beginning, and proceeded from no former being * * * . This being who had no beginning would come to an end. * * * . Evil then should be finally conquered and destroyed, the creation should become as pure as on its first day, and Ahriman should disappear forever." Such, doubtless, was the original doctrine, but the form probably in vogue in the time of Mani was more pantheistic or monotheistic, both Ormuzd and Ahriman proceeding from boundless time (*Zrvan akarana*). See on this matter, Darmsteter: *Introd. to the Zend-Avesta*, p. lxxii, etc., and his art. in *Contemp. Review*; and Lenormant: *Anc. Hist.* as above.

The creation of man is ascribed, on the other hand, to the King of Darkness (or his subordinates), with a view to hindering the escape of the mingled light by diffusion thereof through propagation. Mazdeism derives the creation solely from Ormuzd, from whose hand it issued "as pure and perfect as himself" (LENORMANT, *Anc. Hist.* II. p. 30). It was the work of Ahriman to "spoil it by his evil influence." The appellation "Maker of the material world" is constantly applied to Ormuzd in the *Vendîdâd* and other sacred books. The most instructive Mazdean account of the creation that has come down to us is that contained in the *Vendîdâd*, Fargard I. Ahura Mazda (Ormuzd) is represented here as naming one by one the sixteen good lands that he had created. Angra Mainyu (Ahriman) is represented as coming to each, one by one, and creating in it noxious things. Examples of these counter-creations are, the serpents, winter, venomous flies, sinful lusts, musquitos, pride, unnatural sin, burying the dead, witchcraft, the sin of unbelief, the burning of corpses, abnormal issues in women, oppression of foreign rulers, excessive heat, etc. This jumble of physical evils and sins is characteristic of Mazdeism.

According to Mani matter is inherently evil, and it only ceases to be absolutely evil by the mixture with it of the elements of the Kingdom of Light. Creation is a process forced upon the King of Light by the ravages of the King of Darkness, and is at best only partially good. Zoroastrianism looked upon earth, fire, water, as sacred elements, to defile which was sin of the most heinous kind. Manichæism regarded actual fire and water as made up of a mixture of elements of light and darkness, and so, as by no means wholly pure. Manichæans regarded earth, so far as it consisted of dead matter, with the utmost contempt. The life-giving light in it was alone thought of with respect. Zoroastrianism somewhat arbitrarily divided animals and plants between the kingdoms of Ormuzd and Ahriman; but the idea that all material things, so far as they are material, are evil, seems never to have occurred to the early Mazdeists. Manichæans agreed with Mazdeists in their veneration for the sun, but the principles underlying this veneration seem to have been widely different in the two cases. The most radical opposition of the two systems is seen in their views of human propagation. Mani regarded the procreation of children as ministering directly to the designs of the King of Darkness to imprison the light, and so absolutely condemned it. The *Zend-Avesta* says: (*Vendîdâd*, Fargard IV.): "Verily I say unto thee, O Spitama Zarathustra; the man who has a wife is far above him who begets no sons; he who keeps a house is far above him who has none; he who has children is far above a childless man." Mani made great merit of voluntary poverty. The *Zend-Avesta* (*ibid.*) says: "He who has riches is far above him who has none." Mani forbade the use of animal food as preventing the escape of the light contained in the bodies of animals. The *Zend-Avesta* (*ibid.*): "And of two men, he who fills himself with meat is filled with the good spirit much more than he who does not do so; the latter is all but dead; the former is above him by the worth of an Asperena, by the worth of a sheep, by the worth of an ox, by the worth of a man." [1]

The eschatology of the two systems might be shown to present just as striking contrasts, and just as marked resemblances. In both systems the consummation of the age is effected by means of a conflagration, the aim of the conflagration in Mazdeism being the punishment and the purging of wicked men, the destruction of wicked spirits, the renovation of the earth, and the inauguration of the sole sovereignty of Ormuzd, while in Manichæism the aim of the conflagration is to liberate the portions of light which the processes of animal and vegetable growth, with the aid of sun and the moon have proved unable to liberate.

---

[1] That meat is used in the sense of flesh may be inferred from Darmsteter's comment on this passage, which he suggests may be a bit of religious polemics against Manichæism. See his *Introd. to the Zend-Avesta*, p. xl. sq.

But enough has been said to make it evident that Manichæism was by no means a slightly altered edition of Zoroastrianism. The points of similarity between the two are certainly more apparent than real, though the historical relationship can by no means be denied.

CHAPTER V.—THE RELATION OF MANICHÆISM TO THE OLD BABYLONIAN RELIGION AS SEEN IN MANDÆISM AND SABEANISM.

It would have been strange indeed if the old Babylonian religion, after dominating the minds of the inhabitants of Mesopotamia for so many centuries, had given place completely to the religion of the Medo-Persian conquerors of the country. Magism itself was a mixture of old Babylonian, Medic and Persian elements. But there is much reason for believing that the primitive Babylonian faith, in a more or less pure form, persisted until long after the time of Mani, nay, that it has maintained its ground even till the present day. The researches of Chwolson, Nöldeke, Kessler and others, in the literature and history of the Mandæans and the Sabeans, combined in the last case at least with accurate knowledge of old Babylonian literature and religion, have rendered it highly probable that representatives of the old Babylonian faith were numerous in Mesopotomia and the adjoining regions at the time of Mani, and that Mani himself was more or less closely connected with it. The Mandæans were a Gnostic sect of the Ophitic type, without Christian elements. It is the opinion of Kessler, who has devoted much attention to this sect and to the relations of occult religious matters in general in Mesopotomia, that "the source of all Gnosis, and especially the immediate source of Ophitic Gnosis, is not the doctrine of the Persian Zoroaster, not Phœnicean heathenism, not the theory and practise of Greek mysteries, but the old Babylonian-Chaldaic national religion, which maintained itself in Mesopotomia and Babylonia, the abode of the Ophites, Perates, Mandæans, until the post-Christian centuries, and was now opposed by the Gentiles in a mystical-ascetical form to Christianity." The close connection of the Mandæans with the Ophites, and of both with the old Babylonian religion, would seem to be established beyond question. The relation of Manichæism to Mandæism has been by no means so clearly shown. Let us look at some of the supposed points of contact. Mani's connection with the Mugtasilah sect (or Baptizers) has already been mentioned. Kessler seeks to identify this party with the Mandæans, or at least to establish a community of origin and of fundamental principles in the two parties. He would connect with the old Babylonian sect, of which ceremonial baptism seems to have been a common characteristic, the Palestinian Hemero-baptists, Elkesaites, Nazareans, Ebionites, etc. There is nothing improbable about this supposition. Certainly we find elements in Palestinian heresy during the early Christian centuries, which we can hardly suppose to have been indigenous. And there is no more likely source of occult religious influence than Babylonia, unless it be Egypt, and there is much reason for supposing that even in Alexandria Babylonian influences were active before and after the beginning of the Christian era. Besides, a large number of Gnostic elements different from these can be traced to Egypt. How far the Mandæans of modern times, and as they are described in extant literature, correspond with representatives of the old Babylonian religion in the third century, cannot be determined with complete certainty. Yet there is much about this party that has a primitive appearance, and the tenacity with which it has held aloof from Judaism, Manichæism, Mohammedanism, and Oriental Christianity, during centuries of conflict and oppression, says much for its conservatism. It would extend this chapter unduly to describe the elaborate cosmogony, mythology, hierarchy, ceremonial, etc., of this interesting party. For the illustration of Christian Gnosticism the facts that have been brought out are of the utmost value. As compared with Manichæism, there is a remarkable parallelism between the two kingdoms and their subordinates or æons; the conflict between Primordial Man and the King of Darkness has its counterpart in Mandæism. The close connection of the Mandæan and the Manichæan cosmogony, together with similar views about water in the two parties, would make it highly probable that the Manichæans, like the Mandæans, practised some kind of ceremonial ablutions.

What, now, are the grounds on which the connection of these systems with the old Babylonian religion is based? The dualistic element in the old Babylonian system was pointed out above. Kessler seeks to establish an almost complete parallelism between the Mandæan and Manichæan cosmological and mythological systems on the one hand, and the old Babylonian on the other. That there are points of striking resemblance it is certain. There is ground to suspect, however, that he has been led by partiality for a theory of his own to minimize unduly the Zoroastrian and Buddhist influence and to magnify unduly the old Babylonian. Be that as it may, there remains an important residuum of solid fact which must be taken account of by all future students of Manichæism. There is reason to hope that future work along the lines of Kessler's researches will bring to light much additional material.

CHAPTER VI.—THE RELATION OF MANICHÆISM TO BUDDHISM.

The extent of Mani's dependence on Buddhism is a matter that has been much disputed. The attention of scholars was first directed to this possible source of Manichæism by the discovery of important features that are radically opposed to Zoroastrianism, Judaism and Christianity, and by the traditional historical connection of Mani with India and Turkestan. The antagonism of spirit and matter, of light and darkness, the mixture of spirit and light with matter and darkness in the formation of the world, the final catastrophe in which complete simplicity shall be re-established, only inert matter and darkness remaining to represent the Kingdom of Darkness, abstinence from bloody sacrifices, from marriage, from killing or eating animals—points in which Manichæism differs widely from the other systems with which it stands historically related—find their counterpart in Buddhism. It is certain, moreover, that they were fully developed in Buddhism centuries before the time of Mani. Baur,[1] though not the first to suggest a connection of the two systems, was the first to show by a somewhat detailed comparison the close parallelism that exists between Manichæism and Buddhism. Baur's reasonings were still further elaborated and confirmed by Neander.[2] External grounds in favor of Mani's dependence on Buddhism are the traditions of Mani's journey to India and China, and of his prolonged stay in Turkestan, where Buddhism flourished at that time. But it is on internal grounds that we chiefly rely.

If space permitted we could illustrate the close parallelism that undoubtedly exists between Manichæism and Buddhism, from Buddhist documents which have been made accessible through Professor Max Müller and his collaborators in *The Sacred Book of the East*, far more completely than was possible to Baur and Neander. It is certain that parallels can be found in Buddhism for almost every feature of Manichæism that is sharply antagonistic to Zoroastrianism. The Buddhist view of matter as antagonistic to spirit is fundamental. It is the world of matter that deludes. It is the body and its passions that prevent the longed-for *Nirvana*. Buddhist asceticism is the direct outgrowth of the doctrine of the evil and delusive nature of matter. The Buddhist doctrine of metempsychosis has its precise counterpart in Manichæism, but it should be said that this doctrine was widely diffused in the West, through Pythagoreanism, before the time of Mani. The Buddhist tenderness for animal and plant life is paralleled by the Manichæan. But there is

---

[1] *Das Manichäische Religionssystem*, p. 433 sq.

[2] *Church Hist*. vol. I.

considerable difference between the views on which this tenderness is based. The Buddhist feeling was based, in part at least, upon the doctrine of metempsychosis, animals and plants being regarded as the abodes of human spirits awaiting their release into *Nirvana.* The Manichæan looked upon the elements of light (life) contained in animals and plants as particles of God, and any injury done to them as a hindrance to the escape of these elements, to be conveyed away into the Kingdom of Light. Both looked upon sexual intercourse as among the greatest of evils, though the theory in the two cases was slightly different. So of the drinking of wine, the eating of animal food, etc. The final state was conceived of in substantially the same way in the two systems. *Nirvana*, the blowing out of man's life as an individual entity, is quite paralleled by the Manichæan view of the gradual escape of the imprisoned particles of light into the Kingdom of Light. In both cases the divine *pleroma* is to be restored in such a way as to destroy individual consciousness.

The Buddhist *Bhikkhus* (or ascetical monks) correspond very closely with the Manichæan Truthful Ones (Elect), and the relations of these to ordinary adherents of the parties was much the same in the two cases. Both systems (like Christianity) had the proselyting spirit fully developed. The position of Mani as a preacher or prophet corresponds with the Buddhist idea of the manifestations of Buddha. The statement is attributed to Mani that "as Buddha came in the land of India, Zoroaster in the land of Persia, and Jesus in the land of the West, so at last in the epoch of the present this preaching came through me [Mani] in the land of Babylonia." In the interest of his theory, which makes the old Babylonian religion the chief source of Manichæism, Kessler has attempted to detract from the significance of the Buddhist influence. Yet he grants that the morality of the Manichæans (including many of the features mentioned above) was Buddhist. The close connection of the two systems cannot, it would seem, be successfully gainsaid.[1]

CHAPTER VII.—THE RELATION OF MANICHÆISM TO JUDAISM.

So far as a relation existed it was one of the intensest hostility. Like the Gnostics in general, Manichæism looked upon the God of the Old Testament as an evil, or at least imperfect being. On this matter we do not learn so much from the Oriental as from the Western sources, but even from the former the radical antagonism is manifest.

The statement in the *Fihrist's* narrative, that "Mani treated all the prophets disparagingly in his books, degraded them, accused them of lying, and maintained that devils had possessed them and that these spoke out of their mouths; nay, he goes so far as expressly to assert in some passages of his books that the prophets were themselves devils," is precisely in the line of the later Manichæan polemics against the Judaistic element in Christianity.

The Manichæan account of the creation shows some acquaintance with the Jewish Scriptures or with Jewish tradition, yet the complete perversion of the Biblical account is

[1] CUNNINGHAM, *St. Austin and his Place in the History of Christian Thought* (1886), has these remarks on the relation of Mani to Buddhism: "Mani was indeed a religious reformer: deeply impregnated with the belief and practice which Buddhist monks were spreading in the East, he tried with some success to reform the religion of Zoroaster in Persia [*i. e.* the Persian Empire], his native land. While his fundamental doctrine, the root of his system, was of Persian origin, and he figured the universe to himself as if it were given over to the unending conflict between the Powers of Light and Darkness, in regard to discipline his system very closely resembles that founded by Buddha; the *elect* of the Manichæans correspond to the Buddhist *monks*; the precepts about abstinence from meat and things of sense are, if not borrowed from the rules Gotama gave for the conduct of his followers, the outcome of the same principles about the nature of man." HARNACK, art. Manichæism in *Ency. Britannica*, follows Kessler in attaching slight importance to the Buddhist influence on Manichæism, preferring, with him, to derive nearly all of the features ascribed by Baur, Neander and others to Buddhist influence, to the old Babylonian religion, the precise character of which, in the time of Mani, is imperfectly understood. Harnack's (and Kessler's) statements must therefore be taken with some allowance. There is no objection, however, to supposing that Mani derived from the old Babylonian party or parties with which he came in contact religious principles which were wrought out in detail under the influence of Buddhism. This is in fact what probably occurred.

one of the clearest indications of hostility. It may be said in general that it is impossible to conceive of two systems of religion that have less in common, or more that is sharply antagonistic. One of the principal points of controversy between Manichæans and Christians was the defense of the Jewish Scriptures and religion by the latter. The Manichæans demanded the elimination from the current Christianity, and from the New Testament itself, of every vestige of Judaism. Their objections to the Old Testament Scriptures and religion were in general substantially the same as those made by other Gnostics, especially by the Marcionites. The Old Testament anthropomorphic representations seem to have been offensive to them, notwithstanding their own crude conceptions of the conflict between light and darkness, of the creation, etc. The relation of God to the conquest of Canaan is a point that those inclined to cavil have never failed to make the most of. The Old Testament encouragement of race propagation, the narratives of polygamy as practised by those that enjoyed the favor of the God of the Old Testament, the seeming approval of prevarication in several well-known cases, the institution of animal sacrifices, the allowing of the use of animal food, were among the standard objections that they raised against Judaism and against Christians who accepted the Old Testament. Judaism had, since the captivity, had many representatives in Mesopotamia, and Mani was doubtless brought up to abominate the Jews. Some of his extreme positions may have been primarily due to his radical anti-Judaistic tendencies. We shall see hereafter how Augustin met the Manichæan objections to the Old Testament.

CHAPTER VIII.—THE RELATION OF MANICHÆISM TO CHRISTIANITY.

Far more superficial are the relations of Manichæism to Christianity than to any of the heathen systems to which we have adverted. In fact no Christian idea has been introduced into the system without being completely perverted. If Christian language is used, it is utterly emptied of its meaning. If Christian practices are introduced, a completely different motive lies at the basis. Indeed the wildest of the Christian Gnostic systems kept immeasurably nearer to historical Christianity than did the Manichæans. While he blasphemed against the historical Jesus, Mani claimed to believe in Christ, a purely spiritual and divine manifestation, whose teachings had been sadly perverted by the Jews. It is scarcely possible to determine with any certainty what view Mani actually took of New Testament history. That he claimed to be a follower of Christ, and the Paraclete whom Christ had promised to send, or at least the organ of the Paraclete, Eastern and Western authorities agree. Mani is said, by Augustin, to have begun his *Fundamental Epistle* as follows: "Manichæus, an Apostle of Jesus Christ, by the providence of God the Father. These are wholesome words from the perennial and living fountain." So also in the *Act. Archel.*, Mani is represented as introducing a letter: "Manichæus, an Apostle of Jesus Christ, and all the saints who are with me, and the virgins, to Marcellus, my beloved son: Grace, mercy, and peace be with you from God the Father, and from our Lord Jesus Christ." There can be no doubt but that Mani and his followers, whether from designed imposture or from less sinister motives, attempted to palm themselves off as Christians, nay, as the only true Christians. It is certain, moreover, that in this guise they gained many proselytes from the Christian ranks. As previously remarked, Mani and his followers professed to accept the New Testament Scriptures, yet they treated them in a purely subjective manner, eliminating as Judaistic interpolation whatever they could not reconcile with their own tenets. Their adherence to the New Testament, as well as their adherence to Christ, was, therefore, virtually a mere pretence. In common with Christianity, Manichæism laid much stress on redemption, yet there was nothing in common between the Christian idea of redemption through the atoning suffering of Jesus Christ and the Manichæan notion of redemption through the escape of imprisoned light. Manichæans and Christians were at one in advocating self-denial and the due subordination of the flesh. It need not be pointed out how radically different the Christian view was from the Manichæan view, already expounded. Yet pagan ascetical ideas had already invaded the Church long before the time of Mani, and many Christians were in a position to be attracted strongly by the Manichæan theory and practice. The later asceticism as it appeared in the hermit life of the fourth and following centuries was essentially pagan and had much in common with the Manichæan. Still more manifest is the anatagonism between Manichæism and Christianity on the great fundamental principles of religion. The Manichæan and Christian ideas of God are mutually contradictory. Christianity holds fast at the same time to the unity, the omnipotence, the omniscience, the perfect wisdom, the holiness and the goodness of God. If He permits sin to exist in the world it is not because He looks upon it with complacency, nor because He lacked wisdom to provide against its rise or power to annihilate it at once when it appeared, nor because He did not foresee its rise and its ravages, but because the permission of sin forms part of His all-wise plan for the education of moral and spiritual beings. If the forces of nature are under certain circumstances hurtful or destructive to man, Christianity does not regard them as the operations of a malevolent power thwarting God's purposes, but it sees underneath the destructive violence purposes of goodness and of grace; or if it fails to see them in any given instance it yet believes that God doeth all things well. Christianity admits the existence of evil in men and in demons, yet of evil that ministers to the purposes of the Most High. Christianity is the only religion that has been able to arrive at a perfectly satisfactory theology, cosmology, anthropology, and eschatology, and this is because Christianity alone has a true and satisfying soteriology. It is God manifest in the flesh that meets all the conditions for the solution of the problem of human existence. Manichæism openly antagonized Christianity in its adherence to Old Testament revelation, including the Jewish and Christian monotheism. The good God could not, they maintained, be the creator of this world and of the universe of being. That God should be looked upon as in any sense the creator of the devil and his angels, and of the material world, was in their view an absurdity—a monstrosity. The unchristian character of the Manichæan view of matter, leading to unchristian asceticism, has already been sufficiently indicated. The reader will only need to compare the principles and practices of Manichæism, as delineated above, with those of Christianity as they are delineated in the New Testament and in the evangelical churches of to-day, to be impressed with the completely anti-Christian character of the former.

How then, it may well be asked, could Manichæism succeed as it did in fascinating so many intelligent members of the Catholic Church during the third, fourth and fifth centuries? In attempting to answer this question it should be premised that the later Western Manichæism took far more account of historical Christianity than did Mani and his immediate followers. In the West, at least, Manichæism set itself up as the only genuine exponent of Christianity. The Jewish-Alexandrian philosophy, and Gnosticism its product, had done much towards discrediting the Old Testament Scriptures, and the moral and religious teachings therein contained. Devout Jewish and Christian thinkers who had adopted this mode of thought, had attempted by means of the allegorical method of interpretation to reconcile the seeming antagonism between Judaism and philosophy. But the process was so forced that its results could not be expected to satisfy those that felt no special interest in the removal of the difficulties. Marcionism represents a stern refusal to apply the allegory, and a determination to exhibit the antagonism between Judaism and current thought, and especially the seeming antagonism between Judaism and Christianity, in the harshest manner. Marcionism was still vigorous in the East when Manichæism arose, and through this party unfavorable views of the Old Testament were widely disseminated. Many Christians doubtless felt that the Old Testament and its religion were burdensome and trammelling to Christianity. The very fact that Mani set aside so summarily every element of Judaism that he encountered in the current Christianity, doubtless commended his views to a large and influential element in the East and the West alike. Mani claimed to set forth a spiritual religion as opposed to a carnal. The asceticism of Manichæism was in the line of a wide-spread popular ascetical movement that was already in progress, and so commended it to many. The question as to the origin of evil, and as to the relation of the good, wise and powerful God to the evil that appears in the world, in man and in demons, was never asked with more interest than during the early Christian centuries, and any party that should advance a moderately plausible theory was sure to receive its share of public attention. Mani professed to have a solution and the only possible solution of questions of this class, and however fantastic may have been the forms in which his speculations were set forth, they were doubtless all the more acceptable on this account in that semi-pagan age to many intelligent people. The fact that these forms satisfied so able a thinker as Mani undoubtedly was, would guarantee their acceptance by a large number both East and West. There was in the West at this time, and had been for centuries, a hankering after Oriental theosophy, the more extravagant the better. The wide-spread worship of Mithra was an excellent preparation for the more complete system of Mani. Manichæism and Neo-Platonism antagonized the Christianity of the fourth and fifth centuries from opposite sides, and those minds for whom Platonism had no charms were almost sure to be attracted by the theosophy of Mani. "How are we to explain," asks Harnack,[1] "the rapid spread of Manichæism, and the fact that it really became one of the great religions? Our answer is, that Manichæism was the most complete Gnosis, the richest, most consequent and most artistic system formed on the basis of the ancient Babylonian religion. . . What gave strength to Manichæism was . . that it united its ancient mythology and a thoroughgoing materialistic dualism with an exceedingly simple spiritual worship and a strict morality. On comparing it with the Semitic religions of nature, we perceive that it retained their mythologies, after transforming them into doctrines, but abolished all their sensuous cultus, substituting instead a spiritual worship as well as a strict morality. Manichæism was thus able to satisfy the new wants of an old world. It offered revelation, redemption, moral virtue, and immortality [this last is very doubtful, if conscious immortality be meant], spiritual benefits on the basis of the religion of nature. A further source of strength lay in the simple, yet firm social organization which was given by Mani himself to his new institution. The wise man and the ignorant, the enthusiast and the man of the world, could all find acceptance here, and there was laid on no one more than he was able and willing to bear."

The question as to the secret of the fascination that Manichæism was able to exercise even over the most intelligent Western minds, may receive a more concrete answer from the autobiographical account of Augustin's own relations to the party. What was it that attracted and enthralled, for nine years, him who was to become the greatest theologian of the age? In his *Confessions* (Book III. ch. 6) he gives this impassioned account of his first connection with Manichæism: "Therefore I fell among men proudly railing, very carnal and voluble, in whose mouth were the snares of the devil—the bird lime being composed of a mixture of the syllables of Thy Name, and of our Lord Jesus Christ, and of the Paraclete, the Holy Ghost, the Comforter. These names departed not out of their mouths, but so far forth as the sound and clatter of the tongue; for the heart was empty of truth. Still

1 *Encyclopædia Britannica*, art. Manichæism.

they cried 'Truth, Truth,' and spoke much about it to me, yet it was not in them, but they spake falsely not of Thee only—who, verily art the Truth—but also of the elements of this world, Thy creatures . . . O Truth, Truth! how inwardly even then did the marrow of my soul pant after Thee, when they frequently and in a multiplicity of ways, and in numerous and huge books, sounded out Thy Name to me, though it was but a voice. And these were the dishes in which to me, hungering for Thee, they, instead of Thee, served up the sun and the moon, Thy beauteous works—but yet Thy works, not Thyself, nay, nor Thy first works . . . Woe, woe, by what steps was I dragged down to the depths of hell!—toiling and turmoiling through want of Truth, when I sought after Thee, my God,—to Thee I confess it, who hadst mercy on me when I had not yet confessed, sought after Thee not according to the understanding of the mind in which Thou desiredst that I should excel the beasts, but according to the sense of the flesh."

CHAPTER IX.—AUGUSTIN AND THE MANICHÆANS.

In the preceding Chapter we have given in Augustin's own words some account of the process by which he became ensnared in Manichæan error. In reading Augustin's account of his experience among the Manichæans, we can not escape the conviction that he was never wholly a Manichæan, that he never surrendered himself absolutely to the system. He held it rather as a matter of opinion than as a matter of heart-attachment. Doubtless the fact that he continued to occupy himself with rhetorical and philosophical studies prevented his complete enthrallment. His mind was not naturally of an Oriental cast, and the study of the hard, common-sense philosophy of Aristotle, and of the Eclecticism of Cicero, could hardly have failed to make him more or less conscious of the absurdity of Manichæism. The influence of scientific studies on his mind is very manifest from *Confessions*, Book V. ch. 3, where he compares the accurate astronomical knowledge with which he had become acquainted, with the absurd cosmological fancies of Faustus, the great Manichæan teacher who appeared at Carthage in Augustin's twenty-ninth year. "Many truths, however, concerning the creation did I retain from these men [the philosophers], and the cause appeared to confirm calculations, the succession of seasons, and the visible manifestations of the stars; and I compared them with the sayings of Manichæus, who in his frenzy has written most extensively on these subjects, but discovered not any account either of the solstices, or the equinoxes, the eclipses of the luminaries, or anything of the kind I had learned in the books of secular philosophy. But therein I was ordered to believe, and yet it corresponded not with those rules acknowledged by calculation and by our light, but was far different."

From this time Augustin's faith was shaken, and he was soon able to throw off completely the yoke that had become too grievous to be borne. But to reject Manichæism was not necessarily to become an orthodox Christian. Augustin finds himself still greatly perplexed about the nature of God and the origin of evil, problems the somewhat plausible Manichæan solutions of which had ensnared him. It was through Platonism, or rather Neo-Platonism, that he was led to more just and satisfying views, and through Platonism, along with other influences, he was enabled at last to find peace in the bosom of the Catholic church. "And Thou, willing to show me how Thou 'resistest the proud, but givest grace unto the humble,' and by how great an act of mercy Thou hadst pointed out to men the path of humility, in that 'Thy Word was made flesh and dwelt among men,'—Thou procuredst for me, by the instrumentality of one inflated with monstrous pride, certain books of the Platonists, translated from Greek into Latin. And therein I read, not indeed in the same words but to the self-same effect, enforced by many and divers reasons, that 'In the beginning was the Word, and the Word was with God, and the Word was God. The same was in the beginning with God. All things were made by Him; and without Him was not anything made that was made.' "[1] In other words, Augustin thought that he discerned complete harmony between the prologue of John's gospel and the teachings of the Platonists, and in this teaching, thus corroborated, he found the solution of the problem that had caused him such anguish of soul. In this connection Augustin points out in some detail the features that Platonism and Christianity have in common. Thus Neo-Platonism, not blindly followed, but adapted to his Christian purpose, became not only a means of deliverance to Augustin himself, but a mighty weapon for the combating of Manichæan error.

Neo-Platonism enters so largely and influentially into Augustin's polemics against Manichæism that it will be apposite here to inquire into the extent and the nature of Augustin's dependence on this system of thought. Much has been written on this subject, especially by German and French scholars. A brief statement of some of the more important points of contact is all that is allowable in an essay like this. Premising, therefore, that Platonism essentially influenced the entire circle of Augustin's theological and philosophical thinking, let us first examine the Neo-Platonic and Augustinian conceptions of God. With Augustin God is absolutely simple and immutable, incomprehensible by men in their present state of existence, exalted above all human powers of thought or expression. All things may be said of God, and yet nothing worthily; God is honored more by reverential silence than by any human voice. He is better known by not being known; it is easier to say what He is not, than what He is. God is wanting in qualities; has no variety and multitude of properties and attributes; is absolutely simple. By no means is God to be called substance, for the word substance pertains to a certain accident; nor is it allowable to think of Him as composed of substance and of accidents. Divine qualities are therefore purely subjective. There is no discrimination in God of substance and accidents, of potency and act, of matter and form, of universal and singular, of superior and inferior. To know, to will, to do, to be, are in God equivalent and identical. Eternity itself is the substance of God, which has nothing mutable, nothing past, nothing future. God makes new things, without being Himself new, unchangeable He makes changeable things, He always works and always rests. The changes that take place in the world do not fall in the will of God, but solely in the things moved by God. God changes them out of His unchangeable counsel. For nearly every one of these statements an almost exact parallel can be pointed out in the writings of Plotinus, the Neo-Platonic writer with whom Augustin was most conversant.[2] It would be easy to point out that Augustin here goes to a dangerous extreme, and narrowly escapes fatalism on the one hand, and denial of the true personality of God on the other. But the effectiveness of this type of teaching against Manichæism is what chiefly interests us in this connection. Readers of the following treatises will have no difficulty in seeing for themselves how confidently and with what telling effect Augustin employs this view of God against the crudities of Manichæism, which thought of God as mutable, as capable of being successfully assailed by evil, as rent asunder, as suffering miserable contamination and imprisonment by mixture with matter, as painfully struggling for freedom, as suffering with the suffering of plants and animals, as liberated by their decay and by the digestive operations of the faithful, etc., etc.

Again, while still a Manichæan Augustin had thought and written much about beauty. On this point also, the throwing off of Manichæism and the adoption of a Platonizing Christianity brought about a revolution in his conceptions. The exactness with which he has followed Plotinus in his ideas of the beauty of God and of his creatures is remarkable. This we could fully illustrate by the citation of parallel passages. But we must content our-

---

[1] Confessions, Book. VII. ch. 9, vol. I. p. 108, of the present series.

[2] See G. LOESCHE: *De Augustino Plotinizante in Doctrina de Deo Disserenda*, Jenæ, 1880. Also, DORNER: *Augustinus*, ZELLER, UEBERWEG, RITTER, and ERDMANN: *Histories of Philosophy*, sections on Augustin and Neo-Platonism.

selves with remarking that Augustin himself acknowledged his indebtedness, and that his idea of beauty was an important factor in his polemics against Manichæism. According to Augustin (and Plotinus) God is the most beautiful and splendid of all beings. He is the beauty of all beauties; all the beautiful things that are the objects of our vision and love He Himself made. If these are beautiful what is He? All beauty is from the highest beauty, which is God. Augustin follows Plato and Plotinus even in neglecting the distinction between the good and the beautiful. The idea of Divine beauty Augustin applies to Christ also. He speaks of Him as beautiful God, beautiful Word with God, beautiful on earth, beautiful in the womb, beautiful in the hands of his parents, beautiful in miracles, beautiful in being scourged, beautiful when inciting to life, beautiful when not caring for death, beautiful when laying down his life, beautiful when taking it up again, beautiful in the sepulchre, beautiful in Heaven. The beauty of the creation, which is simply a reflection of the beauty of God, is not even disturbed by evil or sin. Beauty is with Augustin (and the Platonists) a comprehensive term, and is almost equivalent to perfect harmonv or symmetry of parts, perfect adaptation of beings to the ends for which they exist.

It is patent that this view of the beauty of God and His creation is diametrically opposed to the crude conceptions of Mani, with reference to the disorder of the universe, a disorder not confined even to the Kingdom of Darkness, but invading the Realm of Light itself. So also Augustin's Platonizing views of the creation must be taken into consideration in judging of his attitude towards Manichæism. It goes without saying that from Augustin's theological point of view, to account for creation is a matter of grave difficulty. How can there be a relation between the infinite and the finite? Any substantial connection is unthinkable. The only thing left is a relation of causality. The finite, according to Plotinus, is an accident, an image and shadow of God. It is constituted, established, sustained, and nourished by the Divine potency, and is therefore absolutely dependent upon God. The power that flows from God permeates each and every finite thing. God as one, whole, and indivisible, is perpetually present with his eternal process, to everything, everywhere. When Augustin teaches that God of his own free will, subject to no necessity, by His own Word created the world out of nothing, this statement might be taken in connection with his view of the absolute simplicity of God and the consequent denial of distinction between being, willing, doing, etc. The easiest way to get over the difficulty involved in creation was to maintain the simultaneous creation of all things. The six days of creation in Genesis are an accommodation to human modes of thinking. In some expressions Augustin approaches the Platonic doctrine of the ideal or archetypal world. Finite things, so far as they exist, are essence, *i.e.*, God; so far as they are not essence they do not exist at all. Thus the distinction between God and the world is almost obliterated. Again, whatever is finite and derivative is subject to negation or nothingness. Thus he goes along with Plato and Plotinus to the verge of denying the reality of derived existence, and so narrowly escapes pantheism.

It is easy to see how effectively this conception of creation might be employed against the Manichæan notion of the creation as something forced upon God by the powers of evil, and as a mere expedient for the gradual liberation of his imprisoned elements. The Manichæan limitation of God and his domain by the bordering Kingdom of Darkness, was in sheer opposition to Augustin's view of the indivisibility of God and his presence as a whole everywhere and always. Augustin's theory that nature or essence, as far as it has existence is God, is quite the antithesis of Mani's dualism, especially of his supposition that the Kingdom of Darkness is essentially and wholly evil. Augustin argued that even the inhabitants of the Kingdom of Darkness, and the King of Darkness himself, according to Mani's own representations, are good so far as they have essence or nature, and evil only so far as they are non-existent.

With Augustin's Platonizing view of creation is closely connected his theory of evil and his doctrine of divine providence. Evil with him, as with the Platonists, has no substantial existence. It is only privation of good. It is wanting in essence, substance, truth,—is in short mere negation, and so cannot have God for its efficient cause or author, or be referred to God. God would not have permitted evil unless by His own supreme power he had been able to make good use of it. He attempts, with some success, to show the advantages of the permission of evil in the world. God made all things good from the angels of heaven to the lowest beasts and herbs of the earth. Augustin delighted, with the Platonists, in dwelling upon the goodness of nature as shown in the animal and vegetable worlds, as well as in the great cosmical phenomena. Each creature of God has its place, some a higher, some a lower, but all so far as they conform to the idea of their creation, or to their nature, are good. So far as they fall short of this idea they are evil.

This principle Augustin applied with great force to the confutation of the Manichæan view of the substantiality and permanence of evil. This may be regarded as the central point in Augustin's controversies with the Manichæans. He evidently felt that the Manichæan view of evil was the citadel of their system, and he never wearied of assailing it. It would be beyond the scope of the present essay to inquire whether and how far Augustin himself became involved in error, in his efforts to dislodge the Manichæans. Far less satisfactory than his confutation of the fundamental principles of the Manichæan system were his answers to the Manichæan cavils against the Old Testament. If we may judge from the prominence given in the extant literature to the Old Testament question, this must have been the favorite point of attack with the Manichæans. The importance of the questions raised and the necessity of answering them was fully recognized by Augustin. His principal reliance is the allegorical or typological method of interpretation. It would be hard to find examples of more perverse allegorizing than Augustin's Anti-Manichæan treatises furnish. It will not be needful to adduce instances here, as readers of the treatises will discover them in abundance. Nothing more wearisome and disgusting in Biblical interpretation can well be conceived of than certain sections of *The Reply to Faustus, the Manichæan.* Yet Augustin did not fail entirely to recognize the distinction between Old Testament times and New, and he even suggests the theory "that God could in a former age and to a people of a lower moral standard, give commands to do actions, which we should think it wrong to do now. . . . There was a certain inward want, an unenlightenment, a rudeness of moral conception, in those to whom such commands were given; otherwise they would not have been given. God would not have given a command to slaughter a whole nation to an enlightened people."[1]

Yet with all the defects of Augustin's polemics against the Manichæans, they seem to have been adapted to the needs of the time. Well does Canon Mozley declare Augustin to have been "the most marvellous controversial phenomenon which the whole history of the Church from first to last presents. . . . Armed with superabundant facility of expression,—so that he himself observes that one who had written so much must have a good deal to answer for,—he was able to hammer any point of view which he wanted, and which was desirable as a counteracting one to a pervading heresy, with endless repetition upon the ear of the Church; at the same time varying the forms of speech sufficiently to please and enliven." Certainly he was one of the greatest debaters of any age. He doubtless deserves the credit of completely checking the progress of Manichæism in the West, and of causing its gradual but almost complete overthrow. His arguments were probably more effective in guarding Christians against perversion by Manichæan proselytizers, than in converting

[1] See J. B. Mozley's *Ruling Ideas in Early Ages*, art. The Manichæans and the Jewish Fathers. The sentence quoted above is Mozley's.

those that were already ensnared by Manichæan error. Other controversies of a completely different character, especially the Pelagian, caused Augustin to look to other aspects of truth and so led to certain modifications in his own statements, nay led him on some occasions to the verge of Manichæan error itself. But we are chiefly interested at present in knowing that his earnest efforts against the Manichæans from A.D. 388, the year of his baptism, to A.D. 405, were not in vain.[1]

CHAPTER X.—OUTLINE OF MANICHÆAN HISTORY.[2]

In the *East* Mani's followers were involved in the persecution that resulted in his death, and many of them fled to Transoxiania. Their headquarters and the residence of the chief of the sect continued to be Babylon. They returned to Persia in 661, but were driven back, 908–32. They seem to have become very numerous in the Transoxiania. Albîrûnî, 973–1048, speaks of the Manichæans as still existing in large numbers throughout all Mohammedan lands, and especially in the region of Samarkand, where they were known as Sabeans. He also relates that they were prevalent among the Eastern Turks, in China, Thibet and India. In Armenia and Cappadocia they gained many followers, and thence made their way into Europe. The Paulicians are commonly represented as a Manichæan party, but the descriptions that have come down to us would seem to indicate Marcionitic rather than Manichæan elements. Yet contemporary Catholic writers such as Peter Siculus and Photius constantly assail them as Manichæans.

In the *West* we have traces of their existence from 287 onwards. Diocletian, according to a somewhat doubtful tradition, condemned its leaders to the stake, and its adherents to decapitation with confiscation of goods. The edict is supposed to have been directed to the pro-consul of Africa where Manichæans were making great progress. According to an early account, Mani sent a special envoy to Africa. Valentinian (372) and Theodosius (381) issued bloody edicts against them, yet we find them still aggressive in the time of Augustin. From Africa Manichæism spread into Spain, Gaul and Aquitaine. Leo the Great and Valentinian III. took measures against them in Italy (440 sq.) They appear, however, to have continued their work, for Gregory the Great mentions them (590 sq.). From this time onwards their influence is to be traced in such parties as the Euchites, Enthusiasts, Bogomiles, Catharists, Beghards, etc. But it is not safe to attach too much importance to the mere fact that these parties were stigmatized as Manichæans by their enemies. Even in the Reformation time and since, individuals and small parties have appeared which in some features strongly resembled the ancient Manichæans. Manichæism was a product of the East, and in the East it met with most acceptance. To the spirit of the West it was altogether foreign, and only in a greatly modified form could it ever have flourished there. It might persist for centuries as a secret society, but it could not endure the light.

---

[1] For an account of the controversies in which Augustin was engaged with the Manichæans, and for the chronological order of the Anti-Manichæan treatises, see the Preface of the Edinburgh editor. Cf. BINDEMANN, on the various controversies, in his *Der h. Augustinus, passim.* See also, a good chronological list of St. Augustin's works in CUNNINGHAM: *St. Austin*, p. 277 sq.

[2] Compare Professor George T. Stokes' excellent article *Manichæans*, in SMITH and WACE: *Dict. of Chr. Biography*, vol. III. p. 798 sq.

PREFACE TO THE ANTI-MANICHÆAN WRITINGS.

No reader of the accompanying volume can be expected to take a very lively interest in its contents, unless he has before his mind some facts regarding the extraordinary genius to whom the heresy of Manichæism owes its origin and its name. His history is involved in considerable obscurity, owing to the suspicious nature of the documents from which it is derived, and the difficulty of constructing a consistent and probable account out of the contradictory statements of the Asiatics and the Greeks. The ascertained facts, therefore, are few, and may be briefly stated.[1]

According to the Chronicle of Edessa, Mani was born A.D. 240.[2] From his original name, Corbicius or Carcubius, Beausobre conjectures that he was born in Carcub, a town of Chaldæa. He belonged to a Magian family, and while still a youth won a distinguished place among the sages of Persia. He was master of all the lore peculiar to his class, and was, besides, so proficient a mathematician and geographer, that he was able to construct a globe. He was a skilled musician, and had some knowledge of the Greek language,—an accomplishment rare among his countrymen. But his fame, and even his ultimate success as a teacher, was due in great measure to his skill in painting, which was so considerable as to earn for him among the Persians the distinctive title, Mani the painter. His disposition was ardent and lively but patient and self-restrained. His appearance was striking, as he wore the usual dress of a Persian sage: the high-soled shoes, the one red, the other green; the mantle of azure blue, that changed color as he moved; the ebony staff in his right hand, and the Babylonish book under his left arm.

The meaning of his name, Mani, Manes, or Manichæus, has been the subject of endless conjectures. Epiphanius supposes that he was providentially so named, that men might be warned against the mania of his heresy.[3] Hyde, whose opinion on any Oriental subject must have weight, tells us that in Persian *mani* means painter, and that he was so called from his profession. Archbishop Usher conjectured that it was a form of *Manaem* or *Menahem*, which means Paraclete or Comforter; founding this conjecture on the fact that Sulpicius Severus calls the Israelitish king Menahem,[4] Mane. Gataker supplements this idea by the conjecture that Mani took this name at his own instance, and in pursuance of his claim to be the Paraclete. It is more probable that, if his name was really given on account of this meaning, he received it from the widow who seems to have adopted him when a boy, and may have called him her Consolation. But it is also possible that Mani was not an uncommon Persian name, and that he adopted it for some reason too trifling to discover.[5]

While still a young man he was ordained as a Christian priest, and distinguished himself in that capacity by his knowledge of Scripture, and the zeal with which he discharged his sacred functions.[6] His heretical tendencies, however, were very soon manifested, stimulated, we may suppose, by his anxiety to make the Christian religion more acceptable to those who adhered to the Eastern systems. Excommunicated from the Christian Church, Mani found asylum with Sapor, and won his confidence by presenting only the Magian side of his system. But no sooner did he permit the Christian element to appear, and call himself the apostle of the Lord, and show a desire to reform Magianism, than his sovereign determined to put him to death as a revolutionist. Forced to flee, he took refuge in Turkestan, and gained influence there, partly by decorating the temples with paintings. To lend his doctrines the appearance of divine authority, he adopted the same device as Zoroaster

---

1 Beausobre (*Histoire Critique de Manichée et du Manichéisme*, Amst. 1734, 2 vols.) has collected everything that is known of Mani. The original sources are here sifted with unusual acuteness, and with great and solid learning, though the author's strong "bias in favor of a heretic" frequently leads him to make unwarranted statements. Burton's estimate of this entertaining and indispensable work (*Heresies of Apostol. Age*, p. xxi.), is much fairer than Pusey's (*Aug. Conf.* p. 314). A brief account of Mani and his doctrines is given by Milman with his usual accuracy, impartiality and lucidity (*Hist. of Christianity*, ii. 259, ed. 1867). For any one who wishes to investigate the subject further, ample references are there given. A specimen of the confusion that involves the history of Mani will be found in the account given by Socrates (*Hist.* i. 22).

2 [For the Oriental accounts of Mani's parentage and youth, see the *Introductory Essay*, and the works there referred to.—A.H.N.]

3 See also EUSEBIUS: *Hist. Eccl.* vii. 31, with Heinichen's note.

4 Kings xv. 14.

5 "*Peut-être cherchons nous du mystere, ou il n'y en a point.*"—Beausobre, i. 79.

6 [This is in the highest degree improbable.—A.H.N.]

and Mohammed. Having discovered a cave through which there ran a rill of water, he laid up in it a store of provisions, and retired there for a year, giving out that he was on a visit to heaven. In this retirement he produced his *Gospel*,[1]—a work illustrated with symbolical drawings the ingenuity of which has been greatly praised. This book Mani presented to Hormizdas, the son and successor of Sapor, who professed himself favorable to his doctrine, and even built him a castle as a place of shelter and retirement. Unfortunately for Mani, Hormizdas died in the second year of his reign; and though his successor, Varanes, was at first willing to shield him from persecution, yet, finding that the Magians were alarmed for their religion, he appointed a disputation to be held between the opposing parties. Such trials of dialectic in Eastern courts have not unfrequently resulted in very serious consequences to the parties engaged in them. In this instance the result was fatal to Mani. Worsted in argument, he was condemned to die, and thus perished in some sense as a martyr. The mode of his death is uncertain,[2] but it seems that his skin was stuffed with chaff, and hung up in public *in terrorem*. This occurred in the year 277, and the anniversary was commemorated as the great religious festival of the Manichæans.

This is not the place to attempt any account or criticism of the strange eclecticism of Mani.[3] An adequate idea of the system may be gathered from the accompanying treatises. It may, however, be desirable to give some account of the original sources of information regarding it.

We study the systems of heresiarchs at a disadvantage when our only means of ascertaining their opinions is from the fragmentary quotations and hostile criticism which occur in the writings of their adversaries. Such, however, is our only source of information regarding the teaching of Mani. Originally, indeed, this heresy was specially active in a literary direction, assailing the Christian Scriptures with an ingenuity of unbelief worthy of a later age, and apparently ambitious of promulgating a rival canon. Certainly the writings of its early supporters were numerous;[4] and from the care and elegance with which they were transcribed, the sumptuous character of the manuscripts, and the mysterious emblems with which they were adorned, we should fancy it was intended to inspire the people with respect for an authoritative though as yet undefined code. It is, indeed, nowhere said or implied that the sacred books of the Manichæans were reserved for the eye only of the initiated or elect; and their reception of the New Testament Scriptures (subject to their own revision and emendation) would make it difficult for them to establish any secret code apart from these writings. They were certainly, however, doctrines of an esoteric kind, which were not divulged to the catechumens or hearers; and many of their books, being written in Persian, Syriac, or Greek, were practically unavailable for the instruction of the Latin speaking population. It was not always easy, therefore, to obtain an accurate knowledge of their opinions. Commentaries on the whole of the Old and New Testaments were written by Hierax;[5] a *Theosophy* by Aristocritus; a book of memoirs, or rather *Memorabilia*, of Mani, and other works, by Heraclides, Aphthonius, Adas, and Agapius. Unfortunately all of these books have perished, whether in the flames to which the Christian authorities commanded that all Manichæan books should be consigned, or by the slower if not more critical and impartial processes of time.

Mani himself was the author of several works: a *Gospel*, the *Treasury of Life* (and probably an abridgment of the same), the *Mysteries*, the *Foundation Epistle*, a book of *Articles* or heads of doctrine, one or two works on astronomy or astrology, and a collection of letters so dangerous, that Manichæans who sought restoration to the Church were required to anathematize them.

Probably the most important of these writings was the *Foundation Epistle*, so called because it contained the leading articles of doctrine on which the new system was built. This letter was written in Greek or Syriac; but a Latin version of it was current in Africa, and came into the hands of Augustin, who undertook its refutation. To accomplish this with the greater precision and effect, he quotes the entire text of each passage of the *Epistle* before proceeding to criticise it. Had Augustin accomplished the whole of his task, we should accordingly have been in possession of the whole of this important document. Unfortunately, for reasons unknown, Augustin stops short at an early point in the *Epistle;* and though he tells us he had notes on the remainder, and would some day expand and publish them, this promise lay unredeemed for thirty years till the day of his death. Extracts from the same *Epistle* and from the *Treasury* are also given by Augustin in the treatise *De Natura Boni*.[6]

---

1 Called Erteng or Arzeng, *i. e.*, according to Renaudot, an illustrated book.

2 Böhringer adopts the more horrible tradition. "*Sein Schicksal war, dass er von den Christen, von den Magiern verfolgt, nach mannigfachem Wechsel unter Bahram lebendig geschunden wurde*" (p. 386).

3 Böhringer characterizes it briefly in the words: "*Es ist der alte heidnische Dualismus mit seiner Naturtheologie, der in Mani's Systeme seine letzten Kräfte sammelt und unter der gleissenden Hülle christlicher Worte und Formen an den reinen Monotheismus des Christenthums und dessen reine Ethik sich heranwagt.*"

4 Aug. *c. Faustum*, xiii. 6 and 18. [See full list of Mani's writings in Kessler's art. in *Herzog*, R. E.—A.H.N.]

5 Lardner, however, seems to prove that Hierax was not a Manichæan, though some of his opinions approximated to this heresy. The whole subject of the Manichæan literature is treated by Lardner (*Works*, iii. p. 374), with the learning of Beausobre and more than Beausobre's impartiality.

6 The *De Natura Boni*, written in the year 405, is necessarily very much a reproduction of what is elsewhere affirmed, that all natures are good, and created by God, who alone is immutable and incorruptible. It presents concisely the leading positions of Augus-

Next, we have in the *Opus Imperfectum* of Augustin some extracts from a letter of Mani to Menoch, which Julian had unearthed and republished to convict Augustin of being still tainted with Manichæan sentiments. These extracts give us some insight into the heresiarch's opinions regarding the corruption of nature and the evils of sexual love.

Again, we have Mani's letter to Marcel, preserved by Epiphanius, and given in full by Beausobre;[1] which, however, merely reiterates two of the doctrines most certainly identified with Mani,—the assertion of two principles, and the tenet that the Son of God was man only in appearance.

Finally, Fabricius has inserted in the fifth volume of his *Bibliotheca Græca* the fragments, such as they are, collected by Grabe.

Such is the fragmentary character of the literary remains of Mani: for fuller information regarding his opinions we must depend on Theodoret, Epiphanius, Alexander of Lycopolis, Titus of Bostra, and Augustin. Beausobre is of opinion that the Fathers derived all that they knew of Manichæus from the *Acts of Archelaus*.[2] This professes to be a report of a disputation held between Manes and Archelaus, bishop of Caschar in Mesopotamia. Grave doubts have been cast on the authenticity of this document, and Burton and Milman seem inclined to consider it an imaginary dialogue, and use it on the understanding that while some of its statements are manifestly untrustworthy, a discriminating reader may gather from it some reliable material.[3]

In the works of Augustin there are some other pieces which may well be reckoned among the original sources. In the reply to Faustus, which is translated in this volume, the book of Faustus is not indeed reproduced; but there is no reason for doubting that his arguments are fairly represented, and we think there is evidence that even the original expression of them is preserved.[4] Augustin had been acquainted with Faustus for many years. He first met him at Carthage in 383, and found him nothing more than a clever and agreeable talker, making no pretension to science or philosophy, and with only slender reading.[5] His cleverness is sufficiently apparent in his debate with Augustin; the objections he leads are plausible, and put with acuteness, but at the same time with a flippancy which betrays a want of earnestness and real interest in the questions. In his reply to Faustus, Augustin is very much on the defensive, and his statements are apologetic rather than systematic.[6]

But in an age when the ability to read was by no means commensurate with the interest taken in theological questions, written discussions were necessarily supplemented by public disputations. These theological contests seem to have been a popular entertainment in North Africa; the people attending in immense crowds, while reporters took down what was said on either side for the sake of appeal as well as for the information of the absent. In tw such disputations Augustin engaged in connection with Manichæism.[7] The first was held on the 28th and 29th of August, 392, with a Manichæan priest, Fortunatus. To this encounter Augustin was invited by a deputation of Donatists and Catholics,[8] who were alike alarmed at the progress which this heresy was making in the district of Hippo. Fortunatus at first showed some reluctance to meet so formidable an antagonist, but was prevailed upon by his own sectaries, and shows no nervousness during the debate. His incompetence, however, was manifest to the Manichæans themselves; and so hopeless was it to think of any further proselytizing in Hippo, that he left that city, and was too much ashamed of himself ever to return. The character of his reasoning is shifty; he evades Augustin's questions and starts fresh ones. Augustin pushes his usual and fundamental objection to the Manichæan system. If God is impassable and incorruptible, how could He be injured by the assaults of the kingdom of darkness? In opposition to the statement of Fortunatus, that the Almighty produces no evil, he explains that God made no nature evil, but made man free, and that voluntary

---

tin in this controversy, and concludes with an eloquent prayer that his efforts may be blessed to the conversion of the heretics,—not the only passage which demonstrates that he wrote not for the glory of victory so much as for the deliverance of men from fatal error.

1 *Histoire*, i. 91.

2 Published by Zaccagni in his *Collectanea Monumentorum Veterum*, Romæ, 1698; and by Routh in his *Reliquiæ Sacræ*, vol. v., in which all the material for forming an opinion regarding it is collected.

3 Any one who consults Beausobre on this point will find that historical criticism is not of so recent an origin as some persons seem to think. It is worth transcribing his own account of the spirit in which he means to do his work: "*Je traiterai mon sujet en Critique, suivant la Regle de S. Paul, Examinez toutes choses, et ne retenez que ce qui est bon. L'Histoire en general, et l'Histoire Ecclesiastique en particulier, n'est bien souvent qu'un mélange confus de faux et de vrai, entasse par des Ecrivains mal instruits, credules ou passionez. Cela convient surtout a l'Histoire des Heretiques et des Heresies. C'est au Lecteur attentif et judicieux d'en faire le discernement, a l'aide d'une critique, qui ne soit trop timide, ni temeraire. Sans le secours de cet art, on erre dans l'Histoire comme un Pilote sur les mers, lorsqu'il n'a ni boussole, ni carte marine*" (i. 7).

4 Beausobre and Cave suppose that we have the whole of Faustus' book embodied in Augustin's review of it. Lardner is of opinion that the commencement, and perhaps the greater part, of the work is given, but not the whole.

5 See the interesting account of Faustus in the *Confessions*, v. 10.

6 [This estimate of Faustus is somewhat too disparaging. For fuller bibliography, see *Introductory Essay*.—A. H. N.]

7 His willingness to do so, and the success with which he encountered the most renowned champions of this heresy, should have prevented Beausobre from charging him with misunderstanding or misrepresenting the Manichæan doctrine. The retractation of Felix tells strongly against this view of Augustin's incompetence to deal with Manichæism.

8 Possidius, *Vita Aug.* vi.

sin is the grand original evil. The most remarkable circumstance in the discussion is the desire of Fortunatus to direct the conversation to the conduct of the Manichæans, and the refusal of Augustin to make good the charges which had been made against them, or to discuss anything but the doctrine.[1]

Twelve years after this, a similar disputation was held between Augustin and one of the elect among the Manichæans, who had come to Hippo to propagate his religion. This man, Felix, is described by Augustin[2] as being ill-educated, but more adroit and subtle than Fortunatus. After a keen discussion, which occupied two days, the proceedings terminated by Felix signing a recantation of his errors in the form of an anathema on Mani, his doctrines, and the seducing spirit that possessed him. These two disputations are valuable, as exhibiting the points of the Manichæan system to which its own adherents were accustomed to direct attention, and the arguments on which they specially relied for their support.

The works given in the accompanying volume comprehend by no means the whole of Augustin's writings against this heresy. Before his ordination he wrote five anti-Manichæan books, entitled, *De Libero Arbitrio*, *De Genesi contra Manichæos*, *De Moribus Ecclesiæ Catholicæ*, *De Moribus Manichæorum*, and *De Vera Religione*. These Paulinus called his anti-Manichæan Pentateuch. After his ordination he was equally diligent, publishing a little treatise in the year 391, under the title *De Utilitate Credendi*,[3] which was immediately followed by a small work, *De Duabus Animabus*. In the following year the report of the *Disputatio contra Fortunatum* was published; and after this, at short intervals, there appeared the books *Contra Adimantum*, *Contra Epistolam Manichæi quam vocant Fundamenti*, *Contra Faustum*, *Disputatio contra Felicem*, *De Natura Boni*, and *Contra Secundinum*.

Besides these writings, which are exclusively occupied with Manichæism, there are others in which the Manichæan doctrines are handled with more or less directness. These are the *Confessions*, the 79th and 236th Letters, the Lecture on Psalm 140, Sermons 1, 2, 12, 50, 153, 182, 237, the *Liber de Agone Christiano*, and the *De Continentia*.

Of these writings, Augustin himself professed a preference for the reply to the letter of Secundinus.[4] It is a pleasing feature of the times, that a heretic whom he did not know even by sight should write to Augustin entreating him to abstain from writing against the Manichæans, and reconsider his position, and ally himself with those whom he had till now fancied to be in error. His language is respectful, and illustrates the esteem in which Augustin was held by his contemporaries; though he does not scruple to insinuate that his conversion from Manichæism was due to motives not of the highest kind. We have not given this letter and its reply, because the preference of Augustin has not been ratified by the judgment of his readers.

The present volume gives a fair sample of Augustin's controversial powers. His nine years' personal experience of the vanity of Manichæism made him thoroughly earnest and sympathetic in his efforts to disentangle other men from its snares, and also equipped him with the knowledge requisite for this task. No doubt the Pelagian controversy was more congenial to his mind. His logical acuteness and knowledge of Scripture availed him more in combating men who fought with the same weapons, than in dealing with a system which threw around its positions the mist of Gnostic speculation, or veiled its doctrine under a grotesque mythology, or based itself on a cosmogony too fantastic for a Western mind to tolerate.[5] But however Augustin may have misconceived the strange forms in which this system was presented, there is no doubt that he comprehended and demolished its fundamental principles;[6] that he did so as a necessary part of his own personal search for the truth; and that in doing so he gained possession, vitally and permanently of ideas and principles which subsequently entered into all he thought and wrote. In finding his way through the mazes of the obscure region into which Mani had led him, he once for all ascertained the true relation subsisting between God and His creatures, formed his opinion regarding the respective provinces of reason and faith, and the connection of the Old and New Testaments, and found the root of all evil in the created will. THE EDITOR.

Some knowledge of the Magianism of the time of Mani may be obtained from the sacred books of the Parsis, especially from the *Vendidad Sade*, an account of which is given by Dr. Wilson, of Bombay, in his book on the Parsi Religion.—TR.

---

1 This cannot but make us cautious in receiving the statements of the tract, *On the Morals of the Manichæans*. There can be little doubt that many of the Manichæans practiced the ascetic virtues, and were recognizable by the gauntness and pallor of their looks, so that *Manichæan* became a by-word for any one who did not appreciate the felicity of good living. Thus Jerome says of a certain class of women, "*quam viderint pallentem atque tristem, Miseram, Monacham, et Manichæan vocant*" (*De Custod. Virg. Ep.* 18). Lardner throws light on the practices of the Manichæans, and effectually disposes of some of the calumnies uttered regarding them. Pusey's appendix to his translation of the *Confessions* may also be referred to with advantage.

2 *Retract.* ii. 8.

3 *Epist. August.* xxv.

4 *Retract.* ii. 10: "*quod, mea sententia, omnibus quæ adversus illam pestem scribere potui, facile præpono.*" The reason of this preference is explained by Bindemann, *Der heilige Augustinus*, iii. 168.

5 "*Wo Entwickelungen, dialektische Begriffe sein sollten, stellt sich ein Bild, ein Mythus ein.*"—Böhringer, p. 390.

6 Some have thought Augustin more successful here than elsewhere. Cassiodorus may have thought so when he said: "*diligentius atque vivacius adversus eos quam contra hæreses alias disseruit*" (*Instit.* i. quoted by Lardner).

ST. AUGUSTIN:

ON THE

MORALS OF THE CATHOLIC CHURCH.

[DE MORIBUS ECCLESIÆ CATHOLICÆ].

A.D. 388.

TRANSLATED BY

REV. RICHARD STOTHERT, M.A.,

BOMBAY

CONTENTS OF THE MORALS OF THE CATHOLIC CHURCH.

OF THE

MORALS OF THE CATHOLIC CHURCH.[1]

[DE MORIBUS ECCLESIÆ CATHOLICÆ]. A.D. 388.

IT IS LAID DOWN AT THE OUTSET THAT THE CUSTOMS OF THE HOLY LIFE OF THE CHURCH SHOULD BE REFERRED TO THE CHIEF GOOD OF MAN, THAT IS, GOD. WE MUST SEEK AFTER GOD WITH SUPREME AFFECTION; AND THIS DOCTRINE IS SUPPORTED IN THE CATHOLIC CHURCH BY THE AUTHORITY OF BOTH TESTAMENTS. THE FOUR VIRTUES GET THEIR NAMES FROM DIFFERENT FORMS OF THIS LOVE. THEN FOLLOW THE DUTIES OF LOVE TO OUR NEIGHBOR. IN THE CATHOLIC CHURCH WE FIND EXAMPLES OF CONTINENCE AND OF TRUE CHRISTIAN CONDUCT.

CHAP. I.—HOW THE PRETENSIONS OF THE MANICHÆANS ARE TO BE REFUTED. TWO MANICHÆAN FALSEHOODS.

1. ENOUGH, probably, has been done in our other books[2] in the way of answering the ignorant and profane attacks which the Manichæans make on the law, which is called the Old Testament, in a spirit of vainglorious boasting, and with the approval of the uninstructed. Here, too, I may shortly touch upon the subject. For every one with average intelligence can easily see that the explanation of the Scriptures should be sought for from those who are the professed teachers of the Scriptures; and that it may happen, and indeed always happens, that many things seem absurd to the ignorant, which, when they are explained by the learned, appear all the more excellent, and are received in the explanation with the greater pleasure on account of the obstructions which made it difficult to reach the meaning. This commonly happens as regards the holy books of the Old Testament, if only the man who meets with difficulties applies to a pious teacher, and not to a profane critic, and if he begins his inquiries from a desire to find truth, and not in rash opposition. And should the inquirer meet with some, whether bishops or presbyters, or any officials or ministers of the Catholic Church, who either avoid in all cases opening up mysteries, or, content with simple faith, have no desire for more recondite knowledge, he must not despair of finding the knowledge of the truth in a case where neither are all able to teach to whom the inquiry is addressed, nor are all inquirers worthy of learning the truth. Diligence and piety are both necessary: on the one hand, we must have knowledge to find truth, and, on the other hand, we must deserve to get the knowledge.

2. But as the Manichæans have two tricks for catching the unwary, so as to make them take them as teachers,—one, that of finding fault with the Scriptures, which they either misunderstand or wish to be misunderstood, the other, that of making a show of chastity and of notable abstinence,—this book shall

---

[1] Written in the year 388. In his *Retractations* (i. 7) Augustin says· "When I was at Rome after my baptism, and could not bear in silence the vaunting of the Manichæans about their pretended and misleading continence or abstinence, in which, to deceive the inexperienced, they claim superiority over true Christians, to whom they are not to be compared, I wrote two books, one on the morals of the Catholic Church, the other on the morals of the Manichæans."

[2] [This is commonly supposed to have been the first work of any importance written by the Author against Manichæism. What he here refers to it is not easy to conjecture.—A. H. N.]

contain our doctrine of life and morals according to Catholic teaching, and will perhaps make it appear how easy it is to pretend to virtue, and how difficult to possess virtue. I will refrain, if I can, from attacking their weak points, which I know well, with the violence with which they attack what they know nothing of; for I wish them, if possible, to be cured rather than conquered. And I will quote such testimonies from the Scriptures as they are bound to believe, for they shall be from the New Testament; and even from this I will take none of the passages which the Manichæans when hard pressed are accustomed to call spurious, but passages which they are obliged to acknowledge and approve. And for every testimony from apostolic teaching I will bring a similar statement from the Old Testament, that if they ever become willing to wake up from their persistent dreams, and to rise towards the light of Christian faith, they may discover both how far from being Christian is the life which they profess, and how truly Christian is the Scripture which they cavil at.

CHAP. 2.—HE BEGINS WITH ARGUMENTS, IN COMPLIANCE WITH THE MISTAKEN METHOD OF THE MANICHÆANS.

3. Where, then, shall I begin? With authority, or with reasoning? In the order of nature, when we learn anything, authority precedes reasoning. For a reason may seem weak, when, after it is given, it requires authority to confirm it. But because the minds of men are obscured by familiarity with darkness, which covers them in the night of sins and evil habits, and cannot perceive in a way suitable to the clearness and purity of reason, there is most wholesome provision for bringing the dazzled eye into the light of truth under the congenial shade of authority. But since we have to do with people who are perverse in all their thoughts and words and actions, and who insist on nothing more than on beginning with argument, I will, as a concession to them, take what I think a wrong method in discussion. For I like to imitate, as far as I can, the gentleness of my Lord Jesus Christ, who took on Himself the evil of death itself, wishing to free us from it.

CHAP. 3.—HAPPINESS IS IN THE ENJOYMENT OF MAN'S CHIEF GOOD. TWO CONDITIONS OF THE CHIEF GOOD: 1ST, NOTHING IS BETTER THAN IT; 2D, IT CANNOT BE LOST AGAINST THE WILL.

4. How then, according to reason, ought man to live? We all certainly desire to live happily; and there is no human being but assents to this statement almost before it is made. But the title happy cannot, in my opinion, belong either to him who has not what he loves, whatever it may be, or to him who has what he loves if it is hurtful, or to him who does not love what he has, although it is good in perfection. For one who seeks what he cannot obtain suffers torture, and one who has got what is not desirable is cheated, and one who does not seek for what is worth seeking for is diseased. Now in all these cases the mind cannot but be unhappy, and happiness and unhappiness cannot reside at the same time in one man; so in none of these cases can the man be happy. I find, then, a fourth case, where the happy life exists,—when that which is man's chief good is both loved and possessed. For what do we call enjoyment but having at hand the objects of love? And no one can be happy who does not enjoy what is man's chief good, nor is there any one who enjoys this who is not happy. We must then have at hand our chief good, if we think of living happily.

5. We must now inquire what is man's chief good, which of course cannot be anything inferior to man himself. For whoever follows after what is inferior to himself, becomes himself inferior. But every man is bound to follow what is best. Wherefore man's chief good is not inferior to man. Is it then something similar to man himself? It must be so, if there is nothing above man which he is capable of enjoying. But if we find something which is both superior to man, and can be possessed by the man who loves it, who can doubt that in seeking for happiness man should endeavor to reach that which is more excellent than the being who makes the endeavor. For if happiness consists in the enjoyment of a good than which there is nothing better, which we call the chief good, how can a man be properly called happy who has not yet attained to his chief good? or how can that be the chief good beyond which something better remains for us to arrive at? Such, then, being the chief good, it must be something which cannot be lost against the will. For no one can feel confident regarding a good which he knows can be taken from him, although he wishes to keep and cherish it. But if a man feels no confidence regarding the good which he enjoys, how can he be happy while in such fear of losing it?

CHAP. 4.—MAN—WHAT?

6. Let us then see what is better than man. This must necessarily be hard to find, unless

we first ask and examine what man is. I am not now called upon to give a definition of man. The question here seems to me to be, —since almost all agree, or at least, which is enough, those I have now to do with are of the same opinion with me, that we are made up of soul and body,—What is man? Is he both of these? or is he the body only, or the soul only? For although the things are two, soul and body, and although neither without the other could be called man (for the body would not be man without the soul, nor again would the soul be man if there were not a body animated by it), still it is possible that one of these may be held to be man, and may be called so. What then do we call man? Is he soul and body, as in a double harness, or like a centaur? Or do we mean the body only, as being in the service of the soul which rules it, as the word lamp denotes not the light and the case together, but only the case, yet it is on account of the light that it is so called? Or do we mean only the mind, and that on account of the body which it rules, as horseman means not the man and the horse, but the man only, and that as employed in ruling the horse? This dispute is not easy to settle; or, if the proof is plain, the statement requires time. This is an expenditure of time and strength which we need not incur. For whether the name man belongs to both, or only to the soul, the chief good of man is not the chief good of the body; but what is the chief good either of both soul and body, or of the soul only, that is man's chief good.

CHAP. 5.—MAN'S CHIEF GOOD IS NOT THE CHIEF GOOD OF THE BODY ONLY, BUT THE CHIEF GOOD OF THE SOUL.

7. Now if we ask what is the chief good of the body, reason obliges us to admit that it is that by means of which the body comes to be in its best state. But of all the things which invigorate the body, there is nothing better or greater than the soul. The chief good of the body, then, is not bodily pleasure, not absence of pain, not strength, not beauty, not swiftness, or whatever else is usually reckoned among the goods of the body, but simply the soul. For all the things mentioned the soul supplies to the body by its presence, and, what is above them all, life. Hence I conclude that the soul is not the chief good of man, whether we give the name of man to soul and body together, or to the soul alone. For as, according to reason, the chief good of the body is that which is better than the body, and from which the body receives vigor and life, so whether the soul itself is man, or soul and body both, we must discover whether there is anything which goes before the soul itself, in following which the soul comes to the perfection of good of which it is capable in its own kind. If such a thing can be found, all uncertainty must be at an end, and we must pronounce this to be really and truly the chief good of man.

8. If, again, the body is man, it must be admitted that the soul is the chief good of man. But clearly, when we treat of morals, —when we inquire what manner of life must be held in order to obtain happiness,—it is not the body to which the precepts are addressed, it is not bodily discipline which we discuss. In short, the observance of good *customs* belongs to that part of us which inquires and learns, which are the prerogatives of the soul; so, when we speak of attaining to virtue, the question does not regard the body. But if it follows, as it does, that the body which is ruled over by a soul possessed of virtue is ruled both better and more honorably, and is in its greatest perfection in consequence of the perfection of the soul which rightfully governs it, that which gives perfection to the soul will be man's chief good, though we call the body man. For if my coachman, in obedience to me, feeds and drives the horses he has charge of in the most satisfactory manner, himself enjoying the more of my bounty in proportion to his good conduct, can any one deny that the good condition of the horses, as well as that of the coachman, is due to me? So the question seems to me to be not, whether soul and body is man, or the soul only, or the body only, but what gives perfection to the soul; for when this is obtained, a man cannot but be either perfect, or at least much better than in the absence of this one thing.

CHAP. 6.—VIRTUE GIVES PERFECTION TO THE SOUL; THE SOUL OBTAINS VIRTUE BY FOLLOWING GOD; FOLLOWING GOD IS THE HAPPY LIFE.

9. No one will question that virtue gives perfection to the soul. But it is a very proper subject of inquiry whether this virtue can exist by itself or only in the soul. Here again arises a profound discussion, needing lengthy treatment; but perhaps my summary will serve the purpose. God will, I trust, assist me, so that, notwithstanding our feebleness, we may give instruction on these great matters briefly as well as intelligibly. In either case, whether virtue can exist by itself without the soul, or can exist only in the soul, undoubtedly in the pursuit of virtue the soul follows after something, and this must be

either the soul itself, or virtue, or something else. But if the soul follows after itself in the pursuit of virtue, it follows after a foolish thing; for before obtaining virtue it is foolish. Now the height of a follower's desire is to reach that which he follows after. So the soul must either not wish to reach what it follows after, which is utterly absurd and unreasonable, or, in following after itself while foolish, it reaches the folly which it flees from. But if it follows after virtue in the desire to reach it, how can it follow what does not exist? or how can it desire to reach what it already possesses? Either, therefore, virtue exists beyond the soul, or if we are not allowed to give the name of virtue except to the habit and disposition of the wise soul, which can exist only in the soul, we must allow that the soul follows after something else in order that virtue may be produced in itself; for neither by following after nothing, nor by following after folly, can the soul, according to my reasoning, attain to wisdom.

10. This something else then, by following after which the soul becomes possessed of virtue and wisdom, is either a wise man or God. But we have said already that it must be something that we cannot lose against our will. No one can think it necessary to ask whether a wise man, supposing we are content to follow after him, can be taken from us in spite of our unwillingness or our persistence. God then remains, in following after whom we live well, and in reaching whom we live both well and happily. If any deny God's existence, why should I consider the method of dealing with them, when it is doubtful whether they ought to be dealt with at all? At any rate, it would require a different starting-point, a different plan, a different investigation from what we are now engaged in. I am now addressing those who do not deny the existence of God, and who, moreover, allow that human affairs are not disregarded by Him. For there is no one, I suppose, who makes any profession of religion but will hold that divine Providence cares at least for our souls.

CHAP. 7.—THE KNOWLEDGE OF GOD TO BE OBTAINED FROM THE SCRIPTURE. THE PLAN AND PRINCIPAL MYSTERIES OF THE DIVINE SCHEME OF REDEMPTION.

11. But how can we follow after Him whom we do not see? or how can we see Him, we who are not only men, but also men of weak understanding? For though God is seen not with the eyes but with the mind, where can such a mind be found as shall, while obscured by foolishness, succeed or even attempt to drink in that light? We must therefore have recourse to the instructions of those whom we have reason to think wise. Thus far argument brings us. For in human things reasoning is employed, not as of greater certainty, but as easier from use. But when we come to divine things, this faculty turns away; it cannot behold; it pants, and gasps, and burns with desire; it falls back from the light of truth, and turns again to its wonted obscurity, not from choice, but from exhaustion. What a dreadful catastrophe is this, that the soul should be reduced to greater helplessness when it is seeking rest from its toil! So, when we are hasting to retire into darkness, it will be well that by the appointment of adorable Wisdom we should be met by the friendly shade of authority, and should be attracted by the wonderful character of its contents, and by the utterances of its pages, which, like shadows, typify and attemper the truth.

12. What more could have been done for our salvation? What can be more gracious and bountiful than divine providence, which, when man had fallen from its laws, and, in just retribution for his coveting mortal things, had brought forth a mortal offspring, still did not wholly abandon him? For in this most righteous government, whose ways are strange and inscrutable, there is, by means of unknown connections established in the creatures subject to it, both a severity of punishment and a mercifulness of salvation. How beautiful this is, how great, how worthy of God, in fine, how true, which is all we are seeking for, we shall never be able to perceive, unless, beginning with things human and at hand, and holding by the faith and the precepts of true religion, we continue without turning from it in the way which God has secured for us by the separation of the patriarchs, by the bond of the law, by the foresight of the prophets, by the witness of the apostles, by the blood of the martyrs, and by the subjugation of the Gentiles. From this point, then, let no one ask me for my opinion, but let us rather hear the oracles, and submit our weak inferences to the announcements of Heaven.[1]

CHAP. 8.—GOD IS THE CHIEF GOOD, WHOM WE ARE TO SEEK AFTER WITH SUPREME AFFECTION.

13. Let us see how the Lord Himself in the gospel has taught us to live; how, too, Paul the apostle,—for the Manichæans dare not reject these Scriptures. Let us hear, O Christ, what chief end Thou dost prescribe to us; and that is evidently the chief end

[1] [Augustin's transition from his fine Platonizing discussion of virtue, the chief good, etc., to the patriarchs, the law, and the prophets is very fine rhetorically and apologetically.—A. H. N.]

after which we are told to strive with supreme affection. "Thou shalt love," He says, "the Lord thy God." Tell me also, I pray Thee, what must be the measure of love; for I fear lest the desire enkindled in my heart should either exceed or come short in fervor. "With all thy heart," He says. Nor is that enough. "With all thy soul." Nor is it enough yet. "With all thy mind."[1] What do you wish more? I might, perhaps, wish more if I could see the possibility of more. What does Paul say on this? "We know," he says, "that all things issue in good to them that love God." Let him, too, say what is the measure of love. "Who then," he says, "shall separate us from the love of Christ? shall tribulation, or distress, or persecution, or famine, or nakedness, or peril, or the sword?"[2] We have heard, then, what and how much we must love; this we must strive after, and to this we must refer all our plans. The perfection of all our good things and our perfect good is God. We must neither come short of this nor go beyond it: the one is dangerous, the other impossible.

CHAP. 9.—HARMONY OF THE OLD AND NEW TESTAMENT ON THE PRECEPTS OF CHARITY.[3]

14. Come now, let us examine, or rather let us take notice,—for it is obvious and can be seen, at once,—whether the authority of the Old Testament too agrees with those statements taken from the gospel and the apostle. What need to speak of the first statement, when it is clear to all that it is a quotation from the law given by Moses? For it is there written, "Thou shalt love the Lord thy God with all thy heart, and with all thy soul, and with all thy mind."[4] And not to go farther for a passage of the Old Testament to compare with that of the apostle, he has himself added one. For after saying that no tribulation, no distress, no persecution, no pressure of bodily want, no peril, no sword, separates us from the love of Christ, he immediately adds, "As it is written, For Thy sake we are in suffering all the day long; we are accounted as sheep for the slaughter."[5] The Manichæans are in the habit of saying that this is an interpolation,—so unable are they to reply, that they are forced in their extremity to say this. But every one can see that this is all that is left for men to say when it is proved that they are wrong.

15. And yet I ask them if they deny that this is said in the Old Testament, or if they hold that the passage in the Old Testament does not agree with that of the apostle. For the first, the books will prove it; and as for the second, those prevaricators who fly off at a tangent will be brought to agree with me, if they will only reflect a little and consider what is said, or else I will press upon them the opinion of those who judge impartially. For what could agree more harmoniously than these passages? For tribulation, distress, persecution, famine, nakedness, peril, cause great suffering to man while in this life. So all these words are implied in the single quotation from the law, where it is said, "For Thy sake we are in suffering."[6] The only other thing is the sword, which does not inflict a painful life, but removes whatever life it meets with. Answering to this are the words, "We are accounted as sheep for the slaughter." And love could not have been more plainly expressed than by the words, "For Thy sake." Suppose, then, that this testimony is not found in the Apostle Paul, but is quoted by me, must you not prove, you heretic, either that this is not written in the old law, or that it does not harmonize with the apostle? And if you dare not say either of these things (for you are shut up by the reading of the manuscript, which will show that it is written, and by common sense, which sees that nothing could agree better with what is said by the apostle), why do you imagine that there is any force in accusing the Scriptures of being corrupted? And once more, what will you reply to a man who says to you, This is what I understand, this is my view, this is my belief, and I read these books only because I see that everything in them agrees with the Christian faith? Or tell me at once if you will venture deliberately to tell me to the face that we are not to believe that the apostles and martyrs are spoken of as having endured great sufferings for Christ's sake, and as having been accounted by their persecutors as sheep for the slaughter? If you cannot say this, why should you bring a charge against the book in which I find what you acknowledge I ought to believe?

---

1 Matt. xxii. 37.
2 Rom. viii. 28, 35.
3 [The most satisfactory feature of Augustin's apology for the Old Testament Scriptures is his demonstration of the substantial agreement of the Old Testament with undisputed portions of the New Testament.—A. H. N.]
4 Deut. vi. 5.
5 Rom. viii. 36; cf. Ps. xliv. 22.

6 *Retract.* i. 7, § 2:—"In the book on the morals of the Catholic Church, where I have quoted the words, 'For Thy sake we are in suffering all day long, we are accounted as sheep for the slaughter,' the inaccuracy of my manuscript misled me; for my recollection of the Scriptures was defective from my not being at that time familiar with them. For the reading of the other manuscripts has a different meaning: not, we suffer, but we suffer death, or, in one word, we are killed. That this is the true reading is shown by the Greek text of the Septuagint, from which the Old Testament was translated into Latin. I have indeed made a good many remarks on the words, 'For thy sake we suffer,' and the things said are not wrong in themselves; but, as regards the harmony of the Old and New Testaments, this case certainly does not prove it. The error originated in the way mentioned above, and this harmony is afterwards abundantly proved from other passages."

CHAP. 10.—WHAT THE CHURCH TEACHES ABOUT GOD. THE TWO GODS OF THE MANICHÆANS.

16. Will you say that you grant that we are bound to love God, but not the God worshipped by those who acknowledge the authority of the Old Testament? In that case you refuse to worship the God who made heaven and earth, for this is the God set forth all through these books. And you admit that the whole of the world, which is called heaven and earth, had God and a good God for its author and maker. For in speaking to you about God we must make a distinction. For you hold that there are two gods, one good and the other bad.

But if you say that you worship and approve of worshipping the God who made heaven and earth, but not the God supported by the authority of the Old Testament, you act impertinently in trying, though vainly, to attribute to us views and opinions altogether unlike the wholesome and profitable doctrine we really hold. Nor can your silly and profane discourses be at all compared with the expositions in which learned and pious men of the Catholic Church open up those Scriptures to the willing and worthy. Our understanding of the law and the prophets is quite different from what you suppose. Mistake us no longer. We do not worship a God who repents, or is envious, or needy, or cruel, or who takes pleasure in the blood of men or beasts, or is pleased with guilt and crime, or whose possession of the earth is limited to a little corner of it. These and such like are the silly notions you are in the habit of denouncing at great length. Your denunciation does not touch us. The fancies of old women or of children you attack with a vehemence that is only ridiculous. Any one whom you persuade in this way to join you shows no fault in the teaching of the Church, but only proves his own ignorance of it.

17. If, then, you have any human feeling,—if you have any regard for your own welfare,—you should rather examine with diligence and piety the meaning of these passages of Scripture. You should examine, unhappy beings that you are; for we condemn with no less severity and copiousness any faith which attributes to God what is unbecoming Him, and in those by whom these passages are literally understood we correct the mistake of ignorance, and look upon persistence in it as absurd. And in many other things which you cannot understand there is in the Catholic teaching a check on the belief of those who have got beyond mental childishness, not in years, but in knowledge and understanding—old in the progress towards wisdom. For we learn the folly of believing that God is bounded by any amount of space, even though infinite; and it is held unlawful to think of God, or any part of Him, as moving from one place to another. And should any one suppose that anything in God's substance or nature can suffer change or conversion, he will be held guilty of wild profanity. There are thus among us children who think of God as having a human form, which they suppose He really has, which is a most degrading idea; and there are many of full age to whose mind the majesty of God appears in its inviolableness and unchangeableness as not only above the human body, but above their own mind itself. These ages, as we said, are distinguished not by time, but by virtue and discretion. Among you, again, there is no one who will picture God in a human form; but neither is there one who sets God apart from the contamination of human error. As regards those who are fed like crying babies at the breast of the Catholic Church, if they are not carried off by heretics, they are nourished according to the vigor and capacity of each, and arrive at last, one in one way and another in another, first to a perfect man, and then to the maturity and hoary hairs of wisdom, when they may get life as they desire, and life in perfect happiness.

CHAP. 11.—GOD IS THE ONE OBJECT OF LOVE; THEREFORE HE IS MAN'S CHIEF GOOD. NOTHING IS BETTER THAN GOD. GOD CANNOT BE LOST AGAINST OUR WILL.

18. Following after God is the desire of happiness; to reach God is happiness itself. We follow after God by loving Him; we reach Him, not by becoming entirely what He is, but in nearness to Him, and in wonderful and immaterial contact with Him, and in being inwardly illuminated and occupied by His truth and holiness. He is light itself; we get enlightenment from Him. The greatest commandment, therefore, which leads to happy life, and the first, is this: "Thou shalt love the Lord thy God with all thy heart, and soul, and mind." For to those who love the Lord all things issue in good. Hence Paul adds shortly after, "I am persuaded that neither death, nor life, nor angels, nor virtue, nor things present, nor things future, nor height, nor depth, nor any other creature,

[1] [Augustin's *virtus* takes the place of the Greek δυνάμεις and the Vulgate *virtutes*. It is not quite certain what meaning he attached to the expression. He seems to waver between the idea of *power* and that of *virtue* in the ethical sense, and finally settles down to the use of the term in the latter sense. That this does not accord with the meaning of the Apostle is evident.—A. H. N.]

shall be able to separate us from the love of God, which is in Christ Jesus our Lord."[1] If, then, to those who love God all things issue in good, and if, as no one doubts, the chief or perfect good is not only to be loved, but to be loved so that nothing shall be loved better, as is expressed in the words, "With all thy soul, with all thy heart, and with all thy mind," who, I ask, will not at once conclude, when these things are all settled and most surely believed, that our chief good which we must hasten to arrive at in preference to all other things is nothing else than God? And then, if nothing can separate us from His love, must not this be surer as well as better than any other good?

19. But let us consider the points separately. No one separates us from this by threatening death. For that with which we love God cannot die, except in not loving God; for death is not to love God, and that is when we prefer anything to Him in affection and pursuit. No one separates us from this in promising life; for no one separates us from the fountain in promising water. Angels do not separate us; for the mind cleaving to God is not inferior in strength to an angel. Virtue does not separate us; for if what is here called virtue is that which has power in this world, the mind cleaving to God is far above the whole world. Or if this virtue is perfect rectitude of our mind itself, this in the case of another will favor our union with God, and in ourselves will itself unite us with God. Present troubles do not separate us; for we feel their burden less the closer we cling to Him from whom they try to separate us. The promise of future things does not separate us; for both future good of every kind is surest in the promise of God, and nothing is better than God Himself, who undoubtedly is already present to those who truly cleave to Him. Height and depth do not separate us; for if the height and depth of knowledge are what is meant, I will rather not be inquisitive than be separated from God; nor can any instruction by which error is removed separate me from Him, by separation from whom it is that any one is in error. Or if what is meant are the higher and lower parts of this world, how can the promise of heaven separate me from Him who made heaven? Or who from beneath can frighten me into forsaking God, when I should not have known of things beneath but by forsaking Him? In fine, what place can remove me from His love, when He could not be all in every place unless He were contained in none?

[1] Rom. viii. 38, 39.

CHAP. 12.—WE ARE UNITED TO GOD BY LOVE, IN SUBJECTION TO HIM.

20. "No other creature," he says, separates us. O man of profound mysteries! He thought it not enough to say, no creature: but he says no other creature; teaching that that with which we love God and by which we cleave to God, our mind, namely, and understanding, is itself a creature. Thus the body is another creature; and if the mind is an object of intellectual perception, and is known only by this means, the other creature is all that is an object of sense, which as it were makes itself known through the eyes, or ears, or smell, or taste, or touch, and this must be inferior to what is perceived by the intellect alone. Now, as God also can be known by the worthy, only intellectually,[2] exalted though He is above the intelligent mind as being its Creator and Author, there was danger lest the human mind, from being reckoned among invisible and immaterial things, should be thought to be of *the same* nature with Him who created it, and so should fall away by pride from Him to whom it should be united by love. For the mind becomes like God, to the extent vouchsafed by its subjection of itself to Him for information and enlightenment. And if it obtains the greatest nearness by that subjection which produces likeness, it must be far removed from Him by that presumption which would make the likeness greater. It is this presumption which leads the mind to refuse obedience to the laws of God, in the desire to be sovereign, as God is.

21. The farther, then, the mind departs from God, not in space, but in affection and lust after things below Him, the more it is filled with folly and wretchedness. So by love it returns to God,—a love which places it not along with God, but under Him. And the more ardor and eagerness there is in this, the happier and more elevated will the mind be, and with God as sole governor it will be in perfect liberty. Hence it must know that it is a creature. It must believe what is the truth,—that its Creator remains ever possessed of the inviolable and immutable nature of truth and wisdom, and must confess, even in view of the errors from which it desires deliverance, that it is liable to folly and falsehood. But then again, it must take care that it be not separated by the love of the other creature, that is, of this visible world, from the love of God Himself, which sanctifies it in order to lasting happiness. No

[2] [*I. e.* only by the use of the mental faculty of which God Himself is the Creator and Author; not by any independently existing power "of the same nature with Him who created it."—A. H. N.]

other creature, then,—for we are ourselves a creature,—separates us from the love of God which is in Christ Jesus our Lord.

CHAP. 13.—WE ARE JOINED INSEPARABLY TO GOD BY CHRIST AND HIS SPIRIT.

22. Let this same Paul tell us who is this Christ Jesus our Lord. "To them that are called," he says, "we preach Christ the virtue of God, and the wisdom of God."[1] And does not Christ Himself say, "I am the truth?" If, then, we ask what it is to live well,—that is, to strive after happiness by living well,—it must assuredly be to love virtue, to love wisdom, to love truth, and to love with all the heart, with all the soul, and with all the mind; virtue which is inviolable and immutable, wisdom which never gives place to folly, truth which knows no change or variation from its uniform character. Through this the Father Himself is seen; for it is said, "No man cometh unto the Father but by me."[2] To this we cleave by sanctification. For when sanctified we burn with full and perfect love, which is the only security for our not turning away from God, and for our being conformed to Him rather than to this world; for "He has predestinated us," says the same apostle, "that we should be conformed to the image of His Son."[3]

23. It is through love, then, that we become conformed to God; and by this conformation, and configuration, and circumcision from this world we are not confounded with the things which are properly subject to us. And this is done by the Holy Spirit. "For hope," he says, "does not confound us; for the love of God is shed abroad in our hearts by the Holy Spirit, which is given unto us."[4] But we could not possibly be restored to perfection by the Holy Spirit, unless He Himself continued always perfect and immutable. And this plainly could not be unless He were of the nature and of the very substance of God, who alone is always possessed of immutability and invariableness. "The creature," it is affirmed, not by me but by Paul, "has been made subject to vanity."[5] And what is subject to vanity is unable to separate us from vanity, and to unite us to the truth. But the Holy Spirit does this for us. He is therefore no creature. For whatever is, must be either God or the creature.

CHAP. 14.—WE CLEAVE TO THE TRINITY, OUR CHIEF GOOD, BY LOVE.

24. We ought then to love God, the Trinity in unity, Father, Son, and Holy Spirit; for this must be said to be God Himself, for it is said of God, truly and in the most exalted sense, "Of whom are all things, by whom are all things, in whom are all things." Those are Paul's words. And what does he add? "To Him be glory."[6] All this is exactly true. He does not say, To them; for God is one. And what is meant by, To Him be glory, but to Him be chief and perfect and wide-spread praise? For as the praise improves and extends, so the love and affection increases in fervor. And when this is the case, mankind cannot but advance with sure and firm step to a life of perfection and bliss. This, I suppose, is all we wish to find when we speak of the chief good of man, to which all must be referred in life and conduct. For the good plainly exists; and we have shown by reasoning, as far as we were able, and by the divine authority which goes beyond our reasoning, that it is nothing else but God Himself. For how can any thing be man's chief good but that in cleaving to which he is blessed? Now this is nothing but God, to whom we can cleave only by affection, desire, and love.

CHAP. 15.—THE CHRISTIAN DEFINITION OF THE FOUR VIRTUES.

25. As to virtue leading us to a happy life, I hold virtue to be nothing else than perfect love of God. For the fourfold division of virtue I regard as taken from four forms of love. For these four virtues (would that all felt their influence in their minds as they have their names in their mouths!), I should have no hesitation in defining them: that temperance is love giving itself entirely to that which is loved; fortitude is love readily bearing all things for the sake of the loved object; justice is love serving only the loved object, and therefore ruling rightly; prudence is love distinguishing with sagacity between what hinders it and what helps it. The object of this love is not anything, but only God, the chief good, the highest wisdom, the perfect harmony. So we may express the definition thus: that temperance is love keeping itself entire and incorrupt for God; fortitude is love bearing everything readily for the sake of God; justice is love serving God only, and therefore ruling well all else, as subject to man; prudence is love making a right distinction between what helps it towards God and what might hinder it.[7]

---

1 1 Cor. i. 23, 24. 2 John xiv. 6. 3 Rom. viii. 29. 4 Rom. v. 5. 5 Rom. viii. 20.

6 Rom. xi. 36.

7 [It would be difficult to find in Christian literature a more beautiful and satisfactory exposition of love to God. The Neo-Platonic influence is manifest, but it is Neo-Platonism thoroughly Christianized.—A. H. N.]

CHAP. 16.—HARMONY OF THE OLD AND NEW TESTAMENTS.

26. I will briefly set forth the manner of life according to these virtues, one by one, after I have brought forward, as I promised, passages from the Old Testament parallel to those I have been quoting from the New Testament. For is Paul alone in saying that we should be joined to God so that there should be nothing between to separate us? Does not the prophet say the same most aptly and concisely in the words, "It is good for me to cleave to God?"[1] Does not this one word *cleave* express all that the apostle says at length about love? And do not the words, It is good, point to the apostle's statement, "All things issue in good to them that love God?" Thus in one clause and in two words the prophet sets forth the power and the fruit of love.

27. And as the apostle says that the Son of God is the virtue of God and the wisdom of God,—virtue being understood to refer to action, and wisdom to teaching (as in the gospel these two things are expressed in the words, "All things were made by Him," which belongs to action and virtue; and then, referring to teaching and the knowledge of the truth, he says, "The life was the light of men"[2]),—could anything agree better with these passages than what is said in the Old Testament[3] of wisdom, "She reaches from end to end in strength, and orders all things sweetly?" For reaching in strength expresses virtue, while ordering sweetly expresses skill and method. But if this seems obscure, see what follows: "And of all," he says, "God loved her; for she teaches the knowledge of God, and chooses His works." Nothing more is found here about action; for choosing works is not the same as working, so this refers to teaching. There remains action to correspond with the virtue, to complete the truth we wish to prove. Read then what comes next: "But if," he says, "the possession which is desired in life is honorable, what is more honorable than wisdom, which works all things?" Could anything be brought forward more striking or more distinct than this, or even more fully expressed? Or, if you wish more, hear another passage of the same meaning. "Wisdom," he says, "teaches sobriety, and justice, and virtue."[4] Sobriety refers, I think, to the knowledge of the truth, or to teaching; justice and virtue to work and action. And I know nothing comparable to these two things, that is, to efficiency in action and sobriety in contemplation, which the virtue of God and the wisdom of God, that is, the Son of God, gives to them that love Him, when the same prophet goes on to show their value; for it is thus stated: "Wisdom teaches sobriety, and justice, and virtue, than which nothing is more useful in life to man."[5]

28. Perhaps some may think that those passages do not refer to the Son of God. What, then, is taught in the following words: "She displays the nobility of her birth, having her dwelling with God?"[6] To what does birth refer but to parentage? And does not dwelling with the Father claim and assert equality? Again, as Paul says that the Son of God is the wisdom of God,[7] and as the Lord Himself says, "No man knoweth the Father save the only-begotten Son,"[8] what could be more concordant than those words of the prophet: "With Thee is wisdom which knows Thy works, which was present at the time of Thy making the world, and knew what would be pleasing in Thine eyes?"[9] And as Christ is called the truth, which is also taught by His being called the brightness of the Father[10] (for there is nothing round about the sun but its brightness which is produced from it), what is there in the Old Testament more plainly and obviously in accordance with this than the words, "Thy truth is round about Thee?"[11] Once more, Wisdom herself says in the gospel, "No man cometh unto the Father but by me;"[12] and the prophet says, "Who knoweth Thy mind, unless Thou givest wisdom?" and a little after, "The things pleasing to Thee men have learned, and have been healed by wisdom."[13]

29. Paul says, "The love of God is shed abroad in our hearts by the Holy Spirit which is given unto us;"[14] and the prophet says, "The Holy Spirit of knowledge will shun guile."[15] For where there is guile there is no love. Paul says that we are "conformed to the image of the Son of God;"[16] and the

1 Ps. lxxiii. 28.

2 John i. 3, 4.

3 [Augustin seems to make no distinction between Apocryphal and Canonical books. The book of Wisdom was evidently a favorite with him, doubtless on account of its decided Platonic quality.—A. H. N.]

4 Wisd. viii. 1, 4, 7.

5 *Retract.* i. 7, § 3:—"The quotation from the book of Wisdom is from my manuscript, where the reading is, 'Wisdom teaches sobriety, justice, and virtue.' From these words I have made some remarks true in themselves, but occasioned by a false reading. It is perfectly true that wisdom teaches truth of contemplation, as I have explained sobriety; and excellence of action, which is the meaning I give to justice and virtue. And the reading in better manuscripts has the same meaning: 'It teaches sobriety, and wisdom, and justice, and virtue.' These are the names given by the Latin translator to the four virtues which philosophers usually speak about. Sobriety is for temperance, wisdom for prudence, virtue for fortitude, and justice only has its own name. It was long after that we found these virtues called by their proper names in the Greek text of this book of Wisdom."

6 Wisd. viii. 3.

7 1 Cor. i. 24.

8 Matt. xi. 27.

9 Wisd. ix. 9.

10 Heb. i. 3.

11 Ps. lxxxix. 8.

12 John xiv. 6.

13 Wisd. ix. 17-19.

14 Rom. v. 5.

15 Wisd. i. 5.

16 Rom. viii. 29.

prophet says, "The light of Thy countenance is stamped upon us."[1] Paul teaches that the Holy Spirit is God, and therefore is no creature; and the prophet says, "Thou sendest Thy Spirit from the highest."[2] For God alone is the highest, than whom nothing is higher. Paul shows that the Trinity is one God, when he says, "To Him be glory;"[3] and in the Old Testament it is said, "Hear, O Israel, the Lord thy God is one God."[4]

CHAP. 17.—APPEAL TO THE MANICHÆANS, CALLING ON THEM TO REPENT.

30. What more do you wish? Why do you resist ignorantly and obstinately? Why do you pervert untutored minds by your mischievous teaching? The God of both Testaments is one. For as there is an agreement in the passages quoted from both, so is there in all the rest, if you are willing to consider them carefully and impartially. But because many expressions are undignified, and so far adapted to minds creeping on the earth, that they may rise by human things to divine,[5] while many are figurative, that the inquiring mind may have the more profit from the exertion of finding their meaning, and the more delight when it is found, you pervert this admirable arrangement of the Holy Spirit for the purpose of deceiving and ensnaring your followers. As to the reason why divine Providence permits you to do this, and as to the truth of the apostle's saying, "There must needs be many heresies, that they which are approved may be made manifest among you,"[6] it would take long to discuss these things, and you, with whom we have now to do, are not capable of understanding them. I know you well. To the consideration of divine things, which are far higher than you suppose, you bring minds quite gross and sickly, from being fed with material images.

31. We must therefore in your case try not to make you understand divine things, which is impossible, but to make you desire to understand. This is the work of the pure and guileless love of God, which is seen chiefly in the conduct, and of which we have already said much. This love, inspired by the Holy Spirit, leads to the Son, that is, to the wisdom of God, by which the Father Himself is known. For if wisdom and truth are not sought for with the whole strength of the mind, it cannot possibly be found. But when it is sought as it deserves to be, it cannot withdraw or hide itself from its lovers. Hence its words, which you too are in the habit of repeating, "Ask, and ye shall receive; seek, and ye shall find; knock, and it shall be opened unto you:"[7] "Nothing is hid which shall not be revealed."[8] It is love that asks, love that seeks, love that knocks, love that reveals, love, too, that gives continuance in what is revealed. From this love of wisdom, and this studious inquiry, we are not debarred by the Old Testament, as you always say most falsely, but are exhorted to this with the greatest urgency.

32. Hear, then, at length, and consider, I pray you, what is said by the prophet: "Wisdom is glorious, and never fadeth away; yea, she is easily seen of them that love her, and found of such as seek her. She preventeth them that desire her, in making herself first known unto them. Whoso seeketh her early shall have no great travail; for he shall find her sitting at his doors. To think, therefore, upon her is perfection of wisdom; and whoso watcheth for her shall quickly be without care. For she goeth about seeking such as are worthy of her, showeth herself favorably unto them in the ways, and meeteth them in every thought. For the very true beginning of her is the desire of discipline; and the care of discipline is love; and love is the keeping of her laws; and the giving heed unto her laws is the assurance of incorruption; and incorruption maketh us near unto God. Therefore the desire of wisdom bringeth to a kingdom."[9] Will you still continue in dogged hostility to these things? Do not things thus stated, though not yet understood, make it evident to every one that they contain something deep and unutterable? Would that you could understand the things here said! Forthwith you would abjure all your silly legends and your unmeaning material imaginations, and with great alacrity, sincere love, and full assurance of faith, would betake yourselves bodily to the shelter of the most holy bosom of the Catholic Church.

CHAP. 18.—ONLY IN THE CATHOLIC CHURCH IS PERFECT TRUTH ESTABLISHED ON THE HARMONY OF BOTH TESTAMENTS.

33. I could, according to the little ability I have, take up the points separately, and could expound and prove the truths I have learned, which are generally more excellent and lofty than words can express; but this

1 Ps. iv. 6.
2 Wisd. ix. 17.
3 Rom. xi. 36.
4 Deut. vi. 4.
5 [Here we have the key to all that is best in Augustin's defense of the anthropomorphisms and the seemingly imperfect ethical representations of the Old Testament. See Mozley's essay on "The Manichæans and the Jewish Fathers," in his *Ruling Ideas in Early Ages*. The entire volume represents an attempt to account for the elements in the Old Testament that offend the Christian consciousness.—A. H. N.]
6 1 Cor. xi. 19.
7 Matt. vii. 7.
8 Matt. x. 26.
9 Wisd. vi. 12-20.

cannot be done while you bark at it. For not in vain is it said, "Give not that which is holy to dogs."[1] Do not be angry. I too barked and was a dog; and then, as was right, instead of the food of teaching, I got the rod of correction. But were there in you that love of which we are speaking, or should it ever be in you as much as the greatness of the truth to be known requires, may God vouchsafe to show you that neither is there among the Manichæans the Christian faith which leads to the summit of wisdom and truth, the attainment of which is the true happy life, nor is it anywhere but in the Catholic teaching. Is not this what the Apostle Paul appears to desire when he says, "For this cause I bow my knees to the Father of our Lord Jesus Christ, from whom the whole family in heaven and earth is named, that He would grant unto you, according to the riches of His glory, to be strengthened with might by His Spirit in the inner man; that Christ may dwell in your hearts by faith; that ye, being rooted and grounded in love, may be able to comprehend with all saints what is the height, and length, and breadth, and depth, and to know the love of Christ, which passeth knowledge, that ye may be filled with all the fullness of God?"[2] Could anything be more plainly expressed?

34. Wake up a little, I beseech you, and see the harmony of both Testaments, making it quite plain and certain what should be the manner of life in our conduct, and to what all things should be referred. To the love of God we are incited by the gospel, when it is said, "Ask, seek, knock;"[3] by Paul, when he says, "That ye, being rooted and grounded in love, may be able to comprehend;"[4] by the prophet also, when he says that wisdom can easily be known by those who love it, seek for it, desire it, watch for it, think about it, care for it. The salvation of the mind[5] and the way of happiness is pointed out by the concord of both Scriptures; and yet you choose rather to bark at these things than to obey them. I will tell you in one word what I think. Do you listen to the learned men of the Catholic Church with as peaceable a disposition, and with the same zeal, that I had when for nine years I attended on you:[6] there will be no need of so long a time as that during which you made a fool of me. In a much, a very much, shorter time you will see the difference between truth and vanity.

1 Matt. vii. 6.
2 Eph. iii. 14-19.
3 Matt. vii. 7.
4 Eph. iii. 7.
5 [*Animi* not *mentis*.—A. H. N.]
6 From his 19th to his 28th year.

CHAP. 19.—DESCRIPTION OF THE DUTIES OF TEMPERANCE, ACCORDING TO THE SACRED SCRIPTURES.

35. It is now time to return to the four virtues, and to draw out and prescribe a way of life in conformity with them, taking each separately. First, then, let us consider temperance, which promises us a kind of integrity and incorruption in the love by which we are united to God. The office of temperance is in restraining and quieting the passions which make us pant for those things which turn us away from the laws of God and from the enjoyment of His goodness, that is, in a word, from the happy life. For there is the abode of truth; and in enjoying its contemplation, and in cleaving closely to it, we are assuredly happy; but departing from this, men become entangled in great errors and sorrows. For, as the apostle says, "The root of all evils is covetousness; which some having followed, have made shipwreck of the faith, and have pierced themselves through with many sorrows."[7] And this sin of the soul is quite plainly, to those rightly understanding, set forth in the Old Testament in the transgression of Adam in Paradise. Thus, as the apostle says, "In Adam we all die, and in Christ we shall all rise again."[8] Oh, the depth of these mysteries! But I refrain; for I am now engaged not in teaching you the truth, but in making you unlearn your errors, if I can, that is, if God aid my purpose regarding you.

36. Paul then says that covetousness is the root of all evils; and by covetousness the old law also intimates that the first man fell. Paul tells us to put off the old man and put on the new.[9] By the old man he means Adam who sinned, and by the new man him whom the Son of God took to Himself in consecration for our redemption. For he says in another place, "The first man is of the earth, earthy; the second man is from heaven, heavenly. As is the earthy, such are they also that are earthy; and as is the heavenly, such are they also that are heavenly. And as we have borne the image of the earthy, let us also bear the image of the heavenly,"[10]—that is, put off the old man, and put on the new. The whole duty of temperance, then, is to put off the old man, and to be renewed in God,—that is, to scorn all bodily delights, and the popular applause, and to turn the whole love to things divine and unseen. Hence that following passage which is so admirable: "Though our outward man perish,

7 1 Tim. vi. 10.
8 1 Cor. xv. 22.
9 Col. iii. 9, 10.
10 1 Cor. xv. 47-49.

our inward man is renewed day by day."[1] Hear, too, the prophet singing, "Create in me a clean heart, O God, and renew a right spirit within me."[2] What can be said against such harmony except by blind barkers?

CHAP. 20.—WE ARE REQUIRED TO DESPISE ALL SENSIBLE THINGS, AND TO LOVE GOD ALONE.

37. Bodily delights have their source in all those things with which the bodily sense comes in contact, and which are by some called the objects of sense; and among these the noblest is light, in the common meaning of the word, because among our senses also, which the mind uses in acting through the body, there is nothing more valuable than the eyes, and so in the Holy Scriptures all the objects of sense are spoken of as visible things. Thus in the New Testament we are warned against the love of these things in the following words: "While we look not at the things which are seen, but at the things which are not seen; for the things which are seen are temporal, but the things which are not seen are eternal."[3] This shows how far from being Christians those are who hold that the sun and moon are to be not only loved but worshipped. For what is seen if the sun and moon are not? But we are forbidden to regard things which are seen. The man, therefore, who wishes to offer that incorrupt love to God must not love these things too. This subject I will inquire into more particularly elsewhere. Here my plan is to write not of faith, but of the life by which we become worthy of knowing what we believe. God then alone is to be loved; and all this world, that is, all sensible things, are to be despised,—while, however, they are to be used as this life requires.

CHAP. 21.—POPULAR RENOWN AND INQUISITIVENESS ARE CONDEMNED IN THE SACRED SCRIPTURES.

38. Popular renown is thus slighted and scorned in the New Testament: "If I wished," says St. Paul, "to please men, I should not be the servant of Christ."[4] Again, there is another production of the soul formed by imaginations derived from material things, and called the knowledge of things. In reference to this we are fitly warned against inquisitiveness to correct which is the great function of temperance. Thus it is said, "Take heed lest any one seduce you by philosophy." And because the word philosophy originally means the love and pursuit of wisdom, a thing of great value and to be sought with the whole mind, the apostle, with great prudence, that he might not be thought to deter from the love of wisdom, has added the words, "And the elements of this world."[5] For some people, neglecting virtues, and ignorant of what God is, and of the majesty of the nature which remains always the same, think that they are engaged in an important business when searching with the greatest inquisitiveness and eagerness into this material mass which we call the world. This begets so much pride, that they look upon themselves as inhabitants of the heaven of which they often discourse. The soul, then, which purposes to keep itself chaste for God must refrain from the desire of vain knowledge like this. For this desire usually produces delusion, so that the soul thinks that nothing exists but what is material; or if, from regard to authority, it confesses that there is an immaterial existence, it can think of it only under material images, and has no belief regarding it but that imposed by the bodily sense. We may apply to this the precept about fleeing from idolatry.

39. To this New Testament authority, requiring us not to love anything in this world,[6] especially in that passage where it is said, "Be not conformed to this world,"[7]—for the point is to show that a man is conformed to whatever he loves,—to this authority, then, if I seek for a parallel passage in the Old Testament, I find several; but there is one book of Solomon, called Ecclesiastes, which at great length brings all earthly things into utter contempt. The book begins thus: "Vanity of the vain, saith the Preacher, vanity of the vain; all is vanity. What profit hath a man of all his labor which he taketh under the sun?"[8] If all these words are considered, weighed, and thoroughly examined, many things are found of essential importance to those who seek to flee from the world and to take shelter in God; but this requires time and our discourse hastens on to other topics. But, after this beginning, he goes on to show in detail that the vain[9] are those who are deceived by things of this sort; and he calls this which deceives them vanity,—not that God did not create those things, but because men choose to subject themselves by their sins to those things, which the divine law has made subject to them in well-doing. For when you consider things beneath your-

[1] 2 Cor. iv. 16.
[2] Ps. li. 10.
[3] 2 Cor. iv. 18
[4] Gal. i. 10.
[5] Coll. ii. 8.
[6] 1 John ii. 15.
[7] Rom. xii. 2.
[8] Eccles. i. 2, 3.
[9] *Retract.* i. 7, § 3:—"I found in many manuscripts the reading, 'Vanity of the vain.' But this is not in the Greek, which has 'Vanity of vanities.' This I saw afterwards. And I found that the best Latin manuscripts had vanities and not vain. But the truths I have drawn from this false reading are self-evident."

self to be admirable and desirable, what is this but to be cheated and misled by unreal goods? The man, then, who is temperate in such mortal and transient things has his rule of life confirmed by both Testaments, that he should love none of these things, nor think them desirable for their own sakes, but should use them as far as is required for the purposes and duties of life, with the moderation of an employer instead of the ardor of a lover. These remarks on temperance are few in proportion to the greatness of the theme, but perhaps too many in view of the task on hand.

CHAP. 22.—FORTITUDE COMES FROM THE LOVE OF GOD.

40. On fortitude we must be brief. The love, then, of which we speak, which ought with all sanctity to burn in desire for God, is called temperance, in not seeking for earthly things, and fortitude, in bearing the loss of them. But among all things which are possessed in this life, the body is, by God's most righteous laws, for the sin of old, man's heaviest bond, which is well known as a fact, but most incomprehensible in its mystery. Lest this bond should be shaken and disturbed, the soul is shaken with the fear of toil and pain; lest it should be lost and destroyed, the soul is shaken with the fear of death. For the soul loves it from the force of habit, not knowing that by using it well and wisely its resurrection and reformation will, by the divine help and decree, be without any trouble made subject to its authority. But when the soul turns to God wholly in this love, it knows these things, and so will not only disregard death, but will even desire it.

41. Then there is the great struggle with pain. But there is nothing, though of iron hardness, which the fire of love cannot subdue. And when the mind is carried up to God in this love, it will soar above all torture free and glorious, with wings beauteous and unhurt, on which chaste love rises to the embrace of God. Otherwise God must allow the lovers of gold, the lovers of praise, the lovers of women, to have more fortitude than the lovers of Himself, though love in those cases is rather to be called passion or lust. And yet even here we may see with what force the mind presses on with unflagging energy, in spite of all alarms, towards that it loves; and we learn that we should bear all things rather than forsake God, since those men bear so much in order to forsake Him.

CHAP. 23.—SCRIPTURE PRECEPTS AND EXAMPLES OF FORTITUDE.

42. Instead of quoting here authorities from the New Testament, where it is said, "Tribulation worketh patience; and patience, experience and experience, hope;"[1] and where, in addition to these words, there is proof and confirmation of them from the example of those who spoke them; I will rather summon an example of patience from the Old Testament, against which the Manichæans make fierce assaults. Nor will I refer to the man who, in the midst of great bodily suffering, and with a dreadful disease in his limbs, not only bore human evils, but discoursed of things divine. Whoever gives considerate attention to the utterances of this man, will learn from every one of them what value is to be attached to those things which men try to keep in their power, and in so doing are themselves brought by passion into bondage, so that they become the slaves of mortal things, while seeking ignorantly to be their masters. This man, in the loss of all his wealth, and on being suddenly reduced to the greatest poverty, kept his mind so unshaken and fixed upon God, as to manifest that these things were not great in his view, but that he was great in relation to them, and God to him.[2] If this mind were to be found in men in our day, we should not be so strongly cautioned in the New Testament against the possession of these things in order that we may be perfect; for to have these things without cleaving to them is much more admirable than not to have them at all.[3]

43. But since we are speaking here of bearing pain and bodily sufferings, I pass from this man, great as he was, indomitable as he was: this is the case of a man. But these Scriptures present to me a woman of amazing fortitude, and I must at once go on to her case. This woman, along with seven children, allowed the tyrant and executioner to extract her vitals from her body rather than a profane word from her mouth, encouraging her sons by her exhortations, though she suffered in the tortures of their bodies, and was herself to undergo what she called on them to bear.[4] What patience could be greater than this? And yet why should we be astonished that the love of God, implanted in her inmost heart, bore up against tyrant, and executioner, and pain, and sex, and natural affection? Had she not heard, "Precious in the sight of the Lord is the death of His saints?"[5] Had she not heard, "A patient man is better than the mightiest?"[6] Had she not heard, "All that is appointed

---

1 Rom. v. 3, 4.
2 Job. i. 2.
3 [It is interesting to observe how remote Augustin was from attaching superior merit to voluntary poverty, or to other forms of asceticism as ends in themselves. What he prized was the ability to use without abusing, to have without cleaving to the good things which God provides.—A. H. N.]
4 2 Mac. vii.
5 Ps. cxvi. 15.
6 Prov. xvi. 32.

thee receive; and in pain bear it; and in abasement keep thy patience: for in fire are gold and silver tried?"[1] Had she not heard, "The fire tries the vessels of the potter, and for just men is the trial of tribulation?"[2] These she knew, and many other precepts of fortitude written in these books, which alone existed at that time, by the same divine Spirit who writes those in the New Testament.

CHAP. 24.—OF JUSTICE AND PRUDENCE.

44. What of justice that pertains to God? As the Lord says, "Ye cannot serve two masters,"[3] and the apostle denounces those who serve the creature rather than the Creator,[4] was it not said before in the Old Testament, "Thou shalt worship the Lord thy God, and Him only shalt thou serve?"[5] I need say no more on this, for these books are full of such passages. The lover, then, whom we are describing, will get from justice this rule of life, that he must with perfect readiness serve the God whom he loves, the highest good, the highest wisdom, the highest peace;[6] and as regards all other things, must either rule them as subject to himself, or treat them with a view to their subjection. This rule of life, is, as we have shown, confirmed by the authority of both Testaments.

45. With equal brevity we must treat of prudence, to which it belongs to discern between what is to be desired and what to be shunned. Without this, nothing can be done of what we have already spoken of. It is the part of prudence to keep watch with most anxious vigilance, lest any evil influence should stealthily creep in upon us. Thus the Lord often exclaims, "Watch;"[7] and He says, "Walk while ye have the light, lest darkness come upon you."[8] And then it is said, "Know ye not that a little leaven leaveneth the whole lump?"[9] And no passage can be quoted from the Old Testament more expressly condemning this mental somnolence, which makes us insensible to destruction advancing on us step by step, than those words of the prophet, "He who despiseth small things shall fall by degrees."[10] On this topic I might discourse at length did our haste allow of it. And did our present task demand it, we might perhaps prove the depth of these mysteries, by making a mock of which profane men in their perfect ignorance fall, not certainly by degrees, but with a headlong overthrow.

CHAP. 25.—FOUR MORAL DUTIES REGARDING THE LOVE OF GOD, OF WHICH LOVE THE REWARD IS ETERNAL LIFE AND THE KNOWLEDGE OF THE TRUTH.

46. I need say no more about right conduct. For if God is man's chief good, which you cannot deny, it clearly follows, since to seek the chief good is to live well, that to live well is nothing else but to love God with all the heart, with all the soul, with all the mind; and, as arising from this, that this love must be preserved entire and incorrupt, which is the part of temperance; that it give way before no troubles, which is the part of fortitude; that it serve no other, which is the part of justice; that it be watchful in its inspection of things lest craft or fraud steal in, which is the part of prudence. This is the one perfection of man, by which alone he can succeed in attaining to the purity of truth. This both Testaments enjoin in concert; this is commended on both sides alike. Why do you continue to cast reproaches on Scriptures of which you are ignorant? Do you not see the folly of your attack upon books which only those who do not understand them find fault with, and which only those who find fault fail in understanding? For neither can an enemy know them, nor can one who knows them be other than a friend to them.

47. Let us then, as many as have in view to reach eternal life, love God with all the heart, with all the soul, with all the mind. For eternal life contains the whole reward in the promise of which we rejoice; nor can the reward precede desert, nor be given to a man before he is worthy of it. What can be more unjust than this, and what is more just than God? We should not then demand the reward before we deserve to get it. Here, perhaps, it is not out of place to ask what is eternal life; or rather let us hear the Bestower of it: "This," He says, "is life eternal, that they should know Thee, the true God, and Jesus Christ whom Thou hast sent."[11] So eternal life is the knowledge of the truth. See, then, how perverse and preposterous is the character of those who think that their teaching of the knowledge of God will make us perfect, when this is the reward of those already perfect! What else, then, have we to do but first to love with full affection Him whom we desire to know?[12] Hence arises that principle on which we have all

---

[1] Ecclus. ii. 4, 5. [2] Ecclus. xxvii. 6. [3] Matt. vi. 24.
[4] Rom. i. 25. [5] Deut. vi. 13.
[6] A name given by Augustin to the Holy Spirit, *v.* xxx.
[7] Matt. xxiv. 42. [8] John xii. 35. [9] 1 Cor. v. 6.
[10] Ecclus. xix. 1.

[11] John xvii. 3.
[12] *Retract.* i. -, § 4:—"I should have said *sincere* affection rather than full; or it might be thought that the love of God will be no greater when we shall see Him face to face. Full, then, must be here understood as meaning that it cannot be greater while we walk by faith. There will be greater, yea, perfect fullness, but only by sight."

along insisted, that there is nothing more wholesome in the Catholic Church than using authority[1] before argument.

CHAP. 26.—LOVE OF OURSELVES AND OF OUR NEIGHBOR.

48. To proceed to what remains. It may be thought that there is nothing here about man himself, the lover. But to think this, shows a want of clear perception. For it is impossible for one who loves God not to love himself. For he alone has a proper love for himself who aims diligently at the attainment of the chief and true good; and if this is nothing else but God, as has been shown, what is to prevent one who loves God from loving himself? And then, among men should there be no bond of mutual love? Yea, verily; so that we can think of no surer step towards the love of God than the love of man to man.

49. Let the Lord then supply us with the other precept in answer to the question about the precepts of life; for He was not satisfied with one as knowing that God is one thing and man another, and that the difference is nothing less than that between the Creator and the thing created in the likeness of its Creator. He says then that the second precept is, "Thou shalt love thy neighbor as thyself."[2] Now you love yourself suitably when you love God better than yourself. What, then, you aim at in yourself you must aim at in your neighbor, namely, that he may love God with a perfect affection. For you do not love him as yourself, unless you try to draw him to that good which you are yourself pursuing. For this is the one good which has room for all to pursue it along with thee. From this precept proceed the duties of human society, in which it is hard to keep from error. But the first thing to aim at is, that we should be benevolent, that is, that we cherish no malice and no evil design against another. For man is the nearest neighbor of man.

50. Hear also what Paul says: "The love of our neighbor," he says, "worketh no ill."[3] The testimonies here made use of are very short, but, if I mistake not, they are to the point, and sufficient for the purpose. And every one knows how many and how weighty are the words to be found everywhere in these books on the love of our neighbor. But as a man may sin against another in two ways, either by injuring him or by not helping him when it is in his power, and as it is for these things which no loving man would do that men are called wicked, all that is required is, I think, proved by these words, "The love of our neighbor worketh no ill." And if we cannot attain to good unless we first desist from working evil, our love of our neighbor is a sort of cradle of our love to God, so that, as it is said, "the love of our neighbor worketh no ill," we may rise from this to these other words, "We know that all things issue in good to them that love God."[4]

51. But there is a sense in which these either rise together to fullness and perfection, or, while the love of God is first in beginning, the love of our neighbor is first in coming to perfection. For perhaps divine love takes hold on us more rapidly at the outset, but we reach perfection more easily in lower things. However that may be, the main point is this, that no one should think that while he despises his neighbor he will come to happiness and to the God whom he loves. And would that it were as easy to seek the good of our neighbor, or to avoid hurting him, as it is for one well trained and kind-hearted to love his neighbor! These things require more than mere good-will, and can be done only by a high degree of thoughtfulness and prudence, which belongs only to those to whom it is given by God, the source of all good. On this topic—which is one, I think, of great difficulty--I will try to say a few words such as my plan admits of, resting all my hope in Him whose gifts these are.

CHAP. 27.—ON DOING GOOD TO THE BODY OF OUR NEIGHBOR.

52. Man, then, as viewed by his fellow-man, is a rational soul with a mortal and earthly body in its service. Therefore he who loves his neighbor does good partly to the man's body, and partly to his soul. What benefits the body is called medicine; what benefits the soul, discipline. Medicine here includes everything that either preserves or restores bodily health. It includes, therefore, not only what belongs to the art of medical men, properly so called, but also food and drink, clothing and shelter, and every means of covering and protection to guard our bodies against injuries and mishaps from without as well as from within. For hunger and thirst, and cold and heat, and all violence from without, produce loss of that health which is the point to be considered.

53. Hence those who seasonably and wisely supply all the things required for warding off

---

1 [By *authority* Augustin does not mean the authority of the Church or of Scripture, but he refers to the loving recognition of the authority of God as the condition of true discipleship.—A. H. N.]

2 Matt. xxii. 39.

3 Rom. xiii. 10.

4 Rom. viii. 28.

these evils and distresses are called compassionate, although they may have been so wise that no painful feeling disturbed their mind in the exercise of compassion.[1] No doubt the word compassionate implies suffering in the heart of the man who feels for the sorrow of another. And it is equally true that a wise man ought to be free from all painful emotion when he assists the needy, when he gives food to the hungry and water to the thirsty, when he clothes the naked, when he takes the stranger into his house, when he sets free the oppressed, when, lastly, he extends his charity to the dead in giving them burial. Still the epithet compassionate is a proper one, although he acts with tranquillity of mind, not from the stimulus of painful feeling, but from motives of benevolence. There is no harm in the word compassionate when there is no passion in the case.

54. Fools, again, who avoid the exercise of compassion as a vice, because they are not sufficiently moved by a sense of duty without feeling also distressful emotion, are frozen into hard insensibility, which is very different from the calm of a rational serenity. God, on the other hand, is properly called compassionate; and the sense in which He is so will be understood by those whom piety and diligence have made fit to understand. There is a danger lest, in using the words of the learned, we harden the souls of the unlearned by leading them away from compassion instead of softening them with the desire of a charitable disposition. As compassion, then, requires us to ward off these distresses from others, so harmlessness forbids the infliction of them.

CHAP. 28.—ON DOING GOOD TO THE SOUL OF OUR NEIGHBOR. TWO PARTS OF DISCIPLINE, RESTRAINT AND INSTRUCTION. THROUGH GOOD CONDUCT WE ARRIVE AT THE KNOWLEDGE OF THE TRUTH.

55. As regards discipline, by which the health of the mind is restored, without which bodily health avails nothing for security against misery, the subject is one of great difficulty. And as in the body we said it is one thing to cure diseases and wounds, which few can do properly, and another thing to meet the cravings of hunger and thirst, and to give assistance in all the other ways in which any man may at any time help another; so in the mind there are some things in which the high and rare offices of the teacher are not much called for,—as, for instance, in advice and exhortation to give to the needy the things already mentioned as required for the body. To give such advice is to aid the mind by discipline, as giving the things themselves is aiding the body by our resources. But there are other cases where diseases of the mind, many and various in kind, are healed in a way strange and indescribable. Unless His medicine were sent from heaven to men, so heedlessly do they go on in sin, there would be no hope of salvation; and, indeed, even bodily health, if you go to the root of the matter, can have come to men from none but God, who gives to all things their being and their well-being.

56. This discipline, then, which is the medicine of the mind, as far as we can gather from the sacred Scriptures, includes two things, restraint and instruction. Restraint implies fear, and instruction love, in the person benefited by the discipline; for in the giver of the benefit there is the love without the fear. In both of these God Himself, by whose goodness and mercy it is that we are anything, has given us in the two Testaments a rule of discipline. For though both are found in both Testaments, still fear is prominent in the Old, and love in the New; which the apostle calls bondage in the one, and liberty in the other. Of the marvellous order and divine harmony of these Testaments it would take long to speak, and many pious and learned men have discoursed on it. The theme demands many books to set it forth and explain it as far as is possible for man. He, then, who loves his neighbor endeavors all he can to procure his safety in body and in soul, making the health of the mind the standard in his treatment of the body. And as regards the mind, his endeavors are in this order, that he should first fear and then love God. This is true excellence of conduct, and thus the knowledge of the truth is acquired which we are ever in the pursuit of.

57. The Manichæans agree with me as regards the duty of loving God and our neighbor, but they deny that this is taught in the Old Testament. How greatly they err in this is, I think, clearly shown by the passages quoted above on both these duties. But, in a single word, and one which only stark madness can oppose, do they not see the unreasonableness of denying that these very two precepts which they commend are quoted by the Lord in the Gospel from the Old Testament, "Thou shalt love the Lord thy God with all thy heart, and with all thy soul, and with all thy mind;" and the other, "Thou

[1] *Retract.* i. 7. § 4:—"This does not mean that there are actually in this life wise men such as are here spoken of. My words are not, 'although they are so wise,' but 'although they were so wise.'" [Augustin's ideal wise man was evidently the "Gnostic" of Clement of Alexandria. The conception is Stoical and Neo-Platonic.—A. H. N.]

shalt love thy neighbor as thyself?"[1] Or if they dare not deny this, from the light of truth being too strong for them, let them deny that these precepts are salutary; let them deny, if they can, that they teach the best morality; let them assert that it is not a duty to love God, or to love our neighbor; that all things do not issue in good to them that love God; that it is not true that the love of our neighbor worketh no ill (a two-fold regulation of human life which is most salutary and excellent). By such assertions they cut themselves off not only from Christians, but from mankind. But if they dare not speak thus, but must confess the divinity of the precepts, why do they not desist from assailing and maligning with horrible profanity the books from which they are quoted?

58. Will they say, as they often do, that although we find these precepts in the books, it does not follow that all is good that is found there? How to meet and refute this quibble I do not well see. Shall I discuss the words of the Old Testament one by one, to prove to stubborn and ignorant men their perfect agreement with the New Testament? But when will this be done? When shall I have time, or they patience? What, then, is to be done? Shall I desert the cause, and leave them to escape detection in an opinion which, though false and impious, is hard to disprove? I will not. God will Himself be at hand to aid me; nor will He suffer me in those straits to remain helpless or forsaken.

CHAP. 29.—OF THE AUTHORITY OF THE SCRIPTURES.

59. Attend, then, ye Manichæans, if perchance there are some of you of whom your superstition has hold so as to allow you yet to escape. Attend, I say, without obstinacy, without the desire to oppose, otherwise your decision will be fatal to yourselves. No one can doubt, and you are not so lost to the truth as not to understand that if it is good, as all allow, to love God and our neighbor, whatever hangs on these two precepts cannot rightly be pronounced bad. What it is that hangs on them it would be absurd to think of learning from me. Hear Christ Himself; hear Christ, I say; hear the Wisdom of God: "On these two commandments," He says, "hang all the law and the prophets."[2]

60. What can the most shameless obstinacy say to this? That these are not Christ's words? But they are written in the Gospel as His words. That the writing is false? Is not this most profane blasphemy? Is it not most presumptuous to speak thus? Is it not most foolhardy? Is it not most criminal? The worshippers of idols, who hate even the name of Christ, never dared to speak thus against these Scriptures. For the utter overthrow of all literature will follow, and there will be an end to all books handed down from the past, if what is supported by such a strong popular belief and established by the uniform testimony of so many men and so many times, is brought into such suspicion, that it is not allowed to have the credit and the authority of common history. In fine, what can you quote from any writings of which I may not speak in this way, if it is quoted against my opinion and my purpose?[3]

61. And is it not intolerable that they forbid us to believe a book widely known and placed now in the hands of all, while they insist on our believing the book which they quote? If any writing is to be suspected, what should be more so than one which has not merited notoriety, or which may be throughout a forgery, bearing a false name? If you force such a writing on me against my will, and make a display of authority to drive me into belief, shall I, when I have a writing which I see spread far and wide for a length of time, and sanctioned by the concordant testimony of churches scattered over all the world, degrade myself by doubting, and, worse degradation, by doubting at your suggestion? Even if you brought forward other readings, I should not receive them unless supported by general agreement; and this being the case, do you think that now, when you bring forward nothing to compare with the text except your own silly and inconsiderate statement, mankind are so unreasonable and so forsaken by divine Providence as to prefer to those Scriptures not others quoted by you in refutation, but merely your own words? You ought to bring forward another manuscript with the same contents, but incorrupt and more correct, with only the passage wanting which you charge with being spurious. For example, if you hold that the Epistle of Paul to the Romans is spurious, you must bring forward another incorrupt, or rather another manuscript with the same epistle of the same apostle, free from error and corruption. You say you will not, lest you be suspected of corrupting it. This is your usual reply, and a true one. Were you to do this, we should assuredly have this very suspicion; and all men of any sense would have it too. See then

[1] Deut. vi. 5; Lev. xix. 18; Matt. xxii. 37, 39.
[2] Matt. xxii. 40.

[3] [The strong testimony borne by Augustin against the perverse subjective criticism of the Manichæans has an important application to the present time.—A. H. N.]

what you are to think of your own authority; and consider whether it is right to believe your words against these Scriptures, when the simple fact that a manuscript is brought forward by you makes it dangerous to put faith in it.

CHAP. 30.—THE CHURCH APOSTROPHISED AS TEACHER OF ALL WISDOM. DOCTRINE OF THE CATHOLIC CHURCH.

62. But why say more on this? For who but sees that men who dare to speak thus against the Christian Scriptures, though they may not be what they are suspected of being, are at least no Christians? For to Christians this rule of life is given, that we should love the Lord our God with all the heart, with all the soul, and with all the mind, and our neighbor as ourselves; for on these two commandments hang all the law and the prophets. Rightly, then, Catholic Church, most true mother of Christians, dost thou not only teach that God alone, to find whom is the happiest life, must be worshipped in perfect purity and chastity, bringing in no creature as an object of adoration whom we should be required to serve; and from that incorrupt and inviolable eternity to which alone man should be made subject, in cleaving to which alone the rational soul escapes misery, excluding everything made, everything liable to change, everything under the power of time; without confounding what eternity, and truth, and peace itself keeps separate, or separating what a common majesty unites: but thou dost also contain love and charity to our neighbor in such a way, that for all kinds of diseases with which souls are for their sins afflicted, there is found with thee a medicine of prevailing efficacy.

63. Thy training and teaching are childlike for children, forcible for youths, peaceful for the aged, taking into account the age of the mind as well as of the body. Thou subjectest women to their husbands in chaste and faithful obedience, not to gratify passion, but for the propagation of offspring,[1] and for domestic society. Thou givest to men authority over their wives, not to mock the weaker sex, but in the laws of unfeigned love. Thou dost subordinate children to their parents in a kind of free bondage, and dost set parents over their children in a godly rule. Thou bindest brothers to brothers in a religious tie stronger and closer than that of blood. Without violation of the connections of nature and of choice, thou bringest within the bond of mutual love every relationship of kindred, and every alliance of affinity. Thou teachest servants to cleave to their masters from delight in their task rather than from the necessity of their position. Thou renderest masters forbearing to their servants, from a regard to God their common Master, and more disposed to advise than to compel. Thou unitest citizen to citizen, nation to nation, yea, man to man, from the recollection of their first parents, not only in society but in fraternity. Thou teachest kings to seek the good of their peoples; thou counsellest peoples to be subject to their kings. Thou teachest carefully to whom honor is due, to whom regard, to whom reverence, to whom fear, to whom consolation, to whom admonition, to whom encouragement, to whom discipline, to whom rebuke, to whom punishment; showing both how all are not due to all, and how to all love is due, and how injury is due to none.[2]

64. Then, after this human love has nourished and invigorated the mind cleaving to thy breast, and fitted it for following God, when the divine majesty has begun to disclose itself as far as suffices for man while a dweller on the earth, such fervent charity is produced, and such a flame of divine love is kindled, that by the burning out of all vices, and by the purification and sanctification of the man, it becomes plain how divine are these words, "I am a consuming fire,"[3] and, "I have come to send fire on the earth."[4] These two utterances of one God stamped on both Testaments, exhibit with harmonious testimony the sanctification of the soul, pointing forward to the accomplishment of that which

[1] [This view of the marriage relation seems to have been almost universal in the ancient Church. Tertullian and Clement of Alexandria are fond of dwelling upon it. For Augustin's views more fully stated see his *De Bono Conjugali*, 6. See also an interesting excursus on "Continence in Married Life" in CUNNINGHAM'S *St. Austin*, p. 168. sq.—A. H. N.]

[2] [If this apostrophe had been addressed to "Christianity" rather than to the "Catholic Church," no Christian could fail to see in it one of the noblest tributes ever bestowed on the religion of Christ. Augustin identified Christianity with the organized body which was far from realizing the ideal that he here sets forth. As an apostrophe to ideal Christianity nothing could be finer.—A. H. N.]

[3] Deut. iv. 24. *Retract.* i. 7, § 5:—"The Pelagians may think that I have spoken of perfection as attainable in this life. But they must not think so. For the fervor of charity which is fitted for following God, and of force enough to consume all vices, can have its origin and growth in this life; but it does not follow that it can here accomplish the purpose of its origin, so that no vice shall remain in the man; although this great effect is produced by this same fervor of charity, when and where this is possible, that as the laver of regeneration purifies from the guilt of all the sins which attach to man's birth, or come from his evil conduct, so this perfection may purify him from all stain from the vices which necessarily attend human infirmity in this world. So we must understand the words of the apostle: 'Christ loved the Church, and gave himself for it; cleansing it with the washing of water by the word, that He might present it to Himself a glorious Church, not having spot, or wrinkle, or any such thing' (Eph. v. 25-27). For in this world there is the washing of water by the word which purifies the Church. But as the whole Church, as long as it is here, says, 'Forgive us our debts,' it certainly is not while here without spot, or wrinkle, or any such thing; but from that which it here receives, it is led on to the glory which is not here, and to perfection.

[4] Luke xii. 49.

is also quoted in the New Testament from the Old: "Death is swallowed up in victory. O death, where is thy sting? Where, O death, is thy contest?"[1] Could these heretics understand this one saying, no longer proud but quite reconciled, they would worship God nowhere but with thee and in thy bosom. In thee, as is fit, divine precepts are kept by widely-scattered multitudes. In thee, as is fit, it is well understood how much more heinous sin is when the law is known than when it is unknown. For "the sting of death is sin, and the strength of sin is the law,"[2] which adds to the force with which the consciousness of disregard of the precept strikes and slays. In thee it is seen, as is fit, how vain is effort under the law, when lust lays waste the mind, and is held in check by fear of punishment, instead of being overborne by the love of virtue. Thine, as is fit, are the many hospitable, the many friendly, the many compassionate, the many learned, the many chaste, the many saints, the many so ardent in their love to God, that in perfect continence and amazing indifference to this world they find happiness even in solitude.

CHAP. 31.—THE LIFE OF THE ANACHORETES AND CŒNOBITES SET AGAINST THE CONTINENCE OF THE MANICHÆANS.

65. What must we think is seen by those who can live without seeing their fellow-creatures, though not without loving them? It must be something transcending human things in contemplating which man can live without seeing his fellow-man. Hear now, ye Manichæans, the customs and notable continence of perfect Christians, who have thought it right not only to praise but also to practise the height of chastity, that you may be restrained, if there is any shame in you, from vaunting your abstinence before uninstructed minds as if it were the hardest of all things. I will speak of things of which you are not ignorant, though you hide them from us. For who does not know that there is a daily increasing multitude of Christian men of absolute continence spread all over the world, especially in the East and in Egypt, as you cannot help knowing?

66. I will say nothing of those to whom I just now alluded, who, in complete seclusion from the view of men, inhabit regions utterly barren, content with simple bread, which is brought to them periodically, and with water, enjoying communion with God, to whom in purity of mind they cleave, and most blessed in contemplating His beauty, which can be seen only by the understanding of saints. I will say nothing of them, because some people think them to have abandoned human things more than they ought, not considering how much those may benefit us in their minds by prayer, and in their lives by example, whose bodies we are not permitted to see. But to discuss this point would take long, and would be fruitless; for if a man does not of his own accord regard this high pitch of sanctity as admirable and honorable, how can our speaking lead him to do so? Only the Manichæans, who make a boast of nothing, should be reminded that the abstinence and continence of the great saints of the Catholic Church has gone so far, that some think it should be checked and recalled within the limits of humanity,—so far above men, even in the judgment of those who disapprove, have their minds soared.

67. But if this is beyond our tolerance, who can but admire and commend those who, slighting and discarding the pleasures of this world, living together in a most chaste and holy society, unite in passing their time in prayers, in readings, in discussions, without any swelling of pride, or noise of contention, or sullenness of envy; but quiet, modest, peaceful, their life is one of perfect harmony and devotion to God, an offering most acceptable to Him from whom the power to do those things is obtained? No one possesses anything of his own; no one is a burden to another. They work with their hands in such occupations as may feed their bodies without distracting their minds from God. The product of their toil they give to the decans or tithesmen,—so called from being set over the tithes,—so that no one is occupied with the care of his body, either in food or clothes, or in anything else required for daily use or for the common ailments. These decans, again, arranging everything with great care, and meeting promptly the demands made by that life on account of bodily infirmities, have one called "father," to whom they give in their accounts. These fathers are not only more saintly in their conduct, but also distinguished for divine learning, and of high character in every way; and without pride they superintend those whom they call their children, having themselves great authority in giving orders, and meeting with willing obedience from those under their charge. At the close of the day they assemble from their separate dwellings before their meal to hear their father, assembling to the number of three thousand at least for one father; for one may have even a much larger number than this. They listen with astonishing

[1] Hos. xiii. 14; 1 Cor. xv. 54, 55.
[2] 1 Cor. xv. 56

eagerness in perfect silence, and give expression to the feelings of their minds as moved by the words of the preacher, in groans, or tears, or signs of joy without noise or shouting. Then there is refreshment for the body, as much as health and a sound condition of the body requires, every one checking unlawful appetite, so as not to go to excess even in the poor, inexpensive fare provided. So they not only abstain from flesh and wine, in order to gain the mastery over their passions, but also from those things which are only the more likely to whet the appetite of the palate and of the stomach, from what some call their greater cleanness, which often serves as a ridiculous and disgraceful excuse for an unseemly taste for exquisite viands, as distant from animal food. Whatever they possess in addition to what is required for their support (and much is obtained, owing to their industry and frugality), they distribute to the needy with greater care than they took in procuring it for themselves. For while they make no effort to obtain abundance, they make every effort to prevent their abundance remaining with them,—so much so, that they send shiploads to places inhabited by poor people. I need say no more on a matter known to all.[1]

68. Such, too, is the life of the women, who serve God assiduously and chastely, living apart and removed as far as propriety demands from the men, to whom they are united only in pious affection and in imitation of virtue. No young men are allowed access to them, nor even old men, however respectable and approved, except to the porch, in order to furnish necessary supplies. For the women occupy and maintain themselves by working in wool, and hand over the cloth to the brethren, from whom, in return, they get what they need for food. Such customs, such a life, such arrangements, such a system, I could not commend as it deserves, if I wished to commend it; besides, I am afraid that it would seem as if I thought it unlikely to gain acceptance from the mere description of it, if I considered myself obliged to add an ornamental eulogium to the simple narrative. Ye Manichæans, find fault here if you can. Do not bring into prominence our tares before men too blind to discriminate.

CHAP. 32.—PRAISE OF THE CLERGY.

69. There is not, however, such narrowness in the moral excellence of the Catholic Church as that I should limit my praise of it to the life of those here mentioned. For how many bishops have I known most excellent and holy men, how many presbyters, how many deacons, and ministers of all kinds of the divine sacraments, whose virtue seems to me more admirable and more worthy of commendation on account of the greater difficulty of preserving it amidst the manifold varieties of men, and in this life of turmoil! For they preside over men needing cure as much as over those already cured. The vices of the crowd must be borne with in order that they may be cured, and the plague must be endured before it is subdued. To keep here the best way of life and a mind calm and peaceful is very hard. Here, in a word, we are among people who are learning to live. There they live.

CHAP. 33.—ANOTHER KIND OF MEN LIVING TOGETHER IN CITIES. FASTS OF THREE DAYS.

70. Still I would not on this account cast a slight upon a praiseworthy class of Christians,—those, namely, who live together in cities, quite apart from common life. I saw at Milan a lodging-house of saints, in number not a few, presided over by one presbyter, a man of great excellence and learning. At Rome I knew several places where there was in each one eminent for weight of character, and prudence, and divine knowledge, presiding over all the rest who lived with him, in Christian charity, and sanctity, and liberty. These, too, are not burdensome to any one; but, in the Eastern fashion, and on the authority of the Apostle Paul, they maintain themselves with their own hands. I was told that many practised fasts of quite amazing severity, not merely taking only one meal daily towards night, which is everywhere quite common, but very often continuing for three days or more in succession without food or drink. And this among not men only, but women, who also live together in great numbers as widows or virgins, gaining a livelihood by spinning and weaving, and presided over in each case by a woman of the greatest judgment and experience, skilled and accomplished not only in directing and forming moral conduct, but also in instructing the understanding.[2]

71. With all this, no one is pressed to endure hardships for which he is unfit; nothing is imposed on any one against his will; nor is he condemned by the rest because he con-

[1] [This picture of cœnobitic life, even in its purest form, is doubtless idealized. It is certain that the monasteries very soon became hot-beds of vice, and the refuge of the scum of society.—A. H. N.]

[2] [Augustin ascribes a broadmindedness and charitableness to the ascetics of his time which was doubtless quite subjective. The ascetics of that age with whose history we are acquainted were not of this type. Jerome is an example.—A. H. N.]

fesses himself too feeble to imitate them: for they bear in mind how strongly Scripture enjoins charity on all: they bear in mind, "To the pure all things are pure,"[1] and "Not that which entereth into your mouth defileth you, but that which cometh out of it."[2] Accordingly, all their endeavors are concerned not about the rejection of kinds of food as polluted, but about the subjugation of inordinate desire and the maintenance of brotherly love. They remember, "Meats for the belly, and the belly for meats; but God shall destroy both it and them;"[3] and again, "Neither if we eat shall we abound, nor if we refrain from eating shall we be in want;"[4] and, above all, this: "It is good, my brethren, not to eat flesh, nor drink wine, nor anything whereby thy brother is offended;" for this passage shows that love is the end to be aimed at in all these things. "For one man," he says, "believes that he can eat all things: another, who is weak, eateth herbs. He that eateth, let him not despise him that eateth not; and let not him that eateth not judge him that eateth: for God hath approved him. Who art thou that thou shouldest judge another man's servant? To his own master he stands or falls; but he shall stand: for God is able to make him to stand." And a little after: "He that eateth, to the Lord he eateth, and giveth God thanks; and he that eateth not, to the Lord he eateth not, and giveth God thanks." And also in what follows: "So every one of us shall give account of himself to God. Let us not, then, any more judge one another: but judge this rather, that ye place no stumbling-block, or cause of offence, in the way of a brother. I know, and am confident in the Lord Jesus, that there is nothing common in itself: but to him that thinketh anything to be common, to him it is common." Could he have shown better that it is not in the things we eat, but in the mind, that there is a power able to pollute it, and therefore that even those who are fit to think lightly of these things, and know perfectly that they are not polluted if they take any food in mental superiority, without being gluttons, should still have regard to charity? See what he adds: "For if thy brother be grieved with thy meat, now walkest thou not charitably."[5]

72. Read the rest: it is too long to quote all. You will find that those able to think lightly of such things,—that is, those of greater strength and stability,—are told that they must nevertheless abstain, lest those should be offended who from their weakness are still in need of such abstinence. The people I was describing know and observe these things; for they are Christians, not heretics. They understand Scripture according to the apostolic teaching, not according to the presumptuous and fictitious name of apostle.[6] Him that eats not no one despises; him that eats no one judges; he who is weak eats herbs. Many who are strong, however, do this for the sake of the weak; with many the reason for so doing is not this, but that they may have a cheaper diet, and may lead a life of the greatest tranquillity, with the least expensive provision for the support of the body. "For all things are lawful for me," he says; "but I will not be brought under the power of any."[7] Thus many do not eat flesh, and yet do not superstitiously regard it as unclean. And so the same people who abstain when in health take it when unwell without any fear, if it is required as a cure. Many drink no wine; but they do not think that wine defiles them; for they cause it to be given with the greatest propriety and moderation to people of languid temperament, and, in short, to all who cannot have bodily health without it. When some foolishly refuse it, they counsel them as brothers not to let a silly superstition make them weaker instead of making them holier. They read to them the apostle's precept to his disciple to "take a little wine for his many infirmities."[8] Then they diligently exercise piety; bodily exercise, they know, profiteth for a short time, as the same apostle says.[9]

73. Those, then who are able, and they are without number, abstain both from flesh and from wine for two reasons: either for the weakness of their brethren, or for their own liberty. Charity is principally attended to. There is charity in their choice of diet, charity in their speech, charity in their dress, charity in their looks. Charity is the point where they meet, and the plan by which they act. To transgress against charity is thought criminal, like transgressing against God. Whatever opposes this is attacked and expelled; whatever injures it is not allowed to continue for a single day. They know that it has been so enjoined by Christ and the apostles; that without it all things are empty, with it all are fulfilled.

CHAP. 34.—THE CHURCH IS NOT TO BE BLAMED FOR THE CONDUCT OF BAD CHRISTIANS, WORSHIPPERS OF TOMBS AND PICTURES.

74. Make objections against these, ye

1 Tit. i. 15. 2 Matt. xv. 11. 3 1 Cor. vi. 13. 4 1 Cor. viii. 8. 5 Rom. xiv. 2-21.

6 See title of the Epistle of Manichæus, *Contra Faust.* xiii. 4. 7 1 Cor. vi. 12. 8 1 Tim. v. 23. 9 1 Tim. iv. 8.

Manichæans, if you can. Look at these people, and speak of them reproachfully, if you dare, without falsehood. Compare their fasts with your fasts, their chastity with yours; compare them to yourselves in dress, food, self-restraint, and, lastly, in charity. Compare, which is most to the point, their precepts with yours. Then you will see the difference between show and sincerity, between the right way and the wrong, between faith and imposture, between strength and inflatedness, between happiness and wretchedness, between unity and disunion; in short, between the sirens of superstition and the harbor of religion.

75. Do not summon against me professors of the Christian name, who neither know nor give evidence of the power of their profession.[1] Do not hunt up the numbers of ignorant people, who even in the true religion are superstitious, or are so given up to evil passions as to forget what they have promised to God. I know that there are many worshippers of tombs and pictures. I know that there are many who drink to great excess over the dead, and who, in the feasts which they make for corpses, bury themselves over the buried, and give to their gluttony and drunkenness the name of religion. I know that there are many who in words have renounced this world, and yet desire to be burdened with all the weight of worldly things, and rejoice in such burdens. Nor is it surprising that among so many multitudes you should find some by condemning whose life you may deceive the unwary and seduce them from Catholic safety; for in your small numbers you are at a loss when called on to show even one out of those whom you call the elect who keeps the precepts, which in your indefensible superstition you profess. How silly those are, how impious, how mischievous, and to what extent they are neglected by most, nearly all of you, I have shown in another volume.

76. My advice to you now is this: that you should at least desist from slandering the Catholic Church, by declaiming against the conduct of men whom the Church herself condemns, seeking daily to correct them as wicked children. Then, if any of them by good will and by the help of God are corrected, they regain by repentance what they had lost by sin. Those, again, who with wicked will persist in their old vices, or even add to them others still worse, are indeed allowed to remain in the field of the Lord, and to grow along with the good seed; but the time for separating the tares will come.[2] Or if, from their having at least the Christian name, they are to be placed among the chaff rather than among thistles, there will also come One to purge the floor and to separate the chaff from the wheat, and to assign to each part (according to its desert) the due reward.[3]

CHAP. 35.—MARRIAGE AND PROPERTY ALLOWED TO THE BAPTIZED BY THE APOSTLES.

77. Meanwhile, why do you rage? why does party spirit blind your eyes? Why do you entangle yourselves in a long defence of such great error? Seek for fruit in the field, seek for wheat in the floor: they will be found easily, and will present themselves to the inquirer. Why do you look so exclusively at the dross? Why do you use the roughness of the hedge to scare away the inexperienced from the fatness of the garden? There is a proper entrance, though known to but a few; and by it men come in, though you disbelieve it, or do not wish to find it. In the Catholic Church there are believers without number who do not use the world, and there are those who "use it," in the words of the apostle, "as not using it,"[4] as was proved in those times when Christians were forced to worship idols. For then, how many wealthy men, how many peasant householders, how many merchants, how many military men, how many leading men in their own cities, and how many senators, people of both sexes, giving up all these empty and transitory things, though while they used them they were not bound down by them, endured death for the salutary faith and religion, and proved to unbelievers that instead of being possessed by all these things they really possessed them?

78. Why do you reproach us by saying that men renewed in baptism ought no longer to beget children, or to possess fields, and houses, and money? Paul allows it. For, as cannot be denied, he wrote to believers, after recounting many kinds of evil-doers who shall not possess the kingdom of God: "And such were you," he says: "but ye are washed, but ye are sanctified, but ye are justified in

1 [Augustin says nothing of the encouragement given to such pagan practices by men regarded in that age as possessed of almost superhuman sanctity, such as Sulpicius Severus, Paulinus of Nola, etc. He speaks of corruptions as if they were exceptional, whereas they seem to have been the rule. Yet there is force in his contention that Christianity be judged by its best products rather than by the worst elements associated with it.—A. H. N.]

2 [Augustin's ideal representation of Christianity and his identification of the organized Catholic Church with Christianity is quite inconsistent with the practice of the Church which he here seeks to justify. No duty is more distinctly enjoined upon believers in the New Testament than separation from unbelievers and evil doers. But such separation is impracticable in an established Church such as that to which Augustin rejoiced to belong.—A. H. N.]

3 Matt. iii. 13, and xiii. 24–43.

4 1 Cor. vii. 31.

the name of the Lord Jesus Christ and by the Spirit of our God." By the washed and sanctified, no one, assuredly, will venture to think any are meant but believers, and those who have renounced this world. But, after showing to whom he writes, let us see whether he allows these things to them. He goes on: "All things are lawful for me, but all things are not expedient: all things are lawful for me, but I will not be brought under the power of any. Meat for the belly, and the belly for meats: but God will destroy both it and them. Now the body is not for fornication, but for the Lord, and the Lord for the body. But God raised up the Lord, and will raise us up also by His own power. Know ye not that your bodies are the members of Christ? shall I then take the members of Christ, and make them the members of an harlot? God forbid. Know ye not that he which is joined to an harlot is made one body? for the twain, saith He, shall be one flesh. But he that is joined to the Lord is one spirit. Flee fornication. Whatever sin a man doeth is without the body: but he that committeth fornication sinneth against his own body. Know ye not that your members are the temple of the Holy Spirit which is in you, which ye have of God, and ye are not your own? For ye are bought with a great price: glorify God, and carry Him in your body."[1] "But of the things concerning which ye wrote to me: it is good for a man not to touch a woman. Nevertheless, to avoid fornication, let every man have his own wife, and let every woman have her own husband. Let the husband render unto the wife due benevolence: and likewise also the wife unto the husband. The wife hath not power of her own body, but the husband: and likewise also the husband hath not power of his own body, but the wife. Defraud ye not one the other, except it be with consent for a time, that ye may have leisure for prayer; and come together again, that Satan tempt you not for your incontinency. But I speak this by permission, and not of commandment. For I would that all men were even as I myself: but every man hath his proper gift of God, one after this manner, and another after that."[2]

79. Has the apostle, think you, both shown sufficiently to the strong what is highest, and permitted to the weaker what is next best? Not to touch a woman he shows is highest when he says, "I would that all men were even as I myself." But next to this highest is conjugal chastity, that man may not be the prey of fornication. Did he say that these people were not yet believers because they were married? Indeed, by this conjugal chastity he says that those who are united are sanctified by one another, if one of them is an unbeliever, and that their children also are sanctified. "The unbelieving husband," he says, "is sanctified by the believing wife, and the unbelieving woman by the believing husband: otherwise your children would be unclean; but now are they holy."[3] Why do you persist in opposition to such plain truth? Why do you try to darken the light of Scripture by vain shadows?

80. Do not say that catechumens are allowed to have wives, but not believers; that catechumens may have money, but not believers. For there are many who use as not using. And in that sacred washing the renewal of the new man is begun so as gradually to reach perfection, in some more quickly, in others more slowly. The progress, however, to a new life is made in the case of many, if we view the matter without hostility, but attentively. As the apostle says of himself, "Though the outward man perish, the inward man is renewed day by day."[4] The apostle says that the inward man is renewed day by day that it may reach perfection; and you wish it to begin with perfection! And it were well if you did wish it. In reality, you aim not at raising the weak, but at misleading the unwary. You ought not to have spoken so arrogantly, even if it were known that you are perfect in your childish precepts. But when your conscience knows that those whom you bring into your sect, when they come to a more intimate acquaintance with you, will find many things in you which nobody hearing you accuse others would suspect, is it not great impertinence to demand perfection in the weaker Catholics, to turn away the inexperienced from the Catholic Church, while you show nothing of the kind in yourself to those thus turned away? But not to seem to inveigh against you without reason, I will now close this volume, and will proceed at last to set forth the precepts of your life and your notable customs.

[1] 1 Cor. vi. 11-20.
[2] 1 Cor. vii. 1-7.
[3] 1 Cor. vii. 14.
[4] 2 Cor. iv. 16.

ST. AUGUSTIN:

ON THE

MORALS OF THE MANICHÆANS.

[DE MORIBUS MANICHÆORUM].

A.D. 388.

TRANSLATED BY

REV. RICHARD STOTHERT, M.A.,

BOMBAY.

CONTENTS OF THE MORALS OF THE MANICHÆANS.

ON THE

MORALS OF THE MANICHÆANS.

[DE MORIBUS MANICHÆORUM.] A. D. 388.

CONTAINING A PARTICULAR REFUTATION OF THE DOCTRINE OF THESE HERETICS REGARDING THE ORIGIN AND NATURE OF EVIL; AN EXPOSURE OF THEIR PRETENDED SYMBOLICAL CUSTOMS OF THE MOUTH, OF THE HANDS, AND OF THE BREAST; AND A CONDEMNATION OF THEIR SUPERSTITIOUS ABSTINENCE AND UNHOLY MYSTERIES. LASTLY, SOME CRIMES BROUGHT TO LIGHT AMONG THE MANICHÆANS ARE MENTIONED.

CHAP. 1.—THE SUPREME GOOD IS THAT WHICH IS POSSESSED OF SUPREME EXISTENCE.

1. EVERY one, I suppose, will allow that the question of things good and evil belongs to moral science, in which such terms are in common use. It is therefore to be wished that men would bring to these inquiries such a clear intellectual perfection as might enable them to see the chief good, than which nothing is better or higher, next in order to which comes a rational soul in a state of purity and perfection.[1] If this were clearly understood, it would also become evident that the chief good is that which is properly described as having supreme and original existence. For that exists in the highest sense of the word which continues always the same, which is throughout like itself, which cannot in any part be corrupted or changed, which is not subject to time, which admits of no variation in its present as compared with its former condition. This is existence in its true sense. For in this signification of the word existence there is implied a nature which is self-contained, and which continues immutably. Such things can be said only of God, to whom there is nothing contrary in the strict sense of the word. For the contrary of existence is non-existence. There is therefore no nature contrary to God. But since the minds with which we approach the study of these subjects have their vision damaged and dulled by silly notions, and by perversity of will, let us try as we can to gain some little knowledge of this great matter by degrees and with caution, making our inquiries not like men able to see, but like men groping the dark.

CHAP. 2.—WHAT EVIL IS. THAT EVIL IS THAT WHICH IS AGAINST NATURE. IN ALLOWING THIS, THE MANICHÆANS REFUTE THEMSELVES.

2. You Manichæans often, if not in every case, ask those whom you try to bring over to your heresy, Whence is evil? Suppose I had now met you for the first time, I would ask you, if you please, to follow my example in putting aside for a little the explanation you suppose yourselves to have got of these subjects, and to commence this great inquiry with me as if for the first time. You ask me, Whence is evil? I ask you in return, What is evil? Which is the more reasonable question? Are those right who ask whence a thing is, when they do not know what it is; or he who thinks it necessary to inquire first what it is, in order to avoid the gross absurdity of searching for the origin of a thing unknown? Your answer is quite correct, when you say that evil is that which is contrary to nature; for no one is so mentally blind as not to see that, in every kind, evil is that which is contrary to the nature of the kind. But the establishment of this doctrine is the overthrow of your heresy. For evil is no nature,

[1] [This statement has a complete parallel in Clement of Alexandria, and along with what follows, is Neo-Platonic.—A. H. N.]

if it is contrary to nature. Now, according to you, evil is a certain nature and substance. Moreover, whatever is contrary to nature must oppose nature and seek its destruction. For nature means nothing else than that which anything is conceived of as being in its own kind. Hence is the new word which we now use derived from the word for being,—essence namely, or, as we usually say, substance,—while before these words were in use, the word nature was used instead. Here, then, if you will consider the matter without stubbornness, we see that evil is that which falls away from essence and tends to non-existence.

3. Accordingly, when the Catholic Church declares that God is the author of all natures and substances, those who understand this understand at the same time that God is not the author of evil. For how can He who is the cause of the being of all things be at the same time the cause of their not being,—that is, of their falling off from essence and tending to non-existence? For this is what reason plainly declares to be the definition of evil. Now, how can that race of evil of yours, which you make the supreme evil, be against nature, that is, against substance, when it, according to you, is itself a nature and substance? For if it acts against itself, it destroys its own existence; and when that is completely done, it will come at last to be the supreme evil. But this cannot be done, because you will have it not only to be, but to be everlasting. That cannot then be the chief evil which is spoken of as a substance.[1]

4. But what am I to do? I know that many of you can understand nothing of all this. I know, too, that there are some who have a good understanding and can see these things, and yet are so stubborn in their choice of evil,—a choice that will ruin their understanding as well,—that they try rather to find what reply they can make in order to impose upon inactive and feeble minds, instead of giving their assent to the truth. Still I shall not regret having written either what one of you may come some day to consider impartially, and be led to abandon your error, or what men of understanding and in allegiance to God, and who are still untainted with your errors, may read and so be kept from being led astray by your addresses.

CHAP. 3.—IF EVIL IS DEFINED AS THAT WHICH IS HURTFUL, THIS IMPLIES ANOTHER REFUTATION OF THE MANICHÆANS.

5. Let us then inquire more carefully, and, if possible, more plainly. I ask you again, What is evil? If you say it is that which is hurtful, here, too, you will not answer amiss. But consider, I pray you; be on your guard, I beg of you; be so good as to lay aside party spirit, and make the inquiry for the sake of finding the truth, not of getting the better of it. Whatever is hurtful takes away some good from that to which it is hurtful; for without the loss of good there can be no hurt. What, I appeal to you, can be plainer than this? what more intelligible? What else is required for complete demonstration to one of average understanding, if he is not perverse? But, if this is granted, the consequence seems plain. In that race which you take for the chief evil, nothing can be liable to be hurt, since there is no good in it. But if, as you assert, there are two natures,—the kingdom of light and the kingdom of darkness; since you make the kingdom of light to be God, attributing to it an uncompounded nature,[2] so that it has no part inferior to another, you must grant, however decidedly in opposition to yourselves, you must grant, nevertheless, that this nature, which you not only do not deny to be the chief good, but spend all your strength in trying to show that it is so, is immutable, incorruptible, impenetrable, inviolable, for otherwise it would not be the chief good; for the chief good is that than which there is nothing better, and for such a nature to be hurt is impossible. Again, if, as has been shown, to hurt is to deprive of good, there can be no hurt to the kingdom of darkness, for there is no good in it. And as the kingdom of light cannot be hurt, as it is inviolable, what can the evil you speak of be hurtful to?

CHAP. 4.—THE DIFFERENCE BETWEEN WHAT IS GOOD IN ITSELF AND WHAT IS GOOD BY PARTICIPATION.

6. Now, compare with this perplexity, from which you cannot escape, the consistency of the statements in the teaching of the Catholic Church, according to which there is one good which is good supremely and in itself, and not by the participation of any good, but by its own nature and essence; and another good which is good by participation, and by having something bestowed. Thus it has its being as good from the supreme good, which, however, is still self-contained, and loses nothing.

---

1 [On Augustin's view of negativity of evil and on the relation of this view to Neo-Platonism, see Introduction, chapter IX. Augustin's view seems to exclude the permanence of evil in the world, and so everlasting punishment and everlasting rebellion against God.—A. H. N.]

2 [It is probable that Mani thought of the Kingdom of Light pantheistically, and that the principles personified in his mythological system were the result of efforts on his part to connect the infinite with the finite.—A. H. N.]

This second kind of good is called a creature, which is liable to hurt through falling away. But of this falling away God is not the author, for He is author of existence and of being. Here we see the proper use of the word evil; for it is correctly applied not to essence, but to negation or loss. We see, too, what nature it is which is liable to hurt. This nature is not the chief evil, for when it is hurt it loses good; nor is it the chief good, for its falling away from good is because it is good not intrinsically, but by possessing the good. And a thing cannot be good by nature when it is spoken of as being made, which shows that the goodness was bestowed. Thus, on the one hand, God is the good, and all things which He has made are good, though not so good as He who made them. For what madman would venture to require that the works should equal the workman, the creatures the Creator? What more do you want? Could you wish for anything plainer than this?

CHAP. 5.—IF EVIL IS DEFINED TO BE CORRUPTION, THIS COMPLETELY REFUTES THE MANICHÆAN HERESY.

7. I ask a third time, What is evil? Perhaps you will reply, Corruption. Undeniably this is a general definition of evil; for corruption implies opposition to nature, and also hurt. But corruption exists not by itself, but in some substance which it corrupts; for corruption itself is not a substance. So the thing which it corrupts is not corruption, is not evil; for what is corrupted suffers the loss of integrity and purity. So that which has no purity to lose cannot be corrupted; and what has, is necessarily good by the participation of purity. Again, what is corrupted is perverted; and what is perverted suffers the loss of order, and order is good. To be corrupted, then, does not imply the absence of good; for in corruption it can be deprived of good, which could not be if there was the absence of good. Therefore that race of darkness, if it was destitute of all good, as you say it was, could not be corrupted, for it had nothing which corruption could take from it; and if corruption takes nothing away, it does not corrupt. Say now, if you dare, that God and the kingdom of God can be corrupted, when you cannot show how the kingdom of the devil, such as you make it, can be corrupted.

CHAP. 6.—WHAT CORRUPTION AFFECTS AND WHAT IT IS.

8. What further does the Catholic light say? What do you suppose, but what is the actual truth, that it is the created substance which can be corrupted, for the uncreated, which is the chief good, is incorruptible; and corruption, which is the chief evil, cannot be corrupted; besides, that it is not a substance? But if you ask what corruption is, consider to what it seeks to bring the things which it corrupts; for it affects those things according to its own nature. Now all things by corruption fall away from what they were, and are brought to non-continuance, to non-existence; for existence implies continuance. Thus the supreme and chief existence is so called because it continues in itself, or is self-contained. In the case of a thing changing for the better, the change is not from continuance, but from perversion to the worse, that is, from falling away from essence; the author of which falling away is not He who is the author of the essence. So in some things there is change for the better, and so a tendency towards existence. And this change is not called a perversion, but reversion or conversion; for perversion is opposed to orderly arrangement. Now things which tend towards existence tend towards order, and, attaining order they attain existence, as far as that is possible to a creature. For order reduces to a certain uniformity that which it arranges; and existence is nothing else than being one. Thus, so far as anything acquires unity, so far it exists. For uniformity and harmony are the effects of unity, and by these compound things exist as far as they have existence. For simple things exist by themselves, for they are one. But things not simple imitate unity by the agreement of their parts; and so far as they attain this, so far they exist. This arrangement is the cause of existence, disorder of non-existence; and perversion or corruption are the other names for disorder. So whatever is corrupted tends to non-existence. You may now be left to reflect upon the effect of corruption, that you may discover what is the chief evil; for it is that which corruption aims at accomplishing.

CHAP. 7.—THE GOODNESS OF GOD PREVENTS CORRUPTION FROM BRINGING ANYTHING TO NON-EXISTENCE. THE DIFFERENCE BETWEEN CREATING AND FORMING.

9. But the goodness of God does not permit the accomplishment of this end, but so orders all things that fall away that they may exist where their existence is most suitable, till in the order of their movements they return to that from which they fell away.[1]

[1] In *Retract.* i. 7, § 6, it is said: "This must not be understood to mean that all things return to that from which they fell away,

Thus, when rational souls fall away from God, although they possess the greatest amount of free-will, He ranks them in the lower grades of creation, where their proper place is. So they suffer misery by the divine judgment, while they are ranked suitably to their deserts. Hence we see the excellence of that saying which you are always inveighing against so strongly, "I make good things, and create evil things."[1] To create is to form and arrange. So in some copies it is written, "I make good things and form evil things." To make is used of things previously not in existence; but to form is to arrange what had some kind of existence, so as to improve and enlarge it. Such are the things which God arranges when He says, "I form evil things," meaning things which are falling off, and so tending to non-existence,—not things which have reached that to which they tend. For it has been said, Nothing is allowed in the providence of God to go the length of non-existence.[2]

10. These things might be discussed more fully and at greater length, but enough has been said for our purpose in dealing with you. We have only to show you the gate which you despair of finding, and make the uninstructed despair of it too. You can be made to enter only by good-will, on which the divine mercy bestows peace, as the song in the Gospel says, "Glory to God in the highest, and on earth peace to men of good-will."[3] It is enough, I say, to have shown you that there is no way of solving the religious question of good and evil, unless whatever is, as far as it is, is from God; while as far as it falls away from being it is not of God, and yet is always ordered by Divine Providence in agreement with the whole system. If you do not yet see this, I know nothing else that I can do but to discuss the things already said with greater particularity. For nothing save piety and purity can lead the mind to greater things.

CHAP. 8.—EVIL IS NOT A SUBSTANCE, BUT A DISAGREEMENT HOSTILE TO SUBSTANCE.

11. For what other answer will you give to the question, What is evil? but either that it is against nature, or that it is hurtful, or that it is corruption, or something similar? But I have shown that in these replies you make shipwreck of your cause, unless, indeed, you will answer in the childish way in which you generally speak to children, that evil is fire, poison, a wild beast, and so on. For one of the leaders of this heresy, whose instructions we attended with great familiarity and frequency, used to say with reference to a person who held that evil was not a substance, "I should like to put a scorpion in the man's hand, and see whether he would not withdraw his hand; and in so doing he would get a proof, not in words but in the thing itself, that evil is a substance, for he would not deny that the animal is a substance." He said this not in the presence of the person, but to us, when we repeated to him the remark which had troubled us, giving, as I said, a childish answer to children. For who with the least tincture of learning or science does not see that these things hurt by disagreement with the bodily temperament, while at other times they agree with it, so as not only not to hurt, but to produce the best effects? For if this poison were evil in itself, the scorpion itself would suffer first and most. In fact, if the poison were quite taken from the animal, it would die. So for its body it is evil to lose what it is evil for our body to receive; and it is good for it to have what it is good for us to want. Is the same thing then both good and evil? By no means; but evil is what is against nature, for this is evil both to the animal and to us. This evil is the disagreement, which certainly is not a substance, but hostile to substance. Whence then is it? See what it leads to, and you will learn, if any inner light lives in you. It leads all that it destroys to non-existence. Now God is the author of existence; and there is no existence which, as far as it is existing, leads to non-existence. Thus we learn whence disagreement is not; as to whence it is, nothing can be said.

12. We read in history of a female criminal in Athens, who succeeded in drinking the quantity of poison allotted as a fatal draught for the condemned with little or no injury to her health, by taking it at intervals. So being condemned, she took the poison in the prescribed quantity like the rest, but rendered it powerless by accustoming herself to it, and did not die like the rest. And as this excited great wonder, she was banished. If poison is an evil, are we to think that she made it to be no evil to her? What could be more absurd than this? But because disagreement is an evil, what she did was to make the poisonous matter agree with her own body by a process of habituation. For how could she by any amount of cunning have brought it

as Origen believed, but only those which do return. Those who shall be punished in everlasting fire do not return to God, from whom they fell away. Still they are in order as existing in punishment where their existence is most suitable." [This does not really meet the difficulty suggested on a preceding page.—A. H. N.]

[1] Isa. xlv. 7.

[2] [That is to say nothing is absolutely evil, and conversely what is absolutely evil is *ipso facto* non-existent.—A. H. N.]

[3] Luke ii. 14.

about that disagreement should not hurt her? Why so? Because what is truly and properly an evil is hurtful both always and to all. Oil is beneficial to our bodies, but very much the opposite to many six-footed animals. And is not hellebore sometimes food, sometimes medicine, and sometimes poison. Does not every one maintain that salt taken in excess is poisonous? And yet the benefits to the body from salt are innumerable and most important. Sea-water is injurious when drunk by land animals, but it is most suitable and useful to many who bathe their bodies in it; and to fish it is useful and wholesome in both ways. Bread nourishes man, but kills hawks. And does not mud itself, which is offensive and noxious when swallowed or smelt, serve as cooling to the touch in hot weather, and as a cure for wounds from fire? What can be nastier than dung, or more worthless than ashes? And yet they are of such use to the fields, that the Romans thought divine honors due to the discoverer, Stercutio, from whose name the word for dung [*stercus*] is derived.

13. But why enumerate details which are countless? We need not go farther than the four elements themselves, which, as every one knows, are beneficial when there is agreement, and bitterly opposed to nature when there is disagreement in the objects acted upon. We who live in air die under earth or under water, while innumerable animals creep alive in sand or loose earth, and fish die in our air. Fire consumes our bodies, but, when suitably applied, it both restores from cold, and expels diseases without number. The sun to which you bow the knee, and than which, indeed, there is no fairer object among visible things, strengthens the eyes of eagles, but hurts and dims our eyes when we gaze on it; and yet we too can accustom ourselves to look upon it without injury. Will you, then, allow the sun to be compared to the poison which the Athenian woman made harmless by habituating herself to it? Reflect for once, and consider that if a substance is an evil because it hurts some one, the light which you worship cannot be acquitted of this charge. See the preferableness of making evil in general to consist in this disagreement, from which the sun's ray produces dimness in the eyes, though nothing is pleasanter to the eyes than light.[1]

CHAP. 9.—THE MANICHÆAN FICTIONS ABOUT THINGS GOOD AND EVIL ARE NOT CONSISTENT WITH THEMSELVES.

14. I have said these things to make you cease, if that is possible, giving the name of evil to a region boundless in depth and length; to a mind wandering through the region; to the five caverns of the elements,—one full of darkness, another of waters, another of winds, another of fire, another of smoke; to the animals born in each of these elements,—serpents in the darkness, swimming creatures in the waters, flying creatures in the winds, quadrupeds in the fire, bipeds in the smoke. For these things, as you describe them, cannot be called evil; for all such things, as far as they exist, must have their existence from the most high God, for as far as they exist they are good. If pain and weakness is an evil, the animals you speak of were of such physical strength that their abortive offspring, after, as your sect believes, the world was formed of them, fell from heaven to earth, according to you, and could not die. If blindness is an evil, they could see; if deafness, they could hear. If to be nearly or altogether dumb is an evil, their speech was so clear and intelligible, that, as you assert, they decided to make war against God in compliance with an address delivered in their assembly. If sterility is an evil, they were prolific in children. If exile is an evil, they were in their own country, and occupied their own territories. If servitude is an evil, some of them were rulers. If death is an evil, they were alive, and the life was such that, by your statement, even after God was victorious, it was impossible for the mind ever to die.

15. Can you tell me how it is that in the chief evil so many good things are to be found, the opposites of the evils above mentioned? and if these are not evils, can any substance be an evil, as far as it is a substance? If weakness is not an evil, can a weak body be an evil? If blindness is not an evil, can darkness be an evil? If deafness is not an evil, can a deaf man be an evil? If dumbness is not an evil, can a fish be an evil? If sterility is not an evil, how can we call a barren animal an evil? If exile is not an evil, how can we give that name to an animal in exile, or to an animal sending some one into exile? If servitude is not an evil, in what sense is a subject animal an evil, or one enforcing subjection? If death is not an evil, in what sense is a mortal animal an evil, or one causing death? Or if these are evils, must we not give the name of good things to bodily strength, sight, hearing, persuasive speech, fertility, native land, liberty, life, all which you hold to exist in that kingdom of evil, and yet venture to call it the perfection of evil?

16. Once more, if, as has never been de-

[1] [The reasoning here is admirably adapted to Augustin's purpose, which is to refute the Manichæan notion of the evil nature of material substances.—A. H. N.]

nied, unsuitableness is an evil, what can be more suitable than those elements to their respective animals,—the darkness to serpents, the waters to swimming creatures, the winds to flying creatures, the fire to voracious animals, the smoke to soaring animals? Such is the harmony which you describe as existing in the race of strife; such the order in the seat of confusion. If what is hurtful is an evil, I do not repeat the strong objection already stated, that no hurt can be suffered where no good exists; but if that is not so clear, one thing at least is easily seen and understood as following from the acknowledged truth, that what is hurtful is an evil. The smoke in that region did not hurt bipeds: it produced them, and nourished and sustained them without injury in their birth, their growth, and their rule. But now, when the evil has some good mixed with it, the smoke has become more hurtful, so that we, who certainly are bipeds, instead of being sustained by it, are blinded, and suffocated, and killed by it. Could the mixture of good have given such destructiveness to evil elements? Could there be such confusion in the divine government?

17. In the other cases, at least, how is it that we find that congruity which misled your author and induced him to fabricate falsehoods? Why does darkness agree with serpents, and waters with swimming creatures, and winds with flying creatures, though the fire burns up quadrupeds, and smoke chokes us? Then, again, have not serpents very sharp sight, and do they not love the sunshine, and abound most where the calmness of the air prevents the clouds from gathering much or often? How very absurd that the natives and lovers of darkness should live most comfortably and agreeably where the clearest light is enjoyed! Or if you say that it is the heat rather than the light that they enjoy, it would be more reasonable to assign to fire serpents, which are naturally of rapid motion, than the slow-going asp.[1] Besides, all must admit that light is agreeable to the eyes of the asp, for they are compared to an eagle's eyes. But enough of the lower animals. Let us, I pray, attend to what is true of ourselves without persisting in error, and so our minds shall be disentangled from silly and mischievous falsehoods. For is it not intolerable perversity to say that in the race of darkness, where there was no mixture of light, the biped animals had so sound and strong, so incredible force of eyesight, that even in their darkness they could see the perfectly pure light (as you represent it) of the kingdom of God? for, according to you, even these beings could see this light, and could gaze at it, and study it, and delight in it, and desire it; whereas our eyes, after mixture with light, with the chief good, yea, with God, have become so tender and weak, that we can neither see anything in the dark, nor bear to look at the sun, but, after looking, lose sight of what we could see before.

18. The same remarks are applicable if we take corruption to be an evil, which no one doubts. The smoke did not corrupt that race of animals, though it corrupts animals now. Not to go over all the particulars, which would be tedious, and is not necessary, the living creatures of your imaginary description were so much less liable to corruption than animals are now, that their abortive and premature offspring, cast headlong from heaven to earth, both lived and were productive, and could band together again, having, forsooth, their original vigor, because they were conceived before good was mixed with the evil; for, after this mixture, the animals born are, according to you, those which we now see to be very feeble and easily giving way to corruption. Can any one persist in the belief of error like this, unless he fails to see these things, or is affected by your habit and association in such an amazing way as to be proof against all the force of reasoning?

Chap. 10.—Three Moral Symbols Devised by the Manichæans for No Good.

19. Now that I have shown, as I think, how much darkness and error is in your opinions about good and evil things in general, let us examine now those three symbols which you extol so highly, and boast of as excellent observances. What then are those three symbols? That of the mouth, that of the hands, and that of the breast. What does this mean? That man, we are told, should be pure and innocent in mouth, in hands, and in breast. But what if he sins with eyes, ears, or nose? What if he hurts some one with his heels, or perhaps kills him? How can he be reckoned criminal when he has not sinned with mouth, hands, or breast? But, it is replied, by the mouth we are to understand all the organs of sense in the head; by the hands, all bodily actions; by the breast, all lustful tendencies. To what, then, do you assign blasphemies? To the mouth or to the hand? For blasphemy is an action of the tongue. And if all actions are to be classed under one head, why should you join together the actions of the hands and the feet, and not those of the tongue. Do you wish to separate the action

[1] [The text has *asinum* in this sentence but *aspidem* in the next. The former is evidently a mistake.—A. H. N.]

of the tongue, as being for the purpose of expressing something, from actions which are not for this purpose, so that the symbol of the hands should mean abstinence from all evil actions which are not for the purpose of expressing something? But then, what if some one sins by expressing something with his hands, as is done in writing or in some significant gesture? This cannot be assigned to the tongue and the mouth, for it is done by the hands. When you have three symbols of the mouth, the hands, and the breast, it is quite inadmissible to charge against the mouth sins found in the hands. And if you assign action in general to the hands, there is no reason for including under this the action of the feet and not that of the tongue. Do you see how the desire of novelty, with its attendant error, lands you in great difficulties? For you find it impossible to include purification of all sins in these three symbols, which you set forth as a kind of new classification.

CHAP. 11.—THE VALUE OF THE SYMBOL OF THE MOUTH AMONG THE MANICHÆANS, WHO ARE FOUND GUILTY OF BLASPHEMING GOD.

20. Classify as you please, omit what you please, we must discuss the doctrines you insist upon most. You say that the symbol of the mouth implies refraining from all blasphemy. But blasphemy is speaking evil of good things. So usually the word blasphemy is applied only to speaking evil of God; for as regards man there is uncertainty, but God is without controversy good. If, then, you are proved guilty of saying worse things of God than any one else says, what becomes of your famous symbol of the mouth? The evidence is not obscure, but clear and obvious to every understanding, and irresistible, the more so that no one can remain in ignorance of it, that God is incorruptible, immutable, liable to no injury, to no want, to no weakness, to no misery. All this the common sense of rational beings perceives, and even you assent when you hear it.

21. But when you begin to relate your fables, that God is corruptible, and mutable, and subject to injury, and exposed to want and weakness, and not secure from misery, this is what you are blind enough to teach, and what some are blind enough to believe. And this is not all; for, according to you, God is not only corruptible, but corrupted; not only changeable, but changed; not only subject to injury, but injured; not only liable to want, but in want; not only possibly, but actually weak; not only exposed to misery, but miserable. You say that the soul is God, or a part of God. I do not see how it can be part of God without being God. A part of gold is gold; of silver silver; of stone stone; and, to come to greater things, part of earth is earth, part of water is water, and of air air; and if you take part from fire, you will not deny it to be fire; and part of light can be nothing but light. Why then should part of God not be God? Has God a jointed body, like man and the lower animals? For part of man is not man.

22. I will deal with each of these opinions separately. If you view God as resembling light, you must admit that part of God is God. Hence, when you make the soul part of God, though you allow it to be corrupted as being foolish, and changed as having once been wise, and in want as needing health, and feeble as needing medicine, and miserable as desiring happiness, all these things you profanely attribute to God. Or if you deny these things of the mind, it follows that the Spirit is not required to lead the soul into truth, since it is not in folly; nor is the soul renewed by true religion, since it does not need renewal; nor is it perfected by your symbols, since it is already perfect; nor does God give it assistance, since it does not need it; nor is Christ its physician, since it is in health; nor does it require the promise of happiness in another life. Why then is Jesus called the deliverer, according to His own words in the Gospel, "If the Son shall make you free, ye shall be free indeed?"[1] And the Apostle Paul says, "Ye have been called to liberty."[2] The soul, then, which has not attained this liberty is in bondage. Therefore, according to you, God, since part of God is God, is both corrupted by folly, and is changed by falling, and is injured by the loss of perfection, and is in need of help, and is weakened by disease, and bowed down with misery, and subject to disgraceful bondage.

23. Again, if part of God is not God, still He is not incorrupt when His part is corrupted, nor unchanged when there is change in any part, nor uninjured when He is not perfect in every part, nor free from want when He is busily endeavoring to recover part of Himself, nor quite whole when He has a weak part, nor perfectly happy when any part is suffering misery, nor entirely free when any part is under bondage. These are conclusions to which you are driven, because you say that the soul, which you see to be in such a calamitous condition, is part of God. If you can succeed in making your sect abandon these and many similar opinions, then you may speak of your mouth being free from blas-

---

[1] John viii. 36.

[2] Gal. v. 13

phemies. Better still, leave the sect; for if you cease to believe and to repeat what Manichæus has written, you will be no longer Manichæans.

24. That God is the supreme good, and that than which nothing can be or can be conceived better, we must either understand or believe, if we wish to keep clear of blasphemy. There is a relation of numbers which cannot possibly be impaired or altered, nor can any nature by any amount of violence prevent the number which comes after one from being the double of one. This can in no way be changed; and yet you represent God as changeable! This relation preserves its integrity inviolable; and you will not allow God an equality even in this! Let some race of darkness take in the abstract the number three, consisting of indivisible units, and divide it into two equal parts. Your mind perceives that no hostility could effect this. And can that which is unable to injure a numerical relation injure God? If it could not, what possible necessity could there be for a part of him to be mixed with evil, and driven into such miseries?

CHAP. 12.—MANICHÆAN SUBTERFUGE.

25. For this gives rise to the question, which used to throw us into great perplexity even when we were your zealous disciples, nor could we find any answer,—what the race of darkness would have done to God, supposing He had refused to fight with it at the cost of such calamity to part of Himself. For if God would not have suffered any loss by remaining quiet, we thought it hard that we had been sent to endure so much. Again, if He would have suffered, His nature cannot have been incorruptible, as it behoves the nature of God to be. Sometimes the answer was, that it was not for the sake of escaping evil or avoiding injury, but that God in His natural goodness wished to bestow the blessing of order on a disturbed and disordered nature. This is not what we find in the Manichæan books: there it is constantly implied and constantly asserted that God guarded against an invasion of His enemies. But supposing this answer, which was given from want of a better, to represent the opinion of the Manichæans, is God, in their view, vindicated from the charge of cruelty or weakness? For this goodness of His to the hostile race proved most pernicious to His own subjects. Besides, if God's nature could not be corrupted nor changed, neither could any destructive influence corrupt or change us; and the order to be bestowed on the race of strangers might have been bestowed without robbing us of it.

26. Since those times, however, another answer has appeared which I heard recently at Carthage. For one, whom I wish much to see brought out of this error, when reduced to this same dilemma, ventured to say that the kingdom had its own limits, which might be invaded by a hostile race, though God Himself could not be injured. But this is a reply which your founder would never consent to give; for he would be likely to see that such an opinion would lead to a still speedier demolition of his heresy. And in fact any one of average intellect, who hears that in this nature part is subject to injury and part not, will at once perceive that this makes not two but three natures,—one violable, a second inviolable, and a third violating.

CHAP. 13.—ACTIONS TO BE JUDGED OF FROM THEIR MOTIVE, NOT FROM EXTERNALS. MANICHÆAN ABSTINENCE TO BE TRIED BY THIS PRINCIPLE.

27. Having every day in your mouth these blasphemies which come from your heart, you ought not to continue holding up the symbol of the mouth as something wonderful, to ensnare the ignorant. But perhaps you think the symbol of the mouth excellent and admirable because you do not eat flesh or drink wine. But what is your end in this? For according as the end we have in view in our actions, on account of which we do whatever we do, is not only not culpable but also praiseworthy, so only can our actions merit any praise. If the end we have regard to in any performance is unlawful and blameworthy, the performance itself will be unhesitatingly condemned as improper.

28. We are told of Catiline that he could bear cold, thirst, and hunger.[1] This the vile miscreant had in common with our apostles. What then distinguishes the parricide from our apostles but the precisely opposite end which he followed? He bore these things in order to gratify his fierce and ungoverned passions; they, on the other hand, in order to restrain these passions and subdue them to reason. You often say, when you are told of the great number of Catholic virgins, a she-mule is a virgin. This, indeed, is said in ignorance of the Catholic system, and is not applicable. Still, what you mean is that this continence is worthless unless it leads, on right principles, to an end of high excellence. Catholic Christians might also compare your abstinence from wine and flesh to that of cattle and many small birds, as likewise of countless sorts of worms. But, not

1 Sallust, *in prolog. Catilin.* § 3.

to be impertinent like you, I will not make this comparison prematurely, but will first examine your end in what you do. For I suppose I may safely take it as agreed on, that in such customs the end is the thing to look to. Therefore, if your end is to be frugal and to restrain the appetite which finds gratification in eating and drinking, I assent and approve. But this is not the case.

29. Suppose, what is quite possible, that there is one so frugal and sparing in his diet, that, instead of gratifying his appetite or his palate, he refrains from eating twice in one day, and at supper takes a little cabbage moistened and seasoned with lard, just enough to keep down hunger; and quenches his thirst, from regard to his health, with two or three draughts of pure wine; and this is his regular diet: whereas another of different habits never takes flesh or wine, but makes an agreeable repast at two o'clock on rare and foreign vegetables, varied with a number of courses, and well sprinkled with pepper, and sups in the same style towards night; and drinks honey-vinegar, mead, raisin-wine, and the juices of various fruits, no bad imitation of wine, and even surpassing it in sweetness; and drinks not for thirst but for pleasure; and makes this provision for himself daily, and feasts in this sumptuous style, not because he requires it, but only gratifying his taste;—which of these two do you regard as living most abstemiously in food and drink? You cannot surely be so blind as not to put the man of the little lard and wine above this glutton!

30. This is the true view; but your doctrine sounds very differently. For one of your elect distinguished by the three symbols may live like the second person in this description, and though he may be reproved by one or two of the more sedate, he cannot be condemned as abusing the symbols. But should he sup with the other person, and moisten his lips with a morsel of rancid bacon, or refresh them with a drink of spoilt wine, he is pronounced a transgressor of the symbol, and by the judgment of your founder is consigned to hell, while you, though wondering, must assent. Will you not discard these errors? Will you not listen to reason? Will you not offer some little resistance to the force of habit? Is not such doctrine most unreasonable? Is it not insanity? Is it not the greatest absurdity that one, who stuffs and loads his stomach every day to gratify his appetite with mushrooms, rice, truffles, cake, mead, pepper, and assafœtida, and who fares thus every day, cannot be convicted of transgressing the three symbols, that is, the rule of sanctity; whereas another, who seasons his dish of the commonest herbs with some smoky morsel of meat, and takes only so much of this as is needed for the refreshment of his body, and drinks three cups of wine for the sake of keeping in health, should, for exchanging the former diet for this, be doomed to certain punishment?

CHAP. 14.—THREE GOOD REASONS FOR ABSTAINING FROM CERTAIN KINDS OF FOOD.

31. But, you reply, the apostle says, "It is good, brethren, neither to eat flesh, nor to drink wine."[1] No one denies that this is good, provided that it is for the end already mentioned, of which it is said, "Make not provision for the flesh to fulfill the lusts thereof;"[2] or for the ends pointed out by the apostle, namely, either to check the appetite, which is apt to go to a more wild and uncontrollable excess in these things than in others, or lest a brother should be offended, or lest the weak should hold fellowship with an idol. For at the time when the apostle wrote, the flesh of sacrifices was often sold in the market. And because wine, too, was used in libations to the gods of the Gentiles, many weaker brethren, accustomed to purchase such things, preferred to abstain entirely from flesh and wine rather than run the risk of having fellowship, as they considered it, with idols, even ignorantly. And, for their sakes, even those who were stronger, and had faith enough to see the insignificance of these things, knowing that nothing is unclean except from an evil conscience, and holding by the saying of the Lord, "Not that which entereth into your mouth defileth you, but that which cometh out of it,"[3] still, lest these weaker brethren should stumble, were bound to abstain from these things. And this is not a mere theory, but is clearly taught in the epistles of the apostle himself. For you are in the habit of quoting only the words, "It is good, brethren, neither to eat flesh, nor to drink wine," without adding what follows, "nor anything whereby thy brother stumbleth, or is offended or is made weak." These words show the intention of the apostle in giving the admonition.

32. This is evident from the preceding and succeeding context. The passage is a long one to quote, but, for the sake of those who are indolent in reading and searching the sacred Scriptures, we must give the whole of it. "Him that is weak in the faith," says the apostle, "receive ye, but not to doubtful disputations. For one believeth that he may eat

1 Rom. xiv. 21. 2 Rom. xiii. 14. 3 Matt. xv. 2.

all things: another, who is weak, eateth herbs. Let not him that eateth despise him that eateth not; and let not him that eateth not judge him that eateth, for God hath received him. Who art thou that judgest another man's servant? to his own master he standeth or falleth; yea, he shall be holden up: for God is able to make him stand. One man esteemeth one day above another; another esteemeth every day alike. Let every man be fully persuaded in his own mind. He that regardeth the day, regardeth it to the Lord. He that eateth, eateth to the Lord, for he giveth God thanks; and he that eateth not, to the Lord he eateth not, and giveth God thanks. For none of us liveth to himself, and no man dieth to himself. For whether we live, we live unto the Lord; and whether we die, we die unto the Lord: whether we live, therefore, or die, we are the Lord's. For to this end Christ both lived, and died, and rose again, that He might be Lord both of the dead and living. But why dost thou judge thy brother? or why dost thou set at nought thy brother? for we shall all stand before the judgment-seat of God. For it is written, As I live, saith the Lord, every knee shall bow to me, and every tongue shall confess to God.[1] So then every one of us shall give account of himself to God. Let us not, therefore, judge one another any more: but judge this rather, that no man put a stumbling-block, or occasion to fall, in his brother's way. I know, and am persuaded in the Lord Jesus, that there is nothing common of itself: but to him that esteemeth anything to be common, to him it is common. But if thy brother be grieved with thy meat, now walkest thou not charitably. Destroy not him with thy meat, for whom Christ died. Let not then our good be evil spoken of. For the kingdom of God is not meat and drink; but righteousness, and peace, and joy in the Holy Ghost. For he who in this serveth Christ is acceptable to God, and approved of men. Let us therefore follow after the things which make for peace, and things whereby one may edify another. For meat destroys not the work of God. All things indeed are pure; but it is evil for that man who eateth with offense. It is good neither to eat flesh, nor to drink wine, nor anything whereby thy brother stumbleth, or is offended, or is made weak. Hast thou faith? have it to thyself before God. Happy is he who condemneth not himself in that thing which he alloweth. And he that distinguishes is damned if he eats, because he eateth not of faith: for whatsoever is not of faith is sin. We then that are strong ought to bear the infirmities of the weak, and not to please ourselves. Let every one of us please his neighbor for his good to edification. For even Christ pleased not Himself."[2]

33. Is it not clear that what the apostle required was, that the stronger should not eat flesh nor drink wine, because they gave offense to the weak by not going along with them, and made them think that those who in faith judged all things to be pure, did homage to idols in not abstaining from that kind of food and drink? This is also set forth in the following passage of the Epistle to the Corinthians: "As concerning, therefore, the eating of those things that are offered in sacrifice unto idols, we know that an idol is nothing in the world, and that there is none other God but one. For though there be that are called gods, whether in heaven or in earth, but to us there is but one God, the Father, of whom are all things, and we in Him; and one Lord Jesus Christ, by whom are all things, and we by Him. Howbeit there is not in every man that knowledge: for some, with conscience of the idol unto this hour, eat it as a thing offered to an idol; and their conscience being weak is defiled. But meat commendeth us not to God: for neither, if we eat, shall we abound; neither, if we eat not, shall we suffer want. But take heed, lest by any means this liberty of yours become a stumbling-block to them that are weak. For if any man see one who has knowledge sit at meat in the idol's temple, shall not his conscience being weak be emboldened to eat those things which are offered to idols; and through thy knowledge shall the weak brother perish, for whom Christ died? But when ye sin so against the brethren, and wound their weak conscience, ye sin against Christ. Wherefore, if meat make my brother to offend, I will eat no flesh forever, lest I make my brother to offend."[3]

34. Again, in another place: "What say I then? that the idol is anything? or that which is offered in sacrifice to idols is anything? But the things which the Gentiles sacrifice they sacrifice to devils, and not to God: and I would not that ye should have fellowship with devils. Ye cannot drink the cup of the Lord, and the cup of devils: ye cannot be partakers of the Lord's table and of the table of devils. Do we provoke the Lord to jealousy? are we stronger than He? All things are lawful for me, but all things are not expedient: all things are lawful for me, but all things edify not. Let no man seek his own, but every man what is another's. Whatso-

[1] Isa. xlv. 23, 24.

[2] Rom. xiv. and xv. 1-3.

[3] 1 Cor. viii. 4, etc.

ever is sold in the shambles, that eat, asking no question for conscience sake. But if any man say unto you, This is offered in sacrifice unto idols, eat not for his sake that shows it, and for conscience sake: conscience, I say, not thine own, but another's: for why is my liberty judged of another man's conscience? For if I be a partaker with thanksgiving, why am I evil spoken of for that for which I give thanks? Whether, therefore, ye eat or drink, or whatsoever ye do, do all to the glory of God. Give none offence, neither to the Jews, nor to the Greeks, nor to the Church of God: even as I please all men in all things not seeking mine own profit, but the profit of many that they may be saved. Be ye followers of me, even as I also am of Christ." [1]

35. It is clear, then, I think, for what end we should abstain from flesh and wine. The end is threefold: to check indulgence, which is mostly practised in this sort of food, and in this kind of drink goes the length of intoxication; to protect weakness, on account of the things which are sacrificed and offered in libation; and, what is most praiseworthy of all, from love, not to offend the weakness of those more feeble than ourselves, who abstain from these things. You, again, consider a morsel of meat unclean; whereas the apostle says that all things are clean, but that it is evil to him that eateth with offence. And no doubt you are defiled by such food, simply because you think it unclean. For the apostle says, "I know, and am persuaded by the Lord Jesus, that there is nothing common of itself: but to him that esteemeth anything common, to him it is common." And every one can see that by common he means unclean and defiled. But it is folly to discuss passages of Scripture with you; for you both mislead people by promising to prove your doctrines, and those books which possess authority to demand our homage you affirm to be corrupted by spurious interpolations. Prove then to me your doctrine that flesh defiles the eater, when it is taken without offending any one, without any weak notions, and without any excess. [2]

CHAP. 15.—WHY THE MANICHÆANS PROHIBIT THE USE OF FLESH.

36. It is worth while to take note of the whole reason for their superstitious abstinence, which is given as follows:—Since, we are told, the member of God has been mixed with the substance of evil, to repress it and to keep it from excessive ferocity,—for that is what you say,—the world is made up of both natures, of good and evil, mixed together. But this part of God is daily being set free in all parts of the world, and restored to its own domain. But in its passage upwards as vapor from earth to heaven, it enters plants, because their roots are fixed in the earth, and so gives fertility and strength to all herbs and shrubs. From these animals get their food, and, where there is sexual intercourse, fetter in the flesh the member of God, and, turning it from its proper course, they come in the way and entangle it in errors and troubles. So then, if food consisting of vegetables and fruits comes to the saints, that is, to the Manichæans by means of their chastity, and prayers, and psalms, whatever in it is excellent and divine is purified, and so is entirely perfected, in order to restoration, free from all hindrance, to its own domain. Hence you forbid people to give bread or vegetables, or even water, which would cost nobody anything, to a beggar, if he is not a Manichæan, lest he should defile the member of God by his sins, and obstruct its return.

37. Flesh, you say, is made up of pollution itself. For, according to you, some portion of that divine part escapes in the eating of vegetables and fruits: it escapes while they undergo the infliction of rubbing, grinding, or cooking, as also of biting or chewing. It escapes, too, in all motions of animals, in the carriage of burdens, in exercise, in toil, or in any sort of action. It escapes, too, in our rest, when digestion is going on in the body by means of internal heat. And as the divine nature escapes in all these ways, some very unclean dregs remain, from which, in sexual intercourse, flesh is formed. These dregs, however, fly off, in the motions above mentioned, along with what is good in the soul; for though it is mostly, it is not entirely good. So, when the soul has left the flesh, the dregs are utterly filthy, and the soul of those who eat flesh is defiled.

CHAP. 16.—DISCLOSURE OF THE MONSTROUS TENETS OF THE MANICHÆANS.

38. O the obscurity of the nature of things! How hard to expose falsehood! Who that hears these things, if he is one who has not learned the causes of things, and who, not yet illuminated by any ray of truth, is deceived by material images, would not think them true, precisely because the things spoken of are invisible, and are presented to the mind under the form of visible things, and can be eloquently expressed? Men of this description exist in numbers and in droves, who are kept from being led away into these errors

[1] 1 Cor. x. 19-25 and 28, xi. 1.

[2] [Augustin's comparison of Manichæan with Christian asceticism is thoroughly just and admirable.—A. H. N.]

more by a fear grounded on religious feeling than by reason. I will therefore endeavor, as God may please to enable me, so to refute these errors, as that their falsehood and absurdity will be manifest not only in the judgment of the wise, who reject them on hearing them, but also to the intelligence of the multitude.

39. Tell me then, first, where you get the doctrine that part of God, as you call it, exists in corn, beans, cabbage, and flowers and fruits. From the beauty of the color, say they, and the sweetness of the taste; this is evident; and as these are not found in rotten substances, we learn that their good has been taken from them. Are they not ashamed to attribute the finding of God to the nose and the palate? But I pass from this. For I will speak, using words in their proper sense; and, as the saying is, this is not so easy in speaking to you. Let us see rather what sort of mind is required to understand this; how, if the presence of good in bodies is shown by their color, the dung of animals, the refuse of flesh itself, has all kinds of bright colors, sometimes white, often golden, and so on, though these are what you take in fruits and flowers as proofs of the presence and indwelling of God. Why is it that in a rose you hold the red color to be an indication of an abundance of good, while the same color in blood you condemn? Why do you regard with pleasure in a violet the same color which you turn away from in cases of cholera, or of people with jaundice, or in the excrement of infants? Why do you believe the light, shining appearance of oil to be a sign of a plentiful admixture of good, which you readily set about purifying by taking the oil into your throats and stomachs, while you are afraid to touch your lips with a drop of fat, though it has the same shining appearance as oil? Why do you look upon a yellow melon as part of the treasures of God, and not rancid bacon fat or the yolk of an egg? Why do you think that whiteness in a lettuce proclaims God, and not in milk? So much for colors, as regards which (to mention nothing else) you cannot compare any flower-clad meadow with the wings and feathers of a single peacock, though these are of flesh and of fleshly origin.

40. Again, if this good is discovered also by smell, perfumes of excellent smell are made from the flesh of some animals. And the smell of food, when cooked along with flesh of delicate flavor, is better than if cooked without it. Once more, if you think that the things that have a better smell than others are therefore cleaner, there is a kind of mud which you ought to take to your meals instead of water from the cistern; for dry earth moistened with rain has an odor most agreeable to the sense, and this sort of mud has a better smell than rain-water taken by itself. But if we must have the authority of taste to prove the presence in any object of part of God, he must dwell in dates and honey more than in pork, but more in pork than in beans. I grant that He dwells more in a fig than in a liver; but then you must allow that He is more in liver than in beet. And, on this principle, must you not confess that some plants, which none of you can doubt to be cleaner than flesh, receive God from this very flesh, if we are to think of God as mixed with the flavor? For both cabbages taste better when cooked along with flesh; and, while we cannot relish the plants on which cattle feed, when these are turned into milk we think them improved in color, and find them very agreeable to the taste.

41. Or must we think that good is to be found in greater quantity where the three good qualities—a good color, and smell, and taste—are found together? Then you must not admire and praise flowers so much, as you cannot admit them to be tried at the tribunal of the palate. At least you must not prefer purslain to flesh, since flesh when cooked is superior in color, smell, and taste. A young pig roasted (for your ideas on this subject force us to discuss good and evil with you as if you were cooks and confectioners, instead of men of reading or literary taste) is bright in color, and agreeable in smell, and pleasant in taste. Here is a perfect evidence of the presence of the divine substance. You are invited by this threefold testimony, and called on to purify this substance by your sanctity. Make the attack. Why do you hold back? What objection have you to make. In color alone the excrement of an infant surpasses lentils; in smell alone a roast morsel surpasses a soft green fig; in taste alone a kid when slaughtered surpasses the plant which it fed on when alive: and we have found a kind of flesh in flavor of which all three give evidence. What more do you require? What reply will you make? Why should eating meat make you unclean, if using such monstrosities in discussion does not? And, above all, the rays of the sun, which you surely think more of than all animal or vegetable food, have no smell or taste, and are remarkable among other substances only by their eminently bright color; which is a loud call to you, and an obligation, in spite of yourselves, to place nothing higher than a bright color among the evidences of an admixture of good.

42. Thus you are forced into this difficulty, that you must acknowledge the part of God as dwelling more in blood, and in the filthy but bright-colored animal refuse which is thrown out in the streets, than in the pale leaves of the olive. If you reply, as you actually do, that olive leaves when burnt give out a flame, which proves the presence of light, while flesh when burnt does not, what will you say of oil, which lights nearly all the lamps in Italy? What of cow dung (which surely is more unclean than the flesh), which peasants use when dry as fuel, so that the fire is always at hand, and the liberation of the smoke is always going on? And if brightness and lustre prove a greater presence of the divine part, why do you yourselves not purify it, why not appropriate it, why not liberate it? For it is found chiefly in flowers, not to speak of blood and countless things almost the same as blood in flesh or coming from it, and yet you cannot feed on flowers. And even if you were to eat flesh, you would certainly not take with your gruel the scales of fish, or some worms and flies, though these all shine with a light of their own in the dark.

43. What then remains, but that you should cease saying that you have in your eyes, nose, and palate sufficient means of testing the presence of the divine part in material objects? And, without these means, how can you tell not only that there is a greater part of God in plants than in flesh, but that there is any part in plants at all? Are you led to think this by their beauty—not the beauty of agreeable color, but that of agreement of parts? An excellent reason, in my opinion. For you will never be so bold as to compare twisted pieces of wood with the bodies of animals, which are formed of members answering to one another. But if you choose the testimony of the senses, as those must do who cannot see with their mind the full force of existence, how do you prove that the substance of good escapes from bodies in course of time, and by some kind of attrition, but because God has gone out of it, according to your view, and has left one place for another? The whole is absurd. But, as far as I can judge, there are no marks or appearances to give rise to this opinion. For many things plucked from trees, or pulled out of the ground, are the better of some interval of time before we use them for food, as leeks and endive, lettuce, grapes, apples, figs, and some pears; and there are many other things which get a better color when they are not used immediately after being plucked, besides being more wholesome for the body, and having a finer flavor to the palate. But these things should not possess all these excellent and agreeable qualities, if, as you say, they become more destitute of good the longer they are kept after separation from their mother earth. Animal food itself is better and more fit for use the day after the animal is killed; but this should not be, if, as you hold, it possessed more good immediately after the slaughter than next day, when more of the divine substance had escaped.

44. Who does not know that wine becomes purer and better by age? Nor is it, as you think, more tempting to the destruction of the senses, but more useful for invigorating the body,—only let there be moderation, which ought to control everything. The senses are sooner destroyed by new wine. When the must has been only a short time in the vat, and has begun to ferment, it makes those who look down into it fall headlong, affecting their brain, so that without assistance they would perish. And as regards health, every one knows that bodies are swollen up and injuriously distended by new wine? Has it these bad properties because there is more good in it? Are they not found in wine when old because a good deal of the divine substance has gone? An absurd thing to say, especially for you, who prove the divine presence by the pleasing effect produced on your eyes, nose, and palate! And what a contradiction it is to make wine the poison of the princes of darkness, and yet to eat grapes! Has it more of the poison when in the cup than when in the cluster? Or if the evil remains unmixed after the good is gone, and that by the process of time, how is it that the same grapes, when hung up for awhile, become milder, sweeter, and more wholesome? or how does the wine itself, as already mentioned, become purer and brighter when the light has gone, and more wholesome by the loss of the beneficial substance?

45. What are we to say of wood and leaves, which in course of time become dry, but cannot be the worse on that account in your estimation? For while they lose that which produces smoke, they retain that from which a bright flame arises; and, to judge by the clearness, which you think so much of, there is more good in the dry than in the green. Hence you must either deny that there is more of God in the pure light than in the smoky one, which will upset all your evidences; or you must allow it to be possible that, when plants are plucked up, or branches plucked off, and kept for a time, more of the nature of evil may escape from them than

of the nature of good. And, on the strength of this, we shall hold that more evil may go off from plucked fruits; and so more good may remain in animal food. So much on the subject of time.

46. As for motion, and tossing, and rubbing, if these give the divine nature the opportunity of escaping from these substances, many things of the same kind are against you, which are improved by motion. In some grains the juice resembles wine, and is excellent when moved about. Indeed, as must not be overlooked, this kind of drink produces intoxication rapidly; and yet you never called the juice of grain the poison of the princes of darkness. There is a preparation of water, thickened with a little meal, which is the better of being shaken, and, strange to say, is lighter in color when the light is gone. The pastrycook stirs honey for a long time to give it this light color, and to make its sweetness milder and less unwholesome: you must explain how this can come from the loss of good. Again, if you prefer to test the presence of God by the agreeable effects on the hearing, and not sight, or smell, or taste, harps get their strings and pipes their bones from animals; and these become musical by being dried, and rubbed, and twisted. So the pleasures of music, which you hold to have come from the divine kingdom, are obtained from the refuse of dead animals, and that, too, when they are dried by time, and lessened by rubbing, and stretched by twisting. Such rough treatment, according to you, drives the divine substance from living objects; even cooking them, you say, does this. Why then are boiled thistles not unwholesome? Is it because God, or part of God, leaves them when they are cooked?

47. Why mention all the particulars, when it is difficult to enumerate them? Nor is it necessary; for every one knows how many things are sweeter and more wholesome when cooked. This ought not to be, if, as you suppose, things lose the good by being thus moved about. I do not suppose that you will find any proof from your bodily senses that flesh is unclean, and defiles the souls of those who eat it, because fruits, when plucked and shaken about in various ways, become flesh; especially as you hold that vinegar, in its age and fermentation, is cleaner than wine, and the mead you drink is nothing else than cooked wine, which ought to be more impure than wine, if material things lose the divine members by being moved about and cooked. But if not, you have no reason to think that fruits, when plucked, kept, handled, cooked, and digested, are forsaken by the good, and therefore supply most unclean matter for the formation of bodies.

48. But if it is not from their color and appearance, and smell and taste, that you think the good to be in these things, what else can you bring forward? Do you prove it from the strength and vigor which those things seem to lose when they are separated from the earth and put to use? If this is your reason (though its erroneousness is seen at once, from the fact that the strength of some things is increased after their separation from the earth, as in the case already mentioned of wine, which becomes stronger from age),—if the strength, then, is your reason, it would follow that the part of God is to be found in no food more abundantly than in flesh. For athletes, who especially require vigor and energy, are not in the habit of feeding on cabbage and fruit without animal food.

49. Is your reason for thinking the bodies of trees better than our bodies, that flesh is nourished by trees and not trees by flesh. You forget the obvious fact that plants, when manured with dung, become richer and more fertile and crops heavier, though you think it your gravest charge against flesh that it is the abode of dung. This then gives nourishment to things you consider clean, though it is, according to you, the most unclean part of what you consider unclean. But if you dislike flesh because it springs from sexual intercourse, you should be pleased with the flesh of worms, which are bred in such numbers, and of such a size, in fruits, in wood, and in the earth itself, without any sexual intercourse. But there is some insincerity in this. For if you were displeased with flesh because it is formed from the cohabitation of father and mother, you would not say that those princes of darkness were born from the fruits of their own trees; for no doubt you think worse of these princes than of flesh, which you refuse to eat.

50. Your idea that all the souls of animals come from the food of their parents, from which confinement you pretend to liberate the divine substance which is held bound in your viands, is quite inconsistent with your abstinence from flesh, and makes it a pressing duty for you to eat animal food. For if souls are bound in the body by those who eat animal food, why do you not secure their liberation by being beforehand in eating the food? You reply, it is not from the animal food that the good part comes which those people bring into bondage, but from the vegetables which they take with their meat. What will you say then of the souls of lions, who feed only on flesh? They drink, is the reply, and so

the soul is drawn in from the water and confined in flesh. But what of birds without number? What of eagles, which eat only flesh, and need no drink? Here you are at a loss, and can find no answer. For if the soul comes from food, and there are animals which neither drink anything nor have any food but flesh, and yet bring forth young, there must be some soul in flesh; and you are bound to try your plan of purifying it by eating the flesh. Or will you say that a pig has a soul of light, because it eats vegetables, and drinks water; and that the eagle, because it eats only flesh, has a soul of darkness, though it is so fond of the sun?[1]

51. What a confusion of ideas! What amazing fatuity! All this you would have escaped, if you had rejected idle fictions, and had followed what truth sanctions in abstinence from food, which would have taught you that sumptuous eating is to be avoided, not to escape pollution, as there is nothing of the kind, but to subdue the sensual appetite. For should any one, from inattention to the nature of things, and the properties of the soul and body, allow that the soul is polluted by animal food, you will admit that it is much much more defiled by sensuality. Is it reasonable, then, or rather, is it not most unreasonable, to expel from the number of the elect a man who, perhaps for his health's sake, takes some animal food without sensual appetite; while, if a man eagerly devours peppered truffles, you can only reprove him for excess, but cannot condemn him as abusing your symbol? So one who has been induced, not by sensuality, but for health, to eat part of a fowl, cannot remain among your elect; though one may remain who has yielded voluntarily to an excessive appetite for comfits and cakes without animal matter. You retain the man plunged in the defilements of sensuality, and dismiss the man polluted, as you think, by the mere food; though you allow that the defilement of sensuality is far greater than that of meat. You keep hold of one who gloats with delight over highly-seasoned vegetables, unable to keep possession of himself; while you shut out one who, to satisfy hunger, takes whatever comes, if suitable for nourishment, ready either to use the food, or to let it go. Admirable customs! Excellent morals! Notable temperance!

52. Again, the notion that it is unlawful for any one but the elect to touch as food what is brought to your meals for what you call purification, leads to shameful and sometimes to criminal practices. For sometimes so much is brought that it cannot easily be eaten up by a few; and as it is considered sacrilege to give what is left to others, or, at least, to throw it away, you are obliged to eat to excess, from the desire to purify, as you call it, all that is given. Then, when you are full almost to bursting, you cruelly use force in making the boys of your sect eat the rest. So it was charged against some one at Rome that he killed some poor children, by compelling them to eat for this superstitious reason. This I should not believe, did I not know how sinful you consider it to give this food to those who are not elect, or, at any rate, to throw it away. So the only way is to eat it; and this leads every day to gluttony, and may sometimes lead to murder.

53. For the same reason you forbid giving bread to beggars. By way of showing compassion, or rather of avoiding reproach, you advise to give money. The cruelty of this is equalled by its stupidity. For suppose a place where food cannot be purchased: the beggar will die of starvation, while you, in your wisdom and benevolence, have more mercy on a cucumber than on a human being! This is in truth (for how could it be better designated) pretended compassion, and real cruelty. Then observe the stupidity. What if the beggar buys bread for himself with the money you give him? Will the divine part, as you call it, not suffer the same in him when he buys the food as it would have suffered if he had taken it as a gift from you? So this sinful beggar plunges in corruption part of God eager to escape, and is aided in this crime by your money! But you in your great sagacity think it enough that you do not give to one about to commit murder a man to kill, though you knowingly give him money to procure somebody to be killed. Can any madness go beyond this? The result is, that either the man dies if he cannot get food for his money, or the food itself dies if he gets it. The one is true murder; the other what you call murder: though in both cases you incur the guilt of real murder. Again, there is the greatest folly and absurdity in allowing your followers to eat animal food, while you forbid them to kill animals. If this food does not defile, take it yourselves. If it defiles, what can be more unreasonable than to think it more sinful to separate the soul of a pig from its body than to defile the soul of a man with the pig's flesh.

CHAP. 17.—DESCRIPTION OF THE SYMBOL OF THE HANDS AMONG THE MANICHÆANS.

54. We must now notice and discuss the

[1] [Much of the foregoing, as well as of what follows, seems to the modern reader like mere trifling, but Augustin's aim was by introducing many familiar illustrations to show the utter absurdity of the Manichæan distinctions between clean and unclean. It must be confessed that he does this very effectively.—A. H. N.]

symbol of the hands. And, in the first place, your abstaining from the slaughter of animals and from injuring plants is shown by Christ to be mere superstition; for, on the ground that there is no community of rights between us and brutes and trees, He both sent the devils into an herd of swine,[1] and withered by His curse a tree in which He had found no fruit.[2] The swine assuredly had not sinned, nor had the tree. We are not so insane as to think that a tree is fruitful or barren by its own choice. Nor is it any reply to say that our Lord wished in these actions to teach some other truths; for every one knows that. But assuredly the Son of God would not commit murder to illustrate truth,—if you call the destruction of a tree or of an animal murder. The signs which Christ wrought in the case of men, with whom we certainly have a community of rights, were in healing, not in killing them. And it would have been the same in the case of beasts and trees, if we had that community with them which you imagine.

55. I think it right to refer here to the authority of Scripture, because we cannot here enter on a profound discussion about the soul of animals, or the kind of life in trees. But as you preserve the right to call the Scriptures corrupted, in case you should find them too strongly opposed to you,—although you have never affirmed the passages about the tree and the herd of swine to be spurious,—still, lest some day you should wish to say this of them too, when you find how much they are against you, I will adhere to my plan, and will ask you, who are so liberal in your promises of evidence and truth, to tell me first what harm is done to a tree, I say not by plucking a leaf or an apple,—for which, however, one of you would be condemned at once as having abused the symbol, if he did it intentionally, and not accidentally,—but if you tear it up by the root. For the soul in trees, which, according to you, is a rational soul, is, in your theory, freed from bondage when the tree is cut down,—a bondage, too, where it suffered great misery and got no profit. For it is well known that you, in the words of your founder, threaten as a great, though not the greatest punishment, the change from a man to a tree; and it is not probable that the soul in a tree can grow in wisdom as it does in a man. There is the best reason for not killing a man, in case you should kill one whose wisdom or virtue might be of use to many, or one who might have attained to wisdom, whether by the advice of another without himself, or by divine illumination in his own mind. And the more wisdom the soul has when it leaves the body, the more profitable is its departure, as we know both from well-grounded reasoning and from wide-spread belief. Thus to cut down a tree is to set free the soul from a body in which it makes no progress in wisdom. You—the holy men, I mean—ought to be mainly occupied in cutting down trees, and in leading the souls thus emancipated to better things by prayers and psalms. Or can this be done only with the souls which you take into your belly, instead of aiding them by your understanding?

56. And you cannot escape the admission that the souls in trees make no progress in wisdom while they are there, when you are asked why no apostle was sent to teach trees as well as men, or why the apostle sent to men did not preach the truth to trees also. Your reply must be, that the souls while in such bodies cannot understand the divine precepts. But this reply lands you in great difficulties; for you declare that these souls can hear your voices and understand what you say, and see bodies and their motions, and even discern thoughts. If this is true, why could they learn nothing from the apostle of light? Why could they not learn even much better than we, since they can see into the mind? Your master, who, as you say, has difficulty in teaching you by speech, might have taught these souls by thought; for they could see his ideas in his mind before he expressed them. But if this is untrue, consider into what errors you have fallen.

57. As for your not plucking fruits or pulling up vegetables yourselves, while you get your followers to pluck and pull and bring them to you, that you may confer benefits not only on those who bring the food but on the food which is brought, what thoughtful person can bear to hear this? For, first, it matters not whether you commit a crime yourself, or wish another to commit it for you. You deny that you wish this! How then can relief be given to the divine part contained in lettuce and leeks, unless some one pull them and bring them to the saints to be purified. And again, if you were passing through a field where the right of friendship permitted you to pluck anything you wished, what would you do if you saw a crow on the point of eating a fig? Does not, according to your ideas, the fig itself seem to address you and to beg of you piteously to pluck it yourself and give it burial in a holy belly, where it may be purified and restored, rather than that the crow should swallow it and make it

[1] Matt. viii. 32.
[2] Matt. xxi. 19.

part of his cursed body, and then hand it over to bondage and torture in other forms? If this is true, how cruel you are! If not, how silly! What can be more contrary to your opinions than to break the symbol? What can be more unkind to the member of God than to keep it?

58. This supposes the truth of your false and vain ideas. But you can be shown guilty of plain and positive cruelty flowing from the same error. For were any one lying on the road, his body wasted with disease, weary with journeying, and half-dead from his sufferings, and able only to utter some broken words, and if eating a pear would do him good as an astringent, and were he to beg you to help him as you passed by, and were he to implore you to bring the fruit from a neighboring tree, with no divine or human prohibition to prevent your doing so, while the man is sure to die for the want of it, you, a Christian man and a saint, will rather pass on and abandon a man thus suffering and entreating, lest the tree should lament the loss of its fruit, and you should be doomed to the punishment threatened by Manichæus for breaking the symbol. Strange customs, and strange harmlessness!

59. Now, as regards killing animals, and the reasons for your opinion, much that has been said will apply also to this. For what harm will be done to the soul of a wolf by killing the wolf, since the wolf, as long as it lives, will be a wolf, and will not listen to any preacher, or give up, in the least, shedding the blood of sheep; and, by killing it, the rational soul, as you think, will be set free from its confinement in the body? But you make this slaughter unlawful even for your followers; for you think it worse than that of trees. And in this there is not much fault to be found with your senses,—that is, your bodily senses. For we see and hear by their cries that animals die with pain, although man disregards this in a beast, with which, as not having a rational soul, we have no community of rights. But as to your senses in the observation of trees, you must be entirely blind. For not to mention that there are no movements in the wood expressive of pain, what is clearer than that a tree is never better than when it is green and flourishing, gay with flowers, and rich in fruit? And this comes generally and chiefly from pruning. But if it felt the iron, as you suppose, it ought to die of wounds so many, so severe, instead of sprouting at the places, and reviving with such manifest delight.

60. But why do you think it a greater crime to destroy animals than plants, although you hold that plants have a purer soul than animals? There is a compensation, we are told, when part of what is taken from the fields is given to the elect and the saints to be purified. This has already been refuted; and it has, I think, been proved sufficiently that there is no reason for saying that more of the good part is found in vegetables than in flesh. But should any one support himself by selling butcher-meat, and spend the whole profit of his business in purchasing food for your elect, and bring larger supplies for those saints than any peasant or farmer, will he not plead this compensation as a warrant for his killing animals? But there is, we are told, some other mysterious reason; for a cunning man can always find some resource in the secrets of nature when addressing unlearned people. The story, then, is that the heavenly princes who were taken from the race of darkness and bound, and have a place assigned them in this region by the Creator of the world, have animals on the earth specially belonging to them, each having those coming from his own stock and class; and they hold the slaughterers of those animals guilty, and do not allow them to leave the earth, but harass them as much as they can with pains and torments. What simple man will not be frightened by this, and, seeing nothing in the darkness shrouding these things, will not think that the fact is as described? But I will hold to my purpose, with God's help, to rebut mysterious falsehood by the plainest truth.

61. Tell me, then, if animals on land and in water come in regular succession by ordinary generation from this race of princes, since the origin of animal life is traced to the abortive births in that race;—tell me, I say, whether bees and frogs, and many other creatures not sprung from sexual intercourse,[1] may be killed with impunity. We are told they cannot. So it is not on account of their relation to certain princes that you forbid your followers to kill animals. Or if you make a general relationship to all bodies, the princes would be equally concerned about trees, which you do not require your followers to spare. You are brought back to the weak reply, that the injuries done in the case of plants are atoned for by the fruits which your followers bring to your church. For this implies that those who slaughter animals, and sell their flesh in the market, if they are your followers, and if they bring to you vegetables bought with their gains, may think nothing

1 [This is, of course, a physiological blunder, but Augustin doubtless states what was the common view at the time.—A. H. N.]

of the daily slaughter, and are cleared of any sin that may be in it by your repasts.

62. But if you say that, in order to expiate the slaughter, the thing must be given as food, as in the case of fruits and vegetables,—which cannot be done, because the elect do not eat flesh, and so your followers must not slaughter animals,—what reply will you give in the case of thorns and weeds, which farmers destroy in clearing their fields, while they cannot bring any food to you from them? How can there be pardon for such destruction, which gives no nourishment to the saints? Perhaps you also put away any sin committed, for the benefit of the fruits and vegetables, by eating some of these. What then if the fields are plundered by locusts, mice, or rats, as we see often happen? Can your rustic follower kill these with impunity, because he sins for the good of his crops? Here you are at a loss; for you either allow your followers to kill animals, which your founder prohibited, or you forbid them to be cultivators, which he made lawful. Indeed, you sometimes go so far as to say that an usurer is more harmless than a cultivator,—you feel so much more for melons than for men. Rather than hurt the melons, you would have a man ruined as a debtor. Is this desirable and praiseworthy justice, or not rather atrocious and damnable error? Is this commendable compassion, or not rather detestable barbarity?

63. What, again, of your not abstaining yourselves from the slaughter of lice, bugs, and fleas? You think it a sufficient excuse for this to say that these are the dirt of our bodies. But this is clearly untrue of fleas and bugs; for every one knows that these animals do not come from our bodies. Besides, if you abhor sexual intercourse as much as you pretend to do, you should think those animals all the cleaner which come from our bodies without any other generation; for although they produce offspring of their own, they are not produced in ordinary generation from us. Again, if we must consider as most filthy the production of living bodies, still worse must be the production of dead bodies. There must be less harm, therefore, in killing a rat, a snake, or a scorpion, which you constantly say come from our dead bodies. But to pass over what is less plain and certain, it is a common opinion regarding bees that they come from the carcases of oxen; so there is no harm in killing them. Or if this too is doubted, every one allows that beetles, at least, are bred in the ball of mud which they make and bury.[1] You ought therefore to consider these animals, and others that it would be tedious to specify, more unclean than your lice; and yet you think it sinful to kill them, though it would be foolish not to kill the lice. Perhaps you hold the lice cheap because they are small. But if an animal is to be valued by its size, you must prefer a camel to a man.

64. Here we may use the gradation which often perplexed us when we were your followers. For if a flea may be killed on account of its small size, so may the fly which is bred in beans. And if this, so also may one of a little larger size, for its size at birth is even less. Then again, a bee may be killed, for its young is no larger than a fly. So on to the young of a locust, and to a locust; and then to the young of a mouse, and to a mouse. And, to cut short, it is clear we may come at last to an elephant; so that one who thinks it no sin to kill a flea, because of its small size, must allow that it would be no sin in him to kill this huge creature. But I think enough has been said of these absurdities.

CHAP. 18.—OF THE SYMBOL OF THE BREAST, AND OF THE SHAMEFUL MYSTERIES OF THE MANICHÆANS.

65. Lastly, there is the symbol of the breast, in which your very questionable chastity consists. For though you do not forbid sexual intercourse, you, as the apostle long ago said, forbid marriage in the proper sense, although this is the only good excuse for such intercourse. No doubt you will exclaim against this, and will make it a reproach against us that you highly esteem and approve perfect chastity, but do not forbid marriage, because your followers—that is, those in the second grade among you—are allowed to have wives. After you have said this with great noise and heat, I will quietly ask, Is it not you who hold that begetting children, by which souls are confined in flesh, is a greater sin than cohabitation? Is it not you who used to counsel us to observe as much as possible the time when a woman, after her purification, is most likely to conceive, and to abstain from cohabitation at that time, lest the soul should be entangled in flesh? This proves that you approve of having a wife, not for the procreation of children, but for the gratification of passion. In marriage, as the marriage law declares, the man and woman come together for the procreation of children. Therefore whoever makes the procreation of children a greater sin than copulation, forbids marriage, and makes the woman not a wife, but a mistress, who for some gifts presented

[1] *V. Retract.* i. 7, § 6, where Augustin allows that this is doubtful, and that many have not even heard of it.

to her is joined to the man to gratify his passion. Where there is a wife there must be marriage. But there is no marriage where motherhood is not in view; therefore neither is there a wife. In this way you forbid marriage. Nor can you defend yourselves successfully from this charge, long ago brought against you prophetically by the Holy Spirit.

66. Moreover, when you are so eager in your desire to prevent the soul from being confined in flesh by conjugal intercourse, and so eager in asserting that the soul is set free from seed by the food of the saints, do you not sanction, unhappy beings, the suspicion entertained about you? For why should it be true regarding corn and beans and lentils and other seeds, that when you eat them you wish to set free the soul, and not true of the seeds of animals? For what you say of the flesh of a dead animal, that it is unclean because there is no soul in it, cannot be said of the seed of the animal; for you hold that it keeps confined the soul which will appear in the offspring, and you avow that the soul of Manichæus himself is thus confined. And as your followers cannot bring these seeds to you for purification, who will not suspect that you make this purification secretly among yourselves, and hide it from your followers, in case they should leave you?[1] If you do not these things, as it is to be hoped you do not, still you see how open to suspicion your superstition is, and how impossible it is to blame men for thinking what your own profession suggests, when you maintain that you set free souls from bodies and from senses by eating and drinking. I wish to say no more about this: you see yourselves what room there is here for denunciation. But as the matter is one rather to repress than to invite remark, and also as throughout my discourse my purpose appears of exaggerating nothing, and of keeping to bare facts and arguments, we shall pass on to other matters.

CHAP. 19.—CRIMES OF THE MANICHÆANS.

67. We see then, now, the nature of your three symbols. These are your customs. This is the end of your notable precepts, in which there is nothing sure, nothing steadfast, nothing consistent, nothing irreproachable, but all doubtful, or rather undoubtedly and entirely false, all contradictory, abominable, absurd. In a word, evil practices are detected in your customs so many and so serious, that one wishing to denounce them all, if he were at all able to enlarge, would require at least a separate treatise for each. Were you to observe these, and to act up to your profession, no childishness, or folly, or absurdity would go beyond yours; and when you praise and teach these things without doing them, you display craft and deceit and malevolence equal to anything that can be described or imagined.

68. During nine full years that I attended you with great earnestness and assiduity, I could not hear of one of your elect who was not found transgressing these precepts, or at least was not suspected of doing so. Many were caught at wine and animal food, many at the baths; but this we only heard by report. Some were proved to have seduced other men's wives, so that in this case I could not doubt the truth of the charge. But suppose this, too, a report rather than a fact. I myself saw, and not I only, but others who have either escaped from that superstition, or will, I hope, yet escape,—we saw, I say, in a square in Carthage, on a road much frequented, not one, but more than three of the elect walking behind us, and accosting some women with such indecent sounds and gestures as to outdo the boldness and insolence of all ordinary rascals. And it was clear that this was quite habitual, and that they behaved in this way to one another, for no one was deterred by the presence of a companion,—showing that most of them, if not all, were affected with this evil tendency. For they did not all come from one house, but lived in quite different places, and quite accidentally left together the place where they had met. It was a great shock to us, and we lodged a complaint about it. But who thought of inflicting punishment,—I say not by separation from the church, but even by severe rebuke in proportion to the heinousness of the offence?

69. All the excuse given for the impunity of those men was that, at that time, when their meetings were forbidden by law, it was feared that the persons suffering punishment might retaliate by giving information. What then of their assertion that they will always have persecution in this world, for which they suppose that they will be thought the more of? for this is the application they make of the words about the world hating them.[2] And they will have it that truth must be sought for among them, because, in the promise of the Holy Spirit, the Paraclete, it is said that the world cannot receive Him.[3] This is not the place to discuss this question. But clearly,

[1] [Compare what is said about the disgusting ceremonial of Ischas by Cyril of Jerusalem (*Cat.* vi.), Augustin (*Haeres.* xlvi.), Pope Leo X. (*Serm. V. de Jejuniis, X. Mens.*). These charges were probably unfounded, though they are not altogether out of harmony with the Manichæan principles.—A. H. N.]

[2] John xv. 18.

[3] John xiv. 17.

if you are always to be persecuted, even to the end of the world, there will be no end to this laxity, and to the unchecked spread of all this immorality, from your fear of giving offence to men of this character.

70. This answer was also given to us, when we reported to the very highest authorities that a woman had complained to us that in a meeting, where she was along with other women, not doubting of the sanctity of these people, some of the elect came in, and when one of them had put out the lamp, one, whom she could not distinguish, tried to embrace her, and would have forced her into sin, had she not escaped by crying out. How common must we conclude the practice to have been which led to the misdeed on this occasion! And this was done on the night when you keep the feast of vigils. Forsooth, besides the fear of information being given, no one could bring the offender before the bishop, as he had so well guarded against being recognized. As if all who entered along with him were not implicated in the crime; for in their indecent merriment they all wished the lamp to be put out.

71. Then what wide doors were opened for suspicions, when we saw them full of envy, full of covetousness, full of greed for costly foods, constantly at strife, easily excited about trifles! We concluded that they were not competent to abstain from the things they professed to abstain from, if they found an opportunity in secret or in the dark. There were two of sufficiently good character, of active minds, and leaders in their debates, with whom we had a more particular and intimate acquaintance than with the rest. One of them was much associated with us, because he was also engaged in liberal studies; he is said to be now an elder there. These two were very jealous of one another, and one accused the other—not openly, but in conversation, as he had opportunity, and in whispers—of having made a criminal assault on the wife of one of the followers. He again, in clearing himself to us, brought the same charge against another of the elect, who lived with this follower as his most trusted friend. He had, going in suddenly, caught this man with the woman, and his enemy and rival had advised the woman and her paramour to raise this false report about him, that he might not be believed if he gave any information. We were much distressed, and took it greatly to heart, that although there was a doubt about the assault on the woman, the jealous feeling in those two men, than whom we found none better in the place, showed itself so keenly, and inevitably raised a suspicion of other things.[1]

72. Another thing was, that we very often saw in theatres men belonging to the elect, men of years and, it was supposed, of character, along with a hoary-headed elder We pass over the youths, whom we used to come upon quarrelling about the people connected with the stage and the races; from which we may safely conclude how they would be able to refrain in secret, when they could not subdue the passion by which they were exposed in the eyes of their followers, bringing on them disgrace and flight. In the case of the saint, whose discussions we attended in the street of the fig-sellers, would his atrocious crime have been discovered if he had been able to make the dedicated virgin his wife without making her pregnant? The swelling womb betrayed the secret and unthought-of iniquity. When her brother, a young man, heard of it from his mother, he felt keenly the injury, but refrained, from regard to religion, from a public accusation. He succeeded in getting the man expelled from that church, for such conduct cannot always be tolerated; and that the crime might not be wholly unpunished, he arranged with some of his friends to have the man well beaten and kicked. When he was thus assailed, he cried out that they should spare him, from regard to the authority of the opinion of Manichæus, that Adam the first hero had sinned, and was a greater saint after his sin.

73. This, in fact, is your notion about Adam and Eve.[2] It is a long story; but I will touch only on what concerns the present matter. You say that Adam was produced from his parents, the abortive princes of darkness; that he had in his soul the most part of light, and very little of the opposite race. So while he lived a holy life, on account of the prevalence of good, still the opposite part in him was stirred up, so that he was led away into conjugal intercourse. Thus he fell and sinned, but afterwards lived in greater holiness. Now, my complaint is not so much about this wicked man, who, under the garb of an elect and holy man, brought such shame and reproach on a family of strangers by his shocking immorality. I do not charge you with this. Let it be attributed to the abandoned character of the man, and not to your habits. I blame the man for the atrocity, and not you. Still there is

[1] Doubtless Augustin exaggerates the immorality of the Manichæans; but there must have been a considerable basis of fact for his charges.—A. H. N.]

[2] Compare the account from the *Fihrist*, in our Introduction, Chapter III.—A. H. N.]

this in you all that cannot, as far as I can see, be admitted or tolerated, that while you hold the soul to be part of God, you still maintain that the mixture of a little evil prevailed over the superior force and quantity of good. Who that believes this, when incited by passion, will not find here an excuse, instead of checking and controlling his passion?

CHAP. 20.—DISGRACEFUL CONDUCT DISCOVERED AT ROME.

74. What more shall I say of your customs? I have mentioned what I found myself when I was in the city when the things were done. To go through all that happened at Rome in my absence would take a long time. I will, however, give a short account of it; for the matter became so notorious, that even the absent could not remain in ignorance of it. And when I was afterwards in Rome, I ascertained the truth of all I had heard, although the story was told me by an eye-witness whom I knew so well and esteemed so highly, that I could not feel any doubt about it. One of your followers, then, quite equal to the elect in their far-famed abstinence, for he was both liberally educated, and was in the habit of defending your sect with great zeal, took it very ill that he had cast in his teeth the vile conduct of the elect, who lived in all kinds of places, and went hither and thither for lodging of the worst description. He therefore desired, if possible, to assemble all who were willing to live according to the precepts into his own house, and to maintain them at his own expense; for he was above the average in carelessness as to spending money, besides being above the average in the amount he had to spend. He complained that his efforts were hindered by the remissness of the bishops, whose assistance he required for success. At last one of your bishops was found,—a man, as I know, very rude and unpolished, but somehow, from his very moroseness, the more inclined to strict observance of morality. The follower eagerly lays hold of this man as the person he had long wished for and found at last, and relates his whole plan. He approves and assents, and agrees to be the first to take up his abode in the house. When this was done, all the elect who could be at Rome were assembled there. The rule of life in the epistle of Manichæus was laid before them. Many thought it intolerable, and left; not a few felt ashamed, and stayed. They began to live as they had agreed, and as this high authority enjoined. The follower all the time was zealously enforcing everything on everybody, though never, in any case, what he did not undertake himself. Meanwhile quarrels constantly arose among the elect. They charged one another with crimes, all which he lamented to hear, and managed to make them unintentionally expose one another in their altercations. The revelations were vile beyond description. Thus appeared the true character of those who were unlike the rest in being willing to bend to the yoke of the precepts. What then is to be suspected, or rather, concluded, of the others? To come to a close, they gathered together on one occasion and complained that they could not keep the regulations. Then came rebellion. The follower stated his case most concisely, that either all must be kept, or the man who had given such a sanction to such precepts, which no one could fulfill, must be thought a great fool. But, as was inevitable, the wild clamor of the mob prevailed over the opinion of one man. The bishop himself gave way at last, and took to flight with great disgrace; and he was said to have got in provisions by stealth, contrary to rule, which were often discovered. He had a supply of money from his private purse, which he carefully kept concealed.

75. If you say these things are false, you contradict what is too clear and public. But you may say so if you like. For, as the things are certain, and easily known by those who wish to know them, those who deny that they are true show what their habit of telling the truth is. But you have other replies with which I do not find fault. For you either say that some do keep your precepts, and that they should not be mixed up with the guilty in condemning the others; or that the whole inquiry into the character of the members of your sect is wrong, for the question is of the character of the profession. Should I grant both of these (although you can neither point out those faithful observers of the precepts, nor clear your heresy of all those frivolities and iniquities), still I must insist on knowing why you heap reproaches on Christians of the Catholic name on seeing the immoral life of some, while you either have the effrontery to repel inquiry about your members, or the still greater effrontery not to repel it, wishing it to be understood that in your scanty membership there are some unknown individuals who keep the precepts they profess, but that among the multitudes in the Catholic Church there are none.

ST. AUGUSTIN:

ON TWO SOULS,

AGAINST THE MANICHÆANS.

[DE DUABUS ANIMABUS CONTRA MANICHÆOS].

A.D. 391.

TRANSLATED BY

ALBERT H. NEWMAN, D.D., LL.D.,

PROFESSOR OF CHURCH HISTORY AND COMPARATIVE RELIGION, IN TORONTO BAPTIST (THEOLOGICAL) COLLEGE, TORONTO, CANADA.

CONTENTS ON TWO SOULS AGAINST THE MANICHÆANS.

CONCERNING

TWO SOULS, AGAINST THE MANICHÆANS.

[DE DUABUS ANIMABUS CONTRA MANICHÆOS.] A.D. 391.[1]

ONE BOOK.

CHAP. 1.—BY WHAT COURSE OF REASONING THE ERROR OF THE MANICHÆANS CONCERNING TWO SOULS, ONE OF WHICH IS NOT FROM GOD, IS REFUTED. EVERY SOUL, INASMUCH AS IT IS A CERTAIN LIFE, CAN HAVE ITS EXISTENCE ONLY FROM GOD THE SOURCE OF LIFE.

1. Through the assisting mercy of God, the snares of the Manichæans having been broken to pieces and left behind, having been restored at length to the bosom of the Catholic Church, I am disposed now at least to consider and to deplore my recent wretchedness. For there were many things that I ought to have done to prevent the seeds of the most true religion wholesomely implanted in me from boyhood, from being banished from my mind, having been uprooted by the error and fraud of false and deceitful men. For, in the first place, if I had soberly and diligently considered, with prayerful and pious mind, those two kinds of souls to which they attributed natures and properties so distinct that they wished one to be regarded as of the very substance of God, but were not even willing that God should be accepted as the author of the other; perhaps it would have appeared to me, intent on learning, that there is no life whatsoever, which, by the very fact of its being life and in so far as it is life at all, does not pertain to the supreme source and beginning of life,[2] which we must acknowledge to be nothing else than the supreme and only and true God. Wherefore there is no reason why we should not confess, that those souls which the Manichæans call evil are either devoid of life and so not souls, neither will anything positively or negatively, neither follow after nor flee from anything; or, if they live so that they can be souls, and act as the Manichæans suppose, in no way do they live unless by life, and if it be an established fact, as it is, that Christ has said: "I am the life,"[3] that all souls seeing that they cannot be souls except by living were created and fashioned by Christ, that is, by the Life.

CHAP. 2.—IF THE LIGHT THAT IS PERCEIVED BY SENSE HAS GOD FOR ITS AUTHOR, AS THE MANICHÆANS ACKNOWLEDGE, MUCH MORE THE SOUL WHICH IS PERCEIVED BY INTELLECT ALONE.

2. But if at that time[4] my thought was not able to bear and sustain the question concern-

---

[1] Scarcely any one of his earlier treatises was more unsatisfactory to Augustin in his later Anti-Pelagian years than that *Concerning Two Souls*. In his *Retractations*, Book I., chapter xv., he recognizes the rashness of some of his statements and points out the sense in which they are tenable or the reverse. As regards the occasion of the writing, the following may be quoted: "After this book [*De Utilitate Credendi*] I wrote, while still a presbyter, against the Manichæans *Concerning Two Souls*, of which they say that one part is of God, the other from the race of darkness, which God did not found, and which is coeternal with God, and they rave about both these souls, the one good, the other evil, being in one man, saying forsooth that the evil soul on the one hand belongs to the flesh, which flesh also they say is of the race of darkness; but that the good soul is from the part of God that came forth, combated the race of darkness, and mingled with the latter; and they attribute all good things in man to that good soul, and all evil things to that evil soul."—A. H. N.

[2] In his *Retractations*, Augustin explains this proposition as follows: "I said this in the sense in which the creature is known to pertain to the Creator, but not in the sense that it is of Him, so as to be regarded as part of Him."—A. H. N.

[3] John xiv. 6.

[4] It will aid the reader in following the thread of Augustin's argu-

ing life and partaking of life, which is truly a great question, and one that requires much calm discussion among the learned, I might perchance have had power to discover that which to every man considering himself, without a study of the individual parts, is perfectly evident, namely, that everything we are said to know and to understand, we comprehend either by bodily sense or by mental operation. That the five bodily senses are commonly enumerated as sight, hearing, smell, taste, touch, than all of which intellect is immeasurably more noble and excellent, who would have been so ungrateful and impious as not to concede to me; which being established and confirmed, we should have seen how it follows, that whatsoever things are perceived by touch or sight or in any bodily manner at all, are by so much inferior to those things that we comprehend intellectually as the senses are inferior to the intellect. Wherefore, since all life, and so every soul, can be perceived by no bodily sense, but by the intellect alone, whereas while yonder sun and moon and every luminary that is beheld by these mortal eyes, the Manichæans themselves also say must be attributed to the true and good God, it is the height of madness to claim that that belongs to God which we observe bodily; but, on the other hand, to think that what we receive not only by the mind, but by the highest form of mind,[1] namely, reason and intellect,[2] that is life, whatsoever it may be called, nevertheless life, should be deprived and bereft of the same God as its author. For if having invoked God, I had asked myself what living is, how inscrutable it is to every bodily sense, how absolutely incorporeal it is, could not I have answered? Or would not the Manichæans also confess not only that the souls they detest live, but that they live also immortally? and that Christ's saying: "Send the dead to bury their dead,"[3] was uttered not with reference to those not living at all, but with reference to sinners, which is the only death of the immortal soul; as when Paul writes: "The widow that giveth herself to pleasure is dead while she liveth,"[4] he says that she at the same time is dead, and alive. Wherefore I should have directed attention not to the great degree of contamination in which the sinful soul lives, but only to the fact itself that it lives. But if I cannot perceive except by an act of intelligence, I believe it would have come into the mind, that by as much as any mind whatever is to be preferred to the light which we see through these eyes, by so much we should give to intellect the preference over the eyes themselves.

CHAP. 3.—HOW IT IS PROVED THAT EVERY BODY ALSO IS FROM GOD. THAT THE SOUL WHICH IS CALLED EVIL BY THE MANICHÆANS IS BETTER THAN LIGHT.

They also affirm that the light is from the Father of Christ: should I then have doubted that every soul is from Him? But not even then, as a man forsooth so inexperienced and so youthful as I was, should I have been in doubt as to the derivation not only of the soul, but also of the body, nay of everything whatsoever, from Him, if I had reverently and cautiously reflected on what form is, or what has been formed, what shape is and what has been endued with shape.

3. But not to speak at present concerning the body, I lament concerning the soul, concerning spontaneous and vivid movement, concerning action, concerning life, concerning immortality; in fine, I lament that I, miserable, should have believed that anything could have all these properties apart from the goodness of God, which properties, great as they are, I sadly neglected to consider; this I think, should be to me a matter of groaning and of weeping. I should have inwardly pondered these things, I should have discussed them with myself, I should have referred them to others, I should have propounded the inquiry, what the power of knowing is, seeing there is nothing in man that we can compare to this excellency? And as men, if only they had been men, would have granted me this, I should have inquired whether seeing with these eyes is knowing? In case they had answered negatively, I should first have concluded, that mental intelligence is vastly inferior to ocular sensation; then I should have added, that what we perceive by means of a better thing must needs be judged to be itself better. Who would not grant this? I should have gone on to inquire, whether that soul which they call evil is an object of ocular sensation or of mental intelligence? They would have acknowledged that the latter is the case. All which things having been agreed upon and confirmed between us, I should have shown how it follows, that that soul forsooth which they execrate, is better than that light which

ment, if he will bear in mind that throughout this treatise the writer considers the points of antagonism between Manichæism and Catholicism from the point of view of his early entanglement in Manichæan error. Considering the opportunities that he had for knowing the truth, the helps to have been expected from God in answer to prayer, the capacities of the unperverted intellect to arrive at truth, he inquires how he should have guarded himself from the insinuation of Manichæan error, how he should have defended the truth, and how he should have been the means of liberating others.—A. H. N.

[1] *Sublimitate animi.*
[2] *Mente atque intelligentia.*
[3] Matt. viii. 22.
[4] 1 Tim. v. 6.

they venerate, since the former is an object of mental knowledge, the latter an object of corporeal sense perception. But here perhaps they would have halted, and would have refused to follow the lead of reason, so great is the power of inveterate opinion and of falsehood long defended and believed. But I should have pressed yet more upon them halting, not harshly, not in puerile fashion, not obstinately; I should have repeated the things that had been conceded, and have shown how they must be conceded. I should have exhorted that they consult in common, that they may see clearly what must be denied to us; whether they think it false that intellectual perception is to be preferred to these carnal organs of sight, or that what is known by means of the excellency of the mind is more excellent than what is known by vile corporeal sensation; whether they would be unwilling to confess that those souls which they think heterogenous, can be known only by intellectual perception, that is, by the excellency itself of the mind; whether they would wish to deny that the sun and the moon are made known to us only by means of these eyes. But if they had replied that no one of these things could be denied otherwise than most absurdly and most impudently, I should have urged that they ought not to doubt but that the light whose worthiness of worship they proclaim, is viler than that soul which they admonish men to flee.

CHAP. 4.—EVEN THE SOUL OF A FLY IS MORE EXCELLENT THAN THE LIGHT.

4. And here, if perchance in their confusion they had inquired of me whether I thought that the soul even of a fly[1] surpasses that light, I should have replied, yes, nor should it have troubled me that the fly is little, but it should have confirmed me that it is alive. For it is inquired, what causes those members so diminutive to grow, what leads so minute a body here and there according to its natural appetite, what moves its feet in numerical order when it is running, what regulates and gives vibration to its wings when flying? This thing whatever it is in so small a creature towers up so prominently to one well considering, that it excels any lightning flashing upon the eyes.

CHAP. 5.—HOW VICIOUS SOULS, HOWEVER WORTHY OF CONDEMNATION THEY MAY BE, EXCEL THE LIGHT WHICH IS PRAISEWORTHY IN ITS KIND.

Certainly nobody doubts that whatever is an object of intellectual perception, by virtue of divine laws surpasses in excellence every sensible object and consequently also this light. For what, I ask, do we perceive by thought, if not that it is one thing to know with the mind, and another thing to experience bodily sensations, and that the former is incomparably more sublime than the latter, and so that intelligible things must needs be preferred to sensible things, since the intellect itself is so highly exalted above the senses?

5. Hence this also I should perchance have known, which manifestly follows, since injustice and intemperance and other vices of the mind are not objects of sense, but of intellect, how it comes about that these too which we detest and consider condemnable, yet in as much as they are objects of intellect, can outrank this light however praiseworthy it may be in its kind. For it is borne in upon the mind subjecting itself well to God, that, first of all, not everything that we praise is to be preferred to everything that we find fault with. For in praising the purest lead, I do not therefore put a higher value upon it than upon the gold that I find fault with. For everything must be considered in its kind. I disapprove of a lawyer ignorant of many statutes, yet I so prefer him to the most approved tailor, that I should think him incomparably superior. But I praise the tailor because he is thoroughly skilled in his own craft, while I rightly blame the lawyer because he imperfectly fulfills the functions of his profession. Wherefore I should have found out that the light which in its own kind is perfect, is rightly to be praised; yet because it is included in the number of sensible things, which class must needs yield to the class of intelligible things, it must be ranked below unjust and intemperate souls, since these are intelligible; although we may without injustice judge these to be most worthy of condemnation. For in the case of these we ask that they be reconciled to God, not that they be preferred to that lightning. Wherefore, if any one had contended that this luminary is from God, I should not have opposed; but rather I should have said, that souls, even vicious ones, not in so far as they are vicious, but in so far as they are souls, must be acknowledged to be creatures of God.

CHAP. 6.—WHETHER EVEN VICES THEMSELVES AS OBJECTS OF INTELLECTUAL APPREHENSION ARE TO BE PREFERRED TO LIGHT AS AN OBJECT OF SENSE PERCEPTION, AND ARE TO BE ATTRIBUTED TO GOD AS THEIR

[1] Neither Augustin nor the Manichæans seem to have recognized the distinction in kind between the human soul and animal life.—A. H. N.

AUTHOR. VICE OF THE MIND AND CERTAIN DEFECTS ARE NOT RIGHTLY TO BE COUNTED AMONG INTELLIGIBLE THINGS. DEFECTS THEMSELVES EVEN IF THEY SHOULD BE COUNTED AMONG INTELLIGIBLE THINGS SHOULD NEVER BE PUT BEFORE SENSIBLE THINGS. IF LIGHT IS VISIBLE BY GOD, MUCH MORE IS THE SOUL, EVEN IF VICIOUS, WHICH IN SO FAR AS IT LIVES IS AN INTELLIGIBLE THING. PASSAGES OF SCRIPTURE ARE ADDUCED BY THE MANICHÆANS TO THE CONTRARY.

At this point, in case some one of them, cautious and watchful, now also more studious than pertinacious, had admonished me that the inquiry is not about vicious souls, but about vices themselves, which, seeing that they are not known by corporeal sense, and yet are known, can only be received as objects of intellectual apprehension, which if they excel all objects of sense, why can we not agree in attributing light to God as its author, but only a sacrilegious person would say that God is the author of vices; I should have replied to the man, if either on the spur of the moment, as is customary to the worshippers of the good God, a solution of this question had darted like lightning from on high, or a solution had been previously prepared. If I had not deserved or was unable to avail myself of either of these methods, I should have deferred the undertaking, and should have confessed that the thing propounded was difficult to discern and arduous. I should have withdrawn to myself, prostrated myself before God, groaned aloud asking Him not to suffer me to halt in mid space, when I should have moved forward with assured arguments, asking Him that I might not be compelled by a doubtful question either to subordinate intelligible things to sensible, and to yield, or to call Himself the author of vices; since either of these alternatives would have been absolutely full of falsehood and impiety. I can by no means suppose that He would have deserted me in such a frame of mind. Rather, in His own ineffable way, He would have admonished me to consider again and again whether vices of mind concerning which I was so troubled should be reckoned among intelligible things. But that I might find out, on account of the weakness of my inner eye, which rightly befell me on account of my sins, I should have devised some sort of stage for gazing upon spiritual things in visible things themselves, of which we have by no means a surer knowledge, but a more confident familiarity. Therefore I should straightway have inquired, what properly pertains to the sensation of the eyes. I should have found that it is the color, the dominion of which the light holds. For these are the things that no other sense touches, for the motions and magnitudes and intervals and figures of bodies, although they also can be perceived by the eyes, yet to perceive such is not their peculiar function, but belongs also to touch. Whence I should have gathered that by as much as yonder light excels other corporeal and sensible things, by so much is sight more noble than the other senses. The light therefore having been selected from all the things that are perceived by bodily sense, by this [light] I should have striven, and in this of necessity I should have placed that stage of my inquiry. I should have gone on to consider what might be done in this way, and thus I should have reasoned with myself: If yonder sun, conspicuous by its brightness and sufficing for day by its light, should little by little decline in our sight into the likeness of the moon, would we perceive anything else with our eyes than light however refulgent, yet seeking light by reason of not seeing what had been, and using it for seeing what was present? Therefore we should not see the decline, but the light that should survive the decline. But since we should not see, we should not perceive; for whatever we perceive by sight must necessarily be seen; wherefore if that decline were perceived neither by sight nor by any other sense, it cannot be reckoned among objects of sense. For nothing is an object of sense that cannot be perceived by sense. Let us apply now the consideration to virtue, by whose intellectual light we most fittingly say the mind shines. Again, a certain decline from this light of virtue, not destroying the soul, but obscuring it, is called vice. Therefore also vice can by no means be reckoned among objects of intellectual perception, as that decline of light is rightly excluded from the number of objects of sense perception. Yet what remains of soul, that is, that which lives and is soul, is just as much an object of intellectual perception as that is an object of sense perception which should shine in this visible luminary after any imaginable degree of decline. And so the soul, in so far as it is soul and partakes of life, without which it can in no way be soul, is most correctly to be preferred to all objects of sense perception. Wherefore it is most erroneous to say that any soul is not from God, from whom you boast that the sun and moon have their existence.

7. But if now it should be thought fit to designate as objects of sense perception not

only all those things that we perceive by the senses, but also all those things that though not perceiving by the senses we judge of by means of the body, as of darkness through the eyes, of silence through the ears,—for not by seeing darkness and not by hearing silence do we know of their existence,—and again, in the case of objects of intellectual perception, not those things only which we see illuminated by the mind, as is wisdom itself, but also those things which by the illumination itself we avoid, such as foolishness, which I might fittingly designate mental darkness; I should have made no controversy about a word, but should have dissolved the whole question by an easy division, and straightway I should have proved to those giving good attention, that by the divine law of truth intelligible subsistences are to be preferred to sensible subsistences, not the decline of these subsistences, even though we should choose to call these intelligible, those sensible. Wherefore, that those who acknowledge that these visible luminaries and those intelligible souls are subsistences, are in every way compelled to grant and to attribute the sublimer part to souls; but that defects of either kind cannot be preferred the one to the other, for they are only privative and indicate non-existence, and therefore have precisely the same force as negations themselves. For when we say, It is not gold, and, It is not virtue, although there is the greatest possible difference between gold and virtue, yet there is no difference between the negations that we adjoin to them. But that it is worse indeed not to be virtue than not to be gold, no sane man doubts. Who does not know that the difference lies not in the negations themselves, but in the things to which they are adjoined? For by as much as virtue is more excellent than gold, by so much is it more wretched to be in want of virtue than of gold. Wherefore, since intelligible things excel sensible things, we rightly feel greater repugnance towards defect in intelligible than in sensible things, esteeming not the defects, but the things that are deficient more or less precious. From which now it appears, that defect of light, which is intelligible, is far more wretched than defect of the sensible light, because, forsooth, life which is known is by far more precious than yonder light which is seen.

8. This being the case, who will dare, while attributing sun and moon, and whatever is refulgent in the stars, nay in this fire of ours and in this visible earthly life, to God, to decline to grant that any souls whatsoever, which are not souls except by the fact of their being perfectly alive, since in this fact alone life has the precedence of light, are from God. And since he speaks truth who says, In as far as a thing shines it is from God, would I speak falsely, mighty God, if I should say, In so far as a thing lives it is from God? Let not, I beseech thee, blindness of intellect and perversions of mind be increased to such an extent that men may fail to know these things. But however great their error and pertinacity might have been, trusting in these arguments and armed therewith, I believe that when I should have laid the matter before them thus considered and canvassed, and should have calmly conferred with them, I should have feared lest any one of them should have seemed to me to be of any consequence, should he endeavor to subordinate or even to compare to bodily sense, or to those things that pertain to bodily sense as objects of knowledge, either intellect or those things that are perceived (not by way of defect) by the intellect. Which point having been settled, how would he or any other have dared to deny that such souls as he would consider evil, yet since they are souls, are to be reckoned in the number of intelligible things, nor are objects of intellectual perception by way of defect? This is on the supposition that souls are souls only by being alive. For if they were intellectually perceived as vicious through defect, being vicious by lack of virtue, yet they are perceived as souls not through defect, for they are souls by reason of being alive. Nor can it be maintained that presence of life is a cause of defect, for by as much as anything is defective, by so much is it severed from life.

9. Since therefore it would have been every way evident that no souls can be separated from that Author from whom yonder light is not separated, whatever they might have now adduced I should not have accepted, and should rather have admonished them that they should choose with me to follow those who maintain that whatever is, since it is, and in whatever degree it is, has its existence from the one God.

CHAP. 7.—HOW EVIL MEN ARE OF GOD, AND NOT OF GOD.

They might have cited against me those words of the gospel: "Ye therefore do not hear, because ye are not of God;" "Ye are of your father the devil."[1] I also should have cited: "All things were made by Him and without Him was not anything made,"[2] and this of the Apostle: "One God of whom are all things, and one Lord Jesus Christ

[1] John viii. 47 and 44.

[2] John i. 3.

through whom are all things,"[1] and again from the same Apostle: "Of whom are all things, through whom are all things, in whom are all things, to Him be glory."[2] I should have exhorted those men (if indeed I had found them men), that we should presume upon nothing as if we had found it out, but should rather inquire of the masters who would demonstrate the agreement and harmony of those passages that seem to be discordant. For when in one and the same Scriptural authority we read: "All things are of God,"[3] and elsewhere: "Ye are not of God," since it is wrong rashly to condemn books of Scripture, who would not have seen that a skilled teacher should be found who would know a solution of this problem, from whom assuredly if endowed with good intellectual powers, and a "spiritual man," as is said by divine inspiration[4] (for he would necessarily have favored the true arguments concerning the intelligible and sensible nature, which, as far as I can, I have conducted and handled, nay he would have disclosed them far better and more convincingly); we should have heard nothing else concerning this problem, except, as might happen, that there is no class of souls but has its existence from God, and that it is yet rightly said to sinners and unbelievers: "Ye are not of God." For we also, perchance, Divine aid having been implored, should have been able easily to see, that it is one thing to live and another to sin, and (although life in sin may be called death in comparison with just life,[5] and while in one man it may be found, that he is at the same time alive and a sinner) that so far as he is alive, he is of God, so far as he is a sinner he is not of God. In which division we use that alternative that suits our sentiment; so that when we wish to insist upon the omnipotence of God as Creator, we may say even to sinners that they are of God. For we are speaking to those who are contained in some class, we are speaking to those having animal life, we are speaking to rational beings, we are speaking lastly—and this applies especially to the matter in hand—to living beings, all which things are essentially divine functions. But when our purpose is to convict evil men, we rightly say: "Ye are not of God." For we speak to them as averse to truth, unbelieving, criminal, infamous, and, to sum up all in one term—sinners, all of which things are undoubtedly not of God. Therefore what wonder is it, if Christ says to sinners, convicting them of this very thing that they were sinners and did not believe in Him: "Ye are not of God;" and on the other hand, without prejudice to the former statement: "All things were made through Him," and "All things are of God?" For if not to believe Christ, to repudiate Christ's advent, not to accept Christ, was a sure mark of souls that are not of God; and so it was said: "Ye therefore hear not, because ye are not of God;" how would that saying of the apostle be true that occurs in the memorable beginning of the gospel: "He came unto his own things, and his own people did not receive him?"[6] Whence his own if they did not receive him; or whence therefore not his own because they did not receive him, unless that sinners by virtue of being men belong to God, but by virtue of being sinners belong to the devil? He who says: "His own people received him not" had reference to nature; but he who says: "Ye are not of God," had reference to will; for the evangelist was commending the works of God, Christ was censuring the sins of men

CHAP. 8.—THE MANICHÆANS INQUIRE WHENCE IS EVIL AND BY THIS QUESTION THINK THEY HAVE TRIUMPHED. LET THEM FIRST KNOW, WHICH IS MOST EASY TO DO, THAT NOTHING CAN LIVE WITHOUT GOD. CONSUMMATE EVIL CANNOT BE KNOWN EXCEPT BY THE KNOWLEDGE OF CONSUMMATE GOOD, WHICH IS GOD.

Here perchance some one may say: Whence are sins themselves, and whence is evil in general? If from man, whence is man? if from an angel, whence is the angel? When it is said, however truly and rightly, that these are from God, it nevertheless seems to those unskillful and possessed of little power to look into recondite matters, that evils and sins are thereby connected, as by a sort of chain, to God. By this question they think themselves triumphant, as if forsooth to ask were to know;—would it were so, for in that case no one would be more knowing than myself. Yet very often in controversy the propounder of a great question, while impersonating the great teacher, is himself more ignorant in the matter concerning which he would frighten his opponent, than he whom he would frighten.

These therefore suppose that they are superior to the common run, because the former ask questions that the latter cannot answer. If therefore when I most unfortunately was associated with them, not in the position in which I have now for some time been, they had raised these objections when I

[1] 1 Cor. viii. 6.
[2] Rom. xi. 36.
[3] 1 Cor. xi. 12.
[4] 1 Cor. ii. 15.
[5] 1 Tim. v. 6.
[6] John i. 11.

had brought forward this argument, I should have said: I ask that you meanwhile agree with me, which is most easy, that if nothing can shine without God, much less can anything live without God. Let us not persist in such monstrous opinions as to maintain that any souls whatsoever have life apart from God. For perchance it may so happen that with me you are ignorant as to this thing, namely whence is evil, let us then learn either simultaneously or in any order, I care not what. For what if knowledge of the perfection of evil is impossible to man without knowledge of the perfection of good? For we should not know darkness if we were always in darkness. But the notion of light does not allow its opposite to be unknown. But the highest good is that than which there is nothing higher. But God is good and than Him nothing can be higher. God therefore is the highest good. Let us therefore together so recognize God, and thus what we seek too hastily will not be hidden from us. Do you suppose then that the knowledge of God is a matter of small account or desert. For what other reward is there for us than life eternal, which is to know God? For God the Master says: "But this is life eternal, that they might know Thee the only and true God, and Jesus Christ whom thou hast sent."[1] For the soul, although it is immortal, yet because aversion from the knowledge of God is rightly called its death, when it is converted to God, the reward of eternal life to be attained is that knowledge; so that this is, as has been said, eternal life. But no one can be converted to God, except he turn himself away from this world. This for myself I feel to be arduous and exceedingly difficult, whether it is easy to you, God Himself would have seen. I should have been inclined to think it easy to you, had I not been moved by the fact, that, since the world from which we are commanded to turn away is visible, and the apostle says: "The things that are seen are temporal, but the things that are unseen are eternal,"[2] you ascribe more importance to the judgment of these eyes than to that of the mind, asserting and believing as you do that there is no shining feather that does not shine from God, and that there are living souls that do not live from God. These and like things I should either have said to them or considered with myself, for even then, supplicating God with all my bowels, so to speak, and examining as attentively as possible the Scriptures, I should perchance have been able either to say such things or to think them, so far as was necessary for my salvation.

CHAP. 9.—AUGUSTIN DECEIVED BY FAMILIARITY WITH THE MANICHÆANS, AND BY THE SUCCESSION OF VICTORIES OVER IGNORANT CHRISTIANS REPORTED BY THEM. THE MANICHÆANS ARE LIKEWISE EASILY REFUTED FROM THE KNOWLEDGE OF SIN AND THE WILL.

But two things especially, which easily lay hold upon that unwary age, urged me through wonderful circuits. One of these was familiarity, suddenly, by a certain false semblance of goodness, wrapped many times around my neck as a certain sinuous chain. The other was, that I was almost always noxiously victorious in arguing with ignorant Christians who yet eagerly attempted, each as he could, to defend their faith.[3] By which frequent success the ardor of youth was kindled, and by its own impulse rashly verged upon the great evil of stubbornness. For this kind of wrangling, after I had become an auditor among them, whatever I was able to do either by my own genius, such as it was, or by reading the works of others, I most gladly devoted to them alone. Accordingly from their speeches ardor in disputations was daily increased, from success in disputations love for them [the Manichæans]. Whence it resulted that whatever they said, as if affected by certain strange disorders, I approved of as true, not because I knew it to be true, but because I wished it to be. So it came about that, however slowly and cautiously, yet for a long time I followed men that preferred a sleek straw to a living soul.

12. So be it, I was not able at that time to distinguish and discern sensible from intelligible things, carnal forsooth from spiritual. It did not belong to age, nor to discipline, nor even to any habit, nor, finally, to any deserts; for it is a matter of no small joy and felicitation: had I not thus been able at length even to grasp that which in the judgment of all men nature itself by the laws of the most High God has established?

CHAP. 10.—SIN IS ONLY FROM THE WILL. HIS OWN LIFE AND WILL BEST KNOWN TO EACH INDIVIDUAL. WHAT WILL IS.

For let any men whatever, if only no madness has broken them loose from the common

[1] John xvii. 3.

[2] 2 Cor. iv. 13.

[3] Nothing is more certain than that Christianity has suffered more at the hands of injudicious and ignorant defenders than from its most astute and determined foes. Little attention would be paid to the blatant infidels of the present day were it not for the interest aroused and sustained by weak attempts to refute their arguments. And as the youthful, ardent Augustin was encouraged and confirmed in his errors by the inability of his opponents, so

sense of the human race, bring whatever zeal they like for judging, whatever ignorance, nay whatever slowness of mind, I should like to find out what they would have replied to me had I asked, whether a man would seem to them to have sinned by whose hand while he was asleep another should have written something disgraceful? Who doubts that they would have denied that it is a sin, and have exclaimed against it so vehemently that they might perchance have been enraged that I should have thought them proper objects of such a question? Of whom reconciled and restored to equanimity, as best I could do it, I should have begged that they would not take it amiss if I asked them another thing just as manifest, just as completely within the knowledge of all. Then I should have asked, if some stronger person had done some evil thing by the hand of one not sleeping but conscious, yet with the rest of his members bound and in constraint, whether because he knew it, though absolutely unwilling, he should be held guilty of any sin? And here all marvelling that I should ask such questions, would reply without hesitation, that he had absolutely not sinned at all. Why so? Because whoever has done anything evil by means of one unconscious or unable to resist, the latter can by no means be justly condemned. And precisely why this is so, if I should inquire of the human nature in these men, I should easily bring out the desired answer, by asking in this manner: Suppose that the sleeper already knew what the other would do with his hand, and of purpose aforethought, having drunk so much as would prevent his being awakened, should go to sleep, in order to deceive some one with an oath. Would any amount of sleep suffice to prove his innocence? What else than a guilty man would one pronounce him? But if he has also willingly been bound that he may deceive some one by this pretext, in what respect then would those chains profit as a means of relieving him of sin? Although bound by these he was really not able to resist, as in the other case the sleeper was absolutely ignorant of what he was then doing. Is there therefore any possibility of doubting that both should be judged to have sinned? Which things having been conceded, I should have argued, that sin is indeed nowhere but in the will,[1] since this consideration also would have helped me, that justice holds guilty those sinning by evil will alone, although they may have been unable to accomplish what they willed.

13. For who could have said that, in adducing these considerations, I was dwelling upon obscure and recondite things, where on account of the fewness of those able to understand, either fraud or suspicion of ostentation is accustomed to arise? Let that distinction between intelligible and sensible things withdraw for a little: let me not be found fault with for following up slow minds with the stimuli of subtle disputations. Permit me to know that I live, permit me to know that I will to live. If in this the human race agrees, as our life is known to us, so also is our will. Nor when we become possessed of this knowledge, is there any occasion to fear lest any one should convince us that we may be deceived; for no one can be deceived as to whether he does not live, or wishes nothing. I do not think that I have adduced anything obscure, and my concern is rather lest some should find fault with me for dwelling on things that are too manifest. But let us consider the bearing of these things.

14. Sinning therefore takes place only by exercise of will. But our will is very well known to us; for neither should I know that I will, if I did not know what will itself is. Accordingly, it is thus defined: will is a movement of mind, no one compelling, either

are errors confirmed at the present day. The philosophical defence of Christianity is a matter of the utmost delicacy, and should be undertaken with fear and trembling.—A. H. N.

[1] The Pelagians used this statement with considerable effect in their polemics against its author. In his *Retractations* Augustin has this to say by way of explanation: "The Pelagians may think that this was said in their interest, on account of young children whose sin which is remitted to them in baptism they deny on the ground that they do not yet use the power of will. As if indeed the sin, which we say they derive originally from Adam, that is, that they are implicated in his guilt and on this account are held obnoxious to punishment, could ever be otherwise than in will, by which will it was committed when the transgression of the divine precept was accomplished. Our statement, that 'there is never sin but in will,' may be thought false for the reason that the apostle says: 'If what I will not this I do, it is no longer I that do it, but sin that dwelleth in me.' For this sin is to such an extent involuntary, that he says: 'What I will not this I do.' How, therefore, is there never sin but in the will? But this sin concerning which the apostle has spoken is called sin, because by sin it was done, and it is the penalty of sin; since this is said concerning carnal concupiscence, which he discloses in what follows saying: 'I know that in me, that is in my flesh, dwelleth no good; for to will is present to me, but to accomplish that which is good, is not." (Rom. vii. 16–18). Since the perfection of good is, that not even the concupiscence of sin should be in man, to which indeed when one lives well the will does not consent; nevertheless man does not accomplish the good because as yet concupiscence is in him, to which the will is antagonistic, the guilt of which concupiscence is loosed by baptism, but the infirmity remains, against which until it is healed every believer who advances well most earnestly struggles. But sin, which is never but in will, must especially be known as that which is followed by just condemnation. For this through one man entered into the world; although that sin also by which consent is yielded to concupiscence is not committed but by will. Wherefore also in another place I have said: 'Not therefore except by will is sin committed.'"—A. H. N.

On this matter Augustin's still earlier treatise *De Libero Arbitrio*, and his interesting *Retractations* on the same, should be compared. The reader of these earlier treatises in comparison with the Anti-Pelagian treatises can hardly fail to recognize a marked change of base on Augustin's part. His efforts to show the consistency of his earlier with his later modes of thought are to be pronounced only partially successful. The fact is, that in the Anti-Manichæan time he went too far in maintaining the absolute freedom of the will and the impossibility of sin apart from personal will in the sinner; while in the Anti-Pelagian time he ventured too near to the fatalism that he so earnestly combated in the Manichæans.—A. H. N.

for not losing or for obtaining something.[1] Why therefore could not I have so defined it then? Was it difficult to see that one unwilling is contrary to one willing, just as the left hand is contrary to the right, not as black to white? For the same thing cannot be at the same time black and white. But whoever is placed between two men is on the left hand with reference to one, on the right with reference to the other. One man is both on the right hand and on the left hand at the same time, but by no means both to the one man. So indeed one mind may be at the same time unwilling and willing, but it cannot be at the same time unwilling and willing with reference to one and the same thing. For when any one unwillingly does anything; if you ask him whether he wished to do it, he says that he did not. Likewise if you ask whether he wished not to do it, he replies that he did. So you will find him unwilling with reference to doing, willing with reference to not doing, that is to say, one mind at the same time having both attitudes, but each referring to different things. Why do I say this? Because if we should again ask wherefore though unwilling he does this, he will say that he is compelled. For every one also who does a thing unwillingly is compelled, and every one who is compelled, if he does a thing, does it only unwillingly. It follows that he that is willing is free from compulsion, even if any one thinks himself compelled. And in this manner every one who willingly does a thing is not compelled, and whoever is not compelled, either does it willingly or not at all. Since nature itself proclaims these things in all men whom we can interrogate without absurdity, from the boy even to the old man, from literary sport even to the throne of the wise, why then should I not have seen that in the definition of will should be put, "no one compelling," which now as if with greater experience most cautiously I have done. But if this is everywhere manifest, and promptly occurs to all not by instruction but by nature, what is there left that seems obscure, unless perchance it be concealed from some one, that when we wish for something, we will, and our mind is moved towards it, and we either have it or do not have it, and if we have it we will to retain it, if we have it not, to acquire it? Wherefore everyone who wills, wills either not to lose something or to obtain it. Hence if all these things are clearer than day, as they are, nor are they given to my conception alone, but by the liberality of truth itself to the whole human race, why could I not have said even at that time: Will is a movement of the mind, no one compelling, either for not losing or for obtaining something?

CHAP. 11.—WHAT SIN IS.

Some one will say: What assistance would this have furnished you against the Manichæans? Wait a moment; permit me first also to define sin, which, every mind reads divinely written in itself, cannot exist apart from will. Sin therefore is the will to retain and follow after what justice forbids, and from which it is free to abstain.[2] Although if it be not free, it is not will. But I have preferred to define more roughly than precisely. Should I not also have carefully examined those obscure books, whence I might have learned that no one is worthy of blame or punishment who either wills what justice does not prohibit him from willing, or does not do what he is not able to do? Do not shepherds on mountains, poets in theatres, unlearned in social intercourse, learned in libraries, masters in schools, priests in consecrated places, and the human race throughout the whole world, sing out these things? But if no one is worthy of blame and condemnation, who either does not act against the prohibition of justice, or who does not do what he cannot do, yet every sin is blameworthy and condemnable, who doubts then that it is sin, when willing is unjust, and not willing is free. And hence that definition is both true and easy to understand, and not only now but then also could have been spoken by me: Sin is the will of retaining or of obtaining, what justice forbids, and whence it is free to abstain?

[1] This dictum also Augustin thought it needful to explain: "This was said that by this definition a willing person might be distinguished from one not willing, and so the intention might be referred to those who first in Paradise were the origin of evil to the human race, by sinning no one compelling, that is by sinning with free will, because also knowingly they sinned against the command, and the tempters persuaded, did not compel, that this should be done. For he who ignorantly sinned may not incongruously be said to have sinned unwillingly, although not knowing what he did, yet willingly he did it. So not even the sin of such a one could be without will, which will assuredly, as it has been defined, was a 'movement of the mind, no one compelling, either for not losing or for obtaining something.' For he was not compelled to do what if he had been unwilling he would not have done. Because he willed, therefore he did it, even if he did not sin because he willed, being ignorant that what he did is sin. So not even such a sin could be without will, but by will of deed not by will of sin, which deed was yet sin; for this deed is what ought not to have taken place. But whoever knowingly sins, if he can without sin resist the one compelling him to sin, yet resists not, assuredly sins willingly. For he who can resist is not compelled to yield. But he who cannot by good will resist cogent covetousness, and therefore does what is contrary to the precepts of righteousness, this now is sin in the sense of being the penalty of sin. Wherefore it is most true that sin cannot be apart from will."

It is needless to say that such reasoning would not have answered Augustin's purpose in writing against the Manichæans. --A. H. N.

[2] Here also Augustin guards himself in his *Retractations*: "The definition is true, inasmuch as that is defined which is only sin, and not also that which is the penalty of sin."—A. H. N.

CHAP. 12.—FROM THE DEFINITIONS GIVEN OF SIN AND WILL, HE OVERTHROWS THE ENTIRE HERESY OF THE MANICHÆANS. LIKEWISE FROM THE JUST CONDEMNATION OF EVIL SOULS IT FOLLOWS THAT THEY ARE EVIL NOT BY NATURE BUT BY WILL. THAT SOULS ARE GOOD BY NATURE, TO WHICH THE PARDON OF SINS IS GRANTED.

16. Come now, let us see in what respect these things would have aided us. Much every way, so that I should have desired nothing more; for they end the whole cause; for whoever consulting in the inner mind, where they are more pronounced and assured, the secrets of his own conscience, and the divine laws absolutely imposed upon nature, grants that these two definitions of will and sin are true, condemns without any hesitation by the fewest and the briefest, but plainly the most invincible reasons, the whole heresy of the Manichæans. Which can be thus considered. They say that there are two kinds of souls, the one good, which is in such a way from God, that it is said not to have been made by Him out of any material or out of nothing, but to have proceeded as a certain part from the very substance itself of God; the other evil, which they believe and strive to get others to believe pertains to God in no way whatever; and so they maintain that the one is the perfection of good, but the other the perfection of evil, and that these two classes were at one time distinct but are now commingled. The character and the cause of this commingling I had not yet heard; but nevertheless I could have inquired whether that evil kind of souls, before it was mingled with the good, had any will. For if not, it was without sin and innocent, and so by no means evil.[1] But if evil in such a way, that though without will, as fire, yet if it should touch the good it would violate and corrupt it; how impious it is to believe that the nature of evil is powerful enough to change any part of God, and that the Highest Good is corruptible and violable! But if the will was present, assuredly there was present, no one compelling, a movement of the mind either towards not losing something or obtaining something. But this something was either good, or was thought to be good, for not otherwise could it be earnestly desired. But in supreme evil, before the commingling which they maintain, there never was any good. Whence then could there be in it either the knowledge or the thought of good? Did they wish for nothing that was in themselves, and earnestly desire that true good which was without? That will must truly be declared worthy of distinguished and great praise by which is earnestly desired the supreme and true good. Whence then in supreme evil was this movement of mind most worthy of so great praise? Did they seek it for the sake of injuring it? In the first place, the argument comes to the same thing. For he who wishes to injure, wishes to deprive another of some good for the sake of some good of his own. There was therefore in them either a knowledge of good or an opinion of good, which ought by no means to belong to supreme evil. In the second place, whence had they known, that good placed outside of themselves, which they designed to injure, existed at all. If they had intellectually perceived it, what is more excellent than such a mind? Is there anything else for which the whole energy of good men is put forth except the knowledge of that supreme and sincere good? What therefore is now scarcely conceded to a few good and just men, was mere evil, no good assisting, then able to accomplish? But if those souls bore bodies and saw the supreme good with their eyes, what tongues, what hearts, what intellects suffice for lauding and proclaiming those eyes, with which the minds of just men can scarcely be compared? How great good things we find in supreme evil! For if to see God is evil, God is not a good; but God is a good; therefore to see God is good; and I know not what can be compared to this good. Since to see anything is good, whence can it be made out that to be able to see is evil? Therefore whatever in those eyes or in those minds brought it about, that the divine essence could be seen by them, brought about a great thing and a good thing most worthy of ineffable praise. But if it was not brought about, but it was such in itself and eternal, it is difficult to find anything better than this evil.

17. Lastly, that these souls may have nothing of these praiseworthy things which by the reasonings of the Manichæans they are compelled to have, I should have asked, whether God condemns any or no souls. If none, there is no judgment of rewards and punishments, no providence, and the world is administered by chance rather than by reason, or rather is not administered at all. For the name administration must not be given to chances. But if it is impious for all those that are bound by any religion to believe

[1] In his *Retractations*, Augustin replies to the Pelagian denial of the sinfulness of infants, in support of which they had quoted the above sentence. "They [infants] are held guilty not by propriety of will but by origin. For what is every earthly man in origin but Adam?" The will of the whole human race was in Adam, and when Adam sinned the whole race voluntarily sinned, seems to be his meaning.—A. H. N.

this, it remains either that there is condemnation of some souls, or that there are no sins. But if there are no sins, neither is there any evil. Which if the Manichæans should say, they would slay their heresy with a single blow. Therefore they and I agree that some souls are condemned by divine law and judgment. But if these souls are good, what is that justice? If evil, are they so by nature, or by will? But by nature souls can in no way be evil. Whence do we teach this. From the above definitions of will and sin. For to speak of souls, and that they are evil, and that they do not sin, is full of madness; but to say that they sin without will, is great craziness, and to hold any one guilty of sin for not doing what he could not do, belongs to the height of iniquity and insanity. Wherefore whatever these souls do, if they do it by nature not by will, that is, if they are wanting in a movement of mind free both for doing and not doing, if finally no power of abstaining from their work is conceded to them; we cannot hold that the sin is theirs.[1] But all confess both that evil souls are justly, and souls that have not sinned are unjustly condemned; therefore they confess that those souls are evil that sin. But these, as reason teaches, do not sin. Therefore the extraneous class of evil souls of the Manichæans, whatever it may be, is a non-entity.

18. Let us now look at that good class of souls, which again they exalt to such a degree as to say that it is the very substance of God. But how much better it is that each one should recognize his own rank and merit, nor be so puffed up with sacrilegious pride as to believe that as often as he experiences a change in himself it is the substance of that supreme good, which devout reason holds and teaches to be unchangeable! For behold! since it is manifest that souls do not sin in not being such as they cannot be; it follows that these supposititious souls, whatever they may be, do not sin at all, and moreover that they are absolutely non-existent; it remains that since there are sins, they find none to whom to attribute them except the good class of souls and the substance of God. But especially are they pressed by Christian authority; for never have they denied that forgiveness of sins is granted when any one has been converted to God; never have they said (as they have said of many other passages) that some corrupter has interpolated this into the divine Scriptures. To whom then are sins attributed? If to those evil souls of the alien class, these also can become good, can possess the kingdom of God with Christ. Which denying, they [the Manichæans] have no other class except those souls which they maintain are of the substance of God. It remains that they acknowledge that not only these latter also, but these alone sin. But I make no contention about their being alone in sinning; yet they sin. But are they compelled to sin by being commingled with evil? If so compelled that there was no power of resisting, they do not sin. If it is in their power to resist, and they voluntarily consent, we are compelled to find out through their [the Manichæan] teaching, why so great good things in supreme evil, why this evil in supreme good, unless it be that neither is that which they bring into suspicion evil, nor is that which they pervert by superstition supreme good?

CHAP. 13.—FROM DELIBERATION ON THE EVIL AND ON THE GOOD PART IT RESULTS THAT TWO CLASSES OF SOULS ARE NOT TO BE HELD TO. A CLASS OF SOULS ENTICING TO SHAMEFUL DEEDS HAVING BEEN CONCEDED, IT DOES NOT FOLLOW THAT THESE ARE EVIL BY NATURE, THAT THE OTHERS ARE SUPREME GOOD.

19. But if I had taught, or at any rate had myself learned, that they rave and err regarding those two classes of souls, why should I have thenceforth thought them worthy of being heard or consulted about anything? That I might learn hence, that these two kinds of souls are pointed out, which in the course of deliberation assent puts now on the evil side, now on the good? Why is not this rather the sign of one soul which by free will can be borne here and there, swayed hither and thither? For it was my own experience to feel that I am one, considering evil and good and choosing one or the other, but for the most part the one pleases, the other is fitting, placed in the midst of which we fluctuate. Nor is it to be wondered at, for we are now so constituted that through the flesh we can be affected by sensual pleasure, and through the spirit by honorable considerations. Am I not therefore compelled to acknowledge two souls? Nay, we can better and with far less difficulty recognize two classes of good things, of which neither is alien from God as its author, one soul acted upon from diverse directions, the lower and the higher, or to speak more correctly, the external and the internal. These are the two

[1] In his *Retractations*, Augustin explains that by nature is to be understood the state in which we were created without vice. He transfers the entire argument from the actual condition of man to the primitive Adamic condition. It is evident, however, that this was not his meaning when he combated the Manichæans. The question of infant sinfulness arises here also, and is discussed in the usual Anti-Pelagian way.—A. H. N.

classes which a little while ago we considered under the names *sensible* and *intelligible*, which we now prefer to call more familiarly carnal and spiritual. But it has been made difficult for us to abstain from carnal things, since our truest bread is spiritual. For with great labor we now eat this bread. For neither without punishment for the sin of transgression have we been changed from immortal into mortal. So it happens, that when we strive after better things, habit formed by connection with the flesh and our sins in some way begin to militate against us and to put obstacles in our way, some foolish persons with most obtuse superstition suspect that there is another kind of souls which is not of God.

20. However even if it be conceded to them that we are enticed to shameful deeds by another inferior kind of souls, they do not thence make it evident that those enticing are evil by nature, or those enticed, supremely good. For it may be, the former of their own will, by striving after what was not lawful, that is, by sinning, from being good have become evil; and again they may be made good, but in such manner that for a long time they remain in sin, and by a certain occult suasion traduce to themselves other souls. Then, they may not be absolutely evil, but in their own kind, however inferior, they may exercise their own functions without any sin. But those superior souls to whom justice, the directress of things, has assigned a far more excellent activity, if they should wish to follow and to imitate those inferior ones, become evil, not because they imitate evil souls, but because they imitate in an evil way. By the evil souls is done what is proper to them, by the good what is alien to them is striven after. Hence the former remain in their own grade, the latter are plunged into a lower. It is as when men copy after beasts. For the four-footed horse walks beautifully, but if a man on all fours should imitate him, who would think him worthy even of chaff for food? Rightly therefore we generally disapprove of one who imitates, while we approve of him whom he imitates. But we disapprove not because he has not succeeded, but for wishing to succeed at all. For in the horse we approve of that to which by as much as we prefer man, by so much are we offended that he copies after inferior creatures. So among men, however well the crier may do in sending forth his voice, would not the senator be insane, if he should do it even more clearly and better than the crier? Take an illustration from the heavenly bodies: The moon when shining is praised, and by its course and its changes is quite pleasing to those that pay attention to such things. But if the sun should wish to imitate it (for we may feign that it has desires of this sort [1]), who would not be greatly and rightly displeased. From which illustrations I wish it to be understood, that even if there are souls (which meanwhile is left an open question [2]) devoted to bodily offices not by sin but by nature, and even if they are related to us, however inferior they may be, by some inner affinity, they should not be esteemed evil simply because we are evil ourselves in following them and in loving corporeal things. For we sin by loving corporeal things, because by justice we are required and by nature we are able to love spiritual things, and when we do this we are, in our kind, the best and the happiest.[3]

21. Wherefore what proof does deliberation, violently urged in both directions, now prone to sin, now borne on toward right conduct, furnish, that we are compelled to accept two kinds of souls, the nature of one of which is from God, of the other not; when we are free to conjecture so many other causes of alternating states of mind? But that these things are obscure and are to no purpose pried into by blear-eyed minds, whoever is a good judge of things sees. Wherefore those things rather which have been said regarding the will and sin, those things, I say, that supreme justice permits no man using his reason to be ignorant of, those things which if they were taken from us, there is nothing whence the discipline of virtue may begin, nothing whence it may rise from the death of vices, those things I say considered again and again with sufficient clearness and lucidity convince us that the heresy of the Manichæans is false.

CHAP. 14.—AGAIN IT IS SHOWN FROM THE UTILITY OF REPENTING THAT SOULS ARE NOT BY NATURE EVIL. SO SURE A DEMONSTRATION IS NOT CONTRADICTED EXCEPT FROM THE HABIT OF ERRING.

22. Like the foregoing considerations is what I shall now say about repenting. For as among all sane people it is agreed, and this the Manichæans themselves not only confess but also teach, that to repent of sin is useful. Why shall I now, in this matter, collect the testimonies of the divine Scriptures, which

1 Augustin's carefulness to explain that he is only indulging in personification is doubtless due to the fact that with the Manichæans the sun and the moon were objects of worship.—A. H. N.

2 In his *Retractations*, Augustin explains that he did not really regard this as an open question, but speaks of it as such only so far as this particular discussion is concerned. He simply declines to enter upon a consideration of it in this connection.—A. H. N.

3 Here also the use of the word "nature" gave Augustin trouble in his later years. He claims in the *Retractations* that he uses the word in the sense of "nature that has been healed' and that "cannot be vitiated," and seeks to show that he did not mean to exclude divine grace.—A. H. N.

are scattered throughout their pages? It is also the voice of nature; notice of this thing has escaped no fool. We should be undone, if this were not deeply imbedded in our nature. Some one may say that he does not sin; but no barbarity will dare to say, that if one sins he should not repent of it. This being the case, I ask to which of the two kinds of souls does repenting pertain? I know indeed that it can pertain neither to him who does ill nor to him who cannot do well. Wherefore, that I may use the words of the Manichæans, if a soul of darkness repent of sin, it is not of the substance of supreme evil, if a soul of light, it is not of the substance of supreme good; that disposition of repenting which is profitable testifies alike that the penitent has done ill, and that he could have done well. How, therefore, is there from me nothing of evil, if I have acted unadvisedly, or how can I rightly repent if I have not so done? Hear the other part. How is there from me nothing of good, if in me there is good will, or how do I rightly repent if there is not? Wherefore, either let them deny that there is great utility in repenting, so that they may be driven not only from the Christian name, but from every even imaginary argument for their views, or let them cease to say and to teach that there are two kinds of souls, one of which has nothing of evil, the other nothing of good; for that whole sect is propped up by this two-headed[1] or rather headlong[2] variety of souls.

23. And to me indeed it is sufficient thus to know that the Manichæans err, that I know that sin must be repented of; and yet if now by right of friendship I should accost some one of my friends who still thinks that they are worthy of being listened to, and should say to him: Do you not know that it is useful, when any one has sinned, to repent? Without hesitation he will swear that he knows. If then I shall have convinced you that Manichæism is false, will you not desire anything more? Let him reply what more he can desire in this matter. Very well, so far. But when I shall have begun to show the sure and necessary arguments which, bound to it with adamantine chains, as the saying is, follow that proposition, and shall have conducted to its conclusion the whole process by which that sect is overthrown, he will deny perhaps that he knows the utility of repenting, which no learned man, no unlearned, is ignorant of, and will rather contend, when we hesitate and deliberate, that two souls in us furnish each its own proper help to the solution of the different parts of the question. O habit of sin! O accompanying penalty of sin! Then you turned me away from the consideration of things so manifest, but you injured me when I did not discern. But now, among my most familiar acquaintances who do not discern, you wound and torment me discerning.

[1] *Bicipiti.*

[2] *Præcipiti.*

CHAP. 15.—HE PRAYS FOR HIS FRIENDS WHOM HE HAS HAD AS ASSOCIATES IN ERROR.

24. Give heed to these things, I beseech you, dearly beloved. Your dispositions I have well known. If you now concede to me the mind and the reason of any sort of man, these things are far more certain than the things that we seemed to learn or rather were compelled to believe. Great God, God omnipotent, God of supreme goodness, whose right it is to be believed and known to be inviolable and unchangeable. Trinal Unity, whom the Catholic Church worships, as one who have experienced in myself Thy mercy, I supplicate Thee, that Thou wilt not permit those with whom from boyhood I have lived most harmoniously in every relation to dissent from me in Thy worship. I see how it was especially to be expected in this place that I should either even then have defended the Catholic Scriptures attacked by the Manichæans, if as I say, I had been cautious; or I should now show that they can be defended. But in other volumes God will aid my purpose, for the moderate length of this, as I suppose, already asks to be spared.[3]

[3] This purpose Augustin accomplished in several works. See especially *Contra Adimantum*, and *Contra Faustum Manichæum*. On Augustin's defense of the Old Testament Scriptures, see MOZLEY'S *Ruling Ideas in Early Ages*, last chapter.— A. H. N.

ST. AUGUSTIN:

ACTS OR DISPUTATION

AGAINST

FORTUNATUS THE MANICHÆAN.

[ACTA SEU DISPUTATIO CONTRA FORTUNATUM MANICHÆUM].

A.D. 392.

TRANSLATED BY

ALBERT H. NEWMAN, D.D., L.L.D.,

PROFESSOR OF CHURCH HISTORY AND COMPARATIVE RELIGION, IN TORONTO BAPTIST (THEOLOGICAL) COLLEGE, TORONTO, CANADA.

CONTENTS OF ACTS OR DISPUTATION AGAINST FORTUNATUS THE MANICHÆAN.

ACTS OR DISPUTATION

AGAINST FORTUNATUS, THE MANICHÆAN.

[ACTA SEU DISPUTATIO CONTRA FORTUNATUM MANICHÆUM.] A.D. 392.[1]

DISPUTATION OF THE FIRST DAY.

ON THE FIFTH OF SEPTEMBER, THE MOST RENOWNED MEN ARCADIUS AUGUSTUS (THE SECOND TIME) AND RUFINUS BEING CONSULS, A DISPUTATION AGAINST FORTUNATUS, AN ELDER OF THE MANICHÆANS, WAS HELD IN THE CITY OF HIPPO REGIUS, IN THE BATHS OF SOSSIUS, IN THE PRESENCE OF THE PEOPLE.

1. AUGUSTIN said: I now regard as error what formerly I regarded as truth. I desire to hear from you who are present whether my supposition is correct. First of all I regard it as the height of error to believe that Almighty God, in whom is our one hope, is in any part either violable, or contaminable, or corruptible. This I know your heresy affirms, not indeed in the words that I now use; for when you are questioned you confess that God is incorruptible, and absolutely inviolable, and incontaminable; but when you begin to expound the rest of your system, we are compelled to declare Him corruptible, penetrable, contaminable. For you say that another race of darkness, whatever it may be, has rebelled against the kingdom of God; but that Almighty God, when He saw what ruin and desolation threatened his domains, unless he should make some opposition to the adverse race and resist it, sent this virtue, from whose commingling with evil and the race of darkness the world was framed. Hence it is that here good souls labor, serve, err, are corrupted: that they may see the need of a liberator, who should purge them from error, loose them from this commingling with evil, and liberate them from servitude. I think it impious to believe that Almighty God ever feared any adverse race, or was under necessity to precipitate us into afflictions.

FORTUNATUS said: Because I know that you have been in our midst, that is, have lived as an adherent among the Manichæans, these are the principles of our faith. The matter now to be considered is our mode of living, the falsely alleged crimes for which we are maltreated. Therefore let the good men present hear from you whether these things with which we are charged and which we have thrown in our teeth are true or false. For from your instruction, and from your exposition and explanation, they will have been able to gain more correct information about our

[1] This *Disputation* seems to have occurred shortly after the writing of the preceding treatise. It appears from the *Retractations* that Fortunatus had lived for a considerable time at Hippo, and had secured so large a number of followers that it was a delight to him to dwell there. The *Disputation* is supposed to be a verbatim report of what Augustin and Fortunatus said during a two days' discussion. The subject is the origin of evil. Augustin maintains that evil, so far as man is concerned, has arisen from a free exercise of the will on man's part; Fortunatus, on the other hand, maintains that the nature of evil is co-eternal with God. Fortunatus shows considerable knowledge of the New Testament, but no remarkable dialectic powers. He appears at great disadvantage beside his great antagonist. In fact, he is far from saying the best that can be said in favor of dualism. We may say that he was fairly vanquished in the argument, and at the close confessed himself at a loss what to say, and expressed an intention of more carefully examining the problems discussed, in view of what Augustin had said. Augustin is more guarded in this treatise than in the preceding in his statements about free will. He found little occasion here, therefore, to retract or explain. Fortunatus often expresses himself vaguely and obscurely. If some sentences are difficult to understand in the translation, they will be found equally so in the Latin.—A. H. N.

mode of life, if it shall have been set forth by you.

2. AUGUSTIN said: I was among you, but faith and morals are different questions. I proposed to discuss faith. But if those present prefer to hear about morals, I do not decline that question.

FORTUNATUS said: I wish first to purge myself in your conscience in which we are polluted, by the testimony of a competent man, (who even now is competent for me), and in view of the future examination of Christ, the just judge, whether he saw in us, or himself practiced by imitation, the things that are now thrown in our teeth?

3. AUGUSTIN said: You call me to something else, when I had proposed to discuss faith, but concerning your morals only those who are your Elect can fully know. But you know that I was not your Elect, but an Auditor. Hence though I was present at your prayer meetings,[1] as you have asked (whether separately among yourselves you have any prayer meetings, God alone and yourselves can know); yet in your prayer meetings where I have been present I have seen nothing shameful take place; but only that the faith that I afterwards learned and approved is denounced, and that you perform your services facing the sun. Besides this I found out nothing new in your meetings, but whoever raises any question of morals against you, raises it against your Elect. But what you who are Elect do among yourselves, I have no means of knowing. For I have often heard from you that you receive the Eucharist. But since the time of receiving it was concealed from me, how could I know what you receive?[2] So keep the question about morals, if you please, for discussion among your Elect, if it can be discussed. You gave me a faith that I to-day disapprove. This I proposed to discuss. Let a response be made to my proposition.

FORTUNATUS said: And our profession is this very thing: that God is incorruptible, lucid, unapproachable, intenible, impassible, that He inhabits His own eternal lights, that nothing corruptible proceeds from Him, neither darkness, demons, Satan, nor anything adverse can be found in His kingdom. But that He sent forth a Saviour like Himself; that the Word born from the foundation of the world, when He had formed the world, after the formation of the world came among men; that He has chosen souls worthy of Himself according to His own holy will, sanctified by celestial command, imbued with the faith and reason of celestial things; that under His leadership those souls will return hence again to the kingdom of God according to the holy promise of Him who said: "I am the way, the truth, and the door;"[3] and "No one can come unto the Father, except through me." These things we believe because otherwise, that is, through another mediator, souls cannot return to the kingdom of God, unless they find Him as the way, the truth, and the door. For Himself said: "He that hath seen me, hath seen my Father also;"[4] and "whosoever shall have believed on me shall not taste death forever, but has passed from death unto life, and shall not come into judgment."[5] These things we believe and this is the reason of our faith, and according to the strength of our mind we endeavor to act according to His commandments, following after the one faith of this Trinity, Father and Son and Holy Spirit.[6]

4. AUGUSTIN said: What was the cause of those souls being precipitated into death, whom you confess come through Christ from death to life?

FORTUNATUS said: Hence now deign to go on and to contradict, if there is nothing besides God.

5. AUGUSTIN said: Nay, do you deign to answer the question put to you: What cause has given these souls to death?

FORTUNATUS said: Nay but do you deign to say whether there is anything besides God, or all things are in God.

6. AUGUSTIN said: This I can reply, that the Lord wished me to know that God cannot suffer any necessity, nor be violated or corrupted in any part. Which, since you also acknowledge, I ask by what necessity He sent hither souls that you say return through Christ?

FORTUNATUS said: What you have said: that thus far God has revealed to you, that He is incorruptible, as He has also revealed to me; the reason must be sought, how and wherefore souls have come into this world, so that now of right God should liberate them

[1] The word used is *oratio*, by which is evidently meant the religious services to which Auditors were admitted, prayer (*oratio*) being the prominent feature.—A. H. N.

[2] The allusion here is doubtless to the probably slanderous charge that the Manichæans were accustomed to partake of human semen as a Eucharist. The Manichæan view of the relation of the substance mentioned to the light, and their well-known opposition to procreation, give a slight plausibility to the charge. Compare the *Morals of the Manichæans*, ch. xviii., where Augustin expresses his suspicions of Manichæan shamelessness. See also further references in the *Introduction*.—A. H. N.

[3] This is, of course, a mixture of two passages of Scripture.—A. H. N.

[4] John xiv. 8, 9.

[5] John v. 24.

[6] As remarked in the *Introduction*, the Manichæans of the West, in Augustin's time, sustained a far more intimate relation to Christianity than did Mani and his immediate followers. Far as Fortunatus may have been from using the above language in the ordinary Christian sense, yet he held, by profession at least, enough of Christian truth to beguile the unwary.—A. H. N.

from this world through his Son only begotten and like Himself, if besides Himself there is nothing?

7. AUGUSTIN said: We ought not to disappoint those present, being men of note, and from the question proposed for discussion go to another. So we both confess, so we concede to ourselves, that God is incorruptible and inviolable, and could have in no way suffered. From which it follows, that your heresy is false, which says that God, when He saw desolation and ruin threaten His kingdom, sent forth a power that should do battle with the race of darkness, and that out of this commingling our souls are laboring. My argument is brief, and as I suppose, perfectly clear to any one. If God could have suffered nothing from the race of darkness because He is inviolable, without cause He sent us hither that we might here suffer distress. But if anything can suffer, it is not inviolable, and you deceive those to whom you say that God is inviolable. For this your heresy denies when you expound the rest of it.

FORTUNATUS said: We are of that mind in which the Apostle Paul instructs us, who says: "Let this mind be in you that was also in Christ Jesus, who when He had been constituted in the form of God, thought it not robbery to be equal with God; but emptied Himself receiving the form of a servant, having been made in the likeness of men, and having been found in fashion as a man, He humbled Himself, and was made obedient even unto death."[1] We have this mind therefore about ourselves, which we have also about Christ, who when He was constituted in the form of God, was made obedient even unto death that He might show the similitude of our souls. And like as He showed in Himself the similitude of death, and having been raised from the midst of the dead showed that He was from the Father, in the same manner we think it will be with our souls, because through Him we shall have been able to be freed from this death, which is either alien from God, or if it belongs to God, His mercy ceases, and the name of liberator, and the works of Him who liberates.[2]

8. AUGUSTIN said: I ask how we came into death, and you tell how we may be liberated from death.

FORTUNATUS said: So the apostle said that we ought to have that mind concerning ourselves which Christ has shown us. If Christ was in suffering and death, so also are we.

9. AUGUSTIN said: It is known to all that the Catholic faith is to the effect that our Lord, that is the Power and Wisdom of God,[3] and the Word through whom all things have been made and without whom was not anything made,[4] took upon Himself man to liberate us. In the man whom He took upon Himself, He demonstrated those things that you spoke of. But we now ask concerning the substance of God Himself and of Unspeakable Majesty, whether anything can injure it or not. For if anything can injure it, He is not inviolable. If nothing can injure the substance of God, what was the race of darkness about to do to it, against which you say war was waged by God before the foundation of the world, in which war you assert that we, that is souls that are now manifestly in need of a liberator, have been commingled with every evil and implicated in death. For I return to that very brief statement: If He could be injured, He is not inviolable; if He could not, He acted cruelly in sending us hither to suffer these things.

FORTUNATUS said: Does the soul belong to God, or not?

10. AUGUSTIN said: If it is just that you should fail to respond to my questions, and that I should be questioned, I will reply.

FORTUNATUS said: Does the soul act independently? This I ask of you.

11. AUGUSTIN said: I indeed will tell what you have asked; only remember this, that while you have refused to respond to my questions, I have responded to yours. If you ask whether the soul descended from God, it is indeed a great question; but whether it descends from God or not, I make this reply concerning the soul, that it is not God; that God is one thing, the soul another. That God is inviolable, incorruptible, and impenetrable, and incontaminable, who also could be corrupted in no part and to whom no injury can be done in any part. But we see also that the soul is sinful, and is conversant with misery, and seeks the truth, and is in want of a liberator. This changing condition of the soul shows me that the soul is not God. For if the soul is the substance of God, the substance of God errs, the substance of God is corrupted, the substance of God is violated, the substance of God is deceived; which it is impious to say.

FORTUNATUS said: Therefore you have denied that the soul is of God, so long as it serves sins, and vices, and earthly things, and is led by error, because it cannot happen that either God or His substance should suffer

[1] Philipp. ii. 5–8.

[2] Fortunatus could not surely have used this language with any proper conception of its meaning. He seems, against Mani, to have identified in some sense the Jesus that suffered with Christ. Yet even in this statement his docetism is manifest.—A. H. N.

[3] 1 Cor. i. 24.

[4] John i. 3.

this thing. For God is incorruptible and His substance immaculate and holy. But here it is inquired of you whether the soul is of God, or not? Which we confess, and show from the advent of the Saviour, from His holy preaching, from His election; while He pitied souls, and the soul is said to have come according to His will, that He might free it from death and might bring it to eternal glory, and restore it to the Father. But what do you say and hope concerning the soul; is it from God or not? Can the substance of God, from which you deny that the soul has its being, be subject to no passions?

12. AUGUSTIN said: I have denied that the soul is the substance of God in the sense of its being God; but yet I hold that it is from God as its author, because it was made by God. The Maker is one thing, the thing made is another. He who made cannot be corruptible at all, but what He made cannot be at all equal to Him who made it.

FORTUNATUS said: Nor have I said that the soul is like God. But because you have said that the soul is an artificial thing, and that there is nothing besides God, I ask whence then God invented the substance of the soul?

13. AUGUSTIN said: Only bear in mind that I reply to your interrogations, but that you do not reply to mine. I say that the soul was made by God as all other things that were made by God; and that among the things that God Almighty made the principal place was given to the soul. But if you ask whence God made the soul, remember that you and I agree in confessing that God is almighty. But he is not almighty who seeks the assistance of any material whence he may make what he will. From which it follows, that according to our faith, all things that God made through His Word and Wisdom, He made out of nothing. For so we read: He ordered and they were made; He commanded and they were created."[1]

FORTUNATUS said: Do all things have their existence from God's command?

14. AUGUSTIN said: So I believe, but all things which were made.

FORTUNATUS said: As things made they agree, but because they are unsuitable to themselves, therefore on this account it follows, that there is not one substance, although from the same order of the One they came to the composition and fashioning of this world. But it is plain in the things themselves that there is no similarity between darkness and light, truth and falsehood, death and life, soul and body, and other similar things which differ from each other both in names and appearances. And for good reason did our Lord say: "The tree which my heavenly Father has not planted shall be rooted up and cast into the fire, because it brings not forth good fruit:"[2] and that the tree has been rooted up. Hence truly it follows from the reason of things that there are two substances in this world which agree in forms and in names, of which one belongs to corporeal natures, but the other is the eternal substance of the omnipotent Father, which we believe to be God's substance.

15. AUGUSTIN said: Those contrary things that move you so that we think adversely, have happened on account of our sin, that is, on account of the sin of man. For God made all things good, and ordered them well; but He did not make sin, and our voluntary sin is the only thing that is called evil. There is another kind of evil, which is the penalty of sin. Since therefore there are two kinds of evil, sin and the penalty of sin, sin does not pertain to God; the penalty of sin pertains to the avenger. For as God is good who constituted all things, so He is just in taking vengeance on sin. Since therefore all things are ordered in the best possible way, which seem to us now to be adverse, it has deservedly happened to fallen man who was unwilling to keep the law of God. For God gave free will to the rational soul which is in man. For thus it would have been possible to have merit, if we should be good voluntarily and not of necessity. Since therefore it behooves us to be good not of necessity but voluntarily, it behooved God to give to the soul free will. But to this soul obeying His laws, He subjected all things without adversity, so that the rest of the things that God made should serve it, if also the soul itself had willed to serve God. But if it should refuse to serve God, those things that served it should be converted into its punishment. Wherefore if all things are rightly ordered by God, and are good, neither does God suffer evil.

FORTUNATUS said: He does not suffer, but prevents evil.

16. AUGUSTIN said: From whom then was He about to suffer it?

FORTUNATUS said: This is my point, that He wished to prevent it, not rashly, but by power and prescience. But deny evil to be apart from God, when other precepts can be shown which are done apart from His will. A precept is not introduced, unless where there is contrariety. The free faculty of liv-

[1] Ps. cxlviii. 5.

[2] Matt. xv. 13, and iii. 10.

ing is not given except where there is a fall, according to the argument of the apostle who says: "And you did he quicken, when ye were dead in your trespasses and sins, wherein aforetime ye walked according to the rulership of this world, according to the prince of the power of the air, of the spirit that now worketh in the souls of disobedience; among whom we also all once lived in the lusts of our flesh, doing the desires of the counsels of the flesh, and were by nature children of wrath, even as the rest: but God, who is rich in all mercy, had mercy on us. And when we were dead by sins, quickened us together in Christ, by whose grace ye have been saved; and at the same time also raised us up, and made us to sit with Him in the heavenly places with Christ Jesus, that in the ages to come He might show the exceeding riches of his grace in kindness toward us in Christ Jesus. For by grace have ye been saved through faith; and that not of yourselves, for it is a gift of God; not of works, lest any one should glory. For we are his workmanship created in Christ Jesus in good works, which God prepared that we should walk in them. Wherefore remember, that aforetime ye were Gentiles in the flesh, who are called uncircumcision, by that which is called circumcision in flesh made by hands, because ye were at that time without Christ, alienated from the commonwealth of Israel, and strangers of the covenant, having no hope of the promise, and without God in this world. But now in Christ Jesus, ye that once were far off are made nigh in the blood of Christ. For He is our peace, who made both one, and breaking down the middle wall of partition, the enmities in His flesh, making void by His decrees the law of commandments, that in Himself He might unite the two into one new man, making peace, that He might reconcile them both in one body unto God through the cross, slaying the enmities in Himself. And He came and preached peace unto you that were far off, and peace to them that were nigh. For through Him we both have our access in one Spirit unto the Father."[1]

17. AUGUSTIN said: This passage from the apostle, which you have thought fit to recite, if I mistake not, makes very strongly for my faith and against yours. In the first place, because free will itself, on which I have said that the possibility of the soul's sinning depends, is here sufficiently expressed, when sins are mentioned, and it is said that our reconciliation with God takes place through Jesus Christ. For by sinning we were brought into opposition to God; but by holding to the precepts of Christ we are reconciled to God; so that we who were dead in sins may be made alive by keeping His precepts, and may have peace with Him in one Spirit, from whom we were alienated, by failure to keep His precepts; as is set forth in our faith concerning the man who was first created. I ask of you, therefore, according to that passage which has been read, how can we have sins if contrary nature compels us to do what we do? For he who is compelled by nature to do anything, does not sin. But he who sins, sins by free will. Wherefore would repentance be enjoined upon us, if we have done nothing evil, but only the race of darkness? Likewise, I ask, to whom is forgiveness of sins granted, to us or to the race of darkness? If to the race of darkness, their race will also reign with Him, receiving the forgiveness of sin; but if to us it is manifest that we have sinned voluntarily. For it is the height of folly for him to be pardoned who has done no evil. But he has done no evil, who has done nothing of his own will. Therefore the soul that to-day promises itself forgiveness of sins and reconciliation to God, if it should cease to sin, and repent of past sins; if it should answer according to your faith and should say: In what have I sinned? In what am I guilty? Why hast Thou expelled me from Thy domains, that I might do battle with some sort of race? I have been trodden under foot, I have been mixed up, I have been corrupted, I am worn out,[2] my free will has not been preserved. Thou knowest the necessity by which I am preserved: Why dost Thou impute to me the wounds that I have received? Wherefore dost Thou compel me to repentance when Thou art the cause of my wounds; when Thou knowest what I have suffered, what the race of darkness has done against me, Thou being the author who couldst suffer no harm and yet wishing to save the domains which nothing could injure, Thou didst thrust me down into these miseries. If indeed I am a part of Thee, who have proceeded from Thy bowels, if I am from Thy kingdom and Thy mouth, I ought not to suffer anything in this race of darkness, so that I being uncorrupted that race should be subjected, if I was a part of the Lord. But now since it cannot be controlled except by my corruption, how can I either be said to be a part of Thee, or Thou remain

[1] Eph. ii. 1–18. There are several somewhat important variations from the Greek text in this long extract. The attentive reader can get a good idea of the nature of the variations by comparing this literal translation with the revised English version.—A. H. N.

[2] There are three readings here, "wearied out," "deceived," and "worn out." The latter is preferred by the Benedictine editors.—A. H. N.

inviolable, or not be cruel in wishing me to suffer for those domains, that could in no way be injured by that race of darkness? Respond to this if you please, and deign also to explain to me how it was said by the apostle, "We were by nature children of wrath," who, he says, have been reconciled to God. If therefore they were by nature children of wrath, how do you say that the soul is by nature a daughter and portion of God?

FORTUNATUS said: If with regard to the soul the apostle had said that we are by nature children of wrath, the soul would have been alienated by the mouth of the apostle from God. From this argument you only show that the soul does not belong to God, because, the apostle says, "We are by nature children of wrath." But if it is said in view of the fact that the apostle[1] was held by the law, descending as he himself testifies, from the seed of Abraham, it follows that he has said corporeally, that we [*i.e.*, Jews] were children of wrath even as the rest of mankind. But he shows that the substance of the soul is of God, and that the soul cannot otherwise be reconciled to God than through the Master, who is Christ Jesus. For the enmity having been slain, the soul seemed to God unworthy to have existed. But that it was sent, this we confess, by God yet omnipotent, both deriving its origin from Him and sent for the sealing of His will. In the same way we believe also that Christ the Saviour came from heaven to fulfill the will of the Father. Which will of the Father was this, to free our souls from the same enmity, this enmity having been slain, which if it had not been opposed to God could neither be called enmity where there was unity, nor could slaying be spoken of or take place where there was life.

18. AUGUSTIN said: Remember that the apostle said that we are alienated from God by our manner of life.

FORTUNATUS said: I submit, that there were two substances. In the substance of light, as we have above said, God is to be held incorruptible; but that there was a contrary nature of darkness, that which I also to-day confess is vanquished by the power of God, and that Christ has been sent forth as a Saviour for my restoration, as previously the same apostle says.

19. AUGUSTIN said· That we should discuss on rational grounds the belief in two natures, has been made obligatory by those who are hearing us. But inasmuch as you have again betaken yourself to the Scriptures, I descend to them, and demand that nothing be passed by, lest using certain statements we should bring confusion into the minds of those to whom the Scriptures are not well known. Let us therefore consider a statement that the apostle has in his epistle to the Romans. For on the first page is what is strongly against you. For he says: "Paul, a servant of Jesus Christ, called to be an apostle, separated unto the gospel of God, which He promised aforetime by His prophets in the Holy Scriptures, concerning his Son, who was made unto Him of the seed of David according to the flesh, who was predestinated to be the Son of God with power, according to the spirit of holiness from the resurrection from the dead of our Lord Jesus Christ."[2] We see that the apostle teaches us concerning our Lord Jesus Christ that before the flesh he was predestinated by the power of God, and according to the flesh was made unto Him of the seed of David. Since you have always denied and always will deny this, how do you so earnestly demand the Scriptures that we should discuss rather according to them.

FORTUNATUS said: You assert that according to the flesh Christ was of the seed of David, when it should be asserted that he was born of a virgin,[3] and should be magnified as Son of God. For this cannot be, unless as what is from spirit may be held to be spirit, so also what is from flesh may be known to be flesh.[4] Against which is the authority of the Gospel in which it is said, that "flesh and blood shall not inherit the kingdom of God, neither shall corruption inherit incorruption."[5]

Here a clamor was made by the audience who wished the argument to be conducted on rational grounds, because they saw that Fortunatus was not willing to receive all things that are written in the *Codex* of the apostle. Then little discussions began to be held here and there by all, until Fortunatus said that the Word of God has been fettered in the race of darkness. At which, when those present had expressed their horror, the meeting was closed.[6]

---

1 Rom. xi. 1.
2 Rom. i. 1–4.
3 Isa. vii. 14.
4 John iii. 6.
5 1 Cor. xv. 50.
6 This little side remark lends reality to the discussion, and enables us to form a vivid conception of what doctrinal debates were in the age of Augustin.—A. H. N.

DISPUTATION OF THE SECOND DAY.

THE NEXT DAY, A NOTARY HAVING AGAIN BEEN SUMMONED, THE DISCUSSION WAS CONDUCTED AS FOLLOWS:

FORTUNATUS said: I say that God Almighty brings forth from Himself nothing evil, and that the things that are His remain incorrupt, having sprung and being born from an inviolable source; but other contrary things which have their being in this world, do not flow from God nor have appeared in this world with God as their author; that is to say, they do not derive their origin from God. These things therefore we have received in the belief that evil things are foreign to God.

20. AUGUSTIN said: And our faith is this, that God is not the progenitor of evil things, neither has He made any evil nature. But since both of us agree that God is incorruptible and incontaminable, it is the part of the prudent and faithful to consider, which faith is purer and worthier of the majesty of God; that in which it is asserted that either the power of God, or some part of God, or the Word of God, can be changed, violated, corrupted, fettered; or that in which it is said that Almighty God and His entire nature and substance can never be corrupted in any part, but that evils have their being by the voluntary sin of the soul, to which God gave free will. Which free will if God had not given, there could be no just penal judgment, nor merit of righteous conduct, nor divine instruction to repent of sins, nor the forgiveness of sins itself which God has bestowed upon us through our Lord Jesus Christ. Because he who sins not voluntarily, sins not at all. This I suppose to be open and perspicuous to all. Wherefore it ought not to trouble us if according to our deserts we suffer some inconveniences in the things God has made. For as He is good, that He should constitute all things; so He is just, that He may not spare sins, which sins, as I have said, unless free will were in us, would not be sins. For if any one, so to speak, should be bound by some one in his other members, and with his hand something false should be written without his own will, I ask whether if this were laid open before a judge, he could condemn this one for the crime of falsehood. Wherefore, if it is manifest that there is no sin where there is not free exercise of will,[1] I wish to hear what evil the soul which you call either part, or power, or word, or something else, of God, has done, that it should be punished by God, or repent of sin, or merit forgiveness, since it has in no way sinned?

FORTUNATUS said: I proposed concerning substances, that God is to be regarded as creator only of good things, but as the avenger of evil things, for the reason that evil things are not of Him. Therefore for good reason I think this, and that God avenges evil things because they are not of Himself. But if they were from Him, either He would give them license to sin, as you say that God has given free will, He would be already found a participator in my fault, because He would be the author of my fault; or ignorant what I should be, he left me whom he did not constitute worthy of Himself. This therefore is proposed by me, and what I ask now is, whether God instituted evil or not? and whether He Himself instituted the end of evils. For it appears from these things, and the evangelical faith teaches, that the things which we have said were made by God Himself as God the Creator, as having been created and begotten by Him, are to be esteemed incorruptible. These things I also proposed which belong to our belief, and which can be confirmed by you in that profession of ours, without prejudice to the authority of the Christian faith. And because I can in no way show that I rightly believe, unless I should confirm that belief by the authority of the Scriptures, this is therefore what I have insinuated, what I have said. Either if evil things have appeared in the world with God as their author, deign to say so yourself; or if it is right to believe that evil things are not of God, this also the contemplation of those present ought to honor and receive. I have spoken about substances, not about sin that dwells in us. For if what we think to make faults had no origin, we should not be compelled to come to sin or to fault. For because we sinned unwillingly, and are compelled by a substance contrary and hostile to ourselves, therefore we follow the knowledge of things. By which knowledge the soul admonished and restored to pristine memory, recognizes the source from which it derives its existence, in what evil it dwells, by what good works emending again that in which unwillingly it sinned, it may be able through the emendation of its faults, for

[1] *Liberum voluntatis arbitrium.*

the sake of good works, to secure for itself the merit of reconciliation with God, our Saviour being the author of it, who teaches us also to practice good things and to flee from evil. For you ask us to believe that not by some contrary nature, but by his own choice, man either serves righteousness or becomes involved in sins; since, no contrary race existing, if the soul, to which as you say God has given free will, having been constituted in the body, dwells alone, it would be without sin, nor would it become involved in sins.

21. AUGUSTIN said: I say it is not sin, if it be not committed by one's own will; hence also there is reward, because of our own will we do right. Or if he who sins unwillingly deserves punishment, he who unwillingly does well ought to deserve reward. But who doubts that reward is only bestowed upon him who does something of good will? From which we know that punishment also is inflicted upon him who does something of ill will. But since you recall me to primordial natures and substances, my faith is that God Almighty—which must especially be attended to and fixed in the mind—that God Almighty has made good things. But the things made by Him cannot be such as is He who made them. For it is unjust and foolish to believe that works are equal to the workman, things made to the maker. Wherefore if it is reverential to believe that God made all good things, than which nevertheless He is by far more excellent and by far more pre-eminent; the origin and head of evil is sin, as the apostle said: "Covetousness is the root of all evils; which some following after have made shipwreck of the faith, and have pierced themselves through with many sorrows."[1] For if you seek the root of all evils, you have the apostle saying that covetousness is the root of all evils. But the root of a root I cannot seek. Or if there is another evil, whose root covetousness is not, covetousness will not be the root of all evils. But if it is true that covetousness is the root of all evils, in vain do we seek some other kind of evil. But as regards that contrary nature of yours which you introduce, since I have responded to your objections, I ask that you deign to tell me whether it is wholly evil, whether there can be no sin apart from it, whether by this alone punishment is deserved, not by the soul by which no sin has been committed. But if you say that this contrary nature alone deserves punishment, and not the soul, I ask to which is repentance, which is commanded, vouchsafed. If the soul is commanded to repent, sin is from the soul, and the soul has sinned voluntarily. For if the soul is compelled to do evil, that which it does is not evil. Is it not foolish and most absurd to say that the race of darkness has sinned and that I repent of the sins. Is it not most absurd to say that the race of darkness has sinned and that forgiveness of sins is vouchsafed to me, who according to your faith may well say: What have I done? What have I committed? I was with Thee, I was in a state of integrity, I was contaminated with no pollution. Thou didst send me hither, Thou didst suffer necessity, Thou didst protect Thy domains when great pollution and desolation threatened them. Since therefore Thou knowest the necessity by which I have been here oppressed, by reason of which I could not breathe, which I could not resist; why dost Thou accuse me as if sinning? or why dost Thou promise forgiveness of sins? Reply to this without evasion, if you please, as I have replied to you.

FORTUNATUS said: We say this, that the soul is compelled by contrary nature to transgress, for which transgression you maintain there is no root save the evil that dwells in us; for it is certain that apart from our bodies evil things dwell in the whole world. For not those things alone that we have in our bodies, dwell in the whole world, and are known by their names as good; an evil root also inheres. For your dignity said that this covetousness that dwells in our bodies is the root of evils; since therefore there is no desire of evil out of our bodies, from that source contrary nature dwells in the whole world. For the apostle designated that, namely covetousness, as the root of evils, not one evil which you have called the root of all evils. But not in one manner is covetousness, which you have said is the root of all evils, understood, as if of that which dwells in our bodies alone; for it is certain that this evil which dwells in us descends from an evil author and that this root as you call it is a small portion of evil, so that it is not the root itself, but is a small portion of evil, of that evil which dwells everywhere. Which root and tree our Lord called evil, as never bearing good fruit, which his Father did not plant, and which is deservedly rooted up and cast into the fire.[2] For as you say, that sin ought to be imputed to the contrary nature, that nature belongs to evil; and that this is sin of the soul, if after the warning of our Saviour and his wholesome instruction, the soul shall have segregated itself from its contrary and hostile race, adorning itself also

[1] 1 Tim. vi. 10.

[2] Matt. xv. 13, and iii. 10.

with purer things; that otherwise it cannot be restored to its own substance. For it is said: "If I had not come and spoken unto them, they had not had sin. But now that I have come and spoken, and they have refused to believe me, they shall have no excuse for their sin."[1] Whence it is perfectly plain, that repentance has been given after the Saviour's advent, and after this knowledge of things, by which the soul can, as if washed in a divine fountain from the filth and vices as well of the whole world as of the bodies in which the same soul dwells, be restored to the kingdom of God whence it has gone forth. For it is said by the apostle, that "the mind of the flesh is hostile to God; is not subject to the law of God, neither indeed can be."[2] Therefore it is evident from these things that the good soul seems to sin not voluntarily, but by the doing of that which is not subject to the law of God. For it likewise follows that "the flesh lusteth against the spirit and the spirit against the flesh; so that ye may not do the things that ye will."[3] Again: "I see another law in my members, warring against the law of my mind and leading me captive in the law of sin and of death. Therefore I am a miserable man; who shall deliver me from the body of this death, unless it be the grace of God through our Lord Jesus Christ,"[4] "through whom the world has been crucified to me and I to the world?"[5]

22. AUGUSTIN said: I recognize and embrace the testimonies of the divine Scriptures, and I will show in a few words, as God may deign to grant, how they are consistent with my faith. I say that there was free exercise of will in that man who was first formed. He was so made that absolutely nothing could resist his will, if he had willed to keep the precepts of God. But after he voluntarily sinned, we who have descended from his stock were plunged into necessity. But each one of us can by a little consideration find that what I say is true. For to-day in our actions before we are implicated by any habit, we have free choice of doing anything or not doing it. But when by that liberty we have done something and the pernicious sweetness and pleasure of that deed has taken hold upon the mind, by its own habit the mind is so implicated that afterwards it cannot conquer what by sinning it has fashioned for itself. We see many who do not wish to swear, but because the tongue has already become habituated, they are not able to prevent those things from going forth from the mouth which we cannot but ascribe to the root of evil. For that I may discuss with you those words, which as they do not withdraw from your mouth so may they be understood by your heart: you swear by the Paraclete. If therefore you wish to find out experimentally whether what I say is true, determine not to swear. You will see, that that habit is borne along as it has become accustomed to be. And this is what wars against the soul, habit formed in the flesh. This is indeed the mind of the flesh, which, as long as it cannot thus be subject to the law of God, so long is it the mind of the flesh; but when the soul has been illuminated it ceases to be the mind of the flesh. For thus it is said the mind of the flesh cannot be subject to the law of God, just as if it were said, that snow cannot be warm. For so long as it is snow, it can in no way be warm. But as the snow is melted by heat, so that it may become warm, so the mind of the flesh, that is, habit formed with the flesh, when our mind has become illuminated, that is, when God has subjected for Himself the whole man to the choice of the divine law, instead of the evil habit of the soul, makes a good habit. Accordingly it is most truly said by the Lord of the two trees, the one good and the other evil, which you have called to mind, that they have their own fruits; that is, neither can the good tree yield evil fruit, nor the evil tree good fruit, but so long as it is evil. Let us take two men, a good and a bad. As long as he is good he cannot yield evil fruit; as long as he is bad he cannot yield good fruit. But that you may know that those two trees are so placed by the Lord, that free choice may be there signified, that these two trees are not natures but our wills, He Himself says in the gospel: "Either make the tree good, or make the tree evil."[6] Who is it that can make nature? If therefore we are commanded to make a tree either good or evil, it is ours to choose what we will. Therefore concerning that sin of man and concerning that habit of soul formed with the flesh the apostle says: "Let no one seduce you;"[7] "Every creature that has been made by God is good."[8] The same apostle whom you also have cited says: "As through the disobedience of the one the many were constituted sinners; so also through the obedience of the one the many are constituted righteous."[9] "Since through man is death, through man also is resurrection of the dead." As long therefore as we bear the image of the earthly man,[10] that is, as long as we live according to the flesh, which is also called the old man, we have the neces-

[1] John xv. 22.
[2] Rom. viii. 7.
[3] Gal. v. 17.
[4] Rom. vii. 23–25.
[5] Gal. v. 14.
[6] Matt. xii. 35.
[7] Eph. v. 6.
[8] 1 Tim. iv. 4.
[9] Rom. v. 19.
[10] 1 Cor. xv. 21, 49.

sity of our habit, so that we may not do what we will. But when the grace of God has breathed the divine love into us and has made us subject to His will, to us it is said: "Ye are called for freedom,"[1] and "the grace of God has made me free from the law of sin and of death."[2] But the law of sin is that whoever has sinned shall die. From this law we are freed when we have begun to be righteous. The law of death is that by which it was said to man: "Earth thou art and into earth thou shalt go."[3] For from this very fact we are all so born, because we are earth, and from the fact that we are all so born because we are earth, we shall all go into earth on account of the desert of the sins of the first man. But on account of the grace of God, which frees us from the law of sin and of death, having been converted to righteousness we are freed; so that afterwards this same flesh tortures us with its punishment so long as we remain in sins, is subjected to us in resurrection, and shakes us by no adversity from keeping the law of God and His precepts. Whence, since I have replied to your questions, deign to reply as I desire, how it can happen, that if nature is contrary to God, sin should be imputed to us, who were sent into that nature not voluntarily, but by God Himself, whom nothing could injure?

FORTUNATUS said: Just as also the Lord said to His disciples: Behold I send you as sheep in the midst of wolves."[4] Hence it must be known that not with hostile intent did our Saviour send forth His lambs, that is His disciples, into the midst of wolves, unless there had been some contrariety, which He would indicate by the similitude of wolves, where also He had sent His disciples; that the souls which perchance might be deceived in the midst of wolves might be recalled to their proper substance. Hence also may appear the antiquity of our times to which we return, and of our years, that before the foundation of the world souls were sent in this way against the contrary nature, that subjecting the same by their passion, victory might be restored to God. For the same apostle said, that not only there should be a struggle against flesh and blood, but also against principalities and powers, and the spiritual things of wickedness, and the domination of darkness."[5] If therefore in both places evils dwell and are esteemed wickednesses, not only now is evil in our bodies, but in the whole world, where souls appear to dwell, which dwell beneath yonder heaven and are fettered.

23. AUGUSTIN said: The Lord sent His lambs into the midst of wolves, that is, just men into the midst of sinners for the preaching of the gospel received in the time of man from the inestimable divine Wisdom, that He might call us from sin to righteousness. But what the apostle says, that our struggle is not against flesh and blood, but against principalities and powers, and the other things that have been quoted, this signifies that the devil and his angels, as also we, have fallen and lapsed by sin, and have secured possession of earthly things, that is, sinful men, who, as long as we are sinners, are under their yoke, just as when we shall be righteous, we shall be under the yoke of righteousness; and against them we have a struggle, that passing over to righteousness we may be freed from their dominion. Do you also therefore deign to reply to the one question that I ask: Could God suffer injury, or not? But I ask you to reply: He could not.

FORTUNATUS said: He could not suffer injury.

24. AUGUSTIN said: Wherefore then did He send us hither, according to your faith?

FORTUNATUS said: My profession is this, that God could not be injured, and that He directed us hither. But since this is contrary to your view, do you tell how you account for the soul being here, which our God desires to liberate both by His commandments and by His own Son whom He has sent.

25. AUGUSTIN said: Since I see that you cannot answer my inquiries, and wish to ask me something, behold I satisfy you, provided only that you bear in mind that you have not replied to my question. Why the soul is here in this world involved in miseries has been explained by me not just now, but again and again a little while ago. The soul sinned, and therefore is miserable. It accepted free choice, used free choice, as it willed; it fell, was cast out from blessedness, was implicated in miseries. As bearing upon this I recited to you the testimony of the apostle who says: "As through one man death, so also through one man came the resurrection of the dead." What more do you ask? Hence do you reply, wherefore did He, who could not suffer injury, send us hither?

FORTUNATUS said: The cause must be sought, why the soul came hither, or wherefore God desires hence to liberate the soul that lives in the midst of evils?

26. AUGUSTIN said: This cause I ask of you, that is, if God could not suffer injury, wherefore He sent us hither?

FORTUNATUS said: It is inquired of us, if evil cannot injure God, wherefore the soul was sent hither, or for what reason was it

[1] Gal. v. 13. [2] Rom. viii. 2. [3] Gen. iii. 19. [4] Matt. x. 16. [5] Eph. v. 12.

mingled with the world? Which is manifest in what the apostle says: "Shall the thing formed say to him that formed it, why hast thou formed me thus?"[1] If therefore this cause must be pleaded, He must be asked, why He sent the soul, no necessity compelling Him. But if there was necessity for sending the soul, of right is there also the will of liberating it.

27. AUGUSTIN said: Then God is pressed by necessity, is He?

FORTUNATUS said: Now this is it. Do not seek to bring odium upon what has been said; because we do not make God subject to necessity, but to have voluntarily sent the soul.

28. AUGUSTIN said: Recall what was said above. And it runs: "But if there was necessity for sending the soul, of right is there also the will of liberating it. Augustin said: We have heard: But if there was necessity for sending the soul, of right is there also the will of liberating it." You, therefore, said that there was necessity for sending the soul. But if you only wish to say "a will to send," I add this also: He who could suffer no injury, had the cruel will to send the soul to so great miseries. Because I speak for the sake of refuting this statement, I ask pardon from the mercy of that One in whom we have hope of liberation from all the errors of heretics.

FORTUNATUS said: You asseverate that we say that God is cruel in sending the soul, but that God made man, breathed into him a soul which assuredly He foreknew to be involved in future misery, and not to be able by reason of evils to be restored to its inheritance. This belongs either to one who is ignorant, or who gives the soul up to these aforesaid evils. This I have cited because you said not long since, that God adopted the soul, not that it is from Him; for to adopt is a different matter.

29. AUGUSTIN said: Concerning adoption I remember that I spoke some days ago according to the testimony of the apostle, who says that we have been called into the adoption of sons.[2] This was not my reply, therefore, but the apostle's, concerning which thing, that is, that adoption, we may inquire, if we please, in its own time; and concerning that I will reply without delay, when you shall have answered my objections.

FORTUNATUS said: I say that there was a going forth of the soul against a contrary nature, which nature could not injure God.

30. AUGUSTIN said: What need was there for that going forth, when God whom nothing could injure had nothing to protect?

FORTUNATUS said: Do you conscientiously hold that Christ came from God?

31. AUGUSTIN said: Again you are questioning me. Reply to my inquiries.

FORTUNATUS said: So I have received in faith, that by the will of God He came hither.

32. AUGUSTIN said: And I say: Why did God, omnipotent, inviolable, immutable, whom nothing could injure, send hither the soul, to miseries, to error, to those things that we suffer?

FORTUNATUS said: For it has been said: "I have power to lay down my soul and I have power to take it again."[3] Now He said that by the will of God the soul went forth.

33. AUGUSTIN said: I ask for the reason why God, when He can in no way suffer injury, sent the soul hither?

FORTUNATUS said: We have already said that God can in no way suffer injury, and we have said that the soul is in a contrary nature, therefore that it imposes a limit on the contrary nature. The restraint having been imposed on the contrary nature, God takes the same. For He Himself said, "I have power to lay down my soul and power to take it." The Father gave to me the power of laying down my soul, and of taking it. To what soul, therefore, did God who spoke in the Son refer? Evidently our soul, which is held in these bodies, which came of His will, and of His will is again taken up.

34. AUGUSTIN said: Why our Lord said: "I have power to lay down my soul and power to take it," is known to all; because He was about to suffer and to rise again. But I ask of you again and again, If God could in no way suffer injury, why did he send souls hither?

FORTUNATUS said: To impose a limit on contrary nature.

35. AUGUSTIN said: And did God omnipotent, merciful and supreme, that He might impose a restraint on contrary nature, wish it to be limited so that He might make us unrestrained?

FORTUNATUS said: But so He calls us back to Himself.

36. AUGUSTIN said: If He recalls to Himself from an unrestrained state, if from sin, from error, from misery, what need was there for the soul to suffer so great evils through so long a time till the world ends? since God by whom you say it was sent could in no way suffer injury.

FORTUNATUS said: What then am I to say?

37. AUGUSTIN said: I know that you have nothing to say, and that I, when I was among

[1] Rom. ix. 20.
[2] Eph. i. 5.
[3] John x. 18.

you, never found anything to say on this question, and that I was thus admonished from on high to leave that error and to be converted to the Catholic faith or rather to recall it, by the indulgence of Him who did not permit me to inhere forever in this fallacy. But if you confess that you have nothing to reply, I will expound the Catholic faith to all those hearing and investigating, seeing that they are believers, if they permit and wish.

FORTUNATUS said: Without prejudice to my profession I might say: when I shall have reconsidered with my superiors the things that have been opposed by you, if they fail to respond to this question of mine, which is now in like manner proposed to me by you, it will be in my contemplation (since I desire my soul to be liberated by an assured faith) to come to the investigation of this thing that you have proposed to me and that you promise you will show.

AUGUSTIN said: Thanks be to God.

ST. AUGUSTIN:

AGAINST

THE EPISTLE OF MANICHÆUS

CALLED FUNDAMENTAL.

[CONTRA EPISTOLAM MANICHÆI QUAM VOCANT FUNDAMENTUM].

A.D. 397.

TRANSLATED BY

REV. RICHARD STOTHERT, M.A.,

BOMBAY.

CONTENTS OF AGAINST THE EPISTLE OF MANICHÆUS CALLED FUNDAMENTAL.

AGAINST THE EPISTLE OF MANICHÆUS CALLED FUNDAMENTAL.[1]

[CONTRA EPISTOLAM MANICHÆI QUAM VACANT FUNDAMENTI.] A.D. 397.

CHAP. 1.—TO HEAL HERETICS IS BETTER THAN TO DESTROY THEM.

1. My prayer to the one true, almighty God, of whom, and through whom, and in whom are all things, has been, and is now, that in opposing and refuting the heresy of you Manichæans, as you may after all be heretics more from thoughtlessness than from malice, He would give me a mind calm and composed, and aiming at your recovery rather than at your discomfiture. For while the Lord, by His servants, overthrows the kingdoms of error, His will concerning erring men, as far as they are men, is that they should be amended rather than destroyed. And in every case where, previous to the final judgment, God inflicts punishment, whether through the wicked or the righteous, whether through the unintelligent or through the intelligent, whether in secret or openly, we must believe that the designed effect is the healing of men, and not their ruin; while there is a preparation for the final doom in the case of those who reject the means of recovery. Thus, as the universe contains some things which serve for bodily punishment, as fire, poison, disease, and the rest, and other things, in which the mind is punished, not by bodily distress, but by the entanglements of its own passions, such as loss, exile, bereavement, reproach, and the like; while other things, again, without tormenting are fitted to comfort and soothe the languishing, as, for example, consolations, exhortations, discussions, and such things; in all these the supreme justice of God makes use sometimes even of wicked men, acting in ignorance, and sometimes of good men, acting intelligently. It is ours, accordingly, to desire in preference the better part, that we might attain our end in your correction, not by contention, and strife, and persecutions, but by kindly consolation, by friendly exhortation, by quiet discussion; as it is written, "The servant of the Lord must not strive; but be gentle toward all men, apt to teach, patient; in meekness instructing those that oppose themselves."[2] It is ours, I say, to desire to obtain this part in the work; it belongs to God to give what is good to those who desire it and ask for it.

CHAP. 2.—WHY THE MANICHÆANS SHOULD BE MORE GENTLY DEALT WITH.

2. Let those rage against you who know not with what labor the truth is to be found and with what difficulty error is to be avoided. Let those rage against you who know not how rare and hard it is to overcome the fancies of the flesh by the serenity of a pious disposition. Let those rage against you who know not the difficulty of curing the eye of the inner man that he may gaze upon his Sun,—not that sun

---

[1] Written about the year 397. In his *Retractations* (ii. 2) Augustin says: "The book against the Epistle of Manichæus, called Fundamental, refutes only its commencement; but on the other parts of the epistle I have made notes, as required, refuting the whole, and sufficient to recall the argument, had I ever had leisure to write against the whole." [The *Fundamental Epistle* seems to have been a sort of hand-book for Manichæan catechumens or Auditors. In making this document the basis of his attack, Augustin felt that he had selected the best-known and most generally accepted standard of the Manichæan faith. The tone of the work is conciliatory, yet some very sharp thrusts are made at Manichæan error. The claims of Mani to be the Paraclete are set aside, and the absurd cosmological fancies of Mani are ruthlessly exposed. Dualism is combated with substantially the same weapons as in the treatise *Concerning Two Souls*. We could wish that the author had found time to finish the treatise, and had thus preserved for us more of the *Fundamental Epistle* itself. This work was written after the author had become Bishop of Hippo.—A. H. N.]

[2] 2 Tim. ii. 24, 25.

which you worship, and which shines with the brilliance of a heavenly body in the eyes of carnal men and of beasts,—but that of which it is written through the prophet, "The Sun of righteousness has arisen upon me;"[1] and of which it is said in the gospel, "That was the true Light, which lighteth every man that cometh into the world."[2] Let those rage against you who know not with what sighs and groans the least particle of the knowledge of God is obtained. And, last of all, let those rage against you who have never been led astray in the same way that they see that you are.

CHAP. 3.—AUGUSTIN ONCE A MANICHÆAN.

3. For my part, I,—who, after much and long-continued bewilderment, attained at last to the discovery of the simple truth, which is learned without being recorded in any fanciful legend; who, unhappy that I was, barely succeeded, by God's help, in refuting the vain imaginations of my mind, gathered from theories and errors of various kinds; who so late sought the cure of my mental obscuration, in compliance with the call and the tender persuasion of the all-merciful Physician; who long wept that the immutable and inviolable Existence would vouchsafe to convince me inwardly of Himself, in harmony with the testimony of the sacred books; by whom, in fine, all those fictions which have such a firm hold on you, from your long familiarity with them, were diligently examined, and attentively heard, and too easily believed, and commended at every opportunity to the belief of others, and defended against opponents with determination and boldness,—I can on no account rage against you; for I must bear with you now as formerly I had to bear with myself, and I must be as patient towards you as my associates were with me, when I went madly and blindly astray in your beliefs.

4. On the other hand, all must allow that you owe it to me, in return, to lay aside all arrogance on your part too, that so you may be the more disposed to gentleness, and may not oppose me in a hostile spirit, to your own hurt. Let neither of us assert that he has found truth; let us seek it as if it were unknown to us both. For truth can be sought with zeal and unanimity if by no rash presumption it is believed to have been already found and ascertained. But if I cannot induce you to grant me this, at least allow me to suppose myself a stranger now for the first time hearing you, for the first time examining your doctrines. I think my demand a just one. And it must be laid down as an understood thing that I am not to join you in your prayers, or in holding conventicles, or in taking the name of Manichæus, unless you give me a clear explanation, without any obscurity, of all matters touching the salvation of the soul.

CHAP. 4.—PROOFS OF THE CATHOLIC FAITH.

5. For in the Catholic Church, not to speak of the purest wisdom, to the knowledge of which a few spiritual men attain in this life, so as to know it, in the scantiest measure, indeed, because they are but men, still without any uncertainty (since the rest of the multitude derive their entire security not from acuteness of intellect, but from simplicity of faith,)—not to speak of this wisdom, which you do not believe to be in the Catholic Church, there are many other things which most justly keep me in her bosom. The consent of peoples and nations keeps me in the Church; so does her authority, inaugurated by miracles, nourished by hope, enlarged by love, established by age. The succession of priests keeps me, beginning from the very seat of the Apostle Peter, to whom the Lord, after His resurrection, gave it in charge to feed His sheep, down to the present episcopate. And so, lastly, does the name itself of Catholic, which, not without reason, amid so many heresies, the Church has thus retained; so that, though all heretics wish to be called Catholics, yet when a stranger asks where the Catholic Church meets, no heretic will venture to point to his own chapel or house. Such then in number and importance are the precious ties belonging to the Christian name which keep a believer in the Catholic Church, as it is right they should, though from the slowness of our understanding, or the small attainment of our life, the truth may not yet fully disclose itself. But with you, where there is none of these things to attract or keep me, the promise of truth is the only thing that comes into play. Now if the truth is so clearly proved as to leave no possibility of doubt, it must be set before all the things that keep me in the Catholic Church; but if there is only a promise without any fulfillment, no one shall move me from the faith which binds my mind with ties so many and so strong to the Christian religion.

CHAP. 5.—AGAINST THE TITLE OF THE EPISTLE OF MANICHÆUS.

6. Let us see then what Manichæus teaches me; and particularly let us examine that treatise which he calls the Fundamental Epistle,

[1] Mal. iv. 2.
[2] John i. 9.

in which almost all that you believe is contained. For in that unhappy time when we read it we were in your opinion enlightened. The epistle begins thus:—"Manichæus, an apostle of Jesus Christ, by the providence of God the Father. These are wholesome words, from the perennial and living fountain." Now, if you please, patiently give heed to my inquiry. I do not believe Manichæus to be an apostle of Christ. Do not, I beg of you, be enraged and begin to curse. For you know that it is my rule to believe none of your statements without consideration. Therefore I ask, who is this Manichæus? You will reply, An apostle of Christ. I do not believe it. Now you are at a loss what to say or do; for you promised to give knowledge of the truth, and here you are forcing me to believe what I have no knowledge of. Perhaps you will read the gospel to me, and will attempt to find there a testimony to Manichæus. But should you meet with a person not yet believing the gospel, how would you reply to him were he to say, I do not believe? For my part, I should not believe the gospel except as moved by the authority of the Catholic Church.[1] So when those on whose authority I have consented to believe in the gospel tell me not to believe in Manichæus, how can I but consent? Take your choice. If you say, Believe the Catholics: their advice to me is to put no faith in you; so that, believing them, I am precluded from believing you;—If you say, Do not believe the Catholics: you cannot fairly use the gospel in bringing me to faith in Manichæus; for it was at the command of the Catholics that I believed the gospel;—Again, if you say, You were right in believing the Catholics when they praised the gospel, but wrong in believing their vituperation of Manichæus: do you think me such a fool as to believe or not to believe as you like or dislike, without any reason? It is therefore fairer and safer by far for me, having in one instance put faith in the Catholics, not to go over to you, till, instead of bidding me believe, you make me understand something in the clearest and most open manner. To convince me, then, you must put aside the gospel. If you keep to the gospel, I will keep to those who commanded me to believe the gospel; and, in obedience to them, I will not believe you at all. But if haply you should succeed in finding in the gospel an incontrovertible testimony to the apostleship of Manichæus, you will weaken my regard for the authority of the Catholics who bid me not to believe you; and the effect of that will be, that I shall no longer be able to believe the gospel either, for it was through the Catholics that I got my faith in it; and so, whatever you bring from the gospel will no longer have any weight with me. Wherefore, if no clear proof of the apostleship of Manichæus is found in the gospel, I will believe the Catholics rather than you. But if you read thence some passage clearly in favor of Manichæus, I will believe neither them nor you: not them, for they lied to me about you; nor you, for you quote to me that Scripture which I had believed on the authority of those liars. But far be it that I should not believe the gospel; for believing it, I find no way of believing you too. For the names of the apostles, as there recorded,[2] do not include the name of Manichæus. And who the successor of Christ's betrayer was we read in the Acts of the Apostles;[3] which book I must needs believe if I believe the gospel, since both writings alike Catholic authority commends to me. The same book contains the well-known narrative of the calling and apostleship of Paul.[4] Read me now, if you can, in the gospel where Manichæus is called an apostle, or in any other book in which I have professed to believe. Will you read the passage where the Lord promised the Holy Spirit as a Paraclete, to the apostles? Concerning which passage, behold how many and how great are the things that restrain and deter me from believing in Manichæus.

CHAP. 6.—WHY MANICHÆUS CALLED HIMSELF AN APOSTLE OF CHRIST.

7. For I am at a loss to see why this epistle begins, "Manichæus, an apostle of Jesus Christ," and not Paraclete, an apostle of Jesus Christ. Or if the Paraclete sent by Christ sent Manichæus, why do we read, "Manichæus, an apostle of Jesus Christ," instead of Manichæus, an apostle of the Paraclete? If you say that it is Christ Himself who is the Holy Spirit, you contradict the very Scripture, where the Lord says, "And I will send you another Paraclete."[5] Again, if you justify your putting of Christ's name, not because it is Christ Himself who is also the Paraclete, but because they are both of the same substance,—that is, not because they are one person, but one existence [*non quia unus est, sed quia unum sunt*],—Paul too might have used the words, Paul, an apostle of God the Father; for the Lord said, "I and the Father are one."[6] Paul nowhere uses these words; nor does any of the apos-

[1] [This is one of the earliest distinct assertions of the dependence of the Scriptures for authority on the Church.—A. H. N.]

[2] Matt. x. 2-4; Mark iii. 13-19; Luke vi. 13-18.
[3] Acts i. 26.
[4] Acts ix.
[5] John xiv. 16.
[6] John x. 30.

tles write himself an apostle of the Father. Why then this new fashion? Does it not savor of trickery of some kind or other? For if he thought it made no difference, why did he not for the sake of variety in some epistles call himself an apostle of Christ, and in others of the Paraclete? But in every one that I know of, he writes, of Christ; and not once, of the Paraclete. What do we suppose to be the reason of this, but that pride, the mother of all heretics, impelled the man to desire to seem to have been sent by the Paraclete, but to have been taken into so close a relation as to get the name of Paraclete himself? As the man Jesus Christ was not sent by the Son of God, that is, the power and wisdom of God—by which all things were made, but, according to the Catholic faith, was taken into such a relation as to be Himself the Son of God—that is, that in Himself the wisdom of God was displayed in the healing of sinners,—so Manichæus wished it to be thought that he was so taken up by the Holy Spirit, whom Christ promised, that we are henceforth to understand that the names Manichæus and Holy Spirit alike signify the apostle of Jesus Christ,—that is, one sent by Jesus Christ, who promised to send him. Singular audacity this! and unutterable sacrilege!

CHAP. 7.—IN WHAT SENSE THE FOLLOWERS OF MANICHÆUS BELIEVE HIM TO BE THE HOLY SPIRIT.

8. Besides, you should explain how it is that, while the Father, Son, and Holy Spirit are united in equality of nature, as you also acknowledge, you are not ashamed to speak of Manichæus, a man taken into union with the Holy Spirit, as born of ordinary generation; and yet you shrink from believing that the man taken into union with the only-begotten Wisdom of God was born of a Virgin. If human flesh, if generation [*concubitus viri*], if the womb of a woman could not contaminate the Holy Spirit, how could the Virgin's womb contaminate the Wisdom of God? This Manichæus, then, who boasts of a connection with the Holy Spirit, and of being spoken of in the gospel, must produce his claim to either of these two things,—that he was sent by the Spirit, or that he was taken into union with the Spirit. If he was sent, let him call himself the apostle of the Paraclete; if taken into union, let him allow that He whom the only-begotten Son took upon Himself had a human mother, since he admits a human father as well as mother in the case of one taken up by the Holy Spirit. Let him believe that the Word of God was not defiled by the virgin womb of Mary, since he exhorts us to believe that the Holy Spirit could not be defiled by the married life of his parents. But if you say that Manichæus was united to the Spirit, not in the womb or before conception, but after his birth, still you must admit that he had a fleshly nature derived from man and woman. And since you are not afraid to speak of the blood and the bodily substance of Manichæus as coming from ordinary generation, or of the internal impurities contained in his flesh, and hold that the Holy Spirit, who took on Himself, as you believe, this human being, was not contaminated by all those things, why should I shrink from speaking of the Virgin's womb and body undefiled, and not rather believe that the Wisdom of God in union with the human being in his mother's flesh still remained free from stain and pollution? Wherefore, as, whether your Manichæus professes to be sent by or to be united with the Paraclete, neither statement can hold good, I am on my guard, and refuse to believe either in his mission or in his susception.

CHAP. 8.—THE FESTIVAL OF THE BIRTH-DAY OF MANICHÆUS.

9. In adding the words, "by the providence of God the Father," what else did Manichæus design but that, having got the name of Jesus Christ, whose apostle he calls himself, and of God the Father, by whose providence he says he was sent by the Son, we should believe himself, as the Holy Spirit, to be the third person? His words are: "Manichæus, an apostle of Jesus Christ, by the providence of God the Father." The Holy Spirit is not named, though He ought specially to have been named by one who quotes to us in favor of his apostleship the promise of the Paraclete, that he may prevail upon ignorant people by the authority of the gospel. In reply to this, you of course say that in the name of the Apostle Manichæus we have the name of the Holy Spirit, the Paraclete, because He condescended to come into Manichæus. Why then, I ask again, should you cry out against the doctrine of the Catholic Church, that He in whom divine Wisdom came was born of a virgin, when you do not scruple to affirm the birth by ordinary generation of him in whom you say the Holy Spirit came? I cannot but suspect that this Manichæus, who uses the name of Christ to gain access to the minds of the ignorant, wished to be worshipped instead of Christ Himself. I will state briefly the reason of this conjecture. At the time when I was a student of your doctrines, to my frequent inquiries why it was that the Paschal feast of the Lord was

celebrated generally with no interest, though sometimes there were a few languid worshippers, but no watchings, no prescription of any unusual fast,—in a word, no special ceremony,—while great honor is paid to your Bema, that is, the day on which Manichæus was killed, when you have a platform with fine steps, covered with precious cloth, placed conspicuously so as to face the votaries,—the reply was, that the day to observe was the day of the passion of him who really suffered, and that Christ, who was not born, but appeared to human eyes in an unreal semblance of flesh, only feigned suffering, without really bearing it. Is it not deplorable, that men who wish to be called Christians are afraid of a virgin's womb as likely to defile the truth, and yet are not afraid of falsehood? But to go back to the point, who that pays attention can help suspecting that the intention of Manichæus in denying Christ's being born of a woman, and having a human body, was that His passion, the time of which is now a great festival all over the world, might not be observed by the believers in himself, so as to lessen the devotion of the solemn commemoration which he wished in honor of the day of his own death? For to us it was a great attraction in the feast of the Bema that it was held during Pascha, since we used all the more earnestly to desire that festal day [the Bema], that the other which was formerly most sweet had been withdrawn.

CHAP. 9.—WHEN THE HOLY SPIRIT WAS SENT.

10. Perhaps you will say to me, When, then, did the Paraclete promised by the Lord come? As regards this, had I nothing else to believe on the subject, I should rather look for the Paraclete as still to come, than allow that He came in Manichæus. But seeing that the advent of the Holy Spirit is narrated with perfect clearness in the Acts of the Apostles, where is the necessity of my so gratuitously running the risk of believing heretics? For in the Acts it is written as follows: "The former treatise have we made, O Theophilus, of all that Jesus began both to do and teach, in the day in which He chose the apostles by the Holy Spirit, and commanded them to preach the gospel. By those to whom He showed Himself alive after His passion by many proofs in the daytime, He was seen forty days, teaching concerning the kingdom of God. And how He conversed with them, and commanded them that they should not depart from Jerusalem, but wait for the promise of the Father, which, saith He, ye have heard of me. For John indeed baptized with water, but ye shall begin to be baptized with the Holy Spirit, whom also ye shall receive after not many days, that is, at Pentecost. When they had come, they asked him, saying, Lord, wilt Thou at this time manifest Thyself? And when will be the kingdom of Israel? And He said unto them, No one can know the time which the Father hath put in His own power. But ye shall receive the power of the Holy Ghost coming upon you, and ye shall be witnesses unto me both in Jerusalem, and in all Judæa, and in Samaria, and unto the uttermost part of the earth."[1] Behold you have here the Lord reminding His disciples of the promise of the Father, which they had heard from His mouth, of the coming of the Holy Spirit. Let us now see when He was sent; for shortly after we read as follows: "And when the day of Pentecost was fully come, they were all with one accord in one place. And suddenly there came a sound from heaven, as of a rushing mighty wind, and it filled all the house where they were sitting. And there appeared unto them cloven tongues, like as of fire, and it sat upon each of them. And they were all filled with the Holy Ghost, and began to speak with other tongues, as the Spirit gave them utterance. And there were dwelling at Jerusalem Jews, devout men, out of every nation under heaven. And when the sound was heard, the multitude came together, and were confounded, because every man heard them speak in his own language. And they were all amazed, and marvelled, saying one to another, Are not all these which speak Galilæans? and how heard we every man in our own tongue, wherein we were born? Parthians, and Medes, and Elamites, and the dwellers in Mesopotamia, in Armenia, and in Cappadocia, in Pontus, Asia, Phrygia, and Pamphylia, in Egypt, and in the regions of Africa about Cyrene, and strangers of Rome, Jews, natives, Cretes, and Arabians, they heard them speak in their own tongues the wonderful works of God. And they were all amazed, and were in doubt on account of what had happened, saying, What meaneth this? But others, mocking, said, These men are full of new wine."[2] You see when the Holy Spirit came. What more do you wish? If the Scriptures are credible, should not I believe most readily in these Acts, which have the strongest testimony in their support, and which have had the advantage of becoming generally known, and of being handed down and of being publicly taught along with the gospel itself, which contains the promise of the Holy Spirit, which also we believe? On

[1] Acts i. 1-8.
[2] Acts ii. 1-13.

reading, then, these Acts of the Apostles, which stand, as regards authority, on a level with the gospel, I find that not only was the Holy Spirit promised to these true apostles, but that He was also sent so manifestly, that no room was left for errors on this subject.

CHAP. 10.—THE HOLY SPIRIT TWICE GIVEN.

11. For the glorification of our Lord among men is His resurrection from the dead and His ascension to heaven. For it is written in the Gospel according to John: "The Holy Ghost was not yet given, because that Jesus was not yet glorified."[1] Now if the reason why He was not given was that Jesus was not yet glorified, He was given immediately on the glorification of Jesus. And since that glorification was twofold, as regards man and as regards God, twice also was the Holy Spirit given: once, when, after His resurrection from the dead, He breathed on the face of His disciples, saying, "Receive ye the Holy Ghost;"[2] and again, ten days after His ascension to heaven. This number ten signifies perfection; for to the number seven, which embraces all created things, is added the trinity of the Creator.[3] On these things there is much pious and sober discourse among spiritual men. But I must keep to my point; for my business at present is not to teach you, which you might think presumptuous, but to take the part of an inquirer, and learn from you, as I tried to do for nine years without success. Now, therefore, I have a document to believe on the subject of the Holy Spirit's advent; and if you bid me not to believe this document, as your usual advice is not to believe ignorantly, without consideration,[4] much less will I believe your documents. Away, then, with all books, and disclose the truth with logical clearness, so as to leave no doubt in my mind; or bring forward books where I shall find not an imperious demand for my belief, but a trustworthy statement of what I may learn. Perhaps you say this epistle is also of this character. Let me, then, no longer stop at the threshold: let us see the contents.

CHAP. 11.—MANICHÆUS PROMISES TRUTH, BUT DOES NOT MAKE GOOD HIS WORD.

12. "These," he says, "are wholesome words from the perennial and living fountain; and whoever shall have heard them, and shall have first believed them, and then shall have observed the truths they set forth, shall never suffer death, but shall enjoy eternal life in glory. For he is to be judged truly blessed who has been instructed in this divine knowledge, by which he is made free and shall abide in everlasting life." And this, as you see, is a promise of truth, but not the bestowal of it. And you yourselves can easily see that any errors whatever might be dressed up in this fashion, so as under cover of a showy exterior to steal in unawares into the minds of the ignorant. Were he to say, These are pestiferous words from a poisonous fountain; and whoever shall have heard them, and shall have first believed them, and then have observed what they set forth, shall never be restored to life, but shall suffer a woful death as a criminal: for assuredly he is to be pronounced miserable who falls into this infernal error, in which he will sink so as to abide in everlasting torments;—were he to say this, he would say the truth; but instead of gaining any readers for his book, he would excite the greatest aversion in the minds of all into whose hands the book might come. Let us then pass on to what follows; nor let us be deceived by words which may be used alike by good and bad, by learned and unlearned. What, then, comes next?

13. "May the peace," he says, "of the invisible God, and the knowledge of the truth, be with the holy and beloved brethren who both believe and also yield obedience to the divine precepts." Amen, say we. For the prayer is a most amiable and commendable one. Only we must bear in mind that these words might be used by false teachers as well as by good ones. So, if he said nothing more than this, all might safely read and embrace it. Nor should I disapprove of what follows: "May also the right hand of light protect you, and deliver you from every hostile assault, and from the snares of the world." In fact, I have no fault to find with the beginning of this epistle, till we come to the main subject of it. For I wish not to spend time on minor points. Now, then, for this writer's plain statement of what is to be expected from him.

CHAP 12.—THE WILD FANCIES OF MANICHÆUS. THE BATTLE BEFORE THE CONSTITUTION OF THE WORLD.

14. "Of that matter," he says, "beloved brother of Patticus, of which you told me, saying that you desired to know the manner of the birth of Adam and Eve, whether they

---

[1] John vii. 39.
[2] John xx. 22.
[3] [This is, of course, fanciful; but is quite in accordance with the exegetical methods of the time.—A. H. N.]
[4] [The Manichæans assumed the rôle of rationalists, and scorned the credulity of ordinary believers. Yet they required in their followers an amount of credulity which only persons of a peculiar turn of mind could furnish. The same thing applies to modern rationalistic anti-Christian systems. The fact is, that it requires infinitely less credulity to believe in historical Christianity than to disbelieve in it.—A. H. N.]

were produced by a word or sprung from matter, I will answer you as is fit. For in various writings and narratives we find different assertions made and different descriptions given by many authors. Now the real truth on the subject is unknown to all peoples, even to those who have long and frequently treated of it. For had they arrived at a clear knowledge of the generation of Adam and Eve, they would not have remained liable to corruption and death." Here, then, is a promise to us of clear knowledge of this matter, so that we shall not be liable to corruption and death. And if this does not suffice, see what follows: "Necessarily," he says, "many things have to be said by way of preface, before a discovery of this mystery free from all uncertainty can be made." This is precisely what I asked for, to have such evidence of the truth as to free my knowledge of it from all uncertainty. And even were the promise not made by this writer himself, it was proper for me to demand and to insist upon this, so that no opposition should make me ashamed of becoming a Manichæan from a Catholic Christian, in view of such a gain as that of perfectly clear and certain truth. Now, then, let us hear what he has to state.

15. "Accordingly," he says, "hear first, if you please, what happened before the constitution of the world, and how the battle was carried on, that you may be able to distinguish the nature of light from that of darkness." Such are the utterly false and incredible statements which this writer makes. Who can believe that any battle was fought before the constitution of the world? And even supposing it credible, we wish now to get something to know, not to believe. For to say that the Persians and Scythians long ago fought with one another is a credible statement; but while we believe it when we read or hear it, we cannot know it as a fact of experience or as a truth of the understanding. So, then, as I would repudiate any such statement on the ground that I have been promised something, not that I must believe on authority, but that I shall understand without any ambiguity; still less will I receive statements which are not only uncertain, but incredible. But what if he have some evidence to make these things clear and intelligible? Let us hear, then, if we can, what follows with all possible patience and forbearance.

CHAP. 13.—TWO OPPOSITE SUBSTANCES. THE KINGDOM OF LIGHT. MANICHÆUS TEACHES UNCERTAINTIES INSTEAD OF CERTAINTIES.

16. "In the beginning, then," he says, "these two substances were divided. The empire of light was held by God the Father, who is perpetual in holy origin, magnificent in virtue, true in His very nature, ever rejoicing in His own eternity, possessing in Himself wisdom and the vital senses, by which He also includes the twelve members of His light, which are the plentiful resources of his kingdom. Also in each of His members are stored thousands of untold and priceless treasures. But the Father Himself, chief in praise, incomprehensible in greatness, has united to Himself happy and glorious worlds, incalculable in number and duration, along with which this holy and illustrious Father and Progenitor resides, no poverty or infirmity being admitted in His magnificent realms. And these matchless realms are so founded on the region of light and bliss, that no one can ever move or disturb them."[1]

17. Where is the proof of all this? And where did Manichæus learn it? Do not frighten me with the name of the Paraclete. For, in the first place, I have come not to put faith in unknown things, but to get the knowledge of undoubted truths, according to the caution enjoined on me by yourselves. For you know how bitterly you taunt those who believe without consideration. And what is more, this writer, who here begins to tell of very doubtful things, himself promised a little before to give complete and well-grounded knowledge.

CHAP. 14.—MANICHÆUS PROMISES THE KNOWLEDGE OF UNDOUBTED THINGS, AND THEN DEMANDS FAITH IN DOUBTFUL THINGS.

In the next place, if faith is what is required of me, I should prefer to keep to the Scripture, which tells me that the Holy Spirit came and inspired the apostles, to whom the Lord had promised to send Him. You must therefore prove, either that what Manichæus says is true, and so make clear to me what I am unable to believe; or that Manichæus is the Holy Spirit, and so lead me to believe in what you cannot make clear. For I profess the Catholic faith, and by it I expect to attain certain knowledge. Since, then, you try to overthrow my faith, you must supply me with certain knowledge, if you can, that you may convict me of having adopted my present belief without consideration. You make two distinct propositions,—one when you say that the speaker is the Holy Spirit, and another when you say that what the speaker teaches is

[1] [Compare the fuller account from the *Fihrist* in the Introduction.—A. H. N.]

evidently true. I might fairly ask undeniable proof for both propositions. But I am not greedy and require to be convinced only of one. Prove this person to be the Holy Spirit, and I will believe what he says to be true, even without understanding it; or prove that what he says is true, and I will believe him to be the Holy Spirit, even without evidence. Could anything be fairer or kinder than this? But you cannot prove either one or other of these propositions. You can find nothing better than to praise your own faith and ridicule mine. So, after having in my turn praised my belief and ridiculed yours, what result do you think we shall arrive at as regards our judgment and our conduct, but to part company with those who promise the knowledge of indubitable things, and then demand from us faith in doubtful things? while we shall follow those who invite us to begin with believing what we cannot yet fully perceive, that, strengthened by this very faith, we may come into a position to know what we believe by the inward illumination and confirmation of our minds, due no longer to men, but to God Himself.

18. And as I have asked this writer to prove these things to me, I ask him now where he learned them himself. If he replies that they were revealed to him by the Holy Spirit, and that his mind was divinely enlightened that he might know them to be certain and evident, he himself points to the distinction between knowing and believing. The knowledge is his to whom these things are fully made known as proved; but in the case of those who only hear his account of these things, there is no knowledge imparted, but only a believing acquiescence required. Whoever thoughtlessly yields this becomes a Manichæan, not by knowing undoubted truth, but by believing doubtful statements. Such were we when in our inexperienced youth we were deceived. Instead, therefore, of promising knowledge, or clear evidence, or the settlement of the question free from all uncertainty, Manichæus ought to have said that these things were clearly proved to him, but that those who hear his account of them must believe him without evidence. But were he to say this, who would not reply to him, If I must believe without knowing, why should I not prefer to believe those things which have a wide-spread notoriety from the consent of learned and unlearned, and which among all nations are established by the weightiest authority? From fear of having this said to him, Manichæus bewilders the inexperienced by first promising the knowledge of certain truths, and then demanding faith in doubtful things. And then, if he is asked to make it plain that these things have been proved to himself, he fails again, and bids us believe this too. Who can tolerate such imposture and arrogance?

Chap. 15.—The Doctrine of Manichæus Not Only Uncertain, But False. His Absurd Fancy of a Land and Race of Darkness Bordering on the Holy Region and the Substance of God. The Error, First of All, of Giving to the Nature of God Limits and Borders, as If God Were a Material Substance, Having Extension in Space.

19. What if I shall have shown, with the help of God and of our Lord, that this writer's statements are false as well as uncertain? What more unfortunate thing can be found than that superstition which not only fails to impart the knowledge and the truth which it promises, but also teaches what is directly opposed to knowledge and truth? This will appear more clearly from what follows: "In one direction on the border of this bright and holy land there was a land of darkness deep and vast in extent, where abode fiery bodies, destructive races. Here was boundless darkness, flowing from the same source in immeasurable abundance, with the productions properly belonging to it. Beyond this were muddy turbid waters with their inhabitants; and inside of them winds terrible and violent with their prince and their progenitors. Then again a fiery region of destruction, with its chiefs and peoples. And similarly inside of this a race full of smoke and gloom, where abode the dreadful prince and chief of all, having around him innumerable princes, himself the mind and source of them all. Such are the five natures of the pestiferous land."

20. To speak of God as an aerial or even as an ethereal body is absurd in the view of all who, with a clear mind, possessing some measure of discernment, can perceive the nature of wisdom and truth as not extended or scattered in space, but as great, and imparting greatness without material size, nor confined more or less in any direction, but throughout co-extensive with the Father of all, nor having one thing here and another there, but everywhere perfect, everywhere present.[1]

Chap. 16.—The Soul, Though Mutable, Has No Material Form. It Is All Present in Every Part of the Body.

But why speak of truth and wisdom which

[1] [This exalted view of God Augustin held in common with the Neo-Platonists.—A. H. N.]

surpass all the powers of the soul, when the nature of the soul itself, which is known to be mutable, still has no kind of material extension in space? For whatever consists of any kind of gross matter must necessarily be divisible into parts, having one in one place, and another in another. Thus, the finger is less than the whole hand, and one finger is less than two; and there is one place for this finger, and another for that, and another for the rest of the hand. And this applies not to organized bodies only, but also to the earth, each part of which has its own place, so that one cannot be where the other is. So in moisture, the smaller quantity occupies a smaller space, and the larger quantity a larger space; and one part is at the bottom of the cup, and another part near the mouth. So in air, each part has its own place; and it is impossible for the air in this house to have along with itself, in the same house at the same moment, the air that the neighbors have. And even as regards light itself, one part pours through one window, and another through another; and a greater through the larger, and a smaller through the smaller. Nor, in fact, can there be any bodily substance, whether celestial or terrestrial, whether aerial or moist, which is not less in part than in whole, or which can possibly have one part in the place of another at the same time; but, having one thing in one place and another in another, its extension in space is a substance which has distinct limits and parts, or, so to speak, sections. The nature of the soul, on the other hand, though we leave out of account its power of perceiving truth, and consider only its inferior power of giving unity to the body, and of sensation in the body, does not appear to have any material extension in space. For it is all present in each separate part of its body when it is all present in any sensation. There is not a smaller part in the finger, and a larger in the arm, as the bulk of the finger is less than that of the arm; but the quantity everywhere is the same, for the whole is present everywhere. For when the finger is touched, the whole mind feels, though the sensation is not through the whole body. No part of the mind is unconscious of the touch, which proves the presence of the whole. And yet it is not so present in the finger or in the sensation as to abandon the rest of the body, or to gather itself up into the one place where the sensation occurs. For when it is all present in the sensation in a finger, if another part, say the foot, be touched, it does not fail to be all present in this sensation too: so that at the same moment it is all present in different places, without leaving one in order to be in the other, and without having one part in one, and another in the other; but by this power showing itself to be all present at the same moment in separate places. Since it is all present in the sensations of these places, it proves that it is not bound by the conditions of space.[1]

CHAP. 17.—THE MEMORY CONTAINS THE IDEAS OF PLACES OF THE GREATEST SIZE.

Again, if we consider the mind's power of remembering not the objects of the intellect, but material objects, such as we see brutes also remembering (for cattle find their way without mistake in familiar places, and animals return to their cribs, and dogs recognize the persons of their masters, and when asleep they often growl, or break out into a bark, which could not be unless their mind retained the images of things before seen or perceived by some bodily sense), who can conceive rightly where these images are contained, where they are kept, or where they are formed? If, indeed, these images were no larger than the size of our body, it might be said that the mind shapes and retains them in the bodily space which contains itself. But while the body occupies a small material space, the mind revolves images of vast extent, of heaven and earth, with no want of room, though they come and go in crowds; so that clearly, the mind is not diffused through space: for instead of being contained in images of the largest spaces, it rather contains them; not, however, in any material receptacle, but by a mysterious faculty or power, by which it can increase or diminish them, can contract them within narrow limits, or expand them indefinitely, can arrange or disarrange them at pleasure, can multiply them or reduce them to a few or to one.

CHAP. 18.—THE UNDERSTANDING JUDGES OF THE TRUTH OF THINGS, AND OF ITS OWN ACTION.

What, then, must be said of the power of perceiving truth, and of making a vigorous resistance against these very images which take their shape from impressions on the bodily senses, when they are opposed to the truth? This power discerns the difference between, to take a particular example, the true Carthage and its own imaginary one, which it changes as it pleases with perfect ease. It

1 [Modern mental physiologists differ among themselves as regards the presence of the mind throughout the entire nervous system; some maintaining the view here presented, and others making the brain to be the seat of sensation, and the nerves telegraphic lines, so to speak, for the communication of impressions from the various parts of the body to the brain. Compare CARPENTER: *Mental Physiology*, and CALDERWOOD: *Mind and Brain.*—A. H. N.]

shows that the countless worlds of Epicurus, in which his fancy roamed without restraint, are due to the same power of imagination, and, not to multiply examples, that we get from the same source that land of light, with its boundless extent, and the five dens of the race of darkness, with their inmates, in which the fancies of Manichæus have dared to usurp for themselves the name of truth. What then is this power which discerns these things? Clearly, whatever its extent may be, it is greater than all these things, and is conceived of without any such material images. Find, if you can, space for this power; give it a material extension; provide it with a body of huge size. Assuredly if you think well, you cannot. For of everything of this corporeal nature your mind forms an opinion as to its divisibility, and you make of such things one part greater and another less, as much as you like; while that by which you form a judgment of these things you perceive to be above them, not in local loftiness of place, but in dignity of power.

Chap. 19.—If the Mind Has No Material Extension, Much Less Has God.

21. So then, if the mind, so liable to change, whether from a multitude of dissimilar desires, or from feelings varying according to the abundance or the want of desirable things, or from these endless sports of the fancy, or from forgetfulness and remembrance, or from learning and ignorance; if the mind, I say, exposed to frequent change from these and the like causes, is perceived to be without any local or material extension, and to have a vigor of action which surmounts these material conditions, what must we think or conclude of God Himself, who remains superior to all intelligent beings in His freedom from perturbation and from change, giving to every one what is due? Him the mind dares to express more easily than to see; and the clearer the sight, the less is the power of expression. And yet this God, if, as the Manichæan fables are constantly asserting, He were limited in extension in one direction and unlimited in others, could be measured by so many subdivisions or fractions of greater or less size, as every one might fancy; so that, for example, a division of the extent of two feet would be less by eight parts than one of ten feet. For this is the property of all natures which have extension in space, and therefore cannot be all in one place. But even with the mind this is not the case; and this degrading and perverted idea of the mind is found among people who are unfit for such investigations.

Chap. 20.—Refutation of the Absurd Idea of Two Territories.

22. But perhaps, instead of thus addressing carnal minds, we should rather descend to the views of those who either dare not or are as yet unfit to turn from the consideration of material things to the study of an immaterial and spiritual nature, and who thus are unable to reflect upon their own power of reflection, so as to see how it forms a judgment of material extension without itself possessing it. Let us descend then to these material ideas, and let us ask in what direction, and on what border of the shining and sacred territory, to use the expressions of Manichæus, was the region of darkness? For he speaks of one direction and border, without saying which, whether the right or the left. In any case, it is clear that to speak of one side implies that there is another. But where there are three or more sides, either the figure is bounded in all directions, or if it extends infinitely in one direction, still it must be limited in the directions where it has sides. If, then, on one side of the region of light there was the race of darkness, what bounded it on the other side or sides? The Manichæans say nothing in reply to this; but when pressed, they say that on the other sides the region of light, as they call it, is infinite, that is, extends throughout boundless space. They do not see, what is plain to the dullest understanding, that in that case there could be no sides? For the sides are where it is bounded. What, then, he says, though there are no sides? But what you said of one direction or side, implied of necessity the existence of another direction and side, or other directions and sides. For if there was only one side, you should have said, on the side, not *on one side;* as in reference to our body we say properly, By one eye, because there is another; or on one breast, because there is another. But if we spoke of a thing as being on one nose, or one navel, we should be ridiculed by learned and unlearned, since there is only one. But I do not insist on words, for you may have used one in the sense of the only one.

Chap. 21.—This Region of Light Must Be Material if It Is Joined to the Region of Darkness. The Shape of the Region of Darkness Joined to the Region of Light.

What, then, bordered on the side of the region which you call shining and sacred? The region, you reply, of darkness. Do you then allow this latter region to have been material? Of course you must, since you assert that all bodies derive their origin from it. How then is it that, dull and carnal as you are, you do not see that unless both regions were material, they could not have their sides joined to one another? How could you ever be so blinded in mind as to say that only the region of darkness was material, and that the so-called region of light was immaterial and spiritual? My good friends, let us open our eyes for once, and see, now that we are told of it, what is most obvious, that two regions cannot be joined at their sides unless both are material.

23. Or if we are too dull and stupid to see this, let us hear whether the region of darkness too has one side, and is boundless in the other directions, like the region of light. They do not hold this from fear of making it seem equal to God. Accordingly they make it boundless in depth and in length; but upwards, above it, they maintain that there is an infinity of empty space. And lest this region should appear to be a fraction equal in amount to half of that representing the region of light, they narrow it also on two sides. As if, to give the simplest illustration, a piece of bread were made into four squares, three white and one black; then suppose the three white pieces joined as one, and conceive them as infinite upwards and downwards, and backwards in all directions: this represents the Manichæan region of light. Then conceive the black square infinite downwards and backwards, but with infinite emptiness above it: this is their region of darkness. But these are secrets which they disclose to very eager and anxious inquirers.

CHAP. 22.—THE FORM OF THE REGION OF LIGHT THE WORSE OF THE TWO.

Well, then, if this is so, the region of darkness is clearly touched on two sides by the region of light. And if it is touched on two sides, it must touch on two. So much for its being on one side, as we were told before.

24. And what an unseemly appearance is this of the region of light!—like a cloven arch, with a black wedge inserted below, bounded only in the direction of the cleft, and having a void space interposed where the boundless emptiness stretches above the region of darkness. Indeed, the form of the region of darkness is better than that of the region of light: for the former cleaves, the latter is cloven; the former fills the gap which is made in the latter; the former has no void in it, while the latter is undefined in all directions, except that where it is filled up by the wedge of darkness. In an ignorant and greedy notion of giving more honor to a number of parts than to a single one, so that the region of light should have six, three upwards and three downwards, they have made this region be split up, instead of sundering the other. For, according to this figure, though there may be no commixture of darkness with light, there is certainly penetration.

CHAP. 23.—THE ANTHROPOMORPHITES NOT SO BAD AS THE MANICHÆANS.

25. Compare, now, not spiritual men of the Catholic faith, whose mind, as far as is possible in this life, perceives that the divine substance and nature has no material extension, and has no shape bounded by lines, but the carnal and weak of our faith, who, when they hear the members of the body used figuratively, as, when God's eyes or ears are spoken of, are accustomed, in the license of fancy, to picture God to themselves in a human form; compare these with the Manichæans, whose custom it is to make known their silly stories to anxious inquirers as if they were great mysteries: and consider who have the most allowable and respectable ideas of God, —those who think of Him as having a human form which is the most excellent of its kind, or those who think of Him as having boundless material extension, yet not in all directions, but with three parts infinite and solid, while in one part He is cloven, with an empty void, and with undefined space above, while the region of darkness is inserted wedge-like below. Or perhaps the proper expression is, that He is unconfined above in His own nature, but encroached on below by a hostile nature. I join with you in laughing at the folly of carnal men, unable as yet to form spiritual conceptions, who think of God as having a human form. Do you too join me, if you can, in laughing at those whose unhappy conceptions represent God as having a shape cloven or cut in such an unseemly and unbecoming way, with such an empty gap above, and such a dishonorable curtailment below. Besides, there is this difference, that these carnal people, who think of God as having a human form, if they are content to be nourished with milk from the breast of the Catholic Church, and do not rush headlong into rash opinions, but cultivate in the Church the pious habit of inquiry, and there ask that they may receive, and knock that it may be opened to them, begin to understand spiritually the figures and parables of the Scriptures, and gradually to perceive that the divine energies are suitably set forth under the name, sometimes of ears, sometimes of eyes, sometimes of hands or feet, or

even of wings and feathers a shield too, and sword, and helmet, and all the other innumerable things. And the more progress they make in this understanding, the more are they confirmed as Catholics. The Manichæans, on the other hand, when they abandon their material fancies, cease to be Manichæans. For this is the chief and special point in their praises of Manichæus, that the divine mysteries which were taught figuratively in books from ancient times were kept for Manichæus, who was to come last, to solve and demonstrate; and so after him no other teacher will come from God, for he has said nothing in figures or parables, but has explained ancient sayings of that kind, and has himself taught in plain, simple terms. Therefore, when the Manichæans hear these words of their founder, on one side and border of the shining and sacred region was the region of darkness, they have no interpretations to fall back on. Wherever they turn, the wretched bondage of their own fancies brings them upon clefts or sudden stoppages and joinings or sunderings of the most unseemly kind, which it would be shocking to believe as true of any immaterial nature, even though mutable, like the mind, not to speak of the immutable nature of God. And yet if I were unable to rise to higher things, and to bring my thoughts from the entanglement of false imaginations which are impressed on the memory by the bodily senses, into the freedom and purity of spiritual existence, how much better would it be to think of God as in the form of a man, than to fasten that wedge of darkness to His lower edge, and, for want of a covering for the boundless vacuity above to leave it void and unoccupied throughout infinite space! What notion could be worse than this? What darker error can be taught or imagined?

Chap. 24.—Of the Number of Natures in the Manichæan Fiction.

26. Again, I wish to know, when I read of God the Father and His kingdoms founded on the shining and happy region, whether the Father and His kingdoms, and the region, are all of the same nature and substance. If they are, then it is not another nature or sort of body of God which the wedge of the race of darkness cleaves and penetrates, which itself is an unspeakably revolting thing, but it is actually the very nature of God which undergoes this. Think of this, I beseech you: as you are men, think of it, and flee from it; and if by tearing open your breasts you can cast out by the roots such profane fancies from your faith, I pray you to do it. Or will you say that these three are not of one and the same nature, but that the Father is of one, the kingdoms of another, and the region of another, so that each has a peculiar nature and substance, and that they are arranged according to their degree of excellence? If this is true, Manichæus should have taught that there are four natures, not two; or if the Father and the kingdoms have one nature, and the region only one of its own, he should have made three. Or if he made only two, because the region of darkness does not belong to God, in what sense does the region of light belong to God? For if it has a nature of its own, and if God neither generated nor made it, it does not belong to Him, and the seat of His kingdom is in what belongs to another. Or if it belongs to Him because of its vicinity, the region of darkness must do so too; for it not only borders on the region of light, but penetrates it so as to sever it in two. Again, if God generated it, it cannot have a separate nature. For what is generated by God must be what God is, as the Catholic Church believes of the only begotten Son. So you are brought back of necessity to that shocking and detestable profanity, that the wedge of darkness sunders not a region distinct and separate from God, but the very nature of God. Or if God did not generate, but make it, of what did He make it? Or if of Himself, what is this but to generate? If of some other nature, was this nature good or evil? If good, there must have been some good nature not belonging to God; which you will scarcely have the boldness to assert. If evil, the race of darkness cannot have been the only evil nature. Or did God take a part of that region and turn it into a region of light, in order to found His kingdom upon it? If He had, He would have taken the whole, and there would have been no evil nature left. If God, then, did not make the region of light of a substance distinct from His own, He must have made it of nothing.[1]

Chap. 25.—Omnipotence Creates Good Things Differing in Degree. In Every Description Whatsoever of the Junction of the Two Regions There is Either Impropriety or Absurdity.

27. If, then, you are now convinced that God is able to create some good thing out of nothing, come into the Catholic Church, and learn that all the natures which God has created and founded in their order of excel-

[1] [There is sufficient reason to think that Mani identified God with the kingdom and the region of light. See Introduction.—A. H. N.]

lence from the highest to the lowest are good, and some better than others; and that they were made of nothing, though God, their Maker, made use of His own wisdom as an instrument, so to speak, to give being to what was not, and that as far as it had being it might be good, and that the limitation of its being might show that it was not begotten by God, but made out of nothing. If you examine the matter, you will find nothing to keep you from agreeing to this. For you cannot make your region of light to be what God is, without making the dark section an infringement on the very nature of God. Nor can you say that it was generated by God, without being reduced to the same enormity, from the necessity of concluding that as begotten of God, it must be what God is. Nor can you say that it was distinct from Him, lest you should be forced to admit that God placed His kingdom in what did not belong to Him, and that there are three natures. Nor can you say that God made it of a substance distinct from His own, without making something good besides God, or something evil besides the race of darkness. It remains, therefore that you must confess that God made the region of light out of nothing: and you are unwilling to believe this; because if God could make out of nothing some great good which yet was inferior to Himself, He could also, since He is good, and grudges no good, make another good inferior to the former, and again a third inferior to the second, and so on, in order down to the lowest good of created natures, so that the whole aggregate, instead of extending indefinitely without number or measure, should have a fixed and definite consistency. Again, if you will not allow this either, that God made the region of light out of nothing, you will have no escape from the shocking profanities to which your opinions lead.

28. Perhaps, since the carnal imagination can fancy any shapes it likes, you might be able to devise some other form for the junction of the two regions, instead of presenting to the mind such a disagreeable and painful description as this, that the region of God, whether it be of the same nature as God or not, where at least God's kingdoms are founded, lies through immensity in such a huge mass that its members stretch loosely to an infinite extent, and that on their lower part that wedge of the region of darkness, itself of boundless size encroaches upon them. But whatever other form you contrive for the junction of these two regions, you cannot erase what Manichæus has written. I refer not to other treatises where a more particular description is given,—for perhaps, because they are in the hands of only a few, there might not be so much difficulty with them,—but to this Fundamental Epistle which we are now considering, with which all of you who are called enlightened are usually quite familiar. Here the words are: "On one side the border of the shining and sacred region was the region of darkness, deep and boundless in extent."

CHAP. 26.—THE MANICHÆANS ARE REDUCED TO THE CHOICE OF A TORTUOUS, OR CURVED, OR STRAIGHT LINE OF JUNCTION. THE THIRD KIND OF LINE WOULD GIVE SYMMETRY AND BEAUTY SUITABLE TO BOTH REGIONS.

What more is to be got? we have now heard what is on the border. Make what shape you please, draw any kind of lines you like, it is certain that the junction of this boundless mass of the region of darkness to the region of light must have been either by a straight line, or a curved, or a tortuous one. If the line of junction is tortuous the side of the region of light must also be tortuous; otherwise its straight side joined to a tortuous one would leave gaps of infinite depth, instead of having vacuity only above the land of darkness, as we were told before. And if there were such gaps, how much better it would have been for the region of light to have been still more distant, and to have had a greater vacuity between, so that the region of darkness might not touch it at all! Then there might have been such a gap of bottomless depth, that, on the rise of any mischief in that race, although the chiefs of darkness might have the foolhardy wish to cross over, they would fall headlong into the gap (for bodies cannot fly without air to support them); and as there is infinite space downwards, they could do no more harm, though they might live for ever, for they would be for ever falling. Again, if the line of junction was a curved one, the region of light must also have had the disfigurement of a curve to answer it. Or if the land of darkness were curved inwards like a theatre, there would be as much disfigurement in the corresponding line in the region of light. Or if the region of darkness had a curved line, and the region of light a straight one, they cannot have touched at all points. And certainly, as I said before, it would have been better if they had not touched, and if there was such a gap between that the regions might be kept distinctly separate, and that rash evildoers might fall headlong so as to be harmless. If, then, the line of junction was a straight one, there remain, of course, no more gaps or grooves, but, on the contrary, so perfect a junction as to make the greatest possible peace and harmony between the two regions. What more beautiful or more suitable than that one side should meet the other in a straight line, without bends or breaks to disturb the natural and permanent connection throughout endless space and endless duration? And even though there was a separation, the straight sides of both regions would be beautiful in themselves, as being straight; and besides, even in spite of an interval, their correspondence, as running parallel, though not meeting, would give a symmetry to both. With the addition of the junction, both regions become perfectly regular and harmonious; for nothing can be devised more beautiful in description or in conception than this junction of two straight lines.[1]

CHAP. 27.—THE BEAUTY OF THE STRAIGHT LINE MIGHT BE TAKEN FROM THE REGION OF DARKNESS WITHOUT TAKING ANYTHING FROM ITS SUBSTANCE. SO EVIL NEITHER TAKES FROM NOR ADDS TO THE SUBSTANCE OF THE SOUL. THE STRAIGHTNESS OF ITS SIDE WOULD BE SO FAR A GOOD BESTOWED ON THE REGION OF DARKNESS BY GOD THE CREATOR.

29. What is to be done with unhappy minds, perverse in error, and held fast by custom? These men do not know what they say when they say those things; for they do not consider. Listen to me; no one forces you, no one quarrels with you, no one taunts you with past errors, unless some one who has not experienced the div ne mercy in deliverance from error: all we desire is that the errors should some time or other be abandoned. Think a little without animosity or bitterness. We are all human beings: let us hate, not one another, but errors and lies. Think a little, I pray you. God of mercy, help them to think, and kindle in the minds of inquirers the true light. If anything is plain, is not this, that right is better than wrong? Give me, then, a calm and quiet answer to this, whether making crooked the right line of the region of darkness which joins on to the right line of the region of light, would not detract from its beauty. If you will not be dogged, you must confess that not only is beauty taken from it by its being made crooked, but also the beauty which it might have had from connection with the right line of the region of light. Is it the case, then, that in this loss of beauty, in which right is made crooked, and harmony becomes discord, and agreement disagreement, there is any loss of substance? Learn, then, from this that substance is not evil; but as in the body, by change of form for the worse, beauty is lost, or rather lessened, and what was called fair before is said to be ugly, and what was pleasing becomes displeasing, so in the mind the seemliness of a right will, which makes a just and pious life, is injured when the will changes for the worse; and by this sin the mind becomes miserable, instead of enjoying as before the happiness which comes from the ornament of a right will, without any gain or loss of substance.

30. Consider, again, that though we admit that the border of the region of darkness was evil for other reasons, such as that it was dim and dark, or any other reason, still it was not evil in being straight. So, if I admit that there was some evil in its color, you must admit that there was some good in its straightness. Whatever the amount of this good, it is not allowable to attribute it to any other than God the Maker, from whom we must believe that all good in whatsoever nature comes, if we are to escape deadly error. It is absurd, then, to say that this region is perfect evil, when in its straightness of border is found the good of not a little beauty of a material kind; and also to make this region to be altogether estranged from the almighty and good God, when this good which we find in it can be attributed to no other but the author of all good things. But this border, too, we are told, was evil. Well, suppose it evil: it would surely have been worse had it been crooked instead of straight. And how can that be the perfection of evil than which something worse than itself can be thought of? And to be worse implies that there is some good, the want of which makes the thing worse. Here the want of straightness would make the line worse. Therefore its straightness is something good. And you will never answer the question whence this goodness comes, without reference to Him from whom we must acknowledge that all good things come, whether small or great. But now we shall pass on from considering this border to something else.

CHAP. 28.—MANICHÆUS PLACES FIVE NATURES IN THE REGION OF DARKNESS.

31. "There dwelt," he says, "in that region fiery bodies, destructive races." By speaking of dwelling, he must mean that those bodies were animated and in life. But, not to appear to cavil at a word, let us see how he divides into five classes all these inhabitants of this region. "Here," he says, "was boundless darkness, flowing from the same source in immeasurable abundance, with the productions properly belonging to it.

[1] [This discussion of the lines bounding the Kingdom of Light and the Kingdom of Darkness seems very much like trifling, but Augustin's aim was to bring the Manichæan representations into ridicule.—A. H. N.]

Beyond this were muddy turbid waters, with their inhabitants; and inside of them winds terrible and violent, with their prince and their progenitors. Then, again, a fiery region of destruction, with its chiefs and peoples. And, similarly, inside of this a race full of smoke and gloom, where abode the dreadful prince and chief of all, having around him innumerable princes, himself the mind and source of them all. Such are the five natures of the pestiferous region." We find here five natures mentioned as part of one nature, which he calls the pestiferous region. The natures are darkness, waters, winds, fire, smoke; which he so arranges as to make darkness first, beginning at the outside. Inside of darkness he puts the waters; inside of the waters, the winds; inside of the winds, the fire; inside of the fire, the smoke. And each of these natures had its peculiar kind of inhabitants, which were likewise five in number. For to the question, Whether there was only one kind in all, or different kinds corresponding to the different natures; the reply is, that they were different: as in other books we find it stated that the darkness had serpents; the waters swimming creatures, such as fish; the winds flying creatures, such as birds; the fire quadrupeds, such as horses, lions, and the like; the smoke bipeds, such as men.

CHAP. 29.—THE REFUTATION OF THIS ABSURDITY.

32. Whose arrangement, then, is this? Who made the distinctions and the classification? Who gave the number, the qualities, the forms, the life? For all these things are in themselves good, nor could each of the natures have them except from the bestowal of God, the author of all good things. For this is not like the descriptions or suppositions of poets about an imaginary chaos, as being a shapeless mass, without form, without quality, without measurement, without weight and number, without order and variety; a confused something, absolutely destitute of qualities, so that some Greek writers call it ἄποιον. So far from being like this is the Manichæan description of the region of darkness, as they call it, that, in a directly contrary style, they add side to side, and join border to border; they number five natures; they separate, arrange, and assign to each its own qualities. Nor do they leave the natures barren or waste, but people them with their proper inhabitants; and to these, again, they give suitable forms, and adapted to their place of habitation, besides giving the chief of all endowments, life. To recount such good things as these, and to speak of them as having no connection with God, the author of all good things, is to lose sight of the excellence of the order in the things, and of the great evil of the error which leads to such a conclusion.

CHAP. 30.—THE NUMBER OF GOOD THINGS IN THOSE NATURES WHICH MANICHÆUS PLACES IN THE REGION OF DARKNESS.

33. "But," is the reply, "the orders of beings inhabiting those five natures were fierce and destructive." As if I were praising their fierceness and destructiveness. I, you see, join with you in condemning the evils you attribute to them; join you with me in praising the good things which you ascribe to them: so it will appear that there is a mixture of good and evil in what you call the last extremity of evil. If I join you in condemning what is mischievous in this region, you must join with me in praising what is beneficial. For these beings could not have been produced, or nourished, or have continued to inhabit that region, without some salutary influence. I join with you in condemning the darkness; join with me in praising the productiveness. For while you call the darkness immeasurable, you speak of "suitable productions." Darkness, indeed, is not a real substance, and means no more than the absence of light, as nakedness means the want of clothing, and emptiness the want of material contents: so that darkness could produce nothing, although a region in darkness—that is, in the absence of light—might produce something. But passing over this for the present, it is certain that where productions arise there must be a beneficent adaptation of substances, as well as a symmetrical arrangement and construction in unity of the members of the beings produced,—a wise adjustment making them agree with one another. And who will deny that all these things are more to be praised than darkness is to be condemned? If I join with you in condemning the muddiness of the waters, you must join with me in praising the waters as far as they possessed the form and quality of water, and also the agreement of the members of the inhabitants swimming in the waters, their life sustaining and directing their body, and every particular adaptation of substances for the benefit of health. For though you find fault with the waters as turbid and muddy, still, in allowing them the quality of producing and maintaining their living inhabitants, you imply that there was some kind of bodily form, and similarity of parts, giving unity and congruity of character; otherwise there could be no body at all: and,

as a rational being, you must see that all these things are to be praised. And however great you make the ferocity of these inhabitants, and their massacrings and devastations in their assaults, you still leave them the regular limits of form, by which the members of each body are made to agree together, and their beneficial adaptations, and the regulating power of the living principle binding together the parts of the body in a friendly and harmonious union. And if all these are regarded with common sense it will be seen that they are more to be commended than the faults are to be condemned. I join with you in condemning the frightfulness of the winds; join with me in praising their nature, as giving breath and nourishment, and their material form in its continuousness and diffusion by the connection of its parts: for by these things these winds had the power of producing and nourishing, and sustaining in vigor these inhabitants you speak of; and also in these inhabitants—besides the other things which have already been commended in all animated creatures—this particular power of going quickly and easily whence and whither they please, and the harmonious stroke of their wings in flight, and their regular motion. I join with you in condemning the destructiveness of fire; join with me in commending the productiveness of this fire, and the growth of these productions, and the adaptation of the fire to the beings produced, so that they had coherence, and came to perfection in measure and shape, and could live and have their abode there: for you see that all these things deserve admiration and praise, not only in the fire which is thus habitable, but in the inhabitants too. I join with you in condemning the denseness of smoke, and the savage character of the prince who, as you say, abode in it; join with me in praising the similarity of all the parts in this very smoke, by which it preserves the harmony and proportion of its parts among themselves, according to its own nature, and has an unity which makes it what it is: for no one can calmly reflect on these things without wonder and praise. Besides, even to the smoke you give the power and energy of production, for you say that princes inhabited it; so that in that region the smoke is productive, which never happens here, and, moreover, affords a wholesome dwelling place to its inhabitants.

CHAP. 31.—THE SAME SUBJECT CONTINUED.

34. And even in the prince of smoke himself, instead of mentioning only his ferocity as a bad quality, ought you not to have taken notice of the other things in his nature which you must allow to be commendable? For he had a soul and a body; the soul life-giving, and the body endowed with life. Since the soul governed and the body obeyed, the soul took the lead and the body followed; the soul gave consistency, the body was not dissolved; the soul gave harmonious motion, and the body was constructed of a well-proportioned framework of members. In this single prince are you not induced to express approval of the orderly peace or the peaceful order? And what applies to one applies to all the rest. You say he was fierce and cruel to others. This is not what I commend, but the other important things which you will not take notice of. Those things, when perceived and considered,—after advice by any one who has without consideration put faith in Manichæus,—lead him to a clear conviction that, in speaking of those natures, he speaks of things good in a sense, not perfect and uncreated, like God the one Trinity, nor of the higher rank of created things, like the holy angels and the ever-blessed powers; but of the lowest class, and ranked according to the small measure of their endowments. These things are thought to be blameworthy by the uninstructed when they compare them with higher things; and in view of their want of some good, the good they have gets the name of evil, because it is defective. My reason also for thus discussing the natures enumerated by Manichæus is that the things named are things familiar to us in this world. We are familiar with darkness, waters, winds, fire, smoke; we are familiar, too, with animals, creeping, swimming, flying; with quadrupeds and biped. With the exception of darkness (which, as I have said already, is nothing but the absence of light, and the perception of it is only the absence of sight, as the perception of silence is the absence of hearing; not that darkness is anything, but that light is not, as neither that silence is anything, but that sound is not), all the other things are natural qualities and are familiar to all; and the form of those natures, which is commendable and good as far as it exists, no wise man attributes to any other author than God, the author of all good things.[1]

CHAP. 32.—MANICHÆUS GOT THE ARRANGEMENT OF HIS FANCIFUL NOTIONS FROM VISIBLE OBJECTS.

35. For in giving to these natures which he has learned from visible things, an arrange-

[1] [This portion of the argument is conducted with great adroitness. Augustin takes the inhabitants of the region of darkness, as Mani describes them, and proves that they possess so much of good that they can have no other author than God.—A. H. N.]

ment according to his fanciful ideas, to represent the race of darkness, Manichæus is clearly in error. First of all, he makes darkness productive, which is impossible. But, he replies, this darkness was unlike what you are familiar with. How, then, can you make me understand about it? After so many promises to give knowledge, will you force me to take your word for it? Suppose I believe you, this at least is certain, that if the darkness had no form, as darkness usually has not, it could produce nothing; if it had form, it was better than ordinary darkness: whereas, when you call it different from the ordinary kind, you wish us to believe that it is worse. You might as well say that silence, which is the same to the ear as darkness to the eyes, produced some deaf or dumb animals in that region; and then, in reply to the objection that silence is not a nature, you might say that it was different silence from ordinary silence; in a word, you might say what you pleased to those whom you have once misled into believing you. No doubt, the obvious facts relating to the origin of animal life led Manichæus to say that serpents were produced in darkness. However, there are serpents which have such sharp sight, and such pleasure in light, that they seem to give evidence of the most weighty kind against this idea. Then the idea of swimming things in the water might easily be got here, and applied to the fanciful objects in that region; and so of flying things in the winds, for the motion of the lower air in this world, where birds fly, is called wind. Where he got the idea of the quadrupeds in fire, no one can tell. Still he said this deliberately, though without sufficient thought, and from great misconception. The reason usually given is, that quadrupeds are voracious and salacious. But many men surpass any quadruped in voracity, though they are bipeds, and are called children of the smoke, and not of fire. Geese, too, are as voracious as any animal; and though he might place them in fire as bipeds, or in the water because they love to swim, or in the winds because they have wings and sometimes fly, they certainly have nothing to do with fire in this classification. As regards salaciousness, I suppose he was thinking of neighing horses, which sometimes bite through the bridle and rush at the mares; and writing hastily, with this in his mind, he forgot the common sparrow, in comparison of which the hottest stallion is cold. The reason they give for assigning bipeds to the smoke is, that bipeds are conceited and proud, for men are derived from this class; and the idea, which is a plausible one, is that smoke resembles proud people in rising up into the air, round and swelling. This idea might warrant a figurative description of proud men, or an allegorical expression or explanation, but not the belief that bipeds are born in smoke and of smoke. They might with equal reason be said to be born in dust, for it often rises up to the heaven with a similar circling and lofty motion; or in the clouds, for they are often drawn up from the earth in such a way, that those looking from a distance are uncertain whether they are clouds or smoke. Once more, why, in the case of the waters and the winds, does he suit the inhabitants to the character of the place, as we see swimming things in water, and flying things in the wind; whereas, in the face of fire and smoke, this bold liar is not ashamed to assign to these places the most unlikely inhabitants? For fire burns quadrupeds, and consumes them, and smoke suffocates and kills bipeds. At least he must acknowledge that he has made these natures better in the race of darkness than they are here, though he wishes us to think everything to be worse. For, according to this, the fire there produced and nourished quadrupeds, and gave them a lodging not only harmless, but most convenient. The smoke, too, provided room for the offspring of its own benign bosom, and cherished them up to the rank of prince. Thus we see that these lies, which have added to the number of heretics, arose from the perception by carnal sense, only without care or discernment, of visible objects in this world, and when thus conceived, were brought forth by fancy, and then presumptuously written and published.

CHAP. 33.—EVERY NATURE, AS NATURE, IS GOOD.

36. But the consideration we wish most to urge is the truth of the Catholic doctrine, if they can understand it, that God is the author of all natures. I urged this before when I said, I join with you in your condemnation of destructiveness, of blindness, of dense muddiness, of terrific violence, of perishableness, of the ferocity of the princes, and so on; join with me in commending form, classification, arrangement, harmony, unity of structure, symmetry and correspondence of members, provision for vital breath and nourishment, wholesome adaptation, regulation and control by the mind, and the subjection of the bodies, and the assimilation and agreement of parts in the natures, both those inhabiting and those inhabited, and all the other things of the same kind. From this, if they would only think honestly, they would

understand that it implies a mixture of good and evil, even in the region where they suppose evil to be alone and in perfection: so that if the evils mentioned were taken away, the good things will remain, without anything to detract from the commendation given to them; whereas, if the good things are taken away, no nature is left. From this every one sees, who can see, that every nature, as far as it is nature, is good; since in one and the same thing in which I found something to praise, and he found something to blame, if the good things are taken away, no nature will remain; but if the disagreeable things are taken away, the nature will remain unimpaired. Take from waters their thickness and muddiness, and pure clear water remains; take from them the consistence of their parts, and no water will be left. If then, after the evil is removed, the nature remains in a purer state, and does not remain at all when the good is taken away, it must be the good which makes the nature of the thing in which it is, while the evil is not nature, but contrary to nature. Take from the winds their terribleness and excessive force, with which you find fault, you can conceive of winds as gentle and mild; take from them the similarity of their parts which gives them continuity of substance, and the unity essential to material existence, and no nature remains to be conceived of. It would be tedious to go through all the cases; but all who consider the subject free from party spirit must see that in their list of natures the disagreeable things mentioned are additions to the nature; and when they are removed, the natures remain better than before. This shows that the natures, as far as they are natures, are good; for when you take from them the good instead of the evil, no natures remain. And attend, you who wish to arrive at a correct judgment, to what is said of the fierce prince himself. If you take away his ferocity, see how many excellent things will remain; his material frame, the symmetry of the members on one side with those on the other, the unity of his form, the settled continuity of his parts, the orderly adjustment of the mind as ruling and animating, and the body as subject and animated. The removal of these things, and of others I may have omitted to mention, will leave no nature remaining.

CHAP. 34.—NATURE CANNOT BE WITHOUT SOME GOOD. THE MANICHÆANS DWELL UPON THE EVILS.

37. But perhaps you will say that these evils cannot be removed from the natures, and must therefore be considered natural. The question at present is not what can be taken away, and what cannot; but it certainly helps to a clear perception that these natures, as far as they are natures, are good, when we see that the good things can be thought of without these evil things, while without these good things no nature can be conceived of. I can conceive of waters without muddy commotion; but without settled continuity of parts no material form is an object of thought or of sensation in any way. Therefore even these muddy waters could not exist without the good which was the condition of their material existence. As to the reply that these evil things cannot be taken from such natures, I rejoin that neither can the good things be taken away. Why, then, should you call these things natural evils, on account of the evil things which you suppose cannot be taken away, and yet refuse to call them natural good things, on account of the good things which, as has been proved, cannot be taken away?

38. You may next ask, as you usually do for a last resource, whence come these evils which I have said that I too disapprove of. I shall perhaps tell you, if you first tell me whence are those good things which you too are obliged to commend, if you would not be altogether unreasonable. But why should I ask this, when we both acknowledge that all good things whatever, and how great soever, are from the one God, who is supremely good? You must therefore yourselves oppose Manichæus who has placed all these important good things which we have mentioned and justly commended,—the continuity and agreement of parts in each nature, the health and vigor of the animated creatures, and the other things which it would be wearisome to repeat,—(in an imaginary region of darkness, so as to separate them altogether from that God whom he allows to be the author of all good things.) He lost sight of those good things, while taking notice only of what was disagreeable; as if one, frightened by a lion's roaring, and seeing him dragging away and tearing the bodies of cattle or human beings which he had seized, should from childish pusillanimity be so overpowered with fear as to see nothing but the cruelty and ferocity of the lion; and overlooking or disregarding all the other qualities, should exclaim against the nature of this animal as not only evil, but a great evil, his fear adding to his vehemence. But were he to see a tame lion, with its ferocity subdued, especially if he had never been frightened by a lion, he would have leisure, in the absence of danger and terror, to observe and admire the beauty of the animal. My

only remark on this is one closely connected with our subject: that any nature may be in some case disagreeable, so as to excite hatred towards the whole nature; though it is clear that the form of a real living beast, even when it excites terror in the woods, is far better than that of the artificial imitation which is commended in a painting on the wall. We must not then be misled into this error by Manichæus, or be hindered from observing the forms of the natures, by his finding fault with some things in them in such a way as to make us disapprove of them entirely, when it is impossible to show that they deserve entire disapproval. And when our minds are thus composed and prepared to form a just judgment, we may ask whence come those evils which I have said that I condemn. It will be easier to see this if we class them all under one name.

CHAP. 35.—EVIL ALONE IS CORRUPTION. CORRUPTION IS NOT NATURE, BUT CONTRARY TO NATURE. CORRUPTION IMPLIES PREVIOUS GOOD.

39. For who can doubt that the whole of that which is called evil is nothing else than corruption? Different evils may, indeed, be called by different names; but that which is the evil of all things in which any evil is perceptible is corruption. So the corruption of an educated mind is ignorance; the corruption of a prudent mind is imprudence; the corruption of a just mind, injustice; the corruption of a brave mind, cowardice; the corruption of a calm, peaceful mind, cupidity, fear, sorrow, pride. Again, in a living body, the corruption of health is pain and disease; the corruption of strength is exhaustion; the corruption of rest is toil. Again, in any corporeal thing, the corruption of beauty is ugliness; the corruption of straightness is crookedness; the corruption of order is confusion; the corruption of entireness is disseverance, or fracture, or diminution. It would be long and laborious to mention by name all the corruptions of the things here mentioned, and of countless other things; for in many cases the words may apply to the mind as well as to the body, and in innumerable cases the corruption has a distinct name of its own. But enough has been said to show that corruption does harm only as displacing the natural condition; and so, that corruption is not nature, but against nature. And if corruption is the only evil to be found anywhere, and if corruption is not nature, no nature is evil.

40. But if, perchance, you cannot follow this, consider again, that whatever is corrupted is deprived of some good: for if it were not corrupted, it would be incorrupt; or if it could not in any way be corrupted, it would be incorruptible. Now, if corruption is an evil, both incorruption and incorruptibility must be good things. We are not, however, speaking at present of incorruptible nature, but of things which admit of corruption, and which, while not corrupted, may be called incorrupt, but not incorruptible. That alone can be called incorruptible which not only is not corrupted, but also cannot in any part be corrupted. Whatever things, then, being incorrupt, but liable to corruption, begin to be corrupted, are deprived of the good which they had as incorrupt. Nor is this a slight good, for corruption is a great evil. And the continued increase of corruption implies the continued presence of good, of which they may be deprived. Accordingly, the natures supposed to exist in the region of darkness must have been either corruptible or incorruptible. If they were incorruptible, they were in possession of a good than which nothing is higher. If they were corruptible, they were either corrupted or not corrupted. If they were not corrupted, they were incorrupt, to say which of anything is to give it great praise. If they were corrupted, they were deprived of this great good of incorruption; but the deprivation implies the previous possession of the good they are deprived of; and if they possessed this good, they were not the perfection of evil, and consequently all the Manichæan story is a falsehood.

CHAP. 36.—THE SOURCE OF EVIL OR OF CORRUPTION OF GOOD.

41. After thus inquiring what evil is, and learning that it is not nature, but against nature, we must next inquire whence it is. If Manichæus had done this, he might have escaped falling into the snare of these serious errors. Out of time and out of order, he began with inquiring into the origin of evil, without first asking what evil was; and so his inquiry led him only to the reception of foolish fancies, of which the mind, much fed by the bodily senses, with difficulty rids itself. Perhaps, then, some one, desiring no longer argument, but delivery from error, will ask, Whence is this corruption which we find to be the common evil of good things which are not incorruptible? Such an inquirer will soon find the answer if he seeks for truth with great earnestness, and knocks reverently with sustained assiduity. For while man can use words as a kind of sign for the expression of his thoughts, teaching is the work of the incorruptible Truth itself, who is the one true, the one internal Teacher. He became ex-

ternal also, that He might recall us from the external to the internal; and taking on Himself the form of a servant, that He might bring down His height to the knowledge of those rising up to Him, He condescended to appear in lowliness to the low. In His name let us ask, and through Him let us seek mercy of the Father while making this inquiry. For to answer in a word the question, Whence is corruption? it is hence, because these natures that are capable of corruption were not begotten by God, but made by Him out of nothing; and as we already proved that those natures are good, no one can say with propriety that they were not good as made by God. If it is said that God made them perfectly good, it must be remembered that the only perfect good is God Himself, the maker of those good things.

CHAP. 37.—GOD ALONE PERFECTLY GOOD.

42. What harm, you ask, would follow if those things too were perfectly good? Still, should any one, who admits and believes the perfect goodness of God the Father, inquire what source we should reverently assign to any other perfectly good thing, supposing it to exist, our only correct reply would be, that it is of God the Father, who is perfectly good. And we must bear in mind that what is of Him is born of Him, and not made by Him out of nothing, and that it is therefore perfectly, that is, incorruptibly, good like God Himself. So we see that it is unreasonable to require that things made out of nothing should be as perfectly good as He who was begotten of God Himself, and who is one as God is one, otherwise God would have begotten something unlike Himself. Hence it shows ignorance and impiety to seek for brethren for this only-begotten Son through whom all good things were made by the Father out of nothing, except in this, that He condescended to appear as man. Accordingly in Scripture He is called both only-begotten and first-begotten; only-begotten of the Father, and first-begotten from the dead. "And we beheld," says John, "His glory, the glory as of the only-begotten of the Father, full of grace and truth."[1] And Paul says, "that He might be the first-born among many brethren."[2]

43. But should we say, These things made out of nothing are not good things, but only God's nature is good, we shall be unjust to good things of great value. And there is impiety in calling it a defect in anything not to be what God is, and in denying a thing to be good because it is inferior to God. Pray submit then, thou nature of the rational soul, to be somewhat less than God, but only so far less, that after Him nothing else is above thee. Submit, I say, and yield to Him, lest He drive thee still lower into depths where the punishment inflicted will continually detract more and more from the good which thou hast. Thou exaltest thyself against God, if thou art indignant at His preceding thee; and thou art very contumacious in thy thoughts of Him, if thou dost not rejoice unspeakably in the possession of this good, that He alone is above thee. This being settled as certain, thou art not to say, God should have made me the only nature: there should be no good thing after me. It could not be that the next good thing to God should be the last. And in this is seen most clearly how great dignity God conferred on thee, that He who in the order of nature alone rules over thee, made other good things for thee to rule over. Nor be surprised that they are not now in all respects subject to thee, and that sometimes they pain thee; for thy Lord has greater authority over the things subject to thee than thou hast, as a master over the servants of his servants. What wonder, then, if, when thou sinnest, that is, disobeyest thy Lord, the things thou before ruledst over are made instrumental in thy punishment? For what is so just, or what is more just than God? For this befell human nature in Adam, of whom this is not the place to speak. Suffice it to say, the righteous Ruler acts in character both in just rewards and in just punishments, in the happiness of those who live rightly, and in the penalty inflicted on sinners. Nor yet art thou[3] left without mercy, since by an appointed distribution of things and times thou art called to return. Thus the righteous control of the supreme Creator extends even to earthly good things, which are corrupted and restored, that thou mightest have consolations mingled with punishments; that thou mightest both praise God when delighted by the order of good things, and mightest take refuge in Him when tried by experience of evils. So, as far as earthly things are subject to thee, they teach thee that thou art their ruler; as far as they distress thee, they teach thee to be subject to thy Lord.

CHAP. 38.—NATURE MADE BY GOD; CORRUPTION COMES FROM NOTHING.

44. In this way, though corruption is an

[1] John i. 14.

[2] Rom. viii. 29.

[3] [Augustin still addresses himself to the "nature of the rational soul."—A. H. N.]

evil, and though it comes not from the Author of natures, but from their being made out of nothing, still, in God's government and control over all that He has made, even corruption is so ordered that it hurts only the lowest natures, for the punishment of the condemned, and for the trial and instruction of the returning, that they may keep near to the incorruptible God, and remain incorrupt, which is our only good; as is said by the prophet, "But it is good for me that I keep near to God."[1] And you must not say, God did not make corruptible natures: for, as far as they are natures, God made them; but as far as they are corruptible, God did not make them: for corruption cannot come from Him who alone is incorruptible. If you can receive this, give thanks to God; if you cannot, be quiet and do not condemn what you do not yet understand, but humbly wait on Him who is the light of the mind that thou mayest know. For in the expression "corruptible nature" there are two words, and not one only. So, in the expression, God made out of nothing, "God" and "nothing" are two separate words. Render therefore to each of these words that which belongs to each, so that the word "nature" may go with the word "God," and the word "corruptible" with the word "nothing." And yet even the corruptions, though they have not their origin from God, are to be overruled by Him in accordance with the order of inanimate things and the deserts of His intelligent creatures. Thus we say rightly that reward and punishment are both from God. For God's not making corruption is consistent with His giving over to corruption the man who deserves to be corrupted, that is, who has begun to corrupt himself by sinning, that he who has wilfully yielded to the allurements of corruption may, against his will, suffer its pains.

CHAP. 39.—IN WHAT SENSE EVILS ARE FROM GOD.

45. Not only is it written in the Old Testament, "I make good, and create evil;"[2] but more clearly in the New Testament, where the Lord says, "Fear not them which kill the body, and have no more that they can do; but fear him who, after he has killed the body, has power to cast the soul into hell."[3] And that to voluntary corruption penal corruption is added in the divine judgment, is plainly declared by the Apostle Paul, when he says, "The temple of God is holy, which temple ye are; whoever corrupts the temple of God, him will God corrupt."[4] If this had been said in the Old Law, how vehemently would the Manichæans have denounced it as making God a corrupter! And from fear of the word, many Latin translators make it, "him shall God destroy," instead of corrupt, avoiding the offensive word without any change of meaning. Although these would inveigh against any passage in the Old Law or the prophets if God was called in it a destroyer. But the Greek original here shows that corrupt is the true word; for it is written distinctly, "Whoever corrupts the temple of God, him will God corrupt." If the Manichæans are asked to explain the words, they will say, to escape making God a corrupter, that corrupt here means to give over to corruption, or some such explanation. Did they read the Old Law in this spirit, they would both find many admirable things in it; and instead of spitefully attacking passages which they did not understand, they would reverently postpone the inquiry.

CHAP. 40.—CORRUPTION TENDS TO NON-EXISTENCE.

46. But if any one does not believe that corruption comes from nothing, let him place before himself existence and non-existence—one, as it were, on one side, and the other on the other (to speak so as not to outstrip the slow to understand); then let him set something, say the body of an animal, between them, and let him ask himself whether, while the body is being formed and produced, while its size is increasing, while it gains nourishment, health, strength, beauty, stability, it is tending, as regards its duration and permanence, to this side or that, to existence or non-existence. He will see without difficulty, that even in the rudimentary form there is an existence, and that the more the body is established and built up in form, and figure and strength, the more does it come to exist, and to tend to the side of existence. Then, again, let the body begin to be corrupted; let its whole condition be enfeebled, let its vigor languish, its strength decay, its beauty be defaced, its framework be sundered, the consistency of its parts give way and go to pieces; and let him ask now where the body is tending in this corruption, whether to existence or non-existence: he will not surely be so blind or stupid as to doubt how to answer himself, or as not to see that, in proportion as anything is corrupted, in that proportion it approaches decease. But whatever tends to decease tends to non-existence. Since, then, we must believe that God exists immutably and incorruptibly, while what is called nothing is clearly altogether non-

[1] Ps. lxxiii. 28.
[2] Ps. xlv. 7.
[3] Matt. x. 28, and Luke xii. 4.
[4] 1 Cor. iii. 17.

existent; and since, after setting before yourself existence and non-existence, you have observed that the more a visible object increases the more it tends towards existence, while the more it is corrupted the more it tends towards non-existence, why are you at a loss to tell regarding any nature what in it is from God, and what from nothing; seeing that visible form is natural, and corruption against nature? The increase of form leads to existence, and we acknowledge God as supreme existence; the increase of corruption leads to non-existence, and we know that what is non-existent is nothing. Why then, I say, are you at a loss to tell regarding a corruptible nature, when you have both the words *nature* and *corruptible*, what is from God, and what from nothing? And why do you inquire for a nature contrary to God, since, if you confess that He is the supreme existence, it follows that non-existence is contrary to Him?[1]

CHAP. 41.—CORRUPTION IS BY GOD'S PERMISSION, AND COMES FROM US.

47. You ask, Why does corruption take from nature what God has given to it? It takes nothing but where God permits; and He permits in righteous and well-ordered judgment, according to the degrees of non-intelligent and the deserts of intelligent creatures. The word uttered passes away as an object of sense, and perishes in silence; and yet the coming and going of these passing words make our speech, and the regular intervals of silence give pleasing and appropriate distinction; and so it is with temporal natures which have this lowest form of beauty, that transition gives them being, and the death of what they give birth to gives them individuality. And if our sense and memory could rightly take in the order and proportions of this beauty, it would so please us, that we should not dare to give the name of corruptions to those imperfections which give rise to the distinction. And when distress comes to us through their peculiar beauty, by the loss of beloved temporal things passing away, we both pay the penalty of our sins, and are exhorted to set our affection on eternal things.

CHAP. 42.—EXHORTATION TO THE CHIEF GOOD.

48. Let us, then, not seek in this beauty for what has not been given to it (and from not having what we seek for, this is the lowest form of beauty); and in that which has been given to it, let us praise God, because He has bestowed this great good of visible form even on the lowest degree of beauty. And let us not cleave as lovers to this beauty, but as praisers of God let us rise above it; and from this superior position let us pronounce judgment on it, instead of so being bound up in it as to be judged along with it. And let us hasten on to that good which has no motion in space or advancement in time, from which all natures in space and time receive their sensible being and their form. To see this good let us purify our heart by faith in our Lord Jesus Christ, who says, "Blessed are the pure in heart, for they shall see God."[2] For the eyes needed in order to see this good are not those with which we see the light spread through space, which has part in one place and part in another, instead of being all in every place. The sight and the discernment we are to purify is that by which we see, as far as is allowed in this life, what is just, what is pious, what is the beauty of wisdom. He who sees these things, values them far above the fullness of all regions in space, and finds that the vision of these things requires not the extension of his perception through distances in space, but its invigoration by an immaterial influence.[3]

CHAP. 43.—CONCLUSION.

49. And as this vision is greatly hindered by those fancies which are originated by the carnal sense, and are retained and modified by the imagination, let us abhor this heresy which has been led by faith in its fancies to represent the divine substance as extended and diffused through space, even through infinite space, and to cut short one side so as to make room for evil,—not being able to perceive that evil is not nature, but against nature; and to beautify this very evil with such visible appearance, and forms, and consistency of parts prevailing in its several natures, not being able to conceive of any nature without those good things, that the evils found fault with in it are buried under a countless abundance of good things.

Here let us close this part of the treatise. The other absurdities of Manichæus will be exposed in what follows, by the permission and help of God.[4]

---

1 [We have already encountered in the treatise *Concerning two Souls*, substantially the same course of argumentation here pursued. The doctrine of the negativity of evil may be said to have been fundamental with Augustin, and he uses it very effectually against Manichæan dualism.—A. H. N.]

2 Matt. v. 8.

3 [The Neo-Platonic quality of this section cannot escape the attention of the philosophical student.—A. H. N.]

4 *Vide* Preface.

ST. AUGUSTIN:

REPLY TO

FAUSTUS THE MANICHÆAN.

[CONTRA FAUSTUM MANICHÆUM].

A.D. 400.

TRANSLATED BY

REV. RICHARD STOTHERT, M.A.,

BOMBAY.

CONTENTS OF REPLY TO FAUSTUS THE MANICHÆAN.

REPLY TO FAUSTUS THE MANICHÆAN.

[CONTRA FAUSTUM MANICHÆUM.] A.D. 400.

Written about the year 400. [Faustus was undoubtedly the acutest, most determined and most unscrupulous opponent of orthodox Christianity in the age of Augustin. The occasion of Augustin's great writing against him was the publication of Faustus' attack on the Old Testament Scriptures, and on the New Testament so far as it was at variance with Manichæan error. Faustus seems to have followed in the footsteps of Adimantus, against whom Augustin had written some years before, but to have gone considerably beyond Adimantus in the recklessness of his statements. The incarnation of Christ, involving his birth from a woman, is one of the main points of attack. He makes the variations in the genealogical records of the Gospels a ground for rejecting the whole as spurious. He supposed the Gospels, in their present form, to be not the works of the Apostles, but rather of later Judaizing falsifiers. The entire Old Testament system he treats with the utmost contempt, blaspheming the Patriarchs, Moses, the Prophets, etc., on the ground of their private lives and their teachings. Most of the objections to the morality of the Old Testament that are now current were already familiarly used in the time of Augustin. Augustin's answers are only partially satisfactory, owing to his imperfect view of the relation of the old dispensation to the new; but in the age in which they were written they were doubtless very effective. The writing is interesting from the point of view of Biblical criticism, as well as from that of polemics against Manichæism.—A. H. N.]

BOOK I.

WHO FAUSTUS WAS. FAUSTUS'S OBJECT IN WRITING THE POLEMICAL TREATISE THAT FORMS THE BASIS OF AUGUSTIN'S REPLY. AUGUSTIN'S REMARKS THEREON

1. FAUSTUS was an African by race, a citizen of Mileum; he was eloquent and clever, but had adopted the shocking tenets of the Manichæan heresy. He is mentioned in my *Confessions*,[1] where there is an account of my acquaintance with him. This man published a certain volume against the true Christian faith and the Catholic truth. A copy reached us, and was read by the brethren, who called for an answer from me, as part of the service of love which I owe to them. Now, therefore, in the name and with the help of our Lord and Saviour Jesus Christ, I undertake the task, that all my readers may know that acuteness of mind and elegance of style are of no use to a man unless the Lord directs his steps.[3] In the mysterious equity of divine mercy, God often bestows His help on the slow and the feeble; while from the want of this help, the most acute and eloquent run into error only

---

[1] *Confessions*, v. 3, 6.

[2] Ps. xxxvii. 23.

with greater rapidity and willfulness. I will give the opinions of Faustus as if stated by himself, and mine as if in reply to him.

2. Faustus said: As the learned Adimantus, the only teacher since the sainted Manichæus deserving of our attention, has plentifully exposed and thoroughly refuted the errors of Judaism and of semi-Christianity, I think it not amiss that you should be supplied in writing with brief and pointed replies to the captious objections of our adversaries, that when, like children of the wily serpent, they try to bewilder you with their quibbles, you may be prepared to give intelligent answers. In this way they will be kept to the subject, instead of wandering from one thing to another. And I have placed our opinions and those of our opponent over against one another, as plainly and briefly as possible, so as not to perplex the reader with a long and intricate discourse.

3. Augustin replies: You warn against semi-Christians, which you say we are; but we warn against pseudo-Christians, which we have shown you to be. Semi-Christianity may be imperfect without being false. So, then, if the faith of those whom you try to mislead is imperfect, would it not be better to supply what is lacking than to rob them of what they have? It was to imperfect Christians that the apostle wrote, "joying and beholding your conversation," and "the deficiency in your faith in Christ."[1] The apostle had in view a spiritual structure, as he says elsewhere, "Ye are God's building;"[2] and in this structure he found both a reason for joy and a reason for exertion. He rejoiced to see part already finished; and the necessity of bringing the edifice to perfection called for exertion. Imperfect Christians as we are, you pursue us with the desire to pervert what you call our semi-Christianity by false doctrine; while even those who are so deficient in faith as to be unable to reply to all your sophisms, are wise enough at least to know that they must not have anything at all to do with you. You look for semi-Christians to deceive: we wish to prove you pseudo-Christians, that Christians may learn something from your refutation, and that the less advanced may learn to avoid you. Do you call us children of the serpent? You have surely forgotten how often you have found fault with the prohibition in Paradise, and have praised the serpent for opening Adam's eyes. You have the better claim to the title which you give us. The serpent owns you as well when you blame him as when you praise him.

[1] Col. ii. 5; cf. 1 Thess. iii. 10.

[2] 1 Cor. iii. 9.

BOOK II.

FAUSTUS CLAIMS TO BELIEVE THE GOSPEL, YET REFUSES TO ACCEPT THE GENEALOGICAL TABLES ON VARIOUS GROUNDS WHICH AUGUSTIN SEEKS TO SET ASIDE.

1. Faustus said: Do I believe the gospel? Certainly. Do I therefore believe that Christ was born? Certainly not. It does not follow that because I believe the gospel, as I do, I must therefore believe that Christ was born. This I do not believe; because Christ does not say that He was born of men, and the gospel, both in name and in fact, begins with Christ's preaching. As for the genealogy, the author himself does not venture to call it the gospel. For what did he write? "The book of the generation of Jesus Christ the Son of David."[1] The book of the generation is not the book of the gospel. It is more like a birth-register, the star confirming the event. Mark, on the other hand, who recorded the preaching of the Son of God, without any genealogy, begins most suitably with the words, "The gospel of Jesus Christ the Son of God." It is plain that the genealogy is not the gospel. Matthew himself says, that after John was put in prison, Jesus began to preach the gospel of the kingdom; so that what is mentioned before this is the genealogy, and not the gospel. Why did not Matthew begin with, "The gospel of Jesus Christ the Son of God," but because he thought it sinful to call the genealogy the gospel? Understand, then, what you have hitherto overlooked—the distinction between the genealogy and the gospel. Do I then admit the truth of the gospel? Yes; understanding by the gospel the preaching of Christ. I have plenty to say about the generations too, if you wish. But you seem to me now to wish to know not whether I accept the gospel, but whether I accept the generations.

2. Augustin replied: Well, in answer to your

[1] Matt. i. 1.

own questions, you tell us first that you believe the gospel, and next, that you do not believe in the birth of Christ; and your reason is, that the birth of Christ is not in the gospel. What, then, will you answer the apostle when he says, "Remember that Christ Jesus rose from the dead, of the seed of David, according to my gospel?"[1] You surely are ignorant, or pretend to be ignorant, what the gospel is. You use the word, not as the apostle teaches, but as suits your own errors. What the apostles call the gospel you depart from; for you do not believe that Christ was of the seed of David. This was Paul's gospel; and it was also the gospel of the other apostles, and of all faithful stewards of so great a mystery. For Paul says elsewhere, "Whether, therefore, I or they, so we preach, and so ye believed."[2] They did not all write the gospel, but they all preached it. The name evangelist is properly given to the narrators of the birth, the actions, the words, the sufferings of our Lord Jesus Christ. The word gospel means good news, and might be used of any good news, but is properly applied to the narrative of the Saviour. If, then, you teach something different, you must have departed from the gospel. Assuredly those babes whom you despise as semi-Christians will oppose you, when they hear their mother Charity declaring by the mouth of the apostle, "If any one preach another gospel than that which we have preached to you, let him be accursed."[3] Since, then, Paul, according to his gospel, preached that Christ was of the seed of David, and you deny this and preach something else, may you be accursed! And what can you mean by saying that Christ never declares Himself to have been born of men, when on every occasion He calls Himself the Son of man?

3. You learned men, forsooth, dress up for our benefit some wonderful First Man, who came down from the race of light to war with the race of darkness, armed with his waters against the waters of the enemy, and with his fire against their fire, and with his winds against their winds. And why not with his smoke against their smoke, and with his darkness against their darkness? According to you, he was armed against smoke with air, and against darkness with light. So it appears that smoke and darkness are bad, since they could not belong to his goodness. The other three, again—water, wind, and fire—are good. How, then, could these belong to the evil of the enemy? You reply that the water of the race of darkness was evil, while that which the First Man brought was good; and so, too, his good wind and fire fought against the evil wind and fire of the adversary. But why could he not bring good smoke against evil smoke? Your falsehoods seem to vanish in smoke. Well, your First Man warred against an opposite nature. And yet only one of the five things he brought was the opposite of what the hostile race had. The light was opposed to the darkness, but the four others are not opposed to one another. Air is not the opposite of smoke, and still less is water the opposite of water, or wind of wind, or fire of fire.

4. One is shocked at your wild fancies about this First Man changing the elements which he brought, that he might conquer his enemies by pleasing them. So you make what you call the kingdom of falsehood keep honestly to its own nature, while truth is changeable in order to deceive. Jesus Christ, according to you, is the son of this First Man. Truth springs, forsooth, from your fiction. You praise this First Man for using changeable and delusive forms in the contest. If you, then, speak the truth, you do not imitate him. If you imitate him, you deceive as he did. But our Lord and Saviour Jesus Christ, the true and truthful Son of God, the true and truthful Son of man, both of which He testifies of Himself, derived the eternity of His godhead from true God, and His incarnation from true man. Your First Man is not the first man of the apostle. "The first man," he says, "was of the earth, earthy; the second man is from heaven, heavenly. As is the earthy, such are they also that are earthy; as is the heavenly, such are they also that are heavenly. As we have borne the image of the earthy, let us also bear the image of the heavenly."[4] The first man of the earth, earthy, is Adam, who was made of dust. The second man from heaven, heavenly, is the Lord Jesus Christ; for, being the Son of God, He became flesh that He might be a man outwardly, while He remained God within; that He might be both the true Son of God, by whom we were made, and the true Son of man, by whom we are made anew. Why do you conjure up this fabulous First Man of yours, and refuse to acknowledge the first man of the apostle? Is this not a fulfillment of what the apostle says: "Turning away their ears from the truth, they will give heed to fables?"[5] According to Paul, the first man is of the earth, earthy; according to Manichæus, he is not earthy, and is equipped with five elements of some unreal, unintelligible kind. Paul says: "If any one should

[1] 2 Tim. ii. 8.
[2] 1 Cor. xv. 11.
[3] Gal. i. 8, 9.
[4] 1 Cor. xv. 47-49.
[5] 2 Tim. iv. 4.

have announced to you differently from what we have announced let him be accursed." Therefore lest Paul be a liar, let Manichæus be accursed.

5. Again, you find fault with the star by which the Magi were led to worship the infant Christ, which you should be ashamed of doing, when you represent your fabulous Christ, the son of your fabulous First Man, not as announced by a star, but as bound up in all the stars.[1] For you say that he mingled with the principles of darkness in his conflict with the race of darkness, that by capturing these principles the world might be made out of the mixture. So that, by your profane fancies, Christ is not only mingled with heaven and all the stars, but conjoined and compounded with the earth and all its productions,[2]—a Saviour no more, but needing to be saved by you, by your eating and disgorging Him.

This foolish custom of making your disciples bring you food, that your teeth and stomach may be the means of relieving Christ, who is bound up in it, is a consequence of your profane fancies. You declare that Christ is liberated in this way—not, however, entirely; for you hold that some tiny particles of no value still remain in the excrement, to be mixed up and compounded again and again in various material forms, and to be released and purified at any rate by the fire in which the world will be burned up, if not before. Nay, even then, you say, Christ is not entirely liberated; but some extreme particles of His good and divine nature, which have been so defiled that they cannot be cleansed, are condemned to stay for ever in the horrid mass of darkness. And these people pretend to be offended with our saying that a star announced the birth of the Son of God, as if this were placing His birth under the influence of a constellation; while they subject Him not to stars only, but to such polluting contact with all material things, with the juices of all vegetables, and with the decay of all flesh, and with the decomposition of all food, in which He is bound up, that the only way of releasing Him, at least one great means, is that men, that is the Elect of the Manichæans, should succeed in digesting their dinner.

We, too, deny the influence of the stars upon the birth of any man; for we maintain that, by the just law of God, the free-will of man, which chooses good or evil, is under no constraint of necessity. How much less do we subject to any constellation the incarnation of the eternal Creator and Lord of all! When Christ was born after the flesh, the star which the Magi saw had no power as governing, but attended as a witness. Instead of assuming control over Him, it acknowledged Him by the homage it did. Besides, this star was not one of those which from the beginning of the world continue in the course ordained by the Creator. Along with the new birth from the Virgin appeared a new star, which served as a guide to the Magi who were themselves seeking for Christ; for it went before them till they reached the place where they found the Word of God in the form of a child. But what astrologer ever thought of making a star leave its course, and come down to the child that is born, as they imagine, under it? They think that the stars affect the birth, not that the birth changes the course of the stars; so, if the star in the Gospel was one of those heavenly bodies, how could it determine Christ's action, when it was compelled to change its own action at Christ's birth? But if, as is more likely, a star which did not exist before appeared to point out Christ, it was the effect of Christ's birth, and not the cause of it. Christ was not born because the star was there; but the star was there because Christ was born. If there was any fate, it was in the birth, and not in the star. The word fate is derived from a word which means to speak; and since Christ is the Word of God by which all things were spoken before they were, the conjunction of stars is not the fate of Christ, but Christ is the fate of the stars. The same will that made the heavens took our earthly nature. The same power that ruled the stars laid down His life and took it again.

6. Why, then, should the narrative of the birth not be the gospel, since it conveys such good news as heals our malady? Is it because Matthew begins, not like Mark, with the words, "The beginning of the gospel of Jesus Christ," but, "The book of the generation of Jesus Christ?" In this way, John, too, might be said not to have written the gospel, for he has not the words, Beginning of the gospel, or Book of the gospel, but, "In the beginning was the Word." Perhaps the clever word-maker Faustus will call the introduction in John a *Verbidium*, as he called that in Matthew a *Genesidium*. The wonder is, that you are so impudent as to give the name of gospel to your silly stories. What good

[1] [This mixture of the substance of Primordial Man, with the kingdom of darkness, and the formation of stars out of portions thereof, was probably a part of primitive Manichæan teaching.—A. H. N.]

[2] [Compare Book xx. 2, where Faustus states the Manichæan doctrine of the *Jesus patabilis*. Beausobre, Mosheim and Baur agree in thinking that Augustin has not distinguished accurately in these two passages between names *Christ* and *Jesus*, as used by the Manichæans. See Baur: *Das Manichäische Religionssystem*, p. 72.—A. H. N.]

news is there in telling us that, in the conflict against some strange hostile nation, God could protect His own kingdom only by sending part of His own nature into the greedy jaws of the former, and to be so defiled, that after all those toils and tortures it cannot all be purged? Is this bad news the gospel? Every one who has even a slender knowledge of Greek knows that gospel means good news. But where is your good news, when your God himself is said to weep as under eclipse till the darkness and defilement are removed from his members? And when he ceases to weep, it seems he becomes cruel. For what has that part of him which is to be involved in the mass done to deserve this condemnation? This part must go on weeping for ever. But no; whoever examines this news will not weep because it is bad, but will laugh because it is not true.

BOOK III.

FAUSTUS OBJECTS TO THE INCARNATION OF GOD ON THE GROUND THAT THE EVANGELISTS ARE AT VARIANCE WITH EACH OTHER, AND THAT INCARNATION IS UNSUITABLE TO DEITY. AUGUSTIN ATTEMPTS TO REMOVE THE CRITICAL AND THEOLOGICAL DIFFICULTIES.

1. FAUSTUS said: Do I believe in the incarnation? For my part, this is the very thing I long tried to persuade myself of, that God was born; but the discrepancy in the genealogies of Luke and Matthew stumbled me, as I knew not which to follow. For I thought it might happen that, from not being omniscient, I might take the true for false, and the false for true. So, in despair of settling this dispute, I betook myself to Mark and John, two authorities still, and evangelists as much as the others. I approved with good reason of the beginning of Mark and John, for they have nothing of David, or Mary, or Joseph. John says, "In the beginning was the Word, and the Word was with God, and the Word was God," meaning Christ. Mark says, "The gospel of Jesus Christ, the Son of God," as if correcting Matthew, who calls him the Son of David. Perhaps, however, the Jesus of Matthew is a different person from the Jesus of Mark. This is my reason for not believing in the birth of Christ. Remove this difficulty, if you can, by harmonizing the accounts, and I am ready to yield. In any case, however, it is hardly consistent to believe that God, the God of Christians, was born from the womb.

2. AUGUSTIN replied: Had you read the Gospel with care, and inquired into those places where you found opposition, instead of rashly condemning them, you would have seen that the recognition of the authority of the evangelists by so many learned men all over the world, in spite of this most obvious discrepancy, proves that there is more in it than appears at first sight. Any one can see, as well as you, that the ancestors of Christ in Matthew and Luke are different; while Joseph appears in both, at the end in Matthew and at the beginning in Luke. Joseph, it is plain, might be called the father of Christ, on account of his being in a certain sense the husband of the mother of Christ; and so his name, as the male representative, appears at the beginning or end of the genealogies. Any one can see as well as you that Joseph has one father in Matthew and another in Luke, and so with the grandfather and with all the rest up to David. Did all the able and learned men, not many Latin writers certainly, but innumerable Greek, who have examined most attentively the sacred Scriptures, overlook this manifest difference? Of course they saw it. No one can help seeing it. But with a due regard to the high authority of Scripture, they believed that there was something here which would be given to those that ask, and denied to those that snarl; would be found by those that seek, and taken away from those that criticise; would be open to those that knock, and shut against those that contradict. They asked, sought, and knocked; they received, found, and entered in.

3. The whole question is how Joseph had two fathers. Supposing this possible, both genealogies may be correct. With two fathers, why not two grandfathers, and two great-grandfathers, and so on, up to David, who was the father both of Solomon, who is mentioned in Matthew's list, and of Nathan, who occurs in Luke? This is the difficulty with many people who think it impossible that two men should have one and the same son, forgetting the very obvious fact that a man may be called the son of the person who adopted him as well as of the person who begot him.

Adoption, we know, was familiar to the ancients, for even women adopted the children of other women, as Sarah adopted Ishmael, and Leah her handmaid's son, and Pharaoh's daughter Moses. Jacob, too, adopted his grandsons, the children of Joseph. Moreover, the word adoption is of great importance in the system of our faith, as is seen from the apostolic writings. For the Apostle Paul, speaking of the advantages of the Jews, says: "Whose are the adoption, and the glory, and the covenants, and the giving of the law; whose are the fathers, and of whom, according to the flesh, Christ came, who is over all, God blessed for ever."[1] And again: "We ourselves also groan within ourselves, waiting for the adoption of the sons of God, even the redemption of the body."[2] Again, elsewhere: "But in the fullness of time, God sent His Son, made of a woman, made under the law, that we might receive the adoption of sons."[3] These passages show clearly that adoption is a significant symbol. God has an only Son, whom He begot from His own substance, of whom it is said, "Being in the form of God, He thought it not robbery to be equal to God."[4] Us He begot not of His own substance, for we belong to the creation which is not begotten, but made; but that He might make us the brothers of Christ, He adopted us. That act, then, by which God, when we were not born of Him, but created and formed, begot us by His word and grace, is called adoption. So John says, "He gave them power to become the sons of God."[5]

Since, therefore, the practice of adoption is common among our fathers, and in Scripture, is there not irrational profanity in the hasty condemnation of the evangelists as false because the genealogies are different, as if both could not be true, instead of considering calmly the simple fact that frequently in human life one man may have two fathers, one of whose flesh he is born, and another of whose will he is afterwards made a son by adoption? If the second is not rightly called father, neither are we right in saying, "Our Father which art in heaven," to Him of whose substance we were not born, but of whose grace and most merciful will we were adopted, according to apostolic doctrine, and truth most sure. For one is to us God, and Lord, and Father: God, for by Him we are created, though of human parents; Lord, for we are His subjects; Father, for by His adoption we are born again. Careful students of sacred Scripture easily saw, from a little consideration, how, in the different genealogies of the two evangelists, Joseph had two fathers, and consequently two lists of ancestors. You might have seen this too, if you had not been blinded by the love of contradiction. Other things far beyond your understanding have been discovered in the careful investigation of all parts of these narratives. The familiar occurrence of one man begetting a son and another adopting him, so that one man has two fathers, you might, in spite of Manichæan error, have thought of as an explanation, if you had not been reading in a hostile spirit.

4. But why Matthew begins with Abraham and descends to Joseph, while Luke begins with Joseph and ascends, not to Abraham, but to God, who made man, and, by giving a commandment, gave him power to become, by believing, a son of God; and why Matthew records the generations at the commencement of his book, Luke after the baptism of the Saviour by John; and what is the meaning of the number of the generations in Matthew, who divides them into three sections of fourteen each, though in the whole sum there appears to be one wanting; while in Luke the number of generations recorded after the baptism amount to seventy-seven, which number the Lord Himself enjoins in connection with the forgiveness of sins, saying, "Not only seven times, but seventy-seven times;"—these things you will never understand, unless either you are taught by some Catholic of superior stamp, who has studied the sacred Scriptures, and has made all the progress possible, or you yourselves turn from your error, and in a Christian spirit ask that you may receive, seek that you may find, and knock that it may be opened to you.

5. Since, then, this double fatherhood of nature and adoption removes the difficulty arising from the discrepancy of the genealogies, there is no occasion for Faustus to leave the two evangelists and betake himself to the other two, which would be a greater affront to those he betook himself to than to those he left. For the sacred writers do not desire to be favored at the expense of their brethren. For their joy is in union, and they are one in Christ; and if one says one thing, and another another, or one in one way and another in another, still they all speak truth, and in no way contradict one another; only let the reader be reverent and humble, not in an heretical spirit seeking occasion for strife, but with a believing heart desiring edification. Now, in this opinion that the evangelists give the ancestors of different fathers, as it is quite possible for a man to have two fathers, there is nothing inconsistent with truth. So the evangelists are harmonized, and you, by Faustus's promise are bound to yield at once.

1 Rom. ix. 4, 5. 2 Rom. viii. 23. 3 Gal. iv. 4, 5. 4 Phil. ii. 6. 5 John i. 12.

6. You may perhaps be troubled by that additional remark which he makes: "In any case, however, it is hardly consistent to believe that God, the God of Christians, was born from the womb." As if we believed that the divine nature came from the womb of a woman. Have I not just quoted the testimony of the apostle, speaking of the Jews: "Whose are the fathers, and of whom, according to the flesh, Christ came, who is God over all, blessed for ever?" Christ, therefore, our Lord and Saviour, true Son of God in His divinity, and true son of man according to the flesh, not as He is God over all was born of a woman, but in that feeble nature which He took of us, that in it He might die for us, and heal it in us: not as in the form of God, in which He thought it not robbery to be equal to God, was He born of a woman, but in the form of a servant, in taking which He emptied Himself. He is therefore said to have emptied Himself because He took the form of a servant, not because He lost the form of God. For in the unchangeable possession of that nature by which in the form of God He is equal to the Father, He took our changeable nature, by which He might be born of a virgin. You, while you protest against putting the flesh of Christ in a virgin's womb, place the very divinity of God in the womb not only of human beings, but of dogs and swine. You refuse to believe that the flesh of Christ was conceived in the Virgin's womb, in which God was not found nor even changed; while you assert that in all men and beasts, in the seed of male and in the womb of female, in all conceptions on land or in water, an actual part of God and the divine nature is continually bound, and shut up, and contaminated, never to be wholly set free.[1]

[1] [It cannot be said that Augustin adequately meets the difficulty that Faustus finds in the genealogies of our Lord. Cf. HERVEY: *The Genealogies of Our Lord*, and the recent commentaries, such as Meyer's, Lange's, The International Revision, and especially Broadus on *Matthew*.—A.H.N.]

BOOK IV.

FAUSTUS'S REASONS FOR REJECTING THE OLD TESTAMENT, AND AUGUSTIN'S ANIMADVERSIONS THEREON.

1. FAUSTUS said: Do I believe the Old Testament? If it bequeaths anything to me, I believe it; if not, I reject it. It would be an excess of forwardness to take the documents of others which pronounce me disinherited. Remember that the promise of Canaan in the Old Testament is made to Jews, that is, to the circumcised, who offer sacrifice, and abstain from swine's flesh, and from the other animals which Moses pronounces unclean, and observe Sabbaths, and the feast of unleavened bread, and other things of the same kind which the author of the Testament enjoined. Christians have not adopted these observances, and no one keeps them; so that if we will not take the inheritance, we should surrender the documents. This is my first reason for rejecting the Old Testament, unless you teach me better. My second reason is, that this inheritance is such a poor fleshly thing, without any spiritual blessings, that after the New Testament, and its glorious promise of the kingdom of heaven and eternal life, I think it not worth the taking.

2. AUGUSTIN replied: No one doubts that promises of temporal things are contained in the Old Testament, for which reason it is called the Old Testament; or that the kingdom of heaven and the promise of eternal life belong to the New Testament. But that in these temporal things were figures of future things which should be fulfilled in us upon whom the ends of the ages are come, is not my fancy, but the judgment of the apostle, when he says of such things, "These things were our examples;" and again, "These things happened to them for an example, and they are written for us on whom the ends of the ages are come."[1] We receive the Old Testament, therefore, not in order to obtain the fulfillment of these promises, but to see in them predictions of the New Testament; for the Old bears witness to the New. Whence the Lord, after He rose from the dead, and allowed His disciples not only to see but to handle Him, still, lest they should doubt their mortal and fleshly senses, gave them further confirmation from the testimony of the ancient books, saying, "It was necessary that all things should be fulfilled which were written in the law of Moses, and in the Prophets and Psalms, concerning me."[2] Our hope, therefore, rests not on the promise of temporal

[1] 1 Cor. x. 6, 11.
[2] Luke xxiv. 44.

things. Nor do we believe that the holy and spiritual men of these times—the patriarchs and prophets—were taken up with earthly things. For they understood, by the revelation of the Spirit of God, what was suitable for that time, and how God appointed all these sayings and actions as types and predictions of the future. Their great desire was for the New Testament; but they had a personal duty to perform in those predictions, by which the new things of the future were foretold. So the life as well as the tongue of these men was prophetic. The carnal people, indeed, thought only of present blessings, though even in connection with the people there were prophecies of the future.

These things you do not understand, because, as the prophet said, "Unless you believe, you shall not understand."[1] For you are not instructed in the kingdom of heaven,—that is, in the true Catholic Church of Christ. If you were, you would bring forth from the treasure of the sacred Scriptures things old as well as new. For the Lord Himself says, "Therefore every scribe instructed in the kingdom of heaven is like an householder who brings forth from his treasure things new and old."[2] And so, while you profess to receive only the new promises of God, you have retained the oldness of the flesh, adding only the novelty of error; of which novelty the apostle says, "Shun profane novelties of words, for they increase unto more ungodliness, and their speech eats like a cancer. Of whom is Hymenæus and Philetus, who concerning the faith have erred, saying that the resurrection is past already, and have overthrown the faith of some."[3] Here you see the source of your false doctrine, in teaching that the resurrection is only of souls by the preaching of the truth, and that there will be no resurrection of the body. But how can you understand spiritual things of the inner man, who is renewed in the knowledge of God, when in the oldness of the flesh, if you do not possess temporal things, you concoct fanciful notions about them in those images of carnal things of which the whole of your false doctrine consists? You boast of despising as worthless the land of Canaan, which was an actual thing, and actually given to the Jews; and yet you tell of a land of light cut asunder on one side, as by a narrow wedge, by the land of the race of darkness,—a thing which does not exist, and which you believe from the delusion of your minds; so that your life is not supported by having it, and your mind is wasted in desiring it.[4]

1 Isa. vii. 9.

2 Matt. xiii. 52.

3 2 Tim. ii. 16-18.

4 [A good *argumentum ad hominem*, a species of argument which Augustin is fond of using.—A. H. N.]

BOOK V.

FAUSTUS CLAIMS THAT THE MANICHÆANS AND NOT THE CATHOLICS ARE CONSISTENT BELIEVERS IN THE GOSPEL, AND SEEKS TO ESTABLISH THIS CLAIM BY COMPARING MANICHÆAN AND CATHOLIC OBEDIENCE TO THE PRECEPTS OF THE GOSPEL. AUGUSTIN EXPOSES THE HYPOCRISY OF THE MANICHÆANS AND PRAISES THE ASCETICISM OF CATHOLICS.

1. Faustus said: Do I believe the gospel? You ask me if I believe it, though my obedience to its commands shows that I do. I should rather ask you if you believe it, since you give no proof of your belief. I have left my father, mother, wife, and children, and all else that the gospel requires;[1] and do you ask if I believe the gospel? Perhaps you do not know what is called the gospel. The gospel is nothing else than the preaching and the precept of Christ. I have parted with all gold and silver, and have left off carrying money in my purse; content with daily food; without anxiety for to-morrow; and without solicitude about how I shall be fed, or wherewithal I shall be clothed: and do you ask if I believe the gospel? You see in me the blessings of the gospel;[2] and do you ask if I believe the gospel? You see me poor, meek, a peacemaker, pure in heart, mourning, hungering, thirsting, bearing persecutions and enmity for righteousness' sake; and do you doubt my belief in the gospel? One can understand now how John the Baptist, after seeing Jesus, and also hearing of His works, yet asked whether He was Christ. Jesus properly and justly did not deign to reply that He was; but reminded him of the works of which he had already heard: "The blind see, the deaf hear, the dead are raised."[3]

1 Matt. xix. 29.

2 Matt. v. 3-11.

3 Matt. xi. 2-6.

In the same way, I might very well reply to your question whether I believe the gospel, by saying, I have left all, father, mother, wife, children, gold, silver, eating, drinking, luxuries, pleasures; take this as a sufficient answer to your questions, and believe that you will be blessed if you are not offended in me.[1]

2. But, according to you, to believe the gospel is not only to obey its commands, but also to believe in all that is written in it; and, first of all, that God was born. But neither is believing the gospel only to believe that Jesus was born, but also to do what He commands. So, if you say that I do not believe the gospel because I disbelieve the incarnation, much more do you not believe because you disregard the commandments. At any rate, we are on a par till these questions are settled. If your disregard of the precepts does not prevent you from professing faith in the gospel, why should my rejection of the genealogy prevent me? And if, as you say, to believe the gospel includes both faith in the genealogies and obedience to the precepts, why do you condemn me, since we both are imperfect? What one wants the other has. But if, as there can be no doubt, belief in the gospel consists solely in obedience to the commands of God, your sin is twofold. As the proverb says, the deserter accuses the soldier. But suppose, since you will have it so, that there are these two parts of perfect faith, one consisting in word, or the confession that Christ was born, the other in deed, or the observance of the precepts; it is plain that my part is hard and painful, yours light and easy. It is natural that the multitude should flock to you and away from me, for they know not that the kingdom of God is not in word, but in power. Why, then, do you blame me for taking the harder part, and leaving to you, as to a weak brother, the easy part? You have the idea that your part of faith, or confessing that Christ was born, has more power to save the soul than the other parts.

3. Let us then ask Christ Himself, and learn from His own mouth, what is the chief means of our salvation. Who shall enter, O Christ, into Thy kingdom? He that doeth the will of my Father in heaven,[2] is His reply; not, "He that confesses that I was born." And again, He says to His disciples, "Go, teach all nations, baptizing them in the name of the Father, and of the Son, and of the Holy Ghost, teaching them to observe all things which I have commanded you."[3] It is not, "teaching them that I was born," but, "to observe my commandments." Again, "Ye are my friends if ye do what I command you;"[4] not, "if you believe that I was born." Again, "If ye keep my commandments, ye shall abide in my love,"[5] and in many other places. Also in the sermon on the mount, when He taught, "Blessed are the poor, blessed are the meek, blessed are the peacemakers, blessed are the pure in heart, blessed are they that mourn, blessed are they that hunger, blessed are they that are persecuted for righteousness' sake,"[6] He nowhere says, "Blessed are they that confess that I was born." And in the separation of the sheep from the goats in the judgment, He says that He will say to them on the right hand, "I was hungry, and ye gave me meat; I was thirsty, and ye gave me drink,"[7] and so on; therefore "inherit the kingdom." Not, "Because ye believe that I was born, inherit the kingdom." Again, to the rich man seeking for eternal life, He says, "Go, sell all that thou hast, and follow me;"[8] not, "Believe that I was born, that you may have eternal life." You see, the kingdom, life, happiness, are everywhere promised to the part I have chosen of what you call the two parts of faith, and nowhere to your part. Show, if you can, a place where it is written that whoso confesses that Christ was born of a woman is blessed, or shall inherit the kingdom, or have eternal life. Even supposing, then, that there are two parts of faith, your part has no blessing. But what if we prove that your part is not a part of faith at all? It will follow that you are foolish, which indeed will be proved beyond a doubt. At present, it is enough to have shown that our part is crowned with the beatitudes. Besides, we have also a beatitude for a confession in words: for we confess that Jesus Christ is the Son of the living God; and Jesus declares with His own lips that this confession has a benediction, when He says to Peter, "Blessed art thou, Simon Barjona; for flesh and blood hath not revealed this unto thee, but my Father which is in heaven."[9] So that we have not one, but both these parts of faith, and in both alike are we pronounced blessed by Christ; for in one we reduce faith to practice, while in the other our confession is unmixed with blasphemy.

4. Augustin replied: I have already said that the Lord Jesus Christ repeatedly calls Himself the Son of man, and that the Manichæans have contrived a silly story about some fabulous First Man, who figures in their impious heresy, not earthly, but combined

[1] [This is a good description of ideal Manichæan religious life. Whether Faustus lived up to the claims here set forth is another question.—A. H. N.]
[2] Matt. vii. 21.
[3] Matt. xxviii. 19, 20.
[4] John xv. 14.
[5] John xv. 10.
[6] Matt. v. 3-10.
[7] Matt. xxv. 35.
[8] Matt. xix. 21.
[9] Matt. xvi. 7.

with spurious elements, in opposition to the apostle, who says, "The first man is of the earth, earthy;"[1] and that the apostle carefully warns us, "If any one preaches to you differently from what we have preached, let him be accursed."[2] So that we must believe Christ to be the Son of man according to apostolic truth, not according to Manichæan error. And since the evangelists assert that Christ was born of a woman, of the seed of David, and Paul writing to Timothy says, "Remember that Jesus Christ, of the seed of David, was raised from the dead, according to my gospel,"[3] it is clear in what sense we must believe Christ to be the Son of man; for being the Son of God by whom we were made, He also by His incarnation became the Son of man, that He might die for our sins, and rise again for our justification.[4] Accordingly He calls Himself both Son of God and Son of man. To take only one instance out of many, in the Gospel of John it is written, "Verily, verily, I say unto you, The hour cometh, and now is, when the dead shall hear the voice of the Son of God; and they that hear shall live. For as the Father hath life in Himself, so He hath given to the Son to have life in Himself; and hath given Him power to execute judgment also, because He is the Son of man."[5] He says, "They shall hear the voice of the Son of God;" and He says, "because He is the Son of man." As the Son of man, He has received power to execute judgment, because He will come to judgment in human form, that He may be seen by the good and the wicked. In this form He ascended into heaven, and that voice was heard by His disciples, "He shall so come as ye have seen Him go into heaven."[6] As the Son of God, as God equal to and one with the Father, He will not be seen by the wicked; for "blessed are the pure in heart, for they shall see God." Since, then, He promises eternal life to those that believe in Him, and since to believe in Him is to believe in the true Christ, such as He declares Himself and His apostles declare Him to be, true Son of God and true Son of man; you, Manichæans, who believe on a false and spurious son of a false and spurious man, and teach that God Himself, from fear of the assault of the hostile race, gave up His own members to be tortured, and after all not to be wholly liberated, are plainly far from that eternal life which Christ promises to those who believe in Him. It is true, He said to Peter when he confessed Him to be the Son of God, "Blessed art thou, Simon Barjona." But does He promise nothing to those who believe Him to be the Son of man, when the Son of God and the Son of man are the same? Besides, eternal life is expressly promised to those who believe in the Son of man. "As Moses," He says, "lifted up the serpent in the wilderness, so must the Son of man be lifted up, that whosoever believeth in Him should not perish, but have eternal life."[7] What more do you wish? Believe then in the Son of man, that you may have eternal life; for He is also the Son of God, who can give eternal life: for He is "the true God and eternal life," as the same John says in his epistle. John also adds, that he is antichrist who denies that Christ has come in the flesh.[8]

5. There is no need, then, that you should extol so much the perfection of Christ's commands, because you obey the precepts of the gospel. For the precepts, supposing you really to fulfill them, would not profit you without true faith. Do you not know that the apostle says, "If I distribute all my goods to the poor, and give my body to be burned, and have not charity, it profiteth me nothing?"[9] Why do you boast of having Christian poverty, when you are destitute of Christian charity? Robbers have a kind of charity to one another, arising from a mutual consciousness of guilt and crime; but this is not the charity commended by the apostle. In another passage he distinguishes true charity from all base and vicious affections, by saying, "Now the end of the commandment is charity out of a pure heart, and a good conscience, and faith unfeigned."[10] How then can you have true charity from a fictitious faith?[11] You persist in a faith corrupted by falsehood: for your First Man, according to you, used deceit in the conflict by changing his form, while his enemies remained in their own nature; and, besides, you maintain that Christ, who says, "I am the truth," feigned His incarnation, His death on the cross, the wounds of His passion, the marks shown after His resurrection. If you speak the truth, and your Christ speaks falsehood, you must be better than he. But if you really follow your own Christ, your truthfulness may be doubted, and your obedience to the precepts you speak of may be only a pretence. Is it true, as Faustus says, that you have no money in your purses? He means, probably, that your money is in boxes and bags; nor would we blame you for this, if you did not profess one thing and practise

1 1 Cor. xv. 47.
2 Gal. i. 8, 9.
3 2 Tim. ii. 8.
4 Rom. iv. 25.
5 John v. 25-27.
6 Acts. i. 14.
7 John iii. 14, 15.
8 1 John v. 20, iv. 3.
9 1 Cor. xiii. 3.
10 1 Tim. i. 5.
11 [Augustin confounds saving faith with orthodox doctrine, as has been too commonly done since.—A. H. N.]

another. Constantius, who is still alive, and is now our brother in Catholic Christianity, once gathered many of your sect into his house at Rome, to keep these precepts of Manichæus, which you think so much of, though they are very silly and childish. The precepts proved too much for your weakness, and the gathering was entirely broken up. Those who persevered separated from your communion, and are called Mattarians, because they sleep on mats,—a very different bed from the feathers of Faustus and his goatskin coverlets, and all the grandeur that made him despise not only the Mattarians, but also the house of his poor father in Mileum. Away, then, with this accursed hypocrisy from your writing, if not from your conduct; or else your language will conflict with your life by your deceitful words, as your First Man with the race of darkness by his deceitful elements.

6. I am, however, addressing not merely men who fail to do what they are commanded, but the members of a deluded sect. For the precepts of Manichæus are such that, if you do not keep them, you are deceivers; if you do keep them, you are deceived. Christ never taught you that you should not pluck a vegetable for fear of committing homicide; for when His disciples were hungry when passing through a field of corn, He did not forbid them to pluck the ears on the Sabbath-day; which was a rebuke to the Jews of the time, since the action was on Sabbath; and a rebuke in the action itself to the future Manichæans. The precept of Manichæus, however, only requires you to do nothing while others commit homicide for you; though the real homicide is that of ruining miserable souls by such doctrines of devils.

7. The language of Faustus has the typhus of heresy in it, and is the language of overweening arrogance. "You see in me," he says, "the beatitudes of the gospel; and do you ask if I believe the gospel? You see me poor, meek, a peacemaker, pure in heart, mourning, hungering, thirsting, bearing persecution and enmity for righteousness' sake; and do you doubt my belief in the gospel?" If to justify oneself were to be just, Faustus would have flown to heaven while uttering these words. I say nothing of the luxurious habits of Faustus, known to all the followers of the Manichæans, and especially to those at Rome. I shall suppose a Manichæan such as Constantius sought for, when he enforced the observance of these precepts with the sincere desire to see them observed. How can I see him to be poor in spirit, when he is so proud as to believe that his own soul is God, and is not ashamed to speak of God as in bondage? How can I see him meek, when he affronts all the authority of the evangelists rather than believe? How a peacemaker, when he holds that the divine nature itself by which God is whatever is, and is the only true existence, could not remain in lasting peace? How pure in heart, when his heart is filled with so many impious notions? How mourning, unless it is for his God captive and bound till he be freed and escape, with the loss, however, of a part which is to be united by the Father to the mass of darkness, and is not to be mourned for? How hungering and thirsting for righteousness, which Faustus omits in his writings lest, no doubt, he should be thought destitute of righteousness? But how can they hunger and thirst after righteousness, whose perfect righteousness will consist in exulting over their brethren condemned to darkness, not for any fault of their own, but for being irremediably contaminated by the pollution against which they were sent by the Father to contend?

8. How do you suffer persecution and enmity for righteousness' sake, when, according to you, it is righteous to preach and teach these impieties? The wonder is, that the gentleness of Christian times allows such perverse iniquity to pass wholly or almost unpunished. And yet, as if we were blind or silly, you tell us that your suffering reproach and persecution is a great proof of your righteousness. If people are just according to the amount of their suffering, atrocious criminals of all kinds suffer much more than you. But, at any rate, if we are to grant that suffering endured on account of any sort of profession of Christianity proves the sufferer to be in possession of true faith and righteousness, you must admit that any case of greater suffering that we can show proves the possession of truer faith and greater righteousness. Of such cases you know many among our martyrs, and chiefly Cyprian himself, whose writings also bear witness to his belief that Christ was born of the Virgin Mary. For this faith, which you abhor, he suffered and died along with many Christian believers of that day, who suffered as much, or more. Faustus, when shown to be a Manichæan by evidence, or by his own confession, on the intercession of the Christians themselves, who brought him before the proconsul, was, along with some others, only banished to an island, which can hardly be called a punishment at all, for it is what God's servants do of their own accord every day when they wish to retire from the tumult of the world. Besides, earthly sovereigns often by a public decree

give release from this banishment as an act of mercy. And in this way all were afterwards released at once. Confess, then, that they were in possession of a truer faith and a more righteous life, who were accounted worthy to suffer for it much more than you ever suffered. Or else, cease boasting of the abhorrence which many feel for you, and learn to distinguish between suffering for blasphemy and suffering for righteousness. What it is you suffer for, your own books will show in a way that deserves your most particular attention.

9. Those evangelical precepts of peculiar sublimity which you make people who know no better believe that you obey, are really obeyed by multitudes in our communion. Are there not among us many of both sexes who have entirely refrained from sexual intercourse, and many formerly married who practise continence? Are there not many others who give largely of their property, or give it up altogether, and many who keep the body in subjection by fasts, either frequent or daily, or protracted beyond belief? Then there are fraternities whose members have no property of their own, but all things common, including only things necessary for food and clothing, living with one soul and one heart towards God, inflamed with a common feeling of charity. In all such professions many turn out to be deceivers and reprobates, while many who are so are never discovered; many, too, who at first walk well, fall away rapidly from willfulness. Many are found in times of trial to have adopted this kind of life with another intention than they professed; and again, many in humility and steadfastness persevere in their course to the end, and are saved. There are apparent diversities in these societies; but one charity unites all who, from some necessity, in obedience to the apostle's injunction, have their wives as if they had them not, and buy as if they bought not, and use this world as if they used it not. With these are joined, in the abundant riches of God's mercy, the inferior class of those to whom it is said, "Defraud not one another, except it be with consent for a time, that ye may give yourselves to prayer; and come together again, that Satan tempt you not for your incontinency. But I speak this by permission, and not of commandment."[1] To such the same apostle also says, "Now therefore there is utterly a fault among you, that ye go to law one with another;" while, in consideration of their infirmity, he adds, "If ye have judgments of things pertaining to this life, set them to judge who are least esteemed in the Church."[2] For in the kingdom of heaven there are not only those who, that they may be perfect, sell or leave all they have and follow the Lord; but others in the partnership of charity are joined like a mercenary force to the Christian army, to whom it will be said at last, "I was hungry, and ye gave me meat," and so on. Otherwise, there would be no salvation for those to whom the apostle gives so many anxious and particular directions about their families, telling the wives to be obedient to their husbands, and husbands to love their wives; children to obey their parents, and parents to bring up their children in the instruction and admonition of the Lord; servants to obey with fear their masters according to the flesh, and masters to render to their servants what is just and equal. The apostle is far from condemning such people as regardless of gospel precepts, or unworthy of eternal life. For where the Lord exhorts the strong to attain perfection, saying, "If any man take not up his cross and follow me, he cannot be my disciple," He immediately adds, for the consolation of the weak, "Whoso receiveth a just man in the name of a just man shall receive a just man's reward; and whoso receiveth a prophet in the name of a prophet, shall receive a prophet's reward." So that not only he who gives Timothy a little wine for his stomach's sake, and his frequent infirmities, but he who gives to a strong man a cup of cold water only in the name of a disciple, shall not lose his reward.[3]

10. If it is true that a man cannot receive the gospel without giving up everything, why do you delude your followers, by allowing them to keep in your service their wives, and children, and households, and houses, and fields? Indeed, you may well allow them to disregard the precepts of the gospel: for all you promise them is not a resurrection, but a change to another mortal existence, in which they shall live the silly, childish, impious life of those you call the Elect, the life you live yourself, and are so much praised for; or if they possess greater merit, they shall enter into melons or cucumbers, or some eatables which you will masticate, that they may be quickly purified by your digestion. Least of all should you who teach such doctrines profess any regard for the gospel. For if the faith of the gospel had any connection with such nonsense, the Lord should have said, not, "I was hungry, and ye gave me meat;" but, "Ye were hungry, and ye ate me," or, "I was hungry, and I ate you."

[1] 1 Cor. vii. 5, 6.

[2] 1 Cor. vi. 7, 4.

[3] Matt. x. 38–42.

For, by your absurdities, a man will not be received into the kingdom of God for the service of giving food to the saints, but, because he has eaten them and belched them out, or has himself been eaten and belched into heaven. Instead of saying, "Lord, when saw we Thee hungry, and fed Thee?" the righteous must say, "When saw we Thee hungry, and were eaten by Thee?" And He must answer, not, "When ye gave food to one of the least of these my brethren, you gave to me;" but, "When you were eaten by one of the least of these my brethren, you were eaten by me."

11. Believing and teaching such monstrosities, and living accordingly, you yet have the boldness to say that you obey the precepts of the gospel, and to decry the Catholic Church, which includes many weak as well as strong, both of whom the Lord blesses, because both according to their measure obey the precepts of the gospel and hope in its promises. The blindness of hostility makes you see only the tares in our harvest: for you might easily see wheat too, if you were willing that there should be any. But among you, those who are pretended Manichæans are wicked, and those who are really Manichæans are silly. For where the faith itself is false, he who hypocritically professes it acts deceitfully, while he who truly believes is deceived. Such a faith cannot produce a good life, for every man's life is good or bad according as his heart is engaged. If your affections were set upon spiritual and intellectual good, instead of material forms, you would not pay homage to the material sun as a divine substance, and as the light of wisdom, which every one knows you do, though I now only mention it in passing.

BOOK VI.

FAUSTUS AVOWS HIS DISBELIEF IN THE OLD TESTAMENT AND HIS DISREGARD OF ITS PRECEPTS, AND ACCUSES CATHOLICS OF INCONSISTENCY IN NEGLECTING ITS ORDINANCES, WHILE CLAIMING TO ACCEPT IT AS AUTHORITATIVE. AUGUSTIN EXPLAINS THE CATHOLIC VIEW OF THE RELATION OF THE OLD TESTAMENT TO THE NEW.

1. FAUSTUS said: You ask if I believe the Old Testament. Of course not, for I do not keep its precepts. Neither, I imagine, do you. I reject circumcision as disgusting; and if I mistake not, so do you. I reject the observance of Sabbaths as superfluous: I suppose you do the same. I reject sacrifice as idolatry, as doubtless you also do. Swine's flesh is not the only flesh I abstain from; nor is it the only flesh you eat. I think all flesh unclean: you think none unclean. Both alike, in these opinions, throw over the Old Testament. We both look upon the weeks of unleavened bread and the feast of tabernacles as unnecessary and useless. Not to patch linen garments with purple; to count it adultery to make a garment of linen and wool; to call it sacrilege to yoke together an ox and an ass when necessary; not to appoint as priest a bald man, or a man with red hair, or any similar peculiarity, as being unclean in the sight of God, are things which we both despise and laugh at, and rank as of neither first nor second importance; and yet they are all precepts and judgments of the Old Testament. You cannot blame me for rejecting the Old Testament; for whether it is right or wrong to do so, you do it as much as I. As for the difference between your faith and mine, it is this, that while you choose to act deceitfully, and meanly to praise in words what in your heart you hate, I, not having learned the art of deception, frankly declare that I hate both these abominable precepts and their authors.

2. AUGUSTIN replied: How and for what purpose the Old Testament is received by the heirs of the New Testament has been already explained.[1] But as the remarks of Faustus were then about the promises of the Old Testament, and now he speaks of the precepts, I reply that he displays ignorance of the difference between moral and symbolical precepts. For example, "Thou shalt not covet" is a moral precept; "Thou shalt circumcise every male on the eighth day" is a symbolical precept. From not making this distinction, the Manichæans, and all who find fault with the writings of the Old Testament, not seeing that whatever observance God appointed for the former dispensation was a shadow of future things, because these observances are now discontinued, condemn them, though no doubt what is unsuitable

[1] Book iv.

now was perfectly suitable then as prefiguring the things now revealed. In this they contradict the apostle who says, "All these things happened to them for an example, and they were written for our learning, on whom the end of the world is come."[1] The apostle here explains why these writings are to be received, and why it is no longer necessary to continue the symbolical observances. For when he says, "They were written for our learning," he clearly shows that we should be very diligent in reading and in discovering the meaning of the Old Testament Scriptures, and that we should have great veneration for them, since it was for us that they were written. Again, when he says, "They are our examples," and "these things happened to them for an example," he shows that, now that the things themselves are clearly revealed, the observance of the actions by which these things were prefigured is no longer binding. So he says elsewhere, "Let no man judge you in meat, or in drink, or in respect of an holy day, or of the new moon, or of the sabbath-days, which are a shadow of things to come."[2] Here also, when he says, "Let no one judge you" in these things, he shows that we are no longer bound to observe them. And when he says, "which are a shadow of things to come," he explains how these observances were binding at the time when the things fully disclosed to us were symbolized by these shadows of future things.

3. Assuredly, if the Manichæans were justified by the resurrection of the Lord,—the day of whose resurrection, the third after His passion, was the eighth day, coming after the Sabbath, that is, after the seventh day,—their carnal minds would be delivered from the darkness of earthly passions which rests on them; and rejoicing in the circumcision of the heart, they would not ridicule it as prefigured in the Old Testament by circumcision in the flesh, although they should not enforce this observance under the New Testament. But, as the apostle says, "To the pure all things are pure. But to the impure and unbelieving nothing is pure, but both their mind and conscience are defiled."[3] So these people, who are so pure in their own eyes, that they regard, or pretend to regard, as impure these members of their bodies, are so defiled with unbelief and error, that, while they abhor the circumcision of the flesh,—which the apostle calls a seal of the righteousness of faith,—they believe that the divine members of their God are subjected to restraint and contamination in these very carnal members of theirs. For they say that flesh is unclean; and it follows that God, in the part which is detained by the flesh, is made unclean: for they declare that He must be cleansed, and that till this is done, as far as it can be done, He undergoes all the passions to which flesh is subject, not only in suffering pain and distress, but also in sensual gratification. For it is for His sake, they say, that they abstain from sexual intercourse, that He may not be bound more closely in the bondage of the flesh, nor suffer more defilement. The apostle says, "To the pure all things are pure." And if this is true of men, who may be led into evil by a perverse will, how much more must all things be pure to God, who remains for ever immutable and immaculate! In those books which you defile with your violent reproaches, it is said of the divine wisdom, that "no defiled thing falleth into it, and it goeth everywhere by reason of its pureness."[4] It is mere prurient absurdity to find fault with the sign of human regeneration appointed by that God, to whom all things are pure, to be put on the organ of human generation, while you hold that your God, to whom nothing is pure, is in a part of his nature subjected to taint and corruption by the vicious actions in which impure men employ the members of their body. For if you think there is pollution in conjugal intercourse, what must there be in all the practices of the licentious? If you ask, then, as you often do, whether God could not find some other way of sealing the righteousness of faith, the answer is, Why not this way, since all things are pure to the pure, much more to God? And we have the authority of the apostle for saying that circumcision was the seal of the righteousness of the faith of Abraham. As for you, you must try not to blush when you are asked whether your God had nothing better to do than to entangle part of his nature with these members that you revile so much. These are delicate subjects to speak of, on account of the penal corruption attending the propagation of man. They are things which call into exercise the modesty of the chaste, the passions of the impure, and the justice of God.

4. The rest of the Sabbath we consider no longer binding as an observance, now that the hope of our eternal rest has been revealed. But it is a very useful thing to read of, and to reflect on. In prophetic times, when things now manifested were prefigured and predicted by actions as well as words, this

1 1 Cor. x. 6. 2 Col. ii. 16, 17. 3 Tit. i. 15. 4 Wisd. vii. 24, 25.

sign of which we read was a presage of the reality which we possess. But I wish to know why you observe a sort of partial rest. The Jews, on their Sabbath, which they still keep in a carnal manner, neither gather any fruit in the field, nor dress and cook it at home. But you, in your rest, wait till one of your followers takes his knife or hook to the garden, to get food for you by murdering the vegetables, and brings back, strange to say, living corpses. For if cutting plants is not murder, why are you afraid to do it? And yet, if the plants are murdered, what becomes of the life which is to obtain release and restoration from your mastication and digestion? Well, you take the living vegetables, and certainly you ought, if it could be done, to swallow them whole; so that after the one wound your follower has been guilty of inflicting in pulling them, of which you will no doubt consent to absolve him, they may reach without loss or injury your private laboratory, where your God may be healed of his wound. Instead of this, you not only tear them with your teeth, but, if it pleases your taste, mince them, inflicting a multitude of wounds in the most criminal manner. Plainly it would be a most advantageous thing if you would rest at home too, and not only once a week, like the Jews, but every day of the week. The cucumbers suffer while you are cooking them, without any benefit to the life that is in them; for a boiling pot cannot be compared to a saintly stomach. And yet you ridicule as superfluous the rest of the Sabbath. Would it not be better, not only to refrain from finding fault with the fathers for this observance, in whose case it was not superfluous, but, even now that it is superfluous, to observe this rest yourselves instead of your own, which has no symbolical use, and is condemned as grounded on falsehood? According to your own foolish opinions, you are guilty of a defective observance of your own rest, though the observance itself is foolish in the judgment of truth. You maintain that the fruit suffers when it is pulled from the tree, when it is cut and scraped, and cooked, and eaten. So you are wrong in eating anything that can not be swallowed raw and unhurt, so that the wound inflicted might not be from you, but from your follower in pulling them. You declare that you could not give release to so great a quantity of life, if you were to eat only things which could be swallowed without cooking or mastication. But if this release compensates for all the pains you inflict, why is it unlawful for you to pull the fruit? Fruit may be eaten raw, as some of your sect make a point of eating raw vegetables of all kinds. But before it can be eaten at all, it must be pulled or fall off, or be taken in some way from the ground or from the tree. You might well be pardoned for pulling it, since nothing can be done without that, but not for torturing the members of your God to the extent you do in dressing your food. One of your silly notions is that the tree weeps when the fruit is pulled. Doubtless the life in the tree knows all things, and perceives who it is that comes to it. If the elect were to come and pull the fruit, would not the tree rejoice to escape the misery of having its fruit plucked by others, and to gain felicity by enduring a little momentary pain? And yet, while you multiply the pains and troubles of the fruit after it is plucked, you will not pluck it. Explain that, if you can! Fasting itself is a mistake in your case. There should be no intermission in the task of purging away the dross of the excrements from the spiritual gold, and of releasing the divine members from confinement. The most merciful man among you is he who keeps himself always in good health, takes raw food, and eats a great deal. But you are cruel when you eat, in making your food undergo so much suffering; and you are cruel when you fast, in desisting from the work of liberating the divine members.[1]

5. With all this, you venture to denounce the sacrifices of the Old Testament, and to call them idolatry, and to attribute to us the same impious notion. To answer for ourselves in the first place, while we consider it no longer a duty to offer sacrifices, we recognize sacrifices as part of the mysteries of Revelation, by which the things prophesied were foreshadowed. For they were our examples, and in many and various ways they all pointed to the one sacrifice which we now commemorate. Now that this sacrifice has been revealed, and has been offered in due time, sacrifice is no longer binding as an act of worship, while it retains its symbolical authority. For these things "were written for our learning, upon whom the end of the world is come."[2] What you object to in sacrifice is the slaughter of animals, though the whole animal creation is intended conditionally in some way for the use of man. You are merciful to beasts, believing them to contain the souls of human beings, while you refuse a piece of bread to a hungry beggar. The Lord Jesus, on the other hand, was cruel to the swine when He granted the request of the devils to

[1] [In bringing to notice the absurdities of the Manichæan moral system, Augustin may seem to be trifling, but he is in reality striking at the root of the heresy.—A. H. N.]

[2] 1 Cor. x. 11.

be allowed to enter into them.[1] The same Lord Jesus, before the sacrifice of His passion, said to a leper whom He had cured, "Go, show thyself to the priest, and give the offering, as Moses commanded, for a testimony unto them."[2] When God, by the prophets, repeatedly declares that He needs no offering, as indeed reason teaches us that offerings cannot be needed by Him who stands in need of nothing, the human mind is led to inquire what God wished to teach us by these sacrifices. For, assuredly, He would not have required offerings of which He had no need, except to teach us something that it would profit us to know, and which was suitably set forth by means of these symbols. How much better and more honorable it would be for you to be still bound by these sacrifices, which have an instructive meaning, though they are not now necessary, than to require your followers to offer to you as food what you believe to be living victims. The Apostle Paul says most appropriately of some who preached the gospel to gratify their appetite, that their "god was their belly."[3] But the arrogance of your impiety goes much beyond this; for, instead of making your belly your god, you do what is far worse in making your belly the purifier of God. Surely it is great madness to make a pretence of piety in not slaughtering animals, while you hold that the souls of animals inhabit all the food you eat, and yet make what you call living creatures suffer such torture from your hands and teeth.

6. If you will not eat flesh why should you not slay animals in sacrifice to your God, in order that their souls, which you hold to be not only human, but so divine as to be members of God Himself, may be released from the confinement of flesh, and be saved from returning by the efficacy of your prayers? Perhaps, however, your stomach gives more effectual aid than your intellect, and that part of divinity which has had the advantage of passing through your bowels is more likely to be saved than that which has only the benefit of your prayers. Your objection to eating flesh will be that you cannot eat animals alive, and so the operation of your stomach will not avail for the liberation of their souls. Happy vegetables, that, torn up with the hand, cut with knives, tortured in fire, ground by teeth, yet reach alive the altars of your intestines! Unhappy sheep and oxen, that are not so tenacious of life, and therefore are refused entrance into your bodies! Such is the absurdity of your notions. And you persist in making out an opposition in us to the Old Testament, because we consider no flesh unclean: according to the opinion of the apostle, "To the pure all things are pure;"[4] and according to the saying of our Lord Himself, "Not that which goeth into your mouth defileth you, but that which cometh out."[5] This was not said to the crowd only, as your Adimantus, whom Faustus, in his attack on the Old Testament, praises as second only to Manichæus, wishes us to understand; but when retired from the crowd, the Lord repeated this still more plainly and pointedly to His disciples. Adimantus quotes this saying of our Lord in opposition to the Old Testament, where the people are prohibited from eating some animals which are pronounced unclean; and doubtless he was afraid that he should be asked why, since he quotes a passage from the Gospel about man not being defiled by what enters into his mouth and passes into his belly, and out into the draft, he yet considers not some only, but all flesh unclean, and abstains from eating it. It is in order to escape from this strait, when the plain truth is too much for his error, that he makes the Lord say this to the crowd; as if the Lord were in the habit of speaking the truth only in small companies, while He blurted out falsehoods in public. To speak of the Lord in this way is blasphemy. And all who read the passage can see that the Lord said the same thing more plainly to His disciples in private. Since Faustus praises Adimantus so much at the beginning of this book of his, placing him next to Manichæus, let him say in a word whether it is true or false that a man is not defiled by what enters into his mouth. If it is false, why does this great teacher Adimantus quote it against the Old Testament? If it is true, why, in spite of this, do you believe that eating any flesh will defile you? It is true, if you choose this explanation, that the apostle does not say that all things are pure to heretics, but, "to the pure all things are pure." The apostle also goes on to explain why all things are not pure to heretics: "To the impure and unbelieving nothing is pure, but both their mind and conscience are defiled."[6] So to the Manichæans there is absolutely nothing pure; for they hold that the very substance or nature of God not only may be, but has actually been defiled, and so defiled that it can never be wholly restored and purified. What do they mean when they call animals unclean, and refrain from eating them, when it is impossible for them to think anything, whether food or whatever it may be, clean? According to them, vegetables

[1] Matt. viii. 32.
[2] Luke v. 14.
[3] Phil. iii. 19.
[4] Tit. i. 15.
[5] Matt. xvi. 11.
[6] Tit. i. 15.

too, fruits, all kinds of crops, the earth and sky, are defiled by mixture with the race of darkness. Why do they not act up to their opinions about other things as well as about animals? Why do they not abstain altogether, and starve themselves to death, instead of persisting in their blasphemies? If they will not repent and reform, this is evidently the best thing that they could do.

7. The saying of the apostle, that "to the pure all things are pure," and that "every creature of God is good," is not opposed to the prohibitions of the Old Testament; and the explanation, if they can understand it, is this. The apostle speaks of the natures of the things, while the Old Testament calls some animals unclean, not in their nature, but symbolically, on account of the prefigurative character of that dispensation. For instance, a pig and a lamb are both clean in their nature, for every creature of God is good; but symbolically, a lamb is clean, and a pig unclean. So the words *wise* and *fool* are both clean in their nature, as words composed of letters; but *fool* may be called symbolically unclean, because it means an unclean thing. Perhaps a pig is the same among symbols as a fool is among real things. The animal, and the four letters which compose the word, may mean the same thing. No doubt the animal is pronounced unclean by the law, because it does not chew the cud; which is not a fault but its nature. But the men of whom this animal is a symbol are unclean, not by nature, but from their own fault; because, though they gladly hear the words of wisdom, they never reflect on them afterwards. For to recall, in quiet repose, some useful instruction from the stomach of memory to the mouth of reflection, is a kind of spiritual rumination. The animals above mentioned are a symbol of those people who do not do this. And the prohibition of the flesh of these animals is a warning against this fault. Another passage of Scripture speaks of the precious treasure of wisdom, and describes ruminating as clean, and not ruminating as unclean: "A precious treasure resteth in the mouth of a wise man; but a foolish man swallows it up."[1] Symbols of this kind, either in words or in things, give useful and pleasant exercise to intelligent minds in the way of inquiry and comparison. But formerly people were required not only to hear, but to practise many such things. For at that time it was necessary that, by deeds as well as by words, those things should be foreshadowed which were in after times to be revealed. After the revelation by Christ and in Christ, the community of believers is not burdened with the practice of the observances, but is admonished to give heed to the prophecy. This is our reason for accounting no animals unclean, in accordance with the saying of the Lord and of the apostle, while we are not opposed to the Old Testament, where some animals are pronounced unclean. Now let us hear why you consider all animal food unclean.

8. One of your false doctrines is, that flesh is unclean on account of mixture with the race of darkness. But this would make not only flesh unclean, but your God himself, in that part which he sent to become subject to absorption and contamination, in order that the enemy might be conquered and taken captive. Besides, on account of this mixture, all that you eat must be unclean. But you say flesh is especially unclean. It requires patience to listen to all their absurd reasons for this peculiar impurity of flesh. I will mention only what will suffice to show the inveterate folly of these critics of the Old Testament, who, while they denounce flesh, savor only fleshly things, and have no sort of spiritual perception. And a lengthy discussion of this question may perhaps enable us to dispense with saying much on some other points. The following, then, is an account of their vain delusions in this matter:—In that battle, when the First Man ensnared the race of darkness by deceitful elements, princes of both sexes belonging to this race were taken. By means of these princes the world was constructed; and among those used in the formation of the heavenly bodies, were some pregnant females. When the sky began to rotate, the rapid circular motion made these females give birth to abortions, which, being of both sexes, fell on the earth, and lived, and grew, and came together, and produced offspring. Hence sprang all animal life in earth, air, and sea.[2] Now if the origin of flesh is from heaven, that is no reason for thinking it especially unclean. Indeed, in this construction of the world, they hold that these principles of darkness were arranged higher or lower, according to the greater or less amount of good mixed with them in the construction of the various parts of the world. So flesh ought to be cleaner than vegetables which come out of the earth, for it comes from heaven. And how irrational to suppose that the abortions, before becoming animate, were so lively, though in an abortive state, that after falling from the sky, they could live and multiply; whereas, after becoming animate, they die if brought

[1] Prov. xxi. 20.

[2] [Compare the *Introduction*, where an abstract is given of the *Fihrist's* account of the creation.—A. H. N.]

forth prematurely, and a fall from a very moderate height is enough to kill them! The kingdom of life in contest with the kingdom of death ought to have improved them, by giving them life instead of making them more perishable than before. If the perishableness is a consequence of a change of nature, it is wrong to say that there is a bad nature. The change is the only cause of the perishableness. Both natures are good, though one is better than the other. Whence then comes the peculiar impurity of flesh as it exists in this world, sprung, as they say, from heaven? They tell us, indeed, of the first bodies of these principles of darkness being generated like worms from trees of darkness; and the trees, they say, are produced from the five elements. But supposing that the bodies of animals come in the first place from trees, and afterwards from heaven, why should they be more unclean than the fruit of trees? Perhaps it will be said that what remains after death is unclean, because the life is no longer there. For the same reason fruits and vegetables must be unclean, for they die when they are pulled or cut. As we saw before, the elect get others to bring their food to them, that they may not be guilty of murder. Perhaps, since they say that every living being has two souls, one of the race of light, and the other of the race of darkness, the good soul leaves at death, and the bad soul remains. But, in that case, the animal would be as much alive as it was in the kingdom of darkness, when it had only the soul of its own race, with which it had rebelled against the kingdom of God. So, since both souls leave at death, why call the flesh unclean, as if only the good soul had left? Any life that remains must be of both kinds; for some remains of the members of God are found, we are told, even in filth. There is therefore no reason for making flesh more unclean than fruits. The truth is, they pretend to great chastity in holding flesh unclean because it is generated. But if the divine body is more grossly shut in by flesh, there is all the more reason that they should liberate it by eating. And there are innumerable kinds of worms not produced from sexual intercourse; some in the neighborhood of Venice come from trees, which they should eat, since there is not the same reason for their being unclean. Besides, there are the frogs produced by the earth after a shower of rain.[1] Let them liberate the members of their God from these. Let them rebuke the mistake of mankind in preferring fowls and pigeons produced from males and females to the pure frogs, daughters of heaven and earth. By this theory, the first principles of darkness produced from trees must be purer than Manichæus, who was produced by generation; and his followers, for the same reason, must be less pure than the lice which spring from the perspiration of their bodies. But if everything that comes from flesh is unclean, because the origin of flesh itself is unclean, fruits and vegetables must also be unclean, because they are manured with dung. After this, what becomes of the notion that fruits are cleaner than flesh? Dung is the most unclean product of flesh, and also the most fertilizing manure. Their doctrine is, that the life escapes in the mastication and digestion of the food, so that only a particle remains in the excrement. How is it, then, that this particle of life has such an effect on the growth and the quality of your favorite food? Flesh is nourished by the productions of the earth, not by its excrements; while the earth is nourished by the excrements of flesh, not by its productions. Let them say which is the cleaner. Or let them turn from being unbelieving and impure to whom nothing is clean, and join with us in embracing the doctrine of the apostle, that to the pure all things are pure; that the earth is the Lord's, and the fullness thereof; that every creature of God is good. All things in nature are good in their own order; and no one sins in using them, unless, by disobedience to God, he transgresses his own order, and disturbs their order by using them amiss.

9. The elders who pleased God kept their own order by their obedience, in observing, according to God's arrangement, what was appointed as suitable to certain times. So, although all animals intended for food are by nature clean, they abstained from some which had then a symbolical uncleanness, in preparation for the future revelation of the things signified. And so with regard to unleavened bread and all such things, in which the apostle says there was a shadow of future things, neglect of their observance under the old dispensation, when this observance was enjoined, and was employed to prefigure what was afterwards to be revealed, would have been as criminal, as it would now be foolish in us, after the light of the New Testament has arisen, to think that these predictive observances could be of any use to us. On the other hand, since the Old Testament teaches us that the things now revealed were so long ago prefigured, that we may be firm and faithful in our adherence to them, it would be blasphemy and impiety to discard these

[1] [These biological blunders belong to the age, and are not Augustin's peculiar fancies. Of course, the argumentative value of them depends on their general acceptance.—A. H. N.]

books, simply because the Lord requires of us now not a literal, but a spiritual and intelligent regard to their contents. They were written, as the apostle says, for our admonition, on whom the end of the world is come.[1] "For whatsoever things were written aforetime were written for our learning."[2] Not to eat unleavened bread in the appointed seven days was a sin in the time of the Old Testament; in the time of the New Testament it is not a sin. But having the hope of a future world through Christ, who makes us altogether new by clothing our souls with righteousness and our bodies with immortality, to believe that the bondage and infirmity of our original corruption will prevail over us or over our actions, must continue to be a sin, till the seven days of the course of time are accomplished. In the time of the Old Testament, this, under the disguise of a type, was perceived by some saints. In the time of the New Testament it is fully declared and publicly preached.[3]

What was then a precept of Scripture is now a testimony. Formerly, not to keep the feast of tabernacles was a sin, which is not the case now. But not to form part of the building of God's tabernacle, which is the Church, is always a sin. Formerly this was acted in a figure; now the record serves as testimony. The ancient tabernacle, indeed, would not have been called the tabernacle of the testimony, unless as an appropriate symbol it had borne testimony to some truth which was to be revealed in its own time. To patch linen garments with purple, or to wear a garment of woollen and linen together, is not a sin now. But to live intemperately, and to wish to combine opposite modes of life,—as when a woman devoted to religion wears the ornaments of married women, or when one who has not abstained from marriage dresses like a virgin,—is always sin. So it is sin whenever inconsistent things are combined in any man's life. This, which is now a moral truth, was then symbolized in dress. What was then a type is now revealed truth. So the same Scripture which then required symbolical actions, now testifies to the things signified. The prefigurative observance is now a record for the confirmation of our faith. Formerly it was unlawful to plough with an ox and an ass together; now it is lawful. The apostle explains this when he quotes the text about not muzzling the ox that is treading out the corn. He says, "Does God care for oxen?" What, then, have we to do with an obsolete prohibition? The apostle teaches us in the following words, "For our sakes it is written."[4] It must be impiety in us not to read what was written for our sakes; for it is more for our sakes, to whom the revelation belongs, than for theirs who had only the figure. There is no harm in joining an ox with an ass where it is required. But to put a wise man and a fool together, not that one should teach and the other obey, but that both with equal authority should declare the word of God, cannot be done without causing offence. So the same Scripture which was once a command enjoining the shadow in which future things were veiled, is now an authoritative witness to the unveiled truth.

In what he says of the uncleanness of a man that is bald or has red hair, Faustus is inaccurate, or the manuscript he has used is incorrect.[5] Would that Faustus were not ashamed to bear on his forehead the cross of Christ, the want of which is baldness, instead of maintaining that Christ, who says, "I am the truth," showed unreal marks, after His resurrection, of unreal wounds! Faustus says he has not learned the art of deceiving, and speaks what he thinks. He cannot therefore be a disciple of his Christ, whom he madly declares to have shown false marks of wounds to his disciples when they doubted. Are we to believe Faustus, not only in his other absurdities, but also when he tells us that he does not deceive us in calling Christ a deceiver? Is he better than Christ? Is he not a deceiver, while Christ is? Or does he prove himself to be a disciple not of the truthful Christ, but of the deceiver Manichæus, by this very falsehood, when he boasts that he has not learned the art of deceiving?

---

1 1 Cor. x. 11.
2 Rom. xv. 4.
3 [It will be seen in subsequent portions of this treatise that Augustin carries the typological idea to an absurd extreme.—A. H. N.]
4 1 Cor. ix. 9, 10.
5 Cf. Lev. xxi. 18.

BOOK VII.

THE GENEALOGICAL QUESTION IS AGAIN TAKEN UP AND ARGUED ON BOTH SIDES.

1. Faustus said: You ask why I do not believe in the genealogy of Jesus. There are many reasons; but the principal is, that He never declares with His own lips that He had an earthly father or descent, but on the contrary, that he is not of this world, that He came forth from God the Father, that He descended from heaven, that He has no mother or brethren except those who do the will of His Father in heaven. Besides, the framers of these genealogies do not seem to have known Jesus before His birth or soon after it, so as to have the credibility of eye-witnesses of what they narrate. They became acquainted with Jesus as a young man of about thirty years of age, if it is not blasphemy to speak of the age of a divine being. Now the question regarding a witness is always whether he has seen or heard what he testifies to. But the writers of these genealogies never assert that they heard the account from Jesus Himself, nor even the fact of His birth; nor did they see Him till they came to know Him after his baptism, many years after the time of His birth. To me, therefore, and to every sensible man, it appears as foolish to believe this account, as it would be to call into court a blind and deaf witness.

2. Augustin replied: As regards what Faustus calls his principal reason for not receiving the genealogy of Jesus Christ, a complete refutation is found in the passages formerly quoted, where Christ declares Himself to be the Son of man, and in what we have said of the identity of the Son of man with the Son of God: that in His Godhead He has no earthly descent, while after the flesh He is of the seed of David, as the apostle teaches. We are to believe, therefore, that He came forth from the Father, that He descended from heaven, and also that the Word was made flesh and dwelt amongst men. If the words, "Who is my mother, and who are my brethren?"[1] are quoted to show that Christ had no earthly mother or descent, it follows that we must believe that His disciples, whom He here teaches by His own example to set no value on earthly relationship, as compared with the kingdom of heaven, had no fathers, because Christ says to them, "Call no man father upon earth; for one is your Father, even God."[2] What He taught them to do with reference to their fathers, He Himself first did in reference to His own mother and brethren; as in many other things He condescended to set us an example, and to go before that we might follow in His footsteps. Faustus' principal objection to the genealogy fails completely; and after the defeat of this invincible force, the rest is easily routed. He says that the apostles who declared Christ to be the Son of man as well as the Son of God are not to be believed, because they were not present at the birth of Christ, whom they joined when He had reached manhood, nor heard of it from Christ Himself. Why then do they believe John when he says, "In the beginning was the Word, and the Word was with God, and the Word was God. The same was in the beginning with God. All things were made by Him, and without Him was not anything made,"[3] and such passages, which they agree to, without understanding them? Where did John see this, or did he ever hear it from the Lord Himself? In whatever way John learned this, those who narrate the nativity may have learned also. Again, how do they know that the Lord said, "Who is my mother, and who are my brethren?" If on the authority of the evangelist, why do they not also believe that the mother and the brethren of Christ were seeking for Him? They believe that Christ said these words, which they misunderstand, while they deny a fact resting on the same authority. Once more, if Matthew could not know that Christ was born, because he knew Him only in His manhood, how could Manichæus, who lived so long after, know that He was not born? They will say that Manichæus knew this from the Holy Spirit which was in him. Certainly the Holy Spirit would make him speak the truth. But why not rather believe what Christ's own disciples tell us, who were personally acquainted with Him, and who not only had the gift of inspiration to supply defects in their knowledge, but in a purely natural way obtained information of the birth of Christ, and of His descent, when the event was fresh in memory? And yet he dares to call the apostles deaf and blind. Why were you not deaf and blind, to prevent you from learning such profane nonsense, and dumb too, to prevent you from uttering it?

1 Matt. xii. 48.

2 Matt. xxiii. 9.

3 John i. 1-5.

BOOK VIII.

FAUSTUS MAINTAINS THAT TO HOLD TO THE OLD TESTAMENT AFTER THE GIVING OF THE NEW IS PUTTING NEW CLOTH ON AN OLD GARMENT. AUGUSTIN FURTHER EXPLAINS THE RELATION OF THE OLD TESTAMENT TO THE NEW, AND REPROACHES THE MANICHÆANS WITH CARNALITY.

1. FAUSTUS said: Another reason for not receiving the Old Testament is, that I am provided with the New; and Scripture says that old and new do not agree. For "no one putteth a piece of new cloth unto an old garment, otherwise the rent is made worse."[1] To avoid making a worse rent, as you have done, I do not mix Christian newness with Hebrew oldness. Every one accounts it mean, when a man has got a new dress, not to give the old one to his inferiors. So, even if I were a Jew by birth, as the apostles were, it would be proper for me, on receiving the New Testament, to discard the Old, as the apostles did. And having the advantage of being born free from the yoke of bondage, and being early introduced into the full liberty of Christ, what a foolish and ungrateful wretch I should be to put myself again under the yoke! This is what Paul blames the Galatians for; because, going back to circumcision, they turned again to the weak and beggarly elements, whereunto they desired again to be in bondage.[2] Why should I do what I see another blamed for doing? My going into bondage would be worse than their returning to it.

2. AUGUSTIN replied: We have already shown sufficiently why and how we maintain the authority of the Old Testament, not for the imitation of Jewish bondage, but for the confirmation of Christian liberty. It is not I, but the apostle, who says, "All these things happened to them as an example, and they were written for our admonition, on whom the ends of the world are come."[3] We do not therefore, as bondmen, observe what was enjoined as predictive of us; but as free, we read what was written to confirm us. So any one may see that the apostle remonstrates with the Galatians not for devoutly reading what Scripture says of circumcision, but for superstitiously desiring to be circumcised. We do not put a new cloth to an old garment, but we are instructed in the kingdom of heaven, like the householder, whom the Lord describes as bringing out of his treasure things new and old.[4] He who puts a new cloth to an old garment is the man who attempts spiritual self-denial before he has renounced fleshly hope. Examine the passage, and you will see that, when the Lord was asked about fasting, He replied, "No man putteth a new cloth to an old garment." The disciples had still a carnal affection for the Lord; for they were afraid that, if He died, they would lose Him. So He calls Peter Satan for dissuading Him from suffering, because he understood not the things of God, but the things of men.[5] The fleshly character of your hope is evident from your fancies about the kingdom of God, and from your paying homage and devotion to the light of the sun, which the carnal eye perceives, as if it were an image of heaven. So your carnal mind is the old garment to which you join your fasts. Moreover, if a new cloth and an old garment do not agree, how do the members of your God come to be not only joined or fastened, but to be united far more intimately by mixture and coherence to the principles of darkness? Perhaps both are old, because both are false, and both of the carnal mind. Or perhaps you wish to prove that one was new and the other old, by the rent being made worse, in tearing away the unhappy piece of the kingdom of light, to be doomed to eternal imprisonment in the mass of darkness. So this pretended artist in the fashions of the sacred Scriptures is found stitching together absurdities, and dressing himself in the rags of his own invention.

1 Matt. ix. 16. 2 Gal. iv. 9. 3 1 Cor. x. 11. 4 Matt. xiii. 52. 5 Matt. xvi. 23.

BOOK IX.

FAUSTUS ARGUES THAT IF THE APOSTLES BORN UNDER THE OLD COVENANT COULD LAWFULLY DEPART FROM IT, MUCH MORE CAN HE HAVING BEEN BORN A GENTILE. AUGUSTIN EXPLAINS THE RELATION OF JEWS AND GENTILES ALIKE TO THE GOSPEL.

1. FAUSTUS said: Another reason for not receiving the Old Testament is, that if it was allowable for the apostles, who were born under it, to abandon it, much more may I, who was not born under it, be excused for not thrusting myself into it. We Gentiles are

not born Jews, nor Christians either. Out of the same Gentile world some are induced by the Old Testament to become Jews, and some by the New Testament to become Christians. It is as if two trees, a sweet and a bitter, drew from one soil the sap which each assimilates to its own nature. The apostle passed from the bitter to the sweet; it would be madness in me to change from the sweet to the bitter.

2. Augustin replied: You say that the apostle, in leaving Judaism, passed from the bitter to the sweet. But the apostle himself says that the Jews, who would not believe in Christ, were branches broken off, and that the Gentiles, a wild olive tree, were graffed into the good olive, that is, the holy stock of the Hebrews, that they might partake of the fatness of the olive. For, in warning the Gentiles not to be proud on account of the fall of the Jews, he says: "For I speak to you Gentiles, inasmuch as I am the apostle of the Gentiles, I magnify my office; if by any means I may provoke to emulation them which are my flesh, and might save some of them. For if the casting away of them be the reconciling of the world, what shall the receiving of them be, but life from the dead? For if the first fruit be holy, the lump is also holy; and if the root be holy, so are the branches. And if some of the branches are broken off, and thou, being a wild olive tree, were graffed in among them, and with them partakest of the root and fatness of the olive tree; boast not against the branches: but if thou boast, thou bearest not the root, but the root thee. Thou wilt say then, The branches were broken off, that I might be graffed in. Well; because of unbelief they were broken off, and thou standest by faith. Be not high-minded, but fear; for if God spared not the natural branches, take heed lest He also spare not thee. Behold therefore the goodness and severity of God: on them which fell, severity; but toward thee, goodness, if thou continue in His goodness; otherwise thou also shalt be cut off. And they also, if they abide not still in unbelief, shall be graffed in; for God is able to graff them in again. For if thou wert cut out of the olive tree, which is wild by nature, and wert graffed contrary to nature into a good olive tree; how much more shall these, which be the natural branches, be graffed into their own olive tree? For I would not, brethren, that ye should be ignorant of this mystery (lest ye should be wise in your own conceits), that blindness in part is happened to Israel, until the fullness of the Gentiles be come in; and so all Israel shall be saved."[1] It appears from this, that you, who do not wish to be graffed into this root, though you are not broken off, like the carnal unbelieving Jews, remain still in the bitterness of the wild olive. Your worship of the sun and moon has the true Gentile flavor. You are none the less in the wild olive of the Gentiles, because you have added thorns of a new kind, and worship along with the sun and moon a false Christ, the fabrication not of your hands, but of your perverse heart. Come, then, and be graffed into the root of the olive tree, in his return to which the apostle rejoices, after by unbelief he had been among the broken branches. He speaks of himself as set free, when he made the happy transition from Judaism to Christianity. For Christ was always preached in the olive tree, and those who did not believe on Him when He came were broken off, while those who believed were graffed in. These are thus warned against pride: "Be not high-minded, but fear; for if God spared not the natural branches, neither will He spare thee." And to prevent despair of those broken off, he adds: "And they also, if they abide not still in unbelief, shall be graffed in; for God is able to graff them in again. For if thou wert cut out of the olive tree, which is wild by nature, and wert graffed contrary to nature into a good olive tree, how much more shall these, which be the natural branches, be graffed into their own olive tree." The apostle rejoices in being delivered from the condition of a broken branch, and in being restored to the fatness of the olive tree. So you who have been broken off by error should return and be graffed in again. Those who are still in the wild olive should separate themselves from its barrenness, and become partakers of fertility.

[1] Rom. xi. 16–26.

BOOK X.

FAUSTUS INSISTS THAT THE OLD TESTAMENT PROMISES ARE RADICALLY DIFFERENT FROM THOSE OF THE NEW. AUGUSTIN ADMITS A DIFFERENCE, BUT MAINTAINS THAT THE MORAL PRECEPTS ARE THE SAME IN BOTH.

1. Faustus said: Another reason for not receiving the Old Testament is, that both the Old and the New teach us not to covet what belongs to others. Everything in the Old Testament is of this kind. It promises riches, and plenty, and children, and children's children,

and long life, and withal the land of Canaan; but only to the circumcised, the Sabbath observers, those offering sacrifices, and abstaining from swine's flesh. Now I, like every other Christian, pay no attention to these things, as being trifling and useless for the salvation of the soul. I conclude, therefore, that the promises do not belong to me. And mindful of the commandment, Thou shalt not covet, I gladly leave to the Jews their own property, and content myself with the gospel, and with the bright inheritance of the kingdom of heaven. If a Jew were to claim part in the gospel, I should justly reproach him with claiming what he had no right to, because he does not obey its precepts. And a Jew might say the same to me if I professed to receive the Old Testament while I disregard its requirements.

2. AUGUSTIN replied: Faustus is not ashamed to repeat the same nonsense again and again. But it is tiresome to repeat the same answers, though it is to repeat truth. What Faustus says here has already been answered.[1] But if a Jew asks me why I profess to believe the Old Testament while I do not observe its precepts, my reply is this: The moral precepts of the law are observed by Christians; the symbolical precepts were properly observed during the time that the things now revealed were prefigured. Accordingly, those observances, which I regard as no longer binding, I still look upon as a testimony, as I do also the carnal promises from which the Old Testament derives its name. For although the gospel teaches me to hope for eternal blessings, I also find a confirmation of the gospel in those things which "happened to them for an example, and were written for our admonition, on whom the ends of the world are come." So much for our answer to the Jews. And now we have something to say to the Manichæans.

3. By showing the way in which we regard the authority of the Old Testament we have answered the Jews, by whose question about our not observing the precepts Faustus thought we would be puzzled. But what answer can you give to the question, why you deceive simple-minded people by professing to believe in the New Testament, while you not only do not believe it, but assail it with all your force? It will be more difficult for you to answer this than it was for us to answer the Jews. We hold all that is written in the Old Testament to be true, and enjoined by God for suitable times. But in your inability to find a reason for not receiving what is written in the New Testament, you are obliged, as a last resource, to pretend that the passages are not genuine. This is the last gasp of a heretic in the clutches of truth; or rather it is the breath of corruption itself. Faustus, however, confesses that the Old Testament as well as the New teaches him not to covet. His own God could never have taught him this. For if this God did not covet what belonged to another, why did he construct new worlds in the region of darkness? Perhaps the race of darkness first coveted his kingdom. But this would be to imitate their bad example. Perhaps the kingdom of light was previously of small extent, and war was desirable in order to enlarge it by conquest. In that case, no doubt, there was covetousness, though the hostile race was allowed to begin the wars to justify the conquest. If there had been no such desire, there was no necessity to extend the kingdom beyond its old limits into the region of the conquered foe. If the Manichæans would only learn from these Scriptures the moral precepts, one of which is, Do not covet, instead of taking offence at the symbolical precept, they would acknowledge in meekness and candor that they suited the time then present. We do not covet what belongs to another, when we read in the Old Testament what "happened to them for examples, and was written for our admonition, on whom the ends of the world are come." It is surely not coveting when a man reads what is written for his benefit.

[1] Book vi. 2.

BOOK XI.

FAUSTUS QUOTES PASSAGES TO SHOW THAT THE APOSTLE PAUL ABANDONED BELIEF IN THE INCARNATION, TO WHICH HE EARLIER HELD. AUGUSTIN SHOWS THAT THE APOSTLE WAS CONSISTENT WITH HIMSELF IN THE UTTERANCES QUOTED.

1. FAUSTUS said: Assuredly I believe the apostle. And yet I do not believe that the Son of God was born of the seed of David according to the flesh,[1] because I do not believe that God's apostle could contradict himself, and have one opinion about our Lord at one time, and another at another. But, granting that he wrote this,—since you will not hear of anything being spurious in his

[1] Rom. i. 3.

writings,—it is not against us. For this seems to be Paul's old belief about Jesus, when he thought, like everybody else, that Jesus was the son of David. Afterwards, when he learned that this was false, he corrects himself; and in his Epistle to the Corinthians he says: "We know no man after the flesh; yea, though we have known Christ after the flesh, yet now henceforth know we Him no more."[1] Observe the difference between these two verses. In one he asserts that Jesus was the son of David after the flesh; in the other he says that now he knows no man after the flesh. If Paul wrote both, it can only have been in the way I have stated. In the next verse he adds: "Therefore, if any man be in Christ, he is a new creature; old things are passed away; behold, all things are become new." The belief that Jesus was born of the seed of David according to the flesh is of this old transitory kind; whereas the faith which knows no man after the flesh is new and permanent. So, he says elsewhere: "When I was a child, I spoke as a child, I understood as a child, I thought as a child; but when I became a man, I put away childish things."[2] We are thus warranted in preferring the new and amended confession of Paul to his old and faulty one. And if you hold by what is said in the Epistle to the Romans, why should not we hold by what is said to the Corinthians? But it is only by your insisting on the correctness of the text that we are made to represent Paul as building again the things which he destroyed, in spite of his own repudiation of such prevarication. If the verse is Paul's, he has corrected himself. If Paul should not be supposed to have written anything requiring correction, the verse is not his.

2. Augustin replied: As I said a little ago, when these men are beset by clear testimonies of Scripture, and cannot escape from their grasp, they declare that the passage is spurious. The declaration only shows their aversion to the truth, and their obstinacy in error. Unable to answer these statements of Scripture, they deny their genuineness. But if this answer is admitted, or allowed to have any weight, it will be useless to quote any book or any passage against your errors. It is one thing to reject the books themselves, and to profess no regard for their authority, as the Pagans reject our Scriptures, and the Jews the New Testament, and as we reject any books peculiar to your sect, or any other heretical sect, and also the apocryphal books, which are so called, not because of any mysterious regard paid to them, but because they are mysterious in their origin, and in the absence of clear evidence, have only some obscure presumption to rest upon; and it is another thing to say, This holy man wrote only the truth, and this is his epistle, but some verses are his, and some are not. And then, when you are asked for a proof, instead of referring to more correct or more ancient manuscripts, or to a greater number, or to the original text, your reply is, This verse is his, because it makes for me; and this is not his, because it is against me. Are you, then, the rule of truth? Can nothing be true that is against you? But what answer could you give to an opponent as insane as yourself, if he confronts you by saying, The passage in your favor is spurious, and that against you is genuine? Perhaps you will produce a book, all of which can be explained so as to support you. Then, instead of rejecting a passage, he will reply by condemning the whole book as spurious. You have no resource against such an opponent. For all the testimony you can bring in favor of your book from antiquity or tradition will avail nothing. In this respect the testimony of the Catholic Church is conspicuous, as supported by a succession of bishops from the original seats of the apostles up to the present time, and by the consent of so many nations. Accordingly, should there be a question about the text of some passage, as there are a few passages with various readings well known to students of the sacred Scriptures, we should first consult the manuscripts of the country where the religion was first taught; and if these still varied, we should take the text of the greater number, or of the more ancient. And if any uncertainty remained, we should consult the original text. This is the method employed by those who, in any question about the Scriptures, do not lose sight of the regard due to their authority, and inquire with the view of gaining information, not of raising disputes.[3]

3. As regards the passage from Paul's epistle which teaches, in opposition to your *heresy*, that the Son of God was born of the seed of David, it is found in all manuscripts both new and old of all Churches, and in all languages. So the profession which Faustus makes of believing the apostle is hypocritical. Instead of saying, "Assuredly I believe," he should have said, Assuredly I do not believe, as he would have said if he had not wished to deceive people. What part of his belief does

[1] 2 Cor. v. 16.

[2] 1 Cor. xiii. 11.

[3] [The extremely subjective method of dealing with Scripture, which Augustin ascribes to Faustus, was characteristic of Manichæism in general.—A. H. N.]

he get from the apostle? Not the first man, of whom the apostle says that he is of the earth, earthy; and again, "The first man Adam was made a living soul." Faustus' First Man is neither of the earth, earthy, nor made a living soul, but of the substance of God, and the same in essence as God; and this being is said to have mixed up with the race of darkness his members, or vesture, or weapons, that is, the five elements, which also are part of the substance of God, so that they became subject to confinement and pollution. Nor does Faustus get from Paul his Second Man, of whom Paul says that He is from heaven, and that He is the last Adam, and a quickening spirit; and also that He was born of the seed of David after the flesh, that He was made of a woman, made under the law, that He might redeem them that were under the law.[1] Of Him Paul says to Timothy: "Remember that Jesus Christ, of the seed of David, was raised from the dead, according to my gospel."[2] And this resurrection he quotes as an example of our resurrection: "I delivered unto you first of all that which I also received, how that Christ died for our sins, according to the Scriptures; and that He was buried, and that He rose again the third day, according to the Scriptures." And a little further on he draws an inference from this doctrine: "Now, if Christ be preached that He rose from the dead, how say some among you that there is no resurrection of the dead?"[3] Our professed believer in Paul believes nothing of all this. He denies that Jesus was born of the seed of David, that He was made of a woman (by the word woman is not meant a wife in the common sense of the word, but merely one of the female sex, as in the book of Genesis, where it is said that God made a woman before she was brought to Adam[4]); he denies His death, His burial, and His resurrection. He holds that Christ had not a mortal body, and therefore could not really die; and that the marks of His wounds which He showed to His disciples when He appeared to them alive after His resurrection, which Paul also mentions,[5] were not real. He denies, too, that our mortal body will be raised again, changed into a spiritual body; as Paul teaches: "It is sown a natural body, it is raised a spiritual body." To illustrate this distinction between the natural and the spiritual body, the apostle adds what I have quoted already about the first and the last Adam. Then he goes on: "But this I say, brethren, that flesh and blood cannot inherit the kingdom of God." And to explain what he means by flesh and blood, that it is not the bodily substance, but corruption, which will not enter into the resurrection of the just, he immediately says, "Neither shall corruption inherit incorruption." And in case any one should still suppose that it is not what is buried that is to rise again, but that it is as if one garment were laid aside and a better taken instead, he proceeds to show distinctly that the same body will be changed for the better, as the garments of Christ on the mount were not displaced, but transfigured: "Behold, I show you a mystery; we shall not all be changed, but we shall all rise."[6] Then he shows who are to be changed: "In a moment, in the twinkling of an eye, at the last trumpet: for the trumpet shall sound, and the dead shall rise incorruptible, and we shall be changed." And if it should be said that it is not as regards our mortal and corruptible body, but as regards our soul, that we are to be changed, it should be observed that the apostle is not speaking of the soul, but of the body, as is evident from the question he starts with: "But some one will say, How are the dead raised, and with what body do they come?" So also, in the conclusion of his argument, he leaves no doubt of what he is speaking: "This corruptible must put on incorruption, and this mortal must put on immortality."[7] Faustus denies this; and the God whom Paul declares to be "immortal, incorruptible, to whom alone is glory and honor,"[8] he makes corruptible. For in this monstrous and horrible fiction of theirs, the substance and nature of God was in danger of being wholly corrupted by the race of darkness, and to save the rest part actually was corrupted. And to crown all this, he tries to deceive the ignorant who are not learned in the sacred Scriptures, by making this profession: I assuredly believe the Apostle Paul; when he ought to have said, I assuredly do not believe.

4. But Faustus has a proof to show that Paul changed his mind, and, in writing to the Corinthians, corrected what he had written to the Romans; or else that he never wrote the passage which appears as his, about Jesus Christ being born of the seed of David according to the flesh. And what is this proof? If the passage, he says, in the Epistle to the Romans is true, "the Son of God, who was made of the seed of David according to the flesh," what he says to the Corinthians cannot be true, "Henceforth know we no man after the flesh; yea, though we have known Christ after the flesh, yet now henceforth know we

1 Gal. iv. 4, 5. 2 2 Tim. ii. 8. 3 1 Cor. xv. 3, 4, 12. 4 Gen. ii. 22. 5 1 Cor. xi. 5.

6 Vulg. 7 1 Cor. xv. 35-53. 8 1 Tim. i. 17.

Him no more." We must therefore show that both these passages are true, and not opposed to one another. The agreement of the manuscripts proves both to be genuine. In some Latin versions the word "born"[1] is used instead of "made,"[2] which is not so literal a rendering, but gives the same meaning. For both these translations, as well as the original, teach that Christ was of the seed of David after the flesh. We must not for a moment suppose that Paul corrected himself on account of a change of opinion. Faustus himself felt the impropriety and impiety of such an explanation, and preferred to say that the passage was spurious, instead of that Paul was mistaken.

5. As regards our writings, which are not a rule of faith or practice, but only a help to edification, we may suppose that they contain some things falling short of the truth in obscure and recondite matters, and that these mistakes may or may not be corrected in subsequent treatises. For we are of those of whom the apostle says: "And if ye be otherwise minded, God shall reveal even this unto you."[3] Such writings are read with the right of judgment, and without any obligation to believe. In order to leave room for such profitable discussions of difficult questions, there is a distinct boundary line separating all productions subsequent to apostolic times from the authoritative canonical books of the Old and New Testaments. The authority of these books has come down to us from the apostles through the successions of bishops and the extension of the Church, and, from a position of lofty supremacy, claims the submission of every faithful and pious mind. If we are perplexed by an apparent contradiction in Scripture, it is not allowable to say, The author of this book is mistaken; but either the manuscript is faulty, or the translation is wrong, or you have not understood. In the innumerable books that have been written latterly we may sometimes find the same truth as in Scripture, but there is not the same authority. Scripture has a sacredness peculiar to itself. In other books the reader may form his own opinion, and perhaps, from not understanding the writer, may differ from him, and may pronounce in favor of what pleases him, or against what he dislikes. In such cases, a man is at liberty to withhold his belief, unless there is some clear demonstration or some canonical authority to show that the doctrine or statement either must or may be true. But in consequence of the distinctive peculiarity of the sacred writings, we are bound to receive as true whatever the canon shows to have been said by even one prophet, or apostle, or evangelist. Otherwise, not a single page will be left for the guidance of human fallibility, if contempt for the wholesome authority of the canonical books either puts an end to that authority altogether, or involves it in hopeless confusion.[4]

6. With regard, then, to this apparent contradiction between the passage which speaks of the Son of God being of the seed of David, to the words, "Though we have known Christ after the flesh, yet now henceforth know we Him no more," even though both quotations were not from the writings of one apostle,—though one were from Paul, and the other from Peter, or Isaiah, or any other apostle or prophet,—such is the equality of canonical authority, that it would not be allowable to doubt of either. For the utterances of Scripture, harmonious as if from the mouth of one man, commend themselves to the belief of the most accurate and clear-sighted piety, and demand for their discovery and confirmation the calmest intelligence and the most ingenious research. In the case before us both quotations are from the canonical, that is, the genuine epistles of Paul. We cannot say that the manuscript is faulty, for the best Latin translations substantially agree; or that the translations are wrong, for the best texts have the same reading. So that, if any one is perplexed by the apparent contradiction, the only conclusion is that he does not understand. Accordingly it remains for me to explain how both passages, instead of being contradictory, may be harmonized by one rule of sound faith. The pious inquirer will find all perplexity removed by a careful examination.

7. That the Son of God was made man of the seed of David, is not only said in other places by Paul, but is taught elsewhere in sacred Scripture. As regards the words, "Though we have known Christ after the flesh, yet now henceforth know we Him no more," the context shows what is the apostle's meaning. Here, or elsewhere, he views with an assured hope, as if it were already present and in actual possession, our future life, which is now fulfilled in our risen Head and Mediator, the man Christ Jesus. This life will certainly not be after the flesh, even as Christ's life is now not after the flesh. For by flesh the apostle here means not the substance of our bodies, in which sense the Lord used the

[1] *Natus.* [2] *Factus.* [3] Phil. iii. 15.

[4] [This is an excellent statement of the doctrine of Scriptural authority, that has been held to by Protestants with far more consistency than by Catholics.—A. H. N.]

word when, after His resurrection, He said, "Handle me, and see, for a spirit hath not flesh and bones, as ye see me have,"[1] but the corruption and mortality of flesh, which will then not be in us, as now it is not in Christ. The apostle uses the word *flesh* in the sense of corruption in the passage about the resurrection quoted before: "Flesh and blood cannot inherit the kingdom of God, neither shall corruption inherit incorruption." So, after the event described in the next verse, "Behold, I show you a mystery; we shall all rise, but we shall not all be changed. In a moment, in the twinkling of an eye, at the last trump (for the trumpet shall sound); and the dead shall be raised incorruptible, and we shall be changed. For this corruptible must put on incorruption, and this mortal must put on immortality,"[2]—then flesh, in the sense of the substance of the body, will, after this change, no longer have flesh, in the sense of the corruption of mortality; and yet, as regards its own nature, it will be the same flesh, the same which rises and which is changed. What the Lord said after His resurrection is true, "Handle me, and see; for a spirit hath not flesh and bones, as ye see me have;" and what the apostle says is true, "Flesh and blood cannot inherit the kingdom of God." The first is said of the bodily substance, which exists as the subject of the change: the second is said of the corruption of the flesh, which will cease to exist, for, after its change, flesh will not be corrupted. So, "we have known Christ after the flesh," that is, after the mortality of flesh, before His resurrection; "now henceforth we know Him no more," because, as the same apostle says, "Christ being risen from the dead, dieth no more, and death hath no more dominion over Him."[3] The words, "we have known Christ after the flesh," strictly speaking, imply that Christ was after the flesh, for what never was cannot be known. And it is not "we have supposed," but "we have known." But not to insist on a word, in case some one should say that *known* is used in the sense of *supposed*, it is astonishing, if one could be surprised at want of sight in a blind man, that these blind people do not perceive that if what the apostle says about not knowing Christ after the flesh proves that Christ had not flesh, then what he says in the same place of not knowing any one henceforth after the flesh proves that all those here referred to had not flesh. For when he speaks of not knowing any one, he cannot intend to speak only of Christ; but in his realization of the future life with those who are to be changed at the resurrection, he says, "Henceforth we know no man after the flesh;" that is, we have such an assured hope of our future incorruption and immortality, that the thought of it makes us rejoice even now. So he says elsewhere: "If ye then be risen with Christ, seek those things that are above, where Christ sitteth at the right hand of God. Set your affections upon things above, and not on things on the earth."[4] It is true we have not yet risen as Christ has, but we are said to have risen with Him on account of the hope which we have in Him. So again he says: "According to His mercy He saved us, by the washing of regeneration."[5] Evidently what we obtain in the washing of regeneration is not the salvation itself, but the hope of it. And yet, because this hope is certain, we are said to be saved, as if the salvation were already bestowed. Elsewhere it is said explicitly: "We groan within ourselves, waiting for the adoption, even the redemption of our body. For we are saved by hope. But hope which is seen is not hope; for what a man seeth, why doth he yet hope for? But if we hope for what we see not, then do we with patience wait for it."[6] The apostle says not, "we are to be saved," but, "we are now saved," that is, in hope, though not yet in reality. And in the same way it is in hope, though not yet in reality, that we now know no man after the flesh. This hope is in Christ, in whom what we hope for as promised to us has already been fulfilled. He is risen, and death has no more dominion over Him. Though we have known Him after the flesh, before His death, when there was in His body that mortality which the apostle properly calls flesh, now henceforth know we Him no more; for that mortal of His has now put on immortality, and His flesh, in the sense of mortality, no longer exists.

8. The context of the passage containing this clause of which our adversaries make such a bad use, brings out its real meaning. "The love of Christ," we read, "constrains us, because we thus judge, that if one died for all, then all died; and He died for all, that they which live should not henceforth live unto themselves, but to Him who died for them, and rose again. Therefore henceforth know we no man after the flesh; and though we have known Christ after the flesh, yet now henceforth know we Him no more." The words, "that they which live should not henceforth live unto themselves, but unto

[1] Luke xxiv. 39. [2] 1 Cor. xv. 50-53. [3] Rom. vi. 9.

[4] Col. iii. 1, 2. [5] Tit. iii. 5. [6] Rom. viii. 23-25.

Him who died for them, and rose again," show plainly that the resurrection of Christ is the ground of the apostle's statement. To live not to themselves, but to Him, must mean to live not after the flesh, in the hope of earthly and perishable goods, but after the spirit, in the hope of resurrection,—a resurrection already accomplished in Christ. Of those, then, for whom Christ died and rose again, and who live henceforth not to themselves, but to Him, the Apostle says that he knows no one after the flesh, on account of the hope of future immortality to which they were looking forward,—a hope which in Christ was already a reality. So, though he has known Christ after the flesh, before His death, now he knows Him no more; for he knows that He has risen, and that death has no more dominion over Him. And because in Christ we all are even now in hope, though not in reality, what Christ is, he adds: "Therefore if any man be in Christ, he is a new creature: old things are passed away; behold, all things are become new. And all things are of God, who has reconciled us to Himself by Christ."[1] What the new creature —that is, the people renewed by faith—hopes for regarding itself, it has already in Christ; and the hope will also hereafter be actually realized. And, as regards this hope, old things have passed away, because we are no longer in the times of the Old Testament, expecting a temporal and carnal kingdom of God; and all things are become new, making the promise of the kingdom of heaven, where there shall be no death or corruption, the ground of our confidence. But in the resurrection of the dead it will not be as a matter of hope, but in reality, that old things shall pass away, when the last enemy, death, shall be destroyed; and all things shall become new when this corruptible has put on incorruption, and this mortal has put on immortality. This has already taken place in Christ, whom Paul accordingly, in reality, knew no longer after the flesh. But not yet in reality, but only in hope, did he know no one after the flesh of those for whom Christ died and rose again. For, as he says to the Ephesians, we are already saved by grace. The whole passage is to the purpose: "But God, who is rich in mercy, for His great love wherewith He loved us, even when we were dead in sins, hath quickened us together with Christ, by whose grace we have been saved." The words, "hath quickened us together with Christ," correspond to what he said to the Corinthians, "that they which live should no longer live to themselves, but to Him that died for them and rose again." And in the words, "by whose grace we have been saved," he speaks of the thing hoped for as already accomplished. So, in the passage quoted above, he says explicitly, "We have been saved by hope." And here he proceeds to specify future events as if already accomplished. "And has raised us up together," he says, "and has made us sit together in heavenly places in Christ Jesus." Christ is certainly already seated in heavenly places, but we not yet. But as in an assured hope we already possess the future, he says that we sit in heavenly places, not in ourselves, but in Him. And to show that it is still future, in case it should be thought that what is spoken of as accomplished in hope has been accomplished in reality, he adds, "that He might show in the ages to come the exceeding riches of His grace in His kindness towards us in Christ Jesus."[2] So also we must understand the following passage: "For when we were in the flesh, the motions of sins, which were by the law, did work in our members to bring forth fruit unto death."[3] He says, "when we were in the flesh," as if they were no longer in the flesh. He means to say, when we were in the hope of fleshly things, referring to the time when the law, which can be fulfilled only by spiritual love, was in force, in order that by transgression the offence might abound, that after the revelation of the New Testament, grace and the gift by grace might much more abound. And to the same effect he says elsewhere, "They which are in the flesh cannot please God;" and then, to show that he does not mean those not yet dead, he adds, "But ye are not in the flesh, but in the Spirit."[4] The meaning is, those who are in the hope of fleshly good cannot please God; but you are not in the hope of fleshly things, but in the hope of spiritual things, that is, of the kingdom of heaven, where the body itself, which now is natural, will, by the change in the resurrection, be, according to the capacity of its nature, a spiritual body. For "it is sown a natural body, it will be raised a spiritual body." If, then, the apostle knew no one after the flesh of those who were said to be not in the flesh, because they were not in the hope of fleshly things, although they still were burdened with corruptible and mortal flesh; how much more significantly could he say of Christ that he no longer knew Him after the flesh, seeing that in the body of Christ what they hoped for had already been accomplished! Surely it is better and more

[1] 2 Cor. v. 14-18.

[2] Eph. ii. 4-7. [3] Rom. vii. 5. [4] Rom. viii. 8, 9.

reverential to examine the passages of sacred Scripture so as to discover their agreement with one another, than to accept some as true, and condemn others as false, whenever any difficulty occurs beyond the power of our weak intellect to solve. As to the apostle in his childhood understanding as a child, this is said merely as an illustration.[1] And when he was a child he was not a spiritual man, as he was when he produced for the edification of the churches those writings which are not, as other books, merely a profitable study, but which authoritatively claim our belief as part of the ecclesiastical canon.

[1] 1 Cor. xiii. 11.

BOOK XII.

FAUSTUS DENIES THAT THE PROPHETS PREDICTED CHRIST. AUGUSTIN PROVES SUCH PREDICTION FROM THE NEW TESTAMENT, AND EXPOUNDS AT LENGTH THE PRINCIPAL TYPES OF CHRIST IN THE OLD TESTAMENT.

1. Faustus said: Why do I not believe the prophets? Rather why do you believe them? On account, you will reply, of their prophecies about Christ. For my part, I have read the prophets with the most eager attention, and have found no such prophecies. And surely it shows a weak faith not to believe in Christ without proofs and testimonies. Indeed, you yourselves are accustomed to teach that Christian faith is so simple and absolute as not to admit of laborious investigations. Why, then, should you destroy the simplicity of faith by buttressing it with evidences, and Jewish evidences too? Or if you are changing your opinion about evidences, what more trustworthy witness could you have than God Himself testifying to His own Son when He sent Him on earth,—not by a prophet or an interpreter,—by a voice immediately from heaven: "This is my beloved Son, believe Him?"[1] And again He testifies of Himself: "I came forth from the Father, and am come into the world;"[2] and in many similar passages. When the Jews quarrelled with this testimony, saying "Thou bearest witness of thyself, thy witness is not true," He replied: "Although I bear witness of myself, my witness is true. It is written in your law, The witness of two men is true. I am one that bear witness of myself, and the Father who sent me beareth witness of me."[3] He does not mention the prophets. Again He appeals to the testimony of His own works, saying, "If ye believe not me, believe the works;"[4] not, "If ye believe not me, believe the prophets." Accordingly we require no testimonies concerning our Saviour. All we look for in the prophets is prudence and virtue, and a good example, which, you are well aware, are not to be found in the Jewish prophets. This, no doubt, explains your referring me at once to their predictions as a reason for believing them, without a word about their actions. This may be good policy, but it is not in harmony with the declaration of Scripture, that it is impossible to gather grapes from thorns, or figs from thistles. This may serve meanwhile as a brief and sufficient reply to the question, why we do not believe the prophets. The fact that they did not prophesy of Christ is abundantly proved in the writings of our fathers. I shall only add this, that if the Hebrew prophets knew and preached Christ, and yet lived such vicious lives, what Paul says of the wise men among the Gentiles might be applied to them: "Though they knew God, they glorified Him not as God, nor were thankful; but they became vain in their imaginations, and their foolish heart was darkened."[5] You see the knowledge of great things is worth little, unless the life corresponds.

2. Augustin replied: The meaning of all this is, that the Hebrew prophets foretold nothing of Christ, and that, if they did, their predictions are of no use to us, and they themselves did not live suitably to the dignity of such prophecies. We must therefore prove the fact of the prophecies; and their use for the truth and steadfastness of our faith; and that the lives of the prophets were in harmony with their words. In this threefold discussion, it would take a long time under the first head to quote from all the books the passages in which Christ may be shown to have been predicted. Faustus' frivolity may be met effectually by the weight of one great authority. Although Faustus does not believe the prophets, he professes to believe the apostles. Above, as if to satisfy the doubts of some opponent, he declares that he assuredly believes the Apostle Paul.[6] Let us then hear what Paul says of the prophets. His words are: "Paul, a servant of Jesus Christ,

[1] Matt. iii. 17.
[2] John xvi. 28.
[3] John viii. 13-18.
[4] John x. 38.
[5] Rom. i. 21.
[6] Lib. xi.

called to be an apostle, separated unto the gospel of God, which He had promised before by His prophets in the holy Scriptures, concerning His Son, who was made of the seed of David according to the flesh."[1] What more does Faustus wish? Will he maintain that the apostle is speaking of some other prophets, and not of the Hebrew prophets? In any case, the gospel spoken of as promised was concerning the Son of God, who was made for Him of the seed of David according to the flesh: and to this gospel the apostle says that he was separated. So that the Manichæan heresy is opposed to faith in the gospel, which teaches that the Son of God was made of the seed of David according to the flesh. Besides, there are many passages where the apostle plainly testifies in behalf of the Hebrew prophets, with an authority by which the necks of these proud Manichæans are broken.

3. "I speak the truth in Christ," says the apostle, "I lie not, my conscience bearing me witness in the Holy Ghost, that I have great heaviness and continual sorrow of heart. For I could wish that myself were accursed from Christ, for my brethren, my kinsmen according to the flesh: who are Israelites; to whom pertaineth the adoption, and the glory, and the covenants, and the giving of the law, and the service and the promises; whose are the fathers, and of whom, as concerning the flesh, Christ came, who is over all, God blessed for ever."[2] Here is the most abundant and express testimony and the most solemn commendation. The adoption here spoken of is evidently through the Son of God; as the apostle says to the Galatians: "In the fullness of time, God sent forth His Son, made of a woman, made under the law, that He might redeem them that were under the law, that we might receive the adoption of sons."[3] And the glory spoken of is chiefly that of which he says in the same Epistle to the Romans: "What advantage hath the Jew? or what profit is there in circumcision? Much every way: chiefly, because unto them were committed the oracles of God."[4] Can the Manichæans tell us of any oracles of God committed to the Jews besides those of the Hebrew prophets? And why are the covenants said to belong especially to the Israelites, but because not only was the Old Testament given to them, but also the New was prefigured in the Old? Our opponents often display much ignorant ferocity in attacking the dispensation of the law given to the Israelites, not understanding that God wishes us to be not under the law, but under grace. They are here answered by the apostle himself, who, in speaking of the advantages of the Jews, mentions this as one, that they had the giving of the law. If the law had been bad, the apostle would not have referred to it in praise of the Jews. And if Christ had not been preached by the law, the Lord Himself would not have said, "If ye believe Moses, ye would have believed me, for he wrote of me;"[5] nor would He have borne the testimony He did after His resurrection, saying, "All things must needs be fulfilled that were written in the law of Moses, and in the Prophets, and in the Psalms, concerning me."[6]

4. But because the Manichæans preach another Christ, and not Him whom the apostles preached, but a false Christ of their own false contrivance, in imitation of whose falsehood they themselves speak lies, though they may perhaps be believed when they are not ashamed to profess to be the followers of a deceiver, that has befallen them which the apostle asserts of the unbelieving Jews: "When Moses is read, a veil is upon their heart." Neither will this veil which keeps them from understanding Moses be taken away from them till they turn to Christ; not a Christ of their own making, but the Christ of the Hebrew prophets. For, as the apostle says, "When thou shalt turn to the Lord, the veil shall be taken away."[7] We cannot wonder that they do not believe in the Christ who rose from the dead, and who said, "All things must needs be fulfilled which were written in the law of Moses, and in the prophets, and in the Psalms, concerning me;" for this Christ has Himself told us what Abraham said to a hard-hearted rich man when he was in torment in hell, and asked Abraham to send some one to his brothers to teach them, that they might not come too into that place of torment. Abraham's reply was: "They have Moses and the prophets, let them hear them." And when the rich man said that they would not believe unless some one rose from the dead, he received this most truthful answer: "If they hear not Moses and the prophets, neither will they believe even though one rose from the dead."[8] Wherefore, the Manichæans will not hear Moses and the prophets, and so they do not believe Christ, though He rose from the dead. Indeed, they do not even believe that Christ rose from the dead. For how can they believe that He rose, when they do not believe that He died? For, again, how

[1] Rom. i. 1-3.
[2] Rom. ix. 1-5.
[3] Gal. iv. 4, 5.
[4] Rom. iii. 1, 2.
[5] John v. 46.
[6] Luke xxiv. 44.
[7] 2 Cor. iii. 15, 16.
[8] Luke xvi. 27-31.

can they believe that He died, when they deny that He had a mortal body?

5. But we reject those false teachers whose Christ is false, or rather, whose Christ never existed. For we have a Christ true and truthful, foretold by the prophets, preached by the apostles, who in innumerable places refer to the testimonies of the law and the prophets in support of their preaching. Paul, in one short sentence, gives the right view of this subject. "Now," he says, "the righteousness of God without the law is manifested, being witnessed by the law and the prophets."[1] What prophets, if not of Israel, to whom, as he expressly says, pertain the covenants, and the giving of the law, and the promises? And what promises, but about Christ? Elsewhere, speaking of Christ, he says concisely: "All the promises of God are in Him yea."[2] Paul tells me that the giving of the law pertained to the Israelites. He also tells me that Christ is the end of the law for righteousness to every one that believeth. He also tells me that all the promises of God are in Christ yea. And you tell me that the prophets of Israel foretold nothing of Christ. Shall I believe the absurdities of Manichæus relating a vain and long fable in opposition to Paul? or shall I believe Paul when he forewarns us: "If any man preach to you another gospel than that which we have preached, let him be accursed?"

6. Our opponents may perhaps ask us to point out passages where Christ is predicted by the prophets of Israel. One would think they might be satisfied with the authority of the apostles, who declare that what we read in the writings of the Hebrew prophets was fulfilled in Christ, or with that of Christ Himself, who says that these things were written of Him. Whoever is unable to point out the passages should lay the blame on his own ignorance; for the apostles and Christ and the sacred Scriptures are not chargeable with falsehood. However, one instance out of many may be adduced. The apostle, in the verses following the passage quoted above, says: "The word of God cannot fail. For they are not all Israel which are of Israel; neither, because they are the seed of Abraham, are they all children: but, In Isaac shall thy seed be called: that is, they which are the children of the flesh, these are not the children of God; but the children of promise are counted for the seed."[3] What can our opponent says against this, in view of the declaration made to Abraham: "In thy seed shall all the nations of the earth be blessed?" At the time when the apostle gave the following exposition of this promise, "To Abraham and to his seed were the promises made. He saith not, To seed, as of many, but as of one, To thy seed, which is Christ,"[4] a doubt on this point might then have been less inexcusable, for at that time all nations had not yet believed on Christ, who is preached as of the seed of Abraham. But now that we see the fulfillment of what we read in the ancient prophecy,—now that all nations are actually blessed in the seed of Abraham, to whom it was said thousands of years ago, "In thy seed shall all nations be blessed,"—it is mere obstinate folly to try to bring in another Christ, not of the seed of Abraham, or to hold that there are no predictions of Christ in the prophetical books of the children of Abraham.

7. To enumerate all the passages in the Hebrew prophets referring to our Lord and Saviour Jesus Christ, would exceed the limits of a volume, not to speak of the brief replies of which this treatise consists. The whole contents of these Scriptures are either directly or indirectly about Christ. Often the reference is allegorical or enigmatical, perhaps in a verbal allusion, or in a historical narrative, requiring diligence in the student, and rewarding him with the pleasure of discovery. Other passages, again, are plain; for, without the help of what is clear, we could not understand what is obscure. And even the figurative passages, when brought together, will be found so harmonious in their testimony to Christ as to put to shame the obtuseness of the sceptic.

8. In the creation God finished His works in six days, and rested on the seventh. The history of the world contains six periods marked by the dealings of God with men. The first period is from Adam to Noah; the second, from Noah to Abraham; the third, from Abraham to David; the fourth, from David to the captivity in Babylon; the fifth, from the captivity to the advent of lowliness of our Lord Jesus Christ; the sixth is now in progress, and will end in the coming of the exalted Saviour to judgment. What answers to the seventh day is the rest of the saints,—not in this life, but in another, where the rich man saw Lazarus at rest while he was tormented in hell; where there is no evening, because there is no decay. On the sixth day, in Genesis, man is formed after the image of God; in the sixth period of the world there is the clear discovery of our transformation in the renewing of our mind, according to the

---

1 Rom. iii. 21.

2 2 Cor. i. 20.

3 Rom. ix. 6-8.

4 Gal. iii. 16.

image of Him who created us, as the apostle says.[1] As a wife was made for Adam from his side while he slept, the Church becomes the property of her dying Saviour, by the sacrament of the blood which flowed from His side after His death. The woman made out of her husband's side is called Eve, or Life, and the mother of living beings; and the Lord says in the Gospel: "Except a man eat my flesh and drink my blood, he has no life in him."[2] The whole narrative of Genesis, in the most minute details, is a prophecy of Christ and of the Church with reference either to the good Christians or to the bad. There is a significance in the words of the apostle when he calls Adam "the figure of Him that was to come;"[3] and when he says, "A man shall leave his father and mother, and shall cleave to his wife, and they two shall be one flesh. This is a great mystery; but I speak concerning Christ and the Church."[4] This points most obviously to the way in which Christ left His Father; for "though He was in the form of God, and thought it not robbery to be equal with God, He emptied Himself, and took upon Him the form of a servant."[5] And so, too, He left His mother, the synagogue of the Jews which cleaved to the carnality of the Old Testament, and was united to the Church His holy bride, that in the peace of the New Testament they two might be one flesh. For though with the Father He was God, by whom we were made, He became in the flesh partaker of our nature, that we might become the body of which He is the head.

9. As Cain's sacrifice of the fruit of the ground is rejected, while Abel's sacrifice of his sheep and the fat thereof is accepted, so the faith of the New Testament praising God in the harmless service of grace is preferred to the earthly observances of the Old Testament. For though the Jews were right in practising these things, they were guilty of unbelief in not distinguishing the time of the New Testament when Christ came, from the time of the Old Testament. God said to Cain, "If thou offerest well, yet if thou dividest not well, thou hast sinned."[6] If Cain had obeyed God when He said, "Be content, for to thee shall be its reference, and thou shalt rule over it," he would have referred his sin to himself, by taking the blame of it, and confessing it to God; and so assisted by supplies of grace, he would have ruled over his sin, instead of acting as the servant of sin in killing his innocent brother. So also the Jews, of whom all these things are a figure, if they had been content, instead of being turbulent, and had acknowledged the time of salvation through the pardon of sins by grace, and heard Christ saying, "They that are whole need not a physician, but they that are sick; I came not to call the righteous, but sinners to repentance;"[7] and, "Every one that committeth sin is the servant of sin;" and, "If the Son make you free, ye shall be free indeed,"[8]—they would in confession have referred their sin to themselves, saying to the Physician, as it is written in the Psalm, "I said, Lord, be merciful to me; heal my soul, for I have sinned against Thee."[9] And being made free by the hope of grace, they would have ruled over sin as long as it continued in their mortal body. But now, being ignorant of God's righteousness, and wishing to establish a righteousness of their own, proud of the works of the law, instead of being humbled on account of their sins, they have not been content; and in subjection to sin reigning in their mortal body, so as to make them obey it in the lusts thereof, they have stumbled on the stone of stumbling, and have been inflamed with hatred against him whose works they grieved to see accepted by God. The man who was born blind, and had been made to see, said to them, "We know that God heareth not sinners; but if any man serve Him, and do His will, him He heareth;"[10] as if he had said, God regardeth not the sacrifice of Cain, but he regards the sacrifice of Abel. Abel, the younger brother, is killed by the elder brother; Christ, the head of the younger people, is killed by the elder people of the Jews. Abel dies in the field; Christ dies on Calvary.

10. God asks Cain where his brother is, not as if He did not know, but as a judge asks a guilty criminal. Cain replies that he knows not, and that he is not his brother's keeper. And what answer can the Jews give at this day, when we ask them with the voice of God, that is, of the sacred Scriptures, about Christ, except that they do not know the Christ that we speak of? Cain's ignorance was pretended, and the Jews are deceived in their refusal of Christ. Moreover, they would have been in a sense keepers of Christ, if they had been willing to receive and keep the Christian faith. For the man who keeps Christ in his heart does not ask, like Cain, Am I my brother's keeper? Then God says to Cain, "What hast thou done? The voice of thy brother's blood crieth unto me from the ground." So the voice of God in the Holy Scriptures accuses the Jews. For the blood

[1] Col. iii. 10.
[2] John vi. 53.
[3] Rom. v. 14.
[4] Eph. v. 31, 32.
[5] Phil. ii. 6, 7.
[6] Vulg.
[7] Matt. ix. 12, 13.
[8] John viii. 34, 36.
[9] Ps. xli. 4.
[10] John ix. 31.

of Christ has a loud voice on the earth, when the responsive Amen of those who believe in Him comes from all nations. This is the voice of Christ's blood, because the clear voice of the faithful redeemed by His blood is the voice of the blood itself.

11. Then God says to Cain: "Thou art cursed from the earth, which hath opened its mouth to receive thy brother's blood at thy hand. For thou shalt till the earth, and it shall no longer yield unto thee its strength. A mourner and an abject shalt thou be on the earth." It is not, Cursed is the earth, but, Cursed art thou from the earth, which hath opened its mouth to receive thy brother's blood at thy hand. So the unbelieving people of the Jews is cursed from the earth, that is, from the Church, which in the confession of sins has opened its mouth to receive the blood shed for the remission of sins by the hand of the people that would not be under grace, but under the law. And this murderer is cursed by the Church; that is, the Church admits and avows the curse pronounced by the apostle: "Whoever are of the works of the law are under the curse of the law."[1] Then, after saying, Cursed art thou from the earth, which has opened its mouth to receive thy brother's blood at thy hand, what follows is not, For thou shalt till it, but, Thou shalt till the earth, and it shall not yield to thee its strength. The earth he is to till is not necessarily the same as that which opened its mouth to receive his brother's blood at his hand. From this earth he is cursed, and so he tills an earth which shall no longer yield to him its strength. That is, the Church admits and avows the Jewish people to be cursed, because after killing Christ they continue to till the ground of an earthly circumcision, an earthly Sabbath, an earthly passover, while the hidden strength or virtue of making known Christ, which this tilling contains, is not yielded to the Jews while they continue in impiety and unbelief, for it is revealed in the New Testament. While they will not turn to God, the veil which is on their minds in reading the Old Testament is not taken away. This veil is taken away only by Christ, who does not do away with the reading of the Old Testament, but with the covering which hides its virtue. So, at the crucifixion of Christ, the veil was rent in twain, that by the passion of Christ hidden mysteries might be revealed to believers who turn to Him with a mouth opened in confession to drink His blood. In this way the Jewish people, like Cain, continue tilling the ground, in the carnal observance of the law, which does not yield to them its strength, because they do not perceive in it the grace of Christ. So too, the flesh of Christ was the ground from which by crucifying Him the Jews produced our salvation, for He died for our offences. But this ground did not yield to them its strength, for they were not justified by the virtue of His resurrection, for He arose again for our justification. As the apostle says: "He was crucified in weakness, but He liveth by the power of God."[2] This is the power of that ground which is unknown to the ungodly and unbelieving. When Christ rose, He did not appear to those who had crucified Him. So Cain was not allowed to see the strength of the ground which he tilled to sow his seed in it; as God said, "Thou shalt till the ground, and it shall no longer yield unto thee its strength."

12. "Groaning and trembling shalt thou be on the earth." Here no one can fail to see that in every land where the Jews are scattered they mourn for the loss of their kingdom, and are in terrified subjection to the immensely superior number of Christians. So Cain answered, and said: "My case is worse, if Thou drivest me out this day from the face of the earth, and from Thy face shall I be hid, and I shall be a mourner and an outcast on the earth; and it shall be that every one that findeth me shall slay me." Here he groans indeed in terror, lest after losing his earthly possession he should suffer the death of the body. This he calls a worse case than that of the ground not yielding to him its strength, or than that of spiritual death. For his mind is carnal; for he thinks little of being hid from the face of God, that is, of being under the anger of God, were it not that he may be found and slain. This is the carnal mind that tills the ground, but does not obtain its strength. To be carnally minded is death; but he, in ignorance of this, mourns for the loss of his earthly possession, and is in terror of bodily death. But what does God reply? "Not so," He says; "but whosoever shall kill Cain, vengeance shall be taken on him sevenfold." That is, It is not as thou sayest; not by bodily death shall the ungodly race of carnal Jews perish. For whoever destroys them in this way shall suffer sevenfold vengeance, that is, shall bring upon himself the sevenfold penalty under which the Jews lie for the crucifixion of Christ. So to the end of the seven days of time, the continued preservation of the Jews will be a proof to believing Christians of the subjection merited

[1] Gal. iii. 10.

[2] 2 Cor. xiii. 4.

by those who, in the pride of their kingdom, put the Lord to death.

13. "And the Lord God set a mark upon Cain, lest any one finding him should slay him." It is a most notable fact, that all the nations subjugated by Rome adopted the heathenish ceremonies of the Roman worship; while the Jewish nation, whether under Pagan or Christian monarchs, has never lost the sign of their law, by which they are distinguished from all other nations and peoples. No emperor or monarch who finds under his government the people with this mark kills them, that is, makes them cease to be Jews, and as Jews to be separate in their observances, and unlike the rest of the world. Only when a Jew comes over to Christ, he is no longer Cain, nor goes out from the presence of God, nor dwells in the land of Nod, which is said to mean commotion. Against this evil of commotion the Psalmist prays, "Suffer not my feet to be moved;"[1] and again, "Let not the hands of the wicked remove me;"[2] and, "Those that trouble me will rejoice when I am moved:"[3] and, "The Lord is at my right hand, that I should not be moved;"[4] and so in innumerable places. This evil comes upon those who leave the presence of God, that is, His loving-kindness. Thus the Psalmist says, "I said in my prosperity, I shall never be moved." But observe what follows, "Lord, by Thy favor Thou hast given strength to my honor; Thou didst hide Thy face, and I was troubled;"[5] which teaches us that not in itself, but by participation in the light of God, can any soul possess beauty, or honor, or strength. The Manichæans should think of this, to keep them from the blasphemy of identifying themselves with the nature and substance of God. But they cannot think, because they are not content. The Sabbath of the heart they are strangers to. If they were content, as Cain was told to be, they would refer their sin to themselves; that is, they would lay the blame on themselves, and not on a race of darkness that no one ever heard of, and so by the grace of God they would prevail over their sin. But now the Manichæans, and all who oppose the truth by their various heresies, leave the presence of God, like Cain and the scattered Jews, and inhabit the land of commotion, that is, of carnal disquietude, instead of the enjoyment of God, that is instead of Eden, which is interpreted Feasting, where Paradise was planted. But not to depart too much from the argument of this treatise I must limit myself to a few short remarks under this head.

14. Omitting therefore many passages in these Books where Christ may be found, but which require longer explanation and proof, although the most hidden meanings are the sweetest, convincing testimony may be obtained from the enumeration of such things as the following:—That Enoch, the seventh from Adam, pleased God, and was translated, as there is to be a seventh day of rest into which all will be translated who, during the sixth day of the world's history, are created anew by the incarnate Word. That Noah, with his family is saved by water and wood, as the family of Christ is saved by baptism, as representing the suffering of the cross. That this ark is made of beams formed in a square, as the Church is constructed of saints prepared unto every good work: for a square stands firm on any side. That the length is six times the breadth, and ten times the height, like a human body, to show that Christ appeared in a human body. That the breadth reaches to fifty cubits; as the apostle says, "Our heart is enlarged,"[6] that is, with spiritual love, of which he says again, "The love of God is shed abroad in our heart by the Holy Ghost, which is given unto us."[7] For in the fiftieth day after His resurrection, Christ sent His Holy Spirit to enlarge the hearts of His disciples. That it is three hundred cubits long, to make up six times fifty; as there are six periods in the history of the world during which Christ has never ceased to be preached,—in five foretold by the prophets, and in the sixth proclaimed in the gospel. That it is thirty cubits high, a tenth part of the length; because Christ is our height, who in his thirtieth year gave His sanction to the doctrine of the gospel, by declaring that He came not to destroy the law, but to fulfil it. Now the ten commandments are to be the heart of the law; and so the length of the ark is ten times thirty. Noah himself, too, was the tenth from Adam. That the beams of the ark are fastened within and without with pitch, to signify by compact union the forbearance of love, which keeps the brotherly connection from being impaired, and the bond of peace from being broken by the offences which try the Church either from without or from within. For pitch is a glutinous substance, of great energy and force, to represent the ardor of love which, with great power of endurance, beareth all things in the maintenance of spiritual communion.

15. That all kinds of animals are inclosed in the ark; as the Church contains all nations, which was also set forth in the vessel shown

[1] Ps. lxvi. 9. [2] Ps. xxxvi. 11. [3] Ps. xiii. 4. [4] Ps. xvi. 8. [5] Ps. xxx. 6, 7.

[6] 2 Cor. vi. 11. [7] Rom. v. 5.

to Peter. That clean and unclean animals are in the ark; as good and bad take part in the sacraments of the Church. That the clean are in sevens, and the unclean in twos; not because the bad are fewer than the good, but because the good preserve the unity of the Spirit in the bond of peace; and the Spirit is spoken of in Scripture as having a sevenfold operation, as being "the Holy Spirit of wisdom and understanding, of counsel and might, of knowledge and piety, and of the fear of God."[1] So also the number fifty, which is connected with the advent of the Holy Spirit, is made up of seven times seven, and one over; whence it is said, "Endeavoring to keep the unity of the Spirit in the bond of peace."[2] The bad, again, are in twos, as being easily divided, from their tendency to schism. That Noah, counting his family, was the eighth; because the hope of our resurrection has appeared in Christ, who rose from the dead on the eighth day, that is, on the day after the seventh, or Sabbath day. This day was the third from His passion; but in the ordinary reckoning of days, it is both the eighth and the first.

16. That the whole ark together is finished in a cubit above; as the Church, the body of Christ gathered into unity, is raised to perfection. So Christ says in the Gospel: "He that gathereth not with me, scattereth."[3] That the entrance is on the side; as no man enters the Church except by the sacrament of the remission of sins which flowed from Christ's opened side. That the lower spaces of the ark are divided into two and three chambers: as the multitude of all nations in the Church is divided into two, as circumcised and uncircumcised; or into three, as descended from the three sons of Noah. And these parts of the ark are called lower, because in this earthly state there is a difference of races, and above we are completed in one. *Above* there is no diversity; for Christ is all and in all, finishing us, as it were, in one cubit above with heavenly unity.

17. That the flood came seven days after Noah entered the ark; as we are baptized in the hope of the future rest, which was denoted by the seventh day. That all flesh on the face of the earth, outside the ark, was destroyed by the flood; as, beyond the communion of the Church, though the water of baptism is the same, it is efficacious only for destruction, and not for salvation. That it rained for forty days and forty nights; as the sacrament of heavenly baptism washes away all the guilt of the sins against the ten commandments throughout all the four quarters of the world (four times ten is forty), whether that guilt has been contracted in the day of prosperity or in the night of adversity.

18. That Noah was five hundred years old when God told him to make the ark, and six hundred when he entered the ark; which shows that the ark was made during one hundred years, which seem to correspond to the years of an age of the world. So the sixth age is occupied with the construction of the Church by the preaching of the gospel. The man who avails himself of the offer of salvation is made like a square beam, fitted for every good work, and forms part of the sacred fabric. Again, it was the second month of the six hundredth year when Noah entered the ark, and in two months there are sixty days; so that here, as in every multiple of six, we have the number denoting the sixth age.

19. That mention is made of the twenty-seventh day of the month; as we have already seen the significance of the square in the beams. Here especially it is significant; for as twenty-seven is the cube of three, there is a trinity in the means by which we are, as it were, squared, or fitted for every good work. By the memory we remember God; by the understanding we know Him; by the will we love Him. That in the seventh month the ark rested; reminding us again of the seventh day of rest. And here again, to denote the perfection of those at rest, the twenty-seventh day of the month is mentioned for the second time. So what is promised in hope is realized in experience. There is here a combination of seven and eight; for the water rose fifteen cubits above the mountains, pointing to a profound mystery in baptism,—the sacrament of our regeneration. For the seventh day of rest is connected with the eighth of resurrection. For when the saints receive again their bodies after the rest of the intermediate state, the rest will not cease; but rather the whole man, body and soul united, renewed in the immortal health, will attain to the realization of his hope in the enjoyment of eternal life. Thus the sacrament of baptism, like the waters of Noah, rises above all the wisdom of the proud. Seven and eight are also combined in the number of one hundred and fifty, made up of seventy and eighty, which was the number of days during which the water prevailed, pointing out the deep import of baptism in consecrating the new man to hold the faith of rest and resurrection.

20. That the raven sent out after forty days did not return, being either prevented

[1] Isa. xi. 2, 3. [2] Eph. iv. 3. [3] Matt. xii. 30.

by the water or attracted by some floating carcase; as men defiled by impure desire, and therefore eager for things outside in the world, are either baptized, or are led astray into the company of those to whom, as they are outside the ark, that is, outside the Church, baptism is destructive. That the dove when sent forth found no rest, and returned; as in the New Testament rest is not promised to the saints in this world. The dove was sent forth after forty days, a period denoting the length of human life. When again sent forth after seven days, denoting the sevenfold operation of the Spirit, the dove brought back a fruitful olive branch; as some even who are baptized outside of the Church, if not destitute of the fatness of charity, may come after all, as it were in the evening, and be brought into the one communion by the mouth of the dove in the kiss of peace. That, when again sent forth after seven days, the dove did not return; as, at the end of the world, the rest of the saints shall no longer be in the sacrament of hope, as now, while in the communion of the Church, they drink what flowed from the side of Christ, but in the perfection of eternal safety, when the kingdom shall be delivered up to God and the Father, and when, in that unclouded contemplation of unchangeable truth, we shall no longer need natural symbols.

21. There are many other points which we cannot take notice of even in this cursory manner. Why in the six hundred and first year of Noah's life—that is, after six hundred years were completed—the covering of the ark is removed, and the hidden mystery, as it were, disclosed. Why the earth is said to have dried on the twenty-seventh day of the second month; as if the number fifty-seven denoted the completion of the rite of baptism. For the twenty-seventh day of the second month is the fifty-seventh day of the year; and the number fifty-seven is seven times eight, which are the numbers of the spirit and the body, with one over, to denote the bond of unity. Why they leave the ark together, though they entered separately. For it is said: "Noah went in, and his sons, and his wife, and his sons' wives with him, into the ark;" the men and the women being spoken of separately; which denotes the time when the flesh lusteth against the spirit, and the spirit against the flesh. But they go forth, Noah and his wife, and his sons and their wives,—the men and women together. For in the end of the world, and in the resurrection of the just, the body will be united to the spirit in perfect harmony, undisturbed by the wants and the passions of mortality. Why, after leaving the ark, only clean animals are offered in sacrifice to God, though both clean and unclean were in the ark.

22. Then, again, it is significant that when God speaks to Noah, and begins anew, as it were, in order, by repetition in various forms, to draw attention to the figure of the Church, the sons of Noah are blessed, and told to replenish the earth, and all animals are given to them for food; as was said to Peter of the vessel, "Kill and eat." That they are told to pour out the blood when they eat; that the former life may not be kept shut up in the conscience, but may be, as it were, poured out in confession. That God makes the bow, which appears in the clouds only when the sun shines, the sign of His covenant with men, and with every living thing, that He will not destroy them with a flood; as those do not perish by the flood, in separation from the Church, who in the clouds of God—that is, in the prophets and in all the sacred Scriptures—discern the glory of Christ, instead of seeking their own glory. The worshippers of the sun, however, need not pride themselves on this; for they must understand that the sun, as also a lion, a lamb, and a stone, are used as types of Christ because they have some resemblance, not because they are of the same substance.

23. Again, the sufferings of Christ from His own nation are evidently denoted by Noah being drunk with the wine of the vineyard he planted, and his being uncovered in his tent. For the mortality of Christ's flesh was uncovered, to the Jews a stumbling-block, and to the Greeks foolishness; but to them that are called, both Jews and Greeks, both Shem and Japhet, the power of God and the wisdom of God. Because the foolishness of God is wiser than men, and the weakness of God is stronger than men.[1]

Moreover, the two sons, the eldest and the youngest, carrying the garment backwards, are a figure of the two peoples, and the sacrament of the past and completed passions of the Lord. They do not see the nakedness of their father, because they do not consent to Christ's death; and yet they honor it with a covering, as knowing whence they were born. The middle son is the Jewish people, for they neither held the first place with the apostles, nor believed subsequently with the Gentiles. They saw the nakedness of their father, because they consented to Christ's death; and they told it to their brethren outside, for what was hidden in the prophets was disclosed by the Jews. And thus they are the

[1] 1 Cor. i. 23-25.

servants of their brethren. For what else is this nation now but a desk for the Christians, bearing the law and the prophets, and testifying to the doctrine of the Church, so that we honor in the sacrament what they disclose in the letter?

24. Again, every one must be impressed, and be either enlightened or confirmed in the faith, by the blessing of the two sons who honored the nakedness of their father, though they turned away their faces, as displeased with the evil done by the vine. "Blessed," he says, "be the Lord God of Shem." For although God is the God of all nations, even the Gentiles acknowledge Him to be in a peculiar sense the God of Israel. And how is this to be explained but by the blessing of Japhet? The occupation of all the world by the Church among the Gentiles was exactly foretold in the words: "Let God enlarge Japhet, and let him dwell in the tents of Shem." That is for the Manichæan to attend to. You see what the state of the world actually is. The very thing that you are astonished and grieved at in us is this, that God is enlarging Japhet. Is He not dwelling in the tents of Shem?—that is, in the churches built by the apostles, the sons of the prophets. Hear what Paul says to the believing Gentiles: "Ye were at that time without Christ, being aliens from the commonwealth of Israel, and strangers from the covenants; having no hope of the promise, and without God in the world." In these words there is a description of the state of Japhet before he dwelt in the tents of Shem. But observe what follows: "Now then," he says, "ye are no more strangers and foreigners, but fellow-citizens with the saints, and of the household of God, being built upon the foundation of the apostles and prophets, Jesus Christ Himself being the chief corner-stone."[1] Here we have Japhet enlarged, and dwelling in the tents of Shem. These testimonies are taken from the epistles of the apostles, which you yourselves acknowledge, and read, and profess to follow. You occupy an unhappy middle position in a building of which Christ is not the chief corner-stone. For you do not belong to the wall of those who, like the apostles, being of the circumcision, believed in Christ; nor to the wall of those who, being of the uncircumcision, like all the Gentiles, are joined in the unity of faith, as in the fellowship of the corner-stone. However, all who accept and read any books of our canon in which Christ is spoken of as having been born and having suffered in the flesh, and who do not unite with us in a common veiling with the sacrament of the mortality, uncovered by the passion, but without the knowledge of piety and charity make known that from which we all are born,—although they differ among themselves, whether as Jews and heretics, or as heretics of one kind or other,—are still all useful to the Church, as being all alike servants, either in bearing witness to or in proving some truth. For of heretics it is said: "There must be heresies, that those who are approved among you may be manifested."[2] Go on, then, with your objections to the Old Testament Scriptures! Go on, ye servants of Ham! You have despised the flesh from which you were born when uncovered. For you could not have called yourselves Christians unless Christ had come into the world, as foretold by the prophets, and had drunk of His own vine that cup which could not pass from Him, and had slept in His passion, as in the drunkenness of the folly which is wiser than men; and so, in the hidden counsel of God, the disclosure had been made of that infirmity of mortal flesh which is stronger than men. For unless the Word of God had taken on Himself this infirmity, the name of Christian, in which you also glory, would not exist in the earth. Go on, then, as I have said. Declare in mockery what we may honor with reverence. Let the Church use you as her servants to make manifest those members who are approved. So particular are the predictions of the prophets regarding the state and the sufferings of the Church, that we can find a place even for you in what is said of the destructive error by which the reprobate are to perish, while the approved are to be manifested.

25. You say that Christ was not foretold by the prophets of Israel, when, in fact, their Scriptures teem with such predictions, if you would only examine them carefully, instead of treating them with levity. Who in Abraham leaves his country and kindred that he may become rich and prosperous among strangers, but He who, leaving the land and country of the Jews, of whom He was born in the flesh, is now extending His power, as we see, among the Gentiles? Who in Isaac carried the wood for His own sacrifice, but He who carried His own cross? Who is the ram for sacrifice, caught by the horns in a bush, but He who was fastened to the cross as an offering for us?

26. Who in the angel striving with Jacob, on the one hand is constrained to give him a blessing, as the weaker to the stronger, the conquered to the conqueror, and on the other

[1] Eph. ii. 12, 19, 20.

[2] 1 Cor. xi. 19.

hand puts his thigh-bone out of joint, but He who, when He suffered the people of Israel to prevail against Him, blessed those among them who believed, while the multitude, like Jacob's thigh-bone, halted in their carnality? Who is the stone placed under Jacob's head, but Christ the head of man? And in its anointing the very name of Christ is expressed, for, as all know, Christ means anointed. Christ refers to this in the Gospel, and declares it to be a type of Himself, when He said of Nathanael that he was an Israelite indeed, in whom was no guile, and when Nathanael, resting his head, as it were, on this Stone, or on Christ, confessed Him as the Son of God and the King of Israel, anointing the Stone by his confession, in which he acknowledged Jesus to be Christ. On this occasion the Lord made appropriate mention of what Jacob saw in his dream: "Verily I say unto you, Ye shall see heaven opened, and the angels of God ascending and descending upon the Son of man."[1] This Jacob saw, who in the blessing was called Israel, when he had the stone for a pillow, and had the vision of the ladder reaching from earth to heaven, on which the angels of God were ascending and descending.[2] The angels denote the evangelists, or preachers of Christ. They ascend when they rise above the created universe to describe the supreme majesty of the divine nature of Christ as being in the beginning God with God, by whom all things were made. They descend to tell of His being made of a woman, made under the law, that He might redeem them that were under the law. Christ is the ladder reaching from earth to heaven, or from the carnal to the spiritual: for by His assistance the carnal ascend to spirituality; and the spiritual may be said to descend to nourish the carnal with milk when they cannot speak to them as to spiritual, but as to carnal.[3] There is thus both an ascent and a descent upon the Son of man. For the Son of man is above as our head, being Himself the Saviour; and He is below in His body, the Church. He is the ladder, for He says, "I am the way." We ascend to Him to see Him in heavenly places; we descend to Him for the nourishment of His weak members. And the ascent and descent are by Him as well as to Him. Following His example, those who preach Him not only rise to behold Him exalted, but let themselves down to give a plain announcement of the truth. So the apostle ascends, "Whether we be beside ourselves, it is to God;" and descends, "Whether we be sober, it is for your sake." And by whom did he ascend and descend? "For the love of Christ constraineth us: for we thus judge, that if one died for all, then all died; and that He died for all, that they which live should no longer live unto themselves, but unto Him that died for them, and rose again."[4]

27. The man who does not find pleasure in these views of sacred Scripture is turned away to fables, because he cannot bear sound doctrine. The fables have an attraction for childish minds in people of all ages; but we who are of the body of Christ should say with the Psalmist; "O Lord, the wicked have spoken to me pleasing things, but they are not after Thy law."[5] In every page of these Scriptures, while I pursue my search as a son of Adam in the sweat of my brow, Christ either openly or covertly meets and refreshes me. Where the discovery is laborious my ardor is increased, and the spoil obtained is eagerly devoured, and is hidden in my heart for my nourishment.

28. Christ appears to me in Joseph, who was persecuted and sold by his brethren, and after his troubles obtained honor in Egypt. We have seen the troubles of Christ in the world, of which Egypt was a figure, in the sufferings of the martyrs. And now we see the honor of Christ in the same world which He subdues to Himself, in exchange for the food which He bestows. Christ appears to me in the rod of Moses, which became a serpent when cast on the earth as a figure of His death, which came from the serpent. Again, when caught by the tail it became a rod, as a figure of His return after the accomplishment of His work in His resurrection to what He was before, destroying death by His new life, so as to leave no trace of the serpent. We, too, who are His body, glide along in the same mortality through the folds of time; but when at last the tail of this course of things is laid hold of by the hand of judgment that it shall go no further, we shall be renewed, and rising from the destruction of death, the last enemy, we shall be the sceptre of government in the right hand of God.

29. Of the departure of Israel from Egypt, let us hear what the apostle himself says: "I would not, brethren, that ye should be ignorant that all our fathers were under the cloud, and all passed through the sea, and were all baptized into Moses in the cloud and in the sea, and did all eat the same spiritual meat, and did all drink of the same spiritual drink. For they drank of the spiritual rock which followed them, and that rock was Christ."[6]

---

[1] John i. 47-51. [2] Gen. xxviii. 11-18. [3] 1 Cor. iii. 1-3. [4] 2 Cor. v. 13-15. [5] Ps. cxix. 83. [6] 1 Cor. x. 1-4.

The explanation of one thing is a key to the rest. For if the rock is Christ from its stability, is not the manna Christ, the living bread which came down from heaven, which gives spiritual life to those who truly feed on it? The Israelites died because they received the figure only in its carnal sense. The apostle, by calling it spiritual food, shows its reference to Christ, as the spiritual drink is explained by the words, "That rock was Christ," which explain the whole. Then is not the cloud and the pillar Christ, who by His uprightness and strength supports our feebleness; who shines by night and not by day, that they who see not may see, and that they who see may be made blind? In the clouds and the Red Sea there is the baptism consecrated by the blood of Christ. The enemies following behind perish, as past sins are put away.

30. The Israelites are led through the wilderness, as those who are baptized are in the wilderness while on the way to the promised land, hoping and patiently waiting for that which they see not. In the wilderness are severe trials, lest they should in heart return to Egypt. Still Christ does not leave them; the pillar does not go away. The bitter waters are sweetened by wood, as hostile people become friendly by learning to honor the cross of Christ. The twelve fountains watering the seventy palm trees are a figure of apostolic grace watering the nations. As seven is mutiplied by ten, so the decalogue is fulfilled in the sevenfold operation of the Spirit. The enemy attempting to stop them in their way is overcome by Moses stretching out his hands in the figure of the cross. The deadly bites of serpents are healed by the brazen serpent, which was lifted up that they might look at it. The Lord Himself gives the explanation of this: "As Moses lifted up the serpent in the wilderness, so must the Son of man be lifted up, that whosoever believeth in Him may not perish, but have everlasting life."[1] So in many other things we may find a protest against the obstinacy of unbelieving hearts. In the passover a lamb is killed, representing Christ, of whom it is said in the Gospel, "Behold the Lamb of God, who taketh away the sin of the world!"[2] In the passover the bones of the lamb were not to be broken; and on the cross the bones of the Lord were not broken. The evangelist, in reference to this, quotes the words, "A bone of Him shall not be broken."[3] The posts were marked with blood to keep away destruction, as people are marked on their foreheads with the sign of the Lord's passion for their salvation. The law was given on the fiftieth day after the passover; so the Holy Spirit came on the fiftieth day after the passion of the Lord. The law is said to have been written with the finger of God; and the Lord says of the Holy Spirit, "With the finger of God I cast out devils."[4] Such are the Scriptures in which Faustus, after shutting his eyes, declares that he can see no prediction of Christ. But we need not wonder that he should have eyes to read and yet no heart to understand, since, instead of knocking in devout faith at the door of the heavenly secret, he dares to act in profane hostility. So let it be, for so it ought to be. Let the gate of salvation be shut to the proud. The meek, to whom God teaches His ways, will find all these things in the Scriptures, and those things which he does not see he will believe from what he sees.

31. He will see Jesus leading the people into the land of promise; for this name was given to the leader of Israel, not at first, or by chance, but on account of the work to which he was called. He will see the cluster from the land of promise hanging from a wooden pole. He will see in Jericho, as in this perishing world, an harlot, one of those of whom the Lord says that they go before the proud into the kingdom of heaven, putting out of her window a scarlet line symbolical of blood, as confession is made with the mouth for the remission of sins. He will see the walls of Jericho, like the frail defences of the world, fall when compassed seven times by the ark of the covenant; as now in the course of the seven days of time the covenant of God compasses the whole globe, that in the end, death, the last enemy, may be destroyed, and the Church, like one single house, be saved from the destruction of the ungodly, purified from the defilement of fornication by the window of confession in the blood of remission.

32. He will see the times of the judges precede those of the kings, as the judgment will precede the kingdom. And under both the judges and the kings he will see Christ and the Church repeatedly prefigured in many and various ways. Who was in Samson, when he killed the lion that met him as he went to get a wife among strangers, but He who, when going to call His Church from among the Gentiles, said, "Be of good cheer, I have overcome the world?"[5] What means the hive in the mouth of the slain lion, but that, as we see, the very laws of the earthly king-

[1] John iii. 14. [2] John i. 29. [3] John xix. 36. [4] Luke xi. 20. [5] John xvi. 33.

dom which once raged against Christ have now lost their fierceness, and have become a protection for the preaching of gospel sweetness? What is that woman boldly piercing the temples of the enemy with a wooden nail, but the faith of the Church casting down the kingdom of the devil by the cross of Christ? What is the fleece wet while the ground was dry, and again the fleece dry while the ground was wet, but the Hebrew nation at first possessing alone in its typical institution Christ the mystery of God, while the whole world was in ignorance? And now the whole world has this mystery revealed, while the Jews are destitute of it.

33. To mention only a few things in the times of the kings, at the very outset does not the change in the priesthood when Eli was rejected and Samuel chosen, and in the kingdom when Saul was rejected and David chosen, clearly predict the new priesthood and kingdom to come in our Lord Jesus Christ, when the old, which was a shadow of the new, was rejected? Did not David, when he ate the shew-bread, which it was not lawful for any but the priests to eat, prefigure the union of the kingdom and priesthood in one person, Jesus Christ? In the separation of the ten tribes from the temple while two were left, is there not a figure of what the apostle asserts of the whole nation: "A remnant is saved by the election of grace."?[1]

34. In the time of famine, Elijah is fed by ravens bringing bread in the morning and flesh in the evening; but the Manichæans cannot in this perceive Christ, who, as it were, hungers for our salvation, and to whom sinners come in confession, having now the first-fruits of the Spirit, while in the end, that is to say in the evening of the age, they will have the resurrection of their bodies also. Elijah is sent to be fed by a widow woman of another nation, who was going to gather two sticks before she died, denoting the two wooden beams of the cross. Her meal and oil are blessed, as the fruit and cheerfulness of charity do not diminish by expenditure, for God loveth a cheerful giver.[2]

35. The children that mocked Elisha by calling out Baldhead, are devoured by wild beasts, as those who in childish folly scoff at Christ crucified on Calvary are destroyed by devils. Elisha sends his servants to lay his staff on the dead body, but it does not revive; he comes himself, and lays himself exactly upon the dead body, and it revives: as the Word of God sent the law by His servant, without any profit to mankind dead in sins; and yet it was not sent without purpose by Him who knew the necessity of its being first sent. Then He Himself came, conformed Himself to us by participation in our death, and we were revived. When they were cutting down wood with axes, the iron, flying off the wood, sank to the bottom of the river, and came up again when the wood was thrown in by Elisha. So, when Christ's bodily presence was cutting down the unfruitful trees among the unbelieving Jews, according to the saying of John, "Behold, the axe is laid to the roots of the tree,"[3] by the death they inflicted, Christ was separated from His body, and descended to the depths of the infernal world; and then, when His body was laid in the tomb, like the wood on the water, His spirit returned, like the iron to the handle, and He rose. The reader will observe how many things of this kind are omitted for the sake of brevity.

36. As regards the departure to Babylon, where the Spirit of God by the prophet Jeremiah enjoins them to go, telling them to pray for the people in whose land they dwell as strangers, because in their peace they would find peace, and to build houses, and plant vineyards and gardens,—the figurative meaning is plain, when we consider that the true Israelites, in whom is no guile, passed over in the ministry of the apostles with the ordinances of the gospel into the kingdom of the Gentiles. So the apostle, like an echo of Jeremiah, says to us, "I will first of all that prayer, supplications, intercessions and giving of thanks be made for all men, and for those in authority, that we may live a quiet and peaceable life in all godliness and charity; for this is good and acceptable in the sight of God our Saviour, who will have all men to be saved, and to come to the knowledge of the truth."[4] Accordingly the basilicas of Christian congregations have been built by believers as abodes of peace, and vineyards of the faithful have been renewed, and gardens planted, where chief among the plants is the mustard tree, in whose wide-spreading branches the pride of the Gentiles, like the birds of heaven, in its soaring ambition, takes shelter. Again, in the return from captivity after seventy years, according to Jeremiah's prophecy, and in the restoration of the temple, every believer in Christ must see a figure of our return as the Church of God from the exile of this world to the heavenly Jerusalem, after the seven days of time have fulfilled their course. Joshua the high priest, after the captivity, who rebuilt the temple, was a

[1] Rom. xi. 5.
[2] 2 Cor. ix. 7.
[3] Matt. iii. 10.
[4] 1 Tim. ii. 1–4.

figure of Jesus Christ, the true High Priest of our restoration. The prophet Zechariah saw this Joshua in a filthy garment; and after the devil who stood by to accuse him was defeated, the filthy garment was taken from him, and a dress of honor and glory given him. So the body of Jesus Christ, which is the Church, when the adversary is conquered in the judgment at the end of the world, will pass from the pains of exile to the glory of everlasting safety. This is the song of the Psalmist at the dedication of his house: "Thou hast turned for me my mourning into gladness; Thou hast removed my sackcloth, and girded me with gladness, that my glory may sing praise unto Thee, and not be silent."[1]

37. It is impossible, in a digression like this, to refer, however briefly, to all the figurative predictions of Christ which are to be found in the law and the prophets. Will it be said that these things happened in the regular course of things, and that it is a mere ingenious fancy to make them typical of Christ? Such an objection might come from Jews and Pagans; but those who wish to be considered Christians must yield to the authority of the apostle when he says, "All these things happened to them for an example;" and again, "These things are our examples."[2] For if two men, Ishmael and Isaac, are types of the two covenants, can it be supposed that there is no significance in the vast number of particulars which have no historical or natural value? Suppose we were to see some Hebrew characters written on the wall of a noble building, should we be so foolish as to conclude that, because we cannot understand the characters, they are not intended to be read, and are mere painting, without any meaning? So, whoever with a candid mind reads all these things that are contained in the Old Testament Scriptures, must feel constrained to acknowledge that they have a meaning.

38. As an example of those particulars which have no meaning at all if not a symbolical one: Granting that it was necessary that woman should be made as an help meet for man, what natural reason can be assigned for her being taken from his side while he slept? Granting that an ark was required in order to escape from the flood, why should it have precisely these dimensions, and why should they be recorded for the devout study of future generations? Granting that the animals were brought into the ark to preserve the various races, why should there be seven clean and two unclean? Granting that the ark must have a door, why should it be in the side, and why should this fact be committed to writing? Abraham is commanded to sacrifice his son: we may allow that this proof of his obedience was required in order to make it conspicuous in all ages; we may allow, too, that it was a proper thing for the son to carry the wood instead of the aged father, and that in the end the fatal stroke was forbidden, lest the father should be left childless. But what had the shedding of the ram's blood to do with Abraham's trial? or if it was necessary to complete the sacrifice, was the ram any the better of being caught by the horns in a bush? The human mind, that is to say, a rational mind, is led by the consideration of the way in which these apparently superfluous things are blended with what is necessary, first to acknowledge their significance, and then to try to discover it.

39. The Jews themselves, who scoff at the crucified Saviour in whom we believe, and who consequently will not allow that Christ is predicted in the sayings and actions recorded in the Old Testament, are compelled to come to us for an explanation of those things which, if not explained, must appear trifling and ridiculous. This led Philo, a Jew of great learning, whom the Greeks speak of as rivalling Plato in eloquence, to attempt to explain some things without any reference to Christ, in whom he did not believe. His attempt only shows the inferiority of all ingenious speculations, when made without keeping Christ in view, to whom all the predictions really point. So true is that saying of the apostle: "When they shall turn to the Lord, the veil shall be taken away."[3] For instance, Noah's ark is, according to Philo, a type of the human body, member by member: with this view, he shows that the numerical proportions agree perfectly. For there is no reason why a type of Christ should not be a type of the human body, too, since the Saviour of mankind appeared in a human body, though what is typical of a human body is not necessarily typical of Christ. Philo's explanation fails, however, as regards the door in the side of the ark. He actually, for the sake of saying something, makes this door represent the lower apertures of the body. He has the hardihood to put this in words, and on paper. Indeed, he knew not the door and could not understand the symbol. Had he turned to Christ the veil would have been taken away, and he would have found the sacraments of the Church flowing from the side of Christ's human body. For,

---

[1] Ps. xxx. 11, 12.

[2] 1 Cor. x. 10, 6.

[3] 2 Cor. iii. 16.

according to the announcement, "They two shall be one flesh," some things in the ark, which is a type of Christ, refer to Christ, and some to the Church. This contrast between the explanations which keep Christ in view, and all other ingenious perversions, is the same in every particular of all the figures in Scripture.

40. The Pagans, too, cannot deny our right to give a figurative meaning to both words and things, especially as we can point to the fulfillment of the types and figures. For the Pagans themselves try to find in their own fables figures of natural and religious truth. Sometimes they give clear explanations, while at other times they disguise their meaning, and what is sacred in the temples becomes a jest in the theatres. They unite a disgraceful licentiousness to a degrading superstition.

41. Besides this wonderful agreement between the types and the things typified, the adversary may be convinced by plain prophetic intimations, such as this: "In thy seed shall all nations be blessed." This was said to Abraham,[1] and again to Isaac,[2] and again to Jacob.[3] Hence the significance of the words, "I am the God of Abraham, and Isaac, and Jacob."[4] God fulfills His promise to their seed in blessing all nations. With a like significance, Abraham himself, when he made his servant swear, told him to put his hand under his thigh;[5] for he knew that thence would come the flesh of Christ, in whom we have now, not the promise of blessing to all nations, but the promise fulfilled.

42. I should like to know, or rather, it would be well not to know, with what blindness of mind Faustus reads the passage where Jacob calls his sons, and says, "Assemble, that I may tell you the things that are to happen in the last day. Assemble and hear, ye sons of Jacob; give ear to Israel, your father." Surely these are the words of a prophet. What, then, does he say of his son Judah, of whose tribe Christ came of the seed of David according to the flesh, as the apostle teaches? "Judah," he says, "thy brethren shall praise thee: thy hand shall be upon the backs of thine enemies; the sons of thy father shall bow down to thee. Judah is a lion's whelp; my son and offspring: bowing down, thou hast gone up: thou sleepest as a lion, and as a young lion, who will rouse him up? A prince shall not depart from Judah, nor a leader from his loins, till those things come which have been laid up for him. He also is the desire of nations: binding his foal unto the vine, and his ass's colt with sackcloth, he shall wash his garment in wine, and his clothes in the blood of grapes: his eyes are bright with wine, and his teeth whiter than milk."[6] There is no falsehood or obscurity in these words when we read them in the clear light of Christ. We see His brethren the apostles and all His joint-heirs praising Him, seeking, not their own glory, but His. We see His hands on the backs of His enemies, who are bent and bowed to the earth by the growth of the Christian communities in spite of their opposition. We see Him worshipped by the sons of Jacob, the remnant saved according to the election of grace. Christ, who was born as an infant, is the lion's whelp, as it is added, My son and offspring, to show why this whelp, in whose praise it is said, "The lion's whelp is stronger than the herd,"[7] is even in infancy stronger than its elders. We see Christ ascending the cross, and bowing down when He gave up His spirit. We see Him sleeping as a lion, because in death itself He was not the conquered, but the conqueror, and as a lion's whelp; for the reason of His birth and of His death was the same. And He is raised from the dead by Him whom no man hath seen or can see; for the words, "Who will raise Him up?" point to an unknown power. A prince did not depart from Judah, nor a leader from his loins, till in due time those things came which had been laid up in the promise. For we learn from the authentic history of the Jews themselves, that Herod, under whom Christ was born, was their first foreign king. So the sceptre did not depart from the seed of Judah till the things laid up for him came. Then, as the promise is not only to the believing Jews, it is added: "He is the desire of the nations." Christ bound His foal—that is, His people—to the vine, when He preached in sackcloth, crying, "Repent, for the kingdom of heaven is at hand." The Gentiles made subject to Him are represented by the ass's colt, on which He also sat, leading it into Jerusalem, that is, the vision of peace teaching the meek His ways. We see Him washing His garments in wine; for He is one with the glorious Church, which He presents to Himself, not having spot or wrinkle; to whom also it is said by Isaiah: "Though your sins be as scarlet, I will make them white as snow."[8] How is this done but by the remission of sins? And the wine is none other than that of which it is said that it is "shed for many, for the remission of sins." Christ is the cluster that hung on the

[1] Gen. xxii. 18. [2] Gen. xxvi. 4. [3] Gen. xxviii. 14. [4] Ex. iii. 6. [5] Gen. xxiv. 2.

[6] Gen. xlix. 1, 2, 8–12. [7] Prov. xxx. 30. [8] Isa. i. 18.

pole. So it is added, "and His clothes in the blood of the grape." Again, what is said of His eyes being bright with wine, is understood by those members of His body who are enabled, in holy aberration of mind from the current of earthly things, to gaze on the eternal light of wisdom. So Paul says in a passage quoted before: "If we be beside ourselves, it is to God." Those are the eyes bright with wine. But he adds: "If we be sober, it is for your sakes." The babes needing to be fed with milk are not forgotten, as is denoted by the words, "His teeth are whiter than milk."

43. What can our deluded adversaries say to such plain examples, which leave no room for perverse denial, or even for sceptical uncertainty? I call on the Manichæans to begin to inquire into these subjects, and to admit the force of these evidences, on which I have no time to dwell; nor do I wish to make a selection, in case the ignorant reader should think there are no others, while the Christian student might blame me for the omission of many points more striking than those which occur to me at the moment. You will find many passages which require no such explanation as has been given here of Jacob's prophecy. For instance, every reader can understand the words, "He was led as a lamb to the slaughter," and the whole of that plain prophecy, "With His stripes we are healed"—"He bore our sins."[1] We have a poetical gospel in the words: "They pierced my hands and feet. They have told all my bones. They look and stare upon me. They divided my garments among them, and cast lots on my vesture."[2] The blind even may now see the fulfillment of the words: "All the ends of the earth shall remember and turn unto the Lord, and all kingdoms of the nations shall worship before Him." The words in the Gospel, "My soul is sorrowful, even unto death," "My soul is troubled," are a repetition of the words in the Psalm, "I slept in trouble."[3] And who made Him sleep? Whose voices cried, Crucify him, crucify him? The Psalm tells us: "The sons of men, their teeth are spears and arrows, and their tongue a sharp sword."[4] But they could not prevent His resurrection, or His ascension above the heavens, or His filling the earth with the glory of His name; for the Psalm says: "Be Thou exalted, O God, above the heavens, and let Thy glory be above all the earth." Every one must apply these words to Christ: "The Lord said unto me, Thou art my Son, this day have I begotten Thee. Ask of me, and I will give Thee the heathen for Thine inheritance, and the uttermost parts of the earth for Thy possession."[5] And what Jeremiah says of wisdom plainly applies to Christ: "Jacob delivered it to his son, and Israel to his chosen one. Afterwards He appeared on earth, and conversed with men."[6]

44. The same Saviour is spoken of in Daniel, where the Son of man appears before the Ancient of days, and receives a kingdom without end, that all nations may serve Him.[7] In the passage quoted from Daniel by the Lord Himself, "When ye shall see the abomination of desolation, spoken of by Daniel the prophet, standing in the holy place, let him that readeth understand,"[8] the number of weeks points not only to Christ, but to the very time of His advent. With the Jews, who look to Christ for salvation as we do, but deny that He has come and suffered, we can argue from actual events. Besides the conversion of the heathen, now so universal, as prophesied of Christ in their own Scriptures, there are the events in the history of the Jews themselves. Their holy place is thrown down, the sacrifice has ceased, and the priest, and the ancient anointing; which was all clearly foretold by Daniel when he prophesied of the anointing of the Most Holy.[9] Now, that all these things have taken place, we ask the Jews for the anointed Most Holy, and they have no answer to give. But it is from the Old Testament that the Jews derive all the knowledge they have of Christ and His advent. Why do they ask John whether he is Christ? Why do they say to the Lord, 'How long dost thou make us to doubt? If thou art the Christ, tell us plainly." Why do Peter and Andrew and Philip say to Nathanael, "We have found Messias, which is interpreted Christ," but because this name was known to them from the prophecies of their Scriptures? In no other nation were the kings and priests anointed, and called Anointed or Christs. Nor could this symbolical anointing be discontinued till the coming of Him who was thus prefigured. For among all their anointed ones the Jews looked for one who was to save them. But in the mysterious justice of God they were blinded; and thinking only of the power of the Messiah, they did not understand His weakness, in which He died for us. In the book of Wisdom it is prophesied of the Jews: "Let us condemn him to an ignominious death; for he will be proved in his words. If he is truly the Son of God, He will aid him, and deliver him from the hand of his

[1] Isa. liii.
[2] Ps. xxii.
[3] Ps. lvii. 4 (Vulg.).
[4] Ps. lvii. 4.
[5] Ps. ii. 8, 9.
[6] Baruch iii. 37, 38.
[7] Dan. vii. 13, 14.
[8] Matt. xxiv. 15.
[9] Dan. ix. 24-27.

enemies. Thus they thought, and erred; for their wickedness blinded them."[1] These words apply also to those who, in spite of all these evidences, in spite of such a series of prophecies, and of their fulfillment, still deny that Christ is foretold in the Scriptures. As often as they repeat this denial, we can produce fresh proofs, with the help of Him who has made such provision against human perversity, that proofs already given need not be repeated.

45. Faustus has an evasive objection, which he no doubt thinks a most ingenious way of eluding the force of the clearest evidence of prophecy, but of which one is unwilling to take any notice, because answering it may give it an appearance of importance which it does not really possess. What could be more irrational than to say that it is weak faith which will not believe in Christ without evidence? Do our adversaries, then, believe in testimony about Christ? Faustus wishes us to believe the voice from heaven as distinguished from human testimony. But did they hear this voice? Has not the knowledge of it come to us through human testimony? The apostle describes the transmission of this knowledge, when he says: "How shall they call on Him on whom they have not believed? and how shall they believe on Him of whom they have not heard? and how shall they hear without a preacher? and how shall they preach except they be sent? As it is written, "How beautiful are the feet of them who publish peace, who bring good tidings!"[2] Clearly, in the preaching of the apostles there was a reference to prophetic testimony. The apostles quoted the predictions of the prophets, to prove the truth and importance of their doctrines. For although their preaching was accompanied with the power of working miracles, the miracles would have been ascribed to magic, as some even now venture to insinuate, unless the apostles had shown that the authority of the prophets was in their favor. The testimony of prophets who lived so long before could not be ascribed to magical arts. Perhaps the reason why Faustus will not have us believe the Hebrew prophets as witnesses of the true Christ, is because he believes Persian heresies about a false Christ.

46. According to the teaching of the Catholic Church, the Christian mind must first be nourished in simple faith, in order that it may become capable of understanding things heavenly and eternal. Thus it is said by the prophet: "Unless ye believe, ye shall not understand."[3] Simple faith is that by which, before we attain to the height of the knowledge of the love of Christ, that we may be filled with all the fullness of God, we believe that not without reason was the dispensation of Christ's humiliation, in which He was born and suffered as man, foretold so long before by the prophets through a prophetic race, a prophetic people, a prophetic kingdom. This faith teaches us, that in the foolishness which is wiser than men, and in the weakness which is stronger than men, is contained the hidden means of our justification and glorification. There are hid all the treasures of wisdom and knowledge, which are opened to no one who despises the nourishment transmitted through the breast of his mother, that is, the milk of apostolic and prophetic instruction; or who, thinking himself too old for infantile nourishment, devours heretical poison instead of the food of wisdom, for which he rashly thought himself prepared. To require simple faith is quite consistent with requiring faith in the prophets. The very use of simple faith is to believe the prophets at the outset, while the understanding of the person who speaks in the prophets is attained after the mind has been purified and strengthened.

47. But, it is said, if the prophets foretold Christ, they did not live in a way becoming their office. How can you tell whether they did or not? You are bad judges of what it is to live well or ill, whose justice consists in giving relief to an inanimate melon by eating it, instead of giving food to the starving beggar. It is enough for the babes in the Catholic Church, who do not yet know the perfect justice of the human soul, and the difference between the justice aimed at and that actually attained, to think of those men according to the wholesome doctrine of the apostles, that the just lives by faith. "Abraham believed God, and it was counted to him for righteousness. For the scripture, foreseeing that God would justify the Gentiles by faith, preached before the gospel unto Abraham, saying, In thy seed shall all nations be blessed."[4] These are the words of the apostle. If you would, at his clear well-known voice, wake up from your unprofitable dreams, you would follow in the footsteps of our father Abraham, and would be blessed, along with all nations, in his seed. For, as the apostle says, "He received the sign of circumcision, a seal of the righteousness of the faith which he had, yet being uncircumcised, that he might be the father of all that believe in uncircumcision; that he might be the father of circumcision not only to those who are of the circumcision, but also to those who follow the

[1] Wisd. ii. 18-21.
[2] Rom. x. 14, 15.
[3] Isa. vii. 9 (Vulg.).
[4] Gal. iii. 6, 8.

footsteps of the faith of our father Abraham in uncircumcision."[1] Since the righteousness of Abraham's faith is thus set forth as an example to us, that we too, being justified by faith, may have peace with God, we ought to understand his manner of life, without finding fault with it; lest, by a premature separation from mother-Church, we prove abortions, instead of being brought forth in due time, when the conception has arrived at completeness.

48. This is a brief reply to Faustus in behalf of the character of the patriarchs and prophets. It is the reply of the babes of our faith, among whom I would reckon myself, inasmuch as I would not find fault with the life of the ancient saints, even if I did not understand its mystical character. Their life is proclaimed to us with approval by the apostles in their Gospel, as they themselves in their prophecy foretold the future apostles, that the two Testaments, like the seraphim, might cry to one another, "Holy, holy, holy is the Lord God of hosts."[2] When Faustus, instead of the vague general accusation which he makes here, condemns particular actions in the lives of the patriarchs and the prophets, the Lord their God, and ours also, will assist me to reply suitably and appropriately to the separate charges. For the present, the reader must choose whether to believe the commendation of the Apostle Paul or the accusations of Faustus the Manichæan.[3]

[1] Rom. iv. 11, 12.

[2] Isa. vi. 3.

[3] [It is unnecessary to point out in detail the vicious elements in Augustin's allegorizing and typologizing. It should be said that his exegetical fancies were not original, but were derived from Philo, Origen, and their followers.—A. H. N.]

BOOK XIII.

FAUSTUS ASSERTS THAT EVEN IF THE OLD TESTAMENT COULD BE SHOWN TO CONTAIN PREDICTIONS, IT WOULD BE OF INTEREST ONLY TO THE JEWS, PAGAN LITERATURE SUBSERVING THE SAME PURPOSE FOR GENTILES. AUGUSTIN SHOWS THE VALUE OF PROPHESY FOR GENTILES AND JEWS ALIKE.

1. FAUSTUS said: We are asked how we worship Christ when we reject the prophets, who declared the promise of His advent. It is doubtful whether, on examination, it can be shown that the Hebrew prophets foretold our Christ, that is, the Son of God. But were it so, what does it matter to us? If these testimonies of the prophets that you speak of were the means of converting any one from Judaism to Christianity, and if he should afterwards neglect these prophets, he would certainly be in the wrong, and would be chargeable with ingratitude. But we are by nature Gentiles, of the uncircumcision; as Paul says, born under another law. Those whom the Gentiles call poets were our first religious teachers, and from them we were afterwards converted to Christianity. We did not first become Jews, so as to reach Christianity through faith in their prophets; but were attracted solely by the fame, and the virtues, and the wisdom of our liberator Jesus Christ. If I were still in the religion of my fathers, and a preacher were to come using the prophets as evidence in favor of Christianity, I should think him mad for attempting to support what is doubtful by what is still more doubtful to a Gentile of another religion altogether. He would require first to persuade me to believe the prophets, and then through the prophets to believe Christ. And to prove the truth of the prophets, other prophets would be necessary. For if the prophets bear witness to Christ, who bears witness to the prophets? You will perhaps say that Christ and the prophets mutually support each other. But a Pagan, who has nothing to do with either, would believe neither the evidence of Christ to the prophets, nor that of the prophets to Christ. If the Pagan becomes a Christian, he has to thank his own faith, and nothing else. Let us, for the sake of illustration, suppose ourselves conversing with a Gentile inquirer. We tell him to believe in Christ, because He is God. He asks for proof. We refer him to the prophets. He asks, What prophets? We reply, The Hebrew. He smiles, and says that he does not believe them. We remind him that Christ testifies to them. He replies, laughing, that we must first make him believe in Christ. The result of such a conversation is that we are silenced, and the inquirer departs, thinking us more zealous than wise. Again, I say, the Christian Church, which consists more of Gentiles than of Jews, can owe nothing to Hebrew witnesses. If, as is said, any prophecies of Christ are to be found

in the Sibyl,[1] or in Hermes,[2] called Trismegistus, or Orpheus, or any heathen poet, they might aid the faith of those who, like us, are converts from heathenism to Christianity. But the testimony of the Hebrews is useless to us before conversion, for then we cannot believe them; and superfluous after, for we believe without them.

2. Augustin replied: After the long reply of last book, a short answer may suffice here. To one who has read that reply, it must seem insanity in Faustus to persist in denying that Christ was foretold by the Hebrew prophets, when the Hebrew nation was the only one in which the name Christ had a peculiar sacredness as applied to kings and priests; in which sense it continued to be applied till the coming of Him whom those kings and priests typified. Where did the Manichæan learn the name of Christ? If from Manichæus, it is very strange that Africans, not to speak of others, should believe the Persian Manichæus, since Faustus finds fault with the Romans and Greeks, and other Gentiles, for believing the Hebrew prophets as belonging to another race. According to Faustus, the predictions of the Sibyl, or Orpheus, or any heathen poet, are more suitable for leading Gentiles to believe in Christ. He forgets that none of these are read in the churches, whereas the voice of the Hebrew prophets, sounding everywhere, draws swarms of people to Christianity. When it is so evident that men are everywhere led to Christ by the Hebrew prophets, it is great absurdity to say that those prophets are not suitable for the Gentiles.

3. Christ as foretold by the Hebrew prophets does not please you; but this is the Christ in whom the Gentile nations believe, with whom, according to you, Hebrew prophecy should have no weight. They receive the gospel which, as Paul says, "God had promised before by His prophets in the Holy Scriptures of His Son, who was made of the seed of David according to the flesh."[3] So we read in Isaiah: "There shall be a Root of Jesse, which shall rise to reign in the nations; in Him shall the Gentiles trust."[4] And again: "Behold, a virgin shall conceive and bear a son, and they shall call His name Emmanuel,"[5] which is, being interpreted, God with us. Nor let the Manichæan think that Christ is foretold only as a man by the Hebrew prophets; for this is what Faustus seems to insinuate when he says, "Our Christ is the Son of God," as if the Christ of the Hebrews was not the Son of God. We can prove Christ the virgin's son of Hebrew prophecy to be God. For the Lord Himself teaches the carnal Jews not to think that, because He is foretold as the son of David, He is therefore no more than that. He asks: "What think ye of Christ? Whose son is He?" They reply: "Of David." Then, to remind them of the name Emmanuel, God with us, He says: "How does David in the Spirit call Him Lord, saying, The Lord said unto my Lord, Sit Thou at my right hand, till I make Thine enemies Thy footstool?"[6] Here, then, Christ appears as God in Hebrew prophecy. What prophecy can the Manichæans show with the name of Christ in it?

4. Manichæus indeed was not a prophet of Christ, but calls himself an apostle, which is a shameless falsehood; for it is well known that this heresy began not only after Tertullian, but after Cyprian. In all his letters Manichæus begins thus: "Manichæus, an apostle of Jesus Christ." Why do you believe what Manichæus says of Christ? What evidence does he give of his apostleship? This very name of Christ is known to us only from the Jews, who, in their application of it to their kings and priests, were not individually, but nationally, prophets of Christ and Christ's kingdom. What right has he to use this name, who forbids you to believe the Hebrew prophets, that he may make you the heretical disciples of a false Christ, as he himself is a false and heretical apostle? And if Faustus quotes as evidence in his own support some prophets who, according to him, foretell Christ, how will he satisfy his supposed inquirer, who will not believe either the prophets or Faustus? Will he take our apostles as witnesses? Unless he can find some apostles in life, he must read their writings; and these are all against him. They teach our doctrine that Christ was born of the Virgin Mary, that He was the Son of God, of the

[1] [On the Sibylline books, see article by G. H. Schodde in the *Schaff-Hertzog Encyclopædia of Religious Knowledge*, and the works there referred to. The Christian writers of the first three centuries seem not to have suspected the real character of these pseudo-prophetical writings, and to have regarded them as remarkable testimonies from the heathen world to the Truth of the Christian religion.—A. H. N.]

[2] ["The Mercurius or Hermes Trismegistus of legend was a personage, an Egyptian sage or succession of sages, who, since the time of Plato, has been identified with the Thoth (the name of the month September), of that people. . . . He was considered to be the impersonation of the religion, art, learning and sacerdotal discipline of the Egyptian priesthood. He was by several of the Fathers, and, in modern times, by three of his earliest editors, supposed to have existed before the time of Moses, and to have obtained the appellation of 'Thrice greatest,' from his threefold learning and rank of Philosopher, Priest and King, and that of 'Hermes,' or Mercurius, as messenger and authoritative interpreter of divine things." The author of the books that go under the name of Hermes Trismegistus is thought to have lived about the beginning of the second century, and was a Christian Neo-Platonist. See J. C. Chambers: *The Theological and Philosophical Works of Hermes Trismegistus, translated from the original Greek, with Preface, Notes and Index, Edinburgh*, 1882.—A. H. N.]

[3] Rom. i. 2, 3.
[4] Isa. xi. 10.
[5] Isa. vii. 14.
[6] Matt. xxii. 42-44.

seed of David according to the flesh. He cannot pretend that the writings have been tampered with, for that would be to attack the credit of his own witnesses. Or if he produces his own manuscripts of the apostolic writings, he must also obtain for them the authority of the churches founded by the apostles themselves, by showing that they have been preserved and transmitted with their sanction. It will be difficult for a man to make me believe him on the evidence of writings which derive all their authority from his own word, which I do not believe.

5. But perhaps you believe the common report about Christ. Faustus makes a feeble suggestion of this kind as a last resource, to escape being obliged either to produce his worthless authorities, or to come under the power of those opposed to him. Well, if report is your authority, you should consider the consequences of trusting to such evidence. There are many bad things reported of you which you do not wish people to believe. Is it reasonable to make the same evidence true about Christ and false about yourselves? In fact, you deny the common report about Christ. For the report most widely spread, and which every one has heard repeated, is that which distinctly asserts that Christ was born of the seed of David, according to the promise made in the Hebrew Scriptures to Abraham and Isaac and Jacob: "In thy seed shall all nations be blessed." You will not admit this Hebrew testimony, but you do not seem to have any other. The authority of our books, which is confirmed by the agreement of so many nations, supported by a succession of apostles, bishops, and councils, is against you. Your books have no authority, for it is an authority maintained by only a few, and these the worshippers of an untruthful God and Christ. If they are not following the example of the beings they worship, their testimony must be against their own false doctrine. And, once more, common report gives a very bad account of you, and invariably asserts, in opposition to you, that Christ was of the seed of David. You did not hear the voice of the Father from heaven. You did not see the works by which Christ bore witness to Himself. The books which tell of these things you profess to receive, that you may maintain a delusive appearance of Christianity; but when anything is quoted against you, you say that the books have been tampered with. You quote the passage where Christ says, "If ye believe not me, believe the works;" and again, "I am one that bear witness of myself, and the Father that sent me beareth witness of me;" but you will not let us quote in reply such passages as these: "Search the Scriptures; for in them ye think that ye have eternal life, and they are they that testify of me;" "If ye believed Moses, ye would believe me, for he wrote of me;" "They have Moses and the prophets, let them hear them;" "If they hear not Moses and the prophets, neither will they believe though one rose from the dead." What have you to say for yourselves? Where is your authority? If you reject these passages of Scripture, in spite of the weighty authority in their favor, what miracles can you show? However, if you did work miracles, we should be on our guard against receiving their evidence in your case; for the Lord has forewarned us: "Many false Christs and false prophets shall arise, and shall do many signs and wonders, that they may deceive, if it were possible, the very elect: behold, I have told you before."[1] This shows that the established authority of Scripture must outweigh every other; for it derives new confirmation from the progress of events which happen, as Scripture proves, in fulfillment of the predictions made so long before their occurrence.

6. Are, then, your doctrines so manifestly true, that they require no support from miracles or from any testimony? Show us these self-evident truths, if you have anything of the kind to show. Your legends, as we have already seen, are long and silly, old wives' fables for the amusement of women and children. The beginning is detached from the rest, the middle is unsound, and the end is a miserable failure. If you begin with the immortal, invisible, incorruptible God, what need was there of His fighting with the race of darkness? And as for the middle of your theory, what becomes of the incorruptibility and unchangeableness of God, when His members in fruits and vegetables are purified by your mastication and digestion? And for the end, is it just that the wretched soul should be punished with lasting confinement in the mass of darkness, because its God is unable to cleanse it of the defilement contracted from evil external to itself in the fulfillment of His own commission? You are at a loss for a reply. See the worthlessness of your boasted manuscripts, numerous and valuable as you say they are! Alas for the toils of the antiquaries! Alas for the property of the unhappy owners! Alas for the food of the deluded followers! Destitute as you are of Scripture authority, of the power of miracles, of moral excellence, and of sound doctrine,

[1] Matt. xxiv. 24, 25.

depart ashamed, and return penitent, confessing that true Christ, who is the Saviour of all who believe in Him, whose name and whose Church are now displayed as they were of old foretold, not by some being issuing from subterranean darkness, but by a nation in a distinct kingdom established for this purpose, that there those things might be figuratively predicted of Christ which are now in reality fulfilled, and the prophets might foretell in writing what the apostles now exhibit in their preaching.

7. Let us suppose, then, a conversation with a heathen inquirer, in which Faustus described us as making a poor appearance, though his own appearance was much more deplorable. If we say to the heathen, Believe in Christ, for He is God, and, on his asking for evidence, produce the authority of the prophets, if he says that he does not believe the prophets, because they are Hebrew and he is a Gentile, we can prove the truth of the prophets from the actual fulfillment of their prophecies. He could scarcely be ignorant of the persecutions suffered by the early Christians from the kings of this world; or if he was ignorant, he could be informed from history and the records of imperial laws. But this is what we find foretold long ago by the prophet, saying, "Why do the heathen rage, and the people imagine a vain thing? The kings of the earth set themselves, and the princes take counsel together against the Lord, and against His Christ." The rest of the Psalm shows that this is not said of David. For what follows might convince the most stubborn unbeliever: "The Lord said unto me, Thou art my Son; this day have I begotten Thee. Ask of me, and I will give Thee the heathen for Thine inheritance, and the ends of the earth for Thy possession."[1] This never happened to the Jews, whose king David was, but is now plainly fulfilled in the subjection of all nations to the name of Christ. This and many similar prophecies, which it would take too long to quote, would surely impress the mind of the inquirer. He would see these very kings of the earth now happily subdued by Christ, and all nations serving Him; and he would hear the words of the Psalm in which this was so long before predicted: "All the kings of the earth shall bow down to Him; all nations shall serve Him."[2] And if he were to read the whole of that Psalm, which is figuratively applied to Solomon, he would find that Christ is the true King of peace, for Solomon means peaceful; and he would find many things in the Psalm applicable to Christ, which have no reference at all to the literal King Solomon. Then there is that other Psalm where God is spoken of as anointed by God, the very word anointed pointing to Christ, showing that Christ is God, for God is represented as being anointed.[3] In reading what is said in this Psalm of Christ and of the Church, he would find that what is there foretold is fulfilled in the present state of the world. He would see the idols of the nations perishing from off the earth, and he would find that this is predicted by the prophets, as in Jeremiah, "Then shall ye say unto them, The gods that have not made the heavens and the earth shall perish from the earth, and from under heaven;"[4] and again, "O Lord, my strength, and my fortress, and my refuge in the day of affliction, the Gentiles shall come unto Thee from the ends of the earth, and shall say, Surely our fathers have inherited lies, vanity, and things wherein there is no profit. Shall a man make gods unto himself, and they are no gods? Therefore, behold, I will at that time cause them to know, I will cause them to know mine hand and my might; and they shall know that I am the Lord."[5] Hearing these prophecies, and seeing their actual fulfillment, I need not say that he would be affected; for we know by experience how the hearts of believers are confirmed by seeing ancient predictions now receiving their accomplishment.

8. In the same prophet the inquirer would find clear proof that Christ is not merely one of the great men that have appeared in the world. For Jeremiah goes on to say: "Cursed be the man that trusteth in man, and maketh flesh his arm, and whose heart departeth from the Lord: for he shall be like the heath in the desert, and shall not see when good cometh; but shall inhabit the parched places of the wilderness, in a salt land not inhabited. Blessed is the man that trusteth in the Lord, and whose hope the Lord is: for he shall be as a tree beside the water, that spreadeth out its roots by the river: he shall not fear when heat cometh, but his leaf shall be green; he shall not be careful in the year of drought, neither shall cease from yielding fruit."[6] On hearing this curse pronounced in the figurative language of prophecy on him that trusts in man, and the blessing in similar style on him that trusts in God, the inquirer might have doubts about our doctrine, in which we teach not only that Christ is God, so that our trust is not in man, but also that He is man because He took our

[1] Ps. ii. 7, 8.
[2] Ps. lxxii. 10.
[3] Ps. xlv. 7.
[4] Jer. x, 11.
[5] Jer. xvi. 19-21.
[6] Jer. xvii. 5-8.

nature. So some err by denying Christ's humanity, while they allow His divinity. Others, again, assert His humanity, but deny His divinity, and so either become infidels or incur the guilt of trusting in man. The inquirer, then, might say that the prophet says only that Christ is God, without any reference to His human nature; whereas, in our apostolic doctrine, Christ is not only God in whom we may safely trust, but the Mediator between God and man—the man Jesus. The prophet explains this in the words in which he seems to check himself, and to supply the omission: "His heart," he says "is sorrowful throughout; and He is man, and who shall know Him?"[1] He is man, in order that in the form of a servant He might heal the hard in heart, and that they might acknowledge as God Him who became man for their sakes, that their trust might be not in man, but in God-man. He is man taking the form of a servant. And who shall know Him? For "He was in the form of God, and thought it not robbery to be equal to God."[2] He is man, for "the Word was made flesh, and dwelt among us." And who shall know Him? For "in the beginning was the Word, and the Word was with God, and the Word was God."[3] And truly His heart was sorrowful throughout. For even as regards His own disciples His heart was sorrowful, when He said, "Have I been so long time with you, and yet have ye not known me?" "Have I been so long time with you" answers to the words "He is man," and "Have ye not known me?" to "Who shall know Him?" And the person is none other but He who says, "He that hath seen me hath seen the Father."[4] So that our trust is not in man, to be under the curse of the prophet, but in God-man, that is, in the Son of God, the Saviour Jesus Christ, the Mediator between God and man. In the form of a servant the Father is greater than He; in the form of God He is equal with the Father.

9. In Isaiah we read: "The pride of man shall be brought low; and the Lord alone shall be exalted in that day. And they shall hide the workmanship of their hands in the clefts of the rocks, and in dens and caves of the earth, from fear of the Lord, and from the glory of His power, when He shall arise to shake terribly the earth. For in that day a man shall cast away his idols of gold and silver, which they have made to worship, as useless and hurtful."[5] Perhaps the inquirer himself, who, as Faustus supposes, would laugh and say that he does not believe the Hebrew prophets, has hid idols made with hands in some cleft, or cave, or den. Or he may know a friend, or neighbor, or fellow-citizen who has done this from the fear of the Lord, who by the severe prohibition of the kings of the earth, now serving and bowing down to him, as the prophet predicted, shakes the earth, that is, breaks the stubborn heart of worldly men. The inquirer is not likely to disbelieve the Hebrew prophets, when he finds their predictions fulfilled, perhaps in his own person.

10. One might rather fear that the inquirer, in the midst of such copious evidence, would say that the Christians composed those writings when the events described had already begun to take place, in order that those occurrences might appear to be not due to a merely human purpose, but as if divinely foretold. One might fear this, were it not for the widely spread and widely known people of the Jews; that Cain, with the mark that he should not be killed by any one; that Ham, the servant of his brethren, carrying as a load the books for their instruction. From the Jewish manuscripts we prove that these things were not written by us to suit the event, but were long ago published and preserved as prophecies in the Jewish nation. These prophecies are now explained in their accomplishment: for even what is obscure in them—because these things happened to them as an example, and were written for our benefit, on whom the ends of the world are come—is now made plain; and what was hidden in the shadows of the future is now visible in the light of actual experience.

11. The inquirer might bring forward as a difficulty the fact that those in whose books these prophecies are found are not united with us in the gospel. But when convinced that this also is foretold, he would feel how strong the evidence is. The prophecies of the unbelief of the Jews no one can avoid seeing, no one can pretend to be blind to them. No one can doubt that Isaiah spoke of the Jews when he said, "The ox knoweth his owner, and the ass his master's crib; but Israel hath not known, and my people hath not considered;"[6] or again, in the words quoted by the apostle, "I have stretched out my hands all the day to a wicked and gainsaying people;"[7] and especially where he says, "God has given them the spirit of remorse, eyes that they should not see, and ears that they should not hear, and should not understand,"[8] and many similar passages. If the

1 Jer. xvii. 9.
2 Phil. ii. 6.
3 John i. 1.
4 John xiv. 9.
5 Isa. ii. 17-20.
6 Isa. i. 3.
7 Isa. lxv. 2; cf. Rom. x. 21.
8 Isa. vi. 10; cf. Rom. xi.

inquirer objected that it was not the fault of the Jews if God blinded them so that they did not know Christ, we should try in the simplest manner possible to make him understand that this blindness is the just punishment of other secret sins known to God. We should prove that the apostle recognizes this principle when he says of some persons, "God gave them up to the lusts of their own hearts, and to a reprobate mind, to do things not convenient;"[1] and that the prophets themselves speak of this. For, to revert to the words of Jeremiah, "He is man, and who shall know Him?" lest it should be an excuse for the Jews that they did not know,—for if they had known, as the apostle says, "they would not have crucified the Lord of glory,"[2] —the prophet goes on to show that their ignorance was the result of secret criminality; for he says: "I the Lord search the heart, and try the reins, to give to every one according to his ways, and according to the fruits of his doings."

12. If the next difficulty in the mind of the inquirer arose from the divisions and heresies among those called Christians, he would learn that this too is taken notice of by the prophets. For, as if it was natural that, after being satisfied about the blindness of the Jews, this objection from the divisions among Christians should occur, Jeremiah, observing this order in his prophecy, immediately adds in the passage already quoted: "The partridge is clamorous, gathering what it has not brought forth, making riches without judgment." For the partridge is notoriously quarrelsome, and is often caught from its eagerness in quarreling. So the heretics discuss not to find the truth, but with a dogged determination to gain the victory one way or another, that they may gather, as the prophet says, what they have not brought forth. For those whom they lead astray are Christians already born of the gospel, whom the Christian profession of the heretics misleads. Thus they make riches not with judgment, but with inconsiderate haste. For they do not consider that the followers whom they gather as their riches are taken from the genuine original Christian society, and deprived of its benefits; and as the apostle describes these heretics in the words: "As Jannes and Jambres withstood Moses, so they also resist the truth: men of corrupt minds, reprobate concerning the faith. But they shall proceed no further: for their folly shall be manifest to all men, as theirs also was."[3] So the prophet goes on to say of the partridge, which gathers what it has not brought forth: "In the midst of his days they shall leave him, and in the end he shall be a fool;" that is, he who at first misled people by a promising display of superior wisdom, shall be a fool, that is, shall be seen to be a fool. He will be seen when his folly is manifest to all men, and to those to whom he was at first a wise man he will then be a fool.

13. As if anticipating that the inquirer would ask next by what plain mark a young disciple, not yet able to distinguish the truth among so many errors, might find the true Church of Christ, since the clear fulfillment of so many predictions compelled him to believe in Christ, the prophet answers this question in what follows, and teaches that the Church of Christ, which he describes prophetically, is conspicuously visible. His words are: "A glorious high throne is our sanctuary."[4] This glorious throne is the Church of which the apostle says: "The temple of God is holy, which temple ye are."[5] The Lord also, foreseeing the conspicuousness of the Church as a help to young disciples who might be misled, says, "A city that is set on an hill cannot be hid."[6] Since, then, a glorious high throne is our sanctuary, no attention is to be paid to those who would lead us into sectarianism, saying, "Lo, here is Christ," or "Lo there." Lo here, lo there, speaks of division; but the true city is on a mountain, and the mountain is that which, as we read in the prophet Daniel, grew from a little stone till it filled the whole earth.[7] And no attention should be paid to those who, professing some hidden mystery confined to a small number, say, Behold, He is in the chamber; behold, in the desert: for a city set on an hill cannot be hid, and a glorious high throne is our sanctuary.

14. After considering these instances of the fulfillment of prophecy about kings and people acting as persecutors, and then becoming believers, about the destruction of idols, about the blindness of the Jews, about their testimony to the writings which they have preserved, about the folly of heretics, about the dignity of the Church of true and genuine Christians, the inquirer would most reasonably receive the testimony of these prophets about the divinity of Christ. No doubt, if we were to begin by urging him to believe prophecies yet unfulfilled, he might justly answer, What have I to do with these prophets, of whose truth I have no evidence? But, in view of the manifest accomplishment of so many remarkable predictions, no candid per-

[1] Rom. i. 28.
[2] 1 Cor. ii. 8.
[3] 2 Tim. iii. 8.
[4] Jer. xvii. 12.
[5] 1 Cor. iii. 17.
[6] Matt. v. 14.
[7] Dan. ii. 34, 35.

son would despise either the things which were thought worthy of being predicted in those early times with so much solemnity, or those who made the predictions. To none can we trust more safely, as regards either events long past or those still future, than to men whose words are supported by the evidence of so many notable predictions having been fulfilled.

15. If any truth about God or the Son of God is taught or predicted in the Sibyl or Sibyls, or in Orpheus, or in Hermes, if there ever was such a person, or in any other heathen poets, or theologians, or sages, or philosophers, it may be useful for the refutation of Pagan error, but cannot lead us to believe in these writers. For while they spoke, because they could not help it, of the God whom we worship, they either taught their fellow-countrymen to worship idols and demons, or allowed them to do so without daring to protest against it. But our sacred writers, with the authority and assistance of God, were the means of establishing and preserving among their people a government under which heathen customs were condemned as sacrilege. If any among this people fell into idolatry or demon-worship, they were either punished by the laws, or met by the awful denunciations of the prophets. They worshipped one God, the maker of heaven and earth. They had rites; but these rites were prophetic, or symbolical of things to come, and were to cease on the appearance of the things signified. The whole state was one great prophet, with its king and priest symbolically anointed, which was discontinued, not by the wish of the Jews themselves, who were in ignorance through unbelief, but only on the coming of Him who was God, anointed with spiritual grace above His fellows, the holy of holies, the true King who should govern us, the true Priest who should offer Himself for us. In a word, the predictions of heathen ingenuity regarding Christ's coming are as different from sacred prophecy as the confession of devils from the proclamation of angels.

16. By such arguments, which might be expanded if we were discussing with one brought up in heathenism, and might be supported by proofs in still greater number, the inquirer whom Faustus has brought before us would certainly be led to believe, unless he preferred his sins to his salvation. As a believer, he would be taken to be cherished in the bosom of the Catholic Church, and would be taught in due course the conduct required of him. He would see many who do not practise the required duties; but this would not shake his faith, even though these people should belong to the same Church and partake of the same sacraments as himself. He would understand that few share in the inheritance of God, while many partake in its outward signs; that few are united in holiness of life, and in the gift of love shed abroad in our hearts by the Holy Spirit who is given to us, which is a hidden spring that no stranger can approach; and that many join in the solemnity of the sacrament, which he that eats and drinks unworthily eats and drinks judgment to himself, while he who neglects to eat it shall not have life in him,[1] and so shall never reach eternal life. He will understand, too, that the good are called few as compared with the multitude of the evil, but that as scattered over the world there are very many growing among the tares, and mixed with the chaff, till the day of harvest and of purging. As this is taught in the Gospel, so is it foretold by the prophets. We read, "As a lily among thorns, so is my beloved among the daughters;"[2] and again, "I have dwelt in the tabernacles of Kedar; peaceful among them that hated peace;"[3] and again, "Mark in the forehead those who sigh and cry for the iniquities of my people, which are done in the midst of them."[4] The inquirer would be confirmed by such passages; and being now a fellow-citizen with the saints and of the household of God, no longer an alien from Israel, but an Israelite indeed, in whom is no guile, would learn to utter from a guileless heart the words which follow in the passage of Jeremiah already quoted, "O Lord, the patience of Israel: let all that forsake Thee be dismayed." After speaking of the partridge that is clamorous, and gathers what it has not brought forth; and after extolling the city set on an hill which cannot be hid, to prevent heretics from drawing men away from the Catholic Church; after the words, "A glorious high throne is our sanctuary," he seems to ask himself, What do we make of all those evil men who are found mixed with the Church, and who become more numerous as the Church extends, and as all nations are united in Christ? And then follow the words, "O Lord, the patience of Israel." Patience is necessary to obey the command, "Suffer both to grow together till the harvest."[5] Impatience towards the evil might lead to forsaking the good, who in the strict sense are the body of Christ, and to forsake them would be to forsake Him. So the prophet goes on to say, "Let all that forsake Thee be dismayed; let those who have departed to the earth be confounded." The earth is man trusting in himself, and induc-

[1] John vi. 54. [2] Cant. ii. 2. [3] Ps. cxx. 7.
[4] Ezek. ix. 1. [5] Matt. xiii. 30.

ing others to trust in him. So the prophet adds: "Let them be overthrown, for they have forsaken the Lord, the fountain of life." This is the cry of the partridge, that it has got the fountain of life, and will give it; and so men are gathered to it, and depart from Christ, as if Christ, whose name they had professed, had not fulfilled His promise. The partridge gathers those whom it has not brought forth. And in order to do this, it declares, The salvation which Christ promises is with me; I will give it. In opposition to this the prophet says: "Heal me, O Lord, and I shall be healed; save me, and I shall be saved." So we read in the apostle, "Let no man glory in men;"[1] or in the words of the prophet, "Thou art my praise."[2] Such is a specimen of instruction in apostolic and prophetic doctrine, by which a man may be built on the foundation of the apostles and prophets.

17. Faustus has not told us how he would prove the divinity of Christ to the heathen, whom he makes to say: I believe neither the prophets in support of Christ, nor Christ in support of the prophets. It would be absurd to suppose that such a man would believe what Christ says of Himself, when he disbelieves what He says of others. For if he thinks Him unworthy of credit in one case, he must think Him so in all, or at least more so when speaking of Himself than when speaking of others. Perhaps, failing this, Faustus would read to him the Sibyls and Orpheus, and any heathen prophecies about Christ that he could find. But how could he do this, when he confesses that he knows none? His words are: "If, as is said, any prophecies of Christ are to be found in the Sibyl, or in Hermes, called Trismegistus, or Orpheus, or any heathen poet." How could he read writings of which he knows nothing, and which he supposes to exist only from report, to one who will not believe either the prophets or Christ? What, then, would he do? Would he bring forward Manichæus as a witness to Christ? The opposite of this is what the Manichæans do. They take advantage of the widespread fragrance of the name of Christ to gain acceptance for Manichæus, that the edge of their poisoned cup may be sweetened with this honey. Taking hold of the promises of Christ to His disciples that He would send the Paraclete, that is, the Comforter or Advocate, they say that this Paraclete is Manichæus, or in Manichæus, and so steal an entrance into the minds of men who do not know when He who was promised by Christ really came. Those who have read the canonical book called the Acts of the Apostles find a reference to Christ's promise, and an account of its fulfillment. Faustus, then, has no proof to give to the inquirer. It is not likely that any one will be so infatuated as to take the authority of Manichæus when he rejects that of Christ. Would he not reply in derision, if not in anger, Why do you ask me to believe Persian books, when you forbid me to believe Hebrew books? The Manichæan has no hold on the inquirer, unless he is already in some way convinced of the truth of Christianity. When he finds him willing to believe Christ, then he deludes him with the representation of Christ given by Manichæus. So the partridge gathers what it has not brought forth. When will you whom he gathers leave him? When will you see him to be a fool, who tells you that Hebrew testimony is worthless in the case of unbelievers, and superfluous to believers?

18. If believers are to throw away all the books which have led them to believe, I see no reason why they should continue reading the Gospel itself. The Gospel, too, must be worthless to this inquirer, who, according to Faustus' pitiful supposition, rejects with ridicule the authority of Christ. And to the believer it must be superfluous, if true notices of Christ are superfluous to believers. And if the Gospel should be read by the believer, that he may not forget what he has believed, so should the prophets, that he may not forget why he believed. For if he forgets this his faith cannot be firm. By this principle, you should throw away the books of Manichæus, on the authority of which you already believe that light—that is, God—fought with darkness, and that, in order to bind darkness, the light was first swallowed up and bound, and polluted and mangled by darkness, to be restored, and liberated, and purified, and healed by your eating, for which you are rewarded by not being condemned to the mass of darkness for ever, along with that part of the light which cannot be extricated. This fiction is sufficiently published by your practice and your words. Why do you seek for the testimony of books, and add to the embarrassment of your God by the consumption of strength in the needless task of writing manuscripts? Burn all your parchments, with their finely-ornamented binding; so you will be rid of a useless burden, and your God who suffers confinement in the volume will be set free. What a mercy it would be to the members of your God, if you could boil your books and eat them! There might be a difficulty, however, from the prohibition of animal food. Then the writing must share in the impurity

[1] 1 Cor. iii. 21. [2] Jer. xvii. 14.

of the sheepskin. Indeed, you are to blame for this, for, like what you say was done in the first war between light and darkness, you brought what was clean in the pen in contact with the uncleanness of the parchment. Or perhaps, for the sake of the colors, we may put it the other way; and so the darkness would be yours, in the ink which you brought against the light of the white pages. If these remarks irritate you, you should rather be angry with yourselves for believing doctrines of which these are the necessary consequences. As for the books of the apostles and prophets, we read them as a record of our faith, to encourage our hope and animate our love. These books are in perfect harmony with one another; and their harmony, like the music of a heavenly trumpet, wakens us from the torpor of worldliness, and urges us on to the prize of our high calling. The apostle, after quoting from the prophets the words, "The reproaches of them that reproached Thee fell on me," goes on to speak of the benefit of reading the prophets: "For whatsoever things were written beforetime were written for our learning; that we, through patience and comfort of the Scriptures, might have hope."[1] If Faustus denies this, we can only say with Paul, "If any one shall preach to you another doctrine than that ye have received, let him be accursed."[2]

[1] Rom. xv. 4. [2] Gal. i. 9.

BOOK XIV.

FAUSTUS ABHORS MOSES FOR THE AWFUL CURSE HE HAS PRONOUNCED UPON CHRIST. AUGUSTIN EXPOUNDS THE CHRISTIAN DOCTRINE OF THE SUFFERING SAVIOUR BY COMPARING OLD AND NEW TESTAMENT PASSAGES.

1. FAUSTUS said: If you ask why we do not believe Moses, it is on account of our love and reverence for Christ. The most reckless man cannot regard with pleasure a person who has cursed his father. So we abhor Moses, not so much for his blasphemy of everything human and divine, as for the awful curse he has pronounced upon Christ the Son of God, who for our salvation hung on the tree. Whether Moses did this intentionally or not is your concern. Either way, he cannot be excused, or considered worthy of belief. His words are, "Cursed is every one that hangeth on a tree."[1] You tell me to believe this man, though, if he was inspired, he must have cursed Christ knowingly and intentionally; and if he did it in ignorance, he cannot have been divine. Take either alternative. Moses was no prophet, and while cursing in his usual manner, he fell ignorantly into the sin of blasphemy against God. Or he was indeed divine, and foresaw the future; and from ill-will to our salvation, he directs the venom of his malediction against Him who was to accomplish that salvation on a tree. He who thus injures the Son cannot surely have seen or known the Father. He who knew nothing of the final ascension of the Son, cannot surely have foretold His advent. Moreover, the extent of the injury inflicted by this curse is to be considered. For it denounces all the righteous men and martyrs, and sufferers of every kind, who have died in this way, as Peter and Andrew, and the rest. Such a cruel denunciation could never have come from Moses if he had been a prophet, unless he was a bitter enemy of these sufferers. For he pronounces them cursed not only of men but of God. What hope, then, of blessing remains to Christ, or his apostles, or to us if we happen to be crucified for Christ's sake? It indicates great thoughtlessness in Moses, and the want of all divine inspiration, that he overlooked the fact that men are hung on a tree for very different reasons, some for their crimes, and others who suffer in the cause of God and of righteousness. In this thoughtless way he heaps all together without distinction under the same curse; whereas if he had had any sense, not to say inspiration, if he wished to single out the punishment of the cross from all others as specially detestable, he would have said, Cursed is every guilty and impious person that hangeth on a tree. This would have made a distinction between the guilty and the innocent. And yet even this would have been incorrect, for Christ took the malefactor from the cross along with himself into the Paradise of his Father. What becomes of the curse on every one that hangeth on a tree? Was Barabbas, the notorious robber, who certainly was not hung on a tree, but was set free from prison at the request of the Jews, more blessed than the thief who accompanied Christ from the cross to heaven? Again, there is a curse on the man that worships the sun or the moon. Now if under a heathen monarch I am forced to worship the sun, and if from fear of this curse I refuse,

[1] Deut. xxi. 23.

shall I incur this other curse by suffering the punishment of crucifixion? Perhaps Moses was in the habit of cursing everything good. We think no more of his denunciation than of an old wife's scolding. So we find him pronouncing a curse on all youths of both sexes, when he says: "Cursed is every one that raiseth not up a seed in Israel."[1] This is aimed directly at Jesus, who, according to you, was born among the Jews, and raised up no seed to continue his family. It points too at his disciples, some of whom he took from the wives they had married, and some who were unmarried he forbade to take wives. We have good reason, you see, for expressing our abhorrence of the daring style in which Moses hurls his maledictions against Christ, against light, against chastity, against everything divine. You cannot make much of the distinction between hanging on a tree and being crucified, as you often try to do by way of apology; for Paul repudiates such a distinction when he says, "Christ hath redeemed us from the curse of the law, being made a curse for us; as it is written, Cursed is every one that hangeth on a tree."[2]

2. Augustin replied: The pious Faustus is pained because Christ is cursed by Moses. His love for Christ makes him hate Moses. Before explaining the sacred import and the piety of the words, "Cursed is every one that hangeth on a tree," I would ask these pious people why they are angry with Moses, since his curse does not affect their Christ. If Christ hung on the tree, He must have been fastened to it with nails, the marks of which He showed to His doubting disciple after His resurrection. Accordingly He must have had a vulnerable and mortal body, which the Manichæans deny. Call the wounds and the marks false, and it follows that His hanging on the tree was false. This Christ is not affected by the curse, and there is no occasion for this indignation against the person uttering the curse. If they pretend to be angry with Moses for cursing what they call the false death of Christ, what are we to think of themselves, who do not curse Christ, but, what is much worse, make Him a liar? If it is wrong to curse mortality, it is a much more heinous offense to sully the purity of truth. But let us make these heretical cavils an occasion for explaining this mystery to believers.

3. Death comes upon man as the punishment of sin, and so is itself called sin; not that a man sins in dying, but because sin is the cause of his death. So the word tongue, which properly means the fleshy substance between the teeth and the palate, is applied in a secondary sense to the result of the tongue's action. In this sense we speak of a Latin tongue and a Greek tongue. The word hand, too, means both the members of the body we use in working, and the writing which is done with the hand. In this sense we speak of writing as being proved to be the hand of a certain person, or of recognizing the hand of a friend. The writing is certainly not a member of the body, but the name hand is given to it because it is the hand that does it. So sin means both a bad action deserving punishment, and death the consequence of sin. Christ has no sin in the sense of deserving death, but He bore for our sakes sin in the sense of death as brought on human nature by sin. This is what hung on the tree; this is what was cursed by Moses. Thus was death condemned that its reign might cease, and cursed that it might be destroyed. By Christ's taking our sin in this sense, its condemnation is our deliverance, while to remain in subjection to sin is to be condemned.

4. What does Faustus find strange in the curse pronounced on sin, on death, and on human mortality, which Christ had on account of man's sin, though He Himself was sinless? Christ's body was derived from Adam, for His mother the Virgin Mary was a child of Adam. But God said in Paradise, "On the day that ye eat, ye shall surely die." This is the curse which hung on the tree. A man may deny that Christ was cursed who denies that He died. But the man who believes that Christ died, and acknowledges that death is the fruit of sin, and is itself called sin, will understand who it is that is cursed by Moses, when he hears the apostle saying "For our old man is crucified with Him."[3] The apostle boldly says of Christ, "He was made a curse for us;" for he could also venture to say, "He died for all." "He died," and "He was cursed," are the same. Death is the effect of the curse; and all sin is cursed, whether it means the action which merits punishment, or the punishment which follows. Christ, though guiltless, took our punishment, that He might cancel our guilt, and do away with our punishment.

5. These things are not my conjectures, but are affirmed constantly by the apostle, with an emphasis sufficient to rouse the careless and to silence the gainsayers. "God," he says, "sent His Son in the likeness of sinful flesh, that by sin He might condemn sin in the flesh."[4] Christ's flesh was not sin-

[1] Deut. xxv. 5-10.

[2] Gal. iii. 10.

[3] Rom. vi. 6.

[4] Rom. viii. 3.

ful, because it was not born of Mary by ordinary generation; but because death is the effect of sin, this flesh, in being mortal, had the likeness of sinful flesh. This is called sin in the following words, "that by sin He might condemn sin in the flesh." Again he says: "He hath made Him to be sin for us who knew no sin, that we might be made the righteousness of God in Him."[1] Why should not Moses call accursed what Paul calls sin? In this prediction the prophet claims a share with the apostle in the reproach of the heretics. For whoever finds fault with the word cursed in the prophet, must find fault with the word sin in the apostle; for curse and sin go together.

6. If we read, "Cursed of God is every one that hangeth on a tree," the addition of the words "of God" creates no difficulty. For had not God hated sin and our death, He would not have sent His Son to bear and to abolish it. And there is nothing strange in God's cursing what He hates. For His readiness to give us the immortality which will be had at the coming of Christ, is in proportion to the compassion with which He hated our death when it hung on the cross at the death of Christ. And if Moses curses every one that hangeth on a tree, it is certainly not because he did not foresee that righteous men would be crucified, but rather because He foresaw that heretics would deny the death of the Lord to be real, and would try to disprove the application of this curse to Christ, in order that they might disprove the reality of His death. For if Christ's death was not real, nothing cursed hung on the cross when He was crucified, for the crucifixion cannot have been real. Moses cries from the distant past to these heretics: Your evasion in denying the reality of the death of Christ is useless. Cursed is every one that hangeth on a tree; not this one or that, but absolutely every one. What! the Son of God? Yes, assuredly. This is the very thing you object to, and that you are so anxious to evade. You will not allow that He was cursed for us, because you will not allow that He died for us. Exemption from Adam's curse implies exemption from his death. But as Christ endured death as man, and for man; so also, Son of God as He was, ever living in His own righteousness, but dying for our offences, He submitted as man, and for man, to bear the curse which accompanies death. And as He died in the flesh which He took in bearing our punishment, so also, while ever blessed in His own righteousness, He was cursed for our offences, in the death which He suffered in bearing our punishment. And these words "every one" are intended to check the ignorant officiousness which would deny the reference of the curse to Christ, and so, because the curse goes along with death, would lead to the denial of the true death of Christ.

7. The believer in the true doctrine of the gospel will understand that Christ is not reproached by Moses when he speaks of Him as cursed, not in His divine majesty, but as hanging on the tree as our substitute, bearing our punishment, any more than He is praised by the Manichæans when they deny that He had a mortal body, so as to suffer real death. In the curse of the prophet there is praise of Christ's humility, while in the pretended regard of the heretics there is a charge of falsehood. If, then, you deny that Christ was cursed, you must deny that He died; and then you have to meet, not Moses, but the apostles. Confess that He died, and you may also confess that He, without taking our sin, took its punishment. Now the punishment of sin cannot be blessed, or else it would be a thing to be desired. The curse is pronounced by divine justice, and it will be well for us if we are redeemed from it. Confess then that Christ died, and you may confess that He bore the curse for us; and that when Moses said, "Cursed is every one that hangeth on a tree," he said in fact, To hang on a tree is to be mortal, or actually to die. He might have said, "Cursed is every one that is mortal," or "Cursed is every one dying;" but the prophet knew that Christ would suffer on the cross, and that heretics would say that He hung on the tree only in appearance, without really dying. So he exclaims, Cursed; meaning that He really died. He knew that the death of sinful man, which Christ though sinless bore, came from that curse, "If ye touch it, ye shall surely die." Thus also, the serpent hung on the pole was intended to show that Christ did not feign death, but that the real death into which the serpent by his fatal counsel cast mankind was hung on the cross of Christ's passion. The Manichæans turn away from the view of this real death, and so they are not healed of the poison of the serpent, as we read that in the wilderness as many as looked were healed.

8. It is true, some ignorantly distinguish between hanging on a tree and being crucified. So some explain this passage as referring to Judas. But how do they know whether he hung himself from wood or from stone? Faustus is right in saying that the apostle obliges us to refer the words to Christ. Such ignorant Catholics are the prey of the Manichæans. Such they get hold of and entangle

[1] 2 Cor. v. 21.

in their sophistry. Such were we when we fell into this heresy, and adhered to it. Such were we, when, not by our own strength, but by the mercy of God, we were rescued.

9. What attacks on divine things does Faustus speak of when he charges Moses with sparing nothing human or divine? He makes the charge without stopping to prove it. We know, on the contrary, that Moses gave due praise to everything really divine, and in human affairs was a just ruler, considering his times and the grace of his dispensation. It will be time to prove this when we see any proof of Faustus' charges. It may be clever to make such charges cautiously, but there is great incaution in the cleverness which ruins its possessor. It is good to be clever on the side of truth, but it is a poor thing to be clever in opposition to the truth. Faustus says that Moses spared nothing human or divine; not that he spared no god or man. If he said that Moses did not spare God, it could easily be shown in reply that Moses everywhere does honor to the true God, whom he declares to be the Maker of heaven and earth. Again, if he said that Moses spared none of the gods, he would betray himself to Christians as a worshipper of the false gods that Moses denounces; and so he would be prevented from gathering what he has not brought forth, by the brood taking refuge under the wings of the Mother Church. Faustus tries to ensnare the babes, by saying that Moses spared nothing divine, wishing not to frighten Christians with a profession of belief in the gods, which would be plainly opposed to Christianity, and at the same time appearing to take the side of the Pagans against us; for they know that Moses has said many plain and pointed things against the idols and gods of the heathen, which are devils.

10. If the Manichæans disapprove of Moses on this account, let them confess that they are worshippers of idols and devils. This, indeed, may be the case without their being aware of it. The apostle tells us that "in the last days some shall depart from the faith, giving heed to seducing spirits, and to doctrines of devils, speaking lies in hypocrisy."[1] Whence but from devils, who are fond of falsehood, could the idea have come that Christ's sufferings and death were unreal, and that the marks which He showed of His wounds were unreal? Are these not the doctrines of lying devils, which teach that Christ, the Truth itself, was a deceiver? Besides, the Manichæans openly teach the worship, if not of devils, still of created things, which the apostle condemns in the words, "They worshipped and served the creature rather than the Creator."[2]

11. As there is an unconscious worship of idols and devils in the fanciful legends of the Manichæans, so they knowingly serve the creature in their worship of the sun and moon. And in what they call their service of the Creator they really serve their own fancy, and not the Creator at all. For they deny that God created those things which the apostle plainly declares to be the creatures of God, when he says of food, "Every creature of God is good, and nothing to be refused, if it is received with thanksgiving."[3] This is sound doctrine, which you cannot bear, and so turn to fables. The apostle praises the creature of God, but forbids the worship of it; and in the same way Moses gives due praise to the sun and moon, while at the same time he states the fact of their having been made by God, and placed by Him in their courses, —the sun to rule the day, and the moon to rule the night. Probably you think Moses spared nothing divine, simply because he forbade the worship of the sun and moon, whereas you turn towards them in all directions in your worship. But the sun and moon take no pleasure in your false praises. It is the devil, the transgressor, that delights in false praises. The powers of heaven, who have not fallen by sin, wish their Creator to be praised in them; and their true praise is that which does no wrong to their Creator. He is wronged when they are said to be His members, or parts of His substance. For He is perfect and independent, underived, not divided or scattered in space, but unchangeably self-existent, self-sufficient, and blessed in Himself. In the abundance of His goodness, He by His word spoke, and they were made; He commanded, and they were created. And if earthly bodies are good, of which the apostle spoke when he said that no food is unclean, because every creature of God is good, much more the heavenly bodies, of which the sun and moon are the chief; for the apostle says again, "The glory of the terrestrial is one, and the glory of the celestial is another."[4]

12. Moses, then, casts no reproach on the sun and moon when he prohibits their worship. He praises them as heavenly bodies; while he also praises God as the Creator of both heavenly and earthly, and will not allow of His being insulted by giving the worship due to Him to those who are praised only as

[1] 1 Tim. iv. 1, 2.

[2] Rom. i. 25.

[3] 1 Tim. iv. 4.

[4] 1 Cor. xv. 40.

dependent upon Him. Faustus prides himself on the ingenuity of his objection to the curse pronounced by Moses on the worship of the sun and moon. He says, "If under a heathen monarch I am forced to worship the sun, and if from fear of this curse I refuse, shall I incur this other curse by suffering the punishment of crucifixion?" No heathen monarch is forcing you to worship the sun; nor would the sun itself force you, if it were reigning on the earth, as neither does it now wish to be worshipped. As the Creator bears with blasphemers till the judgment, so these celestial bodies bear with their deluded worshippers till the judgment of the Creator. It should be observed that no Christian monarch could enforce the worship of the sun. Faustus instances a heathen monarch, for he knows that their worship of the sun is a heathen custom. Yet, in spite of this opposition to Christianity, the partridge takes the name of Christ, that it may gather what it has not brought forth. The answer to this objection is easy, and the force of truth will soon break the horns of this dilemma. Suppose, then, a Christian threatened by royal authority with being hung on a tree if he will not worship the sun. If I avoid, you say, the curse pronounced by the law on the worshipper of the sun, I incur the curse pronounced by the same law on him that hangs on a tree. So you will be in a difficulty; only that you worship the sun without being forced by anybody. But a true Christian, built on the foundation of the apostles and prophets, distinguishes the curses, and the reasons of them. He sees that one refers to the mortal body which is hung on the tree, and the other to the mind which worships the sun. For though the body bows in worship,—which also is a heinous offence,—the belief or imagination of the object worshipped is an act of the mind. The death implied in both curses is in one case the death of the body, and in the other the death of the soul. It is better to have the curse in bodily death,—which will be removed in the resurrection,—than the curse in the death of the soul, condemning it along with the body to eternal fire. The Lord solves this difficulty in the words: "Fear not them that kill the body, but cannot kill the soul; but fear him who has power to cast both soul and body into hell-fire."[1] In other words, fear not the curse of bodily death, which in time is removed; but fear the curse of spiritual death, which leads to the eternal torment of both soul and body. Be assured, Cursed is every one that hangeth on a tree is no old wife's railing, but a prophetical utterance. Christ, by the curse, takes the curse away, as He takes away death by death, and sin by sin. In the words, "Cursed is every one that hangeth on a tree," there is no more blasphemy than in the words of the apostle, "He died," or, "Our old man was crucified along with Him,"[2] or, "By sin He condemned sin,"[3] or, "He made Him to be sin for us who knew no sin,"[4] and in many similar passages. Confess, then, that when you exclaim against the curse of Christ, you exclaim against His death. If this is not an old wife's railing on your part, it is devilish delusion, which makes you deny the death of Christ because your own souls are dead. You teach people that Christ's death was feigned, making Christ your leader in the falsehood with which you use the name of Christian to mislead men.

13. If Faustus thinks Moses an enemy of continence or virginity because he says, "Cursed is every one that raiseth not up seed in Israel," let them hear the words of Isaiah: "Thus saith the Lord to all eunuchs; To them who keep my precepts, and choose the things that please me, and regard my covenant, will I give in my house and within my walls a place and a name better than of sons and of daughters; I will give them an everlasting name, that shall not be cut off."[5] Though our adversaries disagree with Moses, if they agree with Isaiah it is something gained. It is enough for us to know that the same God spoke by both Moses and Isaiah, and that every one is cursed who raiseth not up seed in Israel, both then when begetting children in marriage (for the continuation of the people was a civil duty), and now because no one spiritually born should rest content without seeking spiritual increase in the production of Christians by preaching Christ, each one according to his ability. So that the times of both Testaments are briefly described in the words, "Cursed is every one that raiseth not up seed in Israel."[6]

---

[1] Matt. x. 28.

[2] Rom. vi. 6.

[3] Rom. viii. 3.

[4] 2 Cor. v. 21.

[5] Isa. lvi. 4, 5.

[6] [In scarcely any other Manichæan record do we find the Manichæan hostility to Judaism expressed with so much ardor and with so much precision as in the blasphemous statements of Faustus in this treatise.—A. H. N.]

BOOK XV.

FAUSTUS REJECTS THE OLD TESTAMENT BECAUSE IT LEAVES NO ROOM FOR CHRIST. CHRIST THE ONE BRIDEGROOM SUFFICES FOR HIS BRIDE THE CHURCH. AUGUSTIN ANSWERS AS WELL AS HE CAN, AND REPROVES THE MANICHÆANS WITH PRESUMPTION IN CLAIMING TO BE THE BRIDE OF CHRIST.

1. Faustus said: Why do we not receive the Old Testament? Because when a vessel is full, what is poured on it is not received, but allowed to run over; and a full stomach rejects what it cannot hold. So the Jews, satisfied with the Old Testament, reject the New; and we who have received the New Testament from Christ, reject the Old. You receive both because you are only half filled with each, and the one is not completed, but corrupted by the other. For vessels half filled should not be filled up with anything of a different nature from what they already contain. If it contains wine, it should be filled up with wine, honey with honey, vinegar with vinegar. For to pour gall on honey, or water on wine, or alkalies on vinegar, is not addition, but adulteration. This is why we do not receive the Old Testament. Our Church, the bride of Christ, the poor bride of a rich bridegroom, is content with the possession of her husband, and scorns the wealth of inferior lovers, and despises the gifts of the Old Testament and of its author, and from regard to her own character, receives only the letters of her husband. We leave the Old Testament to your Church, that, like a bride faithless to her spouse, delights in the letters and gifts of another. This lover who corrupts your chastity, the God of the Hebrews in his stone tablets promises you gold and silver, and abundance of food, and the land of Canaan. Such low rewards have tempted you to be unfaithful to Christ, after all the rich dowry bestowed by him. By such attractions the God of the Hebrews gains over the bride of Christ. You must know that you are cheated, and that these promises are false. This God is in poverty and beggary, and cannot do what he promises. For if he cannot give these things to the synagogue, his proper wife, who obeys him in all things like a servant, how can he bestow them on you who are strangers, and who proudly throw off his yoke from your necks? Go on, then, as you have begun, join the new cloth to the old garment, put the new wine in old bottles, serve two masters without pleasing either, make Christianity a monster, half horse and half man; but allow us to serve only Christ, content with his immortal dower, and imitating the apostle who says, "Our sufficiency is of God, who has made us able ministers of the New Testament."[1] In the God of the Hebrews we have no interest whatever; for neither can he perform his promises, nor do we desire that he should. The liberality of Christ has made us indifferent to the flatteries of this stranger. This figure of the relation of the wife to her husband is sanctioned by Paul, who says: "The woman that has a husband is bound to her husband as long as he liveth; but if her husband die, she is freed from the law of her husband. So, then, if while her husband liveth she be joined to another man, she shall be called an adulteress; but if her husband be dead, she is not an adulteress, though she be married to another man."[2] Here he shows that there is a spiritual adultery in being united to Christ before repudiating the author of the law, and counting him, as it were, as dead. This applies chiefly to the Jews who believe in Christ, and who ought to forget their former superstition. We who have been converted to Christ from heathenism, look upon the God of the Hebrews not merely as dead, but as never having existed, and do not need to be told to forget him. A Jew, when he believes, should regard Adonai as dead; a Gentile should regard his idol as dead; and so with everything that has been held sacred before conversion. One who, after giving up idolatry, worships both the God of the Hebrews and Christ, is like an abandoned woman, who after the death of one husband marries two others.

2. Augustin replied: Let all who have given their hearts to Christ say whether they can listen patiently to these things, unless Christ Himself enable them. Faustus, full of the new honey, rejects the old vinegar; and Paul, full of the old vinegar, has poured out half that the new honey may be poured in, not to be kept, but to be corrupted. When the apostle calls himself a servant of Jesus Christ, called to be an apostle, separated unto the gospel of God, this is the new honey. But when he adds, "which He promised before by His prophets in the Holy Scriptures of His Son, who was made of the seed of David according to the flesh,"[3] this is the old vinegar. Who could bear to hear this, unless

[1] 2 Cor. iii. 5, 6. [2] Rom. vii. 2, 3. [3] Rom. i. 1-3.

the apostle himself consoled us by saying: "There must be heresies, that they which are approved may be made manifest among you?"[1] Why should we repeat what we said already?[2]—that the new cloth and the old garment, the new wine and the old bottles, mean not two Testaments, but two lives and two hopes,—that the relation of the two Testaments is figuratively described by the Lord when He says: "Therefore every scribe instructed in the kingdom of God is like an householder bringing out of his treasure things new and old."[3] The reader may remember this as said before, or he may find it on looking back. For if any one tries to serve God with two hopes, one of earthly felicity, and the other of the kingdom of heaven, the two hopes cannot agree; and when the latter is shaken by some affliction, the former will be lost too. Thus it is said, No man can serve two masters; which Christ explains thus: "Ye cannot serve God and Mammon."[4] But to those who rightly understand it, the Old Testament is a prophecy of the New. Even in that ancient people, the holy patriarchs and prophets, who understood the part they performed, or which they were instrumental in performing, had this hope of eternal life in the New Testament. They belonged to the New Testament, because they understood and loved it, though revealed only in figure. Those belonging to the Old Testament were the people who cared for nothing else but the temporal promises, without understanding them as significant of eternal things. But all this has already been more than enough insisted on.

3. It is amazingly bold in the impious and impure sect of the Manichæans to boast of being the chaste bride of Christ. All the effect of such a boast on the really chaste members of the holy Church is to remind them of the apostle's warning against deceivers: "I have joined you to one husband, to present you as a chaste virgin to Christ. But I fear lest, as the serpent deceived Eve by his guile, so your minds also should be corrupted from the purity which is in Christ."[5] What else do those preachers of another gospel than that which we have received try to do, but to corrupt us from the purity which we preserve for Christ, when they stigmatize the law of God as old, and praise their own falsehoods as new, as if all that is new must be good, and all that is old bad? The Apostle John, however, praises the old commandment, and the Apostle Paul bids us avoid novelties in doctrine. As an unworthy son and servant of the Catholic Church, the true bride of the true Christ, I too, as appointed to give out food to my fellow-servants, would speak to her a word of counsel. Continue ever to shun the profane errors of the Manichæans, which have been tried by the experience of thine own children, and condemned by their recovery. By that heresy I was once separated from thy fellowship, and after running into danger which ought to have been avoided, I escaped. Restored to thy service, my experience may perhaps be profitable to thee. Unless thy true and truthful Bridegroom, from whose side thou wert made, had obtained the remission of sins through His own real blood, the gulf of error would have swallowed me up; I should have become dust, and been devoured by the serpent. Be not misled by the name of truth. The truth is in thine own milk, and in thine own bread. They have the name only, and not the thing. Thy full-grown children, indeed, are secure; but I speak to thy babes, my brothers, and sons, and masters, whom thou, the virgin mother, fertile as pure, dost cherish into life under thine anxious wings, or dost nourish with the milk of infancy. I call upon these, thy tender offspring, not to be seduced by noisy vanities, but rather to pronounce accursed any one that preaches to them another gospel than that which they have received in thee. I call upon these not to leave the true and truthful Christ, in whom are hid all the treasures of wisdom and knowledge; not to forsake the abundance of His goodness which He has laid up for them that fear Him, and has wrought for them that trust in Him.[6] How can they expect to find truthful words in one who preaches an untruthful Christ? Scorn the reproaches cast on thee, for thou knowest well that the gift which thou desirest from thy Bridegroom is eternal life, for He Himself is eternal life.

4. It is a silly falsehood that thou hast been seduced to another God, who promises abundance of food and the land of Canaan. For thou canst perceive how the saints of old, who were also thy children, were enlightened by these figures which were prophecies of thee. Thou needest not regard the poor jest against the stone tablets, for the stony heart of which they were in old times a figure is not in thee. For thou art an epistle of the apostles, "written not with ink, but with the Spirit of the living God; not on tables of stone, but on the fleshy tables of the heart."[7] Our opponents ignorantly think that these words are in their favor, and that the apostle finds fault with the dispensation of the Old Testament, where-

[1] 1 Cor. xi. 19. [2] Lib. viii. [3] Matt. xiii. 52.
[4] Matt. vi. 24. [5] 2 Cor. xi. 2, 3.

[6] Ps. xxxi. 19. [7] 2 Cor. iii. 2, 3.

as they are the words of the prophet. This utterance of the apostles was a fulfillment of the long anterior utterances of the prophet whom the Manichæans reject, for they believe the apostles without understanding them. The prophet says: "I will take away from them the stony heart, and I will give them a heart of flesh."[1] What is this but "Not on tables of stone, but on the fleshy tables of the heart"? For by the heart of flesh and the fleshy tables is not meant a carnal understanding: but as flesh feels, whereas a stone cannot, the insensibility of stone signifies an unintelligent heart, and the sensibility of flesh signifies an intelligent heart. Instead, then, of scoffing at thee, they deserve to be ridiculed who say that earth, and wood, and stones have sense, and that their life is more intelligent than animal life. So, not to speak of the truth, even their own fiction obliges them to confess that the law written on tables of stone was purer than their sacred parchments. Or perhaps they prefer sheepskin to stone, because their legends make stones the bones of princes. In any case, the ark of the Old Testament was a cleaner covering for the tables of stone than the goatskin of their manuscripts. Laugh at these things, while pitying them, to show their falsehood and absurdity. With a heart no longer stony, thou canst see in these stone tablets a suitableness to that hard-hearted people; and at the same time thou canst find even there the stone, thy Bridegroom, described by Peter as "a living stone, rejected by men, but chosen of God, and precious." To them He was "a stone of stumbling and a rock of offence;" but to thee, "the stone which the builders rejected has become the head of the corner."[2] This is all explained by Peter, and is quoted from the prophets, with whom these heretics have nothing to do. Fear not, then, to read these tablets—they are from thy Husband; to others the stone was a sign of insensibility, but to thee of strength and stability. With the finger of God these tablets were written; with the finger of God thy Lord cast out devils; with the finger of God drive thou away the doctrines of lying devils which sear the conscience. With these tablets thou canst confound the seducer who calls himself the Paraclete, that he may impose upon thee by a sacred name. For on the fiftieth day after the passover the tables were given; and on the fiftieth day after the passion of thy Bridegroom—of whom the passover was a type—the finger of God, the Holy Spirit, the promised Paraclete, was given. Fear not the tablets which convey to thee ancient writings now made plain. Only be not under the law, lest fear prevent thy fulfilling it; but be under grace, that love, which is the fulfilling of the law, may be in thee. For it was in a review of these very tablets that the friend of thy Bridegroom said: "For thou shalt not commit adultery, Thou shalt not murder, Thou shalt not covet, and if there be any other commandment, it is contained in this word, Thou shalt love thy neighbor as thyself. Love worketh no ill to his neighbor; therefore love is the fulfilling of the law."[3] One table contains the precept of love to God, and the other of love to man. And He who first sent these tablets Himself came to enjoin those precepts on which hang the law and the prophets.[4] In the first precept is the chastity of thy espousals; in the second is the unity of thy members. In the one thou art united to divinity; in the other thou dost gather a society. And these two precepts are identical with the ten, of which three relate to God, and seven to our neighbor. Such is the chaste tablet in which thy Lover and thy Beloved of old prefigured to thee the new song on a psaltery of ten strings; Himself to be extended on the cross for thee, that by sin He might condemn sin in the flesh, and that the righteouness of the law might be fulfilled in thee. Such is the conjugal tablet, which may well be hated by the unfaithful wife.

5. I turn now to thee, thou deluded and deluding congregation of Manichæus,—wedded to so many elements, or rather prostituted to so many devils, and impregnated with blasphemous falsehoods,—dost thou dare to slander as unchaste the marriage of the Catholic Church with thy Lord? Behold thy lovers, one balancing creation, and the other bearing it up like Atlas. For one, by thy account, holds the sources of the elements, and hangs the world in space; while the other keeps him up by kneeling down and carrying the weight on his shoulders. Where are those beings? And if they are so occupied, how can they come to visit thee, to spend an idle hour in getting their shoulders or their fingers relieved by thy soft, soothing touch? But thou art deceived by evil spirits which commit adultery with thee, that thou mayest conceive falsehoods and bring forth vanities. Well mayest thou reject the message of the true God, as opposed to thy parchments, where in the vain imaginations of a wanton mind thou hast gone after so many false gods. The fictions of the poets are more respectable than thine, in this at least, that they

[1] Ezek. xi. 19.

[2] 1 Pet. ii. 4-8.

[3] Rom. xiii. 9, 10.

[4] Matt. xxii. 37-40.

deceive no one; while the fables in thy books, by assuming an appearance of truth, mislead the childish, both young and old, and pervert their minds. As the apostle says, they have itching ears, and turn away from hearing the truth to listen to fables.[1] How shouldest thou bear the sound doctrine of these tables, where the first commandment is, "Hear, O Israel, the Lord thy God is one Lord,"[2] when thy corrupt affections find shameful delight in so many false deities? Dost thou not remember thy love-song, where thou describest the chief ruler in perennial majesty, crowned with flowers, and of fiery countenance? To have even one such lover is shameful; for a chaste wife seeks not a husband crowned with flowers. And thou canst not say that this description or representation has a typical meaning, for thou art wont to praise Manichæus for nothing more than for speaking to thee the simple naked truth without the disguise of figures. So the God of thy song is a real king, bearing a sceptre and crowned with flowers. When he wears a crown of flowers, he ought to put aside his sceptre; for effeminacy and majesty are incongruous. And then he is not thy only lover; for the song goes on to tell of twelve seasons clothed in flowers, and filled with song, throwing their flowers at their father's face. These are twelve great gods of thine, three in each of the four regions surrounding the first deity. How this deity can be infinite, when he is thus circumscribed, no one can say. Besides, there are countless principalities, and hosts of gods, and troops of angels, which thou sayest were not created by God, but produced from His substance.

6. Thou art thus convicted of worshipping gods without number; for thou canst not bear the sound doctrine which teaches that there is one Son of one God, and one Spirit of both. And these, instead of being without number, are not three Gods; for not only is their substance one and the same, but their operation by means of this substance is also one and the same, while they have a separate manifestation in the material creation. These things thou dost not understand, and canst not receive. Thou art full, as thou sayest, for thou art steeped in blasphemous absurdities. Wilt thou continue burying thyself under such crudities? Sing on, then, and open thine eyes, if thou canst, to thine own shame. In this doctrine of lying devils thou art invited to fabulous dwellings of angels in a happy clime, and to fragrant fields where nectar flows for ever from trees and hills, in seas and rivers. These are the fictions of thy foolish heart, which revels in such idle fancies. Such expressions are sometimes used as figurative descriptions of the abundance of spiritual enjoyments; and they lead the mind of the student to inquire into their hidden meaning. Sometimes there is a material representation to the bodily senses, as the fire in the bush, the rod becoming a serpent, and the serpent a rod, the garment of the Lord not divided by His persecutors, the anointing of His feet or of His head by a devout woman, the branches of the multitude preceding and following Him when riding on the ass. Sometimes, either in sleep or in a trance, the spirit is informed by means of figures taken from material things, as Jacob's ladder, and the stone in Daniel cut out without hands and growing into a mountain, and Peter's vessel, and all that John saw. Sometimes the figures are only in the language; as in the Song of Songs, and in the parable of a householder making a marriage for his son, or that of the prodigal son, or that of the man who planted a vineyard and let it out to husbandmen. Thou boastest of Manichæus as having come last, not to use figures, but to explain them. His expositions throw light on ancient types, and leave no problem unsolved. This idea is supported by the assertion that the ancient types, in vision or in action or in words, had in view the coming of Manichæus, by whom they were all to be explained; while he, knowing that no one is to follow him, makes use of a style free from all figurative expressions. What, then, are those fields, and shady hills, and crowns of flowers, and fragrant odors, in which the desires of thy fleshly mind take pleasure? If they are not significant figures, they are either idle fancies or delirious dreams. If they are figures, away with the impostor who seduces thee with the promise of naked truth, and then mocks thee with idle tales. His ministers and his wretched deluded followers are wont to bait their hook with that saying of the apostle, "Now we see through a glass in a figure, but then face to face."[3] As if, forsooth, the Apostle Paul knew in part, and prophesied in part, and saw through a glass in a figure; whereas all this is removed at the coming of Manichæus, who brings that which is perfect, and reveals the truth face to face. O fallen and shameless! still to continue uttering such folly, still feeding on the wind, still embracing the idols of thine own heart. Hast thou, then, seen face to face the king with the sceptre, and the crown of flowers, and the hosts of gods, and the great world-

---

[1] 2 Tim. iv. 4.

[2] Deut. vi. 4.

[3] 1 Cor. xiii. 9.

holder with six faces and radiant with light, and that other exalted ruler surrounded with troops of angels, and the invincible warrior with a spear in his right hand and a shield in his left, and the famous sovereign who moves the three wheels of fire, water, and wind, and Atlas, chief of all, bearing the world on his shoulders, and supporting himself on his arms? These, and a thousand other marvels, hast thou seen face to face, or are thy songs doctrines learned from lying devils, though thou knowest it not? Alas! miserable prostitute to these dreams, such are the vanities which thou drinkest up instead of the truth; and, drunk with this deadly poison, thou darest with this jest of the tablets to affront the matronly purity of the spouse of the only Son of God; because no longer under the tutorship of the law, but under the control of grace, neither proud in activity nor crouching in fear, she lives by faith, and hope, and love, the Israel in whom there is no guile, who hears what is written: "The Lord thy God is one God." This thou hearest not, and art gone a whoring after a multitude of false gods.

7. Of necessity these tables are against thee, for the second commandment is, "Thou shalt not take the name of the Lord thy God in vain;" whereas thou dost attribute the vanity of falsehood to Christ Himself, who, to remove the vanity of the fleshly mind, rose in a true body, visible to the bodily eye. So also the third commandment about the rest of the Sabbath is against thee, for thou art tossed about by a multitude of restless fancies. How these three commandments relate to the love of God, thou hast neither the power nor the will to understand. Shamefully headstrong and turbulent, thou hast reached the height of folly, vanity, and worthlessness; thy beauty is spoiled, and thine order perished. I know thee, for I was once the same. How shall I now teach thee that these three precepts relate to the love of God, of whom, and by whom, and in whom are all things? How canst thou understand this, when thy pernicious doctrines prevent thee from understanding and from obeying the seven precepts relating to the love of our neighbor, which is the bond of human society? The first of these precepts is, "Honor thy father and mother;" which Paul quotes as the first commandment with promise, and himself repeats the injunction. But thou art taught by thy doctrine of devils to regard thy parents as thine enemies, because their union brought thee into the bonds of flesh, and laid impure fetters even on thy god. The doctrine that the production of children is an evil, directly opposes the next precept, "Thou shalt not commit adultery;" for those who believe this doctrine, in order that their wives may not conceive, are led to commit adultery even in marriage. They take wives, as the law declares, for the procreation of children; but from this erroneous fear of polluting the substance of the deity, their intercourse with their wives is not of a lawful character; and the production of children, which is the proper end of marriage, they seek to avoid. As the apostle long ago predicted of thee, thou dost indeed forbid to marry, for thou seekest to destroy the purpose of marriage. Thy doctrine turns marriage into an adulterous connection, and the bed-chamber into a brothel. This false doctrine leads in a similar way to the transgression of the commandment, "Thou shalt not kill." For thou dost not give bread to the hungry, from fear of imprisoning in flesh the member of thy God. From fear of fancied murder, thou dost actually commit murder. For if thou wast to meet a beggar starving for want of food, by the law of God to refuse him food would be murder; while to give food would be murder by the law of Manichæus. Not one commandment in the decalogue dost thou observe. If thou wert to abstain from theft, thou wouldst be guilty of allowing bread or food, whatever it might be, to undergo the misery of being devoured by a man of no merit, instead of running off with it to the laboratory of the stomach of thine elect; and so by theft saving thy god from the imprisonment with which he is threatened, and also from that from which he already suffers. Then, if thou art caught in the theft, wilt thou not swear by this god that thou art not guilty? For what will he do to thee when thou sayest to him, I swore by thee falsely, but it was for thy benefit; a regard for thine honor would have been fatal to thee? So the precept, Thou shalt not bear false witness, will be broken, not only in thy testimony, but in thine oath, for the sake of the liberation of the members of thy god. The commandment, "Thou shalt not covet thy neighbor's wife," is the only one which thy false doctrine does not oblige thee to break. But if it is unlawful to covet our neighbor's wife, what must it be to excite covetousness in others? Remember thy beautiful gods and goddesses presenting themselves with the purpose of exciting desire in the male and female leaders of darkness, in order that the gratification of this passion might effect the liberation of this god, who is in confinement everywhere, and who requires the assistance of such self-degradation. The last commandment, "Thou shalt not covet the possessions

of thy neighbor," it is wholly impossible for thee to obey. Does not this god of thine delude thee with the promise of making new worlds in a region belonging to another, to be the scene of thine imaginary triumph after thine imaginary conquest? In the desire for the accomplishment of these wild fancies, while at the same time thou believest that this land of darkness is in the closest neighborhood with thine own substance, thou certainly covetest the possessions of thy neighbor. Well indeed mayest thou dislike the tables which contain such good precepts in opposition to thy false doctrine. The three relating to the love of God thou dost entirely set aside. The seven by which human society is preserved thou keepest only from a regard to the opinion of men, or from fear of human laws; or good customs make thee averse to some crimes; or thou art restrained by the natural principle of not doing to another what thou wouldst not have done to thyself. But whether thou doest what thou wouldst not have done to thyself, or refrainest from doing what thou wouldst not have done to thyself, thou seest the opposition of the heresy to the law, whether thou actest according to it or not.

8. The true bride of Christ, whom thou hast the audacity to taunt with the stone tablets, knows the difference between the letter and the spirit, or in other words, between law and grace; and serving God no longer in the oldness of the letter, but in newness of spirit, she is not under the law, but under grace. She is not blinded by a spirit of controversy, but learns meekly from the apostle what is this law which we are not to be under; for "it was given," he says, "on account of transgression, till the seed should come to whom the promise was made."[1] And again: "It entered, that the offence might abound; but where sin abounded, grace has much more abounded."[2] Not that the law is sin, though it cannot give life without grace, but rather increases the guilt; for "where there is no law, there is no transgression."[3] The letter without the spirit, the law without grace, can only condemn. So the apostle explains his meaning, in case any should not understand: "What shall we say then? Is the law sin? God forbid. For I had not known sin but by the law. For I had not known lust unless the law had said, Thou shalt not covet. But sin, taking occasion by the commandment, deceived me, and by it slew me. Therefore the law is holy, and the commandment holy, and just, and good. Was then that which is good made death unto me? God forbid. But sin, that it might appear sin, wrought death in me by that which is good."[4] She at whom thou scoffest knows what this means; for she asks earnestly, and seeks humbly, and knocks meekly. She sees that no fault is found with the law, when it is said, "The letter killeth, but the spirit giveth life," any more than with knowledge, when it is said, "Knowledge puffeth up, but love edifieth."[5] The passage runs thus: "We know that we all have knowledge. Knowledge puffeth up, but love edifieth." The apostle certainly had no desire to be puffed up; but he had knowledge, because knowledge joined with love not only does not puff up, but strengthens. So the letter when joined with the spirit, and the law when joined with grace, is no longer the letter and the law in the same sense as when by itself it kills by abounding sin. In this sense the law is even called the strength of sin, because its strict prohibitions increase the fatal pleasure of sin. Even thus, however, the law is not evil; but "sin, that it may appear sin, works death by that which is good." So things that are not evil may often be hurtful to certain people. The Manichæans, when they have sore eyes, will shut out their god the sun. The bride of Christ, then, is dead to the law, that is, to sin, which abounds more from the prohibition of the law; for the law apart from grace commands, but does not enable. Being dead to the law in this sense, that she may be married to another who rose from the dead, she makes this distinction without any reproach to the law, which would be blasphemy against its author. This is thy crime; for though the apostle tells thee that the law is holy, and the commandment holy, and just, and good, thou dost not acknowledge it as the production of a good being. Its author thou makest to be one of the princes of darkness. Here the truth confronts thee. They are the words of the Apostle Paul: "The law is holy, and the commandment holy, and just, and good." Such is the law given by Him who appointed for a great symbolical use the tablets which thou foolishly deridest. The same law which was given by Moses becomes through Jesus Christ grace and truth; for the spirit is joined to the letter, that the righteousness of the law might begin to be fulfilled, which when unfulfilled only added the guilt of transgression. The law which is holy, and just, and good, is the same law by which sin works death, and to which we must die, that we may be married to another who rose from the dead. Hear what the apostle adds: "But sin, that it

[1] Gal. iii. 19 [2] Rom. v. 20 [3] Rom. iv. 15. [4] Rom. vii. 7-13. [5] 1 Cor. viii. 1.

might appear sin, wrought death in me by that which is good, that sin by the commandment might become exceeding sinful." Deaf and blind, dost thou not now hear and see? "Sin wrought death in me," he says, "by that which is good." The law is always good: whether it hurts those who are destitute of grace, or benefits those who are filled with grace, itself is always good; as the sun is always good, for every creature of God is good, whether it hurts weak eyes or gladdens the sight of the healthy. Grace fits the mind for keeping the law, as health fits the eyes for seeing the sun. And as healthy eyes die not to the pleasure of seeing the sun, but to that painful effect of the rays which beat upon the eye so as to increase the darkness; so the mind, healed by the love of the spirit, dies not to the justice of the law, but to the guilt and transgression which followed on the law in the absence of grace. So it is said, "The law is good, if used lawfully;" and immediately after of the same law, "Knowing this, that the law is not made for a righteous man." The man who delights in righteousness itself, does not require the restraint of the letter.

9. The bride of Christ rejoices in the hope of full salvation, and desires for thee a happy conversion from fables to truth. She desires that the fear of Adoneus, as if he were a strange lover, may not prevent thy escape from the seductions of the wily serpent. Adonai is a Hebrew word, meaning Lord, as applied only to God. In the same way the Greek word *latria* means service, in the sense of the service of God; and Amen means true, in a special sacred sense. This is to be learned only from the Hebrew Scriptures, or from a translation. The Church of Christ understands and loves these names, without regarding the evils of those who scoff because they are ignorant. What she does not yet understand, she believes may be explained, as similar things have already been explained to her. If she is charged with loving Emmanuel, she laughs at the ignorance of the accuser, and holds fast by the truth of this name. If she is charged with loving Messiah, she scorns her powerless adversary, and clings to her anointed Master. Her prayer for thee is, that thou also mayest be cured of thy errors, and be built upon the foundation of the apostles and prophets. The monstrosity with which thou ignorantly chargest the true doctrine, is really to be found in the world which, according to thy fanciful stories, is made partly of thy god and partly of the world of darkness. This world, half savage and half divine, is worse than monstrous. The view of such follies should make thee humble and penitent, and should lead thee to shun the serpent, who seduces thee into such errors. If thou dost not believe what Moses says of the guile of the serpent, thou mayest be warned by Paul, who, when speaking of presenting the Church as a chaste virgin to Christ, says, "I fear lest, as the serpent beguiled Eve through his craftiness, your minds also should be corrupted from the simplicity and purity which is in Christ."[1] In spite of this warning, thou hast been so misled, so infatuated by the serpent's fatal enchantments, that while he has persuaded other heretics to believe various falsehoods, he has persuaded thee to believe that he is Christ. Others, though fallen into the maze of manifold error, still admit the truth of the apostle's warning. But thou art so far gone in corruption, and so lost to shame, that thou holdest as Christ the very being by whom the apostle declares that Eve was beguiled, and against whom he thus seeks to put the virgin bride of Christ on her guard. Thy heart is darkened by the deceiver, who intoxicates thee with dreams of glittering groves. What are these promises but dreams? What reason is there to believe them true? O drunken, but not with wine!

10. Thou hast the impious audacity to accuse the God of the prophets of not fulfilling His promises even to His servants the Jews. Thou dost not mention, however, any promise that is unfulfilled; otherwise it might be shown, either that the promise has been fulfilled, and so that thou dost not understand it, or that it is yet to be fulfilled, and so that thou dost not believe it. What promise has been fulfilled to thee, to make it probable that thou wilt obtain new worlds gained from the region of darkness? If there are prophets who predict the Manichæans with praise, and if it is said that the existence of the sect is a fulfillment of this prediction, it must first be proved that these predictions were not forged by Manichæus in order to gain followers. He does not consider falsehood sinful. If he declares in praise of Christ that He showed false marks of wounds in His body, he can have no scruple about showing false predictions in his sheepskin volumes. Assuredly there are predictions of the Manichæans, less clear in the prophets, and most explicit in the apostle. For example: "The Spirit," he says, "speaketh expressly, that in the last times some shall depart from the faith, giving heed to seducing spirits, and to doctrines of devils, speaking lies in hypocrisy,

[1] 2 Cor. xi. 2, 3.

having their conscience seared, forbidding to marry, abstaining from meats, which God has created to be received with thanksgiving by believers, and those who know the truth. For every creature of God is good, and nothing to be refused, if it be received with thanksgiving."[1] The fulfillment of this in the Manichæans is as clear as day to all that know them, and has already been proved as fully as time permits.

11. She whom the apostle warns against the guile of the serpent by which thou hast been corrupted, that he may present her as a chaste virgin to Christ, her only husband, acknowledges the God of the prophets as the true God, and her own God. So many of His promises have already been fulfilled to her, that she looks confidently for the fulfillment of the rest. Nor can any one say that these prophecies have been forged to suit the present time, for they are found in the books of the Jews. What could be more unlikely than that all nations should be blessed in Abraham's seed, as it was promised? And yet how plainly is this promise now fulfilled! The last promise is made in the following short prophecy: "Blessed are they that dwell in Thy house: they shall ever praise Thee."[2] When trial is past, and death, the last enemy, is destroyed, there will be rest in the constant occupation of praising God, where there shall be no arrivals and no departures. So the prophet says elsewhere: "Praise the Lord, O Jerusalem; celebrate thy God, O Zion: for He hath strengthened the bars of thy gates; He hath blessed thy children within thee."[3] The gates are shut, so that none can go in or out. The Bridegroom Himself says in the Gospel, that He will not open to the foolish virgins though they knock. This Jerusalem, the holy Church, the bride of Christ, is described fully in the Revelation of John. And that which commends the promises of future bliss to the belief of this chaste virgin is, that now she is in possession of what was foretold of her by the same prophets. For she is thus described: "Hearken, O daughter, and regard, and incline thine ear; forget also thine own people, and thy father's house. For the King hath greatly desired thy beauty; and He is thy God. The daughters of Tyre shall worship Him with gifts; the rich among the people shall entreat thy favor. The daughter of the King is all glorious within; her clothing is of wrought gold. The virgins following her shall be brought unto the King: her companions shall be brought unto thee; with gladness and rejoicing shall they be brought into the temple of the King. Instead of thy fathers, children shall be born to thee, whom thou shalt make princes over all the earth. Thy name shall be remembered to all generations: therefore shall the people praise thee for ever and ever."[4] Unhappy victim of the serpent's guile, the inward beauty of the daughter of the King is not for thee even to think of. For this purity of mind is that which thou hast lost in opening thine eyes to love and worship the sun and moon. And so by the just judgment of God thou art estranged from the tree of life, which is eternal and internal wisdom; and with thee nothing is called or accounted truth or wisdom but that light which enters the eyes opened to evil, and which in thy impure mind expands and shapes itself into fanciful images. These are thy abominable whoredoms. Still the truth calls on thee to reflect and return. Return to me, and thou shalt be cleansed and restored, if thy shame leads thee to repentance. Hear these words of the true Truth, who neither with feigned shapes fought against the race of darkness, nor with feigned blood redeemed thee.

[1] 1 Tim. iv. 1-4. [2] Ps. lxxxiv. 4. [3] Ps. cxlviii. 1. [4] Ps. xlv. 10-17.

BOOK XVI.

FAUSTUS WILLING TO BELIEVE NOT ONLY THAT THE JEWISH BUT THAT ALL GENTILE PROPHETS WROTE OF CHRIST, IF IT SHOULD BE PROVED; BUT HE WOULD NONE THE LESS INSIST UPON REJECTING THEIR SUPERSTITIONS. AUGUSTIN MAINTAINS THAT ALL MOSES WROTE IS OF CHRIST, AND THAT HIS WRITINGS MUST BE EITHER ACCEPTED OR REJECTED AS A WHOLE.

1. FAUSTUS said: You ask why we do not believe Moses, when Christ says, "Moses wrote of me; and if ye believed Moses, ye would also believe me." I should be glad if not only Moses, but all prophets, Jew and Gentile, had written of Christ. It would be no hindrance, but a help to our faith, if we could cull testimonies from all hands agreeing in favor of our God. You could extract the prophecies of Christ out of the superstition which we should hate as much as ever. I am quite willing to believe that Moses, though so

much the opposite of Christ, may seem to have written of Him. No one but would gladly find a flower in every thorn, and food in every plant, and honey in every insect, although we would not feed on insects or on grass, nor wear thorns as a crown. No one but would wish pearls to be found in every deep, and gems in every land, and fruit on every tree. We may eat fish from the sea without drinking the water. We may take the useful, and reject what is hurtful. And why may we not take the prophecies of Christ from a religion the rites of which we condemn as useless? This need not make us liable to be led into the bondage of the errors; for we do not hate the unclean spirits less because they confessed plainly and openly that Jesus was the Son of God. If any similar testimony is found in Moses, I will accept it. But I will not on this account be brought into subjection to his law, which to my mind is pure Paganism. There is no reason whatever for thinking that I can have any objections to receiving prophecies of Christ from every spirit.

2. Since you have proved that Christ declared that Moses wrote of him, I should be very grateful if you would show me what he has written. I have searched the Scriptures, as we are told to do, and have found no prophecies of Christ, either because there are none, or because I could not understand them. The only escape from this perplexity was in one or other of two conclusions. Either this verse must be spurious, or Jesus a liar. As it is not consistent with piety to suppose God a liar, I preferred to attribute falsehood to the writers, rather than to the Author of truth. Moreover, He Himself tells that those who came before him were thieves and robbers, which applies first of all to Moses. And when, on the occasion of His speaking of His own majesty, and calling Himself the light of the world, the Jews angrily rejoined, "Thou bearest witness of thyself, thy witness is not true," I do not find that He appealed to the prophecies of Moses, as might have been expected. Instead of this, as having no connection with the Jews, and receiving no testimony from their fathers, He replied: "It is written in your law, that the testimony of two men is true. I am one who bear witness of myself, and the Father who sent me beareth witness of me."[1] He referred to the voice from heaven which all had heard: "This is my beloved Son, believe Him." I think it likely that if Christ had said that Moses wrote of Him, the ingenious hostility of the Jews would have led them at once to ask what He supposed Moses to have written. The silence of the Jews is a proof that Jesus never made such a statement.

3. My chief reason, however, for suspecting the genuineness of this verse is what I said before, that in all my search of the writings of Moses I have found no prophecy of Christ. But now that I have found in you a reader of superior intelligence, I hope to learn something; and I promise to be grateful if no feeling of ill-will prevents you from giving me the benefit of your higher attainments, as your lofty style of reproof entitles me to expect from you. I ask for instruction in whatever the writings of Moses contain about our God and Lord which has escaped me in reading. I beseech you not to use the ignorant argument that Christ affirms Moses to have written of Him. For suppose you had not to deal with me, as in my case there is an obligation to believe Him whom I profess to follow, but with a Jew or a Gentile, in reply to the statement that Moses wrote of Christ, they will ask for proofs. What shall we say to them? We cannot quote Christ's authority, for they do not believe in Him. We must point out what Moses wrote.

4. What, then, shall we point to? Shall it be that passage which you often quote where the God of Moses says to him: "I will raise up unto them from among their brethren a prophet like unto thee?"[2] But the Jew can see that this does not refer to Christ, and there is every reason against our thinking that it does. Christ was not a prophet, nor was He like Moses: for Moses was a man, and Christ was God; Moses was a sinner, and Christ sinless; Moses was born by ordinary generation, and Christ of a virgin according to you, or, as I hold, not born at all: Moses, for offending his God, was put to death on the mountain; and Christ suffered voluntarily, and the Father was well pleased in Him. If we were to assert that Christ was a prophet like Moses, the Jew would either deride us as ignorant or pronounce us untruthful.

5. Or shall we take another favorite passage of yours: "They shall see their life hanging, and shall not believe their life?"[3] You insert the words "on a tree," which are not in the original. Nothing can be easier than to show that this has no reference to Christ. Moses is uttering dire threatenings in case the people should depart from his law, and says among other things that they would be taken captive by their enemies, and would be expecting death day and night, having no confidence in the life allowed them by their

[1] John viii. 13, 17, 18.

[2] Deut. xviii. 15.

[3] Deut. xxviii. 66.

conquerors, so that their life would hang in uncertainty from fear of impending danger. This passage will not do, we must try others. I cannot admit that the words, "Cursed is every one that hangeth on a tree," refer to Christ, or when it is said that the prince or prophet must be killed who should try to turn away the people from their God, or should break any of the commandments.[1] That Christ did this I am obliged to grant. But if you assert that these things were written of Christ, it may be asked in reply, What spirit dictated these prophecies in which Moses curses Christ and orders him to be killed? If he had the Spirit of God, these things are not written of Christ; if they are written of Christ, he had not the Spirit of God. The Spirit of God would not curse Christ, or order Him to be killed. To vindicate Moses, you must confess that these passages too have no reference to Christ. So, if you have no others to show, there are none. If there are none, Christ could not have said that there were; and if Christ did not say so, that verse is spurious.

6. The next verse too is suspicious, "If ye believed Moses, ye would also believe me;" for the religion of Moses is so entirely different from that of Christ, that if the Jews believed one, they could not believe the other. Moses strictly forbids any work to be done on Sabbath, and gives as a reason for this prohibition that God made the world and all that is therein in six days, and rested on the seventh day, which is Sabbath; and therefore blessed or sanctified it as His haven of repose after toil, and commanded that breaking the Sabbath should be punished with death. The Jews, in obedience to Moses, insisted strongly on this, and so would not even listen to Christ when He told them that God always works, and that no day is appointed for the intermission of His pure and unwearied energy, and that accordingly He Himself had to work incessantly even on Sabbath. "My Father," he says, "worketh always, and I too must work."[2] Again, Moses places circumcision among the rites pleasing to God, and commands every male to be circumcised in the foreskin of his flesh, and declares that this is a necessary sign of the covenant which God made with Abraham, and that every male not circumcised would be cut off from his tribe, and from his part in the inheritance promised to Abraham and to his seed.[3] In this observance, too, the Jews were very zealous, and consequently could not believe in Christ, who made light of these things, and declared that a man when circumcised became twofold a child of hell.[4] Again, Moses is very particular about the distinction in animal foods, and discourses like an epicure on the merits of fish, and birds, and quadrupeds, and orders some to be eaten as clean, and others which are unclean not to be touched. Among the unclean he reckons the swine and the hare, and fish without scales, and quadrupeds that neither divide the hoof nor chew the cud. In this also the Jews carefully obeyed Moses, and so could not believe in Christ, who taught that all food is alike, and though he allowed no animal food to his own disciples, gave full liberty to the laity to eat whatever they pleased, and taught that men are polluted not by what goes into the mouth, but by the evil things which come out of it. In these and many other things the doctrine of Jesus, as everybody knows, contradicts that of Moses.

7. Not to enumerate all the points of difference, it is enough to mention this one fact, that most Christian sects, and, as is well known, the Catholics, pay no regard to what is prescribed in the writings of Moses. If this does not originate in some error, but in the doctrine correctly transmitted from Christ and His disciples, you surely must acknowledge that the teaching of Jesus is opposed to that of Moses, and that the Jews did not believe in Christ on account of their attachment to Moses. How can it be otherwise than false that Jesus said to the Jews, "If ye believed Moses, ye would believe me also," when it is perfectly clear that their belief in Moses prevented them from believing in Jesus, which they might have done if they had left off believing in Moses? Again I ask you to show me anything that Moses wrote of Christ.

8. Elsewhere Faustus says: When you find no passage to point to, you use this weak and inappropriate argument, that a Christian is bound to believe Christ when he says that Moses wrote of Him, and that whoever does not believe this is not a Christian. It would be far better to confess at once that you cannot find any passage. This argument might be used with me, because my reverence for Christ compels me to believe what He says. Still it may be a question whether this is Christ's own declaration, requiring absolute belief, or only the writer's, to be carefully examined. And disbelief in falsehood is no offence to Christ, but to impostors. But of whatever use this argument may be with Christians, it is wholly inapplicable in the case of the Jew or Gentile, with whom we are

[1] Deut. xiii. 5. [2] John v. 17. [3] Gen. xvii. 9-14. [4] Matt. xxiii. 15.

supposed to be discussing. And even with Christians the argument is objectionable. When the Apostle Thomas was in doubt, Christ did not spurn him from Him. Instead of saying, "Believe, if thou art a disciple; whoever does not believe is not a disciple," Christ sought to heal the wounds of his mind by showing him the marks of the wounds in His own body. Does it become you then to tell me that I am not a Christian because I am in doubt, not about Christ, but about the genuineness of a remark attributed to Christ? But, you say, He calls those especially blessed who have not seen, and yet have believed. If you think that this refers to believing without the use of judgment and reason, you are welcome to this blind blessedness. I shall be content with rational blessedness.

9. Augustin replied: Your idea of taking any prophecies of Christ to be found in Moses, as a fish out of the sea, while you throw away the water from which the fish is taken, is a clever one. But since all that Moses wrote is of Christ, or relates to Christ, either as predicting Him by words and actions, or as illustrating His grace and glory, you, with your faith in the untrue and untruthful Christ from the writings of Manichæus, and your unbelief in Moses, will not even eat the fish. Moreover, though you are sincere in your hostility to Moses, you are hypocritical in your praise of fish. For how can you say that there is no harm in eating a fish taken out of the sea, when your doctrine is that such food is so hurtful, that you would rather starve than make use of it? If all flesh is unclean, as you say it is, and if the wretched life of your god is confined in all water or plants, from which it is liberated by your using them for food, according to your own vile superstition, you must throw away the fish you have praised, and drink the water and eat the thistles you speak of as useless. As for your comparison of the servant of God to devils, as if his prophecies of Christ resembled their confession, the servant does not refuse to bear the reproach of his master. If the Master of the house was called Beelzebub, how much more they of His household![1] You have learned this reproach from Christ's enemies; and you are worse than they were. They did not believe that Jesus was Christ, and therefore thought Him an impostor. But the only doctrine you believe in is that which dares to make Christ a liar.

10. What reason have you for saying that the law of Moses is pure Paganism? Is it because it speaks of a temple, and an altar of sacrifices, and priests? But all these names are found also in the New Testament. "Destroy," Christ says, "this temple, and in three days I will raise it up;"[2] and again, "When thou offerest thy gift at the altar;"[3] and again, "Go, show thyself to the priest, and offer for thyself a sacrifice as Moses commanded, for a testimony unto them."[4] What these things prefigured the Lord Himself partly tells us, when He calls His own body the temple; and we learn also from the apostle, who says, "The temple of God is holy, which temple ye are;"[5] and again, "I beseech you therefore by the mercies of God, that ye present your bodies a living sacrifice, holy, acceptable to God;"[6] and in similar passages. As the same apostle says, in words which cannot be too often quoted, these things were our examples, for they were not the work of devils, but of the one true God who made heaven and earth, and who, though not needing such things, yet, suiting His requirements to the time, made ancient observances significant of future realities. Since you pretend to abhor Paganism, though it is only that you may lead astray by your deception unlearned Christians or those not established in the faith, show us any authority in Christian books for your worship and service of the sun and moon. Your heresy is liker Paganism than the law of Moses is. For you do not worship Christ, but only something that you call Christ, a fiction of your own fancy; and the gods you serve are either the bodies visible in the heavens, or hosts of your own contrivance. If you do not build shrines for these worthless idols, the creatures of the imagination, you make your hearts their temple.

11. You ask me to show what Moses wrote of Christ. Many passages have already been pointed out. But who could point out all? Besides, when any quotation is made, you are ready perversely to try to give the words another meaning; or if the evidence is too strong to be resisted, you will say that you take the passage as a sweet fish out of the salt water, and that you will not therefore consent to drink all the brine of the books of Moses. It will be enough, then, to take those passages in the Hebrew law which Faustus has chosen for criticism, and to show that, when rightly understood, they apply to Christ. For if the things which our adversary ridicules and condemns are made to prove that he himself is condemned by Christian truth, it will be evident that either the mere quotation or the careful examination of the other passages will

[1] Matt. x. 25.

[2] John ii. 19.
[3] Matt. v. 24.
[4] Matt. viii. 4.
[5] 1 Cor. iii. 17.
[6] Rom. xii. 1.

be enough to show their agreement with Christian faith. Well, then, O thou full of all subtilty, when the Lord in the Gospel says, "If ye believed Moses, ye would believe me also, for he wrote of me,"[1] there is no occasion for the great perplexity you pretend to be in, or for the alternative of either pronouncing this verse spurious or calling Jesus a liar. The verse is as genuine as its words are true. I preferred, says Faustus, to attribute falsehood to the writers, rather than to the Author of truth. What sort of faith can you have in Christ as the author of truth, when your doctrine is that His flesh and His death, His wounds and their marks, were feigned? And where is your authority for saying that Christ is the author of truth, if you dare to attribute falsehood to those who wrote of Him, whose testimony has come down to us with the confirmation of those immediately succeeding them? You have not seen Christ, nor has He conversed with you as with the apostles, nor called you from heaven as He did Saul. What knowledge or belief can we have of Christ, but on the authority of Scripture? Or if there is falsehood in the Gospel which has been widely published among all nations, and has been held in such high sacredness in all churches since the name of Christ was first preached, where shall we find a trustworthy record of Christ? If the Gospel is called in question in spite of the general consent regarding it, there can be no writing which a man may not call spurious if he does not wish to believe it.

12. You go on to quote Christ's words, that all who came before Him were thieves and robbers. How do you know that these were Christ's words, but from the Gospel? You profess faith in these words, as if you had heard them from the mouth of the Lord Himself. But if any one declares the verse to be spurious, and denies that Christ said this, you will have, in reply, to exert yourself in vindication of the authority of the Gospel. Unhappy being! what you refuse to believe is written in the same place as that which you quote as spoken by the Lord Himself. We believe both, for we believe the sacred narrative in which both are contained. We believe both that Moses wrote of Christ, and that all that came before Christ were thieves and robbers. By their coming He means their not being sent. Those who were sent, as Moses and the holy prophets, came not before Him, but with Him. They did not proudly wish to precede Him, but were the humble bearers of the message which He uttered by them. According to the meaning which you give to the Lord's words, it is plain that with you there can be no prophets. And so you have made a Christ for yourselves who should prophesy a Christ to come. If you have any prophets of your own, they will have, of course, no authority, as not being recognized by any others; but if there are any that you dare to quote as prophesying that Christ would come in an unreal body, and would suffer an unreal death, and would show to His doubting disciples unreal marks of wounds, not to speak of the abominable nature of such prophecies, and of the evident untruthfulness of those who commend falsehood in Christ, by your own interpretation those prophets must have been thieves and robbers, for they could not have spoken of Christ as coming in any manner unless they had come before Him. If by those who came before Christ we understand those who would not come with Him, —that is, with the Word of God,—but without being sent byGod brought their own falsehoods to men, you yourselves, although you are born in this world after the death and the resurrection of Christ, are thieves and robbers. For, without waiting for His illumination that you might preach His truth, you have come before Him to preach up your own deceits.

13. In the passage where we read of the Jews saying to Christ, Thou bearest witness of thyself, thy witness is not true, you do not see that Christ replies by saying that Moses wrote of Him, simply because you have not got the eye of piety to see with. The answer of Christ is this: "It is written in your law, that the testimony of two men is true; I am one who bear witness of myself, and the Father that sent me beareth witness of me."[2] What does this mean, if rightly understood, but that this number of witnesses required by the law was fixed upon and consecrated in the spirit of prophecy, that even thus might be prefigured the future revelation of the Father and Son, whose spirit is the Holy Spirit of the inseparable Trinity? So it is written: "In the mouth of two or three witnesses shall every word be established."[3] As a matter of fact, one witness generally speaks the truth, while a number tell lies. And the world, in its conversion to Christianity, believed one apostle preaching the gospel rather than the mistaken multitude who persecuted him. There was a special reason for requiring this number of witnesses, and in His answer the Lord implied that Moses prophesied of Him. Do you carp at His saying *your law* instead

[1] John v. 46.

[2] John viii. 17, 18.

[3] Deut. xix. 15.

of the law of God? But, as every one knows, this is the common expression in Scripture. Your law means the law given to you. So the apostle speaks of his gospel, while at the same time he declares that he received it not from man, but by the revelation of Jesus Christ. You might as well say that Christ denies God to be His Father, when He uses the words your Father instead of our Father. Again, you should refuse to believe the voice which you allude to as having come from heaven, This is my beloved Son, believe Him, because you did not hear it. But if you believe this because you find it in the sacred Scriptures, you will also find there what you deny, that Moses wrote of Christ, besides many other things that you do not acknowledge as true. Do you not see that your own mischievous argument may be used to prove that this voice never came from heaven? To your own destruction, and to the detriment of the welfare of mankind, you try to weaken the authority of the gospel, by arguing that it cannot be true that Christ said that Moses wrote of Him; because if He had said this, the ingenious hostility of the Jews would have led them at once to ask what He supposed Moses to have written of Him. In the same way, it might be impiously argued that if that voice had really come from heaven, all the Jews who heard it would have believed. Why are you so unreasonable as not to consider that, as it was possible for the Jews to remain hardened in unbelief after hearing the voice from heaven, so it was possible for them, when Christ said that Moses wrote of Him, to refrain from asking what Moses wrote, because in their ingenious hostility they were afraid of being proved to be in the wrong?

14. Besides that this argument is an impious assault on the gospel, Faustus himself is aware of its feebleness, and therefore insists more on what he calls his chief difficulty,—that in all his search of the writings of Moses he has found no prophecies of Christ. The obvious reply is, that he does not understand. And if any one asks why he does not understand, the answer is that he reads with a hostile, unbelieving mind; he does not search in order to know, but thinks he knows when he is ignorant. This vainglorious presumption either blinds the eye of his understanding so as to prevent his seeing anything, or distorts his vision, so that his remarks of approval or disapproval are misdirected. I ask, he says, for instruction in whatever the writings of Moses contain about our God and Lord, which has escaped me in reading. I reply at once that it has all escaped him, for all is written of Christ. As we cannot go through the whole, I will, with the help of God, comply with your request, to the extent I have already promised, by showing that the passages which you specially criticise refer to Christ. You tell me not to use the ignorant argument that Christ affirms Moses to have written of Him. But if I use this argument, it is not because I am ignorant, but because I am a believer. I acknowledge that this argument will not convince a Gentile or a Jew. But, in spite of all your evasions, you are obliged to confess that it tells against you, who boast of possessing a kind of Christianity. You say, Suppose you had not to deal with me, as in my case there is an obligation to believe Him whom I profess to follow, but with a Jew or a Gentile. This is as much as to say that you, at any rate, with whom I have at present to do, are satisfied that Moses wrote of Christ; for you are not bold enough to discard altogether the well-grounded authority of the Gospel where Christ's own declaration is recorded. Even when you attack this authority indirectly, you feel that you are attacking your own position. You are aware that if you refuse to believe the Gospel, which is so generally known and received, you must fail utterly in the attempt to substitute for it any trustworthy record of the sayings and doings of Christ. You are afraid that the loss of the Christian name might lead to the exposure of your absurdities to universal scorn and condemnation. Accordingly you try to recover yourself, by saying that your profession of Christianity obliges you to believe these words of the Gospel. So you, at any rate, which is all that we need care for just now, are caught and slain in this death-blow to your errors. You are forced to confess that Moses wrote of Christ, because the Gospel, which your profession obliges you to believe, states that Christ said so. As regards a discussion with a Jew or a Gentile, I have already shown as well as I could how I think it should be conducted.

15. I still hold that there is a reference to Christ in the passage which you select for refutation, where God says to Moses, "I will raise up unto them from among their brethren a prophet like unto thee."[1] The string of showy antitheses with which you try to ornament your dull discourse does not at all affect my belief of this truth. You attempt to prove, by a comparison of Christ and Moses, that they are unlike, and that therefore the words, "I will raise up a prophet like unto thee," cannot be understood of Christ. You specify a number of particulars in which you

1 Deut. xviii. 15.

find a diversity: that the one is man, and the other God; that one is a sinner, the other sinless; that one is born of ordinary generation, the other, as we hold, of a virgin, and, as you hold, not even of a virgin; the one incurs God's anger, and is put to death on a mountain, the other suffers voluntarily, having throughout the approval of His Father. But surely things may be said to be like, although they are not like in every respect. Besides the resemblance between things of the same nature, as between two men, or between parents and children, or between men in general, or any species of animals, or in trees, between one olive and another, or one laurel and another, there is often a resemblance in things of a different nature, as between a wild and a tame olive, or between wheat and barley. These things are to some extent allied. But there is the greatest possible distance between the Son of God, by whom all things were made, and a beast or a stone. And yet in the Gospel we read, "Behold the Lamb of God,"[1] and in the apostle, "That rock was Christ."[2] This could not be said except on the supposition of some resemblance. What wonder, then, if Christ condescended to become like Moses, when He was made like the lamb which God by Moses commanded His people to eat as a type of Christ, enjoining that its blood should be used as a means of protection, and that it should be called the Passover, which every one must admit to be fulfilled in Christ? The Scripture, I acknowledge, shows points of difference; and the Scripture also, as I call on you to acknowledge, shows points of resemblance. There are points of both kinds, and one can be proved as well as the other. Christ is unlike man, for He is God; and it is written of Him that He is "over all, God blessed for ever."[3] Christ is also like man, for He is man; and it is likewise written of Him, that He is the "Mediator between God and man, the man Christ Jesus."[4] Christ is unlike a sinner, for He is ever holy; and He is like a sinner, for "God sent His Son in the likeness of sinful flesh, that by sin He might condemn sin in the flesh."[5] Christ is unlike a man born in ordinary generation, for He was born of a virgin; and yet He is like, for He too was born of a woman, to whom it was said, "That holy thing which shall be born of thee shall be called the Son of God."[6] Christ is unlike a man, who dies on account of his own sin, for He died without sin, and of His own freewill; and again, He is like, for He too died a real death of the body.

16. You ought not to say, in disparagement of Moses, that he was a sinner, and that he was put to death on a mountain because his God was angry with him. For Moses could glory in the Lord as his Saviour, who is also the Saviour of him who says, "Christ Jesus came into the world to save sinners, of whom I am chief."[7] Moses, indeed, is accused by the voice of God, because his faith showed signs of weakness when he was commanded to draw water out of the rock.[8] In this he may have sinned as Peter did, when from the weakness of his faith he became afraid in the midst of the waves.[9] But we cannot think from this, that he who, as the Gospel tells us, was counted worthy to be present with the Lord along with holy Elias on the mount of transfiguration, was separated from the eternal fellowship of the saints. The sacred history shows in what favor he was with God even after his sin. But since you may ask why God speaks of this sin as deserving the punishment of death, and as I have promised to point out prophecies of Christ in those passages which you select for criticism, I will try, with the Lord's help, to show that what you object to in the death of Moses is, when rightly understood, prophetical of Christ.

17. We often find in the symbolical passages of Scripture, that the same person appears in different characters on different occasions. So, on this occasion, Moses represents and prefigures the Jewish people as placed under the law. As, then, Moses, when he struck the rock with his rod, doubted the power of God, so the people who were under the law given by Moses, when they nailed Christ to the cross, did not believe Him to be the power of God. And as water flowed from the smitten rock for those that were athirst, so life comes to believers from the stroke of the Lord's passion. The testimony of the apostle is clear and decisive on this point, when he says, "This rock was Christ."[10] In the command of God, that the death of the flesh of Moses should take place on the mountain, we see the divine appointment that the carnal doubt of the divinity of Christ should die on Christ's exaltation. As the rock is Christ, so is the mountain. The rock is the fortitude of His humiliation; the mountain the height of His exaltation. For as the apostle says, "This rock was Christ," so Christ Himself says, "A city set upon an hill cannot be hid,"[11] showing that He is the hill, and believers the city built upon the glory of His name. The carnal mind lives when, like the smitten rock, the humiliation of Christ on

[1] John i. 29. [2] 1 Cor. x. 4. [3] Rom. ix. 5. [4] 1 Tim. ii. 5. [5] Rom. viii. 3. [6] Luke i. 35.

[7] 1 Tim. i. 15. [8] Num. ix. 10–12. [9] Matt. xiv. 30. [10] 1 Cor. x. 4. [11] Matt. v. 14.

the cross is despised. For Christ crucified is to the Jews a stumbling-block, and to the Greeks foolishness. And the carnal mind dies when, like the mountain-top, Christ is seen in His exaltation. "For to them that are called, both Jews and Greeks, Christ is the power of God, and the wisdom of God."[1] Moses therefore ascended the mount, that in the death of the flesh he might be received by the living spirit. If Faustus had ascended, he would not have uttered carnal objections from a dead mind. It was the carnal mind that made Peter dread the smiting of the rock, when, on the occasion of the Lord's foretelling His passion, he said, "Be it far from Thee, Lord; spare Thyself." And this sin too was severely rebuked, when the Lord replied, "Get thee behind me, Satan; thou art an offense unto me: for thou savorest not the things which be of God, but those which be of men."[2] And where did this carnal distrust die but in the glorification of Christ, as on a mountain height? If it was alive when Peter timidly denied Christ, it was dead when he fearlessly preached Him. It was alive in Saul, when, in his aversion to the offense of the cross, he made havoc of the Christian faith, and where but on this mountain had it died, when Paul was able to say, "I live no longer, but Christ liveth in me?"[3]

18. What other reason has your heretical folly to give for thinking that there is no prophecy of Christ in the words, "I will raise up unto them a Prophet from among their brethren, like unto thee?" Your showing Christ to be unlike Moses is no reason; for we can show that in other respects He is like. How can you object to Christ's being called a prophet, since He condescended to be a man, and actually foretold many future events? What is a prophet, but one who predicts events beyond human foresight? So Christ says of Himself: "A prophet is not without honor, save in his own country."[4] But, turning from you, since you have already acknowledged that your profession of Christianity obliges you to believe the Gospel, I address myself to the Jew, who enjoys the poor privilege of liberty from the yoke of Christ, and who therefore thinks it allowable to say: Your Christ spoke falsely; Moses wrote nothing of him.

19. Let the Jews say what prophet is meant in this promise of God to Moses: "I will raise up unto them a Prophet from among their brethren, like unto thee." Many prophets appeared after Moses; but one in particular is here pointed out. The Jews will perhaps naturally think of the successor of Moses, who led into the promised land the people that Moses had brought out of Egypt. Having this successor of Moses in his mind, he may perhaps laugh at me for asking to what prophet the words of the promise refer, since it is recorded who followed Moses in ruling and leading the people. When he has laughed at my ignorance, as Faustus supposes him to do, I will still continue my inquiries, and will desire my laughing opponent to give me a serious answer to the question why Moses changed the name of this successor, who was preferred to himself as the leader of the people into the promised land, to show that the law given by Moses not to save, but to convince the sinner, cannot lead us into heaven, but only the grace and truth which are by Jesus Christ. This successor was called Osea, and Moses gave him the name of Jesus. Why then did he give him this name when he sent him from the valley of Pharan into the land into which he was to lead the people?[5] The true Jesus says, "If I go and prepare a place for you, I will come again, and receive you unto myself."[6] I will ask the Jew if the prophet does not show the prophetical meaning of these things when he says, "God shall come from Africa, and the Holy One from Pharan." Does this not mean that the holy God would come with the name of him who came from Africa by Pharan, that is, with the name of Jesus? Then, again, it is the Word of God Himself who speaks when He promises to provide this successor to Moses, speaking of him as an angel,—a name commonly given in Scripture to those carrying any message. The words are: "Behold I send my angel before thy face, to preserve thee in the way, and to bring thee into the land which I have sworn to give thee. Take heed unto him, and obey, and beware of unbelief in him; for he will not take anything from thee wrongfully, for my name is in him."[7] Consider these words. Let the Jew, not to speak of the Manichæan, say what other angel he can find in Scripture to whom these words apply, but this leader who was to bring the people into the land of promise. Then let him inquire who it was that succeeded Moses, and brought in the people. He will find that it was Jesus, and that this was not his name at first, but after his name was changed. It follows that He who said, "My name is in him," is the true Jesus, the leader who brings His people into the inheritance of eternal life, according to the New Testament, of which the Old was a figure. No event or action could have a more distinctly prophetical character than this, where the very name is a prediction.

1 1 Cor. i. 23, 24.
2 Matt. xvi. 22, 23.
3 Gal. ii. 20.
4 Matt. xiii. 57.
5 Num. xiii, 9, xiv. 6.
6 John xiv. 3.
7 Ex. xxiii. 20, 21.

20. It follows that this Jew, if he wishes to be a Jew inwardly, in the spirit, and not in the letter, if he wishes to be thought a true Israelite, in whom is no guile, will recognize in this dead Jesus, who led the people into the land of mortality, a figure of the true living Jesus, whom he may follow into the land of life. In this way, he will no longer in a hostile spirit resist so plain a prophecy, but, influenced by the allusion to the Jesus of the Old Testament, he will be prepared to listen meekly to Him whose name he bore, and who leads to the true land of promise; for He says, "Blessed are the meek, for they shall inherit the land."[1] The Gentile also, if his heart is not too stony, if he is one of those stones from which God raises up children unto Abraham, must allow it to be wonderful that in the ancient books of the people of whom Jesus was born, so plain a prophecy, including His very name, is found recorded; and must remark at the same time, that it is not any man of the name of Jesus who is prophesied of, but a divine person, because God said that His name was in that man who was appointed to rule the people, and to lead them into the kingdom, and who by a change of name was called Jesus. In His being sent with this new name, He brings a great and divine message, and is therefore called an Angel, which, as every tyro in Greek knows, means messenger. No Gentile, therefore, if he were not perverse and obstinate, would despise these books merely because he is not subject to the law of the Hebrews, to whom the books belong; but would think highly of the books, no matter whose they were, on finding in them prophecies of such ancient date, and of what he sees now taking place. Instead of despising Christ Jesus because He is foretold in the Hebrew Scriptures, he would conclude that one thought worthy of being the subject of prophetic description, whoever the writers might be, for so many ages before His coming into the world,—sometimes in plain announcements, sometimes in figure by symbolic actions and utterances,—must claim to be regarded with profound admiration and reverence, and to be followed with implicit reliance. Thus the facts of Christian history would prove the truth of the prophecy, and the prophecy would prove the claims of Christ. Call this fancy, if it is not actually the case that men all over the world have been led, and are now led, to believe in Christ by reading these books.

21. In view of the multitudes from all nations who have become zealous believers in these books, it is laughably absurd to tell us that it is impossible to persuade a Gentile to learn the Christian faith from Jewish books. Indeed, it is a great confirmation of our faith that such important testimony is borne by enemies. The believing Gentiles cannot suppose these testimonies to Christ to be recent forgeries; for they find them in books held sacred for so many ages by those who crucified Christ, and still regarded with the highest veneration by those who every day blaspheme Christ. If the prophecies of Christ were the production of the preachers of Christ, we might suspect their genuineness. But now the preacher expounds the text of the blasphemer. In this way the Most High God orders the blindness of the ungodly for the profit of the saint, in His righteous government bringing good out of evil, that those who by their own choice live wickedly may be, in His just judgment, made the instruments of His will. So, lest those that were to preach Christ to the world should be thought to have forged the prophecies which speak of Christ as to be born, to work miracles, to suffer unjustly, to die, to rise again, to ascend to heaven, to publish the gospel of eternal life among all nations, the unbelief of the Jews has been made of signal benefit to us; so that those who do not receive in their heart for their own good these truths, carry in their *hands* for our benefit the writings in which these truths are contained. And the unbelief of the Jews increases rather than lessens the authority of the books, for this blindness is itself foretold. They testify to the truth by their not understanding it. By not understanding the books which predict that they would not understand, they prove these books to be true.

22. In the passage, "Thou shalt see thy life hanging, and shalt not believe thy life,"[2] Faustus is deceived by the ambiguity of the words. The words may be differently interpreted; but that they cannot be understood of Christ is not said by Faustus, nor can be said by any one who does not deny that Christ is life, or that He was seen by the Jews hanging on the cross, or that they did not believe Him. Since Christ Himself says, "I am the life,"[3] and since there is no doubt that He was seen hanging by the unbelieving Jews, I see no reason for doubting that this was written of Christ; for, as Christ says, Moses wrote of Him. Since we have already refuted Faustus' arguments by which he tries to show that the words, "I will raise up from among their brethren a prophet like unto thee," do not

---

[1] Matt. v. 4.

[2] Deut. xxviii. 16.

[3] John xiv. 6.

apply to Christ, because Christ is not like Moses, we need not insist on this other prophecy. Since, in the one case, his argument is that Christ is unlike Moses, so here he ought to argue that Christ is not the life, or that He was not seen hanging by the unbelieving Jews. But as he has not said this, and as no one will now venture to say so, there should be no difficulty in accepting this too as a prophecy of our Lord and Saviour Jesus Christ, uttered by His servant. These words, says Faustus, occur in a chapter of curses. But why should it be the less a prophecy because it occurs in the midst of prophecies? Or why should it not be a prophecy of Christ, although the context does not seem to refer to Christ? Indeed, among all the curses which the Jews brought on themselves by their sinful pride, nothing could be worse than this, that they should see their Life--that is, the Son of God —hanging, and should not believe their Life. For the curses of prophecy are not hostile imprecations, but announcements of coming judgment. Hostile imprecations are forbidden, for it is said, "Bless, and curse not." [1] But prophetic announcements are often found in the writings of the saints, as when the Apostle Paul says: "Alexander the coppersmith has done me much evil; the Lord shall reward him according to his works." [2] So it might be thought that the apostle was prompted by angry feeling to utter this imprecation: "I would that they were even made eunuchs that trouble you." [3] But if we remember who the writer is, we may see in this ambiguous expression an ingenious style of benediction. For there are eunuchs which have made themselves eunuchs for the kingdom of heaven's sake.[4] If Faustus had a pious appetite for Christian food, he would have found a similar ambiguity in the words of Moses. By the Jews the declaration, "Thou shalt see thy life hanging, and shalt not believe thy life," may have been understood to mean that they would see their life to be in danger from the threats and plots of their enemies, and would not expect to live. But the child of the Gospel, who has heard Christ say, "He wrote of me." distinguishes in the ambiguity of the prophecy between what is thrown to swine and what is addressed to man. To his mind the thought immediately suggests itself of Christ hanging as the life of man, and of the Jews not believing in Him for this very reason, that they saw Him hanging. As to the objection that these words, "Thou shalt see thy life hanging, and shalt not believe thy life," are the only words referring to Christ in a passage containing maledictions not applicable to Christ, some might grant that this is true. For this prophecy might very well occur among the curses pronounced by the prophet upon the ungodly people, for these curses are of different kinds. But I, and those who with me consider more closely the saying of the Lord in His Gospel, which is not, He wrote also of me, as admitting that Moses wrote other things not referring to Christ, but, "He wrote of me," as teaching that in searching the Scriptures we should view them as intended solely to illustrate the grace of Christ, see a reference to Christ in the rest of the passage also. But it would take too much time to explain this here.

23. So far from these words of Faustus' quotation being proved not to refer to Christ by their occurring among the other curses, these curses cannot be rightly understood except as prophecies of the glory of Christ, in which lies the happiness of man. And what is true of these curses is still more true of this quotation. If it could be said of Moses that his words have a different meaning from what was in his mind, I would rather suppose him to have prophesied without knowing it, than allow that the words, "Thou shalt see thy life hanging, and shalt not believe thy life," are not applicable to Christ. So the words of Caiaphas had a different meaning from what he intended, when, in his hostility to Christ, he said that it was expedient that one man should die for the people, and that the whole nation should not perish, where the Evangelist added that he said this not of himself, but, since he was high priest, he prophesied.[5] But Moses was not Caiaphas; and therefore when Moses said to the Hebrew people, "Thou shalt see thy life hanging, and shalt not believe thy life," he not only spoke of Christ, as he certainly did, even though he spoke without knowing the meaning of what he said, but he knew that he spoke of Christ. For he was a most faithful steward of the prophetic mystery, that is, of the priestly unction which gives the knowledge of the name of Christ; and in this mystery even Caiaphas, wicked as he was, was able to prophesy without knowing it. The prophetic unction enabled him to prophesy, though his wicked life prevented him from knowing it. Who then can say that there are no prophecies of Christ in Moses, with whom began that unction to which we owe the knowledge of Christ's name, and by which even Caiaphas, the persecutor of Christ, prophesied of Christ without knowing it?

24. We have already said as much as ap-

1 Rom. xii. 14.
2 2 Tim. iv. 14.
3 Gal. v. 12.
4 Matt. xix. 12.
5 John xi. 49-51.

peared desirable of the curse pronounced on every one that hangs on a tree. Enough has been said to show that the command to kill any prophet or prince who tried to turn away the children of Israel from their God, or to break any commandment, is not directed against Christ. The more we consider the words and actions of our Lord Jesus Christ, the more clearly will this appear; for Christ never tried to turn away any of the Israelites from their God. The God whom Moses taught the people to love and serve, is the God of Abraham, of Isaac, and of Jacob, whom the Lord Jesus Christ speaks of by this name, using the name in refutation of the Sadducees, who denied the resurrection of the dead. He says, "Of the resurrection of the dead, have ye not read what God said from the bush to Moses, I am the God of Abraham, the God of Isaac, and the God of Jacob? God is not the God of the dead, but of the living; for all live unto Him."[1] In the same words with which Christ answered the Sadducees we may answer the Manichæans, for they too deny the resurrection, though in a different way. Again, when Christ said, in praise of the centurion's faith, "Verily I say unto you, I have not found so great faith, no, not in Israel," He added, "And I say unto you, that many shall come from the east and from the west, and shall sit down with Abraham, and Isaac, and Jacob, in the kingdom of heaven; but the children of the kingdom shall go into outer darkness."[2] If, then, as Faustus must admit, the God of whom Moses spoke was the God of Abraham, and Isaac, and Jacob, of whom Christ also spoke, as these passages prove, it follows that Christ did not try to turn away the people from their God. On the contrary, He warned them that they would go into outer darkness, because He saw that they were turned away from their God, in whose kingdom He says the Gentiles called from the whole world will sit down with Abraham, and Isaac, and Jacob; implying that they would believe in the God of Abraham, and of Isaac, and of Jacob. So the apostle also says: "The Scripture, foreseeing that God would justify the Gentiles by faith, preached the gospel beforehand to Abraham, saying, In thy seed shall all nations be blessed."[3] It is implied that those who are blessed in the seed of Abraham shall imitate the faith of Abraham. Christ, then, did not try to turn away the Israelites from their God, but rather charged them with being turned away. The idea that Christ broke one of the commandments given by Moses is not a new one, for the Jews thought so; but it is a mistake, for the Jews were in the wrong. Let Faustus mention the commandment which he supposes the Lord to have broken, and we will point out his mistake, as we have done already, when it was required. Meanwhile it is enough to say, that if the Lord had broken any commandment, He could not have found fault with the Jews for doing so. For when the Jews blamed His disciples for eating with unwashen hands, in which they transgressed not a commandment of God, but the traditions of the elders, Christ said, "Why do ye also transgress the commandment of God, that ye may observe your traditions?" He then quotes a commandment of God, which we know to have been given by Moses. "For God said," He adds, "Honor thy father and mother, and he that curseth father or mother shall die the death. But ye say, Whoever shall say to his father or mother, It is a gift, by whatsoever thou mightest be profited by me, is not obliged to honor his father. So ye make the word of God of none effect by your traditions."[4] From this several things may be learned: that Christ did not turn away the Jews from their God; that He not only did not Himself break God's commandments, but found fault with those who did so; and that it was God Himself who gave these commandments by Moses.

25. In fulfillment of our promise that we would prove the reference to Christ in those passages selected by Faustus from the writings of Moses for adverse criticism, since we cannot here point out the reference to Christ which we believe to exist in all the writings of Moses, it becomes our duty to show that this commandment of Moses, that every prophet or prince should be killed who tried to turn away the people from their God, or to break any commandment, refers to the preservation of the faith which is taught in the Church of Christ. Moses no doubt knew in the spirit of prophecy, and from what he himself heard from God, that many heretics would arise to teach errors of all kinds against the doctrine of Christ, and to preach another Christ than the true Christ. For the true Christ is He that was foretold in the prophecies uttered by Moses himself, and by the other holy men of that nation. Moses accordingly commanded that whoever tried to teach another Christ should be put to death. In obedience to this command, the voice of the Catholic Church, as with the spiritual two-edged sword of both Testaments, puts to death all who try to turn us away from our God, or to break any of the

1 Matt. xxii. 31, 32, and Luke xx. 37, 38. 2 Matt. viii. 10-12. 3 Gal. iii. 8.

4 Matt. xv. 3-6.

commandments. And chief among these is Manichæus himself; for the truth of the law and the prophets convinces him of error as trying to turn us away from our God, the God of Abraham, and Isaac, and Jacob, whom Christ acknowledges, and as trying to break the commandments of the law, which, even when they are only figurative, we regard as prophetic of Christ.

26. Faustus uses an argument which is either very deceitful or very stupid. And as Faustus is not stupid, it is probable that he used the argument intentionally, with the design of misleading the careless reader. He says: If these things are not written of Christ, and if you cannot show any others, it follows that there are none at all. The proposition is true; but it remains to be proved, both that these things are not written of Christ, and that no other can be shown. Faustus has not proved this; for we have shown both how these things are to be understood of Christ, and that there are many other things which have no meaning but as applied to Christ. So it does not follow, as Faustus says, that nothing was written by Moses of Christ. Let us repeat Faustus' argument: If these things are not written of Christ, and if you cannot show any others, it follows that there are none at all. Perfectly so. But as both these things and many others have been shown to be written of Christ, or with reference to Christ, the true conclusion is that Faustus' argument is worthless. In the passages quoted by Faustus, he has tried, though without success, to show that they were not written of Christ. But in order to draw the conclusion that there are none at all, he should first have proved that no others can be shown. Instead of this, he takes for granted that the readers of his book will be blind, or the hearers deaf, so that the omission will be overlooked, and runs on thus: If there are none, Christ could not have asserted that there were any. And if Christ did not make this assertion, it follows that this verse is spurious. Here is a man who thinks so much of what he says himself, that he does not consider the possibility of another person saying the opposite. Where is your wit? Is this all you could say for a bad cause? But if the badness of the cause made you utter folly, the bad cause was your own choice. To prove your antecedent false, we have only to show some other things written of Christ. If there are some, it will not be true that there are none. And if there are some, Christ may have asserted that there were. And if Christ may have asserted this, it follows that this verse of the Gospel is not spurious. Coming back, then, to Faustus' proposition, If you cannot show any other, it follows that there are none at all, it requires to be proved that we cannot show any other. We need only refer to what we showed before, as sufficient to prove the truth of the text in the Gospel, in which Christ says, "If ye believed Moses, ye would also believe me; for he wrote of me." And even though from dullness of mind we could find nothing written of Christ by Moses, still, so strong is the evidence in support of the authority of the Gospel, that it would be incumbent on us to believe that not only some things, but everything written by Moses, refers to Christ; for He says not, He wrote also of me, but, He wrote of me. The truth then is this, that even though there were doubts, which God forbid, of the genuineness of this verse, the doubt would be removed by the number of testimonies to Christ which we find in Moses; while, on the other hand, even if we could find none, we should still be bound to believe that these are to be found, because no doubts can be admitted regarding any verse in the Gospel.

27. As to your argument that the doctrine of Moses was unlike that of Christ, and that therefore it was improbable that if they believed Moses, they would believe Christ too; and that it would rather follow that their belief in one would imply of necessity opposition to the other,—you could not have said this if you had turned your mind's eye for a moment to see men all the world over, when they are not blinded by a contentious spirit, learned and unlearned, Greek and barbarian, wise and unwise, to whom the apostle called himself a debtor,[1] believing in both Christ and Moses. If it was improbable that the Jews would believe both Christ and Moses, it is still more improbable that all the world would do so. But as we see all nations believing both, and in a common and well-grounded faith holding the agreement of the prophecy of the one with the gospel of the other, it was no impossible thing to which this one nation was called, when Christ said to them, "If ye believed Moses, ye would also believe me." Rather we should be amazed at the guilty obstinacy of the Jews, who refused to do what we see the whole world has done.

28. Regarding the Sabbath and circumcision, and the distinction in foods, in which you say the teaching of Moses differs from what Christians are taught by Christ, we have already shown that, as the apostle says, "all those things were our examples."[2] The dif-

[1] Rom. i. 14.
[2] 1 Cor. x. 6.

ference is not in the doctrine, but in the time. There was a time when it was proper that these things should be figuratively predicted; and there is now a different time, when it is proper that they should be openly declared and fully accomplished. It is not surprising that the Jews, who understood the Sabbath in a carnal sense, should oppose Christ, who began to open up its spiritual meaning. Reply, if you can, to the apostle, who declares that the rest of the Sabbath was a shadow of something future.[1] If the Jews opposed Christ because they did not understand what the true Sabbath is, there is no reason why you should oppose Him, or refuse to learn what true innocence is. For on that occasion when Jesus appears especially to set aside the Sabbath, when His disciples were hungry, and pulled the ears of corn through which they were passing, and ate them, Jesus, in replying to the Jews, declared His disciples to be innocent. "If you knew," He said, "what this meaneth, I will have mercy, and not sacrifice, you would not have condemned the innocent."[2] They should rather have pitied the wants of the disciples, for hunger forced them to do what they did. But pulling ears of corn, which is innocence in the teaching of Christ, is murder in the teaching of Manichæus. Or was it an act of charity in the apostles to pull the ears of corn, that they might in eating set free the members of God, as in your foolish notions? Then it must be cruelty in you not to do the same. Faustus' reason for setting aside the Sabbath is because he knows that God's power is exercised without cessation, and without weariness. It is for those to say this, who believe that all times are the production of an eternal act of God's will. But you will find it difficult to reconcile this with your doctrine, that the rebellion of the race of darkness broke your god's rest, which was also disturbed by a sudden attack of the enemy; or perhaps God never had rest, as he foresaw this from eternity, and could not feel at ease in the prospect of so dire a conflict, with such loss and disaster to his members.

29. Unless Christ had considered this Sabbath—which in your want of knowledge and of piety you laugh at—one of the prophecies written of Himself, He would not have borne such a testimony to it as He did. For when, as you say in praise of Christ, He suffered voluntarily, and so could choose His own time for suffering and for resurrection, He brought it about that His body rested from all its works on Sabbath in the tomb, and that His resurrection on the third day, which we call the Lord's day, the day after the Sabbath, and therefore the eighth, proved the circumcision of the eighth day to be also prophetical of Him. For what does circumcision mean, but the eradication of the mortality which comes from our carnal generation? So the apostle says: "Putting off from Himself His flesh, He made a show of principalities and powers, triumphing over them in Himself."[3] The flesh here said to be put off is that mortality of flesh on account of which the body is properly called flesh. The flesh is the mortality, for in the immortality of the resurrection there will be no flesh; as it is written, "Flesh and blood shall not inherit the kingdom of God." You are accustomed to argue from these words against our faith in the doctrine of the resurrection of the body, which has already taken place in the Lord Himself. You keep out of view the following words, in which the apostle explains his meaning. To show what he here means by flesh, he adds, "Neither shall corruption inherit incorruption." For this body, which from its mortality is properly called flesh, is changed in the resurrection, so as to be no longer corruptible and mortal. This is the apostle's statement, and not a supposition of ours, as his next words prove. "Lo," he says, "I show you a mystery: we shall all rise again, but we shall not all be changed. In a moment, in the twinkling of an eye, at the last trump; for the last trumpet shall sound, and the dead shall rise incorruptible, and we shall be changed. For this corruptible must put on incorruption, and this mortal must put on immortality."[4] To put on immortality, the body puts off mortality. This is the mystery of circumcision, which by the law took place on the eighth day; and on the eighth day, the Lord's day, the day after the Sabbath, was fulfilled in its true meaning by the Lord. Hence it is said, "Putting off His flesh, He made a show of principalities and powers." For by means of this mortality the hostile powers of hell ruled over us. Christ is said to have made a show or example of these, because in Himself, our Head, He gave an example which will be fully realized in the liberation of His whole body, the Church, from the power of the devil at the last resurrection. This is our faith. And according to the prophetic declaration quoted by Paul, "The just shall live by faith." This is our justification.[5] Even Pagans believe that Christ died. But only Christians believe that Christ rose again. "If thou con-

[1] Col. ii. 16, 17.
[2] Matt. xii. 7.
[3] Col. ii. 15.
[4] 1 Cor. xv. 50–59.
[5] Hab. ii. 4, and Rom. i. 17.

fess with thy mouth," says the apostle, "that Jesus is the Lord, and believest in thy heart that God raised Him from the dead, thou shalt be saved."[1] Again, because we are justified by faith in Christ's resurrection, the apostle says, "He died for our offenses, and rose again for our justification."[2] And because this resurrection by faith in which we are justified was prefigured by the circumcision of the eighth day, the apostle says of Abraham, with whom the observance began, "He received the sign of circumcision, a seal of the righteousness of faith."[3] Circumcision, then, is one of the prophecies of Christ, written by Moses, of whom Christ said, "He wrote of me." In the words of the Lord, "Woe unto you, scribes and Pharisees, hypocrites! for ye compass sea and land to make one proselyte; and when he is made, ye make him twofold more the child of hell than yourselves,"[4] it is not the circumcision of the proselyte which is meant, but his imitation of the conduct of the scribes and Pharisees, which the Lord forbids His disciples to imitate, when He says: "The scribes and Pharisees sit on Moses' seat: what they say unto you, do; but do not after their works, for they say, and do not."[5] These words of the Lord teach us both the honor due to the teaching of Moses, in whose seat even bad men were obliged to teach good things, and the reason of the proselyte becoming a child of hell, which was not that he heard from the Pharisees the words of the law, but that he copied their example. Such a circumcised proselyte might have been addressed in the words of Paul: "Circumcision verily profiteth, if thou keep the law."[6] His imitation of the Pharisees in not keeping the law made him a child of hell. And he was twofold more than they, probably because of his neglecting to fulfill what he voluntarily undertook, when, not being born a Jew, he chose to become a Jew.

30. Your scoff is very inappropriate, when you say that Moses discusses like a glutton what should be eaten, and commands some things to be freely used as clean, and other things as unclean to be not even touched. A glutton makes no distinction, except in choosing the sweetest food. Perhaps you wish to commend to the admiration of the uninitiated the innocence of your abstemious habits, by appearing not to know, or to have forgotten, that swine's flesh tastes better than mutton. But as this too was written by Moses of Christ in figurative prophecy, in which the flesh of animals signifies those who are to be united to the body of Christ, which is the Church, or who are to be cast out, you are typified by the unclean animals; for your disagreement with the Catholic faith shows that you do not ruminate on the word of wisdom, and that you do not divide the hoof, in the sense of making a correct distinction between the Old Testament and the New. But you show still more audacity in adopting the erroneous opinions of your Adimantus.

31. You follow Adimantus in saying that Christ made no distinction in food, except in entirely prohibiting the use of animal food to His disciples, while He allowed the laity to eat anything that is eatable; and declared that they were not polluted by what enters into the mouth, but that the unseemly things which come out of the mouth are the things which defile a man. These words of yours are unseemly indeed, for they express notorious falsehood. If Christ taught that the evil things which come out of the mouth are the only things that defile a man, why should they not be the only things to defile His disciples, so as to make it unnecessary that any food should be forbidden or unclean? Is it only the laity that are not polluted by what goes into the mouth, but by what comes out of it? In that case, they are better protected from impurity than the saints, who are polluted both by what goes in and by what comes out. But as Christ, comparing Himself with John, who came neither eating nor drinking, says that He came eating and drinking, I should like to know what He ate and drank. When exposing the perversity which found fault with both, He says: "John came neither eating nor drinking; and ye say, He hath a devil. The Son of man cometh eating and drinking; and ye say, Behold a glutton and a wine-bibber, a friend of publicans and sinners."[7] We know what John ate and drank. For it is not said that he drank nothing, but that he drank no wine or strong drink; so he must have drunk water. He did not live without food, but his food was locusts and wild honey.[8] When Christ says that John did not eat or drink, He means that he did not use the food which the Jews used. And because the Lord used this food, He is spoken of, in contrast with John, as eating and drinking. Will it be said that it was bread and vegetables which the Lord ate, and which John did not eat? It would be strange if one was said not to eat, because he used locusts and honey, while the other is said to eat simply because he used bread and vegetables. But whatever may be thought of the eating, certainly no one could be called a

---

[1] Rom. x. 9. [2] Rom. iv. 25. [3] Rom. iv. 11.
[4] Matt. xxiii. 15. [5] Matt. xxiii. 2, 3. [6] Rom. ii. 26.

[7] Matt. xi. 18, 19. [8] Matt. iii. 4.

wine-bibber unless he used wine. Why then do you call wine unclean? It is not in order to subdue the body by abstinence that you prohibit these things, but because they are unclean, for you say that they are the poisonous filth of the race of darkness; whereas the apostle says, "To the pure all things are pure."[1] Christ, according to this doctrine, taught that all food was alike, but forbade His disciples to use what the Manichæans call unclean. Where do you find this prohibition? You are not afraid to deceive men by falsehood; but in God's righteous providence, you are so blinded that you provide us with the means of refuting you. For I cannot resist quoting for examination the whole of that passage of the Gospel which Faustus uses against Moses; that we may see from it the falsehood of what was said first by Adimantus, and here by Faustus, that the Lord Jesus forbade the use of animal food to His disciples, and allowed it to the laity. After Christ's reply to the accusation that His disciples ate with unwashen hands, we read in the Gospel as follows: "And He called the multitude, and said unto them, Hear and understand. Not that which goeth into the mouth defileth a man: but that which cometh out of the mouth, this defileth a man. Then came His disciples, and said unto Him, Knowest Thou that the Pharisees were offended after they heard this saying?" Here, when addressed by His disciples, He ought certainly, according to the Manichæans, to have given them special instructions to abstain from animal food, and to show that His words, "Not that which goeth into the mouth defileth a man, but that which goeth out of the mouth," applied to the multitude only. Let us hear, then, what, according to the evangelist, the Lord replied, not to the multitude, but to His disciples: "But He answered and said, Every plant which my heavenly Father hath not planted shall be rooted up. Let them alone: they be blind leaders of the blind. And if the blind lead the blind, both shall fall into the ditch." The reason of this was, that in their desire to observe their own traditions, they did not understand the commandments of God. As yet the disciples had not asked the Master how they were to understand what He had said to the multitude. But now they do so; for the evangelist adds: "Then answered Peter and said unto Him, Declare unto us this parable." This shows that Peter thought that when the Lord said, "Not that which goeth into the mouth defileth a man, but that which goeth out of the mouth," He did not speak plainly and literally, but, as usual, wished to convey some instruction under the guise of a parable. When His disciples, then, put this question in private, does He tell them, as the Manichæans say, that all animal food is unclean, and that they must never touch it? Instead of this, He rebukes them for not understanding His plain language, and for thinking it a parable when it was not. We read: "And Jesus said, Are ye also yet without understanding? Do not ye yet understand, that whatsoever entereth in at the mouth goeth into the belly, and is cast out into the draught? But those things which proceed out of the mouth come forth from the heart, and they defile the man. For out of the heart proceed evil thoughts, murders, adulteries, fornications, thefts, false witness, blasphemies. These are the things which defile a man: but to eat with unwashen hands defileth not a man."[2]

32. Here we have a complete exposure of the falsehood of the Manichæans: for it is plain that the Lord did not in this matter teach one thing to the multitude, and another in private to His disciples. Here is abundant evidence that the error and deceit are in the Manichæans, and not in Moses, nor in Christ, nor in the doctrine taught figuratively in one Testament and plainly in the other,—prophesied in one, and fulfilled in the other. How can the Manichæans say that the Catholics regard none of the things that Moses wrote, when in fact they observe them all, not now in the figures, but in what the figures were intended to foretell? No one would say that one who reads the Scripture subsequently to its being written does not observe it because he does not form the letters which he reads. The letters are the figures of the sounds which he utters; and though he does not form the letters, he cannot read without examining them. The reason why the Jews did not believe in Christ, was because they did not observe even the plain literal precepts of Moses. So Christ says to them: "Ye pay tithe of mint and cummin, and omit the weightier matters of the law, mercy and judgment. Ye strain out a gnat and swallow a camel. These ought ye to have done, and not to leave the other undone."[3] So also He told them that by their traditions they made of none effect the commandment of God to give honor to parents. On account of this pride and perversity in neglecting what they understood, they were justly blinded, so that they could not understand the other things.

33. You see, my argument is not that if

[1] Tit. i. 15.

[2] Matt. xv. 16-20.

[3] Matt. xxiii. 23, 24.

you are a Christian you must believe Christ when He says that Moses wrote of Him, and that if you do not believe this you are no Christian. The account you give of yourself in asking to be dealt with as a Jew or a Gentile is your own affair. My endeavor is to leave no avenue of error open to you. I have shut you out, too, from that precipice to which you rush as a last resort, when you say that these are spurious passages in the Gospel; so that, freed from the pernicious influence of this opinion, you may be reduced to the necessity of believing in Christ. You say you wish to be taught like the Christian Thomas, whom Christ did not spurn from Him because he doubted of Him, but, in order to heal the wounds of his mind, showed him the marks of the wounds in His own body. These are your own words. It is well that you desire to be taught as Thomas was. I feared you would make out this passage too to be spurious. Believe, then, the marks of Christ's wounds. For if the marks were real, the wounds must have been real. And the wounds could not have been real, unless His body had been capable of real wounds; which upsets at once the whole error of the Manichæans. If you say that the marks were unreal which Christ showed to His doubting disciple, it follows that He must be a deceitful teacher, and that you wish to be deceived in being taught by Him. But as no one wishes to be deceived, while many wish to deceive, it is probable that you would rather imitate the teaching which you ascribe to Christ than the learning you ascribe to Thomas. If, then, you believe that Christ deceived a doubting inquirer by false marks of wounds, you must yourself be regarded, not as a safe teacher, but as a dangerous impostor. On the other hand, if Thomas touched the real marks of Christ's wounds, you must confess that Christ had a real body. So, if you believe as Thomas did, you are no more a Manichæan. If you do not believe even with Thomas, you must be left to your infidelity.

BOOK XVII.

FAUSTUS REJECTS CHRIST'S DECLARATION THAT HE CAME NOT TO DESTROY THE LAW AND THE PROPHETS BUT TO FULFILL THEM, ON THE GROUND THAT IT IS FOUND ONLY IN MATTHEW, WHO WAS NOT PRESENT WHEN THE WORDS PURPORT TO HAVE BEEN SPOKEN. AUGUSTIN REBUKES THE FOLLY OF REFUSING TO BELIEVE MATTHEW AND YET BELIEVING MANICHÆUS, AND SHOWS WHAT THE PASSAGE OF SCRIPTURE REALLY MEANS.

1. Faustus said: You ask why we do not receive the law and the prophets, when Christ said that he came not to destroy them, but to fulfill them. Where do we learn that Jesus said this? From Matthew, who declares that he said it on the mount. In whose presence was it said? In the presence of Peter, Andrew, James, and John—only these four; for the rest, including Matthew himself, were not yet chosen. Is it not the case that one of these four—John, namely—wrote a Gospel? It is. Does he mention this saying of Jesus? No. How, then, does it happen that what is not recorded by John, who was on the mount, is recorded by Matthew, who became a follower of Christ long after He came down from the mount? In the first place, then, we must doubt whether Jesus ever said these words, since the proper witness is silent on the matter, and we have only the authority of a less trustworthy witness. But, besides this, we shall find that it is not Matthew that has imposed upon us, but some one else under his name, as is evident from the indirect style of the narrative. Thus we read: "As Jesus passed by, He saw a man, named Matthew, sitting at the receipt of custom, and called him; and he immediately rose up, and followed Him."[1] No one writing of himself would say, He saw a man, and called him, and he followed Him; but, He saw me, and called me, and I followed Him. Evidently this was written not by Matthew himself, but by some one else under his name. Since, then, the passage already quoted would not be true even if it had been written by Matthew, since he was not present when Jesus spoke on the mount; much more is its falsehood evident from the fact that the writer was not Matthew himself, but some one borrowing the names both of Jesus and of Matthew.

2. The passage itself, in which Christ tells the Jews not to think that He came to destroy the law, is rather designed to show that He did destroy it. For, had He not done something of the kind, the Jews would not have suspected Him. His words are: "Think not that I am come to destroy the law." Sup-

[1] Matt. ix. 9.

pose the Jews had replied, What actions of thine might lead us to suspect this? Is it because thou exposest circumcision, breakest the Sabbath, discardest sacrifices, makest no distinction in foods? this would be the natural answer to the words, Think not. The Jews had the best possible reason for thinking that Jesus destroyed the law. If this was not to destroy the law, what is? But, indeed, the law and the prophets consider themselves already so faultlessly perfect, that they have no desire to be fulfilled. Their author and father condemns adding to them as much as taking away anything from them; as we read in Deuteronomy: "These precepts which I deliver unto thee this day, O Israel, thou shalt observe to do; thou shalt not turn aside from them to the right hand or to the left; thou shalt not add thereto nor diminish from it, that thy God may bless thee."[1] Whether, therefore, Jesus turned aside to the right by adding to the law and the prophets in order to fulfill them, or to the left in taking away from them to destroy them, either way he offended the author of the law. So this verse must either have some other meaning, or be spurious.

3. AUGUSTIN replied: What amazing folly, to disbelieve what Matthew records of Christ, while you believe Manichæus! If Matthew is not to be believed because he was not present when Christ said, "I came not to destroy the law and the prophets, but to fulfill," was Manichæus present, was he even born, when Christ appeared among men? According, then, to your rule, you should not believe anything that Manichæus says of Christ. On the other hand, we refuse to believe what Manichæus says of Christ; not because he was not present as a witness of Christ's words and actions, but because he contradicts Christ's disciples, and the Gospel which rests on their authority. The apostle, speaking in the Holy Spirit, tells us that such teachers would arise. With reference to such, he says to believers: "If any man preaches to you another gospel than that ye have received, let him be accursed."[2] If no one can say what is true of Christ unless he has himself seen and heard Him, no one now can be trusted. But if believers can now say what is true of Christ because the truth has been handed down in word or writing by those who saw and heard, why might not Matthew have heard the truth from his fellow-disciple John, if John was present and he himself was not, as from the writings of John both we who are born so long after and those who shall be born after us can learn the truth about Christ? In this way, the Gospels of Luke and Mark, who were companions of the disciples, as well as the Gospel of Matthew, have the same authority as that of John. Besides, the Lord Himself might have told Matthew what those called before him had already been witnesses of. Your idea is, that John should have recorded this saying of the Lord, as he was present on the occasion. As if it might not happen that, since it was impossible to write all that he heard from the Lord, he set himself to write some, omitting this among others. Does he not say at the close of his Gospel: "And there are also many other things which Jesus did, the which, if they should be written every one, I suppose that even the world itself could not contain the books that should be written"?[3] This proves that he omitted many things intentionally. But if you choose John as an authority regarding the law and the prophets, I ask you only to believe his testimony to them. It is John who writes that Isaiah saw the glory of Christ.[4] It is in his Gospel we find the text already treated of: "If ye believed Moses, ye would also believe me; for he wrote of me."[5] Your evasions are met on every side. You ought to say plainly that you do not believe the gospel of Christ. For to believe what you please, and not to believe what you please, is to believe yourselves, and not the gospel.

4. Faustus thinks himself wonderfully clever in proving that Matthew was not the writer of this Gospel, because, when speaking of his own election, he says not, He saw me, and said to me, Follow me; but, He saw him, and said to him, Follow me. This must have been said either in ignorance or from a design to mislead. Faustus can hardly be so ignorant as not to have read or heard that narrators, when speaking of themselves, often use a construction as if speaking of another. It is more probable that Faustus wished to bewilder those more ignorant than himself, in the hope of getting hold on not a few unacquainted with these things. It is needless to resort to other writings to quote examples of this construction from profane authors for the information of our friends, and for the refutation of Faustus. We find examples in passages quoted above from Moses by Faustus himself, without any denial, or rather with the assertion, that they were written by Moses, only not written of Christ. When Moses, then, writes of himself, does he say, I said this, or I did that, and not rather,

[1] Deut. xii. 32.

[2] Gal. i. 9.

[3] John xxi. 25.

[4] John xii. 41.

[5] John v. 46.

Moses said, and Moses did? Or does he say, The Lord called me, The Lord said to me, and not rather, The Lord called Moses, The Lord said to Moses, and so on? So Matthew, too, speaks of himself in the third person. And John does the same; for towards the end of his book he says: "Peter, turning, saw the disciple whom Jesus loved, who also lay on His breast at supper, and who said to the Lord, Who is it that shall betray Thee?" Does he say, Peter, turning, saw me? Or will you argue from this that John did not write this Gospel? But he adds a little after: "This is the disciple that testifies of Jesus, and has written these things; and we know that his testimony is true."[1] Does he say, I am the disciple who testify of Jesus, and who have written these things, and we know that my testimony is true? Evidently this style is common in writers of narratives. There are innumerable instances in which the Lord Himself uses it. "When the Son of man," He says, "cometh, shall He find faith on the earth?"[2] Not, When I come, shall I find? Again, "The Son of man came eating and drinking;"[3] not, I came. Again, "The hour shall come, and now is, when the dead shall hear the voice of the Son of God, and they that hear shall live;"[4] not, My voice. And so in many other places. This may suffice to satisfy inquirers and to refute scoffers.

5. Every one can see the weakness of the argument that Christ could not have said, "Think not that I am come to destroy the law and the prophets: I came not to destroy, but to fulfill," unless He had done something to create a suspicion of this kind. Of course, we grant that the unenlightened Jews may have looked upon Christ as the destroyer of the law and the prophets; but their very suspicion makes it certain that the true and truthful One, in saying that He came not to destroy the law and the prophets, referred to no other law than that of the Jews. This is proved by the words that follow: "Verily, verily, I say unto you, Till heaven and earth pass, one jot or one tittle shall in no wise pass from the law till all be fulfilled. Whosoever therefore shall break one of the least of these commandments, and shall teach men so, shall be called the least in the kingdom of heaven. But whosoever shall do and teach them, shall be called great in the kingdom of heaven." This applied to the Pharisees, who taught the law in word, while they broke it in deed. Christ says of the Pharisees in another place, "What they say, that do; but do not after their works: for they say, and do not."[5] So here also He adds, "For I say unto you, Except your righteousness exceed the righteousness of the scribes and Pharisees, ye shall not enter into the kingdom of heaven;"[6] that is, Unless ye shall both do and teach what they teach without doing, ye shall not enter into the kingdom of heaven. This law, therefore, which the Pharisees taught without keeping it, Christ says He came not to destroy, but to fulfill; for this was the law connected with the seat of Moses in which the Pharisees sat, who, because they said without doing, are to be heard, but not to be imitated.

6. Faustus does not understand, or pretends not to understand, what it is to fulfill the law. He supposes the expression to mean the addition of words to the law, regarding which it is written that nothing is to be added to or taken away from the Scriptures of God. From this Faustus argues that there can be no fulfillment of what is spoken of as so perfect that nothing can be added to it or taken from it. Faustus requires to be told that the law is fulfilled by living as it enjoins. "Love is the fulfilling of the law,"[7] as the apostle says. The Lord has vouchsafed both to manifest and to impart this love, by sending the Holy Spirit to His believing people. So it is said by the same apostle: "The love of God is shed abroad in our heart by the Holy Ghost, which is given unto us."[8] And the Lord Himself says: "By this shall all men know that ye are my disciples, if ye have love one to another."[9] The law, then, is fulfilled both by the observance of its precepts and by the accomplishment of its prophecies. For "the law was given by Moses, but grace and truth came by Jesus Christ."[10] The law itself, by being fulfilled, becomes grace and truth. Grace is the fulfillment of love, and truth is the accomplishment of the prophecies. And as both grace and truth are by Christ, it follows that He came not to destroy the law, but to fulfill it; not by supplying any defects in the law, but by obedience to what is written in the law. Christ's own words declare this. For He does not say, One jot or one tittle shall in no wise pass from the law till its defects are supplied, but "till all be fulfilled."

---

[1] John xxi. 2:-24.
[2] Luke xviii. 8.
[3] Matt. xi. 19.
[4] John v. 25.
[5] Matt. xxiii. 3.
[6] Matt. v. 17-20.
[7] Rom. xiii. 10.
[8] Rom. v. 5.
[9] John xiii. 35.
[10] John i. 7.

BOOK XVIII.

THE RELATION OF CHRIST TO PROPHECY, CONTINUED.

1. FAUSTUS said: "I came not to destroy the law, but to fulfill it." If these are Christ's words, unless they have some other meaning, they are as much against you as against me. Your Christianity as well as mine is based on the belief that Christ came to destroy the law and the prophets. Your actions prove this, even though in words you deny it. It is on this ground that you disregard the precepts of the law and the prophets. It is on this ground that we both acknowledge Jesus as the founder of the New Testament, in which is implied the acknowledgment that the Old Testament is destroyed. How, then, can we believe that Christ said these words without first confessing that hitherto we have been wholly in error, and without showing our repentance by entering on a course of obedience to the law and the prophets, and of careful observance of their requirements, whatever they may be? This done, we may honestly believe that Jesus said that he came not to destroy the law, but to fulfill it. As it is, you accuse me of not believing what you do not believe yourself, and what therefore is false.

2. But grant that we have been in the wrong hitherto. What is to be done now? Shall we come under the law, since Christ has not destroyed, but fulfilled it? Shall we by circumcision add shame to shame, and believe that God is pleased with such sacraments? Shall we observe the rest of the Sabbath, and bind ourselves in the fetters of Saturn? Shall we glut the demon of the Jews, for he is not God, with the slaughter of bulls, rams, and goats, not to say of men; and adopt, only with greater cruelty, in obedience to the law and the prophets, the practices on account of which we abandoned idolatry? Shall we, in fine, call the flesh of some animals clean, and that of others unclean, among which, according to the law and the prophets, swine's flesh has a particular defilement? Of course you will allow that as Christians we must not do any of these things, for you remember that Christ says that a man when circumcised becomes twofold a child of hell.[1] It is plain also that Christ neither observed the Sabbath himself, nor commanded it to be observed. And regarding foods, he says expressly that man is not defiled by anything that goes into his mouth, but rather by the things which come out of it.[2] Regarding sacrifices, too, he often says that God desires mercy, and not sacrifice.[3] What becomes, then, of the statement that he came not to destroy the law, but to fulfill it? If Christ said this, he must have meant something else, or, what is not to be thought of, he told a lie, or he never said it. No Christian will allow that Jesus spoke falsely; therefore he must either not have said this, or said it with another meaning.

3. For my part, as a Manichæan, this verse has little difficulty for me, for at the outset I am taught to believe that many things which pass in Scripture under the name of the Saviour are spurious, and that they must therefore be tested to find whether they are true, and sound, and genuine; for the enemy who comes by night has corrupted almost every passage by sowing tares among the wheat. So I am not alarmed by these words, notwithstanding the sacred name affixed to them; for I still claim the liberty to examine whether this comes from the hand of the good sower, who sows in the day-time, or of the evil one, who sows in the night. But what escape from this difficulty can there be for you, who receive everything without examination, condemning the use of reason, which is the prerogative of human nature, and thinking it impiety to distinguish between truth and falsehood, and as much afraid of separating between what is good and what is not as children are of ghosts? For suppose a Jew or any one acquainted with these words should ask you why you do not keep the precepts of the law and the prophets, since Christ says that he came not to destroy but to fulfill them: you will be obliged either to join in the superstitious follies of the Jews, or to declare this verse false, or to deny that you are a follower of Christ.

4. AUGUSTIN replied: Since you continue repeating what has been so often exposed and refuted, we must be content to repeat the refutation. The things in the law and the prophets which Christians do not observe, are only the types of what they do observe. These types were figures of things to come, and are necessarily removed when the things themselves are fully revealed by Christ, that in this very removal the law and the prophets may be fulfilled. So it is written in the prophets that God would give a new covenant,

[1] Matt. xxiii 15.

[2] Matt. xv. 11.

[3] Matt. ix. 13.

"not as I gave to their fathers."[1] Such was the hardness of heart of the people under the Old Testament, that many precepts were given to them, not so much because they were good, as because they suited the people. Still, in all these things the future was foretold and prefigured, although the people did not understand the meaning of their own observances. After the manifest appearance of the things thus signified, we are not required to observe the types; but we read them to see their meaning. So, again, it is foretold in the prophets, "I will take away their stony heart, and will give them a heart of flesh,"[2]—that is, a sensible heart, instead of an insensible one. To this the apostle alludes in the words: "Not in tables of stone, but in the fleshy tables of the heart."[3] The fleshy tables of the heart are the same as the heart of flesh. Since, then, the removal of these observances is foretold, the law and the prophets could not have been fulfilled but by this removal. Now, however, the prediction is accomplished, and the fulfillment of the law and the prophets is found in what at first sight seems the very opposite.

5. We are not afraid to meet your scoff at the Sabbath, when you call it the fetters of Saturn. It is a silly and unmeaning expression, which occurred to you only because you are in the habit of worshipping the sun on what you call Sunday. What you call Sunday we call the Lord's day, and on it we do not worship the sun, but the Lord's resurrection. And in the same way, the fathers observed the rest of the Sabbath, not because they worshipped Saturn, but because it was incumbent at that time; for it was a shadow of things to come, as the apostle testifies.[4] The Gentiles, of whom the apostle says that they "worshipped and served the creature rather than the Creator,"[5] gave the names of their gods to the days of the week. And so far you do the same, except that you worship only the two brightest luminaries, and not the rest of the stars, as the Gentiles did. Besides, the Gentiles gave the names of their gods to the months. In honor of Romulus, whom they believed to be the son of Mars, they dedicated the first month to Mars, and called it March. The next month, April, is named not from any god, but from the word for opening, because the buds generally open in this month. The third month is called May, in honor of Maia the mother of Mercury. The fourth is called June, from Juno. The rest to December used to be named according to their number The fifth and sixth, however, got the names of July and August from men to whom divine honors were decreed; while the others, from September to December, continued to be named from their number. January, again, is named from Janus, and February from the rites of the Luperci called Februæ. Must we say that you worship the god Mars in the month of March? But that is the month in which you hold the feast you call Bema with great pomp. But if you think it allowable to observe the month of March without thinking of Mars, why do you try to bring in the name of Saturn in connection with the rest of the seventh day enjoined in Scripture, merely because the Gentiles call the day Saturday? The Scripture name for the day is Sabbath, which means rest. Your scoff is as unreasonable as it is profane.

6. As regards animal sacrifices, every Christian knows that they were enjoined as suitable to a perverse people, and not because God had any pleasure in them. Still, even in these sacrifices there were types of what we enjoy; for we cannot obtain purification or the propitiation of God without blood. The fulfillment of these types is in Christ, by whose blood we are purified and redeemed. In these figures of the divine oracles, the bull represents Christ, because with the horns of His cross He scatters the wicked; the lamb, from His matchless innocence; the goat, from His being made in the likeness of sinful flesh, that by sin He might condemn sin.[6] Whatever kind of sacrifice you choose to specify, I will show you a prophecy of Christ in it. Thus we have shown regarding circumcision, and the Sabbath, and the distinction of food, and the sacrifice of animals, that all these things were our examples, and our prophecies, which Christ came not to destroy, but to fulfill, by fulfilling what was thus foretold. Your opponent is the apostle, whose opinion I give in his own words: "All these things were our examples."[7]

7. If you have learned from Manichæus the willful impiety of admitting only those parts of the Gospel which do not contradict your errors, while you reject the rest, we have learned from the apostle the pious caution of looking on every one as accursed that preaches to us another gospel than that which we have received. Hence Catholic Christians look upon you as among the tares; for, in the Lord's exposition of the meaning of the tares, they are not falsehood mixed with truth in the Scriptures, but children of the wicked one,—that is, people who imitate the deceit-

1 Jer. xxxi. 32.
2 Ezek. xi. 19.
3 2 Cor. ii. 3.
4 Col. ii. 17.
5 Rom. i. 25.
6 Rom. viii. 3.
7 1 Cor. x. 6.

fulness of the devil. It is not true that Catholic Christians believe everything; for they do not believe Manichæus or any of the heretics. Nor do they condemn the use of human reason; but what you call reasoning they prove to be fallacious. Nor do they think it profane to distinguish truth from falsehood; for they distinguish between the truth of the Catholic faith and the falsehood of your doctrines. Nor do they fear to separate good from evil; but they contend that evil, instead of being natural, is unnatural. They know nothing of your race of darkness, which, you say, is produced from a principle of its own, and fights against the kingdom of God, and of which your god seems really to be more frightened than children are of ghosts; for, according to you, he covered himself with a veil, that he might not see his own members taken and plundered by the assault of the enemy. To conclude, Catholic Christians are in no difficulty regarding the words of Christ, though in one sense they may be said not to observe the law and the prophets; for by the grace of Christ they keep the law by their love to God and man; and on these two commandments hang all the law and the prophets.[1] Besides, they see in Christ and the Church the fulfillment of all the prophecies of the Old Testament, whether in the form of actions, or of symbolic rites, or of figurative language. So we neither join in superstitious follies, nor declare this verse false, nor deny that we are followers of Christ; for on those principles which I have set forth to the best of my power, the law and the prophets which Christ came not to destroy, but to fulfill, are no other than those recognized by the Church.

[1] Matt. xxii. 40.

BOOK XIX.

FAUSTUS IS WILLING TO ADMIT THAT CHRIST MAY HAVE SAID THAT HE CAME NOT TO DESTROY THE LAW AND THE PROPHETS, BUT TO FULFILL THEM; BUT IF HE DID, IT WAS TO PACIFY THE JEWS AND IN A MODIFIED SENSE. AUGUSTIN REPLIES, AND STILL FURTHER ELABORATES THE CATHOLIC VIEW OF PROPHECY AND ITS FULFILLMENT.

1. Faustus said: I will grant that Christ said that he came not to destroy the law and the prophets, but to fulfill them. But why did Jesus say this? Was it to pacify the Jews, who were enraged at seeing their sacred institutions trampled upon by Christ, and regarded him as a wild blasphemer, not to be listened to, much less to be followed? Or was it for our instruction as Gentile believers, that we might learn meekly and patiently to bear the yoke of commandment laid on our necks by the law and the prophets of the Jews? You yourself can hardly suppose that Christ's words were intended to bring us under the authority of the law and the prophets of the Hebrews. So that the other explanation which I have given of the words must be the true one. Every one knows that the Jews were always ready to attack Christ, both with words and with actual violence. Naturally, then, they would be enraged at the idea that Christ was destroying their law and their prophets; and, to appease them, Christ might very well tell them not to think that he came to destroy the law, but that he came to fulfill it. There was no falsehood or deceit in this, for he used the word law in a general sense, not of any particular law.

2. There are three laws. One is that of the Hebrews, which the apostle calls the law of sin and death.[1] The second is that of the Gentiles, which he calls the law of nature. "For the Gentiles," he says, "do by nature the things contained in the law; and, not having the law, they are a law unto themselves; who show the work of the law written on their hearts."[2] The third law is the truth of which the apostle speaks when he says, "The law of the spirit of life in Christ Jesus hath made me free from the law of sin and death."[3] Since, then, there are three laws, we must carefully inquire which of the three Christ spoke of when He said that He came not to destroy the law, but to fulfill it. In the same way, there are prophets of the Jews, and prophets of the Gentiles, and prophets of truth. With the prophets of the Jews, of course, every one is acquainted. If any one is in doubt about the prophets of the Gentiles, let him hear what Paul says when writing of the Cretans to Titus: "A prophet of their own has said, The Cretans are always liars, evil beasts, slow bellies."[4] This proves that the Gentiles also had their prophets. The truth also has its prophets, as we learn from Jesus as well as from Paul. Jesus says:

[1] Rom. viii. 2.
[2] Rom. ii. 14, 15.
[3] Rom. viii. 2.
[4] Tit. i. 12.

"Behold, I send unto you wise men and prophets, and some of them ye shall kill in divers places."[1] And Paul says: "The Lord Himself appointed first apostles, and then prophets."[2]

3. As "the law and the prophets" may have three different meanings, it is uncertain in what sense the words are used by Jesus, though we may form a conjecture from what follows. For if Jesus had gone on to speak of circumcision, and Sabbaths, and sacrifices, and the observances of the Hebrews, and had added something as a fulfillment, there could have been no doubt that it was the law and the prophets of the Jews of which He said that He came not to destroy, but to fulfill them. But Christ, without any allusion to these, speaks only of commandments which date from the earliest times: "Thou shalt not kill; Thou shalt not commit adultery; Thou shalt not bear false witness." These, it can be proved, were of old promulgated in the world by Enoch and Seth, and the other righteous men, to whom the precepts were delivered by angels of lofty rank, in order to tame the savage nature of men. From this it appears that Jesus spoke of the law and the prophets of truth. And so we find him giving a fulfillment of those precepts already quoted. "Ye have heard," He says, "that it was said by them of old time, Thou shalt not kill; but I say unto you, Be not even angry." This is the fulfillment. Again: "Ye have heard that it was said, Thou shalt not commit adultery; but I say unto you, Do not lust even." This is the fulfillment. Again: "It has been said, Thou shalt not bear false witness; but I say unto you, Swear not." This too is the fulfillment. He thus both confirms the old precepts and supplies their defects. Where He seems to speak of some Jewish precepts, instead of fulfilling them, He substitutes for them precepts of an opposite tendency. He proceeds thus: "Ye have heard that it has been said, An eye for an eye, and a tooth for a tooth; but I say unto you, Whosoever shall smite thee on thy right cheek, turn to him the other also." This is not fulfillment, but destruction. Again: "It has been said, Thou shalt love thy friend, and hate thine enemy; but I say unto you, Love your enemies, and pray for your persecutors." This too is destruction. Again: "It has been said, Whosoever shall put away his wife, let him give her a writing of divorcement; but I say unto you, That whosoever shall put away his wife, saving for the cause of fornication, causeth her to commit adultery, and is himself an adulterer if he afterwards marries another woman."[3] These precepts are evidently destroyed because they are the precepts of Moses; while the others are fulfilled because they are the precepts of the righteous men of antiquity. If you agree to this explanation, we may allow that Jesus said that he came not to destroy the law, but to fulfill it. If you disapprove of this explanation, give one of your own. Only beware of making Jesus a liar, and of making yourself a Jew, by binding yourself to fulfill the law because Christ did not destroy it.

4. If one of the Nazareans, or Symmachians, as they are sometimes called, were arguing with me from these words of Jesus that he came not to destroy the law, I should find some difficulty in answering him. For it is undeniable that, at his coming, Jesus was both in body and mind subject to the influence of the law and the prophets. Those people, moreover, whom I allude to, practise circumcision, and keep the Sabbath, and abstain from swine's flesh and such like things, according to the law, although they profess to be Christians. They are evidently misled, as well as you, by this verse in which Christ says that he came not to destroy the law, but to fulfill it. It would not be easy to reply to such opponents without first getting rid of this troublesome verse. But with you I have no difficulty, for you have nothing to go upon; and instead of using arguments, you seem disposed, in mere mischief, to induce me to believe that Christ said what you evidently do not yourself believe him to have said. On the strength of this verse you accuse me of dullness and evasiveness, without yourself giving any indication of keeping the law instead of destroying it. Do you too, like a Jew or a Nazarean, glory in the obscene distinction of being circumcised? Do you pride yourself in the observance of the Sabbath? Can you congratulate yourself on being innocent of swine's flesh? Or can you boast of having gratified the appetite of the Deity by the blood of sacrifices and the incense of Jewish offerings? If not, why do you contend that Christ came not to destroy the law, but to fulfill it?

5. I give unceasing thanks to my teacher, who prevented me from falling into this error, so that I am still a Christian. For I, like you, from reading this verse without sufficient consideration, had almost resolved to become a Jew. And with reason; for if Christ came not to destroy the law, but to fulfill it, and as a vessel in order to be filled full must not be

[1] Matt. xxiii. 34.

[2] Eph. iv. 11.

[3] Matt. v. 21-44.

empty, but partly filled already, I concluded that no one could become a Christian but an Israelite, nearly filled already with the law and the prophets, and coming to Christ to be filled to the full extent of his capacity. I concluded, too, that in thus coming he must not destroy what he already possesses; otherwise it would be a case, not of fulfilling, but of emptying. Then it appeared that I, as a Gentile, could get nothing by coming to Christ, for I brought nothing that he could fill up by his additions. This preparatory supply is found, on inquiry, to consist of Sabbaths, circumcision, sacrifices, new moons, baptisms, feasts of unleavened bread, distinctions of foods, drink, and clothes, and other things, too many to specify. This, then, it appeared, was what Christ came not to destroy, but to fulfill. Naturally it must appear so: for what is a law without precepts, or prophets without predictions? Besides, there is that terrible curse pronounced upon those who abide not in all things that are written in the book of the law to do them.[1] With the fear of this curse appearing to come from God on the one side, and with Christ on the other side, seeming, as the Son of God, to say that he came not to destroy these things, but to fulfill them, what was to prevent me from becoming a Jew? The wise instruction of Manichæus saved me from this danger.

6. But how can you venture to quote this verse against me? Or why should it be against me only, when it is as much against yourself? If Christ does not destroy the law and the prophets, neither must Christians do so. Why then do you destroy them? Do you begin to perceive that you are no Christian? How can you profane with all kinds of work the day pronounced sacred in the law and in all the prophets, on which they say that God, the maker of the world, himself rested, without dreading the penalty of death pronounced against Sabbath-breakers, or the curse on the transgressor? How can you refuse to receive in your person the unseemly mark of circumcision, which the law and all the prophets declare to be honorable, especially in the case of Abraham, after what was thought to be his faith; for does not the God of the Jews proclaim that whosoever is without this mark of infamy shall perish from his people? How can you neglect the appointed sacrifices, which were made so much of both by Moses and the prophets under the law, and by Abraham in his faith? And how can you defile your souls by making no distinction in foods, if you believe that Christ came not to destroy these things, but to fulfill them? Why do you discard the annual feast of unleavened bread, and the appointed sacrifice of the lamb, which, according to the law and the prophets, is to be observed for ever? Why, in a word, do you treat so lightly the new moons, the baptisms, and the feast of tabernacles, and all the other carnal ordinances of the law and the prophets, if Christ did not destroy them? I have therefore good reason for saying that, in order to justify your neglect of these things, you must either abandon your profession of being Christ's disciple, or acknowledge that Christ himself has already destroyed them; and from this acknowledgment it must follow, either that this text is spurious in which Christ is made to say that he came not to destroy the law, but to fulfill it, or that the words have an entirely different meaning from what you suppose.

7. AUGUSTIN replied: If you allow, in consideration of the authority of the Gospel, that Christ said that He came not to destroy the law and the prophets, but to fulfill them, you should show the same consideration to the authority of the apostle, when he says, "All these things were our examples;" and again of Christ, "He was not yea and nay, but in Him was yea; for all the promises of God are in Him yea;"[2] that is, they are set forth and fulfilled in Him. In this way you will see in the clearest light both what law Christ fulfilled, and how He fulfilled it. It is a vain attempt that you make to escape by your three kinds of law and your three kinds of prophets. It is quite plain, and the New Testament leaves no doubt on the matter, what law and what prophets Christ came not to destroy, but to fulfill. The law given by Moses is that which by Jesus Christ became grace and truth.[3] The law given by Moses is that of which Christ says, "He wrote of me."[4] For undoubtedly this is the law which entered that the offence might abound;[5] words which you often ignorantly quote as a reproach to the law. Read what is there said of this law: "The law is holy, and the commandment holy, and just, and good. Was then that which is good made death unto me? God forbid. But sin, that it might appear sin, wrought death in me by that which is good."[6] The entrance of the law made the offense abound, not because the law required what was wrong, but because the proud and self-confident incurred additional guilt as transgressors after their acquaintance with the holy, and just, and good commandments of the law; so that, being thus humbled, they

1 Deut. xxvii. 15.

2 2 Cor. i. 19, 20. 3 John i. 17. 4 John v. 46. 5 Rom. v. 20. 6 Rom. vii. 12, 13.

might learn that only by grace through faith could they be freed from subjection to the law as transgressors, and be reconciled to the law as righteous. So the same apostle says: "For before faith came, we were kept under the law, shut up unto the faith which was afterwards revealed. Therefore the law was our schoolmaster in Christ Jesus; but after faith came, we are no longer under a schoolmaster."[1] That is, we are no longer subject to the penalty of the law, because we are set free by grace. Before we received in humility the grace of the Spirit, the letter was only death to us, for it required obedience which we could not render. Thus Paul also says: "The letter killeth, but the spirit giveth life."[2] Again, he says: "For if a law had been given which could have given life, verily righteousness should have been by the law; but the Scripture hath concluded all under sin, that the promise by faith of Jesus Christ might be given to them that believe."[3] And once more: "What the law could not do, in that it was weak through the flesh, God sent His Son in the likeness of sinful flesh, that by sin He might condemn sin in the flesh, that the righteousness of the law might be fulfilled in us, who walk not after the flesh, but after the Spirit."[4] Here we see Christ coming not to destroy the law, but to fulfill it. As the law brought the proud under the guilt of transgression, increasing their sin by commandments which they could not obey, so the righteousness of the same law is fulfilled by the grace of the Spirit in those who learn from Christ to be meek and lowly in heart; for Christ came not to destroy the law, but to fulfill it. Moreover, because even for those who are under grace it is difficult in this mortal life perfectly to keep what is written in the law, Thou shalt not covet, Christ, by the sacrifice of His flesh, as our Priest obtains pardon for us. And in this also He fulfills the law; for what we fail in through weakness is supplied by His perfection, who is the Head, while we are His members. Thus John says: "My little children, these things write I unto you, that ye sin not; and if any man sin, we have an Advocate with the Father, Jesus Christ the righteous: He is the propitiation for our sins."[5]

8. Christ also fulfilled the prophecies, because the promises of God were made good in Him. As the apostle says in the verse quoted above, "The promises of God are in Him yea." Again, he says: "Now I say that Jesus Christ was a minister of the circumcision for the truth of God, to confirm the promises made unto the fathers."[6] Whatever, then, was promised in the prophets, whether expressly or in figure, whether by words or by actions, was fulfilled in Him who came not to destroy the law and the prophets, but to fulfill them. You do not perceive that if Christians were to continue in the use of acts and observances by which things to come were prefigured, the only meaning would be that the things prefigured had not yet come. Either the thing prefigured has not come, or if it has, the figure becomes superfluous or misleading. Therefore, if Christians do not practise some things enjoined in the Hebrews by the prophets, this, so far from showing, as you think, that Christ did not fulfill the prophets, rather shows that He did. So completely did Christ fulfill what these types prefigured, that it is no longer prefigured. So the Lord Himself says: "The law and the prophets were until John."[7] For the law which shut up transgressors in increased guilt, and to the faith which was afterwards revealed, became grace through Jesus Christ, by whom grace superabounded. Thus the law, which was not fulfilled in the requirement of the letter, was fulfilled in the liberty of grace. In the same way, everything in the law that was prophetic of the Saviour's advent, whether in words or in typical actions, became truth in Jesus Christ. For "the law was given by Moses, but grace and truth came by Jesus Christ."[8] At Christ's advent the kingdom of God began to be preached; for the law and the prophets were until John: the law, that its transgressors might desire salvation; the prophets, that they might foretell the Saviour. No doubt there have been prophets in the Church since the ascension of Christ. Of these prophets Paul says: "God hath set some in the Church, first apostles, secondarily prophets, thirdly teachers," and so on.[9] It is not of these prophets that it was said, "The law and the prophets were until John," but of those who prophesied the first coming of Christ, which evidently cannot be prophesied now that it has taken place.

9. Accordingly, when you ask why a Christian is not circumcised if Christ came not to destroy the law, but to fulfill it, my reply is, that a Christian is not circumcised precisely for this reason, that what was prefigured by circumcision is fulfilled in Christ. Circumcision was the type of the removal of our fleshly nature, which was fulfilled in the resurrection of Christ, and which the sacrament of baptism teaches us to look forward to in our own resurrection. The sacrament of the new

1 Gal. iii. 23, 25. 2 2 Cor. iii. 6. 3 Gal. iii. 21, 22. 4 Rom. viii. 3, 4. 5 1 John ii. 1, 2.

6 Rom. xv. 8. 7 Luke xvi. 16. 8 John i. 17. 9 1 Cor. xii. 28.

life is not wholly discontinued, for our resurrection from the dead is still to come; but this sacrament has been improved by the substitution of baptism for circumcision, because now a pattern of the eternal life which is to come is afforded us in the resurrection of Christ, whereas formerly there was nothing of the kind. So, when you ask why a Christian does not keep the Sabbath, if Christ came not to destroy the law, but to fulfill it, my reply is, that a Christian does not keep the Sabbath precisely because what was prefigured in the Sabbath is fulfilled in Christ. For we have our Sabbath in Him who said, "Come unto me, all ye that labor and are heavy laden, and I will give you rest. Take my yoke upon you, and learn of me; for I am meek and lowly in heart, and ye shall find rest unto your souls."[1]

10. When you ask why a Christian does not observe the distinction in food as enjoined in the law, if Christ came not to destroy the law, but to fulfill it, I reply, that a Christian does not observe this distinction precisely because what was thus prefigured is now fulfilled in Christ, who admits into His body, which in His saints He has predestined to eternal life, nothing which in human conduct corresponds to the characteristics of the forbidden animals. When you ask, again, why a Christian does not offer sacrifices to God of the flesh and blood of slain animals, if Christ came not to destroy the law, but to fulfill it, I reply, that it would be improper for a Christian to offer such sacrifices, now that what was thus prefigured has been fulfilled in Christ's offering of His own body and blood. When you ask why a Christian does not keep the feast of unleavened bread as the Jews did, if Christ came not to destroy the law, but to fulfill it, I reply, that a Christian does not keep this feast precisely because what was thus prefigured is fulfilled in Christ, who leads us to a new life by purging out the leaven of the old life.[2] When you ask why a Christian does not keep the feast of the paschal lamb, if Christ came not to destroy the law, but to fulfill it, my reply is, that he does not keep it precisely because what was thus prefigured has been fulfilled in the sufferings of Christ, the Lamb without spot. When you ask why a Christian does not keep the feasts of the new moon appointed in the law, if Christ came not to destroy the law, but to fulfill it, I reply, that he does not keep them precisely because what was thus prefigured is fulfilled in Christ. For the feast of the new moon prefigured the new creature, of which the apostle says: "If therefore there is any new creature in Christ Jesus, the old things have passed away; behold, all things are become new."[3] When you ask why a Christian does not observe the baptisms for various kinds of uncleanness according to the law, if Christ came not to destroy the law, but to fulfill it, I reply, that he does not observe them precisely because they were figures of things to come, which Christ has fulfilled. For He came to bury us with Himself by baptism into death, that as Christ rose again from the dead, so we also should walk in newness of life.[4] When you ask why Christians do not keep the feast of tabernacles, if the law is not destroyed, but fulfilled by Christ, I reply that believers are God's tabernacle, in whom, as they are united and built together in love, God condescends to dwell, so that Christians do not keep this feast precisely because what was thus prefigured is now fulfilled by Christ in His Church.

11. I touch upon these things merely in passing with the utmost brevity, rather than omit them altogether. The subjects, taken separately, have filled many large volumes, written to prove that these observances were typical of Christ. So it appears that all the things in the Old Testament which you think are not observed by Christians because Christ destroyed the law, are in fact not observed because Christ fulfilled the law. The very intention of the observances was to prefigure Christ. Now that Christ has come, instead of its being strange or absurd that what was done to prefigure His advent should not be done any more, it is perfectly right and reasonable. The typical observances intended to prefigure the coming of Christ would be observed still, had they not been fulfilled by the coming of Christ; so far is it from being the case that our not observing them now is any proof of their not being fulfilled by Christ's coming. There can be no religious society, whether the religion be true or false, without some sacrament or visible symbol to serve as a bond of union. The importance of these sacraments cannot be overstated, and only scoffers will treat them lightly. For if piety requires them, it must be impiety to neglect them.

12. It is true, the ungodly may partake in the visible sacraments of godliness, as we read that Simon Magus received holy baptism. Such are they of whom the apostle says that "they have the form of godliness, but deny the power of it."[5] The power of godliness is the end of the commandment,

[1] Matt. xi. 28, 29.
[2] 1 Cor. v. 7.
[3] 2 Cor. v. 17.
[4] Rom. vi. 4.
[5] 2 Tim. iii. 5.

that is, love out of a pure heart, and of a good conscience, and of faith unfeigned.[1] So the Apostle Peter, speaking of the sacrament of the ark, in which the family of Noah was saved from the deluge, says, "So by a similar figure baptism also saves you." And lest they should rest content with the visible sacrament, by which they had the form of godliness, and should deny its power in their lives by profligate conduct, he immediately adds, "Not the putting away of the filth of the flesh, but the answer of a good conscience."[2]

13. Thus the sacraments of the Old Testament, which were celebrated in obedience to the law, were types of Christ who was to come; and when Christ fulfilled them by His advent they were done away, and were done away because they were fulfilled. For Christ came not to destroy, but to fulfill. And now that the righteousness of faith is revealed, and the children of God are called into liberty, and the yoke of bondage which was required for a carnal and stiffnecked people is taken away, other sacraments are instituted, greater in efficacy, more beneficial in their use, easier in performance, and fewer in number.

14. And if the righteous men of old, who saw in the sacraments of their time the promise of a future revelation of faith, which even then their piety enabled them to discern in the dim light of prophecy, and by which they lived, for the just can live only by faith;[3] if, then, these righteous men of old were ready to suffer, as many actually did suffer, all trials and tortures for the sake of those typical sacraments which prefigured things in the future; if we praise the three children and Daniel, because they refused to be defiled by meat from the king's table, from their regard for the sacrament of their day; if we feel the strongest admiration for the Maccabees, who refused to touch food which Christians lawfully use;[4] how much more should a Christian in our day be ready to suffer all things for Christ's baptism, for Christ's Eucharist, for Christ's sacred sign, since these are proofs of the accomplishment of what the former sacraments only pointed forward to in the future! For what is still promised to the Church, the body of Christ, is both clearly made known, and in the Saviour Himself, the Head of the body, the Mediator between God and men, the man Christ Jesus, has already been accomplished. Is not the promise of eternal life by resurrection from the dead? This we see fulfilled in the flesh of Him of whom it is said, that the Word became flesh and dwelt among us.[5] In former days faith was dim, for the saints and righteous men of those times all believed and hoped for the same things, and all these sacraments and ceremonies pointed to the future; but now we have the revelation of the faith to which the people were shut up under the law;[6] and what is now promised to believers in the judgment is already accomplished in the example of Him who came not to destroy the law and the prophets, but to fulfill them.

15. It is a question among the students of the sacred Scriptures, whether the faith in Christ before His passion and resurrection, which the righteous men of old learned by revelation or gathered from prophecy, had the same efficacy as faith has now that Christ has suffered and risen; or whether the actual shedding of the blood of the Lamb of God, which was, as He Himself says, for many for the remission of sins,[7] conferred any benefit in the way of purifying or adding to the purity of those who looked forward in faith to the death of Christ, but left the world before it took place; whether, in fact, Christ's death reached to the dead, so as to effect their liberation. To discuss this question here, or to prove what has been ascertained on the subject, would take too long, besides being foreign from our present purpose.

16. Meanwhile it is sufficient to prove, in opposition to Faustus' ignorant cavils, how greatly they mistake who conclude, from the change in signs and sacraments, that there must be a difference in the things which were prefigured in the rites of a prophetic dispensation, and which are declared to be accomplished in the rites of the gospel; or those, on the other hand, who think that as the things are the same, the sacraments which announce their accomplishment should not differ from the sacraments which foretold that accomplishment. For if in language the form of the verb changes in the number of letters and syllables according to the tense, as *done* signifies the past, and *to be done* the future, why should not the symbols which declare Christ's death and resurrection to be accomplished, differ from those which predicted their accomplishment, as we see a difference in the form and sound of the words, past and future, suffered and to suffer, risen and to rise? For material symbols are nothing else than visible speech, which, though sacred, is changeable and transitory. For while God is eternal, the water of baptism, and all that is material in the sacrament, is transitory: the very word "God," which must be pronounced in the consecration, is a sound which

[1] 1 Tim. i. 5.
[2] 1 Pet. iii. 21.
[3] Rom. i. 17.
[4] 2 Macc. vii.
[5] John i. 14.
[6] Gal. iii. 23.
[7] Matt. xxvi. 28.

passes in a moment. The actions and sounds pass away, but their efficacy remains the same, and the spiritual gift thus communicated is eternal. To say, therefore, that if Christ had not destroyed the law and the prophets, the sacraments of the law and the prophets would continue to be observed in the congregations of the Christian Church, is the same as to say that if Christ had not destroyed the law and the prophets, He would still be predicted as about to be born, to suffer, and to rise again; whereas, in fact, it is proved that He did not destroy, but fulfill those things, because the prophecies of His birth, and passion, and resurrection, which were represented in these ancient sacraments, have ceased, and the sacraments now observed by Christians contain the announcement that He has been born, has suffered, has risen. He who came not to destroy the law and the prophets, but to fulfill them, by this fulfillment did away with those things which foretold the accomplishment of what is thus shown to be now accomplished. Precisely in the same way, he might substitute for the expressions, "He is to be born, is to suffer, is to rise," which were in these times appropriate, the expressions, "He has been born, has suffered, has risen," which are appropriate now that the others are accomplished, and so done away.

17. Corresponding to this change in words is the change which naturally took place in the substitution of new sacraments instead of those of the Old Testament. In the case of the first Christians, who came to the faith as Jews, it was by degrees that they were brought to change their customs, and to have a clear perception of the truth; and permission was given them by the apostle to preserve their hereditary worship and belief, in which they had been born and brought up; and those who had to do with them were required to make allowance for this reluctance to accept new customs. So the apostle circumcised Timothy, the son of a Jewish mother and a Greek father, when they went among people of this kind; and he himself accommodated his practice to theirs, not hypocritically, but for a wise purpose. For these practices were harmless in the case of those born and brought up in them, though they were no longer required to prefigure things to come. It would have done more harm to condemn them as hurtful in the case of those to whose time it was intended that they should continue. Christ, who came to fulfill all these prophecies, found those people trained in their own religion. But in the case of those who had no such training, but were brought to Christ, the corner-stone, from the opposite wall of circumcision, there was no obligation to adopt Jewish customs. If, indeed, like Timothy, they chose to accommodate themselves to the views of those of the circumcision who were still wedded to their old sacraments, they were free to do so. But if they supposed that their hope and salvation depended on these works of the law, they were warned against them as a fatal danger. So the apostle says: "Behold, I Paul say unto you, that if ye be circumcised, Christ shall profit you nothing;"[1] that is, if they were circumcised, as they were intending to be, in compliance with some corrupt teachers, who told them that without these works of the law they could not be saved. For when, chiefly through the preaching of the Apostle Paul, the Gentiles were coming to the faith of Christ, as it was proper that they should come, without being burdened with Jewish observances,—for those who were grown up were deterred from the faith by fear of ceremonies to which they were not accustomed, especially of circumcision; and if they who had not been trained from their birth to such observances had been made proselytes in the usual way, it would have implied that the coming of Christ still required to be predicted as a future event;—when, then, the Gentiles were admitted without these ceremonies, those of the circumcision who believed, not understanding why the Gentiles were not required to adopt their customs, nor why they themselves were still allowed to retain them, began to disturb the Church with carnal contentions, because the Gentiles were admitted into the people of God without being made proselytes in the usual way by circumcision and the other legal observances. Some also of the converted Gentiles were bent on these ceremonies, from fear of the Jews among whom they lived. Against these Gentiles the Apostle Paul often wrote, and when Peter was carried away by their hypocrisy, he corrected him with a brotherly rebuke.[2] Afterwards, when the apostles met in council, decreed that these works of the law were not obligatory in the case of the Gentiles,[3] some Christians of the circumcision were displeased, because they failed to understand that these observances were permissible only in those who had been trained in them before the revelation of faith, to bring to a close the prophetic life in those who were engaged in it before the prophecy was fulfilled, lest by a compulsory abandonment it should seem to be condemned rather than closed; while to lay these things on the Gentiles would imply either that they

---

1 Gal. v. 2. 2 Gal. ii. 14. 3 Acts. xv. 6-11.

were not instituted to prefigure Christ, or that Christ was still to be prefigured. The ancient people of God, before Christ came to fulfill the law and the prophets, were required to observe all these things by which Christ was prefigured. It was freedom to those who understood the meaning of the observance, but it was bondage to those who did not. But the people in those latter times who come to believe in Christ as having already come, and suffered, and risen, in the case of those whom this faith found trained to those sacraments, are neither required to observe them, nor prohibited from doing so; while there is a prohibition in the case of those who were not bound by the ties of custom, or by any necessity, to accommodate themselves to the practice of others, so that it might become manifest that these things were instituted to prefigure Christ, and that after His coming they were to cease, because the promises had been fulfilled. Some believers of the circumcision who did not understand this were displeased with this tolerant arrangement which the Holy Spirit effected through the apostles, and stubbornly insisted on the Gentiles becoming Jews. These are the people of whom Faustus speaks under the name of Symmachians or Nazareans. Their number is now very small, but the sect still continues.

18. The Manichæans, therefore, have no ground for saying, in disparagement of the law and the prophets, that Christ came to destroy rather than to fulfill them, because Christians do not observe what is there enjoined: for the only things which they do not observe are those that prefigured Christ, and these are not observed because their fulfillment is in Christ, and what is fulfilled is no longer prefigured; the typical observances having properly come to a close in the time of those who, after being trained in such things, had come to believe in Christ as their fulfillment. Do not Christians observe the precept of Scripture "Hear, O Israel; the Lord thy God is one God;" "Thou shalt not make unto thee an image," and so on? Do Christians not observe the precept, "Thou shalt not take the name of the Lord thy God in vain?" Do Christians not observe the Sabbath, even in the sense of a true rest? Do Christians not honor their parents, according to the commandment? Do Christians not abstain from fornication, and murder, and theft, and false witness, from coveting their neighbor's wife, and from coveting his property,—all of which things are written in the law? These moral precepts are distinct from typical sacraments: the former are fulfilled by the aid of divine grace, the latter by the accomplishment of what they promise. Both are fulfilled in Christ, who has ever been the bestower of this grace, which is also now revealed in Him, and who now makes manifest the accomplishment of what He in former times promised; for "the law was given by Moses, but grace and truth came by Jesus Christ."[1] Again, these things which concern the keeping of a good conscience are fulfilled in the faith which worketh by love;[2] while types of the future pass away when they are accomplished. But even the types are not destroyed, but fulfilled; for Christ, in bringing to light what the types signified, does not prove them vain or illusory.

19. Faustus, therefore, is wrong in supposing that the Lord Jesus fulfilled some precepts of righteous men who lived before the law of Moses, such as, "Thou shalt not kill," which Christ did not oppose, but rather confirmed by His prohibition of anger and abuse; and that He destroyed some things apparently peculiar to the Hebrew law, such as, "An eye for an eye, and a tooth for a tooth," which Christ seems rather to abolish than to confirm, when He says, "But I say unto you, that ye resist not evil; but if any one smite thee on thy right cheek, turn to him the other also,"[3] and so on. But we say that even these things which Faustus thinks Christ destroyed by enjoining the opposite, were suitable to the times of the Old Testament, and were not destroyed, but fulfilled by Christ.

20. In the first place let me ask our opponents if these ancient righteous men, Enoch and Seth, whom Faustus mentions particularly, and any others who lived before Moses, or even, if you choose, before Abraham, were angry with their brother without a cause, or said to their brother, Thou fool. If not, why may they not have taught these things as well as preached them? And if they taught these things, how can Christ be said to have fulfilled their righteousness or their teaching, any more than that of Moses, by adding, "But I say unto you, if any man is angry with his brother, or if he says Racha, or if he says, Thou fool, he shall be in danger of the judgment, or of the council, or of hell-fire," since these men did these very things themselves, and enjoined them upon others? Will it be said that they were ignorant of its being the duty of a righteous man to restrain his passion, and not to provoke his brother with angry abuse; or that, knowing this, they were unable to act accordingly? In that case, they deserved the punishment of hell,

[1] John i. 17. [2] Gal. v. 6. [3] Matt. v. 38, 39.

and could not have been righteous. But no one will venture to say that in their righteousness there was such ignorance of duty, and such a want of self-control, as to make them liable to the punishment of hell. How, then, can Christ be said to have fulfilled the law, by which these men lived by means of adding things without which they could have had no righteousness at all? Will it be said that a hasty temper and bad language are sinful only since the time of Christ, while formerly such qualities of the heart and speech were allowable; as we find some institutions vary according to the times, so that what is proper at one time is improper at another, and *vice versa?* You will not be so foolish as to make this assertion. But even were you to do so, the reply will be that, according to this idea, Christ came not to fulfill what was defective in the old law, but to institute a law which did not previously exist; if it is true that with the righteous men of old it was not a sin to say to their brother, Thou fool, which Christ pronounces so sinful, that whoever does so is in danger of hell. So, then, you have not succeeded in finding any law of which it can be said that Christ supplied its defect by these additions.

21. Will it be said that the law in these early times was incomplete as regards not committing adultery, till it was completed by the Lord, who added that no one should look on a woman to lust after her? This is what you imply in the way you quote the words, "Ye have heard that it has been said, Thou shalt not commit adultery; but I say unto you, Do not lust even." "Here," you say, "is the fulfillment." But let us take the words as they stand in the Gospel, without any of your modifications, and see what character you give to those righteous men of antiquity. The words are: "Ye have heard that it has been said, thou shalt not commit adultery; but I say unto you, that whosoever looketh on a woman to lust after her, hath committed adultery with her already in his heart."[1] In your opinion, then, Enoch and Seth, and the rest, committed adultery in their hearts; and either their heart was not the temple of God, or they committed adultery in the temple of God. But if you dare not say this, how can you say that Christ, when He came, fulfilled the law, which was already in the time of those men complete?

22. As regards not swearing, in which also you say that Christ completed the law given to these righteous men of antiquity, I cannot be certain that they did not swear, for we find that Paul the apostle swore. With you, swearing is still a common practice, for you swear by the light, which you love as flies do; for the light of the mind which lighteth every man that cometh into the world, as distinct from mere natural light, you know nothing of. You swear, too, by your master Manichæus, whose name in his own tongue was Manes. As the name Manes seemed to be connected with the Greek word for madness, you have changed it by adding a suffix, which only makes matters worse, by giving the new meaning of pouring forth madness. One of your own sect told me that the name Manichæus was intended to be derived from the Greek words for pouring forth manna; for χέειν means to pour. But, as it is, you only express the idea of madness with greater emphasis. For by adding the two syllables, while you have forgotten to insert another letter in the beginning of the word, you make it not Mannichæus, but Manichæus; which must mean that he pours forth madness in his long unprofitable discourses. Again, you often swear by the Paraclete,—not the Paraclete promised and sent by Christ to His disciples, but this same madness-pourer himself. Since, then, you are constantly swearing, I should like to know in what sense you make Christ to have fulfilled this part of the law, which is one you mention as belonging to the earliest times. And what do you make of the oaths of the apostle? For as to your authority, it cannot weigh much with yourselves, not to speak of me or any other person. It is therefore evident that Christ's words, "I am come not to destroy the law, but to fulfill it," have not the meaning which you give them. Christ makes no reference in these words to His comments on the ancient sayings which He quotes, and of which His discourse was an explanation, but not a fulfillment.

23. Thus, as regards murder, which was understood to mean merely the destruction of the body, by which a man is deprived of life, the Lord explained that every unjust disposition to injure our brother is a kind of murder. So John also says, "He that hateth his brother is a murderer."[2] And as it was thought that adultery meant only the act of unlawful intercourse with a woman, the Master showed that the lust He describes is also adultery. Again, because perjury is a heinous sin, while there is no sin either in not swearing at all or in swearing truly, the Lord wished to secure us from departing from the truth by not swearing at all, rather than that

[1] Matt. v. 27, 28.

[2] 1 John iii. 15.

we should be in danger of perjury by being in the habit of swearing truly. For one who never swears is less in danger of swearing falsely than one who is in the habit of swearing truly. So, in the discourses of the apostle which are recorded, he never used an oath, lest he should ever fall unawares into perjury from being in the habit of swearing. In his writings, on the other hand, where he had more leisure and opportunity for caution, we find him using oaths in several places,[1] to teach us that there is no sin in swearing truly, but that, on account of the infirmity of human nature, we are best preserved from perjury by not swearing at all. These considerations will also make it evident that the things which Faustus supposes to be peculiar to Moses were not destroyed by Christ, as he says they were.

24. To take, for instance, this saying of the ancients, "Thou shalt love thy neighbor, and hate thine enemy," how does Faustus make out that this is peculiar to Moses? Does not the Apostle Paul speak of some men as hateful to God?[2] And, indeed, in connection with this saying, the Lord enjoins on us that we should imitate God. His words are: "That ye may be the children of your Father in heaven, who maketh the sun to rise upon the evil and the good, and sendeth rain on the just and the unjust."[3] In one sense we must hate our enemies, after the example of God, to whom Paul says some men are hateful; while, at the same time, we must also love our enemies after the example of God, who makes the sun to rise on the evil and the good, and sendeth rain on the just and the unjust. If we understand this, we shall find that the Lord, in explaining to those who did not rightly understand the saying, Thou shalt hate thine enemy, made use of it to show that they should love their enemy, which was a new idea to them. It would take too long to show the consistency of the two things here. But when the Manichæans condemn without exception the precept, Thou shalt hate thine enemy, they may easily be met with the question whether their god loves the race of darkness. Or, if we should love our enemies now, because they have a part of good, should we not also hate them as having a part of evil? So even in this way it would appear that there is no opposition between the saying of ancient times, Thou shalt hate thine enemy, and that of the Gospel, Love your enemies. For every wicked man should be hated as far as he is wicked; while he should be loved as a man. The vice which we rightly hate in him is to be condemned, that by its removal the human nature which we rightly love in him may be amended. This is precisely the principle we maintain, that we should hate our enemy for what is evil in him, that is, for his wickedness; while we also love our enemy for that which is good in him, that is, for his nature as a social and rational being. The difference between us and the Manichæans is, that we prove the man to be wicked, not by nature, either his own or any other, but by his own will; whereas they think that a man is evil on account of the nature of the race of darkness, which, according to them, was an object of dread to God when he existed entire, and by which also he was partly conquered, so that he cannot be entirely set free. The intention of the Lord, then, is to correct those who, from knowing without understanding what was said by them of old time, Thou shalt hate thine enemy, hated their fellow-men instead of only hating their wickedness; and for this purpose He says, Love your enemies. Instead of destroying what is written about hatred of enemies in the law, of which He said, "I am come not to destroy the law, but to fulfill it," He would have us learn, from the duty of loving our enemies, how it is possible in the case of one and the same person, both to hate him for his sin, and to love him for his nature. It is too much to expect our perverse opponents to understand this. But we can silence them, by showing that by their irrational objection they condemn their own god, of whom they cannot say that he loves the race of darkness; so that in enjoining on every one to love his enemy, they cannot quote his example. There would appear to be more love of their enemy in the race of darkness than in the god of the Manichæans. The story is, that the race of darkness coveted the domain of light bordering on their territory, and, from a desire to possess it, formed the plan of invading it. Nor is there any sin in desiring true goodness and blessedness. For the Lord says, "The kingdom of heaven suffereth violence, and the violent take it by force."[4] This fabulous race of darkness, then, wished to take by force the good they desired, for its beautiful and attractive appearance. But God, instead of returning the love of those who wished to possess Him, hated it so as to endeavor to annihilate them. If, therefore, the evil love the good in the desire to possess it, while the good hate the evil in fear of being defiled, I ask the Manichæans, which of these obeys the precept of the Lord, "Love your enemies"? If you insist on making these precepts opposed to one

[1] Rom. i. 9; Phil. i. 8, and 2 Cor. i. 23.
[2] Rom. i. 30.
[3] Matt. v. 45.
[4] Matt. xi. 12.

another, it will follow that your god obeyed what is written in the law of Moses, "Thou shalt hate thine enemy"; while the race of darkness obeyed what is written in the Gospel, "Love your enemies." However, you have never succeeded in explaining the difference between the flies that fly in the day-time and the moths that fly at night; for both, according to you, belong to the race of darkness. How is it that one kind love the light, contrary to their nature; while the other kind avoid it, and prefer the darkness from which they sprung? Strange, that filthy sewers should breed a cleaner sort than dark closets!

25. Nor, again, is there any opposition between that which was said by them of old time, "An eye for an eye, a tooth for a tooth," and what the Lord says, "But I say unto you, that ye resist not evil; but if any one smiteth thee on thy right cheek, turn to him the other also," and so on[1] The old precept as well as the new is intended to check the vehemence of hatred, and to curb the impetuosity of angry passion. For who will of his own accord be satisfied with a revenge equal to the injury? Do we not see men, only slightly hurt, eager for slaughter, thirsting for blood, as if they could never make their enemy suffer enough? If a man receives a blow, does he not summon his assailant, that he may be condemned in the court of law? Or if he prefers to return the blow, does he not fall upon the man with hand and heel, or perhaps with a weapon, if he can get hold of one? To put a restraint upon a revenge so unjust from its excess, the law established the principle of compensation, that the penalty should correspond to the injury inflicted. So the precept, "an eye for an eye, a tooth for a tooth," instead of being a brand to kindle a fire that was quenched, was rather a covering to prevent the fire already kindled from spreading. For there is a just revenge due to the injured person from his assailant; so that when we pardon, we give up what we might justly claim. Thus, in the Lord's prayer, we are taught to forgive others their debts that God may forgive us our debts. There is no injustice in asking back a debt, though there is kindness in forgiving it. But as, in swearing, one who swears, even though truly, is in danger of perjury, of which one is in no danger who never swears; and while swearing truly is not a sin, we are further from sin by not swearing; so that the command not to swear is a guard against perjury: in the same way since it is sinful to wish to be revenged with an unjust excess, though there is no sin in wishing for revenge within the limits of justice, the man who wishes for no revenge at all is further from the sin of an unjust revenge. It is sin to demand more than is due, though it is no sin to demand a debt. And the best security against the sin of making an unjust demand is to demand nothing, especially considering the danger of being compelled to pay the debt to Him who is indebted to none. Thus, I would explain the passage as follows: It has been said by them of old time, Thou shalt not take unjust revenge; but I say, Take no revenge at all: here is the fulfillment. It is thus that Faustus, after quoting, "It has been said, Thou shalt not swear falsely; but I say unto you, swear not at all," adds: here is the fulfillment. I might use the same expression if I thought that by the addition of these words Christ supplied a defect in the law, and not rather that the intention of the law to prevent unjust revenge is best secured by not taking revenge at all, in the same way as the intention to prevent perjury is best secured by not swearing at all. For if "an eye for an eye" is opposed to "If any one smite thee on the cheek, turn to him the other also," is there not as much opposition between "Thou shalt perform unto the Lord thine oath," and "Swear not at all?"[2] If Faustus thinks that there is not destruction, but fulfillment, in the one case, he ought to think the same of the other. For if "Swear not" is the fulfillment of "Swear truly," why should not "Take no revenge" be the fulfillment of "Take revenge justly"?

So, according to my interpretation, there is in both cases a guard against sin, either of false swearing or of unjust revenge; though, as regards giving up the right to revenge, there is the additional consideration that, by forgiving such debts, we shall obtain the forgiveness of our debts. The old precept was required in the case of a self-willed people, to teach them not to be extravagant in their demands. Thus, when the rage eager for unrestrained vengeance, was subdued, there would be leisure for any one so disposed to consider the desirableness of having his own debt cancelled by the Lord, and so to be led by this consideration to forgive the debt of his fellow-servant.

26. Again, we shall find on examination, that there is no opposition between the precept of the Lord about not putting away a wife, and what was said by them of old time: "Whosoever putteth away his wife, let him give her a writing of divorcement."[3] The Lord explains the intention of the law, which

[1] Ex. xxi. 24, and Matt. v. 39.

[2] Matt. v. 33, 34.

[3] Deut. xxiv. 1, and Matt. v. 31, 32.

required a bill of divorce in every case where a wife was put away. The precept not to put away a wife is the opposite of saying that a man may put away his wife if he pleases; which is not what the law says. On the contrary, to prevent the wife from being put away, the law required this intermediate step, that the eagerness for separation might be checked by the writing of the bill, and the man might have time to think of the evil of putting away his wife; especially since, as it is said, among the Hebrews it was unlawful for any but the scribes to write Hebrew: for the scribes claimed the possession of superior wisdom; and if they were men of upright and pious character, their pursuits might justly entitle them to make this claim. In requiring, therefore, that in putting away his wife, a man should give her a writing of divorcement, the design was that he should be obliged to have recourse to those from whom he might expect to receive a cautious interpretation of the law, and suitable advice against separation. Having no other way of getting the bill written, the man should be obliged to submit to their direction, and to allow of their endeavors to restore peace and harmony between him and his wife. In a case where the hatred could not be overcome or checked, the bill would of course be written. A wife might with reason be put away when wise counsel failed to restore the proper feeling and affection in the mind of her husband. If the wife is not loved, she is to be put away. And that she may not be put away, it is the husband's duty to love her. Now, while a man cannot be forced to love against his will, he may be influenced by advice and persuasion. This was the duty of the scribe, as a wise and upright man; and the law gave him the opportunity, by requiring the husband in all cases of quarrel to go to him, to get the bill of divorcement written. No good or prudent man would write the bill unless it were a case of such obstinate aversion as to make reconciliation impossible. But according to your impious notions, there can be nothing in putting away a wife; for matrimony, according to you, is a criminal indulgence. The word "matrimony" shows that a man takes a wife in order that she may become a mother, which would be an evil in your estimation. According to you, this would imply that part of your god is overcome and captured by the race of darkness, and bound in the fetters of flesh.

27. But, to explain the point in hand: If Christ, in adding the words, "But I say unto you," to the quotations He makes of ancient sayings, neither fulfilled the law of primitive times by His additions, nor destroyed the law given to Moses by opposite precepts, but rather paid such deference to the Hebrew law in all the quotations He made from it, as to make His own remarks chiefly explanatory of what the law stated less distinctly, or a means of securing the design intended by the law, it follows that from the words, "I came not to destroy the law, but to fulfill it," we are not to understand that Christ by His precepts filled up what was wanting in the law; but that what the literal command failed in doing from the pride and disobedience of men, is acccomplished by grace in those who are brought to repentance and humility. The fulfillment is not in additional words, but in acts of obedience. So the apostle says "Faith worketh by love;"[1] and again, He that loveth another hath fulfilled the law."[2] This love, by which also the righteousness of the law can be fulfilled was bestowed in its significance by Christ in His coming, through the spirit which He sent according to His promise; and therefore He said, "I came not to destroy the law, but to fulfill it." This is the New Testament in which the promise of the kingdom of heaven is made to this love; which was typified in the Old Testament, suitably to the times of that dispensation. So Christ says again; "A new commandment I give unto you, that ye love one another."[3]

28. So we find in the Old Testament all or nearly all the counsels and precepts which Christ introduces with the words "But I say unto you.' Against anger it is written, "Mine eye is troubled because of anger;"[4] and again, "Better is he that conquers his anger, than he that taketh a city."[5] Against hard words, 'The stroke of a whip maketh a wound; but the stroke of the tongue breaketh the bones."[6] Against adultery in the heart, "Thou shalt not covet thy neighbor's wife."[7] It is not, "Thou shalt not commit adultery;" but, "Thou shalt not covet." The apostle, in quoting this, says: "I had not known lust, unless the law had said, Thou shalt not covet."[8] Regarding patience in not offering resistance, a man is praised who "giveth his cheek to him that smiteth him, and who is filled full with reproach."[9] Of love to enemies it is said: "If thine enemy hunger, feed him; if he thirst, give him drink."[10] This also is quoted by the apostle.[11] In the Psalm, too, it is said, "I was a peace

1 Gal. v. 6. 2 Rom. xiii. 8. 3 John xiii. 34.
4 Ps. vi. 7. 5 Prov. xvi. 32.
6 Ecclus. xxviii. 21. [Augustin makes no distinction between the Old Testament Apocrypha and the canonical books. Indeed, the Platonizing Apocryphal writings, such as *Ecclesiasticus* and *Wisdom*, seem to have been his favorites.—A. H. N.]
7 Ex. xx. 17. 8 Rom. vii. 7. 9 Lam. iii. 30.
10 Prov. xxv. 21. 11 Rom. xii. 20.

maker among them that hated peace;"[1] and in many similar passages. In connection also with our imitating God in refraining from taking revenge, and in loving even the wicked, there is a passage containing a full description of God in this character; for it is written: "To Thee alone ever belongeth great strength, and who can withstand the power of Thine arm? For the whole world before Thee is as a little grain of the balance; yea, as a drop of the morning dew that falleth down upon the earth. But Thou hast mercy upon all, for Thou canst do all things, and winkest at the sins of men, because of repentance. For Thou lovest all things that are, and abhorrest nothing which Thou hast made; for never wouldest Thou have made anything if Thou hadst hated it. And how could anything have endured, if it had not been Thy will? or been preserved, if not called by Thee? But Thou sparest all; for they are Thine, O Lord, Thou lover of souls. For Thy good Spirit is in all things; therefore chastenest Thou them by little and little that offend, and warnest them by putting them in remembrance wherein they have offended, that learning their wickedness, they may believe in Thee, O Lord."[2] Christ exhorts us to imitate this long-suffering goodness of God, who maketh the sun to rise upon the evil and the good, and sendeth rain on the just and on the unjust; that we may not be careful to revenge, but may do good to them that hate us, and so may be perfect, even as our Father in heaven is perfect.[3] From another passage in these ancient books we learn that, by not exacting the vengeance due to us, we obtain the remission of our own sins; and that by not forgiving the debts of others, we incur the danger of being refused forgiveness when we pray for the remission of our own debts: "He that revengeth shall find vengeance from the Lord, and He will surely keep his sin in remembrance. Forgive thy neighbor the hurt that he hath done to thee; so shall thy sins also be forgiven when thou prayest. One man beareth hatred against another, and doth he seek pardon of the Lord? He showeth no mercy to a man who is like himself; and doth he ask forgiveness of his own sins? If he that is but flesh nourishes hatred, and asks for favor from the Lord, who will entreat for the pardon of his sins?"[4]

29. As regards not putting away a wife, there is no need to quote any other passage of the Old Testament than that referred to most appropriately in the Lord's reply to the Jews when they questioned Him on this subject. For when they asked whether it is lawful for a man to put away his wife for any reason, the Lord answered: "Have ye not read, that He that made them at the beginning made them male and female, and said, For this cause shall a man leave his father and mother, and shall cleave to his wife, and they two shall be one flesh? Therefore they are no longer twain, but one flesh. What therefore God hath joined, let no man put asunder."[5] Here the Jews, who thought that they acted according to the intention of the law of Moses in putting away their wives, are made to see from the book of Moses that a wife should not be put away. And, by the way, we learn here, from Christ's own declaration, that God made and joined male and female; so that by denying this, the Manichæans are guilty of opposing the gospel of Christ as well as the writings of Moses. And supposing their doctrine to be true, that the devil made and joined male and female, we see the diabolical cunning of Faustus in finding fault with Moses for dissolving marriages by granting a bill of divorce, and praising Christ for strengthening the union by the precept in the Gospel. Instead of this, Faustus, consistently with his own foolish and impious notions, should have praised Moses for separating what was made and joined by the devil, and should have blamed Christ for ratifying a bond of the devil's workmanship. To return, let us hear the good Master explain how Moses, who wrote of the conjugal chastity in the first union of male and female as so holy and inviolable, afterwards allowed the people to put away their wives. For when the Jews replied, "Why did Moses then command to give a writing of divorcement, and to put her away?" Christ said unto them, "Moses, because of the hardness of your heart, suffered you to put away your wives."[6] This passage we have already explained.[7] The hardness must have been great indeed which could not be induced to admit the restoration of wedded love, even though by means of the writing an opportunity was afforded for advice to be given to this effect by wise and upright men. Ther the Lord quoted the same law, to show both what was enjoined on the good and what was permitted to the hard; for, from what is written of the union of male and female, He proved that a wife must not be put away, and pointed out the divine authority for the union; and shows from the same Scriptures that a bill of divorcement was to be given because of the hardness of the heart, which might be subdued or might not.

1 Ps. cxx. 6. 2 Wisd. xi. 21, xii. 2.
3 Matt. v. 44, 48. 4 Ecclus. xxviii. 1-5.
5 Matt. xix. 4-6. 6 Matt. xix. 7, 8. 7 Sec. 26.

30. Since, then, all these excellent precepts of the Lord, which Faustus tries to prove to be contrary to the old books of the Hebrews, are found in these very books, the only sense in which the Lord came not to destroy the law, but to fulfill it, is this, that besides the fulfillment of the prophetic types, which are set aside by their actual accomplishment, the precepts also, in which the law is holy, and just, and good, are fulfilled in us, not by the oldness of the letter which commands, and increases the offence of the proud by the additional guilt of transgression, but by the newness of the Spirit, who aids us, and by the obedience of the humble, through the saving grace which sets us free. For, while all these sublime precepts are found in the ancient books, still the end to which they point is not there revealed; although the holy men who foresaw the revelation lived in accordance with it, either veiling it in prophecy as suited the time, or themselves discovering the truth thus veiled.

31. I am disposed, after careful examination, to doubt whether the expression so often used by the Lord, "the kingdom of heaven," can be found in these books. It is said, indeed, "Love wisdom, that ye may reign for ever."[1] And if eternal life had not been clearly made known in the Old Testament, the Lord would not have said, as He did even to the unbelieving Jews: "Search the Scriptures, for in them ye think that ye have eternal life, and they are they that testify of me."[2] And to the same effect are the words of the Psalmist: "I shall not die, but live, and declare the works of the Lord."[3] And again: "Enlighten mine eyes, lest I sleep the sleep of death."[4] Again, we read, "The souls of the righteous are in the hand of the Lord, and pain shall not touch them;" and immediately following: "They are in peace; and if they have suffered torture from men, their hope is full of immortality; and after a few troubles, they shall enjoy many rewards."[5] Again, in another place: "The righteous shall live for ever, and their reward is with the Lord, and their concern with the Highest; therefore shall they receive from the hand of the Lord a kingdom of glory and a crown of beauty."[6] These and many similar declarations of eternal life, in more or less explicit terms, are found in these writings. Even the resurrection of the body is spoken of by the prophets. The Pharisees, accordingly, were fierce opponents of the Sadducees, who disbelieved the resurrection. This we learn not only from the canonical Acts of the Apostles, which the Manichæans reject, because it tells of the advent of the Paraclete promised by the Lord, but also from the Gospel, when the Sadducees question the Lord about the woman who married seven brothers, one dying after the other, whose wife she would be in the resurrection.[7] As regards, then, eternal life and the resurrection of the dead, numerous testimonies are to be found in these Scriptures. But I do not find there the expression, "the kingdom of heaven." This expression belongs properly to the revelation of the New Testament, because in the resurrection our earthly bodies shall, by that change which Paul fully describes, become spiritual bodies, and so heavenly, that thus we may possess the kingdom of heaven. And this expression was reserved for Him whose advent as King to govern and Priest to sanctify His believing people, was ushered in by all the symbolism of the old covenant, in its genealogies, its typical acts and words, its sacrifices and ceremonies and feasts, and in all its prophetic utterances and events and figures. He came full of grace and truth, in His grace helping us to obey the precepts, and in His truth securing the accomplishment of the promises. He came not to destroy the law, but to fulfill it.

1 Wisd. vi. 22.
2 John v. 39.
3 Ps. cxviii. 16.
4 Ps. xii. 3.
5 Wisd. iii. 1-5.
6 Wisd. v. 16, 17.
7 Matt. xxii. 23-28.

BOOK XX.

FAUSTUS REPELS THE CHARGE OF SUN-WORSHIP, AND MAINTAINS THAT WHILE THE MANICHÆANS BELIEVE THAT GOD'S POWER DWELLS IN THE SUN AND HIS WISDOM IN THE MOON, THEY YET WORSHIP ONE DEITY, FATHER, SON, AND HOLY SPIRIT. THEY ARE NOT A SCHISM OF THE GENTILES, NOR A SECT. AUGUSTIN EMPHASIZES THE CHARGE OF POLYTHEISM, AND GOES INTO AN ELABORATE COMPARISON OF MANICHÆAN AND PAGAN MYTHOLOGY.

1. Faustus said: You ask why we worship the sun, if we are a sect or separate religion, and not Pagans, or merely a schism of the Gentiles. It may therefore be as well to inquire into the matter, that we may see whether the name of Gentiles is more applicable to you or to us. Perhaps, in giving you in a friendly way this simple account of my faith,

I shall appear to be making an apology for it, as if I were ashamed, which God forbid, of doing homage to the divine luminaries. You may take it as you please; but I shall not regret what I have done if I succeed in conveying to some at least this much knowledge, that our religion has nothing in common with that of the Gentiles.

2. We worship, then, one deity under the threefold appellation of the Almighty God the Father, and his son Christ, and the Holy Spirit. While these are one and the same, we believe also that the Father properly dwells in the highest or principal light, which Paul calls "light inaccessible,"[1] and the Son in his second or visible light. And as the Son is himself twofold, according to the apostle, who speaks of Christ as the power of God and the wisdom of God,[2] we believe that His power dwells in the sun, and His wisdom in the moon. We also believe that the Holy Spirit, the third majesty, has His seat and His home in the whole circle of the atmosphere. By His influence and spiritual infusion, the earth conceives and brings forth the mortal Jesus, who, as hanging from every tree, is the life and salvation of men.[3] Though you oppose these doctrines so violently, your religion resembles ours in attaching the same sacredness to the bread and wine that we do to everything. This is our belief, which you will have an opportunity of hearing more of, if you wish to do so. Meanwhile there is some force in the consideration that you or any one that is asked where his God dwells, will say that he dwells in light; so that the testimony in favor of my worship is almost universal.

3. As to your calling us a schism of the Gentiles, and not a sect, I suppose the word schism applies to those who have the same doctrines and worship as other people, and only choose to meet separately. The word sect, again, applies to those whose doctrine is quite unlike that of others, and who have made a form of divine worship peculiar to themselves. If this is what the words mean, in the first place, in our doctrine and worship we have no resemblance to the Pagans. We shall see presently whether you have. The Pagan doctrine is, that all things good and evil, mean and glorious, fading and unfading, changeable and unchangeable, material and divine, have only one principle. In opposition to this, my belief is that God is the principle of all good things, and *Hyle* [matters] of the opposite. *Hyle* is the name given by our master in divinity to the principle or nature of evil. The Pagans accordingly think it right to worship God with altars, and shrines, and images, and sacrifices, and incense. Here also my practice differs entirely from theirs: for I look upon myself as a reasonable temple of God, if I am worthy to be so; and I consider Christ his Son as the living image of his living majesty; and I hold a mind well cultivated to be the true altar, and pure and simple prayers to be the true way of paying divine honors and of offering sacrifices. Is this being a schism of the Pagans?

4. As regards the worship of the Almighty God, you might call us a schism of the Jews, for all Jews are bold enough to profess this worship, were it not for the difference in the form of our worship, though it may be questioned whether the Jews really worship the Almighty. But the doctrine I have mentioned is common to the Pagans in their worship of the sun, and to the Jews in their worship of the Almighty. Even in relation to you, we are not properly a schism, though we acknowledge Christ and worship Him; for our worship and doctrine are different from yours. In a schism, little or no change is made from the original; as, for instance, you, in your schism from the Gentiles, have brought with you the doctrine of a single principle, for you believe that all things are of God. The sacrifices you change into love-feasts, the idols into martyrs, to whom you pray as they do to their idols. You appease the shades of the departed with wine and food. You keep the same holidays as the Gentiles; for example, the calends and the solstices. In your way of living you have made no change. Plainly you are a mere schism; for the only difference from the original is that you meet separately. In this you have followed the Jews, who separated from the Gentiles, but differed only in not having images. For they used temples, and sacrifices, and altars, and a priesthood, and the whole round of ceremonies the same as those of the Gentiles, only more superstitious. Like the Pagans, they believe in a single principle; so that both you and the Jews are schisms of the Gentiles, for you have the same faith, and nearly the same worship, and you call yourselves sects only because you meet separately. The fact is, there are only two sects, the Gentiles and ourselves. We and the Gentiles are as contrary in our belief as truth and falsehood, day and night, poverty and wealth, health and sickness. You, again, are not a sect in relation either to truth or to error. You are merely

[1] 1 Tim. vi. 16. [2] 1 Cor. i. 24.

[3] [The Manichæan doctrine of the *Jesus patabilis* is more fully expounded in this book than elsewhere. Of course, this is only a way of expressing the familiar Manichæan notion that the divine life which is imprisoned in the world and which is trying to escape through the growth of plants, etc., suffers from any sort of injury done to plants. Compare BAUR: *Das Manichäische Religionssystem*, pp. 72-77.—A. H. N.]

a schism and a schism not of truth, but of error.

5. Augustin replied: O hateful mixture of ignorance and cunning! Why do you put arguments in the mouth of your opponent, which no one that knows you would use? We do not call you Pagans, or a schism of Pagans; but we say that you resemble them in worshipping many gods. But you are far worse than Pagans, for they worship things which exist, though they should not be worshipped: for idols have an existence, though for salvation they are nought. So, to worship a tree with prayers, instead of improving it by cultivation, is not to worship nothing, but to worship in a wrong way. When the apostle says that "the things which the Gentiles sacrifice, they sacrifice to demons, and not to God,"[1] he means that these demons exist to whom the sacrifices are made, and with whom he wishes us not to be partakers. So, too, heaven and earth, the sea and air, the sun and moon, and the other heavenly bodies, are all objects which have a sensible existence. When the Pagans worship these as gods, or as parts of one great God (for some of them identify the universe with the Supreme Deity), they worship things which have an existence. In arguing with Pagans, we do not deny the existence of these things, but we say that they should not be worshipped; and we recommend the worship of the invisible Creator of all these things, in whom alone man can find the happiness which all allow that he desires. To those, again, who worship what is invisible and immaterial, but still is created, as the soul or mind of man, we say that happiness is not to be found in the creature even under this form, and that we must worship the true God, who is not only invisible, but unchangeable; for He alone is to be worshipped, in the enjoyment of whom the worshipper finds happiness, and without whom the soul must be wretched, whatever else it possesses. You, on the other hand, who worship things which have no existence at all except in your fictitious legends, would be nearer true piety and religion if you were Pagans, or if you were worshippers of what has an existence, though not a proper object of worship. In fact, you do not properly worship the sun, though he carries your prayers with him in his course round the heavens.

6. Your statements about the sun himself are so false and absurd, that if he were to repay you for the injury done to him, he would scorch you to death. First of all, you call the sun a ship, so that you are not only astray worlds off, as the saying is, but adrift. Next, while every one sees that the sun is round, which is the form corresponding from its perfection to his position among the heavenly bodies, you maintain that he is triangular, that is, that his light shines on the earth through a triangular window in heaven. Hence it is that you bend and bow your heads to the sun, while you worship not this visible sun, but some imaginary ship which you suppose to be shining through a triangular opening. Assuredly this ship would never have been heard of, if the words required for the composition of heretical fictions had to be paid for, like the wood required for the beams of a ship. All this is comparatively harmless, however ridiculous or pitiable. Very different is your wicked fancy about youths of both sexes proceeding from this ship, whose beauty excites eager desire in the princes and princesses of darkness; and so the members of your god are released from this humiliating confinement in the members of the race of darkness, by means of sinful passion and sensual appetite. And to these filthy rags of yours you would unite the mystery of the Trinity; for you say that the Father dwells in a secret light, the power of the Son in the sun, and His wisdom in the moon, and the Holy Spirit in the air.

7. As for this threefold or rather fourfold fiction, what shall I say of the secret light of the Father, but that you can think of no light except what you have seen? From your knowledge of visible light, with which beasts and insects as well as men are familiar, you form some vague idea in your mind, and call it the light in which God the Father dwells with His subjects. How can you distinguish between the light by which we see, and that by which we understand, when, according to your ideas, to understand truth is nothing else than to form the conception of material forms, either finite or in some cases infinite; and you actually believe in these wild fancies? It is manifest that the act of my mind in thinking of your region of light which has no existence, is entirely different from my conception of Alexandria, which exists, though I have not seen it. And, again, the act of forming a conception of Alexandria, which I have never seen, is very different from thinking of Carthage, which I know. But this difference is insignificant as compared with that between my thinking of material things which I know from seeing them, and my understanding justice, chastity, faith, truth, love, goodness, and things of this nature. Can you describe this intellectual light, which gives us a clear perception of the distinction between

[1] 1 Cor. x. 20.

itself and other things, as well as of the distinction between those things themselves? And yet even this is not the sense in which it can be said that God is light, for this light is created, whereas God is the Creator; the light is made, and He is the Maker; the light is changeable. For the intellect changes from dislike to desire, from ignorance to knowledge, from forgetfulness to recollection; whereas God remains the same in will, in truth, and in eternity. From God we derive the beginning of existence, the principle of knowledge, the law of affection. From God all animals, rational and irrational, derive the nature of their life, the capacity of sensation, the faculty of emotion. From God all bodies derive their subsistence in extension, their beauty in number, and their order in weight. This light is one divine being, in an inseparable triune existence; and yet, without supposing the assumption of any bodily form, you assign to separate places parts of the immaterial, spiritual, and unchangeable substance. And instead of three places for the Trinity, you have four: one, the light inaccessible, which you know nothing about, for the Father; two, the sun and moon, for the Son; and again one, the circle of the atmosphere, for the Holy Spirit. Of the inaccessible light of the Father I shall say nothing further at present, for orthodox believers do not separate the Son and the Spirit from the Father in relation to this light.

8. It is difficult to understand how you have been taken with the absurd idea of placing the power of the Son in the sun, and His wisdom in the moon. For, as the Son remains inseparably in the Father, His wisdom and power cannot be separated from one another, so that one should be in the sun and the other in the moon. Only material things can be thus assigned to separate places. If you only understood this, it would have prevented you from taking the productions of a diseased fancy as the material for so many fictions. But there is inconsistency and improbability as well as falsehood in your ideas. For, according to you, the seat of wisdom is inferior in brightness to the seat of power. Now energy and productiveness are the qualities of power, whereas light teaches and manifests; so that if the sun had the greater heat, and the moon the greater light, these absurdities might appear to have some likelihood to men of carnal minds, who know nothing except through material conceptions. From the connection between great heat and motion, they might identify power with heat; while light from its brightness, and as making things discernible, they might represent wisdom. But what folly as well as profanity, in placing power in the sun, which excels so much in light, and wisdom in the moon, which is so inferior in brightness! And while you separate Christ from Himself, you do not distinguish between Christ and the Holy Spirit; whereas Christ is one, the power of God, and the wisdom of God, and the Spirit is a distinct person. But according to you, the air, which you make the seat of the Spirit, fills and pervades the universe. So the sun and moon in their course are always united to the air. But the moon approaches the sun at one time, and recedes from it at another. So that, if we may believe you, or rather, if we may allow ourselves to be imposed on by you, wisdom recedes from power by half the circumference of a circle, and again approaches it by the other half. And when wisdom is full, it is at a distance from power. For when the moon is full, the distance between the two bodies is so great, that the moon rises in the east while the sun is setting in the west. But as the loss of power produces weakness, the fuller the moon is, the weaker must wisdom be. If, as is certainly true, the wisdom of God is unchangeable in power, and the power of God unchangeable in wisdom, how can you separate them so as to assign them to different places? And how can the place be different when the substance is the same? Is this not the infatuation of subjection to material fancies; showing such a want of power and wisdom that your wisdom is as weak as your power is foolish? This execrable absurdity would divide Christ between the sun and the moon,—His power in one, and His wisdom in the other; so that He would be incomplete in both, lacking wisdom in the sun, and power in the moon, while in both He supplies youths, male and female, to excite the affection of the princes and princesses of darkness. Such are the tenets which you learn and profess. Such is the faith which directs your conduct. And can you wonder that you are regarded with abhorrence?

9. But besides your errors regarding these conspicuous and familiar luminaries, which you worship not for what they are, but for what your wild fancy makes them to be, your other absurdities are still worse than this. Your illustrious World-bearer, and Atlas who helps to hold him up, are unreal beings. Like innumerable other creatures of your fancy, they have no existence, and yet you worship them. For this reason we say that you are worse than Pagans, while you resemble them in worshipping many gods. You are worse, because, while they worship things which exist though they are not gods, you worship

things which are neither gods nor anything else, for they have no existence. The Pagans, too, have fables, but they know them to be fables; and either look upon them as amusing poetical fancies, or try to explain them as representing the nature of things, or the life of man. Thus they say that Vulcan is lame, because flame in common fire has an irregular motion: that Fortune is blind, because of the uncertainty of what are called fortuitous occurrences: that there are three Fates, with distaff, and spindle, and fingers spinning wool into thread, because there are three times,—the past, already spun and wound on the spindle; the present, which is passing through the fingers of the spinner; and the future, still in wool bound to the distaff, and soon to pass through the fingers to the spindle, that is, through the present into the future: and that Venus is the wife of Vulcan, because pleasure has a natural connection with heat; and that she is the mistress of Mars, because pleasure is not properly the companion of warriors: and that Cupid is a boy with wings and a bow, from the wounds inflicted by thoughtless, inconstant passion in the hearts of unhappy beings: and so with many other fables. The great absurdity is in their continuing to worship these beings, after giving such explanations; for the worship without the explanations, though criminal, would be a less heinous crime. The very explanations prove that they do not worship that God, the enjoyment of whom can alone give happiness, but things which He has created. And even in the creature they worship not only the virtues, as in Minerva, who sprang from the head of Jupiter, and who represents prudence,—a quality of reason which, according to Plato, has its seat in the head,—but their vices, too, as in Cupid. Thus one of their dramatic poets says, "Sinful passion, in favor of vice, made Love a god."[1] Even bodily evils had temples in Rome, as in the case of pallor and fever. Not to dwell on the sin of the worshippers of these idols, who are in a way affected by the bodily forms, so that they pay homage to them as deities, when they see them set up in some lofty place, and treated with great honor and reverence, there is greater sin in the very explanations which are intended as apologies for these dumb, and deaf, and blind, and lifeless objects. Still, though, as I have said, these things are nothing in the way of salvation or of usefulness, both they and the things they are said to represent are real existences. But your First Man, warring with the five elements; and your Mighty Spirit, who constructs the world from the captive bodies of the race of darkness, or rather from the members of your god in subjection and bondage; and your World-holder, who has in his hand the remains of these members, and who bewails the capture and bondage and pollution of the rest; and your giant Atlas, who keeps up the World-holder on his shoulders, lest he should from weariness throw away his burden, and so prevent the completion of the final imitation of the mass of darkness, which is to be the last scene in your drama;—these and countless other absurdities are not represented in painting or sculpture, or in any explanation; and yet you believe and worship things which have no existence, while you taunt the Christians with being credulous for believing in realities with a faith which pacifies the mind under its influence. The objects of your worship can be shown to have no existence by many proofs, which I do not bring forward here, because, though I could without difficulty discourse philosophically on the construction of the world, it would take too long to do so here. One proof suffices. If these things are real, God must be subject to change, and corruption, and contamination; a supposition as blasphemous as it is irrational. All these things, therefore, are vain, and false, and unreal. Thus you are much worse than those Pagans, with whom all are familiar, and who still preserve traces of their old customs, of which they themselves are ashamed; for while they worship things which are not gods, you worship things which do not exist.

10. If you think that your doctrines are true because they are unlike the errors of the Pagans, and that we are in error because we perhaps differ more from you than from them, you might as well say that a dead man is in good health because he is not sick; or that good health is undesirable, because it differs less from sickness than from death. Or if the Pagans should be viewed in many cases as rather dead than sick, you might as well praise the ashes in the tomb because they have no longer the human shape, as compared with the living body, which does not differ so much from a corpse as from ashes. It is thus we are reproached for having more resemblance to the dead body of Paganism than to the ashes of Manichæism. But in division, it often happens that a thing is placed in different classes, according to the point of resemblance on which the division proceeds. For instance, if animals are divided into those that fly and those that cannot fly, in this division men and beasts are classed together as

[1] Sen. Hipp. vv. 194, 195.

distinct from birds, because they are both unable to fly. But if they are divided into rational and irrational, beasts and birds are classed together as distinct from men, for they are both destitute of reason. Faustus did not think of this when he said: There are in fact only two sects, the Gentiles and ourselves, for we are directly opposed to them in our belief. The opposition he means is this, that the Gentiles believe in a single principle, whereas the Manichæans believe also in the principle of the race of darkness. Certainly, according to this division we agree in general with the Pagans. But if we divide all who have a religion into those who worship one God and those who worship many gods, the Manichæans must be classed along with the Pagans, and we along with the Jews. This is another distinction, which may be said to make only two sects. Perhaps you will say that you hold all your gods to be of one substance, which the Pagans do not. But you at least resemble them in assigning to your gods different powers, and functions, and employments. One does battle with the race of darkness; another constructs the world from the part which is captured; another, standing above, has the world in his hand; another holds him up from below; another turns the wheels of the fires and winds and waters beneath; another, in his circuit of the heavens, gathers with his beams the members of your god from cesspools. Indeed, your gods have innumerable occupations, according to your fabulous descriptions, which you neither explain nor represent in a visible form. But again, if men were divided into those who believe that God takes an interest in human affairs and those who do not, the Pagans and Jews, and you and all heretics that have anything of Christianity, will be classed together, as opposed to the Epicureans, and any others holding similar views. As this is a principle of importance, here again we may say that there are only two sects, and you belong to the same sect as we do. You will hardly venture to dissent from us in the opinion that God is concerned in human affairs, so that in this matter your opposition to the Epicureans makes you side with us. Thus, according to the nature of the division, what is in one class at one time, is in another at another time: things joined here are separated there: in some things we are classed with others, and they with us; in other things we are classed separately, and stand alone. If Faustus thought of this, he would not talk such eloquent nonsense.

11. But what are we to make of these words of Faustus: The Holy Spirit, by his influence and spiritual infusion, makes the earth conceive and bring forth the mortal Jesus, who, as hanging from every tree, is the life and salvation of men? Letting pass for a moment the absurdity of this statement, we observe the folly of believing that the mortal Jesus can be conceived through the power of the Holy Spirit by the earth, but not by the Virgin Mary. Dare you compare the holiness of that chaste virgin's womb with any piece of ground where trees and plants grow? Do you pretend to look with abhorrence upon a pure virgin, while you do not shrink from believing that Jesus is produced in gardens watered by the filthy drains of a city? For plants of all kinds spring up and are nourished in such moisture. You will have Jesus to be born in this way, while you cry out against the idea of His being born of a virgin. Do you think flesh more unclean than the excrements which its nature rejects? Is the filth cleaner than the flesh which expels it? Are you not aware how fields are manured in order to make them productive? Your folly comes to this, that the Holy Spirit, who, according to you, despised the womb of Mary, makes the earth conceive more fruitfully in proportion as it is carefully enriched with animal offscourings. Do you reply that the Holy Spirit preserves His incorruptible purity everywhere? I ask again, Why not also in the virgin's womb? Passing from the conception, you maintain in regard to the mortal Jesus—who, as you say, is born from the earth, which has conceived by the power of the Holy Spirit—that He hangs in the shape of fruit from every tree: so that, besides this pollution, He suffers additional defilement from the flesh of the countless animals that eat the fruit; except, indeed, the small amount that is purified by your eating it. While we believe and confess Christ the Son of God, and the Word of God, to have become flesh without suffering defilement, because the divine substance is not defiled by flesh, as it is not defiled by anything, your fanciful notions would make Jesus to be defiled even as hanging on the tree, before entering the flesh of any animal; for if He were not defiled, there would be no need of His being purified by your eating Him. And if all trees are the cross of Christ, as Faustus seems to imply when he says that Jesus hangs from every tree, why do you not pluck the fruit, and so take Jesus down from hanging on the tree to bury Him in your stomach, which would correspond to the good deed of Joseph of Arimathea, when he took down the true Jesus from the cross to bury Him?[1]

[1] John xix. 38.

Why should it be impious to take Christ from the tree, while it is pious to lay Him in the tomb? Perhaps you wish to apply to yourselves the words quoted from the prophet by Paul, "Their throat is an open sepulchre:"[1] and so you wait with open mouth till some one comes to use your throat as the best sepulchre for Christ. Once more, how many Christs do you make? Is there one whom you call the mortal Christ, whom the earth conceives and brings forth by the power of the Holy Spirit; and another crucified by the Jews under Pontius Pilate; and a third whom you divide between the sun and the moon? Or is it one and the same person, part of whom is confined in the trees, to be released by the help of the other part which is not confined? If this is the case, and you allow that Christ suffered under Pontius Pilate, though it is difficult to see how he could have suffered without flesh, as you say he did, the great question is, with whom he left those ships you speak of, that he might come down and suffer these things, which he certainly could not have suffered without having a body of some kind. A mere spiritual presence could not have made him liable to these sufferings, and in his bodily presence he could not be at the same time in the sun, in the moon, and on the cross. So, then, if he had not a body, he was not crucified; and if he had a body, the question is, where he got it: for, according to you, all bodies belong to the race of darkness, though you cannot think of the divine substance except as being material. Thus you must say either that Christ was crucified without a body, which is utterly absurd; or that he was crucified in appearance and not in reality, which is blasphemy; or that all bodies do not belong to the race of darkness, but that the divine substance has also a body, and that not an immortal body, but liable to crucifixion and death, which, again, is altogether erroneous; or that Christ had a mortal body from the race of darkness, so that, while you will not allow that Christ's body came from the Virgin Mary, you derive it from the race of demons. Finally, as in Faustus' statement, in which he alludes in the briefest manner possible to the lengthy stories of Manichæan invention, the earth by the power of the Holy Spirit conceives and brings forth the mortal Jesus, who, hanging from every tree, is the life and salvation of men, why should this Saviour be represented by whatever is hanging, because he hung on the tree, and not by whatever is born, because he was born? But if you mean that the Jesus on the trees, and the Jesus crucified under Pontius Pilate, and the Jesus divided between the sun and the moon, are all one and the same substance, why do you not give the name of Jesus to your whole host of deities? Why should not your World-holder be Jesus too, and Atlas, and the King of Honour, and the Mighty Spirit, and the First Man, and all the rest, with their various names and occupations?

12. So, with regard to the Holy Spirit, how can you say that he is the third person, when the persons you mention are innumerable? Or why is he not Jesus himself? And why does Faustus mislead people, in trying to make out an agreement between himself and true Christians, from whom he differs only too widely, by saying, We worship one God under the threefold appellation of the Almighty God the Father, Christ his Son, and the Holy Spirit? Why is the appellation only threefold, instead of being manifold? And why is the distinction in appellation only, and not in reality, if there are as many persons as there are names? For it is not as if you gave three names to the same thing, as the same weapon may be called a short sword, a dagger, or a dirk; or as you give the name of moon, and the lesser ship, and the luminary of night, and so on, to the same thing. For you cannot say that the First Man is the same as the Mighty Spirit, or as the World-Holder, or as the giant Atlas. They are all distinct persons, and you do not call any of them Christ. How can there be one Deity with opposite functions? Or why should not Christ himself be the single person, if in one substance Christ hangs on the trees, and was persecuted by the Jews, and exists in the sun and moon? The fact is, your fancies are all astray, and are no better than the dreams of insanity.

13. How can Faustus think that we resemble the Manichæans in attaching sacredness to bread and wine, when they consider it sacrilege to taste wine? They acknowledge their god in the grape, but not in the cup; perhaps they are shocked at his being trampled on and bottled. It is not any bread and wine that we hold sacred as a natural production, as if Christ were confined in corn or in vines, as the Manichæans fancy, but what is truly consecrated as a symbol. What is not consecrated, though it is bread and wine, is only nourishment or refreshment, with no sacredness about it; although we bless and thank God for every gift, bodily as well as spiritual. According to your notion, Christ is confined in everything you eat, and is released by digestion from the additional confinement of your intestines. So, when you eat, your god

[1] Rom. iii. 13.

suffers; and when you digest, you suffer from his recovery. When he fills you, your gain is his loss. This might be considered kindness on his part, because he suffers in you for your benefit, were it not that he gains freedom by escaping and leaving you empty. There is not the least resemblance between our reverence for the bread and wine, and your doctrines, which have no truth in them. To compare the two is even more foolish than to say, as some do, that in the bread and wine we worship Ceres and Bacchus. I refer to this now, to show where you got your silly idea that our fathers kept the Sabbath in honor of Saturn. For as there is no connection with the worship of the Pagan deities Ceres and Bacchus in our observance of the sacrament of the bread and wine, which you approve so highly that you wish to resemble us in it, so there was no subjection to Saturn in the case of our fathers, who observed the rest of the Sabbath in a manner suitable to prophetic times.

14. You might have found a resemblance in your religion to that of the Pagans as regards *Hyle* [matter], which the Pagans often speak of. You, on the contrary, maintain that you are directly opposed to them in your belief in the evil principle which your teacher in theology calls *Hyle*. But here you only show your ignorance, and, with an affectation of learning, use this word without knowing what it means. The Greeks, when speaking of nature, give the name *Hyle* to the subject-matter of things, which has no form of its own, but admits of all bodily forms, and is known only through these changeable phenomena, not being itself an object of sensation or perception. Some Gentiles, indeed, erroneously make this matter co-eternal with God, as not being derived from Him, though the bodily forms are. In this manifest error you resemble the Pagans, for you hold that *Hyle* has a principle of its own, and does not come from God. It is only ignorance that leads you to deny this resemblance. In saying that *Hyle* has no form of its own, and can take its forms only from God, the Pagans come near to the truth which we believe in contradistinction from your errors. Not knowing what *Hyle* or the subject-matter of things is, you make it the race of darkness, in which you place not only innumerable bodily forms of five different kinds, but also a formative mind. Such, indeed, is your ignorance or insanity, that you call this mind *Hyle*, and make it give forms instead of taking them. If there were such a formative mind as you speak of, and bodily elements capable of form, the word *Hyle* would properly be applicable to the bodily elements, which would be the matter to be formed by the mind, which you make the principle of evil. Even this would not be a quite accurate use of the word *Hyle*, which has no form of any kind; whereas these elements, although capable of new forms, have already the form of elements, and belong to different kinds. Still this use of the word would not be so much amiss, notwithstanding your ignorance; for it would thus be applied, as it properly is, to that which takes form, and not to that which gives it. Even here, however, your folly and impiety would appear in tracing so much that is good to the evil principle, from your not knowing that all natures of every kind, all forms in their proportion, and all weights in their order, can come only from the Father, the Son, and the Holy Spirit. As it is, you know neither what *Hyle* is, nor what evil is. Would that I could persuade you to refrain from misleading people still more ignorant than yourselves!

15. Every one must see the folly of your boasting of superiority to the Pagans because they use altars and temples, images and sacrifices and incense, in the worship of God, which you do not. As if it were not better to build an altar and offer sacrifice to a stone, which has some kind of existence, than to employ a heated imagination in worshipping things which have no existence at all. And what do you mean by saying that you are a rational temple of God? Can that be God's temple which is partly the construction of the devil? And is this not true of you, as you say that all your members and your whole body were formed by the evil principle which you call *Hyle*, and that part of this formative mind dwells in the body along with part of your god? And as this part of your god is bound and confined, you should be called the prison of God rather than his temple. Perhaps it is your soul that is the temple of God, as you have it from the region of light. But you generally call your soul not a temple, but a part or member of God. So, when you say you are the temple of God, it must be in your body, which, you say, was formed by the devil. Thus you blaspheme the temple of God, calling it not only the workmanship of Satan, but the prison-house of God. The apostle, on the other hand, says: "The temple of God is holy, which temple ye are." And to show that this refers not merely to the soul, he says expressly: "Know ye not that your bodies are the temple of the Holy Ghost, which is in you, which ye have of God?"[1] You call the workmanship of devils

[1] 1 Cor. iii. 17, and vi. 19.

the temple of God, and there, to use Faustus' words, you place Christ, the Son of God, the living image of living majesty. Your impiety may well contrive a fabulous temple for a fabulous Christ. The image you speak of must be so called, because it is the creature of your imagination.

16. If your mind is an altar, you see whose altar it is. You may see from the very doctrines and duties in which you say you are trained. You are taught not to give food to a beggar; and so your altar smokes with the sacrifice of cruelty. Such altars the Lord destroys; for in words quoted from the law He tells us what offering pleases God: "I desire mercy, and not sacrifice." Observe on what occasion the Lord uses these words. It was when, in passing through a field, the disciples plucked the ears of corn because they were hungry. Your doctrine would lead you to call this murder. Your mind is an altar, not of God, but of lying devils, by whose doctrines the evil conscience is seared as with a hot iron,[1] calling murder what the truth calls innocence. For in His words to the Jews, Christ by anticipation deals a fatal blow to you: "If ye had known what this meaneth, I desire mercy, and not sacrifice, ye would not have condemned the guiltless."[2]

17. Nor can you say that you honor God with sacrifices in the shape of pure and simple prayers: for, in your low, dishonoring notions about the divine nature and substance, you make your god to be the victim in the sacrifices of Pagans; so far are you from pleasing the true God with your sacrifices. For you hold that God is confined not only in trees and plants, or in the human body, but also in the flesh of animals, which contaminates Him with its impurity. And how can your soul give praise to God, when you actually reproach Him by calling your soul a particle of His substance taken captive by the race of darkness; as if God could not maintain the conflict except by this corruption of His members, and this dishonorable captivity? Instead of honoring God in your prayers, you insult Him. For what sin did you commit, when you belonged to Him, that you should be thus punished by the god you cry to, not because you left Him sinfully of your own choice; for he himself gave you to His enemies, to obtain peace for His kingdom? You are not even given as hostages to be honorably guarded. Nor is it as when a shepherd lays a snare to catch a wild beast: for he does not put one of his own members in the snare, but some animal from his flock; and generally, so that the wild beast is caught before the animal is hurt. You, though you are the members of your god, are given to the enemy, whose ferocity you keep off from your god only by being contaminated with their impurity, infected with their corruptions, without any fault of your own. You cannot in your prayers use the words: "Free us, O Lord, for the glory of Thy name; and for Thy name's sake pardon our sins."[3] Your prayer is: "Free us by Thy skill, for we suffer here oppression, and torture, and pollution, only that Thou mayest mourn unmolested in Thy kingdom." These are words of reproach, not of entreaty. Nor can you use the words taught us by the Master of truth: "Forgive us our debts, as we forgive our debtors."[4] For who are the debtors who have sinned against you? If it is the race of darkness, you do not forgive their debts, but make them be utterly cast out and shut up in eternal imprisonment. And how can God forgive your debts, when He rather sinned against you by sending you into such a state, than you against Him, whom you obeyed by going? If this was not a sin in Him, because He was compelled to do it, this excuse must apply to you, now that you have been overthrown in the conflict, more than to Him before the conflict began. You suffer now from the mixture of evil, which was not the case with Him when nevertheless He was compelled to send you. So either He requires that you should forgive Him his debt; or, if He is not in debt to you, still less are you to Him. It appears that your sacrifices and your pure and simple prayers are false and vile blasphemies.

18. How is it, by the way, that you use the words temple, altar, sacrifice, for the purpose of commending your own practices? If such things can be spoken of as properly belonging to true religion, they must constitute the true worship of the true God. And if there is such a thing as true sacrifice to the true God, which is implied in the expression divine honors, there must be some one true sacrifice of which the rest are imitations. On the one hand, we have the spurious imitations in the case of false and lying gods, that is, of devils, who proudly demand divine honors from their deluded votaries, as is or was the case in the temples and idols of the Gentiles. On the other hand, we have the prophetic intimations of one most true sacrifice to be offered for the sins of all believers, as in the sacrifices enjoined by God on our fathers; along with which there was also the symbolical anointing

[1] 1 Tim. iv. 2.
[2] Matt. xii. 7.
[3] Ps. lxxix. 9.
[4] Matt. vi. 12.

typical of Christ, as the name Christ itself means anointed. The animal sacrifices, therefore, presumptuously claimed by devils, were an imitation of the true sacrifice which is due only to the one true God, and which Christ alone offered on His altar. Thus the apostle says: "The sacrifices which the Gentiles offer, they offer to devils, and not to God."[1] He does not find fault with sacrifices, but with offering to devils. The Hebrews, again, in their animal sacrifices, which they offered to God in many varied forms, suitably to the significance of the institution, typified the sacrifice offered by Christ. This sacrifice is also commemorated by Christians, in the sacred offering and participation of the body and blood of Christ. The Manichæans understand neither the sinfulness of the Gentile sacrifices, nor the importance of the Hebrew sacrifices, nor the use of the ordinance of the Christian sacrifice. Their own errors are the offering they present to the devil who has deceived them. And thus they depart from the faith, giving heed to seducing spirits, and to doctrines of devils, speaking lies in hypocrisy.

19. It may be well that Faustus, or at least that those who are charmed with Faustus' writings, should know that the doctrine of a single principle did not come to us from the Gentiles; for the belief in one true God, from whom every kind of nature is derived, is a part of the original truth retained among the Gentiles, notwithstanding their having fallen away to many false gods. For the Gentile philosophers had the knowledge of God, because, as the apostle says, "the invisible things of God, from the creation of the world, are clearly seen, being understood by the things that are made, even His eternal power and Godhead; so that they are without excuse." But, as the apostle adds, "when they knew God, they glorified Him not as God, neither were thankful; but became vain in their imaginations, and their foolish heart was darkened. Professing themselves to be wise, they became fools, and changed the glory of the incorruptible God into an image made like to corruptible man, and to birds, and four-footed beasts, and creeping things."[2] These are the idols of the Gentiles, which they cannot explain except by referring to the creatures made by God; so that this very explanation of their idolatry, on which the more enlightened Gentiles were wont to pride themselves as a proof of their superiority, shows the truth of the following words of the apostle: "They worshipped and served the creature rather than the Creator, who is blessed forever."[3] Where you differ from the Gentiles, you are in error; where you resemble them, you are worse than they. You do not believe, as they do, in a single principle; and so you fall into the impiety of believing the substance of the one true God to be liable to subjugation and corruption. As regards the worship of a plurality of gods. the doctrine of lying devils has led the Gentiles to worship many idols, and you to worship many phantasms.

20. We do not turn the sacrifices of the Gentiles into love-feasts, as Faustus says we do. Our love-feasts are rather a substitute for the sacrifice spoken of by the Lord, in the words already quoted: "I will have mercy, and not sacrifice." At our love-feasts the poor obtain vegetable or animal food; and so the creature of God is used, as far as it is suitable, for the nourishment of man, who is also God's creature. You have been led by lying devils, not in self-denial, but in blasphemous error, "to abstain from meats which God hath created to be received with thanksgiving of them which believe and know the truth. For every creature of God is good, and nothing to be refused, if it be received with thanksgiving."[4] In return for the bounties of the Creator, you ungratefully insult Him with your impiety; and because in our love-feasts flesh is often given to the poor, you compare Christian charity to Pagan sacrifices. This indeed, is another point in which you resemble some Pagans. You consider it a crime to kill animals, because you think that the souls of men pass into them; which is an idea found in the writings of some Gentile philosophers, although their successors appear to have thought differently. But here again you are most in error: for they dreaded slaughtering a relative in the animal; but you dread the slaughter of your god, for you hold even the souls of animals to be his members.

21. As to our paying honor to the memory of the martyrs, and the accusation of Faustus, that we worship them instead of idols, I should not care to answer such a charge, were it not for the sake of showing how Faustus, in his desire to cast reproach on us, has overstepped the Manichæan inventions, and has fallen heedlessly into a popular notion found in Pagan poetry, although he is so anxious to be distinguished from the Pagans. For in saying that we have turned the idols into martyrs, he speaks of our worshipping them with similar rites, and appeasing the shades of the departed with wine and food. Do you, then,

[1] 1 Cor. x. 30.
[2] Rom. i. 20–23.
[3] Rom. i. 25.
[4] 1 Tim. iv. 3, 4.

believe in shades? We never heard you speak of such things, nor have we read of them in your books. In fact, you generally oppose such ideas: for you tell us that the souls of the dead, if they are wicked, or not purified, are made to pass through various changes, or suffer punishment still more severe; while the good souls are placed in ships, and sail through heaven to that imaginary region of light which they died fighting for. According to you, then, no souls remain near the burying-place of the body; and how can there be any shades of the departed? What and where are they? Faustus' love of evil-speaking has made him forget his own creed; or perhaps he spoke in his sleep about ghosts, and did not wake up even when he saw his words in writing. It is true that Christians pay religious honor to the memory of the martyrs, both to excite us to imitate them, and to obtain a share in their merits, and the assistance of their prayers. But we build altars not to any martyr, but to the God of martyrs, although it is to the memory of the martyrs. No one officiating at the altar in the saints' burying-place ever says, We bring an offering to thee, O Peter! or O Paul! or O Cyprian! The offering is made to God, who gave the crown of martyrdom, while it is in memory of those thus crowned. The emotion is increased by the associations of the place, and love is excited both towards those who are our examples, and towards Him by whose help we may follow such examples. We regard the martyrs with the same affectionate intimacy that we feel towards holy men of God in this life, when we know that their hearts are prepared to endure the same suffering for the truth of the gospel. There is more devotion in our feeling towards the martyrs, because we know that their conflict is over; and we can speak with greater confidence in praise of those already victors in heaven, than of those still combating here. What is properly divine worship, which the Greeks call *latria*, and for which there is no word in Latin, both in doctrine and in practice, we give only to God. To this worship belongs the offering of sacrifices; as we see in the word idolatry, which means the giving of this worship to idols. Accordingly we never offer, or require any one to offer, sacrifice to a martyr, or to a holy soul, or to any angel. Any one falling into this error is instructed by doctrine, either in the way of correction or of caution. For holy beings themselves, whether saints or angels, refuse to accept what they know to be due to God alone. We see this in Paul and Barnabas, when the men of Lycaonia wished to sacrifice to them as gods, on account of the miracles they performed. They rent their clothes, and restrained the people, crying out to them, and persuading them that they were not gods. We see it also in the angels, as we read in the Apocalypse that an angel would not allow himself to be worshipped, and said to his worshipper, "I am thy fellow-servant, and of thy brethen."[1] Those who claim this worship are proud spirits, the devil and his angels, as we see in all the temples and rites of the Gentiles. Some proud men, too, have copied their example; as is related of some kings of Babylon. Thus the holy Daniel was accused and persecuted, because when the king made a decree that no petition should be made to any god, but only to the king, he was found worshipping and praying to his own God, that is, the one true God.[2] As for those who drink to excess at the feasts of the martyrs, we of course condemn their conduct; for to do so even in their own houses would be contrary to sound doctrine. But we must try to amend what is bad as well as prescribe what is good, and must of necessity bear for a time with some things that are not according to our teaching. The rules of Christian conduct are not to be taken from the indulgences of the intemperate or the infirmities of the weak. Still, even in this, the guilt of intemperance is much less than that of impiety. To sacrifice to the martyrs, even fasting, is worse than to go home intoxicated from their feast: to sacrifice to the martyrs, I say, which is a different thing from sacrificing to God in memory of the martyrs, as we do constantly, in the manner required since the revelation of the New Testament, for this belongs to the worship or *latria* which is due to God alone. But it is vain to try to make these heretics understand the full meaning of these words of the Psalmist: "He that offereth the sacrifice of praise glorifieth me, and in this way will I show him my salvation."[3] Before the coming of Christ, the flesh and blood of this sacrifice were foreshadowed in the animals slain; in the passion of Christ the types were fulfilled by the true sacrifice; after the ascension of Christ, this sacrifice is commemorated in the sacrament. Between the sacrifices of the Pagans and of the Hebrews there is all the difference that there is between a false imitation and a typical anticipation. We do not despise or denounce the virginity of holy women because there were vestal virgins. And, in the same way, it is no reproach to the sacrifices of our fathers that the Gentiles

1 Rev. xix. 10. 2 Dan. vi. 3 Ps. l. 23.

also had sacrifices. The difference between the Christian and vestal virginity is great, yet it consists wholly in the being to whom the vow is made and paid; and so the difference in the being to whom the sacrifices of the Pagans and Hebrews are made and offered makes a wide difference between them. In the one case they are offered to devils, who presumptuously make this claim in order to be held as gods, because sacrifice is a divine honor. In the other case they are offered to the one true God, as a type of the true sacrifice, which also was to be offered to Him in the passion of the body and blood of Christ.

22. Faustus is wrong in saying that our Jewish forefathers, in their separation from the Gentiles, retained the temple, and sacrifices, and altars, and priesthood, and abandoned only graven images or idols, for they might have sacrificed, as some do, without any graven image, to trees and mountains, or even to the sun and moon and the stars. If they had thus rendered to these objects the worship called *latria*, they would have served the creature instead of the Creator, and so would have fallen into the serious error of heathenish superstition; and even without idols, they would have found devils ready to take advantage of their error, and to accept their offerings. For these proud and wicked spirits feed not, as some foolishly suppose, on the smell of the sacrifice, and the smoke, but on the errors of men. They enjoy not bodily refreshment, but a malevolent gratification, when they in any way deceive people, or when, with a bold assumption of borrowed majesty, they boast of receiving divine honors. It was not, therefore, only the idols of the Gentiles that our Jewish forefathers abandoned. They sacrificed neither to the earth nor to any earthly thing, nor to the sea, nor to heaven, nor to the hosts of heaven, but laid the victims on the altar of the one God, Creator of all, who required these offerings as a means of foreshadowing the true victim, by whom He has reconciled us to Himself in the remission of sins through our Lord Jesus Christ. So Paul, addressing believers, who are made the body of which Christ is the Head, says: "I beseech you, therefore, brethren, by the mercies of God, that ye present your bodies a living sacrifice, holy, acceptable to God."[1] The Manichæans, on the other hand, say that human bodies are the workmanship of the race of darkness, and the prison in which the captive deity is confined. Thus Faustus' doctrine is very different from Paul's. But since whosover preaches to you another gospel than that ye have received must be accursed, what Christ says in Paul is the truth, while Manichæus in Faustus is accursed.

23. Faustus says also, without knowing what he says, that we have retained the manners of the Gentiles. But seeing that the just lives by faith, and that the end of the commandment is love out of a pure heart, and a good conscience, and faith unfeigned, and that these three, faith, hope, and love, abide to form the life of believers, it is impossible that there should be similarity in the manners of those who differ in these three things. Those who believe differently, and hope differently, and love differently, must also live differently. And if we resemble the Gentiles in our use of such things as food and drink, and houses and clothes and baths, and those of us who marry, in taking and keeping wives, and in begetting and bringing up children as our heirs, there is still a great difference between the man who uses these things for some end of his own, and the man who, in using them, gives thanks to God, having no unworthy or erroneous ideas about God. For as you, according to your own heresy, though you eat the same bread as other men, and live upon the produce of the same plants and the water of the same fountain, and are clothed like others in wool and linen, yet lead a different life, not because you eat or drink, or dress differently, but because you differ from others in your ideas and in your faith, and in all these things have in view an end of your own—the end, namely, set forth in your false doctrines; in the same way we, though we resemble the Gentiles in the use of this and other things, do not resemble them in our life; for while the things are the same, the end is different: for the end we have in view is, according to the just commandment of God, love out of a pure heart, and a good conscience, and faith unfeigned; from which some having erred, are turned to vain jangling. In this vain jangling you bear the palm, for you do not attend to the fact that so great is the difference of life produced by a different faith, even when the things in possession and use are the same, that though your followers have wives, and in spite of themselves get children, for whom they gather and store up wealth; though they eat flesh, drink wine, bathe, reap harvests, gather vintages, engage in trade, and occupy high official positions, you nevertheless reckon them as belonging to you, and not to the Gentiles, though in their actions they approach nearer to the Gentiles than to you. And though some of the Gentiles in some things resemble

[1] Rom. xii. 1.

you more than your own followers,—those, for instance, who in superstitious devotion abstain from flesh, and wine, and marriage,—you still count your own followers, even though they use all these things, and so are unlike you, as belonging to the flock of Manichæus rather than those who resemble you in their practices. You consider as belonging to you a woman that believes in Manichæus, though she is a mother, rather than a Sibyl, though she never marries. But you will say that many who are called Catholic Christians are adulterers, robbers, misers, drunkards, and whatever else is contrary to sound doctrine. I ask if none such are to be found in your company, which is almost too small to be called a company. And because there are some among the Pagans who are not of this character, do you consider them as better than yourselves? And yet, in fact, your heresy is so blasphemous, that even your followers who are not of such a character are worse than the Pagans who are. It is therefore no impeachment to sound doctrine, which alone is Catholic, that many wish to take its name, who will not yield to its beneficial influence. We must bear in mind the true meaning of the contrast which the Lord makes between the little company and the mass of mankind, as spread over all the world; for the company of saints and believers is small, as the amount of grain is small when compared with the heap of chaff; and yet the good grain is quite sufficient far to outnumber you, good and bad together, for good and bad are both strangers to the truth. In a word, we are not a schism of the Gentiles, for we differ from them greatly for the better; nor are you, for you differ from them greatly for the worse.[1]

[1] [Augustin's exposure of the paganism of Manichæism is an admirable and effective piece of *argumentum ad hominem.* That the Christianity of Augustin's time was becoming paganized is undoubted, but Manichæism was pure paganism.—A. H. N.]

BOOK XXI.

FAUSTUS DENIES THAT MANICHÆANS BELIEVE IN TWO GODS. HYLE NO GOD. AUGUSTIN DISCUSSES AT LARGE THE DOCTRINE OF GOD AND HYLE, AND FIXES THE CHARGE OF DUALISM UPON THE MANICHÆANS.

1. Faustus said: Do we believe in one God or in two? In one, of course. If we are accused of making two gods, I reply that it cannot be shown that we ever said anything of the kind. Why do you suspect us of this? Because, you say, you believe in two principles, good and evil. It is true, we believe in two principles; but one we call God, and the other *Hyle*, or, to use common popular language, the devil. If you think this means two gods, you may as well think that the health and sickness of which doctors speak are two kinds of health, or that good and evil are two kinds of good, or that wealth and poverty are two kinds of wealth. If I were describing two things, one white and the other black, or one hot and the other cold, or one sweet and the other bitter, it would appear like idiocy or insanity in you to say that I was describing two white things, or two hot things, or two sweet things. So, when I assert that there are two principles, God and *Hyle*, you have no reason for saying that I believe in two gods. Do you think that we must call them both gods because we attribute, as is proper, all the power of evil to *Hyle*, and all the power of good to God? If so, you may as well say that a poison and the antidote must both be called antidotes, because each has a power of its own, and certain effects follow from the action of both. So also, you may say that a physician and a poisoner are both physicians; or that a just and an unjust man are both just, because both do something. If this is absurd, it is still more absurd to say that God and *Hyle* must both be gods, because they both produce certain effects. It is a very childish and impotent way of arguing, when you cannot refute my statements, to make a quarrel about names. I grant that we, too, sometimes call the hostile nature God; not that we believe it to be God, but that this name is already adopted by the worshippers of this nature, who in their error suppose it to be God. Thus the apostle says: "The god of this world has blinded the minds of them that believe not."[1] He calls him God, because he would be so called by his worshippers; adding that he blinds their minds, to show that he is not the true God.

2. Augustin replied: You often speak in your discourses of two gods, as indeed you acknowledge, though at first you denied it. And you give as a reason for thus speaking the words of the apostle: "The god of this world has blinded the minds of them that believe not." Most of us punctuate this sentence differently, and explain it as meaning

[1] 2 Cor. iv. 4.

that the true God has blinded the minds of unbelievers. They put a stop after the word God, and read the following words together. Or without this punctuation you may, for the sake of exposition, change the order of the words, and read, "In whom God has blinded the minds of unbelievers of this world," which gives the same sense. The act of blinding the minds of unbelievers may in one sense be ascribed to God, as the effect not of malice, but of justice. Thus Paul himself says elsewhere, "Is God unjust, who taketh vengeance?"[1] and again, "What shall we say then? Is there unrighteousness with God? God forbid. For Moses saith, I will have mercy on whom I will have mercy, and will have compassion on whom I will have compassion." Observe what he adds, after asserting the undeniable truth that there is no unrighteousness with God: "But what if God, willing to show His wrath, and to make His power known, endured with much long-suffering the vessels of wrath fitted for destruction, and that He might manifest the riches of His grace towards the vessels of mercy, which He hath before prepared unto glory?"[2] etc. Here it evidently cannot be said that it is one God who shows his wrath, and makes known his power in the vessels of wrath fitted for destruction, and another God who shows his riches in the vessels of mercy. According to the apostle's doctrine, it is one and the same God who does both. Hence he says again, "For this cause God gave them up to the lusts of their own heart, to uncleanness, to dishonor their own bodies between themselves;" and immediately after, "For this cause God gave them up unto vile affections;" and again, "And even as they did not like to retain God in their knowledge, God gave them over to a reprobate mind."[3] Here we see how the true and just God blinds the minds of unbelievers. For in all these words quoted from the apostle no other God is understood than He whose Son, sent by Him, came saying, "For judgment am I come into this world, that they which see not might see, and that they which see might be made blind."[4] Here, again, it is plain to the minds of believers how God blinds the minds of unbelievers. For among the secret things, which contain the righteous principles of God's judgment, there is a secret which determines that the minds of some shall be blinded, and the minds of some enlightened. Regarding this, it is well said of God, "Thy judgments are a great deep."[5] The apostle, in admiration of the unfathomable depth of this abyss, exclaims: "O the depth of the riches both of the wisdom and of the knowledge of God! How unsearchable are His judgments, and His ways past finding out!"[6]

3. You cannot distinguish between what God does in mercy and what He does in judgment, because you can neither understand nor use the words of our Psalter: "I will sing of mercy and judgment unto Thee, O Lord."[7] Accordingly, whatever in the feebleness of your frail humanity seems amiss to you, you separate entirely from the will and judgment of God: for you are provided with another evil god, not by a discovery of truth, but by an invention of folly; and to this god you attribute not only what you do unjustly, but also what you suffer justly. Thus you assign to God the bestowal of blessings, and take from Him the infliction of judgments, as if He of whom Christ says that He has prepared everlasting fire for the wicked were a different being from Him who makes His sun to rise upon the evil and the good, and sends rain on the just and on the unjust. Why do you not understand that this great goodness and great severity belong to one God, but because you have not learned to sing of mercy and judgment? Is not He who causes the sun to rise on the evil and the good, and sends rain on the just and on the unjust, the same who also breaks off the natural branches, and engrafts contrary to nature the wild olive tree? Does not the apostle, in reference to this, say of this one God: "Thou seest, then, the goodness and severity of God: to them which were broken off, severity; but toward thee, goodness, if thou continue in His goodness?"[8] Here it is to be observed how the apostle takes away neither judicial severity from God, nor free-will from man. It is a profound mystery, impenetrable by human thought, how God both condemns the ungodly and justifies the ungodly; for both these things are said of Him in the truth of the Holy Scriptures. But is the mysteriousness of the divine judgments any reason for taking pleasure in cavilling against them? How much more becoming, and more suitable to the limitation of our powers, to feel the same awe which the apostle felt, and to exclaim, "O the depth of the riches both of the wisdom and of the knowledge of God! How unsearchable are His judgments, and His ways past finding out!" How much better thus to admire what you cannot explain, than to try to make an evil god in addition to the true God, simply because you cannot under-

---

1 Rom. iii. 5.
2 Rom. ix. 14, 15, 22, 23.
3 Rom. i. 24, 25, 28.
4 John ix. 39.
5 Ps. xxxvi. 6.
6 Rom. xi. 33.
7 Ps. ci. 1.
8 Rom. xi. 17-24.

stand the one good God! For it is not a question of names, but of actions.

4. Faustus glibly defends himself by saying, "We speak not of two gods, but of God and *Hyle*." But when you ask for the meaning of *Hyle*, you find that it is in fact another god. If the Manichæans gave the name of *Hyle*, as the ancients did, to the unformed matter which is susceptible of bodily forms, we should not accuse them of making two gods. But it is pure folly and madness to give to matter the power of forming bodies, or to deny that what has this power is God. When you give to some other being the power which belongs to the true God of making the qualities and forms, by which bodies, elements, and animals exist, according to their respective modes, whatever name you choose to give to this being, you are chargeable with making another god. There are indeed two errors in this blasphemous doctrine. In the first place, you ascribe the act of God to a being whom you are ashamed to call god; though you must call him god as long as you make him do things which only God can do. In the second place, the good things done by a good God you call bad, and ascribe to an evil god, because you feel a childish horror of whatever shocks the frailty of fallen humanity, and a childish pleasure in the opposite. So you think snakes are made by an evil being; while you consider the sun so great a good, that you believe it to be not the creature of God, but an emission from His substance. You must know that the true God, in whom, alas, you have not yet come to believe, made both the snake along with the lower creatures, and the sun along with other exalted creatures. Moreover, among still more exalted creatures, not heavenly bodies, but spiritual beings, He has made what far surpasses the light of the sun, and what no carnal man can perceive, much less you, who, in your condemnation of flesh, condemn the very principle by which you determine good and evil. For your only idea of evil is from the disagreeableness of some things to the fleshly sense; and your only idea of good is from sensual gratification.

5. When I consider the things lowest in the scale of nature, which are within our view, and which, though earthly, and feeble, and mortal, are still the works of God, I am lost in admiration of the Creator, who is so great in the great works and no less great in the small. For the divine skill seen in the formation of all creatures in heaven and earth is always like itself, even in those things that differ from one another; for it is everywhere perfect, in the perfection which it gives to everything in its own kind. We see each creature made not as a whole by itself, but in relation to the rest of the creation; so that the whole divine skill is displayed in the formation of each, arranging each in its proper place and order, and providing what is suitable for all, both separately and unitedly. See here, lowest in the scale, the animals which fly, and swim, and walk, and creep. These are mortal creatures, whose life, as it is written, "is as a vapor which appeareth for a little time."[1] Each of these, according to the capacity of its kind, contributes the measure appointed in the goodness of the Creator to the completeness of the whole, so that the lowest partake in the good which the highest possess in a greater degree. Show me, if you can, any animal, however despicable, whose soul hates its own flesh, and does not rather nourish and cherish it, by its vital motion minister to its growth and direct its activity, and exercise a sort of management over a little universe of its own, which it makes subservient to its own preservation. Even in the discipline of his own body by a rational being, who brings his body under, that earthly passion may not hinder his perception of wisdom, there is love for his own flesh, which he then reduces to obedience, which is its proper condition. Indeed, you yourselves, although your heresy teaches you a fleshly abhorrence of the flesh, cannot help loving your own flesh, and caring for its safety and comfort, both by avoiding all injury from blows, and falls, and inclement weather, and by seeking for the means of keeping it in health. Thus the law of nature is too strong for your false doctrine.

6. Looking at the flesh itself, do we not see in the construction of its vital parts, in the symmetry of form, in the position and arrangement of the limbs of action and the organs of sensation, all acting in harmony; do we not see in the adjustment of measures, in the proportion of numbers, in the order of weights, the handiwork of the true God, of whom it is truly said, "Thou hast ordered all things in measure, and number, and weight"?[2] If your heart was not hardened and corrupted by falsehood, you would understand the invisible things of God from the things which He has made, even in these feeble creatures of flesh. For who is the author of the things I have mentioned, but He whose unity is the standard of all measure, whose wisdom is the model of all beauty, and whose law is the rule of all order? If you are blind to these things, hear at least the words of the apostle.

[1] Jas. iv. 15.

[2] Wisd. xi. 21.

7. For the apostle, in speaking of the love which husbands ought to have for their wives, gives, as an example, the love of the soul for the body. The words are: "He that loveth his wife, loveth himself: for no man ever yet hated his own flesh, but nourisheth and cherisheth it, even as Christ the Church."[1] Look at the whole animal creation, and you find in the instinctive self-preservation of every animal this natural principle of love to its own flesh. It is so not only with men, who, when they live aright, both provide for the safety of their flesh, and keep their carnal appetites in subjection to the use of reason; the brutes also avoid pain, and shrink from death, and escape as rapidly as they can from whatever might break up the construction of their bodies, or dissolve the connection of spirit and flesh; for the brutes, too, nourish and cherish their own flesh. "For no one ever yet," says the apostle, "hated his own flesh, but nourisheth and cherisheth it, even as Christ the Church." See where the apostle begins, and to what he ascends. Consider, if you can, the greatness which creation derives from its Creator, embracing as it does the whole extent from the host of heaven down to flesh and blood, with the beauty of manifold form, and the order of successive gradations.

8. The same apostle again, when speaking of spiritual gifts as diverse, and yet tending to harmonious action, to illustrate a matter so great, and divine, and mysterious, makes a comparison with the human body,—thus plainly intimating that this flesh is the handiwork of God. The whole passage, as found in the Epistle to the Corinthians, is so much to the point, that though it is long, I think it not amiss to insert it all: "Now concerning spiritual gifts, brethren, I would not have you ignorant. Ye know that ye were Gentiles, carried away unto these dumb idols, even as ye were led. Wherefore I give you to understand, that no man speaking by the Spirit of God calleth Jesus accursed; and that no man can say that Jesus is the Lord, but by the Holy Ghost. Now there are diversities of gifts, but the same Spirit. And there are diversities of administrations, but the same Lord. And there are diversities of operations, but it is the same God which worketh all in all. But the manifestation of the Spirit is given to every man to profit withal. For to one is given by the Spirit the word of wisdom; to another the word of knowledge by the same Spirit; to another faith by the same Spirit; to another the gifts of healing by the same Spirit; to another the working of miracles; to another prophecy; to another discerning of spirits; to another divers kinds of tongues; to another the interpretation of tongues: but all these worketh that one and the self-same Spirit, dividing to every man severally as He will. For as the body is one, and hath many members, and all the members of that one body, being many, are one body: so also is Christ. For by one Spirit are we all baptized into one body, whether we be Jews or Gentiles, whether we be bond or free; and have been all made to drink into one Spirit. For the body is not one member, but many. If the foot shall say, Because I am not the hand, I am not of the body; is it therefore not of the body? And if the ear shall say, Because I am not the eye, I am not of the body; is it therefore not of the body? If the whole body were an eye, where were the hearing? If the whole were hearing, where were the smelling? But now hath God set the members every one of them in the body, as it hath pleased Him. And if they were all one member, where were the body? But now are they many members, yet but one body. And the eye cannot say unto the hand, I have no need of thee; nor again the head to the feet, I have no need of you. Nay, much more those members of the body, which seem to be more feeble, are necessary; and those members of the body which we think to be less honorable, upon these we bestow more abundant honor; and our uncomely parts have more abundant comeliness. For our comely parts have no need; but God hath tempered the body together, having given more abundant honor to that part which lacked: that there should be no schism in the body, but that the members should have the same care one for another. And whether one member suffer, all the members suffer with it; or one member be honored, all the members rejoice with it."[2] Apart altogether from Christian faith, which would lead you to believe the apostle, if you have common sense to perceive what is self-evident, let each examine and see for himself the plain truth regarding those things of which the apostle speaks,—what greatness belongs to the least, and what goodness to the lowest; for these are the things which the apostle extols, in order to illustrate by means of these common and visible bodily objects, unseen spiritual realities of the most exalted nature.

9. Whoever, then, denies that our body and its members, which the apostle so approves and extols, are the handiwork of God,

[1] Eph. v. 28, 29.

[2] 1 Cor. xii. 1–26.

you see whom he contradicts, preaching contrary to what you have received. So, instead of refuting his opinions, I may leave him to be accursed of all Christians. The apostle says, God tempered the body. Faustus says, Not God, but *Hyle*. Anathemas are more suitable than arguments to such contradictions. You cannot say that God is here called the God of this world. And if any one understands the passage where this expression does occur to mean that the devil blinds the minds of unbelievers, we grant that he does so by his evil suggestions, from yielding to which, men lose the light of righteousness in God's righteous retribution. This is all in accordance with sacred Scripture. The apostle himself speaks of temptation from without: "I fear lest, as the serpent beguiled Eve through his subtilty, so your minds should be corrupted from the simplicity and purity that is in Christ."[1] To the same purpose are the words, "Evil communications corrupt good manners;"[2] and when he speaks of a man deceiving himself, "Whoever thinketh himself to be anything, when he is nothing, deceiveth himself;"[3] or again, in the passage already quoted of the judgment of God, "God gave them over to a reprobate mind, to do those things which are not convenient."[4] Similarly, in the Old Testament, after the words, "God did not create death, nor hath He pleasure in the destruction of the living," we read, "By the envy of the devil death entered into the world."[5] And again of death, that men may not put the blame from themselves, "The wicked invite her with hands and voice; and thinking her a friend, they are drawn down."[6] Elsewhere, however, it is said, "Good and evil, life and death, riches and poverty, are from the Lord God."[7] This seems perplexing to people who do not understand that, apart from the manifest judgment to follow hereafter upon every evil work, there is an actual judgment at the time; so that in one action, besides the craft of the deceiver and the wickedness of the voluntary agent, there is also the just penalty of the judge: for while the devil suggests, and man consents, God abandons. So, if you join the words, *God of this world*, and understand that the devil blinds unbelievers by his mischievous delusions, the meaning is not a bad one. For the word God is not used by itself, but with the qualification *of this world*, that is, of wicked men, who seek to prosper only in this age. In this sense the world is also called evil, where it is written, "that He might deliver us from this present evil age."[8] In the same way, in the expression, "whose god is their belly," it is only in connection with the word *whose* that the belly is called god. So also, in the Psalms, the devils would not be called gods without adding "of the nations."[9] But in the passage we are now considering it is not said, The god of this world, or, Whose god is their belly, or, The gods of the nations are devils; but simply, God has tempered the body, which can be understood only of the true God, the Creator of all. There is no disparaging addition here, as in the other cases. But perhaps Faustus will say that God tempered the body, not as the maker of it, in the arrangement of its members, but by mixing His light with it. Thus Faustus would attribute to some other being than God the construction of the body, and the arrangement of its members, while God tempered the evil of the construction by the mixture of His goodness. Such are the inventions with which the Manichæans cram feeble minds. But God, in aid of the feeble, by the mouth of the sacred writers rebukes this opinion. For we read a few verses before: "God has placed the members every one of them in the body, as it has pleased Him." Evidently, God is said to have tempered the body, because He has constructed it of many members, which in their union preserve the variety of their respective functions.

10. Do the Manichæans suppose that the animals which, according to their wild notions, were constructed by *Hyle* in the race of darkness, had not this harmonious action of their members, commended by the apostle, before God mixed His light with them; so that then the head did say to the feet, or the eye to the hand, I have no need of thee? This is not and cannot be the Manichæan doctrine, for they describe the animals as using all these members, and speak of them as creeping, walking, swimming, flying, each in its own kind. They could all see, too, and hear, and use the other senses, and nourish and cherish their own bodies with appropriate means and appliances. Hence, moreover, they had the power of reproduction, for they are spoken of as having offspring. All these things, of which Faust speaks disparagingly as the works of *Hyle*, could not be done without that harmonious arrangement which the apostle praises and ascribes to God. Is it not now plain who is to be followed, and who is to be pronounced accursed? Indeed, the Manichæans tell us of animals that could speak;

[1] 2 Cor. xi. 3. [2] 1 Cor. xv. 33. [3] Gal. vi. 3.
[4] Rom. i. 28. [5] Wisd. i. 13, and ii. 24. [6] Wisd. i. 16.
[7] Ecclus. xi. 14.

[8] Gal. i. 4. [9] Ps. xcvi. 5.

and their speeches were heard and understood and approved of by all creatures, whether creeping things, or quadrupeds, or birds, or fish. Amazing and supernatural eloquence! Especially as they had no grammarian or elocutionist to teach them, and had not passed through the painful experience of the cane and the birch. Why, Faustus himself began late in life to learn oratory, that he might discourse eloquently on these absurdities; and with all his cleverness, after ruining his health by study, his preaching has gained a mere handful of followers. What a pity that he was born in the light, and not in that region of darkness! If he had discoursed there against the light, the whole animal creation, from the biped to the centipede, from the dragon to the shell-fish, would have listened eagerly, and obeyed at once; whereas, when he discourses here against the race of darkness, he is oftener called eloquent than learned, and oftener still a false teacher of the worst kind. And among the few Manichæans who extol him as a great teacher, he has none of the lower animals as his disciples; and not even his horse is any the wiser for his master's instructions, so that the mixture of a part of deity seems only to make the animals more stupid. What absurdity is this! When will these deluded beings have the sense to compare the description in the Manichæan fiction of what the animals were formerly in their own region, with what they are now in this world? Then their bodies were strong, now they are feeble; then their power of vision was such that they were induced to invade the region of God on account of the beauty which they saw, now it is too weak to face the rays of the sun; then they had intelligence sufficient to understand a discourse addressed to them, now they have no ability of the kind; then this astonishing and effective eloquence was natural, now eloquence of the most meagre kind requires diligent study and preparation. How many good things did the race of darkness lose by the mixture of good!

11. Faustus has displayed his ingenuity, in the remarks to which I am now replying, by making for himself a long list of opposites—health and sickness, riches and poverty, white and black, cold and hot, sweet and bitter. We need not say much about black and white. Or, if there is a character for good or evil in colors, so that white must be ascribed to God and black to *Hyle;* if God threw a white color on the wings of birds, when *Hyle*, as the Manichæans say, created them, where had the crows gone to when the swans got whitened? Nor need we discuss heat and cold, for both are good in moderation, and dangerous in excess. With regard to the rest, Faustus probably intended that good and evil, which he might as well have put first, should be understood as including the rest, so that health, riches, white, hot, sweet, should belong to good; and sickness, poverty, black, cold, bitter, to evil. The ignorance and folly of this is obvious. It might look like reviling if I were to take up separately white and black, hot and cold, sweet and bitter, health and sickness. For if white and sweet are both good, and black and bitter evil, how is it that most grapes and all olives become black as they become sweet, and so get good by getting evil? And if heat and health are both good, and cold and sickness evil, why do bodies become sick when heated? Is it healthy to have fever? But I let these things pass, for they may have been put down hastily, or they may have been given as merely instances of opposition, and not as being good and bad, especially as it is nowhere stated that the fire among the race of darkness is cold, so that heat in this case must unquestionably be evil.

12. We pass on, then, to health, riches, sweetness, which Faustus evidently accounts good in his contrasts. Was there no health of body in the race of darkness where animals were born and grew up and brought forth, and had such vitality, that when some that were with child were taken, as the story is, and were put in bonds in heaven, even the abortive offspring of a premature birth, falling from heaven to earth, nevertheless lived, and grew, and produced the innumerable kinds of animals which now exist? Or were there no riches where trees could grow not only in water and wind, but in smoke and fire, and could bear such a rich produce, that animals, according to their several kinds, sprang from the fruit, and were provided with the means of subsistence from those fertile trees, and showed how well fed they were by a numerous progeny? And all this where there was no toil in cultivation, and no inclement change from summer to winter, for there was no sun to give variety to the seasons by his annual course. There must have been perennial productiveness where the trees were not only born in their own element, but had a supply of appropriate nourishment to make them constantly fertile; as we see orange-trees bearing fruit all the year round if they are well watered. The riches must have been abundant, and they must have been secure from harm; for there could be no fear of hailstorms when there were no light-gatherers who, in your fable, set the thunder in motion.

13. Nor would the beings in this race of

darkness have sought for food if it had not been sweet and pleasant, so that they would have died from want. For we find that all bodies have their peculiar wants, according to which food is either agreeable or offensive. If it is agreeable, it is said to be sweet or pleasant; if it is offensive, it is said to be bitter or sour, or in some way disagreeable. In human beings we find that one desires food which another dislikes, from a difference in constitution or habit or state of health. Still more, animals of quite different make can find pleasure in food which is disagreeable to us. Why else should the goats feed so eagerly on the wild olives? This food is sweet to them, as in some sicknesses honey tastes bitter to us. To a thoughtful inquirer these things suggest the beauty of the arrangement in which each finds what suits it, and the greatness of the good which extends from the lowest to the highest, and from the material to the spiritual. As for the race of darkness, if an animal sprung from any element fed on what was produced by that element, doubtless the food must have been sweet from its appropriateness. Again, if this animal had found food of another element, the want of appropriateness would have appeared in its offensiveness to the taste. Such offensiveness is called sourness, or bitterness, or disagreeableness, or something of the kind; or if its adverse nature is such as to destroy the harmony of the bodily constitution, and so take away life or reduce the strength, it is called poison, simply on account of this want of appropriateness, while it may nourish the kind of life to which it is appropriate. So, if a hawk eat the bread which is our daily food, it dies; and we die if we eat hellebore, which cattle often feed on, and which may itself in a certain form be used as a medicine. If Faustus had known or thought of this, he would not have given poison and antidote as an example of the two natures of good and evil, as if God were the antidote and *Hyle* the poison. For the same thing, of one and the same nature, kills or cures, as it is used appropriately or inappropriately. In the Manichæan legends, their god might be said to have been poison to the race of darkness; for he so injured their bodies, that from being strong, they became utterly feeble. But then again, as the light was itself taken, and subjected to loss and injury, it may be said to have been poison to itself.

14. Instead of one good and one evil principle, you seem to make both good or both evil, or rather two good and two evil; for they are good in themselves, and evil to one another. We may see afterwards which is the better or the worse; but meanwhile we may think of them as both good in themselves. Thus God reigned in one region, while *Hyle* reigned in the other. There was health in both kingdoms, and rich produce in both; both had a numerous progeny, and both tasted the sweetness of pleasures suitable to their respective natures. But the race of darkness, say the Manichæans, excepting the part which was evil to the light which it bordered on, was also evil to itself. As, however, I have already pointed out many good things in it, if you can point out its evils, there will still be two good kingdoms, though the one where there are no evils will be the better of the two. What, then, do you call its evils? They plundered, and killed, and devoured one another, according to Faustus. But if they did nothing else than this, how could such numerous hosts be born and grow up to maturity? They must have enjoyed peace and tranquillity too. But, allowing the kingdom where there is no discord to be the better of the two, still they should both be called good, rather than one good and the other bad. Thus the better kingdom will be that where they killed neither themselves nor one another; and the worse, or less good, where, though they fought with one another, each separate animal preserved its own nature in health and safety. But we cannot make much difference between your god and the prince of darkness, whom no one opposed, whose reign was acknowledged by all, and whose proposals were unanimously agreed to. All this implies great peace and harmony. Those kingdoms are happy where all agree heartily in obedience to the king. Moreover, the rule of this prince extended not only to his own species, or to bipeds whom you make the parents of mankind, but to all kinds of animals, who waited in his presence, obeying his commands, and believing his declarations. Do you think people are so stupid as not to recognize the attributes of deity in your description of this prince, or to think it possible that you can have another? If the authority of this prince rested on his resources, he must have been very powerful; if on his fame, he must have been renowned; if on love, the regard must have been universal; if on fear, he must have kept the strictest order. If some evils, then, were mixed with so many good things, who that knows the meaning of words would call this the nature of evil? Besides, if you call this the nature of evil, because it was not only evil to the other nature, but was also evil in itself, was there no evil, think you, in the dire necessity to which your god was subjected before the mixture with

the opposite nature, so that he was compelled to fight with it, and to send his own members to be swallowed up so mercilessly as to be beyond the hope of complete recovery? This was a great evil in that nature before its mixture with the only thing you allow to be evil. Your god must either have had it in his power not to be injured and sullied by the race of darkness, in which case his own folly must have brought him into trouble; or if his substance was liable to corruption, the object of your worship is not the incorruptible God of whom the apostle speaks.[1] Does not, then, this liability to corruption, even apart from the actual experience, seem to you to be an evil in your god?

15. It is plain, moreover, that either he must have been destitute of prescience,—a great defect, surely, in the Deity, not to know what is coming; or if he had prescience, he can never have felt secure, but must have been in constant terror, which you must allow to be a serious evil. There must have been the fear at every moment, that the time might be come for that conflict in which his members suffered such loss and contamination, that to liberate and purify them costs infinite labor, and, after all, can be done only partially. If it is going too far to attribute this state of alarm to the Deity himself, his members at least must have dreaded the prospect of suffering all these evils. Then, again, if they were ignorant of what was to happen, the substance of your god must have been so far wanting in prescience. How many evils do you reckon in your chief good? Perhaps you will say that they had no fear, because they foresaw, along with the suffering, their ultimate liberation and triumph. But still they must have feared for their companions, if they knew that they were to be cut off from their own kingdom, and bound for ever in the mass of darkness.

16. Had they not the charity to feel a kindly sympathy for those who were doomed to suffer eternal punishment, without having committed any sin? These souls that were to be bound up with the mass, were not they too part of your god? Were they not of the same origin, the same substance? They at least must have felt grief or fear in the prospect of their own eternal bondage. To say that they did not know what was to happen, while the others did, is to make one and the same substance partly acquainted with the future, and partly ignorant. How can you call this substance the pure, and perfect, and supreme good, if there were such evils in it, even before its mixture with the evil principle? You will have to confess your two principles either both good or both evil. If you make two evils, you may make either of them the worse, as you please. But if you make two goods, we shall have to inquire which you make the better. Meanwhile there is an end to your doctrine of two principles, one good and the other evil, which are in fact two gods, one good and the other evil. But if hurting another is evil, they both hurt one another. Perhaps the greater evil was in the principle that first began the attack. But if one began the injury, the other returned it; and not by the law of compensation, an eye for an eye, which you are foolish enough to find fault with, but with far greater severity. You must choose which you will call the worse,—the one that began the injury, or the one that had the will and the power to do still greater injury. The one tried to get a share in the enjoyment of light; the other effected the entire overthrow of its opponent. If the one had got what it desired, it would certainly have done no harm to itself. But the other, in the discomfiture of its adversary, did great mischief to part of itself; reminding us of the well-known passionate exclamation, which is on record as having been actually used, "Perish our friends, if that will rid us of our enemies."[2] For part of your god was sent to suffer hopeless contamination, that there might be a covering for the mass in which the enemy is to be buried for ever alive. So much will he continue to be dreaded even when conquered and bound, that the security, such as it is, of one part of the deity must be purchased by the eternal misery of the other parts. Such is the harmlessness of the good principle! Your god, it appears, is guilty of the crime with which you charge the race of darkness—of injuring both friends and enemies. The charge is proved in the case of your god, by that final mass in which his enemies are confined, while his own subjects are involved in it. In fact, the principle that you call god is the more injurious of the two, both to friends and to enemies. In the case of *Hyle,* there was no desire to destroy the opposite kingdom, but only to possess it; and though some of its subjects were put to death by the violence of others, they appeared again in other forms, so that in the alternation of life and death they had intervals of enjoyment in their history. But your god, with all the omnipotence and perfect excellence that you ascribe to him, dooms his enemies to eternal destruction, and his

[1] 1 Tim. i. 17.

[2] Quoted Cic. *pro Dejor.* § 9

friends to eternal punishment. And the height of insanity is in believing that while internal contest occasions the injury of the members of *Hyle*, victory brings punishment to the members of God. What means this folly? To use Faustus' comparison of God and *Hyle* to the antidote and poison, the antidote seems to be more mischievous than the poison. We do not hear of Hyle shutting up God for ever in a mass of darkness, or driving its own members into it; or, which is worst of all, slandering this unfortunate remnant, as an excuse for not effecting its purification. For Manichæus, in his Fundamental Epistle, says that these souls deserved to be thus punished, because they allowed themselves to be led away from their original brightness, and became enemies of holy light; whereas it was God himself that sent them to lose themselves in the region of darkness, that light might be opposed to light: which was unjust, if he forced them against their will; while, if they went willingly, he is ungrateful in punishing them. These souls can never have been happy, if they were tormented with fear before the conflict, from knowing that they were to become enemies to their original principle, and then in the conflict were hopelessly contaminated, and afterwards eternally condemned. On the other hand, they can never have been divine, if before the conflict they were unaware of what was coming, from want of prescience, and then showed feebleness in the conflict, and suffered misery afterwards. And what is true of them must be true of God, since they are of the same substance. Is there any hope of your seeing the folly of these blasphemies? You attempt, indeed, to vindicate the goodness of God, by asserting that *Hyle* when shut up is prevented from doing any more injury to itself. *Hyle*, it seems, is to get some good, when it has no longer any good mixed with it. Perhaps, as God before the conflict had the evil of necessity, when the good was unmixed with evil, so *Hyle* after the conflict is to have the good of rest, when the evil is unmixed with good. Your principles are thus either two evils, one worse than the other; or two goods, both imperfect, but one better than the other. The better, however, is the more miserable; for if the issue of this great conflict is that the enemy gets some good by the cessation of mutual injuries in *Hyle*, while God's own subjects suffer the serious evil of being driven into the mass of darkness, we may ask who has got the victory. The poison, we are to understand, is *Hyle*, where, nevertheless, animal life found a plentiful supply of the means of growth and productiveness; while the antidote is God, who could condemn his own members, but could not restore them. In reality, it is as absurd to call the one *Hyle*, as it is to call the other God. These are the follies of men who turn to fables because they cannot bear sound doctrine.[1]

[1] [This is one of Augustin's most effective refutations of Manichæan dualism.—A. H. N.]

BOOK XXII.

FAUSTUS STATES HIS OBJECTIONS TO THE MORALITY OF THE LAW AND THE PROPHETS, AND AUGUSTIN SEEKS BY THE APPLICATION OF THE TYPE AND THE ALLEGORY TO EXPLAIN AWAY THE MORAL DIFFICULTIES OF THE OLD TESTAMENT.

1. Faustus said: You ask why we blaspheme the law and the prophets. We are so far from professing or feeling any hostility to the law and the prophets, that we are ready, if you will allow us, to declare the falsehood of all the writings which make the law and the prophets appear objectionable. But this you refuse to admit, and by maintaining the authority of your writers, you bring a perhaps unmerited reproach upon the prophets; you slander the patriarchs, and dishonor the law. You are so unreasonable as to deny that your writers are false, while you uphold the piety and sanctity of those who are described in these writings as guilty of the worst crimes, and as leading wicked lives. These opinions are inconsistent; for either these were bad characters, or the writers were untruthful.

2. Supposing, then, that we agree in condemning the writers, we may succeed in vindicating the law and the prophets. By the law must be understood not circumcision, or Sabbaths, or sacrifices, or the other Jewish observances, but the true law, viz., Thou shalt not kill, Thou shalt not commit adultery, Thou shalt not bear false witness, and so on. To this law, promulgated throughout the world, that is, at the commencement of the present constitution of the world, the Hebrew writers did violence, by infecting it with the pollution of their disgusting precepts about circumcision and sacrifice. As a friend of

the law, you should join with me in condemning the Jews for injuring the law by this mixture of unsuitable precepts. Plainly, you must be aware that these precepts are not the law, or any part of the law, since you claim to be righteous, though you make no attempt to keep the precepts. In seeking to lead a righteous life, you pay great regard to the commandments which forbid sinful actions, while you take no notice of the Jewish observances; which would be unjustifiable if they were one and the same law. You resent as a foul reproach being called negligent of the precept, "Thou shalt not kill," or "Thou shalt not commit adultery." And if you showed the same resentment at being called uncircumcised, or negligent of the Sabbath, it would be evident that you considered both to be the law and the commandment of God. In fact, however, you consider the honor and glory of keeping the one no way endangered by disregard of the other. It is plain, as I have said, that these observances are not the law, but a disfigurement of the law. If we condemn them, it is not as being genuine, but as spurious. In this condemnation there is no reproach of the law, or of God its author, but only of those who published their shocking superstitions under these names. If we sometimes abuse the venerable name of law in attacking the Jewish precepts, the fault is yours, for refusing to distinguish between Hebrew observances and the law. Only restore to the law its proper dignity, by removing these foul Israelitish blots; grant that these writers are guilty of disfiguring the law, and you will see at once that we are the enemies not of the law, but of Judaism. You are misled by the word law; for you do not know to what that name properly belongs.

3. For my part, I see no reason for your thinking that we blaspheme your prophets and patriarchs. There would indeed be some ground for the charge, if we had been directly or remotely the authors of the account given of their actions. But as this account is written either by themselves, in a criminal desire to be famous for their misdeeds, or by their companions and coevals, why should you blame us? You condemn them in abhorrence of the wicked actions of which they have voluntarily declared themselves guilty, though there was no occasion for such a confession. Or if the narrative is only a malicious fiction, let its authors be punished, let the books be condemned, let the prophetic name be cleared from this foul reproach, let the patriarchs recover the respect due to their simplicity and purity of manners.

4. These books, moreover, contain shocking calumnies against God himself. We are told that he existed from eternity in darkness, and admired the light when he saw it; that he was so ignorant of the future, that he gave Adam a command, not foreseeing that it would be broken; that his perception was so limited that he could not see Adam when, from the knowledge of his nakedness, he hid himself in a corner of Paradise; that envy made him afraid lest his creature man should taste of the tree of life, and live for ever; that afterwards he was greedy for blood, and fat from all kinds of sacrifices, and jealous if they were offered to any one but himself; that he was enraged sometimes against his enemies, sometimes against his friends; that he destroyed thousands of men for a slight offense, or for nothing; that he threatened to come with a sword and spare nobody, righteous or wicked. The authors of such bold libels against God might very well slander the men of God. You must join with us in laying the blame on the writers if you wish to vindicate the prophets.

5. Again, we are not responsible for what is said of Abraham, that in his irrational craving to have children, and not believing God, who promised that his wife Sara should have a son, he defiled himself with a mistress, with the knowledge of his wife, which only made it worse;[1] or that, in sacrilegious profanation of his marriage, he on different occasions, from avarice and greed, sold his wife Sara for the gratification of the kings Abimelech and Pharas, telling them that she was his sister, because she was very fair.[2] The narrative is not ours, which tells how Lot, Abraham's brother, after his escape from Sodom, lay with his two daughters on the mountain[3] (better for him to have perished in the conflagration of Sodom, than to have burned with incestuous passion); or how Isaac imitated his father's conduct, and called his wife Rebecca his sister, that he might gain a shameful livelihood by her;[4] or how his son Jacob, husband of four wives—two full sisters, Rachel and Leah, and their handmaids—led the life of a goat among them, so that there was a daily strife among his women who should be the first to lay hold of him when he came from the field, ending sometimes in their hiring him from one another for the night;[5] or, again, how his son Judah slept with his daughter-in-law Tamar, after she had been married to two of his sons, deceived, we are told, by the harlot's dress which Tamar put on, knowing that her father-in-law was in the

[1] Gen. xvi. 2-4. [2] Gen. xii. 13, and xx. 2.
[3] Gen. xix. 33, 35. [4] Gen. xxvi. 7. [5] Gen. xxix. and xxx.

habit of associating with such characters;[1] or how David, after having a number of wives, seduced the wife of his soldier Uriah, and caused Uriah himself to be killed in the battle;[2] or how his son Solomon had three hundred wives, and seven hundred concubines, and princesses without number;[3] or how the first prophet Hosea got children from a prostitute, and, what is worse, it is said that this disgraceful conduct was enjoined by God;[4] or how Moses committed murder,[5] and plundered Egypt,[6] and waged wars, and commanded, or himself perpetrated, many cruelties.[7] And he too was not content with one wife. We are neither directly nor remotely the authors of these and similar narratives, which are found in the books of the patriarchs and the prophets. Either your writers forged these things, or the fathers are really guilty. Choose which you please; the crime in either case is detestable, for vicious conduct and falsehood are equally hateful.

6. Augustin replied: You understand neither the symbols of the law nor the acts of the prophets, because you do not know what holiness or righteousness means. We have repeatedly shown at great length, that the precepts and symbols of the Old Testament contained both what was to be fulfilled in obedience through the grace bestowed in the New Testament, and what was to be set aside as a proof of its having been fulfilled in the truth now made manifest. For in the love of God and of our neighbor is secured the accomplishment of the precepts of the law, while the accomplishment of its promises is shown in the abolition of circumcision, and of other typical observances formerly practised. By the precept men were led, through a sense of guilt, to desire salvation; by the promise they were led to find in the typical observances the assurance that the Saviour would come. The salvation desired was to be obtained through the grace bestowed on the appearance of the New Testament; and the fulfillment of the expectation rendered the types no longer necessary. The same law that was given by Moses became grace and truth in Jesus Christ. By the grace in the pardon of sin, the precept is kept in force in the case of those supported by divine help. By the truth the symbolic rites are set aside, that the promise might, in those who trust in the divine faithfulness, be brought to pass.

7. Those, accordingly, who, finding fault with what they do not understand, call the typical institutions of the law disfigurements and excrescences, are like men displeased with things of which they do not know the use. As if a deaf man, seeing others move their lips in speaking, were to find fault with the motion of the mouth as needless and unsightly; or as if a blind man, on hearing a house commended, were to test the truth of what he heard by passing his hand over the surface of the wall, and on coming to the windows were to cry out against them as flaws in the level, or were to suppose that the wall had fallen in.

8. How shall I make those whose minds are full of vanity understand that the actions of the prophets were also mystical and prophetic? The vanity of their minds is shown in their thinking that we believe God to have once existed in darkness, because it is written, "Darkness was over the deep."[8] As if we called the deep God, where there was darkness, because the light did not exist there before God made it by His word. From their not distinguishing between the light which is God, and the light which God made, they imagine that God must have been in darkness before He made light, because darkness was over the deep before God said, "Let there be light, and there was light." In the New Testament both these things are ascribed to God. For we read, "God is light, and in Him is no darkness at all;"[9] and again, "God, who commanded the light to shine out of darkness, hath shined in our hearts."[10] So also, in the Old Testament, the name "Brightness of eternal light"[11] is given to the wisdom of God, which certainly was not created, for by it all things were made; and of the light which exists only as the production of this wisdom it is said, "Thou wilt light my candle, O Lord; my God, Thou wilt enlighten my darkness."[12] In the same way, in the beginning, when darkness was over the deep, God said, "Let there be light, and there was light," which only the light-giving light, which is God Himself, could have made.

9. For as God is His own eternal happiness, and is besides the bestower of happiness, so He is His own eternal light, and is also the bestower of light. He envies the good of none, for He is Himself the source of happiness to all good beings; He fears the evil of none, for the loss of all evil beings is in their being abandoned by Him. He can neither be benefited by those on whom He Himself bestows happiness, nor is He afraid of those whose misery is the doom awarded by His own judgment. Very different, O Manichæus, is the object of your worship.

1 Gen. xxxviii. 2 2 Sam. xi. 4, 15. 3 1 Kings xi. 1–3. 4 Hos. i. 2, 3. 5 Ex. ii. 12. 6 Ex. xii. 35, 36. 7 Ex. xvii. 9.

8 Gen. i. 2. 9 1 John. i. 5. 10 2 Cor. iv. 6. 11 Wisd. vii. 26. 12 Ps. xviii. 28.

You have departed from God in the pursuit of your own fancies, which of all kinds have increased and multiplied in your foolish roving hearts, drinking in through the sense of sight the light of the heavenly bodies. This light, though it too is made by God, is not to be compared to the light created in the minds of the pious, whom God brings out of darkness into light, as He brings them out of sinfulness into righteousness. Still less can it be compared to that inaccessible light from which all kinds of light are derived. Nor is this light inaccessible to all; for "blessed are the pure in heart, for they shall see God."[1] "God is light, and in Him is no darkness at all;" but the wicked shall not see light, as is said in Isaiah.[2] To them the light-giving light is inaccessible. From the light comes not only the spiritual light in the minds of the pious, but also the material light, which is not denied to the wicked, but is made to rise on the evil and on the good.

10. So, when darkness was over the deep, He who was light said, "Let there be light." From what light this light came is clear; for the words are, "God said." What light is that which was made, is not so clear. For there has been a friendly discussion among students of the sacred Scriptures, whether God then made the light in the minds of the angels, or, in other words, these rational spirits themselves, or some material light which exists in the higher regions of the universe beyond our ken. For on the fourth day He made the visible luminaries of heaven. And it is also a question whether these bodies were made at the same time as their light, or were somehow kindled from the light made already. But whoever reads the sacred writings in the pious spirit which is required to understand them, must be convinced that whatever the light was which was made when, at the time that darkness was over the deep, God said, "Let there be light," it was created light, and the creating Light was the maker of it.

11. Nor does it follow that God, before He made light, abode in darkness, because it is said that darkness was over the deep, and then that the Spirit of God moved on the waters. The deep is the unfathomable abyss of the waters. And the carnal mind might suppose that the Spirit abode in the darkness which was over the deep, because it is said that He moved on the waters. This is from not understanding how the light shineth in darkness, and the darkness comprehendeth it not, till by the word of God those who were darkness are made light, and it is said to them, "Ye were once darkness, but now are ye light in the Lord."[3] But if rational minds which are in darkness through a sinful will cannot comprehend the light of the wisdom of God, though it is present everywhere, because they are separated from it not in place, but in disposition: why may not the Spirit of God have moved on the darkness of the waters, when He moved on the waters, though at an immeasurable distance from it, not in place, but in nature?

12. In all this I know I am singing to deaf ears; but the Lord, from whom is the truth which we speak, can open some ears to catch the strain. But what shall we say of those critics of the Holy Scriptures who object to God's being pleased with His own works, and find fault with the words, "God saw the light that it was good," as if this meant that God admired the light as something new? God's seeing His works that they were good, means that the Creator approved of His own works as pleasing to Himself. For God cannot be forced to do anything against His will, so that He should not be pleased with His own work; nor can He do anything by mistake, so that He should regret having done it. Why should the Manichæans object to our God seeing His work that it was good, when their god placed a covering before himself when he mingled his own members with the darkness? For instead of seeing his work that it is good, he refuses to look at it because it is evil.

13. Faustus speaks of our God as astonished, which is not said in Scripture; nor does it follow that one must be astonished when he sees anything to be good. There are many good things which we see without being astonished, as if they were better than we expected; we merely approve of them as being what they ought to be. We can, however, give an instance of God being astonished, not from the Old Testament, which the Manichæans assail with undeserved reproach, but from the New Testament, which they profess to believe in order to entrap the unwary. For they acknowledge Christ as God, and use this as a bait to entice Christ's followers into their snares. God, then, was astonished when Christ was astonished. For we read in the Gospel, that when Christ heard the faith of a certain centurion, He was astonished, and said to His disciples, "Verily I have not found so great faith, no, not in Israel."[4] We have already given our explanation of the words, "God saw that it was good." Better men may give a better explanation. Mean-

[1] Matt. v. 8.
[2] Isa. viii. 20.
[3] Eph. v. 8
[4] Matt. viii. 10.

while let the Manichæans explain Christ's being astonished at what He foresaw before it happened, and knew before He heard it. For though seeing a thing to be good is quite different from being astonished at it, in this case there is some resemblance, for Jesus was astonished at the light of faith which He Himself had created in the heart of the centurion; for Jesus is the true light, which enlighteneth every man that cometh into the world.

14. Thus an irreligious Pagan might bring the same reproaches against Christ in the Gospel, as Faustus brings against God in the Old Testament. He might say that Christ lacked foresight, not only because He was astonished at the faith of the centurion, but because He chose Judas as a disciple who proved disobedient to His commands; as Faustus objects to the precept given in Paradise, which, as it turned out, was not obeyed. He might also cavil at Christ's not knowing who touched Him, when the woman suffering from an issue of blood touched the hem of His garment; as Faustus blames God for not knowing where Adam had hid himself. If this ignorance is implied in God's saying, "Where art thou, Adam?"[1] the same may be said of Christ's asking, "Who touched me?"[2] The Pagans also might call Christ timid and envious, in not wishing five of the ten virgins to gain eternal life by entering into His kingdom, and in shutting them out, so that they knocked in vain in their entreaty to have the door opened, as if forgetful of His own promise, "Knock, and it shall be opened unto you;"[3] as Faustus charges God with fear and envy in not admitting man after his sin to eternal life. Again, he might call Christ greedy of the blood, not of beasts, but of men, because he said, "He that loseth his life for my sake, shall keep it unto life eternal;"[4] as Faustus reproaches God in reference to those animal sacrifices which prefigured the sacrifice of blood-shedding by which we are redeemed. He might also accuse Christ of jealousy, because in narrating His driving the buyers and sellers out of the temple, the evangelist quotes as applicable to Him the words, "The jealousy of Thine house hath eaten me up;"[5] as Faustus accuses God of jealousy in forbidding sacrifices to be offered to other gods. He might say that Christ was angry with both His friends and His enemies: with His friends, because He said, "The servant that knows his lord's will, and doeth it not, shall be beaten with many stripes;" and with His enemies, because He said, "If any one shall not receive you, shake off against him the dust of your shoes; verily I say unto you, that it shall be more tolerable for Sodom in the day of judgment than for that city;"[6] as Faustus accuses God of being angry at one time with His friends, and at another with His enemies; both of whom are spoken of thus by the apostle: "They that have sinned without law shall perish without law, and they that have sinned in the law shall be judged by the law."[7] Or he might say that Christ shed the blood of many without mercy, for a slight offense or for nothing. For to a Pagan there would appear to be little or no harm in not having a wedding garment at the marriage feast, for which our King in the Gospel commanded a man to be bound hand and foot, and cast into outer darkness;[8] or in not wishing to have Christ for a king, which is the sin of which Christ says, "Those that would not have me to reign over them, bring hither and slay before me;"[9] as Faustus blames God in the Old Testament for slaughtering thousands of human beings for slight offenses, as Faustus calls them, or for nothing. Again, if Faustus finds fault with God's threatening to come with the sword, and to spare neither the righteous nor the wicked, might not the Pagan find as much fault with the words of the Apostle Paul, when he says of our God, "He spared not His own Son, but gave Him up for us all;"[10] or of Peter, when, in exhorting the saints to be patient in the midst of persecution and slaughter, he says, "It is time that judgment begin from the house of God; and if it first begin at us, what shall the end be of them that believe not the gospel of the Lord? And if the righteous scarcely be saved, where shall the ungodly and sinner appear?"[11] What can be more righteous than the Only-Begotten, whom nevertheless the Father did not spare? And what can be plainer than that the righteous also are not spared, but chastised with manifold afflictions, as is clearly implied in the words, "If the righteous scarcely are saved"? As it is said in the Old Testament, "Whom the Lord loveth He correcteth, and chastiseth every son whom He receiveth;"[12] and, "If we receive good at the hand of the Lord, shall we not also receive evil?"[13] So we read also in the New Testament, "Whom I love I rebuke and chasten;"[14] and, "If we judge ourselves, we shall not be judged of the Lord; but when we are judged, we are corrected of the Lord, that we may not be condemned with the world."[15] If a Pagan were

1 Gen. iii. 9. 2 Luke viii. 44, 45. 3 Matt. vii. 7. 4 Matt. x. 39. 5 John ii. 17.

6 Matt. x. 14, 15. 7 Rom. ii. 12. 8 Matt. xxii. 11, 15. 9 Luke xix. 27. 10 Rom. viii. 32. 11 1 Pet. iv. 17, 18. 12 Prov. iii. 12. 13 Job ii. 10. 14 Rev. iii. 19. 15 1 Cor. xi. 31, 32.

to make such objections to the New Testament, would not the Manichæans try to answer them, though they themselves make similar objections to the Old Testament? But supposing them able to answer the Pagan, how absurd it would be to defend in the one Testament what they find fault with in the other! But if they could not answer the objections of the Pagan, why should they not allow in both Testaments, instead of in one only, that what appears wrong to unbelievers, from their ignorance, should be believed to be right by pious readers even when they also are ignorant?

15. Perhaps our opponents will maintain that these parallel passages quoted from the New Testament are themselves neither authoritative nor true: for they claim the impious liberty of holding and teaching, that whatever they deem favorable to their heresy was said by Christ and the apostles; while they have the profane boldness to say, that whatever in the same writings is unfavorable to them is a spurious interpolation I have already at some length, as far as the intention of the present work required, exposed the unreasonableness of this assault upon the authority of the whole of Scripture.

16. At present I would call attention to the fact, that when the Manichæans, although they disguise their blasphemous absurdities under the name of Christianity, bring such objections against the Christian Scriptures, we have to defend the authority of the divine record in both Testaments against the Manichæans as much as against the Pagans. A Pagan might find fault with passages in the New Testament in the same way as Faustus does with what he calls unworthy representations of God in the Old Testament; and the Pagan might be answered by the quotation of similar passages from his own authors, as in Paul's speech at Athens.[1] Even in Pagan writings we might find the doctrine that God created and constructed the world, and that He is the giver of light, which does not imply that before light was made He abode in darkness; and that when His work was finished He was elated with joy, which is more than saying that He saw that it was good; and that He made a law with rewards for obedience, and punishments for disobedience, by which they do not mean to say that God was ignorant of the future, because He gave a law to those by whom it was to be broken. Nor could they make asking questions a proof of a want of foresight even in a human being; for in their books many questions are asked only for the purpose of using the answers for the conviction of the persons addressed: for the questioner knows not only what answer he desires, but what will actually be given. Again, if the Pagan tried to make out God to be envious of any one, because He will not give happiness to the wicked, he would find many passages in the writings of his own authors in support of this principle of the divine government.

17. The only objection that a Pagan would make on the subject of sacrifice would refer to our reason for finding fault with Pagan sacrifices, when in the Old Testament God is described as requiring men to offer sacrifice to Him. If I were to reply at length on this subject, I might prove to him that sacrifice is due only to the one true God, and that this sacrifice was offered by the one true Priest, the Mediator of God and man; and that it was proper that this sacrifice should be prefigured by animal sacrifices, in order to foreshadow the flesh and blood of the one sacrifice for the remission of sins contracted by flesh and blood, which shall not inherit the kingdom of God: for the natural body will be endowed with heavenly attributes, as the fire in the sacrifice typified the swallowing up of death in victory. Those observances properly belonged to the people whose kingdom and priesthood were prophetic of the King and Priest who should come to govern and to consecrate believers in all nations, and to lead them into the kingdom of heaven, and the holy society of angels and eternal life. And as this true sacrifice was piously set forth in the Hebrew observances, so it was impiously caricatured by the Pagans, because, as the apostle says, what they offer they offer to devils, and not to God.[2] The typical rite of blood-shedding in sacrifice dates from the earliest ages, pointing forward from the outset of human history to the passion of the Mediator. For Abel is mentioned in the sacred Scripture as the first who offered such sacrifices.[3] We need not therefore wonder that fallen angels who occupy the air, and whose chief sins are pride and falsehood, should demand from their worshippers by whom they wished to be considered as gods what they knew to be due to God only. This deception was favored by the folly of the human heart, especially when regret for the dead led to the making of likenesses, and so to the use of images.[4] By the increase of this homage, divine honors came to be paid to the dead as dwelling in heaven, while devils took their place on earth as the objects of worship,

[1] Acts xvii. 28.

[2] 1 Cor. x. 20.

[3] Gen. iv. 4.

[4] Wisd. xiv. 15.

and required that their deluded and degraded votaries should present sacrifices to them. Thus the nature of sacrifice as due only to God appears not only when God righteously claims it, but also when a false god proudly arrogates it. If the Pagan was slow to believe these things, I should argue from the prophecies, and point out that, though uttered long ago, they are now fulfilled. If he still remained in unbelief, this is rather to be expected than to be wondered at; for the prophecy itself intimates that all would not believe.

18. If the Pagan, in the next place, were to find fault with both Testaments as attributing jealousy to God and Christ, he would only show his own ignorance of literature, or his forgetfulness. For though their philosophers distinguish between desire and passion, joy and gratification, caution and fear, gentleness and tender-heartedness, prudence and cunning, boldness and daring, and so on, giving the first name in each pair to what is good, and the second to what is bad, their books are notwithstanding full of instances in which, by the abuse of these words, virtues are called by the names which properly belong to vices; as passion is used for desire, gratification for joy, fear for caution, tender-heartedness for gentleness, cunning for prudence, daring for boldness. The cases are innumerable in which speech exhibits similar inaccuracies. Moreover, each language has its own idioms. For in religious writings I remember no instance of the word tender-heartedness being used in a bad sense. And common usage affords examples of similar peculiarities in the use of words. In Greek, one word stands for two distinct things, labor and pain; while we have a separate name for each. Again, we use the word in two senses, as when we say of what is not dead, that it has life; and again, of any one that he is a man of good life, whereas in Greek each of these meanings has a word of its own. So that, apart from the abuse of words which prevails in all languages, it may be an Hebrew idiom to use jealousy in two senses, as a man is called jealous when he suffers from a diseased state of mind caused by distress on account of the faithlessness of his wife, in which sense the word cannot be applied to God; or as when diligence is manifested in guarding conjugal chastity, in which sense it is profitable for us not only unhesitatingly to admit, but thankfully to assert, that God is jealous of His people when He calls them His wife, and warns them against committing adultery with a multitude of false gods. The same may be said of the anger of God. For God does not suffer perturbation when He visits men in anger; but either by an abuse of the word, or by a peculiarity of idiom, anger is used in the sense of punishment.

19. The slaughter of multitudes would not seem strange to the Pagan, unless he denied the judgment of God, which Pagans do not; for they allow that all things in the universe, from the highest to the lowest, are governed by God's providence. But if he would not allow this, he would be convinced either by the authority of Pagan writers, or by the more tedious method of demonstration; and if still obstinate and perverse, he would be left to the judgment which he denies. Then, if he were to give instances of the destruction of men for no offense, or for a very slight one, we should show that these were offenses, and that they were not slight. For instance, to take the case already referred to of the wedding garment, we should prove that it was a great crime in a man to attend the sacred feast, seeking not the bridegroom's glory, but his own, or whatever the garment may be found on better interpretation to signify. And in the case of the slaughter before the king of those who would not have him to reign over them, we might perhaps easily prove that, though it may be no sin in a man to refuse to obey his fellow-man, it is both a fault and a great one to reject the reign of Him in whose reign alone is there righteousness, and happiness, and continuance.

20. Lastly, as regards Faustus' crafty insinuation, that the Old Testament misrepresents God as threatening to come with a sword which will spare neither the righteous nor the wicked, if the words were explained to the Pagan, he would perhaps disagree neither with the Old Testament nor with the New; and he might see the beauty of the parable in the Gospel, which people who pretend to be Christians either misunderstand from their blindness, or reject from their perversity. The great husbandman of the vine uses his pruning-hook differently in the fruitful and in the unfruitful branches; yet he spares neither good nor bad, pruning one and cutting off the other.[1] There is no man so just as not to require to be tried by affliction to advance, or to establish, or to prove his virtue. Do the Manichæans not reckon Paul as righteous, who, while confessing humbly and honestly his past sins, still gives thanks for being justified by faith in Jesus Christ? Was Paul then spared by Him whom fools misunderstand, when He says, "I will spare neither the righteous nor the sinner"? Hear the

[1] John xv. 1-3.

apostle himself: "Lest I should be exalted above measure by the abundance of the revelation, there was given me a thorn in the flesh, a messenger of Satan to buffet me. For this I besought the Lord thrice, that He would remove it from me; and He said unto me, My grace is sufficient for thee: for strength is perfected in weakness."[1] Here a just man is not spared that his strength might be perfected in weakness by Him who had given him an angel of Satan to buffet him. If you say that the devil gave this angel, it follows that the devil sought to prevent Paul's being exalted above measure by the abundance of the revelation, and to perfect his strength. This is impossible. Therefore He who gave up this righteous man to be buffeted by the messenger of Satan, is the same as He who, through Paul, gave up to Satan himself the wicked persons of whom Paul says: "I have delivered them to Satan, that they may learn not to blaspheme."[2] Do you see now how the Most High spares neither the righteous nor the wicked? Or is it the sword that frightens you? For to be buffeted is not so bad as to be put to death. But did not the thousands of martyrs suffer death in various forms? And could their persecutors have had this power against them except it had been given them by God, who thus spared neither the righteous nor the wicked? For the Lord Himself, the chief martyr, says expressly to Pilate: "Thou couldst have no power at all against me, except it were given thee from above."[3] Paul also, besides recording his own experience, says that the afflictions and persecutions of the righteous exhibit the judgment of God.[4] This truth is set forth at length by the Apostle Peter in the passage already quoted, where he says: "It is time that judgment should begin at the house of the Lord. And if it first begin at us, what shall the end be of those that believe not the gospel of God? And if the righteous scarcely are saved, where shall the ungodly and the sinner appear?"[5] Peter also explains how the wicked are not spared, for they are branches broken off to be burnt; while the righteous are not spared, because their purification is to be brought to perfection. He ascribes these things to the will of Him who says in the Old Testament, I will spare neither the righteous nor the wicked; for he says: "It is better, if the will of the Spirit of God be so, that we suffer for well-doing than for evil-doing."[6] So, when by the will of the Spirit of God men suffer for well-doing, the righteous are not spared; when they suffer for evil-doing, the wicked are not spared. In both cases it is according to the will of Him who says: I will spare neither the righteous nor the wicked; correcting the one as a son, and punishing the other as a transgressor.

21. I have thus shown, to the best of my power, that the God we worship did not abide from eternity in darkness, but is Himself light, and in Him is no darkness at all; and in Himself dwells in light inaccessible; and the brightness of this light is His coeternal wisdom. From what we have said, it appears that God was not taken by surprise by the unexpected appearance of light, but that light owes its existence to Him as its Creator, as its owes its continued existence to His approval. Neither was God ignorant of the future, but the author of the precept as well as the punisher of disobedience; that by showing His righteous anger against transgression, He might provide a restraint for the time, and a warning for the future Nor does He ask questions from ignorance, but by His very inquiry declares His judgment. Nor is He envious or timid, but excludes the transgressor from eternal life, which is the just reward of obedience. Nor is He greedy for blood and fat; but by requiring from a carnal people sacrifices, suited to their character, He by certain types prefigures the true sacrifice. Nor is His jealousy an emotion of pale anxiety, but of quiet benevolence, in desire to keep the soul, which owes chastity to the one true God, from being defiled and prostituted by serving many false gods. Nor is He enraged with a passion similar to human anger, but is angry, not in the sense of desiring vengeance, but in the peculiar sense of giving full effect to the sentence of a righteous retribution. Nor does He destroy thousands of men for trifling offenses, or for nothing, but manifests to the world the benefit to be obtained from fearing Him, by the temporal death of those already mortal. Nor does He punish the righteous and sinners indiscriminately, but chastises the righteous for their good, in order to perfect them, and gives to sinners the punishment justly due to them. Thus, ye Manichæans, do your suspicions lead you astray, when, by misunderstanding our Scriptures, or by hearing bad interpreters, you form a mistaken judgment of Catholics. Hence you leave sound doctrine, and turn to impious fables; and in your perversity and estrangement from the society of saints, you reject the instruction of the New Testament, which, as we have shown, contains statements similar to those which you condemn in the Old Testament. So we are

1 2 Cor. xii. 7–9. 2 1 Tim. i. 20. 3 John xix. 11.
4 2 Thess. i. 5. 5 1 Pet. iv. 17, 18 6 1 Pet. iii. 17.

obliged to defend both Testaments against you as well as against the Pagans.

22. But supposing that there is some one so deluded by carnality as to worship not the God whom we worship, who is one and true, but the fiction of your suspicions or your slanders, whom you say we worship, is not even this god better than yours? Observe, I beseech you, what must be plain to the feeblest understanding; for here there is no need of great perspicacity. I address all, wise and unwise. I appeal to the common sense and judgment of all alike. Hear, consider, judge. Would it not have been better for your god to have remained in darkness from eternity, than to have plunged the light coeternal with him and cognate to him into darkness? Would it not have been better to have expressed admiration in surprise at the appearance of a new light coming to scatter the darkness, than to have been unable to baffle the assault of darkness except by the concession of his own light? Unhappy if he did this in alarm, and cruel if there was no need of it. Surely it would have been better to see light, made by himself, and to admire it as good, than to make the light begotten by himself evil; better than that his own light should become hostile to himself in repelling the forces of darkness. For this will be the accusation against those who will be condemned for ever to the mass of darkness, that they suffered themselves to lose their original brightness, and became the enemies of sacred light. If they did not know from eternity that they would be thus condemned, they must have suffered the darkness of eternal ignorance; or if they did know, the darkness of eternal fear. Thus part of the substance of your god really did remain from eternity in its own darkness; and instead of admiring new light on its appearance, it only met with another and a hostile darkness, of which it had always been in fear. Indeed, God himself must have been in the darkness of fear for this part of himself, if he was dreading the evil coming upon it. If he did not foresee the evil, he must have been in the darkness of ignorance. If he foresaw it, and was not in fear, the darkness of such cruelty is worse than the darkness either of ignorance or of fear. Your god appears to be destitute of the quality which the apostle commends in the body, which you insanely believe to be made not by God, but by *Hyle*: "If one member suffers, all the members suffer with it."[1] But suppose he did suffer; he foresaw, he feared, he suffered, but he could not help himself. Thus he remained from eternity in the darkness of his own misery; and then, instead of admiring a new light which was to drive away the darkness, he came in contact, to the injury of his own light, with another darkness which he had always dreaded. Again, would it not have been much better, I say, not to have given a commandment like God, but even to have received a commandment like Adam, which he would be rewarded for keeping and punished for breaking, acting either way by his own free-will, than to be forced by inevitable necessity to admit darkness into his light in spite of himself? Surely it would have been better to have given a precept to human nature, not knowing that it would become sinful, than to have been driven by necessity to sin contrary to his own divine nature. Think for a moment, and say how darkness could be conquered by one who was himself conquered by necessity. Conquered already by this greater enemy, he fought under his conqueror's orders against a less formidable opponent. Would it not have been better not to know where Adam had hid himself, than to have been himself destitute of any means of escape, first from a hard and hateful necessity, and then from a dissimilar and hostile race? Would it not have been better to grudge eternal life to human nature, than to consign to misery the divine nature; to desire the blood and fat of sacrifices, than to be himself slaughtered in so many forms, on account of his mixture with the blood and fat of every victim; to be disturbed by jealousy at these sacrifices being offered to other gods as well as to himself, than to be himself offered on all altars to all devils, as mixed up not only with all fruits, but also with all animals? Would it not have been much better to be affected even with human anger, so as to be enraged against both his friends and his enemies for their sins, than to be himself influenced by fear as well as by anger wherever these passions exist, or than to share in all the sin that is committed, and in all punishment that is suffered? For this is the doom of that part of your god which is in confinement everywhere, condemned to this by himself, not as guilty, but in order to conquer his dreaded enemy. Doomed himself to such a fatal necessity, the part of himself which he has given over to condemnation might pardon him, if he were as humble as he is miserable. But how can you pretend to find fault with God for His anger against both friends and enemies when they sin, when the god of your fancies first under compulsion compels his own members to go to be devoured by sin, and then condemns them to remain in dark-

[1] 1 Cor. xii. 26.

ness? Though he does this, you say that it will not be in anger. But will he not be ashamed to punish, or to appear to punish, those from whom he should ask pardon in words such as these: "Forgive me, I beseech you. You are my members; could I treat you thus, except from necessity? You know yourselves, that you were sent here because a formidable enemy had arisen; and now you must remain here to prevent his rising again"? Again, is it not better to slay thousands of men for trifling faults, or for nothing, than to cast into the abyss of sin, and to condemn to the punishment of eternal imprisonment, God's own members, his substance—in fact, God himself? It cannot properly be said of the real substance of God that it has the choice of sinning or not sinning, for God's substance is absolutely unchangeable. God cannot sin, as He cannot deny Himself. Man, on the contrary, can sin and deny God, or he can choose not to do so. But suppose the members of your god had, like a rational human soul, the choice of sinning or not sinning; they might perhaps be justly punished for heinous offenses by confinement in the mass of darkness. But you cannot attribute to these parts a liberty which you deny to God himself. For if God had not given them up to sin, he would have been forced to sin himself, by the prevalence of the race of darkness. But if there was no danger of being thus forced, it was a sin to send these parts to a place where they incurred this danger. To do so, indeed, from free choice is a crime deserving the torment which your god unnaturally inflicts upon his own parts, more than the conduct of these parts in going by his command to a place where they lost the power of living in righteousness. But if God himself was in danger of being forced to sin by invasion and capture, unless he had secured himself first by the misconduct and then by the punishment of his own parts, there can have been no free-will either in your god or in his parts. Let him not set himself up as judge, but confess himself a criminal. For though he was forced against his own will, he professes to pass a righteous sentence in condemning those whom he knows to have suffered evil rather than done it; making this profession that he may not be thought of as having been conquered; as if it could do a beggar any good to be called prosperous and happy. Surely it would have been better for your god to have spared neither righteous nor wicked in indiscriminate punishment (which is Faustus' last charge against our God), than to have been so cruel to his own members,—first giving them up to incurable contamination, and then, as if that was not enough, accusing them falsely of misconduct. Faustus declares that they justly suffer this severe and eternal punishment, because they allowed themselves to be led astray from their original brightness, and became hostile to sacred light. But the reason of this, as Faustus says, was that they were so greedily devoured in the first assault of the princes of darkness, that they were unable to recover themselves, or to separate themselves from the hostile principle. These souls, therefore, did no evil themselves, but in all this were innocent sufferers. The real agent was he who sent them away from himself into this wretchedness. They suffered more from their father than from their enemy. Their father sent them into all this misery; while their enemy desired them as something good, wishing not to hurt them, but to enjoy them. The one injured them knowingly, the other in ignorance. This god was so weak and helpless that he could not otherwise secure himself first against an enemy threatening attack, and then against the same enemy in confinement. Let him, then, not condemn those parts whose obedience defended him, and whose death secures his safety. If he could not avoid the conflict, why slander his defenders? When these parts allowed themselves to be led astray from their original brightness, and became hostile to sacred light, this must have been from the force of the enemy; and if they were forced against their will, they are innocent; while, if they could have resisted had they chosen, there is no need of the origin of evil in an imaginary evil nature, since it is to be found in free-will. Their not resisting, when they could have done so, is plainly their own fault, and not owing to any force from without For, supposing them able to do a thing, to do which is right, while not to do it is great and heinous sin, their not doing it is their own choice. So, then, if they choose not to do it, the fault is in their will not in necessity. The origin of sin is in the will; therefore in the will is also the origin of evil, both in the sense of acting against a just precept, and in the sense of suffering under a just sentence. There is thus no reason why, in your search for the origin of evil, you should fall into so great an evil as that of calling a nature so rich in good things the nature of evil, and of attributing the terrible evil of necessity to the nature of perfect good, before any commixture with evil. The cause of this erroneous belief is your pride, which you need not have unless you choose; but in your wish to defend at all hazards the error into which you have fallen, you take away the origin of evil from free-will, and place it in a fabulous nature of evil. And thus you come at last to say, that the souls which are to be doomed to eternal confinement in the mass of darkness became enemies to sacred light not from choice, but by necessity; and to make your god a judge with whom it is of no use to prove, in behalf of your clients, that they were under compulsion, and a king who will make no allowance for your brethren, his own sons and members, whose hostility against you and against himself you ascribe not to choice, but to necessity. What shocking cruelty! unless you proceed in the next place to defend your god, as also acting not from choice, but by necessity. So, if there could be found another judge free from necessity, who could decide the question on the principles of equity, he would sentence your god to be bound to this mass, not by being fastened on the outside, but by being shut up inside along with the formidable enemy. The first in the guilt of necessity ought to be first in the sentence of condemnation. Would it not be much better, then, in comparison with such a god as this, to choose the god whom we indeed do not worship, but whom you think or pretend to think we worship? Though he spares not his servants, whether righteous or sinful, making no proper separation, and not distinguishing between punishment and discipline, is he not better than the god who spares not his own members though innocent, if necessity is no crime, or guilty from their obedience to him, if necessity itself is criminal; so that they are condemned eternally by him, along with whom they should have been released, if any liberty was recovered by the victory, while he should have been condemned along with them if the victory reduced the force of necessity even so far as to give this small amount of force to justice? Thus the god whom you represent us as worshipping, though he is not the one true God whom we really worship, is far better than your god. Neither, indeed, has any existence; but both are the creatures of your imaginations. But, according to your own representations, the one whom you call ours, and find fault with, is better than the one whom you call your own, and whom you worship.[1]

23. So also the patriarchs and prophets whom you cry out against are not the men whom we honor, but men whose characters are drawn from your fancy, prompted by ill-will. And yet even thus as you paint them, I will not be content with showing them to be superior to your elect, who keep all the precepts of Manichæus, but will prove their superiority to your god himself. Before proving this, however, I must, with the help of God, defend our holy fathers the patriarchs and prophets against your accusations, by a clear exposition of the truth as opposed to the carnality of your hearts. As for you Manichæans, it would be enough to say that the faults you impute to our fathers are preferable to what you praise in your own, and to complete your shame by adding that your god can be proved far inferior to our fathers as you describe them. This would be a sufficient reply for you. But as, even apart from your perversities, some minds are of themselves disturbed when comparing the life of the prophets in the Old Testament with that of the apostles in the New,—not discerning between the manner of the time when the promise was under a veil, and that of the time when the promise is revealed,—I must first of all reply to those who either have the boldness to pride themselves as superior in *temperance* to the prophets, or quote the prophets in defence of their own bad conduct.

24. First of all, then, not only the speech of these men, but their life also, was prophetic; and the whole kingdom of the Hebrews was like a great prophet, corresponding to the greatness of the Person prophesied. So, as regards those Hebrews who were made wise in heart by divine instruction, we may discover a prophecy of the coming of Christ and of the Church, both in what they said and in what they did; and the same is true as regards the divine procedure towards the whole nation as a body. For, as the apostle says, "all these things were our examples."

25. Those who find fault with the prophets, accusing them of adultery for instance, in actions which are above their comprehension, are like those Pagans who profanely charge Christ with folly or madness because He looked for fruit from a tree out of the season;[2] or with childishness, because He stooped down and wrote on the ground, and, after answering the people who were questioning Him, began writing again.[3] Such critics are incapable of understanding that certain virtues in great minds resemble closely the vices of little minds, not in reality, but in appearance. Such criticism of the great is like that of boys at school, whose learning consists in the important rule, that if the nominative is in the singular, the verb must also be in the singular; and so they find fault with the best Latin

[1] [Augustin certainly makes it appear that the God in the Old Testament is not so bad as the God of the Manichæans, yet he cannot be said to reach a complete theodicy.—A. H. N.]

[2] Matt. xxi. 19.

[3] John viii. 6-8.

author, because he says, *Pars in frusta secant.*[1] He should have written, say they, *secat.* And again, knowing that *religio* is spelt with one *l*, they blame him for writing *relligio*, when he says, *Relligione patrum.*[2] Hence it may with reason be said, that as the poetical usage of words differs from the solecisms and barbarisms of the unlearned, so, in their own way, the figurative actions of the prophets differ from the impure actions of the vicious. Accordingly, as a boy guilty of a barbarism would be whipped if he pled the usage of Virgil; so any one quoting the example of Abraham begetting a son from Hagar, in defence of his own sinful passion for his wife's handmaid, ought to be corrected not by caning only, but by severe scourging, that he may not suffer the doom of adulterers in eternal punishment. This indeed is a comparison of great and important subjects with trifles; and it is not intended that a peculiar usage in speech should be put on a level with a sacrament, or a solecism with adultery. Still, allowing for the difference in the character of the subjects, what is called learning or ignorance in the proprieties and improprieties of speech, resembles wisdom or the want of it in reference to the grand moral distinction between virtue and vice.[3]

26. Instead of entering on the distinctions between the praiseworthy and the blameworthy, the criminal and the innocent, the dangerous and the harmless, the guilty and the guiltless, the desirable and the undesirable, which are all illustrations of the distinction between sin and righteousness, we must first consider what sin is, and then examine the actions of the saints as recorded in the holy books, that, if we find these saints described as sinning, we may if possible discover the true reason for keeping these sins in memory by putting them on record. Again, if we find things recorded which, though they are not sins, appear so to the foolish and the malevolent, and in fact do not exhibit any virtues, here also we have to see why these things are put into the Scriptures which we believe to contain wholesome doctrine as a guide in the present life, and a title to the inheritance of the future. As regards the examples of righteousness found among the acts of the saints, the propriety of recording these must be plain even to the ignorant. The question is about those actions the mention of which may seem useless if they are neither righteous nor sinful, or even dangerous if the actions are really sinful, as leading people to imitate them, because they are not condemned in these books, and so may be supposed not to be sinful, or because, though they are condemned, men may copy them from the idea that they must be venial if saints did them.

27. Sin, then, is any transgression in deed, or word, or desire, of the eternal law. And the eternal law is the divine order or will of God, which requires the preservation of natural order, and forbids the breach of it. But what is this natural order in man? Man, we know, consists of soul and body; but so does a beast. Again, it is plain that in the order of nature the soul is superior to the body. Moreover, in the soul of man there is reason, which is not in a beast. Therefore, as the soul is superior to the body, so in the soul itself the reason is superior by the law of nature to the other parts which are found also in beasts; and in reason itself, which is partly contemplation and partly action, contemplation is unquestionably the superior part. The object of contemplation is the image of God, by which we are renewed through faith to sight. Rational action ought therefore to be subject to the control of contemplation, which is exercised through faith while we are absent from the Lord, as it will be hereafter through sight, when we shall be like Him, for we shall see Him as He is.[4] Then in a spiritual body we shall by His grace be made equal to angels, when we put on the garment of immortality and incorruption, with which this mortal and corruptible shall be clothed, that death may be swallowed up of victory, when righteousness is perfected through grace. For the holy and lofty angels have also their contemplation and action. They require of themselves the performance of the commands of Him whom they contemplate, whose eternal government they freely because sweetly obey. We, on the other hand, whose body is dead because of sin, till God quicken also our mortal bodies by His Spirit dwelling in us, live righteously in our feeble measure, according to the eternal law in which the law of nature is preserved, when we live by that faith unfeigned which works by love, having in a good conscience a hope of immortality and incorruption laid up in heaven, and of the perfecting of righteousness to the measure of an inexpressible satisfaction, for which in our pilgrimage we must hunger and thirst, while we walk by faith and not by sight.

28. A man, therefore, who acts in obedience to the faith which obeys God, restrains all mortal affections, and keeps them within the natural limit, regulating his desires so as to

1 *Æn.* i. 212.
2 *Æn.* ii. 715.
3 [This comparison of the objectors to the Old Testament to blundering school-boys is very fine.—A. H. N.]

4 1 John iii. 2.

put the higher before the lower. If there was no pleasure in what is unlawful, no one would sin. To sin is to indulge this pleasure instead of restraining it. And by unlawful is meant what is forbidden by the law in which the order of nature is preserved. It is a great question whether there is any rational creature for which there is no pleasure in what is unlawful. If there is such a class of creatures, it does not include man, nor that angelic nature which abode not in the truth. These rational creatures were so made, that they had the potentiality of restraining their desires from the unlawful; and in not doing this they sinned. Great, then, is the creature man, for he is restored by this potentiality, by which, if he had so chosen, he would not have fallen. And great is the Lord, and greatly to be praised, who created man. For He created also inferior natures which cannot sin, and superior natures which will not sin. Beasts do not sin, for their nature agrees with the eternal law from being subject to it, without being in possession of it. And again, angels do not sin, because their heavenly nature is so in possession of the eternal law that God is the only object of its desire, and they obey His will without any experience of temptation. But man, whose life on this earth is a trial on account of sin, subdues to himself what he has in common with beasts, and subdues to God what he has in common with angels; till, when righteousness is perfected and immortality attained, he shall be raised from among beasts and ranked with angels.

29. The exercise or indulgence of the bodily appetites is intended to secure the continued existence and the invigoration of the individual or of the species. If the appetites go beyond this, and carry the man, no longer master of himself, beyond the limits of temperance, they become unlawful and shameful lusts, which severe discipline must subdue. But if this unbridled course ends in plunging the man into such a depth of evil habits that he supposes that there will be no punishment of his sinful passions, and so refuses the wholesome discipline of confession and repentance by which he might be rescued; or, from a still worse insensibility, justifies his own indulgences in profane opposition to the eternal law of Providence; and if he dies in this state, that unerring law sentences him now not to correction, but to damnation.

30. Referring, then, to the eternal law which enjoins the preservation of natural order and forbids the breach of it, let us see how our father Abraham sinned, that is, how he broke this law, in the things which Faustus has charged him with as highly criminal. In his irrational craving to have children, says Faustus, and not believing God, who promised that his wife Sara should have a son, he defiled himself with a mistress. But here Faustus, in his irrational desire to find fault, both discloses the impiety of his heresy, and in his error and ignorance praises Abraham's intercourse with the handmaid. For as the eternal law—that is, the will of God the Creator of all—for the preservation of the natural order, permits the indulgence of the bodily appetite under the guidance of reason in sexual intercourse, not for the gratification of passion, but for the continuance of the race through the procreation of children; so, on the contrary, the unrighteous law of the Manichæans, in order to prevent their god, whom they bewail as confined in all seeds, from suffering still closer confinement in the womb, requires married people not on any account to have children, their great desire being to liberate their god. Instead, therefore, of an irrational craving in Abraham to have children, we find in Manichæus an irrational fancy against having children. So the one preserved the natural order by seeking in marriage only the production of a child; while the other, influenced by his heretical notions, thought no evil could be greater than the confinement of his god.

31. So, again, when Faustus says that the wife's being privy to her husband's conduct made the matter worse, while he is prompted only by the uncharitable wish to reproach Abraham and his wife, he really, without intending it, speaks in praise of both. For Sara did not connive at any criminal action in her husband for the gratification of his unlawful passions; but from the same natural desire for children that he had, and knowing her own barrenness, she warrantably claimed as her own the fertility of her handmaid; not consenting with sinful desires in her husband, but requesting of him what it was proper in him to grant. Nor was it the request of proud assumption; for every one knows that the duty of a wife is to obey her husband. But in reference to the body, we are told by the apostle that the wife has power over her husband's body, as he has over hers;[1] so that, while in all other social matters the wife ought to obey her husband, in this one matter of their bodily connection as man and wife their power over one another is mutual,—the man over the woman, and the woman over the man. So, when Sara could not have children of her own, she wished to have them by her handmaid, and of the same seed from

[1] 1 Cor. vii. 4.

which she herself would have had them, if that had been possible. No woman would do this if her love for her husband were merely an animal passion; she would rather be jealous of a mistress than make her a mother. So here the pious desire for the procreation of children was an indication of the absence of criminal indulgence.

32. Abraham, indeed, cannot be defended, if, as Faustus says, he wished to get children by Hagar, because he had no faith in God, who promised that he should have children by Sara. But this is an entire mistake: this promise had not yet been made. Any one who reads the preceding chapters will find that Abraham had already got the promise of the land with a countless number of inhabitants,[1] but that it had not yet been made known to him how the seed spoken of was to be produced, whether by generation from his own body, or from his choice in the adoption of a son, or, in the case of its being from his own body, whether it would be by Sara or another. Whoever examines into this will find that Faustus has made either an imprudent mistake or an impudent misrepresentation. Abraham, then, when he saw that he had no children, though the promise was to his seed, thought first of adoption. This appears from his saying of his slave, when speaking to God, "This is mine heir;" as much as to say, As Thou hast not given me a seed of my own, fulfill Thy promise in this man. For the word seed may be applied to what has not come out of a man's own body, else the apostle could not call us the seed of Abraham: for we certainly are not his descendants in the flesh; but we are his seed in following his faith, by believing in Christ, whose flesh did spring from the flesh of Abraham. Then Abraham was told by the Lord: "This shall not be thine heir; but he that cometh out of thine own bowels shall be thine heir."[2] The thought of adoption was thus removed; but it still remained uncertain whether the seed which was to come from himself would be by Sara or another. And this God was pleased to keep concealed, till a figure of the Old Testament had been supplied in the handmaid. We may thus easily understand how Abraham, seeing that his wife was barren, and that she desired to obtain from her husband and her handmaid the offspring which she herself could not produce, acted not in compliance with carnal appetite, but in obedience to conjugal authority, believing that Sara had the sanction of God for her wish; because God had already promised him an heir from his own body, but had not foretold who was to be the mother. Thus, when Faustus shows his own infidelity in accusing Abraham of unbelief, his groundless accusation only proves the madness of the assailant. In other cases, Faustus' infidelity has prevented him from understanding; but here, in his love of slander, he has not even taken time to read.

33. Again, when Faustus accuses a righteous and faithful man of a shameless profanation of his marriage from avarice and greed, by selling his wife Sara at different times to the two kings Abimelech and Pharaoh, telling them that she was his sister, because she was very fair, he does not distinguish justly between right and wrong, but unjustly condemns the whole transaction. Those who think that Abraham sold his wife cannot discern in the light of the eternal law the difference between sin and righteousness; and so they call perseverance obstinacy, and confidence presumption, as in these and similar cases men of wrong judgment are wont to blame what they suppose to be wrong actions. Abraham did not become partner in crime with his wife by selling her to others: but as she gave her handmaid to her husband, not to gratify his passion, but for the sake of offspring, in the authority she had consistently with the order of nature, requiring the performance of a duty, not complying with a sinful desire; so in this case, the husband, in perfect assurance of the chaste attachment of his wife to himself, and knowing her mind to be the abode of modest and virtuous affection, called her his sister, without saying that she was his wife, lest he himself should be killed, and his wife fall into the hands of strangers and evil-doers: for he was assured by his God that He would not allow her to suffer violence or disgrace. Nor was he disappointed in his faith and hope; for Pharaoh, terrified by strange occurrences, and after enduring many evils on account of her, when he was informed by God that Sara was Abraham's wife, restored her with honor uninjured. Abimelech also did the same, after learning the truth in a dream.

34. Some people, not scoffers and evil-speakers like Faustus, but men who pay due honor to the Scriptures, which Faustus finds fault with because he does not understand them, or which he fails to understand because of his fault-finding, in commenting on this act of Abraham, are of opinion that he stumbled from weakness of faith, and denied his wife from fear of death, as Peter denied the Lord. If this is the correct view, we must allow that Abraham sinned; but the sin should

[1] Gen. xii. 3.

[2] Gen. xv. 3, 4.

not cancel or obliterate all his merits, any more than in the case of the apostle. Besides, to deny his wife is not the same as to deny the Saviour. But when there is another explanation, why not abide by it, instead of giving blame without cause, since there is no proof that Abraham told a lie from fear? He did not deny that Sara was his wife in answer to any question on the subject; but when asked who she was, he said she was his sister, without denying her to be his wife: he concealed part of the truth, but said nothing false.

35. It is waste of time to observe Faustus' remark, that Abraham falsely called Sara his sister; as if Faustus had discovered the family of Sara, though it is not mentioned in Scripture. In a matter which Abraham knew, and we do not, it is surely better to believe the patriarch when he says what he knows, than to believe Manichæus when he finds fault with what he knows nothing about. Since, then, Abraham lived at that period in human history, when, though marriage had become unlawful between children of the same parents, or of the same father or mother, no law or authority interfered with the custom of marriage between the children of brothers, or any less degree of consanguinity, why should he not have had as wife his sister, that is, a woman descended from his father? For he himself told the king, when he restored Sara, that she was his sister by his father, and not by his mother. And on this occasion he could not have been led to tell a falsehood from fear, for the king knew that she was his wife, and was restoring her with honor, because he had been warned by God. We learn from Scripture that, among the ancients, it was customary to call cousins brothers and sisters. Thus Tobias says in his prayer to God, before having intercourse with his wife, 'And now, O Lord, Thou knowest that not in wantonness I take to wife my sister;"[1] though she was not sprung immediately from the same father or the same mother, but only belonged to the same family. And Lot is called the brother of Abraham, though Abraham was his uncle.[2] And, by the same use of the word, those called in the Gospel the Lord's brothers are certainly not children of the Virgin Mary, but all the blood relations of the Lord.[3]

36. Some may say, Why did not Abraham's confidence in God prevent his being afraid to confess his wife? God could have warded off from him the death which he feared, and could have protected both him and his wife while among strangers, so that Sara, although very fair, should not have been desired by any one, nor Abraham killed on account of her. Of course, God could have done this; it would be absurd to deny it. But if, in reply to the people, Abraham had told them that Sara was his wife, his trust in God would have included both his own life and the chastity of Sara. Now it is part of sound doctrine, that when a man has any means in his power, he should not tempt the Lord his God. So it was not because the Saviour was unable to protect His disciples that He told them, "When ye are persecuted in one city, flee to another."[4] And He Himself set the example. For though He had the power of laying down His own life, and did not lay it down till He chose to do so, still when an infant He fled to Egypt, carried by His parents;[5] and when He went up to the feast, He went not openly, but secretly, though at other times He spoke openly to the Jews, who in spite of their rage and hostility could not lay hands on Him, because His hour was not come,[6]—not the hour when He would be obliged to die, but the hour when He would consider it seasonable to be put to death. Thus He who displayed divine power by teaching and reproving openly, without allowing the rage of his enemies to hurt Him, did also, by escaping and concealing Himself, exhibit the conduct becoming the feebleness of men, that they should not tempt God when they have any means in their power of escaping threatened danger. So also in the apostle, it was not from despair of divine assistance and protection, or from loss of faith, that he was let down over the wall in a basket, in order to escape being taken by his enemies:[7] not from want of faith in God did he thus escape, but because not to escape, when this escape was possible, would have been tempting God. Accordingly, when Abraham was among strangers, and when, on account of the remarkable beauty of Sara, both his life and her chastity were in danger, since it was in his power to protect not both of these, but one only,—his life, namely,—to avoid tempting God he did what he could; and in what he could not do, he trusted to God. Unable to conceal his being a man, he concealed his being a husband, lest he should be put to death; trusting to God to preserve his wife's purity.

37. There might also be a difference of opinion on the nice point whether Sara's chastity would have been violated even if some one had had intercourse with her, since she submitted to this to save her husband's life,

1 Tob. viii. 9.
2 Gen. xiii. 8, and xi. 31.
3 Matt. xii. 46.
4 Matt. x. 23.
5 Matt. ii. 14.
6 John vii. 10, 30.
7 Acts ix. 25.

both with his knowledge and by his authority. In this there would be no desertion of conjugal fidelity or rebellion against her husband's authority; in the same way as Abraham was not an adulterer, when, in submission to the lawful authority of his wife, he consented to be made a father by his wife's handmaid. But, from the nature of the relationship, for a wife to have two husbands, both in life, is not the same thing as for a man to have two wives: so that we regard the explanation already given of Abraham's conduct as the most correct and unobjectionable; that our father Abraham avoided tempting God by taking what measures he could for the preservation of his own life, and that he showed his hope in God by entrusting to Him the chastity of his wife.

38. But a pleasure which all must feel is obtained from this narrative so faithfully recorded in the Holy Scriptures, when we examine into the prophetic character of the action, and knock with pious faith and diligence at the door of the mystery, that the Lord may open, and show us who was prefigured in the ancient personage, and whose wife this is, who, while in a foreign land and among strangers, is not allowed to be stained or defiled, that she may be brought to her own husband without spot or wrinkle. Thus we find that the righteous life of the Church is for the glory of Christ, that her beauty may bring honor to her husband, as Abraham was honored on account of the beauty of Sara among the inhabitants of that foreign land. To the Church, to whom it is said in the Song of Songs, "O thou fairest among women,"[1] kings offer gifts in acknowledgment of her beauty; as king Abimelech offered gifts to Sara, admiring the grace of her appearance; all the more that, while he loved, he was not allowed to profane it. The holy Church, too is in secret the spouse of the Lord Jesus Christ. For it is secretly, and in the hidden depths of the Spirit, that the soul of man is joined to the word of God, so that they two are one flesh; of which the apostle speaks as a great mystery in marriage, as referring to Christ and the Church.[2] Again, the earthly kingdom of this world, typified by the kings which were not allowed to defile Sara, had no knowledge or experience of the Church as the spouse of Christ, that is, of how faithfully she maintained her relation to her Husband, till it tried to violate her, and was compelled to yield to the divine testimony borne by the faith of the martyrs, and in the person of later monarchs was brought humbly to honor with gifts the Bride whom their predecessors had not been able to humble by subduing her to themselves. What, in the type, happened in the reign of one and the same king, is fulfilled in the earlier monarchs of this era and their successors.

39. Again, when it is said that the Church is the sister of Christ, not by the mother but by the father, we learn the excellence of the relation, which is not of the temporary nature of earthly descent, but of divine grace, which is everlasting. By this grace we shall no longer be a race of mortals when we receive power to be called and to become sons of God. This grace we obtain not from the synagogue, which is the mother of Christ after the flesh, but from God the Father. And when Christ calls us into another life where there is no death, He teaches us, instead of acknowledging, to deny the earthly relationship, where death soon follows upon birth; for He says to His disciples, "Call no man your father upon earth; for you have one Father, who is in heaven."[3] And He set us an example of this when He said, "Who is my mother, and who are my brethren? And stretching forth His hand to His disciples, He said, These are my brethren." And lest any one should think that He referred to an earthly relationship, He added, "Whosoever shall do the will of my Father, the same is my brother, and sister, and mother;"[4] as much as to say, I derive this relationship from God my Father, not from the Synagogue my mother; I call you to eternal life, where I have an immortal birth, not to earthly life, for to call you away from this life I have taken mortality.

40. As for the reason why, though it is concealed among strangers whose wife the Church is, it is not hidden whose sister she is, it is plainly because it is obscure and hard to understand how the human soul and the Word of God are united or mingled, or whatever word may be used to express this connection between God and the creature. It is from this connection that Christ and the Church are called bridegroom and bride, or husband and wife. The other relationship, in which Christ and all the saints are brethren by divine grace and not by earthly consanguinity, or by the father and not by the mother, is more easily expressed in words, and more easily understood. For the same grace makes all the saints to be also brethren of one another; while in their society no one is the bridegroom of all the rest. So also, notwithstanding the surpassing justice and wisdom

[1] Cant. i. 7. [2] Eph. v. 31, 32. [3] Matt. xxiii. 9. [4] Matt. xii. 48-50.

of Christ, His manhood was much more plainly and readily recognized by strangers, who, indeed, were not wrong in believing Him to be man, but they did not understand His being God as well as man. Hence Jeremiah says: "He is both a man, and who shall know Him?"[1] He is a man, for it is made manifest that He is a brother. And who shall know Him? for it is concealed that He is a husband. This must suffice as a defense of our father Abraham against Faustus' impudence and ignorance and malice.

41. Lot also, the brother of Abraham, was just and hospitable in Sodom, and was found worthy to escape the conflagration which prefigured the future judgment; for he was free from all participation in the corruption of the people of Sodom. He was a type of the body of Christ, which in the person of all the saints both groans now among the ungodly and wicked, to whose evil deeds it does not consent, and will at the end of the world be rescued from their society, when they are doomed to the punishment of eternal fire. Lot's wife was the type of a different class of men,—of those, namely, who, when called by the grace of God, look back, instead of, like Paul, forgetting the things that are behind, and looking forward to the things that are before.[2] The Lord Himself says: "No man that putteth his hand to the plough, and looketh back, is fit for the kingdom of Heaven."[3] Nor did He omit to mention the case of Lot's wife; for she, for our warning, was turned into a pillar of salt, that being thus seasoned we might not trifle thoughtlessly with this danger, but be on our guard against it. So, when the Lord was admonishing every one to get rid of the things that are behind by the most strenuous endeavor to reach the things that are before, He said, "Remember Lot's wife."[4] And, in addition to these, there is still a third type in Lot, when his daughters lay with him. For here Lot seems to prefigure the future law; for those who spring from the law, and are placed under the law, by misunderstanding it, stupefy it, as it were, and bring forth the works of unbelief by an unlawful use of the law. "The law is good," says the apostle, "if a man use it lawfully."[5]

42. It is no excuse for this action of Lot or of his daughters that it represented the perversity which was afterwards in certain cases to be displayed. The purpose of Lot's daughters is one thing, and the purpose of God is another, in allowing this to happen that He might make some truth manifest; for God both pronounces judgment on the actions of the people of those times, and arranges in His providence for the prefigurement of the future. As a part of Scripture, this action is a prophecy; as part of the history of those concerned, it is a crime.

43. At the same time there is in this transaction no reason for the torrent of abuse which Faustus' blind hostility discharges on it. By the eternal law which requires the preservation of the order of nature and condemns its violation, the judgment in this case is not what it would have been if Lot had been prompted by a criminal passion to commit incest with his daughters, or if they had been inflamed with unnatural desires. In justice, we must ask not only what was done, but with what motive, in order to obtain a fair view of the action as the effect of that motive. The resolution of Lot's daughters to lie with their father was the effect of the natural desire for offspring in order to preserve the race; for they supposed that there were no other men to be found, thinking that the whole world had been consumed in that conflagration, which, for all they knew, had left no one alive but themselves. It would have been better for them never to have been mothers, than to have become mothers by their own father. But still, the fulfillment of a desire like this is very different from the accursed gratification of lust.

44. Knowing that their father would condemn their design, Lot's daughters thought it necessary to fulfill it without his knowledge. We are told that they made him drunk, so that he was unaware of what happened. His guilt therefore is not that of incest, but of drunkenness. This, too, is condemned by the eternal law, which allows meat and drink only as required by nature for the preservation of health. There is, indeed, a great difference between a drunk man and an habitual drunkard; for the drunkard is not always drunk, and a man may be drunk on one occasion without being a drunkard. However, in the case of a righteous man, we require to account for even one instance of drunkenness. What can have made Lot consent to receive from his daughters all the cups of wine which they went on mixing for him, or perhaps giving him unmixed? Did they feign excessive grief, and did he resort to this consolation in their loneliness, and in the loss of their mother, thinking that they were drinking too, while they only pretended to drink? But this does not seem a proper method for a righteous man to take in consoling his friends when in trouble. Had the daughters learned in Sodom some vile art which enabled them to intoxicate their father

1 Jer. xvii. 9. 2 Phil. iii. 13. 3 Luke ix. 62.
4 Luke xvii. 32. 5 1 Tim. i. 8.

with a few cups, so that in his ignorance he might sin, or rather be sinned against? But it is not likely that the Scripture would have omitted all notice of this, or that God would have allowed His servant to be thus abused without any fault of his own.

45. But we are defending the sacred Scriptures, not man's sins. Nor are we concerned to justify this action, as if our God had either commanded it or approved of it; or as if, when men are called just in Scripture, it meant that they could not sin if they chose. And as, in the books which those critics find fault with, God nowhere expresses approval of this action, what thoughtless folly it is to bring a charge from this narrative against these writings, when in other places such actions are condemned by express prohibitions! In the story of Lot's daughters the action is related, not commended. And it is proper that the judgment of God should be declared in some cases, and concealed in others, that by its manifestation our ignorance may be enlightened, and that by its concealment our minds may be improved by the exercise of recalling what we already know, or our indolence stimulated to seek for an explanation. Here, then, God, who can bring good out of evil, made nations arise from this origin, as He saw good, but did not bring upon His own Scriptures the guilt of man's sin. It is God's writing, but not His doing; He does not propose these things for our imitation, but holds them up for our warning.

46. Faustus' effrontery appears notably in his accusing Isaac also, the son of Abraham, of pretending that his wife Rebecca was his sister.[1] For as regards the family of Rebecca Scripture is not silent, and it appears that she was his sister in the well-known sense of the word. His concealing that she was his wife is not surprising, nor is it insignificant, if he did it in imitation of his father, so that he can be justified on the same grounds. We need only refer to the answer already given to Faustus' charge against Abraham, as being equally applicable to Isaac. Perhaps, however some inquirer will ask what typical significance there is in the foreign king discovering Rebecca to be the wife of Isaac by seeing him playing with her; for he would not have known, had he not seen Isaac playing with Rebecca as it would have been improper to do with a woman not his wife. When holy men act thus as husbands, they do it not foolishly, but designedly: for they accommodate themselves to the nature of the weaker sex in words and actions of gentle playfulness; not in effeminacy, but in subdued manliness. But such behavior towards any woman except a wife would be disgraceful. This is a question in good manners, which is referred to only in case some stern advocate of insensibility should find fault with the holy man even for playing with his wife. For if these men without humanity see a sedate man chatting playfully with children that he may adapt himself to the childish understanding with kindly sympathy, they think that he is insane; forgetting that they themselves were once children, or unthankful for their maturity. The typical meaning, as regards Christ and His Church, which is to be found in this great patriarch playing with his wife, and in the conjugal relation being thus discovered, will be seen by every one who, to avoid offending the Church by erroneous doctrine, carefully studies in Scripture the secret of the Church's Bridegroom. He will find that the Husband of the Church concealed for a time in the form of a servant the majesty in which He was equal to the Father, as being in the form of God, that feeble humanity might be capable of union with Him, and that so He might accommodate Himself to His spouse. So far from being absurd, it has a symbolic suitableness that the prophet of God should use a playfulness which is of the flesh to meet the affection of his wife, as the Word of God Himself became flesh that He might dwell among us.

47. Again, Jacob the son of Isaac is charged with having committed a great crime because he had four wives. But here there is no ground for a criminal accusation: for a plurality of wives was no crime when it was the custom; and it is a crime now, because it is no longer the custom. There are sins against nature, and sins against custom, and sins against the laws. In which, then, of these senses did Jacob sin in having a plurality of wives? As regards nature, he used the women not for sensual gratification, but for the procreation of children. For custom, this was the common practice at that time in those countries. And for the laws, no prohibition existed. The only reason of its being a crime now to do this, is because custom and the laws forbid it. Whoever despises these restraints, even though he uses his wives only to get children, still commits sin, and does an injury to human society itself, for the sake of which it is that the procreation of children is required. In the present altered state of customs and laws, men can have no pleasure in a plurality of wives, except from an excess of lust; and so the mistake arises of supposing that no one could ever have had many

[1] Gen. xxvi. 7.

wives but from sensuality and the vehemence of sinful desires. Unable to form an idea of men whose force of mind is beyond their conception, they compare themselves with themselves, as the apostle says,[1] and so make mistakes. Conscious that, in their intercourse though with one wife only, they are often influenced by mere animal passion instead of an intelligent motive, they think it an obvious inference that, if the limits of moderation are not observed where there is only one wife, the infirmity must be aggravated where there are more than one.

48. But those who have not the virtues of temperance must not be allowed to judge of the conduct of holy men, any more than those in fever of the sweetness and wholesomeness of food. Nourishment must be provided not by the dictates of the sickly taste, but rather by the judgment and direction of health, so as to cure the sickness. If our critics, then, wish to attain not a spurious and affected, but a genuine and sound moral health, let them find a cure in believing the Scripture record, that the honorable name of saint is given not without reason to men who had several wives; and that the reason is this, that the mind can exercise such control over the flesh as not to allow the appetite implanted in our nature by Providence to go beyond the limits of deliberate intention. By a similar misunderstanding, this criticism, which consists rather in dishonest slander than in honest judgment, might accuse the holy apostles too of preaching the gospel to so many people, not from the desire of begetting children to eternal life, but from the love of human praise. There was no lack of renown to these our fathers in the gospel, for their praise was spread in numerous tongues through the churches of Christ. In fact, no greater honor and glory could have been paid by men to their fellow-creatures. It was the sinful desire for this glory in the Church which led the reprobate Simon in his blindness to wish to purchase for money what was freely bestowed on the apostles by divine grace.[2] There must have been this desire of glory in the man whom the Lord in the Gospel checks in his desire to follow Him, saying, "The foxes have holes, and the birds of the air have nests, but the Son of man hath not where to lay His Head."[3] The Lord saw that his mind was darkened by false appearances and elated by sudden emotion, and that there was no ground of faith to afford a lodging to the Teacher of humility; for in Christ's discipleship the man sought not Christ's grace, but his own glory. By this love of glory those were led away whom the Apostle Paul characterizes as preaching Christ not sincerely, but of contention and envy; and yet the apostle rejoices in their preaching, knowing that it might happen that, while the preachers gratified their desire for human praise, believers might be born among their hearers,—not as the result of the envious feeling which made them wish to rival or surpass the fame of the apostles, but by means of the gospel which they preached, though not sincerely; so that God might bring good out of their evil. So a man may be induced to marry by sensual desire, and not to beget children; and yet a child may be born, a good work of God, due to the natural power, not to the misconduct of the parent. As, therefore, the holy apostles were gratified when their doctrine met with acceptance from their hearers, not because they were greedy for praise, but because they desired to spread the truth; so the holy patriarchs in their conjugal intercourse were actuated not by the love of pleasure, but by the intelligent desire for the continuance of their family. Thus the number of their hearers did not make the apostles ambitious; nor did the number of their wives make the patriarchs licentious. But why defend the husbands, to whose character the divine word bears the highest testimony, when it appears that the wives themselves looked upon their connection with their husbands only as a means of getting sons? So, when they found themselves barren, they gave their handmaids to their husbands; so that while the handmaids had the fleshly motherhood, the wives were mothers in intention.

49. Faustus makes a most groundless statement when he accuses the four women of quarreling like abandoned characters for the possession of their husband. Where Faustus read this I know not, unless it was in his own heart, as in a book of impious delusions, in which Faustus himself is seduced by that serpent with regard to whom the apostle feared for the Church, which he desired to present as a chaste virgin to Christ; lest, as the serpent had deceived Eve by his subtlety, so he should also corrupt their minds by turning them away from the simplicity of Christ.[4] The Manichæans are so fond of this serpent, that they assert that he did more good than harm. From him Faustus must have got his mind corrupted with the lies instilled into it, which he now reproduces in these infamous calumnies, and is even bold enough to put

[1] 2 Cor. x. 12. [2] Acts viii. 18–20. [3] Matt. viii. 20. [4] 2 Cor. xi. 2, 3.

down in writing. It is not true that one of the handmaids carried off Jacob from the other, or that they quarreled about possessing him. There was arrangement, because there was no licentious passion; and the law of conjugal authority was all the stronger that there was none of the lawlessness of fleshly desire. His being hired by one of his wives proves what is here said, in plain opposition to the libels of the Manichæans. Why should one have hired him, unless by the arrangement he was to have gone in to the other? It does not follow that he would never have gone in to Leah unless she had hired him. He must have gone to her always in her turn, for he had many children by her; and in obedience to her he had children by her handmaid, and afterwards, without any hiring, by herself. On this occasion it was Rachel's turn, so that she had the power so expressly mentioned in the New Testament by the apostle, "The husband hath not power over his own body, but the wife."[1] Rachel had a bargain with her sister, and, being in her sister's debt, she referred her to Jacob, her own debtor. For the apostle uses this figure when he says, "Let the husband render unto the wife what is due."[2] Rachel gave what was in her power as due from her husband, in return for what she had chosen to take from her sister.

50. If Jacob had been of such a character as Faustus in his incurable blindness supposes, and not a servant of righteousness rather than of concupiscence, would he not have been looking forward eagerly all day to the pleasure of passing the night with the more beautiful of his wives, whom he certainly loved more than the other, and for whom he paid the price of twice seven years of gratuitous service? How, then, at the close of the day, on his way to his beloved, could he have consented to be turned aside, if he had been such as the ignorant Manichæans represent him? Would he not have disregarded the wish of the women, and insisted upon going to the fair Rachel, who belonged to him that night not only as his lawful wife, but also as coming in regular order? He would thus have used his power as a husband, for the wife also has not power over her own body, but the husband; and having on this occasion the arrangement in their obedience in favor of the gratification of his love of beauty, he might have enforced his authority the more successfully. In that case it would be to the credit of the women, that while he thought of his own pleasure they contended about having a son. As it was, this virtuous man, in manly control of sensual appetite, thought more of what was due from him than to him, and instead of using his power for his own pleasure, consented to be only the debtor in this mutual obligation. So he consented to pay the debt to the person to whom she to whom it was due wished him to pay it. When, by this private bargain of his wives, Jacob was suddenly and unexpectedly forced to turn from the beautiful wife to the plain one, he did not give way either to anger or to disappointment, nor did he try to persuade his wives to let him have his own way; but, like a just husband and an intelligent parent, seeing his wives concerned about the production of children, which was all he himself desired in marriage, he thought it best to yield to their authority, in desiring that each should have a child: for, since all the children were his, his own authority was not impaired. As if he had said to them: Arrange as you please among yourselves which is to be the mother; it matters not to me, since in any case I am the father. This control over the appetites, and simple desire to beget children, Faustus would have been clever enough to see and approve, unless his mind had been corrupted by the shocking tenets of his sect, which lead him to find fault with everything in the Scripture, and, moreover, teach him to condemn as the greatest crime the procreation of children, which is the proper design of marriage.

51. Now, having defended the character of the patriarch, and refuted an accusation arising from these detestable errors, let us avail ourselves of the opportunity of searching out the symbolical meaning, and let us knock with the reverence of faith, that the Lord may open to us the typical significance of the four wives of Jacob, of whom two were free, and two slaves. We see that, in the wife and bond-slaves of Abraham, the apostle understands the two Testaments.[3] But there, one represents each; here, the application does not suit so well, as there are two and two. There, also, the son of the bond-slave is disinherited; but here the sons of the slaves receive the land of promise along with the sons of the free women: so that this type must have a different meaning.

52. Supposing that the two free wives point to the New Testament, by which we are called to liberty, what is the meaning of there being two? Perhaps because in Scripture, as the attentive reader will find, we are said to have two lives in the body of Christ,—one

[1] 1 Cor. vii. 4.
[2] 1 Cor. vii. 3.
[3] Gal. iv. 22–24.

temporal, in which we suffer pain, and one eternal, in which we shall behold the blessedness of God. We see the one in the Lord's passion, and the other in His resurrection. The names of the women point to this meaning: It is said that Leah means Suffering, and Rachel the First Principle made visible, or the Word which makes the First Principle visible. The action, then, of our mortal human life, in which we live by faith, doing many painful tasks without knowing what benefit may result from them to those in whom we are interested, is Leah, Jacob's first wife. And thus she is said to have had weak eyes. For the purposes of mortals are timid, and our plans uncertain. Again, the hope of the eternal contemplation of God, accompanied with a sure and delightful perception of truth, is Rachel. And on this account she is described as fair and well-formed. This is the beloved of every pious student, and for this he serves the grace of God, by which our sins, though like scarlet, are made white as snow.[1] For Laban means making white; and we read that Jacob served Laban for Rachel.[2] No man turns to serve righteousness, in subjection to the grace of forgiveness, but that he may live in peace in the Word which makes visible the First Principle, or God; that is, he serves for Rachel, not for Leah. For what a man loves in the works of righteousness is not the toil of doing and suffering. No one desires this life for its own sake; as Jacob desired not Leah, who yet was brought to him, and became his wife, and the mother of children. Though she could not be loved of herself, the Lord made her be borne with as a step to Rachel; and then she came to be approved of on account of her children. Thus every useful servant of God, brought into His grace by which his sins are made white, has in his mind, and heart, and affection, when he thus turns to God, nothing but the knowledge of wisdom. This we often expect to attain as a reward for practising the seven precepts of the law which concern the love of our neighbor, that we injure no one: namely, Honor thy father and mother; Thou shalt not commit adultery; Thou shalt not kill; Thou shalt not steal; Thou shalt not bear false witness; Thou shalt not desire thy neighbor's wife; Thou shalt not covet thy neighbor's property. When a man has obeyed these to the best of his ability, and, instead of the bright joys of truth which he desired and hoped for, finds in the darkness of the manifold trials of this world that he is bound to painful endurance, or has embraced Leah instead of Rachel, if there is perseverance in his love, he bears with the one in order to attain the other; and as if it were said to him, Serve seven other years for Rachel, he hears seven new commands,—to be poor in spirit, to be meek, to be a mourner, to hunger and thirst after righteousness, to be merciful, pure, and a peacemaker.[3] A man would desire, if it were possible, to obtain at once the joys of lovely and perfect wisdom, without the endurance of toil in action and suffering; but this is impossible in mortal life. This seems to be meant, when it is said to Jacob: "It is not the custom in our country to marry the younger before the elder."[4] The elder may very well mean the first in order of time. So, in the discipline of man, the toil of doing the work of righteousness precedes the delight of understanding the truth.

53. To this purpose it is written: "Thou hast desired wisdom; keep the commandments, and the Lord shall give it thee."[5] The commandments are those concerning righteousness, and the righteousness is that which is by faith, surrounded with the uncertainty of temptations; so that understanding is the reward of a pious belief of what is not yet understood. The meaning I have given to these words, "Thou hast desired wisdom; keep the commandments, and the Lord shall give it thee," I find also in the passage, "Unless ye believe, ye shall not understand;"[6] showing that as righteousness is by faith, understanding comes by wisdom. Accordingly, in the case of those who eagerly demand evident truth, we must not condemn the desire, but regulate it, so that beginning with faith it may proceed to the desired end through good works. The life of virtue is one of toil; the end desired is unclouded wisdom. Why should I believe, says one, what is not clearly proved? Let me hear some word which will disclose the first principle of all things. This is the one great craving of the rational soul in the pursuit of truth. And the answer is, What you desire is excellent, and well worthy of your love; but Leah is to be married first, and then Rachel. The proper effect of your eagerness is to lead you to submit to the right method, instead of rebelling against it; for without this method you cannot attain what you so eagerly long for. And when it is attained, the possession of the lovely form of knowledge will be in this world accompanied with the toils of righteousness. For however clear and true our perception in this life may be of the unchangeable good,

---

1 Isa. i. 18.
2 Gen. xxix. 17.
3 Matt. v. 3-9.
4 Gen. xxix. 26.
5 Ecclus. i. 33.
6 Isa. vii. 9, Vulg.

the mortal body is still a weight on the mind, and the earthly tabernacle is a clog on the intellect in its manifold activity. The end, then, is one, but many things must be gone through for the sake of it.

54. Thus Jacob has two free wives; for both are daughters of the remission of sins, or of whitening, that is, of Laban. One is loved, the other is borne. But she that is borne is the most and the soonest fruitful, that she may be loved, if not for herself, at least for her children. For the toil of the righteous is specially fruitful in those whom they beget for the kingdom of God, by preaching the gospel amid many trials and temptations; and they call those their joy and crown[1] for whom they are in labors more abundantly, in stripes above measure, in deaths often,[2]— for whom they have fightings without and fears within.[3] Such births result most easily and plentifully from the word of faith, the preaching of Christ crucified, which speaks also of His human nature as far as it can be easily understood, so as not to hurt the weak eyes of Leah. Rachel, again, with clear eye, is beside herself to God,[4] and sees in the beginning the Word of God with God, and wishes to bring forth, but cannot; for who shall declare His generation? So the life devoted to contemplation, in order to see with no feeble mental eye things invisible to flesh, but understood by the things that are made, and to discern the ineffable manifestation of the eternal power and divinity of God, seeks leisure from all occupation, and is therefore barren. In this habit of retirement, where the fire of meditation burns bright, there is a want of sympathy with human weakness, and with the need men have of our help in their calamities. This life also burns with the desire for children (for it wishes to teach what it knows, and not to go with the corruption of envy[5]), and sees its sister-life fully occupied with work and with bringing forth; and it grieves that men run after that virtue which cares for their wants and weaknesses, instead of that which has a divine imperishable lesson to impart. This is what is meant when it is said, "Rachel envied her sister."[6] Moreover, as the pure intellectual perception of that which is not matter, and so is not the object of the bodliy sense, cannot be expressed in words which spring from the flesh, the doctrine of wisdom prefers to get some lodging for divine truth in the mind by whatever material figures and illustrations occur, rather than to give up teaching these things; and thus Rachel preferred that her husband should have children by her handmaid, rather than that she should be without any children. Bilhah, the name of her handmaid, is said to mean old; and so, even when we speak of the spiritual and unchangeable nature of God, ideas are suggested relating to the old life of the bodily senses.

55. Leah, too, got children by her handmaid, from the desire of having a numerous family. Zilpah, her handmaid, is, interpreted, an open mouth. So Leah's handmaid represents those who are spoken of in Scripture as engaging in the preaching of the gospel with open mouth, but not with open heart. Thus it is written of some: "This people honor me with their lips, but their heart is far from me."[7] To such the apostle says: "Thou that preachest that a man should not steal, dost thou steal? Thou that sayest a man should not commit adultery, dost thou commit adultery?"[8] But that even by this arrangement the free wife of Jacob, the type of labor or endurance, might obtain children to be heirs of the kingdom, the Lord says: "What they say, do; but do not after their works."[9] And again, the apostolic life, when enduring imprisonment, says: "Whether Christ is preached in pretence or in truth, I therein do rejoice, yea, and will rejoice."[10] It is the joy of the mother over her numerous family, though born of her handmaid.

56. In one instance Leah owed her becoming a mother to Rachel, who, in return for some mandrakes, allowed her husband to give her night to her sister. Some, I know, think that eating this fruit has the effect of making barren women productive, and that Rachel, from her desire for children, was thus bent on getting the fruit from her sister. But I should not agree to this, even had Rachel conceived at the time. As Leah then conceived, and, besides, had two other children before God opened Rachel's womb, there is no reason for supposing any such quality in the mandrake, without any experience to prove it. I will give my explanation; those better able than I may give a better. Though this fruit is not often met with, I had once, to my great satisfaction, on account of its connection with this passage of Scripture, an opportunity of seeing it. I examined the fruit as carefully as I could, not with the help of any recondite knowledge of the nature of roots or the virtues of plants, but only as to what I or any one might learn from the sight, and smell, and taste. I thought it a nice-looking fruit, and sweet-smelling, but in-

[1] Phil. iv. 1.
[2] 2 Cor. xi. 23.
[3] 2 Cor. vii. 5.
[4] 2 Cor. v. 13.
[5] Wisd. vi. 23.
[6] Gen. xxx. 1.
[7] Isa. xxix. 13.
[8] Rom. ii. 21, 22.
[9] Matt. xxiii. 3.
[10] Phil. i. 18.

sipid; and I confess it is hard to say why Rachel desired it so much, unless it was for its rarity and its sweet smell. Why the incident should be narrated in Scripture, in which the fancies of women would not be mentioned as important unless it was intended that we should learn some important lesson from them, the only thing I can think of is the very simple idea that the fruit represents a good character; not the praise given a man by a few just and wise people, but popular report, which bestows greatness and renown on a man, and which is not desirable for its own sake, but is essential to the success of good men in their endeavors to benefit their fellow-men. So the apostle says, that it is proper to have a good report of those that are without;[1] for though they are not infallible, the lustre of their praise and the odor of their good opinion are a great help to the efforts of those who seek to benefit them. And this popular renown is not obtained by those that are highest in the Church, unless they expose themselves to the toils and hazards of an active life. Thus the son of Leah found the mandrakes when he went out into the field, that is, when walking honestly towards those that are without. The pursuit of wisdom, on the other hand, retired from the busy crowd, and lost in calm meditation, could never obtain a particle of this public approval, except through those who take the management of public business, not for the sake of being leaders, but in order to be useful. These men of action and business exert themselves for the public benefit, and by a popular use of their influence gain the approval of the people even for the quiet life of the student and inquirer after truth; and thus through Leah the mandrakes come into the hands of Rachel. Leah herself got them from her first-born son, that is, in honor of her fertility, which represents all the useful result of a laborious life exposed to the common vicissitudes; a life which many avoid on account of its troublesome engagements, because, although they might be able to take the lead, they are bent on study, and devote all their powers to the quiet pursuit of knowledge, in love with the beauty of Rachel.

57. But as it is right that this studious life should gain public approval by letting itself be known, while it cannot rightly gain this approval if it keeps its follower in retirement, instead of using his powers for the management of ecclesiastical affairs, and so prevents his being generally useful; to this purpose Leah says to her sister, "Is it a small matter that thou hast taken my husband? and wouldest thou take away my son's mandrakes also?"[2] The husband represents all those who, though fit for active life, and able to govern the Church, in administering to believers the mystery of the faith, from their love of learning and of the pursuit of wisdom, desire to relinquish all troublesome occupations, and to bury themselves in the class-room. Thus the words, "Is it a small matter that thou hast taken my husband? and wouldest thou take away my son's mandrakes also?" mean, "Is it a small matter that the life of study keeps in retirement men required for the toils of public life? and does it ask for popular renown as well?"

58. To get this renown justly, Rachel gives her husband to her sister for the night; that is, those who, by a talent for business, are fitted for government, must for the public benefit consent to bear the burden and suffer the hardships of public life; lest the pursuit of wisdom, to which their leisure is devoted, should be evil spoken of, and should not gain from the multitude the good opinion, represented by the fruit, which is necessary for the encouragement of their pupils. But the life of business must be forced upon them. This is clearly shown by Leah's meeting Jacob when coming from the field, and laying hold of him, saying, "Thou shalt come in to me; for I have hired thee with my son's mandrakes."[3] As if she said, Dost thou wish the knowledge which thou lovest to be well thought of? Do not shirk the toil of business. The same thing happens constantly in the Church. What we read is explained by what we meet with in our own experience. Do we not everywhere see men coming from secular employments, to seek leisure for the study and contemplation of truth, their beloved Rachel, and intercepted mid-way by ecclesiastical affairs, which require them to be set to work, as if Leah said to them, You must come in to me? When such men minister in sincerity the mystery of God, so as in the night of this world to beget sons in the faith, popular approval is gained also for that life, in love for which they were led to abandon worldly pursuits, and from the adoption of which they were called away to undertake the benevolent task of government. In all their labors they aim chiefly at this, that their chosen way of life may have greater and wider renown, as having supplied the people with such leaders; as Jacob consents to go with Leah, that Rachel may obtain the sweet-smelling and good-looking fruit. Rachel,

[1] 1 Tim. iii. 7.

[2] Gen. xxx. 15.

[3] Gen. xxx. 16.

too, in course of time, by the mercy of God, brings forth a child herself, but not till after some time; for it seldom happens that there is a sound, though only partial, apprehension, without fleshly ideas, of such sacred lessons of wisdom as this: "In the beginning was the Word, and the Word was with God, and the Word was God."[1]

59. This must suffice as a reply to the false accusations brought by Faustus against the three fathers, Abraham, Isaac, and Jacob, from whom the God whom the Catholic Church worship was pleased to take His name. This is not the place to discourse on the merits and piety of these three men, or on the dignity of their prophetic character, which is beyond the comprehension of carnal minds. It is enough in this treatise to defend them against the calumnious attacks of malevolence and falsehood, in case those who read the Scriptures in a carping and hostile spirit should fancy that they have proved anything against the sacredness and the profitableness of these books, by their attempts to blacken the character of men who are there mentioned so honorably.

60. It should be added that Lot, the brother, that is the blood relation, of Abraham, is not to be ranked as equal to those of whom God says, "I am the God of Abraham, of Isaac, and of Jacob;" nor does he belong to those testified to in Scripture as having continued righteous to the end, although in Sodom he lived a pious and virtuous life, and showed a praiseworthy hospitality, so that he was rescued from the fire, and a land was given by God to his seed to dwell in, for the sake of his uncle Abraham. On these accounts he is commended in Scripture—not for intemperance or incest. But when we find bad and good actions recorded of the same person, we must take warning from the one, and example from the other. As, then, the sin of Lot, of whom we are told that he was righteous previous to this sin, instead of bringing a stain on the character of God, or the truth of Scripture, rather calls on us to approve and admire the record in its resemblance to a faithful mirror, which reflects not only the beauties and perfections, but also the faults and deformities, of those who approach it; still more, in the case of Judah, who lay with his daughter-in-law, we may see how groundless are the reproaches cast on the narrative. The sacred record has an authority which raises it far above not merely the cavils of a handful of Manichæans, but the determined enmity of the whole Gentile world; for, in confirmation of its claims, we see that already it has brought nearly all people from their idolatrous superstitions to the worship of one God, according to the rule of Christianity. It has conquered the world, not by violence and warfare, but by the resistless force of truth. Where, then, is Judah praised in Scripture? Where is anything good said of him, except that in the blessing pronounced by his father he is distinguished above the rest, because of the prophecy that Christ would come in the flesh from his tribe?[2]

61. Judah, as Faustus says, committed fornication; and besides that, we can accuse him of selling his brother into Egypt. Is it any disparagement to light, that in revealing all things it discloses what is unsightly? So neither is the character of Scripture affected by the evil deeds of which we are informed by the record itself. Undoubtedly, by the eternal law, which requires the preservation of natural order, and forbids the transgression of it, conjugal intercourse should take place only for the procreation of children, and after the celebration of marriage, so as to maintain the bond of peace. Therefore, the prostitution of women, merely for the gratification of sinful passion, is condemned by the divine and eternal law. To purchase the degradation of another, disgraces the purchaser; so that, though the sin would have been greater if Judah had knowingly lain with his daughter-in-law (for if, as the Lord says, man and wife are no more two, but one flesh,[3] a daughter-in-law is the same as a daughter); still, it is plain that, as regards his own intention, he was disgraced by his intercourse with an harlot. The woman, on the other hand, who deceived her father-in-law, sinned not from wantonness, or because she loved the gains of iniquity, but from her desire to have children of this particular family. So, being disappointed in two of the brothers, and not obtaining the third, she succeeded by craft in getting a child by their fatner; and the reward which she got was kept, not as an ornament, but as a pledge. It would certainly have been better to have remained childless than to become a mother without marriage. Still, her desire to have her father-in-law as the father of her children was very different from having a criminal affection for him. And when, by his order, she was brought out to be killed, on her producing the staff and necklace and ring, saying that the father of the child was the man who had given her those pledges, Judah acknowledged them, and said, "She hath been more righteous than I"

[1] John i. 1.

[2] Gen. xlix. 8-12.

[3] Matt. xix. 6.

—not praising her, but condemning himself. He blamed her desire to have children less than his own unlawful passion, which had led him to one whom he thought to be an harlot. In a similar sense, it is said of some that they justified Sodom;[1] that is, their sin was so great, that Sodom seemed righteous in comparison. And even allowing that this woman is not spoken of as comparatively less guilty, but is actually praised by her father-in-law, while, on account of her not observing the established rites of marriage, she is a criminal in the eye of the eternal law of right, which forbids the transgression of natural order, both as regards the body, and first and chiefly as regards the mind, what wonder though one sinner should praise another?

62. The mistake of Faustus and of Manichæism generally, is in supposing that these objections prove anything against us, as if our reverence for Scripture, and our profession of regard for its authority, bound us to approve of all the evil actions mentioned in it; whereas the greater our homage for the Scripture, the more decided must be our condemnation of what the truth of Scripture itself teaches us to condemn. In Scripture, all fornication and adultery are condemned by the divine law; accordingly, when actions of this kind are narrated, without being expressly condemned, it is intended not that we should praise them, but that we should pass judgment on them ourselves. Every one execrates the cruelty of Herod in the Gospel, when, in his uneasiness on hearing of the birth of Christ, he commanded the slaughter of so many infants.[2] But this is merely narrated without being condemned. Or if Manichæan absurdity is bold enough to deny the truth of this narrative, since they do not admit the birth of Christ, which was what troubled Herod, let them read the account of the blind fury of the Jews, which is related without any expression of reproach, although the feeling of abhorrence is the same in all.

63. But, it is said, Judah, who lay with his daughter-in-law, is reckoned as one of the twelve patriarchs. And was not Judas, who betrayed the Lord, reckoned among the twelve apostles? And was not this one of them, who was a devil, sent along with them to preach the gospel?[3] In reply to this, it will be said that after his crime Judas hanged himself, and was removed from the number of the apostles; while Judah, after his evil conduct, was not only blessed along with his brethren, but got special honor and approval from his father, who is so highly spoken of in Scripture. But the main lesson to be learned from this is, that this prophecy refers not to Judah, but to Christ, who was foretold as to come in the flesh from his tribe; and the very reason for the mention of this crime of Judah is to be found in the desirableness of teaching us to look for another meaning in the words of his father, which are seen not to be applicable to him in his misconduct, from the praise which they express.

64. Doubtless, the intention of Faustus' calumnies is to damage this very assertion, that Christ was born of the tribe of Judah. Especially, as in the genealogy given by Matthew we find the name of Zara, whom this woman Tamar bore to Judah. Had Faustus wished to reproach Jacob's family merely, and not Christ's birth, he might have taken the case of Reuben the first-born, who committed the unnatural crime of defiling his father's bed, of which fornication the apostle says, that it was not so much as named among the Gentiles.[4] Jacob also mentions this in his blessing, charging his son with the infamous deed. Faustus might have brought up this, as Reuben seems to have been guilty of deliberate incest, and there was no harlot's disguise in this case, were it not that Tamar's conduct in desiring nothing but to have children is more odious to Faustus than if she had acted from criminal passion, and did he not wish to discredit the incarnation, by bringing reproach on Christ's progenitors. Faustus unhappily is not aware that the most true and truthful Saviour is a teacher, not only in His words, but also in His birth. In His fleshly origin there is this lesson for those who should believe on Him from all nations, that the sins of their fathers need be no hindrance to them. Besides, the Bridegroom, who was to call good and bad to His marriage,[5] was pleased to assimilate Himself to His guests, in being born of good and bad. He thus confirms as typical of Himself the symbol of the Passover, in which it was commanded that the lamb to be eaten should be taken from the sheep or from the goats—that is, from the righteous or the wicked.[6] Preserving throughout the indication of divinity and humanity, as man He consented to have both bad and good as His parents, while as God He chose the miraculous birth from a virgin.

65. The impiety, therefore, of Faustus' attacks on Scripture can injure no one but himself; for what he thus assails is now deservedly the object of universal reverence. As has been said already, the sacred record, like a faithful mirror, has no flattery in its

[1] Ezek. xvi. 52. [2] Matt. ii. 16. [3] John vi. 70, 71. [4] 1 Cor. v. 1. [5] Matt. xxii. 10. [6] Ex. xii. 3–5.

portraits, and either itself passes sentence upon human actions as worthy of approval or disapproval, or leaves the reader to do so. And not only does it distinguish men as blameworthy or praiseworthy, but it also takes notice of cases where the blameworthy deserve praise, and the praiseworthy blame. Thus, although Saul was blameworthy, it was not the less praiseworthy in him to examine so carefully who had eaten food during the curse, and to pronounce the stern sentence in obedience to the commandment of God.[1] So, too, he was right in banishing those that had familiar spirits and wizards out of the land.[2] And although David was praiseworthy, we are not called on to approve or imitate his sins, which God rebukes by the prophet. And so Pontius Pilate was not wrong in pronouncing the Lord innocent, in spite of the accusations of the Jews;[3] nor was it praiseworthy in Peter to deny the Lord thrice; nor, again, was he praiseworthy on that occasion when Christ called him Satan, because, not understanding the things of God, he wished to withhold Christ from his passion, that is, from our salvation. Here Peter, immediately after being called blessed, is called Satan.[4] Which character most truly belonged to him, we may see from his apostleship, and from his crown of martyrdom.

66. In the case of David also, we read of both good and bad actions. But where David's strength lay, and what was the secret of his success, is sufficiently plain, not to the blind malevolence with which Faustus assails holy writings and holy men, but to pious discernment, which bows to the divine authority, and at the same time judges correctly of human conduct. The Manichæans will find, if they read the Scriptures, that God rebukes David more than Faustus does.[5] But they will read also of the sacrifice of his penitence, of his surpassing gentleness to his merciless and bloodthirsty enemy, whom David, pious as he was brave, dismissed unhurt when now and again he fell into his hands.[6] They will read of his memorable humility under divine chastisement, when the kingly neck was so bowed under the Master's yoke, that he bore with perfect patience bitter taunts from his enemy, though he was armed, and had armed men with him. And when his companion was enraged at such things being said to the king, and was on the point of requiting the insult on the head of the scoffer, he mildly restrained him, appealing to the fear of God in support of his own royal order, and saying that this had happened to him as a punishment from God, who had sent the man to curse him.[7] They will read how, with the love of a shepherd for the flock entrusted to him, he was willing to die for them, when, after he had numbered the people, God saw good to punish his sinful pride by lessening the number he boasted of. In this destruction, God, with whom there is no iniquity, in His secret judgment, both took away the lives of those whom He knew to be unworthy of life, and by this diminution cured the vainglory which had prided itself on the number of the people. They will read of that scrupulous fear of God in his regard for the emblem of Christ in the sacred anointing, which made David's heart smite him with regret for having secretly cut off a small piece of Saul's garment, that he might prove to him that he had no wish to kill him, when he might have done it. They will read of his judicious behavior as regards his children, and also of his tenderness toward them—how, when one was sick, he entreated the Lord for him with many tears and with much self-abasement, but when he died, an innocent child, he did not mourn for him; and again, how, when his youthful son was carried away with unnatural hostility to an infamous violation of his father's bed, and in a parricidal war, he wished him to live, and wept for him when he was killed; for he thought of the eternal doom of a soul guilty of such crimes, and desired that he should live to escape this doom by being brought to submission and repentance. These, and many other praiseworthy and exemplary things, may be seen in this holy man by a candid examination of the Scripture narrative, especially if in humble piety and unfeigned faith we regard the judgment of God, who knew the secrets of David's heart, and who, in His infallible inspection, so approves of David as to commend him as a pattern to his sons.

67. It must have been on account of this inspection of the depths of David's heart by the Spirit of God that, when on being reproved by the prophet, he said, I have sinned, he was considered worthy to be told, immediately after this brief confession, that he was pardoned—that is, that he was admitted to eternal salvation. For he did not escape the correction of the fatherly rod, of which God spoke in His threatening, that, while by his confession he obtained eternal exemption, he might be tried by temporal chastisement. And it is a remarkable evidence of the strength of David's faith, and of his meek and submissive spirit, that, when

1 1 Sam. xiv. 2 1 Sam. xxviii. 3. 3 John xix. 4, 6.
4 Matt. xvi. 17, 22, 23. 5 2 Sam. xii. 6 1 Sam. xxiv. and xxvi.

7 2 Sam. xvi.

he had been told by the prophet that God had forgiven him, although the threatened consequences were still permitted to follow, he did not accuse the prophet of having deluded him, or murmur against God as having mocked him with a declaration of forgiveness. This deeply holy man, whose soul was lifted up unto God, and not against God, knew that had not the Lord mercifully accepted his confession and repentance, his sins would have deserved eternal punishment. So when, instead of this, he was made to smart under temporal correction, he saw that, while the pardon remained good, wholesome discipline was also provided. Saul, too, when he was reproved by Samuel, said, I have sinned.[1] Why, then, was he not considered fit to be told, as David was, that the Lord had pardoned his sin? Is there acceptance of persons with God? Far from it. While to the human ear the words were the same, the divine eye saw a difference in the heart. The lesson for us to learn from these things is, that the kingdom of heaven is within us,[2] and that we must worship God from our inmost feelings, that out of the abundance of the heart the mouth may speak, instead of honoring Him with our lips, like the people of old, while our hearts are far from Him. We may learn also to judge of men, whose hearts we cannot see, only as God judges, who sees what we cannot, and who cannot be biased or misled. Having, on the high authority of sacred Scripture, the plainest announcement of God's opinion of David, we may regard as absurd or deplorable the rashness of men who hold a different opinion. The authority of Scripture, as regards the character of these men of ancient times, is supported by the evidence from the prophecies which they contain, and which are now receiving their fulfillment.

68. We see the same thing in the Gospel, where the devils confess that Christ is the Son of God in the words used by Peter, but with a very different heart. So, though the words were the same, Peter is praised for his faith, while the impiety of the devils is checked. For Christ, not by human sense, but by divine knowledge, could inspect and infallibly discriminate the sources from which the words came. Besides, there are multitudes who confess that Christ is the Son of the living God, without meriting the same approval as Peter—not only of those who shall say in that day, "Lord, Lord," and shall receive the sentence, "Depart from me," but also of those who shall be placed on the right hand. They may probably never have denied Christ even once; they may never have opposed His suffering for our salvation; they may never have forced the Gentiles to do as the Jews;[3] and yet they shall not be honored equally with Peter, who, though he did all these things, will sit on one of the twelve thrones, and judge not only the twelve tribes, but the angels. So, again, many who have never desired another man's wife, or procured the death of the husband, as David did, will never reach the place which David nevertheless held in the divine favor. There is a vast difference between what is in itself so undesirable that it must be utterly rejected, and the rich and plenteous harvest which may afterwards appear. For farmers are best pleased with the fields from which, after weeding them, it may be, of great thistles, they receive an hundred-fold; not with fields which have never had any thistles, and hardly bear thirty-fold.

69. So Moses, too, who was so faithful a servant of God in all his house; the minister of the holy, just, and good law; of whose character the apostle speaks in the words here quoted;[4] the minister also of the symbols which, though not conferring salvation, promised the Saviour, as the Saviour Himself shows, when He says, "If ye believed Moses, ye would also believe me, for he wrote of me," —from which passage we have already sufficiently answered the presumptuous cavils of the Manichæans;—this Moses, the servant of the living, the true, the most high God, that made heaven and earth, not of a foreign substance, but of nothing—not from the pressure of necessity, but from plenitude of goodness—not by the suffering of His members, but by the power of His word;—this Moses, who humbly put from him this high ministry, but obediently accepted it, and faithfully kept it, and diligently fulfilled it; who ruled the people with vigilance, reproved them with vehemence, loved them with fervor, and bore with them in patience, standing for his subjects before God to receive His counsel, and to appease His wrath;—this great and good man is not to be judged of from Faustus' malicious representations, but from what is said by God, whose word is a true expression of His true opinion of this man, whom He knew because He made him. For the sins of men are also known to God, though He is not their author; but He takes notice of them as a judge in those who refuse to own them, and pardons them as a father in those who make confession. His servant Moses, as thus described, we love and ad-

[1] 1 Sam. xv. 24.
[2] Luke xvii. 28.
[3] Gal. ii. 14.
[4] Heb. iii. 5.

mire, and to the best of our power imitate, coming indeed far short of his merits, though we have killed no Egyptian, nor plundered any one, nor carried on any war; which actions of Moses were in one case prompted by the zeal of the future champion of his people, and in the other cases commanded by God.

70. It might be shown that, though Moses slew the Egyptian, without being commanded by God, the action was divinely permitted, as, from the prophetic character of Moses, it prefigured something in the future. Now, however, I do not use this argument, but view the action as having no symbolical meaning. In the light, then, of the eternal law, it was wrong for one who had no legal authority to kill the man, even though he was a bad character, besides being the aggressor. But in minds where great virtue is to come, there is often an early crop of vices, in which we may still discern a disposition for some particular virtue, which will come when the mind is duly cultivated. For as farmers, when they see land bringing forth huge crops, though of weeds, pronounce it good for corn; or when they see wild creepers, which have to be rooted out, still consider the land good for useful vines; and when they see a hill covered with wild olives, conclude that with culture it will produce good fruit: so the disposition of mind which led Moses to take the law into his own hands, to prevent the wrong done to his brother, living among strangers, by a wicked citizen of the country from being unrequited, was not unfit for the production of virtue, but from want of culture gave signs of its productiveness in an unjustifiable manner. He who afterwards, by His angel, called Moses on Mount Sinai, with the divine commission to liberate the people of Israel from Egypt, and who trained him to obedience by the miraculous appearance in the bush burning but not consumed, and by instructing him in his ministry, was the same who, by the call addressed from heaven to Saul when persecuting the Church, humbled him, raised him up, and animated him; or in figurative words, by this stroke He cut off the branch, grafted it, and made it fruitful. For the fierce energy of Paul, when in his zeal for hereditary traditions he persecuted the Church, thinking that he was doing God service, was like a crop of weeds showing great signs of productiveness. It was the same in Peter, when he took his sword out of its sheath to defend the Lord, and cut off the right ear of an assailant, when the Lord rebuked him with something like a threat, saying, "Put up thy sword into its sheath; for he that taketh the sword shall perish by the sword."[1] To take the sword is to use weapons against a man's life, without the sanction of the constituted authority. The Lord, indeed, had told His disciples to carry a sword; but He did not tell them to use it. But that after this sin Peter should become a pastor of the Church was no more improper than that Moses, after smiting the Egyptian, should become the leader of the congregation. In both cases the trespass originated not in inveterate cruelty, but in a hasty zeal which admitted of correction. In both cases there was resentment against injury, accompanied in one case by love for a brother, and in the other by love, though still carnal, of the Lord. Here was evil to be subdued or rooted out; but the heart with such capacities needed only, like good soil, to be cultivated to make it fruitful in virtue.

71. Then, as for Faustus' objection to the spoiling of the Egyptians, he knows not what he says. In this Moses not only did not sin, but it would have been sin not to do it. It was by the command of God,[2] who, from His knowledge both of the actions and of the hearts of men, can decide on what every one should be made to suffer, and through whose agency. The people at that time were still carnal, and engrossed with earthly affections; while the Egyptians were in open rebellion against God, for they used the gold, God's creature, in the service of idols, to the dishonor of the Creator, and they had grievously oppressed strangers by making them work without pay. Thus the Egyptians deserved the punishment, and the Israelites were suitably employed in inflicting it. Perhaps, indeed, it was not so much a command as a permission to the Hebrews to act in the matter according to their own inclinations; and God, in sending the message by Moses, only wished that they should thus be informed of His permission. There may also have been mysterious reasons for what God said to the people on this matter. At any rate, God's commands are to be submissively received, not to be argued against. The apostle says, "Who hath known the mind of the Lord? or who hath been His counsellor?"[3] Whether, then, the reason was what I have said, or whether in the secret appointment of God, there was some unknown reason for His telling the people by Moses to borrow things from the Egyptians, and to take them away with them, this remains certain, that this was said for some good reason, and that Moses could not lawfully have done otherwise than God told

1 Matt. xxvi. 51, 52.
2 Ex. iii. 21, 22; xi. 2; xii. 35, 36.
3 Rom. xi. 34.

him, leaving to God the reason of the command, while the servant's duty is to obey.

72. But, says Faustus, it cannot be admitted that the true God, who is also good, ever gave such a command. I answer, such a command can be rightly given by no other than the true and good God, who alone knows the suitable command in every case, and who alone is incapable of inflicting unmerited suffering on any one. This ignorant and spurious goodness of the human heart may as well deny what Christ says, and object to the wicked being made to suffer by the good God, when He shall say to the angels, "Gather first the tares into bundles to burn them." The servants, however, were stopped when they wished to do this prematurely: "Lest by chance, when ye would gather the tares, ye root up the wheat also with them."[1] Thus the true and good God alone knows when, to whom, and by whom to order anything, or to permit anything. In the same way, this human goodness, or folly rather, might object to the Lord's permitting the devils to enter the swine, which they asked to be allowed to do with a mischievous intent,[2] especially as the Manichæans believe that not only pigs, but the vilest insects, have human souls. But setting aside these absurd notions, this is undeniable, that our Lord Jesus Christ, the only son of God, and therefore the true and good God, permitted the destruction of swine belonging to strangers, implying loss of life and of a great amount of property, at the request of devils. No one can be so insane as to suppose that Christ could not have driven the devils out of the men without gratifying their malice by the destruction of the swine. If, then, the Creator and Governor of all natures, in His superintendence, which, though mysterious, is ever just, indulged the violent and unjust inclination of those lost spirits already doomed to eternal fire, why should not the Egyptians, who were unrighteous oppressors, be spoiled by the Hebrews, a free people, who would claim payment for their enforced and painful toil, especially as the earthly possessions which they thus lost were used by the Egyptians in their impious rites, to the dishonor of the Creator? Still, if Moses had originated this order, or if the people had done it spontaneously, undoubtedly it would have been sinful; and perhaps the people did sin, not in doing what God commanded or permitted, but in some desire of their own for what they took. The permission given to this action by divine authority was in accordance with the just and good counsel of Him who uses punishments both to restrain the wicked and to educate His own people; who knows also how to give more advanced precepts to those able to bear them, while He begins on a lower scale in the treatment of the feeble. As for Moses, he can be blamed neither for coveting the property, nor for disputing, in any instance, the divine authority.

73. According to the eternal law, which requires the preservation of natural order, and forbids the transgression of it, some actions have an indifferent character, so that men are blamed for presumption if they do them without being called upon, while they are deservedly praised for doing them when required. The act, the agent, and the authority for the action are all of great importance in the order of nature. For Abraham to sacrifice his son of his own accord is shocking madness. His doing so at the command of God proves him faithful and submissive. This is so loudly proclaimed by the very voice of truth, that Faustus, *eagerly* rummaging for some fault, and reduced at last to slanderous charges, has not the boldness to attack this action. It is scarcely possible that he can have forgotten a deed so famous, that it recurs to the mind of itself without any study or reflection, and is in fact repeated by so many tongues, and portrayed in so many places, that no one can pretend to shut his eyes or his ears to it. If, therefore, while Abraham's killing his son of his own accord would have been unnatural, his doing it at the command of God shows not only guiltless but praiseworthy compliance, why does Faustus blame Moses for spoiling the Egyptians? Your feeling of disapproval for the mere human action should be restrained by a regard for the divine sanction. Will you venture to blame God Himself for desiring such actions? Then "Get thee behind me, Satan, for thou understandest not the things which be of God, but those which be of men." Would that this rebuke might accomplish in you what it did in Peter, and that you might hereafter preach the truth concerning God, which you now, judging by feeble sense, find fault with! as Peter became a zealous messenger to announce to the Gentiles what he objected to at first, when the Lord spoke of it as His intention.

74. Now, if this explanation suffices to satisfy human obstinacy and perverse misinterpretation of right actions of the vast difference between the indulgence of passion and presumption on the part of men, and obedience to the command of God, who knows what to permit or to order, and also the time and the persons, and the due action or suffering in

[1] Matt. xiii. 29, 30.

[2] Matt. viii. 31, 32.

each case, the account of the wars of Moses will not excite surprise or abhorrence, for in wars carried on by divine command, he showed not ferocity but obedience; and God, in giving the command, acted not in cruelty, but in righteous retribution, giving to all what they deserved, and warning those who needed warning. What is the evil in war? Is it the death of some who will soon die in any case, that others may live in peaceful subjection? This is mere cowardly dislike, not any religious feeling. The real evils in war are love of violence, revengeful cruelty, fierce and implacable enmity, wild resistance, and the lust of power, and such like; and it is generally to punish these things, when force is required to inflict the punishment, that, in obedience to God or some lawful authority, good men undertake wars, when they find themselves in such a position as regards the conduct of human affairs, that right conduct requires them to act, or to make others act in this way. Otherwise John, when the soldiers who came to be baptized asked, What shall we do? would have replied, Throw away your arms; give up the service; never strike, or wound, or disable any one. But knowing that such actions in battle were not murderous, but authorized by law, and that the soldiers did not thus avenge themselves, but defend the public safety, he replied, "Do violence to no man, accuse no man falsely, and be content with your wages."[1] But as the Manichæans are in the habit of speaking evil of John, let them hear the Lord Jesus Christ Himself ordering this money to be given to Cæsar, which John tells the soldiers to be content with. "Give," He says, "to Cæsar the things that are Cæsar's."[2] For tribute-money is given on purpose to pay the soldiers for war. Again, in the case of the centurion who said, "I am a man under authority, and have soldiers under me: and I say to one, Go, and he goeth; and to another, Come, and he cometh; and to my servant, Do this, and he doeth it," Christ gave due praise to his faith;[3] He did not tell him to leave the service. But there is no need here to enter on the long discussion of just and unjust wars.

75. A great deal depends on the causes for which men undertake wars, and on the authority they have for doing so; for the natural order which seeks the peace of mankind, ordains that the monarch should have the power of undertaking war if he thinks it advisable, and that the soldiers should perform their military duties in behalf of the peace and safety of the community. When war is undertaken in obedience to God, who would rebuke, or humble, or crush the pride of man, it must be allowed to be a righteous war; for even the wars which arise from human passion cannot harm the eternal well-being of God, nor even hurt His saints; for in the trial of their patience, and the chastening of their spirit, and in bearing fatherly correction, they are rather benefited than injured. No one can have any power against them but what is given him from above. For there is no power but of God,[4] who either orders or permits. Since, therefore, a righteous man, serving it may be under an ungodly king, may do the duty belonging to his position in the State in fighting by the order of his sovereign,—for in some cases it is plainly the will of God that he should fight, and in others, where this is not so plain, it may be an unrighteous command on the part of the king, while the soldier is innocent, because his position makes obedience a duty,—how much more must the man be blameless who carries on war on the authority of God, of whom every one who serves Him knows that He can never require what is wrong?

76. If it is supposed that God could not enjoin warfare, because in after times it was said by the Lord Jesus Christ, "I say unto you, That ye resist not evil: but if any one strike thee on the right cheek, turn to him the left also,"[5] the answer is, that what is here required is not a bodily action, but an inward disposition. The sacred seat of virtue is the heart, and such were the hearts of our fathers, the righteous men of old. But order required such a regulation of events, and such a distinction of times, as to show first of all that even earthly blessings (for so temporal kingdoms and victory over enemies are considered to be, and these are the things which the community of the ungodly all over the world are continually begging from idols and devils) are entirely under the control and at the disposal of the one true God. Thus, under the Old Testament, the secret of the kingdom of heaven, which was to be disclosed in due time, was veiled, and so far obscured, in the disguise of earthly promises. But when the fullness of time came for the revelation of the New Testament, which was hidden under the types of the Old, clear testimony was to be borne to the truth, that there is another life for which this life ought to be disregarded, and another kingdom for which the opposition of all earthly kingdoms should be patiently borne. Thus the name martyrs,

[1] Luke iii. 14. [2] Matt. xxii. 21. [3] Matt. viii. 9, 10. [4] Rom. xiii. 1. [5] Matt. v. 39.

which means witnesses, was given to those who, by the will of God, bore this testimony, by their confessions, their sufferings, and their death. The number of such witnesses is so great, that if it pleased Christ—who called Saul by a voice from heaven, and having changed him from a wolf to a sheep, sent him into the midst of wolves—to unite them all in one army, and to give them success in battle, as He gave to the Hebrews, what nation could withstand them? what kingdom would remain unsubdued? But as the doctrine of the New Testament is, that we must serve God not for temporal happiness in this life, but for eternal felicity hereafter, this truth was most strikingly confirmed by the patient endurance of what is commonly called adversity for the sake of that felicity. So in fullness of time the Son of God, made of a woman, made under the law, that He might redeem them that were under the law, made of the seed of David according to the flesh, sends His disciples as sheep into the midst of wolves, and bids them not fear those that can kill the body, but cannot kill the soul, and promises that even the body will be entirely restored, so that not a hair shall be lost.[1] Peter's sword He orders back into its sheath, restoring as it was before the ear of His enemy that had been cut off. He says that He could obtain legions of angels to destroy His enemies, but that He must drink the cup which His Father's will had given Him.[2] He sets the example of drinking this cup, then hands it to His followers, manifesting thus, both in word and deed, the grace of patience. Therefore God raised Him from the dead, and has given Him a name which is above every name; that in the name of Jesus every knee should bow, of things in heaven and of things in earth, and of things under the earth; and that every tongue should confess that Jesus is Lord, to the glory of God the Father.[3] The patriarchs and prophets, then, have a kingdom in this world, to show that these kingdoms, too, are given and taken away by God: the apostles and martyrs had no kingdom here, to show the superior desirableness of the kingdom of heaven. The prophets, however, could even in those times die for the truth, as the Lord Himself says, "From the blood of Abel to the blood of Zacharia;[4] and in these days, since the commencement of the fulfillment of what is prophesied in the psalm of Christ, under the figure of Solomon, which means the peacemaker, as Christ is our peace,[5] "All kings of the earth shall bow to Him, all nations shall serve Him,"[6] we have seen Christian emperors, who have put all their confidence in Christ, gaining splendid victories over ungodly enemies, whose hope was in the rites of idolatry and devil-worship. There are public and undeniable proofs of the fact, that on one side the prognostications of devils were found to be fallacious, and on the other, the predictions of saints were a means of support; and we have now writings in which those facts are recorded.

77. If our foolish opponents are surprised at the difference between the precepts given by God to the ministers of the Old Testament, at a time when the grace of the New was still undisclosed, and those given to the preachers of the New Testament, now that the obscurity of the Old is removed, they will find Christ Himself saying one thing at one time, and another at another. "When I sent you," He says, "without scrip, or purse, or shoes, did ye lack anything? And they said, Nothing. Then saith He to them, But now, he that hath a scrip, let him take it, and also a purse; and he that hath not a sword, let him sell his garment, and buy one." If the Manichæans found passages in the Old and New Testaments differing in this way, they would proclaim it as a proof that the Testaments are opposed to each other. But here the difference is in the utterances of one and the same person. At one time He says, "I sent you without scrip, or purse, or shoes, and ye lacked nothing;" at another, "Now let him that hath a scrip take it, and also a purse; and he that hath a tunic, let him sell it and buy a sword." Does not this show how, without any inconsistency, precepts and counsels and permissions may be changed, as different times require different arrangements? If it is said that there was a symbolical meaning in the command to take a scrip and purse, and to buy a sword, why may there not be a symbolical meaning in the fact, that one and the same God commanded the prophets in old times to make war, and forbade the apostles? And we find in the passage that we have quoted from the Gospel, that the words spoken by the Lord were carried into effect by His disciples. For, besides going at first without scrip or purse, and yet lacking nothing, as from the Lord's question and their answer it is plain they did, now that He speaks of buying a sword, they say, "Lo, here are two swords;" and He replied, "It is enough." Hence we find Peter with a weapon when he cut off the assailant's ear, on which occasion

[1] Matt. x. 16, 28, 30.
[2] Matt. xxvi. 52, 53; Luke xxii. 42, 51; John xviii. 11.
[3] Phil. ii. 9-11 [4] Matt. xxiii. 35. [5] Eph. ii. 14.

[6] Ps. lxxii. 11.

his spontaneous boldness was checked, because, although he had been told to take a sword, he had not been told to use it.[1] Doubtless, it was mysterious that the Lord should require them to carry weapons, and forbid the use of them. But it was His part to give the suitable precepts, and it was their part to obey without reserve.

78. It is therefore mere groundless calumny to charge Moses with making war, for there would have been less harm in making war of his own accord, than in not doing it when God commanded him. And to dare to find fault with God Himself for giving such a command, or not to believe it possible that a just and good God did so, shows, to say the least, an inability to consider that in the view of divine providence, which pervades all things from the highest to the lowest, time can neither add anything nor take away; but all things go, or come, or remain according to the order of nature or desert in each separate case, while in men a right will is in union with the divine law, and ungoverned passion is restrained by the order of divine law; so that a good man wills only what is commanded, and a bad man can do only what he is permitted, at the same time that he is punished for what he wills to do unjustly. Thus, in all the things which appear shocking and terrible to human feebleness, the real evil is the injustice; the rest is only the result of natural properties or of moral demerit. This injustice is seen in every case where a man loves for their own sake things which are desirable only as means to an end, and seeks for the sake of something else things which ought to be loved for themselves. For thus, as far as he can, he disturbs in himself the natural order which the eternal law requires us to observe. Again, a man is just when he seeks to use things only for the end for which God appointed them, and to enjoy God as the end of all, while he enjoys himself and his friend in God and for God. For to love in a friend the love of God is to love the friend for God. Now both justice and injustice, to be acts at all, must be voluntary; otherwise, there can be no just rewards or punishments; which no man in his senses will assert. The ignorance and infirmity which prevent a man from knowing his duty, or from doing all he wishes to do, belong to God's secret penal arrangement, and to His unfathomable judgments, for with Him there is no iniquity. Thus we are informed by the sure word of God of Adam's sin; and Scripture truly declares that in him all die, and that by him sin entered into the world, and death by sin.[2] And our experience gives abundant evidence, that in punishment for this sin our body is corrupted, and weighs down the soul, and the clay tabernacle clogs the mind in its manifold activity;[3] and we know that we can be freed from this punishment only by gracious interposition. So the apostle cries out in distress, "O wretched man that I am! who shall deliver me from the body of this death? The grace of God through Jesus Christ our Lord."[4] So much we know; but the reasons for the distribution of divine judgment and mercy, why one is in this condition, and another in that, though just, are unknown. Still, we are sure that all these things are due either to the mercy or the judgment of God, while the measures and numbers and weights by which the Creator of all natural productions arranges all things are concealed from our view. For God is not the author, but He is the controller of sin; so that sinful actions, which are sinful because they are against nature, are judged and controlled, and assigned to their proper place and condition, in order that they may not bring discord and disgrace on universal nature. This being the case, and as the judgments of God and the movements of man's will contain the hidden reason why the same prosperous circumstances which some make a right use of are the ruin of others, and the same afflictions under which some give way are profitable to others, and since the whole mortal life of man upon earth is a trial,[5] who can tell whether it may be good or bad in any particular case—in time of peace, to reign or to serve, or to be at ease or to die—or in time of war, to command or to fight, or to conquer or to be killed? At the same time, it remains true, that whatever is good is so by the divine blessing, and whatever is bad is so by the divine judgment.

79. Let no one, then, be so daring as to make rash charges against men, not to say against God. If the service of the ministers of the Old Testament, who were also heralds of the New, consisted in putting sinners to death, and that of the ministers of the New Testament, who are also interpreters of the Old, in being put to death by sinners, the service in both cases is rendered to one God, who, varying the lesson to suit the times, teaches both that temporal blessings are to be sought from Him, and that they are to be forsaken for Him, and that temporal distress is both sent by Him and should be endured for Him. There was, therefore, no cruelty in the command, or in the action of Moses,

[1] Luke xxii. 35-38, 50, 51.

[2] Rom. v. 12, 19.
[3] Wisd. ix. 15.
[4] Rom. vii. 24, 25.
[5] Job vii. 4.

when, in his holy jealousy for his people, whom he wished to be subject to the one true God, on learning that they had fallen away to the worship of an idol made by their own hands, he impressed their minds at the time with a wholesome fear, and gave them a warning for the future, by using the sword in the punishment of a few, whose just punishment God, against whom they had sinned, appointed in the depth of His secret judgment to be immediately inflicted. That Moses acted as he did, not in cruelty, but in great love, may be seen from the words in which he prayed for the sins of the people: "If Thou wilt forgive their sin, forgive it; and if not, blot me out of Thy book."[1] The pious inquirer who compares the slaughter with the prayer will find in this the clearest evidence of the awful nature of the injury done to the soul by prostitution to the images of devils, since such love is roused to such anger. We see the same in the apostle, who, not in cruelty, but in love, delivered a man up to Satan for the destruction of the flesh, that the spirit might be saved in the day of the Lord Jesus.[2] Others, too, he delivered up, that they might learn not to blaspheme.[3] In the apocryphal books of the Manichæans there is a collection of fables, published by some unknown authors under the name of the apostles. The books would no doubt have been sanctioned by the Church at the time of their publication, if holy and learned men then in life, and competent to determine the matter, had thought the contents to be true. One of the stories is, that the Apostle Thomas was once at a marriage feast in a country where he was unknown, when one of the servants struck him, and that he forthwith by his curse brought a terrible punishment on this man. For when he went out to the fountain to provide water for the guests, a lion fell on him and killed him, and the hand with which he had given a slight blow to the apostle was torn off, in fulfillment of the imprecation, and brought by a dog to the table at which the apostle was reclining. What could be more cruel than this? And yet, if I mistake not, the story goes on to say, that the apostle made up for the cruelty by obtaining for the man the blessing of pardon in the next world; so that, while the people of this strange country learned to fear the apostle as being so dear to God, the man's eternal welfare was secured in exchange for the loss of this mortal life. It matters not whether the story is true or false. At any rate, the Manichæans, who regard as genuine and authentic books which the canon of the Church rejects, must allow, as shown in the story, that the virtue of patience, which the Lord enjoins when He says, "If any one smite thee on the right cheek, turn to him thy left also," may be in the inward disposition, though it is not exhibited in bodily action or in words. For when the apostle was struck, instead of turning his other side to the man, or telling him to repeat the blow, he prayed to God to pardon his assailant in the next world, but not to leave the injury unpunished at the time. Inwardly he preserved a kindly feeling, while outwardly he wished the man to be punished as an example. As the Manichæans believe this, rightly or wrongly, they may also believe that such was the intention of Moses, the servant of God, when he cut down with the sword the makers and worshippers of the idol; for his own words show that he so entreated for pardon for their sin of idolatry as to ask to be blotted out of God's book if his prayer was not heard. There is no comparison between a stranger being struck with the hand, and the dishonor done to God by forsaking Him for an idol, when He had brought the people out of the bondage of Egypt, had led them through the sea, and had covered with the waters the enemy pursuing them. Nor, as regards the punishment, is there any comparison between being killed with the sword and being torn in pieces by wild beasts. For judges in administering the law condemn to exposure to wild beasts worse criminals than are condemned to be put to death by the sword.

80. Another of Faustus' malicious and impious charges which has to be answered, is about the Lord's saying to the prophet Hosea, "Take unto thee a wife of whoredoms and children of whoredoms."[4] As regards this passage, the impure mind of our adversaries is so blinded that they do not understand the plain words of the Lord in His gospel, when He says to the Jews, "The publicans and harlots shall go into the kingdom of heaven before you."[5] There is nothing contrary to the mercifulness of truth, or inconsistent with Christian faith, in a harlot leaving fornication, and becoming a chaste wife. Indeed, nothing could be more unbecoming in one professing to be a prophet than not to believe that all the sins of the fallen woman were pardoned when she changed for the better. So when the prophet took the harlot as his wife, it was both good for the woman to have her life amended, and the action symbolized a truth of which we shall speak

1 Ex. xxxii. 32. 2 1 Cor. v. 5. 3 1 Tim. i. 20. 4 Hos. i. 2. 5 Matt. xxi. 31.

presently. But it is plain what offends the Manichæans in this case; for their great anxiety is to prevent harlots from being with child. It would have pleased them better that the woman should continue a prostitute, so as not to bring their god into confinement, than that she should become the wife of one man, and have children.

81. As regards Solomon, it need only be said that the condemnation of his conduct in the faithful narrative of holy Scripture is much more serious than the childish vehemence of Faustus' attacks. The Scripture tells us with faithful accuracy both the good that Solomon had at first, and the evil actions by which he lost the good he began with; while Faustus, in his attacks, like a man closing his eyes, or with no eyes at all, seeks no guidance from the light, but is prompted only by violent animosity. To pious and discerning readers of the sacred Scriptures evidence of the chastity of the holy men who are said to have had several wives is found in this, that Solomon, who by his polygamy gratified his passions, instead of seeking for offspring, is expressly noted as chargeable with being a lover of women. This, as we are informed by the truth which accepts no man's person, led him down into the abyss of idolatry.

82. Having now gone over all the cases in which Faustus finds fault with the Old Testament, and having attended to the merit of each, either defending men of God against the calumnies of carnal heretics, or, where the men were at fault, showing the excellence and the majesty of Scripture, let us again take the cases in the order of Faustus' accusations, and see the meaning of the actions recorded, what they typify, and what they foretell. This we have already done in the case of Abraham, Isaac, and Jacob, of whom God said that He was their God, as if the God of universal nature were the God of none besides them; not honoring them with an unmeaning title, but because He, who could alone have a full and perfect knowledge, knew the sincere and remarkable charity of these men; and because these three patriarchs united formed a notable type of the future people of God, in not only having free children by free women, as by Sarah, and Rebecca, and Leah, and Rachel, but also bond children, as of this same Rebecca was born Esau, to whom it was said, "Thou shalt serve thy brother;"[1] and in having by bond women not only bond children, as by Hagar, but also free children, as by Bilhah and Zilphah. Thus also in the people of God, those spiritually free not only have children born into the enjoyment of liberty, like those to whom it is said, "Be ye followers of me, as I also am of Christ,"[2] but they have also children born into guilty bondage, as Simon was born of Philip.[3] Again, from carnal bondmen are born not only children of guilty bondage, who imitate them, but also children of happy liberty, to whom it is said, "What they say, do; but do not after their works."[4] Whoever rightly observes the fulfillment of this type in the people of God, keeps the unity of the Spirit in the bond of peace, by continuing to the end in union with some, and in patient endurance of others. Of Lot, also, we have already spoken, and have shown what the Scripture mentions as praiseworthy in him, and what as blameworthy and the meaning of the whole narrative.

83. We have next to consider the prophetic significance of the action of Judah in lying with his daughter-in-law. But, for the sake of those whose understanding is feeble, we shall begin with observing, that in sacred Scripture evil actions are sometimes prophetic not of evil, but of good. Divine providence preserves throughout its essential goodness, so that, as in the example given above, from adulterous intercourse a man-child is born, a good work of God from the evil of man, by the power of nature, and not due to the misconduct of the parents; so in the prophetic Scriptures, where both good and evil actions are recorded, the narrative being itself prophetic, foretells something good even by the record of what is evil, the credit being due not to the evil-doer, but to the writer. Judah, when, to gratify his sinful passion, he went in to Tamar, had no intention by his licentious conduct to typify anything connected with the salvation of men, any more than Judas, who betrayed the Lord, intended to produce any result connected with the salvation of men. So then if from the evil deed of Judas the Lord brought the good work of our redemption by His own passion, why should not His prophet, of whom He Himself says "He wrote of me," for the sake of instructing us make the evil action of Judah significant of something good? Under the guidance and inspiration of the Holy Spirit, the prophet has compiled a narrative of actions so as to make a continuous prophecy of the things he designed to foretell. In foretelling good, it is of no consequence whether the typical actions are good or bad. If it is written in red ink that the Ethiopians are black, or in black ink that the Gauls are white, this circumstance does

[1] Gen. xxvii. 40.

[2] 1 Cor. iv. 16. [3] Acts viii. 13. [4] Matt. xxiii. 3.

not affect the information which the writing conveys. No doubt, if it was a painting instead of a writing, the wrong color would be a fault; so when human actions are represented for example or for warning much depends on whether they are good or bad. But when actions are related or recorded as types, the merit or demerit of the agents is a matter of no importance, as long as there is a true typical relation between the action and the thing signified. So in the case of Caiaphas in the Gospel as regards his iniquitous and mischievous intention, and even as regards his words in the sense in which he used them, that a just man should be put to death unjustly, assuredly they were bad; and yet there was a good meaning in his words which he did not know of when he said, "It is expedient that one man should die for the people and that the whole nation perish not." So it is written of Him, "This he spake not of himself; but being the high priest, he prophesied that Jesus should die for the people."[1] In the same way the action of Judah was bad as regards his sinful passion, but it typified a great good he knew nothing of. Of himself he did evil, while it was not of himself that he typified good. These introductory remarks apply not only to Judah, but also to all the other cases where in the narrative of bad actions is contained a prophecy of good.

84. In Tamar, then, the daughter-in-law of Judah, we see the people of the kingdom of Judah, whose kings, answering to Tamar's husbands, were taken from this tribe. Tamar means bitterness; and the meaning is suitable, for this people gave the cup of gall to the Lord.[2] The two sons of Judah represent two classes of kings who governed ill—those who did harm and those who did no good. One of these sons was evil or cruel before the Lord; the other spilled the seed on the ground that Tamar might not become a mother. There are only those two kinds of useless people in the world—the injurious and those who will not give the good they have but lose it or spill it on the ground. And as injury is worse than not doing good, the evil-doer is called the elder and the other the younger. Er, the name of the elder, means a preparer of skins, which were the coats given to our first parents when they were punished with expulsion from paradise.[3] Onan, the name of the younger, means, their grief; that is, the grief of those to whom he does no good, wasting the good he has on the earth. The loss of life implied in the name of the elder is a greater evil than the want of help implied in the name of the younger. Both being killed by God typifies the removal of the kingdom from men of this character. The meaning of the third son of Judah not being joined to the woman, is that for a time the kings of Judah were not of that tribe. So this third son did not become the husband of Tamar; as Tamar represents the tribe of Judah, which continued to exist, although the people received no king from it. Hence the name of this son, Selom, means, his dismission. None of those types apply to the holy and righteous men who, like David, though they lived in those times, belong properly to the New Testament, which they served by their enlightened predictions. Again, in the time when Judah ceased to have a king of its own tribe, the elder Herod does not count as one of the kings typified by the husbands of Tamar; for he was a foreigner, and his union with the people was never consecrated with the holy oil. His was the power of a stranger, given him by the Romans and by Cæsar. And it was the same with his sons, the tetrarchs, one of whom, called Herod, like his father, agreed with Pilate at the time of the Lord's passion.[4] So plainly were these foreigners considered as distinct from the sacred monarchy of Judah, that the Jews themselves, when raging against Christ, exclaimed openly, "We have no king but Cæsar."[5] Nor was Cæsar properly their king, except in the sense that all the world was subject to Rome. The Jews thus condemned themselves, only to express their rejection of Christ, and to flatter Cæsar.

85. The time when the kingdom was removed from the tribe of Judah was the time appointed for the coming of Christ our Lord, the true Saviour, who should come not for harm, but for great good. Thus was it prophesied, "A prince shall not fail from Judah, nor a leader from his loins, till He come for whom it is reserved: He is the desire of nations."[6] Not only the kingdom, but all government, of the Jews had ceased, and also, as prophesied by Daniel, the sacred anointing from which the name Christ or Anointed is derived. Then came He for whom it was reserved, the desire of nations; and the holy of holies was anointed with the oil of gladness above His fellows.[7] Christ was born in the time of the elder Herod, and suffered in the time of Herod the tetrarch. He who thus came to the lost sheep of the house of Israel was typified by Judah when he went to shear his sheep in Thamna, which means, failing. For then the prince had failed from Judah,

[1] John xi. 50, 51.
[2] Matt. xxvii. 34.
[3] Gen. iii. 21.
[4] Luke xxiii. 12.
[5] John xix. 15.
[6] Gen. xlix. 10.
[7] Dan. ix. 24, and Ps. xlv. 7.

with all the government and anointing of the Jews, that He might come for whom it was reserved. Judah, we are told, came with his Adullamite shepherd, whose name was Iras; and Adullamite means, a testimony in water. So it was with this testimony that the Lord came, having indeed greater testimony than that of John;[1] but for the sake of his feeble sheep he made use of the testimony in water. The name Iras, too, means, vision of my brother. So John saw his brother, a brother in the family of Abraham, and from the relationship of Mary and Elisabeth; and the same person he recognised as his Lord and his God, for, as he himself says, he received of His fullness.[2] On account of this vision, among those born of woman, there has arisen no greater than he;[3] because, of all who foretold Christ, he alone saw what many righteous men and prophets desired to see and saw not. He saluted Christ from the womb;[4] he knew Him more certainly from seeing the dove; and therefore, as the Adullamite, he gave testimony by water. The Lord came to shear His sheep, in releasing them from painful burdens, as it is said in praise of the Church in the Song of Songs, that her teeth are like a flock of sheep after shearing.[5]

86. Next, we have Tamar changing her dress; for Tamar also means changing. Still, the name of bitterness must be retained—not that bitterness in which gall was given to the Lord, but that in which Peter wept bitterly.[6] For Judah means confession; and bitterness is mingled with confession as a type of true repentance. It is this repentance which gives fruitfulness to the Church established among all nations. For "it behoved Christ to suffer, and to rise from the dead, and that repentance and the remission of sins be preached among all nations in His name, beginning at Jerusalem."[7] In the dress Tamar put on there is a confession of sins; and Tamar sitting in this dress at the gate of Ænan or Ænaim, which means fountain, is a type of the Church called from among the nations. She ran as a hart to the springs of water, to meet with the seed of Abraham; and there she is made fruitful by one who knows her not, as it is foretold, "A people whom I have not known shall serve me."[8] Tamar received under her disguise a ring, a bracelet, a staff; she is sealed in her calling, adorned in her justification, raised in her glorification. For "whom He predestinated, them He also called: and whom He called, them He also justified: and whom He justified, them He also glorified."[9] This was while she was still disguised, as I have said; and in the same state she conceives, and becomes fruitful in holiness. Also the kid promised is sent to her as to a harlot. The kid represents rebuke for sin, and it is sent by the Adullamite already mentioned, who, as it were, uses the reproachful words, "O generation of vipers!"[10] But this rebuke for sin does not reach her, for she has been changed by the bitterness of confession. Afterwards, by exhibiting the pledges of the ring and bracelet and staff, she prevails over the Jews, in their hasty judgment of her, who are now represented by Judah himself; as at this day we hear the Jews saying that we are not the people of Christ, and have not the seed of Abraham. But when we exhibit the sure tokens of our calling and justification and glorification, they will immediately be confounded, and will acknowledge that we are justified rather than they. I should enter into this more particularly, taking, as it were, each limb and joint separately, as the Lord might enable me, were it not that such minute inquiry is prevented by the necessity of bringing this work to a close, for it is already longer than is desirable.

87. As regards the prophetic significance of David's sin, a single word must suffice. The names occurring in the narrative show what it typifies. David means, strong of hand, or desirable; and what can be stronger than the Lion of the tribe of Judah, who has conquered the world, or more desirable than He of whom the prophet says, "The desire of all nations shall come?"[11] Bersabee means, well of satisfaction, or seventh well: either of these interpretations will suit our purpose. So, in the Song of Songs, the spouse, who is the Church, is called a well of living water;[12] or again, the number seven represents the Holy Spirit, as in the number of days in Pentecost, when the Holy Spirit came from heaven. We learn also from the book of Tobit, that Pentecost was the feast of seven weeks.[13] To forty-nine, which is seven times seven, one is added to denote unity. To this effect is the saying of the apostle: "Bearing with one another in love, endeavoring to keep the unity of the Spirit in the bond of peace."[14] The Church becomes a well of satisfaction by this gift of the Spirit, the number seven denoting its spirituality; for it is in her a fountain of living water springing up unto everlasting life, and he who has it shall never thirst.[15] Uriah, Bersabee's husband, must,

1 John v. 36. 2 John i. 6. 3 Matt. xi. 11. 4 Luke i. 44. 5 Cant. iv. 2. 6 Matt. xxvi. 75. 7 Luke xxiv. 46, 47. 8 Ps. xviii. 43.

9 Rom. viii. 30. 10 Matt. iii. 7. 11 Hag. ii. 8. 12 Cant. iv. 15. 13 Tob. ii. 1. 14 Eph. iv. 2, 3. 15 John iv. 13, 14.

from the meaning of his name, be understood as representing the devil. It is in union to the devil that all are bound whom the grace of God sets free, that the Church without spot or wrinkle may be married to her true Saviour. Uriah means, my light of God; and Hittite means, cut off, referring either to his not abiding in the truth, when he was cut off on account of his pride from the celestial light which he had of God, or to his transforming himself into an angel of light, because, after losing his real strength by his fall, he still dares to say, My light is of God. The literal David, then, was guilty of a heinous crime, which God by the prophet condemned in the rebuke addressed to David, and which David atoned for by his repentance. On the other hand, He who is the desire of all nations loved the Church when washing herself on the roof, that is, when cleansing herself from the pollution of the world, and in spiritual contemplation mounting above her house of clay, and trampling upon it; and after commencing an acquaintance, He puts to death the devil, whom He first entirely removes from her, and joins her to Himself in perpetual union. While we hate the sin, we must not overlook the prophetical significance; and while we love, as is His due, that David who in His mercy has freed us from the devil, we may also love the David who by the humility of his repentance healed the wound made by his transgression.

88. Little need be said of Solomon, who is spoken of in Holy Scripture in terms of the strongest disapproval and condemnation, while nothing is said of his repentance and restoration to the divine favor. Nor can I find in his lamentable fall even a symbolical connection with anything good. Perhaps the strange women he lusted after may be thought to represent the churches chosen from among the Gentiles. This idea might have been admissible, if the women had left their gods for Solomon's sake to worship his God. But as he for their sakes offended his God and worshipped their gods, it seems impossible to think of any good meaning. Doubtless, something is typified, but it is something bad, as in the case already explained of Lot's wife and daughters. We see in Solomon a notable pre-eminence and a notable fall. Now, this good and evil which we see in him at different periods, first good and then evil, are in our day found together in the Church. What is good in Solomon represents, I think, the good members of the Church; and what was bad in him represents the bad members. Both are in one man, as the bad and the good are in the chaff and grain of one floor, or in the tares and wheat of one field. A closer inquiry into what is said of Solomon in Scripture might disclose, either to me or to others of greater learning and greater worth, some more probable interpretation. But as we are now engaged on a different subject, we must not allow this matter to break the connection of our discourse.

89. As regards the prophet Hosea, it is unnecessary for me to explain the meaning of the command, or of the prophet's conduct, when God said to him, "Go and take unto thee a wife of whoredoms and produce children of whoredoms," for the Scripture itself informs us of the origin and purpose of this direction. It proceeds thus: "For the land hath committed great whoredom, departing from the Lord. So he went and took Gomer the daughter of Diblaim; which conceived, and bare him a son. And the Lord said unto him, Call his name Jezreel; for yet a little while, and I will avenge the blood of Jezreel upon the house of Judah, and will cause to cease the kingdom of the house of Israel. And it shall come to pass at that day, that I will break the bow of Israel in the valley of Jezreel. And she conceived again, and bare a daughter. And God said unto him, Call her name No-mercy: for I will no more have mercy upon the house of Israel; but I will utterly take them away. But I will have mercy upon the house of Judah, and will save them by the Lord their God, and will not save them by bow, nor by sword, nor by battle, by horses, nor by horsemen. Now when she had weaned No-mercy, she conceived, and bare a son. Then said God, Call his name Not-my-people: for ye are not my people, and I will not be your God. Yet the number of the children of Israel shall be as the sand of the sea, which cannot be measured for multitude; and it shall come to pass that in the place where it was said unto them, Ye are not my people, there it shall be said unto them, Ye are the sons of the living God. Then shall the children of Israel and the children of Judah be gathered together, and appoint themselves one head, and they shall come up out of the land: for great shall be the day of Jezreel. Say ye unto your brethren, My people; and to your sister, She hath found mercy."[1] Since the typical meaning of the command and of the prophet's conduct is thus explained in the same book by the Lord Himself, and since the writings of the apostles declare the fulfillment of this prophecy in the preaching of the New Testament, every one must accept the explanation thus given of the command

[1] Hos. i. 2—ii. 1.

and of the action of the prophet as the true explanation. Thus it is said by the Apostle Paul, "That He might make known the riches of His glory on the vessels of mercy, which He had afore prepared unto glory, even us, whom He hath called, not of the Jews only, but also of the Gentiles. As He saith also in Hosea, I will call them my people, which were not my people; and her beloved, which was not beloved. And it shall come to pass, that in the place where it was said unto them, Ye are not my people, there shall they be called the children of the living God."[1] Here Paul applies the prophecy to the Gentiles. So also Peter, writing to the Gentiles, without naming the prophet, borrows his expressions when he says, "But ye are a chosen generation, a royal priesthood, a holy nation, a peculiar people; that ye might show forth the praises of Him who has called you out of darkness into His marvellous light; which in time past were not a people, but are now the people of God: which had not obtained mercy, but now have obtained mercy."[2] From this it is plain that the words of the prophet, "And the number of the children of Israel shall be as the sand of the sea, which cannot be measured for multitude," and the words immediately following, "And it shall be that in the place where it was said unto them, Ye are not my people, there they shall be called the children of the living God," do not apply to that Israel which is after the flesh, but to that of which the apostle says to the Gentiles, "Ye therefore are the seed of Abraham, and heirs according to the promise."[3] But, as many Jews who were of the Israel after the flesh have believed, and will yet believe; for of these were the apostles, and all the thousands in Jerusalem of the company of the apostles, as also the churches of which Paul speaks, when he says to the Galatians, "I was unknown by face to the churches of Judæa which were in Christ;"[4] and again, he explains the passage in the Psalms, where the Lord is called the cornerstone,[5] as referring to His uniting in Himself the two walls of circumcision and uncircumcision, "that He might make in Himself of twain one new man, so making peace; and that He might reconcile both unto God in one body by the cross, having slain the enmity thereby: and that He might come and preach peace to them that are far off, and to them that are nigh," that is, to the Gentiles and to the Jews; "for He is our peace, who hath made of both one;"[6] to the same purpose we find the prophet speaking of the Jews as the children of Judah, and of the Gentiles as children of Israel, where he says, "The children of Judah and the children of Israel shall be gathered together, and shall make to themselves one head, and shall go up from the land." Therefore, to speak against a prophecy thus confirmed by actual events, is to speak against the writings of the apostles as well as those of the prophets; and not only to speak against writings, but to impugn in the most reckless manner the evidence clear as noonday of established facts. In the case of the narrative of Judah, it is perhaps not so easy to recognize, under the disguise of the woman called Tamar, the harlot representing the Church gathered from among the corruption of Gentile superstition; but here, where Scripture explains itself, and where the explanation is confirmed by the writings of the apostles, instead of dwelling longer on this, we may proceed at once to inquire into the meaning of the very things to which Faustus objects in Moses the servant of God.

90. Moses killing the Egyptian in defending one of his brethren reminds us naturally of the destruction of the devil, our assailant in this land of strangers, by our defender the Lord Christ. And as Moses hid the dead body in the sand, even so the devil, though slain, remains concealed in those who are not firmly settled. The Lord, we know, builds the Church on a rock; and those who hear His word and do it, He compares to a wise man who builds his house upon a rock, and who does not yield or give way before temptation; and those who hear and do not, He compares to a foolish man who builds on the sand, and when his house is tried its ruin is great.[7]

91. Of the prophetic significance of the spoiling of the Egyptians, which was done by Moses at the command of the Lord his God, who commands nothing but what is most just, I remember to have set down what occurred to me at the time in my book entitled On Christian Doctrine;[8] to the effect that the gold and silver and garments of the Egyptians typified certain branches of learning which may be profitably learned or taught among the Gentiles. This may be the true explanation; or we may suppose that the vessels of gold and silver represent the precious souls, and the garments the bodies, of those from among the Gentiles who join themselves to the people of God, that along with them they may be freed from the Egypt of this world. Whatever the true interpretation may be, the pious student of the Scriptures will feel certain

[1] Rom. ix. 23–26. [2] 1 Pet. ii. 9, 10. [3] Gal. iii. 29. [4] Gal. i. 22. [5] Ps. cxviii. 22. [6] Eph. ii. 11–22.

[7] Matt. vii. 24–27. [8] ii. sec. 40.

that in the command, in the action, and in the narrative there is a purpose and a symbolic meaning.

92. It would take too long to go through all the wars of Moses. It is enough to refer to what has already been said, as sufficient for the purpose in this reply to Faustus of the prophetic and symbolic character of the war with Amalek.[1] There is also the charge of cruelty made against Moses by the enemies of Scriptures, or by those who have never read anything. Faustus does not make any specific charge, but speaks of Moses as commanding and doing many cruel things. But, knowing the things they are in the habit of bringing forward and of misrepresenting, I have already taken a particular case and have defended it, so that any Manichæans who are willing to be corrected, and all other ignorant and irreligious people, may see that there is no ground for their accusations. We must now inquire into the prophetic significance of the command, that many of those who, while Moses was absent, made an idol for themselves should be slain without regard to relationship. It is easy to see that the slaughter of these men represents the warfare against the evil principles which led the people into the same idolatry. Against such evil we are commanded to wage war in the words of the psalm, "Be ye angry and sin not.[2] And a similar command is given by the apostle, when he says, "Mortify your members which are on earth; fornication, uncleanness, luxury, evil concupiscence, and covetousness, which is idolatry."[3]

93. It requires closer examination to see the meaning of the first action of Moses in burning the calf in fire, and grinding it to powder, and sprinkling it in the water for the people to drink. The tables given to him, written with the finger of God, that is, by the agency of the Holy Spirit, he may have broken, because he judged the people unworthy of having them read to them; and he may have burned the calf, and ground it, and scattered it so as to be carried away by the water, in order to let nothing of it remain among the people. But why should he have made them drink it? Every one must feel anxious to discover the typical significance of this action. Pursuing the inquiry, we may find that in the calf there was an embodiment of the devil, as there is in men of all nations who have the devil as their head or leader in their impious rites. The calf is gold, because there is a semblance of wisdom in the institution of idolatrous worship. Of this the apostle says, "Knowing God, they glorified Him not as God, nor were thankful; but they became vain in their imaginations, and their foolish heart was darkened. Professing themselves to be wise they became foolish, and changed the glory of the incorruptible God into the likeness of corruptible man, and of birds, and of four-footed beasts, and of creeping things."[4] From this so-called wisdom came the golden calf, which was one of the forms of idolatry among the chief men and professed sages of Egypt. The calf, then, represents every body or society of Gentile idolaters. This impious society the Lord Christ burns with that fire of which He says in the Gospel, "I am come to send fire on the earth;"[5] for, as there is nothing hid from His heat,[6] when the Gentiles believe in Him they lose the form of the devil in the fire of divine influence. Then all the body is ground, that is, after the dissolution of the combination in the membership of iniquity comes humiliation under the word of truth. Then the dust is sprinkled in the water, that the Israelites, that is, the preachers of the gospel, may in baptism admit those formerly idolaters into their own body, that is, the body of Christ. To Peter, who was one of those Israelites, it was said of the Gentiles, "Kill, and eat."[7] To kill and eat is much the same as to grind and drink. So this calf, by the fire of zeal, and the keen penetration of the word, and the water of baptism, was swallowed up by the people, instead of their being swallowed up by it.

94. Thus, when the very passages on which the heretics found their objections to the Scriptures are studied and examined, the more obscure they are the more wonderful are the secrets which we discover in reply to our questions; so that the mouths of blasphemers are completely stopped, and the evidence of the truth so stifles them that they cannot even utter a sound. The unhappy men who will not receive into their hearts the sweetness of the truth must feel its force as a gag in their mouths. All those passages speak of Christ. The head now ascended into heaven along with the body still suffering on earth is the full development of the whole purpose of the authors of Scripture, which is well called Sacred Scripture. Every part of the narrative in the prophetical books should be viewed as having a figurative meaning, except what serves merely as a framework for the literal or figurative predictions of this king and of his people. For as in harps and other musical instruments the musical sound does not come from all parts of the instrument, but from the strings, and the rest is

1 L. xii. sec. 30.
2 Ps. iv. 4.
3 Col. iii. 5.
4 Rom. i. 21-23.
5 Luke xii. 49.
6 Ps. xix. 6.
7 Acts x. 13.

only for fastening and stretching the strings so as to tune them, that when they are struck by the musician they may give a pleasant sound; so in these prophetical narratives the circumstances selected by the prophetic spirit either predict some future event, or if they have no voice of their own, they serve to connect together other significant utterances.

95. Should the heretics reject our exposition of those allegorical narratives, or even insist on understanding them only in a literal sense, to dispute about such a difference of understanding would be as useless as to dispute about a difference of taste. Only, the fact that the divine precepts have either a moral and religious character or a prophetic meaning must be believed, whether intelligently or not. Moreover, the figurative interpretations must all be in the interest of morality and religion. So, if the Manichæans or any others disagree with our interpretation, or differ from us in method or in any particular opinion, suffice it that the character of the fathers whom God commends for their conduct and obedience to His precepts is vindicated on a principle which all but those inveterate in their hostility will acknowledge to be true; and that the purity and dignity of the Scriptures are maintained in reference to those passages which the enemies of the truth find fault with, where certain actions are either praised or blamed, or merely narrated for us to form a judgment of them.

96. In fact, nothing could have been devised more likely to instruct and benefit the pious reader of sacred Scripture than that, besides describing praiseworthy characters as examples, and blameworthy characters as warnings, it should also narrate cases where good men have gone back and fallen into evil, whether they are restored to the right path or continue irreclaimable; and also where bad men have changed, and have attained to goodness, whether they persevere in it or relapse into evil; in order that the righteous may be not lifted up in the pride of security, nor the wicked hardened in despair of cure. And even those passages in Scripture which contain no examples or warnings are either required for connection, so as to pass on to essential matters, or, from their very appearance of superfluity, indicate the presence of some secret symbolical meaning. For in the books we speak of, so far from there being a want or a scarcity of prophetical announcements, such announcements are numerous and distinct; and now that the fulfillment has actually taken place, the testimony thus borne to the divine authority of the books is irresistibly strong, so that it is mere madness to suppose that there can be any useless or unmeaning passages in books to which all classes of men and of minds do homage, and which themselves predict what we see thus actually coming to pass.

97. If, then, any one reading of the action of David, of which he repented when the Lord rebuked and threatened him, find in the narrative an encouragement to sin, is Scripture to be blamed for this? Is not the man's own guilt in proportion to the abuse which he makes for his own injury or destruction of what was written for his recovery and release? David is set forth as a great example of repentance, because men who fall into sin either proudly disregard the cure of repentance, or lose themselves in despair of obtaining salvation or of meriting pardon. The example is for the benefit of the sick, not for the injury of those in health. If madmen destroy themselves, or if evil-doers destroy others, with surgical instruments, it is not the fault of surgery.

98. Even supposing that our fathers the patriarchs and prophets, of whose devout and religious habits so good a report is given in that Scripture which every one who knows it, and has not lost entirely the use of his reason, must admit to have been provided by God for the salvation of men, were as lustful and cruel as the Manichæans falsely and fanatically allege, they might still be shown to be superior not only to those whom the Manichæans call the Elect, but also to their god himself. Is there in the licentious intercourse of man with woman anything so bad as the self-abasement of unclouded light by mixture with darkness? Here, is a man prompted by avarice and greed to pass off his wife as his sister and sell her to her lover; but worse still and more shocking, that one should disguise his own nature to gratify criminal passion, and submit gratuitously to pollution and degradation. Why, even one who knowingly lies with his own daughters is not equally criminal with one who lets his members share in the defilement of all sensuality as gross as this, or grosser. And is not the Manichæan god a partaker in the contamination of the most atrocious acts of uncleanness? Again, if it were true, as Faustus says, that Jacob went from one to another of his four wives, not desiring offspring, but resembling a he-goat in licentiousness, he would still not be sunk so low as your god, who must not only have shared in this degradation, from his being confined in the bodies of Jacob and his wives so as to be mixed up with all their movements, but also, in union with this very he-goat of Faustus' coarse comparison, must have endured all the pains of animal appetite,

incurring fresh defilement at every step, as partaking in the passion of the male, the conception of the female, and the birth of the kid. And, in the same way, supposing Judah to have been guilty not only of fornication, but of incest, a share in the heats and impurities of this incestuous passion would also belong to your god. David repented of his sin in loving the wife of another, and in ordering the death of her husband; but when will your god repent of giving up his members to the wanton passion of the male and female chiefs of the race of darkness, and of putting to death not the husband of his mistress, but his own children, whom he confines in the members of the very demons who were his own lovers? Even if David had not repented, nor been thus restored to righteousness, he would still have been better than your god. David may have been defiled by this one act, or to the extent to which one man is capable of such defilement; but your god suffers the pollution of his members in all such actions by whomsoever committed. The prophet Hosea, too, is accused by Faustus: and, supposing him to have taken the harlot to wife because he had a criminal affection for her, if he is licentious and she a prostitute, their souls, according to your own assertion, are parts and members of your god and of his nature. In plain language, the harlot herself must be your god. You cannot pretend that your god is not confined in the contaminated body, or that he is only present, while preserving entire the purity of his own nature; and you acknowledge that the members of your god are so defiled as to require a special purification. This harlot, then, for whom you venture to find fault with the man of God, even if she had not been changed for the better by becoming a chaste wife, would still have been your god; at least you must admit her soul to have been a part, however small, of your god. But one single harlot is not so bad as your god, for he on account of his mixture with the race of darkness shares in every act of prostitution; and wherever such impurities are perpetrated, he goes through the corresponding experiences of abandonment, of release, and of confinement, and this from generation to generation, till this most corrupt part reaches its final state in the mass of darkness, like an irreclaimable harlot. Such are the evils and such the shameful abominations which your god could not ward off from his members, and to which he was brought irresistibly by his merciless enemy; for only by the sacrifice of his own subjects, or rather his own parts, could he effect the destruction of his formidable assailant. Surely, there was nothing so bad as this in killing an Egyptian so as to preserve uninjured a fellow-countryman. Yet Faustus finds fault with this most absurdly, while with amazing infatuation he overlooks the case of his own god. Would it not have been better for him to have carried off the gold and silver vessels of the Egyptians, than to let his members be carried off by the race of darkness? And yet the worshippers of this unfortunate god find fault with the servant of our God for carrying on wars, in which he with his followers were always victorious, so that, under the leadership of Moses, the children of Israel carried captive their enemies, men and women, as your god would have done too, if he had been able. You profess to accuse Moses of doing wrong, while in fact you envy his success. There was no cruelty in punishing with the sword those who had sinned grievously against God. Indeed, Moses entreated pardon for this sin, even offering to bear himself in their stead the divine anger. But even had he been cruel instead of compassionate, he would still have been better than your god. For if any of his followers had been sent to break the force of the enemy and had been taken captive, he would never, if victorious, have condemned him when he had done no wrong, but acted in obedience to orders. And yet this is what your god is to do with the part of himself which is to be fastened in the mass of darkness, because it obeyed orders, and advanced at the risk of its own life in defence of his kingdom against the body of the enemy. But, says the Manichæan, this part, after mixture and combination with evil during the course of ages, has not been obedient.. But why? If the obedience was voluntary, the guilt is real, and the punishment just. But from this it would follow that there is no nature opposed to sin; otherwise it would not sin voluntarily; and so the whole system of Manichæism falls at once. If, again, this part suffers from the power of this enemy against whom it was sent, and is subdued by a force it was unable to resist, the punishment is unjust, and flagrantly cruel. The god who is defended on the plea of necessity is a fit object of worship to those who refuse to worship the one true God. Still, it must be allowed that, however debasing the worship of this god may be, the worshippers are so far better than their deity, that they have an existence, while he is nothing more than a fabulous invention. Proceed we now to the rest of Faustus' vagaries.[1]

---

1 [This book is one of the most unsatisfactory parts of the entire treatise. We have here some of the worst specimens of perverse Scripture interpretation.—A. H. N.]

BOOK XXIII.

FAUSTUS RECURS TO THE GENEALOGICAL DIFFICULTY, AND INSISTS THAT EVEN ACCORDING TO MATTHEW JESUS WAS NOT SON OF GOD UNTIL HIS BAPTISM. AUGUSTIN SETS FORTH THE CATHOLIC VIEW OF THE RELATION OF THE DIVINE AND THE HUMAN IN THE PERSON OF CHRIST.

1. FAUSTUS said: On one occasion, when addressing a large audience, I was asked by one of the crowd, Do you believe that Jesus was born of Mary? I replied, Which Jesus do you mean? for in the Hebrew it is the name of several people. One was the son of Nun, the follower of Moses;[1] another was the son of Josedech the high priest;[2] again, another is spoken of as the son of David;[3] and another is the Son of God.[4] Of which of these do you ask whether I believe him to have been born of Mary? His answer was, The Son of God, of course. On what evidence, said I, oral or written, am I to believe this? He replied, On the authority of Matthew. What, said I, did Matthew write? He replied, "The book of the generation of Jesus Christ, the son of David, the son of Abraham" (Matt. i. 1). Then said I, I was afraid you were going to say, The book of the generation of Jesus Christ, the Son of God; and I was prepared to correct you. Now that you have quoted the verse accurately, you must nevertheless be advised to pay attention to the words. Matthew does not profess to give an account of the generation of the Son of God, but of the son of David.

2. I will, for the present, suppose that this person was right in saying that the son of David was born of Mary. It still remains true, that in this whole passage of the generation no mention is made of the Son of God till we come to the baptism; so that it is an injurious misrepresentation on your part to speak of this writer as making the Son of God the inmate of a womb. The writer, indeed, seems to cry out against such an idea, and in the very title of his book to clear himself of such blasphemy, asserting that the person whose birth he describes is the son of David, not the Son of God. And if you attend to the writer's meaning and purpose, you will see that what he wishes us to believe of Jesus the Son of God is not so much that He was born of Mary, as that He became the Son of God by baptism at the river Jordan. He tells us that the person of whom he spoke at the outset as the son of David was baptized by John, and became the Son of God on this particular occasion, when about thirty years old, according to Luke, when also the voice was heard saying to Him, "Thou art my Son; this day have I begotten Thee."[5] It appears from this, that what was born, as is supposed, of Mary thirty years before, was not the Son of God, but what was afterwards made so by baptism at Jordan, that is, the new man, the same as in us when we were converted from Gentile error, and believe in God. This doctrine may or may not agree with what you call the Catholic faith; at all events, it is what Matthew says, if Matthew is the real author. The words, Thou art my Son, this day I have begotten Thee, or, This is my beloved Son, in whom I am well pleased, do not occur in connection with the story of Mary's motherhood, but with the putting away of sin at Jordan. This is what is written; and if you believe this doctrine, you must be called a Matthæan, for you will no longer be a Catholic. The Catholic doctrine is well known; and it is as unlike Matthew's representations as it is unlike the truth. In the words of your creed, you declare that you believe in Jesus Christ, the Son of God, who was born of the Virgin Mary. According to you, therefore, the Son of God comes from Mary; according to Matthew, from the Jordan; while we believe Him to come from God. Thus the doctrine of Matthew, if we are right in assigning the authorship to him, is as different from yours as from ours; only we acknowledge that he is more cautious than you in ascribing the being born of a woman to the son of David, and not to the Son of God. As for you, your only alternative is to deny that those statements were made, as they appear to be, by Matthew, or to allow that you have abandoned the faith of the apostles.

3. For our part, while no one can alter our conviction that the Son of God comes from God, we might indulge a credulous disposition, to the extent of admitting the fiction, that Jesus became the Son of God at Jordan, but not that the Son of God was born of a woman. Then, again, the son said to have been born

[1] Ex. xxiii. 11.
[2] Hag. i. 1.
[3] Rom. i. 1–3.
[4] Mark i. 1.
[5] Luke iii. 22, 23.

of Mary cannot properly be called the son of David, unless it is ascertained that he was begotten by Joseph. You say he was not, and therefore you must allow him not to have been the son of David, even though he were the son of Mary. The genealogy proceeds in the line of Hebrew fathers from Abraham to David, and from David to Joseph; and as we are told that Joseph was not the real father of Jesus, Jesus cannot be said to be the son of David. To begin with calling Jesus the son of David, and then to go on to tell of his being born of Mary before the consummation of her marriage with Joseph, is pure madness. And if the son of Mary cannot be called the son of David, on account of his not being the son of Joseph, still less can the name be given to the Son of God.

4. Moreover, the Virgin herself appears to have belonged not to the tribe of Judah, to which the Jewish kings belonged, and which all agree was David's tribe, but to the priestly tribe of Levi. This appears from the fact that the Virgin's father Joachim was a priest; and his name does not occur in the genealogy. How, then, can Mary be brought within the pale of relationship to David, when she has neither father nor husband belonging to it? Consequently, Mary's son cannot possibly be the son of David, unless you can bring the mother into some connection with Joseph, so as to be either his wife or his daughter.

5. Augustin replied: The Catholic, which is also the apostolic, doctrine, is, that our Lord and Saviour Jesus Christ is both the Son of God in His divine nature, and the Son of David after the flesh. This we prove from the writings of the evangelists and apostles, so that no one can reject our proofs without also rejecting these writings. Faustus' plan is to represent some one as saying a few words, without bringing forward any evidence in answer to Faustus' fertile sophistry. But with all his ingenuity, the proofs I have to give will leave Faustus no reply, but that these passages are spurious interpolations in the sacred record,—a reply which serves as a means of escaping, or of trying to escape, the force of the plainest statements in Holy Scripture. We have already in this treatise sufficiently exposed the irrational absurdity, as well as the daring profanity, of such criticism; and not to exceed all limits, we must avoid repetition. It cannot be necessary that we should bring together all the passages scattered throughout Scripture, which show, in answer to Faustus, that in the books of the highest and most sacred authority He who is called the only-begotten Son of God, even God with God, is also called the Son of David, on account of His taking the form of a servant from the Virgin Mary, the wife of Joseph. To instance only Matthew, since Faustus' argument refers to this Gospel, as the whole book cannot be quoted here, let whoever choose read it, and see how Matthew carries on to the passion and the resurrection the narrative of Him whom He calls the Son of David in the introduction to the genealogy. Of this same Son of David he speaks as being conceived and born of the Virgin Mary by the Holy Ghost. He also applies to this the declaration of the prophet, "Behold, a virgin shall conceive, and shall bear a son, and they shall call His name Emmanuel, which is being interpreted, God with us."[1] Again, He who was called, even from the Virgin's womb, God-with-us, is said to have heard, when He was baptized by John, a voice from heaven, saying, "This is my beloved Son, in whom I am well pleased."[2] Will Faustus say that to be called God is less than to be called the Son of God? He seems to think so, for he tries to prove that because this voice came from heaven at the time of the baptism, therefore, according to Matthew, He must then have become the Son of God; whereas the same evangelist, in a previous passage, quotes the sacred announcement made by the prophet, in which the child born of the Virgin is called God-with-us.

6. It is remarkable how, amid his wild irrelevancies, this wretched trifler loses no available opportunity of darkening the declarations of Scripture by the fabulous creations of his own fancy. Thus he says of Abraham, that when he took his handmaid to wife he disbelieved God's promise that he should have a child by Sarah; whereas, in fact, this promise had not at that time been given. Then he accuses Abraham of falsehood in calling Sarah his sister, not having read what may be learned on the authority of Scripture about the family of Sarah. Abraham's son Isaac also he accuses of falsely calling his wife his sister, though a distinct account is given of her family. Then he accuses Jacob of there being a daily quarrel among his four wives, which should be the first to appropriate him on his return from the field, while nothing of this is said in Scripture. And this is the man who pretends to hate the writers of the sacred books for their falsehood, and who has the effrontery so to misrepresent even the gospel record, though its authority is admitted by all as possessing the most abundant confirmation, as to try to make it appear, not indeed that Matthew himself,—for in that case

[1] Isa. viii. 14, and Matt. i. 23.
[2] Matt. iii. 17.

he would have been forced to yield to apostolic authority,—but that some one under the name of Matthew, has written about Christ what he refuses to believe, and attempts to refute with a contumelious ingenuity!

7. The voice from heaven at the Jordan should be compared with the voice heard on the Mount.[1] In neither case do the words, "This is my beloved Son, in whom I am well pleased," imply that He was not the Son of God before; for He who from the Virgin's womb took the form of a servant "was in the form of God, and thought it no robbery to be equal with God."[2] And the same Apostle Paul himself says distinctly elsewhere," "But in the fullness of time, God sent His Son, made of a woman, made under the law;"[3] that is, a woman in the Hebrew sense, not a wife, but one of the female sex. The Son of God is both Lord of David in His divine nature, and Son of David as being of the seed of David after the flesh. And if it were not profitable for us to believe this, the same apostle would not have made it so prominent as he does, when he says to Timothy, "Remember that Christ Jesus, of the seed of David, rose from the dead, according to my gospel."[4] And he carefully enjoins believers to regard as accursed whoever preaches another gospel contrary to this.

8. This assailant of the holy Gospel need find no difficulty in the fact that Christ is called the Son of David, though He was born of a virgin, and though Joseph was not His real father; while the genealogy is brought down by the evangelist Matthew, not to Mary, but to Joseph. First of all, the husband, as the man, is the more honorable; and Joseph was Mary's husband, though she did not live with him, for Matthew himself mentions that she was called Joseph's wife by the angel; as it is also from Matthew that we learn that Mary conceived not by Joseph, but by the Holy Spirit. But if this, instead of being a true narrative written by Matthew the apostle, was a false narrative written by some one else under his name, is it likely that he would have contradicted himself in such an apparent manner, and in passages so immediately connected, as to speak of the Son of David as born of Mary without conjugal intercourse, and then, in giving His genealogy, to bring it down to the very man with whom the Virgin is expressly said not to have had intercourse, unless he had some reason for doing so? Even supposing there were two writers, one calling Christ the Son of David, and giving an account of Christ's progenitors from David down to Joseph; while the other does not call Christ the Son of David, and says that He was born of the Virgin Mary without intercourse with any man; those statements are not irreconcilable, so as to prove that one or both writers must be false. It will appear on reflection that both accounts might be true; for Joseph might be called the husband of Mary, though she was his wife only in affection, and in the intercourse of the mind, which is more intimate than that of the body. In this way it might be proper that the husband of the virgin-mother of Christ should have a place in the list of Christ's ancestors. It might also be the case that some of David's blood flowed in Mary herself, so that the flesh of Christ, although produced from a virgin, still owed its origin to David's seed. But as, in fact, both statements are made by one and the same writer, who informs us both that Joseph was the husband of Mary and that the mother of Christ was a virgin, and that Christ was of the seed of David, and that Joseph is in the list of Christ's progenitors in the line of David, those who prefer the authority of the sacred Gospel to that of heretical fiction must conclude that Mary was not unconnected with the family of David, and that she was properly called the wife of Joseph, because being a woman she was in spiritual alliance with him, though there was no bodily connection. Joseph, too, it is plain, could not be omitted in the genealogy; for, from the superiority of his sex, such an omission would be equivalent to a denial of his relation to the woman with whom he was inwardly united; and believers in Christ are taught not to think carnal connection the chief thing in marriage, as if without this they could not be man and wife, but to imitate in Christian wedlock as closely as possible the parents of Christ, that so they may have the more intimate union with the members of Christ.

9. We believe that Mary, as well as Joseph, was of the family of David, because we believe the Scriptures, which assert both that Christ was of the seed of David after the flesh, and that His mother was the Virgin Mary, He having no human father. Therefore, whoever denies the relationship of Mary to David, evidently opposes the pre-eminent authority of these passages of Scripture; and to maintain this opposition he must bring evidence in support of his statement from writings acknowledged by the Church as canonical and catholic, not from any writings he pleases. In the matters of which we are now treating, only the canonical writings have any weight with us; for they only are received

1 Matt. xvii. 5.
2 Phil. ii. 6.
3 Gal. iv. 4.
4 2 Tim. ii. 8.

and acknowledged by the Church spread over all the world, which is itself a fulfillment of the prophecies regarding it contained in these writings. Accordingly, I am not bound to admit the uncanonical account of Mary's birth which Faustus adopts, that her father was a priest of the tribe of Levi, of the name of Joachim. But even were I to admit this account, I should still contend that Joachim must have in some way belonged to the family of David, and had somehow been adopted from the tribe of Judah into that of Levi; or if not he, one of his ancestors; or, at least, that while born in the tribe of Levi, he had still some relation to the line of David; as Faustus himself acknowledges that Mary, though belonging to the tribe of Levi, could be given to a husband of the tribe of Judah; and he expressly says that if Mary were Joseph's daughter, the name Son of David would be applicable to Christ. In this way, by the marriage of Joseph's daughter in the tribe of Levi, her son, though born in the tribe of Levi, might not improperly be called the Son of David. And so, if the mother of that Joachim, who in the passage quoted by Faustus is called the father of Mary, married in the tribe of Levi while she belonged to the tribe of Judah and to the family of David, there would thus be a sufficient reason for speaking of Joachim and Mary and Mary's son as belonging to the seed of David. If I felt obliged to pay any regard to the apocryphal scripture in which Joachim is called the father of Mary, I should adopt some such explanation as the above, rather than admit any falsehood in the Gospel, where it is written both that Jesus Christ, the Son of God, and our Saviour, was of the seed of David after the flesh, and that He was born of the Virgin Mary. It is enough for us that the enemies of these Scriptures, which record these truths and which we believe, cannot prove against them any charge of falsehood.

10. Faustus cannot pretend then I am unable to prove that Mary was of the family of David, as I have shown him unable to prove that she was not. I produce the strongest evidence from Scriptures of established authority, which declare that Christ was of the seed of David, and that He was born without a father of the Virgin Mary. Faustus expresses what he considers a most becoming indignation against impropriety when he says, It is an injurious misrepresentation of the writer to make him speak of the Son of God as the inmate of a womb. Of course, the Catholic doctrine which teaches that Christ the Son of God was born in the flesh of a virgin, does not make the Son of God the inmate of her womb in the sense of having no existence beyond it, as if He had abandoned the government of heaven and earth, or as if He had left the presence of the Father. The mistake is with the Manichæans, whose understanding is so incapable of forming a conception of anything except what is material, that they cannot comprehend how the Word of God, who is the virtue and wisdom of God, while remaining in Himself and with the Father, and while governing the universe, reaches from end to end in strength, and sweetly orders all things.[1] In the faultless procedure of this adorable providence, He appointed for Himself an earthly mother; and to free His servants from the bondage of corruption He took in this mother the form of a servant, that is, a mortal body; and this body which He took He showed openly, and when it had been exposed, even to suffering and death, He raised it again from the dead, and built again the temple which had been destroyed. You who shrink from this doctrine as blasphemous, make the members of your god to be confined not in a virgin's womb, but in the wombs of all female animals, from elephants down to flies. Perhaps you think the less of the true Christ, because the Word is said so to have become incarnate in the Virgin's womb as to provide a temple for Himself in human nature, while His own nature continued unaltered in its integrity; and, on the other hand, you think the more of your god, because in the bonds and pollution of his confinement in flesh, in the part which is to be made fast to the mass of darkness, he seeks for help to no purpose, or is even rendered powerless to ask for help.

[1] Wisd. viii. 1.

BOOK XXIV.

FAUSTUS EXPLAINS THE MANICHÆAN DENIAL THAT MAN WAS MADE BY GOD AS APPLYING TO THE FLESHLY MAN NOT TO THE SPIRITUAL. AUGUSTIN ELUCIDATES THE APOSTLE PAUL'S CONTRASTS BETWEEN FLESH AND SPIRIT SO AS TO EXCLUDE THE MANICHÆAN VIEW.

1. Faustus said: We are asked the reason for our denial that man is made by God. But we do not assert that man is in no sense made by God; we only ask in what sense,

and when, and how. For, according to the apostle, there are two men, one of whom he calls sometimes the outer man, generally the earthy, sometimes, too, the old man: the other he calls the inner or heavenly or new man.[1] The question is, Which of these is made by God? For there are likewise two times of our nativity; one when nature brought us forth into this light, binding us in the bonds of flesh; and the other, when the truth regenerated us on our conversion from error and our entrance into the faith. It is this second birth of which Jesus speaks in the Gospel, when He says, "Except a man be born again, he cannot see the kingdom of God."[2] Nicodemus, not knowing what Christ meant, was at a loss, and inquired how this could be, for an old man could not enter into his mother's womb and be born a second time. Jesus said in reply, "Except a man be born of water and of the Holy Spirit, he cannot see the kingdom of God." Then He adds, "That which is born of the flesh is flesh; and that which is born of the Spirit is spirit." Hence, as the birth in which our bodies originate is not the only birth, but there is another in which we are born again in spirit, an important question arises from this distinction as to which of those births it is in which God makes us. The manner of birth also is twofold. In the humiliating process of ordinary generation, we spring from the heat of animal passion; but when we are brought into the faith, we are formed under good instruction in honor and purity in Jesus Christ, by the Holy Spirit. For this reason, in all religion, and especially in the Christian religion, young children are invited to membership. This is hinted at in the words of His apostle: "My little children, of whom I travail in birth again until Christ be formed in you."[3] The question, then, is not whether God makes man, but what man He makes, and when, and how. For if it is when we are fashioned in the womb that God forms us after His own image, which is the common belief of Gentiles and Jews, and which is also your belief, then God makes the old man, and produces us by means of sensual passion, which does not seem suitable to His divine nature. But if it is when we are converted and brought to a better life that we are formed by God, which is the general doctrine of Christ and His apostles, and which is also our doctrine, in this case God makes us new men, and produces us in honor and purity, which would agree perfectly with His sacred and adorable majesty. If you do not reject Paul's authority, we will prove to you from him what man God makes, and when, and how. He says to the Ephesians, "That ye put off according to your former conversation the old man, which is corrupt through deceitful lusts; and be renewed in the spirit of your mind; and put on the new man, which after God is created in righteousness and holiness of truth."[4] This shows that in the creation of man after the image of God, it is another man that is spoken of, and another birth, and another manner of birth. The putting off and putting on of which he speaks, point to the time of the reception of the truth; and the assertion that the new man is created by God implies that the old man is created neither by God nor after God. And when he adds, that this new man is made in holiness and righteousness and truth, he thus points to another manner of birth of which this is the character, and which, as I have said, differs widely from the manner in which bodily generation is effected. And as he declares that only the former is of God, it follows that the latter is not. Again, writing to the Colossians, he uses words to the same effect: "Put off the old man with his deeds, and put on the new man, which is renewed in the knowledge of God according to the image of Him who created Him in you." Here he not only shows that it is the new man that God makes, but he declares the time and manner of the formation, for the words in the knowledge of God point to the time of believing. Then he adds, according to the image of Him who created him, to make it clear that the old man is not the image of God, nor formed by God. Moreover, the following words, "Where there is neither male nor female, Jew nor Greek, Barbarian nor Scythian,"[5] show more plainly still that the birth by which we are made male and female, Greeks and Jews, Scythians and Barbarians, is not the birth in which God effects the formation of man; but that the birth with which God has to do is that in which we lose the difference of nation and sex and condition, and become one like Him who is one, that is, Christ. So the same apostle says again, "As many as have been baptized in Christ have put on Christ: there is neither Jew nor Greek, there is neither male nor female, there is neither bond nor free; but all are one in Christ."[6] Man, then, is made by God, not when from one he is divided into many, but when from many he becomes one. The division is in the first birth, or that of the body; union comes by the second, which is immaterial and divine. This affords sufficient

[1] Rom. vi., vii.; 1 Cor. xv.; 2 Cor. iv., Eph. iii. iv., and Col. iii.
[2] John iii. 3.
[3] Gal. iv. 19.
[4] Eph. iv. 22-24.
[5] Col. iii. 9-11.
[6] Gal. iii. 27, 28.

ground for our opinion, that the birth of the body should be ascribed to nature, and the second birth to the Supernal Majesty. So the same apostle says again to the Corinthians, "I have begotten you in Christ Jesus by the gospel;"[1] and, speaking of himself, to the Galatians, "When it pleased Him, who separated me from my mother's womb, to reveal His Son in me, that I might preach Him among the Gentiles, immediately I conferred not with flesh and blood."[2] It is plain that everywhere he speaks of the second or spiritual birth as that in which we are made by God, as distinct from the indecency of the first birth, in which we are on a level with other animals as regards dignity and purity, as we are conceived in the maternal womb, and are formed, and brought forth. You may observe that in this matter the dispute between us is not so much about a question of doctrine as of interpretation. For you think that it is the old or outer or earthy man that is said to have been made by God; while we apply this to the heavenly man, giving the superiority to the inner or new man. And our opinion is not rash or groundless, for we have learned it from Christ and His apostles, who are proved to have been the first in the world who thus taught.

2. AUGUSTIN replied: The Apostle Paul certainly uses the expression the inner man for the spirit of the mind, and the outer man for the body and for this mortal life; but we nowhere find him making these two different men, but one, which is all made by God, both the inner and the outer. However, it is made in the image of God only as regards the inner, which, besides being immaterial, is rational, and is not possessed by the lower animals. God, then, did not make one man after His own image, and another man not after that image; but the one man, which includes both the inner and the outer, He made after His own image, not as regards the possession of a body and of mortal life, but as regards the rational mind with the power of knowing God, and with the superiority as compared with all irrational creatures which the possession of reason implies. Faustus allows that the inner man is made by God, when, as he says, it is renewed in the knowledge of God after the image of Him that created him. I readily admit this on the apostle's authority. Why does not Faustus admit on the same authority that "God has placed the members every one in the body, as it has pleased Him"?[3] Here we learn from the same apostle that God is the framer of the outer man too. Why does Faustus take only what he thinks to be in his own favor, while he leaves out or rejects what upsets the follies of the Manichæans? Moreover, in treating of the earthy and the heavenly man, and making the distinction between the mortal and the immortal, between that which we are in Adam and that which we shall be in Christ, the apostle quotes the declaration of the law regarding the earthy or natural body, referring to the very book and the very passage where it is written that God made the earthy man too. Speaking of the manner in which the dead shall rise again, and of the body with which they shall come, after using the similitude of the seeds of corn, that they are sown bare grain, and that God gives them a body as it pleases Him, and to every seed his own body,—thus, by the way, overthrowing the error of the Manichæans, who say that grains and plants, and all roots and shoots, are created by the race of darkness, and not by God, who, according to them, instead of exerting power in the production of these objects, is Himself subject to confinement in them,—he goes on, after this refutation of Manichæan impieties, to describe the different kinds of flesh. "All flesh," he says, "is not the same flesh." Then he speaks of celestial and terrestrial bodies, and then of the change of our body by which it will become spiritual and heavenly. "It is sown," he says, "in dishonor, it shall rise in glory; it is sown in weakness, it shall rise in power; it is sown a natural body, it shall rise a spiritual body." Then, in order to show the origin of the animal body, he says, "There is a natural body, and there is a spiritual body; as it is written, The first man, Adam, was made a living soul."[4] Now this is written in Genesis,[5] where it is related how God made man, and animated the body which He had formed of the earth. By the old man the apostle simply means the old life, which is a life in sin, and is after the manner of Adam, of whom it is said, "By one man sin entered into the world, and death by sin; and so death passed upon all men, in that all have sinned."[6] Thus the whole of this man, both the inner and the outer part, has become old because of sin, and liable to the punishment of mortality. There is, however, a restoration of the inner man, when it is renewed after the image of its Creator, in the putting off of unrighteousness—that is, the old man, and putting on righteousness—that is, the new man. But when that which is sown a natural body shall rise a spiritual body, the outer man too shall attain the dignity of a

[1] 1 Cor. iv. 15. [2] Gal. i. 15, 16. [3] 1 Cor. xii. 18. [4] 1 Cor. xv. 33-45. [5] Gen. ii. 7. [6] Rom. v. 12.

celestial character; so that all that has been created may be created anew, and all that has been made be remade by the Creator and Maker Himself. This is briefly explained in the words: "The body is dead because of sin; but the spirit is life because of righteousness. But if the Spirit of Him who raised up Jesus from the dead dwell in you, He that raised up Christ from the dead will also quicken your mortal bodies by His Spirit dwelling in you."[1] No one instructed in the Catholic doctrine but knows that it is in the body that some are male and some female, not in the spirit of the mind, in which we are renewed after the image of God. But elsewhere the apostle teaches that God is the Maker of both; for he says, "Neither is the woman without the man, nor the man without the woman, in the Lord; for as the woman is of the man, so is the man by the woman; but all things are of God."[2] The only reply given to this, by the perverse stupidity of those who are alienated from the life of God by the ignorance which is in them, on account of the blindness of their heart, is, that whatever pleases them in the apostolic writings is true, and whatever displeases them is false. This is the insanity of the Manichæans, who will be wise if they cease to be Manichæans. As it is, if they are asked whether it is He that remakes and renews the inner man (which they acknowledge to be renewed after the image of God, and they themselves quote the passage in support of this; and, according to Faustus, God makes man when the inner man is renewed in the image of God), they will answer, yes. And if we then go on to ask when God made what He now renews, they must devise some subterfuge to prevent the exposure of their absurdities. For, according to them, the inner man is not formed or created or originated by God, but is part of His own substance sent against His enemies; and instead of becoming old by sin, it is through necessity captured and damaged by the enemy. Not to repeat all the nonsense they talk, the first man they speak of is not the man of the earth earthy that the apostle speaks of,[3] but an invention proceeding from their own magazine of untruths. Faustus, though he chooses man as a subject for discussion, says not a word of this first man; for he is afraid that his opponents in the discussion might come to know something about him.

[1] Rom. viii. 10, 11.

[2] 1 Cor. xi. 11, 12.

[3] 1 Cor. xv. 47.

BOOK XXV.

FAUSTUS SEEKS TO BRING INTO RIDICULE THE ORTHODOX CLAIM TO BELIEVE IN THE INFINITY OF GOD BY CARICATURING THE ANTHROPOMORPHIC REPRESENTATIONS OF THE OLD TESTAMENT. AUGUSTIN EXPRESSES HIS DESPAIR OF BEING ABLE TO INDUCE THE MANICHÆANS TO ADOPT RIGHT VIEWS OF THE INFINITUDE OF GOD SO LONG AS THEY CONTINUE TO REGARD THE SOUL AND GOD AS EXTENDED IN SPACE.

1. Faustus said: Is God finite or infinite? He must be finite unless you are mistaken in addressing Him as the God of Abraham and Isaac and Jacob; unless, indeed, the being thus addressed is different from the God you call infinite. In the case of the God of Abraham and Isaac and Jacob, the mark of circumcision, which separated these men from fellowship with other people, marked also the limit of God's power as extending only to them. And a being whose power is finite cannot himself be infinite. Moreover, in this address, you do not mention even the ancients before Abraham, such as Enoch, Noah, and Shem, and others like them, whom you allow to have been righteous though in uncircumcision; but because they lacked this distinguishing mark, you will not call God their God, but only of Abraham and his seed. Now, if God is one and infinite, what need of such careful particularity in addressing Him, as if it was not enough to name God, without adding whose God He is—Abraham's, namely, and Isaac's and Jacob's; as if Abraham were a landmark to steer by in your invocation, to escape shipwreck among a shoal of deities? The Jews, who are circumcised, may very properly address this deity, as having a reason for it, because they call God the God of circumcision, in contrast to the gods of uncircumcision. But why you should do the same, it is difficult to understand; for you do not pretend to have Abraham's sign, though you invoke his God. If we understand the matter rightly, the Jews and their God seem to have set marks upon one another for the purpose of recognition, that they might not lose each other. So God gave them the disgusting mark of circumcision, that, in whatever land or among whatever people they

might be, they might by being circumcised be known to be His. They again marked God by calling Him the God of their fathers, that, wherever He might be, though among a crowd of gods, He might, on hearing the name God of Abraham, God of Isaac, God of Jacob, know at once that He was addressed. So we often see, in a number of people of the same name, that no one answers till called by his surname. In the same way the shepherd or herdsman makes use of a brand to prevent his property being taken by others. In thus marking God by calling Him the God of Abraham and Isaac and Jacob, you show not only that He is finite, but also that you have no connection with Him, because you have not the mark of circumcision by which He recognizes His own. Therefore, if this is the God you worship, there can be no doubt of His being finite. But if you say that God is infinite, you must first of all give up this finite deity, and by altering your invocation, show your penitence for your past errors. We have thus proved God to be finite, taking you on your own ground. But to determine whether the supreme and true God is infinite or not, we need only refer to the opposition between good and evil. If evil does not exist, then certainly God is infinite; otherwise He must be finite. Evil, however, undoubtedly exists; therefore God is not infinite. It is where good stops that evil begins.

2. Augustin replied: No one that knows you would dream of asking you about the infinitude of God, or of discussing the matter with you. For, before there can be any degree of spirituality in any of your conceptions, you must first have your minds cleared by simple faith, and by some elementary knowledge, from the illusions of carnal and material ideas. This your heresy prevents you from doing, for it invariably represents the body and the soul and God as extended in space, either finite or infinite, while the idea of space is applicable only to the body. As long as this is the case, it will be better for you to leave this matter alone; for you can teach no truth regarding it, any more than in other matters; and in this you are unfit for learning, as you might do in other things, if you were not proud and quarrelsome. For in such questions as how God can be finite, when no space can contain Him; how He can be infinite, when the Son knows Him perfectly; how He can be finite, and yet unbounded; how He can be infinite, and yet perfect; how He can be finite, who is without measure; how He can be infinite, who is the measure of all things—all carnal ideas go for nothing; and if the carnality is to be removed, it must first become ashamed of itself. Accordingly, your best way of ending the matter you have brought forward of God as finite or infinite, is to say no more about it till you cease going so far astray from Christ, who is the end of the law. Of the God of Abraham and Isaac and Jacob we have already said enough to show why He who is the true God of all creatures wished to be familiarly known by His people under this name. On circumcision, too, we have already spoken in several places in answer to ignorant reproaches. The Manichæans would find nothing to ridicule in this sign if they would view it as appointed by God, to be an appropriate symbol of the putting off of the flesh. They ought thus to consider the rite with a Christian instead of a heretical mind; as it is written, "To the pure all things are pure." But, considering the truth of the following words, "To the unclean and unbelieving nothing is pure, but even their mind and conscience are defiled,"[1] we must remind our witty opponents, that if circumcision is indecent, as they say it is, they should rather weep than laugh at it; for their god is exposed to restraint and contamination in conjunction both with the skin which is cut and with the blood which is shed.

[1] Tit. i. 15.

BOOK XXVI.

FAUSTUS INSISTS THAT JESUS MIGHT HAVE DIED THOUGH NOT BORN, BY THE EXERCISE OF DIVINE POWER, YET HE REJECTS BIRTH AND DEATH ALIKE. AUGUSTIN MAINTAINS THAT THERE ARE SOME THINGS THAT EVEN GOD CANNOT DO, ONE OF WHICH IS TO DIE. HE REFUTES THE DOCETISM OF THE MANICHÆANS.

1. Faustus said: You ask, If Jesus was not born, how did He die? Well this is a probability, such as one makes use of in want of proofs. We will, however, answer the question by examples taken from what you generally believe. If they are true, they will prove our case; if they are false, they will help you no more than they will us. You say then,

How could Jesus die, if He were not man? In return, I ask you, How did Elias not die, though he was a man? Could a mortal encroach upon the limits of immortality, and could not Christ add to His immortality whatever experience of death was required? If Elias, contrary to nature, lives for ever, why not allow that Jesus, with no greater contrariety to nature, could remain in death for three days? Besides that, it is not only Elias, but Moses and Enoch you believe to be immortal, and to have been taken up with their bodies to heaven. Accordingly, if it is a good argument that Jesus was a man because He died, it is an equally good argument that Elias was not a man because he did not die. But as it is false that Elias was not a man, notwithstanding his supposed immortality, so it is false that Jesus was a man, though He is considered to have died. The truth is, if you will believe it, that the Hebrews were in a mistake regarding both the death of Jesus and the immortality of Elias. For it is equally untrue that Jesus died and that Elias did not die. But you believe whatever you please; and for the rest, you appeal to nature. And, allowing this appeal, nature is against both the death of the immortal and the immortality of the mortal. And if we refer to the power of effecting their purpose as possessed by God and by man, it seems more possible for Jesus to die than for Elias not to die; for the power of Jesus is greater than that of Elias. But if you exalt the weaker to heaven, though nature is against it, and, forgetting his condition as a mortal, endow him with eternal felicity, why should I not admit that Jesus could die if He pleased, even though I were to grant His death to have been real, and not a mere semblance? For, as from the outset of His taking the likeness of man He underwent in appearance all the experiences of humanity, it was quite consistent that He should complete the system by appearing to die.

2. Moreover, it is to be remembered that this reference to what nature grants as possible, should be made in connection with all the history of Jesus, and not only with His death. According to nature, it is impossible that a man blind from his birth should see the light; and yet Jesus appears to have performed a miracle of this kind, so that the Jews themselves exclaimed that from the beginning of the world it was not seen that one opened the eyes of a man born blind.[1] So also healing a withered hand, giving the power of utterance and expression to those born dumb, restoring animation to the dead, with the recovery of their bodily frame after dissolution had begun, produce a feeling of amazement, and must seem utterly incredible in view of what is naturally possible and impossible. And yet, as Christians, we believe all the things to have been done by the same person; for we regard not the law of nature, but the powerful operation of God. There is a story, too, of Jesus having been cast from the brow of a hill, and having escaped unhurt. If, then, when thrown down from a height He did not die, simply because He chose not to die, why should He not have had the power to die when He pleased? We take this way of answering you, because you have a fancy for discussion, and affect to use logical weapons not properly belonging to you. As regards our own belief, it is no more true that Jesus died than that Elias is immortal.

3. Augustin replied: As to Enoch and Elias and Moses, our belief is determined not by Faustus' suppositions, but by the declarations of Scripture, resting as they do on foundations of the strongest and surest evidence. People in error, as you are, are unfit to decide what is natural, and what contrary to nature. We admit that what is contrary to the ordinary course of human experience is commonly spoken of as contrary to nature. Thus the apostle uses the words, "If thou art cut out of the wild olive, and engrafted contrary to nature in the good olive."[2] Contrary to nature is here used in the sense of contrary to human experience of the course of nature; as that a wild olive engrafted in a good olive should bring forth the fatness of the olive instead of wild berries. But God, the Author and Creator of all natures, does nothing contrary to nature; for whatever is done by Him who appoints all natural order and measure and proportion must be natural in every case. And man himself acts contrary to nature only when he sins; and then by punishment he is brought back to nature again. The natural order of justice requires either that sin should not be committed or that it should not go unpunished. In either case, the natural order is preserved, if not by the soul, at least by God. For sin pains the conscience, and brings grief on the mind of the sinner, by the loss of the light of justice, even should no physical sufferings follow, which are inflicted for correction, or are reserved for the incorrigible. There is, however, no impropriety in saying that God does a thing contrary to nature, when it is contrary to what we know of nature. For we

[1] John ix.

[2] Rom. xi. 24.

give the name nature to the usual common course of nature; and whatever God does contrary to this, we call a prodigy, or a miracle. But against the supreme law of nature, which is beyond the knowledge both of the ungodly and of weak believers, God never acts, any more than He acts against Himself. As regards spiritual and rational beings, to which class the human soul belongs, the more they partake of this unchangeable law and light, the more clearly they see what is possible, and what impossible; and again, the greater their distance from it, the less their perception of the future, and the more frequent their surprise at strange occurrences.

4. Thus of what happened to Elias we are ignorant; but still we believe the truthful declarations of Scripture regarding him. Of one thing we are certain, that what God willed happened, and that except by God's will nothing can happen to any one. So, if I am told that it is possible that the flesh of a certain man shall be changed into a celestial body, I allow the possibility, but I cannot tell whether it will be done; and the reason of my ignorance is, that I am not acquainted with the will of God in the matter. That it will be done if it is God's will, is perfectly clear and indubitable. Again, if I am told that something would happen if God did not prevent it from happening, I reply confidently that what is to happen is the action of God, not the event which might otherwise have happened. For God knows His own future action, and therefore He knows also the effect of that action in preventing the happening of what would otherwise have happened; and, beyond all question, what God knows is more certain than what man thinks. Hence it is as impossible for what is future not to happen, as for what is past not to have happened; for it can never be God's will that anything should, in the same sense, be both true and false. Therefore all that is properly future cannot but happen; what does not happen never was future; even as all things which are properly in the past did indubitably take place.

5. Accordingly, to say, if God is almighty, let Him make what has been done to be undone, is in fact to say, if God is almighty, let Him make a thing to be in the same sense both true and false. God can put an end to the existence of anything, when the thing to be put an end to has a present existence; as when He puts an end by death to the existence of any one who has been brought into existence in birth; for in this case there is an actual existence which may be put a stop to. But when a thing does not exist, the existence cannot be put a stop to. Now, what is past no longer exists, and whatever has an existence which can be put an end to cannot be past. What is truly past is no longer present; and the truth of its past existence is in our judgment, not in the thing itself which no longer exists. The proposition asserting anything to be past is true when the thing no longer exists. God cannot make such a proposition false, because He cannot contradict the truth. The truth in this case, or the true judgment, is first of all in our own mind, when we know and give expression to it. But should it disappear from our minds by our forgetting it, it would still remain as truth. It will always be true that the past thing which is no longer present had an existence; and the truth of its past existence after it has stopped is the same as the truth of its future existence before it began to be. This truth cannot be contradicted by God, in whom abides the supreme and unchangeable truth, and whose illumination is the source of all the truth to be found in any mind or understanding. Now God is not omnipotent in the sense of being able to die; nor does this inability prevent His being omnipotent. True omnipotence belongs to Him who truly exists, and who alone is the source of all existence, both spiritual and corporeal. The Creator makes what use He pleases of all His creatures; and His pleasure is in harmony with true and unchangeable justice, by which, as by His own nature, He, Himself unchangeable, brings to pass the changes of all changeable things according to the desert of their natures or of their actions. No one, therefore, would be so foolish as to deny that Elias being a creature of God could be changed either for the worse or for the better; or that by the will of the omnipotent God he could be changed in a manner unusual among men. So we can have no reason for doubting what on the high authority of Scripture is related of him, unless we limit the power of God to things which we are familiar with.

6. Faustus' argument is, If Elias who was a man could escape death, why might not Christ have the power of dying, since He was more than man? This is the same as to say, If human nature can be changed for the better, why should not the divine nature be changed for the worse?—a weak argument, seeing that human nature is changeable, while the divine nature is not. Such a method of inference would lead to the glaring absurdity, that if God can bestow eternal glory on man, He must also have the power of consigning Himself to eternal misery. Faustus will reply that his argument refers only to three days

of death for God, as compared with eternal life for man. Well, if you understood the three days of death in the sense of the death of the flesh which God took as a part of our mortal nature, you would be quite correct; for the truth of the gospel makes known that the death of Christ for three days was for the eternal life of men. But in arguing that there is no impropriety in asserting a death of three days of the divine nature itself, without any assumption of mortality, because human nature can be endowed with immortality, you display the folly of one who knows neither God nor the gifts of God. And indeed, since you make part of your god to be fastened to the mass of darkness for ever, how can you escape the absurd conclusion already mentioned, that God consigns Himself to eternal misery? You will then require to prove that part of light is light, while part of God is not God. To give you in a word, without argument, the true reason of our faith, as regards Elias having been caught up to heaven from the earth, though only a man, and as regards Christ being truly born of a virgin, and truly dying on the cross, our belief in both cases is grounded on the declaration of Holy Scripture,[1] which it is piety to believe, and impiety to disbelieve. What is said of Elias you pretend to deny, for you will pretend anything. Regarding Christ, although even you do not go the length of saying that He could not die, though He could be born, still you deny His birth from a virgin, and assert His death on the cross to have been feigned, which is equivalent to denying it too, except as a mockery for the delusion of men; and you allow so much merely to obtain indulgence for your own falsehoods from the believers in these fictions.

7. The question which Faustus makes it appear that he is asked by a Catholic, If Jesus was not born, how could He die? could be asked only by one who overlooked the fact that Adam died, though he was not born. Who will venture to say that the Son of God could not, if He had pleased, have made for Himself a true human body in the same way as He did for Adam; for all things were made by Him?[2] or who will deny that He who is the Almighty Son of the Almighty could, if He had chosen, have taken a body from a heavenly substance, or from air or vapor, and have so changed it into the precise character of a human body, as that He might have lived as a man, and have died in it? Or, once more, if He had chosen to take a body of none of the material substances which He had made, but to create for Himself from nothing real flesh, as all things were created by Him from nothing, none of us will oppose this by saying that He could not have done it. The reason of our believing Him to have been born of the Virgin Mary, is not that He could not otherwise have appeared among men in a true body, but because it is so written in the Scripture, which we must believe in order to be Christians, or to be saved. We believe, then, that Christ was born of the Virgin Mary, because it is so written in the Gospel; we believe that He died on the cross, because it is so written in the Gospel; we believe that both His birth and death were real, because the Gospel is no fiction. Why He chose to suffer all these things in a body taken from a woman is a matter known only to Himself. Perhaps He took this way of giving importance and honor to both the sexes which He had created, taking the form of a man, and being born of a woman; or there may have been some other reason, we cannot tell. But this may be confidently affirmed, that what took place was exactly as we are told in the Gospel narrative, and that what the wisdom of God determined upon was exactly what ought to have happened. We place the authority of the Gospel above all heretical discussions; and we admire the counsel of divine wisdom more than any counsel of any creature.

8. Faustus calls upon us to believe him, and says, The truth is, if you will believe it, that the Hebrews were in a mistake regarding both the death of Jesus and the immortality of Elias. And a little after he adds, As from the outset of His taking the likeness of man He underwent in appearance all the experiences of humanity, it was quite consistent that He should seal the dispensation by appearing to die. How can this infamous liar, who declares that Christ feigned death, expect to be believed? Did Christ utter falsehood when He said, "It behoves the Son of man to be killed, and to rise the third day?"[3] And do you tell us to believe what you say, as if you utter no falsehoods? In that case, Peter was more truthful than Christ when he said to Him, "Be it far from Thee, Lord; this shall not be unto Thee;" for which it was said to him, "Get thee behind me, Satan."[4] This rebuke was not lost upon Peter, for, after his correction and full preparation, he preached even to his own death the truth of the death of Christ. But if Peter deserved to be called Satan for thinking that Christ would not die, what should

[1] 2 Kings ii. 11; Matt. i. 25, xvii. 50. [2] John i. 3.

[3] Luke xxiv. 7. [4] Matt. xvi. 22, 23.

you be called, when you not only deny that Christ died, but assert that He feigned death? You give, as a reason for Christ's appearing to die, that He underwent in appearance all the experiences of humanity. But that He feigned all the experiences of humanity is only your opinion in opposition to the Gospel. In reality, when the evangelist says that Jesus slept,[1] that He was hungry,[2] that He was thirsty,[3] that He was sorrowful,[4] or glad, and so on,—these things are all true in the sense of not being feigned, but actual experiences; only that they were undergone, not from a mere natural necessity, but in the exercise of a controlling will, and of divine power. In the case of a man, anger, sorrow, sleeping, being hungry and thirsty, are often involuntary; in Christ they were acts of His own will. So also men are born without any act of their own will, and suffer against their will; while Christ was born and suffered by His own will. Still, the things are true; and the accurate narrative of them is intended to instruct whoever believes in Christ's gospel in the truth, not to delude him with falsehoods.

[1] Matt. viii. 24.
[2] Matt. iv. 2.
[3] John xix. 28.
[4] Matt. xxvi. 37.

BOOK XXVII.

FAUSTUS WARNS AGAINST PRESSING TOO FAR THE ARGUMENT, THAT IF JESUS WAS NOT BORN HE CANNOT HAVE SUFFERED. AUGUSTIN ACCEPTS THE BIRTH AND DEATH ALIKE ON THE TESTIMONY OF THE GOSPEL NARRATIVE, WHICH IS HIGHER AUTHORITY THAN THE FALSEHOOD OF MANICHÆUS.

1. Faustus said: If Jesus was not born, He cannot have suffered; but since He did suffer, He must have been born. I advise you not to have recourse to logical inference in these matters, or else your whole faith will be shaken. For, even according to you, Jesus was born miraculously of a virgin; which the argument from consequents to antecedents shows to be false. For your argument might thus be turned against you: If Jesus was born of a woman, He must have been begotten by a man; but He was not begotten by a man, therefore He was not born of a woman. If, as you believe, He could be born without being begotten, why could He not also suffer without being brought forth?

2. Augustin replied: The argument which you here reply to is one which could be used only by such ignorant people as you succeed in misleading, not by those who know enough to refute you. Jesus could both be born without being begotten and suffer without being brought forth. His being one and not the other was the effect of His own will. He chose to be born without being begotten, and not to suffer without being brought forth. And if you ask how I know that He was brought forth, and that He suffered, I read this in the faithful Gospel narrative. If I ask how you know what you state, you bring forward the authority of Manichæus, and charge the Gospel with falsehood. Even if Manichæus did not set forth falsehood as an excellence in Christ, I should not believe his statements. His praise of falsehood comes from nothing that he found in Christ, but from his own moral character.

BOOK XXVIII.

FAUSTUS RECURS TO THE GENEALOGY AND INSISTS UPON EXAMINING IT AS REGARDS ITS CONSISTENCY WITH ITSELF. AUGUSTIN TAKES HIS STAND ON SCRIPTURE AUTHORITY AND MAINTAINS THAT MATTHEW'S STATEMENTS AS TO THE BIRTH OF CHRIST MUST BE ACCEPTED AS FINAL.

1. Faustus said: Christ, you say, could not have died, had He not been born. I reply, If He was born, He cannot have been God; or if He could both be God and be born, why could He not both be born and die? Plainly, arguments and necessary consequences are not applicable to those matters, where the question is of the account to be given of Jesus. The answer must be obtained from His own statements, or from the statements of His apostles regarding Him. The genealogy must be examined as regards its consistency with itself, instead of arguing from the supposition of Christ's death to the

fact of His birth; for He might have suffered without having been born, or He might have been born, and yet never have suffered; for you yourselves acknowledge that with God nothing is impossible, which is inconsistent with the denial that Christ could have suffered without having been born.

2. Augustin replied: You are always answering arguments which no one uses, instead of our real arguments, which you cannot answer. No one says that Christ could not die if He had not been born; for Adam died though he had not been born. What we say is, Christ was born, because this is said not by this or that heretic, but in the holy Gospel; and He died, for this too is written, not in some heretical production, but in the holy Gospel. You set aside argument on the question of the true account to be given of Jesus, and refer to what He says of Himself, and what His apostles say of Him; and yet, when I begin to quote the Gospel of His apostle Matthew, where we have the whole narrative of Christ's birth, you forthwith deny that Matthew wrote the narrative, though this is affirmed by the continuous testimony of the whole Church, from the days of apostolic presidency to the bishops of our own time. What authority will you quote against this? Perhaps some book of Manichæus, where it is denied that Jesus was born of a virgin. As, then, I believe your book to be the production of Manichæus, since it has been kept and handed down among the disciples of Manichæus, from the time when he lived to the present time, by a regular succession of your presidents, so I ask you to believe the book which I quote to have been written by Matthew, since it has been handed down from the days of Matthew in the Church, without any break in the connection between that time and the present. The question then is, whether we are to believe the statements of an apostle who was in the company of Christ while He was on earth, or of a man away in Persia, born long after Christ. But perhaps you will quote some other book bearing the name of an apostle known to have been chosen by Christ; and you will find there that Christ was not born of Mary. Since, then, one of the books must be false, the question in this case is, whether we are to yield our belief to a book acknowledged and approved as handed down from the beginning in the Church founded by Christ Himself, and maintained through the apostles and their successors in an unbroken connection all over the world to the present day; or to a book which this Church condemns as unknown, and which, moreover, is brought forward by men who prove their veracity by praising Christ for falsehood.

3. Here you will say, Examine the genealogy as given in the two Gospels, and see if it is consistent with itself. The answer to this has been given already.[1] Your difficulty is how Joseph could have two fathers. But even if you could not have thought of the explanation, that one was his own father, and the other adopted, you should not have been so ready to put yourself in opposition to such high authority. Now that this explanation has been given you, I call upon you to acknowledge the truth of the Gospel, and above all to cease your mischievous and unreasonable attacks upon the truth.

4. Faustus most plausibly refers to what Jesus said of Himself. But how is this to be known except from the narratives of His disciples? And if we do not believe them when they tell us that Christ was born of a virgin, how shall we believe what they record as said by Christ of Himself? For, as regards any writing professing to come immediately from Christ Himself, if it were really His, how is it not read and acknowledged and regarded as of supreme authority in the Church, which, beginning with Christ Himself, and continued by His apostles, who were succeeded by the bishops, has been maintained and extended to our own day, and in which is found the fulfillment of many former predictions, while those concerning the last days are sure to be accomplished in the future? In regard to the appearance of such a writing, it would require to be considered from what quarter it issued. Supposing it to have issued from Christ Himself, those in immediate connection with Him might very well have received it, and have transmitted it to others. In this case, the authority of the writing would be fully established by the traditions of various communities, and of their presidents, as I have already said. Who, then, is so infatuated as in our day to believe that the Epistle of Christ issued by Manichæus is genuine, or to disbelieve Matthew's narrative of Christ's words and actions? Or, if the question is of Matthew being the real author, who would not, in this also, believe what he finds in the Church, which has a distinct history in unbroken connection from the days of Matthew to the present time, rather than a Persian interloper, who comes more than two hundred years after, and wishes us to believe his account of Christ's words and actions rather than that of Matthew; whereas, even in the case of the Apostle Paul, who was called from

[1] III. 3.

heaven after the Lord's ascension, the Church would not have believed him, had there not been apostles in life with whom he might communicate, and compare his gospel with theirs, so as to be recognized as belonging to the same society? When it was ascertained that Paul preached what the apostles preached, and that he lived in fellowship and harmony with them, and when God's testimony was added by Paul's working miracles like those done by the apostles, his authority became so great, that his words are now received in the Church, as if, to use his own appropriate words, Christ were speaking in him.[1] Manichæus, on the other hand, thinks that the Church of Christ should believe what he says in opposition to the Scriptures, which are supported by such strong and continuous evidence, and in which the Church finds an emphatic injunction, that whoever preaches to her differently from what she has received must be anathema.[2]

5. Faustus tells us that he has good grounds for concluding that these Scriptures are unworthy of credit. And yet he speaks of not using arguments. But the argument too shall be refuted. The end of the whole argument is to bring the soul to believe that the reason of its misery in this world is, that it is the means of preventing God from being deprived of His kingdom, and that God's substance and nature is so exposed to change, corruption, injury, and contamination, that part of it is incurably defiled, and is consigned by Himself to eternal punishment in the mass of darkness, though, when it was in harmless union with Himself, and guilty of no crime, He knowingly sent it where it was to suffer defilement. This is the end of all your arguments and fictions; and would that there were an end of them as regards your heart and your lips, that you might sometime desist from believing and uttering those execrable blasphemies! But, says Faustus, I prove from the writings themselves that they cannot be in all points trustworthy, for they contradict one another. Why not say, then, that they are wholly untrustworthy, if their testimony is inconsistent and self-contradictory? But, says Faustus, I say what I think to be in accordance with truth. With what truth? The truth is only your own fiction, which begins with God's battle, goes on to His contamination, and ends with His damnation. No one, says Faustus, believes writings which contradict themselves. But if you think they do this, it is because you do not understand them; for your ignorance has been manifested in regard to the passages you have quoted in support of your opinion, and the same will appear in regard to any quotations you may still make. So there is no reason for our not believing these writings, supported as they are by such weighty testimony; and this is itself the best reason for pronouncing accursed those whose preaching differs from what is there written.

[1] 2 Cor. xiii. 3.

[2] Gal. i. 8, 9.

BOOK XXIX.

FAUSTUS SEEKS TO JUSTIFY THE DOCETISM OF THE MANICHÆANS. AUGUSTIN INSISTS THAT THERE IS NOTHING DISGRACEFUL IN BEING BORN.

1. Faustus said: If Christ was visible, and suffered without having been born, this was sorcery. This argument of yours may be turned against you, by replying that it was sorcery if He was conceived or brought forth without being begotten. It is not in accordance with the law of nature that a virgin should bring forth, and still less that she should still be a virgin after bringing forth. Why, then, do you refuse to admit that Christ, in a preternatural manner, suffered without submitting to the condition of birth? Believe me: in substance, both our beliefs are contrary to nature; but our belief is decent, and yours is not. We give an explanation of Christ's passion which is at least probable, while the only explanation you give of His birth is false. In fine, we hold that He suffered in appearance, and did not really die; you believe in an actual birth, and conception in the womb. If it is not so, you have only to acknowledge that the birth too was a delusion, and our whole dispute will be at an end. As to what you frequently allege, that Christ could not have appeared or spoken to men without having been born, it is absurd; for, as our teachers have shown, angels have often appeared and spoken to men.

2. Augustin replied: We do not say that to die without having been born is sorcery; for, as we have said already, this happened in the case of Adam. But, though it had never happened, who will venture to say that Christ could not, if He had so pleased, have come without taking His body from a virgin, and yet appearing in a true body to redeem us by

a true death? However, it was better that He should be, as He actually was, born of a virgin, and, by His condescension, do honor to both sexes, for whose deliverance He was to die, by taking a man's body born of a woman. In this He testifies emphatically against you, and refutes your doctrine, which makes the sexes the work of the devil. What we call sorcery in your doctrine is your making Christ's passion and death to have been only in appearance, so that, by a spectral illusion, He seemed to die when He did not. Hence you must also make His resurrection spectral and illusory and false; for if there was no true death, there could not be a real resurrection. Hence also the marks which He showed to His doubting disciples must have been false; and Thomas was not assured by truth, but cheated by a lie, when he exclaimed, "My Lord, and my God." [1] And yet you would have us believe that your tongue utters truth, though Christ's whole body was a falsehood. Our argument against you is, that the Christ you make is such that you cannot be His true disciples unless you too practise deceit. The fact that Christ's body was the only one born of a virgin does not prove that there was sorcery in His birth, any more than there is sorcery in its being the only body to rise again on the third day, never to die any more. Will you say that there was sorcery in all the Lord's miracles because they were unusual? They really happened, and their appearance, as seen by men, was true, and not an illusion; and when they are said to be contrary to nature, it is not that they oppose nature, but that they transcend the method of nature to which we are accustomed. May God keep the minds of His people who are still babes in Christ from being influenced by Faustus, when he recommends as a duty that we should acknowledge Christ's birth to have been illusory and not real, that so we may end our dispute! Nay, verily, rather let us continue to contend for the truth against them, than agree with them in falsehood.

3. But if we are to end the controversy by saying this, why do not our opponents themselves say it? While they assert the death of Christ to have been not real but feigned, why do they make out that He had no birth at all, not even of the same kind as His death? If they had so much regard for the authority of the evangelist as to oblige them to admit that Christ suffered, at least in appearance, it is the same authority which testifies to His birth. Two evangelists, indeed, give the story of the birth; [2] but in all we read of Jesus having a mother. [3] Perhaps Faustus was unwilling to make the birth an illusion, because the difference of the genealogies given in Matthew and Luke causes an apparent discrepancy. But, supposing a man ignorant, there are many things also relating to the passion of Christ in which he will think the evangelists disagree; suppose him instructed, he finds entire agreement. Can it be right to feign death, and wrong to feign birth? And yet Faustus will have us acknowledge the birth to be feigned, in order to put an end to the dispute. It will appear presently in our reply to another objection what we think to be the reason why Faustus will not admit of any birth, even a feigned one.

4. We deny that there is anything disgraceful in the bodies of saints. Some members, indeed, are called uncomely, because they have not so pleasing an appearance as those constantly in view. [4] But attend to what the apostle says, when from the unity and harmony of the body he enjoins charity on the Church: "Much more those members of the body, which seem to be feeble, are necessary: and those members of the body, which we think to be less honorable, upon these we bestow more abundant honor; and our uncomely parts have more abundant comeliness. For our comely parts have no need: but God hath tempered the body together, having given more abundant honor to that part which lacked: that there should be no schism in the body." [5] The licentious and intemperate use of those members is disgraceful, but not the members themselves; for they are preserved in purity not only by the unmarried, but also by wedded fathers and mothers of holy life, in whose case the natural appetite, as serving not lust, but an intelligent purpose in the production of children, is in no way disgraceful. Still more, in the holy Virgin Mary, who by faith conceived the body of Christ, there was nothing disgraceful in the members which served not for a common natural conception, but for a miraculous birth. In order that we might conceive Christ in sincere hearts, and, as it were, produce Him in confession, it was meet that His body should come from the substance of His mother without injury to her bodily purity. We cannot suppose that the mother of Christ suffered loss by His birth, or that the gift of productiveness displaced the grace of virginity. If

[1] John xx. 28.

[2] Matt. i. 25; Luke ii. 7.

[3] Matt. ii. 11; Mark iii. 32; Luke ii. 33; John ii. 1.

[4] In the *Retractations*, ii. sec. 7, Augustin refers in correction of this remark to his *Reply to the Second Answer of Julian*, iv. sec. 36, where he makes uncomeliness the effect of sin.

[5] 1 Cor. xii. 22-25.

these occurrences, which were real and no illusion, are new and strange, and contrary to the common course of nature, the reason is, that they are great, and amazing, and divine; and all the more on this account are they true, and firm, and sure. Angels, says Faustus, appeared and spoke without having been born. As if we held that Christ could not have appeared or spoken without having been born of a woman! He could, but He chose not; and what He chose was best. And that He chose to do what He did is plain, because He acted, not like your god, from necessity, but voluntarily. That He was born we know, because we put faith not in a heretic, but in Christ's gospel.

BOOK XXX.

FAUSTUS REPELS THE INSINUATION THAT THE PROPHECY OF PAUL WITH REFERENCE TO THOSE THAT SHOULD FORBID TO MARRY, ABSTAIN FROM MEATS, ETC., APPLIES TO THE MANICHÆANS MORE THAN TO THE CATHOLIC ASCETICS, WHO ARE HELD IN THE HIGHEST ESTEEM IN THE CHURCH. AUGUSTIN JUSTIFIES THIS APPLICATION OF THE PROPHECY, AND SHOWS THE DIFFERENCE BETWEEN MANICHÆAN AND CHRISTIAN ASCETICISM.

1. Faustus said: You apply to us the words of Paul: "Some shall depart from the faith, giving heed to lying spirits, and doctrines of devils; speaking lies in hypocrisy; having their consciences seared as with a hot iron; forbidding to marry, abstaining from meats, which God has created to be received with thanksgiving by believers."[1] I refuse to admit that the apostle said this, unless you first acknowledge that Moses and the prophets taught doctrines of devils, and were the interpreters of a lying and malignant spirit; since they enjoin with great emphasis abstinence from swine's flesh and other meats, which they call unclean. This case must first be settled; and you must consider long and carefully how their teaching is to be viewed: whether they said these things from God, or from the devil. As regards these matters, either Moses and the prophets must be condemned along with us, or we must be acquitted along with them. You are unjust in condemning us, as you do now, as followers of the doctrine of devils, because we require the priestly class to abstain from animal food; for we limit the prohibition to the priesthood, while you hold that your prophets, and Moses himself, who forbade all classes of men to eat the flesh of swine, and hares, and conies, besides all varieties of cuttle-fish, and all fish wanting scales, said this not in a lying spirit, nor in the doctrine of devils, but from God, and in the Holy Spirit. Even supposing, then, that Paul said these words, you can convince me only by condemning Moses and the prophets; and so, though you will not do it for reason or truth, you will contradict Moses for the sake of your belly.

2. Besides, you have in your Book of Daniel the account of the three youths, which you will find it difficult to reconcile with the opinion that to abstain from meats is the doctrine of devils. For we are told that they abstained not only from what the law forbade, but even from what it allowed;[2] and you are wont to praise them, and count them as martyrs; though they too followed the doctrine of devils, if this is to be taken as the apostle's opinion. And Daniel himself declares that he fasted for three weeks, not eating flesh or drinking wine, while he prayed for his people.[3] How is it that he boasts of this doctrine of devils, and glories in the falsehood of a lying spirit?

3. Again, what are we to think of you, or of the better class of Christians among you, some of whom abstain from swine's flesh, some from the flesh of quadrupeds, and some from all animal food, while all the Church admires them for it, and regards them with profound veneration, as only not gods? You obstinately refuse to consider that if the words quoted from the apostle are true and genuine, these people too are misled by doctrines of devils. And there is another observance which no one will venture to explain away or to deny, for it is known to all, and is practised yearly with particular attention in the congregation of Catholics all over the world—I mean the fast of forty days, in the due observance of which a man must abstain from all the things which, according to this verse, were created by God that we might receive them, while at the same time he calls this abstinence a doctrine of devils. So, my dear friends, shall we say that you too, during this fast, while celebrating the mysteries of Christ's passion, live after the manner of

[1] 1 Tim. iv. 1-3.

[2] Dan. i. 12

[3] Dan. x. 2, 3.

devils, and are deluded by a seducing spirit, and speak lies in hypocrisy, and have your conscience seared with a hot iron? If this does not apply to you, neither does it apply to us. What is to be thought of this verse, or its author; or to whom does it apply, since it agrees neither with the traditions of the Old Testament, nor with the institutions of the New? As regards the New Testament, the proof is from your own practice; and though the Old requires abstinence only from certain things, still it requires abstinence. On the other hand, this opinion of yours makes all abstinence from animal food a doctrine of devils. If this is your belief, once more I say it, you must condemn Moses, and reject the prophets, and pass the same sentence on yourselves; for, as they always abstained from certain kinds of food, so you sometimes abstain from all food.

4. But if you think that in making a distinction in food, Moses and the prophets established a divine ordinance, and not a doctrine of devils; if Daniel in the Holy Spirit observed a fast of three weeks; if the youths Ananias, Azarias, and Mishael, under divine guidance, chose to live on cabbage or pulse; if, again, those among you who abstain, do it not at the instigation of devils; if your abstinence from wine and flesh for forty days is not superstitious, but by divine command,—consider, I beseech you, if it is not perfect madness to suppose these words to be Paul's, that abstinence from food and forbidding to marry are doctrines of devils. Paul cannot have said that to dedicate virgins to Christ is a doctrine of devils. But you read the words, and inconsiderately, as usual, apply them to us, without seeing that this stamps your virgins too as led away by the doctrine of devils, and that you are the functionaries of the devils in your constant endeavors to induce virgins to make this profession, so that in all your churches the virgins nearly outnumber the married women. Why do you still adhere to such practises? Why do you ensnare wretched young women, if it is the will of devils, and not of Christ, that they fulfill? But, first of all, I wish to know if making virgins is, in all cases, the doctrine of devils, or only the prohibition of marriage. If it is the prohibition, it does not apply to us, for we too hold it equally foolish to prevent one who wishes, as it is criminal and impious to force one who has some reluctance. But if you say that to encourage the proposal, and not to resist such a desire, is all the doctrine of devils, to say nothing of the consequence as regards you, the apostle himself will be thus brought into danger, if he must be considered as having introduced the doctrines of devils into Iconium, when Thecla, after having been betrothed, was by his discourse inflamed with the desire of perpetual virginity.[1] And what shall we say of Jesus, the Master Himself, and the source of all sanctity, who is the unwedded spouse of the virgins who make this profession, and who, when specifying in the Gospel three kinds of eunuchs, natural, artificial, and voluntary, gives the palm to those who have "made themselves eunuchs for the kingdom of heaven,"[2] meaning the youths of both sexes who have extirpated from their hearts the desire of marriage, and who in the Church act as eunuchs of the King's palace? Is this also the doctrine of devils? Are those words, too, spoken in a seducing spirit? And if Paul and Christ are proved to be priests of devils, is not their spirit the same that speaks in God? I do not mention the other apostles of our Lord, Peter, Andrew, Thomas, and the example of celibacy, the blessed John, who in various ways commended to young men and maidens the excellence of this profession, leaving to us, and to you too, the form for making virgins. I do not mention them, because you do not admit them into the canon, and so you will not scruple impiously to impute to them doctrines of devils. But will you say the same of Christ, or of the Apostle Paul, who, we know, everywhere expressed the same preference for unmarried women to the married, and gave an example of it in the case of the saintly Thecla? But if the doctrine preached by Paul to Thecla, and which the other apostles also preached, was not the doctrine of devils, how can we believe that Paul left on record his opinion, that the very exhortation to sanctity is the injunction and the doctrine of devils? To make virgins simply by exhortation, without forbidding to marry, is not peculiar to you. That is our principle too; and he must be not only a fool, but a madman, who thinks that a private law can forbid what the public law allows. As regards marriage, therefore, we too encourage virgins to remain as they are when they are willing to do so; we do not make them virgins against their will. For we know the force of will and of natural appetite when opposed by public law; much more when the law is only private, and every one is at liberty to disobey it. If, then, it is no crime to make virgins in this manner, we are guiltless as well as you. If it is wrong to make virgins in any way, you are guilty as well as we. So that what you mean, or intend, by quoting this verse against us, it is impossible to say.

[1] See the apocryphal book, *Paul and Thecla*.
[2] Matt. xix. 12.

5. Augustin replied: Listen, and you shall hear what we mean and intend by quoting this verse against you, since you say that you do not know. It is not that you abstain from animal food; for, as you observe, our ancient fathers abstained from some kinds of food, not, however, as condemning them, but with a typical meaning, which you do not understand, and of which I have said already in this work all that appeared necessary. Besides, Christians, not heretics, but Catholics, in order to subdue the body, that the soul may be more humbled in prayer, abstain not only from animal food, but also from some vegetable productions, without, however, believing them to be unclean. A few do this always; and at certain seasons or days, as in Lent, almost all, more or less, according to the choice or ability of individuals. You, on the other hand, deny that the creature is good, and call it unclean, saying that animals are made by the devil of the worst impurities in the substance of evil; and so you reject them with horror, as being the most cruel and loathsome places of confinement of your god. You, as a concession, allow your followers, as distinct from the priests, to eat animal food; as the apostle allows, in certain cases, not marriage in the general sense, but the indulgence of passion in marriage.[1] It is only sin which is thus made allowance for. This is the feeling you have toward all animal food; you have learned it from your heresy, and you teach it to your followers. You make allowance for your followers, because, as I said before, they supply you with necessaries; but you grant them indulgence without saying that it is not sinful. For yourselves, you shun contact with this evil and impurity; and hence our reason for quoting this verse against you is found in the words of the apostle which follow those with which you end the quotation. Perhaps it was for this reason that you left out the words, and then say that you do not know what we mean or intend by the quotation; for it suited you better to omit the account of our intention than to express it. For, after speaking of abstaining from meats, which God has created to be received with thanksgiving by believers, the apostle goes on, "And by them who know the truth; for every creature of God is good, and nothing to be refused, if it be received with thanksgiving: for it is sanctified by the word of God and prayer."[2] This you deny; for your idea, and motive, and belief in abstaining from such food is, that they are not typically, but naturally, evil and impure. In this assuredly you blaspheme the Creator; and in this is the doctrine of devils. You need not be surprised that, so long before the event, this prediction regarding you was made by the Holy Spirit.

6. So, again, if your exhortations to virginity resembled the teaching of the apostle, "He who giveth in marriage doeth well, and he who giveth not in marriage doeth better;"[3] if you taught that marriage is good, and virginity better, as the Church teaches which is truly Christ's Church, you would not have been described in the Spirit's prediction as forbidding to marry. What a man forbids he makes evil; but a good thing may be placed second to a better thing without being forbidden. Moreover, the only honorable kind of marriage, or marriage entered into for its proper and legitimate purpose, is precisely that you hate most. So, though you may not forbid sexual intercourse, you forbid marriage; for the peculiarity of marriage is, that it is not merely for the gratification of passion, but, as is written in the contract, for the procreation of children. And, though you allow many of your followers to retain their connection with you in spite of their refusal, or their inability, to obey you, you cannot deny that you make the prohibition. The prohibition is part of your false doctrine, while the toleration is only for the interests of the society. And here we see the reason, which I have delayed till now to mention, for your making not the birth but only the death of Christ feigned and illusory. Death being the separation of the soul, that is, of the nature of your god, from the body which belongs to his enemies, for it is the work of the devil, you uphold and approve of it; and thus, according to your creed, it was meet that Christ, though He did not die, should commend death by appearing to die. In birth, again, you believe your god to be bound instead of released; and so you will not allow that Christ was born even in this illusory fashion. You would have thought better of Mary had she ceased to be a virgin without being a mother, than as being a mother without ceasing to be a virgin. You see, then, that there is a great difference between exhorting to virginity as the better of two good things, and forbidding to marry by denouncing the true purpose of marriage; between abstaining from food as a symbolic observance, or for the mortification of the body, and abstaining from food which God has created for the reason that God did not create it. In one case, we have the doctrine of the prophets and apostles; in the other, the doctrine of lying devils.

[1] 1 Cor. vii. 5, 6.
[2] 1 Tim. iv. 3-5.
[3] 1 Cor. vii. 38.

BOOK XXXI.

THE SCRIPTURE PASSAGE: "TO THE PURE ALL THINGS ARE PURE, BUT TO THE IMPURE AND DEFILED IS NOTHING PURE; BUT EVEN THEIR MIND AND CONSCIENCE ARE DEFILED," IS DISCUSSED FROM BOTH THE MANICHÆAN AND THE CATHOLIC POINTS OF VIEW, FAUSTUS OBJECTING TO ITS APPLICATION TO HIS PARTY AND AUGUSTIN INSISTING ON ITS APPLICATION.

1. Faustus said: "To the pure all things are pure. But to the impure and defiled is nothing pure; but even their mind and conscience are defiled." As regards this verse, too, it is very doubtful whether, for your own sake, you should believe it to have been written by Paul. For it would follow that Moses and the prophets were not only influenced by devils in making so much in their laws of the distinctions in food, but also that they themselves were impure and defiled in their mind and conscience, so that the following words also might properly be applied to them: "They profess to know God, but in works deny Him."[1] This is applicable to no one more than to Moses and the prophets, who are known to have lived very differently from what was becoming in men knowing God. Up to this time I have thought only of adulteries and frauds and murders as defiling the conscience of Moses and the prophets; but now, from what this verse says, it is plain that they were also defiled, because they looked upon something as defiled. How, then, can you persist in thinking that the vision of the divine majesty can have been bestowed on such men, when it is written that only the pure in heart can see God? Even supposing that they had been pure from unlawful crimes, this superstitious abstinence from certain kinds of food, if it defiles the mind, is enough to debar them from the sight of deity. Gone for ever, too, is the boast of Daniel, and of the three youths, who, till now that we are told that nothing is unclean, have been regarded among the Jews as persons of great purity and excellence of character, because, in observance of hereditary customs, they carefully avoided defiling themselves with Gentile food, especially that of sacrifices.[2] Now it appears that they were defiled in mind and conscience most of all when they were closing their mouth against blood and idol-feasts.

2. But perhaps their ignorance may excuse them; for, as this Christian doctrine of all things being pure to the pure had not then appeared, they may have thought some things impure. But there can be no excuse for you in the face of Paul's announcement, that there is nothing which is not pure, and that abstinence from certain food is the doctrine of devils, and that those who think anything defiled are polluted in their mind, if you not only abstain, as we have said, but make a merit of it, and believe that you become more acceptable to Christ in proportion as you are more abstemious, or, according to this new doctrine, as your minds are defiled and your conscience polluted. It should also be observed that, while there are three religions in the world which, though in a very different manner, appoint chastity and abstinence as the means of purification of the mind, the religions, namely, of the Jews, the Gentiles, and the Christians, the opinion that everything is pure cannot have come from any one of the three. It is certainly not from Judaism, nor from Paganism, which also makes a distinction of food; the only difference being, that the Hebrew classification of animals does not harmonize with the Pagan. Then as to the Christian faith, if you think it peculiar to Christianity to consider nothing defiled, you must first of all confess that there are no Christians among you. For things offered to idols, and what dies of itself, to mention nothing else, are regarded by you all as great defilement. If, again, this is a Christian practice, on your part, the doctrine which is opposed to all abstinence from impurities cannot be traced to Christianity either. How, then, could Paul have said what is not in keeping with any religion? In fact, when the apostle from a Jew became a Christian, it was a change of customs more than of religion. As for the writer of this verse, there seems to be no religion which favors his opinion.

3. Be sure, then, whenever you discover anything else in Scripture to assail our faith with, to see, in the first place, that it is not against you, before you commence your attack on us. For instance, there is the passage you continually quote about Peter, that he once saw a vessel let down from heaven in which were all kinds of animals and serpents, and that, when he was surprised and astonished, a voice was heard, saying to him, Peter, kill and eat whatsoever thou seest in the vessel, and that he replied, Lord I will

[1] Tit. i. 16.

[2] Dan. i. 12.

not touch what is common or unclean. On this the voice spoke again, What I have cleansed, call not unclean.[1] This, indeed, seems to have an allegorical meaning, and not to refer to the absence of distinction in food. But as you choose to give it this meaning, you are bound to feed upon all wild animals, and scorpions, and snakes, and reptiles in general, in compliance with this vision of Peter's. In this way, you will show that you are really obedient to the voice which Peter is said to have heard. But you must never forget that you at the same time condemn Moses and the prophets, who considered many things polluted which, according to this utterance, God has sanctified.

4. Augustin replied: When the apostle says, "To the pure all things are pure," he refers to the natures which God had created, —as it is written by Moses in Genesis, "And God made all things; and behold they were very good,"[2]—not to the typical meanings, according to which God, by the same Moses, distinguished the clean from the unclean. Of this we have already spoken at length more than once, and need not dwell on it here. It is clear that the apostle called those impure who, after the revelation of the New Testament, still advocated the observance of the shadows of things to come, as if without them the Gentiles could not obtain the salvation which is in Christ, because in this they were carnally minded; and he called them unbelieving, because they did not distinguish between the time of the law and the time of grace. To them, he says, nothing is pure, because they made an erroneous and sinful use both of what they received and of what they rejected; which is true of all unbelievers, but especially of you Manichæans, for to you nothing whatever is pure. For, although you take great care to keep the food which you use separate from the contamination of flesh, still it is not pure to you, for the only creator of it you allow is the devil. And you hold, that, by eating it, you release your god, who suffers confinement and pollution in it. One would think you might consider yourselves pure, since your stomach is the proper place for purifying your god. But even your own bodies, in your opinion, are of the nature and handiwork of the race of darkness; while your souls are still affected by the pollution of your bodies. What, then, is pure to you? Not the things you eat; not the receptacle of your food; not yourselves, by whom it is purified. Thus you see against whom the words of the apostle are directed; he expresses himself so as to include all who are impure and unbelieving, but first and chiefly to condemn you. To the pure, therefore, all things are pure, in the nature in which they were created; but to the ancient Jewish people all things were not pure in their typical significance; and, as regards bodily health, or the customs of society, all things are not suitable to us. But when things are in their proper places, and the order of nature is preserved, to the pure all things are pure; but to the impure and unbelieving, among whom you stand first, nothing is pure. You might make a wholesome application to yourselves of the following words of the apostle, if you desired a cure for your seared consciences. The words are: "Their very mind and conscience are defiled."

[1] Acts x. 11-15.

[2] Gen. i. 31.

BOOK XXXII.

FAUSTUS FAILS TO UNDERSTAND WHY HE SHOULD BE REQUIRED EITHER TO ACCEPT OR REJECT THE NEW TESTAMENT AS A WHOLE, WHILE THE CATHOLICS ACCEPT OR REJECT THE VARIOUS PARTS OF THE OLD TESTAMENT AT PLEASURE. AUGUSTIN DENIES THAT THE CATHOLICS TREAT THE OLD TESTAMENT ARBITRARILY, AND EXPLAINS THEIR ATTITUDE TOWARDS IT.

1. Faustus said: You say, that if we believe the Gospel, we must believe everything that is written in it. Why, then, since you believe the Old Testament, do you not believe all that is found in any part of it? Instead of that, you cull out only the prophecies telling of a future King of the Jews, for you suppose this to be Jesus, along with a few precepts of common morality, such as, Thou shalt not kill, Thou shalt not commit adultery; and all the rest you pass over, thinking of the other things as Paul thought of the things which he held to be dung.[1] Why, then, should it seem strange or singular in me that I select from the New Testament whatever is purest, and helpful for my salvation, while I set aside the interpolations of your predecessors, which impair its dignity and grace?

2. If there are parts of the Testament of

[1] Phil. iii. 8.

the Father which we are not bound to observe (for you attribute the Jewish law to the Father, and it is well known that many things in it shock you, and make you ashamed, so that in heart you no longer regard it as free from corruption, though, as you believe, the Father Himself partly wrote it for you with His own finger while part was written by Moses, who was faithful and trustworthy), the Testament of the Son must be equally liable to corruption, and may equally well contain objectionable things; especially as it is allowed not to have been written by the Son Himself, nor by His apostles, but long after, by some unknown men, who, lest they should be suspected of writing of things they knew nothing of, gave to their books the names of the apostles, or of those who were thought to have followed the apostles, declaring the contents to be according to these originals. In this, I think, they do grievous wrong to the disciples of Christ, by quoting their authority for the discordant and contradictory statements in these writings, saying that it was according to them that they wrote the Gospels, which are so full of errors and discrepancies, both in facts and in opinions, that they can be harmonized neither with themselves nor with one another. This is nothing else than to slander good men, and to bring the charge of dissension on the brotherhood of the disciples. In reading the Gospels, the clear intention of our heart perceives the errors, and, to avoid all injustice, we accept whatever is useful, in the way of building up our faith, and promoting the glory of the Lord Christ, and of the Almighty God, His Father, while we reject the rest as unbecoming the majesty of God and Christ, and inconsistent with our belief.

3. To return to what I said of your not accepting everything in the Old Testament. You do not admit carnal circumcision, though that is what is written;[1] nor resting from all occupation on the Sabbath, though that is enjoined;[2] and instead of propitiating God, as Moses recommends, by offerings and sacrifices, you cast these things aside as utterly out of keeping with Christian worship, and as having nothing at all to recommend them. In some cases, however, you make a division, and while you accept one part, you reject the other. Thus, in the Passover, which is also the annual feast of the Old Testament, while it is written that in this observance you must slay a lamb to be eaten in the evening, and that you must abstain from leaven for seven days, and be content with unleavened bread and bitter herbs,[3] you accept the feast, but pay no attention to the rules for its observance. It is the same with the feast of Pentecost, or seven weeks, and the accompaniment of a certain kind and number of sacrifices which Moses enjoins:[4] you observe the feast, but you condemn the propitiatory rites, which are part of it, because they are not in harmony with Christianity. As regards the command to abstain from Gentile food, you are zealous believers in the uncleanness of things offered to idols, and of what has died of itself; but you are not so ready to believe the prohibition of swine's flesh, and hares, and conies, and mullets, and cuttle-fish, and all the fish that you have a relish for, although Moses pronounces them all unclean.

4. I do not suppose that you will consent, or even listen, to such things as that a father-in-law should lie with his daughter-in-law, as Judah did; or a father with his daughters, like Lot; or prophets with harlots, like Hosea; or that a husband should sell his wife for a night to her lover, like Abraham; or that a man should marry two sisters, like Jacob; or that the rulers of the people and the men you consider as most inspired should keep their mistresses by hundreds and thousands; or, according to the provision made in Deuteronomy about wives, that the wife of one brother, if he dies without children, should marry the surviving brother, and that he should raise up seed from her instead of his brother; and that if the man refuses to do this, the fair plaintiff should bring her case before the elders, that the brother may be called and admonished to perform this religious duty; and that, if he persists in his refusal, he must not go unpunished, but the woman must loose his shoe from his right foot, and strike him in the face, and send him away, spat upon and accursed, to perpetuate the reproach in his family.[5] These, and such as these, are the examples and precepts of the Old Testament. If they are good, why do you not practise them? If they are bad, why do you not condemn the Old Testament, in which they are found? But if you think that these are spurious interpolations, that is precisely what we think of the New Testament. You have no right to claim from us an acknowledgment for the New Testament which you yourselves do not make for the Old.

5. Since you hold to the divine authorship of the Old as well as of the New Testament, it would surely be more consistent and more becoming, as you do not obey its precepts, to

---

1 Gen. xvii. 9–14. 2 Ex. xxxi. 13. 3 Ex. xii. 4 Lev. xxiii. 5 Deut. xxv. 5–10.

confess that it has been corrupted by improper additions, than to treat it so contemptuously, if it is genuine and uncorrupted. Accordingly, my explanation of your neglect of the requirements of the Old Testament has always been, and still is, that you are either wise enough to reject them as spurious, or that you have the boldness and irreverence to disregard them if they are true. At any rate, when you would oblige me to believe everything contained in the documents of the New Testament because I receive the Testament itself, you should consider that, though you profess to receive the Old Testament, you in your heart disbelieve many things in it. Thus, you do not admit as true or authoritative the declaration of the Old Testament, that every one that hangeth on a tree is accursed,[1] for this would apply to Jesus; or that every man is accursed who does not raise up seed in Israel,[2] for that would include all of both sexes devoted to God; or that whoever is not circumcised in the flesh of his foreskin will be cut off from among his people,[3] for that would apply to all Christians; or that whoever breaks the Sabbath must be stoned to death;[4] or that no mercy should be shown to the man who breaks a single precept of the Old Testament. If you really believe these things as certainly enjoined by God, you would, in the time of Christ, have been the first to assail Him, and you would now have no quarrel with the Jews, who, in persecuting Christ with heart and soul, acted in obedience to their own God.

6. I am aware that instead of boldly pronouncing these passages spurious, you make out that these things were required of the Jews till the coming of Jesus; and that now that He is come, according, as you say, to the predictions of this Old Testament, He Himself teaches what we should receive, and what we should set aside as obsolete. Whether the prophets predicted the coming of Jesus we shall see presently. Meanwhile, I need say no more than that if Jesus, after being predicted in the Old Testament, now subjects it to this sweeping criticism, and teaches us to receive a few things and to throw over many things, in the same way the Paraclete who is promised in the New Testament teaches us what part of it to receive, and what to reject; as Jesus Himself says in the Gospel, when promising the Paraclete, "He shall guide you into all truth, and shall teach you all things, and bring all things to your remembrance."[5] So then, with the help of the Paraclete, we may take the same liberties with the New Testament as Jesus enables you to take with the Old, unless you suppose that the Testament of the Son is of greater value than that of the Father, if it is really the Father's; so that while many parts of the one are to be condemned, the other must be exempted from all disapproval; and that, too, when we know, as I said before, that it was not written by Christ or by His apostles.

7. Hence, as you receive nothing in the Old Testament except the prophecies and the common precepts of practical morality, which we quoted above, while you set aside circumcision, and sacrifices, and the Sabbath and its observance, and the feast of unleavened bread, why should not we receive nothing in the New Testament but what we find said in honor and praise of the majesty of the Son, either by Himself or by His apostles, with the proviso, in the case of the apostles, that it was said by them after reaching perfection, and when no longer in unbelief; while we take no notice of the rest, which, if said at the time, was the utterance of ignorance or inexperience, or, if not, was added by crafty opponents with a malicious intention, or was stated by the writers without due consideration, and so handed down as authentic? Take as examples, the shameful birth of Jesus from a woman, His being circumcised like the Jews, His offering sacrifice like the Gentiles, His being baptized in a humiliating manner, His being led about by the devil in the wilderness, and His being tempted by him in the most distressing way. With these exceptions, besides whatever has been inserted under the pretence of being a quotation from the Old Testament, we believe the whole, especially the mystic nailing to the cross, emblematic of the wounds of the soul in its passion; as also the sound moral precepts of Jesus, and His parables, and the whole of His immortal discourse, which sets forth especially the distinction of the two natures, and therefore must undoubtedly be His. There is, then, no reason for your thinking it obligatory in me to believe all the contents of the Gospels; for you, as has been proved, take so dainty a sip from the Old Testament, that you hardly, so to speak, wet your lips with it.

8. Augustin replied: We give to the whole Old Testament Scriptures their due praise as true and divine; you impugn the Scriptures of the New Testament as having been tampered with and corrupted. Those things in the Old Testament which we do not observe we hold to have been suitable appointments for the time and the people of that dispensation, besides being symbolical to us of truths in which they have still a spiritual use, though

[1] Deut. xxi. 23. [2] Deut. xxv. 5-10. [3] Gen. xvii. 14.
[4] Num. xv. 35. [5] John xvi. 13, xiv. 26.

the outward observance is abolished; and this opinion is proved to be the doctrine of the apostolic writings. You, on the other hand, find fault with everything in the New Testament which you do not receive, and assert that these passages were not spoken or written by Christ or His apostles. In these respects there is a manifest difference between us. When, therefore, you are asked why you do not receive all the contents of the New Testament, but, while you approve of some things, reject a great many in the very same books as false and spurious interpolations, you must not pretend to imitate us in the distinction which we make, reverently and in faith, but must give account of your own presumption.

9. If we are asked why we do not worship God as the Hebrew fathers of the Old Testament worshipped Him, we reply that God has taught us differently by the New Testament fathers, and yet in no opposition to the Old Testament, but as that Testament itself predicted. For it is thus foretold by the prophet: "Behold, the days come, saith the Lord, when I will make a new covenant with the house of Israel, and with the house of Judah; not according to the covenant which I made with their fathers when I took them by the hand to bring them out of the land of Egypt."[1] Thus it was foretold that that covenant would not continue, but that there would be a new one. And to the objection that we do not belong to the house of Israel or to the house of Judah, we answer according to the teaching of the apostle, who calls Christ the seed of Abraham, and says to us, as belonging to Christ's body, "Therefore ye are Abraham's seed."[2] Again, if we are asked why we regard that Testament as authoritative when we do not observe its ordinances, we find the answer to this also in the apostolic writings; for the apostle says, "Let no man judge you in meat or drink, or in respect of a holiday, or a new moon, or of Sabbaths, which are a shadow of things to come."[3] Here we learn both that we ought to read of these observances, and acknowledge them to be of divine institution, in order to preserve the memory of the prophecy, for they were shadows of things to come; and also that we need pay no regard to those who would judge us for not continuing the outward observance; as the apostle says elsewhere to the same purpose, "These things happened to them for an example; and they are written for our admonition, on whom the end of the ages are come."[4] So, when we read anything in the books of the Old Testament which we are not required to observe in the New Testament, or which is even forbidden, instead of finding fault with it, we should ask what it means; for the very discontinuance of the observance proves it to be, not condemned, but fulfilled. On this head we have already spoken repeatedly.

10. To take, for example, this requirement on which Faustus ignorantly grounds his charge against the Old Testament, that a man should take his brother's wife to raise up seed for his brother, to be called by his name; what does this prefigure, but that every preacher of the gospel should so labor in the Church as to raise up seed to his deceased brother, that is, Christ, who died for us, and that this seed should bear His name? Moreover, the apostle fulfills this requirement not now in the typical observance, but in the spiritual reality, when he reproves those of whom he says that he had begotten them in Christ Jesus by the gospel,[5] and points out to them their error in wishing to be of Paul. "Was Paul," he says, "crucified for you? Or were ye baptized in the name of Paul?"[6] As if he should say, I have begotten you for my deceased brother; your name is Christian, not Paulian. Then, too, whoever refuses the ministry of the gospel when chosen by the Church, justly deserves the contempt of the Church. So we see that the spitting in the face is accompanied with a sign of reproach in loosing a shoe from one foot, to exclude the man from the company of those to whom the apostle says, "Let your feet be shod with the preparation of the gospel of peace;"[7] and of whom the prophet thus speaks, "How beautiful are the feet of them who publish peace, who bring good tidings of good!"[8] The man who holds the faith of the gospel so as both to profit himself and to be ready when called to serve the Church, is properly represented as shod on both feet. But the man who thinks it enough to secure his own safety by believing, and shirks the duty of benefiting others, has the reproach of being unshod, not in type, but in reality.

11. Faustus needlessly objects to our observance of the passover, taunting us with differing from the Jewish observance: for in the gospel we have the true Lamb, not in shadow, but in substance; and instead of prefiguring the death, we commemorate it daily, and especially in the yearly festival. Thus also the day of our paschal feast does not correspond with the Jewish observance, for we take in the Lord's day, on which Christ rose. And as to the feast of unleavened bread, all

---

1 Jer. xxxi. 31, 32.
2 Gal. iii. 29.
3 Col. ii. 16, 17.
4 1 Cor. x. 11.
5 1 Cor. iv. 15.
6 1 Cor. ii. 13.
7 Eph. vi. 15.
8 Isa. lii. 7.

Christians sound in the faith keep it, not in the leaven of the old life, that is, of wickedness, but in the truth and sincerity of the faith;[1] not for seven days, but always, as was typified by the number seven, for days are always counted by sevens. And if this observance is somewhat difficult in this world, since the way which leads to life is strait and narrow,[2] the future reward is sure; and this difficulty is typified in the bitter herbs, which are a little distasteful.

12. The Pentecost, too, we observe, that is, the fiftieth day from the passion and resurrection of the Lord, for on that day He sent to us the Holy Paraclete whom He had promised; as was prefigured in the Jewish passover, for on the fiftieth day after the slaying of the lamb, Moses on the mount received the law written with the finger of God.[3] If you read the Gospel, you will see that the Spirit is there called the finger of God.[4] Remarkable events which happened on certain days are annually commemorated in the Church, that the recurrence of this festival may preserve the recollection of things so important and salutary. If you ask, then, why we keep the passover, it is because Christ was then sacrificed for us. If you ask why we do not retain the Jewish ceremonies, it is because they prefigured future realities which we commemorate as past; and the difference between the future and the past is seen in the different words we use for them. Of this we have already said enough.

13. Again, if you ask why, of all the kinds of food prohibited in the former typical dispensation, we abstain only from food offered to idols and from what dies of itself, you shall hear, if for once you will prefer the truth to idle calumnies. The reason why it is not expedient for a Christian to eat food offered to idols is given by the apostle: "I would not," he says, "that ye should have fellowship with demons." Not that he finds fault with sacrifice itself, as offered by the fathers to typify the blood of the sacrifice with which Christ has redeemed us. For he first says, "The things which the Gentiles offer, they offer to demons, and not to God;" and then adds these words: "I would not that ye should have fellowship with demons."[5] If the uncleanness were in the nature of sacrificial flesh, it would necessarily pollute even when eaten in ignorance. But the reason for not partaking knowingly is not in the nature of the food, but, for conscience sake, not to seem to have fellowship with demons. As regards what dies of itself, I suppose the reason why such food was prohibited was that the flesh of animals which have died of themselves is diseased, and is not likely to be wholesome, which is the chief thing in food. The observance of pouring out the blood which was enjoined in ancient times upon Noah himself after the deluge,[6] the meaning of which we have already explained, is thought by many to be what is meant in the Acts of the Apostles, where we read that the Gentiles were required to abstain from fornication, and from things sacrificed, and from blood,[7] that is, from flesh of which the blood has not been poured out. Others give a different meaning to the words, and think that to abstain from blood means not to be polluted with the crime of murder. It would take too long to settle this question, and it is not necessary. For, allowing that the apostles did on that occasion require Christians to abstain from the blood of animals, and not to eat of things strangled, they seem to me to have consulted the time in choosing an easy observance that could not be burdensome to any one, and which the Gentiles might have in common with the Israelities, for the sake of the Corner-stone, who makes both one in Himself;[8] while at the same time they would be reminded how the Church of all nations was prefigured by the ark of Noah, when God gave this command,—a type which began to be fulfilled in the time of the apostles by the accession of the Gentiles to the faith. But since the close of that period during which the two walls of the circumcision and the uncircumcision, although united in the Corner-stone, still retained some distinctive peculiarities, and now that the Church has become so entirely Gentile that none who are outwardly Israelites are to be found in it, no Christian feels bound to abstain from thrushes or small birds because their blood has not been poured out, or from hares because they are killed by a stroke on the neck without shedding their blood. Any who still are afraid to touch these things are laughed at by the rest: so general is the conviction of the truth, that "not what entereth into the mouth defileth you, but what cometh out of it;"[9] that evil lies in the commission of sin, and not in the nature of any food in ordinary use.

14. As regards the deeds of the ancients, both those which seem sinful to foolish and ignorant people, when they are not so, and those which really are sinful, we have already explained why they have been written, and how this rather adds to than impairs the dignity of Scripture. So, too, about the curse

[1] 1 Cor. v. 8. [2] Matt. vii. 13. [3] Ex. xix.-xxxi. [4] Luke xi. 8. [5] 1 Cor. x. 20. [6] Gen. ix. 6. [7] Acts xv. 29. [8] Eph. ii. 11-22. [9] Matt. xv. 11.

on him who hangeth on a tree, and on him who raises not up seed in Israel, our reply has already been given in the proper place, when meeting Faustus' objections.[1] And in reply to all objections whatsoever, whether we have already answered them separately, or whether they are contained in the remarks of Faustus which we are now considering, we appeal to our established principles, on which we maintain the authority of sacred Scripture. The principle is this, that all things written in the books of the Old Testament are to be received with approval and admiration, as most true and most profitable to eternal life; and that those precepts which are no longer observed outwardly are to be understood as having been most suitable in those times, and are to be viewed as having been shadows of things to come, of which we may now perceive the fulfillments. Accordingly, whoever in those times neglected the observance of these symbolical precepts was righteously condemned to suffer the punishment required by the divine statute, as any one would be now if he were impiously to profane the sacraments of the New Testament, which differ from the old observances only as this time differs from that. For as praise is due to the righteous men of old who refused not to die for the Old Testament sacraments, so it is due to the martyrs of the New Testament. And as a sick man should not find fault with the medical treatment, because one thing is prescribed to-day and another to-morrow, and what was at first required is afterwards forbidden, since the method of cure depends on this; so the human race, sick and sore as it is from Adam to the end of the world, as long as the corrupted body weighs down the mind,[2] should not find fault with the divine prescriptions, if sometimes the same observances are enjoined, and sometimes an old observance is exchanged for one of a different kind; especially as there was a promise of a change in the appointments.

15. Hence there is no force in the analogy which Faustus institutes between Christ's pointing out to us what to believe and what to reject in the Old Testament, in which He Himself is predicted, and the Paraclete's doing the same to you as regards the New Testament, where there is a similar prediction of Him. There might have been some plausibility in this, had there been anything in the Old Testament which we denounced as a mistake, or as not of divine authority, or as untrue. We do nothing of the kind; we receive everything, both what we observe as rules of conduct, and what we no longer observe, but still recognize as having been prophetical observances, once enjoined and now fulfilled. And besides, the promise of the Paraclete is found in those books, all the contents of which you do not accept; and His mission is recorded in the book which you shrink from even naming. For, as is stated above, and has been said repeatedly, there is a distinct narrative in the Acts of the Apostles of the mission of the Spirit on the day of Pentecost, and the effect produced showed who it was. For all who first received Him spoke with tongues;[3] and in this sign there was a promise that in all tongues, or in all nations, the Church of after times would faithfully proclaim the doctrine of the Spirit as well as of the Father and of the Son.

16. Why, then, do you not accept everything in the New Testament? Is it because the books have not the authority of Christ's apostles, or because the apostles taught what was wrong? You reply that the books have not the authority of the apostles. That the apostles were wrong in their teaching is what Pagans say. But what can you say to prove that the publication of these books cannot be traced to the apostles? You reply that in many things they contradict themselves and one another. Nothing could be more untrue; the fact is, you do not understand. In every case where Faustus has brought forward what you think a discrepancy, we have shown that there was none; and we will do the same in every other case. It is intolerable that the reader or learner should dare to lay the blame on Scriptures of such high authority, instead of confessing his own stupidity. Did the Paraclete teach you that these writings are not of the apostles' authorship, but written by others under their names? But where is the proof that it was the Paraclete from whom you learned this? If you say that the Paraclete was promised and sent by Christ, we reply that your Paraclete was neither promised nor sent by Christ; and we also show you when He sent the Paraclete whom He promised. What proof have you that Christ sent your Paraclete? Where do you get the evidence in support of your informant, or rather misinformant? You reply that you find the proof in the Gospel. In what Gospel? You do not accept all the Gospel, and you say that it has been tampered with. Will you first accuse your witness of corruption, and then call for his evidence? To believe him when you wish it, and then disbelieve him when you wish it, is to believe nobody but yourself. If we were prepared to believe you, there would

[1] Book XXII.

[2] Wisd. ix. 15.

[3] Acts ii.

be no need of a witness at all. Moreover, in the promise of the Holy Spirit as the Paraclete, it is said, "He shall lead you into all truth;"[1] but how can you be led into all truth by one who teaches you that Christ was a deceiver? And again, if you were to prove that all that is said in the Gospel of the promise of the Paraclete could apply to no one but Manichæus, as the predictions of the prophets are applicable to Christ; and if you quoted passages from those manuscripts which you say are genuine, we might say that on this very point, as proving Manichæus to be the only person intended, the passages have been altered in the interest of your sect. Your only answer to this would be, that you could not possibly alter documents already in the possession of all Christians; for at the very outset of such an attempt, it would be met by an appeal to older copies. But if this proves that the books could not be corrupted by you, it also proves that they could not be corrupted by any one. The first person who ventured to do such a thing would be convicted by a comparison of older manuscripts; especially as the Scripture is to be found not in one language only, but in many. As it is, false readings are sometimes corrected by comparing older copies or the original language. Hence you must either acknowledge these documents as genuine, and then your heresy cannot stand a moment; or if they are spurious, you cannot use their authority in support of your doctrine of the Paraclete, and so you refute yourselves.

17. Further, what is said in the promise of the Paraclete shows that it cannot possibly refer to Manichæus, who came so many years after. For it is distinctly said by John, that the Holy Spirit was to come immediately after the resurrection and ascension of the Lord: "For the Spirit was not yet given, because that Jesus was not yet glorified."[2] Now, if the reason why the Spirit was not given was, that Jesus was not glorified, He would necessarily be given immediately on the glorification of Jesus. In the same way, the Cataphrygians[3] said that they had received the promised Paraclete; and so they fell away from the Catholic faith, forbidding what Paul allowed, and condemning second marriages, which he made lawful. They turned to their own use the words spoken of the Spirit, "He shall lead you into all truth," as if, forsooth, Paul and the other apostles had not taught all the truth, but had left room for the Paraclete of the Cataphrygians. The same meaning they forced from the words of Paul: "We know in part, and we prophesy in part; but when that which is perfect is come, then that which is in part shall be done away;"[4] making out that the apostle knew and prophesied in part, when he said, "Let him do what he will; if he marries, he sinneth not,"[5] and that this is done away by the perfection of the Phrygian Paraclete.[6] And if they are told that they are condemned by the authority of the Church, which is the subject of such ancient promises, and is spread all over the world, they reply that this is in exact fulfillment of what is said of the Paraclete, that the world cannot receive Him.[7] And are not those passages, "He shall lead you into all truth," and, "When that which is perfect is come, that which is in part shall be done away," and, "The world cannot receive Him," precisely those in which you find a prediction of Manichæus? And so every heresy arising under the name of the Paraclete will have the boldness to make an equally plausible application to itself of such texts. For there is no heresy but will call itself the truth; and the prouder it is, the more likely it will be to call itself perfect truth: and so it will profess to lead into all truth; and since that which is perfect has come by it, it will try to do away with the doctrine of the apostles, to which its own errors are opposed. And as the Church holds by the earnest admonition of the apostle, that "whoever preaches another gospel to you than that which ye have received, let him be accursed;"[8] when the heretical preacher begins to be pronounced accursed by all the world, will he not forthwith exclaim, This is what is written, "The world cannot receive Him"?

18. Where, then, will you find the proof required to show that it is from the Paraclete that you have learned that the Gospels were not written by the apostles? On the other hand, we have proof that the Holy Spirit, the Paraclete, came immediately after the glorification of Jesus. For "He was not yet given, because that Jesus was not yet glorified." We have proof also that He leads into all truth, for the only way to truth is by love, and "the love of God," says the apostle, "is shed abroad in our hearts by the Holy Ghost who is given unto us."[9] We show, too, that in the words, "when that which is perfect is come," Paul spoke of the perfection in the enjoyment of eternal life. For in the same place he says: "Now we see through a glass darkly, but then face to face."[10] You

1 John xvi. 13.
2 John vii. 39.
3 [Another name for the Montanists, who arose in Phrygia shortly after the middle of the second century.—A. H. N.]
4 1 Cor. xiii. 9, 10.
5 1 Cor. vii. 36.
6 Montanus.
7 John xiv. 17.
8 Gal. i. 9.
9 Rom. v. 5.
10 1 Cor. xiii. 12.

cannot reasonably maintain that we see God face to face here. Therefore that which is perfect has not come to you. It is thus clear what the apostle thought on this subject. This perfection will not come to the saints till the accomplishment of what John speaks of: "Now we are the sons of God, and it doth not yet appear what we shall be; but we know that when it shall appear we shall be like Him, for we shall see Him as He is."[1] Then we shall be led into all truth by the Holy Spirit, of which we have now received the pledge. Again, the words, "The world cannot receive Him," plainly point to those who are usually called the world in Scripture—the lovers of the world, the wicked, or carnal; of whom the apostle says: "The natural man perceiveth not the things which are of the Spirit of God."[2] Those are said to be of this world who can understand nothing beyond material things, which are the objects of sense in this world; as is the case with you, when, in your admiration of the sun and moon, you suppose all divine things to resemble them. Deceivers, and being deceived, you call the author of this silly theory the Paraclete. But as you have no proof of his being the Paraclete, you have no reliable ground for the statement that the Gospel writings, which you receive only in part, are not of apostolic authorship. Thus your only remaining argument is, that these writings contain things disparaging to the glory of Christ; such as, that He was born of a virgin, that He was circumcised, that the customary sacrifice was offered for Him, that He was baptized, that He was tempted of the devil.

19. With those exceptions, including also the testimonies quoted from the Old Testament, you profess, to use the words of Faustus, to receive all the rest, especially the mystic nailing to the cross, emblematic of the wounds of the soul in its passion; as also the sound moral precepts of Jesus, and the whole of His immortal discourse, which sets forth especially the distinction of the two natures, and therefore must undoubtedly be His. Your design clearly is to deprive Scripture of all authority, and to make every man's mind the judge what passage of Scripture he is to approve of, and what to disapprove of. This is not to be subject to Scripture in matters of faith, but to make Scripture subject to you. Instead of making the high authority of Scripture the reason of approval, every man makes his approval the reason for thinking a passage correct. If, then, you discard authority, to what, poor feeble soul, darkened by the mists of carnality, to what, I beseech you, will you betake yourself? Set aside authority, and let us hear the reason of your beliefs. Is it by a logical process that your long story about the nature of God concludes necessarily with this startling announcement, that this nature is subject to injury and corruption? And how do you know that there are eight continents and ten heavens, and that Atlas bears up the world, and that it hangs from the great world-holder, and innumerable things of the same kind? Who is your authority? Manichæus, of course, you will say. But, unhappy being, this is not sight, but faith. If, then, you submit to receive a load of endless fictions at the bidding of an obscure and irrational authority, so that you believe all those things because they are written in the books which your misguided judgment pronounces trustworthy, though there is no evidence of their truth, why not rather submit to the authority of the Gospel, which is so well founded, so confirmed, so generally acknowledged and admired, and which has an unbroken series of testimonies from the apostles down to our own day, that so you may have an intelligent belief, and may come to know that all your objections are the fruit of folly and perversity; and that there is more truth in the opinion that the unchangeable nature of God should take part of mortality, so as, without injury to itself from this union, to do and to suffer not feignedly, but really, whatever it behoved the mortal nature to do and to suffer for the salvation of the human race from which it was taken, than in the belief that the nature of God is subject to injury and corruption, and that, after suffering pollution and captivity, it cannot be wholly freed and purified, but is condemned by a supreme divine necessity to eternal punishment in the mass of darkness?

20. You say, in reply, that you believe in what Manichæus has not proved, because he has so clearly proved the existence of two natures, good and evil, in this world. But here is the very source of your unhappy delusion; for as in the Gospels, so in the world, your idea of what is evil is derived entirely from the effect on your senses of such disagreeable things as serpents, fire, poison, and so on; and the only good you know of is what has an agreeable effect on your senses, as pleasant flavors, and sweet smells, and sunlight, and whatever else recommends itself strongly to your eyes, or your nostrils, or your palate, or any other organ of sensation. But had you begun with looking on the book of nature as the production of the Creator of all, and had you believed that your own finite

[1] 1 John iii. 2.

[2] 1 Cor. ii. 14.

understanding might be at fault wherever anything seemed to be amiss, instead of venturing to find fault with the works of God, you would not have been led into these impious follies and blasphemous fancies with which, in your ignorance of what evil really is, you heap all evils upon God.

21. We can now answer the question, how we know that these books were written by the apostles. In a word, we know this in the same way that you know that the books whose authority you are so deluded as to prefer were written by Manichæus. For, suppose some one should raise a question on this point, and should contend, in arguing with you, that the books which you attribute to Manichæus are not of his authorship; your only reply would be, to ridicule the absurdity of thus gratuitously calling in question a matter confirmed by successive testimonies of such wide extent. As, then, it is certain that these books are the production of Manichæus, and as it is ridiculous in one born so many years after to start objections of his own, and so raise a discussion on the point; with equal certainty may we pronounce it absurd, or rather pitiable, in Manichæus or his followers to bring such objections against writings originally well authenticated, and carefully handed down from the times of the apostles to our own day through a constant succession of custodians.

22. We have now only to compare the authority of Manichæus with that of the apostles. The genuineness of the writings is equally certain in both cases. But no one will compare Manichæus to the apostles, unless he ceases to be a follower of Christ, who sent the apostles. Who that did not misunderstand Christ's words ever found in them the doctrine of two natures opposed to one another, and having each its own principle? Again, the apostles, as becomes the disciples of truth, declare the birth and passion of Christ to have been real events; while Manichæus, who boasts that he leads into all truth, would lead us to a Christ whose very passion he declares to have been an illusion. The apostles say that Christ was circumcised in the flesh which He took of the seed of Abraham; Manichæus says that God, in his own nature, was cut in pieces by the race of darkness. The apostles say that a sacrifice was offered for Christ as an infant in our nature, according to the institutions of the time; Manichæus, that a member, not of humanity, but of the divine substance itself, must be sacrificed to the whole host of demons by being introduced into the nature of the hostile race. The apostles say that Christ, to set us an example, was baptized in the Jordan; Manichæus, that God immersed himself in the pollution of darkness, and that he will never wholly emerge, but that the part which cannot be purified will be condemned to eternal punishment. The apostles say that Christ, in our nature, was tempted by the chief of the demons; Manichæus, that part of God was taken captive by the race of demons. And in the temptation of Christ He resists the tempter; while in the captivity of God, the part taken captive cannot be restored to its origin even after victory. To conclude, Manichæus, under the guise of an improvement, preaches another gospel, which is the doctrine of devils; and the apostles, after the doctrine of Christ, enjoin that whoever preaches another gospel shall be accursed.[1]

[1] Gal. i. 8.

BOOK XXXIII.

FAUSTUS DOES NOT THINK IT WOULD BE A GREAT HONOR TO SIT DOWN WITH ABRAHAM, ISAAC AND JACOB, WHOSE MORAL CHARACTERS AS SET FORTH IN THE OLD TESTAMENT HE DETESTS. HE JUSTIFIES HIS SUBJECTIVE CRITICISM OF SCRIPTURE. AUGUSTIN SUMS UP THE ARGUMENT, CLAIMS THE VICTORY, AND EXHORTS THE MANICHÆANS TO ABANDON THEIR OPPOSITION TO THE OLD TESTAMENT NOTWITHSTANDING THE DIFFICULTIES THAT IT PRESENTS, AND TO RECOGNIZE THE AUTHORITY OF THE CATHOLIC CHURCH.

1. Faustus said: You quote from the Gospel the words, "Many shall come from the east and the west, and shall sit down with Abraham, and Isaac, and Jacob, in the kingdom of heaven,"[1] and ask why we do not acknowledge the patriarchs. Now, we should be the last to grudge to any human being that God should have compassion on him, and bring him out of perdition to salvation. At the same time, we should acknowledge in such a case the clemency shown in this act of compassion, and not the merit of the person whose

[1] Matt. viii. 11.

life is undeniably blameworthy. Thus, in the case of the Jewish fathers, Abraham, and Isaac, and Jacob, who are mentioned by Christ in this verse, supposing it to be genuine, although they led wicked lives, as we may learn from their descendant Moses, or whoever was the author of the history called Genesis, which describes their conduct as having been most shocking and detestable; we are ready to allow that they may, after all, be in the kingdom of heaven, in the place which they neither believed in, nor hoped for, as is plain enough from their books. But then it must be kept in mind that, as you yourselves confess, if they did attain to what is spoken of in this verse, it was something very different from the nether dungeons of woe to which their own deserts consigned them, and that their deliverance was the work of our Lord Christ, and the result of His mystic passion. Who would grudge to the thief on the cross that deliverance was granted to him by the same Lord, and that Christ said that on that very day he should be with Him in the paradise of His Father?[1] Who is so hard-hearted as to disapprove of this act of benevolence? Still, it does not follow that, because Jesus pardoned a thief, we must approve of the habits and practices of thieves; any more than of the publicans and harlots, whose faults Jesus pardoned, declaring that they would go into the kingdom of heaven before those who behaved proudly.[2] For, when He acquitted the woman accused by the Jews as sinful, and as having been caught in adultery, He told her to sin no more.[3] If, then, He has done something of the same kind in the case of Abraham, and Isaac, and Jacob, all the praise is His; for such actions towards souls are becoming in Him who maketh His sun to rise upon the evil and upon the good, and sendeth rain on the just and on the unjust.[4] One thing perplexes me in your doctrine: why you limit your statements to the fathers of the Jews, and are not of opinion that the Gentile patriarchs had also a share in this grace of our Redeemer; especially as the Christian Church consists of their children more than of the seed of Abraham, Isaac, and Jacob. You will say that the Gentiles worshipped idols, and the Jews the Almighty God, and that therefore Jesus had regard only to the Jews. It would seem from this that the worship of the Almighty God is the sure way to hell, and that the Son must come to the aid of the worshipper of the Father. That is as you please. For my part, I am ready to join you in the belief that the fathers reached heaven, not by any merit of their own, but by that divine mercy which is stronger than sin.

2. However, there is a difficulty in deciding as regards this verse too, whether the words were really spoken to Christ, for there is a discrepancy in the narratives. For while two evangelists, Matthew and Luke, both alike tell of the centurion whose servant was sick, and to whom these words of Jesus are supposed to have applied, that He had not seen so great faith, no, not in Israel, as in this man, though a Gentile and a Pagan, because he said that he was not worthy that Jesus should come under his roof, but wished Him only to speak the word, and his servant should be healed; Matthew alone adds that Jesus went on to say, "Verily I say unto you, that many shall come from the east and from the west, and shall sit down with Abraham, and Isaac, and Jacob, in the kingdom of heaven; but the children of the kingdom shall be cast into outer darkness." By the many who should come are meant the Pagans, on account of the centurion, in whom, although he was a Gentile, so great faith was found; and the children of the kingdom are the Jews, in whom there was no faith found. Luke, again, though he too mentions the occurrence in his Gospel as part of the narrative of the miracles of Christ, says nothing of Abraham, Isaac, and Jacob. If it is said that he omitted it because it had been already said by Matthew, why does he tell the story at all of the centurion and his servant, since that, too, has the advantage of being recorded at length in Matthew's ingenious narrative? But the passage is corrupt. For, in describing the centurion's application to Jesus, Matthew says that he came himself to ask for a cure; while Luke says he did not, but sent elders of the Jews, and that they, in case Jesus should despise the centurion as a Gentile (for they will have Jesus to be a thorough Jew), set about persuading Him, by saying that he was worthy for whom He should do this, because he loved their nation, and had built them a synagogue;[5] here again taking for granted that the Son of God was concerned in a pagan centurion having thought it proper to build a synagogue for the Jews. The words in question are, indeed, found in Luke also, perhaps because on reflection he thought they might be genuine; but they are found in another place, and in a connection altogether different. The passage is where Jesus says to His disciples, "Strive to enter in at the strait gate; for many shall come seeking to

[1] Luke xxiii. 43.
[2] Matt. xxi. 31.
[3] John viii. 3-11.
[4] Matt. v. 45.
[5] Matt. viii. 5-13; Luke vii. 2-10.

enter in, and shall not be able. When once the Master of the house has entered in, and has shut to the door, ye shall begin to stand without, and to knock, saying Lord, open to us. And He shall answer and say, I know you not. Then ye shall begin to say, We have eaten and drunk in Thy presence, and Thou hast taught in our streets and synagogues; but He shall say unto you, I know not whence ye are; depart from me, all ye workers of iniquity. There shall be weeping and gnashing of teeth, when ye shall see Abraham, and Isaac, and Jacob, and all the prophets, entering into the kingdom of God, and you yourselves cast out. And they shall come from the east, and from the west, and from the north, and from the south, and shall sit down in the kingdom of God."[1] The part where it is said that many shall be shut out of the kingdom of God, who have only borne the name of Christ, without doing His works, is not left out by Matthew; but he makes no mention here of Abraham, and Isaac, and Jacob. In the same way, Luke mentions the centurion and his servant, without alluding in that connection to Abraham, and Isaac, and Jacob. Since it is uncertain when the words were spoken, we are at liberty to doubt whether they were spoken at all.

3. It is not without reason that we bring a critical judgment to the study of Scriptures where there are such discrepancies and contradictions. By thus examining everything, and comparing one passage with another, we determine which contains Christ's actual words, and what may or may not be genuine. For your predecessors have made many interpolations in the words of our Lord, which thus appear under His name, while they disagree with His doctrine. Besides, as we have proved again and again, the writings are not the production of Christ or of His apostles, but a compilation of rumors and beliefs, made, long after their departure, by some obscure semi-Jews, not in harmony even with one another, and published by them under the name of the apostles, or of those considered the followers of the apostles, so as to give the appearance of apostolic authority to all these blunders and falsehoods. But whatever you make of that, as regards this verse, I repeat that I do not insist on rejecting it. It is enough for my position, that, as I said before, and as you are obliged to confess, before the coming of our Lord all the patriarchs and prophets of Israel lay in infernal darkness for their sins. Even though they may have been restored to light and liberty by Christ, that has nothing to do with the hateful character of their lives. We hate and eschew not their persons, but their characters; not as they are now, when they are purified, but as they were, when impure. So, whatever you think of this verse, it does not affect us: for if it is genuine, it only illustrates Christ's goodness and compassion; and if it is spurious, those who wrote it are to blame. Our cause is as safe as it always is.

4. Augustin replied: Poor safety, indeed! when you contradict yourself by hating the patriarchs as impure, at the same time that you grieve for your impure god. You allow that, since the advent of the Saviour, the patriarchs have had purity restored, and have enjoyed the rest of the blessed; while your god, even after the Saviour's advent, still lies in darkness, is still sunk in the ocean of iniquity, still wallows in the mire of all uncleanness. These men, therefore, were not only better than your god in their lives, but also happier in their death. Where was the abode of the just who departed from this life before Christ's coming in the flesh, and whether their condition also was improved by the passion of Christ, in whom they had believed as to come, and to suffer, and to rise again, and had, moreover, foretold this in suitable language under the guidance of the Spirit of prophecy, is to be discovered from the Holy Scriptures, if any clear discovery in this matter is possible; we are not called on to adopt the crude notions of all and sundry, still less the heretical opinions of men who have gone astray into such egregious error. There is a vain attempt here on the part of Faustus to introduce by a side-door the idea that we may obtain something after this life besides the due reward of our conduct in this life. It will be better for you to abandon your error while you are still alive, and to embrace and hold the truths of the Catholic faith. Otherwise the expectations of the unrighteous will be sadly disappointed when God begins to fulfill His threatenings to the unrighteous.

5. I have already given what I considered a sufficient answer to Faustus' calumnies of the lives of the patriarchs. That they were punished at their death, or that they were justified after the Lord's passion, is not what we learn from His commendation of them, when He admonished the Jews that, if they were Abraham's children, they should do the works of Abraham, and said that Abraham desired to see His day, and was glad when he saw it;[2] and that it was into his bosom, that is, some deep recess of blissful repose,

[1] Luke xiii. 24-29.

[2] John viii. 39, 56.

that the angels carried the poor sufferer who was despised by the proud rich man.[1] And what are we to make of the Apostle Paul? Is there any idea of justification after death in his praise of Abraham, when he says that before he was circumcised he believed God, and that it was counted to him for righteousness?[2] And so much importance does he attach to this, that the single ground which he specifies for our becoming Abraham's children, though not descended from him in the flesh, is, that we follow the footsteps of his faith.

6. You are so hardened in your errors against the testimonies of Scripture, that nothing can be made of you; for whenever anything is quoted against you, you have the boldness to say that it is written not by the apostle, but by some pretender under his name. The doctrine of demons which you preach is so opposed to Christian doctrine, that you could not continue, as professing Christians, to maintain it, unless you denied the truth of the apostolic writings. How can you thus do injury to your own souls? Where will you find any authority, if not in the Gospel and apostolic writings? How can we be sure of the authorship of any book, if we doubt the apostolic origin of those books which are attributed to the apostles by the Church which the apostles themselves founded, and which occupies so conspicuous a place in all lands, and if at the same time we acknowledge as the undoubted production of the apostles what is brought forward by heretics in opposition to the Church, whose authors, from whom they derive their name, lived long after the apostles? And do we not see in profane literature that there are well-known authors under whose names many things have been published after their time which have been rejected, either from inconsistency with their ascertained writings, or from their not having been known in the lifetime of the authors, so as to be handed down with the confirmatory statement of the authors themselves, or of their friends? To give a single example, were not some books published lately under the name of the distinguished physician Hippocrates, which were not received as authoritative by physicians? And this decision remained unaltered in spite of some similarity in style and matter: for, when compared to the genuine writings of Hippocrates, these books were found to be inferior; besides that they were not recognized as his at the time when his authorship of his genuine productions was ascertained. Those books, again, from a comparison with which the productions of questionable origin were rejected, are with certainty attributed to Hippocrates; and any one who denies their authorship is answered only by ridicule, simply because there is a succession of testimonies to the books from the time of Hippocrates to the present day, which makes it unreasonable either now or hereafter to have any doubt on the subject. How do we know the authorship of the works of Plato, Aristotle, Cicero, Varro, and other similar writers, but by the unbroken chain of evidence? So also with the numerous commentaries on the ecclesiastical books, which have no canonical authority, and yet show a desire of usefulness and a spirit of inquiry. How is the authorship ascertained in each case, except by the author's having brought his work into public notice as much as possible in his own lifetime, and, by the transmission of the information from one to another in continuous order, the belief becoming more certain as it becomes more general, up to our own day; so that, when we are questioned as to the authorship of any book, we have no difficulty in answering? But why speak of old books? Take the books now before us: should any one, after some years, deny that this book was written by me, or that Faustus' was written by him, where is evidence for the fact to be found but in the information possessed by some at the present time, and transmitted by them through successive generations even to distant times? From all this it follows, that no one who has not yielded to the malicious and deceitful suggestions of lying devils, can be so blinded by passion as to deny the ability of the Church of the apostles—a community of brethren as numerous as they were faithful—to transmit their writings unaltered to posterity, as the original seats of the apostles have been occupied by a continuous succession of bishops to the present day, especially when we are accustomed to see this happen in the case of ordinary writings both in the Church and out of it.

7. But Faustus finds contradictions in the Gospels. Say, rather, that Faustus reads the Gospels in a wrong spirit, that he is too foolish to understand, and too blind to see. If you were animated with piety instead of being misled by party spirit, you might easily, by examining these passages, discover a wonderful and most instructive harmony among the writers. Who, in reading two narratives of the same event, would think of charging one or both of the authors with error or falsehood, because one omits what the other mentions, or one tells concisely, but with sub-

[1] Luke xvi. 23.

[2] Rom. iv. 3.

stantial agreement, what the other relates in detail, so as to indicate not only what was done, but also how it was done? This is what Faustus does in his attempt to impeach the truth of the Gospels; as if Luke's omitting some saying of Christ recorded in Matthew implied a denial on the part of Luke of Matthew's statement. There is no real difficulty in the case; and to make a difficulty shows want of thought, or of the ability to think. There is, indeed, a point in the narrative of the centurion which is discussed among believers, and on which objections are raised by unbelievers of no great learning, who prove their quarrelsomeness, when, after being instructed, they do not give up their errors. The point is, that Matthew says that the centurion came to Jesus "beseeching Him, and saying;" while Luke says that he sent to Jesus the elders of the Jews with this same request, that He would heal his servant who was sick; and that when He came near the house he sent others, through whom he said that he was not worthy that Jesus should come into his house, and that he was not worthy to come himself to Jesus. How, then, do we read in Matthew, "He came to Him, beseeching Him, and saying, My servant lieth at home sick of the palsy, and grievously tormented?"[1] The explanation is, that Matthew's narrative is correct, but brief, mentioning the centurion's coming to Jesus, without saying whether he came himself or by others, or whether the words about his servant were spoken by himself or through others. But is it not common to speak of a person as coming near to a thing, although he may not reach it? And even the word *reach*, which is the strongest form of expression, is frequently used in cases where the person spoken of acts through others, as when we say he took his case to court, he reached the presence of the judge; or, again, he reached the presence of some man in power, although it may probably have been through his friends, and the person may not have seen him whose presence he is said to have reached. And from the word for *to reach* we give the name of Perventors to those who by ambitious arts gain access, either personally or through friends, to the, so to speak, inaccessible minds of the great. Are we, then, in reading to forget the common usage of speech? Or must the sacred Scripture have a language of its own? The cavils of forward critics are thus met by a reference to the usual forms of speech.

8. Those who examine this matter not in a disputatious but in a calm believing spirit are invited to come to Jesus, not outwardly but in heart, not in bodily presence but in the power of faith, as the centurion did, and then they will better understand Matthew's narrative. To such it is said in the Psalm "Come unto Him, and be enlightened; and your faces shall not be ashamed."[2] Hence we learn that the centurion, whose faith was so highly spoken of, came to Christ more truly than the people who carried his message. We find an analogous case in the woman with the issue of blood, who was healed by touching the hem of Christ's garment, when Christ said, "Some one hath touched me." The disciples wondered what Christ meant by saying, "Who hath touched me?" "Some one hath touched me," when the crowd was thronging Him. In fact, they made this reply: "The crowd throngeth Thee, and sayest Thou, Who hath touched me?"[3] Now, as the people thronged Christ while the woman touched Him, so the messengers were sent to Christ, but the centurion really came to Him. In Matthew we have a not infrequent form of expression, and at the same time a symbolical import; while in Luke there is a simple narrative of the whole event, such as to draw our attention to the manner in which Matthew has recorded it. I wish one of those people who found their silly objections to the Gospels on such trifling difficulties would himself tell a story twice over, honestly giving a true account of what happened, and that his words were written down and read over to him. We should then see whether he would not say more or less at one time than at another; and whether the order would not be changed, not only of words, but of things; and whether he would not put some opinion of his own into the mouth of another, because, though he never heard him say it, he knew it perfectly well to be in his mind; and whether he would not sometimes put in a few words what he had before related at length. In these and other ways, which might perhaps be reduced to rule, the narratives of the same thing by two persons, or two narratives by the same person, might differ in many things without being opposed, might be unlike without being contradictory. Thus are undone all the bandages with which poor Manichæans stifle themselves to keep in the spirit of error, and to keep out all that might lead to their salvation.

9. Now that all Faustus' calumnies have been refuted, those at least on the subjects here treated of at large and explained fully

[1] Matt. viii. 5-13; Luke vii. 2-10.

[2] Ps. xxxiv. 5.

[3] Luke viii. 43, 46.

as the Lord has enabled me, I close with a word of counsel to you who are implicated in those shocking and damnable errors, that, if you acknowledge the supreme authority of Scripture, you should recognise that authority which from the time of Christ Himself, through the ministry of His apostles, and through a regular succession of bishops in the seats of the apostles, has been preserved to our own day throughout the whole world, with a reputation known to all. There the Old Testament too has its difficulties solved, and its predictions fulfilled. If you ask for demonstration, consider first what you are, how unfit for comprehending the nature of your own soul, not to speak of God; I mean an intelligent comprehension, such as you profess to desire, or to have once desired, and not the notions of a credulous fancy. Admitting this incompetency, which must continue while you remain as you are, you may at least be referred to the natural conviction of every human mind, unless it is corrupted by error, of the perfect unchangeableness and incorruptibility of the nature and substance of God. Admit this, or believe it, and you will no longer be Manichæans, so that in course of time you may become Catholics.

ST. AUGUSTIN:

CONCERNING THE NATURE OF GOOD, AGAINST THE MANICHÆANS.

[DE NATURA BONI CONTRA MANICHÆOS.]

CIRCA A.D. 495.

TRANSLATED BY

ALBERT H. NEWMAN, D.D., L.L.D.,

PROFESSOR OF CHURCH HISTORY AND COMPARATIVE RELIGION, IN TORONTO BAPTIST (THEOLOGICAL) COLLEGE, TORONTO, CANADA.

CONTENTS ON CONCERNING THE NATURE OF GOOD.

CONCERNING THE NATURE OF GOOD, AGAINST THE MANICHÆANS.

[DE NATURA BONI CONTRA MANICHÆOS.] *c.* A.D. 405.

IN ONE BOOK.

Written after the year 404. It is put in the *Retractations* immediately after the *De Actis cum Felice Manichæo*, which was written about the end of the year 404. It is one of the most argumentative of the Anti-Manichæan treatises, and so one of the most abstruse and difficult. The lines of argument here pursued have already been employed in part in the earlier treatises. The most interesting portions of the contents of the treatise, and the most damaging to the Manichæans, are the long extracts from Mani's *Thesaurus*, and his *Fundamental Epistle*.—A. H. N.

CHAP. 1.—GOD THE HIGHEST AND UNCHANGEABLE GOOD, FROM WHOM ARE ALL OTHER GOOD THINGS, SPIRITUAL AND CORPOREAL.

THE highest good, than which there is no higher, is God, and consequently He is unchangeable good, hence truly eternal and truly immortal. All other good things are only from Him, not of Him. For what is of Him, is Himself. And consequently if He alone is unchangeable, all things that He has made, because He has made them out of nothing, are changeable. For He is so omnipotent, that even out of nothing, that is out of what is absolutely non-existent, He is able to make good things both great and small, both celestial and terrestrial, both spiritual and corporeal. But because He is also just, He has not put those things that He has made out of nothing on an equality with that which He begat out of Himself. Because, therefore, no good things whether great or small, through whatever gradations of things, can exist except from God; but since every nature, so far as it is nature, is good, it follows that no nature can exist save from the most high and true God: because all things even not in the highest degree good, but related to the highest good, and again, because all good things, even those of most recent origin, which are far from the highest good, can have their existence only from the highest good. Therefore every spirit, though subject to change, and every corporeal entity, is from God, and all this, having been made, is nature. For every nature is either spirit or body. Unchangeable spirit is God, changeable spirit, having been made, is nature, but is better than body; but body is not spirit, unless when the wind, because it is invisible to us and yet its power is felt as something not inconsiderable, is in a certain sense called spirit.

CHAP. 2.—HOW THIS MAY SUFFICE FOR CORRECTING THE MANICHÆANS.

But for the sake of those who, not being able to understand that all nature, that is, every spirit and every body, is naturally good, are moved by the iniquity of spirit and the mortality of body, and on this account endeavor to bring in another nature of wicked spirit and mortal body, which God did not make, we determine thus to bring to their understanding what we say can be brought. For they acknowledge that no good thing can exist save from the highest and true God, which also is true and suffices for correcting them, if they are willing to give heed.

CHAP. 3.—MEASURE, FORM, AND ORDER, GENERIC GOODS IN THINGS MADE BY GOD.

For we Catholic Christians worship God, from whom are all good things whether great or small; from whom is all measure great or small; from whom is all form great or small; from whom is all order great or small. For all things in proportion as they are better measured, formed, and ordered, are assuredly good in a higher degree; but in proportion as they are measured, formed, and ordered in an inferior degree, are they the less good. These three things, therefore, measure, form, and order,—not to speak of innumerable other things that are shown to pertain to these three,—these three things, therefore, measure, form, order, are as it were generic goods in things made by God, whether in spirit or in body. God is, therefore, above every measure of the creature, above every form, above every order, nor is He above by local spaces, but by ineffable and singular potency, from whom is every measure, every form, every order. These three things, where they are great, are great goods, where they are small, are small goods; where they are absent, there is no good. And again where these things are great, there are great natures, where they are small, there are small natures, where they are absent, there is no nature. Therefore all nature is good.

CHAP. 4.—EVIL IS CORRUPTION OF MEASURE, FORM, OR ORDER.

When accordingly it is inquired, whence is evil, it must first be inquired, what is evil, which is nothing else than corruption, either of the measure, or the form, or the order, that belong to nature. Nature therefore which has been corrupted, is called evil, for assuredly when incorrupt it is good; but even when corrupt, so far as it is nature it is good, so far as it is corrupted it is evil.

CHAP. 5.—THE CORRUPTED NATURE OF A MORE EXCELLENT ORDER SOMETIMES BETTER THAN AN INFERIOR NATURE EVEN UNCORRUPTED.

But it may happen, that a certain nature which has been ranked as more excellent by reason of natural measure and form, though corrupt, is even yet better than another incorrupt which has been ranked lower by reason of an inferior natural measure and form: as in the estimation of men, according to the quality which presents itself to view, corrupt gold is assuredly better than incorrupt silver, and corrupt silver than incorrupt lead; so also in more powerful spiritual natures a rational spirit even corrupted through an evil will is better than an irrational though incorrupt, and better is any spirit whatever even corrupt than any body whatever though incorrupt. For better is a nature which, when it is present in a body, furnishes it with life, than that to which life is furnished. But however corrupt may be the spirit of life that has been made, it can furnish life to a body, and hence, though corrupt, it is better than the body though incorrupt.

CHAP. 6.—NATURE WHICH CANNOT BE CORRUPTED IS THE HIGHEST GOOD; THAT WHICH CAN, IS SOME GOOD.

But if corruption take away all measure, all form, all order from corruptible things, no nature will remain. And consequently every nature which cannot be corrupted is the highest good, as is God. But every nature that can be corrupted is also itself some good; for corruption cannot injure it, except by taking away from or diminishing that which is good.

CHAP. 7.—THE CORRUPTION OF RATIONAL SPIRITS IS ON THE ONE HAND VOLUNTARY, ON THE OTHER PENAL.

But to the most excellent creatures, that is, to rational spirits, God has offered this, that if they will not they cannot be corrupted; that is, if they should maintain obedience under the Lord their God, so should they adhere to his incorruptible beauty; but if they do not will to maintain obedience, since willingly they are corrupted in sins, unwillingly they shall be corrupted in punishment, since God is such a good that it is well for no one who deserts Him, and among the things made by God the rational nature is so great a good, that there is no good by which it may be blessed except God. Sinners, therefore, are ordained to punishment; which ordination is punishment for the reason that it is not conformable to their nature, but it is justice because it is conformable to their fault.

CHAP. 8.—FROM THE CORRUPTION AND DESTRUCTION OF INFERIOR THINGS IS THE BEAUTY OF THE UNIVERSE.

But the rest of things that are made of nothing, which are assuredly inferior to the rational soul, can be neither blessed nor miserable. But because in proportion to their fashion and appearance are things themselves good, nor could there be good things in a less or the least degree except from God, they are so ordered that the more infirm yield to the firmer, the weaker to the stronger, the more impotent to the more powerful; and so earthly things harmonize with celestial, as being subject to the things that are pre-eminent. But to things falling away, and succeeding, a certain temporal beauty in its kind belongs, so that neither those things that die, or cease to be what they were, degrade or disturb the fashion and appearance and order of the universal creation; as a speech well composed is assuredly beautiful, although in it syllables and all sounds rush past as it were in being born and in dying.

CHAP. 9.—PUNISHMENT IS CONSTITUTED FOR THE SINNING NATURE THAT IT MAY BE RIGHTLY ORDERED.

What sort of punishment, and how great, is due to each fault, belongs to Divine judgment, not to human; which punishment assuredly when it is remitted in the case of the converted, there is great goodness on the part of God, and when it is deservedly inflicted, there is no injustice on the part of God; because nature is better ordered by justly smarting under punishment, than by rejoicing with impunity in sin; which nature nevertheless, even thus having some measure, form, and order, in whatever extremity there is as yet some good, which things, if they were absolutely taken away, and utterly consumed, there will be accordingly no good, because no nature will remain.

CHAP. 10.—NATURES CORRUPTIBLE, BECAUSE MADE OF NOTHING.

All corruptible natures therefore are natures at all only so far as they are *from* God, nor would they be corruptible if they were *of* Him; because they would be what He himself is. Therefore of whatever measure, of whatever form, of whatever order, they are, they are so because it is God by whom they were made; but they are not immutable, because it is nothing of which they were made. For it is sacrilegious audacity to make nothing and God equal, as when we wish to make what has been born of God such as what has been made by Him out of nothing.

CHAP. 11.—GOD CANNOT SUFFER HARM, NOR CAN ANY OTHER NATURE EXCEPT BY HIS PERMISSION.

Wherefore neither can God's nature suffer harm, nor can any nature under God suffer harm unjustly: for when by sinning unjustly some do harm, an unjust will is imputed to them; but the power by which they are permitted to do harm is from God alone, who knows, while they themselves are ignorant, what they ought to suffer, whom He permits them to harm.

CHAP. 12.—ALL GOOD THINGS ARE FROM GOD ALONE.

All these things are so perspicuous, so assured, that if they who introduce another nature which God did not make, were willing to give attention, they would not be filled with so great blasphemies, as that they should place so great good things in supreme evil, and so great evil things in God. For what the truth compels them to acknowledge, namely, that all good things are from God alone, suffices for their correction, if they were willing to give heed, as I said above. Not, therefore, are great good things from one, and small good things from another; but good things great and small are from the supremely good alone, which is God.

CHAP. 13.—INDIVIDUAL GOOD THINGS, WHETHER SMALL OR GREAT, ARE FROM GOD.

Let us, therefore, bring before our minds good things however great, which it is fitting that we attribute to God as their author, and these having been eliminated let us see whether any nature will remain. All life both great and small, all power great and small, all safety great and small, all memory great and small, all virtue great and small, all intellect great and small, all tranquillity great and small, all plenty great and small, all sensation great and small, all light great and small, all suavity[1] great and small, all measure great and small, all beauty great and small, all peace great and small, and whatever other like things may occur, especially such as are found throughout all things, whether spiritual or corporeal, every measure, every form, every order both great and small, are from the Lord God. All which good things whoever should wish to abuse, pays the penalty by divine judgment; but where none of these things shall have been present at all, no nature will remain.

CHAP. 14.—SMALL GOOD THINGS IN COMPARISON WITH GREATER ARE CALLED BY CONTRARY NAMES.

But in all these things, whatever are small are called by contrary names in comparison with greater things; as in the form of a man

[1] Or *sanity*, according to another reading.—A. H. N.

because the beauty is greater, the beauty of the ape in comparison with it is called deformity. And the imprudent are deceived, as if the former is good, and the latter evil, nor do they regard in the body of the ape its own fashion, the equality of members on both sides, the agreement of parts, the protection of safety, and other things which it would be tedious to enumerate.

CHAP. 15.—IN THE BODY OF THE APE THE GOOD OF BEAUTY IS PRESENT, THOUGH IN A LESS DEGREE.

But that what we have said may be understood, and may satisfy those too slow of comprehension, or that even the pertinacious and those repugnant to the most manifest truth may be compelled to confess what is true, let them be asked, whether corruption can harm the body of an ape? But if it can, so that it may become more hideous, what diminishes but the good of beauty? Whence as long as the nature of the body subsists, so long something will remain. If, accordingly, good having been consumed, nature is consumed, the nature is therefore good. So also we say that slow is contrary to swift, but yet he who does not move at all cannot even be called slow. So we say that a heavy voice is contrary to a sharp voice, or a harsh to a musical; but if you completely remove any kind of voice, there is silence where there is no voice, which silence, nevertheless, for the simple reason that there is no voice, is usually opposed to voice as something contrary thereto. So also lucid and obscure are called as it were two contrary things, yet even obscure things have something of light, which being absolutely wanting, darkness is the absence of light in the same way in which silence is the absence of voice.

CHAP. 16.—PRIVATIONS IN THINGS ARE FITTINGLY ORDERED BY GOD.

Yet even these privations of things are so ordered in the universe of nature, that to those wisely considering they not unfittingly have their vicissitudes. For by not illuminating certain places and times, God has also made the darkness as fittingly as the day. For if we by restraining the voice fittingly interpose silence in speaking, how much more does He, as the perfect framer of all things, fittingly make privations of things? Whence also in the hymn of the three children, light and darkness alike praise God,[1] that is, bring forth praise in the hearts of those who well consider.

CHAP. 17.—NATURE, IN AS FAR AS IT IS NATURE, NO EVIL.

No nature, therefore, as far as it is nature, is evil; but to each nature there is no evil except to be diminished in respect of good. But if by being diminished it should be consumed so that there is no good, no nature would be left; not only such as the Manichæans introduce, where so great good things are found that their exceeding blindness is wonderful, but such as any one can introduce.

CHAP. 18.—HYLE, WHICH WAS CALLED BY THE ANCIENTS THE FORMLESS MATERIAL OF THINGS, IS NOT AN EVIL.

For neither is that material, which the ancients called *Hyle*, to be called an evil. I do not say that which Manichæus with most senseless vanity, not knowing what he says, denominates *Hyle*, namely, the former of corporeal beings; whence it is rightly said to him, that he introduces another god. For nobody can form and create corporeal beings but God alone; for neither are they created unless there subsist with them measure, form, and order, which I think that now even they themselves confess to be good things, and things that cannot be except from God. But by *Hyle* I mean a certain material absolutely formless and without quality, whence those qualities that we perceive are formed, as the ancients said. For hence also wood is called in Greek ὕλη, because it is adapted to workmen, not that itself may make anything, but that it is the material of which something may be made. Nor is that *Hyle*, therefore, to be called an evil which cannot be perceived through any appearance, but can scarcely be thought of through any sort of privation of appearance. For this has also a capacity of forms; for if it cannot receive the form imposed by the workman, neither assuredly may it be called material. Hence if form is some good, whence those who excel in it are called beautiful,[2] as from appearance they are called handsome,[3] even the capacity of form is undoubtedly something good. As because wisdom is a good, no one doubts that to be capable of wisdom is a good. And because every good is from God, no one ought to doubt that even matter, if there is any, has its existence from God alone.

CHAP. 19.—TO HAVE TRUE EXISTENCE IS AN EXCLUSIVE PREROGATIVE OF GOD.

Magnificently and divinely, therefore, our God said to his servant: "I am that I am,"

[1] Dan. iii. 72.

[2] *Forma—formosus.*

[3] *Species—speciosus.*

and "Thou shalt say to the children of Israel, He who is sent me to you."[1] For He truly is because He is unchangeable. For every change makes what was not, to be: therefore He truly is, who is unchangeable; but all other things that were made by Him have received being form Him each in its own measure. To Him who is highest, therefore, nothing can be contrary, save what is not; and consequently as from Him everything that is good has its being, so from Him is everything that by nature exists; since everything that exists by nature is good. Thus every nature is good, and everything good is from God; therefore every nature is from God.

CHAP. 20.—PAIN ONLY IN GOOD NATURES.

But pain which some suppose to be in an especial manner an evil, whether it be in mind or in body, cannot exist except in good natures. For the very fact of resistance in any being leading to pain, involves a refusal not to be what it was, because it was something good; but when a being is compelled to something better, the pain is useful, when to something worse, it is useless. Therefore in the case of the mind, the will resisting a greater power causes pain; in the case of the body, sensation resisting a more powerful body causes pain. But evils without pain are worse: for it is worse to rejoice in iniquity than to bewail corruption; yet even such rejoicing cannot exist save from the attainment of inferior good things. But iniquity is the desertion of better things. Likewise in a body, a wound with pain is better than painless putrescence, which is especially called the corruption which the dead flesh of the Lord did not see, that is, did not suffer, as was predicted in prophecy: "Thou shalt not suffer Thy Holy one to see corruption."[2] For who denies that He was wounded by the piercing of the nails, and that He was stabbed with the lance?[3] But even what is properly called by men corporeal corruption, that is, putrescence itself, if as yet there is anything left to consume, increases by the diminution of the good. But if corruption shall have absolutely consumed it, so that there is no good, no nature will remain, for there will be nothing that corruption may corrupt; and so there will not even be putrescence, for there will be nowhere at all for it to be.

CHAP. 21.—FROM MEASURE THINGS ARE SAID TO BE MODERATE-SIZED.[4]

Therefore now by common usage things small and mean are said to have measure, because some measure remains in them, without which they would no longer be moderate-sized, but would not exist at all. But those things that by reason of too much progress are called immoderate, are blamed for very excessiveness; but yet it is necessary that those things themselves be restrained in some manner under God who has disposed all things in extension, number, and weight.[5]

CHAP. 22.—MEASURE IN SOME SENSE IS SUITABLE TO GOD HIMSELF.

But God cannot be said to have measure, lest He should seem to be spoken of as limited. Yet He is not immoderate by whom measure is bestowed upon all things, so that they may in any measure exist. Nor again ought God to be called measured, as if He received measure from any one. But if we say that He is the highest measure, by chance we say something; if indeed in speaking of the highest measure we mean the highest good. For every measure in so far as it is a measure is good; whence nothing can be called measured, modest, modified, without praise, although in another sense we use *measure* for *limit*, and speak of no *measure* where there is no *limit*, which is sometimes said with praise as when it is said: "And of His kingdom there shall be no limit."[6] For it might also be said, "There shall be no measure," so that measure might be used in the sense of limit; for He who reigns in no measure, assuredly does not reign at all.

CHAP. 23.—WHENCE A BAD MEASURE, A BAD FORM, A BAD ORDER MAY SOMETIMES BE SPOKEN OF.

Therefore a bad measure, a bad form, a bad order, are either so called because they are less than they should be, or because they are not adapted to those things to which they should be adapted; so that they may be called bad as being alien and incongruous; as if any one should be said not to have done in a good measure because he has done less than he ought, or because he has done in such a thing as he ought not to have done, or more than was fitting, or not conveniently; so that the very fact of that being reprehended which is done in a bad measure, is justly reprehended for no other cause than that the measure is not there maintained. Likewise a form is called bad either in comparison with something more handsome or more beautiful, this form being less, that greater, not in size but

[1] Ex. iii. 14.
[2] Ps. xvl. 10.
[3] John xix. 18, 34.
[4] *Modus*, *modica*.
[5] Wisd. xi. 21.
[6] Luke i. 33.

in comeliness; or because it is out of harmony with the thing to which it is applied, so that it seems alien and unsuitable. As if a man should walk forth into a public place naked, which nakedness does not offend if seen in a bath. Likewise also order is called bad when order itself is maintained in an inferior degree. Hence not order, but rather disorder, is bad; since either the ordering is less than it should be, or not as it should be. Yet where there is any measure, any form, any order, there is some good and some nature; but where there is no measure, no form, no order, there is no good, no nature.

CHAP. 24.—IT IS PROVED BY THE TESTIMONIES OF SCRIPTURE THAT GOD IS UNCHANGEABLE. THE SON OF GOD BEGOTTEN, NOT MADE.

Those things which our faith holds and which reason in whatever way has traced out, are fortified by the testimonies of the divine Scriptures, so that those who by reason of feebler intellect are not able to comprehend these things, may believe the divine authority, and so may deserve to know. But let not those who understand, but are less instructed in ecclesiastical literature, suppose that we set forth these things from our own intellect rather than what are in those Books. Accordingly, that God is unchangeable is written in the Psalms: "Thou shalt change them and they shall be changed; but Thou thyself art the same."[1] And in the book of Wisdom, concerning wisdom: "Remaining in herself, she renews all things."[2] Whence also the Apostle Paul: "To the invisible, incorruptible, only God."[3] And the Apostle James: "Every best giving and every perfect gift is from above, descending from the Father of light, with whom there is no changeableness, neither obscuring of influence."[4] Likewise because what He begat of Himself is what He Himself is, it is said in brief by the Son Himself: "I and the Father are one."[5] But because the Son was not made, since through Him were all things made, thus it is written: "In the beginning was the Word, and the Word was with God, and God was the Word; this was in the beginning with God. All things were made through Him, and without Him was made nothing;"[6] that is, without Him was not anything made.

CHAP. 25.—THIS LAST EXPRESSION MISUNDERSTOOD BY SOME.

For no attention should be paid to the ravings of men who think that *nothing* should be understood to mean *something*, and moreover think to compel any one to vanity of this kind on the ground that *nothing* is placed at the end of the sentence. Therefore, they say, it was made, and because it was made, nothing is itself something. They have lost their senses by zeal in contradicting, and do not understand that it makes no difference whether it be said: "Without Him was made nothing," or "without Him nothing was made." For even if the order were the last mentioned, they could nevertheless say, that nothing is itself something because it was made. For in the case of what is in truth something, what difference does it make if it be said "Without him a house was made," so long as it is understood that something was made without him, which something is a house? So also because it is said: "Without Him was made nothing," since nothing is assuredly not anything, when it is truly and properly spoken, it makes no difference whether it be said: "Without Him was made nothing or Without Him nothing was made," or "nothing was made." But who cares to speak with men who can say of this very expression of mine "It makes no difference," "Therefore it makes some difference, for nothing itself is something?" But those whose brains are not addled, see it as a thing most manifest that this something is to be understood when it says "It makes no difference," as when I say "It matters in no respect." But these, if they should say to any one, "What hast thou done?" and he should reply that he has done nothing, would, according to this mode of disputation, falsely accuse him saying, "Thou hast done something, therefore, because thou hast done nothing; for nothing is itself something." But they have also the Lord Himself placing this word at the end of a sentence, when He says: "And in secret have I spoken nothing."[7] Let them read, therefore, and be silent.[8]

CHAP. 26.—THAT CREATURES ARE MADE OF NOTHING.

Because therefore God made all things which He did not beget of Himself, not of those things that already existed, but of those things that did not exist at all, that is, of nothing," the Apostle Paul says: "Who calls the things that are not as if they are."[9] But still more plainly it is written in the book of Maccabees: "I pray thee, son, look at the

1 Ps. cii. 27. 2 Wisd. vii. 27. 3 1 Tim. i. 17. 4 James i. 17. 5 John x. 30. 6 John i. 1-3.

7 John xviii. 20.

8 It is difficult for us to understand why Augustin should have thought it worth while to refute so elaborately an argument so puerile. But it is his way to be prolix in such matters.—A. H. N.

9 Rom. iv. 17.

heaven and the earth and all the things that are in them; see and know that it was not these of which the Lord God made us."[1] And from this that is written in the Psalm: "He spake, and they were made."[2] It is manifest, that not of Himself He begat these things, but that He made them by word and command. But what is not of Himself is assuredly of nothing. For there was not anything of which he should make them, concerning which the apostle says most openly: "For from Him, and through Him, and in Him are all things."[3]

CHAP. 27.—"FROM HIM" AND "OF HIM" DO NOT MEAN THE SAME THING.

But "from Him" does not mean the same as "of Him."[4] For what is of Him may be said to be from Him; but not everything that is from Him is rightly said to be of Him. For from Him are heaven and earth, because He made them; but not of Him because they are not of His substance. As in the case of a man who begets a son and makes a house, from himself is the son, from himself is the house, but the son is of him, the house is of earth and wood. But this is so, because as a man he cannot make something even of nothing; but God of whom are all things, through whom are all things, in whom are all things, had no need of any material which He had not made to assist His omnipotence.

CHAP. 28.—SIN NOT FROM GOD, BUT FROM THE WILL OF THOSE SINNING.

But when we hear: "All things are from Him, and through Him, and in Him," we ought assuredly to understand all natures which naturally exist. For sins, which do not preserve but vitiate nature, are not from Him; which sins, Holy Scripture in many ways testifies, are from the will of those sinning, especially in the passage where the apostle says: "But dost thou suppose this, O man, that judgest those who do such things, and doest them, that thou shalt escape the judgment of God? Or dost thou despise the riches of His goodness, and patience, and long-suffering, not knowing that the patience of God leadeth thee to repentance? But according to the hardness of thy heart and thy impenitent heart, thou treasurest up for thyself wrath against the day of wrath and of the revelation of the just judgment of God, who will render unto every one according to his works."[5]

CHAP. 29.—THAT GOD IS NOT DEFILED BY OUR SINS.

And yet, though all things that He established are in Him, those who sin do not defile Him, of whose wisdom it is said: "She touches all things by reason of her purity, and nothing defiled assails her."[6] For it behooves us to believe that as God is incorruptible and unchangeable, so also is He consequently undefilable.

CHAP. 30.—THAT GOOD THINGS, EVEN THE LEAST, AND THOSE THAT ARE EARTHLY, ARE BY GOD.

But that God made even the least things, that is, earthly and mortal things, must undoubtedly be understood from that passage of the apostle, where, speaking of the members of our flesh: "For if one member is glorified, all the members rejoice with it, and if one member suffers, all the members suffer with it;" also this he then says: "God has placed the members each one of them in the body as he willed;" and "God has tempered the body, giving to that to which it was wanting greater honor, that there should be no schism in the body, but that the members should have the same care one for another."[7] But what the apostle thus praises in the measure and form and order of the members of the flesh, you find in the flesh of all animals, alike the greatest and the least; for all flesh is among earthly goods, and consequently is esteemed among the least.

CHAP. 31.—TO PUNISH AND TO FORGIVE SINS BELONG EQUALLY TO GOD.

Likewise because it belongs to divine judgment, not human, what sort of punishment and how great is due to every fault, it is thus written: "O the height of the riches of the wisdom and the knowledge of God! how inscrutable are His judgments and his ways past finding out!"[8] Likewise because by the goodness of God sins are forgiven to the converted, the very fact that Christ was sent sufficiently shows, who not in His own nature as God, but in our nature, which He assumed from a woman, died for us; which goodness of God with reference to us, and which love of God, the apostle thus sets forth: "But God commendeth His love toward us, in that while we were yet sinners Christ died for us; much more now being justified in His blood we shall be saved from wrath through Him. For if when we were enemies we were reconciled to

1 Mac. vii. 28. 2 Ps. cxlviii. 5. 3 Rom. xi. 36.
4 *Ex ipso* and *de ipso*. 5 Rom. ii. 3-6.
6 Wisd. vii. 24, 25. 7 1 Cor. xii. 26, 18, 24, 25.
8 Rom. xi. 33.

God through the death of His Son, much more being reconciled we shall be saved in His life."[1] But because even when due punishment is rendered to sinners, there is no unrighteousness on God's part, he thus says: "What shall we say? Is God unrighteous who visiteth with wrath?"[2] But in one place he has briefly admonished that goodness and severity are alike from Him, saying: "Thou seest then the goodness and severity of God; toward them that have fallen, severity, but towards thee goodness, if thou shouldst continue in goodness.[3]

CHAP. 32.—FROM GOD ALSO IS THE VERY POWER TO BE HURTFUL.

Likewise because the power even of those that are hurtful is from God alone, thus it stands written, Wisdom speaking: "Through me kings reign and tyrants hold the land through me."[4] The apostle also says: "For there is no power but of God."[5] But that it is worthily done is written in the book of Job: "Who maketh to reign a man that is a hypocrite, on account of the perversity of the people."[6] And concerning the people of Israel God says: "I gave them a king in my wrath."[7] For it is not unrighteous, that the wicked receiving the power of being hurtful, both the patience of the good should be proved and the iniquity of the evil punished. For through power given to the Devil both Job was proved so that he might appear righteous,[8] and Peter was tempted lest he should be presumptuous,[9] and Paul was buffeted lest he should be exalted,[10] and Judas was damned so that he should hang himself.[11] When, therefore, through the power which He has given the Devil, God Himself shall have done all things righteously, nevertheless punishment shall at last be rendered to the Devil not for these things justly done, but for the unrighteous willing to be hurtful, which belonged to himself, when it shall be said to the impious who persevered in consenting to his wickedness, "Go ye into everlasting fire which my God has prepared for the Devil and his angels."[12]

CHAP. 33.—THAT EVIL ANGELS HAVE BEEN MADE EVIL, NOT BY GOD, BUT BY SINNING.

But because evil angels also were not constituted evil by God, but were made evil by sinning, Peter in his epistle says: "For if God spared not angels when they sinned, but casting them down into the dungeons of smoky hell, He delivered them to be reserved for punishment in judgment."[13] Hence Peter shows that there is still due to them the penalty of the last judgment, concerning which the Lord says: "Go ye into everlasting fire, which has been prepared for the Devil and his angels." Although they have already penally received this hell, that is, an inferior smoky air as a prison, which nevertheless since it is also called heaven, is not that heaven in which there are stars, but this lower heaven by the smoke of which the clouds are conglobulated, and where the birds fly; for both a cloudy heaven is spoken of, and flying things are called heavenly. As when the Apostle Paul calls those evil angels, against whom as enemies by living piously we contend, "spiritual things of wickedness in heavenly places."[14] That this may not be understood of the upper heavens, he plainly says elsewhere: "According to the presence of the prince of this air, who now worketh in the sons of disobedience."[15]

CHAP. 34.—THAT SIN IS NOT THE STRIVING FOR AN EVIL NATURE, BUT THE DESERTION OF A BETTER.

Likewise because sin, or unrighteousness, is not the striving after evil nature but the desertion of better, it is thus found written in the Scriptures: "Every creature of God is good."[16] And accordingly every tree also which God planted in Paradise is assuredly good. Man did not therefore strive after an evil nature when he touched the forbidden tree; but by deserting what was better, he committed an evil deed. Since the Creator is better than any creature which He has made, His command should not have been deserted, that the thing forbidden, however good, might be touched; since the better having been deserted, the good of the creature was striven for, which was touched contrary to the command of the Creator. God did not plant an evil tree in Paradise; but He Himself was better who prohibited its being touched.

CHAP. 35.—THE TREE WAS FORBIDDEN TO ADAM NOT BECAUSE IT WAS EVIL, BUT BECAUSE IT WAS GOOD FOR MAN TO BE SUBJECT TO GOD.

For besides, He had made the prohibition, in order to show that the nature of the rational soul ought not to be in its own power, but in subjection to God, and that it guards the order of its salvation through obedience,

1 Rom. v. 8-10. 2 *Ibid.* iii. 5. 3 *Ibid.* xi. 22.
4 Prov. viii. 15. 5 Rom. xiii. 1.
6 Job xxxiv. 30. Compare the Revised English Version. The sense seems to be completely missed in Augustin's text.—A. H. N.
7 Hos. xiii. 11. 8 Job i. and ii. 9 Matt. xxvi. 31-35, 69-75.
10 2 Cor. xii. 7. 11 Matt. xxvii. 5. 12 Matt. xxv. 41.

13 2 Pet. ii. 4. 14 Eph. vi. 12.
15 *Ibid.* ii. 2. 16 1 Tim. iv. 4.

corrupting it through disobedience. Hence also He called the tree, the touching of which He forbade, the tree "of the knowledge of good and evil;"[1] because when man should have touched it in the face of the prohibition, he would experience the penalty of sin, and so would know the difference between the good of obedience, and the evil of disobedience.

CHAP. 36.—NO CREATURE OF GOD IS EVIL, BUT TO ABUSE A CREATURE OF GOD IS EVIL.

For who is so foolish as to think a creature of God, especially one planted in Paradise, blameworthy; when indeed not even thorns and thistles, which the earth brought forth, according to the judiciary judgment of God, for wearing out the sinner in labor, should be blamed? For even such herbs have their measure and form and order, which whoever considers soberly will find praiseworthy; but they are evil to that nature which ought thus to be restrained as a recompense for sin. Therefore, as I have said, sin is not the striving after an evil nature, but the desertion of a better, and so the deed itself is evil, not the nature which the sinner uses amiss. For it is evil to use amiss that which is good. Whence the apostle reproves certain ones as condemned by divine judgment, "Who have worshipped and served the creature more than the Creator."[2] He does not reprove the creature, which he who should do would act injuriously towards the Creator, but those who, deserting the better, have used amiss the good.

CHAP. 37.—GOD MAKES GOOD USE OF THE EVIL DEEDS OF SINNERS.

Accordingly, if all natures should guard their own proper measure and form and order, there would be no evil: but if any one should wish to misuse these good things, not even thus does he vanquish the will of God, who knows how to order righteously even the unrighteous; so that if they themselves through the iniquity of their will should misuse His good things, He through the righteousness of His power may use their evil deeds, rightly ordaining to punishment those who have perversely ordained themselves to sins.

CHAP 38.—ETERNAL FIRE TORTURING THE WICKED, NOT EVIL.

For neither is eternal fire itself, which is to torture the impious, an evil nature, since it has its measure, its form and its order depraved by no iniquity; but it is an evil torture for the damned, to whose sins it is due. For neither is yonder light, because it tortures the blear-eyed, an evil nature.

CHAP. 39.—FIRE IS CALLED ETERNAL, NOT AS GOD IS, BUT BECAUSE WITHOUT END.

But fire is eternal, not as God is eternal, because, though without end, yet it is not without beginning; but God is also without beginning. Then, although it may be employed perpetually for the punishment of sinners, yet it is mutable nature. But that is true eternity which is true immortality, that is that highest immutability, which cannot be changed at all. For it is one thing not to suffer change, when change is possible, and another thing to be absolutely incapable of change. Therefore, just as man is called good, yet not as God, of whom it was said, "There is none good save God alone;"[3] and just as the soul is called immortal, yet not as God, of whom it was said, "Who alone hath immortality;"[4] and just as a man is called wise, yet not as God, of whom it was said, "To God the only wise;"[5] so fire is called eternal, yet not as God, whose alone is immortality itself and true eternity.

CHAP. 40.—NEITHER CAN GOD SUFFER HURT, NOR ANY OTHER, SAVE BY THE JUST ORDINATION OF GOD.

Since these things are so, according to the Catholic faith, and wholesome doctrine, and truth perspicuous to those of good understanding, neither can any one hurt the nature of God, nor can the nature of God unrighteously hurt any one, or suffer any one to do hurt with impunity. "For he that doeth hurt shall receive," says the apostle, "according to the hurt that he has done; and there is no accepting of persons with God."[6]

CHAP. 41.—HOW GREAT GOOD THINGS THE MANICHÆANS PUT IN THE NATURE OF EVIL, AND HOW GREAT EVIL THINGS IN THE NATURE OF GOOD.

But if the Manichæans were willing, without pernicious zeal for defending their error, and with the fear of God, to think, they would not most criminally blaspheme by supposing two natures, the one good, which they call God, the other evil, which God did not make: so erring, so delirious, nay so insane, are they that they do not see, that even in what they call the nature of supreme evil they place so great good things: life, power, safety, mem-

[1] Gen. ii. 9.
[2] Rom. i. 25.
[3] Mark x. 18.
[4] 1 Tim. vi. 16.
[5] Rom. xvi. 27.
[6] Col. iii. 25.

ory, intellect, temperance, virtue, plenty, sense, light, suavity, extensions, numbers, peace, measure, form, order; but in what they call supreme good, so many evil things: death, sickness, forgetfulness, foolishness, confusion, impotence, need, stolidity, blindness, pain, unrighteousness, disgrace, war, intemperance, deformity, perversity. For they say that the princes of darkness also have been alive in their own nature, and in their own kingdom were safe, and remembered and understood. For they say that the Prince of Darkness harangued in such a manner, that neither could he have said such things, nor could he have been heard by those by whom he was said to have been heard, without memory and understanding; and to have had a temper suitable to his mind and body, and to have ruled by virtue of power, and to have had abundance and fruitfulness with respect to his elements, and they are said to have perceived themselves mutually and the light as near at hand, and to have had eyes by which they could see the light afar off; which eyes assuredly could not have seen the light without some light (whence also they are rightly called light); and they are said to have enjoyed exceedingly the sweetness of their pleasures, and to have been determined by measured members and dwelling-places. But unless there had been some sort of beauty there, they would not have loved their wives, nor would their bodies have been steady by adaptation of parts; without which, those things could not have been done there which the Manichæans insanely say were done. And unless some peace had been there, they would not have obeyed their Prince. Unless measure had been there, they would have done nothing else than eat or drink, or rage, or whatever they might have done, without any society: although not even those that did these things would have had determinate forms, unless measure had been there. But now the Manichæans say that they did such things that they cannot be denied to have had in all their actions measures suitable to themselves. But if form had not been there, no natural quality would have there subsisted. But if there had been no order there, some would not have ruled, others been ruled; they would not have lived harmoniously in their elements; in fine, they would not have had their members adapted to their places, so that they could not do all those things that the Manichæans vainly fable. But if they say that God's nature does not die, what according to their vanity does Christ raise from the dead? If they say that it does not grow sick, what does He cure? If they say that it is not subject to forgetfulness, what does He remind? If they say that it is not deficient in wisdom, what does He teach? If they say that it is not confused, what does He restore? If they say that it was not vanquished and taken captive, what does He liberate? If they say that it was not in need, to what does He minister aid? If they say that it did not lose feeling, what does He animate? If they say that it has not been blinded, what does He illuminate? If it is not in pain, to what does He give relief? If it is not unrighteous, what does He correct through precepts? If it is not in disgrace, what does He cleanse? If it is not in war, to what does He promise peace? If it is not deficient in moderation, upon what does He impose the measure of law? If it is not deformed, what does He reform? If it is not perverse, what does He emend? For all these things done by Christ, they say, are to be attributed not to that thing which was made by God, and which has become depraved by its own free choice in sinning, but to the very nature, yea to the very substance of God, which is what God Himself is.

CHAP. 42.—MANICHÆAN BLASPHEMIES CONCERNING THE NATURE OF GOD.

What can be compared to those blasphemies? Absolutely nothing, unless the errors of other sectaries be considered; but if that error be compared with itself in another aspect, of which we have not yet spoken, it will be convicted of far worse and more execrable blasphemy. For they say that some souls, which they will have to be of the substance of God and of absolutely the same nature, which have not sinned of their own accord, but have been overcome and oppressed by the race of darkness, which they call evil, for combating which they descended not of their own accord, but at the command of the Father, are fettered forever in the horrible sphere of darkness. So according to their sacrilegious vaporings, God liberated Himself in a certain part from a great evil, but again condemned Himself in another part, which He could not liberate, and triumphed over the enemy itself as if it had been vanquished from above. O criminal, incredible audacity, to believe, to speak, to proclaim such things about God! Which when they endeavor to defend, that with their eyes shut they may rush headlong into yet worse things, they say that the commingling of the evil nature does these things, in order that the good nature of God may suffer so great evils: for that this good nature in its own sphere could or can suffer no one of these things. As if a nature were lauded as incorruptible, because it does not hurt itself, and not because it cannot suffer hurt from another. Then if the nature of God hurt the nature of darkness, and the nature of darkness hurt the nature of God, there are therefore two evil things which hurt each other in turn, and the race of darkness was the better disposed, because if it committed hurt it did it unwillingly; for it did not wish to commit hurt, but to enjoy the good which belonged to God. But God wished to extinguish it, as Manichæus most openly raves forth in his epistle of the ruinous *Foundation*. For forgetting that he had shortly before said: "But His most resplendent realms were so founded upon the shining and happy land, that they could never be either moved or shaken by any one;" he afterwards said: "But the Father of the most blessed light, knowing that great ruin and desolation which would arise from the darkness, threaten his holy worlds, unless he should send in opposition a deity excellent and renowned, mighty in strength, by whom he might at the same time overcome and destroy the race of darkness, which having been extinguished, the inhabitants of light would enjoy perpetual rest." Behold, he feared ruin and desolation that threatened his worlds! Assuredly they were so founded upon the shining and happy land that they never could be either moved or shaken by any one? Behold, from fear he wished to hurt the neighboring race, which he endeavored to destroy and extinguish, in order that the inhabitants of light might enjoy perpetual rest. Why did he not add, and perpetual bondage? Were not these souls that he fettered forever in the sphere of darkness, the inhabitants of light, of whom he says plainly, that "they have suffered themselves to err from their former bright nature?" when against his will he is compelled to say, that they sinned by free will, while he wishes to ascribe sin only to the necessity of the contrary nature: everywhere ignorant what to say, and as if he were himself already in the sphere of darkness which he invented, seeking, and not finding, how he may escape. But let him say what he will to the seduced and miserable men by whom he is honored far more highly than Christ, that at this price he may sell to them such long and sacrilegious fables. Let him say what he will, let him shut up, as it were, in a sphere, as in a prison, the race of darkness, and let him fasten outside the nature of light, to which he promised perpetual rest on the extinction of the enemy: behold, the penalty of light is worse than that of darkness; the penalty of the divine nature is worse than that of the adverse race. But since although the latter is in the midst of darkness it pertains to its nature to dwell in darkness; but souls which are the very same thing that God is, cannot be received, he says, into those peaceful realms, and are alienated from the life and liberty of the holy light, and are fettered in the aforesaid horrible sphere: whence he says, "Those souls shall adhere to the things that they have loved, having been left in the same sphere of darkness, bringing this upon themselves by their own deserts." Is not this assuredly free voluntary choice? See how insanely he ignores what he says, and by making self-contradictory statements wages a worse war against himself than against the God of the race of darkness itself. Accordingly, if the souls of light are damned, because they loved darkness, the race of darkness, which loved light, is unjustly damned. And the race of darkness indeed loved light from the beginning, violently, it may be, but yet so as to wish for its possession, not its extinction: but the nature of light wished to extinguish in war the darkness; therefore when vanquished it loved darkness. Choose which you will: whether it was compelled by necessity to love darkness, or seduced by free will. If by necessity, wherefore is it damned? if by free will, wherefore is the nature of God involved in so great iniquity? If the nature of God was compelled by necessity to love darkness, it did not vanquish, but was vanquished: if by free will, why do the wretches hesitate any longer to attribute the will to sin to the nature which God made out of nothing, lest they should thereby attribute it to the light which He begat?

CHAP. 43.—MANY EVILS BEFORE HIS COMMINGLING WITH EVIL ARE ATTRIBUTED TO THE NATURE OF GOD BY THE MANICHÆANS.

What if we should also show that before the commingling of evil, which stupid fable they have most madly believed, great evils were in what they call the nature of light? what will it seem possible to add to these blasphemies? For before the conflict, there was the hard and inevitable necessity of fighting: here is truly a great evil, before evil is commingled with good. Let them say whence this is, when as yet no commingling had taken place? But if there was no necessity, there was therefore free will: whence also this so great evil, that God himself should wish to hurt his own nature, which could not be hurt by the enemy, by sending it to be cruelly commingled, to be basely purged, to be unjustly damned? Behold, the great evil of a pernicious, noxious, and savage will, before any evil from the contrary nature was mingled with it! Or perchance he did not know that this would happen to his members, that they should love darkness and become hostile to holy light, as Manichæus says, that is, not only to their own God, but also to the Father from whom they had their being? Whence therefore this so great evil of ignorance, before any evil from the nature of darkness was mingled with it? But if he knew that this would happen, either there was in him everlasting cruelty, if he did not grieve over the contamination and damnation of his own nature that was to take place, or everlasting misery, if he did so grieve: whence also this so great evil of your supreme good before any commingling with your supreme evil? Assuredly that part of the nature itself which was fettered in the eternal chain of that sphere, if it knew not that this fate awaited it, even so was there everlasting ignorance in the nature of God, but if it knew, then everlasting misery: whence this so great evil before any evil from the contrary nature was commingled? Or perchance did it, in the greatness of its love (charity), rejoice that through its punishment perpetual rest was prepared for the residue of the inhabitants of light? Let him who sees how abominable it is to say this, pronounce an anathema. But if this should be done so that at least the good nature itself should not become hostile to the light, it might be possible, perchance, not for the nature of God indeed, but for some man, as it were, to be regarded as praiseworthy, who for the sake of his country should be willing to suffer something of evil, which evil indeed could be only for a time, and not forever: but now also they speak of that fettering in the sphere of darkness as eternal, and not indeed of a certain thing but of the nature of God; and assuredly it were a most unrighteous, and execrable, and ineffably sacrilegious joy, if the nature of God rejoiced that it should love darkness, and should become hostile to holy light. Whence this so monstrous and abominable evil before any evil from the contrary nature was commingled? Who can endure insanity so perverse and so impious, as to attribute so great good things to supreme evil, and so great evils to supreme good, which is God?

Chap. 44.—Incredible Turpitudes in God Imagined by Manichæus.

But now when they speak of that part of the nature of God as everywhere mixed up in heaven, in earth, in all bodies dry and moist, in all sorts of flesh, in all seeds of trees, herbs, men, and animals: not as present by the power of divinity, for administering and ruling all things, undefilably, inviolably, incorruptibly, without any connection with them, which we say of God; but fettered, oppressed, polluted, to be loosed and liberated, as they say, not only through the running to and fro of the sun and the moon, and through the powers of light, but also through their Elect: what sacrilegious and incredible turpitudes this kind of error recommends to them even if it does not induce them to accept, it is horrible to speak of. For they say that the powers of light are transformed into beautiful males and are set over against the women of the race of darkness; and that the same powers again are transformed into beautiful females and are set over against the males of the race of darkness; that through their beauty they enkindle the foulest lust of the princes of darkness, and in this manner vital substance, that is, the nature of God, which they say is held fettered in their bodies, having been loosed from their members relaxed through lust, flies away, and when it has been taken up or cleansed, is liberated. This the wretches read, this they say, this they hear, this they believe, this they put as follows, in the seventh book of their *Thesaurus* (for so they call a certain writing of Manichæus, in which these blasphemies stand written): "Then the blessed Father, who has bright ships, little apartments, dwelling-places, or magnitudes, according to his indwelling clemency, brings the help by which he is drawn out and liberated from the impious bonds, straits, and torments of his vital substance. And so by his own invisible nod he transforms those powers of his, which are held in this most brilliant ship, and makes them to bring forth adverse powers, which have been arranged in the various tracts of the heavens. Since these consist of both sexes, male and female, he orders the aforesaid powers to bring forth partly in the form of beardless youths, for the adverse race of females, partly in the form of bright maidens, for the contrary race of males: knowing that all these hostile powers on account of the deadly and most foul lust innate in them, are very easily taken captive, delivered up to these most beautiful forms which appear, and in this manner they are dissolved. But you may know that this same blessed Father of ours is identical with his powers, which for a necessary reason he transforms into the undefiled likeness of youths and maidens. But these he uses as his own arms, and through them he accomplishes his will. But there are bright ships full of these divine powers, which are stationed after the likeness of marriage over against the infernal races, and who with alacrity and ease effect at the very moment what they have planned. Therefore, when reason demands that these same holy powers should appear to males, straightway also they show by their dress the likeness of most beautiful maidens. Again when females are to be dealt with, putting aside the forms of maidens, they show the forms of beardless youths. But by this handsome appearance of theirs, ardor and lust increase, and in this way the chain of their worst thoughts is loosed, and the living soul which was held by their members, relaxed by this occasion, escapes, and is mingled with its own most pure air; when the souls thoroughly cleansed ascend to the bright ships, which have been prepared for conveying them and for ferrying them over to their own country. But that which still bears the stains of the adverse race, descends little by little through billows and fires, and is mingled with trees and other plants and with all seeds, and is plunged into divers fires. And in what manner the figures of youths and maidens from that great and most glorious ship appear to the contrary powers which live in the heavens and have a fiery nature; and from that handsome appearance, part of the life which is held in their members having been released is conducted away through fires into the earth: in the same manner also, that most high power, which dwells in the ship of vital waters appears in the likeness of youths and holy maidens to those powers whose nature is cold and moist, and which are arranged in the heavens. And indeed to those that are females, among these the form of youths appears, but to the males, the form of maidens. By his changing and diversity of divine and most beautiful persons, the princes male and female of the moist and cold race are loosed, and what is vital in them escapes; but whatever should remain, having been relaxed, is conducted into the earth through cold, and is mingled with all the races of darkness." Who can endure this? Who can believe, not indeed that it is true, but that it could even be said? Behold those who fear to anathematize Manichæus teaching these things, and do not fear to believe in a God doing them and suffering them!

CHAP. 45.—CERTAIN UNSPEAKABLE TURPITUDES BELIEVED, NOT WITHOUT REASON, CONCERNING THE MANICHÆANS THEMSELVES.

But they say, that through their own Elect that same commingled part and nature of God is purged, by eating and drinking forsooth, (because they say that it is held fettered in all foods); that when they are taken up by the Elect for the nourishment of the body in eating and drinking, it is loosed, sealed, and liberated through their sanctity. Nor do the wretches pay heed to the fact that this is believed about them not without good reason, and they deny it in vain, so long as they do not anathematize the books of Manichæus and cease to be Manichæans. For if, as they say, a part of God is fettered in all seeds, and is purged by eating on the part of the Elect; who may not properly believe, that they do what they read in the *Thesaurus* was done among the powers of heaven and the princes of darkness; since indeed they say that their flesh is also from the race of darkness, and since they do not hesitate to believe and to affirm that the vital substance fettered in them is a part of God? Which assuredly if it is to be loosed, and purged by eating, as their lamentable error compels them to acknowledge; who does not see, who does not shudder at the greatness and the unspeakableness of what follows?

CHAP. 46.—THE UNSPEAKABLE DOCTRINE OF THE FUNDAMENTAL EPISTLE.

For they even say that Adam, the first man, was created by certain princes of darkness so that the light might be held by them lest it should escape. For in the epistle which they call *Fundamental*, Manichæus wrote as follows respecting the way in which the Prince of Darkness, whom they represent as the father of the first man, spoke to the rest of his allied princes of darkness, and how he acted: "Therefore with wicked inventions he said to those present: What does this huge light that is rising seem to you to be? See how the pole moves, how it shakes most of the powers. Wherefore it is right for me rather to ask you beforehand for whatever light you have in your powers: since thus I will form an image of that great one who has appeared in his glory, through which we may be able to rule, freed in some measure from the conversation of darkness. Hearing these things, and deliberating for a long time among themselves, they thought it most just to furnish what was demanded of them. For they did not have confidence in being able to retain the light that they had forever; hence they thought it better to offer it to their Prince, by no means without hope that in this way they would rule. It must be considered therefore how they furnished the light that they had. For this also is scattered throughout all the divine scriptures and the heavenly secrets; but to the wise it is easy enough to know how it was given: for it is known immediately and openly by him who should truly and faithfully wish to consider. Since there was a promiscuous throng of those who had come together, females and males of course, he impelled them to copulate among themselves: in which copulation the males emitted seed, the females were made pregnant. But the offspring were like those who had begotten them, the first obtaining as it were the largest portion of the parents' strength. Taking these as a special gift their Prince rejoiced. And just as even now we see take place, that the nature of evil taking thence strength forms the fashioner of bodies, so also the aforesaid Prince, taking the offspring of his companions, which had the senses of their parents, sagacity, light, procreated at the same time with themselves in the process of generation, devoured them; and very many powers having been taken from food of this kind, in which there was present not only fortitude, but much more astuteness and depraved sensibilities from the ferocious race of the progenitors, he called his own spouse to himself, springing from the same stock as himself, emitted, like the rest, the abundance of evils that he had devoured, himself also adding something from his own thought and power, so that his disposition became the former and arranger of all the things that he had poured forth; whose consort received these things as soil cultivated in the best way is accustomed to receive seed. For in her were constructed and woven together the images of all heavenly and earthly powers, so that what was formed obtained the likeness, so to speak, of a full orb."

CHAP. 47.—HE COMPELS TO THE PERPETRATION OF HORRIBLE TURPITUDES.

O abominable monster! O execrable perdition and ruin of deluded souls! I am not speaking of the blasphemy of saying these things about the nature of God which is thus fettered. Let the wretches deluded and hunted by deadly error give heed to this at least, that if a part of their God is fettered by the copulation of males and females which they profess to loose and purge by eating it, the necessity of this unspeakable error compels them not only to loose and purge the part of God from bread and vegetables and fruits, which alone they are seen publicly to partake of, but also from that which might be fettered through copulation, if conception should take place. That they do this some are said to have confessed before a public tribunal, not only in Paphlagonia, but also in Gaul, as I heard in Rome from a certain Catholic Christian; and when they were asked by the authority of what writing they did these things, they betrayed this fact concerning the *Thesaurus* that I have just mentioned. But when this is cast in their teeth, they are in the habit of replying, that some enemy or other has withdrawn from their number, that is from the number of their Elect, and has made a schism, and has founded a most foul heresy of this kind. Whence it is manifest that even if they do not themselves practise this thing, some who do practise it do it on the basis of their books. Therefore let them reject the books, if they abhor the crime, which they are compelled to commit, if they hold to the books; or if they do not commit them, they endeavor in opposition to the books to live more purely. But what do they do when it is said to them, either purge the light from whatever seeds you can, so that you cannot refuse to do that which you assert that you do not do; or else anathematize Manichæus, when he says that a part of God is in all seeds, and that it is fettered by copulation, but that whatever of light, that is, of the aforesaid part of God, should become the food of the Elect, is purged by being eaten. Do you see what he compels you to believe, and do you still hesitate to anathematize him? What do they do, I say, when this is said to them? To what subterfuges do they betake themselves, when either so nefarious a doctrine is to be anathematized, or so nefarious a turpitude committed, in comparison with which all those intolerable evils to which I have already called attention, seem tolerable, namely, that they say of the nature of God that it was pressed by necessity to wage war, that it was either secure by everlasting ignorance, or was disturbed by everlasting grief and fear, when the corruption of commingling and the chain of everlasting damnation should come upon it, that finally as a result of the conflict it should be taken captive, oppressed, polluted, that after a false victory it should be fettered forever in a horrible sphere and separated from its original blessedness, while if considered in themselves they cannot be endured?

CHAP. 48.—AUGUSTIN PRAYS THAT THE MANICHÆANS MAY BE RESTORED TO THEIR SENSES.

O great is Thy patience, Lord, full of compassion and gracious, slow to anger, and plenteous in mercy, and true;[1] who makest Thy sun to rise upon the good and the evil, and who sendest rain upon the just and the unjust;[2] who willest not the death of the sinner, so much as that he return and live;[3] who

[1] Ps. ciii. 8. [2] Matt. v. 45. [3] Ezek. xxxiii. 11.

reproving in parts, dost give place to repentance, that wickedness having been abandoned, they may believe on Thee, O Lord;[1] who by Thy patience dost lead to repentance, although many according to the hardness of their heart and their impenitent heart treasure up for themselves wrath against the day of wrath and of the revelation of Thy righteous judgment, who wilt render to every man according to his works;[2] who in the day when a man shall have turned from his iniquity to Thy mercy and truth, wilt forget all his iniquities:[3] stand before us, grant unto us that through our ministry, by which Thou hast been pleased to refute this execrable and too horrible error, as many have already been liberated, many also may be liberated, and whether through the sacrament of Thy holy baptism, or through the sacrifice of a broken spirit and a contrite and humbled heart,[4] in the sorrow of repentance, they may deserve to receive the remission of their sins and blasphemies, by which through ignorance they have offended Thee. For nothing is of any avail, save Thy surpassing mercy and power, and the truth of Thy baptism, and the keys of the kingdom of heaven in Thy holy Church; so that we must not despair of men as long as by Thy patience they live on this earth, who even knowing how great an evil it is to think or to say such things about Thee, are detained in that malign profession on account of the use or the attainment of temporal or earthly convenience, if rebuked by Thy reproaches they in any way flee to Thy ineffable goodness, and prefer to all the enticements of the carnal life, the heavenly and eternal life.

1 Wisd. xii. 2. 2 Rom. ii. 4–6. 3 Ezek. xviii. 21.

4 Ps. li. 17.

WRITINGS

IN CONNECTION WITH THE

DONATIST CONTROVERSY

TRANSLATED BY THE

REV. J. R. KING, M.A.,

VICAR OF ST. PETER'S IN THE EAST, OXFORD; AND LATE FELLOW AND TUTOR OF MERTON COLLEGE, OXFORD.

REVISED, WITH ADDITIONAL NOTES,

BY THE

REV. CHESTER D. HARTRANFT, D.D.,

PROFESSOR OF BIBLICAL AND ECCLESIASTICAL HISTORY, IN THE THEOLOGICAL SEMINARY AT HARTFORD, CONN.

INTRODUCTORY ESSAY.

By Rev. Chester D. Hartranft, D.D.

CHAPTER I.—BIBLIOGRAPHY.

A. Sources.

I. Of course all the Anti-Donatist writings of Augustin are found in the general editions from Amerbach, 1506, to Migne, 1861. A few are also collected in Du Pin's edd. of Optatus Mil. 1. In the *Monumenta vetera ad Donatistarum Historiam pertinentia.* 2. In the *Gesta Collationis Carthagini habitae Honorii Caesaris iussu inter Catholicos et Donatistas.* See also the different *Collections of Councils*, Labbe, Baluze, Harduin, Mansi, etc. Since these works are discussed in Chapter II. it is unnecessary to repeat the titles here. Cp. titles in *Retractationes*: and *Indiculus librorum, tractatuum et epistolarum S. Augustini*, ed. *cura Possidii*, cap. III.

II. Separate editions of Augustin's Anti-Donatist writings. (From Schönemann's *Bibliotheca*, and other bibliographies.)

1. *S. Augustini liber seu Epistola de unitate Ecclesiae contra Petiliani Donat. Epistolam, Argumentis, Notis atque Analysi illustrata, studio Justi Caluini. Moguntiae.* 1602.

2. *SS. Cypriani et Augustini de unitate Ecclesiae tractatus. Accedit Georgii Calixti, S. Theo. Doct. et in Acad. Julia Prof. primarii, in eorundem librorum lectionem Introductionis fragmentum edente Frid. Ulrico Calixto. Georgii filio. Helmæstadii ex typogr. Calixt.* 1657. 8.

3. *Aurelii Augustini, Episcopi Hipponensis, Liber de Unitate Ecclesiae contra Donatistas. Ext. cum Commentariis uberrimis et utillisimis in Melchioris Lydeckeri Historia illustrata Ecclesiae Africanae, cujus totum pæne tomum secundum constituit inscriptum*:

Tomus secundus ad Librum Augustini de Unitate Ecclesiae contra Donatistas, de principiis Ecclesiae Africanae, illiusque fide in Articulis de Capite Christo et Ecclesia, de Unitate et Schismate, plurimisque Religionis Christianae capitibus agit. Ultrajecti apud viduam Guil. Clerck, 1690. 4.

4. *D. Augustini liber de moderate coercendis haereticis ad Bonifacium Comitem. Nic. Bergius Revalensis Holmiae,* 1696, *in* 8.

III. Translations.

1. *Epistre ou le Livre de St. Augustin de l'Unité de l'Eglise, contre Petilien, Evesque Donatiste, avec certaines observations pour entendre les lieux plus difficiles par Jac. Tigeou, imprimé à Reims par Jean de Foigny.* 1567. 8.

2. *L'Epistre à Vincent, Evesque de l'heresie Rogatiane, traduict de latin par Clément Vaillant. A Paris, Mathurin Prevost.* 1573. 8.

3. *Traité du Baptême trad. par l'abbé Dujat, chapelain d'Étampes. Paris.* 1778. 12.

4. Writings in connection with the Donatist controversy, translated by the Rev. J. R. King, M.A. In the Series of Translations of the Works of Augustin. Edinburgh. T. & T. Clark. 1872.

5. *Ausgewählte Schriften des heil. Aurelius Augustinus, Kirchenlehrers, nacn aem Urtexte ubersetzt. Mit einer kurzen Lebensbeschreibung des Heiligen von J. Motzberger.* 1871–1879. *In the Bibliothek der Kirchenväter, Kempten,* 1869 *sqq.*

B. Literature.

This is a selected literature of the Donatist controversy so far as Augustin was connected with it.

I. In the Benedictine editions occur:

1. Their *Vita S. Aurelii Augustini.*
   Tom. XI. Antw., pp. 1–344. *Tom. I. Migne, pp.* 65–578.
2. *Praefatio of Tom. IX.*
   Antw. s. p. Migne, pp. 9–24.
3. *Index opusculorum S. Augustini contra Donatistas.*
   Tom. IX. Antw., pp. 463, 4. *Migne, pp.* 757–760.
4. *Excerpta et scripta vetera ad Donatistarum historiam pertinentia.*
   Tom. IX. Antw., App. pp. 7–50. *Migne, pp.* 773–842.
5. *Epistolarum ordo chronologicus.*
   Tom. II. Antw., s. p. Migne, pp. 13–48.

II. *Possidius: Vita S. Aurelii Augustini.*
Reprinted in Migne Aug. Op. Tom. I., pp. 33–66. *Cp. Migne Pat. Lat. L. p.* 407.

III. *Ecclesiastica Historia. By the Magdeburg Centuriators.* 1559–1574.
Tom. II. and III., Centuria, IV. and V., contain the Donatist history.

IV. *Balduinius, Franc.*

1. *Delibatio Africanae historiae ecclesticae, s. Optati libri VII. de Schismate Donatistarum, etc. Paris,* 1563. A second edition with improved readings. *Ib.,* 1569. In this the prefaces and annotations are of value. Reprinted in Du Pin's ed. of Optatus Mil.

2. *Historia Carthaginensis Collationis sive disputationis de ecclesia, olim habitae inter Catholicos et Donatistas. Paris,* 1566. 8. *Reprinted in Du Pin. ib.*

V. *Baronius. Annales Ecclesiatici.* 1588–1607.
Tom. III.–V., contain the Donatist history.

VI. *Albaspinæus:*
Optati Mel. opera cum notis et observationibus Gabrielis Albaspinæi. Paris, 1631.
Valuable mainly for the observations; reprinted in Du Pin's ed. of Optatus.

VII. *Casaubonus:*
Optati Mel. de schismate Donatistarum libri VII. In eosd. notae et emendationes Merici Casauboni. Lond. 1631.
These notes are of value and are reproducea with those of other editions in the *Annotationes Variorum* of Du Pin's ed

VIII. *Valesius Henricus:*

Eusebii Pamph. Historia ecc., libri de Vita Constantini, Panegyricus, Const. Oratio ad Sanctorum coetum, gr. et lat. cum annotatt. Paris, 1659 and often.

In this is his dissertation: *De schismate Donatistarum.*

IX. Long, Thomas, B.D. History of the Donatists. Lond. 1677. 8.

X. *Du Pin: Nouvelle Bibliothéque des Auteurs Ecclésiastiques.*

1. *St. Augustin. Tom. III. première partie, pp.* 522–839, 1690. Particularly the review of vol. IX. of Augustin's collected works, pp. 792–811.

2. In *Tom. II., Troisième partie*, 1701, there are also many allusions to the history and literature.

3. In his ed. of *Optatus Mel., Historia Donatistarum.*

XI. *Ittig, Thomas: de Haeresiarchis œvi apostolici at apostol. prox. Lips.* 1690–1703. 4.

XII. *Leydecker Melchior; Historia Ecclesiastica Africana.* 2 *Tom.* 4, See above. *Traj.* 1690. 4.

XIII. *Witsius, Hermann: Miscellaneorum Sacrorum libri.* 2 *vols. Amst.* 1692. 4.

In vol. I. *Dissertatio de schismate Donatistarum.*

XIV. *Bernino:*

Historia di tutte l'heresie descritta da Domenico Bernino. Venezia 1711. Tom. I., contains hist. of Donatism.

XV. *Storren, J. Ph.: ansführlicher und gründlicher Bericht von den Namen, Ursprung, v.s.w. der Donatisten. Frankf.* 1723. 8.

XVI. *Norisius, Henricus:*

Opera omnia nunc prim. collecta et ordinata. Veronae, Tumermani, 1729-32, *fol.* 4 *vols.*

The fourth volume contains his posthumous work on *History of Donatism*, as finished by Ballerini.

XVII. *Tillemont: in his Memoires pour servir a l'histoire Ecclésiastique:*

1. *Tom. VI. Histoire du schisme des Donatistes, où l'on marque aussi tout ce qui regarde l'Eglise d'Afrique depuis l'an* 305, *jusques en l'an* 391 *que S. Augustin fut fait Prestre.* 1732.

2. *Tom. XIII. La Vie de Saint Augustin, dans laquelle on trouvera l'histoire des Donatistes de son temps, et celle des Pelagiens.* 1732.

XVIII. *Orsi:*

Della Istoria Ecclesiastica descritta da F. Guiseppe Agostino Orsi. Tom. IV. (1741) and V. (1749) contain the history of the Donatists.

XIX. *Walch, Ch. Wilh. Fr.:*

Entwurf einer vollständigen Historie der Ketzereien, Spaltungen und Religionsstreitigkeiten, bis auf die Zeiten der Reformation. Leipzig, 1768.

Vierter Theil: Von der Spaltung der Donatisten; with its three sections:

(a) *Von der historie der Donatisten.*

(b) *Von den zwischen den Donatisten und ihren Gegnern geführten Religionsstreitigkeiten.*

(c) *Beurtheilung der Donatistichen Streitigkeiten.*

This work was the beginning of a new critical estimate of the documents.

XX. *Schröckh, Johann Mattheus: Christliche Kirchengeschichte. Sechster Theil:* 1784, but particularly *Elfter Theil*, 1786.

A juster estimate of Donatism.

XXI. *Morcellii, Steph. Ant.: Africa christiana in tres partes distributa.* 3 *vols.* 4. *Brixiae*, 1816–17. 4. *P. II.* for Donatism.

XXII. *Bindemann, C.: Der heilige Augustinus*, 1844–1869.

Bdd. II. & III. contain excellent analyses of the works on Donatism, as well as a history during Augustin's life.

XXIII. *Roux, Adrianus:*

Dissertatio de Aurelio Augustino, adversario Donatistarum. Lugduni Batavorum, 1838.

A brief summary of the works and doctrine.

XIV. *Ribbeck:*

Donatus und Augustinus oder der erste entscheidende Kampf zwischen Separatismus und Kirche. Ein Kirchenhistorischer Versuch von Ferdinand Ribbeck. Elberfeld. 1857. 8.

An uncritical history; but a vigorous analysis, apologetic and polemic.

XXV. *Deutsch:*

Drei Actenstücke zur Geschichte des Donatismus. Neu herausgegeben und erklärt von Martin Deutsch. Berlin, 1875.

The first work on the textual and historical criticism of the sources.

XXVI. *Voelter:*

Der Ursprung des Donatismus, nach den Quellen untersucht und dargestellt von Lic Dr. Daniel Voelter. Freiburg i. B. und Tübingen, 1883.

This keen writer, at present Prof. Ord. in Univ. of Amsterdam, has gone still further into textual and historical criticism, and gives fair promise of a more impartial hearing for Donatism. It is to be hoped that he will fulfill his qualified promise of further research.

Among the general church histories particular mention may be made of Gieseler, Neander, Lindner, Niedner, Robertson, Ritter, Hergenröther, Schaff. The articles on Augustin, Donatism and related persons and topics in Ceillier, Ersch und Gruber, Herzog, Schaff-Herzog, Smith's Dictionary of Christian Biography, Wetzer and Welte, Lichtenberger, are more or less noteworthy. Mention must also be made of the Patrologies, the biographies, Hefele's Conciliengeschichte, the Analyses Patrum, etc.

Chapter II.—An Analysis of Augustin's Writings against the Donatists.

The object of this chapter is to present a rudimentary outline and summary of all that Augustin penned or spoke against those traditional North African Christians whom he was pleased to regard as schismatics. It will be arranged, so far as may be, in chronological order, following the dates suggested by the Benedictine edition. The necessary brevity precludes anything but a very meagre treatment of so considerable a theme. The writer takes no responsibility for the ecclesiological tenets of the great Father, nor will he enter here into any criticism of the text and truth of the documents, upon which the historical argument was so laboriously and peremptorily built, to the utter ignoring of the Donatist archives, and the protests of their scholars against the validity and integrity of their opponents' records. Both parties claimed to be the historic Catholic church; both were little apart in doctrine, worship, and polity; both tended toward externalism in piety; both accused one another of fraud in inventing records. Later Romanism in its bright spirit of selection took much spoil from either camp.

The city of Augustin's birth, its neighborhood, indeed the whole ecclesiastical province of Numidia, was a stronghold for this puristic school. Is it not singular, then, that it seems to have made no impression upon his early years? As a child he had witnessed its brief restoration under Julian, and then the severe or lax efforts at suppression under succeeding emperors; the Rogatian schism and the Tychonian reformation were quite familiar to him in his Manichæan period; but the Confessions are silent as to any such stamp or hold upon his mind. His activity begins with his ordination to the presbyterate, a time marked in Donatist annals by the Maximianist separation, and increases as he becomes bishop. From about 392 to near the close of his life, pen and voice were seldom still. In all those years the outlinear thoughts grew in breadth and depth; endless are the forms in which his few and radical conceptions manifest themselves; never does he lose sight of the popular effect, so that he knows when to relax his love of word-play and delight in mysterious inductions, in order to make the chief themes plain to the dullest mind.

How varied the channels through which he struggled for the mastery of his idea of the Church! In the pulpit he made Donatism the occasion of many a polemic, many an appeal; in his correspondence it was an ever-recurrent topic; it was the staple of many a tract and book; verse was not shunned to destroy its fashionableness and popularity; commentaries and manuals for the meditative hour or for the training of the theological student, abounded in warnings against its aggressiveness; no opportunity for debate or conference or epistolary discussion was left unimproved. And no wonder: it was a living thing, of the street, of the market, of the social circle, of the home; it threatened at times to obliterate the transmarine view of the church from North Africa; its spirit of political independence and plea for religious liberty went to the hearts of a people, more and more restive under the decline of the Empire.

The literary creations of Donatism had been somewhat more fertile than that of Cæcilianism. We must not belittle Donatus the Great, Parmenian, Petilian, Gaudentius, and certainly the eminence of Tychonius is confessed by Augustin himself. Up to this time Optatus of Milevis had been the only forcible opponent. But against the great Augustin whom could they bring into the field? And against the great Augustin, backed by the energy of the State, there was little hope of fairness. Augustin found a new and weighty school. Donatism, with its impossible ideal, already began to despise the culture which seemed to help its defeat and withdrew into its sensitive shell after the manner of all puristic tendencies under persecution.

The two prevalent lines of attack are the historical on the origin of the schism, which involved the dissection of the documents, and the doctrinal, or the discussion of the true notes of the Church from the basis of the Scriptures. This latter Augustin preferred, because final; he bowed to no patristic. One or the other or both may be traced in all his works, great or small, against them. Out of so protracted a controversy there grew up a symmetrical and comprehensive theory of the Church and the Sacraments on either side.

Of three fundamental points of Donatism, as perpetuated practices of North Africa, rebaptism and the encouragement of a martyr spirit with its attendant feasts, the continuance of the Seniores in the government of the Church, we find Augustin aiming mainly at the overthrow of the first two. One of his earliest letters suggests to his bishop some means for checking the drunkenness and great excess connected with the Natalitia. Passing to the specific subject in view:

In the early period of his presbyterate, (possibly about 392, others place it later), Augustin journeyed through Mutugenna, which apparently belonged to his bishop's see. He learned how pacifically disposed Maximin, Donatist bishop of Sinaita, was. The friendly feeling thus kindled toward him was shaken by the rumor that he had rebaptized a defecting

Catholic deacon of Mutugenna; not willing to credit the story, he visited the deacon's home. His parents testified to their son's reception into the same office by the Donatists. In the absence of Bishop Valerius, he writes to Maximin with entreaty, refusing to credit the repetition of the rite, and urging him to remain firm in the convictions which had been imputed to him. He solicits a reply, that both letters may be read in the public service, after the dismission of the military. The prominent points of the letter are: while declining to recognize the validity of Maximin's orders, he does not refuse to salute him as *Dominus dulcissimus*, and *Pater venerabilis*. His solicitude as a shepherd to do his duty to all the sheep, constrains him to force himself upon their attention, and to be eager for correspondence or conference with a view to bringing them back to the fold. He is perfectly assured of the absolute and final correctness of his idea of the Church, and of the hopeless error of Donatism, an error so great as to merit eternal destruction. He discriminates, however, between heresy and schism at this time. Rebaptism in any case is a sin, but as applied to apostatizing Catholics, is an *immanissimum scelus*. There is only one baptism, that of Christ; as there was no double circumcision, so the sacrament of the New Testament should not be repeated. The Church is the owner of the nations which are Christ's inheritance, and of the ends of the earth, which are his possession; hence it is universal; the seamless robe should not be rent. Moreover the Lord's threshing-floor has chaff upon it along with the wheat, and therefore he urged the disuse of imputations through unworthy members on either side, whether Macarius or Circumcelliones. The schism made itself disastrously felt in all domestic and social relations. He engages to avoid anything that would look like using the power of the state for coercing conscience, and begs that on Maximin's side the Circumcelliones may be restrained. [*Ep.* xxiii.]

A Plenary council of all Africa was convened in Hippo-Regius in 393, before which Augustin preached the sermon. His subject was Faith and the Creed: his handling made such an impression that he was induced to expand it into the treatise: *De Fide et Symbolo.* In explaining the article *credimus et sanctam ecclesiam, utique catholicam,* he reflects on heretics and schismatics as claiming the title of churches for their congregations; and distinguishes between these two opponents of the Catholic body, heretics erring in doctrine, schismatics, while similar to the Catholic body in views of truth yet transgressing in the rupture of fraternal love. Neither pertain to the true Church of God. (Cp. *Retractt.* I. xvii).

Determined if possible to win the ear of all classes, the presbyter next affected a poem, "*Psalmus contra Partem Donati,*" in the art of an Abecedarium, running the letters to U. The line with which it began was to be chanted as a refrain after each group of usually twelve lines connected with each letter, the whole closing with an extended epilogue. A generally vulgar performance it is, and purposely disclaimed all metrical dignity; and yet it contains the germs of his logical and historical opinions on the controverted points. The Church is a net in the sea of the world, enclosing the good and bad, which are not to be separated until the net is drawn to the shore. Those who accuse the Catholics of tradition, were themselves traditors and broke the net. The history is repeated, and all proof of the Donatist charges declared to be wanting. Unity is a note of the Church, and toleration within the net essential to its preservation. Over against Macarius he puts the violent Circumcelliones. The wicked members of the Church do not contaminate the good by a communion which is only outward and not of the heart. The threshing-floor has chaff upon it; wheat and tares must grow together. The Catholics rear the Elijah altar, the Donatist the Baal altar over against it. Christ endured Judas. Why rebaptize us, he exclaims, when you do not repeat the rite upon your once expelled but now restored Maximianists? Surely it is better to draw life from the real root. The character of him who administers the sacrament has nothing to do with its efficiency; and so he returns to the necessity for toleration within the net, as Judas was forborne in the apostolic company. The epilogue pictures the personified Church expostulating with the Donatists for quarreling with their Mother, and presents a loose summary of the previous arguments

It is doubtful whether, even in the fashion of the times, so lengthy a poem could become a street theme, or find many repeaters in the markets and inns of Hippo or Carthage, although the refrain for peace and truthful judgment might catch the ear of the more zealous. [Cp. *Retractt.* I. xx.].

The Bishop of Carthage, Donatus the Great, the sphinx of Donatism, had written a book to vindicate the claim of his church to the only Christian baptism. The work obtained considerable currency, and maintained its authority, even in Augustin's day, so he answered it during the year 393, most probably, in a treatise of one book now no longer extant, but which has been given the title: "*Contra Epistolam Donati hæretici.*" The Retractations (I. xxi.) correct some points which had been held in this work. (1). According to the Ambrosian view, Augustin here identified Peter with the rock, on which the Church was to be built; but afterwards he regarded that rock as Christ, who was the subject of the Petrine confession; on Christ was the Church to be built, and to the Church as thus reared, were given the keys. (2). The Donatus present at the Roman Synod, he had spoken of as the bishop of Carthage, the author of the book, which error is corrected in the Retractations. (3). He had also charged the writer with falsifying a favorite passage of their side, Ecclus. xxxiv. 30, but afterwards found that some codices read according to the Donatist quotation, and apologizes for his assertions.

Doubtless many of the sermons preached during his presbyterate had reference to the schism, but the chronology of these is too uncertain to allow of any definite arrangement.

We pass to the period of his co-bishopric with the aged Valerius, which dates from 395 A.D.

Evodius, a brother connected with the Church at Hippo Regius, had a chance meeting with Proculeianus, bishop of the Donatist body in that diocese. The two fell into a discussion of their mutual differences. Evodius spoke in rather a lofty and censorious way, after the fashion of his side, and wounded the feelings of the older disputant, for the Donatists, like all kindred bodies, cultivated an undue sensitiveness and were altogether too ready to take offense. Proculeianus, however, expressed a perfect readiness to have a friendly debate with Augustin in the presence of competent men. In view of this suggestion, and in the absence of Valerius, Augustin, always anxious to improve such an opening, addressed a letter to Proculeianus (*c.* 396), with courteous recognition, and no such sharp denial of the episcopal function as in the case of Maximin. He apologizes for the severe language of his friend, and in every way avoids any expression which might cause the tendrils again to be drawn in. The methods suggested for discussion show the anxiety of Augustin to beat out the fire of Donatism; there is the debate before chosen hearers, all the statements to be written out for use; or there is the private discussion through mutual discourse, to be read to one another and corrected, and so given to the people; or the single correspondence with a view to public lections, or any possible way that the aged bishop himself might prefer. He urges that the dead bury their dead, and the past history be left out of the debate; the present with its burning dissensions affords sufficient topics. As the people seek the bishop to arbitrate in their private litigations, let these worthies cultivate peace in this broader field; to this end he invites to prayer and conference. (*Ep.* xxxiii.).

Apparently the letter led to nothing practical. A new turn was given to matters. A son had beaten his mother, and threatened her life; to avoid Catholic discipline, he joined the Donatists and was rebaptized by them: as Augustin says, he wounded also his spiritual mother by contemning her sacrament. Public registration of the facts were made by Augustin, all the more because the reported instructions, given by bishop Proculeianus to his presbyter Victor concerning the affair, had already been denied. The case presented an opportunity for getting at some rule for the recognition of one another's discipline. Accordingly Augustin addresses himself to Eusebius, a judicious Donatist of higher rank. He professes tnat his aim is peace; he emphasizes with impatient vehemence his opposition to coercive measures in matters of conscience: *neque me id agere ut ad communionem catholicam quisquam cogatur invitus*. He asks Eusebius to find out whether Proculeianus had given the order to his presbyter as recorded; whether the bishop would consent to a collation between themselves and ten selected men on each side, agreeably to the original suggestion, so that the whole question might be discussed from the Scriptural grounds, not the historical. Some proposals for a meeting either at the Donatist region of Constantina, or at their projected council at Milevis, he could not accept, because both lay outside of his diocese. If Proculeianus objected to the dialectic and rhetorical skill of his counter bishop, the latter would propose Samsucius, bishop of Turris, an earnest but uncultivated man, as a substitute to lead the Catholic side. (*Ep.* xxxiv.).

Eusebius declined to interfere on the ground that he could not be a judge, so Augustin replies (*Ep.* xxxv.) that he had only asked him to make some inquiries, because the bishop refused to have any direct communication. The need for some adjustment concerning discipline had become very pressing; a Catholic subdeacon and some nuns under rebuke had been received into full standing by the Donatists, yet their subsequent career had been even more scandalous. Augustin claimed that the Catholics always respected the penal enactments of their opponents. To show his own hostility to compulsory conversions, he cites the case of a daughter, who against the paternal will had joined the Donatists, and had professed among them; when the father was about to use violence for her recall, he was dissuaded by Augustin, and when a presbyter of Proculeianus had shouted abusive epithets at him, although upon the property of a Catholic woman, he neither replied nor allowed others to resent the insult.

A practical treatise is ascribed by some to this time, called *de Agone Christiano*. In expounding the faith he warns against different groups of heretics and schismatics. In Chap. xxix. 31, he cautions against listening to the Donatist party, who deny the one holy Catholic church to be diffused throughout the whole world, and claim it to be alone in Africa, and there among themselves, against the plain Scripture teaching of its universality; they affirm that the prophecies of its extension have already been fulfilled, after which the whole church perished outside of their remnant. He alludes to the divisions which have befallen them as a retribution for their separation. If the end shall come after the preaching of the gospel to all nations, how can all nations have lapsed from the faith, when there remain some who are yet to hear and believe? This system robs Christ of His glory, and is to be avoided by all who love the Church. (Cp. *Retractt.* II. iii.).

In 397 A. D., at the death of Valerius, he became sole bishop. In this year, while on a visit to Tibursi, he had met with Glorius and other Donatists, with whom he held a friendly disputation on the origin and history of the schism, during which some Donatist documents were produced which he declared to be false, and from memory recapitulated the archives current on his side. Augustin pursued his journey to Gelizi, where he attended to some episcopal duties, and brought back with him a copy of the Catholic Gesta, and spent a day with these friends in reading them, but could not quite finish. He subsequently reproduces this story with the arguments in a letter. (*Ep.* xliii.). The chief burden is a criticism of the Acts, highly important in its place, but it must be passed by here save to remark that in speaking of Bishop Secundus, he suggests that it would have been better to appeal to the principalities of Rome or of some other apostolic church, than to have proceeded as he did; he should have preserved the unity at all hazards; had the case been inexplicable, he should have left it to God; if definable, he should have addressed the transmarine bishops, after finding that his peers at home could not adjust the difficulty; disobedience on the part of Cæcilian to such an order, would have made him the author of the schism; but now the Donatist altar is set up against the Universal Church. It may be well to note that throughout the survey of these acts, there appears a manifest contradiction as to the beginning of the appellations. In the next place, the Donatists are held guilty of schism, rebaptism, and resistance to civil correction; of non-communion with those churches concerning whom they read in their lections; and of the demand for purism against the Lord's parable. The angels of the churches in the apocalypse are ecclesiastical powers, not heavenly messengers. The Church cannot be charged with the crimes of the evil men in it. Toleration is the only practice by which unity can be conserved; Moses bore with murmurers, David with Saul, Samuel with the sons of Eli, Christ with Judas. They themselves forbear with Circumcelliones, with Optatus bishop of Thamugada. The emphasis, however, is not so much upon those matters as upon schism. He would rather leave the archives and elucidate the doctrine, in which he claims to have the book of the world; that the Catholics are the Lord's inheritance; that they stand in fellowship with the churches of the New Testament; they are the light of the world. A divine rebuke has befallen Donatism in all the tenets of its particularity, by the schism and return of the Maximianists.

No open door was passed by. On a journey to Cirta, possibly about the beginning of 398 A.D., he visited with clerical friends the aged Donatist, bishop Fortunius, at Tibursi. A great company gathered who interrupted the debate; all attempts at taking notes were finally given up. In a letter (*Ep.* xliv.) to the Donatists, Eleusius, Glorius, and the two Felixes, who were of the number of those addressed in the previous epistle, he speaks of their witness to the conciliatory disposition of Fortunius, and recounts the substance of the interview, with the desire that it may be submitted to that bishop for correction. The discussion had opened with the question of the Church. Fortunius regretted that Augustin was not in it; the latter reversed the wish. What is the Church? Is it diffused throughout the whole world, or is it confined to Africa? Can the Donatists send letters of communion to any of the apostolic churches? Thence they dissected the Donatist claim to be the people of God, on account of their subjection to persecution; in which it appears that they recorded the schism of the whole world from themselves as the true Church as due to sympathy with the Macarian persecution; up to that time they had held fellowship with the whole world, and as proof thereof brought forward a letter of a council of Sardica addressed to them. From the condemnation of Athanasius and Julius by this document, Augustin, to whom it was new, concluded that this was an Arian council, and was only the more damaging to their theory. The note of persecution being resumed, he maintained that there was no approved suffering unless for a just cause, and hence the justice of the cause must first be established. Though Ambrose had endured violence at the hand of the soldiery, they would deny him to be a Christian, for they would rebaptize even him. Maximianists on the other hand were confessed to be just, although they had been dispossessed of their basilicas by the Primianist appeal to the state. As an offset, Fortunius urged the curious fact that before the election of Majorinus, an interventor had been chosen, whom the Cæcilianists put out of the way. On the following day Augustin had to confess that there was no example in the New Testament to justify compulsion in matters of faith. The next topic was Discipline. Augustin pleaded for toleration in order to keep unity. A point as to Johannic baptism sprang up, but was not pressed. From this time the debate became miscellaneous and repetitious; in its progress Fortunius confessed reluctantly that rebaptism was a fixed practice among them, and that even a Catholic bishop so highly esteemed among the Donatists for his non-persecuting spirit as was

Genethlius, would have to submit to the rite before he could be recognized by their body. Augustin proposes a further examination of matters, with a view to peace, but the pacific Fortunius doubts whether many of the so-called Catnolics really desire concord, to which Augustin replies that he can find ten men who would heartily enter into such a conference.

On the next day the venerable Donatist calls upon his opponent to resume their talk, until an ordination called Augustin away; we also obtain information of the Cœlicolæ as professing a new sort of baptism, with whose leader he desired to confer. The letter closes with a proposition to meet in the little village of Titia, near Tibursi, where there was no church, and the population pretty equally divided, and where no crowd could disturb the progress of the investigation; thither all documents should be brought and the whole subject canvassed for as long a time as it might take to terminate the discussion.

During the year Augustin issued a weighty work, which stands closely related to these visits to Fortunius. It was in two books named by himself: *Contra partem Donati.* Unhappily it is lost, but in the Retractations (II. v.), he says, that in the first book he had opposed the use of the secular power for compelling the schismatics to return to the communion of the State Church, a form of discipline which experience afterwards persuaded him was necessary and wholesome.

Possibly it was at the close of the year 398 that a hint from the Donatist bishop Honoratus was brought by Herotes to Augustin, to the effect that they carry on a correspondence on the questions in dispute between them, and avoid the uproar of public debates. Augustin acquiesces heartily, and at once plunges (*Ep.* xlix.) into the doctrinal aspect of the matter. He begins with the note of Universality, the Church is diffused through the whole world, to establish which he brings forward some of his key passages, Ps. ii. 7, 8, Matt. xxiv. 14, Rom. i. 5. With all the apostolic churches Catholics communicate, Donatists do not. How then can this universality be limited? Why call the Catholic church Macarian, when the name of Macarius or Donatus is not known in any of these gospel regions? It rests with Donatists to prove how the Church is lost from the whole world and is confined to them. Catholics can rely on the Scriptures only for their theory. Correspondence seems to him also the better plan for discussion. Whether this mutual approach went further is not known.

It may have been in 399 A.D. that the Donatist presbyter Crispinus had met Augustin at Carthage; the two joined words, and both seem to have become heated; the former made promise to resume the parley at a later date, to the fulfillment of which the bishop had occasionally urged him. When Crispinus was elevated to the see of Calama, *c.* 400 A.D., and was not far from Augustin's diocese, the latter addressed him a letter (*Ep.* li.) rehearsing these facts. A new rumor credited Crispinus with being ready to enter the arena once more. All salutation is avoided in Augustin's letter, because the Donatists had accused him of servility. For the sake of accuracy and instruction he proposes simply to correspond, whether by one interchange of letters or by many. He pleads that present interests alone may be touched upon. Schism according to the Old Testament was more severely punished than idolatry or the burning of the sacred scroll. The charge of traditorship is set off by the acceptance of the Maximianists, whom the council of Bagai had condemned in such severe terms. If a mistake was made with regard to them why not in Cæcilian's case? If these were really guilty, you consulted the wider duties of unity and toleration, and why not carry these principles farther and apply them to communion with the Catholics? As to the charge of persecution, Augustin will not enter into the merits of the matter theoretically, nor stop to plead the mildness of the measures used, but at once asks why the Donatists used the State to dislodge the Maximianists, and to deny the Catholics the possession of genuine baptism is made foolish by the recognition of the rite as existing among the Maximianists who had been cut off, and were restored without a renewal of the ceremony. The whole world had been condemned by the Donatists without an opportunity of being heard, and yet they accept the sacrament of the condemned Felicianus and Prætextatus. While they deny the validity of the symbol as administered by apostolic communions, and by the missionary churches which brought the light to Africa, they maintain that their little fraction alone is its possessor. Summarizing these arguments as a weight for the bishop to stagger under, he invokes the peace of Christ to conquer his heart.

In this same year one of his relatives, Severinus, who was a Donatist, sent a communication to him at Hippo by a special messenger, with a view of reopening friendly intercourse with his kinsman; and Augustin seizes it as a way to reestablish as well the higher kinship in Christ (*Ep.* lii.). The Church is an unconcealable city set on a hill; it is Catholic, being diffused throughout the whole world. The party of Donatus is cut off from the historic root of the Oriental churches, and therefore cannot bring forth the fruits of peace and love; indeed it suppresses Christ by its rebaptism. Had their charges been genuine the transmarine bishops would have supported them; at any rate they should not have withdrawn from the Unity, but rather have practiced toleration. He hopes that the bonds of custom may be broken by Severinus, and that both may find their truest relationship in Christ, since the state of schism is a despising of the eternal heritage and of perpetual salvation.

Further along in the year, a Donatist presbyter had sent to Generosus an *ordo Christianitatis*, or episcopal succession of Constantina, his native city, asserting that it had been delivered by an angel from heaven. About nothing were the church externalists of every camp so eager as the preservation of the succession in proof of antiquity. Generosus had only laughed at the man's stupidity, but nevertheless wrote to the bishop of Hippo about it. Fortunatus, Alypius and Augustin combine in a reply, undeniably written by the latter, commending him (*Ep.* liii.). The *ordo Christianitatis* of the whole world is theirs, from which the Donatists do not hesitate to separate themselves. This presbyter's fiction would have to be rejected at any rate, even had it come from an angel, since all other gospels than that which teaches the universality of the Church are anathema. That doctrine is in Matt. xxiv. 14, Gen. xii. 3, Gal. iii. 16. The true *ordo* is the Roman, which he gives from Peter to Anastasius, the cotemporary pope; no Donatist is found in this list; yet as Montenses and Cutzupitæ, they have intruded into Rome. Had there been an actual tradition, or any wicked man in the Church, that would not have vitiated the *ordo*, or the Church, for the law of Christ is plain, Matt. xxiii. 3, a passage again and again quoted by Augustin to substantiate this thought. They are separated from the peace of these very churches, concerning which they read in their codices, and sing *pax tecum*. There follows a very full and notable summary of the acts, as a refutation of the schism. He prefers the Scriptural proofs, which certify to the world-wide reach of Christ's inheritance, and its existence among all nations; from this they are separated by a nefarious schism, and charge upon the Catholics the crimes of the chaff on the threshing-floor, which must be mixed with the grain until the winnowing; these accusations do not affect the wheat which grows with the tares in the field until the end. Their divinely appointed retribution is in the history of the Maximianists, with whom they now commune, and affirm that they are not stained thereby; let them apply that lenity of judgment to the inheritance of Christ. The angel then was either Satan, or the man is Satanic, yet his salvation is desired; the sharp writing concerning him is without odium, and seeks only his correction.

Celer was a Donatist, a man of middle age and of considerable estate and civil position.

He afterwards rose to the proconsulship. Augustin expresses (*Ep.* lvi.) a peculiar respect and affection for him, as a man of integrity and seriousness. He had desired direct instruction from the bishop, both in a matter of Christian culture and in the controversies between the two parties. Weighed down with the cares of visitation, Augustin had to delegate his presbyter Optatus to the reading and explanations of the bishop's works and views in Celer's leisure hours. The superior claims of the life beyond are set before him, together with the overwhelming force of the proofs against the schism, so that the dullest with patience and attention can get correction. The sundering of the bonds of custom and of a perversity that has become familiar, is a matter requiring great strength of character, for which step, however, he, under God, would be readily capable.

But Celer was not persuaded to change his church connection by this first endeavor. On the contrary, Augustin thought he saw a laxity in the enforcement of the repressive measures ordered by the government, and so wrote a second time (*Ep.* lvii.). He affirms that there is no just cause for separation from that Catholic church which prophets and evangelists have declared should be diffused through the whole world. A long retained codex of Augustin, which had been loaned to Celer through Cæcilian, his own son, who seems to have been under the special tutelage of the bishop, was designed to convince the state official on this very point (we do not know which writing it may have been), should inclination or leisure lead him to its perusal, and whatever difficulties might occur, Augustin was ready to answer. He desires him also to stir up his subordinates to greater care in restoring the Catholic unity in the region of Hippo; indeed he cautions him to diligence on his own estates; a friend there, who fears to be strict in the carrying out of the statutes, could have his position alleviated by a word from Celer his patron. From this point we notice a decided sympathy with the effort to break up Donatism by force.

Parmenian, the successor of Donatus the Great in the see of Carthage, was one of the brightest disputants on their side. Against him Optatus of Milevis had directed his review of the schism, full indeed of grave historical blunders, but not lacking in that suavity which those who think they have the keys of heaven sometimes affect. When Tychonius had exposed some of the inconsequences and weaknesses of the Donatist theory of the Church, Parmenian undertook a reply, whose main object was to fortify the propositions, (1) that the evil defile the good in the Church, and must therefore be cut off; and (2) that puristic folly, that the Donatist community was absolutely pure in its membership and priesthood. To this much-esteemed work, Augustin replies (*c.* 400 A.D.) in three books: *Contra Epistolam Parmeniani.*

In Book I. the main question is, who really incurred the guilt of schism, and initiated the appeal to the State? He opens with the praise of Tychonius as man and author, but misses the acute drift of that great man's argument. He seeks to answer the data of the origin of the separation as given by Parmenian, who attributes it to the joint movement of Gaul, Spain and Italy in seeking to make their views universal, and to the influence of Hosius over Constantine, in winning him to their opinion; nor does Parmenius cease to deprecate the imperial intervention Augustin defends this use of the secular arm, but accuses the Donatists by their history of beginning it in the appeal to Constantine, in the treatment of the Rogatists and Maximianists, in the abuses of the Circumcelliones, in their petition to Julian.

Book II. discusses the texts alleged by the Donatists in support of the purity of the Church, the need of discipline, the sole validity of their baptism and ordination, the blamelessness of their members and clergy. While both fail in exegetical principles, Parmenian, after the manner of his school, is aggravatingly guilty of using mere catch-words, without regard to text or context. He quotes indiscriminately whatever sounds favorable to his cause. Some of the passages are: Is. v. 20, Prov. xvii. 15, Is. lix. 1–8, Ecclus. x. 2, Is. lxvi. 3, Prov. xxi. 27, and others. Augustin gives his interpretations, and does not fail to prod his opponent with barbs of Optatus, Maximianists, and Circumcelliones.

Book III. handles further the theory of purism in the light of Scriptural proofs. The first part is mainly an endeavor to give the true significance of 1 Cor. v. 12, 13. (Compare his correction in the *Retractt.* II. xvii.). Augustin is constrained to confess the need of some internal discipline, and then enforces with wider range the notes of universality, unity and toleration, especially as illustrated by Cyprian. [Cp. *Retractt.* II. xvii.].

In the work against Parmenian, he had promised to write more fully on this subject of baptism, the frequent persuasions of the brethren also moved him so that in this same year (400 A.D.) he issued the seven books *De Baptismo: Contra Donatistas.* The double purpose is to define that sacrament as the property of Christ, and to overthrow the Donatist appeal to the authority of Cyprian and the famous council of Carthage, with its eighty-seven deliverances in favor of the repetition of the rite. Since this is one of the works translated in the accompanying volume any further analysis may be passed by. [Cp. *Retractt.* II. xviii.].

In this period of frequent and heated controversy, a Donatist layman, Centurius by name, brought some of their quotations and writings, and supported with Scriptural proofs to the Church in Hippo. It seems to have begun with an exposition of Prov. ix. 17. (N. Afr. version and LXX). Augustin answered them briefly in a tractate, which he entitles: *Contra quod attulit Centurius a Donatistis.* It is however not extant. In the Retractations (II. xix.) it is placed immediately after the work on Baptism.

Meanwhile, and as the Retractations tell us, before he had finished his work on the Trinity, and his literal commentary on Genesis, he found it desirable to reply to the pastoral letter of Petilian, Donatist bishop of Constantina; unfortunately only a part of the epistle came into his hand, so strenuous and vigilant were the efforts to hide their literature from the eyes of this ardent foe. He replied with one book to so much as he had received, *c.* 400 A.D. Some of his clergy subsequently obtained and wrote out a complete copy, so that he composed the second book, *c.* 401 A.D. Meanwhile Petilian responded to the first issue, and this necessitated a third book, *c.* 401 or 402 A.D. The three books were collected into one treatise, and are known under the title *Contra Litteras Petiliani.* The main object of the series is the refutation of Petilian's proposition: "*Conscientia namque* (*sancte*) *dantis attenditur, quæ* (*qui*) *abluat accipientis.*" "*Nam qui fidem* (*sciens*) *a perfido sumpserit, non fidem percipit, sed reatum.*" "What we look for is the conscience of the giver (him who gives in holiness), to cleanse that of the recipient." "For he who (wittingly) receives faith from the faithless receives not faith, but guilt." Since the work is also a part of this volume, we need not dwell on it farther. [Cp. *Retractt.* II. xxv.]

The civil restraints were applied with vigor on the one side and resented on the other by the retaliatory Circumcelliones. To Pammachius, a man of senatorial rank, Augustin, in 401 A.D., sends a letter [*Ep.* lviii.] of exuberant congratulations and flatteries, because he had compelled some of his Numidian tenants to return to the mother Church; a converting agency which he condemns unmercifully when practised by the Donatists. The plan, he says, would have been urged upon other landholders, had the clergy not been afraid of the scornful finger of the Donatists, who were in such favor with the proprietors, that an effort like this might have failed. He desires the senator to circulate this letter wherever there was promise of effect. The bishop, now thoroughly committed to these arbitrary procedures, was in some trepidation lest the plausible arguments which the Donatists were urging, might shake the resolution of Pammachius himself, and so he sends a secret commission of instruction.

The coercive measures yielded fruit, and the question about the status of recedent Donatist clergy now became pressing. Augustin had already met with a certain Theodore on this subject, and in a letter addressed to him [*Ep.* lxi.] *c.* 401, recapitulated the proposition then agreed upon, to be used as a basis for treatment with all who wanted to come over. The Catholic church opposed only the schism and the rebaptism among the Donatists; what was good she was ready to acknowledge. Baptism itself, ordination, self-denial, celibacy, doctrinal views, especially as to the Trinity, these were confessedly right, only to reap the profit of them, it was essential for Donatists to be in the unity and in the root.

The Council of Carthage of September 13, 401, adopted this view, Can. 2. There had also been a remarkable scarcity of Catholic clergy, so that application had been made to Rome and Milan for relief; probably this had its influence upon so charitable a view of schismatic ordination.

It was alleged that Crispinus, the bishop of Calama, had bought a state farm at Mappalia, and had rebaptized the tenants. Augustin was roused by this counter-irritant and wrote him a letter, *c.* 402 A.D. [*Ep.* lxvi.], wondering what he would do if the authorities were to impose the fine for every offense. He pleads for an answer to Christ, whose was all the world, because bought with his blood, while the Donatist would affirm that Christ had lost all the world save Africa. He urges a public discussion of the mooted points before these converts, which should be reported and done into Punic as a test of their freedom in this conversion, and frankly enough offers to do the same for any case of coercion on his side. Unless Crispinus and his helpers acquiesce, he will hold them guilty.

The uppermost talk of those times was the extraordinary charity of the Donatists toward the Maximianists. One form of apology for such a seeming vacation of all their tenets was to say, *e.g.*, of Felicianus of Musti, that he was ignorantly condemned when innocent and absent, so in his absence, he was reinstated. This statement was made by a Donatist bishop, Clarentius, in reply to the inquiries of Naucelio. Alypius and Augustin, who were made aware of this defense, urged in criticism [*Ep.* lxx.] that the Council of Bagai was therefore guilty in condemning Felicianus unheard, and all the more in that they afterwards found him to be innocent. Either he ought not to have been condemned if he was innocent, or if guilty, he ought not to have been received back. If the council erred, why not apply such a liability to error to the origin of the schism; might not Cæcilian, unheard, have been condemned although innocent? But, as a matter of fact, Felicianus was found guilty while in thorough and declared sympathy with Maximian, and the state was called upon to enforce his ejection. If he was welcomed without rebaptism, why not treat the Church diffused through the whole world with the same consideration?

It was probably in the year 402 that he addressed a general appeal to the Donatists [*Ep.* lxxvi.], not to endanger their salvation by continuance in schism. If they counted the surrender of the sacred books so great a sin, how much more grievous a transgression ought the refusal to obey the plain commands of these books as to unity be considered. He brings forward the usual array of passages to demonstrate the universality of the Church, and that any limitation of this note, can only be at the end of the world. The attempt to separate the wheat from the tares before the harvest, is only a proof that they are of the tares. A rapid survey of the origin of the schism follows, and all the archives are made to tell against them. He asks how they can hold any theory of purism while they regard Optatus as a martyr and welcome the excommunicated Maximianists? Schism in the Scriptures is punished more severely than the burning of the books. Why complain about traditorship when Maximianists are received? Why abuse the imperial laws directed against them, when they had invoked the same against the Maximianists? If theirs is the only baptism, what is the baptism of these Maximianists, which is without question validated? He challenges the Donatist bishops to discuss these matters with their laity, if they persist in declining to meet the Catholics, and bids the sheep beware of the wolves and their den.

The *ad Catholicos Epistola*, popularly known as *de Unitate Ecclesiæ*, is pretty generally attributed to Augustin, and is addressed to the brethren of his charge; it may be taken as a contrast to the previous letter directed to the Donatists, and not unlikely saw the light in 402 A.D. This book is designed as a continuance of the controversy with Petilian, and indeed a further correspondence is proposed, so that the work must have appeared before that bishop's death, which is generally placed in this year. The chief question between the two parties is, Where is the Church? Is it with Catholic or Donatist? The Church is one and Catholic: it is the body of Christ, consisting of Him as its Head and those in Him as members. The historical issue in any of four possibilities of truth or falsity does not justify separation from this body. The point is, What does the Lord say? The Donatist should believe in the books, which he says were delivered up, and put aside all other documents except the divine canons. Do the Scriptures say that the Church is in Africa only, and in the few Cutzupitanæ or Montenses at Rome, and in the house or patrimony of one woman in Spain, or is it in the whole world? A second time does he start out with a definition of the Church, as having for its head the Only Begotten Son, and for its body the members in Him; as bridegroom and bride, two in one flesh. Any divergence from the Head or the body, whether caused by difference in doctrine or government, is *per se* outside of the Church. He meets the two favorite Donatistic comparisons of the divine institution with the ark and Gideon's fleece, and then enlarges upon the note of universality, with included unity, by Scripture texts from the Law, the Prophets, especially Isaiah, and the Psalms. From the Donatist position these are not fulfilled, because, say they, men are unwilling. Men were created with free will; they believe or disbelieve according to that. When the Church began to increase in the world, men refused to persevere, and the Christian religion was lost from all the nations with the exception of the Donatists. All this, replies Augustin, as if the Spirit of God did not know the future volitions of men. But Christ, after the resurrection, said that the Law, the Prophets and the Psalms testified of Him, and that the fulfillment of his kingdom should begin from Jerusalem. He then follows out the expansion of the Church as given in the Acts, and the foundation of Christian communities as mentioned in the Epistles and the Revelation. The Donatists reply to this theory of development that the Church perished save among them in North Africa. It is among the few: for which they cite a similar state of things under Enoch, Noah, Lot, Abraham, Isaac, and Jacob, and the Kingdom of Judah. The spread of the Church did indeed begin from Jerusalem, but afterwards an apostasy befell it, in the progress of which the communion of the Donatists alone remained faithful. Augustin says the fact that there are evil persons in the Church is simply a proof of the fulfillment of those parables of our Lord, which illustrate the mixed characters in his kingdom. There is indeed a paucity of the good, but within that communion. Then follows a discussion of the geographical limitation, the Donatists maintaining that the Oriental churches and the rest mentioned in the sacred canon had receded from the faith. Especially is their favorite paragraph, a passage from Cant. i. 7, commented upon. He presses the continuous preaching among all nations, after which event the end is to come; there must be such a universal growth to that end. Let us cease drawing from the acts and sayings of men about this great matter, and take the simple testimony of the Scriptures. But the Donatists object: If the Church be among you why do you compel us by force to enter its peace? Or if we are evil why do you desire us? and if we are tares why hinder us from growing until the harvest? Augustin then justifies the system of correction adopted in loving care for their salvation, not failing to remind them of the Circumcelliones and their own action with regard to the

Maximianists. Another inquiry of the Donatists was, How will you recognize us if we come to you? Augustin says, as the universally founded Church is wont to receive, put away all hatred and your sacraments are acknowledged. This leads to the discussion of baptism and of that related topic, the effect, of the celebrant's character, upon the recipient. He returns finally to the note of universality as essential to the unity, with the one Head and the one body.

Somewhere about 404 A.D. two official cases of discipline had occurred in Augustin's monasterium, which had grieved the pride of the clergy, because they had boasted of their establishment as really purer than the puristic body gathered about the Donatist bishop Proculeianus. They were more troubled about this than about the sins of the suspected brethren, one of whom, however, seemed to have considerable injustice done him. While discussing this matter [in *Ep.* lxxviii.] he incidentally mentions the lapse of two Donatists, who had been received into Augustin's communion, and whose conduct the clergy had regarded as a proof of the laxity of discipline under Proculeianus.

A sermon on the 95th Ps. (96) may have been preached in the year 404 or thereabouts, in which he rebukes the Donatists for their pride in claiming either that they, the few in Africa, are the ones bought by Christ, or that they are so great because this large gift was bestowed on them alone. And in commenting on v. 10, *dicite in nationibus. Dominus regnavit a ligno*, etc., he twits them with seeking this reign by the wood through the cudgels of the Circumcelliones; and enlarges too upon the theme of universality, against their undiscoverable here and there.

Cæcilianus, whose exact civil office, whether vicar or *præfectus annonæ* is yet undetermined, Augustin addresses as *præses* in *Ep.* lxxxvi., which is ascribed to 405 A.D. The severer edicts of Honorius had just been published. This official had carried them out with telling earnestness. His administration in the greater part of Africa is particularly commended; the bishop begs of him to restore the Catholic unity also in Hippo and the frontiers of Numidia. The ill-success of his own work is not due to lack of episcopal duty, and he asks Cæcilianus to inquire of the clergy, or of the bearer, a commissioned presbyter, about the true state of matters; he would have the State begin with monitions in the hope of preventing a resort to severer remedies.

Emeritus, the bishop of Julia Cæsarea, one of the seven Donatist disputants at the later conference, did not shun correspondence or association with his opponents. He is described as a man of parts and character. Augustin had written a letter to him, which is not preserved, and it had received no reply. He once more seeks to win him to a friendly discussion or correspondence [*Ep.* lxxxvii.], in this time of general return to the mother Church. He would have all men of culture come back to the true fellowship. What Emeritus's particular ground for continuing in separation may be he does not know. He proceeds to discuss universality, purism, the validity of the documents, the heinousness of schism, the paucity of numbers, and the right of coercion.

The enforcement of the civil edicts was followed by violent outbreaks of the Circumcelliones, especially in Augustin's diocese. The clergy united in a protest [*Ep.* lxxxviii.] addressed to the venerable Bishop Januarius, a Donatist, probably in 406 A.D. They claim (1) that they are receiving evil for good. (2) The appeal to the state was begun by the Majorinists, and two full documents are given in proof. (3) All decrees of the empire since, are the simple execution of the edict of Constantine against the party of Donatus, which these had wanted to be issued against Cæcilian. (4) The acts of the Circumcelliones; were the real occasion for sharper efforts at suppression; instances of their cruelty are mentioned. (5) The Catholics have pursued a conciliatory policy by conferences and by desiring a mitigation of the penalties, which were frustrated the one by refusals, the other by a gross assault on the Catholic bishop of Bagai; all who come into the hands of the state clergy, are treated with merciful persuasion. (6) Various proposals for peace are suggested.

Festus, a government official and a landed proprietor apparently in Hippo, had written a letter urging a return of the Donatists to the mother Church. It bore little fruit, and he asks Augustin first to instruct him and also to give him a tractate for general use. Augustin, *c.* 406. [*Ep.* lxxxix.], enforces the duty of perseverance in the civil reclamation of the Donatists; their claim of persecution as a note attesting them to be the true people of God is folly, because it is not the mere suffering but the cause for which one suffers that makes a martyr. He exhorts him to read the archives and see how the schismatics initiated the appeal to the secular power, and how all things that have befallen them through that arm would have been the just fate of the Cæcilianists, had the Donatist course been approved. Besides, why this unjust treatment of the Church universal in condemning it unheard, and rebaptizing its members, who have done them no wrong? The theory that baptism alone is valid when administered by the just, is putting a trust in man which the Scriptures condemn; the sacrament is not man's but Christ's; further, one would prefer to be baptized by a bad man, for then he would receive grace from Christ directly, according to their subterfuge. He is vexed with their active and passive opposition; the mother has to correct, although her obstinate child may not like it. They aver that the Catholics accept them without requiring any change in them, but the change required is great, no less a one than from error to truth. The bishop proposes as a substitute for Festus's plan, the sending of an authorized messenger secretly to himself, and they would devise together a method for the correction of the Donatists.

In the second sermon on Ps. cii. (ci.) preached about this time, when enlarging upon the unity he ridicules the Donatist assertion that the Church which was among all the nations had perished, as the impudent voice of those who are not in it declares. So is their affirmation that Scripture prophecies about the spread of the kingdom have been fulfilled; all nations have believed, but this diffused communion apostatized and perished. He rebukes the conceit that the Lord's saying, I am with you, even to the end of the world, was designed for them alone, the Lord foreseeing that the party of Donatus would be in the earth. If emperors have propounded laws against heretics, it is a part of the predictions which foretold how kings would serve the Lord. Thence he expands the notes of universality and perpetuity.

Cresconius, a layman and philologist, read Augustin's first book in answer to Petilian, and wrote a reply, which, however, was circulated among the Donatists only. Augustin at last secured a copy, and wrote (406 A.D., some say as late as 409) *Contra Cresconium Grammaticum Partis Donati, libri IV* Three of these books controvert the arguments of Cresconius; part of the third and the fourth entire is a detailed polemic history of the Maximian schism.

In Book I. he alludes to the occasion of the writing, and hesitates between being regarded as contumelious if he declined an answer, and arrogant, should he reply. Cresconius had attacked eloquence, which Augustin defends as simply the art of speaking, and as not to be condemned because it has been abused. You do not condemn military armament for your country because others have taken up arms against the country; the physician does not refuse to use all drugs because some are baneful; because there are sophists one is not to deny the value of eloquence. Cresconius seemed to regard its cultivation as injurious to the simplicity of Christian law and teaching. He also had accused Augustin of persistent arrogance in his pertinacious pursuit of the Donatists. Augustin claims to do a good work with good ends in view, and says its fruit has been a rich harvest for the Church. So the discussion passes on to the use of dialectics, which Cresconius assails, but Augustin defends as nothing else than a demonstration of results, either the true from the true or the false from the false. He justifies not disputatiousness, but the arguments by which truth is built up, for Christ employed it, and St. Paul wielded its weapons not only with the Jews but with Epicureans and Stoics. In all this we have an illustration of that unfortunate tendency to undervalue culture whenever a puristic community passes into the fires. Augustin applies the art to one of the points which Cresconius had discussed, *viz.*, rebaptism. He had endeavored to prove that it was solely among them. Augustin concedes that the rite is there, but not its profit; in order to enjoy its profit, it must be administered lawfully. The oneness of baptism as a ceremony is not dependent on the oneness of the Church, whereas its profit is. A reprobate society of heretics can have a good baptism, but it is not properly and not profitably administered among them; the proper and profitable administration is solely in the Church to salvation; the rite outside is to judgment.

In Book II. after a *résumé* of the previous book, he notices first the criticism as to the true construction of the name *Donatistæ*; it should rather be *Donatiani* as Cresconius claimed. He is ready to concede this, and in his controversy with the philologist will use that form, but on all other occasion he would prefer the more familiar termination. Cresconius also protests against the term heretic as applied to them, which he regards as a divergence of views from the Christian faith; while a schism has sprung up among those for whom the same Christ was born, died and rose again, who have one religion, the same sacraments, and no diversity in Christian observance. Augustin, however, while not particularly dwelling on these agreements, presses upon him the articles of divergence, and asks why they rebaptize? The recognition of Donatist ordination concerning which Cresconius had asked, Augustin declares to be a matter of charity. As to the question of Cresconius, Why, if the Donatists are such heretics and so sacrilegious, if they are indeed guilty of a nefarious and inexpiable crime, some purification is not adopted when they come over to the Catholic church? Augustin answers: We do not regard it as inexpiable, and baptism is not to be repeated, it is Christ's; on coming to us the Donatist receives the Spirit signified by that rite; he begins to have healthfully what he previously had hurtfully and unworthily. The relation of the celebrant to the symbol as presented by Cresconius is a modification of Petilianism. "Regard is had," says he, "to the conscience of the giver, not according to its actuality, which cannot be perceived, but according to his reputation, whether that be true or false." Augustin does not fail to crowd him for the change of base. The favorite passages of Ps. cxli. 5, Jer. xv. 18, and Ecclus. xxxiv. 31, are gone over. Then he answers the charge made by Cresconius, as to the right of any sinner to baptize among the Catholics. Finally, he reviews Cyprian's relation to rebaptism, who is not a canonical authority for him; the Scriptures alone are such; but the Donatists ought to consider that decision of his to remain in unity from the fact that the mixed nature of its membership requires toleration.

Book III. Augustin contends that the Donatists by their schism from especially the Eastern churches had violated the principle of toleration, which their boasted leader had so strenuously enforced. There follows then a *seriatim* consideration of the points made by Cresconius, similar to those maintained by Petilian, as to the importance of the origin and the head and root in baptism, or the character of the celebrant, and the rebaptism by Paul of John's disciples. The case of Optatus and the Maximianists next come under review, as witnesses against their testimonies. Cresconius says he will neither absolve nor condemn Optatus, and as to the Maximianists, he professes to have made special inquiry into the whole history. The Synod had granted a season of delay during which all who returned should be held innocent. Of this very many availed themselves; the baptism of these was valid; those who remained outside lost both baptism and the church. Augustin refutes the statement from its inherent contradictions and from the language of the Synod against the Maximianists. Cresconius also brings forward the Sardican council's letter to Donatus as a proof of sustained fellowship. Augustin declares it to be an Arian council; and he insists on paralleling all Cresconius would say about Cæcilianism with the career of the Maximianists. With reference to persecution, he cites *in extenso* their own persecutions, the case of Severus, bishop of Thubursicubur; the acts of Optatus; his own treatment at a collation by the Circumcelliones; the case of Crispinus, the Donatist bishop of Calama; their own invocation of the state against the Maximianists. Thence he returns to the doctrine of the unity as universal with many of the familiar Scripture texts, and asserts by the documents that the Donatists were the occasion of the rupture

Book IV. is a review of Cresconius's work by the light of the Maximianist records. Beginning with a pleasantry as to their eloquence and dialectic spirit, he follows in detail the points of Cresconius whether doctrinal or historical as to Cæcilian, mainly with Maximianist data as offsets. Cresconius charges Augustin with having called Petilian Satan, and so violating the peace he professes. Augustin claims that he only compared the error not the person, to Satan. Nor had Cresconius forgotten to bring out the Manichæism of his opponent. Augustin reminds him both of what he had written against them and also of what sins were forgiven in the return of Maximian, who was an old man when Augustin was but young; these were the sins of his youth. The theories of fellowship, of persecution, of baptism, are all considered in the light of their own council of Bagai and its sequences. [Cp. *Retractt.* II. xxvi.].

After concluding his work against Cresconius, he issued, probably in this same year, a little treatise he had promised, containing a collection of proofs both for Donatist and Catholic popular use. To the pledge itself an unknown Donatist replied, which led to the production of a second book, whose title Augustin designed to be: *Contra nescio quem Donatistam.* The original promise was fulfilled in the publication of the *Probationes et Testimonia contra Donatistas*, embracing all the ecclesiastical and public acts and Scripture proofs bearing on the questions between them. It was designed mainly for public reading in the basilicas. Both were joined in one book, although apparently afterwards separated. In each he confesses to the error of placing the purgation of Felix after instead of before the vindication of Cæcilian. At this writing he still regarded the Donatists as psychics and babes, but in his old age corrects his application of the words to them, since he came to consider them rather as dead and lost. Unfortunately neither treatise has been preserved. [Cp. *Retractt.* II. xxvii. and xxviii.].

He also conceived the plan of preparing a polemic for the people who had little time for extended reading, by refuting the entire theory of the schism through the story of the excision and restoration of the Maximianists. It appeared *c.* 406 A.D. under the name of *Admonitio Donatistarum de Maximianistis:* this too is lost. [Cp. *Retractt.* II. xxix.].

An acquaintance of earlier days in Carthage, Vincentius, had become bishop of the little Rogatist fragment as the immediate successor of Rogatus himself at Cartenna. He, or some one of that little band, had written a letter to Augustin with a pretty strong plea against persecution. This was not unlikely in *c.* 408 A.D., and Augustin answers in one of his most weighty epistles (*Ep.* xciii.), under the supposition that Vincentius was the author, and vindicates the help of the State. Evidently a change had come over Numidia, for he boasts of the multitudes who had been converted, and rejoices in the fruitful use of the secular arm for their salvation. Even Circumcelliones had become steadfast Catholics. Coercion stimulates the thoughtless and those bound by custom, and delivers these held back by fear; it is like a wholesome medicine, or the wounds inflicted by a friend. God chastens in order to better the life and to bring men to repentance. The householder instructs us to compel them to come in. Sarah and Hagar are types; so the mother Church corrects her children. Everything depends on the aim in persecution, whether it be done for oppression or for good; it is the difference between Pharaoh and Moses in their treatment of Israel. The Father gave up the Son, and the Son gave Himself up; while Judas betrayed Him. The righteousness of the end for which one suffers alone constitutes martyrdom. The Rogatist is not suffering for righteousness but for unrighteousness. Augustin is constrained to confess that there are no persecutions recorded in the New Testament as inflicted by Christians, but explains the omission as due to the fact that rulers were not yet members of the Church. He thinks, too, that the moderate and discriminating form of the correction employed, helps to justify a resort thereto. If the Rogatists have nothing to do with the violence of the Circumcelliones, and use no force as the rest of the Donatists do, it is because they are so few and feeble. The Donatists, however, did use the secular arm against the Maximianists, and in the appeal to Julian. He will not allow a distinction between resort to law for the recovery of property and for the coercion of the conscience. He claims that to regain one's own in this way has no apostolic warrant. The Donatists, too, sought imperial aid to coerce Cæcilianus. Why shall not Catholics return in kind? The very edict of confiscation which had hit them they had hoped might fall on the head of Cæcilian and his followers. What Tychonius said describes the very essence of Donatist arbitrariness: *quod volumus sanctum est*. The sin of separation from the whole world followed; the universal church was condemned unheard, and the toleration which Cyprian urged disregarded. He traces his own change of views from the non-coercive to the coercive policy, the success of the method in hastening conversions won him wholly as an enthusiastic and persistent supporter. He bids Vincentius flee from the wrath to come. What is his little handful compared with the universal Church? This note of universality he develops *in extenso* against their limitation, and especially their new definition of Catholic, as obedience to all the laws and the sacraments, and to their childish allegory of Cant. i. 7. He hints that in the ancient times there might have been a little schism which anticipated the Rogatists, and which had called itself exclusively the Church. He thinks it is also the duty of the State to suppress idolatry. The passage quoted from Hilary by Vincentius, as to the few who in Asia in his day were believers in spite of the spread of the Church, Augustin softens into an excited picture of the dark times of persecution. Next, he discusses the position of Cyprian. All patristic testimony, however, is of no final value; the only authority is the Word of God. Moreover, if Cyprian be quoted, why not on the side of his love for unity and toleration? The averment that the Church, with the exception of the Rogatists, perished by fellowship with the unbaptized, is met with the fact that in Cyprian's time men had been received without rebaptism into the Church, and therefore the Church, according to their theory, must have perished before their day; if it, however, survived that condition, then there is no excuse left for a schism on that ground. One is not of higher merit than Cyprian simply because he may abhor that father's error, any more than they who did not fall into Peter's mistake are above him in worth on that account. Indeed Cyprian may have rectified his fault before death; and some say that those passages are interpolations. Augustin, however, concedes their authenticity. Cyprian, in his Epistle to Antonianus, shows how the African bishops maintained unity in spite of the corrupt lives of some colleagues; variations of opinion were allowed; neither were they contaminated by such a fellowship, nor was the Church destroyed. Tychonius states the result of a Donatist council which granted fellowship to those in their own body who had been guilty of tradition, and that without rebaptism, in case the restored should oppose such a repetition of the rite. Deuterius, bishop of Macriana, had admitted traditors to his communion without renewing the sacrament, and many witnesses of both facts were living in Tychonius's own day. Parmenian had indeed replied to the arguments, but could not gainsay the facts. Augustin professes in all sincerity his anxiety for the salvation of the jeopardized Donatists; the Church acknowledges the Sacrament which they have administered, and desires them to have the profit thereof. In defence of rebaptism Vincentius had alleged the case of Paul, repeating the ceremony after John. Augustin asks was John then a heretic? If not, it is for you to say why the ordinance was iterated. Christ's baptism is always the same and must not be iterated; it has nothing to do with the merit or demerit of the individual, or else Paul would not have declined its continuous administration. He begs him to put no confidence in the accident of their being a little company, and not to arrogate to themselves the title of Catholic, in the sense of being keepers of the entire law and all the sacraments, nor to peculiar sanctity as the few who were to have faith at the coming of the Son of Man. The Church does not take pleasure in correction, save for conversion; she abhors those who seek Donatist property out of sheer covetousness, yet all property does belong to the true Church. She has also no delight in any who disregard Donatist discipline, by receiving members who have been ejected from that body for sin. The Catholic Church sustains the unity, and recognizes the mixture of chaff and wheat, good and bad fish, the goats and the sheep. He bids him come to that Church into whose fellowship Vincentius had described Augustin as entering. He closes with reflections on the aggravations in the sin of schism and on the need of repentance.

Olympius had recently been elevated to the dignity of *magister officiorum*. He had written to Augustin soliciting his advice on the best way for the civil authority to help the Church. Augustin, *c.* 408 [*Ep.* xcvii.], welcomes his elevation, commends his devotion to the body of Christ, and is glad to have his own timidity relieved by this invitation to lay before the highest official the exacting needs of the hour. These had become grave; the very success of coercion had precipitated new commotions among the Circumcelliones and their clerical abettors. A commission had sailed in mid-winter to solicit imperial help against their fury. The first point he would suggest, but without having had the opportunity of consultation, save probably with bishop Severus, is to declare by proclamation that the imperial edicts were not the invention of Stilicho, as the Donatists and heathen boasted. As to further plans, the episcopal commission would doubtless consult with him on their return from court. He invites Olympius to rejoice with him on the practical benefits of coercion thus far.

It may have been a little later (*c.* 408 or 409) that Augustin writes to Donatus the proconsul (*Ep.* c.) regretting indeed that the Church must avail herself of the State, but he is gratified that so devoted a son is wielding the sword for her. The crimes against the Church are greater than all other crimes, but in her discipline he deprecates any spirit of revenge, and pleads most beseechingly against the infliction of capital punishment; that would be a deterrent to the bringing in of any charges against the guilty. He asks for a republication of the repressive laws, since the enemy is boasting of their repeal.

Augustin wrote a general letter to the Donatist people in *c.* 409 [*Ep.* cv.], in which he declares that the Catholic effort at their conversion is the work of peacemakers. Some Donatist presbyters had ordered the Catholics to let their people alone, if they did not want to be killed, but Augustin would all the rather ask the people to recede from the schismatics because they were separated from that body for which Christ died. Catholics must seek for the stolen sheep that had on them the mark of Christ. The charge of being traditors, says he, we meet with a like accusation against you, and then you bid us leave. You claim to be the Church on this unproved charge, unmindful of what law, prophecy, Psalms, Apostles and Gospels say as to its universality beginning at Jerusalem. You are not in communion with that universal body, and you prevent the escape of others from a similar perdition. The objection as to persecution he meets with an invitation to look at the deeds of clergy and Circumcelliones, and cites instances of grievous ill-treatment toward voluntary converts: Marcus, presbyter of Casphalia, Restitutus of Victoria, Marcianus of Urga, Maximinus and Possidius, and then protests against their general violence and robberies, and especially against attributing martyrdom to those who had only been punished for their crimes. To all this compulsion we oppose the State, he affirms, and many of your own people rejoice in deliverance from your oppressions. You have filled Africa with false charges as to Cæcilian, Felix, etc., and though we do not place our hope in man, yet we do recognize the State as the servant of the Church. Nebuchadnezzar is an example both of the persecutor and the correctionist. You despise the baptism of Christ; ought this not to be punished? He then reviews the history of the case in the light of the documents; commenting on them as forms of their own appeal to the State. The liberty of error is most deadly to the soul. Christ and the Apostles command unity, and this command the Emperors seek to enforce. Only Julian and the heathen emperors were persecutors; the only martyrs are those who suffer for Catholic truth. The whole imperial legislation against Donatism is the outcome of the original statute of Constantine and sprang after all from their appeal. He next discusses their view of baptism and insists that the rite is independent of the character of the celebrant; were it dependent, then, according to their notion, we should rather desire to be baptized by a bad man, in order to receive the grace directly from Christ. The appeal to unity follows. Make concord with us, he urges; we love you and desire to serve you, even by the aid of the temporal laws; we do not want you to perish as aliens from your Catholic mother. Your charges you are unable to substantiate, and yet you avoid all conference with us, as if to shun fellowship with sinners; a false pride, which is rebuked by Paul's conduct, by the Lord's in his treatment of Judas; the Lord held conference even with the devil. This he follows with extended Scriptural proofs of the universality of the Church. He reminds them again of the unproved charges which apply rather to themselves; but he has no desire for the historical argument, rather for the doctrinal. The Catholic aim is their conversion, whether by the persuasion of argument or the correction of laws. They should remember the mixed nature of the Church, and that mere contact with evil does not defile. If you hold to Christ, hold also to His Church; you kill us who seek to tell you the truth, and do not want you to perish in evil. May God vindicate us and his cause by slaying your errors and making you rejoice with us in the truth.

On the death of Proculeianus, Macrobius succeeded to the see of Hippo Regius. Augustin hears that he is about to rebaptize a subdeacon (Rusticianus) who under discipline left the Catholics. Augustin urges him [*Ep.* cvi.], c. 409, not to do this by his desire to have life in God, and to please God by not making the sacraments vain, and by his hope of not being separated from the body of Christ eternally. The Donatists have admitted the validity of baptism as administered by Felicianus and Primianus, why then rebaptize others? and begs him to search that case as a test of the whole matter.

Maximus and Theodore had been commissioned to deliver the previous letter to Bishop Macrobius. He at first declined to listen to its reading, but was at last persuaded to attend, and in reply said: It was his duty to receive all who came, and to give faith to those who asked it. Into the question about Primian he would not enter, because of his own recent ordination; he was not a judge of his father, and he would remain in what his predecessors had accepted. These replies were conveyed to Augustin in the letter cvii. (*c.* 409) by the two commissioners.

In still further hope of reaching Bishop Macrobius, Augustin addressed another epistle, (cviii.) *c.* 409, to him in answer to the objections offered by him at the interview with the commissioners. 1. As to the point that he must receive those who come and give them the faith they ask: Augustin proposes the case of some one who has received the rite in their communion, but had been separated from it for a time, and having returned, conscientiously desires to be rebaptized; Macrobius, according to his objection, could not repeat the rite, but would proceed to instruct him. Why repeat it when Augustin administers it? May be you will quote, "keep thyself from strange water and do not drink from a strange fountain." How then will you explain the reception of Felicianus? 2. As to the second conclusion, that you would remain in the faith of your predecessors: It is a pity for a young man of good parts to say so; nothing compels you to remain in evil; you had better be in the Church which began in Jerusalem and spread thence through the world. 3. And if you will not judge your fathers why judge my fathers? If not Primian, why Cæcilian? Why deny us to be brethren? why rend the body? why extinguish the baptism of Christ, who baptizes with the Spirit, and who gave Himself for the Church? Yet your colleagues in effect do yield to the truth in their recognition of the Maximianists. Judge not the evil but do judge what was good in Primian. That act of his, the reception of the Maximianists, absolves the nations who are ignorant of what you accuse us. He then traces the whole development of that schism and its overthrow, to show that those schismatics were not rebaptized at their return. That history Augustin considers a divinely appointed refutation of all the Donatist tenets. He proceeds to criticise their Scripture proofs, Prov. ix. 18, Jer. xv. 18, Eccl. xxxiv. 30, Ps. cxli. 5, which he turns against them through the story of the schism. He next addresses himself to their theory of fellowship, and discusses their proof texts, 1 Tim. v. 22, Is. lii. 11, 1 Cor. v. 6; Ezekiel, Daniel, the Apostles, Christ and Paul all rebuke this purism. Cyprian's authority for rebaptism is reviewed. Augustin repeats the doubts of very many as to the authenticity of those parts of his works which favor this view; but granted that they are valid, Cyprian, nevertheless, maintained unity and toleration, and by martyrdom purged his mistake. There is, however, no martyrdom outside of the unity, as that father also testified. Cyprian acknowledged as well the presence of many evil persons in the ministry and in the Church, but stood to it that unity must not be sacrificed on that account. The Church is a mixed society; this is Christ's law. Had Macrobius's associates remembered the parable of the wheat and tares they would not have separated. This argument is concluded with a sort of summary of the points traversed before. As to the note of persecution: that alone is a martyrdom which surrenders the life for a good cause. The Donatists too used the State in the case of the Maximianists, and to them belong the Circumcelliones. The matter of unity and the connected points of toleration and fellowship are again enlarged upon.

A sermon attributed to Augustin, *De Rusticiano subdiacono a Donatistis rebaptizato et in diaconum ordinato,* falls in the same year, 409, with the letter to Bishop Macrobius. There is an outburst of deep grief over the act. It would appear that Rusticianus had been a special favorite of Augustin, on whom he had expended much care; but he had become involved in scurrilous deeds, in feasting and intemperance, day and night, and was plunged in debt, and at last was excommunicated by his presbyter, and so fled to the Donatists, by whom he was rebaptized and made a deacon; this defection happened in the diocese of the bishop Valerius (?); so Augustin interposed through Maximius and Theodorus with Bishop Macrobius, but in vain. He deplores the disgrace done to the sacrament, as dishonor done to the sign of the King. The repetition is contradicted by the procedure with regard to the returning Maximianists. He corrects the misinterpretation of Ecclus. xxxiv. 30. He wishes for the Donatists the experience of the prodigal, that they may be forgiven by return to the Church and so attain to the profit of charity.

Great calamities were befalling the Church in all parts of the world. Victorianus, a presbyter, wrote to Augustin for relief from doubts as to the office of such afflictions; in the bishop's reply, [*Ep.* cxi.] possibly of Nov., 409, he mentions the cruelties of the Donatists at Hippo exceeding those of the barbarians, especially in the resort to acidified lime, clubbing, robberies, and other destructive measures to compel rebaptism; forty-eight in one place were thus forced to a repetition. The coercion policy, in other words, had stimulated some of the Donatists to retaliation.

Donatus had resigned his proconsulship. Augustin writes [*Ep.* cxii.] at the end of 409 or beginning of 410 A.D., to express his regrets at not meeting him on his visit to Tibilis; his retirement would now give leisure for a larger development in graces, and would lead him to esteem the superiority of eternal things. He praises him for his official worth, which indeed was in everybody's mouth, but he urges him not to defer to that popularity, but to seek the higher approbation. After reminding him of the duty of Christian progress, he asks for a reply and an exhortation to be addressed to all his dependents at Sinitis and Hippo to return to the Church. Greetings are sent to his father, whom the son had been instrumental in converting to the faith.

Petilian of Constantina had written a treatise, *de unico baptismo*, which Constantinus had come into possession of through some Donatist presbyter, and then gave it to Augustin while they were in the country, imploring him to answer it. He did so, *c.* 410, in the book bearing the same title. He scorns those who desire secrecy in such matters; when the deeds are public let the discussion be. Petilian claims that the only true baptism is theirs; and therefore it is not repeated by the sacrilegious theorists. Yes, replies Augustin, baptism is indeed one, but it is Christ's, not yours; yours is only a repetition of the rite. We correct what is yours and recognize what is Christ's. Therefore we do not repeat it. So Christ corrected what was evil and recognized what was good among the Jews. So Paul exposed the sin of the heathen world but acknowledged what truth it had. Moreover you perform the ceremony, but it is to destruction: there is no real advantage in baptism outside of the Church. Petilian pleads for rebaptism because Paul rebaptized John's disciples; but, says Augustin, that is to declare John a heretic. These are two different things, as indeed Petilian himself suggests, some might say, and then gives two irrelevant passages, Matt. xii. 30, and vii. 21—23, as if the Catholics had no fellowship with Christ and were not recognized by Him. Augustin, after considering the import of these passages, avers the readiness of the Church to recognize the baptism of Christ as administered by Donatists when they return to the Church; for to deny Christ's baptism because it is administered by heretics, is to say Christ Himself should be denied, when even demons confess Him. There is a belief in God outside of the Church; the devils believe in Him outside of the Church. So there is one baptism of Christ which may exist also outside of the Church. Petilian's declaration that true baptism is where the true faith is, Augustin disproves by citing the case of the unbelieving and schismatic, yet baptized Corinthians. So all the ages of the kingdom bear witness to a like state of things. The action of Agrippinus and Cyprian on the one side, and of Stephen on the other, as to rebaptism is reviewed; differing in this, they yet maintained unity, especially Cyprian. Further, if the contact of evil men within the fellowship really defiles the good, then the Church perished in Cyprian's time; where could Donatus then have been spiritually born? If there is no such pollution, then there is no occasion to rage for separation. The origin of the schism is then denied from documentary testimony, and the charges declared to be not sustained; on the other hand, these archives prove the schismatics to have been traditors. A summary of the main points concludes his plea for the sole baptism as that of Christ. [Cp. *Retractt.* II. xxxiv.].

After this book against Petilian just mentioned had been finished, he wrote another work of larger proportions and with more thoroughness, in refutation of their schism, by the data of the Maximian schism, which he considered a full surrender of all their particularism. This has been styled: *De Maximianistis contra Donatistas.* It is lost, but noticed in the Retractations (II. xxxv.) immediately after *de unico Baptismo.*

At Carthage, about May 15, 411, he preached in praise of peace (Sermo ccclvii.). After its eulogy, he summons his hearers to the love of that peace; and recalls Donatists as alienated from the unity unto the concord which exists in the Church only. Patience and prayer are better means to their conquest than reproof. After the pentecostal fast he bade them exercise hospitality toward the guests who should attend the Conference.

The two edicts concerning the great Conference had been issued by Marcellinus. The Donatists had sent in their protest to the second, while the Catholic bishops sent in their acquiescence in a letter [*Ep.* cxxviii.], which is ascribed to Augustin's hand. It was of course written before June 1, 411, the day appointed for the opening. They agree to all the provisions for maintaining an orderly discussion; to the time and place of meeting; to the numbers to be present; to the requirement that all the delegated disputants sign their deliverances; to the countersignatures; to the order prohibiting the people from access to the Conference. If the Donatists prove the Church universal to have been lost and to be solely with them, the Catholic bishops will resign their sees; if, however, the collation prove the universality of the Church, then they suggest the recognition of the ordination and office of the Donatist clergy, and propose details for the succession in case of any jointure. The conciliatory example of Christ persuades them to this step; the peace of Christ in the Church is higher than the episcopate. The Donatist use of the civil authority against the Maximianists, and their gladness in receiving the returning schismatics without rebaptism, and without any diminution of their honors, give hope of a return to the root.

Before the meeting of the Conference, Augustin preached a sermon (No. ccclviii.) in Carthage, on peace and love, of which the main thoughts were the peace to which the Catholics cling and which they love under the persuasion of the divine testimonies; the victory of truth is love. He presents the Scripture proofs of charity and universality; the inheritance should not be divided. Donatus and Cæcilian were but men, but baptism is Christ's and not man's. The charity spread abroad in the heart is a broad commandment. He invites the Donatists to share in the Church's possessions, and to be bishops along with the Catholics, and pleads for a joint fraternal recognition; the Catholics seek peace and want to build up the Church. He finally requests the people to keep aloof from the place of dispute, but invokes their prayers in its behalf.

The objection to the second edict on the part of the Donatists respecting the restriction upon the number to be present at the collation, led the Catholics to write a second letter to Marcellinus, which is most likely also from the pen of Augustin. [*Ep.* cxxix.]. Solicitude over the opposition is expressed; some seem disposed to present a hindrance to the peaceful progress of the Conference; and yet the writers hope that the thought and suspicion may not prove true, but that the desire of the whole body may after all be to press into the unity of the Catholic Church. Then they go on, very wrongfully in such a document, to discuss their favorite note of the universality of the Church, as the body of Christ was not stolen, so neither are His members outside of the few in Africa, dead. From Jerusalem outward was to be its progress and thence it filled the whole world. The fact that the Donatists have the very same Scriptures as the Catholics which contain these proofs of universality, fills the complainants with grief for them. The Jews who denied the resurrection rejected also the New Testament; but the Donatists receive it, and yet they deny the note of universality, and accuse the Catholics of being traditors of the sacred books. Now at the collation probably they wish to be in full numbers, in order to search completely the Scriptures; and through their innumerable testimonies they long to come *en masse*, not to create a tumult, but to put an end to the old discord. It is true that they have found fault with our use of the State; and yet the Scriptures vindicate such a recourse, and the Donatists themselves appealed to Constantine. The Scriptures too show the mixed character of the Church, wheat and chaff, good and bad fish, to the final harvest, the winnowing, and the further shore. Perhaps they see the wrong of their opposition to the Church. The case of the Maximianists has shown their willingness to use the power of the State and to ignore rebaptism; and probably moved by these things, they want to come in such large numbers in the interest not of tumult but of peace. They desire to show that they are not so few as their enemies report them to be. The Catholic numbers exceed in proconsular Africa, and, except in Numidia, are more numerous than in the rest of the African provinces; and most of all when one comes to compare the whole world with the few Donatists. Why, however, could not the number be just as well certified by the subscription? Even though quiet be preserved, yet at such a Conference the murmur of such a crowd will impede the progress of the work. If they all are allowed to be present, the writers, nevertheless, will limit themselves to the delegation suggested by the Judge, and then no blame for disorder can attach to them. If, however, the protest has been made in behalf of unity, they all will be present joyfully to welcome the Donatists as brethren.

The *Mandatum Catholicorum*, a sort of voucher and letter of instruction for the disputants on the side of the State Church, was undoubtedly the product of Augustin's pen. After a preamble which attests the sufficiency of the Church through her divine proofs against all heretics and schismatics, and the desire of Church and State to settle the long pending controversy in Africa, and the duty to enlighten men as to the eternal salvation, which things had induced them to convene and to select defenders, there follows the note of the universality, which, as the great proposition, is expanded with many proof texts from the Old and the New Testament. This truth is to be defended against the Donatist assertion that the universal Church had perished through contamination with Cæcilian; for the Church is a mixed society of good and evil, and not to be condemned on this account, but its unity is to be preserved by toleration. If they maintain this view, the documents concerning Cæcilian's character must be examined. The contestants must prove that the Church was thus defiled, or else the evil do not defile the good in this unity. The mandate then gives Scriptural and also post-apostolic proofs on this point, especially from Cyprian, and quotes the Donatist action concerning the Maximianists. The next topic is baptism as a sacrament of Christ and not of man, and as independent of the character of the celebrant: the Maximian schism again affords material for the confutation of this Donatistic tenet. They are instructed also to use the archives to show that their opponents initiated civil appellation.

In the session of the second day, Augustin is the speaker, mainly on the matter of delay and adjournment.

In the third session, he appears as the chief disputant on the doctrinal and historical points, and also as answering the letter of the Donatists in reply to the mandate.

In a sermon preached after the close of the Conference, (Sermo cclix. on Ecclus. xxv. 2), he exhorted all Christians to be brethren; the Catholics desire to have the Donatists unite with them in worship in the universal Church. The history of Cæcilian should not affect the doctrine of the body. He claims a triumph indeed for his side and rejoices over the many who are returning to the mother Church, but candidly confesses that many harden themselves in their opposition. His exordium appeals for a restoration of brotherly harmony.

A little later in the year, probably, Augustin preached from Gal. vi. 2–5 (Sermo clxiv.), in which he rebukes those who say: "We are saints, we do not carry your burdens, therefore we do not communicate with you;" and says: "your ancestors carry burdens of separation, burdens of schism, burdens of heresy, burdens of dissension, burdens of animosity, burdens of false proofs, burdens of calumnious accusations." In your boast of non-participation in other's sins, you desert the flock, the threshing-floor and the net. The traditors who had condemned the absent Cæcilian dissolved connection with the whole world. He reminds them of the Maximianists; he charges them with breaking the parables, and yet inculcates patience. The whole sermon indicates that the effect of the conference had been to embitter both sides.

Another sermon (xcix.) on Luke vii. 36, 50, was also preached about this time, in which he conceives that the Puristic *noli me tangere* may develop into a system for sin-pardoning, and justification and sanctification; the men of the *Gesta Collationis* are likely to bring about such a machine religion. Already do they say: if men do not remit sins, then what Christ says is false as to loosing on earth and in heaven. With this conception of the tendency of their tenets he further says against them, that the cleansing in baptism does not depend on the man.

In a fragment of another sermon (ccclx.), preached on the vigils of Maximian, he personates a Donatist, who has returned to the unity, thanking the Lord that the lost is found, and expressing his joy in the vine, the unity, the baptism and peace of Christ.

The authorized acts of the council of 411 were too unwieldy for either general or popular use, and a compendium framed from them was too obscure; so Augustin, about the close of 411, determined to make a digest, called the *Breviculus collationis cum Donatistis.* It gives the collations of the three days, but it is thoroughly disconnected without the official account, for too many links known to the actors alone are not apparent to the uninitiated; too much of what would throw light on the animus of the parties in power is passed over, and a considerable deal of the minor business necessary to the understanding of the spirit of the debate does not appear. A reader would certainly get a still more one-sided and intolerant idea of the Conference from the digest than from the *Gesta.* The analysis of the order of business would require a comparison with the *Gesta Collationis,* and that lies outside of our present purpose. [Cp. *Retractt.* II. xxxix.].

The decision of the Conference again stirred up a counter movement by the Circumcelliones, especially in Augustin's diocese, during which some terrible outrages were perpetrated; the presbyter Restitutus was killed; the presbyter Innocentius was clubbed and mutilated. A trial was instituted by Marcellinus and the crimes confessed. Augustin hastens to write to him [*Ep.* cxxxiii.], somewhere about the opening of 412 A.D., imploring that the punishment be not capital or retaliatory; restraint and labor would be just. He commends the tribune-notary's moderation in the examination, in that he did not resort to torture for extorting evidence, but only to whipping. He commands him, as bishop, not to proceed to extremity, which would be an injury to the Church, or at least to the diocese of Hippo. Since the pronouncing of the sentence presumably belonged to the proconsul, he had also indicted a letter to him.

Apringius, the proconsul, was a brother of Marcellinus. To him Augustin addressed a letter in the same interest, and at the same date. [*Ep.* cxxxiv.] For the use of his newly gained authority, he was accountable to God; he was also a Christian, so that Augustin felt a greater confidence in petitioning and in warning, and begs that he may regard his interference as a part of a bishop's zeal for the welfare of the Church. He repeats the story of the arrest of the Circumcelliones and Donatist clergy, the trial by Apringius's own brother, the tribune-notary, Marcellinus, and the gentleness of the hearing, in which the accused confessed their crime, especially as to the copresbyters. He now begs for a mild punishment; in the one case it cannot be strictly retaliatory; in that of the homicide he fears it may be capital punishment. Apringius must not only consider the State, but the Church, and respect her clemency. He is not only a ruler of exalted power but a son of Christian piety. Our enemies boast of persecution; we must give them no occasion for it. These acts should be read for the cure of the minds which have been perverted. If the extreme penalty has to fall, spare at least the children. He implores him to imitate the patience and mildness of the Church and of Christ.

Augustin, in 412, writes to Marcellinus [*Ep.* cxxxix.] expressing his delight that the proceedings connected with the trial are in preparation, and for the intention of having them read in the churches of tne city, and, if possible, in all the churches of his diocese. The crimes mentioned are the same as before, with added confessions of many who were in some degree abettors. These are the men who refuse to commune with the Catholic Church for fear of pollution from wicked men, and yet refuse to leave a schism debased by such a fellowship. It was a question in Marcellinus's mind whether the *Gesta* should be read in the Donatist church of Theoprepia in Carthage. Augustin urges it, and if it be too small, then in some other quarter, in that region of the city. Augustin pleads for a mild punishment in imitation of the clemency of the Church; however weak it may seem at the outset, men will afterward regard it with favor, and the reading of the *Gesta* will be more welcome and more effective by the contrast between Donatist cruelty and Catholic moderation. He speaks of the commission of the bishop Bonifacius and the bearer Peregrinus, who were empowered to treat upon some new measures for the benefit of the Church. The Donatist Bishop Macrobius was busy reopening the churches of his sect, followed by a band of both sexes. In the absence of Celer, a Donatist, his procurator, Spondeus, a Catholic, had broken their audacity. He is commended to the favorable notice of Marcellinus. While Spondeus was on a visit to Carthage, Macrobius had actually reopened the Donatist churches on the estates of Celer. He was assisted by Donatus, a rebaptized deacon and a leader in the slaughter; from which fact other outrages might be expected. Should the plea for mildness not be granted, Augustin asks that his letters urging clemency [*Epp.* cxxxiii. and cxxxiv.] be read along with the *Gesta*. At least let a remission be granted to give time for an appeal to the Emperors, for no martyrs desire their blood to be avenged by death. In apologizing for his inability to complete his work on the baptism of infants, he urges the variety of his labors; among other things he had completed the *Breviculus Collationis*, as a compend for those who had not the leisure to read the entire proceedings of the Conference; also a letter addressed to the Donatist laity.

The Donatists were charged with circulating the story of the bribery of the cognitor or judge of the Conference. The letter from the council of Zerta, June 14, 412, in refutation of this was written by Augustin, [*Ep.* cxli.] in which it is said that they had become acquainted with this rumor so easily credited by the common people. The vote of the council was to authorize a refutation of it as a falsehood. The Donatists had been convicted of mendacity in the charge which they had made and signed against the Catholics as traditors; they had also invented stories to account for the signature of an absent bishop. How can they be believed in such a charge against the cognitor? Since the acts of the Collation are so voluminous we present herewith a digest. The meeting, the election of disputants and scribes, the matter of the subscriptions, are then recapitulated. In the attempt at discussion, the whole aim of the Donatist disputants was to avoid coming to the point to be debated, while the Catholic representatives exerted themselves to reach just that goal and nothing else. When at last the Donatists were forced to the issue, they were vanquished by the clear testimony of the Scriptures to the universality of the Church. Any one separated from this unity has not life; the wrath of God abides upon him. The communion with the wicked does not defile any one by the mere participation in the sacraments, but only by agreement with their deeds. All these truths they had to acknowledge. The Catholics had prevented a confusion between the doctrinal and historical sides of the question. In the discussion of the documents, the chief offset to all the points was found in the case of the Maximianists, although the Donatists plead that a case should not be prejudged by a case, nor a person by a person. All the accusations which had been concentrated against Cæcilian they were unable to meet with proofs. Defeated men are wont to suggest such a defense as the corruption of the judge. Then says the paper in effect: If you will believe us, let us hold fast to the unity which God commands and loves. But if you are unwilling to believe us, read the proceedings themselves, or allow them to be read to you, and do you yourselves test whether what we have written to you be true. If you decline all these, and will still cleave to the Donatists, we are clear from your judgment. If you will renounce the schism, we will welcome you to the peace of Christ, and you will have the profit of that sacrament which was administered among you to judgment.

The Donatist presbyters Saturninus and Eufrates had joined the Catholic Church and maintained their rank. Augustin writes [*Ep.* cxlii.], *c.* 412 A.D., to express his joy at their arrival and bids them not to grieve at his absence, for they are now in the one Church whose note of universality he expands as the one Body of the one Head, and as the one house in all the earth; in the unity of this house we rejoice as embracive of those transmarine churches, to whom the appeal had vainly been made by the Donatists. He who lives evilly in this Church eats and drinks condemnation to himself, but whoever lives correctly, another case and another person cannot prejudge him. The Donatists had protested against the parallel proofs drawn from the Maximianists, on the ground that a case should not be prejudged by a case nor a person by a person. On the Lord's threshing-floor the chaff must be tolerated. He exhorts them to a faithful discharge of their clerical duties, especially in mercifulness and also in prayer for the removal of the schism.

The hostility of the Donatists was increased by the Collation. Their clergy charged the judge with bribery, and protested against the unfairness of the trial, the compulsion of the meeting, the unjust decision. Augustin felt compelled to write, *c.* 412 A.D., to the people in order to stay the fury of their leaders. The treatise is known as *Ad Donatistas post Collationem.* Why make such a charge? Why does Primian say, it is unworthy for the sons of the martyrs to meet in the same place with the offspring of traditors? Why did they come? Why were they unable to prove the old accusations? And how are they the sons of martyrs? The universality of the Church was demonstrated at the Conference. Donatists do not commune with the churches addressed in those epistles which they read at their services, because they say these perished by communion with the African Cæcilians, and yet they put in the plea that a case should not be prejudged by a case nor a person by a person. He meets the Cæcilian charge by the Maximianists in spite of this caveat. He represents all the New Testament churches and the East as expostulating on the basis of this very plea with the Donatists for separation from them. So the case and the person of the bad does not prejudice the case and the person of the good; they must abide together until the end. He condemns their arrogant pretense to holiness. The wicked must be tolerated in the Church, but their deeds are not to be participated in. Cyprian would not destroy the unity because bad people were in it; frequent are the examples of such forbearance in the Scriptures, and the principle was not changed after the resurrection of Christ; it continued in force in the New Testament Church; the winnowing and severance come at the end of the world. They would perhaps deny their own words as uttered in the Conference were they not written; that was the beauty of requiring subscription. They charge too that the sentence against them was pronounced in the night. Augustin playfully speaks of many good things which have been said and done in the night. He subsequently reminds them of the days in which they tried to prove the origin of heresy, and their defeat at every point of the Cæcilian history. It appears here again that the Donatists had a considerable body of acts of their own. The plea of persecution as a note of the Church and as an experience of the Donatists was one of the points urged at the conference in the Donatist reply to the Catholic mandate, and by Primian, to which we have the usual answer. Another complaint of the Donatists was that they were tried by those who had been condemned by themselves, and were compelled to unite with sinners; to which Augustin gives a little Maximianist parallel and then considers the questions of purism, the paucity of believers, the need of discipline, the fellowship of a mixed community which ought not to degenerate into a participation in the deeds of the wicked therein. These are discussed with considerable detail of quotations from the Old and New Testaments. Some who thought Cæcilian guilty would not break the unity; they imitated Cyprian. He charges their clergy with duplicity. He reminds them of the deception practiced in presenting the signature of a Donatist, who was already dead; so with regard to the show of numbers in attendance and the alleged multitude absent, and also the means adopted for securing delay, the interruptions and turnings of the debate from the true object in view. He vindicates the cognitor's method and rulings. He then renews the discussion concerning the archival origin of the schism. In conclusion he addresses them as brethren and exhorts them to love peace and unity.

The Donatists of Cirta, clergy and people, had returned to the Catholic Church and had written a letter of thanks to Augustin for his preaching, under which they had been persuaded to renounce the schism. Augustin in reply [*Ep.* cxliv.], probably at end of 412 A.D., says that this is not man's work, but God's. Their allusion to the conversion of the drunken and luxurious Polemo by Xenocrates, draws from him the reflection, that such a change of character, though not a Christian repentance, is, nevertheless, a work of God. So he bids them not to give thanks to himself but to God, for their return to the unity. Those who still are alienated, whether from love or fear, he charges to remember the undeceived scrutiny of God; to weigh Scripture testimony as to the universality of the Church; and the documents as to the origin of the schism. The case has been tried or not been tried by the transmarine churches; if not, then there is no existing ground for the separation; if it has, the defeated ones are the separatists. But alas! the obstacles to their persuasion are well-nigh insuperable. He hopes that the mutual desire for his visit to them may be fulfilled.

About the beginning of the year 413, appeared the book *De Fide et Operibus*. In Chap. iv. 6, he speaks of the need of coercion against the Donatists as disturbers of the peace of the Church, as separaters of the tares from the wheat before the time, as those who have blindly preferred to cut themselves off from the unity; commixture of evil and good is a necessity, and we ought to remain in that fellowship which is not at all destitute of discipline. [Cp. *Retractt.* II. xxxviii.]

Donatus, a Donatist presbyter, and another person connected with that body, had been arrested by order of Augustin about the beginning of 416 A.D. Mounted upon a beast against his will, he dashed himself to the ground and so received injuries which his less obstinate companion escaped. Augustin writes [*Ep.* clxxiii.] to vindicate himself as concerned about the salvation of the recusants, and puts the blame of the wounds upon the offender. Donatus urged in opposition to this style of conversion that no one should be compelled to be good. Augustin claims on the other hand that many are compelled to take the good office of a bishop against their will. Donatus argues that God had given us free will, therefore a man should not be compelled even to be good. Augustin replies that the effort of a good will is to restrain and change the evil will, because of the awful results which follow a vitiated will. Why were the Israelites compelled to go to the land of promise? Why was Paul forced to turn from persecution to the embrace of the truth? Why do parents correct children? Why are negligent shepherds blamed? You are an errant sheep, with the Lord's mark upon you, and I as shepherd must save you from perishing. Of your own will you threw yourself into a well, but it would have been wicked to leave you there where you had cast yourself according to your will, and hence the attendants took you out; how much more is it a duty to save you from eternal death. Besides, it is unlawful to inflict death upon yourself. He reminds him that the Scriptures do not allow suicide; and controverts his use of I. Cor. xiii. 3, "though I give my body to be burned." Severed from charity and unity, nothing can profit, not even the surrender of the body to burning. The points of the recent joint Conference are then dwelt upon. Donatus was understood to have criticized the saying of his party as to the Maximianist parallel: do not prejudge a case by a case or a person by a person. Augustin twits him in this wise: If you object to this, then you are deceived concerning it, because you oppose your authority to theirs, and if you say it is not true, the hope of vindicating the great schism falls through entirely. He presses him to weigh all the proceedings. But Donatus objects also that the Lord did not cause the seventy to come back, and did not put a barrier in the way of the twelve when he asked, "Will ye also go away?" Augustin says that was in the beginning of Christianity; kings were not yet converted; now the State helps the Church. Our Lord said prophetically, Compel them to come in. So we hunt you in the hedges; the unwilling sheep is brought to the true pasture.

The series of Tractatus on the Gospel of John, which are ascribed to 416 A.D., contain many reflections on Donatism. We can only notice the passages:

Tractatus IV.	in Jo.	i. 19–33.	
" V.	"	i. 33.	
" VI.	"	i. 32, 33.	Quite fully.
" IX.	"	ii. 1–11.	
" X.	"	ii. 12–21.	
" XI.	"	ii. 23–25, and iii. 1–5.	
" XII.	"	iii. 6–21.	
" XIII.	"	iii. 22–29.	

To the same year are ascribed the Tractatus on the I. *Ep.* of John.

Tractatus I.	1 Jo.	i. and ii. 1–11.
" II.	"	ii. 12–17.
" III.	"	ii. 18–27.
" IV.	"	iii. 1–8.

In the Retractations, II. xlvi., we read of a book addressed to Emeritus, the Donatist bishop of Cæsarea, in the province of Mauritania Cæsariensis. [See *Ep.* lxxxvii.] He speaks of him as the best of the seven Donatist disputants at the Conference. The work marked briefly the lines on which the Donatists were defeated. Its title is: *Ad Emeritum Donatistarum Episcopum, post collationem, liber unus*. Since the Retractations place it before *De Gestis Pelagii*, and *De Correctione Donatistarum*, it was most likely written in the beginning of 417 A.D.

Boniface had requested from Augustin a letter of instructions on the relation of the Donatists to the Arians. The bishop replies, *c.* 417 [*Ep.* clxxxv.], which he himself calls a book *de Correctione Donatistarum.* [Cp. *Retractt.* II. xlviii.]. Since this is translated in the present volume, we will omit any further notice.

The above-mentioned Emeritus was present at a Synod of the Catholics, near Deuterius, September 20, 418. At a service held two days after, Augustin preached the *Sermo ad Cæsariensis Ecclesiæ plebem.* Emeritus was present. In the church during a previous colloquy with Augustin he had said: I cannot will what you will, but I can will what I will. Augustin in this sermon (and the writing has all the abruptness and repetition of an extempore address) urges him to will what God wills, *viz.*, peace, and that now, in response to the cry of the people; and if you ask why I, who call you schismatics and heretics, desire to receive you, it is because you are brethren; because you have the baptism of Christ; because I want you to have salvation: one can have everything outside the Church except salvation; he can have honor, he can have the sacraments, he can sing Allelulia, he can respond Amen, he can hold to the gospels, he can have faith in the name of the Father and the Son and the Holy Spirit, and can preach. Persecution after all is rather of you. The failure of the archival evidence as to Cæcilian is alleged as usual, and hence no reason for separation exists. He recites too the story of the seizure, escape, reseizure, compulsory baptism and ordination of Petilian, while at the time a Catholic catechumen. This occurred at Constantina, when that city and region were largely Donatist. He was seized unto death, do we not draw him to salvation? Here or nowhere, says Augustin, repeating the voice of the people, is the place for peace.

There was a gathering of clergy (the bishops Alypius, Augustinus, Possidius, Rusticus, Palladius, etc., many presbyters and deacons and a considerable number of people) in the exedra of the larger church at Cæsarea, *c.* 418 A.D. Emeritus, the Donatist bishop of the city, was also present. Augustin addresses those devoted to the unity, and says that when he came to the city on the day before yesterday he found Emeritus returned from a journey. Augustin met him in the street and invited him to the Church, and Emeritus consented without any demur. The sermon of Augustin is full of the peace, love and related themes of the Church, in hope of winning Emeritus. He alludes to the many conversions in the city and since the collation; if Emeritus has anything new to say in defense of his side, he invites him to state it. Emeritus had been reported as affirming that at the Conference the Donatists were overcome by power rather than by truth. Augustin then addresses inquiries to Emeritus directly: as to why he had come if he was defeated at the council; or if he thought his party had triumphed, then to state the ground for such an opinion. Emeritus said: The acts show whether I am defeated or not, whether I am defeated by truth or oppressed by power. Augustin: Then why do you come? Emeritus: That I might say this very thing which you ask, and so on. Under some taunting and arrogant observations to the brethren, Emeritus keeps quiet. From Augustin's statement it appears that the Acts were read during Lent, at Thagaste, Constantina, Hippo, and all the faithful churches. Part of these *Gesta* are then read by Alypius, *viz.*, the imperial convocation of the Conference, and comments are made by Augustin. Then follows his application of the lessons afforded by the Maximianist schism, in which he says the Donatists make shipwreck of all their tenets. Emeritus, however, remained a silent hearer. The account of the above meeting is given in the treatise: *De Gestis cum Emerito, Cæsariensi Donatistarum Episcopo liber unus.* [Cp. *Retractt.* II. li.].

The book *de Patientia* is assigned to 418 A.D. In Chapter xiii. he contrasts genuine and false martyrdom.

Dulcitius had been appointed Tribune-notary. The effect of his carrying out of the renewed edicts against the Donatists was signalized by many conversions, but also by many suicides. He had written to Augustin requesting directions about how he ought to proceed against the heretics. Augustin replies [*Ep.* cciv.], *c.* 420 A.D., that his work had indeed persuaded many to return to their salvation, but others were stirred either to kill the Catholics or themselves. We indeed do desire the return of all to unity, yet some are doubtless predestinated to perish by an occult yet just decree of God. They perish not only in their own fires but in that of Gehenna. The Church grieves over them, as David over his son, although they have met the deserved punishment of rebels. Augustin does not find fault with the notary's edict at Thamugada, only with the phrase: You may know that you are to be given over to the death which you deserve; for that is not contained in the rescripts. In the second edict there is a clearer statement of the notary's aim. Augustin also criticizes his courtesy toward Gaudentius, the Donatist bishop of Thamugada. As to a special reply to that bishop Augustin urges a more diligent refutation of the fallacious doctrines by which the Donatists are accustomed to be seduced. He had already done this in very many works, but adds some points by way of suggestion. He alone is a martyr who dies for a true cause. Man's will is free, but nevertheless amenable to divine and human laws. The State can punish not only adulteries and homicides, but also sacrileges. Many think it strange that we do not rebaptize, but the sacrament once given ought not to be repeated. Suicides are utterly prohibited by the Scriptures. The case of Razius gives the Donatist no pretext, for the deed is simply mentioned but not commended. (II. Mac. xiv. 37—46). In conclusion he intimates that in answer to the united wish of the people of Thamugada, of himself and of Eleusinus, the tribune of that place, that Augustin should answer both epistles of Gaudentius, the Donatist bishop, and especially the latter of the two, which contained Scriptural proofs, he will write such a criticism.

Dulcitius had written a pacific letter to Gaudentius, the Donatist bishop of Thamugada, one of the quieter members of the seven Donatist disputants, concerning the enforcement of the imperial edicts. Gaudentius replied in two epistles, one short, the other longer and fortified by Scripture proofs. Augustin was requested to answer these, which he does (*c.* 420) in the work *Contra Gaudentium Donatistarum Episcopum, libri duo.* In Book I. he makes a change of form from the Petilian cast of personal dialogue, because of the captious fault found with that way as savoring of untruth, and takes a duller formula, "*Verba Epistolæ*" and "*ad haec responsio,*" whose dryness and literality the most sensitive Donatist could take no exception to. In the first epistle of Gaudentius, the fairly courteous strain in which he had replied to the tribune-notary, with titles and recognition of character, Augustin rather resents by saying that the Catholic had treated the heretic too kindly and incautiously, and bids Gaudentius consider what he had said at the Collation. Gaudentius proposes to remain in the communion where the name of God and of his Christ is and where the Sacraments are, and pleads for religious liberty against compulsion as to matters of faith; and concludes, by another hand, with wishing him well and desiring his recession from the disquieting of Christians. Augustin objects that Gaudentius had not reproduced the language of Dulcitius correctly, and accuses the Donatists of holding the truth of baptism in the iniquity of human error; he comments on their false eagerness for death; he responds to all the good wishes for the tribune, but not that he should cease from correcting the heretics.

The second epistle of Gaudentius is mainly a protest from Scriptural grounds; against persecution he brings forward the case of Gabinus, who, if bad, should not have been received without correction, that is, baptism; but if innocent, why kill the innocent Donatists from whom he came to you? The false rumor about Emeritus, as having turned Catholic, is another instance of this persecution. The duty of a persecuted pastor is to be a doer of the law and to lay down his life for the sheep; there is no place whither the persecuted may now flee; the divine right of free will is restrained by the arbitrary laws of the emperor; persecution is a note of the Church from the blessings attached to it by Christ and the apostles. The peace of Christ invites the willing but does not compel the unwilling; a thing very different from the war-bearing peace and the bloody unity which their oppressors present. We rejoice in the hatred of the world; there is a martyr host of the apocalypse; Christians may yield up their souls in testimony against sacrilege, as Razius did. He begs Dulcitius to turn to the few who have the solidity and not the semblance of truth. God gave prophets not kings to teach the people: the Saviour sent fishermen not soldiers. God never needs the aid of soldiers. Gaudentius charges the Catholics with coveting the Donatist possessions. The farewell is in another handwriting, in which he wishes Dulcitius well, and advises him to pursue a lenient and temperate course.

The points of Augustin's reply are in no way different save form from those so constantly presented, unless there be an increase of roughness and a more hardened idea of the Church's right to use coercion. As to Gabinus, the Church's course with regard to him is a vindication of the right to receive a convert without rebaptism: in communion with charity and unity he received the profit of that rite which had been administered among the Donatists. In the case of Emeritus, Augustin confesses that the rumor of his having turned Catholic was false; but Emeritus came to Cæsarea of his own will; he came to the Church where a multitude was present; he could say nothing for his or his party's defense; he kept quiet. The argument against suicide from the case of Razius is well made; he died rather in suffering for the state; and besides the narrative does not commend the deed, but only states it; then too the books have not the weight that the Law, the Prophets and the Psalms carry with them. The plea for correction is precisely as usual. The doctrines of universality and unity and charity are incidentally brought forward. Circumcelliones, Secundus and Maximianists furnish the concluding parallels.

Book II. Gaudentius had written a reply to Augustin's first book. He had taken refuge under the example of Cyprian; but Augustin now refers him to the writings of Cyprian on *De Simplicitate Prælatorum seu De Catholicæ Ecclesiæ unitate*, showing Cyprian's belief in the universality of the Church which Augustin expands by the explanation of the term Catholic. Purgation of the Church is not by separation, but by toleration, as Cyprian too held in his letter to Maximus and others. The explanation of the field not as the Church, but rather as the world outside of the Church, had been supported at the Conference and is repeated by Gaudentius; and also its alternative, that were the field the Church then it must have perished from the tares which were in it. If so, says Augustin, then the ancestors of the Donatists would have perished. The period of separation is at the end, when the Gospel shall have been preached in the whole world. As to their theme of rebaptism, Augustin replies that he had already before referred him to his Maximianist practice, so that the action of Agrippinus and Cyprian are vain for him. And then too, according to Cyprian's own confession, and Stephen's testimony, there were crimes in the Church in their day; did the Church perish then? If so where was Donatus born? If not, then why did the party of Donatus separate? They are guilty of the very schism which Cyprian particularly deprecated as a cure, instead of toleration and discipline, for the ills of the Church. As to baptism: The Catholics recognize the Donatist rite, for the sacrament cannot be lost upon those who receive it among Catholics and then pass over to heretics; they have the truth but in iniquity; the truth is not the property of the Donatists. The apostle recognized such truth as he found among the Gentiles. Gaudentius had vindicated his reference to the tribune's letter, as to the Donatists having the names of God and of his Christ, and quoted the passage in proof. Augustin acknowledges his mistake, which, however, was not intentional, and he apologizes for the tribune's error as that of a military man who was not familiar with theology. Since Gaudentius had called the tribune religious in his first letter, Augustin accuses him of insincerity and berates him as superstitious. He also corrects Gaudentius for saying that God sent Jonah not to the king but only to the people of Nineveh, for the king compelled the humiliation of his subjects. In conclusion he quotes from Cyprian's letter to Maximus in behalf of universality and tolerant unity. His exordium is an earnest appeal to the Catholics to maintain all the notes of the Church. [Cp. *Retractt.* II. lix.].

Felicia had been a Donatist originally and was converted by force. She had devoted herself to the virgin life and apparently had become head of a religious house; but by reason of some wicked deeds of the clergy, possibly the extortion and rapacity of Antonius at Fussala, she was much disturbed and seemed inclined to relapse into her earlier puristic notions, if not to return to the body that upheld them. To quiet her doubts Augustin writes *Ep.* ccviii. *c.* 423. The Lord had predicted offenses. There are two kinds of shepherds over the flock, and will be to the end: the flock too has the good and the bad in it. The gathering is the present duty, the separation will be the future one; this latter is the Lord's prerogative. To abide in unity under such circumstances is a duty until the winnowing, and one is to believe what these shepherds teach, not what they do. Good and bad are therefore in the world under the widely diffused Catholic Church; the Donatist has no such note of universality. Love Christ and the Church, and then He will not permit you to lose the fruit of your virginity and to perish with the lost. If you go out of this life, separated from the unity of the body of Christ, this preserved integrity of the body will not profit you. You were compelled to come in; be thankful to those who compelled you. Show your devotion to the Lord, as your only hope, by being unmoved with these offenses, and by cleaving to his body, the Church.

A letter addressed to Pope Cœlestine is ascribed to Augustin [*Ep.* ccix. *c.* 423]; its authenticity has been disputed. The author, in giving an account of the appointment of Antonius as bishop of Fussala, remarks that at Fussala, a castellum about forty miles distant from Hippo, as in all the adjoining region, there had been a Donatist population; in Fussala itself there had not been a solitary Catholic; the Punic was the common language. The coercive measures had converted the whole territory, but the process had also aroused a violent opposition in the form of robbery, beating, blinding, murder. After its conversion, the distance from Hippo and the great numbers to be instructed, required a new bishopric, the history of which and the troubles growing out of it, the author further relates.

In that valuable book *De doctrina christiana*, (begun in 397, but ended in 426, including the part having reference to our subject III. xxx. 42), Augustin quotes approvingly from the book of Tychonius the *De septem regulis*, and prefaces a discussion of these rules by an allusion to the treatise of Tychonius, which had refuted some of the narrow and puristic doctrines of the Church, as held by his own party; this we have already seen was answered by Parmenian, whose letter in turn was dissected by Augustin. The first, second, fourth and seventh of these rules bear especially upon the doctrinal points under discussion. [Cp. *Retractt.* II. iv. and *Tychonius de Septem Regulis* reprinted in Migne. Pat. Lat. xviii.]

In his *de Hœresibus* [*c.* 428 A.D.] Chapter lxix. gives a brief account of the Donatiani or Donatistæ: (*a*) as to origin and progress; (*b*) Donatus's view of the Trinity; (*c*) the Montenses at Rome; (*d*) the Circumcelliones; (*e*) the schism of Maximian.

This was his parting arrow after the thirty-six years of battle. Catholics and Donatists passed under the persecutions of the Arian Vandals. Two years after this treatise Augustin laid aside his weapons to enter the land of eternal peace and unity.

More or less extended allusions are made to Donatism in the following sermons, arranged in the order of the Benedictine editions; for the years in which they were delivered cannot be determined. Want of space prevents the presentation of any analysis.

Sermo X.	1 Kings, iii. 16–28.
" XLV.	Is. lvii. 13 and 2 Cor. vii. 1.
" XLVI.	Ez. xxxiv. 1–16.
" XLVII.	Ez. xxxiv. 17–31.
" LXXI.	Matt. xii. 32.
" LXXXVIII.	Matt. xx. 30–34.

Sermo	XC.	Matt. xxii. 1–14.
"	CVII.	Luc. xii. 13–21.
"	CXXIX.	Jo. v. 39–47.
"	CXXXVII.	Jo. x. 1–16.
"	CXXXVIII.	Jo. x. 11–16.
"	CLXXXIII.	1 Jo. iv. 2.
"	CCXVIII.	Luc. xxiv. 38–47.
"	CCXLIX.	Jo. xxi. 1–14.
"	CCLII.	Jo. xxi. 1–14.
"	CCLXV.	The Ascension.
"	CCLXVI.	Ps. cxli. (cxl.) 5.
"	CCLXVIII.	Pentecost.
"	CCLXIX.	Pentecost.
"	CCLXXXV.	Anniversary of the martyrs Castus and Æmilus.
"	CCXCII.	John the Baptist.
"	CCCXXV.	Anniversary of the Twenty Martyrs.

Similar references are to be found in the expositions and sermons based on the Psalms. The first column is the Hebrew and English order; the second that of LXX. and Vulgate.

Exposition of Psalms XI. (X.)
" " XXVI. (XXV.) Sermon.
" " XXXI. (XXX.) Sermons I. and II.
" " XXXIII. (XXXII.) Sermon II.
" " XXXIV. (XXXIII.) Sermon II.
" " XXXVI. (XXXV.) Sermon.
" " XXXVII. (XXXVI.) Sermons II. (archival) and III
" " XL. (XXXIX.) Sermon.
" " LV. (LIV.) Sermon.
" " LVIII. (LVII.) Sermon.
" " LXXXVI. (LXXXV.) Sermon.
" " XCIX. (XCVIII.) Sermon.
" " CXX. (CXIX.) Sermon.
" " CXXV. (CXXIV.) Sermon.
" " CXXXIII. (CXXXII.) Sermon.
" " CXLVI. (CXLV.) Sermon.
" " CXLVII. 12–20 (CXLVII.) Sermon.
" " CXLIX. Sermon.

The time of writing the *de Utilitate Jejunii* is unknown. Chapter V. 9, contrasts pagan, heretical and Catholic fasts; heretics claim indeed to fast in order to please God; how can they, when they sever the unity? All heretics perish; they are the dividers of the inheritance of Christ.

In conclusion the reviser desires to commend the fidelity and lucidity of the translation made by the Rev. J. R. King, M.A.

No changes made by the reviser have been indicated, since all could not be without confusion. The translation had taken most of its notes and references from the Benedictines. The citations of Cyprian are according to the numerals in Hartel's edition.

PREFACE

THE schism of the Donatists, with which the treatises in the present volume are concerned, arose indirectly out of the persecution under Diocletian at the beginning of the fourth century. At that time Mensurius, bishop of Carthage, and his archdeacon Cæcilianus, had endeavored to check the fanatical spirit in which many of the Christians courted martyrdom; and consequently, on the death of Mensurius in 311, and the elevation of Cæcilianus to the see of Carthage in his place, the opposing party, alleging that Felix, bishop of Aptunga, by whom Cæcilianus had been consecrated, had been a *traditor*, and that therefore his consecration was invalid, set up against him Majorinus, who was succeeded in 315 by Donatus. The party had by this time gained strength, through the professions that they made of extreme purity in the discipline which they maintained, and had gone so far, under the advice of another Donatus, bishop of Casæ Nigræ in Numidia, as to accuse Cæcilianus before the Roman Emperor Constantine,—thus setting the first precedent for referring a spiritual cause to the decision of a civil magistrate. Constantine accepted the appeal, and in 313 the matter was laid for decision before Melchiades, bishop of Rome, and three bishops of the province of Gaul. They decided in favor of the validity of the consecration of Cæcilianus; and a similar verdict was given by a council held at Arles, by direction of the Emperor, in the following year. The party of Majorinus then appealed to the personal judgment of the Emperor, which was likewise given against them, not without strong expressions of his anger at their pertinacity. This was followed by severe laws directed against their schism; but so far from crushing them, the attack seemed only to increase their enthusiasm and develope their resources. And, under the leadership of Donatus, the successor of Majorinus, their influence spread widely throughout Africa, and continued to prevail, in spite of various efforts at their forcible suppression, during the whole of the fourth century. They especially brought on themselves the vengeance of the civil powers, by the turbulence of certain fanatical ascetics who embraced their cause, and who, under the name of Circumcelliones, spread terror through the country, seeking martydom for themselves, and offering violence to every one who opposed them.[1]

Towards the close of the century, this schism attracted the attention of Augustin, then a priest of Hippo Regius in Numidia. The controversy seems to have had for him a special attraction, not merely because of its intrinsic importance, but also because of the field which it presented for his unrivalled powers as a dialectician. These the Donatists had recently provoked, by inconsistently receiving back into their body a deacon of Carthage named Maximianus who had separated himself from them, and by recognizing as valid all baptism administered by his followers. Hence they naturally shrank from engaging in a contest with an antagonist who was sure to make the most of such a deviation from the very principles on which they based their schism; and, on the other hand, Augustin was so firmly convinced that his own position was impregnable, that he seems to have thought that if he could only secure a thorough and dispassionate discussion of the matter, the Donatists must necessarily be brought to acknowledge not only their theoretical errors, but also the practical sinfulness of their separation from the Church. Throughout the controversy, however, he appears to have put out of sight two considerations: first, the influence of party spirit and prejudice in blinding men to argument; and, secondly, the necessity of treating his opponents in a logical discussion as on an equal footing with himself. The first was in some degree an unavoidable element of disappointment; but Augustin made concession yet more difficult on the part of his opponents, by expecting them to acknowledge his superior position as a member of the Catholic Church, whose duty it was to expose the error of their views. He practically begs the very point at issue, by assuming that he, and not the Donatists, was in the Catholic communion; and though his argument is conducted independently of this premiss, yet it naturally rendered them more unwilling to admit its force.

This dogmatism was of less consequence in the first pamphlet which Augustin published on the subject,—his *Alphabetical Psalm*, in which he set forth the history and errors of the Donatists in a popular form,—since it was not intended as a controversial treatise, but only as a means of enlightening the less educated as to the Catholic tenets on the question in dispute. His next work, written in answer to a letter of Donatus of Carthage, in which the latter tried to prove that the baptism of Christ existed only in his communion, is unfortunately lost;

---

[1] Aug. *De Hær.* c. 69; *Enarr. in Ps.* 132, *secs.* 3, 6; *C. Cresc.* iii. c. xlii. 46., c. xliii. 47; *C. Gaudentium*, i. c. xxviii. 32.

and we can only gather hints as to the further part which he took in the controversy during the next few years from certain of his letters, especially those to the Donatist Bishops Honoratus and Crispinus.[1] From the former he claims the admission that the exclusiveness of the Donatists proves that they are not the Church of Christ; and his letter to the latter contains an invitation to discuss the leading points at issue, which Crispinus seems to have declined.

In the year 400 he wrote two books *Against the Party of Donatus*, which are also lost; and about the same time he published his refutation of the letter of Parmenianus in answer to Tichonius, in which he handles and solves the famous question, whether, while abiding in unity in the communion of the same sacraments, the wicked pollute the good by their society.[2]

Then followed his seven books *On Baptism*, included in this volume, in which he shows the emptiness of the arguments of the Donatists for the repetition of baptism; and proves that so far was Cyprian from being on their side, that his letters and conduct are of the highest value as overthrowing their position, and utterly condemning their separation from the Church.

Not long after this, Petilianus, bishop of Cirta or Constantina, the most eminent theologian among the Donatist divines, wrote a letter to his clergy against the Catholics, of which Augustin managed to obtain a copy, though the Donatists used their utmost care to keep it from him; and he replied to it in two books, written at different times,—the first in the year 400, before he was in possession of the whole letter, the remainder in 402. To the first book Petilianus made an answer, of which we gather the main tenor from a third book written by Augustin in reply to it. It appears to have been full of vehement abuse, and to have assumed the question in dispute, that the existence of the true Church, and the catholicity of any branch of it, depended on the purity and orthodoxy of all its ministers; so that the guilt or heresy of any minister would invalidate the whole of his ministerial acts. Hence he argued that Cæcilianus being the spiritual father of the so-called Catholics, and having been a *traditor*, none of them could possibly have been lawfully baptized, much less rightfully ordained.

Augustin admits neither of his assumptions; but, leaving the guilt or innocence of Cæcilianus as a point which was irrelevant (though practically the case against him utterly broke down), he addresses himself to the other point, and argues most conclusively that all the functions of the clergy in celebrating the rites of the Church being purely ministerial, the efficacy of those rites could in no way depend upon the excellence of the individual minister, but was derived entirely from Christ. Hence there was a certainty of the grace bestowed through the several ordinances, which otherwise there could not possibly have been, had their virtue depended on the character of any man, in whom even an unblemished reputation might have been the fruit of a skilled hypocrisy.

The third treatise in this volume belongs to a later period, being a letter written to Bonifacius, the Roman Count of Africa under Valentinian the Third. He had written to Augustin to consult him as to the best means of dealing with the Donatists; and Augustin in his reply points out to him his mistake in supposing that the Donatists shared in the errors of the Arians, whilst he urges him to use moderation in his coercive measures; though both here and in his answer to Petilianus we find him countenancing the theory that the State has a right to interfere in constraining men to keep within the Church. Starting with a forced interpretation of the words, "*Compel* them to come in," in Luke xiv. 23, he enunciates principles of coercion which, though in him they were subdued and rendered practically of little moment by the spirit of love which formed so large an element in his character, yet found their natural development in the despotic intolerance of the Papacy, and the horrors of the Inquisition. It is probable that he was himself in some degree misled by confounding the necessity of repressing the violence of the Circumcelliones, which was a real offense against the State, with the expediency of enforcing spiritual unity by temporal authority.

The Donatist treatises have met with little attention from individual editors. There is a dissertation, *De Aur. Augustino adversario Donatistarum*, by Adrien Roux, published at Louvain in 1838;[3] but it is believed that no treatises of this series have ever before been translated into English, nor are they separately edited. They are in themselves a valuable authority for an important scene in the history of the Church, and afford a good example both of the strength and the weakness of Augustin's writing,—its strength, in the exhaustive way in which he tears to pieces his opponent's arguments, and the clearness with which he exposes the fallacies of their reasoning; its weakness, in the persistency with which he pursues a point long after its discussion might fairly have been closed, as though he hardly knew when he had gained the victory; and his tendency to claim, by right of his position, a vantage-ground which did not in reality belong to him till the superiority of his cause was proved.

J. R. KING

OXFORD, *March*, 1870.

[1] *Epist.* xlix. li.

[2] Bened. Ed. Vol. ix. pp. 7-52. Migne, Vol. ix. pp. 33-108.

[3] The other works bearing on this controversy are mentioned in the exhaustive volume of Ferd. Ribbeck, *Donatus und Augustinus* (Elberfeld, 1858).—ED.

THE

SEVEN BOOKS OF AUGUSTIN,

BISHOP OF HIPPO,

ON

BAPTISM, AGAINST THE DONATISTS

[DE BAPTISIMO CONTRA DONATISTAS.]

CIRCA A.D. 400.

TRANSLATED BY THE

REV. J. R. KING, M.A.,

VICAR OF ST. PETER'S IN THE EAST, OXFORD; AND LATE FELLOW AND TUTOR OF MERTON COLLEGE, OXFORD.

CONTENTS ON BAPTISM, AGAINST THE DONATISTS.

THE

SEVEN BOOKS OF AUGUSTIN,

BISHOP OF HIPPO,

ON BAPTISM, AGAINST THE DONATISTS

This treatise was written about 400 A.D. Concerning it Aug. in *Retract.* Book II. c. xviii., says: I have written seven books on Baptism against the Donatists, who strive to defend themselves by the authority of the most blessed bishop and martyr Cyprian; in which I show that nothing is so effectual for the refutation of the Donatists, and for shutting their mouths directly from upholding their schism against the Catholic Church, as the letters and act of Cyprian.

BOOK I.

HE PROVES THAT BAPTISM CAN BE CONFERRED OUTSIDE THE CATHOLIC COMMUNION BY HERETICS OR SCHISMATICS, BUT THAT IT OUGHT NOT TO BE RECEIVED FROM THEM; AND THAT IT IS OF NO AVAIL TO ANY WHILE IN A STATE OF HERESY OR SCHISM.

CHAP. 1.—1. In the treatise which we wrote against the published epistle of Parmenianus[1] to Tichonius,[2] we promised that at some future time we would treat the question of baptism more thoroughly;[3] and indeed, even if we had not made this promise, we are not unmindful that this is a debt fairly due from us to the prayers of our brethren. Wherefore in this treatise we have undertaken, with the help of God, not only to refute the objections which the Donatists have been wont to urge against us in this matter, but also to advance what God may enable us to say in respect of the authority of the blessed martyr Cyprian, which they endeavor to use as a prop, to prevent their perversity from falling before the attacks of truth.[4] And this we propose to do, in order that all whose judgment is not blinded by party spirit may understand that, so far from Cyprian's authority being in their favor, it tends directly to their refutation and discomfiture.

2. In the treatise above mentioned, it has already been said that the grace of baptism can be conferred outside the Catholic communion, just as it can be also there retained. But no one of the Donatists themselves denies that even apostates retain the grace of baptism; for when they return within the pale of the Church, and are converted through re-

[1] Parmenianus was successor to Donatus the Great in the See of Carthage, circ. 350 A.D., and died circ. 392 A.D.

[2] Tichonius, who flourished circ. 380, was the leader of a reformatory movement in Donatism, which Parmenianus opposed, in the writing here alluded to. The reformer was excommunicated. He had the clearest ideas concerning the church and concerning interpretation of any of the ancients.

[3] *Contra Epist. Parmen.* ii. 14, also written circ. 400 A.D.

[4] Cyprian, in his controversy with Pope Stephen of Rome, denied the validity of heretical or schismatical baptism. The Donatists denied the validity of Catholic baptism. See Schaff, *Church History*, vol. ii. 262 sqq.

pentance, it is never given to them a second time, and so it is ruled that it never could have been lost. So those, too, who in the sacrilege of schism depart from the communion of the Church, certainly retain the grace of baptism, which they received before their departure, seeing that, in case of their return, it is not again conferred on them; whence it is proved, that what they had received while within the unity of the Church, they could not have lost in their separation. But if it can be retained outside, why may it not also be given there? If you say, "It is not rightly given without the pale;" we answer, "As it is not rightly retained, and yet is in some sense retained, so it is not indeed rightly given, but yet it is given." But as, by reconciliation to unity, that begins to be profitably possessed which was possessed to no profit in exclusion from unity, so, by the same reconciliation, that begins to be profitable which without it was given to no profit. Yet it cannot be allowed that it should be said that that was not given which was given, nor that any one should reproach a man with not having given this, while confessing that he had given what he had himself received. For the sacrament of baptism is what the person possesses who is baptized; and the sacrament of conferring baptism is what he possesses who is ordained. And as the baptized person, if he depart from the unity of the Church, does not thereby lose the sacrament of baptism, so also he who is ordained, if he depart from the unity of the Church, does not lose the sacrament of conferring baptism. For neither sacrament may be wronged. If a sacrament necessarily becomes void in the case of the wicked, both must become void; if it remain valid with the wicked, this must be so with both. If, therefore, the baptism be acknowledged which he could not lose who severed himself from the unity of the Church, that baptism must also be acknowledged which was administered by one who by his secession had not lost the sacrament of conferring baptism. For as those who return to the Church, if they had been baptized before their secession, are not rebaptized, so those who return, having been ordained before their secession, are certainly not ordained again; but either they again exercise their former ministry, if the interests of the Church require it, or if they do not exercise it, at any rate they retain the sacrament of their ordination; and hence it is, that when hands are laid on them,[1] to mark their reconciliation, they are not ranked with the laity. For Felicianus,[2] when he separated himself from them with Maximianus, was not held by the Donatists themselves to have lost either the sacrament of baptism or the sacrament of conferring baptism. For now he is a recognized member of their own body, in company with those very men whom he baptized while he was separated from them in the schism of Maximianus. And so others could receive from them, whilst they still had not joined our society, what they themselves had not lost by severance from our society. And hence it is clear that they are guilty of impiety who endeavor to rebaptize those who are in Catholic unity; and we act rightly who do not dare to repudiate God's sacraments, even when administered in schism. For in all points in which they think with us, they also are in communion with us, and only are severed from us in those points in which they dissent from us. For contact and disunion are not to be measured by different laws in the case of material or spiritual affinities. For as union of bodies arises from continuity of position, so in the agreement of wills there is a kind of contact between souls. If, therefore, a man who has severed himself from unity wishes to do anything different from that which had been impressed on him while in the state of unity, in this point he does sever himself, and is no longer a part of the united whole; but wherever he desires to conduct himself as is customary in the state of unity, in which he himself learned and received the lessons which he seeks to follow, in these points he remains a member, and is united to the corporate whole.

Chap. 2.—3. And so the Donatists in some matters are with us; in some matters have gone out from us. Accordingly, those things wherein they agree with us we do not forbid them to do; but in those things in which they differ from us, we earnestly encourage them to come and receive them from us, or return and recover them, as the case may be; and with whatever means we can, we lovingly busy ourselves, that they, freed from faults and corrected, may choose this course. We do not therefore say to them, "Abstain from giving baptism," but "Abstain from giving it in schism." Nor do we say to those whom we see them on the point of baptizing, "Do

1 Comp. v. 23, and iii. 16, note.

2 Felicianus, bishop of Musti, headed the revolt against Primianus, the successor of Parmenianus in the Carthaginian See. Listening to the complaint of the deacon Maximianus, who had been deposed by Primianus, a synod was convened in 393 at Cabarsussis, which ordained Maximianus as bishop of Carthage Hence the title Maximianistæ. Primianus, in 394, at the council of Bagai, was recognized by 310 bishops. The larger fraction, according to the Catholics, was subsequently forced into reunion. Prætextatus, bp. of Assuris, was also one of the leaders in this separation.

not receive the baptism," but "Do not receive it in schism." For if any one were compelled by urgent necessity, being unable to find a Catholic from whom to receive baptism, and so, while preserving Catholic peace in his heart, should receive from one without the pale of Catholic unity the sacrament which he was intending to receive within its pale, this man, should he forthwith depart this life, we deem to be none other than a Catholic. But if he should be delivered from the death of the body, on his restoring himself in bodily presence to that Catholic congregation from which in heart he had never departed, so far from blaming his conduct, we should praise it with the greatest truth and confidence; because he trusted that God was present to his heart, while he was striving to preserve unity, and was unwilling to depart this life without the sacrament of holy baptism, which he knew to be of God, and not of men, wherever he might find it. But if any one who has it in his power to receive baptism within the Catholic Church prefers, from some perversity of mind, to be baptized in schism, even if he afterwards bethinks himself to come to the Catholic Church, because he is assured that there that sacrament will profit him, which can indeed be received but cannot profit elsewhere, beyond all question he is perverse, and guilty of sin, and that the more flagrant in proportion as it was committed wilfully. For that he entertains no doubt that the sacrament is rightly received in the Church, is proved by his conviction that it is there that he must look for profit even from what he has received elsewhere.

CHAP. 3.—4. There are two propositions, moreover, which we affirm,—that baptism exists in the Catholic Church, and that in it alone can it be rightly received,—both of which the Donatists deny. Likewise there are two other propositions which we affirm,—that baptism exists among the Donatists, but that with them it is not rightly received,—of which two they strenuously confirm the former, that baptism exists with them; but they are unwilling to allow the latter, that in their Church it cannot be rightly received. Of these four propositions, three are peculiar to us; in one we both agree. For that baptism exists in the Catholic Church, that it is rightly received there, and that it is not rightly received among the Donatists, are assertions made only by ourselves; but that baptism exists also among the Donatists, is asserted by them and allowed by us. If any one, therefore, is desirous of being baptized, and is already convinced that he ought to choose our Church as a medium for Christian salvation, and that the baptism of Christ is only profitable in it, even when it has been received elsewhere, but yet wishes to be baptized in the schism of Donatus, because not they only, nor we only, but both parties alike say that baptism exists with them, let him pause and look to the other three points. For if he has made up his mind to follow us in the points which they deny, though he prefers what both of us acknowledge to what only we assert, it is enough for our purpose that he prefers what they do not affirm and we alone assert, to what they alone assert. That baptism exists in the Catholic Church, we assert and they deny. That it is rightly received in the Catholic Church, we assert and they deny. That it is not rightly received in the schism of Donatus, we assert and they deny. As, therefore, he is the more ready to believe what we alone assert should be believed, so let him be the more ready to do what we alone declare should be done. But let him believe more firmly, if he be so disposed, what both parties assert should be believed, than what we alone maintain. For he is inclined to believe more firmly that the baptism of Christ exists in the schism of Donatus, because that is acknowledged by both of us, than that it exists in the Catholic Church, an assertion made alone by the Catholics. But again, he is more ready to believe that the baptism of Christ exists also with us, as we alone assert, than that it does not exist with us, as they alone assert. For he has already determined and is fully convinced, that where we differ, our authority is to be preferred to theirs. So that he is more ready to believe what we alone assert, that baptism is rightly received with us, than that it is not rightly so received, since that rests only on their assertion. And, by the same rule, he is more ready to believe what we alone assert, that it is not rightly received with them, than as they alone assert, that it is rightly so received. He finds, therefore, that his confidence in being baptized among the Donatists is somewhat profitless, seeing that, though we both acknowledge that baptism exists with them, yet we do not both declare that it ought to be received from them. But he has made up his mind to cling rather to us in matters where we disagree. Let him therefore feel confidence in receiving baptism in our communion, where he is assured that it both exists and is rightly received; and let him not receive it in a communion, where those whose opinion he has determined to follow acknowledge indeed that it exists, but say that it cannot rightly be received. Nay, even if he should hold it to be a doubtful question, whether or no it is impossible for that to be rightly received among the Donatists which he is assured can rightly be received in the Catholic Church, he would commit a grievous sin, in matters concerning the salvation of his soul, in the mere fact of preferring uncertainty to certainty. At any rate, he must be quite sure that a man can be rightly baptized in the Catholic Church, from the mere fact that he has determined to come over to it, even if he be baptized elsewhere. But let him at least acknowledge it to be matter of uncertainty whether a man be not improperly baptized among the Donatists, when he finds this asserted by those whose opinion he is convinced should be preferred to theirs; and, preferring certainty to uncertainty, let him be baptized here, where he has good grounds for being assured that it is rightly done, in the fact that when he thought of doing it elsewhere, he had still determined that he ought afterwards to come over to this side.

Chap. 4.—5. Further, if any one fails to understand how it can be that we assert that the sacrament is not rightly conferred among the Donatists, while we confess that it exists among them, let him observe that we also deny that it exists rightly among them, just as they deny that it exists rightly among those who quit their communion. Let him also consider the analogy of the military mark, which, though it can both be retained, as by deserters, and, also be received by those who are not in the army, yet ought not to be either received or retained outside its ranks; and, at the same time, it is not changed or renewed when a man is enlisted or brought back to his service. However, we must distinguish between the case of those who unwittingly join the ranks of these heretics, under the impression that they are entering the true Church of Christ, and those who know that there is no other Catholic Church save that which, according to the promise, is spread abroad throughout the whole world, and extends even to the utmost limits of the earth; which, rising amid tares, and seeking rest in the future from the weariness of offenses, says in the Book of Psalms, "From the end of the earth I cried unto Thee, while my heart was in weariness: Thou didst exalt me on a rock."[1] But the rock was Christ, in whom the apostle says that we are now raised up, and set together in heavenly places, though not yet actually, but only in hope.[2] And so the psalm goes on to say, "Thou wast my guide, because Thou art become my hope, a tower of strength from the face of the enemy."[1] By means of His promises, which are like spears and javelins stored up in a strongly fortified place, the enemy is not only guarded against, but overthrown, as he clothes his wolves in sheep's clothing,[3] that they may say, "Lo, here is Christ, or there;"[4] and that they may separate many from the Catholic city which is built upon a hill, and bring them down to the isolation of their own snares, so as utterly to destroy them. And these men, knowing this, choose to receive the baptism of Christ without the limits of the communion of the unity of Christ's body, though they intend afterwards, with the sacrament which they have received elsewhere, to pass into that very communion. For they propose to receive Christ's baptism in antagonism to the Church of Christ, well knowing that it is so even on the very day on which they receive it. And if this is a sin, who is the man that will say, Grant that for a single day I may commit sin? For if he proposes to pass over to the Catholic Church, I would fain ask why. What other answer can he give, but that it is ill to belong to the party of Donatus, and not to the unity of the Catholic Church? Just so many days, then, as you commit this ill, of so many days' sin are you going to be guilty. And it may be said that there is greater sin in more days' commission of it, and less in fewer; but in no wise can it be said that no sin is committed at all. But what is the need of allowing this accursed wrong for a single day, or a single hour? For the man who wishes this license to be granted him, might as well ask of the Church, or of God Himself, that for a single day he should be permitted to apostatize. For there is no reason why he should fear to be an apostate for a day, if he does not shrink from being for that time a schismatic or a heretic.

Chap. 5.—6. I prefer, he says, to receive Christ's baptism where both parties agree that it exists. But those whom you intend to join say that it cannot be received there rightly; and those who say that it can be received there rightly are the party whom you mean to quit. What they say, therefore, whom you yourself consider of inferior authority, in opposition to what those say whom you yourself prefer, is, if not false, at any rate, to use a milder term, at least uncertain. I entreat you, therefore, to prefer what is true to what is false, or what is certain to what is uncertain. For it is not only those whom

[1] Ps. lxi. 2, 3. Cp. Hieron. and LXX. [2] Eph. ii. 6.

[3] Matt. vii. 15. [4] Matt. xxiv. 23.

you are going to join, but you yourself who are going to join them, that confess that what you want can be rightly received in that body which you mean to join when you have received it elsewhere. For if you had any doubts whether it could be rightly received there, you would also have doubts whether you ought to make the change. If, therefore, it is doubtful whether it be not sin to receive baptism from the party of Donatus, who can doubt but that it is certain sin not to prefer receiving it where it is certain that it is not sin? And those who are baptized there through ignorance, thinking that it is the true Church of Christ, are guilty of less sin in comparison than these, though even they are wounded by the impiety of schism; nor do they escape a grievous hurt, because others suffer even more. For when it is said to certain men, "It shall be more tolerable for the land of Sodom in the day of judgment than for you,"[1] it is not meant that the men of Sodom shall escape torment, but only that the others shall be even more grievously tormented.

7. And yet this point had once, perhaps, been involved in obscurity and doubt. But that which is a source of health to those who give heed and receive correction, is but an aggravation of the sin of those who, when they are no longer suffered to be ignorant, persist in their madness to their own destruction. For the condemnation of the party of Maximianus, and their restoration after they had been condemned, together with those whom they had sacrilegiously, to use the language of their own Council,[2] baptized in schism, settles the whole question in dispute, and removes all controversy. There is no point at issue between ourselves and those Donatists who hold communion with Primianus, which could give rise to any doubt that the baptism of Christ may not only be retained, but even conferred by those who are severed from the Church. For as they themselves are obliged to confess that those whom Felicianus baptized in schism received true baptism, inasmuch as they now acknowledge them as members of their own body, with no other baptism than that which they received in schism; so we say that that is Christ's baptism, even without the pale of Catholic communion, which they confer who are cut off from that communion, inasmuch as they had not lost it when they were cut off. And what they themselves think that they conferred on those persons whom Felicianus baptized in schism, when they admitted them to reconcilation with themselves, viz., not that they should receive that which they did not as yet possess, but that what they had received to no advantage in schism, and were already in possession of, should be of profit to them, this God really confers and bestows through the Catholic communion on those who come from any heresy or schism in which they received the baptism of Christ; viz., not that they should begin to receive the sacrament of baptism as not possessing it before, but that what they already possessed should now begin to profit them.

CHAP. 6.—8. Between us, then, and what we may call the genuine[3] Donatists, whose bishop is Primianus at Carthage, there is now no controversy on this point. For God willed that it should be ended by means of the followers of Maximianus, that they should be compelled by the precedent of his case to acknowledge what they would not allow at the persuasion of Christian charity. But this brings us to consider next, whether those men do not seem to have something to say for themselves, who refuse communion with the party of Primianus, contending that in their body there remains greater sincerity of Donatism, just in proportion to the paucity of their numbers. And even if these were only the party of Maximianus, we should not be justified in despising their salvation. How much more, then, are we bound to consider it, when we find that this same party of Donatus is split up into many most minute fractions, all which small sections of the body blame the one much larger portion which has Primianus for its head, because they receive the baptism of the followers of Maximianus; while each endeavors to maintain that it is the sole receptacle of true baptism, which exists nowhere else, neither in the whole of the world where the Catholic Church extends itself, nor in that larger main body of the Donatists, nor even in the other minute sections, but only in itself. Whereas, if all these fragments would listen not to the voice of man, but to the most unmistakable manifestation of the truth, and would be willing to curb the fiery temper of their own perversity, they would return from their own barrenness, not indeed to the main body of Donatus, a mere fragment of which they are a smaller fragment, but to the neverfailing fruitfulness of the root of the Catholic Church. For all of them who are not against us are for us; but when they gather not with us, they scatter abroad.

[1] Matt. xi. 24.
[2] The Council of 310 Donatist bishops, held at Bagai in Numidia, A.D. April 24, 394. Cp. *Contr. Crescon.* iii. 52, 56.
[3] *Quodam modo cardinales Donatistas.*

Chap. 7.—9. For, in the next place, that I may not seem to rest on mere human arguments,—since there is so much obscurity in this question, that in earlier ages of the Church, before the schism of Donatus, it has caused men of great weight, and even our fathers, the bishops, whose hearts were full of charity, so to dispute and doubt among themselves, saving always the peace of the Church, that the several statutes of their Councils in their different districts long varied from each other, till at length the most wholesome opinion was established, to the removal of all doubts, by a plenary Council of the whole world:[1]—I therefore bring forward from the gospel clear proofs, by which I propose, with God's help, to prove how rightly and truly in the sight of God it has been determined, that in the case of every schismatic and heretic, the wound which caused his separation should be cured by the medicine of the Church; but that what remained sound in him should rather be recognized with approbation, than wounded by condemnation. It is indeed true that the Lord says in the gospel, "He that is not with me is against me; and he that gathereth not with me scattereth abroad."[2] Yet when the disciples had brought word to Him that they had seen one casting out devils in His name, and had forbidden him, because he followed not them, He said, "Forbid him not: for he that is not against us is for us. For there is no man which shall do a miracle in my name, that can lightly speak evil of me."[3] If, indeed, there were nothing in this man requiring correction, then any one would be safe who, setting himself outside the communion of the Church, severing himself from all Christian brotherhood, should gather in Christ's name; and so there would be no truth in this, "He that is not with me is against me; and he that gathereth not with me scattereth abroad." But if he required correction in the point where the disciples in their ignorance were anxious to check him, why did our Lord, by saying, "Forbid him not," prevent this check from being given? And how can that be true which He then says, "He that is not against you is for you?" For in this point he was not against, but for them, when he was working miracles of healing in Christ's name. That both, therefore, should be true, as both are true,—both the declaration, that "he that is not with me is against me, and he that gathereth not with me scattereth abroad;" and also the injunction, "Forbid him not; for he that is not against you is for you,"—what must we understand, except that the man was to be confirmed in his veneration for that mighty Name, in respect of which he was not against the Church, but for it; and yet he was to be blamed for separating himself from the Church, whereby his gathering became a scattering; and if it should have so happened that he sought union with the Church, he should not have received what he already possessed, but be made to set right the points wherein he had gone astray?

Chap. 8.—10. Nor indeed were the prayers of the Gentile Cornelius unheard, nor did his alms lack acceptance; nay, he was found worthy that an angel should be sent to him, and that he should behold the messenger, through whom he might assuredly have learned everything that was necessary, without requiring that any man should come to him. But since all the good that he had in his prayers and alms could not benefit him unless he were incorporated in the Church by the bond of Christian brotherhood and peace, he was ordered to send to Peter, and through him learned Christ; and, being also baptized by his orders, he was joined by the tie of communion to the fellowship of Christians, to which before he was bound only by the likeness of good works.[4] And indeed it would have been most fatal to despise what he did not yet possess, vaunting himself in what he had. So too those who, by separating themselves from the society of their fellows, to the overthrow of charity, thus break the bond of unity, if they observe none of the things which they have received in that society, are separated in everything; and so any one whom they have joined to their society, if he afterwards wish to come over to the Church, ought to receive everything which he has not already received. But if they observe some of the same things, in respect of these they have not severed themselves; and so far they are still a part of the framework of the Church, while in all other respects they are cut off from it. Accordingly, any one whom they have associated with themselves is united to the Church in all those points in which they are not separated from it. And therefore, if he wish to come over to the Church, he is made sound in those points in which he was unsound and went astray; but where he was sound in union with the Church, he is not cured, but recognized,—lest in desiring to cure what is sound we should rather inflict a wound. Therefore those whom they baptize they heal from the wound of idolatry or unbelief; but they injure them more seriously with the wound of schism.

[1] See below, on ii. 9.
[2] Matt. xii. 30.
[3] Mark ix. 38, 39; Luke ix. 50.
[4] Acts x.

For idolaters among the people of the Lord were smitten with the sword;[1] but schismatics were swallowed up by the earth opening her mouth.[2] And the apostle says, "Though I have all faith, so that I could remove mountains, and have not charity, I am nothing."[3]

11. If any one is brought to the surgeon, afflicted with a grievous wound in some vital part of the body, and the surgeon says that unless it is cured it must cause death, the friends who brought him do not, I presume, act so foolishly as to count over to the surgeon all his sound limbs, and, drawing his attention to them, make answer to him, "Can it be that all these sound limbs are of no avail to save his life, and that one wounded limb is enough to cause his death?" They certainly do not say this, but they entrust him to the surgeon to be cured. Nor, again, because they so entrust him, do they ask the surgeon to cure the limbs that are sound as well; but they desire him to apply drugs with all care to the one part from which death is threatening the other sound parts too, with the certainty that it must come, unless the wound be healed. What will it then profit a man that he has sound faith, or perhaps only soundness in the sacrament of faith, when the soundness of his charity is done away with by the fatal wound of schism, so that by the overthrow of it the other points, which were in themselves sound, are brought into the infection of death? To prevent which, the mercy of God, through the unity of His holy Church, does not cease striving that they may come and be healed by the medicine of reconciliation, through the bond of peace. And let them not think that they are sound because we admit that they have something sound in them; nor let them think, on the other hand, that what is sound must needs be healed, because we show that in some parts there is a wound. So that in the soundness of the sacrament, because they are not against us, they are for us; but in the wound of schism, because they gather not with Christ, they scatter abroad. Let them not be exalted by what they have. Why do they pass the eyes of pride over those parts only which are sound? Let them condescend also to look humbly on their wound, and give heed not only to what they have, but also to what is wanting in them.

CHAP. 9.—12. Let them see how many things, and what important things, are of no avail, if a certain single thing be wanting, and let them see what that one thing is. And herein let them hear not my words, but those of the apostle: "Though I speak with the tongues of men and of angels, and have not charity, I am become as sounding brass, or a tinkling cymbal. And though I have the gift of prophecy, and understand all mysteries, and all knowledge; and though I have all faith, so that I could remove mountains, and have not charity, I am nothing.[4] What does it profit them, therefore, if they have both the voice of angels in the sacred mysteries, and the gift of prophecy, as had Caiaphas[5] and Saul,[6] that so they may be found prophesying, of whom Holy Scripture testifies that they were worthy of condemnation? If they not only know, but even possess the sacraments, as Simon Magus did;[7] if they have faith, as the devils confessed Christ (for we must not suppose that they did not believe when they said, "What have we to do with Thee, O Son of God? We know Thee who Thou art"[8]); if they distribute of themselves their own substance to the poor, as many do, not only in the Catholic Church, but in the different heretical bodies; if, under the pressure of any persecution, they give their bodies with us to be burned for the faith which they like us confess: yet because they do all these things apart from the Church, not "forbearing one another in love," nor "endeavoring to keep the unity of the spirit in the bond of peace,"[9] insomuch as they have not charity, they cannot attain to eternal salvation, even with all those good things which profit them not.

CHAP. 10.—13. But they think within themselves that they show very great subtlety in asking whether the baptism of Christ in the party of Donatus makes men sons or not; so that, if we allow that it does make them sons, they may assert that theirs is the Church, the mother which could give birth to sons in the baptism of Christ; and since the Church must be one, they may allege that ours is no Church. But if we say that it does not make them sons, "Why then," say they, "do you not cause those who pass from us to you to be born again in baptism, after they have been baptized with us, if they are not thereby born as yet?"

14. Just as though their party gained the power of generation in virtue of what constitutes its division, and not from what causes its union with the Church. For it is severed from the bond of peace and charity, but it is joined in one baptism. And so there is one Church which alone is called Catholic; and

[1] Ex. xxxii. [2] Num. xvi. [3] 1 Cor. xiii. 2.

[4] 1 Cor. xiii. 1, 2. [5] John xi. 51. [6] 1 Sam. xviii. 10. [7] Acts viii. 13. [8] Mark i. 24. [9] Eph. iv. 2, 3.

whenever it has anything of its own in these communions of different bodies which are separate from itself, it is most certainly in virtue of this which is its own in each of them that it, not they, has the power of generation. For neither is it their separation that generates, but what they have retained of the essence of the Church; and if they were to go on to abandon this, they would lose the power of generation. The generation, then, in each case proceeds from the Church, whose sacraments are retained, from which any such birth can alone in any case proceed,—although not all who receive its birth belong to its unity, which shall save those who persevere even to the end. Nor is it those only that do not belong to it who are openly guilty of the manifest sacrilege of schism, but also those who, being outwardly joined to its unity, are yet separated by a life of sin. For the Church had herself given birth to Simon Magus through the sacrament of baptism; and yet it was declared to him that he had no part in the inheritance of Christ.[1] Did he lack anything in respect of baptism, of the gospel, of the sacraments? But in that he wanted charity, he was born in vain; and perhaps it had been well for him that he had never been born at all. Was anything wanting to their birth to whom the apostle says, "I have fed you with milk, and not with meat, even as babes in Christ"? Yet he recalls them from the sacrilege of schism, into which they were rushing, because they were carnal: "I have fed you," he says, "with milk, and not with meat: for hitherto ye were not able to bear it, neither yet now are ye able. For ye are yet carnal: for whereas there is among you envying and strife, are ye not carnal, and walk as men? For while one saith, I am of Paul; and another, I am of Apollos; are ye not men?"[2] For of these he says above: "Now I beseech you, brethren, by the name of our Lord Jesus Christ, that ye all speak the same thing, and that there be no divisions among you; but that ye be perfectly joined together in the same mind, and in the same judgment. For it hath been declared unto me of you, my brethren, by them which are of the house of Chlöe, that there are contentions among you. Now this I say, that every one of you saith, I am of Paul, and I of Apollos, and I of Cephas, and I of Christ. Is Christ divided? was Paul crucified for you? or were ye baptized in the name of Paul?"[3] These, therefore, if they continued in the same perverse obstinacy, were doubtless indeed born, but yet would not belong by the bond of peace and unity to the very Church in respect of which they were born. Therefore she herself bears them in her own womb and in the womb of her handmaids, by virtue of the same sacraments, as though by virtue of the seed of her husband. For it is not without meaning that the apostle says that all these things were done by way of figure.[4] But those who are too proud, and are not joined to their lawful mother, are like Ishmael, of whom it is said, "Cast out this bondwoman and her son: for the son of the bondwoman shall not be heir with my son, even with Isaac."[5] But those who peacefully love the lawful wife of their father, whose sons they are by lawful descent, are like the sons of Jacob, born indeed of handmaids, but yet receiving the same inheritance.[6] But those who are born within the family, of the womb of the mother herself, and then neglect the grace they have received, are like Isaac's son Esau, who was rejected, God Himself bearing witness to it, and saying, "I loved Jacob, and I hated Esau;"[7] and that though they were twin-brethren, the offspring of the same womb.

Chap. 11.—15. They ask also, "Whether sins are remitted in baptism in the party of Donatus:" so that, if we say that they are remitted, they may answer, then the Holy Spirit is there; for when by the breathing of our Lord the Holy Spirit was given to the disciples, He then went on to say, "Baptize all nations in the name of the Father, and of the Son, and of the Holy Ghost."[8] Whose soever sins ye remit, they are remitted unto them; and whose soever sins ye retain, they are retained."[9] And if it is so, they say, then our communion is the Church of Christ; for the Holy Spirit does not work the remission of sins except in the Church. And if our communion is the Church of Christ, then your communion is not the Church of Christ. For that is one, wherever it is, of which it is said, "My dove is but one; she is the only one of her mother;"[10] nor can there be just so many churches as there are schisms. But if we should say that sins are not there remitted, then, say they, there is no true baptism there; and therefore ought you to baptize those whom you receive from us. And since you do not do this, you confess that you are not in the Church of Christ.

16. To these we reply, following the Scriptures, by asking them to answers themselves what they ask of us. For I beg them to tell

[1] Acts viii. 13, 21.
[2] 1 Cor. iii. 1–4.
[3] 1 Cor. i. 10–13.
[4] 1 Cor. x. 11. *In figura*; τυπικῶς; A. V., "for ensamples."
[5] Gen. xxi. 10.
[6] Gen. xxx. 3.
[7] Mal. i. 2, 3; Gen. xxv. 24.
[8] Matt. xxviii. 19.
[9] John xx. 23.
[10] Song of Sol. vi. 9.

us whether there is any remission of sins where there is not charity; for sins are the darkness of the soul. For we find St. John saying, "He that hateth his brother is still in darkness."[1] But none would create schisms, if they were not blinded by hatred of their brethren. If, therefore, we say that sins are not remitted there, how is he regenerate who is baptized among them? And what is regeneration in baptism, except the being renovated from the corruption of the old man? And how can he be so renovated whose past sins are not remitted? But if he be not regenerate, neither does he put on Christ; from which it seems to follow that he ought to be baptized again. For the apostle says, "For as many of you as have been baptized into Christ have put on Christ;"[2] and if he has not so put on Christ, neither should he be considered to have been baptized in Christ. Further, since we say that he has been baptized in Christ, we confess that he has put on Christ; and if we confess this, we confess that he is regenerate. And if this be so, how does St. John say, "He that hateth his brother remaineth still in darkness," if remission of his sins has already taken place? Can it be that schism does not involve hatred of one's brethren? Who will maintain this, when both the origin of, and perseverance in schism consists in nothing else save hatred of the brethren?

17. They think that they solve this question when they say: "There is then no remission of sins in schism, and therefore no creation of the new man by regeneration, and accordingly neither is there the baptism of Christ." But since we confess that the baptism of Christ exists in schism, we propose this question to them for solution: Was Simon Magus endued with the true baptism of Christ? They will answer, Yes; being compelled to do so by the authority of holy Scripture. I ask them whether they confess that he received remission of his sins. They will certainly acknowledge it. So I ask why Peter said to him that he had no part in the lot of the saints. Because, they say, he sinned afterwards, wishing to buy with money the gift of God, which he believed the apostles were able to sell.

CHAP. 12.—18. What if he approached baptism itself in deceit? were his sins remitted, or were they not? Let them choose which they will. Whichever they choose will answer our purpose. If they say they were remitted, how then shall "the Holy Spirit of discipline flee deceit,"[3] if in him who was full of deceit He worked remission of sins? If they say they were not remitted, I ask whether, if he should afterwards confess his sin with contrition of heart and true sorrow, it would be judged that he ought to be baptized again. And if it is mere madness to assert this, then let them confess that a man can be baptized with the true baptism of Christ, and that yet his heart, persisting in malice or sacrilege, may not allow remission of sins to be given; and so let them understand that men may be baptized in communions severed from the Church, in which Christ's baptism is given and received in the said celebration of the sacrament, but that it will only then be of avail for the remission of sins, when the recipient, being reconciled to the unity of the Church, is purged from the sacrilege of deceit, by which his sins were retained, and their remission prevented. For, as in the case of him who had approached the sacrament in deceit there is no second baptism, but he is purged by faithful discipline and truthful confession, which he could not be without baptism, so that what was given before becomes then powerful to work his salvation, when the former deceit is done away by the truthful confession; so also in the case of the man who, while an enemy to the peace and love of Christ, received in any heresy or schism the baptism of Christ, which the schismatics in question had not lost from among them, though by his sacrilege his sins were not remitted, yet, when he corrects his error, and comes over to the communion and unity of the Church, he ought not to be again baptized: because by his very reconciliation to the peace of the Church he receives this benefit, that the sacrament now begins in unity to be of avail for the remission of his sins, which could not so avail him as received in schism.

19. But if they should say that in the man who has approached the sacrament in deceit, his sins are indeed removed by the holy power of so great a sacrament at the moment when he received it, but return immediately in consequence of his deceit: so that the Holy Spirit has both been present with him at his baptism for the removal of his sins, and has also fled before his perseverance in deceit so that they should return: so that both declarations prove true,—both, "As many of you as have been baptized into Christ have put on Christ;" and also, "The holy spirit of discipline will flee deceit;"—that is to say, that both the holiness of baptism clothes him with Christ, and the sinfulness of deceit strips him of

---

[1] 1 John ii. 11.
[2] Gal. iii. 27.
[3] Wisd. i. 5.

Christ; like the case of a man who passes from darkness through light into darkness again, his eyes being always directed towards darkness, though the light cannot but penetrate them as he passes;—if they should say this, let them understand that this is also the case with those who are baptized without the pale of the Church, but yet with the baptism of the Church, which is holy in itself, wherever it may be; and which therefore belongs not to those who separate themselves, but to the body from which they are separated; while yet it avails even among them so far, that they pass through its light back to their own darkness, their sins, which in that moment had been dispelled by the holiness of baptism, returning immediately upon them, as though it were the darkness returning which the light had dispelled while they were passing through it.

20. For that sins which have been remitted do return upon a man, where there is no brotherly love, is most clearly taught by our Lord, in the case of the servant whom He found owing Him ten thousand talents, and to whom He yet forgave all at his entreaty. But when he refused to have pity on his fellow-servant who owed him a hundred pence, the Lord commanded him to pay what He had forgiven him. The time, then, at which pardon is received through baptism is as it were the time for rendering accounts, so that all the debts which are found to be due may be remitted. Yet it was not afterwards that the servant lent his fellow-servant the money, which he had so pitilessly exacted when the other was unable to pay it; but his fellow-servant already owed him the debt, when he himself, on rendering his accounts to his master, was excused a debt of so vast an amount. He had not first excused his fellow-servant, and so come to receive forgiveness from his Lord. This is proved by the words of the fellow-servant: "Have patience with me, and I will pay thee all." Otherwise he would have said, "You forgave me it before; why do you again demand it?" This is made more clear by the words of the Lord Himself. For He says, "But the same servant went out, and found one of his fellow-servants which was owing[1] him a hundred pence."[2] He does not say, "To whom he had already forgiven a debt of a hundred pence." Since then He says, "was owing him," it is clear that he had not forgiven him the debt. And indeed it would have been better, and more in accordance with the position of a man who was going to render an account of so great a debt, and expected forbearance from his lord, that he should first have forgiven his fellow-servant what was due to him, and so have come to render the account when there was such need for imploring the compassion of his lord. Yet the fact that he had not yet forgiven his fellow-servant, did not prevent his lord from forgiving him all his debts on the occasion of receiving his accounts. But what advantage was it to him, since they all immediately returned with redoubled force upon his head, in consequence of his persistent want of charity? So the grace of baptism is not prevented from giving remission of all sins, even if he to whom they are forgiven continues to cherish hatred towards his brother in his heart. For the guilt of yesterday is remitted, and all that was before it, nay, even the guilt of the very hour and moment previous to baptism, and during baptism itself. But then he immediately begins again to be responsible, not only for the days, hours, moments which ensue, but also for the past,—the guilt of all the sins which were remitted returning on him, as happens only too frequently in the Church.

Chap. 13.—21. For it often happens that a man has an enemy whom he hates most unjustly; although we are commanded to love even our unjust enemies, and to pray for them. But in some sudden danger of death he begins to be uneasy, and desires baptism, which he receives in such haste, that the emergency scarcely admits of the necessary formal examination of a few words, much less of a long conversation, so that this hatred should be driven from his heart, even supposing it to be known to the minister who baptizes him. Certainly cases of this sort are still found to occur not only with us, but also with them. What shall we say then? Are this man's sins forgiven or not? Let them choose just which alternative they prefer. For if they are forgiven, they immediately return: this is the teaching of the gospel, the authoritative announcement of truth. Whether, therefore, they are forgiven or not, medicine is necessary afterwards; and yet if the man lives, and learns that his fault stands in need of correction, and corrects it, he is not baptized anew, either with them or with us. So in the points in which schismatics and heretics neither entertain different opinions nor observe different practice from ourselves, we do not correct them when they join us, but rather commend what we find in them. For where they do not differ from us, they are not separated from us. But because these things do them no good so long as they are schismatics or heretics, on account of

---

1 *Debebat.* Hieron. debebat, LXX. ὤφειλεν.
2 Matt. xviii. 23-35.

other points in which they differ from us, not to mention the most grievous sin that is involved in separation itself, therefore, whether their sins remain in them, or return again immediately after remission, in either case we exhort them to come to the soundness of peace and Christian charity, not only that they may obtain something which they had not before, but also that what they had may begin to be of use to them.

CHAP. 14.—22. It is to no purpose, then, that they say to us, "If you acknowledge our baptism, what do we lack that should make you suppose that we ought to think seriously of joining your communion?" For we reply, We do not acknowledge any baptism of yours; for it is not the baptism of schismatics or heretics, but of God and of the Church, wheresoever it may be found, and whithersoever it may be transferred. But it is in no sense yours, except because you entertain false opinions, and do sacrilegious acts, and have impiously separated yourselves from the Church. For if everything else in your practice and opinions were true, and still you were to persist in this same separation, contrary to the bond of brotherly peace, contrary to the union of all the brethren, who have been manifest, according to the promise, in all the world; the particulars of whose history, and the secrets of whose hearts, you never could have known or considered in every case, so as to have a right to condemn them; who, moreover, cannot be liable to condemnation for submitting themselves to the judges of the Church rather than to one of the parties to the dispute,—in this one thing, at least, in such a case, you are deficient, in which he is deficient who lacks charity. Why should we go over our argument again? Look and see yourselves in the apostle, how much there is that you lack. For what does it matter to him who lacks charity, whether he be carried away outside the Church at once by some blast of temptation, or remain within the Lord's harvest, so as to be separated only at the final winnowing? And yet even such, if they have once been born in baptism, need not be born again.

CHAP. 15.—23. For it is the Church that gives birth to all, either within her pale, of her own womb; or beyond it, of the seed of her bridegroom,—(either of herself, or of her handmaid.[1]) But Esau, even though born of the lawful wife, was separated from the people of God because he quarrelled with his brother. And Asher, born indeed by the authority of a wife, but yet of a handmaid, was admitted to the land of promise on account of his brotherly good-will. Whence also it was not the being born of a handmaid, but his quarrelling with his brother, that stood in the way of Ishmael, to cause his separation from the people of God; and he received no benefit from the power of the wife, whose son he rather was, inasmuch as it was in virtue of her conjugal rights that he was both conceived in and born of the womb of the handmaid. Just as with the Donatists it is by the right of the Church, which exists in baptism, that whosoever is born receives his birth; but if they agree with their brethren, through the unity of peace they come to the land of promise, not to be again cast out from the bosom of their true mother, but to be acknowledged in the seed of their father; but if they persevere in discord, they will belong to the line of Ishmael. For Ishmael was first, and then Isaac; and Esau was the elder, Jacob the younger. Not that heresy gives birth before the Church, or that the Church herself gives birth first to those who are carnal or animal, and afterwards to those who are spiritual; but because, in the actual lot of our mortality, in which we are born of the seed of Adam, "that was not first which is spiritual, but that which is natural, and afterward that which is spiritual."[2] But from mere animal sensation, because "the natural man receiveth not the things of the Spirit of God,"[3] arise all dissensions and schisms. And the apostle says[4] that all who persevere in this animal sensation belong to the old covenant, that is, to the desire of earthly promises, which are indeed the type of the spiritual; but "the natural man receiveth not the things of the Spirit of God."[3]

24. At whatever time, therefore, men have begun to be of such a nature in this life, that, although they have partaken of such divine sacraments as were appointed for the dispensation under which they lived, they yet savor of carnal things, and hope for and desire carnal things from God, whether in this life or afterwards, they are yet carnal. But the Church, which is the people of God, is an ancient institution even in the pilgrimage of this life, having a carnal interest in some men, a spiritual interest in others. To the carnal belongs the old covenant, to the spiritual the new. But in the first days both were hidden, from Adam even to Moses. But by Moses the old covenant was made manifest, and in it was hidden the new covenant, because after

[1] The words in parenthesis are wanting in the MSS., and seem to have crept from the margin into the text.

[2] 1 Cor. xv. 46. [3] 1 Cor. ii. 14. [4] Gal. iv.

a secret fashion it was typified. But so soon as the Lord came in the flesh, the new covenant was revealed; yet, though the sacraments of the old covenant passed away; the dispositions peculiar to it did not pass away. For they still exist in those whom the apostle declares to be already born indeed by the sacrament of the new covenant, but yet incapable, as being natural, of receiving the things of the Spirit of God. For, as in the sacraments of the old covenant some persons were already spiritual, belonging secretly to the new covenant, which was then concealed, so now also in the sacrament of the new covenant, which has been by this time revealed, many live who are natural. And if they will not advance to receive the things of the Spirit of God, to which the discourse of the apostle urges them, they will still belong to the old covenant. But if they advance, even before they receive them, yet by their very advance and approach they belong to the new covenant; and if, before becoming spiritual, they are snatched away from this life, yet through the protection of the holiness of the sacrament they are reckoned in the land of the living, where the Lord is our hope and our portion. Nor can I find any truer interpretation of the scripture, "Thine eyes did see my substance, yet being imperfect"[1] considering what follows, "And in Thy book shall all be written."[2]

Chap. 16.—25. But the same mother which brought forth Abel, and Enoch, and Noah, and Abraham, brought forth also Moses and the prophets who succeeded him till the coming of our Lord; and the mother which gave birth to them gave birth also to our apostles and martyrs, and all good Christians. For all these that have appeared have been born indeed at different times, but are included in the society of our people; and it is as citizens of the same state that they have experienced the labors of this pilgrimage, and some of them are experiencing them, and others will experience them even to the end. Again, the mother who brought forth Cain, and Ham, and Ishmael, and Esau, brought forth also Dathan and others like him in the same people; and she who gave birth to them gave birth also to Judas the false apostle, and Simon Magus, and all the other false Christians who up to this time have persisted obstinately in their carnal affections, whether they have been mingled in the unity of the Church, or separated from it in open schism. But when men of this kind have the gospel preached to them, and receive the sacraments at the hand of those who are spiritual, it is as though Rebecca gave birth to them of her own womb, as she did to Esau; but when they are produced in the midst of the people of God through the instrumentality of those who preach the gospel not sincerely,[3] Sarah is indeed the mother, but through Hagar. So when good spiritual disciples are produced by the preaching or baptism of those who are carnal, Leah, indeed, or Rachel, gives birth to them in her right as wife, but from the womb of a handmaid. But when good and faithful disciples are born of those who are spiritual in the gospel, and either attain to the development of spiritual age, or do not cease to strive in that direction, or are only deterred from doing so by want of power, these are born like Isaac from the womb of Sarah, or Jacob from the womb of Rebecca, in the new life and the new covenant.

Chap. 17.—26. Therefore, whether they seem to abide within, or are openly outside, whatsoever is flesh is flesh, and what is chaff is chaff, whether they persevere in remaining in their barrenness on the threshing-floor, or, when temptation befalls them, are carried out as it were by the blast of some wind. And even that man is always severed from the unity of the Church which is without spot or wrinkle,[4] who associates with the congregation of the saints in carnal obstinacy. Yet we ought to despair of no man, whether he be one who shows himself to be of this nature within the pale of the Church, or whether he more openly opposes it from without. But the spiritual, or those who are steadily advancing with pious exertion towards this end, do not stray without the pale; since even when, by some perversity or necessity among men, they seem to be driven forth, they are more approved than if they had remained within, since they are in no degree roused to contend against the Church, but remain rooted in the strongest foundation of Christian charity on the solid rock of unity. For hereunto belongs what is said in the sacrifice of Abraham: "But the birds divided he not."[5]

Chap. 18.—27. On the question of bap-

[1] Ps. cxxxix. 16.

[2] Cf. Hieron. and LXX. A. V. "In Thy book were all my members written."

[3] Non caste; οὐχ ἁγνῶς. Phil. i. 16. Hieron. *non sincere.*

[4] In the *Retractations*, ii. 18, Augustin notes on this passage, that wherever he uses this quotation from the Epistle to the Ephesians, he means it to be understood of the progress of the Church towards this condition, and not of her success in its attainment; for at present the infirmities and ignorance of her members give ground enough for the whole Church joining daily in the petition, "Forgive us our debts."

[5] Gen. xv. 10.

tism, then, I think that I have argued at sufficient length; and since this is a most manifest schism which is called by the name of the Donatists, it only remains that on the subject of baptism we should believe with pious faith what the universal Church maintains, apart from the sacrilege of schism. And yet, if within the Church different men still held different opinions on the point, without meanwhile violating peace, then till some one clear and simple decree should have been passed by an universal Council, it would have been right for the charity which seeks for unity to throw a veil over the error of human infirmity, as it is written "For charity shall cover the multitude of sins."[1] For, seeing that its absence causes the presence of all other things to be of no avail, we may well suppose that in its presence there is found pardon for the absence of some missing things.

28. There are great proofs of this existing on the part of the blessed martyr Cyprian, in his letters,—to come at last to him of whose authority they carnally flatter themselves they are possessed, whilst by his love they are spiritually overthrown. For at that time, before the consent of the whole Church had declared authoritatively, by the decree of a plenary Council,[2] what practice should be followed in this matter, it seemed to him, in common with about eighty of his fellow-bishops of the African churches, that every man who had been baptized outside the communion of the Catholic Church should, on joining the Church, be baptized anew. And I take it, that the reason why the Lord did not reveal the error in this to a man of such eminence, was, that his pious humility and charity in guarding the peace and health of the Church might be made manifest, and might be noticed, so as to serve as an example of healing power, so to speak, not only to Christians of that age, but also to those who should come after. For when a bishop of so important a Church, himself a man of so great merit and virtue, endowed with such excellence of heart and power of eloquence, entertained an opinion about baptism different from that which was to be confirmed by a more diligent searching into the truth; though many of his colleagues held what was not yet made manifest by authority, but was sanctioned by the past custom of the Church, and afterwards embraced by the whole Catholic world; yet under these circumstances he did not sever himself, by refusal of communion, from the others who thought differently, and indeed never ceased to urge on the others that they should "forbear one another in love, endeavoring to keep the unity of the Spirit in the bond of peace."[3] For so, while the framework of the body remained whole, if any infirmity occurred in certain of its members, it might rather regain its health from their general soundness, than be deprived of the chance of any healing care by their death in severance from the body. And if he had severed himself, how many were there to follow! what a name was he likely to make for himself among men! how much more widely would the name of Cyprianist have spread than that of Donatist! But he was not a son of perdition, one of those of whom it is said, "Thou castedst them down while they were elevated;"[4] but he was the son of the peace of the Church, who in the clear illumination of his mind failed to see one thing, only that through him another thing might be more excellently seen. "And yet," says the apostle, "show I unto you a more excellent way: though I speak with the tongues of men and of angels, and have not charity, I am become as sounding brass, or a tinkling cymbal."[5] He had therefore imperfect insight into the hidden mystery of the sacrament. But if he had known the mysteries of all sacraments, without having charity, it would have been nothing. But as he, with imperfect insight into the mystery, was careful to preserve charity with all courage and humility and faith, he deserved to come to the crown of martyrdom; so that, if any cloud had crept over the clearness of his intellect from his infirmity as man, it might be dispelled by the glorious brightness of his blood. For it was not in vain that our Lord Jesus Christ, when He declared Himself to be the vine, and His disciples, as it were, the branches in the vine, gave command that those which bare no fruit should be cut off, and removed from the vine as useless branches.[6] But what is really fruit, save that new offspring, of which He further says, "A new commandment I give unto you, that ye love one another?"[7] This is that very charity, without which the rest profiteth nothing. The apostle also says: "But the fruit of the Spirit is love, joy, peace, long-suffering, gentleness, goodness, faith, meekness, temperance;"[8] which all begin with charity, and with the rest of the combination forms one unity in a kind of wondrous cluster.[9] Nor is it again in vain that our Lord added, "And every branch that beareth fruit, my Father purgeth it, that it may bring forth more fruit,"[10] but because those who are

[1] 1 Pet. iv. 8.
[2] See below, ii. 9.
[3] Eph. iv. 2, 3.
[4] Ps. lxxiii. 18; cp. Hieron.
[5] 1 Cor. xii. 31, xiii. 1.
[6] John xv. 1, 2.
[7] John xiii. 34.
[8] Gal. v. 22, 23.
[9] Botrum.
[10] John xv. 2.

strong in the fruit of charity may yet have something which requires purging, which the Husbandman will not leave untended. Whilst, then, that holy man entertained on the subject of baptism an opinion at variance with the true view, which was afterwards thoroughly examined and confirmed after most diligent consideration, his error was compensated by his remaining in catholic unity, and by the abundance of his charity; and finally it was cleared away by the pruning-hook of martyrdom.

Chap. 19.—29. But that I may not seem to be uttering these praises of the blessed martyr (which, indeed, are not his, but rather those of Him by whose grace he showed himself what he was), in order to escape the burden of proof, let us now bring forward from his letters the testimony by which the mouths of the Donatists may most of all be stopped. For they advance his authority before the unlearned, to show that in a manner they do well when they baptize afresh the faithful who come to them. Too wretched are they—and, unless they correct themselves, even by themselves are they utterly condemned—who choose in the example set them by so great a man to imitate just that fault, which only did not injure him, because he walked with constant steps even to the end in that from which they have strayed who "have not known the way of peace."[1] It is true that Christ's baptism is holy; and although it may exist among heretics or schismatics, yet it does not belong to the heresy or schism; and therefore even those who come from thence to the Catholic Church herself ought not to be baptized afresh. Yet to err on this point is one thing; it is another thing that those who are straying from the peace of the Church, and have fallen headlong into the pit of schism, should go on to decide that any who join them ought to be baptized again. For the former is a speck on the brightness of a holy soul which abundance of charity[2] would fain have covered; the latter is a stain in their nether foulness which the hatred of peace in their countenance ostentatiously brings to light. But the subject for our further consideration, relating to the authority of the blessed Cyprian, we will commence from a fresh beginning.

---

[1] Rom. iii. 17; from which it has been introduced into the Alexandrine MS. of the Septuagint at Ps. xiv. 3, cf. Hieron.; it is also found in the English Prayer-book version of the Psalms.

[2] *Charitatis ubera.*

BOOK II.

IN WHICH AUGUSTIN PROVES THAT IT IS TO NO PURPOSE THAT THE DONATISTS BRING FORWARD THE AUTHORITY OF CYPRIAN, BISHOP AND MARTYR, SINCE IT IS REALLY MORE OPPOSED TO THEM THAN TO THE CATHOLICS. FOR THAT HE HELD THAT THE VIEW OF HIS PREDECESSOR AGRIPPINUS, ON THE SUBJECT OF BAPTIZING HERETICS IN THE CATHOLIC CHURCH WHEN THEY JOIN ITS COMMUNION, SHOULD ONLY BE RECEIVED ON CONDITION THAT PEACE SHOULD BE MAINTAINED WITH THOSE WHO ENTERTAINED THE OPPOSITE VIEW, AND THAT THE UNITY OF THE CHURCH SHOULD NEVER BE BROKEN BY ANY KIND OF SCHISM.

CHAP. I.—1. How much the arguments make for us, that is, for catholic peace, which the party of Donatus profess to bring forward against us from the authority of the blessed Cyprian, and how much they prove against those who bring them forward, it is my intention, with the help of God, to show in the ensuing book. If, therefore, in the course of my argument, I am obliged to repeat what I have already said in other treatises (although I will do so as little as I can,) yet this ought not to be objected to by those who have already read them and agree with them; since it is not only right that those things which are necessary for instruction should be frequently instilled into men of dull intelligence, but even in the case of those who are endowed with larger understanding, it contributes very much both to make their learning easier and their powers of teaching readier, where the same points are handled and discussed in many various ways. For I know how much it discourages a reader, when he comes upon any knotty question in the book which he has in hand, to find himself presently referred for its solution to another which he happens not to have. Wherefore, if I am compelled, by the urgency of the present questions, to repeat what I have already said in other books, I would seek forgiveness from those who know those books already, that those who are ignorant may have their difficulties removed; for it is better to give to one who has already, than to abstain from satisfying any one who is in want.

2. What, then, do they venture to say, when their mouth is closed[1] by the force of truth, with which they will not agree? "Cyprian," say they, "whose great merits and vast learning we all know, decreed in a Council,[2] with many of his fellow-bishops contributing their several opinions, that all heretics and schismatics, that is, all who are severed from the communion of the one Church, are without baptism; and therefore, whosoever has joined the communion of the Church after being baptized by them must be baptized in the Church." The authority of Cyprian does not alarm me, because I am reassured by his humility. We know, indeed, the great merit of the bishop and martyr Cyprian; but is it in any way greater than that of the apostle and martyr Peter, of whom the said Cyprian speaks as follows in his epistle to Quintus? "For neither did Peter, whom the Lord chose first, and on whom He built His Church,[3] when Paul afterwards disputed with him about circumcision, claim or assume anything insolently and arrogantly to himself, so as to say that he held the primacy, and should rather be obeyed of those who were late and newly come. Nor did he despise Paul because he had before been a persecutor of the Church, but he admitted the counsel of truth, and readily assented to the legitimate grounds which Paul maintained; giving us thereby a pattern of concord and patience,

---

1 *Præfocantur.*

2 The Council of Carthage, A.D. 256, in which eighty-seven African bishops declared in favor of rebaptizing heretics. The opinions of the bishops are quoted and answered by Augustin, one by one, in Books vi. and vii.

3 Matt. xvi. 18.

that we should not pertinaciously love our own opinions, but should rather account as our own any true and rightful suggestions of our brethren and colleagues for the common health and weal."[1] Here is a passage in which Cyprian records what we also learn in holy Scripture, that the Apostle Peter, in whom the primacy of the apostles shines with such exceeding grace, was corrected by the later Apostle Paul, when he adopted a custom in the matter of circumcision at variance with the demands of truth. If it was therefore possible for Peter in some point to walk not uprightly according to the truth of the gospel, so as to compel the Gentiles to judaize, as Paul writes in that epistle in which he calls God to witness that he does not lie; for he says, "Now the things which I write unto you, behold, before God, I lie not;"[2] and, after this sacred and awful calling of God to witness, he told the whole tale, saying in the course of it, "But when I saw that they walked not uprightly, according to the truth of the gospel, I said unto Peter before them all, If thou, being a Jew, livest after the manner of the Gentiles, and not as do the Jews, why compellest thou the Gentiles to live as do the Jews?"[3]—if Peter, I say, could compel the Gentiles to live after the manner of the Jews, contrary to the rule of truth which the Church afterwards held, why might not Cyprian, in opposition to the rule of faith which the whole Church afterwards held, compel heretics and schismatics to be baptized afresh? I suppose that there is no slight to Cyprian in comparing him with Peter in respect to his crown of martyrdom; rather I ought to be afraid lest I am showing disrespect towards Peter. For who can be ignorant that the primacy of his apostleship is to be preferred to any episcopate whatever? But, granting the difference in the dignity of their sees, yet they have the same glory in their martyrdom. And whether it may be the case that the hearts of those who confess and die for the true faith in the unity of charity take precedence of each other in different points, the Lord Himself will know, by the hidden and wondrous dispensation of whose grace the thief hanging on the cross once for all confesses Him, and is sent on the selfsame day to paradise,[4] while Peter, the follower of our Lord, denies Him thrice, and has his crown postponed:[5] for us it were rash to form a judgment from the evidence. But if any one were now found compelling a man to be circumcised after the Jewish fashion, as a necessary preliminary for baptism, this would meet with much more general repudiation by mankind, than if a man should be compelled to be baptized again. Wherefore, if Peter, on doing this, is corrected by his later colleague Paul, and is yet preserved by the bond of peace and unity till he is promoted to martyrdom, how much more readily and constantly should we prefer, either to the authority of a single bishop, or to the Council of a single province, the rule that has been established by the statutes of the universal Church? For this same Cyprian, in urging his view of the question, was still anxious to remain in the unity of peace even with those who differed from him on this point, as is shown by his own opening address at the beginning of the very Council which is quoted by the Donatists. For it is as follows:

Chap. 2.—3. "When, on the calends of September, very many bishops from the provinces of Africa,[6] Numidia, and Mauritania, with their presbyters and deacons, had met together at Carthage, a great part of the laity also being present; and when the letter addressed by Jubaianus[7] to Cyprian, as also the answer of Cyprian to Jubaianus, on the subject of baptizing heretics, had been read, Cyprian said: 'Ye have heard, most beloved colleagues, what Jubaianus, our fellow-bishop, has written to me, consulting my moderate ability concerning the unlawful and profane baptism of heretics, and what answer I gave him,—giving a judgment which we have once and again and often given, that heretics coming to the Church ought to be baptized, and sanctified with the baptism of the Church. Another letter of Jubaianus has likewise been read to you, in which, agreeably to his sincere and religious devotion, in answer to our epistle, he not only expressed his assent, but returned thanks also, acknowledging that he had received instruction. It remains that we severally declare our opinion on this subject, judging no one, nor depriving any one of the right of communion if he differ from us. For no one of us sets himself up as a bishop of bishops, or, by tyrannical terror, forces his colleagues to a necessity of obeying, inasmuch as every bishop, in the free use of his liberty and power, has the right of forming his own judgment, and can no more be judged by another than he can himself judge another. But we must all await the judgment of our Lord Jesus Christ, who alone has the power both of setting us in the government of His Church, and of judging of our acts therein.'"

[1] Cypr. *Ep.* lxxi. [2] Gal. i. 20. [3] Gal. ii. 14. [4] Luke xxiii. 40-43. [5] Matt. xxvi. 69-75.

[6] That is, the proconsular province of Africa, or Africa Zeugitana, answering to the northern part of the territory of Tunis.

[7] The letters of Jubaianus, Mauritanian bishop, are not extant.

CHAP. 3.—4. Now let the proud and swelling necks of the heretics raise themselves, if they dare, against the holy humility of this address. Ye mad Donatists, whom we desire earnestly to return to the peace and unity of the holy Church, that ye may receive health therein, what have ye to say in answer to this? You are wont, indeed, to bring up against us the letters of Cyprian, his opinion, his Council; why do ye claim the authority of Cyprian for your schism, and reject his example when it makes for the peace of the Church? But who can fail to be aware that the sacred canon of Scripture, both of the Old and New Testament, is confined within its own limits, and that it stands so absolutely in a superior position to all later letters of the bishops, that about it we can hold no manner of doubt or disputation whether what is confessedly contained in it is right and true; but that all the letters of bishops which have been written, or are being written, since the closing of the canon, are liable to be refuted if there be anything contained in them which strays from the truth, either by the discourse of some one who happens to be wiser in the matter than themselves, or by the weightier authority and more learned experience of other bishops, or by the authority of Councils; and further, that the Councils themselves, which are held in the several districts and provinces, must yield, beyond all possibility of doubt, to the authority of plenary Councils which are formed for the whole Christian world; and that even of the plenary Councils, the earlier are often corrected by those which follow them, when, by some actual experiment, things are brought to light which were before concealed, and that is known which previously lay hid, and this without any whirlwind of sacrilegious pride, without any puffing of the neck through arrogance, without any strife of envious hatred, simply with holy humility, catholic peace, and Christian charity?

CHAP. 4.—5. Wherefore the holy Cyprian, whose dignity is only increased by his humility, who so loved the pattern set by Peter as to use the words, "Giving us thereby a pattern of concord and patience, that we should not pertinaciously love our own opinions, but should rather account as our own any true and rightful suggestions of our brethren and colleagues, for the common health and weal,"[1] —he, I say, abundantly shows that he was most willing to correct his own opinion, if any one should prove to him that it is as certain that the baptism of Christ can be given by those who have strayed from the fold, as that it could not be lost when they strayed; on which subject we have already said much. Nor should we ourselves venture to assert anything of the kind, were we not supported by the unanimous authority of the whole Church, to which he himself would unquestionably have yielded, if at that time the truth of this question had been placed beyond dispute by the investigation and decree of a plenary Council. For if he quotes Peter as an example for his allowing himself quietly and peacefully to be corrected by one junior colleague, how much more readily would he himself, with the Council of his province, have yielded to the authority of the whole world, when the truth had been thus brought to light? For, indeed, so holy and peaceful a soul would have been most ready to assent to the arguments of any single person who could prove to him the truth; and perhaps he even did so,[2] though we have no knowledge of the fact. For it was neither possible that all the proceedings which took place between the bishops at that time should have been committed to writing, nor are we acquainted with all that was so committed. For how could a matter which was involved in such mists of disputation even have been brought to the full illumination and authoritative decision of a plenary Council, had it not first been known to be discussed for some considerable time in the various districts of the world, with many discussions and comparisons of the views of the bishop on every side? But this is one effect of the soundness of peace, that when any doubtful points are long under investigation, and when, on account of the difficulty of arriving at the truth, they produce difference of opinion in the course of brotherly disputation, till men at last arrive at the unalloyed truth; yet the bond of unity remains, lest in the part that is cut away there should be found the incurable wound of deadly error.

CHAP. 5.—6. And so it is that often something is imperfectly revealed to the more learned, that their patient and humble charity, from which proceeds the greater fruit, may be proved, either in the way in which they preserve unity, when they hold different opinions on matters of comparative obscurity, or in the temper with which they receive the truth, when they learn that it has been declared to be contrary to what they thought. And of these two we have a manifestation in the blessed Cyprian of the one, viz., of the

[1] See above, c. i. 2.

[2] Bede asserts that this was the case, Book VIII. qu. 5.

way in which he preserved unity with those from whom he differed in opinion. For he says, 'Judging no one nor depriving any one of the right of communion if he differ from us."[1] And the other, viz., in what temper he could receive the truth when found to be different from what he thought it, though his letters are silent on the point, is yet proclaimed by his merits. If there is no letter extant to prove it, it is witnessed by his crown of martyrdom; if the Council of bishops declare it not, it is declared by the host of angels. For it is no small proof of a most peaceful soul, that he won the crown of martyrdom in that unity from which he would not separate, even though he differed from it. For we are but men; and it is therefore a temptation incident to men that we should hold views at variance with the truth on any point. But to come through too great love for our own opinion, or through jealousy of our betters, even to the sacrilege of dividing the communion of the Church, and of founding heresy or schism, is a presumption worthy of the devil But never in any point to entertain an opinion at variance with the truth is perfection found only in the angels. Since then we are men, yet forasmuch as in hope we are angels, whose equals we shall be in the resurrection,[2] at any rate, so long as we are wanting in the perfection of angels, let us at least be without the presumption of the devil. Accordingly the apostle says, "There hath no temptation taken you but such as is common to man."[3] It is therefore part of man's nature to be sometimes wrong. Wherefore he says in another place, "Let us therefore, as many as be perfect, be thus minded: and if in anything ye be otherwise minded, God shall reveal even this unto you."[4] But to whom does He reveal it when it is His will (be it in this life or in the life to come), save to those who walk in the way of peace, and stray not aside into any schism? Not to such as those who have not known the way of peace,[5] or for some other cause have broken the bond of unity. And so, when the apostle said, "And if in anything ye be otherwise minded, God shall reveal even this unto you," lest they should think that besides the way of peace their own wrong views might be revealed to them, he immediately added, "Nevertheless, whereto we have already attained, let us walk by the same rule."[6] And Cyprian, walking by this rule, by the most persistent tolerance, not simply by the shedding of his blood, but because it was shed in unity (for if he gave his body to be burned, and had not charity, it would profit him nothing[7]), came by the confession of martyrdom to the light of the angels, and if not before, at least then, acknowledged the revelation of the truth on that point on which, while yet in error, he did not prefer the maintenance of a wrong opinion to the bond of unity.

Chap. 6.—7. What then, ye Donatists, what have ye to say to this? If our opinion about baptism is true, yet all who thought differently in the time of Cyprian were not cut off from the unity of the Church, till God revealed to them the truth of the point on which they were in error, why then have ye by your sacrilegious separation broken the bond of peace? But if yours is the true opinion about baptism, Cyprian and the others, in conjunction with whom ye set forth that he held such a Council, remained in unity with those who thought otherwise; why, therefore, have ye broken the bond of peace? Choose which alternative ye will, ye are compelled to pronounce an opinion against your schism. Answer me, wherefore have ye separated yourselves? Wherefore have ye erected an altar in opposition to the whole world? Wherefore do ye not communicate with the Churches to which apostolic epistles have been sent, which you yourselves read and acknowledge, in accordance with whose tenor you say that you order your lives? Answer me, wherefore have ye separated yourselves? I suppose in order that ye might not perish by communion with wicked men. How then was it that Cyprian, and so many of his colleagues, did not perish? For though they believed that heretics and schismatics did not possess baptism, yet they chose rather to hold communion with them when they had been received into the Church without baptism, although they believed that their flagrant and sacrilegious sins were yet upon their heads, than to be separated from the unity of the Church, according to the words of Cyprian, "Judging no one, nor depriving any one of the right of communion if he differ from us."

8. If, therefore, by such communion with the wicked the just cannot but perish, the Church had already perished in the time of Cyprian. Whence then sprang the origin of Donatus? where was he taught, where was he baptized, where was he ordained, since the Church had been already destroyed by the contagion of communion with the wicked? But if the Church still existed, the wicked could do no harm to the good in one com-

[1] See above, c. ii. 3. [2] Matt. xxii. 30. [3] 1 Cor x. 13.
[4] Phil. iii. 15. [5] Rom. iii. 17; see on i. 19, 29
[6] Phil. iii. 16.

[7] 1 Cor. xiii. 3.

munion with them. Wherefore did ye separate yourselves? Behold, I see in unity Cyprian and others, his colleagues, who, on holding a council, decided that those who have been baptized without the communion of the Church have no true baptism, and that therefore it must be given them when they join the Church. But again, behold I see in the same unity that certain men think differently in this matter, and that, recognizing in those who come from heretics and schismatics the baptism of Christ, they do not venture to baptize them afresh. All of these catholic unity embraces in her motherly breast, bearing each other's burdens by turns, and endeavoring to keep the unity of the Spirit in the bond of peace,[1] till God should reveal to one or other of them any error in their views. If the one party held the truth, were they infected by the others, or no? If the others held the truth, were they infected by the first, or no? Choose which ye will. If there was contamination, the Church even then ceased to exist; answer me, therefore, whence came ye forth hither? But if the Church remained, the good are in no wise contaminated by the bad in such communion; answer me, therefore, why did ye break the bond?

9. Or is it perhaps that schismatics, when received without baptism, bring no infection, but that it is brought by those who deliver up the sacred books?[2] For that there were *traditors* of your number is proved by the clearest testimony of history. And if you had then brought true evidence against those whom you were accusing, you would have proved your cause before the unity of the whole world, so that you would have been retained whilst they were shut out. And if you endeavored to do this, and did not succeed, the world is not to blame, which trusted the judges of the Church rather than the beaten parties in the suit; whilst, if you would not urge your suit, the world again is not to blame, which could not condemn men without their cause being heard. Why, then, did you separate yourselves from the innocent? You cannot defend the sacrilege of your schism. But this I pass over. But so much I say, that if the *traditors* could have defiled you, who were not convicted by you, and by whom, on the contrary, you were beaten, much more could the sacrilege of schismatics and heretics, received into the Church, as you maintain, without baptism, have defiled Cyprian. Yet he did not separate himself. And inasmuch as the Church continued to exist, it is clear that it could not be defiled. Wherefore, then, did you separate yourselves, I do not say from the innocent, as the facts proved them, but from the *traditors*, as they were never proved to be? Are the sins of *traditors*, as I began to say, heavier than those of schismatics? Let us not bring in deceitful balances, to which we may hang what weights we will and how we will, saying to suit ourselves, "This is heavy and this is light;" but let us bring forward the sacred balance out of holy Scripture, as out of the Lord's treasure-house, and let us weigh them by it, to see which is the heavier; or rather, let us not weigh them for ourselves, but read the weights as declared by the Lord. At the time when the Lord showed, by the example of recent punishment, that there was need to guard against the sins of olden days, and an idol was made and worshipped, and the prophetic book was burned by the wrath of a scoffing king, and schism was attempted, the idolatry was punished with the sword,[3] the burning of the book by slaughter in war and captivity in a foreign land,[4] schism by the earth opening, and swallowing up alive the leaders of the schism while the rest were consumed with fire from heaven.[5] Who will now doubt that that was the worse crime which received the heavier punishment? If men coming from such sacrilegious company, without baptism, as you maintain, could not defile Cyprian, how could those defile you who were not convicted but supposed betrayers of the sacred books?[6] For if they had not only given up the books to be burned, but had actually burned them with their own hands, they would have been guilty of a less sin than if they had committed schism; for schism is visited with the heavier, the other with the lighter punishment, not at man's discretion, but by the judgment of God.

CHAP. 7.—10. Wherefore, then, have ye severed yourselves? If there is any sense left in you, you must surely see that you can find no possible answer to these arguments. "We are not left," they say, "so utterly without resource, but that we can still answer, It is our will. 'Who art thou that judgest another man's servant? to his own master he standeth or falleth.'"[7] They do not understand that this was said to men who were wishing to judge, not of open facts, but of the hearts of other men. For how does the apostle himself come to say so much about the sins of schisms and heresies? Or how comes that verse in the Psalms, "If of a truth ye love justice, judge uprightly, O ye sons of

---

[1] Eph. iv. 3

[2] *Traditores sanctorum librorum.*

[3] Ex. xxxii.

[4] Jer. xxxvi.

[5] Num. xvi.

[6] *Non convicti sed conficti traditores.*

[7] Rom. xiv. 4.

men?"[1] But why does the Lord Himself say, "Judge not according to the appearance, but judge righteous judgment,"[2] if we may not judge any man? Lastly, why, in the case of those *traditors*, whom they have judged unrighteously, have they themselves ventured to pass any judgments at all on another man's servants? To their own master they were standing or falling. Or why, in the case of the recent followers of Maximianus, have they not hesitated to bring forward the judgment delivered with the infallible voice, as they aver, of a plenary Council, in such terms as to compare them with those first schismatics whom the earth swallowed up alive? And yet some of them, as they cannot deny, they either condemned though innocent, or received back again in their guilt. But when a truth is urged which they cannot gainsay, they mutter a truly wholesome murmuring: "It is our will: 'Who art thou that judgest another man's servant? to his own master he standeth or falleth.'" But when a weak sheep is espied in the desert, and the pastor who should reclaim it to the fold is nowhere to be seen, then there is setting of teeth, and breaking of the weak neck: "Thou wouldst be a good man, wert thou not a *traditor*. Consult the welfare of thy soul; be a Christian." What unconscionable madness! When it is said to a Christian, "Be a Christian," what other lesson is taught, save a denial that he is a Christian? Was it not the same lesson which those persecutors of the Christians wished to teach, by resisting whom the crown of martyrdom was gained? Or must we even look on crime as lighter when committed with threatening of the sword than with treachery of the tongue?

11. Answer me this, ye ravening wolves, who, seeking to be clad in sheep's clothing,[3] think that the letters of the blessed Cyprian are in your favor. Did the sacrilege of schismatics defile Cyprian, or did it not? If it did, the Church perished from that instant, and there remained no source from which ye might spring. If it did not, then by what offense on the part of others can the guiltless possibly be defiled, if the sacrilege of schism cannot defile them? Wherefore, then, have ye severed yourselves? Wherefore, while shunning the lighter offenses, which are inventions of your own, have ye committed the heaviest offense of all, the sacrilege of schism? Will ye now perchance confess that those men were no longer schismatics or heretics who had been baptized without the communion of the Church, or in some heresy or schism, because by coming over to the Church, and renouncing their former errors, they had ceased to be what formerly they were? How then was it, that though they were not baptized, their sins remained not on their heads? Was it that the baptism was Christ's, but that it could not profit them without the communion of the Church; yet when they came over, and, renouncing their past error, were received into the communion of the Church by the laying on of hands, then, being now rooted and founded in charity, without which all other things are profitless, they began to receive profit for the remission of sins and the sanctification of their lives from that sacrament, which, while without the pale of the Church, they possessed in vain?

12. Cease, then, to bring forward against us the authority of Cyprian in favor of repeating baptism, but cling with us to the example of Cyprian for the preservation of unity. For this question of baptism had not been as yet completely worked out, but yet the Church observed the most wholesome custom of correcting what was wrong, not repeating what was already given, even in the case of schismatics and heretics: she healed the wounded part, but did not meddle with what was whole. And this custom, coming, I suppose, from apostolical tradition (like many other things which are held to have been handed down under their actual sanction, because they are preserved throughout the whole Church, though they are not found either in their letters, or in the Councils of their successors), —this most wholesome custom, I say, according to the holy Cyprian, began to be what is called amended by his predecessor Agrippinus.[4] But, according to the teaching which springs from a more careful investigation into the truth, which, after great doubt and fluctuation, was brought at last to the decision of a plenary Council, we ought to believe that it rather began to be corrupted than to receive correction at the hands of Agrippinus. Accordingly, when so great a question forced itself upon him, and it was difficult to decide the point, whether remission of sins and man's spiritual regeneration could take place among heretics or schismatics, and the authority of Agrippinus was there to guide him, with that of some few men who shared in his misapprehension of this question, having pre-

[1] Ps. lviii. 1. Aug.: *Si vere justitiam diligitis, recte judicate filii hominum.* Cp. Hieron.: *Si vere utique justitiam loquimini, recta judicate filii hominum.*

[2] John vii. 24.

[3] Matt. vii. 15.

[4] Agrippinus was probably the second (some place him still earlier) bishop before Cyprian. He convened the council of 70 (disputed date), who were the first to take action in favor of rebaptism. Cp. Cypr. Ep. lxxi. 4, *bonæ memoriæ vir.* Cp. lxxiii. 3.

ferred attempting something new to maintaining a custom which they did not understand how to defend; under these circumstances, considerations of probability forced themselves into the eyes of his soul, and barred the way to the thorough investigation of the truth.

CHAP. 8.—13. Nor do I think that the blessed Cyprian had any other motive in the free expression and earlier utterance of what he thought in opposition to the custom of the Church, save that he should thankfully receive any one that could be found with a fuller revelation of the truth, and that he should show forth a pattern for imitation, not only of diligence in teaching, but also of modesty in learning; but that, if no one should be found to bring forward any argument by which those considerations of probability should be refuted, then he should abide by his opinion, with the full consciousness that he had neither concealed what he conceived to be the truth, nor violated the unity which he loved. For so he understood the words of the apostle: "Let the prophets speak two or three, and let the other judge. If anything be revealed to another that sitteth by, let the first hold his peace."[1] "In which passage he has taught and shown, that many things are revealed to individuals for the better, and that we ought not each to strive pertinaciously for what he has once imbibed and held, but if anything has appeared better and more useful, he should willingly embrace it."[2] At any rate, in these words he not only advised those to agree with him who saw no better course, but also exhorted any who could to bring forward arguments by which the maintenance of the former custom might rather be established; that if they should be of such a nature as not to admit of refutation, he might show in his own person with what sincerity he said "that we ought not each to strive pertinaciously for what he has once imbibed and held, but that, if anything has appeared better and more useful, he should willingly embrace it."[2] But inasmuch as none appeared, except such as simply urged the custom against him, and the arguments which they produced in its favor were not of a kind to bring conviction to a soul like his, this mighty reasoner was not content to give up his opinions, which, though they were not true, as he was himself unable to see, were at any rate not confuted, in favor of a custom which had truth on its side, but had not yet been confirmed. And yet, had not his predecessor Agrippinus, and some of his fellow-bishops throughout Africa, first tempted him to desert this custom, even by the decision of a Council, he certainly would not have dared to argue against it. But, amid the perplexities of so obscure a question, and seeing everywhere around him a strong universal custom, he would rather have put restraint upon himself by prayer and stretching forth his mind towards God, so as to have perceived or taught that for truth which was afterwards decided by a plenary Council. But when he had found relief amid his weariness in the authority of the former Council[3] which was held by Agrippinus, he preferred maintaining what was in a manner the discovery of his predecessors, to expending further toil in investigation. For, at the end of his letter to Quintus, he thus shows how he has sought repose, if one may use the expression, for his weariness, in what might be termed the resting-place of authority.[4]

CHAP. 9.—14. "This, moreover," says he, "Agrippinus, a man of excellent memory, with the rest, bishops with him, who at that time governed the Church of the Lord in the province of Africa and Numidia, did establish and, after the investigation of a mutual Council had weighed it, confirm; whose sentence, being both religious and legitimate and salutary in accordance with the Catholic faith and Church, we also have followed."[5] By this witness he gives sufficient proof how much more ready he would have been to bear his testimony, had any Council been held to discuss this matter which either embraced the whole Church, or at least represented our brethren beyond the sea.[6] But such a Council had not yet been held, because the whole world was bound together by the powerful bond of custom; and this was deemed sufficient to oppose to those who wished to introduce what was new, because they could not comprehend the truth. Afterwards, however, while the question became matter for discussion and investigation amongst many on either side, the new practice was not only invented, but even submitted to the authority and power of a plenary Council,—after the martyrdom of Cyprian, it is true, but before we were born.[7] But that this was indeed the

---

1 1 Cor. xiv. 29, 30.

2 Cypr. *Ep.* lxxi.

3 The former Council of Carthage was held by Agrippinus early in the third century, the ordinary date given being 215-7 A.D.; others 186-7.

4 *Tanquam lectulo auctoritatis.*

5 Cypr. *Ep.* lxxi. 4.

6 *Transmarinum vel universale Concilium.*

7 The plenary Council, on whose authority Augustin relies in many places in this work, was either that of Arles, in 314 A.D., or of Nicæa, in 325 A.D., both of them being before his birth, in 354 A.D. He quotes the decision of the same council, *contra Parmenianum*, ii. 13, 30; *de Hæresibus*, 69; *Ep.* xliii. 7, 19. *Contra Parmenianum*, iii. 4, 21: "They condemned," he says, "some few in Africa, by whom they were in turn vanquished by the judgment of the whole world;" and he adds, that "the Catholics

custom of the Church, which afterwards was confirmed by a plenary Council, in which the truth was brought to light, and many difficulties cleared away, is plain enough from the words of the blessed Cyprian himself in that same letter to Jubaianus, which was quoted as being read in the Council.[1] For he says, "But some one asks, What then will be done in the case of those who, coming out of heresy to the Church, have already been admitted without baptism?" where certainly he shows plainly enough what was usually done, though he would have wished it otherwise; and in the very fact of his quoting the Council of Agrippinus, he clearly proves that the custom of the Church was different. Nor indeed was it requisite that he should seek to establish the practice by this Council, if it was already sanctioned by custom; and in the Council itself some of the speakers expressly declare, in giving their opinion, that they went against the custom of the Church in deciding what they thought was right. Wherefore let the Donatists consider this one point, which surely none can fail to see, that if the authority of Cyprian is to be followed, it is to be followed rather in maintaining unity than in altering the custom of the Church; but if respect is paid to his Council, it must at any rate yield place to the later Council of the universal Church, of which he rejoiced to be a member, often warning his associates that they should all follow his example in upholding the coherence of the whole body. For both later Councils are preferred among later generations to those of earlier date; and the whole is always, with good reason, looked upon as superior to the parts.

Chap. 10.—15. But what attitude do they assume, when it is shown that the holy Cyprian, though he did not himself admit as members of the Church those who had been baptized in heresy or schism, yet held communion with those who did admit them, according to his express declaration, "Judging no one, nor depriving any one of the right of communion if he differ from us?"[2] If he was polluted by communion with persons of this kind, why do they follow his authority in the question of baptism? But if he was not polluted by communion with them, why do they not follow his example in maintaining unity? Have they anything to urge in their defense except the plea, "We choose to have it so?" What other answer have any sinful or wicked men to the discourse of truth or justice,—the voluptuous, for instance, the drunkards, adulterers, and those who are impure in any way, thieves, robbers, murderers, plunderers, evil-doers, idolaters,—what other answer can they make when convicted by the voice of truth, except "I choose to do it;" "It is my pleasure so"? And if they have in them a tinge of Christianity, they say further, "Who art thou that judgest another man's servant?"[3] Yet these have so much more remains of modesty, that when, in accordance with divine and human law, they meet with punishment for their abandoned life and deeds, they do not style themselves martyrs; while the Donatists wish at once to lead a sacrilegious life and enjoy a blameless reputation, to suffer no punishment for their wicked deeds, and to gain a martyr's glory in their just punishment. As if they were not experiencing the greater mercy and patience of God, in proportion as "executing His judgments upon them by little and little, He giveth them place of repentance,"[4] and ceases not to redouble His scourgings in this life; that, considering what they suffer, and why they suffer it, they may in time grow wise; and that those who have received the baptism of the party of Maximianus in order to preserve the unity of Donatus, may the more readily embrace the baptism of the whole world in order to preserve the peace of Christ; that they may be restored to the root, may be reconciled to the unity of the Church, may see that they have nothing left for them to say, though something yet remains for them to do; that for their former deeds the sacrifice of loving-kindness may be offered to a long-suffering God, whose unity they have broken by their wicked sin, on whose sacraments they have inflicted such a lasting wrong. For "the Lord is merciful and gracious, slow to anger, plenteous in mercy and truth."[5] Let them embrace His mercy and long-suffering in this life, and fear His truth in the next. For He willeth not the death of a sinner, but rather that he should turn from his way and live;[6] because He bends His judgment against the wrongs that have been inflicted on Him. This is our exhortation.

Chap. 9.—16. For this reason, then, we hold them to be enemies, because we speak the truth, because we are afraid to be silent,

trusted ecclesiastical judges like these in preference to the defeated parties in the suit." *Ib.* 6, 30: He says that the Donatists, "having made a schism in the unity of the Church, were refuted, not by the authority of 310 African bishops, but by that of the whole world." And in the sixth chapter of the first book of the same treatise, he says that the Donatists, after the decision at Arles, came again to Constantine, and there were defeated "by a final decision," *i.e.* at Milan, as is seen from *Ep.* xliii. 7, 20, in the year 316 A.D. Substance of note in Benedictine ed. reproduced in Migne.

[1] See above, ch. ii. 3.

[2] *Ib.*

[3] Rom. xiv. 4.

[4] Wisd. xii. 10.

[5] Not Ps. ciii. 8, but lxxxvi. 15.

[6] Ezek. xxiii. 11.

because we fear to shrink from pressing our point with all the force that lies within our power, because we obey the apostle when he says, "Preach the word; be instant in season, out of season; reprove, rebuke, exhort."[1] But, as the gospel says, "They love the praise of men more than the praise of God;"[2] and while they fear to incur blame for a time, they do not fear to incur damnation for ever. They see, too, themselves what wrong they are doing; they see that they have no answer which they can make, but they overspread the inexperienced with mists, whilst they themselves are being swallowed up alive,—that is, are perishing knowingly and willfully. They see that men are amazed, and look with abhorrence on the fact that they have divided themselves into many schisms, especially in Carthage,[3] the capital and most noted city of all Africa; they have endeavored to patch up the disgrace of their rags. Thinking that they could annihilate the followers of Maximianus, they pressed heavily on them through the agency of Optatus the Gildonian;[4] they inflicted on them many wrongs amid the cruellest of persecutions. Then they received back some, thinking that all could be converted under the influence of the same terror; but they were unwilling to do those whom they received the wrong of baptizing afresh those who had been baptized by them in their schism, or rather of causing them to be baptized again within their communion by the very same men by whom they had been baptized outside, and thus they at once made an exception to their own impious custom. They feel how wickedly they are acting in assailing the baptism of the whole world, when they have received the baptism of the followers of Maximianus. But they fear those whom they have themselves rebaptized, lest they should receive no mercy from them, when they have shown it to others; lest these should call them to account for their souls when they have ceased to destroy those of other men.

CHAP. 12.—17. What answer they can give about the followers of Maximianus whom they have received, they cannot divine. If they say, "Those we received were innocent," the answer is obvious, "Then you had condemned the innocent." If they say, "We did it in ignorance," then you judged rashly (just as you passed a rash judgment on the *traditors*), and your declaration was false that "you must know that they were condemned by the truthful voice of a plenary Council."[5] For indeed the innocent could never be condemned by a voice of truth. If they say, "We did not condemn them," it is only necessary to cite the Council, to cite the names of bishops and states alike. If they say, "The Council itself is none of ours," then we cite the records of the proconsular province, where more than once they quoted the same Council to justify the exclusion of the followers of Maximianus from the basilicas, and to confound them by the din of the judges and the force of their allies. If they say that Felicianus of Musti, and Prætextatus of Assavæ, whom they afterwards received, were not of the party of Maximianus, then we cite the records in which they demanded, in the courts of law, that these persons should be excluded from the Council which they held against the party of Maximianus. If they say, "They were received for the sake of peace," our answer is, "Why then do ye not acknowledge the only true and full peace? Who urged you, who compelled you to receive a schismatic whom you had condemned, to preserve the peace of Donatus, and to condemn the world unheard, in violation of the peace of Christ?" Truth hems them in on every side. They see that there is no answer left for them to make, and they think that there is nothing left for them to do; they cannot find out what to say. They are not allowed to be silent. They had rather strive with perverse utterance against truth, than be restored to peace by a confession of their faults.

CHAP. 13.—18. But who can fail to understand what they may be saying in their hearts? "What then are we to do," say they, "with those whom we have already rebaptized?" Return with them to the Church. Bring those whom you have wounded to be healed by the medicine of peace: bring those whom you have slain to be brought to life again by the life of charity. Brotherly union has great power in propitiating God. "If two of you," says our Lord, "shall agree on earth as touching anything that they shall ask, it shall be done for them."[6] If for two men who agree, how much more for two communities? Let us throw ourselves together on our knees

1 2 Tim. iv. 2.
2 John xii. 43.
3 He is alluding to that chief schism among the Donatists, which occurred when Maximianus was consecrated bishop of Carthage, in opposition to Primianus, probably immediately after the Synod of Cabarsussum, 393.
4 Optatus, a Donatist bishop of Thamogade in Numidia, was called Gildonianus from his adherence to Gildo, Count of Africa, and generalissimo of the province under the elder Theodosius. On his death, in 395 A.D., Gildo usurped supreme authority, and by his aid Optatus was enabled to oppress the Catholics in the province, till, in 398 A.D., Gildo was defeated by his brother Mascezel, and destroyed himself, and Optatus was put in prison, where he died soon afterwards. He is not to be confounded with Optatus, Bishop of Milevis, the strenuous opponent of the Donatists.
5 The Council of Bagai. See above, I. v. 7.
6 Matt. xviii. 19.

before the Lord Do you share with us our unity; let us share with you your contrition; and let charity cover the multitude of sins.[1] Seek counsel from the blessed Cyprian himself. See how much he considered to depend upon the blessing of unity, from which he did not sever himself to avoid the communion of those who disagreed with him; how, though he considered that those who were baptized outside the communion of the Church had no true baptism, he was yet willing to believe that, by simple admission into the Church, they might, merely in virtue of the bond of unity, be admitted to a share in pardon. For thus he solved the question which he proposed to himself in writing as follows to Jubaianus: "But some will say, 'What then will become of those who, in times past, coming to the Church from heresy, were admitted without baptism?' The Lord is able of His mercy to grant pardon, and not to sever from the gifts of His Church those who, being out of simplicity admitted to the Church, have in the Church fallen asleep."[2]

Chap. 14.—19. But which is the worse, not to be baptized at all, or to be twice baptized, it is difficult to decide. I see, indeed, which is more repugnant and abhorrent to men's feelings; but when I have recourse to that divine balance, in which the weight of things is determined, not by man's feelings, but by the authority of God, I find a statement by our Lord on either side. For He said to Peter, "He who is washed has no need of washing a second time;"[3] and to Nicodemus, "Except a man be born of water and of the Spirit, he cannot enter into the kingdom of God."[4] What is the purport of the more secret determination of God, it is perhaps difficult for men like us to learn; but as far as the mere words are concerned, any one may see what a difference there is between "has no need of washing," and "cannot enter into the kingdom of heaven." The Church, lastly, herself holds as her tradition, that without baptism she cannot admit a man to her altar at all; but since it is allowed that one who has been rebaptized may be admitted after penance, surely this plainly proves that his baptism is considered valid. If, therefore, Cyprian thought that those whom he considered to be unbaptized yet had some share in pardon, in virtue of the bond of unity, the Lord has power to be reconciled even to the rebaptized by means of the simple bond of unity and peace, and by this same compensating power of peace to mitigate His displeasure against those by whom they were rebaptized, and to pardon all the errors which they had committed while in error, on their offering the sacrifice of charity, which covereth the multitude of sins; so that He looks not to the number of those who have been wounded by their separation, but to the greater number who have been delivered from bondage by their return. For in the same bond of peace in which Cyprian conceived that, through the mercy of God, those whom he considered to have been admitted to the Church without baptism, were yet not severed from the gifts of the Church, we also believe that through the same mercy of God the rebaptized can earn their pardon at His hands.

Chap. 15.—20. Since the Catholic Church, both in the time of the blessed Cyprian and in the older time before him, contained within her bosom either some that were rebaptized or some that were unbaptized, either the one section or the other must have won their salvation only by the force of simple unity. For if those who came over from the heretics were not baptized, as Cyprian asserts, they were not rightly admitted into the Church; and yet he himself did not despair of their obtaining pardon from the mercy of God in virtue of the unity of the Church. So again, if they were already baptized, it was not right to rebaptize them. What, therefore, was there to aid the other section, save the same charity that delighted in unity, so that what was hidden from man's weakness, in the consideration of the sacrament, might not be reckoned, by the mercy of God, as a fault in those who were lovers of peace? Why, then, while ye fear those whom ye have rebaptized, do ye grudge yourselves and them the entrance to salvation? There was at one time a doubt upon the subject of baptism; those who held different opinions yet remained in unity. In course of time, owing to the certain discovery of the truth, that doubt was taken away. The question which, unsolved, did not frighten Cyprian into separation from the Church, invites you, now that it is solved, to return once more within the fold. Come to the Catholic Church in its agreement, which Cyprian did not desert while yet disturbed with doubt; or if now you are dissatisfied with the example of Cyprian, who held communion with those who were received with the baptism of heretics, declaring openly that we should "neither judge any one, nor deprive any one of the right of communion if he differ from us,"[5]

1 1 Pet. iv. 8.

2 Cypr. *Ep.* lxxiii. 23, to Jubaianus.

3 John xiii. 10. "*Qui lotus est, non habet necessitatem iterum lavandi.*" The Latin, with the A.V., loses the distinction between ὁ λελουμένος, "he that has *bathed*," and νίπτειν, "to *wash*:" and further wrongfully introduces the idea of repetition.

4 John iii. 5.

5 See above, cii. 3.

whither are ye going, ye wretched men? What are ye doing? You are bound to fly even from yourselves, because you have advanced beyond the position where he abode. But if neither his own sins nor those of others could stand in his way, on account of the abundance of his charity and his love of brotherly kindness and the bond of peace, do you return to us, where you will find much less hindrance in the way of either us or you from the fictions which your party have invented.

BOOK III.

AUGUSTIN UNDERTAKES THE REFUTATION OF THE ARGUMENTS WHICH MIGHT BE DERIVED FROM THE EPISTLE OF CYPRIAN TO JUBAIANUS, TO GIVE COLOR TO THE VIEW THAT THE BAPTISM OF CHRIST COULD NOT BE CONFERRED BY HERETICS.

CHAP. 1.—1. I think that it may now be considered clear to every one, that the authority of the blessed Cyprian for the maintenance of the bond of peace, and the avoiding of any violation of that most wholesome charity which preserves unity in the Church, may be urged on our side rather than on the side of the Donatists. For if they have chosen to act upon his example in rebaptizing Catholics, because he thought that heretics ought to be baptized on joining the Catholic Church, shall not we rather follow his example, whereby he laid down a manifest rule that one ought in no wise, by the establishment of a separate communion, to secede from the Catholic communion, that is, from the body of Christians dispersed throughout the world, even on the admission of evil and sacrilegious men, since he was unwilling even to remove from the right of communion those whom he considered to have received sacrilegious men without baptism into the Catholic communion, saying, "Judging no one, nor depriving any of the right of communion if he differ from us?"

CHAP. 2.—2. Nevertheless, I see what may still be required of me, viz., that I should answer those plausible arguments, by which, in even earlier times, Agrippinus, or Cyprian himself, or those in Africa who agreed with them, or any others in far distant lands beyond the sea, were moved, not indeed by the authority of any plenary or even regionary Council, but by a mere epistolary correspondence, to think that they ought to adopt a custom which had no sanction from the ancient custom of the Church, and which was expressly forbidden by the most unanimous resolution of the Catholic world in order that an error which had begun to creep into the minds of some men, through discussions of this kind, might be cured by the more powerful truth and universal healing power of unity coming on the side of safety. And so they may see with what security I approach this discourse. If I am unable to gain my point, and show how those arguments may be refuted which they bring forward from the Council and the epistles of Cyprian, to the effect that Christ's baptism may not be given by the hands of heretics, I shall still remain safely in the Church, in whose communion Cyprian himself remained with those who differed from him.

3. But if they say that the Catholic Church existed then, because there were a few, or, if they prefer it, even a considerable number, who denied the validity of any baptism conferred in an heretical body, and baptized all who came from thence, what then? Did the Church not exist at all before Agrippinus, with whom that new kind of system began, at variance with all previous custom? Or how, again after the time of Agrippinus, when, unless there had been a return to the primitive custom, there would have been no need for Cyprian to set on foot another Council? Was there no Church then, because such a custom as this prevailed everywhere, that the baptism of Christ should be considered nothing but the baptism of Christ, even though it were proved to have been conferred in a body of heretics or schismatics? But if the Church existed even then, and had not perished through a breach of its continuity, but was, on the contrary, holding its ground, and receiving increase in every nation, surely it is the safest plan to abide by this same custom, which then embraced good and bad alike in unity. But if there was then no Church in existence, because sacrilegious heretics were received without baptism, and this prevailed by universal custom, whence has Donatus made his appearance? From what land did

[1] See above, II. ii. 3.

he spring? or from what sea did he emerge? or from what sky did he fall? And so we, as I had begun to say, are safe in the communion of that Church, throughout the whole extent of which the custom now prevails, which prevailed in like manner through its whole extent before the time of Agrippinus, and in the interval between Agrippinus and Cyprian, and whose unity neither Agrippinus nor Cyprian ever deserted, nor those who agreed with them, although they entertained different views from the rest of their brethren—all of them remaining in the same communion of unity with the very men from whom they differed in opinion. But let the Donatists themselves consider what their true position is, if they neither can say whence they derived their origin, if the Church had already been destroyed by the plague-spot of communion with heretics and schismatics received into her bosom without baptism; nor again agree with Cyprian himself, for he declared that he remained in communion with those who received heretics and schismatics, and so also with those who were received as well: while they have separated themselves from the communion of the whole world, on account of the charge of having delivered up the sacred books, which they brought against the men whom they maligned in Africa, but failed to convict when brought to trial beyond the sea; although, even had the crimes which they alleged been true, they were much less heinous than the sins of heresy and schism; and yet these could not defile Cyprian in the persons of those who came from them without baptism, as he conceived, and were admitted without baptism into the Catholic communion. Nor, in the very point in which they say that they imitate Cyprian, can they find any answer to make about acknowledging the baptism of the followers of Maximianus, together with those whom, though they belonged to the party that they had first condemned in their own plenary Council, and then gone on to prosecute even at the tribunal of the secular power, they yet received back into their communion, in the episcopate of the very same bishop under whom they had been condemned. Wherefore, if the communion of wicked men destroyed the Church in the time of Cyprian, they have no source from which they can derive their own communion; and if the Church was not destroyed, they have no excuse for their separation from it. Moreover, they are neither following the example of Cyprian, since they have burst the bond of unity, nor abiding by their own Council, since they have recognized the baptism of the followers of Maximianus.

CHAP. 3.—4. Let us therefore, seeing that we adhere to the example of Cyprian, go on now to consider Cyprian's Council. What says Cyprian? "Ye have heard," he says, "most beloved colleagues, what Jubaianus our fellow-bishop has written to me, consulting my moderate ability concerning the unlawful and profane baptism of heretics, and what answer I gave him,—giving a judgment which we have once and again and often given, that heretics coming to the Church ought to be baptized and sanctified with the baptism of the Church. Another letter of Jubaianus has likewise been read to you, in which, agreeably to his sincere and religious devotion, in answer to our epistle, he not only expressed his assent, but returned thanks also, acknowledging that he had received instruction."[1] In these words of the blessed Cyprian, we find that he had been consulted by Jubaianus, and what answer he had given to his questions, and how Jubaianus acknowledged with gratitude that he had received instruction. Ought we then to be thought unreasonably persistent if we desire to consider this same epistle by which Jubaianus was convinced? For till such time as we are also convinced (if there are any arguments of truth whereby this can be done), Cyprian himself has established our security by the right of Catholic communion.

5. For he goes on to say: "It remains that we severally declare our opinion on this same subject, judging no one, nor depriving any one of the right of communion if he differ from us."[1] He allows me, therefore, without losing the right of communion, not only to continue inquiring into the truth, but even to hold opinions differing from his own. "For no one of us," he says, "setteth himself up as a bishop of bishops, or by tyrannical terror forces his colleagues to a necessity of obeying." What could be more kind? what more humble? Surely there is here no authority restraining us from inquiry into what is truth. "Inasmuch as every bishop," he says, "in the free use of his liberty and power, has the right of forming his own judgment, and can no more be judged by another than he can himself judge another,"—that is, I suppose, in those questions which have not yet been brought to perfect clearness of solution; for he knew what a deep question about the sacrament was then occupying the whole Church with every kind of disputation, and gave free liberty of inquiry to every man, that the truth might be made known by investigation. For he was surely not uttering what was false, and trying to catch his simpler colleagues in their

[1] See above, II. ii. 3.

speech, so that, when they should have betrayed that they held op nions at variance with his, he might then propose, in violation of his promise, that they should be excommunicated. Far be it from a soul so holy to entertain such accursed treachery; indeed, they who hold such a view about such a man, thinking that it conduces to his praise, do but show that it would be in accordance with their own nature. I for my part will in no wise believe that Cyprian, a Catholic bishop, a Catholic martyr, whose greatness only made him proportionately humble in all things, so as to find favor before the Lord,[1] should ever, especially in the sacred Council of his colleagues, have uttered with his mouth what was not echoed in his heart, especially as he further adds, "But we must all await the judgment of our Lord Jesus Christ, who alone has the power both of setting us in the government of His Church, and of judging of our acts therein."[2] When, then, he called to their remembrance so solemn a judgment, hoping to hear the truth from his colleagues, would he first set them the example of lying? May God avert such madness from every Christian man, and how much more from Cyprian! We have therefore the free liberty of inquiry granted to us by the most moderate and most truthful speech of Cyprian.

Chap. 4.—6. Next nis colleagues proceed to deliver their several opinions. But first they listened to the letter written to Jubaianus; for it was read, as was mentioned in the preamble. Let it therefore be read among ourselves also, that we too, with the help of God, may discover from it what we ought to think. "What!" I think I hear some one saying, "do you proceed to tell us what Cyprian wrote to Jubaianus?" I have read the letter, I confess, and should certainly have been a convert to his views, had I not been induced to consider the matter more carefully by the vast weight of authority, originating in those whom the Church, distributed throughout the world amid so many nations, of Latins, Greeks, barbarians, not to mention the Jewish race itself, has been able to produce,—that same Church which gave birth to Cyprian himself,—men whom I could in no wise bring myself to think had been unwilling without reason to hold this view,—not because it was impossible that in so difficult a question the opinion of one or of a few might not have been more near the truth than that of more, but because one must not lightly, without full consideration and investigation of the matter to the best of his abilities, decide in favor of a single individual, or even of a few, against the decision of so very many men of the same religion and communion, all endowed with great talent and abundant learning. And so how much was suggested to me on more diligent inquiry, even by the letter of Cyprian himself, in favor of the view which is now held by the Catholic Church, that the baptism of Christ is to be recognized and approved, not by the standard of their merits by whom it is administered, but by His alone of whom it is said, "The same is He which baptizeth,"[3] will be shown naturally in the course of our argument. Let us therefore suppose that the letter which was written by Cyprian to Jubaianus has been read among us, as it was read in the Council.[4] And I would have every one read it who means to read what I am going to say, lest he might possibly think that I have suppressed some things of consequence. For it would take too much time, and be irrelevant to the elucidation of the matter in hand, were we at this moment to quote all the words of this epistle.

Chap. 5.—7. But if any one should ask what I hold in the meantime, while discussing this question, I answer that, in the first place, the letter of Cyprian suggested to me what I should hold till I should see clearly the nature of the question which next begins to be discussed. For Cyprian himself says: "But some will say, 'What then will become of those who in times past, coming to the Church from heresy, were admitted without baptism?'"[5] Whether they were really without baptism, or whether they were admitted because those who admitted them conceived that they had partaken of baptism, is a matter for our future consideration. At any rate, Cyprian himself shows plainly enough what was the ordinary custom of the Church, when he says that in past time those who came to the Church from heresy were admitted without baptism.

8. For in the Council itself Castus of Sicca says: "He who, despising truth, presumes to follow custom, is either envious or evil-disposed towards the brethren to whom the truth is revealed, or is ungrateful towards God, by whose inspiration His Church is instructed."[6] Whether the truth had been revealed, we shall investigate hereafter; at any rate, he acknowledges that the custom of the Church was different.

1 Ecclus. iii. 18.

2 See above, II. ii. 3.

3 John i. 33.

4 The Council of Carthage.

5 *Epist.* lxxiii. 23, to Jubaianus.

6 Seventh Conc. Carth. under Cyprian, the third which dealt with baptism, A.D. 256, sec. 28. These opinions are quoted again in Books VI. and VII.

CHAP. 6.—9. Libosus also of Vaga says: "The Lord says in the gospel, 'I am the Truth.'[1] He does not say, 'I am custom.' Therefore, when the truth is made manifest, custom must give way to truth."[2] Clearly, no one could doubt that custom must give way to truth where it is made manifest. But we shall see presently about the manifestation of the truth. Meanwhile he also makes it clear that custom was on the other side.

CHAP. 7.—10. Zosimus also of Tharassa said: "When a revelation of the truth has been made, error must give way to truth; for even Peter, who at the first circumcised, afterwards gave way to Paul when he declared the truth."[3] He indeed chose to say error, not custom; but in saying "for even Peter, who at the first circumcised, afterwards gave way to Paul when he declared the truth," he shows plainly enough that there was a custom also on the subject of baptism at variance with his views. At the same time, also, he warns us that it was not impossible that Cyprian might have held an opinion about baptism at variance with that required by the truth, as held by the Church both before and after him, if even Peter could hold a view at variance with the truth as taught us by the Apostle Paul.[4]

CHAP. 8—11. Likewise Felix of Buslacene said: "In admitting heretics without the baptism of the Church, let no one prefer custom to reason and truth; because reason and truth always prevail to the exclusion of custom."[5] Nothing could be better, if it be reason, and if it be truth; but this we shall see presently. Meanwhile, it is clear from the words of this man also that the custom was the other way.

CHAP. 9.—12. Likewise Honoratus of Tucca[6] said: "Since Christ is the Truth, we ought to follow truth rather than custom."[7] By all these declarations it is proved that we are not excluded from the communion of the Church, till it shall have been clearly shown what is the nature of the truth, which they say must be preferred to our custom. But if the truth has made it clear that the very regulation ought to be maintained which the said custom had prescribed, then it is evident both that this custom was not established or confirmed in vain, and also that, in consequence of the discussions in question, the most wholesome observance of so great a sacrament, which could never, indeed, have been changed in the Catholic Church, was even more watchfully guarded with the most scrupulous caution, when it had received the further corroboration of Councils.

CHAP. 10.—13. Therefore Cyprian writes to Jubaianus as follows, "concerning the baptism of heretics, who, being placed without, and set down out of the Church," seem to him to "claim to themselves a matter over which they have neither right nor power. Which we," he says, "cannot account valid or lawful, since it is clear that among them it is unlawful."[8] Neither, indeed, do we deny that a man who is baptized among heretics, or in any schism outside the Church, derives no profit from it so far as he is partner in the perverseness of the heretics and schismatics; nor do we hold that those who baptize, although they confer the real true sacrament of baptism, are yet acting rightly, in gathering adherents outside the Church, and entertaining opinions contrary to the Church. But it is one thing to be without a sacrament, another thing to be in possession of it wrongly, and to usurp it unlawfully. Therefore they do not cease to be sacraments of Christ and the Church, merely because they are unlawfully used, not only by heretics, but by all kinds of wicked and impious persons. These, indeed, ought to be corrected and punished, but the sacraments should be acknowledged and revered.

14. Cyprian, indeed, says that on this subject not one, but two or more Councils were held; always, however, in Africa. For indeed in one he mentions that seventy-one bishops had been assembled,[8]—to all whose authority we do not hesitate, with all due deference to Cyprian, to prefer the authority, supported by many more bishops, of the whole Church spread throughout the whole world, of which Cyprian himself rejoiced that he was an inseparable member.

15. Nor is the water "profane and adulterous"[8] over which the name of God is invoked, even though it be invoked by profane and adulterous persons; because neither the creature itself of water, nor the name invoked, is adulterous. But the baptism of Christ, consecrated by the words of the gospel, is necessarily holy, however polluted and unclean its ministers may be; because its inherent sanctity cannot be polluted, and the divine excellence abides in its sacrament, whether to the salvation of those who use it aright, or to the destruction of those who use it wrong. Would you indeed maintain that, while the

1 John xiv. 6. 2 Conc. Carth. sec. 30. 3 *Ib.* sec. 56.
4 Gal. ii. 11-14. 5 Conc. Carth. sec. 63. 6 Thucca.
7 Conc. Carth. sec. 77.

8 Cypr. *Ep.* lxxiii. 1.

light of the sun or of a candle, diffused through unclean places, contracts no foulness in itself therefrom, yet the baptism of Christ can be defiled by the sins of any man, whatsoever he may be? For if we turn our thoughts to the visible materials themselves, which are to us the medium of the sacraments, every one must know that they admit of corruption. But if we think on that which they convey to us, who can fail to see that it is incorruptible, however much the men through whose ministry it is conveyed are either being rewarded or punished for the character of their lives?

Chap. 11.—16. But Cyprian was right in not being moved by what Jubaianus wrote, that "the followers of Novatian[1] rebaptize those who come to them from the Catholic Church."[2] For, in the first place, it does not follow that whatever heretics have done in a perverse spirit of mimicry, Catholics are therefore to abstain from doing, because the heretics do the same. And again, the reasons are different for which heretics and the Catholic Church ought respectively to abstain from rebaptizing. For it would not be right for heretics to do so, even if it were fitting in the Catholic Church; because their argument is, that among the Catholics is wanting that which they themselves received whilst still within the pale, and took away with them when they departed. Whereas the reason why the Catholic Church should not administer again the baptism which was given among heretics, is that it may not seem to decide that a power which is Christ's alone belongs to its members, or to pronounce that to be wanting in the heretics which they have received within her pale, and certainly could not lose by straying outside. For thus much Cyprian himself, with all the rest, established, that if any should return from heresy to the Church, they should be received back, not by baptism, but by the discipline of penitence; whence it is clear that they cannot be held to lose by their secession what is not restored to them when they return. Nor ought it for a moment to be said that, as their heresy is their own, as their error is their own, as the sacrilege of disunion is their own, so also the baptism is their own, which is really Christ's. Accordingly, while the evils which are their own are corrected when they return, so in that which is not theirs His presence should be recognised, from whom it is.

Chap. 12.—17. But the blessed Cyprian shows that it was no new or sudden thing that he decided, because the practice had already begun under Agrippinus. "Many years," he says, "and much time has passed away since, under Agrippinus of honored memory, a large assembly of bishops determined this point." Accordingly, under Agrippinus, at any rate, the thing was new. But I cannot understand what Cyprian means by saying, "And thenceforward to the present day, so many thousand heretics in our provinces, having been converted to our Church, showed no hesitation or dislike, but rather with full consent of reason and will, have embraced the opportunity of the grace of the laver of life and the baptism unto salvation,"[3] unless indeed he says, "thenceforward to the present day," because from the time when they were baptized in the Church, in accordance with the Council of Agrippinus, no question of excommunication had arisen in the case of any of the rebaptized. Yet if the custom of baptizing those who came over from heretics remained in force from the time of Agrippinus to that of Cyprian, why should new Councils have been held by Cyprian on this point? Why does he say to this same Jubaianus that he is not doing anything new or sudden, but only what had been established by Agrippinus? For why should Jubaianus be disturbed by the question of novelty, so as to require to be satisfied by the authority of Agrippinus, if this was the continuous practice of the Church from Agrippinus till Cyprian? Why, lastly, did so many of his colleagues urge that reason and truth must be preferred to custom, instead of saying that those who wished to act otherwise were acting contrary to truth and custom alike?

Chap. 13.—18. But as regards the remission of sins, whether it is granted through baptism at the hands of the heretics, I have already expressed my opinion on this point in a former book;[4] but I will shortly recapitulate it here. If remission of sins is there conferred by the sacredness of baptism, the sins return again through obstinate perseverance in heresy or schism; and therefore such men must needs return to the peace of the Catholic Church, that they may cease to be heretics and schismatics, and deserve that those sins which had returned on them should be cleansed away by love working in the bond of unity. But if, although among heretics and schismatics it be still the same baptism of Christ, it yet cannot work remission of sins owing to this same foulness of discord and

[1] The Novatian bishop, Acesius, was invited by Constantine to attend the Council of Nicæa. Soc., H. E. I. 10.

[2] Cypr. *Ep.* lxxiii. 2.

[3] Cypr. *Ep.* lxxiii. 3.

[4] Above, Book I. c. xi. sqq.

wickedness of dissent, then the same baptism begins to be of avail for the remission of sins when they come to the peace of the Church, —[not][1] that what has been already truly remitted should not be retained; nor that heretical baptism should be repudiated as belonging to a different religion, or as being different from our own, so that a second baptism should be administered; but that the very same baptism, which was working death by reason of discord outside the Church, may work salvation by reason of the peace within. It was, in fact, the same savor of which the apostle says, "We are a sweet savor of Christ in every place;" and yet, says he, "both in them that are saved and in them that perish. To the one we are the savor of life unto life; and to the other the savor of death unto death."[2] And although he used these words with reference to another subject, I have applied them to this, that men may understand that what is good may not only work life to those who use it aright, but also death to those who use it wrong.

CHAP. 14.—19. Nor is it material, when we are considering the question of the genuineness and holiness of the sacrament, "what the recipient of the sacrament believes, and with what faith he is imbued." It is of the very highest consequence as regards the entrance into salvation, but is wholly immaterial as regards the question of the sacrament. For it is quite possible that a man may be possessed of the genuine sacrament and a corrupted faith, as it is possible that he may hold the words of the creed in their integrity, and yet entertain an erroneous belief about the Trinity, or the resurrection, or any other point. For it is no slight matter, even within the Catholic Church itself, to hold a faith entirely consistent with the truth about even God Himself, to say nothing of any of His creatures. Is it then to be maintained, that if any one who has been baptized within the Catholic Church itself should afterwards, in the course of reading, or by listening to instruction, or by quiet argument, find out, through God's own revelation, that he had before believed otherwise than he ought, it is requisite that he should therefore be baptized afresh? But what carnal and natural man is there who does not stray through the vain conceits[3] of his own heart, and picture God's nature to himself to be such as he has imagined out of his carnal sense, and differ from the true conception of God as far as vanity from truth? Most truly, indeed, speaks the apostle, filled with the light of truth: "The natural man," says he, "receiveth not the things of the Spirit of God."[4] And yet herein he was speaking of men whom he himself shows to have been baptized. For he says to them, "Was Paul crucified for you? or were ye baptized in the name of Paul?"[5] These men had therefore the sacrament of baptism; and yet, inasmuch as their wisdom was of the flesh, what could they believe about God otherwise than according to the perception of their flesh, according to which "the natural man receiveth not the things of the Spirit of God?" To such he says: "I could not speak unto you as unto spiritual, but as unto carnal, even as unto babes in Christ. I have fed you with milk, and not with meat: for hitherto ye were not able to bear it, neither yet now are ye able. For ye are yet carnal."[6] For such are carried about with every wind of doctrine, of which kind he says, "That we be no more children, tossed to and fro, and carried about with every wind of doctrine."[7] It is then true that, if these men shall have advanced even to the spiritual age of the inner man, and in the integrity of understanding shall have learned how far different from the requirements of the truth has been the belief which they have been led by the fallacious character of their conceits to entertain of God, they are therefore to be baptized again? For, on this principle, it would be possible for a Catholic catechumen to light upon the writings of some heretic, and, not having the knowledge requisite for discerning truth from error, he might entertain some belief contrary to the Catholic faith, yet not condemned by the words of the creed, just as, under color of the same words, innumerable heretical errors have sprung up. Supposing, then, that the catechumen was under the impression that he was studying the work of some great and learned Catholic, and was baptized with that belief in the Catholic Church, and by subsequent research should discover what he ought to believe, so that, embracing the Catholic faith, he should reject his former error, ought he, on confessing this, to be baptized again? Or supposing that, before learning and confessing this for himself, he should be found to entertain such an opinion, and should be taught what he ought to reject and what he should believe, and it were to become clear that he had held

1 *Non ut jam vere dimissa non retineantur.* One of the negatives here appears to be superfluous, and the former is omitted in Amerbach's edition, and in many of the MSS., which continue the sentence, "*non ut ille baptismus,*" instead of "*neque ut ille,*" etc. If the latter negative were omitted, the sense would be improved. and "*neque*" would appropriately remain.

2 2 Cor. ii. 15, 16.

3 *Phantasmata.*

4 1 Cor. ii. 14.

5 1 Cor. i. 13.

6 1 Cor. iii. 1-3.

7 Eph. iv. 14.

this false belief when he was baptized, ought he therefore to be baptized again? Why should we maintain the contrary? Because the sanctity of the sacrament, consecrated in the words of the gospel, remains upon him in its integrity, just as he received it from the hands of the minister, although he, being firmly rooted in the vanity of his carnal mind, entertained a belief other than was right at the time when he was baptized. Wherefore it is manifest that it is possible that, with defective faith, the sacrament of baptism may yet remain without defect in any man; and therefore all that is said about the diversity of the several heretics is beside the question. For in each person that is to be corrected which is found to be amiss by the man who undertakes his correction. That is to be made whole which is unsound; that is to be given which is wanting, and, above all, the peace of Christian charity, without which the rest is profitless. Yet, as the rest is there, we must not administer it as though it were wanting, only take care that its possession be to the profit, not the hurt of him who has it, through the very bond of peace and excellence of charity.

Chap. 15.—20. Accordingly, if Marcion consecrated the sacrament of baptism with the words of the gospel, "In the name of the Father, and of the Son, and of the Holy Ghost,"[1] the sacrament was complete, although his faith expressed under the same words, seeing that he held opinions not taught by the Catholic truth, was not complete, but stained with the falsity of fables.[2] For under these same words, "In the name of the Father, and of the Son, and of the Holy Ghost," not Marcion only, or Valentinus, or Arius, or Eunomius, but the carnal babes of the Church themselves (to whom the apostle said, "I could not speak unto you as unto spiritual, but as unto carnal"), if they could be individually asked for an accurate exposition of their opinions, would probably show a diversity of opinions as numerous as the persons who held them, "for the natural man receiveth not the things of the Spirit of God." Can it, however, be said on this account that they do not receive the complete sacrament? or that, if they shall advance, and correct the vanity of their carnal opinions, they must seek again what they had received? Each man receives after the fashion of his own faith; yet how much does he obtain under the guidance of that mercy of God, in the confident assurance of which the same apostle says, "If in anything ye be otherwise minded, God shall reveal even this unto you"?[3] Yet the snares of heretics and schismatics prove for this reason only too pernicious to the carnally-minded, because their very progress is intercepted when their vain opinions are confirmed in opposition to the Catholic truth, and the perversity of their dissension is strengthened against the Catholic peace. Yet if the sacraments are the same, they are everywhere complete, even when they are wrongly understood, and perverted to be instruments of discord, just as the very writings of the gospel, if they are only the same, are everywhere complete, even though quoted with a boundless variety of false opinions. For as to what Jeremiah says:—"Why do those who grieve me prevail against me? My wound is stubborn, whence shall I be healed? In its origin it became unto me as lying water, having no certainty,"[4]—if the term "water" were never used figuratively and in the allegorical language of prophecy except to signify baptism, we should have trouble in discovering what these words of Jeremiah meant; but as it is, when "waters" are expressly used in the Apocalypse[5] to signify "peoples," I do not see why, by "lying water having no certainty," I should not understand, a "lying people, whom I cannot trust."

Chap. 16.—21. But when it is said that "the Holy Spirit is given by the imposition of hands in the Catholic Church only, I suppose that our ancestors meant that we should understand thereby what the apostle says, "Because the love of God is shed abroad in our hearts by the Holy Ghost which is given unto us."[6] For this is that very love which is wanting in all who are cut off from the communion of the Catholic Church; and for lack of this, "though they speak with the tongues of men and of angels, though they understand all mysteries and all knowledge, and though they have the gift of prophecy, and all faith, so that they could remove mountains, and though they bestow all their goods to feed the poor, and though they give their bodies to be burned, it profiteth them nothing."[7] But those are wanting in God's love who do not care for the unity of the Church; and consequently we are right in understanding that the Holy Spirit may be said not to be received except in the Catholic

[1] Matt. xxviii. 19.

[2] Cp. *Concilium Arelatense*, A.D. 314, can. 8. "*De Afris, quod propria lege utuntur ut rebaptizent; placuit ut si ad ecclesiam aliquis de hæresi venerit, interrogent eum symbolum; et si perviderint eum in Patre, et Filio, et Spiritu sancto esse baptizatum, manus ei tantum imponatur, ut accipiat Spiritum sanctum. Quod si interrogatus non responderit hanc Trinitatem, baptizetur.*"

[3] Phil. iii. 15.

[4] Jer. xv. 18, cp. LXX.

[5] Rev. xvii 15.

[6] Rom. v. 5.

[7] 1 Cor. xiii. 1-3.

Church. For the Holy Spirit is not only given by the laying on of hands amid the testimony of temporal sensible miracles, as He was given in former days to be the credentials of a rudimentary faith, and for the extension of the first beginnings of the Church. For who expects in these days that those on whom hands are laid that they may receive the Holy Spirit should forthwith begin to speak with tongues? but it is understood that invisibly and imperceptibly, on account of the bond of peace, divine love is breathed into their hearts, so that they may be able to say, "Because the love of God is shed abroad in our hearts by the Holy Ghost which is given unto us." But there are many operations of the Holy Spirit, which the same apostle commemorates in a certain passage at such length as he thinks sufficient, and then concludes: "But all these worketh that one and the selfsame Spirit, dividing to every man severally as He will."[1] Since, then, the sacrament is one thing, which even Simon Magus could have;[2] and the operation of the Spirit is another thing, which is even often found in wicked men, as Saul had the gift of prophecy;[3] and that operation of the same Spirit is a third thing, which only the good can have, as "the end of the commandment is charity out of a pure heart, and of a good conscience, and of faith unfeigned:"[4] whatever, therefore, may be received by heretics and schismatics, the charity which covereth the multitude of sins is the especial gift of Catholic unity and peace; nor is it found in all that are within that bond, since not all that are within it are of it, as we shall see in the proper place. At any rate, outside the bond that love cannot exist, without which all the other requisites, even if they can be recognized and approved, cannot profit or release from sin. But the laying on of hands in reconciliation to the Church is not, like baptism, incapable of repetition; for what is it more than a prayer offered over a man?[5]

CHAP. 17.—22. "For as regards the fact that to preserve the figure of unity the Lord gave the power to Peter that whatsoever he should loose on earth should be loosed,"[6] it is clear that that unity is also described as one dove without fault.[7] Can it be said, then, that to this same dove belong all those greedy ones, whose existence in the same Catholic Church Cyprian himself so grievously bewailed? For birds of prey, I believe, cannot be called doves, but rather hawks. How then did they baptize those who used to plunder estates by treacherous deceit, and increase their profits by compound usury,[8] if baptism is only given by that indivisible and chaste and perfect dove, that unity which can only be understood as existing among the good? Is it possible that, by the prayers of the saints who are spiritual within the Church, as though by the frequent lamentations of the dove, a great sacrament is dispensed, with a secret administration of the mercy of God, so that their sins also are loosed who are baptized, not by the dove but by the hawk, if they come to that sacrament in the peace of Catholic unity? But if this be so, why should it not also be the case that, as each man comes from heresy or schism to the Catholic peace, his sins should be loosed through their prayers? But the integrity of the sacrament is everywhere recognized, though it will not avail for the irrevocable remission of sins outside the unity of the Church. Nor will the prayers of the saints, or, in other words, the groanings of that one dove, be able to help one who is set in heresy or schism; just as they are not able to help one who is placed within the Church, if by a wicked life he himself retain the debts of his sins against himself, and that though he be baptized, not by this hawk, but by the pious ministry of the dove herself.

CHAP. 18.—23. "As my Father hath sent me," says our Lord, "even so send I you. And what He had said this, He breathed on them, and saith unto them, Receive ye the Holy Ghost. Whose soever sins ye remit, they are remitted unto them; and whose soever sins ye retain, they are retained."[9] Therefore, if they represented the Church, and this was said to them as to the Church herself, it follows that the peace of the Church looses sins, and estrangement from the Church retains them, not according to the will of men, but according to the will of God and the prayers of the saints who are spiritual, who "judge all things, but themselves are judged of no man."[10] For the rock retains, the rock remits; the dove retains, the dove remits; unity retains, unity remits. But the peace of this unity exists only in the good, in those who are either already spiritual, or are advancing by the obedience of concord to spiritual things; it exists not in the bad, whether they make disturbances abroad, or are endured within the Church with lamenta-

1 1 Cor. xii. 11.
2 Acts viii. 13.
3 1 Sam. x. 6, 10.
4 1 Tim. i. 5.
5 He refers to laying on of hands such as he mentions below, Book V. c. xxiii.: "If the laying on of hands were not applied to one coming from heresy, he would be, as it were, judged to be wholly blameless."
6 Matt. xvi. 19.
7 Song of Sol. vi. 9.
8 Cypr. *de Lapsis* c vi.
9 John xx. 21-23.
10 1 Cor. ii. 15.

tions, baptizing and being baptized. But just as those who are tolerated with groanings within the Church, although they do not belong to the same unity of the dove, and to that "glorious Church, not having spot or wrinkle, or any such thing,"[1] yet if they are corrected, and confess that they approached to baptism most unworthily, are not baptized again, but begin to belong to the dove, through whose groans those sins are remitted which were retained in them who were estranged from her peace; so those also who are more openly without the Church, if they have received the same sacraments, are not freed from their sins on coming, after correction, to the unity of the Church, by a repetition of baptism, but by the same law of charity and bond of unity. For if "those only may baptize who are set over the Church, and established by the law of the gospel and ordination as appointed by the Lord," were they in any wise of this kind who seized on estates by treacherous frauds, and increased their gains by compound interest? I trow not, since those are established by ordination as appointed of the Lord, of whom the apostle, in giving them a standard, says, "Not greedy, not given to filthy lucre."[2] Yet men of this kind used to baptize in the time of Cyprian himself; and he confesses with many lamentations that they were his fellow-bishops, and endures them with the great reward of tolerance. Yet did they not confer remission of sins, which is granted through the prayers of the saints, that is, the groans of the dove, whoever it be that baptizes, if those to whom it is given belong to her peace. For the Lord would not say to robbers and usurers, "Whose soever sins ye remit, they shall be remitted to him; and whose soever sins ye retain, they shall be retained." "Outside the Church, indeed, nothing can be either bound or loosed, since there there is no one who can either bind or loose;" but he is loosed who has made peace with the dove, and he is bound who is not at peace with the dove, whether he is openly without, or appears to be within.

24. But we know that Dathan, Korah, and Abiram,[3] who tried to usurp to themselves the right of sacrificing, contrary to the unity of the people of God, and also the sons of Aaron who offered strange fire upon the altar,[4] did not escape punishment. Nor do we say that such offenses remain unpunished, unless those guilty of them correct themselves, if the patience of God leading them to repentance[5] give them time for correction.

[1] Eph. v. 27. Cp. *Retract.* ii. 18, quoted above on I. xvii.
[2] Tit. i. 7.
[3] Num. xvi.
[4] Lev. x. 1, 2.
[5] Rom. ii. 4.

Chap. 19.—25. They indeed who say that baptism is not to be repeated, because only hands were laid on those whom Philip the deacon had baptized,[6] are saying what is quite beside the point; and far be it from us, in seeking the truth, to use such arguments as this. Wherefore we are all the further from "yielding to heretics,"[7] if we deny that what they possess of Christ's Church is their own property, and do not refuse to acknowledge the standard of our General because of the crimes of deserters; nay, all the more because "the Lord our God is a jealous God,"[8] let us refuse, whenever we see anything of His with an alien, to allow him to consider it his own. For of a truth the jealous God Himself rebukes the woman who commits fornication against Him, as the type of an erring people, and says that she gave to her lovers what belonged to Him, and again received from them what was not theirs but His. In the hands of the adulterous woman and the adulterous lovers, God in His wrath, as a jealous God, recognizes His gifts; and do we say that baptism, consecrated in the words of the gospel, belongs to heretics? and are we willing, from consideration of their deeds, to attribute to them even what belongs to God, as though they had the power to pollute it, or as though they could make what is God's to be their own, because they themselves have refused to belong to God?

26. Who is that adulterous woman whom the prophet Hosea points out, who said, "I will go after my lovers, that give me my bread and my water, my wool and my flax, and everything that befits me?"[9] Let us grant that we may understand this also of the people of the Jews that went astray; yet whom else are the false Christians (such as are all heretics and schismatics) wont to imitate, except false Israelites? For there were also true Israelites, as the Lord Himself bears witness to Nathanael, "Behold an Israelite indeed, in whom is no guile."[10] But who are true Christians, save those of whom the same Lord said, "He that hath my commandments, and keepeth them, he it is that loveth me?"[11] But what is it to keep His commandments, except to abide in love? Whence also He says, "A new commandment I give unto you, that ye love one another;" and again, "By this shall all men know that ye are my disciples, if ye have love one to another."[12] But who can doubt that this was spoken not only to those

[6] Acts viii 5-17.
[7] Because Cyprian, in his letter to Jubaianus (*Ep.* lxxiii. 10), had urged as following from this, that "there is no reason, dearest brother, why we should think it right to yield to heretics that baptism which was granted to the one and only Church."
[8] Deut. iv. 24.
[9] Hos. ii. 5, cp. LXX.
[10] John i. 47.
[11] John xiv. 21.
[12] John xiii. 34, 35.

who heard His words with their fleshly ears when He was present with them, but also to those who learn His words through the gospel, when He is sitting on His throne in heaven? For He came not to destroy the law, but to fulfill.[1] But the fulfilling of the law is love.[2] And in this Cyprian abounded greatly, insomuch that though he held a different view concerning baptism, he yet did not forsake the unity of the Church, and was in the Lord's vine a branch firmly rooted, bearing fruit, which the heavenly Husbandman purged with the knife of suffering, that it should bear more fruit.[3] But the enemies of this brotherly love, whether they are openly without, or appear to be within, are false Christians, and antichrists. For when they have found an opportunity, they go out, as it is written: "A màn wishing to separate himself from his friends, seeketh opportunities."[4] But even if occasions are wanting, while they seem to be within, they are severed from that invisible bond of love. Whence St. John says, "They went out from us, but they were not of us; for had they been of us, they would no doubt have continued with us."[5] He does not say that they ceased to be of us by going out, but that they went out because they were not of us. The Apostle Paul also speaks of certain men who had erred concerning the truth, and were overthrowing the faith of some; whose word was eating as a canker. Yet in saying that they should be avoided, he nevertheless intimates that they were all in one great house, but as vessels to dishonor, —I suppose because they had not as yet gone out. Or if they had already gone out, how can he say that they were in the same great house with the honorable vessels, unless it was in virtue of the sacraments themselves, which even in the severed meetings of heretics are not changed, that he speaks of all as belonging to the same great house, though in different degrees of esteem, some to honor and some to dishonor? For thus he speaks in his Epistle to Timothy: "But shun profane and vain babblings; for they will increase unto more ungodliness. And their word will eat as doth a canker; of whom is Hymenæus and Philetus; who concerning the truth have erred, saying that the resurrection is past already; and overthrow the faith of some. Nevertheless the foundation of God standeth firm, having this seal, The Lord knoweth them that are His. And, Let every one that nameth the name of Christ depart from iniquity. But in a great house there are not only vessels of gold and of silver, but also of wood and of earth; and some to honor, and some to dishonor. If a man therefore purge himself from these, he shall be a vessel unto honor, sanctified, and meet for the master's use, and prepared unto every good work."[6] But what is it to purge oneself from such as these, except what he said just before, "Let every one that nameth the name of Christ depart from iniquity." And lest any one should think that, as being in one great house with them, he might perish with such as these, he has most carefully forewarned them, "The Lord knoweth them that are His,"—those, namely, who, by departing from iniquity, purge themselves from the vessels made to dishonor, lest they should perish with them whom they are compelled to tolerate in the great house.

27. They, therefore, who are wicked, evildoers, carnal, fleshly, devilish, think that they receive at the hands of their seducers what are the gifts of God alone, whether sacraments, or any spiritual workings about present salvation. But these men have not love towards God, but are busied about those by whose pride they are led astray, and are compared to the adulterous woman, whom the prophet introduces as saying, "I will go after my lovers, that give me my bread and my water, my wool and my flax, and my oil, and everything that befits me." For thus arise heresies and schisms, when the fleshly people which is not founded on the love of God says, "I will go after my lovers," with whom, either by corruption of her faith, or by the puffing up of her pride, she shamefully commits adultery. But for the sake of those who, having undergone the difficulties, and straits, and barriers of the empty reasoning of those by whom they are led astray, afterwards feel the prickings of fear, and return to the way of peace, to seeking God in all sincerity,—for their sake He goes on to say, "Therefore, behold, I will hedge up thy way with thorns, and make a wall, that she shall not find her paths. And she shall follow after her lovers, but she shall not overtake them: and she shall seek them, but she shall not find them: then shall she say, I will go and return to my first husband; for then was it better with me than now." Then, that they may not attribute to their seducers what they have that is sound, and derived from the doctrine of truth, by which they lead them astray to the falseness of their own dogmas and dissensions; that they may not think that what is sound in them belongs to them, he immediately added, "And she did not know that I gave her corn, and

---

1 Matt. v. 17. 2 Rom. xiii. 10. 3 John xv. 1-5.
4 Prov. xviii. 1, cp. Hieron. and LXX. 5 1 John ii. 19.

6 2 Tim. ii. 16-21.

wine, and oil, and multiplied her money; but she made vessels of gold and silver for Baal."[1] For she had said above, "I will go after my lovers, that give me my bread," etc., not at all understanding that all this, which was held soundly and lawfully by her seducers, was of God, and not of men. Nor would even they themselves claim these things for themselves, and as it were assert a right in them, had not they in turn been led astray by a people which had gone astray, when faith is reposed in them, and such honors are paid to them, that they should be enabled thereby to say such things, and claim such things for themselves, that their error should be called truth, and their iniquity be thought righteousness, in virtue of the sacraments and Scriptures, which they hold, not for salvation, but only in appearance. Accordingly, the same adulterous woman is addressed by the mouth of Ezekiel: "Thou hast also taken thy fair jewels of my gold and of my silver, which I had given thee, and madest to thyself images of men, and didst commit whoredom with them; and tookest my[2] broidered garments, and coveredst them: and thou hast set mine oil and mine incense before them. My meat also which I gave thee, fine flour, and oil, and honey, wherewith I fed thee, thou hast even set it before thine idols for a sweet savor: and this thou hast done."[3] For she turns all the sacraments, and the words of the sacred books, to the images of her own idols, with which her carnal mind delights to wallow. Nor yet, because those images are false, and the doctrines of devils, speaking lies in hypocrisy,[4] are those sacraments and divine utterances therefore so to lose their due honor, as to be thought to belong to such as these; seeing that the Lord says, "Of my gold, and my silver, and my broidered garments, and mine oil, and mine incense, and my meat," and so forth. Ought we, because those erring ones think that these things belong to their seducers, therefore not to recognize whose they really are, when He Himself says, "And she did not know that I gave her corn, and wine, and oil, and multiplied her money"? For He did not say that she did not have these things because she was an adulteress; but she is said to have had them, and that not as belonging to herself or her lovers, but to God, whose alone they are. Although, therefore, she had her fornication, yet those things wherewith she adorned it, whether as seduced or in her turn seducing, belonged not to her, but to God. If these things were spoken in a figure of the Jewish nation, when the scribes and Pharisees were rejecting the commandment of God in order to set up their own traditions, so that they were in a manner committing whoredom with a people which was abandoning their God; and yet for all that, whoredom at that time among the people, such as the Lord brought to light by convicting it, did not cause that the mysteries should belong to them, which were not theirs but God's, who, in speaking to the adulteress, says that all these things were His; whence the Lord Himself also sent those whom He cleansed from leprosy to the same mysteries, that they should offer sacrifice for themselves before the priests, because that sacrifice had not become efficacious for them, which He Himself afterwards wished to be commemorated in the Church for all of them, because He Himself proclaimed the tidings to them all;—if this be so, how much the more ought we, when we find the sacraments of the New Testament among certain heretics or schismatics, not to attribute them to these men, nor to condemn them, as though we could not recognize them? We ought to recognize the gifts of the true husband, though in the possession of an adulteress, and to amend, by the word of truth, that whoredom which is the true possession of the unchaste woman, instead of finding fault with the gifts, which belong entirely to the pitying Lord.

28. From these considerations, and such as these, our forefathers, not only before the time of Cyprian and Agrippinus, but even afterwards, maintained a most wholesome custom, that whenever they found anything divine and lawful remaining in its integrity even in the midst of any heresy or schism, they approved rather than repudiated it; but whatever they found that was alien, and peculiar to that false doctrine or division, this they convicted in the light of the truth, and healed. The points, however, which remain to be considered in the letter written by Jubaianus, must, I think, when looking at the size of this book, be taken in hand and treated with a fresh beginning.

[1] Hos. ii. 5-8, cp. LXX.

[2] In Hieron. and LXX., as well as in the English version, this is in the second person, *vestimenta tua multicolaria; τὸν ἱματισμὸν τὸν ποικίλον σου.*

[3] Ezek. xvi. 17–19.

[4] 1 Tim. iv. 1, 2.

BOOK IV.

IN WHICH HE TREATS OF WHAT FOLLOWS IN THE SAME EPISTLE OF CYPRIAN TO JUBAIANUS.

CHAP. 1.—1. The comparison of the Church with Paradise[1] shows us that men may indeed receive her baptism outside her pale, but that no one outside can either receive or retain the salvation of eternal happiness. For, as the words of Scripture testify, the streams from the fountain of Paradise flowed copiously even beyond its bounds. Record indeed is made of their names; and through what countries they flow, and that they are situated beyond the limits of Paradise, is known to all;[2] and yet in Mesopotamia, and in Egypt, to which countries those rivers extended, there is not found that blessedness of life which is recorded in Paradise. Accordingly, though the waters of Paradise are found beyond its boundaries, yet its happiness is in Paradise alone. So, therefore, the baptism of the Church may exist outside, but the gift of the life of happiness is found alone within the Church, which has been founded on a rock, which has received the keys of binding and loosing.[3] "She it is alone who holds as her privilege the whole power of her Bridegroom and Lord;"[4] by virtue of which power as bride, she can bring forth sons even of handmaids. And these, if they be not high-minded, shall be called into the lot of the inheritance; but if they be high-minded, they shall remain outside.

CHAP. 2.—2. All the more, then, because "we are fighting[5] for the honor and unity" of the Church, let us beware of giving to heretics the credit of whatever we acknowledged among them as belonging to the Church; but let us teach them by argument, that what they possess that is derived from unity is of no efficacy to their salvation, unless they shall return to that same unity. For "the water of the Church is full of faith, and salvation, and holiness"[6] to those who use it rightly. No one, however, can use it well outside the Church. But to those who use it perversely, whether within or without the Church, it is employed to work punishment, and does not conduce to their reward. And so baptism "cannot be corrupted and polluted," though it be handled by the corrupt or by adulterers, just as also "the Church herself is uncorrupt, and pure, and chaste."[7] And so no share in it belongs to the avaricious, or thieves, or usurers,—many of whom, by the testimony of Cyprian himself in many places of his letters, exist not only without, but actually within the Church,—and yet they both are baptized and do baptize, with no change in their hearts.

3. For this, too, he says, in one of his epistles[8] to the clergy on the subject of prayer to God, in which, after the fashion of the holy Daniel, he represents the sins of his people as falling upon himself. For among many other evils of which he makes mention, he speaks of them also as "renouncing the world in words only and not in deeds;" as the apostle says of certain men, "They profess that they know God. but in works they deny Him."[9] These, therefore, the blessed Cyprian shows to be contained within the Church herself, who are baptized without their hearts being changed for the better, seeing that they renounce the world in words and not in deeds, as the Apostle Peter says, "The like figure whereunto even baptism doth also now save us, (not the putting away of the filth of the flesh, but the answer of a good conscience),"[10] which certainly they had not of whom it is said that they "renounced the world in words only, and not in deeds;" and yet he does his utmost, by chiding and convincing them, to make them at length walk in the way of Christ, and be His friends rather than friends of the world.

CHAP. 3.—4. And if they would have obeyed him, and begun to live rightly, not as

1 Cypr. *Ep.* lxxiii. ad Jubaian. 10. 2 Gen. ii. 8-14. 3 Matt. xvi. 18, 19. 4 Cypr. *Ep.* lxxiii. 11. 5 *Ib.* 6 *Ib.*

7 Cypr. *Ep.* lxxiii. 11. 8 Cypr. *Ep.* xi. 1. 9 Tit. i. 16. 10 1 Pet. iii. 21.

false but as true Christians, would he have ordered them to be baptized anew? Surely not; but their true conversion would have gained this for them, that the sacrament which availed for their destruction while they were yet unchanged, should begin when they changed to avail for their salvation.

5. For neither are they "devoted to the Church"[1] who seem to be within and live contrary to Christ, that is, act against His commandments; nor can they be considered in any way to belong to that Church, which He so purifies by the washing of water, "that He may present to Himself a glorious Church, not having spot or wrinkle, or any such thing."[2] But if they are not in that Church to whose members they do not belong, they are not in the Church of which it is said, "My dove is but one; she is the only one of her mother;"[3] for she herself is without spot or wrinkle. Or else let him who can assert that those are members of this dove who renounce the world in words but not in deeds. Meantime there is one thing which we see, from which I think it was said, "He that regardeth the day, regardeth it unto the Lord,"[4] for God judgeth every day. For, according to His foreknowledge, who knows whom He has foreordained before the foundation of the world to be made like to the image of His Son, many who are even openly outside, and are called heretics, are better than many good Catholics. For we see what they are to-day, what they shall be to-morrow we know not. And with God, with whom the future is already present, they already are what they shall hereafter be. But we, according to what each man is at present, inquire whether they are to be to-day reckoned among the members of the Church which is called the one dove, and the Bride of Christ without a spot or wrinkle,[5] of whom Cyprian says in the letter which I have quoted above, that "they did not keep in the way of the Lord, nor observe the commandments given unto them for their salvation; that they did not fulfill the will of their Lord, being eager about their property and gains, following the dictates of pride, giving way to envy and dissension, careless about single-mindedness and faith, renouncing the world in words only and not in deeds, pleasing each himself, and displeasing all men."[6] But if the dove does not acknowledge them among her members, and if the Lord shall say to them, supposing that they continue in the same perversity, "I never knew you: depart from me, ye that work iniquity;"[7] then they seem indeed to be in the Church, but are not; "nay, they even act against the Church. How then can they baptize with the baptism of the Church,"[8] which is of avail neither to themselves, nor to those who receive it from them, unless they are changed in heart with a true conversion, so that the sacrament itself, which did not avail them when they received it whilst they were renouncing the world in words and not in deeds, may begin to profit them when they shall begin to renounce it in deeds also? And so too in the case of those whose separation from the Church is open; for neither these nor those are as yet among the members of the dove, but some of them perhaps will be at some future time.

Chap. 4.—6. We do not, therefore, "acknowledge the baptism of heretics,"[9] when we refuse to baptize after them; but because we acknowledge the ordinance to be of Christ even among evil men, whether openly separated from us, or secretly severed whilst within our body, we receive it with due respect, having corrected those who were wrong in the points wherein they went astray. However as I seem to be hard pressed when it is said to me, "Does then a heretic confer remission of sins?" so I in turn press hard when I say, Does then he who violates the commands of Heaven, the avaricious man, the robber, the usurer, the envious man, does he who renounces the world in words and not in deeds, confer such remission? If you mean by the force of God's sacrament, then both the one and the other; if by his own merit, neither of them. For that sacrament, even in the hands of wicked men, is known to be of Christ; but neither the one nor the other of these men is found in the body of the one uncorrupt, holy, chaste dove, which has neither spot nor wrinkle. And just as baptism is of no profit to the man who renounces the world in words and not in deeds, so it is of no profit to him who is baptized in heresy or schism; but each of them, when he amends his ways, begins to receive profit from that which before was not profitable, but was yet already in him.

7. "He therefore that is baptized in heresy does not become the temple of God;"[10] but does it therefore follow that he is not to be considered as baptized? For neither does the avaricious man, baptized within the Church, become the temple of God unless he depart from his avarice; for they who become the temple of God certainly inherit the kingdom of God. But the apostle says, among

[1] Cypr. *Ep.* lxxiii. 11. [2] Eph. v. 26, 27. [3] Song of Sol. vi. 9.
[4] Rom. xiv. 6. [5] *Retract.* ii. 18, quoted on I. 17.
[6] Cypr. *Ep.* xi. 1, first part loosely quoted. [7] Matt. vii. 23.

[8] Cypr. *Ep.* lxxiii. 11.
[9] *Ib.*, lxxiii. 12, *quando a nobis baptisma eorum in acceptum refertur.*
[10] Cypr. *Ep.* lxxvii. 12.

many other things, "Neither the covetous, nor extortioners, shall inherit the kingdom of God."[1] For in another place the same apostle compares covetousness to the worship of idols: "Nor covetous man," he says, "who is an idolater;"[2] which meaning the same Cyprian has so far extended in a letter to Antonianus, that he did not hesitate to compare the sin of covetousness with that of men who in time of persecution had declared in writing that they would offer incense.[3] The man, then, who is baptized in heresy in the name of the Holy Trinity, yet does not become the temple of God unless he abandons his heresy, just as the covetous man who has been baptized in the same name does not become the temple of God unless he abandons his covetousness, which is idolatry. For this, too, the same apostle says: "What agreement hath the temple of God with idols?"[4] Let it not, then, be asked of us "of what God he is made the temple"[5] when we say that he is not made the temple of God at all. Yet he is not therefore unbaptized, nor does his foul error cause that what he has received, consecrated in the words of the gospel, should not be the holy sacrament; just as the other man's covetousness (which is idolatry) and great uncleanness cannot prevent what he receives from being holy baptism, even though he be baptized with the same words of the gospel by another man covetous like himself.

CHAP. 5.—8. "Further," Cyprian goes on to say, "in vain do some, who are overcome by reason, oppose to us custom, as though custom were superior to truth, or that were not to be followed in spiritual things which has been revealed by the Holy Spirit, as the better way."[6] This is clearly true, since reason and truth are to be preferred to custom. But when truth supports custom, nothing should be more strongly maintained. Then he proceeds as follows: "For one may pardon a man who merely errs, as the Apostle Paul says of himself, 'Who was before a blasphemer, a persecutor, and injurious; but I obtained mercy, because I did it ignorantly;'[7] but he who, after inspiration and revelation given, perseveres advisedly and knowingly in his former error, sins without hope of pardon on the ground of ignorance. For he rests on a kind of presumption and obstinacy, when he is overcome by reason." This is most true, that his sin is much more grievous who has sinned wittingly than his who has sinned through ignorance. And so in the case of the holy Cyprian, who was not only learned, but also patient of instruction, which he so fully himself understood to be a part of the praise of the bishop whom the apostle describes,[8] that he said, "This also should be approved in a bishop, that he not only teach with knowledge, but also learn with patience."[9] I do not doubt that if he had had the opportunity of discussing this question, which has been so long and so much disputed in the Church, with the pious and learned men to whom we owe it that subsequently that ancient custom was confirmed by the authority of a plenary Council, he would have shown, without hesitation, not only how learned he was in those things which he had grasped with all the security of truth, but also how ready he was to receive instruction in what he had failed to perceive. And yet, since it is so clear that it is much more grievous to sin wittingly than in ignorance, I should be glad if any one would tell me which is the worse,—the man who falls into heresy, not knowing how great a sin it is, or the man who refuses to abandon his covetousness, knowing its enormity? I might even put the question thus: If one man unwittingly fall into heresy, and another knowingly refuse to depart from idolatry, since the apostle himself says, "The covetous man, which is an idolater;" and Cyprian too understood the same passage in just the same way, when he says, in his letter to Antonianus, "Nor let the new heretics flatter themselves in this, that they say they do not communicate with idolaters, whereas there are amongst them both adulterers and covetous persons, who are held guilty of the sin of idolatry; 'for know this, and understand, that no whoremonger, nor unclean person, nor covetous man, who is an idolater, hath any inheritance in the kingdom of Christ and of God;'[10] and again, 'Mortify therefore your members which are upon the earth; fornication, uncleanness, inordinate affection, evil concupiscence, and covetousness, which is idolatry.'"[11] I ask, therefore, which sins more deeply,—he who ignorantly has fallen into heresy, or he who wittingly has refused to abandon covetousness, that is idolatry? According to that rule by which the sins of those who sin wittingly are placed before those of the ignorant, the man who is covetous with knowledge takes the first place in sin. But as it is possible that the greatness of the actual sin should produce the same effect in the case of heresy that the witting commission of the sin produces in that of covetousness, let us suppose the ignorant heretic to be on

[1] 1 Cor. vi. 10.
[2] Eph. v. 5.
[3] Cypr. *Ep.* lv. 26.
[4] 2 Cor. vi. 16.
[5] Cypr. *Ep.* lxxvii. 12.
[6] Cypr. *Ep.* lxxiii. 13.
[7] 1 Tim. i. 13.
[8] 2 Tim. ii. 24.
[9] Cypr. *Ep.* lxxiv. 10.
[10] Eph. v. 5.
[11] Col. iii. 5. Cypr. *Ep.* lv. 27.

a par in guilt with the consciously covetous man, although the evidence which Cyprian himself has advanced from the apostle does not seem to prove this. For what is it that we abominate in heretics except their blasphemies? But when he wished to show that ignorance of the sin may conduce to ease in obtaining pardon, he advanced a proof from the case of the apostle, when he says; "Who was before a blasphemer, and a persecutor, and injurious; but I obtained mercy, because I did it ignorantly."[1] But if possible, as I said before, let the sins of the two men—the blasphemy of the unconscious, and the idolatry of the conscious sinner—be esteemed of equal weight; and let them be judged by the same sentence,—he who, in seeking for Christ, falls into a truth-like setting forth of what is false, and he who wittingly resists Christ speaking through His apostle, "seeing that no whoremonger, nor unclean person, nor covetous man, which is an idolater, hath any inheritance in the kingdom of Christ and of God,"[2]—and then I would ask why baptism and the words of the gospel are held as naught in the former case, and accounted valid in the latter, when each is alike found to be estranged from the members of the dove. Is it because the former is an open combatant outside, that he should not be admitted, the latter a cunning assenter within the fold, that he may not be expelled?

Chap. 6.—9. But as regards his saying, "Nor let any one affirm that what they have received from the apostles, that they follow; for the apostles handed down only one Church and one baptism, and that appointed only in the same Church:"[3] this does not so much move me to venture to condemn the baptism of Christ when found amongst heretics (just as it is necessary to recognize the gospel itself when I find it with them, though I abominate their error), as it warns me that there were some even in the times of the holy Cyprian who traced to the authority of the apostles that custom against which the African Councils were held, and in respect of which he himself said a little above, "In vain do those who are beaten by reason oppose to us the authority of custom." Nor do I find the reason why the same Cyprian found this very custom, which after his time was confirmed by nothing less than a plenary Council of the whole world, already so strong before his time, that when with all his learning he sought an authority worth following for changing it, he found nothing but a Council of Agrippinus held in Africa a very few years before his own time. And seeing that this was not enough for him, as against the custom of the whole world, he laid hold on these reasons which we just now, considering them with great care, and being confirmed by the antiquity of the custom itself, and by the subsequent authority of a plenary Council, found to be truth-like rather than true; which, however, seemed to him true, as he toiled in a question of the greatest obscurity, and was in doubt about the remission of sins,—whether it could fail to be given in the baptism of Christ, and whether it could be given among heretics. In which matter, if an imperfect revelation of the truth was given to Cyprian, that the greatness of his love in not deserting the unity of the Church might be made manifest, there is yet not any reason why any one should venture to claim superiority over the strong defenses and excellence of his virtues, and the abundance of graces which were found in him, merely because, with the instruction derived from the strength of a general Council, he sees something which Cyprian did not see, because the Church had not yet held a plenary Council on the matter. Just as no one is so insane as to set himself up as surpassing the merits of the Apostle Peter, because, taught by the epistles of the Apostle Paul, and confirmed by the custom of the Church herself, he does not compel the Gentiles to judaize, as Peter once had done.[4]

10. We do not then "find that any one, after being baptized among heretics, was afterwards admitted by the apostles with the same baptism, and communicated;"[5] but neither do we find this, that any one coming from the society of heretics, who had been baptized among them, was baptized anew by the apostles. But this custom, which even then those who looked back to past ages could not find to have been invented by men of a later time, is rightly believed to have been handed down from the apostles. And there are many other things of the same kind, which it would be tedious to recount. Wherefore, if they had something to say for themselves to whom Cyprian, wishing to persuade them of the truth of his own view, says, "Let no one say, What we have received from the apostles, that we follow," with how much more force we now say, What the custom of the Church has always held, what this argument has failed to prove false, and what a plenary Council has confirmed, this we follow! To this we may add that it may also be said, after a careful inquiry into the reasoning on both sides of the discussion, and into the evidence

[1] 1 Tim. i. 13.
[2] Eph. v. 5.
[3] Cypr. *Ep.* lxxiii. 13.
[4] Gal. ii. 14.
[5] Cypr. *Ep.* lxxiii. 13.

of Scripture, What truth has declared, that we follow.

CHAP. 7.—11. For in fact, as to what some opposed to the reasoning of Cyprian, that the apostle says, "Notwithstanding every way, whether in pretence or in truth, let Christ be preached,"[1] Cyprian rightly exposed their error, showing that it has nothing to do with the case of heretics, since the apostle was speaking of those who were acting within the Church, with malicious envy seeking their own profit. They announced Christ, indeed, according to the truth whereby we believe in Christ, but not in the spirit in which He was announced by the good evangelists to the sons of the dove. "For Paul," he says, "in his epistle was not speaking of heretics, or of their baptism, so that it could be shown that he had laid down anything concerning this matter. He was speaking of brethren, whether as walking disorderly and contrary to the discipline of the Church, or as keeping the discipline of the Church in the fear of God. And he declared that some of them spoke the word of God steadfastly and fearlessly, but that some were acting in envy and strife; that some had kept themselves encompassed with kindly Christian love, but that others entertained malice and strife: but yet that he patiently endured all things, with the view that, whether in truth or in pretence, the name of Christ, which Paul preached, might come to the knowledge of the greatest number, and that the sowing of the word, which was as yet a new and unaccustomed work, might spread more widely by the preaching of those that spoke. Furthermore, it is one thing for those who are within the Church to speak in the name of Christ, another thing for those who are without, acting against the Church, to baptize in the name of Christ."[2] These words of Cyprian seem to warn us that we must distinguish between those who are bad outside, and those who are bad within the Church. And those whom he says that the apostle represents as preaching the gospel impurely and of envy, he says truly were within. This much, however, I think I may say without rashness, if no one outside can have anything which is of Christ, neither can any one within have anything which is of the devil. For if that closed garden can contain the thorns of the devil, why cannot the fountain of Christ equally flow beyond the garden's bounds? But if it cannot contain them, whence, even in the time of the Apostle Paul himself, did there arise amongst those who were within so great an evil of envy and malicious strife? For these are the words of Cyprian. Can it be that envy and malicious strife are a small evil? How then were those in unity who were not at peace? For it is not my voice, nor that of any man, but of the Lord Himself; nor did the sound go forth from men, but from angels, at the birth of Christ, "Glory to God in the highest, and on earth peace to men of good will."[3] And this certainly would not have been proclaimed by the voice of angels when Christ was born upon the earth, unless God wished this to be understood, that those are in the unity of the body of Christ who are united in the peace of Christ, and those are in the peace of Christ who are of good will. Furthermore, as good will is shown in kindliness, so is bad will shown in malice.

CHAP. 8—12. In short, we may see how great an evil in itself is envy, which cannot be other than malicious. Let us not look for other testimony. Cyprian himself is sufficient for us, through whose mouth the Lord poured forth so many thunders in most perfect truth, and uttered so many useful precepts about envy and malignity. Let us therefore read the letter of Cyprian about envy and malignity, and see how great an evil it is to envy those better than ourselves,—an evil whose origin he shows in memorable words to have sprung from the devil himself. "To feel jealousy," he says, "of what you regard as good, and to envy those who are better than yourselves, to some, dearest brethren, seems a light and minute offense."[4] And again a little later, when he was inquiring into the source and origin of the evil, he says, "From this the devil, in the very beginning of the world, perished first himself, and led others to destruction."[5] And further on in the same chapter: "What an evil, dearest brethren, is that by which an angel fell! by which that exalted and illustrious loftiness was able to be deceived and overthrown! by which he was deceived who was the deceiver! From that time envy stalks upon the earth, when man, about to perish through malignity, submits himself to the teacher of perdition, —when he who envies imitates the devil, as it is written, 'Through envy of the devil came death into the world, and they that do hold of his side do find it.'"[6] How true, how forcible are these words of Cyprian, in an epistle known throughout the world, we cannot fail to recognize. It was truly fitting for

---

[1] Phil. i. 18. Hieron. "*annuntietur.*"
[2] Cypr. *Ep.* lxxiii. 14.

[3] Luke ii. 14. "*Hominibus bonæ voluntatis;*" and so the Vulgate, following the reading ἐν ἀνθρώποις εὐδοκίας.
[4] Cypr. *de Zel. et Liv.* c. 1. [5] *Ib.* c. 4. [6] Wisd. ii. 24, 25.

Cyprian to argue and warn most forcibly about envy and malignity, from which most deadly evil he proved his own heart to be so far removed by the abundance of his Christian love; by carefully guarding which he remained in the unity of communion with his colleagues, who without ill-feeling entertained different views about baptism, whilst he himself differed in opinion from them, not through any contention of ill will, but through human infirmity, erring in a point which God, in His own good time, would reveal to him by reason of his perseverance in love. For he says openly, "Judging no one, nor depriving any of the right of communion if he differ from us. For no one of us setteth himself up as a bishop of bishops, or by tyrannical terror forces his colleagues to a necessity of obeying."[1] And in the end of the epistle before us he says, "These things I have written to you briefly, dearest brother, according to my poor ability, prescribing to or prejudging no one, so as to prevent each bishop from doing what he thinks right in the free exercise of his own judgment. We, so far as in us lies, do not strive on behalf of heretics with our colleges and fellow-bishops, with whom we hold the harmony that God enjoins, and the peace of our Lord, especially as the apostle says, 'If any man seem to be contentious, we have no such custom, neither the churches of God.'[2] Christian love in our souls, the honor of our fraternity, the bond of faith, the harmony of the priesthood, all these are maintained by us with patience and gentleness. For this cause we have also, so far as our poor ability admitted, by the permission and inspiration of the Lord, written now a treatise on the benefit of patience,[3] which we have sent to you in consideration of our mutual affection."[4]

Chap. 9.—13. By this patience of Christian love he not only endured the difference of opinion manifested in all kindliness by his good colleagues on an obscure point, as he also himself received toleration, till, in process of time, when it so pleased God, what had always been a most wholesome custom was further confirmed by a declaration of the truth in a plenary Council, but he even put up with those who were manifestly bad, as was very well known to himself, who did not entertain a different view in consequence of the obscurity of the question, but acted contrary to their preaching in the evil practices of an abandoned life, as the apostle says of them, "Thou that preachest a man should not steal, dost thou steal?"[5] For Cyprian says in his letter of such bishops of his own time, his own colleagues, and remaining in communion with him, "While they had brethren starving in the Church, they tried to amass large sums of money, they took possession of estates by fraudulent proceedings, they multiplied their gains by accumulated usuries."[6] For here there is no obscure question. Scripture declares openly, "Neither covetous nor extortioners shall inherit the kingdom of God;"[7] and "He that putteth out his money to usury,"[8] and "No whoremonger, nor unclean person, nor covetous man, who is an idolater, hath any inheritance in the kingdom of Christ and of God."[9] He therefore certainly would not, without knowledge, have brought accusations of such covetousness, that men not only greedily treasured up their own goods, but also fraudulently appropriated the goods of others, or of idolatry existing in such enormity as he understands and proves it to exist; nor assuredly would he bear false witness against his fellow-bishops. And yet with the bowels of fatherly and motherly love he endured them, lest that, by rooting out the tares before their time, the wheat should also have been rooted up,[10] imitating assuredly the Apostle Paul, who, with the same love towards the Church, endured those who were ill-disposed and envious towards him.[11]

14. But yet because "by the envy of the devil death entered into the world, and they that do hold of his side do find it,"[12] not because they are created by God, but because they go astray of themselves, as Cyprian also says himself, seeing that the devil, before he was a devil, was an angel, and good, how can it be that they who are of the devil's side are in the unity of Christ? Beyond all doubt, as the Lord Himself says, "an enemy hath done this," who "sowed tares among the wheat."[13] As therefore what is of the devil within the fold must be convicted, so what is of Christ without must be recognized. Has the devil what is his within the unity of the Church, and shall Christ not have what is His without? This, perhaps, might be said of individual men, that as the devil has none that are his among the holy angels, so God has none that are His outside the communion of the Church. But though it may be allowed to the devil to mingle tares, that is, wicked men, with this Church which still wears the mortal nature of

[1] Conc. Carth. *sub in.*
[2] 1 Cor. xi. 16.
[3] This treatise is still extant. See Trans. in Ante-Nicene Fathers, vol. V. 484-490.
[4] Cypr. *Ep.* lxxiii. 26.

[5] Rom. ii. 21.
[6] Cypr. *de Lapsis.* c. vi.
[7] 1 Cor. vi. 10.
[8] Ps. xv. 5.
[9] Eph. v. 5.
[10] Matt. xiii. 29.
[11] Phil. i. 15-18.
[12] Wisd. ii. 24, 25.
[13] Matt. xiii. 28, 25.

flesh, so long as it is wandering far from God, he being allowed this just because of the pilgrimage of the Church herself, that men may desire more ardently the rest of that country which the angels enjoy, yet this cannot be said of the sacraments. For, as the tares within the Church can have and handle them, though not for salvation, but for the destruction to which they are destined in the fire, so also can the tares without, which received them from seceders from within; for they did not lose them by seceding. This, indeed, is made plain from the fact that baptism is not conferred again on their return, when any of the very men who seceded happen to come back again. And let not any one say, Why, what fruit hath the tares? For if this be so, their condition is the same, so far as this goes, both inside and without. For it surely cannot be that grains of corn are found in the tares inside, and not in those without. But when the question is of the sacrament, we do not consider whether the tares bear any fruit, but whether they have any share of heaven; for the tares, both within and without, share the rain with the wheat itself, which rain is in itself heavenly and sweet, even though under its influence the tares grow up in barrenness. And so the sacrament, according to the gospel of Christ, is divine and pleasant; nor is it to be esteemed as naught because of the barrenness of those on whom its dew falls even without.

CHAP. 10.—15. But some one may say that the tares within may more easily be converted into wheat. I grant that it is so; but what has this to do with the question of repeating baptism? You surely do not maintain that if a man converted from heresy, through the occasion and opportunity given by his conversion, should bear fruit before another who, being within the Church, is more slow to be washed from his iniquity, and so corrected and changed, the former therefore needs not to be baptized again, but the churchman to be baptized again, who was outstripped by him who came from the heretics, because of the greater slowness of his amendment. It has nothing, therefore, to do with the question now at issue who is later or slower in being converted from his especial waywardness to the straight path of faith, or hope, or charity. For although the bad within the fold are more easily made good yet it will sometimes happen that certain of the number of those outside will outstrip in their conversion certain of those within; and while these remain in barrenness, the former, being restored to unity and communion, will bear fruit with patience, thirty-fold, or sixty-fold, or a hundred-fold.[1] Or if those only are to be called tares who remain in perverse error to the end, there are many ears of corn outside, and many tares within.

16. But it will be urged that the bad outside are worse than those within. It is indeed a weighty question, whether Nicolaus, being already severed from the Church,[2] or Simon, who was still within it,[3] was the worse,—the one being a heretic, the other a sorcerer. But if the mere fact of division, as being the clearest token of violated charity, is held to be the worse evil, I grant that it is so. Yet many, though they have lost all feelings of charity, yet do not secede from considerations of worldly profit; and as they seek their own, not the things which are Jesus Christ's,[4] what they are unwilling to secede from is not the unity of Christ, but their own temporal advantage. Whence it is said in praise of charity, that she "seeketh not her own."[5]

17. Now, therefore, the question is, how could men of the party of the devil belong to the Church, which has no spot, or wrinkle, or any such thing,[6] of which also it is said, "My dove is one?"[7] But if they cannot, it is clear that she groans among those who are not of her, some treacherously laying wait within, some barking at her gate without. Such men, however, even within, both receive baptism, and possess it, and transmit it holy in itself; nor is it in any way defiled by their wickedness, in which they persevere even to the end. Wherefore the same blessed Cyprian teaches us that baptism is to be considered as consecrated in itself by the words of the gospel, as the Church has received, without joining to it or mingling with it any consideration of waywardness and wickedness on the part of either minister or recipients; since he himself points out to us both truths,—both that there have been some within the Church who did not cherish kindly Christian love, but practised envy and unkind dissension, of whom the Apostle Paul spoke; and also that the envious belong to the devil's party, as he testifies in the most open way in the epistle which he wrote about envy and malignity. Wherefore, since it is clearly possible that in those who belong to the devil's party, Christ's sacrament may yet be holy,—not, indeed, to their salvation, but to their condemnation,—and that not only if they are led astray after they have been baptized, but even if they were such in heart when they received the sacrament, renouncing the world (as the same

---

1 Matt. xiii. 23; Luke viii. 15.
2 Rev. ii. 6.
3 Acts viii. 9–24.
4 Phil. ii. 21.
5 1 Cor. xiii. 5.
6 Eph. v. 27; *Retract.* ii. 18.
7 Song of Sol. vi. 9.

Cyprian shows) in words only and not in deeds;[1] and since even if afterwards they be brought into the right way, the sacrament is not to be again administered which they received when they were astray; so far as I can see, the case is already clear and evident, that in the question of baptism we have to consider, not who gives, but what he gives; not who receives, but what he receives; not who has, but what he has. For if men of the party of the devil, and therefore in no way belonging to the one dove, can yet receive, and have, and give baptism in all its holiness, in no way defiled by their waywardness, as we are taught by the letters of Cyprian himself, how are we ascribing to heretics what does not belong to them? how are we saying that what is really Christ's is theirs, and not rather recognizing in them the signs of our Sovereign, and correcting the deeds of deserters from Him? Wherefore it is one thing, as the holy Cyprian says, "for those within, in the Church, to speak in the name of Christ, another thing for those without, who are acting against the Church, to baptize in His name."[2] But both many who are within act against the Church by evil living, and by enticing weak souls to copy their lives; and some who are without speak in Christ's name, and are not forbidden to work the works of Christ, but only to be without, since for the healing of their souls we grasp at them, or reason with them, or exhort them. For he, too, was without who did not follow Christ with His disciples, and yet in Christ's name was casting out devils, which the Lord enjoined that he should not be prevented from doing;[3] although, certainly, in the point where he was imperfect he was to be made whole, in accordance with the words of the Lord, in which He says, "He that is not with me is against me; and he that gathereth not with me scattereth abroad."[4] Therefore both some things are done outside in the name of Christ not against the Church, and some things are done inside on the devil's part which are against the Church.

Chap. 11.—18. What shall we say of what is also wonderful, that he who carefully observes may find that it is possible that certain persons, without violating Christian charity, may yet teach what is useless, as Peter wished to compel the Gentiles to observe Jewish customs,[5] as Cyprian himself would force heretics to be baptized anew? whence the apostle says to such good members, who are rooted in charity, and yet walk not rightly in some points, "If in anything ye be otherwise minded, God shall reveal even this unto you;"[6] and that some again, though devoid of charity, may teach something wholesome? of whom the Lord says, "The scribes and the Pharisees sit in Moses' seat: all therefore whatsoever they bid you observe, that observe and do; but do not ye after their works: for they say and do not."[7] Whence the apostle also says of those envious and malicious ones who yet preach salvation through Christ, "Whether in pretense, or in truth, let Christ be preached."[8] Wherefore, both within and without, the waywardness of man is to be corrected, but the divine sacraments and utterances are not to be attributed to men. He is not, therefore, a "patron of heretics" who refuses to attribute to them what he knows not to belong to them, even though it be found among them. We do not grant baptism to be theirs; but we recognize His baptism of whom it is said, "The same is He which baptizeth,"[9] wheresoever we find it. But if "the treacherous and blasphemous man" continue in his treachery and blasphemy, he receives no "remission of sins either without" or within the Church; or if, by the power of the sacrament, he receives it for the moment, the same force operates both without and within, as the power of the name of Christ used to work the expulsion of devils even without the Church.

Chap. 12.—19. But he urges that "we find that the apostles, in all their epistles, execrated and abhorred the sacrilegious wickedness of heretics, so as to say that 'their word does spread as a canker.'"[10] What then? Does not Paul also show that those who said, "Let us eat and drink, for to-morrow we die," were corrupters of good manners by their evil communications, adding immediately afterwards, "Evil communications corrupt good manners;" and yet he intimated that these were within the Church when he says, "How say some among you that there is no resurrection of the dead?"[11] But when does he fail to express his abhorrence of the covetous? Or could anything be said in stronger terms, than that covetousness should be called idolatry, as the same apostle declared?[12] Nor did Cyprian understand his language otherwise, inserting it when need required in his letters; though he confesses that in his time there were in the Church not covetous men of an ordinary type, but robbers

1 Cypr. *Ep.* xi. 1.
2 Cypr. *Ep.* lxxiii. 14.
3 Luke ix. 49, 50.
4 Matt. xii. 30.
5 Gal. ii. 14.
6 Phil. iii. 15.
7 Matt. xxiii. 2, 3.
8 Phil. i. 18; see on ch. 7. 10.
9 John i. 33.
10 Cypr. *Ep.* lxxiii. 15; 2 Tim. ii. 17.
11 1 Cor. xv. 32, 33, 12.
12 Eph. v. 5.

and usurers, and these found not among the masses, but among the bishops. And yet I should be willing to understand that those of whom the apostle says, "Their word does spread as a canker," were without the Church, but Cyprian himself will not allow me. For, when showing, in his letter to Antonianus,[1] that no man ought to sever himself from the unity of the Church before the time of the final separation of the just and unjust, merely because of the admixture of evil men in the Church, when he makes it manifest how holy he was, and deserving of the illustrious martyrdom which he won, he says, "What swelling of arrogance it is, what forgetfulness of humility and gentleness, that any one should dare or believe that he can do what the Lord did not grant even to the apostles,—to think that he can distinguish the tares from the wheat, or, as if it were granted to him to carry the fan and purge the floor, to endeavor to separate the chaff from the grain! And whereas the apostle says, 'But in a great house there are not only vessels of gold and of silver, but also of wood and of earth,'[2] that he should seem to choose those of gold and of silver, and despise and cast away and condemn those of wood and of earth, when really the vessels of wood are only to be burned in the day of the Lord by the burning of the divine conflagration, and those of earth are to be broken by Him to whom the 'rod of iron[3] has been given.'"[4] By this argument, therefore, against those who, under the pretext of avoiding the society of wicked men, had severed themselves from the unity of the Church, Cyprian shows that by the great house of which the apostle spoke, in which there were not only vessels of gold and of silver, but also of wood and of earth, he understood nothing else but the Church, in which there should be good and bad, till at the last day it should be cleansed as a threshing-floor by the winnowing-fan. And if this be so, in the Church herself, that is, in the great house itself, there were vessels to dishonor, whose word did spread like a canker. For the apostle, speaking of them, taught as follows: "And their word," he says, "will spread as doth a canker; of whom is Hymenæus and Philetus; who concerning the truth have erred, saying that the resurrection is past already; and overthrow the faith of some. Nevertheless the foundation of God standeth sure, having this seal, The Lord knoweth them that are His. And, Let every one that nameth the name of Christ depart from iniquity. But in a great house there are not only vessels of gold and of silver, but also of wood and of earth."[5] If, therefore, they whose words did spread as doth a canker were as it were vessels to dishonor in the great house, and by that "great house" Cyprian understands the unity of the Church itself, surely it cannot be that their canker polluted the baptism of Christ. Accordingly, neither without, any more than within, can any one who is of the devil's party, either in himself or in any other person, stain the sacrament which is of Christ. It is not, therefore, the case that "the word which spreads as a canker to the ears of those who hear it gives remission of sins;"[6] but when baptism is given in the words of the gospel, however great be the perverseness of understanding on the part either of him through whom, or of him to whom it is given, the sacrament itself is holy in itself on account of Him whose sacrament it is. And if any one, receiving it at the hands of a misguided man, yet does not receive the perversity of the minister, but only the holiness of the mystery, being closely bound to the unity of the Church in good faith and hope and charity, he receives remission of his sins,—not by the words which do eat as doth a canker, but by the sacraments of the gospel flowing from a heavenly source. But if the recipient himself be misguided, on the one hand, what is given is of no avail for the salvation of the misguided man; and yet, on the other hand, that which is received remains holy in the recipient, and is not renewed to him if he be brought to the right way.

CHAP. 13.—20. There is therefore "no fellowship between righteousness and unrighteousness,"[7] not only without, but also within the Church; for "the Lord knoweth them that are His," and "Let every one that nameth the name of Christ depart from iniquity." There is also "no communion between light and darkness,"[8] not only without, but also within the Church; for "he that hateth his brother is still in darkness."[9] And they at any rate hated Paul, who, preaching Christ of envy and malicious strife, supposed that they added affliction to his bonds;[10] and yet the same Cyprian understands these still to have been within the Church. Since, therefore, "neither darkness can enlighten, nor

[1] Antonianus, a bishop of Numidia, wrote 252 A.D., to Cyprian, favoring his milder view in opposition to the purism of Novatian: subsequently Novatian wrote to him, advocating the purist movement and impugning the laxity of Cornelius, bp. of Rome. To overthrow the effect upon A. of this letter, Cyprian wrote Epistle LV. In Ep. LXX., A. is of the number of those Numidian bishops whom Cyprian addresses.

[2] 2 Tim. ii. 20. [3] Ps. ii. 9. [4] Cypr. *Ep.* lv. 25.

[5] 2 Tim. ii. 17-20. [6] Cypr. *Ep.* lxxiii. 15. [7] Cypr. *Ep.* lxxiii. 15; 2 Cor. vi. 14. [8] *Ib.* [9] 1 John ii. 9. [10] Phil. i. 15, 16.

unrighteousness justify,"[1] as Cyprian again says, I ask, how could those men baptize within the very Church herself? I ask, how could those vessels which the large house contains not to honor, but to dishonor, administer what is holy for the sanctifying of men within the great house itself, unless because that holiness of the sacrament cannot be polluted even by the unclean, either when it is given at their hands, or when it is received by those who in heart and life are not changed for the better? of whom, as situated within the Church, Cyprian himself says, "Renouncing the world in word only, and not in deed."[2]

21. There are therefore also within the Church "enemies of God, whose hearts the spirit of Antichrist has possessed;" and yet they "deal with spiritual and divine things,"[3] which cannot profit for their salvation so long as they remain such as they are; and yet neither can they pollute them by their own uncleanness. With regard to what he says, therefore, "that they have no part given them in the saving grace of the Church, who, scattering and fighting against the Church of Christ, are called adversaries by Christ Himself, and antichrists by His apostles,[3] this must be received under the consideration that there are men of this kind both within and without. But the separation of those that are within from the perfection and unity of the dove is not only known in the case of some men to God, but even in the case of some to their fellow-men; for, by regarding their openly abandoned life and confirmed wickedness, and comparing it with the rules of God's commandments, they understand to what a multitude of tares and chaff, situated now some within and some without, but destined to be most manifestly separated at the last day, the Lord will then say, "Depart from me, ye that work iniquity,"[4] and "Depart into everlasting fire, prepared for the devil and his angels."[5]

Chap. 14.—22. But we must not despair of the conversion of any man, whether situated within or without, so long as "the goodness of God leadeth him to repentance,"[6] and "visits their transgressions with the rod, and their inquity with stripes." For in this way "He does not utterly take from them His loving-kindness,"[7] if they will themselves sometimes "love their own soul, pleasing God."[8] But as the good man "that shall endure unto the end, the same shall be saved,"[9] so the bad man, whether within or without, who shall persevere in his wickedness to the end, shall not be saved. Nor do we say that "all, wheresoever and howsoever baptized, obtain the graceof baptism,"[10] if by the grace of baptism is understood the actual salvation which is conferred by the celebration of the sacrament; but many fail to obtain this salvation even within the Church, although it is clear that they possess the sacrament, which is holy in itself. Well, therefore, does the Lord warn us in the gospel that we should not company with ill-advisers,[11] who walk under the pretence of Christ's name; but these are found both within and without, as, in fact, they do not proceed without unless they have first been ill-disposed within. And we know that the apostle said of the vessels placed in the great house, "If a man therefore purge himself from these, he shall be a vessel unto honor, sanctified, and meet for the Master's use, and prepared unto every good work."[12] But in what manner each man ought to purge himself from these he shows a little above, saying, "Let every one that nameth the name of Christ depart from iniquity,"[13] that he may not in the last day, with the chaff, whether with that which has already been driven from the threshing-floor, or with that which is to be separated at the last, hear the command, "Depart from me, ye that work iniquity."[14] Whence it appears, indeed, as Cyprian says, that "we are not at once to admit and adopt whatsoever is professed in the name of Christ, but only what is done in the truth of Christ."[15] But it is not an action done in the truth of Christ that men should "seize on estates by fraudulent pretenses, and increase their gains by accumulated usury,"[16] or that they should "renounce the world in word only;"[17] and yet, that all this is done within the Church, Cyprian himself bears sufficient testimony.

Chap. 15.—23. To go on to the point which he pursues at great length, that "they who blaspheme the Father of Christ cannot be baptized in Christ,"[18] since it is clear that they blaspheme through error (for he who comes to the baptism of Christ will not openly blaspheme the Father of Christ, but he is led to blaspheme by holding a view contrary to the teaching of the truth about the Father of Christ), we have already shown at sufficient length that baptism, consecrated in the words of the gospel, is not affected by the error of

1 Cypr. *l.c.* 2 Cypr. *Ep.* xi. 1. 3 Cypr. *Ep.* lxxiii. 15. 4 Matt. vii. 23. 5 Matt. xxv. 41. 6 Rom. ii. 4. 7 Ps. lxxxix. 32, 33. 8 Ecclus. xxx. 23. The words "*placentes Deo*" are derived from the Latin version only.

9 Matt. xxiv. 13. 10 From a letter of Pope Stephen's, quoted Cypr. *Ep.* lxxiii. 16. 11 Mark xiii. 21. 12 2 Tim. ii. 21. 13 2 Tim. ii. 19. 14 Matt. vii. 23. 15 Cypr. *Ep.* lxxiii. 16. 16 *Ib. de Laps.* c. vi. 17 *Ib. Ep.* xi. 1. 18 *Ib. Ep.* lxxiii. 17.

any man, whether ministrant or recipient, whether he hold views contrary to the revelation of divine teaching on the subject of the Father, or the Son, or the Holy Ghost. For many carnal and natural men are baptized even within the Church, as the apostle expressly says: "The natural man receiveth not the things of the Spirit of God;"[1] and after they had received baptism, he says that they "are yet carnal."[2] But according to it carnal sense, a soul given up to fleshly appetites cannot entertain but fleshly wisdom about God. Wherefore many, progressing after baptism, and especially those who have been baptized in infancy or early youth, in proportion as their intellect becomes clearer and brighter, while "the inward man is renewed day by day,"[3] throw away their former opinions which they held about God while they were mocked with vain imaginings, with scorn and horror and confession of their mistake. And yet they are not therefore considered not to have received baptism, or to have received baptism of a kind corresponding to their error; but in them both the perfection of the sacrament is honored and the delusion of their mind is corrected, even though it had become inveterate through long confirmation, or been, perhaps, maintained in many controversies. Wherefore even the heretic, who is manifestly without, if he has there received baptism as ordained in the gospel, has certainly not received baptism of a kind corresponding to the error which blinds him. And therefore, in returning into the way of wisdom he perceives that he ought to relinquish what he has held amiss, he must not at the same time give up the good which he had received; nor because his error is to be condemned, is the baptism of Christ in him to be therefore extinguished. For it is already sufficiently clear, from the case of those who happen to be baptized within the Church with false views about God, that the truth of the sacrament is to be distinguished from the error of him who believes amiss, although both may be found in the same man. And therefore, when any one grounded in any error, even outside the Church, has yet been baptized with the true sacrament, when he is restored to the unity of the Church, a true baptism cannot take the place of a true baptism, as a true faith takes the place of a false one, because a thing cannot take the place of itself, since neither can it give place. Heretics therefore join the Catholic Church to this end, that what they have evil of themselves may be corrected, not that what they have good of God should be repeated.

[1] 1 Cor. ii. 14. [2] 1 Cor. iii. 3. [3] 2 Cor. iv. 16.

CHAP. 16.—24. Some one says, Does it then make no difference, if two men, rooted in like error and wickedness, be baptized without change of life or heart, one without, the other within the Church? I acknowledge that there is a difference. For he is worse who is baptized without, in addition to his other sin,—not because of his baptism, however, but because he is without; for the evil of division is in itself far from insignificant or trivial. Yet the difference exists only if he who is baptized within has desired to be within not for the sake of any earthly or temporal advantage, but because he has preferred the unity of the Church spread throughout the world to the divisions of schism; otherwise he too must be considered among those who are without. Let us therefore put the two cases in this way. Let us suppose that the one, for the sake of argument, held the same opinions as Photinus[4] about Christ, and was baptized in his heresy outside the communion of the Catholic Church; and that another held the same opinion but was baptized in the Catholic Church, believing that his view was really the Catholic faith. I consider him as not yet a heretic, unless, when the doctrine of the Catholic faith is made clear to him, he chooses to resist it, and prefers that which he already holds; and till this is the case, it is clear that he who was baptized outside is the worse. And so in the one case erroneous opinion alone, in the other the sin of schism also, requires correction; but in neither of them is the truth of the sacrament to be repeated. But if any one holds the same view as the first, and knows that it is only in heresy severed from the Church that such a view is taught or learned, but yet for the sake of some temporal emolument has desired to be baptized in the Catholic unity, or, having been already baptized in it, is unwilling on account of the said emolument to secede from it, he is not only to be considered as seceding, but his offense is aggravated, in so far as to the error of heresy and the division of unity he adds the deceit of hypocrisy. Wherefore the depravity of each man, in proportion as it is more dangerous and wanting in straightforwardness, must be corrected with the more earnestness and energy; and yet, if he has anything that is good in him, especially if it be not of himself, but from God, we ought not to think it of no value because of his depravity, or to be blamed like it, or to be ascribed to it, rather than to His bountiful goodness, who even to a soul that plays the harlot, and

[4] Various Synods from 345 on anathematized Photinus, the bishop of Sirmium. The two of Sirmium, 351 and 357, accused him of constituting two Gods.

goes after her lovers, yet gives His bread, and His wine, and His oil, and other food or ornaments, which are neither from herself nor from her lovers, but from Him who in compassion for her is even desirous to warn her to whom she should return.[1]

Chap. 17.—25. "Can the power of baptism," says Cyprian, "be greater or better than confession? than martyrdom? that a man should confess Christ before men, and be baptized in his own blood? And yet," he goes on to say, "neither does this baptism profit the heretic, even though for confessing Christ he be put to death outside the Church."[2] This is most true; for, by being put to death outside the Chruch, he is proved not to have had charity, of which the apostle says, "Though I give my body to be burned, and have not charity, it profiteth me nothing."[3] But if martyrdom is of no avail for this reason, because it has not charity, neither does it profit those who, as Paul says, and Cyprian further sets forth, are living within the Church without charity in envy and malice; and yet they can both receive and transmit true baptism. "Salvation," he says, "is not without the Church."[4] Who says that it is? And therefore, whatever men have that belongs to the Church, it profits them nothing towards salvation outside the Church. But it is one thing not to have, another to have so as to be of no use. He who has not must be baptized that he may have; but he who has to no avail must be corrected, that what he has may profit him. Nor is the water in the baptism of heretics "adulterous,"[4] because neither is the creature itself which God made evil, nor is fault to be found with the words of the gospel in the mouths of any who are astray; but the fault is theirs in whom there is an adulterous spirit, even though it may receive the adornment of the sacrament from a lawful spouse. Baptism therefore can "be common to us, and the heretics,"[4] just as the gospel can be common to us, whatever difference there may be between our faith and their error,—whether they think otherwise than the truth about the Father, or the Son, or the Holy Spirit; or, being cut away from unity, do not gather with Christ, but scatter abroad,[5]—seeing that the sacrament of baptism can be common to us, if we are the wheat of the Lord, with the covetous within the Church, and with robbers, and drunkards, and other pestilent persons of the same sort, of whom it is said, "They shall not inherit the kingdom of God,"[6] and yet the vices by which they are separated from the kingdom of God are not shared by us.

Chap. 18.—26. Nor indeed, is it of heresies alone that the apostle says "that they which do such things shall not inherit the kingdom of God." But it may be worth while to look for a moment at the things which he groups together. "The works of the flesh," he says "are manifest, which are these; fornication, uncleanness, lasciviousness, idolatry, witchcraft, hatred, variance, emulations, wrath, strife, seditions, heresies, envyings, murders, drunkenness, revellings, and such like: of the which I tell you before, as I have also told you in time past, that they which do such things shall not inherit the kingdom of God."[7] Let us suppose some one, therefore, chaste, continent, free from covetousness, no idolater, hospitable, charitable to the needy, no man's enemy, not contentious, patient, quiet, jealous of none, envying none, sober, frugal, but a heretic; it is of course clear to all that for this one fault only, that he is a heretic, he will fail to inherit the kingdom of God. Let us suppose another, a fornicator, unclean, lascivious, covetous, or even more openly given to idolatry, a student of witchcraft, a lover of strife and contention, envious, hot-tempered, seditious, jealous, drunken, and a reveller, but a Catholic; can it be that for this sole merit, that he is a Catholic, he will inherit the kingdom of God, though his deeds are of the kind of which the apostle thus concludes: "Of the which I tell you before, as I have also told you in time past, that they which do such things shall not inherit the kingdom of God?" If we say this, we lead ourselves astray. For the word of God does not lead us astray, which is neither silent, nor lenient, nor deceptive through any flattery. Indeed, it speaks to the same effect elsewhere: "For this ye know, that no whoremonger, nor unclean person, nor covetous man, which is an idolater, hath any inheritance in the kingdom of Christ and of God. Let no man deceive you with vain words."[8] We have no reason, therefore, to complain of the word of God. It certainly says, and says openly and freely, that those who live a wicked life have no part in the kingdom of God.

Chap. 19.—27.—Let us therefore not flatter the Catholic who is hemmed in with all these vices, nor venture, merely because he is a Catholic Christian, to promise him the impunity which holy Scripture does not prom-

[1] Hos. ii. 5-8
[2] Cypr. *Ep.* lxxiii. 21
[3] 1 Cor. xiii. 3.
[4] Cyp. *l.c.*
[5] Matt. xii. 30.
[6] 1 Cor. vi. 10.
[7] Gal. v. 19-21.
[8] Eph. v. 5, 6.

ise him; nor, if he has any one of the faults above mentioned, ought we to promise him a partnership in that heavenly land. For, in writing to the Corinthians, the apostle enumerates the several sins, under each of which it is implicitly understood that it shall not inherit the kingdom of God: "Be not deceived," he says: "neither fornicators, nor idolaters, nor adulterers, nor effeminate, nor abusers of themselves with mankind, nor thieves, nor covetous, nor drunkards, nor revilers, nor extortioners, shall inherit the kingdom of God."[1] He does not say, those who possess all these vices together shall not inherit the kingdom of God; but neither these nor those: so that, as each is named, you may understand that no one of them shall inherit the kingdom of God. As, therefore, heretics shall not possess the kingdom of God, so the covetous shall not inherit the kingdom of God. Nor can we indeed doubt that the punishments themselves, with which they shall be tortured who do not inherit the kingdom of God, will vary in proportion to the difference of their offences, and that some will be more severe than others; so that in the eternal fire itself there will be different tortures in the punishments, corresponding to the different weights of guilt. For indeed it was not idly that the Lord said, "It shall be more tolerable for the land of Sodom in the day of judgment than for thee."[2] But yet, so far as failing to inherit the kingdom of God is concerned, it is just as certain, if you choose any one of the less heinous of these vices, as if you choose more than one, or some one which you saw was more atrocious; and because those will inherit the kingdom of God whom the Judge shall set on His right hand, and for those who shall not be found worthy to be set at the right hand nothing will remain but to be at the left, no other announcement is left for them to hear like goats from the mouth of the Shepherd, except, "Depart into everlasting fire, prepared for the devil and his angels;"[3] though in that fire, as I said before, it may be that different punishments will be awarded corresponding to the difference of the sins.

CHAP. 20.—28. But on the question whether we ought to prefer a Catholic of the most abandoned character to a heretic in whose life, except that he is a heretic, men can find nothing to blame, I do not venture to give a hasty judgment. But if any one says, because he is a heretic, he cannot be this only without other vices also following,—for he is carnal and natural, and therefore must be also envious, and hot-tempered, and jealous, and hostile to truth itself, and utterly estranged from it,—let him fairly understand, that of those other faults of which he is supposed to have chosen some one less flagrant, a single one cannot exist by itself in any man, because he in turn is carnal and natural; as, to take the case of drunkenness, which people have now become accustomed to talk of not only without horror, but with some degree of merriment, can it possibly exist alone in any one in whom it is found? For what drunkard is not also contentious, and hot-tempered, and jealous, and at variance with all soundness of counsel, and at grievous enmity with those who rebuke him? Further, it is not easy for him to avoid being a fornicator and adulterer, though he may be no heretic; just as a heretic may be no drunkard, nor adulterer, nor fornicator, nor lascivious, nor a lover of money, or given to witchcraft, and cannot well be all these together. Nor indeed is any one vice followed by all the rest. Supposing, therefore, two men,—one a Catholic with all these vices, the other a heretic free from all from which a heretic can be free,—although they do not both contend against the faith, and yet each lives contrary to the faith, and each is deceived by a vain hope, and each is far removed from charity of spirit, and therefore each is severed from connection with the body of the one dove; why do we recognise in one of them the sacrament of Christ, and not in the other, as though it belonged to this or that man, whilst really it is the same in both, and belongs to God alone, and is good even in the worst of men? And if of the men who have it, one is worse than another, it does not follow that the sacrament which they have is worse in the one than in the other, seeing that neither in the case of two bad Catholics, if one be worse than the other, does he possess a worse baptism, nor, if one of them be good and another bad, is baptism bad in the bad one and good in the good one; but it is good in both. Just as the light of the sun, or even of a lamp, is certainly not less brilliant when displayed to bad eyes than when seen by better ones; but it is the same in the case of both, although it either cheers or hurts them differently according to the difference of their powers.

CHAP. 21.—29. With regard to the objection brought against Cyprian, that the catechumens who were seized in martyrdom, and slain for Christ's name's sake, received a crown even without baptism, I do not quite see what it has to do with the matter, unless,

[1] 1 Cor. vi. 9, 10 [2] Matt. xi. 24. [3] Matt. xxv. 41.

indeed, they urged that heretics could much more be admitted with baptism to Christ's kingdom, to which catechumens were admitted without it, since He Himself has said, "Except a man be born of water and of the Spirit, he cannot enter into the kingdom of God."[1] Now, in this matter I do not hesitate for a moment to place the Catholic catechumen, who is burning with love for God, before the baptized heretic; nor yet do we thereby do dishonor to the sacrament of baptism which the latter has already received, the former not as yet; nor do we consider that the sacrament of the catechumen[2] is to be preferred to the sacrament of baptism, when we acknowledge that some catechumens are better and more faithful than some baptized persons. For the centurion Cornelius, before baptism, was better than Simon, who had been baptized. For Cornelius, even before his baptism, was filled with the Holy Spirit;[3] Simon, even after baptism, was puffed up with an unclean spirit.[4] Cornelius, however, would have been convicted of contempt for so holy a sacrament, if, even after he had received the Holy Ghost, he had refused to be baptized. But when he was baptized, he received in no wise a better sacrament than Simon; but the different merits of the men were made manifest under the equal holiness of the same sacrament—so true is it that the good or ill deserving of the recipient does not increase or diminish the holiness of baptism. But as baptism is wanting to a good catechumen to his receiving the kingdom of heaven, so true conversion is wanting to a bad man though baptized. For He who said, "Except a man be born of water and of the Spirit, he cannot enter into the kingdom of God," said also Himself, "except your righteousness shall exceed the righteousness of the scribes and Pharisees, ye shall in no case enter into the kingdom of heaven."[5] For that the righteousness of the catechumens might not feel secure, it is written, "Except a man be born again of water and of the Spirit, he cannot enter into the kingdom of God." And again, that the unrighteousness of the baptized might not feel secure because they had received baptism, it is written, "Except your righteousness shall exceed the righteousness of the scribes and Pharisees, ye shall in no case enter into the kingdom of heaven." The one were too little without the other; the two make perfect the heir of that inheritance. As, then, we ought not to depreciate a man's righteousness, which begins to exist before he is joined to the Church, as the righteousness of Cornelius began to exist before he was in the body of Christian men,—which righteousness was not thought worthless, or the angel would not have said to him, "Thy prayers and thine alms are come up as a memorial before God;" nor did it yet suffice for his obtaining the kingdom of heaven, or he would not have been told to send to Peter,[6]—so neither ought we to depreciate the sacrament of baptism, even though it has been received outside the Church. But since it is of no avail for salvation unless he who has baptism indeed in full perfection be incorporated into the Church, correcting also his own depravity, let us therefore correct the error of the heretics, that we may recognize what in them is not their own but Christ's.

Chap. 22.—30. That the place of baptism is sometimes supplied by martyrdom is supported by an argument by no means trivial, which the blessed Cyprian adduces[7] from the thief, to whom, though he was not baptized, it was yet said, "To-day shalt thou be with me in Paradise."[8] On considering which, again and again, I find that not only martyrdom for the sake of Christ may supply what was wanting of baptism, but also faith and conversion of heart, if recourse may not be had to the celebration of the mystery of baptism for want of time.[9] For neither was that thief crucified for the name of Christ, but as the reward of his own deeds; nor did he suffer because he believed, but he believed while suffering. It was shown, therefore, in the case of that thief, how great is the power, even without the visible sacrament of baptism, of what the apostle says, "With the heart man believeth unto righteousness, and with the mouth confession is made unto salvation."[10] But the want is supplied invisibly only when the administration of baptism is prevented, not by contempt for religion, but by the necessity of the moment. For much more in the case of Cornelius and his friends, than in the case of that robber, might it seem superfluous that they should also be baptized with water, seeing that in them the gift of the Holy Spirit, which, according to the testi-

1 John iii. 5.

2 Another reading, of less authority, is, "*Aut catechumeno sacramentum baptismi præferendum putamus.*" This does not suit the sense of the passage, and probably sprung from want of knowledge of the meaning of the "catechumen's sacrament." It is mentioned in the Council of Carthage, A.D. 397, as "the sacrament of salt" (cap.5). Augustin (*de Peccat. Meritis*, ii. c. 26), says that "what the catechumens receive, though it be not the body of Christ, yet is holy, more holy than the food whereby our bodies are sustained, because it is a sacrament."—Cp. *de Catech. Rudibus*, c. 26 [Bened.]. It appears to have been only a taste of salt, given them as the emblem of purity and incorruption. See Bingham, *Orig. Eccles.* Book x. c. ii. 16.

3 Acts x. 44. 4 Acts viii. 13, 18, 19. 5 Matt. v. 20.

6 Acts x. 4, 5. 7 Cypr. *Ep.* lxxiii. 22. 8 Luke xxiii. 43.

9 In *Retract.* ii. 18, Augustin expresses a doubt whether the thief may not have been baptized.

10 Rom. x. 10.

mony of holy Scripture, was received by other men only after baptism, had made itself manifest by every unmistakable sign appropriate to those times when they spoke with tongues. Yet they were baptized, and for this action we have the authority of an apostle as the warrant. So far ought all of us to be from being induced by any imperfection in the inner man, if it so happen that before baptism a person has advanced, through the workings of a pious heart, to spiritual understanding, to despise a sacrament which is applied to the body by the hands of the minister, but which is God's own means for working spiritually a man's dedication to Himself. Nor do I conceive that the function of baptizing was assigned to John, so that it should be called John's baptism, for any other reason except that the Lord Himself, who had appointed it, in not disdaining to receive the baptism of His servant,[1] might consecrate the path of humility, and show most plainly by such an action how high a value was to be placed on His own baptism, with which He Himself was afterwards to baptize. For He saw, like an excellent physician of eternal salvation, that overweening pride would be found in some, who, having made such progress in the understanding of the truth and in uprightness of character that they would not hesitate to place themselves, both in life and knowledge, above many that were baptized, would think it was unnecessary for them to be baptized, since they felt that they had attained a frame of mind to which many that were baptized were still only endeavoring to raise themselves.

CHAP. 23.—31. But what is the precise value of the sanctification of the sacrament (which that thief did not receive, not from any want of will on his part, but because it was unavoidably omitted) and what is the effect on a man of its material application, it is not easy to say. Still, had it not been of the greatest value, the Lord would not have received the baptism of a servant. But since we must look at it in itself, without entering upon the question of the salvation of the recipient, which it is intended to work, it shows clearly enough that both in the bad, and in those who renounce the world in word and not in deed, it is itself complete, though they cannot receive salvation unless they amend their lives. But as in the thief, to whom the material administration of the sacrament was necessarily wanting, the salvation was complete, because it was spiritually present through his piety, so, when the sacrament itself is present, salvation is complete, if what the thief possessed be unavoidably wanting. And this is the firm tradition of the universal Church, in respect of the baptism of infants, who certainly are as yet unable "with the heart to believe unto righteousness, and with the mouth to make confession unto salvation," as the thief could do; nay, who even, by crying and moaning when the mystery is performed upon them, raise their voices in opposition to the mysterious words, and yet no Christian will say that they are baptized to no purpose.

CHAP. 24.—32. And if any one seek for divine authority in this matter, though what is held by the whole Church, and that not as instituted by Councils, but as a matter of invariable custom, is rightly held to have been handed down by apostolical authority, still we can form a true conjecture of the value of the sacrament of baptism in the case of infants, from the parallel of circumcision, which was received by God's earlier people, and before receiving which Abraham was justified, as Cornelius also was enriched with the gift of the Holy Spirit before he was baptized. Yet the apostle says of Abraham himself, that "he received the sign of circumcision, a seal of the righteousness of the faith," having already believed in his heart, so that "it was counted unto him for righteousness."[2] Why, therefore, was it commanded him that he should circumcise every male child in order on the eighth day,[3] though it could not yet believe with the heart, that it should be counted unto it for righteousness, because the sacrament in itself was of great avail? And this was made manifest by the message of an angel in the case of Moses' son; for when he was carried by his mother, being yet uncircumcised, it was required, by manifest present peril, that he should be circumcised,[4] and when this was done, the danger of death was removed. As therefore in Abraham the justification of faith came first, and circumcision was added afterwards as the seal of faith; so in Cornelius the spiritual sanctification came first in the gift of the Holy Spirit, and the sacrament of regeneration was added afterwards in the laver of baptism. And as in Isaac, who was circumcised on the eighth day after his birth, the seal of this righteousness of faith was given first, and afterwards, as he imitated the faith of his father, the righteousness itself followed as he grew up, of which the seal had been given before when he was an infant; so in infants, who are baptized,

[1] Matt. iii. 6, 13.

[2] Rom. iv. 11, 3.

[3] Gen. xvii. 9-14.

[4] Ex. iv. 24-26.

the sacrament of regeneration is given first, and if they maintain a Christian piety, conversion also in the heart will follow, of which the mysterious sign had gone before in the outward body. And as in the thief the gracious goodness of the Almighty supplied what had been wanting in the sacrament of baptism, because it had been missing not from pride or contempt, but from want of opportunity; so in infants who die baptized, we must believe that the same grace of the Almighty supplies the want, that, not from perversity of will, but from insufficiency of age, they can neither believe with the heart unto righteousness, nor make confession with the mouth unto salvation. Therefore, when others take the vows for them, that the celebration of the sacrament may be complete in their behalf, it is unquestionably of avail for their dedication to God, because they cannot answer for themselves. But if another were to answer for one who could answer for himself, it would not be of the same avail. In accordance with which rule, we find in the gospel what strikes every one as natural when he reads it, "He is of age, he shall speak for himself."[1]

Chap. 25.—33. By all these considerations it is proved that the sacrament of baptism is one thing, the conversion of the heart another; but that man's salvation is made complete through the two together. Nor are we to suppose that, if one of these be wanting, it necessarily follows that the other is wanting also; because the sacrament may exist in the infant without the conversion of the heart; and this was found to be possible without the sacrament in the case of the thief, God in either case filling up what was involuntarily wanting. But when either of these requisites is wanting intentionally, then the man is responsible for the omission. And baptism may exist when the conversion of the heart is wanting; but, with respect to such conversion, it may indeed be found when baptism has not been received, but never when it has been despised. Nor can there be said in any way to be a turning of the heart to God when the sacrament of God is treated with contempt. Therefore we are right in censuring, anathematizing, abhorring, and abominating the perversity of heart shown by heretics; yet it does not follow that they have not the sacrament of the gospel, because they have not what makes it of avail. Wherefore, when they come to the true faith, and by penitence seek remission of their sins, we are not flattering or deceiving them, when we instruct them by heavenly discipline for the kingdom of heaven, correcting and reforming in them their errors and perverseness, to the intent that we may by no means do violence to what is sound in them, nor, because of man's fault, declare that anything which he may have in him from God is either valueless or faulty.

Chap. 26.—34. A few things still remain to be noticed in the epistle to Jubaianus; but since these will raise the question both of the past custom of the Church and of the baptism of John, which is wont to excite no small doubt in those who pay slight attention to a matter which is sufficiently obvious, seeing that those who had received the baptism of John were commanded by the apostle to be baptized again,[2] they are not to be treated in a hasty manner, and had better be reserved for another book, that the dimensions of this may not be inconveniently large.

[1] John ix. 21.

[2] Acts xix. 3-5.

BOOK V.

HE EXAMINES THE LAST PART OF THE EPISTLE OF CYPRIAN TO JUBAIANUS, TOGETHER WITH HIS EPISTLE TO QUINTUS, THE LETTER OF THE AFRICAN SYNOD TO THE NUMIDIAN BISHOPS, AND CYPRIAN'S EPISTLE TO POMPEIUS.

CHAP. 1.—1. We have the testimony of the blessed Cyprian, that the custom of the Catholic Church is at present retained, when men coming from the side of heretics or schismatics, if they have received baptism as consecrated in the words of the gospel, are not baptized afresh. For he himself proposed to himself the question, and that as coming from the mouth of brethren either seeking the truth or contending for the truth. For in the course of the arguments by which he wished to show that heretics should be baptized again, which we have sufficiently considered for our present purpose in the former books, he says: "But some will say, What then will become of those who in times past, coming to the Church from heresy, were admitted without baptism?"[1] In this question is involved the shipwreck of the whole cause of the Donatists, with whom our contest is on this point. For if those had not really baptism who were thus received on coming from heretics, and their sins were still upon them, then, when such men were admitted to communion, either by those who came before Cyprian or by Cyprian himself, we must acknowledge that one of two things occurred,—either that the Church perished then and there from the pollution of communion with such men, or that any one abiding in unity is not injured by even the notorious sins of other men. But since they cannot say that the Church then perished through the contamination arising from communion with those who, as Cyprian says, were admitted into it without baptism—for otherwise they cannot maintain the validity of their own origin if the Church then perished, seeing that the list of consuls proves that more than forty years elapsed between the martyrdom of Cyprian and the burning of the sacred books,[2] from which they took occasion to make a schism, spreading abroad the smoke of their calumnies,—it therefore is left for them to acknowledge that the unity of Christ is not polluted by any such communion, even with known offenders. And, after this confession, they will be unable to discover any reason which will justify them in maintaining that they were bound to separate from the churches of the whole world, which, as we read, were equally founded by the apostles, seeing that, while the others could not have perished from any admixture of offenders, of whatsoever kind, they, though they would not have perished if they had remained in unity with them, brought destruction on themselves in schism, by separating themselves from their brethren, and breaking the bond of peace. For the sacrilege of schism is most clearly evident in them, if they had no sufficient cause for separation. And it is clear that there was no sufficient cause for separation, if even the presence of notorious offenders cannot pollute the good while they abide in unity. But that the good, abiding in unity, are not polluted even by notorious offenders, we teach on the testimony of Cyprian, who says that "men in past times, coming to the Church from heresy, were admitted without baptism;" and yet, if the wickedness of their sacrilege, which was still upon them, seeing it had not been purged away by baptism, could not pollute and destroy the holiness of the Church, it cannot perish by any infection from wicked men. Wherefore, if they allow that Cyprian spoke the truth, they are convicted of schism on his testimony; if they maintain that he does not speak truth, let them not use his testimony on the question of baptism.

[1] Cypr. *Ep.* lxxiii. *ad Jubaian.* 23.

[2] See below, Book VII. c. 2, 3.

Chap. 2.—2. But now that we have begun a disputation with a man of peace like Cyprian, let us go on. For when he had brought an objection against himself, which he knew was urged by his brethren, "What then will become of those who in times past, coming to the Church from heresy, were admitted without baptism? The Lord," he answers, "is able of His mercy to grant indulgence, and not to separate from the gifts of His Church those who, being admitted in all honesty to His Church, have fallen asleep within the Church."[1] Well indeed has he assumed that charity can cover the multitude of sins. But if they really had baptism, and this were not rightly perceived by those who thought that they should be baptized again, that error was covered by the charity of unity so long as it contained, not the discord and spirit of the devil, but merely human infirmity, until, as the apostle says, "if they were otherwise minded, the Lord should reveal it to them."[2] But woe unto those who, being torn asunder from unity by a sacrilegious rupture, either rebaptize, if baptism exists with both us and them, or do not baptize at all, if baptism exist in the Catholic Church only. Whether, therefore, they rebaptize, or fail to baptize, they are not in the bond of peace; wherefore let them apply a remedy to which they please of these two wounds. But if we admit to the Church without baptism, we are of the number of those who, as Cyprian has assumed, may receive pardon because they preserved unity. But if (as is, I think, already clear from what has been said in the earlier books) Christian baptism can preserve its integrity even amid the perversity of heretics, then even though any in those times did rebaptize, yet without departing from the bond of unity, they might still attain to pardon in virtue of that same love of peace, through which Cyprian bears witness that those admitted even without baptism might obtain that they should not be separated from the gifts of the Church. Further, if it is true that with heretics and schismatics the baptism of Christ does not exist, how much less could the sins of others hurt those who were fixed in unity, if even men's own sins were forgiven when they came to it even without baptism! For if, according to Cyprian, the bond of unity is of such efficacy, how could they be hurt by other men's sins, who were unwilling to separate themselves from unity, if even the unbaptized, who wished to come to it from heresy, thereby escaped the destruction due to their own sins?

Chap. 3.—3. But in what Cyprian adds, saying, "Nor yet because men once have erred must there be always error, since it rather befits wise and God-fearing men gladly and unhesitatingly to follow truth, when it is clearly laid before their eyes, than obstinately and persistently to fight for heretics against their brethren and their fellow-priests,"[3] he is uttering the most perfect truth; and the man who resists the manifest truth is opposing himself rather than his neighbors. But, so far as I can judge, it is perfectly clear and certain, from the many arguments which I have already adduced, that the baptism of Christ cannot be invalidated even by the perversity of heretics, when it is given or received among them. But, granting that it is not yet certain, at any rate no one who has considered what has been said, even from a hostile point of view, will assert that the question has been decided the other way. Therefore we are not striving against manifest truth, but either, as I think, we are striving in behalf of what is clearly true, or, at any rate, as those may hold who think that the question has not yet been solved, we are seeking for the truth. And therefore, if the truth be other than we think, yet we are receiving those baptized by heretics with the same honesty of heart with which those received them whom, Cyprian supposed, in virtue of their cleaving to the unity of the Church, to be capable of pardon. But if the baptism of Christ, as is indicated by the many arguments used above, can retain its integrity amid any defect either of life or faith, whether on the part of those who seem to be within, and yet do not belong to the members of the one dove, or on the part of those whose severance from her extends to being openly without, then those who sought its repetition in those former days deserved the same pardon for their charity in clinging to unity, which Cyprian thought that those deserved for charity of the same kind whom he believed to have been admitted without baptism. They therefore who, without any cause (since, as Cyprian himself shows, the bad cannot hurt the good in the unity of the Church), have cut themselves off from the charity which is shown in this unity, have lost all place of pardon, and whilst they would incur destruction by the very crime of schism, even though they did not rebaptize those who had been baptized in the Catholic Church, of how bitter punishment are they deserving, who are either endeavoring to give to the Catholics who have it what Cyprian affirms that they themselves

[1] Cypr. *Ep.* lxxiii. 23.

[2] Phil. iii. 15.

[3] Cypr. *Ep.* lxxiii. 23.

have not, or, as is clear from the facts of the case, are bringing as a charge against the Catholic Church that she has not what even they themselves possess?

CHAP. 4.—4. But since now, as I said before, we have begun a disputation with the epistles of Cyprian, I think that I should not seem even to him, if he were present, "to be contending obstinately and persistently in defense of heretics against my brethren and my fellow-priests," when he learned the powerful reasons which move us to believe that even among heretics, who are perversely obstinate in their malignant error, the baptism of Christ is yet in itself most holy, and most highly to be reverenced. And seeing that he himself, whose testimony has such weight with us, bears witness that they were wont in past times to be admitted without a second baptism, I would have any one, who is induced by Cyprian's arguments to hold it as certain that heretics ought to be baptized afresh, yet consider that those who, on account of weight of the arguments on the other side, are not as yet persuaded that this should be so, hold the same place as those in past time, who in all honesty admitted men who were baptized in heresy on the simple correction of their individual error, and who were capable of salvation with them in virtue of the bond of unity. And let any one, who is led by the past custom of the Church, and by the subsequent authority of a plenary Council, and by so many powerful proofs from holy Scripture, and by much evidence from Cyprian himself, and by the clear reasoning of truth, to understand that the baptism of Christ, consecrated in the words of the gospel, cannot be perverted by the error of any man on earth,—let such an one understand, that they who then thought otherwise, but yet preserved their charity, can be saved by the same bond of unity. And herein he should also understand of those who, in the society of the Church dispersed throughout the world, could not have been defiled by any tares, by any chaff, so long as they themselves desired to be fruitful corn, and who therefore severed themselves from the same bond of unity without any cause for the divorce, that at any rate, whichever of the two opinions be true,—that which Cyprian then held, or that which was maintained by the universal voice of the Catholic Church, which Cyprian did not abandon,—in either case they, having most openly placed themselves outside in the plain sacrilege of schism, cannot possibly be saved, and all that they possess of the holy sacraments, and of the free gifts of the one legitimate Bridegroom, is of avail, while they continue what they are, for their confusion rather than the salvation of their souls.

CHAP. 5.—5. Wherefore, even if heretics should be truly anxious to correct their error and come to the Church, for the very reason that they believed that they had no baptism unless they received it in the Church, even under these circumstances we should not be bound to yield to their desire for the repetition of baptism; but rather they should be taught, on the one hand, that baptism, though perfect in itself, could in no way profit their perversity if they would not submit to be corrected; and, on the other hand, that the perfection of baptism could not be impaired by their perversity, while refusing to be corrected: and again, that no further perfection is added to baptism in them because they are submitting to correction; but that, while they themselves are quitting their iniquity, that which was before within them to their destruction is now beginning to be of profit for salvation. For, learning this, they will both recognize the need of salvation in Catholic unity, and will cease to claim as their own what is really Christ's, and will not confound the sacrament of truth, although existing in themselves, with their own individual error.

6. To this we may add a further reason, that men, by a sort of hidden inspiration from heaven, shrink from any one who for the second time receives baptism which he had already received in any quarter whatsoever, insomuch that the very heretics themselves, when their arguments start with that subject, rub their forehead in perplexity, and almost all their laity, even those who have grown old in their body, and have conceived an obstinate animosity against the Catholic Church, confess that this one point in their system displeases them; and many who, for the sake of gaining some secular advantage, or avoiding some disadvantage, wish to secede to them, strive with many secret efforts that they may have granted to them, as a peculiar and individual privilege, that they should not be rebaptized; and some, who are led to place credence in their other vain delusions and false accusations against the Catholic Church, are recalled to unity by this one consideration, that they are unwilling to associate with them lest they should be compelled to be rebaptized. And the Donatists, through fear of this feeling, which has so thorough possession of all men's hearts, have consented to acknowledge the baptism which was conferred among the followers of Maximianus, whom they had condemned, and so to cut short their own tongues

and close their mouths, in preference to baptizing again so many men of the people of Musti, and Assuræ, and other districts, whom they received with Felicianus and Prætextatus, and the others who had been condemned by them and afterwards returned to them.

Chap. 6.—7. For when this is done occasionally in the case of individuals, at great intervals of time and space, the enormity of the deed is not equally felt; but if all were suddenly to be brought together who had been baptized in course of time by the aforesaid followers of Maximianus, either under pressure of the peril of death or at their Easter solemnities, and it were told them that they must be baptized again, because what they had already received in the sacrilege of schism was null and void, they might indeed say what obstinate perseverance in their error would compel them to say, that they might hide the rigor and iciness of their hardness under any kind of false shade of consistency against the warmth of truth. But in fact, because the party of Maximianus could not bear this, and because the very men who would have to enforce it could not endure what must needs have been done in the case of so many men at once, especially as those very men would be rebaptizing them in the party of Primianus who had already baptized them in the party of Maximianus, for these reasons their baptism was received, and the pride of the Donatists was cut short. And this course they would certainly not have chosen to adopt, had they not thought that more harm would have been done to their cause by the offense men would have taken at the repetition of the baptism, than by the reputation lost in abandoning their defense. And this I would not say with any idea that we ought to be restrained by consideration of human feelings, if the truth compelled those who came from heretics to be baptized afresh. But because the holy Cyprian says, "that heretics might have been all the more impelled to the necessity of coming over, if only they were to be rebaptized in the Catholic Church,"[1] on this account I have wished to place on record the intensity of the repugnance to this act which is seated deeply in the heart of nearly every one,—a repugnance which I can believe was inspired by God Himself, that the Church might be fortified by the instinct of repugnance against any possible arguments which the weak cannot dispel.

Chap. 7.—8. Truly, when I look at the actual words of Cyprian, I am warned to say some things which are very necessary for the solution of this question. "For if they were to see," he says, "that it was settled and established by our formal decision and vote, that the baptism with which they are baptized in heresy is considered just and lawful, they will think that they are in just and lawful possession of the Church also, and all its other gifts."[2] He does not say "that they will think they are in possession," but "in just and lawful possession of the gifts of the Church." But we say that we cannot allow that they are *in just and lawful* possession of baptism. That they are in possession of it we cannot deny, when we recognize the sacrament of the Lord in the words of the gospel. They have therefore lawful baptism, but they do not have it lawfully. For whosoever has it both in Catholic unity, and living worthily of it, both has lawful baptism and has it lawfully; but whosoever has it either within the Catholic Church itself, as chaff mixed with the wheat, or outside, as chaff carried away by the wind, has indeed lawful baptism, but not lawfully. For he has it as he uses it. But the man does not use it lawfully who uses it against the law,—which every one does, who, being baptized, yet leads an abandoned life, whether inside or without the Church.

Chap 8.—9. Wherefore, as the apostle said of the law, "The law is good, if a man use it lawfully,"[3] so we may fairly say of baptism, Baptism is good, if a man use it lawfully. And as they who used the law unlawfully could not in that case cause that it should not be in itself good, or make it null and void, so any one who uses baptism unlawfully, either because he lives in heresy, or because he lives the worst of lives, yet cannot cause that the baptism should be otherwise than good, or altogether null and void. And so, when he is converted either to Catholic unity, or to a mode of living worthy of so great a sacrament, he begins to have not another and a lawful baptism, but that same baptism in a lawful manner. Nor does the remission of irrevocable sins follow on baptism, unless a man not only have lawful baptism, but have it lawfully; and yet it does not follow that if a man have it not lawfully, so that his sins are either not remitted, or, being remitted, are brought on him again, therefore the sacrament of baptism should be in the baptized person either bad or null and void. For as Judas, to whom the Lord gave a morsel, gave a place within himself of the devil, not by re-

[1] Cypr. *Ep.* lxxiii. 24.

[2] *Ib.*

[3] 1 Tim. i. 8.

ceiving what was bad, but by receiving it badly,[1] so each person, on receiving the sacrament of the Lord, does not cause that it is bad because he is bad himself, or that he has received nothing because he has not received it to salvation. For it was none the less the body of the Lord and the blood of the Lord, even in those to whom the apostle said, "He that eateth unworthily, eateth and drinketh damnation to himself."[2] Let the heretics therefore seek in the Catholic Church not what they have, but what they have not,—that is, the end of the commandment, without which many holy things may be possessed, but they cannot profit. "Now, the end of the commandment is charity out of a pure heart, and of a good conscience, and of faith unfeigned."[3] Let them therefore hasten to the unity and truth of the Catholic Church, not that they may have the sacrament of washing, if they have been already bathed in it, although in heresy, but that they may have it to their health.

CHAP. 9.—10. Now we must see what is said of the baptism of John. For "we read in the Acts of the Apostles, that those who had already been baptized with the baptism of John were yet baptized by Paul,"[4] simply because the baptism of John was not the baptism of Christ, but a baptism allowed by Christ to John, so as to be called especially John's baptism; as the same John says, "A man can receive nothing, except it be given him from heaven."[5] And that he might not possibly seem to receive this from God the Father in such wise as not to receive it from the Son, speaking presently of Christ Himself, he says, "Of His fullness have all we received."[6] But by the grace of a certain dispensation John received this, which was to last not for long, but only long enough to prepare for the Lord the way in which he must needs be the forerunner. And as our Lord was presently to enter on this way with all humility, and to lead those who humbly followed Him to perfection, as He washed the feet of His servants,[7] so was He willing to be baptized with the baptism of a servant.[8] For as He set Himself to minister to the feet of those whose guide He was Himself, so He submitted Himself to the gift of John which He Himself had given, that all might understand what sacrilegious arrogance they would show in despising the baptism which they ought each of them to receive from the Lord, when the Lord Himself accepted what He Himself had bestowed upon a servant, that he might give it as his own; and that when John, than whom no greater had arisen among them that are born of women,[9] bore such testimony to Christ, as to confess that he was not worthy to unloose the latchet of His shoe,[10] Christ might both, by receiving his baptism, be found to be the humblest among men, and, by taking away the place for the baptism of John, be believed to be the most high God, at once the teacher of humility and the giver of exaltation.

11. For to none of the prophets, to no one at all in holy Scripture, do we read that it was granted to baptize in the water of repentance for the remission of sins, as it was granted to John; that, causing the hearts of the people to hang upon him through this marvellous grace, he might prepare in them the way for Him whom he declared to be so infinitely greater than himself. But the Lord Jesus Christ cleanses His Church by such a baptism that on receiving it no other is required; while John gave a first washing with such a baptism that on receiving it there was further need of the baptism of the Lord,—not that the first baptism should be repeated, but that the baptism of Christ, for whom he was preparing the way, might be further bestowed on those who had received the baptism of John. For if Christ's humility were not to be commended to our notice, neither would there be any need of the baptism of John; again, if the end were in John, after his baptism there would be no need of the baptism of Christ. But because "Christ is the end of the law for righteousness to every one that believeth,"[11] it was shown by John to whom men should go, and in whom, when they had reached Him, they should rest. The same, John, therefore, set forth both the exalted nature of the Lord, when he placed Him far before himself, and His humility, when he baptized Him as the lowest of the people. But if John had baptized Christ alone, he would be thought to have been the dispenser of a better baptism, in that with which Christ alone was baptized, than the baptism of Christ with which Christians are baptized; and again, if all ought to be baptized first with the baptism of John, and then with that of Christ, the baptism of Christ would deservedly seem to be lacking in fullness and perfection, as not sufficing for salvation. Wherefore the Lord was baptized with the baptism of John, that He might bend the proud necks of men to His own health-giving baptism; and He was not alone baptized with it, lest He should

1 John xiii. 27. 2 1 Cor. xi. 29. 3 1 Tim. i. 5.
4 Cypr. *Ep.* lxxiii. 24; Acts xix. 3-5. 5 John iii. 27.
6 John i. 16. 7 John xiii. 4, 5. 8 Matt. iii. 13.

9 Matt. xi. 11. 10 John i. 27. 11 Rom. x. 4.

show His own to be inferior to this, with which none but He Himself had deserved to be baptized; and He did not allow it to continue longer, lest the one baptism with which He baptizes might seem to need the other to precede it.

Chap. 10.—12. I ask, therefore, if sins were remitted by the baptism of John, what more could the baptism of Christ confer on those whom the Apostle Paul desired to be baptized with the baptism of Christ after they had received the baptism of John? But if sins were not remitted by the baptism of John, were those men in the days of Cyprian better than John, of whom he says himself that they "used to seize on estates by treacherous frauds, and increase their gains by accumulated usuries,"[1] through whose administration of baptism the remission of sins was yet conferred? Or was it because they were contained within the unity of the Church? What then? Was John not contained within that unity, the friend of the Bridegroom, the preparer of the way of the Lord, the baptizer of the Lord Himself? Who will be mad enough to assert this? Wherefore, although my belief is that John so baptized with the water of repentance for the remission of sins, that those who were baptized by him received the expectation of the remission of their sins, the actual remission taking place in the baptism of the Lord,—just as the resurrection which is expected at the last day is fulfilled in hope in us, as the apostle says, that "He hath raised us up together, and made us sit together in heavenly places in Christ Jesus;"[2] and again, "For we are saved by hope;"[3] or as again John himself, while he says, "I indeed baptize you with water unto repentance, for the remission of your sins,"[4] yet says, on seeing our Lord, "Behold the Lamb of God, which taketh away the sin of the world,"[5]—nevertheless I am not disposed to contend vehemently against any one who maintains that sins were remitted even in the baptism of John, but that some fuller sanctification was conferred by the baptism of Christ on those whom Paul ordered to be baptized anew.[6]

Chap. 11.—13. For we must look at the point which especially concerns the matter before us (whatever be the nature of the baptism of John, since it is clear that he belongs to the unity of Christ), viz., what is the reason for which it was right that men should be baptized again after receiving the baptism of the holy John, and why they ought not to be baptized again after receiving the baptism of the covetous bishops. For no one denies that in the Lord's field John was as wheat, bearing an hundred-fold, if that be the highest rate of increase; also no one doubts that covetousness, which is idolatry, is reckoned in the Lord's harvest among the chaff. Why then is a man baptized again after receiving baptism from the wheat, and not after receiving it from the chaff? If it was because he was better than John that Paul baptized after John, why did not also Cyprian baptize after his usurious colleagues, than whom he was better beyond all comparison? If it was because they were in unity with him that he did not baptize after such colleagues, neither ought Paul to have baptized after John, because they were joined together in the same unity. Can it be that defrauders and extortioners belong to the members of that one dove, and that he does not belong to it to whom the full power of the Lord Jesus Christ was shown by the appearance of the Holy Spirit in the form of a dove?[7] Truly he belongs most closely to it; but the others, who must be separated from it either by the occasion of some scandal, or by the winnowing at the last day, do not by any means belong to it, and yet baptism was repeated after John and not after them. What then is the cause, except that the baptism which Paul ordered them to receive was not the same as that which was given at the hands of John? And so in the same unity of the Church, the baptism of Christ cannot be repeated though it be given by an usurious minister; but those who receive the baptism of John, even from the hands of John Himself, ought to be afterwards baptized with the baptism of Christ.

Chap. 12.—14. Accordingly, I too might use the words of the blessed Cyprian to turn the hearts of those that hear me to the consideration of something truly marvellous, if I were to say "that John, who was accounted greater among the prophets,—he who was filled with divine grace while yet in his mother's womb; he who was upheld in the spirit and power of Elias; who was not the adversary, but a forerunner and herald of the Lord; who not only foretold our Lord in words, but also showed Him to the sight; who baptized Christ Himself, through whom all others are baptized,"[8]—he was not worthy to baptize in such wise that those who were baptized by him should not be baptized again

[1] Cypr. *Serm. de Lapsis*, c. vi.
[2] Eph. ii. 6.
[3] Rom. viii. 24.
[4] Matt. iii. 11.
[5] John i. 29.
[6] Acts xix. 3-5.
[7] Matt. iii. 16; John i. 33.
[8] Cypr. *Ep.* lxxiii. 25.

after him; and shall no one think that a man should be baptized in the Church after he had been baptized by the covetous, by defrauders, by extortioners, by usurers? Is not the answer ready to this invidious question, Why do you think this unmeet, as though either John were dishonored, or the covetous man honored? But His baptism ought not to be repeated, of whom John says, "The same is He which baptizeth with the Holy Ghost."[1] For whoever be the minister by whose hands it is given, it is His baptism of whom it was said, "The same is He which baptizeth." But neither was the baptism of John himself repeated, when the Apostle Paul commanded those who had been baptized by him to be baptized in Christ. For what they had not received from the friend of the Bridegroom, this it was right that they should receive from the Bridegroom Himself, of whom that friend had said, "The same is He which baptizeth with the Holy Ghost."

CHAP. 13.—15. For the Lord Jesus might, if He had so thought fit, have given the power of His baptism to some one or more of His chief servants, whom He had already made His friends, such as those to whom He says, "Henceforth I call you not servants, but friends;"[2] that, as Aaron was shown to be the priest by the rod that budded,[3] so in His Church, when more and greater miracles are performed, the ministers of more excellent holiness, and the dispensers of His mysteries, might be made manifest by some sign, as those who alone ought to baptize. But if this had been done, then though the power of baptizing were given them by the Lord, yet it would necessarily be called their own baptism, as in the case of the baptism of John. And so Paul gives thanks to God that he baptized none of those men who, as though forgetting in whose name they had been baptized, were for dividing themselves into factions under the names of different individuals.[4] For when baptism is as valid at the hands of a contemptible man as it was when given by an apostle, it is recognized as the baptism neither of this man nor of that, but of Christ; as John bears witness that he learned, in the case of the Lord Himself, through the appearance of the dove. For in what other respect he said, "And I knew Him not," I cannot clearly see. For if he had not known Him in any sense, he could not have said to Him when He came to his baptism, "I have need to be baptized of Thee."[5] What is it, therefore, that he says, "I saw the Spirit descending from heaven like a dove, and it abode upon Him. And I knew Him not: but He that sent me to baptize with water, the same said unto me, Upon whom thou shalt see the Spirit descending, and remaining on Him, the same is He which baptizeth with the Holy Ghost?"[6] The dove clearly descended on Him after He was baptized. But while He was yet coming to be baptized, John had said, "I have need to be baptized of Thee." He therefore already knew Him. What does he therefore mean by the words, "I knew Him not: but He that sent me to baptize with water, the same said unto me, Upon whom thou shalt see the Spirit descending, and remaining on Him, the same is He which baptizeth with the Holy Ghost," since this took place after He was baptized, unless it were that he knew Him in respect of certain attributes, and in respect of others knew Him not? He knew Him, indeed, as the Son of God, the Bridegroom, of whose fullness all should receive; but whereas of His fullness he himself had so received the power of baptizing that it should be called the baptism of John, he did not know whether He would so give it to others also, or whether He would have His own baptism in such wise, that at whosesoever hands it was given, whether by a man that brought forth fruit a hundredfold, or sixtyfold, or thirtyfold, whether by the wheat or by the chaff, it should be known to be of Him alone; and this he learned through the Spirit descending like a dove, and abiding on Him.

CHAP. 14.—16. Accordingly we find the apostles using the expressions, "My glorying,"[7] though it was certainly in the Lord; and "Mine office,"[8] and "My knowledge,"[9] and "My gospel,"[10] although it was confessedly bestowed and given by the Lord; but no one of them ever once said, "My baptism." For neither is the glorying of all of them equal, nor do they all minister with equal powers, nor are they all endowed with equal knowledge, and in preaching the gospel one works more forcibly than another, and so one may be said to be more learned than another in the doctrine of salvation itself; but one cannot be said to be more or less baptized than another, whether he be baptized by a greater or a less worthy minister. So when "the works of the flesh are manifest, which are these: fornication, uncleanness, lasciviousnness, idolatry, witchcraft, hatred, variance, emulations, strife, seditions, heresies, envyings, drunkenness, revellings, and

[1] John i 33. [2] John xv. 15. [3] Num. xvii. 8. [4] 1 Cor. i. 12-15. [5] Matt. iii. 14.

[6] John i. 32, 33. [7] 1 Cor. ix. 15. [8] Rom. xi. 13. [9] Eph. iii. 4. [10] 2 Tim. ii. 8.

such like;"[1] if it be strange that it should be said, "Men were baptized after John, and are not baptized after heretics," why is it not equally strange that it should be said, "Men were baptized after John, and are not baptized after the envious," seeing that Cyprian himself bears witness in his epistle concerning envy and malignity that the covetous are of the party of the devil, and Cyprian himself makes it manifest from the words of the Apostle Paul, as we have shown above, that in the time of the apostles themselves there were envious persons in the Church of Christ among the very preachers of the name of Christ?

Chap. 15.—17. That therefore the baptism of John was not the same as the baptism of Christ, has, I think, been shown with sufficient clearness; and therefore no argument can be drawn from it that baptism should be repeated after heretics because it was repeated after John: since John was not a heretic, and could have a baptism, which, though granted by Christ, was yet not the very baptism of Christ, seeing that he had the love of Christ; while a heretic can have at once the baptism of Christ and the perversity of the devil, as another within the Church may have at once the baptism of Christ and the envy of the devil.

18. But it will be urged that baptism after a heretic is much more required, because John was not a heretic, and yet baptism was repeated after him. On this principle, a man may say, much more must we rebaptize after a drunkard, because John was sober, and yet baptism was repeated after him. And we shall have no answer to make to such a man, save that the baptism of Christ was given to those who were baptized by John, because they had it not; but where men have the baptism of Christ, no iniquity on their part can possibly effect that the baptism of Christ should fail to be in them.

19. It is not therefore true that "by baptizing first, the heretic obtains the right of baptism;"[2] but because he did not baptize with his own baptism, and though he did not possess the right of baptizing, yet that which he gave is Christ's, and he who received it is Christ's. For many things are given wrongfully, and yet they are not therefore said to be non-existent or not given at all. For neither does he who renounces the world in word only and not in deed receive baptism lawfully, and yet he does receive it. For both Cyprian records that there were such men in the Church in his day, and we ourselves experience and lament the fact.

20. But it is strange in what sense it can be said that "baptism and the Church cannot in any way be separated and detached from one another."[3] For if baptism remains inseparably in him who is baptized, how can it be that he can be separated from the Church, and baptism cannot? But it is clear that baptism does remain inseparably in the baptized person; because into whatever depth of evil, and into whatever fearful whirlpool of sin the baptized person may fall, even to the ruin of apostasy, he yet is not bereft of his baptism. And therefore, if through repentance he returns, it is not given again, because it is judged that he could not have been bereft of it. But who can ever doubt that a baptized person can be separated from the Church? For hence all the heresies have proceeded which deceive by the use of Christian terms.

Chap. 16.—Wherefore, since it is manifest that the baptism remains in the baptized person when he is separated from the Church, the baptism which is in him is certainly separated with him. And therefore not all who retain the baptism retain the Church, just as not all who retain the Church retain eternal life. Or if we say that only those retain the Church who observe the commandments of God, we at once concede that there are many who retain baptism, and do not retain the Church.

21. Therefore the heretic is not "the first to seize baptism," since he has received it from the Church. Nor, though he seceded, could baptism have been lost by him whom we assert no longer to retain the Church, and yet allow to retain baptism. Nor does any one "yield his birthright, and give it to a heretic,"[4] because he says that he took away with him what he could not give lawfully, but what would yet be according to law when given; or that he no longer has lawfully what yet is in accordance with law in his possession. But the birthright rests only in a holy conversation and good life, to which all belong of whom that bride consists as her members which has no spot or wrinkle,[5] or that dove that groans amid the wickedness of the many crows,—unless it be that, while Esau lost his birthright from his lust after a mess of pottage,[6] we are yet to hold that it is retained by defrauders, robbers, usurers, envious persons, drunkards and the like, over whose

[1] Gal. v. 19–21.

[2] Cypr. *Ep.* lxxiii. 25.

[3] *Ib.*

[4] Cypr. *Ep.* lxxiii. 25.

[5] Eph. v. 27. Cp. Aug. *Retract.* ii. 18, quoted above, I. 17, 26.

[6] Gen. xxv. 29–34.

existence in the Church of his time Cyprian groaned in his epistles. Wherefore, either it is not the same thing to retain the Church and to retain the birthright in divine things, or, if every one who retains the Church also retains the birthright, then all those wicked ones do not retain the Church who yet both seem and are allowed by every one of us to give baptism within the Church; for no one, save the man who is wholly ignorant of sacred things, would say that they retain the birthright in sacred things

CHAP. 17.—22. But, having considered and handled all these points, we have now come to that peaceful utterance of Cyprian at the end of the epistle, with which I am never sated, though I read and re-read it again and again, — so great is the pleasantness of brotherly love which breathes forth from it, so great the sweetness of charity in which it abounds. "These things," he says, "we have written unto you, dearest brother, shortly, according to our poor ability, prescribing to or prejudging no one, lest each bishop should not do what he thinks right, in the free exercise of his own will. We, so far as in us lies, do not contend on the subject of heretics with our colleagues and fellow-bishops, with whom we maintain concord and peace in the Lord; especially as the apostle also says, 'If any man seem to be contentious, we have no such custom, neither the churches of God.'[1] We observe patiently and gently charity of spirit, the honor of our brotherhood, the bond of faith, the harmony of the priesthood. For this reason also, to the best of our poor ability, by the permission and the inspiration of God we have written this treatise on 'The Good of Patience,' which we have sent to you in consideration of our mutual love."[2]

23. There are many things to be considered in these words, wherein the brightness of Christian charity shines forth in this man, who "loved the beauty of the Lord's house, and the place of the tabernacle of His habitation."[3] First, that he did not conceal what he felt; then, that he set it forth so gently and peacefully, in that he maintained the peace of the Church with those who thought otherwise, because he understood how great healthfulness was bound up in the bond of peace, loving it so much, and maintaining it with sobriety, seeing and feeling that even men who think differently may entertain their several sentiments with saving charity. For he would not say that he could maintain divine concord or the peace of the Lord with evil men; for the good man can observe peace towards wicked men, but he cannot be united with them in the peace which they have not. Lastly, that prescribing to no one, and prejudging no one, lest each bishop should not do what he thinks right in the free exercise of his own will, he has left for us also, whatsoever we may be, a place for treating peacefully of those things with him. For he is present, not only in his letters, but by that very charity which existed in so extraordinary a degree in him, and which can never die. Longing, therefore, with the aid of his prayers, to cling to and be in union with him, if I be not hindered by the unmeetness of my sins, I will learn if I can through his letters with how great peace and comfort the Lord administered His Church through him; and, putting on the bowels of humility through the moving influence of his discourse, if, in common with the Church at large, I entertain any doctrine more true than his, I will not prefer my heart to his, even in the point in which he, though holding different views, was yet not severed from the Church throughout the world. For in that, when that question was yet undecided for want of full discussion, though his sentiments differed from those of many of his colleagues, yet he observed so great moderation, that he would not mutilate the sacred fellowship of the Church of God by any stain of schism, a greater strength of excellence appeared in him than would have been shown if, without that virtue, he had held views on every point not only true, but coinciding with their own. Nor should I be acting as he would wish, if I were to pretend to prefer his talent and his fluency of discourse and copiousness of learning to the holy Council of all nations, whereat he was assuredly present through the unity of his spirit, especially as he is now placed in such full light of truth as to see with perfect certainty what he was here seeking in the spirit of perfect peace. For out of that rich abundance he smiles at all that here seems eloquence in us, as though it were the first essay of infancy; there he sees by what rule of piety he acted here, that nothing should be dearer in the Church to him than unity. There, too, with unspeakable delight he beholds with what prescient and most merciful providence the Lord, that He might heal our swellings, "chose the foolish things of the world to confound the wise,"[4] and, in the ordering of the members of His Church, placed all things in such a healthful way, that men should not say

[1] 1 Cor. xi. 16. [2] Cypr. *Ep.* lxxiii. 26. [3] Ps. xxvi. 8.

[4] 1 Cor. i. 27.

that they were chosen to the help of the gospel for their own talent or learning, of whose source they yet were ignorant, and so be puffed up with deadly pride. Oh, how Cyprian rejoices! With how much more perfect calmness does he behold how greatly it conduces to the health of the human race, that in the writings even of Christian and pious orators there should be found what merits blame, and in the writings of the fishermen there should nothing of the sort be found! And so I, being fully assured of this joy of that holy soul, neither in any way venture to think or say that my writings are free from every kind of error, nor, in opposing that opinion of his, wherein it seemed to him that those who came from among heretics were to be received otherwise than either they had been in former days, as he himself bears witness, or are now received, as is the reasonable custom, confirmed by a plenary Council of the whole Christian world, do I set against him my own view, but that of the holy Catholic Church, which he so loved and loves, in which he brought forth such abundant fruit with tolerance, whose entirety he himself was not, but in whose entirety he remained; whose root he never left, but, though he already brought forth fruit from its root, he was purged by the heavenly Husbandman that he should bring forth more fruit;[1] for whose peace and safety, that the wheat might not be rooted out together with the tares, he both reproved with the freedom of truth, and endured with the grace of charity, so many evils on the part of men who were placed in unity with himself.

Chap. 18.—24. Whence Cyprian himself[2] again admonishes us with the greatest fullness, that many who were dead in their trespasses and sins, although they did not belong to the body of Christ, and the members of that innocent and guileless dove (so that if she alone baptized, they certainly could not baptize), yet to all appearance seemed both to be baptized and to baptize within the Church. And among them, however dead they are, their baptism nevertheless lives, which is not dead, and death shall have no more dominion over it. Since, therefore, there be dead men within the Church, nor are they concealed, for else Cyprian would not have spoken of them so much, who either do not belong at all to that living dove, or at least do not as yet belong to her; and since there be dead men without, who yet more clearly do not belong to her at all, or not as yet; and since it is true that "another man cannot be quickened by one who himself liveth not,"—it is therefore clear that those who within are baptized by such persons, if they approach the sacrament with true conversion of heart, are quickened by Him whose baptism it is. But if they renounce the world in word and not in deed, as Cyprian declares to be the case with some who are within, it is then manifest that they are not themselves quickened unless they be converted, and yet that they have true baptism even though they be not converted. Whence also it is likewise clear that those who are dead without, although they neither "live themselves, nor quicken others," yet have the living baptism, which would profit them unto life so soon as they should be converted unto peace.

Chap. 19.—25. Wherefore, as regards those who received the persons who came from heresy in the same baptism of Christ with which they had been baptized outside the Church, and said "that they followed ancient custom," as indeed the Church now receives such, it is in vain urged against them "that among the ancients there were as yet only the first beginning of heresy and schisms,[3] so that those were involved in them who were seceders from the Church, and had originally been baptized within the Church, so that it was not necessary that they should be baptized again when they returned and did penance." For so soon as each several heresy existed, and departed from the communion of the Catholic Church, it was possible that, I will not even say the next day, but even on that very day, its votaries might have baptized some who flocked to them. And therefore if this was the old custom, that they should be so received into the Church (as could not be denied even by those who maintained the contrary part in the discussion), there can be no doubt in the mind of any one who pays careful attention to the matter, that those also were so received who had been baptized without in heresy.

26. But I cannot see what show of reason there is in this, that the name of "erring sheep"[4] should be denied to one whose lot it has been that, while seeking the salvation which is in Christ, he has fallen into the error of heretics, and been baptized in their body; while he is held to have become a sheep al-

---

[1] John xv. 2.

[2] In this and the following chapter, Augustin is examining the seventy-first epistle of Cyprian to his brother Quintus, bishop in Mauritania. Here LXXI. 1.

[3] *Apud veteres hæreses et schismata prima adhuc fuisse initia*; that among the ancients heresies and schisms were yet in their very infancy. Benedictines suggest: "*hæresis et schismatum*." Hartel reads: *apud veteres hæreseos et schismatum prima adhuc fuerint initia*.

[4] Cypr. *Ep.* lxxi. 2.

ready within the body of the Catholic Church herself, who has renounced the world in words and not in deeds, and has received baptism in such falseness of heart as this. Or if such an one also does not become a sheep unless after turning to God with a true heart, then, as he is not baptized at the time when he becomes a sheep, if he had been already baptized, but was not yet a sheep; so he too, who comes from the heretics that he may become a sheep, is not then to be baptized if he had been already baptized with the same baptism, though he was not yet a sheep. Wherefore, since even all the bad that are within—the covetous, the envious, the drunkards, and those that live contrary to the discipline of Christ—may be deservedly called liars, and in darkness, and dead, and antichrists, do they yet therefore not baptize, on the ground that "there can be nothing common between truth and falsehood, between light and darkness, between death and immortality, between Antichrist and Christ?"[1]

27. He makes an assumption, then, not "of mere custom," but "of the reason of truth itself,"[2] when he says that the sacrament of God cannot be turned to error by the error of any men, since it is declared to exist even in those who have erred. Assuredly the Apostle John says most plainly, "He that hateth his brother is in darkness even until now;"[3] and again, "Whosoever hateth his brother is a murderer;"[4] and why, therefore, do they baptize those within the Church whom Cyprian himself declares to be in the envy of malice?[5]

CHAP. 20. How does a murderer cleanse and sanctify the water?[6] How can darkness bless the oil? But if God is present in His sacraments to confirm His words by whomsoever the sacraments may be administered, then both the sacraments of God are everywhere valid, and evil men whom they profit not are everywhere perverse.

28. But what kind of argument is this, that "a heretic must be considered not to have baptism, because he has not the Church?" And it must be acknowledged that "when he is baptized, he is questioned about the Church."[7] Just as though the same question about the Church were not put in baptism to him who within the Church renounces the world in word and not in deed. As therefore his false answer does not prevent what he receives from being baptism, so also the false reply of the other about the holy Church does not prevent what he receives from being baptism; and as the former, if he afterwards fulfill with truth what he promised in falsehood, does not receive a second baptism, but only an amended life, so also in the case of the latter, if he come afterwards to the Church about which he gave a false answer to the question put to him, thinking that he had it when he had it not, the Church herself which he did not possess is given him, but what he had received is not repeated. But I cannot tell why it should be, that while God can "sanctify the oil" in answer to the words which proceed out of the mouth of a murderer, "He yet cannot sanctify it on the altar reared by a heretic," unless it be that He who is not hindered by the false conversion of the heart of man within the Church is hindered by the false erection of some wood without from deigning to be present in His sacraments, though no falseness on the part of men can hinder Him. If, therefore, what is said in the gospel, that "God heareth not sinners,"[8] extends so far that the sacraments cannot be celebrated by a sinner, how then does He hear a murderer praying, either over the water of baptism, or over the oil, or over the eucharist, or over the heads of those on whom his hand is laid? All which things are nevertheless done, and are valid, even at the hands of murderers, that is, at the hands of those who hate their brethren, even within, in the Church itself. Since "no one can give what he does not possess himself,"[9] how does a murderer give the Holy Spirit? And yet such an one even baptizeth within the Church. It is God, therefore, that gives the Holy Spirit even when a man of this kind is baptizing.

CHAP. 21.—29. But as to what he says, that "he who comes to the Church is to be baptized and renewed, that within he may be hallowed through the holy,"[9] what will he do, if within also he meets with those who are not holy? Or can it be that the murderer is holy? And if the reason for his being baptized in the Church is that "he should put off this very thing also that he, being a man that sought to come to God, fell, through the deceit of error, on one profane,"[9] where is he afterwards to put off this, that he may chance, while seeking a man of God within the Church itself, to have fallen, through the deceit of error, on a murderer? If "there cannot be in a man something that is void

[1] Cypr. *Ep.* lxxi. 2. [2] Cypr. *Ep.* lxxi. 3.
[3] 1 John ii. 9. [4] 1 John iii. 15. [5] Cypr. *Ep.*lxxiii. 14.
[6] In this and the next two chapters Augustin is examining the seventieth epistle of Cyprian, from himself and thirty other bishops (text of Hartel), to Januarius, Saturninus, Maximus, and fifteen others.
[7] In the question, "Dost thou believe in eternal life and remission of sins through the holy Church?" Cyp. *l.c.* 2.

[8] John ix. 31. [9] Cypr. *Ep.* lxx. 2.

and something that is valid,"[1] why is it possible that in a murderer the sacrament should be holy and his heart unholy? If "whosoever cannot give the Holy Spirit cannot baptize,"[1] why does the murderer baptize within the Church? Or how has the murderer the Holy Spirit, when every one that has the Holy Spirit is filled with light, but "he who hates his brother is still in darkness?"[2] If because "there is one baptism, and one Spirit,"[1] therefore they cannot have the one baptism who have not the one Spirit, why do the innocent man and the murderer within the Church have the one baptism and not have the one Spirit? So therefore the heretic and the Catholic may have the one baptism, and yet not have the one Church, as in the Catholic Church the innocent man and the murderer may have the one baptism, though they have not the one Spirit; for as there is one baptism, so there is one Spirit and one Church. And so the result is, that in each person we must acknowledge what he already has, and to each person we must give what he has not. If "nothing can be confirmed and ratified with God which has been done by those whom God calls His enemies and foes,"[3] why is the baptism confirmed which is given by murderers? Are we not to call murderers the enemies and foes of the Lord? But "he that hateth his brother is a murderer." How then did they baptize who hated Paul, the servant of Jesus Christ, and thereby hated Jesus Himself, since He Himself said to Saul, "Why persecutest thou me?"[4] when he was persecuting His servants, and since at the last He Himself shall say, "Inasmuch as ye did it not to one of the least of these that are mine, ye did it not to me?"[5] Wherefore all who go out from us are not of us, but not all who are with us are of us; just as when men thresh, all that flies from the threshing-floor is shown not to be corn, but not all that remains there is therefore corn. And so John too says, "They went out from us, but they were not of us; for if they had been of us, they would no doubt have continued with us."[6] Wherefore God gives the sacrament of grace even through the hands of wicked men, but the grace itself only by Himself or through His saints. And therefore He gives remission of sins either of Himself, or through the members of that dove to whom He says, "Whosesoever sins ye remit, they are remitted unto them; and whosesoever sins ye retain, they are retained."[7] But since no one can doubt that baptism, which is the sacrament of the remission of sins, is possessed even by murderers, who are yet in darkness because the hatred of their brethren is not excluded from their hearts, therefore either no remission of sins is given to them if their baptism is accompanied by no change of heart for the better, or if the sins are remitted, they at once return on them again. And we learn that the baptism is holy in itself, because it is of God; and whether it be given or whether it be received by men of such like character, it cannot be polluted by any perversity of theirs, either within, or yet outside the Church.

Chap. 22.—30. Accordingly we agree with Cyprian that "heretics cannot give remission of sins;"[3] but we maintain that they can give baptism,—which indeed in them, both when they give and when they receive it, is profitable only to their destruction, as misusing so great a gift of God; just as also the malicious and envious, whom Cyprian himself acknowledges to be within the Church, cannot give remission of sins, while we all confess that they can give baptism. For if it was said of those who have sinned against us, "If ye forgive not men their trespasses, neither will your Father forgive your trespasses,"[8] how much more impossible is it that their sins should be forgiven who hate the brethren by whom they are loved, and are baptized in that very hatred; and yet when they are brought to the right way, baptism is not given them anew, but that very pardon which they did not then deserve is granted them in their true conversion? And so even what Cyprian wrote to Quintus, and what, in conjunction with his colleagues Liberalis, Caldonius, Junius, and the rest, he wrote to Saturninus, Maximus, and others, is all found, on due consideration, to be in no wise meet to be preferred as against the agreement of the whole Catholic Church, of which they rejoiced that they were members, and from which they neither cut themselves away nor allowed others to be cut away who held a contrary opinion, until at length, by the will of the Lord, it was made manifest, by a plenary Council many years afterwards, what was the more perfect way, and that not by the institution of any novelty, but by confirming what was old.

Chap. 23.—31. Cyprian writes also to Pompeius[9] about this selfsame matter, and clearly shows in that letter that Stephen, who, as we learn, was then bishop of the

1 Cypr. *Ep.* lxx. 3. 2 1 John ii. 9. 3 Cypr. *Ep.* lxx. 3.
4 Acts ix. 4. 5 Matt. xxv. 45. 6 1 John ii. 19.
7 John xx. 23.

8 Matt. vi. 15.
9 Cypr. *Ep.* lxxiv., which is examined by Augustin in the remaining chapters of this book.

Roman Church, not only did not agree with him upon the points before us, but even wrote and taught the opposite views. But Stephen certainly did not "communicate with heretics,"[1] merely because he did not dare to impugn the baptism of Christ, which he knew remained perfect in the midst of their perversity. For if none have baptism who entertain false views about God, it has been proved sufficiently, in my opinion, that this may happen even within the Church. "The apostles," indeed, "gave no injunctions on the point;"[1] but the custom, which is opposed to Cyprian, may be supposed to have had its origin in apostolic tradition, just as there are many things which are observed by the whole Church, and therefore are fairly held to have been enjoined by the apostles, which yet are not mentioned in their writings.

32. But it will be urged that it is written of heretics that "they are condemned of themselves."[2] What then? are they not also condemned of themselves to whom it was said, "For wherein thou júdgest another, thou condemnest thyself?"[3] But to these the apostle says, "Thou that preachest a man should not steal, dost thou steal?"[4] and so forth. And such truly were they who, being bishops and established in Catholic unity with Cyprian himself, used to plunder estates by treacherous frauds, preaching all the time to the people the words of the apostle, who says, "Nor shall extortioners inherit the kingdom of God."[5]

33. Wherefore I will do no more than run shortly through the other sentiments founded on the same rules, which are in the aforesaid letter written to Pompeius. By what authority of holy Scripture is it shown that "it is against the commandment of God that persons coming from the society of heretics, if they have already there received the baptism of Christ, are not baptized again?"[6] But it is clearly shown that many pretended Christians, though they are not joined in the same bond of charity with the saints, without which anything holy that they may have been able to possess is of no profit to them, yet have baptism in common with the saints, as has been already sufficiently proved with the greatest fullness. He says "that the Church, and the Spirit, and baptism, are mutually incapable of separation from each other, and therefore" he wishes that "those who are separated from the Church and the Holy Spirit should be understood to be separated also from baptism."[6] But if this is the case, then when any one has received baptism in the Catholic Church, it remains so long in him as he himself remains in the Church, which is not so. For it is not restored to him when he returns, just because he did not lose it when he seceded. But as the disaffected sons have not the Holy Spirit in the same manner as the beloved sons, and yet they have baptism; so heretics also have not the Church as Catholics have, and yet they have baptism. "For the Holy Spirit of discipline will flee deceit,"[7] and yet baptism will not flee from it. And so, as baptism can continue in one from whom the Holy Spirit withdraws Himself, so can baptism continue where the Church is not. But if "the laying on of hands" were not "applied to one coming from heresy,"[8] he would be as it were judged to be wholly blameless; but for the uniting of love, which is the greatest gift of the Holy Spirit, without which any other holy thing that there may be in a man is profitless to his salvation, hands are laid on heretics when they are brought to a knowledge of the truth.[9]

CHAP. 24.—34. I remember that I have already discussed at sufficient length the question of "the temple of God," and how this saying is to be taken, "As many of you as have been baptized into Christ have put on Christ."[10] For neither are the covetous the temple of God, since it is written, "What agreement hath the temple of God with idols?"[11] And Cyprian has adduced the testimony of Paul to the fact that covetousness is idolatry. But men put on Christ, sometimes so far as to receive the sacrament, sometimes so much further as to receive holiness of life. And the first of these is common to good and bad alike; the second, peculiar to the good and pious. Wherefore, if "baptism cannot be without the Spirit," then heretics have the Spirit also,—but to destruction, not to salvation, just as was the case with Saul.[12] For in the Holy Spirit devils are cast out through the name of Christ, which even he was able to do who was without the Church, which called forth a suggestion from the disciples to their Lord.[13] Just as the covetous have the Holy Spirit, who yet are not the temple of God. For "what agreement hath the temple of God with idols?" If therefore the covetous have not the Spirit of God, and yet have baptism, it is possible for baptism to exist without the Spirit of God.

1 Cypr. *Ep.* lxxiv. 2. 2 Tit. iii. 11. 3 Rom. ii. 1.
4 Rom. ii. 21. 5 1 Cor. vi. 10. 6 Cypr. *Ep.* lxxiv. 4.

7 Wisd. i. 5. 8 Cypr. *Ep.* lxxiv. 5.
9 Cyprian, in the laying on of hands, appears to refer to confirmation, but Augustin interprets it of the restoration of penitents. Cp. III. 16, 21.
10 Gal. iii. 27. 11 2 Cor. vi. 16.
12 1 Sam. xix. 23. 13 Mark ix. 38.

35. If therefore heresy is rendered "unable to engender sons to God through Christ, because it is not the bride of Christ,"[1] neither can that crowd of evil men established within the Church, since it is also not the bride of Christ; for the bride of Christ is described as being without spot or wrinkle.[2] Therefore either not all baptized persons are the sons of God, or even that which is not the bride can engender the sons of God. But as it is asked whether "he is spiritually born who has received the baptism of Christ in the midst of heretics,"[3] so it may be asked whether he is spiritually born who has received the baptism of Christ in the Catholic Church, without being turned to God in a true heart, of whom it cannot be said that he has not received baptism.

Chap. 25.—36. I am unwilling to go on to handle again what Cyprian poured forth with signs of irritation against Stephen, as it is, moreover, quite unnecessary. For they are but the selfsame arguments which have already been sufficiently discussed; and it is better to pass over those points which involved the danger of baneful dissension. But Stephen thought that we should even hold aloof from those who endeavored to destroy the primitive custom in the matter of receiving heretics; whereas Cyprian, moved by the difficulty of the question itself, and being most largely endowed with the holy bowels of Christian charity, thought that we ought to remain at unity with those who differed in opinion from ourselves. Therefore, although he was not without excitement, though of a truly brotherly kind, in his indignation, yet the peace of Christ prevailed in their hearts, that in such a dispute no evil of schism should arise between them. But it was not found that "hence grew more abundant heresies and schisms,"[4] because what is of Christ in them is approved, and what is of themselves is condemned: for all the more those who hold this law of rebaptizing were cut into smaller fragments.

Chap. 26.—37. To go on to what he says, "that a bishop should be 'teachable,'"[5] adding, "But he is teachable who is gentle and meek to learn; for a bishop ought not only to teach, but to learn as well, since he is indeed the better teacher who daily grows and advances by learning better things;"[6]—in these words assuredly the holy man, endowed with pious charity, sufficiently points out that we should not hesitate to read his letters in such a sense, that we should feel no difficulty if the Church should afterwards confirm what had been discovered by further and longer discussions; because, as there were many things which the learned Cyprian might teach, so there was still something which the teachable Cyprian might learn. But the admonition that he gives us, "that we should go back to the fountain, that is, to apostolic tradition, and thence turn the channel of truth to our times,"[6] is most excellent, and should be followed without hesitation. It is handed down to us, therefore, as he himself records, by the apostles, that there is "one God, and one Christ, and one hope, and one faith, and one Church, and one baptism."[7] Since then we find that in the times of the apostles themselves there were some who had not the one hope, but had the one baptism, the truth is so brought down to us from the fountain itself, that it is clear to us that it is possible that though there is one Church, as there is one hope, and one baptism, they may yet have the one baptism who have not the one Church; just as even in those early times it was possible that men should have the one baptism who had not the one hope. For how had they one hope with the holy and the just, who used to say, "Let us eat and drink, for to-morrow we die,"[8] asserting that there was no resurrection of the dead? And yet they were among the very men to whom the same apostle says, "Was Paul crucified for you? or were you baptized in the name of Paul?"[9] For he writes most manifestly to them, saying, "How say some among you that there is no resurrection of the dead?"[10]

Chap. 27.—38. And in that the Church is thus described in the Song of Songs, "A garden enclosed is my sister, my spouse; a spring shut up, a fountain sealed, a well of living water; thy plants are an orchard of pomegranates, with pleasant fruits;"[11] I dare not understand this save of the holy and just,—not of the covetous, and defrauders, and robbers, and usurers, and drunkards, and the envious, of whom we yet both learn most fully from Cyprian's letters, as I have often shown, and teach ourselves, that they had baptism in common with the just, in common with whom they certainly had not Christian charity. For I would that some one would tell me how they "crept into the garden enclosed and the

[1] Cypr. *Ep.* lxxiv. 6.
[2] Eph. v. 27. Cp. Aug. *Retract.* ii. 18, quoted above, I. 17, 26.
[3] Cypr. *Ep.* lxxiv. 7.
[4] *Ib.*
[5] "*Docibilis;*" and so the passage (2 Tim. ii. 24) is quoted frequently by Augustin. The English version, "apt to teach," is more true to the original, διδακτικός.
[6] Cypr. *Ep.* lxxiv. 10.
[7] *Ib.* 11, and Eph. iv, 4-6.
[8] 1 Cor. xv. 32.
[9] 1 Cor. i. 13.
[10] 1 Cor. xv. 12.
[11] Cant. iv. 12, 13.

fountain sealed," of whom Cyprian bears witness that they renounced the world in word and not in deed, and that yet they were within the Church. For if they both are themselves there, and are themselves the bride of Christ, can she then be as she is described, "without spot or wrinkle,"[1] and is the fair dove defiled with such a portion of her members? Are these the thorns among which she is a lily, as it is said in the same Song?[2] So far therefore, as the lily extends, so far does "the garden enclosed and the fountain sealed," namely, through all those just persons who are Jews inwardly in the circumcision of the heart[3] (for "the king's daughter is all glorious within"[4]), in whom is the fixed number of the saints predestined before the foundation of the world. But that multitude of thorns, whether in secret or in open separation, is pressing on it from without, above number. "If I would declare them," it is said, "and speak of them, they are more than can be numbered."[5] The number, therefore, of the just persons, "who are the called according to His purpose,"[6] of whom it is said, "The Lord knoweth them that are His,"[7] is itself "the garden enclosed, the fountain sealed, a well of living water, the orchard of pomegranates with pleasant fruits." Of this number some live according to the Spirit, and enter on the excellent way of charity; and when they "restore a man that is overtaken in a fault in the spirit of meekness, they consider themselves, lest they also be tempted."[8] And when it happens that they also are themselves overtaken, the affection of charity is but a little checked, and not extinguished; and again rising up and being kindled afresh, it is restored to its former course. For they know how to say, "My soul melteth for heaviness: strengthen thou me according unto Thy word."[9] But when "in anything they be otherwise minded, God shall reveal even this unto them,"[10] if they abide in the burning flame of charity, and do not break the bond of peace. But some who are yet carnal, and full of fleshly appetites, are instant in working out their progress; and that they may become fit for heavenly food, they are nourished with the milk of the holy mysteries, they avoid in the fear of God whatever is manifestly corrupt even in the opinion of the world, and they strive most watchfully that they may be less and less delighted with worldly and temporal matters. They observe most constantly the rule of faith which has been sought out with diligence; and if in aught they stray from it, they submit to speedy correction under Catholic authority, although, in Cyprian's words, they be tossed about, by reason of their fleshly appetite, with the various conflicts of phantasies. There are some also who as yet live wickedly, or even lie in heresies or the superstitions of the Gentiles, and yet even then "the Lord knoweth them that are His." For, in that unspeakable foreknowledge of God, many who seem to be without are in reality within, and many who seem to be within yet really are without. Of all those, therefore, who, if I may so say, are inwardly and secretly within, is that "enclosed garden" composed, "the fountain sealed, a well of living water, the orchard of pomegranates, with pleasant fruits." The divinely imparted gifts of these are partly peculiar to themselves, as in this world the charity that never faileth, and in the world to come eternal life; partly they are common with evil and perverse men, as all the other things in which consist the holy mysteries.

CHAP. 28.—39. Hence, therefore, we have now set before us an easier and more simple consideration of that ark of which Noah was the builder and pilot. For Peter says that in the ark of Noah, "few, that is, eight souls, were saved by water. The like figure whereunto even baptism doth also now save us, (not the putting away of the filth of the flesh, but the answer of a good conscience towards God)."[11] Wherefore, if those appear to men to be baptized in Catholic unity who renounce the world in words only and not in deeds, how do they belong to the mystery of this ark in whom there is not the answer of a good conscience? Or how are they saved by water, who, making a bad use of holy baptism, though they seem to be within, yet persevere to the end of their days in a wicked and abandoned course of life? Or how can they fail to be saved by water, of whom Cyprian himself records that they were in time past simply admitted to the Church with the baptism which they had received in heresy? For the same unity of the ark saved them, in which no one has been saved except by water. For Cyprian himself says, "The Lord is able of His mercy to grant pardon, and not to sever from the gifts of His Church those who, being in all simplicity admitted to the Church, have fallen asleep within her pale."[12] If not by water, how in the ark? If not in the ark, how in the Church? But if in the Church,

[1] Eph. v. 27. [2] Cant. ii. 2. [3] Rom. ii. 29.
[4] Ps. xlv. 13. [5] Ps. xl. 5. [6] Rom. viii. 28.
[7] 2 Tim. ii. 19. [8] Gal. vi. 1. [9] Ps. cxix. 28.
[10] Phil. iii. 15.

[11] 1 Pet. iii. 20, 21. [12] Cypr. *Ep.* lxxiii. 23.

certainly in the ark; and if in the ark, certainly by water. It is therefore possible that some who have been baptized without may be considered, through the foreknowledge of God, to have been really baptized within, because within the water begins to be profitable to them unto salvation; nor can they be said to have been otherwise saved in the ark except by water. And again, some who seemed to have been baptized within may be considered, through the same foreknowledge of God, more truly to have been baptized without, since, by making a bad use of baptism, they die by water, which then happened to no one who was not outside the ark. Certainly it is clear that, when we speak of within and without in relation to the Church, it is the position of the heart that we must consider, not that of the body, since all who are within in heart are saved in the unity of the ark through the same water, through which all who are in heart without, whether they are also in body without or not, die as enemies of unity. As therefore it was not another but the same water that saved those who were placed within the ark, and destroyed those who were left without the ark, so it is not by different baptisms, but by the same, that good Catholics are saved, and bad Catholics or heretics perish. But what the most blessed Cyprian thinks of the Catholic Church, and how the heretics are utterly crushed by his authority; notwithstanding the much I have already said, I have yet determined to set forth by itself, if God will, with somewhat greater fullness and perspicuity, so soon as I shall have first said about his Council what I think is due from me, which, in God's will, I shall attempt in the following book.

BOOK VI.

IN WHICH IS CONSIDERED THE COUNCIL OF CARTHAGE, HELD UNDER THE AUTHORITY AND PRESIDENCY OF CYPRIAN, TO DETERMINE THE QUESTION OF THE BAPTISM OF HERETICS.

CHAP. I.—1. It might perhaps have been sufficient, that after the reasons have been so often repeated, and considered, and discussed with such variety of treatment, supplemented, too, with the addition of proofs from holy Scripture, and the concurrent testimony of so many passages from Cyprian himself, even those who are slow of heart should thus understand, as I believe they do, that the baptism of Christ cannot be rendered void by any perversity on the part of man, whether in administering or receiving it. And when we find that in those times, when the point in question was decided in a manner contrary to ancient custom, after discussions carried on without violation of saving charity and unity, it appeared to some even eminent men who were bishops of Christ, among whom the blessed Cyprian was specially conspicuous, that the baptism of Christ could not exist among heretics or schismatics, this simply arose from their not distinguishing the sacrament from the effect or use of the sacrament; and because its effect and use were not found among heretics in freeing them from their sins and setting their hearts right, the sacrament itself was also thought to be wanting among them. But if we turn our eyes to the multitude of chaff within the Church, since these also who are perverse and lead an abandoned life in unity itself appear to have no power either of giving or retaining remission of sins, seeing that it is not to the wicked but the good sons that it was said, "Whosesoever sins ye remit, they are remitted unto them; and whosesoever sins ye retain, they are retained,"[1] yet that such persons both have, and give, and receive the sacrament of baptism, was sufficiently manifest to the pastors of the Catholic Church dispersed over the whole world, through whom the original custom was afterwards confirmed by the authority of a plenary Council; so that even the sheep which was straying outside, and had received the mark of the Lord from false plunderers outside, if it seek the salvation of Christian unity, is purified from error, is freed from captivity, is healed of its wound, and yet the mark of the Lord is recognized rather than rejected in it; since the mark itself is often impressed both by wolves and on wolves, who seem indeed to be within the fold, but yet are proved by the fruits of their conduct, in which they persevere even to the end, not to belong to that sheep which is one in many; because, according to the foreknowledge of God, as many sheep wander outside, so many wolves lurk treacherously within, among whom the Lord yet knoweth them that are His, which hear only the voice of the Shepherd, even when He calls by the voice of men like the Pharisees, of whom it was said, "Whatsoever they bid you observe that observe and do."[2]

2. For as the spiritual man, keeping "the end of the commandment," that is, "charity out of a pure heart, and of a good conscience, and of faith unfeigned,"[3] can see some things less clearly out of a body which is yet "corruptible and presseth down the soul,"[4] and is liable to be otherwise minded in some things which God will reveal[5] to him in His own good time if he abide in the same charity, so in a carnal and perverse man something good and useful may be found, whch has its origin not in the man himself, but in some other source. For as in the fruitful branch there is found something which must be purged that it may bring forth more fruit, so also a grape is often found to hang on a cane that is barren and dry or fettered. And so, as it is foolish to love the portions which require purg-

[1] John xx. 23.

[2] Matt. xxiii. 3.

[3] 1 Tim. i. 5.

[4] Wisd. ix. 15.

[5] Phil. iii. 15.

ing in the fruitful branch, while he acts wisely who does not reject the sweet fruit wherever it may hang, so, if any one cuts himself off from unity by rebaptizing, simply because it seemed to Cyprian that one ought to baptize again those who came from the heretics, such a man turns aside from what merits praise in that great man, and follows what requires correction, and does not even attain to the very thing he follows after. For Cyprian, while grievously abhorring, in his zeal for God, all those who severed themselves from unity, thought that thereby they were separated from baptism itself; while these men, thinking it at most a slight offense that they themselves are severed from the unity of Christ, even maintain that His baptism is not in that unity, but issued forth with them. Therefore they are so far from the fruitfulness of Cyprian, as not even to be equal to the parts in him which needed purging.

CHAP. 2.—3. Again, if any one not having charity, and walking in the abandoned paths of a most wicked life, seems to be within while he really is without, and at the same time does not seek for the repetition of baptism even in the case of heretics, it in no wise helps his barrenness, because he is not rendered fruitful with his own fruit, but laden with that of others. But it is possible that some one may flourish in the root of charity, and may be most rightly minded in the point in which Cyprian was otherwise minded, and yet there may be more that is fruitful in Cyprian than in him, more that requires purging in him than in Cyprian. Not only, therefore, do we not compare bad Catholics with the blessed Cyprian, but even good Catholics we do not hastily pronounce to be on an equality with him whom our pious mother Church counts among the few rare men of surpassing excellence and grace, although these others may recognize the baptism of Christ even among heretics, while he thought otherwise; so that, by the instance of Cyprian, who saw one point less clearly, and yet remained most firm in the unity of the Church, it might be shown more clearly to heretics what a sacrilegious crime it was to break the bond of peace. For neither were the blind Pharisees, although they sometimes enjoined what was right to be done, to be compared to the Apostle Peter, though he at times enjoined what was not right. But not only is their dryness not to be compared to his greenness, but even the fruit of others may not be deemed equal to his fertility. For no one now compels the Gentiles to judaize, and yet no one now in the Church, however great his progress in goodness, may be compared with the apostleship of Peter. Wherefore, while rendering due reverence, and paying, so far as I can, the fitting honor to the peaceful bishop and glorious martyr Cyprian, I yet venture to say that his view concerning the baptism of schismatics and heretics was contrary to that which was afterwards brought to light by a decision, not of mine, but of the whole Church, confirmed and strengthened by the authority of a plenary Council: just as, while paying the reverence he deserves to Peter, the first of the apostles and most eminent of martyrs, I yet venture to say that he did not do right in compelling the Gentiles to judaize; for this also, I say, not of my own teaching, but according to the wholesome doctrine of the Apostle Paul, retained and preserved through out the whole Church.[1]

4. Therefore, in discussing the opinion of Cyprian, though myself of far inferior merit to Cyprian, I say that good and bad alike can have, can give, can receive the sacrament of baptism,—the good, indeed, to their health and profit; the bad to their destruction and ruin,—while the sacrament itself is of equal perfectness in both of them; and that it is of no consequence to its equal perfectness in all, how much worse the man may be that has it among the bad, just as it makes no difference how much better he may be that has it among the good. And accordingly it makes no difference either how much worse he may be that confers it, as it makes no difference how much better he may be; and so it makes no difference how much worse he may be that receives it, as it makes no difference how much better he may be. For the sacrament is equally holy, in virtue of its own excellence, both in those who are unequally just, and in those who are unequally unjust.

CHAP. 3.—5. But I think that we have sufficiently shown, both from the canon of Scripture, and from the letters of Cyprian himself, that bad men, while by no means converted to a better mind, can have, and confer, and receive baptism, of whom it is most clear that they do not belong to the holy Church of God, though they seem to be within it, inasmuch as they are covetous, robbers, usurers, envious, evil thinkers, and the like; while she is one dove,[2] modest and chaste, a bride without spot or wrinkle,[3] a garden enclosed, a fountain sealed, an orchard of pomegranates with pleasant fruits,[4] with all similar properties which are attributed to her;

[1] Gal. ii. 14.
[2] Cant. vi. 8, 9.
[3] Eph. v. 27; cp. Aug. *Retract.* ii. 18.
[4] Cant. iv. 12, 13.

and all this can only be understood to be in the good, and holy, and just,—following, that is, not only the operations of the gifts of God, which are common to good and bad alike, but also the inner bond of charity conspicuous in those who have the Holy Spirit, to whom the Lord says, "Whosesoever sins ye remit, they are remitted unto them; and whosesoever sins ye retain, they are retained."[1]

CHAP. 4.—6. And so it is clear that no good ground is shown herein why the bad man, who has baptism, may not also confer it; and as he has it to destruction, so he may also confer it to destruction,—not because this is the character of the thing conferred, nor of the person conferring, but because it is the character of him on whom it is conferred. For when a bad man confers it on a good man, that is, on one in the bond of unity, converted with a true conversion, the wickedness of him who confers it makes no severance between the good sacrament which is conferred, and the good member of the Church on whom it is conferred. And when his sins are forgiven him on his true conversion to God, they are forgiven by those to whom he is united by his true conversion. For the same Spirit forgives them, which is given to all the saints that cling to one another in love, whether they know one another in the body or not. Similarly when a man's sins are retained, they are assuredly retained by those from whom he, in whom they are retained, separates himself by dissimilarity of life, and by the turning away of a corrupt heart, whether they know him in the body or not.

CHAP. 5.—7. Wherefore all bad men are separated in the spirit from the good; but if they are separated in the body also by a manifest dissension, they are made yet worse. But, as it has been said, it makes no difference to the holiness of baptism how much worse the man may be that has it, or how much worse he that confers it: yet he that is separated may confer it, as he that is separated may have it; but as he has it to destruction, so he may confer it to destruction. But he on whom he confers it may receive it to his soul's health, if he, on his part, receive it not in separation; as it has happened to many that, in a catholic spirit, and with heart not alienated from the unity of peace, they have, under some pressure of impending death, turned hastily to some heretic and received from him the baptism of Christ without any share in his perversity, so that, whether dying or restored to life, they by no means remain in communion with those to whom they never passed in heart. But if the recipient himself has received the baptism in separation, he receives it so much the more to his destruction, in proportion to the greatness of the good which he has not received well; and it tends the more to his destruction in his separation, as it would avail the more to the salvation of one in unity. And so, if, reforming himself from his perverseness and turning from his separation, he should come to the Catholic peace, his sins are remitted through the bond of peace and the same baptism under which his sins were retained through the sacrilege of separation, because that is always holy both in the just and the unjust, which is neither increased by the righteousness nor diminished by the unrighteousness of any man.

8. This being the case, what bearing has it on so clear a truth, that many of his fellow-bishops agreed with Cyprian in that opinion, and advanced their own several opinions on the same side, except that his charity towards the unity of Christ might become more and more conspicuous? For if he had been the only one to hold that opinion, with no one to agree with him, he might have been thought, in remaining, to have shrunk from the sin of schism, because he found no companions in his error; but when so many agreed with him, he showed, by remaining in unity with the rest who thought differently from him, that he preserved the most sacred bond of universal catholicity, not from any fear of isolation, but from the love of peace. Wherefore it might indeed seem now to be superfluous to consider the several opinions of the other bishops also in that Council; but since those who are slow in heart think that no answer has been made at all, if to any passage in any discourse the answer which might be brought to bear on the spot be given not there but somewhere else, it is better that by reading much they should be polished into sharpness, than that by understanding little they should have room left for complaining that the argument has not been fairly conducted.

CHAP. 6.—9. First, then, let us record for further consideration the case proposed for decision by Cyprian himself, with which he initiates the proceedings of the Council, and by which he shows a peaceful spirit, abounding in the fruitfulness of Christian charity. "Ye have head," he says, "most beloved colleagues, what Jubaianus, our fellow-bishop, has written to me, consulting my

[1] John xx. 23.

poor ability about the unlawful and profane baptism of heretics, and what I have written back to him, expressing to him the same opinion that I have expressed once and again and often, that heretics coming to the Church ought to be baptized, and sanctified with the baptism of the Church. Another letter also of Jubaianus has been read to you, in which, agreeably to his sincere and religious devotion, in answer to our epistle, he not only expressed his assent to it, but also gratefully acknowledged that he had received instruction. It remains that we should individually express our opinions on this same subject, judging no one, and removing no one from the right of communion if he should entertain a different opinion. For neither does any one of us set himself up as a bishop of bishops, or by tyrannical terror force his colleagues to the necessity of obeying, since every bishop, in the free use of his liberty and power, has the right of free judgment, and can no more be judged by another than he can himself judge another. But we are all awaiting the judgment of our Lord Jesus Christ, who alone has the power both of preferring us in the government of His Church, and of judging of our actions."[1]

Chap. 7.—10. I have already, I think, argued to the best of my power, in the preceding books, in the interests of Catholic unanimity and counsel, in whose unity these continued as pious members, in reply not only to the letter which Cyprian wrote to Jubaianus, but also to that which he sent to Quintus, and that which, in conjunction with certain of his colleagues, he sent to certain other colleagues, and that which he sent to Pompeius. Wherefore it seems now to be fitting to consider also what the others severally thought, and that with the liberty of which he himself would not deprive us, as he says, "Judging no one, nor removing any from the right of communion if he entertain different opinions." And that he did not say this with the object of arriving at the hidden thoughts of his colleagues, extracted as it were from their secret lurking-places, but because he really loved peace and unity, is very easily to be seen from other passages of the same sort, where he wrote to individuals as to Jubaianus himself. "These things," he says, "we have written very shortly in answer to you, most beloved brother, according to our poor ability, not preventing any one of the bishops by our writing or judgment, from acting as he thinks right, having a free exercise of his own judgment."[2] And that it might not seem that any one, because of his entertaining different opinions in this same free exercise of his judgment, should be driven from the society of his brethren, he goes on to say, "We, so far as lies in us, do not strive on behalf of heretics against our colleagues and fellow-bishops, with whom we maintain godly unity and the peace of our Lord;"[2] and a little later he says, "Charity of spirit, respect for our fraternity, the bond of faith, the harmony of the priesthood, are by us maintained with patience and gentleness."[2] And so also in the epistle which he wrote to Magnus, when he was asked whether there was any difference in the efficacy of baptism by sprinkling or by immersion, "In this matter," he says, "I am too modest and diffident to prevent any one by my judgment from thinking as he deems right, and acting as he thinks."[3] By which discourses he clearly shows that these subjects were being handled by them at a time when they were not yet received as decided beyond all question, but were being investigated with great care as being yet unrevealed. We, therefore, maintaining on the subject of the identity of all baptisms what must be acknowledged everywhere to be the custom[4] of the universal Church, and what is confirmed by the decision of general Councils,[5] and taking greater confidence also from the words of Cyprian, which allowed me even then to hold opinions differing from his own without forfeiting the right of communion, seeing that greater importance and praise were attached to unity, such as the blessed Cyprian and his colleagues, with whom he held that Council, maintained with those of different opinions, disturbing and overthrowing thereby the seditious calumnies of heretics and schismatics in the name of the Lord Jesus Christ, who, speaking by His apostle, says, "Forbearing one another in love, endeavoring to keep the unity of the Spirit in the bond of peace;"[6] and again, by the mouth of the same apostle, "If in anything ye be otherwise minded, God shall reveal even this unto you,"[7]—we, I say, propose for consideration and discussion the opinions of the holy bishops, without violating the bond of unity and peace with them, in maintaining which we imitate them so far as we can by the aid of the Lord Himself.

[1] Conc. Carth., the seventh under Cyprian, A.D. 256. Introduction.

[2] Cypr. *Ep.* lxxiii. 26.

[3] Cypr. *Ep.* lxix. 12.

[4] *De baptismi simplicitate ubique agnoscendam consuetudinem.* The Benedictines give the reading of some MSS.: "*De baptismi simplicitate ubique agnoscenda*," etc., "maintaining the custom of the universal Church to acknowledge everywhere the identity of baptism."

[5] *Conciliis universalibus.*

[6] Eph. iv. 2, 3.

[7] Phil. iii. 15.

CHAP. VIII.—11. Cæcilius of Bilta[1] said: "I know of one baptism in the one Church, and of none outside the Church. The one will be where there is true hope and sure faith. For so it is written, 'One faith, one hope, one baptism.'[2] Not among heretics, where there is no hope and a false faith; where all things are done by a lie; where one possessed of a devil exorcises; the question of the sacrament is asked by one from whose mouth and words proceeds a cancer; the faithless gives faith; the guilty gives pardon for sins; and Antichrist baptizes in the name of Christ; one accursed of God blesses; the dead promises life; the unpeaceful gives peace; the blasphemer calls on God; the profane administers the priesthood; the sacrilegious sets up the altar. To all this is added this further evil, that the servant of the devil dares to celebrate the eucharist. If this be not so, let those who stand by them prove that all of it is false concerning heretics. See the kind of things to which the Church is compelled to assent, being forced to communicate without baptism or the remission of sins. This, brethren, we ought to shun and avoid, separating ourselves from so great a sin, and holding to the one baptism which is granted to the Church alone."[3]

12. To this I answer, that all who even within the Church profess that they know God, but deny Him in their deeds, such as are the covetous and envious, and those who, because they hate their brethren, are pronounced to be murderers, not on my testimony, but on that of the holy Apostle John,[4] —all these are both devoid of hope, because they have a bad conscience; and are faithless, because they do not do what they have vowed to God; and liars, because they make false professions; and possessed of devils, because they give place in their heart to the devil and his angels; and their words work corruption, since they corrupt good manners by evil communications; and they are infidels, because they laugh at the threats which God utters against such men; and accursed, because they live wickedly; and antichrists, because their lives are opposed to Christ; and cursed of God, since holy Scripture everywhere calls down curses on such men; and dead, because they are without the life of righteousness; and unpeaceful, because by their contrary deeds they are at variance with God's behests; and blasphemous, because by their abandoned acts despite is done to the name of Christian; and profane, because they are spiritually shut out from that inner sanctuary of God; and sacrilegious, because by their evil life they defile the temple of God within themselves; and servants of the devil, because they do service to fraud and covetousness, which is idolatry. That of such a kind are some, nay very many, even within the Church, is testified both by Paul the apostle and by Cyprian the bishop. Why, then, do they baptize? Why also are some, who "renounce the world in words and not in deeds," baptized without being converted from a life like this, and not rebaptized when they are converted? And as to what he says with such indignation, "See the kind of things to which the Church is compelled to assent, being forced to communicate without baptism or the remission of sins," he could never have used such expressions had there not been the other bishops who elsewhere forced men to such things. Whence also it is shown that at that time those men held the truer views who did not depart from the primitive custom, which is since confirmed by the consent of a general Council.[5] But what does he mean by adding, "This, brethren, we ought to shun and avoid, separating ourselves from so great a sin?" For if he means that he is not to do nor to approve of this, that is another matter; but if he means to condemn and sever from him those that hold the contrary opinion, he is setting himself against the earlier words of Cyprian, "Judging no man, nor depriving any of the right of communion if he differ from us."

CHAP. 9.—13. The elder Felix[6] of Migirpa said: "I think that every one coming from heresy should be baptized. For in vain does any one suppose that he has been baptized there, seeing that there is no baptism save the one true baptism in the Church; for there is one Lord, and one faith, and one Church, in which rests the one baptism, and holiness, and the rest. For the things that are practised without have no power to work salvation."

14. To what Felix of Migirpa said we answer as follows. If the one true baptism did not exist except in the Church, it surely would not exist in those who depart from unity. But it does exist in them, since they do not

1 Bilta (Biltha, Vilta) was in Africa Proconsularis. This Cæcilius is probably the same as the one addressed by Cyprian in Ep. lxiii.; and who unites with Cyprian and other bishops in letters addressed to others. Epp. iv. (to Pomponius), lvii., lxvii., lxx.

2 Eph. iv. 4, 5.

3 Conc. Carth. sec. 1.

4 1 John iii. 15.

5 *Concilii universitate.*

6 This section is wanting in the MSS. and in the edition of Amerbach, so that it has been supposed to have been added by Erasmus from Cyprian (Conc. Carth. sec. 2),—the name of Felix (really Primus), which is not found in Cyprian, being derived from the following section of Augustin. So Hartel: *Primus a Misgirpa dixit.* Migirpa or Misgirpa, was in Zeugitana. This Primus is seemingly identical with the Primus of Cypr. Epp. 67 (following Cæcilius), and 70 (preceding Cæcilius).

receive it when they return, simply because they had not lost it when they departed. But as regards his statement, that "the things that are practised without have no power to work salvation," I agree with him, and think that it is quite true; for it is one thing that baptism should not be there, and another that it should have no power to work salvation. For when men come to the peace of the Catholic Church, then what was in them before they joined it, but did not profit them, begins at once to profit them.

CHAP. 10.—15. To the declaration of Polycarp of Adrumetum,[1] that "those who declare the baptism of heretics to be valid, make ours of none effect," we answer, if that is the baptism of heretics which is given by heretics, then that is the baptism of the covetous and murderers which is given by them within the Church. But if this be not their baptism, neither is the other the baptism of heretics; and so it is Christ's, by whomsoever it be given.

CHAP. 11.—16. Novatus of Thamugadis[2] said: "Though we know that all Scripture gives its testimony respecting saving baptism, yet we ought to express our belief that heretics and schismatics, coming to the Church with the semblance of having been baptized, ought to be baptized in the unfailing fountain; and that therefore, according to the testimony of the Scriptures, and according to the decree of those most holy men, our colleagues,[3] all schismatics and heretics who are converted to the Church ought to be baptized; and that, moreover, all that seemed to have received ordination should be admitted as simple laymen."

17. Novatus of Thamugadis has stated what he has done, but he has brought forward no proofs by which to show that he ought to have acted as he did. For he has made mention of the testimony of the Scriptures, and the decree of his colleagues, but he has not adduced out of them anything which we could consider.

CHAP. 12.—18. Nemesianus of Tubunæ[4] said: "That the baptism which is given by heretics and schismatics is not true is everywhere declared in the holy Scriptures, inasmuch as their very prelates are false Christs and false prophets, as the Lord declares by the mouth of Solomon, 'Whoso trusteth in lies, the same feedeth the winds; he also followeth flying birds. For he deserteth the ways of his own vineyard, and hath strayed from the paths of his own field. For he walketh through pathless and dry places, and a land destined to thirst; and he gathereth fruitless weeds in his hands.'[5] And again, 'Abstain from strange water, and drink not of a strange fountain, that thou mayest live long, and that years may be added to thy life.[6] And in the gospel our Lord Jesus Christ spake with His own voice, saying, 'Except a man be born of water and of the Spirit, he cannot enter into the kingdom of God.'[7] This is the Spirit which from the beginning 'moved upon the face of the waters.'[8] For neither can the Spirit act without the water, nor the water without the Spirit. Ill, therefore, for themselves do some interpret, saying that by imposition of hands they receive the Holy Ghost, and are received into the Church, when it is manifest that they ought to be born again by both sacraments in the Catholic Church. For then indeed will they be able to become the sons of God, as the apostle says, 'Endeavoring to keep the unity of the Spirit in the bond of peace. There is one body, and one Spirit, even as ye are called in one hope of your calling; one Lord, one faith, one baptism, one God.'[9] All this the Catholic Church asserts. And again he says in the gospel, 'That which is born of the flesh is flesh, and that which is born of the Spirit is spirit; for the Spirit is God, and is born of God.'[10] Therefore all things whatsoever all heretics and schismatics do are carnal, as the apostle says, 'Now the works of the flesh are manifest, which are these: fornication, uncleanness, lasciviousness, idolatry, witchcraft,

1 Adrumetum (Hadrumetum) was an ancient Phœnician settlement, made a Roman colony by Trajan, on the coast of the Sinus Neapolitanus, some ninety miles south-east of Carthage, capital of Byzacium. Cyprian writes to Bp. Cornelius, Ep. xlviii., vindicating Polycarp: his name occurs also in the titles of Cypr. Epp. lvii., lxvii. (after Primus), and lxx. (after Cæcilius).

2 Thamugadis (Thamogade), a town in Numidia, on the east side of Mount Aurasius. The whole opinion of Novatus (Conc. Carth. sec. 4), is omitted in the MSS.

3 The words in Cyprian are, "*secundum decretum collegarum nostrorum sanctissimæ memoriæ virorum.*" The decree referred to is one of the Council held by Agrippinus.

4 Tubunæ, a town in Mauritania Cæsariensis. Nemesianus probably same with one of that name in Cypr. Epp. lxii., lxx., lxxvi., lxxvii.

5 Prov. ix. 12, LXX., the passage being altogether absent in the Hebrew, and consequently in the English version. Probably in N. Afr. version. The text in Erasmus is somewhat different, and was revised by the Louvain editors to bring it into harmony with the answer of Augustin and the text of Cyprian (Conc. Carth. sec. 5).

6 Prov. ix. 18, LXX., possibly N. Afr. version also.

7 John iii. 5. 8 Gen. i. 2. 9 Eph. iv. 3-6.

10 *Quoniam Spiritus Deus est, et de Deo natus est.* These words are found at the end of John iii. 6, in the oldest Latin MS. (in the Bodleian Library), and their meaning appears to be, as given in the text, that whatsoever is born of the Spirit is spirit, since the Holy Ghost, being God, and born of, or proceeding from God, in virtue of His supreme power makes those to be spirits whom He regenerates. If the meaning had been (as Bishop Fell takes it), that "he who is born of the Spirit is born of God," the neuter "*de Deo natum est*" would have been required. To refer "*Spiritus Deus est,*" with the Benedictines, to John iv. 24, "God is a Spirit," reverses the grammar and destroys the sense of the passage. The above explanation is taken from the preface to Cyprian by the monk of St. Maur (Maranus), p. xxxvi., quoted by Routh, *Rel. Sac.* iii. 193.

hatred, variance, emulations, wrath, seditions, heresies, and such like: of the which I tell you before, as I have also told you in time past, that they which do such things shall not inherit the kingdom of God.'[1] The apostle condemns, equally with all the wicked, those also who cause divisions, that is, schismatics and heretics. Unless therefore they receive that saving baptism which is one, and found only in the Catholic Church, they cannot be saved, but will be condemned with the carnal in the judgment of the Lord."

19. Nemesianus of Tubunæ has advanced many passages of Scripture to prove his point; but he has in fact said much on behalf of the view of the Catholic Church, which we have undertaken to set forth and maintain. Unless, indeed, we must suppose that he does not "trust in what is false" who trusts in the hope of things temporal, as do all covetous men and robbers, and those "who renounce the world in words but not in deeds," of whom Cyprian yet bears witness that such men not only baptize, but even are baptized within the Church.[2] For they themselves also "follow flying birds,"[3] since they do not attain to what they desire. But not only the heretic, but everyone who leads an evil life, "deserteth the ways of his own vineyard, and hath strayed from the paths of his own field. And he walketh through pathless and dry places, and a land destined to thirst; and he gathereth fruitless weeds in his hands;" because all justice is fruitful, and all iniquity is barren. Those, again, who "drink strange water out of a strange fountain," are found not only among heretics, but among all who do not live according to the teaching of God, and do live according to the teaching of the devil. For if he were speaking of baptism, he would not say, "Do not drink of a strange fountain," but, do not wash thyself in a strange fountain. Again, I do not see at all what aid he gets towards proving his point from the words of our Lord, "Except a man be born of water and of the Spirit, he cannot enter into the kingdom of God."[4] For it is one thing to say that every one who shall enter into the kingdom of heaven is first born again of water and the Spirit, because except a man be born of water and of the Spirit, he shall not enter into the kingdom of heaven, which is the Lord's saying, and is true; another thing to say that every one who is born of water and the Spirit shall enter into the kingdom of heaven, which is assuredly false. For Simon Magus also was born of water and of the Spirit,[5] and yet he did not enter into the kingdom of heaven; and this may possibly be the case with heretics as well. Or if only those are born of the Spirit who are changed with a true conversion, all "who renounce the world in word and not in deed" are assuredly not born of the Spirit, but of water only, and yet they are within the Church, according to the testimony of Cyprian. For we must perforce grant one of two things,—either those who renounce the world deceitfully are born of the Spirit, though it is to their destruction, not to salvation, and therefore heretics may be so born; or if what is written, that "the Holy Spirit of discipline will flee deceit,"[6] extends to proving as much as this, that those who renounce the world deceitfully are not born of the Spirit, then a man may be baptized with water, and not born of the Spirit, and Nemesianus says in vain that neither the Spirit can work without the water, nor the water without the Spirit. Indeed it has been already often shown how it is possible that men should have one baptism in common who have not one Church, as it is possible that in the body of the Church herself those who are sanctified by their righteousness, and those who are polluted through their covetousness, may not have the same one Spirit, and yet have the same one baptism. For it is said "one body," that is, the Church, just as it is said "one Spirit" and "one baptism." The other arguments which he has adduced rather favor our position. For he has brought forward a proof from the gospel, in the words, "That which is born of the flesh is flesh, and that which is born of the Spirit is spirit; for the Spirit is God, and born of God;"[7] and he has advanced the argument that therefore all things that are done by any heretic or schismatic are carnal, as the apostle says, "The works of the flesh are manifest, which are these: fornication, uncleanness;" and so he goes through the list which the apostle there enumerates, amongst which he has reckoned heresies, since "they who do such things shall not inherit the kingdom of God."[8] Then he goes on to add, that "therefore the apostle condemns with all wicked men those also who cause division, that is, schismatics and heretics." And in this he does well, that when he enumerates the works of the flesh, among which are also heresies, he found and declared that the apostle condemns them all alike. Let him therefore question the holy Cyprian himself, and learn from him how many even within the Church live according to the evil works of the flesh, which the apostle condemns in common with the heresies,

[1] Gal. v. 19-21. [2] Cypr. *Ep.* xi. 1.
[3] Prov. ix. 12, cp. LXX. [4] John iii. 5. [5] Acts viii. 13.
[6] Wisd. i. 5. [7] John iii. 6. [8] Gal. v. 19-21.

and yet these both baptize and are baptized. Why then are heretics alone said to be incapable of possessing baptism, which is possessed by the very partners in their condemnation?

Chap. 13.—20. Januarius of Lambæse[1] said: "Following the authority of the holy Scriptures, I pronounce that all heretics should be baptized, and so admitted into the holy Church."[2]

21. To him we answer, that, following the authority of the holy Scriptures, a universal Council of the whole world decreed that the baptism of Christ was not to be disavowed, even when found among heretics. But if he had brought forward any proof from the Scriptures, we should have shown either that they were not against us, or even that they were for us, as we proceed to do with him who follows.

Chap. 14.—21. Lucius of Castra Galbæ[3] said: "Since the Lord hath said in His gospel, 'Ye are the salt of the earth: but if the salt have lost his savor, that which is salted from it shall be thenceforth good for nothing, but to be cast out, and to be trodden under foot of men;'[4] and seeing that again, after His resurrection, when sending forth His apostles, He commanded them, saying, 'All power is given unto me in heaven and in earth: go ye therefore, and teach all nations, baptizing them in the name of the Father, and of the Son, and of the Holy Ghost,'[5]—since then it is plain that heretics, that is, the enemies of Christ, have not the full confession of the sacrament, also that schismatics cannot reason with spiritual wisdom, since they themselves, by withdrawing when they have lost their savor from the Church, which is one, have become contrary to it,[6] let that be done which is written, 'The houses of those that are opposed to the law must needs be cleansed;'[7] and it therefore follows that those who have been polluted by being baptized by men opposed to Christ should first be cleansed, and only then baptized."[8]

23. Lucius of Castra Galbæ has brought forward a proof from the gospel, in the words of the Lord, "Ye are the salt of the earth: but if the salt have lost his savor, that which is salted from it shall be good for nothing, but to be cast out, and to be trodden under foot of men;" just as though we maintained that men when cast out were of any profit for the salvation either of themselves or of any one else. But those also who, though seeming to be within, are yet of such a kind, not only are without spiritually, but will in the end be separated in the body also. For all such are profitable for nothing. But it does not therefore follow that the sacrament of baptism which is in them is nothing. For even in the very men who are cast out, if they return to their senses and come back, the salvation which had departed from them returns; but the baptism does not return, because it never had departed. And in what the Lord says, "Go therefore, and teach all nations, baptizing them in the name of the Father, and of the Son, and of the Holy Ghost," He did not permit any to baptize except the good, inasmuch as He did not say to the bad, "Whosesoever sins ye remit, they are remitted unto them; and whosesoever sins ye retain, they are retained."[9] How then do the wicked baptize within, who cannot remit sins? How also is it that they baptize the wicked whose hearts are not changed, whose sins are yet upon them, as John says, "He that hateth his brother is in darkness even until now?"[10] But if the sins of these men are remitted when they join themselves in the close bonds of love to the good and just, through whom sins are remitted in the Church, though they have been baptized by the wicked, so the sins of those also are remitted who come from without and join themselves by the inner bond of peace to the same framework of the body of Christ. Yet the baptism of Christ should be acknowledged in both, and held invalid in none, whether before they are converted, though then it profit them nothing, or after they are converted, that so it may profit them, as he says, "Since they themselves, by withdrawing when they have lost their savor from the Church, which is one, have become contrary to it, let that be done which is written, 'The houses of those that are opposed to the law must need be cleansed.' And it therefore follows," he goes on to say, "that those who have been polluted by being baptized by men opposed to Christ should first be cleansed, and only then baptized." What then? Are thieves

---

1 Lambæse (Lambese) was one of the chief cities in southern Numidia. This Januarius is not unlikely identical with the first of that name in Cypr. Ep. lxvii., and with the one of Epp. lxii. and lxx. For an opponent of Cyprian in Lambese, see Cypr. Epp. xxxvi. and lix.

2 Conc. Carth. sec. 6.

3 Castra Galbæ was most likely in Numidia. Lucius as bishop occurs in Cypr. Epp. lxvii., lxx., lxxvi. and lxxvii., but it is doubtful to which of the four of this name attendant on this council these references may apply.

4 Matt. v. 13. "*Id quod salietur ex eo, ad nihilum valebit.*"

5 Matt. xxviii. 18, 19.

6 *Recedendo infatuati contrarii facti sunt.* Dr. Routh, from a MS. in his own possession, inserts "*et*" after "*infatuati*,"—"have lost their savor and become contrary to the Church." *Rel. Sac.* iii. p. 194.

7 Prov. xiv. 9, cp. LXX.

8 Conc. Carth. sec. 7.

9 John xx. 23.

10 1 John ii. 9.

and murderers not contrary to the law, which says, "Thou shalt not kill; thou shalt not steal?"[1] "They must therefore needs be cleansed." Who will deny it? And yet not only those who are baptized by such within the Church, but also those who, being such themselves, are baptized without being changed in heart, are nevertheless exempt from further baptism when they are so changed. So great is the force of the sacrament of mere baptism, that though we allow that a man who has been baptized and continues to lead an evil life requires to be cleansed, we yet forbid him to be any more baptized.

CHAP. 15.—24. Crescens of Cirta[2] said: "The letters of our most beloved Cyprian to Jubaianus, and also to Stephen,[3] having been read in so large an assembly of our most holy brethren in the priesthood, containing as they do so large a body of sacred testimony derived from the Scriptures that give us our God,[4] that we have every reason to assent to them, being all united by the grace of God, I give my judgment that all heretics or schismatics who wish to come to the Catholic Church should not enter therein unless they have been first exorcised and baptized; with the obvious exception of those who have been originally baptized in the Catholic Church, these being reconciled and admitted to the penance of the Church by the imposition of hands."[5]

25 Here we are warned once more to inquire why he says, "Except, of course, those who have been originally baptized in the Catholic Church." Is it because they had not lost what they had before received? Why then could they not also transmit outside the Church what they were able to possess outside? Is it that outside it is unlawfully transmitted? But neither is it lawfully possessed outside, and yet it is possessed; so it is unlawfully given outside, but yet it is given. But what is given to the person returning from heresy who had been baptized inside, is given to the person coming to the Church who had been baptized outside,—that is, that he may have lawfully inside what before he had unlawfully outside. But perhaps some one may ask what was said on this point in the letter of the blessed Cyprian to Stephen, which is mentioned in this judgment, though not in the opening address to the Council,—I suppose because it was not considered necessary. For Crescens stated that the letter itself had been read in the assembly, which I have no doubt was done, if I am not mistaken, as is customary, in order that the bishops, being already assembled, might receive some information at the same time on the subject contained in that letter. For it certainly has no bearing on the present subject; and I am more surprised at Crescens having thought fit to mention it at all, than at its having been passed over in the opening address. But if any one thinks that I have shrunk from bringing forward something which has been urged in it that is essential to the present point, let him read it and see that what I say is true; or if he finds it otherwise, let him convict me of falsehood. For that letter contains nothing whatsoever about baptism administered among heretics or schismatics, which is the subject of our present argument.[6]

CHAP. 16.—26. Nicomedes of Segermi[7] said: "My judgment is that heretics coming to the Church should be baptized, because they can obtain no remission of sins among sinners outside."[8]

27. The answer to which is: The judgment of the whole Catholic Church is that heretics, being already baptized with the baptism of Christ, although in heresy, should not be rebaptized on coming to the Church. For if there is no remission of sins among sinners, neither can sinners within the Church remit sins; and yet those who have been baptized by them are not rebaptized.

CHAP. 17.—28. Monnulus of Girba[9] said: "The truth of our mother, the Catholic Church, hath continued, and still continues among us, brethren, especially in the threefold nature[10] of baptism, as our Lord says, 'Go, baptize all nations in the name of the Father, and of the Son, and of the Holy Ghost.'[11] Since, therefore," he goes on to say, "we know clearly that heretics have neither Father, Son, nor Holy Ghost, they

[1] Ex. xx. 13, 15.
[2] Cirta, an inland city of the Massylii in Numidia, was rebuilt by Constantine, and called Constantina.
[3] See below, on sec. 25.
[4] *Ex Scripturis deificis.*
[5] Conc. Carth. sec. 8.

[6] There are two letters extant from Cyprian to Stephen, No. 68, respecting Marcianus of Arles, who had joined Novatian, and No. 72, on a Council concerning heretical baptism. It is clear, however, from *Ep.* lxxiv. 1, that this Council, and consequently the letter to Stephen, was subsequent to the Council under consideration; and consequently Augustin is right in ignoring it, and referring solely to the former. Dr. Routh thinks the words an interpolation, of course before Augustin's time; and they may perhaps have been inserted by some one who had Cyprian's later letter to Stephen before his mind. *Rel. Sac.* iii. p. 194.
[7] Segermi church province of Byzacium. A Nicomedes occurs in Cypr. Epp. lvii., lxvii., lxx.
[8] Conc. Carth. sec. 9.
[9] Girba, formerly Meninx (Lotophagitis), an island to the south-east of the Lesser Syrtis belonged to church province of Tripolis. For Bp. Monnulus, see Cypr. Ep. lvii.
[10] *In baptismi trinitate.* "*Quia trina immersione expediebatur, in nomine Patris, Filii, et S. Spiritus.*"—*Bishop Fell.*
[11] Matt. xxviii. 19.

ought, on coming to our mother, the Church, to be truly regenerated and baptized, that the cancer which they had, and the wrath of condemnation, and the destructive energy of error,[1] may be sanctified by the holy and heavenly laver."[2]

29. To this we answer, That all who are baptized with the baptism that is consecrated in the words of the gospel have the Father, and the Son, and the Holy Ghost in the sacrament alone; but that in heart and in life neither do those have them who live an abandoned and accursed life within.

Chap. 18.—30. Secundinus of Cedias[3] said: "Since our Lord Christ said, 'He that is not with me is against me,'[4] and the Apostle John declares those who go out from the Church to be antichrists,[5] without all doubt the enemies of Christ, and those who are called antichrists, cannot minister the grace of the baptism which gives salvation; and therefore my judgment is that those who take refuge in the Church from the snares of heresy should be baptized by us, who of His condescension are called the friends of God."[6]

31. The answer to which is, That all are the opponents of Christ, to whom, on their saying, "Lord, have we not in Thy name done many wonderful things?" with all the rest that is there recorded, He shall at the last day answer, "I never knew you: depart from me, ye that work iniquity,"[7]—all which kind of chaff is destined for the fire, if it persevere to the last in its wickedness, whether any part of it fly outside before its winnowing, or whether it seem to be within. If, therefore, those heretics who come to the Church are to be again baptized, that they may be baptized by the friends of God, are those covetous men, those robbers, murderers, the friends of God, or must those whom they have baptized be baptized afresh?

Chap. 19.—32. Felix of Bagai[8] said: "As when the blind leads the blind, both fall into the ditch,[9] so when a heretic baptizes a heretic, both fall together into death."

33. This is true, but it does not follow that what he adds is true. "And therefore," he says, "the heretic must be baptized and brought to life, lest we who are alive should hold communion with the dead."[10] Were they not dead who said, "Let us eat and drink, for to-morrow we die?"[11] for they did not believe in the resurrection of the dead. Those then who were corrupted by their evil communications, and followed them, were not they likewise falling with them into the pit? And yet among them there were men to whom the apostle was writing as being already baptized; nor would they, therefore, if they were corrected, be baptized afresh. Does not the same apostle say, "To be carnally-minded is death?"[12] and certainly the covetous, the deceivers, the robbers, in the midst of whom Cyprian himself was groaning, were carnally-minded. What then? Did the dead hurt him who was living in unity? Or who would say, that because such men had or gave the baptism of Christ, that it was therefore violated by their iniquities?

Chap. 20.—34. Polianus of Mileum[13] said: "It is right that a heretic should be baptized in the holy Church."[14]

35. Nothing, indeed, could be expressed more shortly. But I think this too is short: It is right that the baptism of Christ should not be depreciated in the Church of Christ.

Chap. 21.—36. Theogenes of Hippo Regius[15] said: "According to the sacrament of the heavenly grace of God which we have received, we believe in the one only baptism which is in the holy Church."[16]

37. This may be my own judgment also. For it is so balanced, that it contains nothing contrary to the truth. For we also believe in the one only baptism which is in the holy Church. Had he said, indeed, We believe in that which is in the holy Church alone, the same answer must have been made to him as to the rest. But as it is, since he has expressed himself in this wise, "We believe in the one only baptism which is in the holy Church," so that it is asserted that it exists in the holy Church, but not denied that it may be elsewhere as well, whatever his meaning may have been, there is no need to argue against these words. For if I were ques-

1 *Erroris offectura.* Other readings are "*offensa*" and "*effectura.*"

2 Conc. Carth. sec. 10.

3 Cedias (Cedia) has been identified, but without sufficient reason, with Quidias, or Quiza, in Mauritania Cæsariensis for both places have bishops at the Collation of 411. A Bp. Secundinus is mentioned in Cypr. Epp. lvii., lxvii., but whether these refer to him of Cedias or him of Carpos (ch. 31) cannot be decided.

4 Matt. xii. 30.

5 1 John ii. 18

6 Conc. Carth. sec. 11.

7 Matt. vii. 22, 23.

8 Bagai, in church province of Numidia. See on l. 5. 7. Among the many of the name of Felix in the letters of Cyprian, lvi., lvii., lxvii., title 1, 6, lxx., lxxvi. *bis*, lxxvii., lxxix., title and text, it would be unsafe to decide a sure reference to distinguish between this and the other bishops of the same cognomen in this council.

9 Matt. xv. 14.

10 Conc. Carth. sec. 12.

11 1 Cor. xv. 32.

12 Rom. viii. 6.

13 Mileum, Milevis, Mileve, in ecclesiastical province of Numidia, noted as the seat of two Councils 402 A.D. and 416 A.D.; also as the See of Optatus. Polianus is most likely to be identified with the one in Cypr. Epp. lxxvi., lxxix.

14 Conc. Cath. sec. 13.

15 Hippo Regius, the see of Augustin himself, in ecclesiastical province of Numidia.

16 Conc. Carth. sec. 14.—C. D. H.

tioned on the several points, first, whether there was one baptism, I should answer that there was one. Then if I were asked, whether this was in the holy Church, I should answer that it was. In the third place, if it were asked whether I believed in this baptism, I should answer that I did so believe; and consequently I should answer that I believed in the one baptism which is in the holy Church. But if it were asked whether it was found in the holy Church alone, and not among heretics and schismatics, I should answer that, in common with the whole Church, I believed the contrary. But since he did not insert this in his judgment, I should consider that it was mere wantonness if I added words which I did not find there, for the sake of arguing against them. For if he were to say, There is one water of the river Euphrates, which is in Paradise, no one could gainsay the truth of what he said. But if he were asked whether that water were in Paradise and nowhere else, and were to say that this was so, he would be saying what was false. For, besides Paradise, it is also in those lands into which it flows from that source. But who is rash enough to say that he would have been likely to assert what is false, when it is quite possible that he was asserting what is true? Wherefore the words of this judgment require no contradiction, because they in no wise run counter to the truth.

CHAP. 22.—38. Dativus of Badiæ[1] said "We, so far as lies within our power, refuse to communicate with a heretic, unless he has been baptized in the Church, and received remission of his sins."[2]

39. The answer to this is: If your reason for wishing him to be baptized is that he has not received remission of sins, supposing you find a man within the Church who has been baptized, though entertaining hatred towards his brother, since the Lord cannot lie, who says, "If ye forgive not men their trespasses, neither will your Father forgive your trespasses,"[3] will you bid such an one, when corrected, to be baptized afresh? Assuredly not; so neither should you bid the heretic. It is clear that we must not pass unnoticed why he did not briefly say, "We do not communicate with a heretic," but added, "so far as lies within our power." For he saw that a greater number agreed with this view, from whose communion, however, he and his friends could not separate themselves, lest unity should be impaired, and so he added, "so far as lies within our power,"—showing beyond all doubt that he did not willingly communicate with those whom he held to be without baptism, but that yet all things were to be endured for the sake of peace and unity; just as was done also by those who thought that Dativus and his party were in the wrong, and who held what afterwards was taught by a fuller declaration of the truth, and urged by ancient custom, which received the stronger confirmation of a later Council; yet in turn, with anxious piety, they showed toleration towards each other, though without violation of Christian charity they entertained different opinions, endeavoring to keep the unity of the Spirit in the bond of peace,[4] till God should reveal to one of them, were he otherwise minded, even this error of his ways.[5] And to this I would have those give heed, by whom unity is attacked on the authority of this very Council by which it is declared how much unity should be loved.

CHAP. 23.—40. Successus of Abbir Germaniciana[6] said: "Heretics may either do nothing or everything. If they can baptize, they can also give the Holy Spirit; but if they cannot give the Holy Spirit, because they do not possess the Holy Spirit, then can they not either spiritually baptize. Therefore we give our judgment that heretics should be baptized."[7]

41. To this we may answer almost word for word: Murderers may either do nothing or everything. If they can baptize, they can also give the Holy Spirit; but if they cannot give the Holy Spirit, because they do not possess the Holy Spirit, then can they not either spiritually baptize. Therefore we give our judgment that persons baptized by murderers, or murderers themselves who have been baptized without being converted, should, when they have corrected themselves, be baptized. Yet this is not true. For "whosoever hateth his brother is a murderer;"[8] and Cyprian knew such men within the Church, who certainly baptized. Therefore it is to no purpose that words of this sort are used concerning heretics.

CHAP. 24.—42. Fortunatus of Thuccabori[9] said: "Jesus Christ our Lord and God, the Son of God the Father and Creator, built His Church upon a rock, not upon heresy,

1 Badiæ (Vada) in ecclesiastical province of Numidia. For Dativus see Cypr. Epp. lxxvi., lxxvii.

2 Conc. Carth. sec. 15.

3 Matt. vi. 15.

4 Eph. iv. 3.

5 Phil. iii. 15.

6 Abbir Germaniciana was in ecclesiastical province of Zeugitana, or Africa Proconsularis. Successus probably identical with one mentioned in Cypr. Epp. lvii., lxvii., lxx., lxxx.

7 Conc. Carth. sec. 16.

8 1 John iii. 15.

9 Thuccabori, Tucca or Terebrinthina, in ecclesiastical province of Africa Proconsularis or Zeugitana. For Bp. Fortunatus, see Cypr. Epp. xlviii., lvi., lvii. (the first), lxvii., lxx.

and gave the power of baptizing to bishops, not to heretics. Wherefore those who are outside the Church, and stand against Christ, scattering His sheep and flock, cannot baptize outside." [1]

43. He added the word "outside" in order that he might not be answered with a like brevity to Successus. For otherwise he might also have been answered word for word: Jesus Christ our Lord and God, the Son of God the Father and Creator, built His Church upon a rock, not upon iniquity, and gave the power of baptizing to bishops, not to the unrighteous. Wherefore those who do not belong to the rock on which they build, who hear the word of God and do it,[2] but, living contrary to Christ in hearing the word and not doing it, and hereby building on the sand, in this way scatter His sheep and flock by the example of an abandoned character, cannot baptize. Might not this be said with all the semblance of truth? and yet it is false. For the unrighteous do baptize, since those robbers are unrighteous whom Cyprian maintained to be at unity with himself.[3] But for this reason, says the Donatist, he adds "outside." Why therefore can they not baptize outside? Is it because they are worse from the very fact that they are outside? But it makes no difference, in respect of the validity of baptism, how much worse the minister may be. For there is not so much difference between bad and worse as between good and bad; and yet, when the bad baptizes, he gives the selfsame sacrament as the good. Therefore, also, when the worse baptizes, he gives the selfsame sacrament as the less bad. Or is it that it is not in respect of man's merit, but of the sacrament of baptism itself, that it cannot be given outside? If this were so, neither could it be possessed outside, and it would be necessary that a man should be baptized again so often as he left the Church and again returned to it.

44. Further, if we inquire more carefully what is meant by "outside," especially as he himself makes mention of the rock on which the Church is built, are not they in the Church who are on the rock, and they who are not on the rock, not in the Church either? Now, therefore, let us see whether they build their house upon a rock who hear the words of Christ and do them not. The Lord Himself declares the contrary, saying, "Whosoever heareth these sayings of mine, and doeth them, I will liken him unto a wise man, which built his house upon a rock;" and a little later, "Every one that heareth these sayings of mine, and doeth them not, shall be likened unto a foolish man, which built his house upon the sand."[4] If, therefore, the Church is on a rock, those who are on the sand, because they are outside the rock, are necessarily outside the Church. Let us recollect, therefore, how many Cyprian mentions as placed within who build upon the sand, that is, who hear the words of Christ and do them not. And therefore, because they are on the sand, they are proved to be outside the rock, that is, outside the Church; yet even while they are so situated, and are either not yet or never changed for the better, not only do they baptize and are baptized, but the baptism which they have remains valid in them though they are destined to damnation.

45. Neither can it be said in this place,[5] Yet who is there that doeth all the words of the Lord which are written in the evangelic sermon itself,[5] at the end of which He says, that he who heard the said words and did them built upon a rock, and he who heard them and did them not built upon the sand? For, granting that by certain persons all the words are not accomplished, yet in the same sermon He has appointed the remedy, saying, "Forgive, and ye shall be forgiven."[6] And after the Lord's prayer had been recorded in detail in the same sermon, He says, "For I say unto you, if ye forgive men their trespasses, your heavenly Father will also forgive you: but if ye forgive not men their trespasses, neither will your Father forgive your trespasses."[7] Hence also Peter says, "For charity shall cover the multitude of sins;"[8] which charity they certainly did not have, and on this account they built upon the sand, of whom the same Cyprian says, that within the Church they held conversation, even in the time of the apostles, in unkindly hatred alien from Christian charity;[9] and therefore they seemed indeed to be within, but really were without, because they were not on that rock by which the Church is signified.

Chap. 25.—46. Sedatus of Tuburbo [10] said: "Inasmuch as water, sanctified by the prayer of the priest in the Church, washes away sins, just so much does it multiply sins when infected, as by a cancer, with the words of heretics. Wherefore one must strive, with all such efforts as conduce to peace, that no one who has been infected and tainted by

1 Conc. Carth. sec. 17.
2 Matt. vii. 24.
3 Cypr. *Serm. de Laps.*
4 Matt. vii. 24, 26.
5 It is pointed out by the Louvain editors that this passage shows that Augustin considered our Lord's precept to comprehend everything contained in the Sermon on the Mount.
6 Luke vi. 37.
7 Matt. vi. 14, 15.
8 1 Pet. iv. 8.
9 Cypr. *Ep.* lxxiii. 14.
10 Tuburbo (Thuburbo) was in the ecclesiastical province of Zeugitana. Sedatus is not unlikely the same as the one mentioned in Cypr. Epp. iv., lxvii., lxx.

heretical error should refuse to receive the one true baptism, with which whosoever is not baptized shall not inherit the kingdom of heaven."[1]

47. To this we answer, that if the water is not sanctified, when through want of skill the priest who prays utters some words of error, many, not only of the bad, but of the good brethren in the Church itself, fail to sanctify the water. For the prayers of many are corrected every day on being recited to men of greater learning, and many things are found in them contrary to the Catholic faith. Supposing, then, that it were shown that some persons were baptized when these prayers had been uttered over the water, will they be bidden to be baptized afresh? Why not? Because generally the fault in the prayer is more than counterbalanced by the intent of him who offers it; and those fixed words of the gospel, without which baptism cannot be consecrated, are of such efficacy, that, by their virtue, anything faulty that is uttered in the prayer contrary to the rule of faith is made of no effect, just as the devil is excluded by the name of Christ. For it is clear that if a heretic utters a faulty prayer, he has no good intent of love whereby that want of skill may be compensated, and therefore he is like any envious or spiteful person in the Catholic Church itself, such as Cyprian proves to exist within the Church. Or one might offer some prayer, as not unfrequently happens, in which he should speak against the rule of faith, since many rush into the use of prayers which are composed not only by unskillful men who love to talk, but even by heretics, and in the simplicity of ignorance, not being able to discern their true character, use them, thinking they are good; and yet what is erroneous in them does not vitiate what is right, but rather it is rendered null thereby, just as in the man of good hope and approved faith, who yet is but a man, if in anything he be otherwise minded, what he holds aright is not thereby vitiated until God reveal to him also that in which he is otherwise minded.[2] But supposing that the man himself is wicked and perverse, then, if he should offer an upright prayer, in no part contrary to the Catholic faith, it does not follow that because the prayer is right the man himself is also right; and if over some he offer an erroneous prayer, God is present to uphold the words of His gospel, without which the baptism of Christ cannot be consecrated, and He Himself consecrates His sacrament, that in the recipient, either before he is baptized, or when he is baptized, or at some future time when he turns in truth to God, that very sacrament may be profitable to salvation, which, were he not to be converted, would be powerful to his destruction. But who is there who does not know that there is no baptism of Christ, if the words of the gospel in which consists the outward visible sign be not forthcoming? But you will more easily find heretics who do not baptize at all, than any who baptize without those words. And therefore we say, not that every baptism (for in many of the blasphemous rites of idols men are said to be baptized), but that the baptism of Christ, that is, every baptism consecrated in the words of the gospel, is everywhere the same, and cannot be vitiated by any perversity on the part of any men.[3]

48. We must certainly not lightly pass over in this judgment that he here inserted a clause, and says, "Wherefore we must strive, with all such efforts as conduce to peace, that no one who has been infected," etc. For he had regard to those words of the blessed Cyprian in his opening speech, "Judging no man, nor depriving any of the right of communion if he entertain a different view." See of what power is the love of unity and peace in the good sons of the Church, that they should choose rather to show tolerance towards those whom they called sacrilegious and profane, being admitted, as they thought, without the sacrament of baptism, if they could not correct them as they thought was right, than on their account to break that holy bond, lest on account of the tares the wheat also should be rooted out,[4]—permitting, so far as rested with them, as in that noblest judgment of Solomon, that the infant body should rather be nourished by the false mother than be cut in pieces.[5] But this was the opinion both of those who held the truer view about the sacrament of baptism, and of those to whom God, in consideration of their great love, was purposing to reveal any point in which they were otherwise minded.

CHAP. 26.—49 Privatianus of Sufetula[6] said: "He who says that heretics have the power of baptizing should first say who it was that founded heresy. For if heresy is of God, it may have the divine favor; but if it be not of God, how can it either have or confer on any one the grace of God?"[7]

50. This man may thus be answered word

---

1 Conc. Carth sec. 18.

2 Phil. iii. 15.

3 See above, III. cc. 14, 15.

4 Matt. xiii. 29.

5 1 Kings iii. 26.

6 Sufetula was a town in ecclesiastical province of Byzacene, twenty-five miles from Sufes (same province), of which the name is a diminutive. Bp. Privatianus is mentioned in Cypr. Epp. lvi., lvii.

7 Conc. Carth. sec. 19.

for word: He who says that malicious and envious persons have the power of baptizing, should first say who was the founder of malice and envy. For if malice and envy are of God, they may have the divine favor; but if they are not of God, how can they either have or confer on any one the grace of God? But as these words are in the same way most manifestly false, so are also those which these were uttered to confute. For the malicious and envious baptize, as even Cyprian himself allows, because he bears testimony that they also are within. So therefore even heretics may baptize, because baptism is the sacrament of Christ; but envy and heresy are the works of the devil. Yet though a man possesses them, he does not thereby cause that if he have the sacrament of Christ, it also should itself be reckoned in the number of the devil's works.

Chap. 27.—51. Privatus of Sufes[1] said: "What can be said of the man who approves the baptism of heretics, save that he communicates with heretics?"[2]

52. To this we answer: It is not the baptism of heretics which we approve in heretics, as it is not the baptism of the covetous, or the treacherous, or deceitful, or of robbers, or of envious men which we approve in them; for all of these are unjust, but Christ is just, whose sacrament existing in them, they do not in its essence violate. Otherwise another man might say: What can be said of the man who approves the baptism of the unjust, save that he communicates with the unjust. And if this objection were brought against the Catholic Church herself, it would be answered just as I have answered the above.

Chap. 28.—53. Hortensianus of Lares[3] said: "How many baptisms there are, let those who uphold or favor heretics determine. We assert one baptism of the Church, which we only know in the Church. Or how can those baptize any one in the name of Christ whom Christ Himself declares to be His enemies?"[4]

54. Giving answer to this man in a like tenor of words, we say: Let those who uphold or favor the unrighteous see to it: we recall to the Church when we can the one baptism which we know to be of the Church alone, wherever it be found. Or how can they baptize any one in the name of Christ whom Christ Himself declares to be His enemies? For He says to all the unrighteous, "I never knew you: depart from me, ye that work iniquity;"[5] and yet, when they baptize, it is not themselves that baptize, but He of whom John says, "The same is He which baptizeth."[6]

Chap. 29.—55. Cassius of Macomades[7] said: "Since there cannot be two baptisms, he who grants baptism unto heretics takes it away from himself. I therefore declare my judgment that heretics, those objects for our tears, those masses of corruption,[8] should be baptized when they begin to come to the Church, and that so being washed by the sacred and divine laver, and enlightened with the light of life, they may be received into the Church,—as being now made not enemies, but peaceful; not strangers, but of the household of the faith of the Lord; not bastards,[9] but sons of God; partaking not of error, but of salvation,—with the exception of those who, being believers transplanted from the Church, had gone over to heresy, and that these should be restored by the laying on of hands."[10]

56. Another might say: Since there cannot be two baptisms, he who grants baptism to the unrighteous takes it away from himself. But even our opponents would join us in resisting such a man when he says that we grant baptism to the unrighteous, which is not of the unrighteous, like their unrighteousness, but of Christ, of whom is righteousness, and whose sacrament, even among the unrighteous, is not unrighteous. What, therefore, they would join us in saying of the unrighteous, that let them say to themselves of heretics. And therefore he should rather have said as follows: I therefore give my judgment that heretics, those objects for our tears, those masses of corruption, should not be baptized when they begin to come to the Church, if they already have the baptism of Christ, but should be corrected from their error. For we may similarly say of the unrighteous, of whom the heretics are a part: I therefore give

1 See n. 6. p. 475.
2 Conc. Carth. sec. 20.
3 Lares, in ecclesiastical province of Numidia. Hortensianus is very likely the same as the one in Cypr. Epp. lvii., lxx.
4 Conc. Carth. sec. 21.

5 Matt. vii. 23.
6 John i. 33.
7 Macomades [in ecclesiastical province of Numidia. Bp. Cassius is probably to be identified with the one in Cypr. Ep. lxx.
8 *Flebiles et tabidos.* This is otherwise taken of the repentant heretics, "Melting with the grief and wretchedness of penitence;" but Bishop Fell points out that the interpretation in the text is supported by an expression in c. 33, 63: *Mens hæretica, quæ diuturna tabe polluta est.* Routh *Rel. Sac.* iii. p. 199.
9 *Adulteros.* So all the MSS. of Augustin, though in Cyprian is sometimes found "*adulterinos.*" In classical Latin, however, "*adulterit*" is sometimes used in the sense of "*adulterinus.*" Cassius seems to have had in mind Heb. xii. 8, "Then are ye bastards, and not sons."
10 Conc. Carth. sec. 22.

my judgment that the unrighteous, those objects for our tears, and masses of corruption, if they have been already baptized, should not be baptized again when they begin to come to the Church, that is, to that rock outside which are all who hear the words of Christ and do them not; but being already washed with the sacred and divine laver, and now further enlightened with the light of truth, should be received into the Church no longer as enemies but as peaceful, for the unrighteous have no peace; no longer as strangers, but of the household of the faith of the Lord, for to the unrighteous it is said, "How then art thou turned into the degenerate plant of a strange vine unto me?"[1] no longer as bastards, but the sons of God, for the unrighteous are the sons of the devil, partaking not of error but of salvation, for unrighteousness cannot save. And by the Church I mean that rock, that dove, that garden enclosed and fountain sealed, which is recognized only in the wheat, not in the chaff, whether that be scattered far apart by the wind, or appear to be mingled with the corn even till the last winnowing. In vain, therefore, did Cassius add, "With the exception of those who, being believers transplanted from the Church, had gone over to heresy.' For if even they themselves had lost baptism by seceding, to themselves also let it be restored; but if they had not lost it, let what was given by them receive due recognition.

CHAP. 30.—57. Another Januarius of Vicus Cæsaris[2] said: "If error does not obey truth, much more does truth refuse assent to error; and therefore we stand by the Church in which we preside, so that, claiming her baptism for herself alone, we baptize those whom the Church has not baptized."[3]

58. We answer: Whom the Church baptizes, those that rock baptizes outside which are all they who hear the words of Christ and do them not. Let all, therefore, be baptized again who have been baptized by such. But if this is not done, then, as we recognize the baptism of Christ in these, so should we recognize it in heretics, though we either condemn or correct their unrighteousness and error.

CHAP. 31.—59. Another Secundinus of Carpis[4] said: "Are heretics Christians or not? If they are Christians, why are they not in the Church of God? If they are not Christians, let them be made so.[5] Else what will be the reference in the discourse of the Lord, in which He says, 'He that is not with me is against me; and he that gathereth not with me scattereth abroad?'[6] Whence it is clear that on strange children and the offspring of Antichrist the Holy Spirit cannot descend by the laying on of hands alone, since it is clear that heretics have not baptism."[7]

60. To this we answer: Are the unrighteous Christians or not? If they are Christians, why are they not on that rock on which the Church is built? for they hear the words of Christ and do them not. If they are not Christians, let them be made so. Else what will be the reference in the discourse of our Lord, in which He says, "He that is not with me is against me; and he that gathereth not with me scattereth abroad?" For they scatter His sheep who lead them to the ruin of their lives by a false imitation of the Lord. Whence it is clear that upon strange children (as all the unrighteous are called), and upon the offspring of Antichrist (which all are who oppose themselves to Christ), the Holy Spirit cannot descend by the laying on of hands alone, if there be not added a true conversion of the heart; since it is clear that the unrighteous, so long as they are unrighteous, may indeed have baptism, but cannot have the salvation of which baptism is the sacrament. For let us see whether heretics are described in that psalm where the following words are used of strange children: "Deliver me, O Lord, from the hand of strange children, whose mouth speaketh vanity, and their right hand is a right hand of falsehood: whose sons are like young shoots well established, and their daughters polished after the similitude of the temple. Their garners are full, affording all manner of store; their sheep are fruitful, bringing forth plenteously in their streets; their oxen are strong: there is no breaking down of their fence, no opening of a passage out, no complaining in their streets. Men deemed happy the people that is in such a case; rather blessed is the people whose God is the Lord."[8] If, therefore, those are strange children who place their happiness in temporal things, and in the abundance of earthly prosperity, and depsise the commandments of the Lord, let us see whether these are not the very same of whom Cyprian so speaks, transforming them also

---

[1] Jer. ii. 21.
[2] Vicus Cæsaris, probably of ecclesiastical province of Byzacium. This Bp. Januarius may be the second of that name in Cypr. Ep. lxvii., and is to be distinguished from Bp. Januarius of Lambæse, ch. xiii. 20.
[3] Conc. Carth. sec. 23.
[4] Carpis (Carpos) was in ecclesiastical province of Zeugitana. See for Secundinus, note on chap. 13.
[5] *Fiant.* Another reading in some MSS. of Cyprian (not found in those of Augustin) is, "*quomodo Christianos faciunt*," which is less in harmony with the context.
[6] Matt. xii. 30.
[7] Conc. Carth. sec. 24.
[8] Ps. cxliv. 11–15, so LXX. cp. Hieron. Ps. cxliii. 11–15.

into himself, that he may show that he is speaking of men with whom he held communion in the sacraments: "In not keeping," he says, "the way of the Lord, nor observing the heavenly commandments given us for our salvation. Our Lord did the will of His Father, and we do not do the will of the Lord, being eager about our patrimony or our gains, following after pride, and so forth."[1] But if these could both have and transmit baptism, why is it denied that it may exist among strange children, whom he yet exhorts, that, by keeping the heavenly commandments conveyed to them through the only-begotten Son, they should deserve to be His brethren and the sons of God?

Chap. 32.—61. Victoricus of Thabraca[2] said: "If heretics may baptize, and give remission of sins, why do we destroy their credit, and call them heretics?"[3]

62. What if another were to say: If the unrighteous may baptize, and give remission of sins, why do we destroy their credit, and call them unrighteous? The answer which we should give to such an one concerning the unrighteous may also be given to the other concerning heretics,—that is, in the first place, that the baptism with which they baptize is not theirs; and secondly, that it does not follow that whosoever has the baptism of Christ is also certain of the remission of his sins if he has this only in the outward sign, and is not converted with a true conversion of the heart, so that he who gives remission should himself have remission of his sins.

Chap. 33.—63. Another Felix of Uthina[4] said: "No one can doubt, most holy brethren in the priesthood, that human presumption has not so much power as the adorable and venerable majesty of our Lord Jesus Christ. Remembering then the danger, we ought not only to observe this ourselves, but to confirm it by our general consent, that all heretics who come to the bosom of our mother the Church be baptized, that the heretical mind, which has been polluted by long-continued corruption, may be reformed when cleansed by the sanctification of the laver."[5]

64. Perhaps the man who has placed the strength of his case for the baptizing of heretics in the cleansing away of the long-continued corruption, would spare those who, having fallen headlong into some heresy, had remained in it a brief space, and presently being corrected, had passed from thence to the Catholic Church. Furthermore, he has himself failed to observe that it might be said that all unrighteous persons who come to that rock, in which is understood the Church, should be baptized, so that the unrighteous mind, which was building outside the rock upon the sand by hearing the words of Christ and not doing them, might be reformed when cleansed by the sanctification of the laver; and yet this is not done if they have been baptized already, even if it be proved that such was their character when they were baptized, that is, that they "renounced the world in words and not in deeds."

Chap. 34.—65. Quietus of Burug[6] said: "We who live by faith ought with believing observance to obey what has been before foretold for our instruction. For it is written in Solomon, 'He that is washed by one dead, what availeth his washing?'[7] Which assuredly he says of those who are washed by heretics, and of those who wash. For if they who are baptized among them receive eternal life through the remission of their sins, why do they come to the Church? But if no salvation is received from a dead person, and they therefore, acknowledging their former error, return with penance to the truth, they ought to be sanctified with the one life-giving baptism which is in the Catholic Church."[8]

66. What it is to be baptized by the dead, we have already, without prejudice to the more careful consideration of the same scripture, sufficiently declared before.[9] But I would ask why it is that they wish heretics alone to be considered dead, when Paul the apostle has said generally of sin, "The wages of sin is death;"[10] and again, "To be carnally minded is death."[11] And when he says that a widow that liveth in pleasure is dead,[12] how are they not dead "who renounce the world in words and not in deeds"? What, therefore, is the profit of washing in him who is baptized by them, except, indeed, that if he himself also is of the same character, he has the laver indeed, but it does not profit him to salvation? But if he by whom he is baptized

1 Cypr. *Presbyteris et diaconibus fratribus*, Ep. xi. 1.

2 Thabraca was on the coast of Numidia, in ecclesiastical province of that name, the frontier town towards Zeugitana, at the mouth of the Tucca. The name of a Victoricus occurs in Cypr. Epp. lvii., lxvii.

3 Conc. Carth. sec. 25.

4 Uthina was in ecclesiastical province of Zeugitana. This Felix is to be distinguished from the bishop of Bagai, ch. 19: A reference to a bishop of Utina is made by Tert. de Monog. ch. xii., but he cannot have been this Felix, as some assume.

5 Conc. Carth. sec. 26.

6 Burug (Buruc) or Burca was in ecclesiastical province of Numidia. Quietus may be identical with the one mentioned in Cypr. Ep. lxvii.

7 In the English version this is, "He that washeth himself after touching a dead body, if he touch it again, what availeth his washing?"—Ecclus. xxxiv. 25.

8 Conc. Carth. sec. 27.

9 *Contra Parmenianum*, II. 10. 22.

10 Rom. vi. 23.

11 Rom. viii. 6.

12 1 Tim. v. 6.

is such, but the man who is baptized is turned to the Lord with no false heart, he is not baptized by that dead person, but by that living One of whom it is said, "The same is He which baptizeth."[1] But to what he says of heretics, that if they who are baptized among them receive eternal life through the remission of their sins, why do they come to the Church? we answer: They come for this reason, that although they have received the baptism of Christ up to the point of the celebration of the sacrament, yet they cannot attain to life eternal save through the charity of unity; just as neither would those envious and malicious ones attain to life eternal, who would not have their sins forgiven them, even if they entertained hatred only against those from whom they suffered wrong; since the Truth said, "If ye forgive not men their trespasses, neither will your Father forgive your trespasses,"[2] how much less when they were hating those towards whom they were rewarding evil for good?[3] And yet these men, though "renouncing the world in words and not in deeds," would not be baptized again, if they should afterwards be corrected, but they would be made holy by the one living baptism. And this is indeed in the Catholic Church, but not in it alone, as neither is it in the saints alone who are built upon the rock, and of whom that one dove is composed.[4]

CHAP. 35.—67. Castus of Sicca[5] said: He who presumes to follow custom in despite of truth is either envious and evilly disposed towards the brethren to whom the truth is revealed, or else he is ungrateful towards God, by whose inspiration His Church is instructed."[6]

68. If this man proved that those who differed from him, and held the view that has since been held by the whole world under the sanction of a Christian Council, were following custom so as to despise truth, we should have reason for fearing these words; but seeing that this custom is found both to have had its origin in truth and to have been confirmed by truth, we have nothing to fear in this judgment. And yet, if they were envious or evilly disposed towards the brethren, or ungrateful towards God, see with what kind of men they were willing to hold communion; see what kind of men, holding different opinions from their own, they treated as Cyprian enjoined them at the first, not removing them from the right of communion; see by what kind of men they were not polluted in the preservation of unity; see how greatly the bond of peace was to be loved; see what views they hold who bring charges against us, founded on the Council of bishops, their predecessors, whose example they do not imitate, and by whose example, when the rights of the case are considered, they are condemned. If it was the custom, as this judgment bears witness, that heretics coming to the Church should be received with the baptism which they already had, either this was done rightly, or the evil do not pollute the good in unity. If it was rightly done, why do they accuse the world because they are so received? But if the evil do not pollute the good in unity, how do they defend themselves against the charge of sacrilegious separation?

CHAP. 36.—69. Eucratius of Theni[7] said: "Our God and Lord Jesus Christ, teaching the apostles with His own mouth, fully laid down our faith, and the grace of baptism, and the rule of the law of the Church, saying, 'Go ye, and teach all nations, baptizing them in the name of the Father, and of the Son, and of the Holy Ghost.'[8] Therefore the false and unrighteous baptism of heretics is to be repudiated by us, and contradicted with all solemnity of witness, seeing that from their mouth issues not life, but poison, not heavenly grace, but blaspheming of the Trinity. And so it is plain that heretics coming to the Church ought to be baptized with perfect and Catholic baptism, that, being purified from the blasphemy of their presumption, they may be reformed by the grace of the Holy Spirit."[9]

70. Clearly, if the baptism is not consecrated in the name of the Father, and of the Son, and of the Holy Ghost, it should be considered to be of the heretics, and repudiated as unrighteous by us with all solemnity of witness; but if we discern this name in it, we do better to distinguish the words of the gospel from heretical error, and approve what is sound in them, correcting what is faulty.

CHAP. 37.—71. Libosus of Vaga[10] said: "The Lord says in the gospel, 'I am the truth;'[11] He did not say, I am custom. Therefore, when the truth is made manifest, let custom yield to truth; so that, if even in time

---

1 John i. 33.
2 Matt. vi. 15.
3 Ps. xxxv. 12.
4 Cant. vi. 9.
5 Sicca was in ecclesiastical province of Zeugitana. This is certainly not the Castus of Cypr. *de Laps.* c. xiii.
6 Conc. Carth. sec. 28.
7 Theni was in ecclesiastical province of Byzacene. A Eucratius occurs in Cypr. Ep. ii.
8 Matt. xxviii. 19.
9 Conc. Carth. sec. 29.
10 Vaga was in ecclesiastical province of Byzacium. The name of a Libosus occurs in Cypr. Ep. lxvii.
11 John xiv. 6.

past any one did not baptize heretics in the Church, he may now begin to baptize them."[1]

72. Here he has in no way tried to show how that is the truth to which he says that custom ought to yield. But it is of more importance that he helps us against those who have separated themselves from unity, by confessing that the custom existed, than that he thinks it ought to yield to a truth which he does not show. For the custom is of such a nature, that if it admitted sacrilegious men to the altar of Christ without the cleansing of baptism, and polluted none of the good men who remained in unity, then all who have cut themselves off from the same unity, in which they could not be polluted by the contagion of any evil persons whatsoever, have separated themselves without reason, and have committed the manifest sacrilege of schism. But if all perished in pollution through that custom, from what cavern do they issue without the original truth, and with all the cunning of calumny? If, however, the custom was a right one by which heretics were thus received, let them abandon their madness, let them confess their error; let them come to the Catholic Church, not that they may be bathed again with the sacrament of baptism, but that they may be cured from the wound of severance.

Chap. 38.—73. Lucius of Thebaste[2] said: "I declare my judgment that heretics, and blasphemers, and unrighteous men, who with various words pluck away the sacred and adorable words of the Scriptures, should be held accursed, and therefore exorcised and baptized."[3]

74. I too think that they should be held accursed, but not that therefore they should be exorcised and baptized; for it is their own falsehood which I hold accursed, but Christ's sacrament which I venerate.

Chap. 39.—75. Eugenius of Ammedera[4] said: "I too pronounce this same judgment, that heretics should be baptized."[5]

76. To him we answer: But this is not the judgment which the Church pronounces, to which also God has now revealed in a plenary Council the point in which ye were then still otherwise minded,[6] but because saving charity was in you, ye remained in unity.

Chap. 40.—77. Also another Felix of Ammacura[7] said: "I too, following the authority of the holy Scriptures, give my judgment that heretics should be baptized, and with them those also who maintain that they have been baptized among schismatics. For if, according to the warning of Christ, our fountain is sealed to ourselves,[8] let all the enemies of our Church understand that it cannot belong to others; nor can He who is the Shepherd of our flock give the water unto salvation to two different peoples. And therefore it is clear that neither heretics nor schismatics can receive anything heavenly, who dare to accept from men that are sinners and aliens from the Church. When the giver has no ground to stand upon, surely neither can the receiver derive any profit."[9]

78. To him we answer, that the holy Scriptures nowhere have enjoined that heretics baptized among heretics should be baptized afresh, but that they have shown in many places that all are aliens from the Church who are not on the rock, nor belong to the members of the dove, and yet that they baptize and are baptized and have the sacrament of salvation without salvation. But how our fountain is like the fountain of Paradise, in that, like it, it flows forth even beyond the bounds of Paradise, has been sufficiently set forth above;[10] and that "He who is the Shepherd of our flock cannot give the water unto salvation to two different peoples," that is, to one that is His own, and to another that is alien, I fully agree in admitting. But does it follow that because the water is not unto salvation it is not the identical water? For the water of the deluge was for salvation unto those who were placed within the ark, but it brought death to those without, and yet it was the same water. And many aliens, that is to say, envious persons, whom Cyprian declares and proves from Scripture to be of the party of the devil, seem as it were to be within, and yet, if they were not without the ark, they would not perish by water. For such men are slain by baptism, as the sweet savor of Christ was unto death to those of whom the apostle speaks.[11] Why then do not either heretics or schismatics receive anything heavenly, just as thorns or tares, like those who were without the ark received indeed the rain from the floods of heaven, but to destruction, not to salvation? And so I do not take the pains to refute what he said in conclusion: "When the giver has no ground to stand upon, surely neither can the receiver derive

1 Conc. Carth. sec. 30.
2 Thebaste (Thebeste) in ecclesiastical province of Numidia. For Lucius, cp. c. 14.
3 Conc. Carth. sec. 31.
4 Ammedera, probably in ecclesiastical province of Proconsularis Africa.
5 Conc. Carth. sec. 32.
6 Phil. iii. 15.
7 Ammacura (Bamacorra) in ecclesiastical province of Numidia.
8 Cant. iv. 12.
9 Conc. Carth. sec. 33.
10 Ch. 21, 37.
11 2 Cor. ii. 15.

any profit," since we also say that it does not profit the receivers while they receive it in heresy, consenting with the heretics; and therefore they come to Catholic peace and unity, not that they may receive baptism, but that what they had received may begin to profit them.

CHAP. 41.—79. Also another Januarius of Muzuli[1] said: "I wonder that, while all acknowledge that there is one baptism, all do not understand the unity of the same baptism. For the Church and heresy are two distinct things. If heretics have baptism we have it not; but if we have it, heretics cannot have it. But there is no doubt that the Church alone possesses the baptism of Christ, since it alone possesses both the favor and the truth of Christ."[2]

80. Another might equally say, and say with equal want of truth: I wonder that, while all confess there is one baptism, all do not understand the unity of baptism. For righteousness and unrighteousness are two distinct things. If the unrighteous have baptism, the righteous have it not; but if the righteous have it, the unrighteous cannot have it. But there is no doubt that the righteous alone possess the baptism of Christ, since they alone possess both the favor and the truth of Christ. This is certainly false, as they confess themselves. For those envious ones also who are of the party of the devil, though placed within the Church, as Cyprian tells us, and who were well known to the Apostle Paul, had baptism, but did not belong to the members of that dove which is safely sheltered on the rock.

CHAP. 42.—81. Adelphius of Thasbalte[3] said: "It is surely without cause that they find fault with the truth in false and invidious terms, saying that we rebaptize, since the Church does not rebaptize heretics, but baptizes them."[4]

82. Truly enough it does not rebaptize them, because it only baptizes those who were not baptized before; and this earlier custom has only been confirmed in a later Council by a more careful perfecting of the truth.

CHAP. 43.—83. Demetrius of the Lesser Leptis[5] said: "We uphold one baptism, because we claim for the Catholic Church alone what is her own. But those who say that heretics baptize truly and lawfully are themselves the men who make, not two, but many baptisms; for since heresies are many in number, the baptisms, too, will be reckoned according to their number."[6]

84. To him we answer: If this were so, then would as many baptisms be reckoned as there are works of the flesh, of which the apostle says "that they which do such things shall not inherit the kingdom of God;"[7] among which are reckoned also heresies; and so many of those very works are tolerated within the Church as though in the chaff, and yet there is one baptism for them all, which is not vitiated by any work of unrighteousness.

CHAP. 44.—85. Vincentius of Thibari[8] said: "We know that heretics are worse than heathens. If they, being converted, wish to come to God, they have assuredly a rule of truth, which the Lord by His divine precept committed to the apostles, saying, 'Go ye, lay on hands in my name, cast out devils;'[9] and in another place, 'Go ye, and teach all nations, baptizing them in the name of the Father, and of the Son, and of the Holy Ghost.'[10] Therefore, first by the laying on of hands in exorcism, secondly by regeneration in baptism, they may come to the promises of Christ; but my judgment is that in no other way should this be done."[11]

86. By what rule he asserts that heretics are worse than heathens I do not know, seeing that the Lord says, "If he neglect to hear the Church, let him be unto thee as a heathen man and a publican."[12] Is a heretic worse even than such? I do not gainsay it. I do not, however, allow that because the man himself is worse than a heathen, that is, than a Gentile and pagan, therefore whatever the sacrament contains that is Christ's is mingled with his vices and character, and perishes through the corruption of such admixture. For if even those who depart from the Church, and become not the followers but the founders of heresies, have been baptized before their secession, they continue to have baptism, although, according to the above rule, they are worse than heathens; for if on correction they return, they do not receive it, as they certainly would do if they had lost it. It is therefore possible that a man may be worse than a heathen, and yet that the sacrament of Christ

[1] Muzuli is perhaps the same as Muzuca in ecclesiastical province of Byzacium.
[2] Conc. Carth. sec. 34.
[3] Thasbalte (Thasvalthe) was in ecclesiastical province of Byzacene. An Adelphius is mentioned in Cypr. Ep. lxvii.
[4] Conc. Carth. sec. 35.
[5] Leptis the Lesser was in ecclesiastical province of Byzacene, the Greater being in that of Tripolis. A Demetrius occurs in Cypr. Epp. lvii., lxx.
[6] Conc. Carth. sec. 36.
[7] Gal. v. 21.
[8] Thibari, perhaps the same as Tabora, in ecclesiastical province of Mauritania Cæsariensis. A Bp. Vincentius is mentioned in Cypr. Ep. lxvii.
[9] Mark xvi. 15–18.
[10] Matt. xxviii. 19.
[11] Conc. Carth. sec. 37.
[12] Matt. xviii. 17.

may not only be in him, but be not a whit inferior to what it is in a holy and righteous man. For although to the extent of his powers he has not preserved the sacrament, but done it violence in heart and will, yet so far as the sacrament's own nature is concerned, it has remained unhurt in its integrity even in the man who despised and rejected it. Were not the people of Sodom heathens, that is to say, Gentiles? The Jews therefore were worse, to whom the Lord says, "It shall be more tolerable for the land of Sodom in the day of judgment than for thee;"[1] and to whom the prophet says, "Thou hast justified Sodom,"[2] that is to say, in comparison with thee Sodom is righteous. Shall we, however, maintain that on this account the holy sacraments which existed among the Jews partook of the nature of the Jews themselves,—those sacraments which the Lord Himself also accepted, and sent the lepers whom He had cleansed to fulfill them,[3] of which when Zacharias was administering them, the angel stood by him, and declared that his prayer had been heard while he was sacrificing in the temple?[4] These same sacraments were both in the good men of that time, and in those bad men who were worse than are the heathens, seeing that they were ranked before the Sodomites for wickedness, and yet those sacraments were perfect and holy in both.

87. For even if the Gentiles themselves could have anything holy and right in their doctrines, our saints did not condemn it, however much the Gentiles themselves were to be detested for their superstitions and idolatry and pride, and the rest of their corruptions, and to be punished with judgment from heaven unless they submitted to correction. For when Paul the apostle also was saying something concerning God before the Athenians, he adduced as a proof of what he said, that certain of them had said something to the same effect,[5] which certainly would not be condemned but recognized in them if they should come to Christ. And the holy Cyprian uses similar evidence against the same heathens; for, speaking of the magi, he says, "The chief of them, however, Hostanes, asserts both that the form of the true God cannot be seen, and also that true angels stand beside His seat. In which Plato also agrees in like manner, and, maintaining the existence of one God, he calls the others angels or demons. Hermes Trismegistus also speaks of one God, and confesses that He is incomprehensible, and past our powers of estimation."[6] If, therefore, they were to come to the perception of salvation in Christ, it surely would not be said to them, This that ye have is bad, or false; but clearly it would deservedly be said, Though this in you is perfect and true, yet it would profit nothing unless ye came to the grace of Christ. If, therefore, anything that is holy can be found and rightly approved in the very heathens, although the salvation which is of Christ is not yet to be granted to them, we ought not, even though heretics are worse than they, to be moved to the desire of correcting what is bad in them belonging to themselves, without being willing to acknowledge what is good in them of Christ. But we will set forth from a fresh preface to consider the remaining judgments of this Council.

1 Matt. xi. 24.
2 Ezek. xvi. 51.
3 Luke xvii. 14.
4 Luke i. 11, 13.
5 Acts xvii. 28.
6 Cypr. *de Idol. Vanitate*, c. vi.

BOOK VII.

IN WHICH THE REMAINING JUDGMENTS OF THE COUNCIL OF CARTHAGE ARE EXAMINED.

CHAP. 1.—1. Let us not be considered troublesome to our readers, if we discuss the same question often and from different points of view. For although the Holy Catholic Church throughout all nations be fortified by the authority of primitive custom and of a plenary Council against those arguments which throw some darkness over the question about baptism, whether it can be the same among heretics and schismatics that it is in the Catholic Church, yet, since a different opinion has at one time been entertained in the unity of the Church itself, by men who are in no wise to be despised, and especially by Cyprian, whose authority men endeavor to use against us who are far removed from his charity, we are therefore compelled to make use of the opportunity of examining and considering all that we find on this subject in his Council and letters, in order, as it were, to handle at some considerable length this same question, and to show how it has more truly been the decision of the whole body of the Catholic Church, that heretics or schismatics, who have received baptism already in the body from which they came, should be admitted with it into the communion of the Catholic Church, being corrected in their error and rooted and grounded in the faith, that, so far as concerns the sacrament of baptism, there should not be an addition of something that was wanting, but a turning to profit of what was in them. And the holy Cyprian indeed, now that the corruptible body no longer presseth down the soul, nor the earthly tabernacle presseth down the mind that museth upon many things,[1] sees with greater clearness that truth to which his charity made him deserving to attain. May he therefore help us by his prayers, while we labor in the mortality of the flesh as in a darksome cloud, that if the Lord so grant it, we may imitate so far as we can the good that was in him. But if he thought otherwise than right on any point, and persuaded certain of his brethren and colleagues to entertain his views in a matter which he now sees clearly through the revelation of Him whom he loved, let us, who are far inferior to his merits, yet following, as our weakness will allow, the authority of the Catholic Church of which he was himself a conspicuous and most noble member, strive our utmost against heretics and schismatics, seeing that they, being cut off from the unity which he maintained, and barren of the love with which he was fruitful, and fallen away from the humility in which he stood, are disavowed and condemned the more by him, in proportion as he knows that they wish to search out his writings for purposes of treachery, and are unwilling to imitate what he did for the maintainance of peace,—like those who, calling themselves Nazarene Christians, and circumcising the foreskin of their flesh after the fashion of the Jews, being heretics by birth in that error from which Peter, when straying from the truth, was called by Paul[2] persist in the same to the present day. As therefore they have remained in their perversity cut off from the body of the Church, while Peter has been crowned in the primacy of the apostles through the glory of martyrdom, so these men, while Cyprian, through the abundance of his love, has been received into the portion of the saints through the brightness of his passion, are obliged to recognize themselves as exiles from unity, and, in defence of their calumnies, set up a citizen of unity as an opponent against the very home of unity. Let us, therefore, go on to examine the other judgments of that Council after the same fashion.

CHAP. 2.—2. Marcus of Mactaris[3] said:

[1] Wisd. ix. 15.

[2] Gal. ii. 11.

[3] Mactaris (Macthari) was in ecclesiastical province of Byzacium. This bishop is probably the Marcus of Cypr. Ep. lxx.

"It is not to be wondered at if heretics, being enemies and opponents of the truth, claim to themselves what has been entrusted and vouchsafed to other men. What is marvellous is that some of us, traitors to the truth, uphold heretics and oppose Christians; therefore we decree that heretics should be baptized."[1]

3. To him we answer: It is indeed much more to be wondered at, and deserving of expressions of great praise, that Cyprian and his colleagues had such love for unity that they continued in unity with those whom they considered to be traitors to the truth, without any apprehension of being polluted by them. For when Marcus said, "It is marvellous that some of us, traitors to the truth, uphold heretics and oppose Christians," it seemed natural that he should add, Therefore we decree that communion should not be held with them. This he did not say; but what he does say is, "Therefore we decree that heretics should be baptized," adhering to what the peaceful Cyprian had enjoined in the first instance, saying, "Judging no man, nor removing any from the right of communion if he entertain a different opinion." While, therefore, the Donatists calumniate us and call us *traditors*, I should be glad to know, supposing that any Jew or pagan were found, who, after reading the records of that Council should call both us and them, according to their own rules, traitors to the truth, how we should be able to make our joint defense so as to refute and wash away so grave a charge. They give the name of *traditors* to men whom they were never able in times past to convict of the offense, and whom they cannot now show to be involved in it, being themselves rather shown to be liable to the same charge. But what has this to do with us? What shall we say of them who, by their own showing, are unquestionably traitors? For if we, however falsely, are called *traditors*, because, as they allege, we took part in the same communion with *traditors*, we have all taken part with the *traditors* in question, seeing that in the time of the blessed Cyprian the party of Donatus had not yet separated itself from unity. For the delivery of the sacred books, from which they began to be called *traditors*, occurred somewhat more than forty years after his martyrdom. If, therefore, we are *traditors*, because we sprang from *traditors*, as they believe or pretend, we both of us derive our origin from those other traitors. For there is no room for saying that they did not communicate with these traitors, since they call them men of their own party. In the words of the Council which they are most forward to quote, "Some of us," it declares, "traitors to the truth, uphold heretics." To this is added the testimony of Cyprian, showing clearly that he remained in communion with them, when he says, "Judging no man, nor removing any from the right of communion if he entertain a different opinion." For those who entertained a different opinion were the very persons whom Marcus calls traitors to the truth because they upheld heretics, as he maintains, by receiving them into the Church without baptism. That it was, moreover, the custom that they should be so received, is testified both by Cyprian himself in many passages, and by some bishops in this Council. Whence it is evident that, if heretics have not baptism, the Church of Christ of those days was full of traitors, who upheld them by receiving them in this way. I would urge, therefore, that we plead our cause in common against the charge of treason which they cannot disavow, and therein our special case will be argued against the charge of delivering the books, which they could not prove against us. But let us argue the point as though they had convicted us; and what we shall answer jointly to those who urge against both of us the general treason of our forefathers, that we will answer to these men who urge against us that our forefathers gave up the sacred books. For as we were dead because our forefathers delivered up the books, which caused them to divide themselves from us, so both we and they themselves are dead through the treason of our forefathers, from whom both we and they are sprung. But since they say they live, they hold that that treason does not in any way affect them, therefore neither are we affected by the delivery of the books. And it should be observed that, according to them, the treason is indisputable: while, according to us, there is no truth either in the former charge of treason, because we say that heretics also may have the baptism of Christ; nor in the latter charge of delivering the books, because in that they were themselves beaten. They have therefore no reason for separating themselves by the wicked sin of schism, because, if our forefathers were not guilty of delivering up the books, as we say, there is no charge which can affect us at all; but if they were guilty of the sin, as these men say, then it is just as far from affecting us as the sin of those other traitors is from affecting either us or them. And hence, since there is no charge that can implicate us from the unrighteousness of our forefathers, the charge arising against them from their own schism is manifestly proved.

[1] Conc. Carth. sec. 38.

CHAP. 3.—4. Satius of Sicilibba[1] said: "If heretics receive forgiveness of their sins in their own baptism, it is without reason that they come to the Church. For since it is for sins that men are punished in the day of judgment, heretics have nothing to fear in the judgment of Christ if they have obtained remission of their sins."[2]

5. This too might also have been our own judgment; but let its author beware in what spirit it was said. For it is expressed in terms of such import, that I should feel no compunction in consenting and subscribing to it in the same spirit in which I too believe that heretics may indeed have the baptism of Christ, but cannot have the remission of their sins. But he does not say, If heretics baptize or are baptized, but "If heretics," he says, "receive forgiveness of their sins in their own baptism, it is without reason that they come to the Church." For if we were to set in the place of heretics those whom Cyprian knew within the Church as "renouncing the world in words alone and not in deeds," we also might express this same judgment, in just so many words, with the most perfect truth. If those who only seem to be converted receive forgiveness of their sins in their own baptism, it is without reason that they are afterwards led on to a true conversion. For since it is for sins that men are punished in the day of judgment, "those who renounce the world in words and not in deeds" have nothing to fear in the judgment of Christ if they have obtained remission of their sins. But this reasoning is only made perfect by some such context as is formed by the addition of the words, But they ought to fear the judgment of Christ, and to lose no time in being converted in the truth of their hearts; and, when they have done this, it is certainly not necessary that they should be baptized a second time. It was possible, therefore, for them to receive baptism, and either not to receive remission of their sins, or to be burdened again at once with the load of sins which were forgiven them; and so the same is the case also with the heretics.

CHAP. 4.—6. Victor of Gor[3] said: "Seeing that sins are forgiven only in the baptism of the Church, he who admits heretics to communion without baptism is guilty of two errors contrary to reason; for, on the one hand, he does not cleanse the heretics, and, on the other, he defiles the Christians."[4]

7. To this we answer that the baptism of the Church exists even among heretics, though they themselves are not within the Church; just as the water of Paradise was found in the land of Egypt, though that land was not itself in Paradise. We do not therefore admit heretics to communion without baptism; and since they come with their waywardness corrected, we receive not their sins, but the sacraments of Christ. And, in respect of the remission of their sins, we say again here exactly what we said above. And certainly, in regard of what he says at the end of his judgment, declaring that he "is guilty of two errors contrary to reason, seeing that on the one hand he does not cleanse the heretics, and on the other he defiles the Christians," Cyprian himself is the first and the most earnest in repudiating this with the colleagues who agreed with him. For neither did he think that he was defiled, when, on account of the bond of peace, he decreed that it was right to hold communion with such men, when he used the words, "Judging no one, nor removing any from the right of communion if he entertain a different opinion." Or, if heretics defile the Church by being admitted to communion without being baptized, then the whole Church has been defiled in virtue of that custom which has been so often recorded here. And just as those men call us *traditors* because of our forefathers, in whom they were able to prove nothing of the sort when they laid the charge against them, so, if every man partakes of the character of those with whom he may have held communion, all were then made heretics. And if every one who asserts this is mad, it must be false that Victor says, when he declares that "he who admits heretics to communion without baptism, not only fails to cleanse the heretics, but pollutes the Christians as well." Or if this be true, they were then not admitted without baptism, but those men had the baptism of Christ, although it was given and received among heretics, who were so admitted in accordance with that custom which these very men acknowledged to exist; and on the same grounds they are even now rightly admitted in the same manner.

CHAP. ⁓.—8. Aurelius of Utica[5] said:

[1] Sicilibba was in ecclesiastical province of Zeugitana. In the text of this Council the bishop's name is Sattius, and the name occurs in Cypr. Epp. lvii., lxvii., lxx.

[2] Con. Carth. sec. 39.

[3] Gor (Gorduba) is variously supposed to be Garra in ecclesiastical province of Mauritania Cæsariensis, or Garriana in ecclesiastical province of Byzacium. The name of a bishop Victor occurs in Cypr. Epp. iv., lvii., lxii., lxvii. In Ep. lxx. the names of three.

[4] Conc. Carth. sec. 40.

[5] Utica, the well-known city in ecclesiastical province of Zeugitana. The Aurelius of Cypr. Epp. xxvii. 4, lvii. and lxvii. (the first) are more likely to be identical with the bishop of Utica, than with the Aurelius of Chullabis, who delivers his opinion the 81st in order.

"Since the apostle says that we ought not to be partakers with the sins of other men,[1] what else does he do but make himself partaker with the sins of other men, who holds communion with heretics without the baptism of the Church? And therefore I pronounce my judgment that heretics should be baptized, that they may receive remission of their sins, and so communion be allowed to them."[2]

9. The answer is: Therefore Cyprian and all those bishops were partakers in the sins of other men, inasmuch as they remained in communion with such men, when they removed no one from the right of communion who entertained a different opinion. Where, then, is the Church? Then, to say nothing for the moment of heretics,—since the words of this judgment are applicable also to other sinners, such as Cyprian saw with lamentation to be in the Church with him, whom, while he confuted them, he yet tolerated,—where is the Church, which, according to these words, must be held to have perished from that very moment by the contagion of their sins? But if, as is the most firmly established truth, the Church both has remained and does remain, the partaking of the sins of others, which is forbidden by the apostle, must be considered only to consist in consenting to them. But let heretics be baptized again, that they may receive remission of their sins, if the wayward and the envious are baptized again, who, seeing that "they renounced the world in words and not in deeds," were indeed able to receive baptism, but did not obtain remission of their sins, as the Lord says, "If ye forgive not men their trespasses, neither will your Father forgive your trespasses."[3]

Chap. 6—10. Iambus of Germaniciana[4] said: "Those who approve the baptism of heretics disapprove ours, so as to deny that such as are, I will not say washed, but defiled outside the Church, ought to be baptized within the Church."[5]

11. To him we answer, that none of our party approves the baptism of heretics, but all the baptism of Christ, even though it be found in heretics who are as it were chaff outside the Church, as it may be found in other unrighteous men who are as chaff within the Church. For if those who are baptized without the Church are not washed, but defiled, assuredly those who are baptized outside the rock on which the Church is built are not washed, but defiled. But all are without the said rock who hear the words of Christ and do them not. Or if it be the case that they are washed indeed in baptism, but yet continue in the defilement of their unrighteousness, from which they were unwilling to be changed for the better, the same is true also of the heretics.

Chap. 7.—12. Lucianus of Rucuma[6] said: "It is written, 'And God saw the light that it was good, and God divided the light from the darkness.'[7] If light and darkness can agree, then can there be something in common between us and heretics. Therefore I give my judgment that heretics should be baptized."[8]

13. To him the answer is: If light and darkness can agree, then can there be something common between the righteous and unrighteous. Let him therefore declare his judgment that those unrighteous should be baptized afresh whom Cyprian confuted within the Church itself; or let him who can say if those are not unrighteous "who renounce the world in words and not in deeds."

Chap. 8.—14. Pelagianus of Luperciana[9] said: "It is written, 'Either the Lord is God, or Baal is God.'[10] So now either the Church is the Church, or heresy is the Church. Further, if heresy be not the Church, how can the baptism of the Church exist among heretics?"[11]

15. To him we may answer as follows: Either Paradise is Paradise, or Egypt is Paradise. Further, if Eygpt be not Paradise, how can the water of Paradise be in Egypt? But it will be said to us that it extends even thither by flowing forth from Paradise. In like manner, therefore, baptism extends to heretics. Also we say: Either the rock is the Church, or the sand is the Church. Further, since the sand is not the Church, how can baptism exist with those who build upon the sand by hearing the words of Christ and doing them not?[12] And yet it does exist with them; and in like manner also it exists among the heretics.

Chap. 9.—16. Jader of Midila[13] said: "We know that there is but one baptism in the Catholic Church, and therefore we ought not

1 Tim. v. 22. 2 Conc. Carth. sec. 41.
3 Matt. vi. 15.
4 Germaniciana Nova was in ecclesiastical province of Byzacium, and so called after the German veterans settled there. An Iambus is mentioned as bishop in Cypr. Epp. lvii., lxvii.
5 Conc. Carth. sec. 42.
6 Rucuma was in ecclesiastical province of Zeugitana. This Lucianus is probably the same with the one mentioned in Cypr. Epp. lvii., lxx.
7 Gen. i. 4. 8 Conc. Carth. sec. 43.
9 The position of Luperciana is unknown.
10 See 1 Kings xviii. 21. 11 Con. Carth. sec. 44.
12 Matt. vii. 24-27.
13 Midila (Midili) was in ecclesiastical province of Numidia. Jader is Punic name. Occurs as bishop in Cypr. Epp. lxxvi., lxxix.

to admit a heretic unless he has been baptized in our body, lest he should think that he has been baptized outside the Catholic Church."[1]

17. To him our answer is, that if this were said of those unrighteous men who are outside the rock, it certainly would be falsely said. And so it is therefore also in the case of heretics.

CHAP. 10.—18. Likewise another Felix of Marazana[2] said: "There is one faith, one baptism,[3] but of the Catholic Church, to which alone is given authority to baptize."[4]

19. What if another were to say as follows: One faith, one baptism, but of the righteous only, to whom alone authority is given to baptize? As these words might be refuted, so also may the judgment of Felix be refuted. Do even the unrighteous who are not[5] changed in heart in baptism, while "they renounce the world in words and not in deeds" yet belong to the members of the Church? Let them consider whether such a Church is the actual rock, the very dove, the bride herself without spot or wrinkle.[6]

CHAP. 11.—20. Paul of Bobba[7] said: "I for my part am not moved if some fail to uphold the faith and truth of the Church, seeing that the apostle says 'For what if some did not believe? shall their unbelief make the faith of God without effect? God forbid: yea let God be true, but every man a liar.'[8] But if God be true, how can the truth of baptism be in the company of heretics, where God is not?"[9]

21. To him we answer: What, is God among the covetous? And yet baptism exists among them; and so also it exists among heretics. For they among whom God is, are the temple of God. "But what agreement hath the temple of God with idols?"[10] Further, Paul considers, and Cyprian agrees with him, that covetousness is idolatry; and Cyprian himself again associates with his colleagues, who were robbers, but yet baptized, with great reward of toleration.

CHAP. 12.—22. Pomponius of Dionysiana[11] said: "It is manifest that heretics cannot baptize and give remission of sins, seeing that no power is given to them that they should be able either to loose or bind anything on earth."[12]

23. The answer is: This power is not given to murderers either, that is, to those who hate their brothers. For it was not said to such as these, "whosesoever sins ye remit, they are remitted unto them; and whosesoever sins ye retain, they are retained."[13] And yet they baptize, and both Paul tolerates them in the same communion of baptism, and Cyprian acknowledges them.

CHAP. 13.—24. Venantius of Tinisa[14] said: "If a husband, going on a journey into foreign countries, had entrusted the guardianship of his wife to a friend, he would surely keep her that was entrusted to his care with the utmost diligence, that her chastity and holiness might not be defiled by any one. Christ our Lord and God, when going to the Father, committed His bride to our care: do we keep her uncorrupt and undefiled, or do we betray her purity and chastity to adulterers and corrupters? For he who makes the baptism of Christ common with heretics betrays the bride of Christ to adulterers."[15]

25. We answer: What of those who, when they are baptized, turn themselves to the Lord with their lips and not with their heart? do not they possess an adulterous mind? Are not they themselves lovers of the world, which they renounce in words and not in deeds; and they corrupt good manners through evil communications, saying, "Let us eat and drink; for to-morrow we die?"[16] Did not the discourse of the apostle take heed even against such as these, when he says, "But I fear, lest by any means, as the serpent beguiled Eve through his subtilty, so your minds [also] should be corrupted from the simplicity that is in Christ?"[17] When, therefore, Cyprian held the baptism of Christ to be in common with such men, did he therefore betray the bride of Christ into the hands of adulterers, or did he not rather recognize the necklace of the Bridegroom even on an adulteress?

CHAP. 14.—26. Aymnius[18] of Ausuaga[19] said: "We have received one baptism, which same also we administer; but he who says that authority is given to heretics also to baptize, the same makes two baptisms."[20]

1 Conc. Carth. sec. 45.
2 Marazana was in ecclesiastical province of Byzacene. On Felix, see Bk. VI. c. 19, note 2.
3 Eph. iv. 5.
4 Conc. Carth. sec. 46.
5 *Nec . . . mutati.* "*Nec*" is restored by the Benedictines from the MSS.
6 Eph. v. 27. See *Retract.* ii. 18, quoted on I. 17, 26.
7 Bobba (Obba) was in ecclesiastical province of Mauritania Cæsariensis, including Tingitana. A bishop Paul is mentioned in Cypr. Ep. lxvii.
8 Rom. iii. 3, 4.
9 Conc. Carth. sec. 47.
10 2 Cor. vi. 16.
11 Dionysiana was in ecclesiastical province of Byzacium. The name of Pomponius occurs in Cypr. Epp. iv., lvii., lxvii., lxx.
12 Conc. Carth. sec. 48.
13 John xx. 23.
14 Tinisa (Thinisa) was in ecclesiastical province of Zeugitana. In Cypr. Ep. lxvii. the name Venantius is found.
15 Conc. Carth. sec. 49.
16 1 Cor. xv. 33, 32.
17 2 Cor. xi. 3.
18 Ahymmus. See Cypr. Ep. lvi.
19 Ausuaga was in ecclesiastical province of Zeugitana.
20 Conc. Carth. sec. 50.

27. To him we answer: Why does not he also make two baptisms who maintains that the unrighteous also can baptize? For although the righteous and unrighteous are in themselves opposed to one another, yet the baptism which the righteous give, such as was Paul, or such as was also Cyprian, is not contrary to the baptism which those unrighteous men were wont to give who hated Paul, whom Cyprian understands to have been not heretics, but bad Catholics; and although the moderation which was found in Cyprian, and the covetousness which was found in his colleagues, are in themselves opposed to one another, yet the baptism which Cyprian used to give was not contrary to the baptism which his colleagues who opposed him used to give, but one and the same with it, because in both cases it is He that baptizes of whom it is said, "The same is He which baptizeth."[1]

Chap. 15.—28. Saturninus of Victoriana[2] said: "If heretics may baptize, they are excused and defended in doing unlawful things; nor do I see why either Christ called them His adversaries, or the apostle called them antichrists."[3]

29. To him we answer: We say that heretics have no authority to baptize in the same sense in which we say that defrauders have no authority to baptize. For not only to the heretic, but to the sinner, God says, "What hast thou to do to declare my statutes, or that thou shouldest take my covenant in thy mouth?" To the same person He assuredly says, "When thou sawest a thief, then thou consentedst with him."[4] How much worse, therefore, are those who did not consent with thieves, but themselves were wont to plunder farms with treacherous deceits? Yet Cyprian did not consent with them, though he did tolerate them in the corn-field of the Catholic Church, lest the wheat should be rooted out together with it. And yet at the same time the baptism which they themselves conferred was the very selfsame baptism, because it was not of them, but of Christ. As therefore they, although the baptism of Christ be recognized in them, were yet not excused and defended in doing unlawful things, and Christ rightly called those His adversaries who were destined, by persevering in such things, to hear the doom, "Depart from me, ye that work iniquity,"[5] whence also they are called antichrists, because they are contrary to Christ while they live in opposition to His words, so likewise is it the case with heretics.

Chap. 16.—30. Another Saturninus of Tucca[6] said: "The Gentiles, although they worship idols, yet acknowledge and confess the supreme God, the Father and Creator. Against Him Marcion blasphemes, and some men do not blush to approve the baptism of Marcion.[7] How do such priests either maintain or vindicate the priesthood of God, who do not baptize the enemies of God, and hold communion with them while they are thus unbaptized?"[8]

31. The answer is this: Truly when such terms as this are used, all moderation is passed; nor do they take into consideration that even they themselves hold communion with such men, "judging no one, nor removing any from the right of communion if he entertain a contrary opinion." But Saturninus has used an argument in this very judgment of his, which might furnish materials for his admonition (if he would pay attention to it), that in each man what is wrong should be corrected, and what is right should be approved, since he says, "The Gentiles, although they worship idols, yet acknowledge and confess the supreme God, the Father and Creator." If, then, any Gentile of such a kind should come to God, would he wish to correct and change this point in him, that he acknowledged and confessed God the Father and Creator? I trow not. But he would amend in him his idolatry, which was an evil in him; and he would give to him the sacraments of Christ, which he did not possess; and anything that was wayward which he found in him he would correct; and anything which had been wanting he would supply. So also in the Marcionist heretic he would acknowledge the perfectness of baptism, he would correct his waywardness, he would teach him Catholic truth.

Chap. 17.—32. Marcellus of Zama[9] said: "Since sins are remitted only in the baptism of the Church, he who does not baptize a heretic holds communion with a sinner."[10]

33. What, does he who holds communion

1 John i. 33.
2 Victoriana was in ecclesiastical province of Byzacium. [The name Saturninus is found in Cypr. Epp. xxi. 4, xxii. 3, xxvii. 1, 11, lvii. *ter*, lxvii. *bis*, lxx. *quinquies*.
3 Conc. Carth. sec. 51.
4 Ps. l. 16, 18.
5 Matt. vii. 23.

6 Tucca was in ecclesiastical province of Numidia. For Saturninus see, c. 15-28, n. 2.
7 He is alluding to Stephen, bishop of Rome, of whom Cyprian says in his Ep. lxxiv. 7 (to Pompeius): "Why has the perverse obstinacy of our brother Stephen burst out to such a point, that he should even contend that sons of God are born of the baptism of Marcion, also of Valentinus and Apelles, and others who blaspheme against God the Father?"
8 Conc. Carth. sec. 52.
9 Zama was in ecclesiastical province of Numidia. For Marcellus, see Cypr. Ep. lxvii.
10 Conc. Carth. sec. 53.

with one who does this not hold communion with a sinner? But what else did all of them do, "in judging no one, or removing from the right of communion any one who entertained a different opinion"? Where, then, is the Church? Are those things not an obstacle to those who are patient, and tolerate the tares lest the wheat should be rooted out together with them? I would have them therefore say, who have committed the sacrilege of schism by separating themselves from the whole world, how it comes that they have in their mouths the judgment of Cyprian, while they do not have in their hearts the patience of Cyprian. But to this Marcellus we have an answer in what has been said above concerning baptism and the remission of sins, explaining how there can be baptism in a man although there be in him no remission of his sins.

CHAP. 18.—34. Irenæus of Ululi[1] said: "If the Church does not baptize a heretic, because it is said that he has been baptized already, then heresy is the greater."[2]

35. The answer is: On the same principle it might be said, If therefore the Church does not baptize the covetous man, because it is said that he has been baptized already, then covetousness is the greater. But this is false, therefore the other is also false.

CHAP. 19.—36. Donatus of Cibaliana[3] said: "I acknowledge one Church, and one baptism that appertains thereto. If there is any one who says that the grace of baptism exists among heretics, he must first show and prove that the Church exists with them."[4]

37. To him we answer: If you say that the grace of baptism is identical with baptism, then it exists among heretics; but if baptism is the sacrament or outward sign of grace, while the grace itself is the abolition of sins, then the grace of baptism does not exist with heretics. But so there is one baptism and one Church, just as there is one faith. As therefore the good and bad, not having one hope, can yet have one baptism, so those who have not one common Church can have one common baptism.

CHAP. 20.—38. Zozimus of Tharassa[5] said: "When a revelation has been made of the truth, error must give way to truth; inasmuch as Peter also, who before was wont to circumcise, gave way to Paul when he declared the truth."[6]

39. The answer is: This may also be considered as the expression of our judgment too, and this is just what has been done in respect of this question of baptism. For after that the truth had been more clearly revealed, error gave way to truth, when that most wholesome custom was further confirmed by the authority of a plenary Council. It is well, however, that they so constantly bear in mind that it was possible even for Peter, the chief of the apostles, to have been at one time minded otherwise than the truth required; which we believe, without any disrespect to Cyprian, to have been the case with him, and that with all our love for Cyprian, for it is not right that he should be loved with greater love than Peter.

CHAP. 21.—40. Julianus of Telepte[7] said: "It is written, 'A man can receive nothing, except it be given him from heaven;'[8] if heresy is from heaven, it can give baptism."[9]

41. Let him hear another also saying: If covetousness is from heaven, it can give baptism. And yet the covetous do confer it; so therefore also may the heretics.

CHAP. 22.—42. Faustus of Timida Regia[10] said: "Let not these persons flatter themselves who favor heretics. He who interferes with the baptism of the Church on behalf of heretics makes them Christians, and us heretics."[11]

43. To him we answer: If any one were to say that a man who, when he received baptism had not received remission of his sins, because he entertained hatred towards his brother in his heart, was nevertheless not to be baptized again when he dismissed that hatred from his heart, does such a man interfere with the baptism of the Church on behalf of murderers, or does he make them righteous and us murderers? Let him therefore understand the same also in the case of heretics.

CHAP. 23.—44. Geminius of Furni[12] said: "Certain of our colleagues may prefer heretics to themselves, they cannot prefer them to us: and therefore what we have once decreed we hold, that we should baptize those who come to us from heretics."[13]

[1] Ululi (Ullita, Vallita) in ecclesiastical province of Numidia.
[2] Conc. Carth. sec. 54.
[3] [Cibaliana (Cybaliana), most probably in ecclesiastical province of Africa Proconsularis. Donatus, as cotemporary bishop, occurs in Cypr. *Epp.* lvii. *bis*, lxx. *bis*.
[4] Conc. Carth. sec. 55.
[5] Tharassa was in ecclesiastical province of Numidia.
[6] Gal. ii. 11; Conc. Carth. sec. 56.
[7] Telepte (Thelepte) or Thala, was in ecclesiastical province of Byzacium.
[8] John iii. 27. [9] Conc. Carth. sec. 57.
[10] Timida Regia was in ecclesiastical province of Zeugitana. A Faustus is mentioned in Cypr. *Ep.* lxvii.
[11] Conc. Carth. sec. 58.
[12] Furni was in ecclesiastical province of Zeugitana. For Geminius as bishop, see Cypr. *Ep.* lxvii.
[13] Conc. Carth. sec. 59.

45. This man also acknowledges most openly that certain of his colleagues entertained opinions contrary to his own: whence again and again the love of unity is confirmed, because they were separated from one another by no schism, till God should reveal to one or other of them anything wherein they were othewise minded.[1] But to him our answer is, that his colleagues did not prefer heretics to themselves, but that, as the baptism of Christ is acknowledged in the covetous, in the fraudulent, in robbers, in murderers, so also they acknowledged it in heretics.

Chap. 24.—46. Rogatianus of Nova[2] said: "Christ established the Church, the devil heresy: how can the synagogue of Satan have the baptism of Christ?"[3]

47. To him our answer is: Is it true that because Christ established the well-affectioned, and the devil the envious, therefore the party of the devil, which is proved to be among the envious, cannot have the baptism of Christ?

Chap. 25.—48. Therapius of Bulla[4] said: "If a man gives up and betrays the baptism of Christ to heretics, what else can he be said to be but a Judas to the Bride of Christ?"[5]

49. How great a condemnation have we here of all schismatics, who have separated themselves by wicked sacrilege from the inheritance of Christ dispersed throughout the whole world, if Cyprian held communion witn such as was the traitor Judas, and yet was not defiled by them; or if he was defiled, then were all made such as Judas; or if they were not, then the evil deeds of those who went before do not belong to those who came after, even though they were the offspring of the same communion. Why, therefore, do they cast in our teeth the *traditores*, against whom they did not prove their charge, and do not cast in their own teeth Judas, with whom Cyprian and his colleagues held communion? Behold the Council in which these men are wont to boast! We indeed say, that he who approves the baptism of Christ even in heretics, does not betray to heretics the baptism of Christ; just in the same way as he does not betray to murderers the baptism of Christ who approves the baptism of Christ even in murderers: but inasmuch as they profess to prescribe to us from the decrees of this Council what opinions we ought to hold, let them first assent to it themselves. See how therein were compared to the traitor Judas, all who said that heretics, although baptized in heresy, yet should not be baptized again. Yet with such Cyprian was willing to hold communion, when he said, "Judging no man, nor depriving any of the right of communion if he entertain a contrary opinion." But that there had been men of such a sort in former times within the Church, is made clear by the sentence in which he says: "But some one will say, What, then, shall be done with these men who in times past were admitted into the Church without baptism?"[6] That such had been the custom of the Church, is testified again and again by the very men who compose this Council. If, therefore, any one who does this "can be said to be nothing else but a Judas to the Bride of Christ," according to the terms in which the judgment of Therapius is couched; but Judas, according to the teaching of the gospel, was a traitor; then all those men held communion with traitors who at that time uttered those very judgments, and before they uttered them they all had become traitors through that custom which at that time was retained by the Church. All, therefore—that is to say, both we and they themselves who were the offspring of that unity—are traitors. But we defend ourselves in two ways: first, because without prejudice to the right of unity, as Cyprian himself declared in his opening speech, we do not assent to the decrees of this Council in which this judgment was pronounced; and secondly, because we hold that the wicked in no way hurt the good in Catholic unity, until at the last the chaff be separated from the wheat. But our opponents, inasmuch as they both shelter themselves as it were under the decrees of this Council, and maintain that the good perish as by a kind of infection from communion with the wicked, have no resource to save them from allowing both that the earlier Christians, whose offspring they are, were traitors, inasmuch as they are convicted by their own Council; and that the deeds of those who went before them do reflect on them, since they throw in our teeth the deeds of our ancestors.

Chap. 26.—50. Also another Lucius of Membresa[7] said: "It is written, 'God heareth not sinners.'[8] How can he who is a sinner be heard in baptism?"[9]

---

1 Phil. iii. 15.

2 Nova was in ecclesiastical province of Mauritania Cæsariensis. For Rogatianus as bishop, see Cypr. *Epp.* lvii., lxvii., lxx., *bis.*

3 Conc. Carth. sec. 'o.

4 Bulla (Vulla) was in ecclesiastical province of Africa Proconsularis. For Therapius cp. Cypr. *Ep.* lxiv. 1.

5 Conc. Carth. sec. 61.

6 Cypr. *Ep.* lxxiii. 23.

7 Membresa was in ecclesiastical province of Zeugitana. Fo Lucius, See, Bk. VI. c. 38.

8 John ix. 31.

9 Conc. Carth. sec. 62.

51. We answer: How is the covetous man heard, or the robber, and usurer, and murderer? Are they not sinners? And yet Cyprian, while he finds fault with them in the Catholic Church, yet tolerates them.

CHAP. 27.—52. Also another Felix of Buslaceni[1] said: "In admitting heretics to the Church without baptism, let no one place custom before reason and truth; for reason and truth always exclude custom."[2]

53. To him our answer is: You do not show the truth; you confess the existence of the custom. We should therefore do right in maintaining the custom which has since been confirmed by a plenary Council, even if the truth were still concealed, which we believe to have been already made manifest.

CHAP. 28.—54. Another Saturninus of Abitini[3] said: "If Antichrist can give to any one the grace of Christ, then can heretics also baptize, who are called Antichrists."[4]

55. What if another were to say, If a murderer can give the grace of Christ, then can they also baptize that hate their brethren, who are called murderers? For certainly he would seem in a way to speak the truth, and yet they can baptize; in like manner, therefore, can the heretics as well.

CHAP. 29.—56. Quintus of Aggya[5] said: "He who has a thing can give it; but what can the heretics give, who are well known to have nothing?"[6]

57. To him our answer is: If, then, any man can give a thing who has it, it is clear that heretics can give baptism: for when they separate from the Church, they have still the sacrament of washing which they had received while in the Church; for when they return they do not again receive it, because they had not lost it when they withdrew from the Church.

CHAP. 30.—58. Another Julianus of Marcelliana[7] said: "If a man can serve two masters, God and mammon,[8] then baptism also can serve two, the Christian and the heretic."[9]

59. Truly, if it can serve the self-restrained and the covetous man, the sober and the drunken, the well-affectioned and the murderer, why should it not also serve the Christian and the heretic?—whom, indeed, it does not really serve; but it ministers to them, and is administered by them, for salvation to those who use it right, and for judgment to such as use it wrong.

CHAP. 31.—60. Tenax of Horrea Celiæ[10] said: "There is one baptism, but of the Church; and where the Church is not, there baptism also cannot be."[11]

61. To him we answer: How then comes it that it may be where the rock is not, but only sand; seeing that the Church is on the rock, and not on sand?

CHAP. 32.—62. Another Victor of Assuras[12] said: "It is written, that 'there is one God and one Christ, one Church and one baptism.'[13] How then can any one baptize in a place where there is not either God, or Christ, or the Church?"[14]

63. How can any one baptize either in that sand, where the Church is not, seeing that it is on the rock; nor God and Christ, seeing that there is not there the temple of God and Christ?

CHAP. 33.—64. Donatulus of Capse[15] said: "I also have always entertained this opinion, that heretics, who have gained nothing outside the Church, should be baptized when they are converted to the Church."[16]

65. To this the answer is: They have, indeed, gained nothing outside the Church, but that is nothing towards salvation, not nothing towards the sacrament. For salvation is peculiar to the good; but the sacraments are common to the good and bad alike.

CHAP. 34.—66. Verulus of Rusiccade[17] said: "A man that is a heretic cannot give that which he has not; much more is this the case with a schismatic, who has lost what he had."[18]

67. We have already shown that they still have it, because they do not lose it when they separate themselves. For they do not re-

1 Buslaceni (Cussaceni) is probably Byzacium, the capital of province of Byzacium, since we know that it was also called Bizica Lucana; others place it in Africa Proconsularis. For Felix, cp. Bk. VI. cc. 19 and 23.

2 Conc. Carth. sec. 63.

3 Abitini (Avitini) was in ecclesiastical province of Africa Proconsularis. For Saturninus, cp. cc. 15, 16.

4 Conc. Carth. sec. 64.

5 Aggya, probably the same as Aggiva and the Aga in ecclesiastical province of Proconsular Africa. The name Quintas as bishop occurs in Cypr. *Epp.* lvii., lxvii., lxx., lxxi., but this one is of Mauritania, as appears from *Epp.* lxxii. 1, lxxiii. 1.

6 Conc. Carth. sec. 65.

7 Marcelliana (Gyrnmarcelli) in ecclesiastical province of Numidia.

8 Matt. vi. 24.

9 Conc. Carth. sec. 66.

10 Horrea Celiæ (Cæliæ) was a village of ecclesiastical province of Byzacium, ten miles north of Hadrumetum. A Tenax is mentioned as bishop in Cypr. *Ep.* lxvii.

11 Conc. Carth. sec. 67.

12 Assuras was in ecclesiastical province of Zeugitana. For Victor, cp. c. 4.

13 See Eph. iv. 4–6.

14 Conc. Carth. sec. 68.

15 Capse was in ecclesiastical province of Byzacene. This Donatulus is probably to be identified with the one mentioned Cypr. *Ep.* lvi.

16 Conc. Carth. sec. 69.

17 Rusiccade was at the mouth of the Thapsus, in ecclesiastical province of Numidia.

18 Conc. Carth. sec. 70.

ceive it again when they return: wherefore, if it was thought that they could not give it because they were supposed not to have it, let it now be understood that they can give it, because it is understood that they also have it.

Chap. 35.—68. Pudentianus of Cuiculi[1] said: "My recent ordination to the episcopate induced me, brethren, to wait and hear what my elders would decide. For it is plain that heresies have and can have nothing; and so, if any come from them, it is determined righteously that they should be baptized."[2]

69. As, therefore, we have already answered those who went before, for whose judgment this man was waiting, so be it understood that we have answered himself.

Chap. 36.—70. Peter of Hippo Diarrhytus[3] said: "Since there is one baptism in the Catholic Church, it is clear that a man cannot be baptized outside the Church; and therefore I give my judgment, that those who have been bathed in heresy or in schism ought to be baptized on coming to the Church."[4]

71. There is one baptism in the Catholic Church, in such a sense that, when any have gone out from it, it does not become two in those who go out, but remains one and the same. What, therefore, is recognized in those who return, should also be recognized in those who received it from men who have separated themselves, since they did not lose it when they went apart into heresy.

Chap. 37.—72. Likewise another Lucius of Ausafa[5] said: "According to the motion of my mind and of the Holy Spirit, since there is one God, the Father of our Lord Jesus Christ, and one Christ, and one hope, one Spirit, one Church, there ought also to be only one baptism. And therefore I say, both that if anything has been set on foot or done among the heretics, that it ought to be rescinded; and also, that they who come out from among the heretics should be baptized in the Church."[6]

73. Let it therefore be pronounced of no effect that they baptize, who hear the words of God and do them not, when they shall begin to pass from unrighteousness to righteousness, that is, from the sand to the rock. And if this is not done, because what there was in them of Christ was not violated by their unrighteousness, then let this also be understood in the case of heretics: for neither is there the same hope in the unrighteous, so long as they are on the sand, as there is in those who are upon the rock; and yet there is in both the same baptism, although as it is said that there is one hope, so also is it said that there is one baptism.

Chap. 38.—74. Felix of Gurgites[7] said: "I give my judgment, that, according to the precepts of the holy Scriptures, those who have been unlawfully baptized outside the Church by heretics, if they wish to flee to the Church, should obtain the grace of baptism where it is lawfully given."[8]

75. Our answer is: Let them indeed begin to have in a lawful manner to salvation what they before had unlawfully to destruction; because each man is justified under the same baptism, when he has turned himself to God with a true heart, as that under which he was condemned, when on receiving it he "renounced the world in words alone, and not in deeds."

Chap. 39.—76. Pusillus of Lamasba[9] said: "I believe that baptism is not unto salvation except within the Catholic Church. Whatsoever is without the Catholic Church is mere pretense."[10]

77. This indeed is true, that "baptism is not unto salvation except within the Catholic Church." For in itself it can indeed exist outside the Catholic Church as well; but there it is not unto salvation, because there it does not work salvation; just as that sweet savor of Christ is certainly not unto salvation in them that perish,[11] though from a fault not in itself, but in them. But "whatsoever is without the Catholic Church is mere pretense," yet only in so far as it is not Catholic. But there may be something Catholic outside the Catholic Church, just as the name of Christ could exist outside the congregation of Christ, in which name he who did not follow with the disciples was casting out devils.[12] For there may be pretense also within the Catholic Church, as is unquestionable in the case of those "who renounce the world in words and not in deeds," and yet the pretense is not Catholic. As, therefore, there is in the Catholic Church something which is not Catholic, so there may be something which is Catholic outside the Catholic Church.

---

1 Cuiculi was in ecclesiastical province of Numidia.
2 Conc. Carth. sec. 71.
3 Hippo Diarrhytus (Hippozaritus) was on the coast in ecclesiastical province of Zeugitana. For Petrus, cp. Cypr. *Ep.* lxvii.
4 Conc. Carth. sec. 72.
5 Ausafa was in ecclesiastical province of Zeugitana. For Lucius, cp. Bk. VI. cc. 14 and 38, and Bk. VII. c. 26.
6 Conc. Carth. sec. 73.
7 Gurgites was in ecclesiastical province of Byzacium. For Felix, cp. Bk. VI. cc. 19, 33, 40; Bk. VII. cc. 10, 28.
8 Conc. Carth. sec. 74.
9 Lamasba was in ecclesiastical province of Numidia.
10 Conc. Carth. sec. 75.
11 2 Cor. ii. 15.
12 Mark ix. 38.

CHAP. 40.—78. Salvianus of Gazaufala[1] said: "It is generally known that heretics have nothing; and therefore they come to us, that they may receive what previously they did not have."[2]

79. Our answer is: On this theory, the very men who founded heresies are not heretics themselves, because they separated themselves from the Church, and certainly they previously had what they received there. But if it is absurd to say that those are not heretics through whom the rest became heretics, it is therefore possible that a heretic should have what turns to his destruction through his evil use of it.

CHAP. 41.—80. Honoratus of Tucca[3] said: "Since Christ is the truth, we ought to follow the truth rather than custom; that we may sanctify by the baptism of the Church the heretics who come to us, simply because they could receive nothing outside."[4]

81. This man, too, is a witness to the custom, in which he gives us the greatest assistance, whatever else he may appear to say against us. But this is not the reason why heretics come over to us, because they have received nothing outside, but that what they did receive may begin to be of use to them: for this it could not be outside in any wise.

CHAP. 42.—82. Victor of Octavus[5] said: "As ye yourselves also know, I have not been long appointed a bishop, and therefore I waited for the counsel of my seniors. This therefore I express as my opinion, that whosoever comes from heresy should undoubtedly be baptized."[6]

83. What, therefore, has been answered to those for whom he waited, may be taken as the answer also to himself.

CHAP. 43.—84. Clarus of Mascula[7] said: "The sentence of our Lord Jesus Christ is manifest, when He sent forth His apostles, and gave the power which had been given Him of His Father to them alone, whose successors we are, governing the Church of the Lord with the same power, and baptizing those who believe the faith. And therefore heretics, who, being without, have neither power nor the Church of Christ, cannot baptize any one with His baptism."[8]

85. Are, then, ill-affectioned murderers successors of the apostles? Why, then, do they baptize? Is it because they are not outside? But they are outside the rock, to which the Lord gave the keys, and on which He said that He would build His Church.[9]

CHAP. 44.—86. Secundianus of Thambei[10] said: "We ought not to deceive heretics by our too great forwardness, that not having been baptized in the Church of our Lord Jesus Christ, and having therefore not received remission of their sins, they may not impute to us, when the day of judgment comes, that we have been the cause of their not being baptized, and not having obtained the indulgence of the grace of God. On which account, since there is one Church and one baptism, when they are converted to us, let them receive together with the Church the baptism also of the Church."[11]

87. Nay, when they are transferred to the rock, and joined to the society of the Dove, let them receive the remission of their sins, which they could not have outside the rock and outside the Dove, whether they were openly without, like the heretics, or apparently within, like the abandoned Catholics; of whom, however, it is clear that they both have and confer baptism without remission of sins, when even from themselves it is received by men, who, being not changed for the better, honor God with their lips, while their heart is far from Him.[12] Yet it is true that there is one baptism, just as there is one Dove, though those who are not in the one communion of the Dove may yet have baptism in common.

CHAP. 45.—88.—Also another Aurelius of Chullabi[13] said: "The Apostle John has laid down in his epistle the following precept: 'If there come any unto you, and bring not this doctrine, receive him not into your house, neither bid him God speed: for he that biddeth him God speed is partaker of his evil deeds.'[14] How can such men be admitted without consideration into the house of God, who are forbidden to be admitted into our private house? Or how can we hold communion with them without the baptism of Christ, when, if we only so much as bid them

1 Gazaufala (Gazophyla) was in ecclesiastical province of Numidia.
2 Conc. Carth. sec. 76.
3 Tucca (Thucca) was in ecclesiastical province of Numidia. Honoratus occurs as bishop's name in Cypr. *Epp.* lvii., lxii., lxvii., lxx. *bis.* The attempts to distinguish or to identify these are hazardous.
4 Conc. Carth. sec. 77.
5 Octavus was in ecclesiastical province of Numidia. For Victor, cp. cc. 4, 32.
6 Conc. Carth. sec. 78.
7 Mascula was in ecclesiastical province of Numidia.
8 Conc. Carth. *Ibid.* sec. 79.
9 Matt. xvi. 18, 19.
10 Thambei (Thambi, Satambei), was in ecclesiastical province of Byzacium.
11 Conc. Carth. sec. 80.
12 Isa. xxix. 13.
13 Chullabi, or Cululi, was in ecclesiastical province of Byzacium. For Aurelius, cp. c. 5.
14 2 John 10, 11.

God speed, we are partakers of their evil deeds?"[1]

89. In respect of this testimony of John there is no need of further disputation, since it has no reference at all to the question of baptism, which we are at present discussing. For he says, "If any come unto you, and bring not the doctrine of Christ." But heretics leaving the doctrine of their error are converted to the doctrine of Christ, that they may be incorporated with the Church, and may begin to belong to the members of that Dove whose sacrament they previously had; and therefore what previously they lacked belonging to it is given to them, that is to say, peace and charity out of a pure heart, and of a good conscience, and of faith unfeigned.[2] But what they previously had belonging to the Dove is acknowledged, and received without any depreciation; just as in the adulteress God recognises His gifts, even when she is following her lovers; because when after her fornication is corrected she is turned again to chastity, those gifts are not laid to her charge, but she herself is corrected.[3] But just as Cyprian might have defended himself, if this testimony of John had been cast in his teeth whilst he was holding communion with men like these, so let those against whom it is spoken make their own defense. For to the question before us, as I said before, it has no reference at all. For John says that we are not to bid God speed to men of strange doctrine; but Paul the apostle says, with even greater vehemence, "If any man that is called a brother be covetous, or a drunkard," or anything of the sort, with such an one no not to eat;[4] and yet Cyprian used to admit to fellowship, not with his private table, but with the altar of God, his colleagues who were usurers, and treacherous, and fraudulent, and robbers. But in what manner this may be defended has been sufficiently set forth in other books already.

Chap. 46.—90. Litteus[5] of Gemelli[6] said: "'If the blind lead the blind, both shall fall into the ditch.'[7] Since, therefore, it is clear that heretics can give no light[8] to any one, as being blind themselves, therefore their baptism is invalid."[9]

91. Neither do we say that it is valid for salvation so long as they are heretics, just as it is of no value to those murderers of whom we spoke, so long as they hate their brethren: for they also themselves are in darkness, and if any one follows them they fall together into the ditch; and yet it does not follow that they either have not baptism or are unable to confer it.

Chap. 47.—92. Natalis of Oëa[10] said: "It is not only I myself who am present, but also Pompeius of Sabrati,[10] and Dioga of Leptis Magna,[10] who commissioned me to represent their views, being absent indeed in body, but present in spirit, who deliver this same judgment as our colleagues, that heretics cannot have communion with us, unless they have been baptized with the baptism of the Church."[11]

93. He means, I suppose, tnat communion which belongs to the society of the Dove; for in the partaking of the sacraments they doubtless held communion with them, judging no man, nor removing any from the right of communion if he held a different opinion. But with whatever reference he spoke, there is no great need for these words being refuted. For certainly a heretic would not be admitted to communion, unless he had been baptized with the baptism of the Church. But it is clear that the baptism of the Church exists even among heretics if it be consecrated with the words of the gospel; just as the gospel itself belongs to the Church, and has nothing to do with their waywardness, but certainly retains its own holiness.

Chap. 48.—94. Junius of Neapolis[12] said: "I do not depart from the judgment which we once pronounced, that we should baptize heretics on their coming to the Church."[13]

95. Since this man has adduced no argument nor proof from the Scriptures, he need not detain us long.

Chap. 49.—96. Cyprian of Carthage said: "My opinion has been set forth with the greatest fullness in the letter which has been written to our colleague Jubaianus,[14] that heretics being called enemies of Christ and antichrists according to the testimony of the gospel and the apostles, should, when they come to the Church, be baptized with the one baptism of the Church, that from enemies they may be made friends, and that from antichrists they may be made Christians."[15]

1 Conc.Carth. sec. 81.
2 1 Tim. i. 5.
3 Hos. ii.
4 1 Cor. v. 11.
5 Some read Licteus; not unlikely the bishop of Cypr. *Ep.* lxxvi.
6 Gemelli was a Roman colony in ecclesiastical province of Numidia.
7 Matt. xv. 14.
8 *Illuminare;* baptism being often called φωτισμός.
9 Conc. Carth. sec. 82.
10 Sabrati, Oëa and Leptis Magna were the three cities whose combination gave its name to Tripolis, an ecclesiastical province.
11 Conc. Carth. sec. 83–85.
12 Neapolis was in ecclesiastical province of Zeugitana. The name Junius as bishop appears in Cypr. *Epp.* lvii., lxx.
13 Conc. Carth. sec. 86.
14 Cypr. *Ep.* lxxiii.
15 Conc. Carth. sec. 87.

97. What need is there of further disputation here, seeing that we have already handled with the utmost care that very epistle to Jubaianus of which he has made mention? And as to what he has said here, let us not forget that it might be said of all unrighteous men who, as he himself bears witness, are in the Catholic Church, and whose power of possessing and of conferring baptism is not questioned by any of us. For they come to the Church, who pass to Christ from the party of the devil, and build upon the rock, and are incorporated with the Dove, and are placed in security in the garden enclosed and fountain sealed; where none of those are found who live contrary to the precepts of Christ, wherever they may seem to be. For in the epistle which he wrote to Magnus, while discussing this very question, he himself warned us at sufficient length, and in no ambiguous terms, of what kind of society we should understand that the Church consists. For he says, in speaking of a certain man, "Let him become an alien and profane, an enemy to the peace and unity of the Lord, not dwelling in the house of God, that is to say, in the Church of Christ, in which none dwell save those who are of one heart and of one mind."[1] Let those, therefore, who would lay injunctions on us on the authority of Cyprian, pay attention for a time to what we here say. For if only those who are of one heart and of one mind dwell in the Church of Christ, beyond all question those were not dwelling in the Church of Christ, however much they might appear to be within, who of envy and contention were announcing Christ without charity; by whom he understands, not the heretics and schismatics who are mentioned by the Apostle Paul,[2] but false brethren holding conversation with him within, who certainly ought not to have baptized, because they were not dwelling in the Church, in which he himself says that none dwell save those who are of one heart and of one mind: unless, indeed, any one be so far removed from the truth as to say that those were of one heart and of one mind who were envious and malevolent, and contentious without charity; and yet they used to baptize: nor did the detestable waywardness which they displayed in any degree violate or diminish from the sacrament of Christ, which was handled and dispensed by them.

CHAP. 50.—98. It is indeed worth while to consider the whole of the passage in the aforesaid letter to Magnus, which he has put together as follows: "Not dwelling," he says, "in the house of God—that is to say, in the Church of Christ—in which none dwell save those that are of one heart and of one mind, as the Holy Spirit says in the Psalms, speaking of 'God that maketh men to be of one mind in an house.'[3] Finally, the very sacrifices of the Lord declare that Christians are united among themselves by a firm and inseparable love for one another. For when the Lord calls bread, which is compacted together by the union of many grains, His body,[4] He is signifying one people, whom He bore, compacted into one body; and when He calls wine, which is pressed out from a multitude of branches and clusters and brought together into one, His blood,[5] He also signifies one flock joined together by the mingling of a multitude united into one." These words of the blessed Cyprian show that he both understood and loved the glory of the house of God, which house he asserted to consist of those who are of one heart and of one mind, proving it by the testimony of the prophets and the meaning of the sacraments, and in which house certainly were not found those envious persons, those malevolent without charity, who nevertheless used to baptize. From whence it is clear that the sacrament of Christ can both be in and be administered by those who are not in the Church of Christ, in which Cyprian himself bears witness that there are none dwelling save those who are of one heart and of one mind. Nor can it indeed be said that they are allowed to baptize so long as they are undetected, seeing that the Apostle Paul did not fail to detect those of whose ministry he bears unquestionable testimony in his epistle, saying that he rejoices that they also were proclaiming Christ. For he says of them, "Whether in pretense or in truth, Christ is preached; and I therein do rejoice, yea, and will rejoice."[6]

CHAP. 51.—99. Taking all these things, therefore, into consideration, I think that I am not rash in saying that there are some in the house of God after such a fashion as not to be themselves the very house of God, which is said to be built upon a rock,[7] which is called the one dove,[8] which is styled the beauteous bride without spot or wrinkle,[9] and a garden enclosed, a fountain sealed, a well of living water, an orchard of pomegranates with pleasant fruits;[10] which house also received the keys, and the power of binding and loosing.[11] If any one shall neglect this

[1] Cypr. *Ep.* lxix. 5.

[2] Phil. i. 15, 17.

[3] Ps. lxviii. 6; cp. LXX. and Hieron.

[4] John vi. 51.

[5] Matt. xxvi. 26-29.

[6] Phil. i. 18.

[7] Matt. xvi. 18.

[8] Cant. vi. 9.

[9] Eph. v. 27; cp. *Retract.* ii. 18.

[10] Cant. iv. 12, 13.

[11] Matt. xvi. 19.

house when it arrests and corrects him, the Lord says, "Let him be unto thee as an heathen man and a publican."[1] Of this house it is said, "Lord, I have loved the habitation of Thy house, and the place where Thine honor dwelleth;"[2] and, "He maketh men to be of one mind in an house;"[3] and, "I was glad when they said unto me, Let us go into the house of the Lord;"[4] and, "Blessed are they that dwell in Thy house, O Lord; they will be still praising Thee;"[5] with countless other passages to the same effect. This house is also called wheat, bringing forth fruit with patience, some thirtyfold, some sixtyfold, and some an hundredfold.[6] This house is also in vessels of gold and of silver,[7] and in precious stones and imperishable woods. To this house it is said, "Forbearing one another in love, endeavoring to keep the unity of the Spirit in the bond of peace;"[8] and, "For the temple of God is holy, which temple ye are."[9] For this house is composed of those that are good and faithful, and of the holy servants of God dispersed throughout the world, and bound together by the unity of the Spirit, whether they know each other personally or not. But we hold that others are said to be in the house after such a sort, that they belong not to the substance of the house, nor to the society of fruitful and peaceful justice, but only as the chaff is said to be among the corn; for that they are in the house we cannot deny, when the apostle says, "But in a great house there are not only vessels of gold and of silver, but also of wood and of earth; and some to honor, and some to dishonor."[10] Of this countless multitude are found to be not only the crowd which within the Church afflicts the hearts of the saints, who are so few in comparison with so vast a host, but also the heresies and schisms which exist in those who have burst the meshes of the net, and may now be said to be rather out of the house than in the house, of whom it is said, "They went out from us, but they were not of us."[11] For they are more thoroughly separated, now that they are also divided from us in the body, than are those who live within the Church in a carnal and worldly fashion, and are separated from us in the spirit.

[1] Matt. xviii. 17. [2] Ps. xxvi. 8.
[3] Ps. lxviii. 6; cp. LXX. and Hieron. [4] Ps. cxxii. 1.
[5] Ps. lxxxiv. 4. [6] Matt. xiii. 23; Luke viii. 15.
[7] 2 Tim. ii. 20. [8] Eph. iv. 2, 3. [9] 1 Cor. iii. 17.
[10] 2 Tim. ii. 20. In *Retract.* ii. 18, Augustin says that he thinks the meaning of this last passage to be, not as Cyprian took it, *Ep.* liv. 3, that the vessels of gold and silver are the good, which are to honor; the vessels of wood and earth the wicked, which are to dishonor: but that the material of the vessels refers to the outward appearance of the several members of the Church, and that in each class some will be found to honor, and some to dishonor. This interpretation he derives from Tychonius.
[11] 1 John ii. 19.

Chap. 52.—100. Of all these several classes, then, no one doubts respecting those first, who are in the house of God in such a sense as themselves to be the house of God, whether they be already spiritual, or as yet only babes nurtured with milk, but still making progress with earnestness of heart, towards that which is spiritual, that such men both have baptism so as to be of profit to themselves, and transmit it to those who follow their example so as to benefit them; but that in its transmission to those who are false, whom the Holy Spirit shuns, though they themselves, so far as lies with them, confer it so as to be of profit, yet the others receive it in vain, since they do not imitate those from whom they receive it. But they who are in the great house after the fashion of vessels to dishonor, both have baptism without profit to themselves, and transmit it without profit to those who follow their example: those, however, receive it with profit, who are united in heart and character, not to their ministers, but to the holy house of God. But those who are more thoroughly separated, so as to be rather out of the house than in the house, have baptism without any profit to themselves; and, moreover, there is no profit to those who receive it from them, unless they be compelled by urgent necessity to receive it, and their heart in receiving it does not depart from the bond of unity: yet nevertheless they possess it, though the possession be of no avail; and it is received from them, even when it is of no profit to those who so receive it, though, in order that it may become of use, they must depart from their heresy or schism, and cleave to that house of God. And this ought to be done, not only by heretics and schismatics, but also by those who are in the house through communion in the sacraments, yet so as to be outside the house through the perversity of their character. For so the sacrament begins to be of profit even to themselves, which previously was of no avail.

Chap. 53.—101. The question is also commonly raised, whether baptism is to be held valid which is received from one who had not himself received it, if, from some promptings of curiosity, he had chanced to learn how it ought to be conferred; and whether it makes no difference in what spirit the recipient receives it, whether in mockery or in sincerity: if in mockery, whether the difference arises when the mockery is of deceit, as in the Church, or in what is thought to be the Church; or when it is in jest, as in a play: and which is the more accursed, to receive it deceitfully in the Church, or in heresy or schism without deceit, that is to say, with full sincerity of heart: or whether it be worse to receive it deceitfully in heresy or in good faith in a play, if any one were to be moved by a sudden feeling of religion in the midst of his acting. And yet, if we compare such an one even with him who receives it deceitfully in the Catholic Church itself, I should be surprised if any one were to doubt which of the two should be preferred; for I do not see of what avail the intention of him who gives in truth can be to him who receives deceitfully. But let us consider, in the case of some one also giving it in deceit, when both the giver and the recipient are acting deceitfully in the unity of the Catholic Church itself, whether this should rather be acknowledged as baptism, or that which is given in a play, if any one should be found who received it faithfully from a sudden impulse of religion: or whether it be not true that, so far as the men themselves are concerned, there is a very great difference between the believing recipient in a play, and the mocking recipient in the Church; but that in regard to the genuineness of the sacrament there is no difference. For if it makes no difference in respect to the genuineness of the sacrament within the Catholic Church itself, whether certain persons celebrate it in truth or in deceit, so long as both still celebrate the same thing, I cannot see why it should make a difference outside, seeing that he who receives it is not cloaked by his deceit, but he is changed by his religious impulse. Or have those truthful persons among whom it is celebrated more power for the confirmation of the sacrament, than those deceitful men by whom and in whom it is celebrated can exert for its invalidation? And yet, if the deceit be subsequently brought to light, no one seeks a repetition of the sacrament; but the fraud is either punished by excommunication or set right by penitence.

102. But the safe course for us is, not to advance with any rashness of judgment in setting forth a view which has neither been started in any regionary Council of the Catholic Church nor established in a plenary one; but to assert, with all the confidence of a voice that cannot be gainsaid, what has been confirmed by the consent of the universal Church, under the direction of our Lord God and Saviour Jesus Christ. Nevertheless, if any one were to press me—supposing I were duly seated in a Council in which a question were raised on points like these—to declare what my own opinion was, without reference to the previously expressed views of others, whose judgment I would rather follow, if I were under the influence of the same feelings as led me to assert what I have said before, I should have no hesitation in saying that all men possess baptism who have received it in any place, from any sort of men, provided that it were consecrated in the words of the gospel, and received without deceit on their part with some degree of faith; although it would be of no profit to them for the salvation of their souls if they were without charity, by which they might be grafted into the Catholic Church. For "though I have faith," says the apostle, "so that I could remove mountains, but have not charity, I am nothing."[1] Just as already, from the established decrees of our predecessors, I have no hesitation in saying that all those have baptism who, though they receive it deceitfully, yet receive it in the Church, or where the Church is thought to be by those in whose society it is received, of whom it was said, "They went out from us."[2] But when there was no society of those who so believed, and when the man who received it did not himself hold such belief, but the whole thing was done as a farce, or a comedy, or a jest,—if I were asked whether the baptism which was thus conferred should be approved, I should declare my opinion that we ought to pray for the declaration of God's judgment through the medium of some revelation seeking it with united prayer and earnest groanings of suppliant devotion, humbly deferring all the time to the decision of those who were to give their judgment after me, in case they should set forth anything as already known and determined. And, therefore, how much the more must I be considered to have given my opinion now without prejudice to the utterance of more diligent research or authority higher than my own!

CHAP. 54.—103. But now I think that it is fully time for me to bring to their due termination these books also on the subject of baptism, in which our Lord God has shown to us, through the words of the peaceful Bishop Cyprian and his brethren who agreed with him, how great is the love which should be felt for catholic unity; so that even where they were otherwise minded until God should reveal even this to them,[3] they should rather bear with those who thought differently from themselves, than sever themselves from them by a wicked schism; whereby the mouths of the Donatists are wholly closed, even if we say nothing of the followers of Maximian. For if the wicked pollute the good in unity, then even Cyprian himself already found no

[1] 1 Cor. xiii. 2. [2] 1 John ii. 19. [3] Phil. iii. 15.

Church to which he could be joined. But if the wicked do not infect the good in unity, then the sacrilegious Donatist has no ground to set before himself for separation. But if baptism is both possessed and transferred by the multitude of others who work the works of the flesh, of which it is said, that "they which do such things shall not inherit the kingdom of God,"[1] then it is possessed and transferred also by heretics, who are numbered among those works; because they could have transferred it had they remained, and did not lose it by their secession. But men of this kind confer it on their fellows as fruitlessly and uselessly as the others who resemble them, inasmuch as they shall not inherit the kingdom of God. And as, when those others are brought into the right path, it is not that baptism begins to be present, having been absent before, but that it begins to profit them, having been already in them; so is it the case with heretics as well. Whence Cyprian and those who thought with him could not impose limits on the Catholic Church, which they would not mutilate. But in that they were otherwise minded we feel no fear, seeing that we too share in their veneration for Peter; yet in that they did not depart from unity we rejoice, seeing that we, like them, are founded on the rock.

[1] Gal. v. 19-21.

THE

THREE BOOKS OF AUGUSTIN,

BISHOP OF HIPPO,

IN ANSWER

TO THE LETTERS OF PETILIAN, THE DONATIST

BISHOP OF CIRTA.

[CONTRA LITTERAS PETILIANI DONATISTÆ CORTENSIS, EPISCOPI.]

CIRCA A. D. 400.

TRANSLATED BY THE

REV. J. R. KING, M.A.,

VICAR OF ST. PETER'S IN THE EAST, OXFORD; AND LATE FELLOW AND TUTOR OF MERTON COLLEGE, OXFORD.

CONTENTS OF ANSWER TO LETTERS OF PETILIAN

THE

THREE BOOKS OF AUGUSTIN,

BISHOP OF HIPPO.

IN ANSWER TO

THE LETTERS OF PETILIAN, THE DONATIST,

BISHOP OF CIRTA.

Written c. 400 A.D., some say 398 A.D., but Augustin places it some time after the treatise on Baptism: *Retractt.* Bk. ii. xxv. From the same, we gather the following points as to the origin of this treatise: Before A. had finished his books on the Trinity and his word-for-word commentary on Genesis, a reply to a letter which Petilian had addressed to his followers, only a small part of which however had come into A.'s hands, demanded immediate preparation. This constitutes Book First. Subsequently the whole document was obtained, and he was engaged in preparing the second Book, c. 401; but even before the full treatise of Petilian had been secured, the latter had obtained A.'s first book, and afterwards put an epistle abusive of A. in circulation. The answer to this latter is Book Third, c. 402. Petilian was originally an advocate. The opponents charged him with having become a Donatist by compulsion, with assuming the title of Paraclete, and with endeavoring to prevent all access on their part to his writings.

BOOK I.

WRITTEN IN THE FORM OF A LETTER ADDRESSED TO THE CATHOLICS, IN WHICH THE FIRST PORTION OF THE LETTER WHICH PETILIAN HAD WRITTEN TO HIS ADHERENTS IS EXAMINED AND REFUTED.

Augustin, to the well-beloved brethren that belong to the care of our charge, greeting in the Lord:

CHAP. I.—1. Ye know that we have often wished to bring forward into open notoriety, and to confute, not so much from our own arguments as from theirs, the sacrilegious error of the Donatist heretics; whence it came to pass that we wrote letters even to some of their leaders,—not indeed for purposes of communion with them, for of that they had already in times past rendered themselves unworthy by dissenting from the Church; nor yet in terms of reproach, but of a conciliatory character, with the view that, having discussed the question with us which caused them to break off from the holy communion of the whole world, they might, on consideration of the truth, be willing to be corrected, and might not defend the headstrong perversity of their predecessors with a yet more foolish obstinacy, but might be reunited to the Catholic stock, so as to bring forth the fruits of charity. But as it is written, "With those who have hated peace I am more peaceful,"[1] so they rejected my letters, just as they hate the very name of peace, in whose interests they were written. Now, however, as I was in the church of Constantina, Absentius[2] being present, with my colleague Fortunatus, his bishop, the brethren brought before my notice a letter, which they said that a bishop of the said schism had addressed to his presbyters, as was set forth in the superscription of the letter itself. When I had read it, I was so amazed to find that in his very first words he cut away the very roots of the whole claims of his party to communion, that I was unwilling to believe that it could be the letter of a man who, if fame speaks truly, is especially conspicuous among them for learning and eloquence. But some of those who were present when I read it, being acquainted with the polish and embellishment of his composition, gradually persuaded me that it was undoubtedly his address. I thought, however, that whoever the author might be, it required refutation, lest the writer should seem to himself, in the company of the inexperienced, to have written something of weight against the Catholic Church.

2. The first point, then, that he lays down in his letter is the statement, "that we find fault with them for the repetition of baptism, while we ourselves pollute our souls with a laver stained with guilt." But to what profit is it that I should reproduce all his insulting terms? For, since it is one thing to strengthen proofs, another thing to meddle with abusive words by way of refutation, let us rather turn our attention to the mode in which he has sought to prove that we do not possess baptism, and that therefore they do not require the repetition of what was already present, but confer what hitherto was wanting. For he says: "What we look for is the conscience of the giver to cleanse that of the recipient." But supposing the conscience of the giver is concealed from view, and perhaps defiled with sin, how will it be able to cleanse the conscience of the recipient, if, as he says, "what we look for is the conscience of the giver to cleanse that of the recipient?" For if he should say that it makes no matter to the recipient what amount of evil may lie concealed from view in the conscience of the giver, perhaps that ignorance may have such a degree of efficacy as this, that a man cannot be defiled by the guilt of the conscience of him from whom he receives baptism, so long as he is unaware of it. Let it then be granted that the guilty conscience of his neighbor cannot defile a man so long as he is unaware of it, but is it therefore clear that it can further cleanse him from his own guilt?

Chap. 2.—3. Whence, then, is a man to be cleansed who receives baptism, when the conscience of the giver is polluted without the knowledge of him who is to receive it? Especially when he goes on to say, "For he who receives faith from the faithless receives not faith, but guilt." There stands before us one that is faithless ready to baptize, and he who should be baptized is ignorant of his faithlessness: what think you that he will receive? Faith, or guilt? If you answer faith, then you will grant that it is possible that a man should receive not guilt, but faith, from him that is faithless; and the former saying will be false, that "he who receives faith from the faithless receives not faith, but guilt." For we find that it is possible that a man should receive faith even from one that is faithless, if he be not aware of the faithlessness of the giver. For he does not say, He who receives faith from one that is openly and notoriously faithless; but he says, "He who receives faith from the faithless receives not faith, but guilt;" which certainly is false when a person is baptized by one who hides his faithlessness. But if he shall say, Even when the faithlessness of the baptizer is concealed, the recipient receives not faith from him, but guilt, then let them rebaptize those who are well known to have been baptized by men who in their own body have long concealed a life of guilt, but have eventually been detected, convicted, and condemned.

Chap. 3.—For, so long as they escaped detection, they could not bestow faith on any whom they baptized, but only guilt, if it be true that whosoever receives faith from one that is faithless receives not faith, but guilt. Let them therefore be baptized by the good, that they may be enabled to receive not guilt, but faith.

4. But how, again, shall they have any certainty about the good who are to give them faith, if what we look to is the conscience of the giver, which is unseen by the eyes of the proposed recipient? Therefore, according to their judgment, the salvation of the spirit is made uncertain, so long as in opposition to the holy Scriptures, which say, "It is better to trust in the Lord than to put confidence in

[1] Ps. cxx. 7; cf. Hieron.
[2] Probably Alypius.

man,"[1] and, "Cursed be the man that trusteth in man,"[2] they remove the hope of those who are to be baptized from the Lord their God, and persuade them that it should be placed in man; the practical result of which is, that their salvation becomes not merely uncertain, but actually null and void. For "salvation belongeth unto the Lord,"[3] and "vain is the help of man."[4] Therefore, whosoever places his trust in man, even in one whom he knows to be just and innocent, is accursed. Whence also the Apostle Paul finds fault with those who said they were of Paul, saying, "Was Paul crucified for you? or were ye baptized in the name of Paul?"[5]

CHAP. 4.—5. Wherefore, if they were in error, and would have perished had they not been corrected, who wished to be of Paul, what must we suppose to be the hope of those who wished to be of Donatus? For they use their utmost endeavors to prove that the origin, root, and head of the baptized person is none other than the individual by whom he is baptized. The result is, that since it is very often a matter of uncertainty what kind of man the baptizer is, the hope therefore of the baptized being of uncertain origin, of uncertain root, of uncertain head, is of itself uncertain altogether. And since it is possible that the conscience of the giver may be in such a condition as to be accursed and defiled without the knowledge of the recipient, it results that, being of an accursed origin, accursed root, accursed head, the hope of the baptized may prove to be vain and ungrounded. For Petilian expressly states in his epistle, that "everything consists of an origin and root; and if it have not something for a head, it is nothing." And since by the origin and root and head of the baptized person he wishes to be understood the man by whom he is baptized, what good does the unhappy recipient derive from the fact that he does not know how bad a man his baptizer really is? For he does not know that he himself has a bad head, or actually no head at all. And yet what hope can a man have, who, whether he is aware of it or not, has either a very bad head or no head at all? Can we maintain that his very ignorance forms a head, when his baptizer is either a bad head or none at all? Surely any one who thinks this is unmistakeably without a head.

CHAP. 5.—6. We ask, therefore, since he says, "He who receives faith from the faithless receives not faith, but guilt," and immediately adds to this the further statement, that "everything consists of an origin and root; and if it have not something for a head, it is nothing;"—we ask, I say, in a case where the faithlessness of the baptizer is undetected: If, then, the man whom he baptizes receives faith, and not guilt; if, then, the baptizer is not his origin and root and head, who is it from whom he receives faith? where is the origin from which he springs? where is the root of which he is a shoot? where the head which is his starting-point? Can it be, that when he who is baptized is unaware of the faithlessness of his baptizer, it is then Christ who gives faith, it is then Christ who is the origin and root and head? Alas for human rashness and conceit! Why do you not allow that it is always Christ who gives faith, for the purpose of making a man a Christian by giving it? Why do you not allow that Christ is always the origin of the Christian, that the Christian always plants his root in Christ, that Christ is the head of the Christian? Do we then maintain that, even when spiritual grace is dispensed to those that believe by the hands of a holy and faithful minister, it is still not the minister himself who justifies, but that One of whom it is said, that "He justifieth the ungodly?"[6] But unless we admit this, either the Apostle Paul was the head and origin of those whom he had planted, or Apollos the root of those whom he had watered, rather than He who had given them faith in believing; whereas the same Paul says, "I have planted, Apollos watered, but God gave the increase: so then neither is he that planteth anything, nor he that watereth, but God that giveth the increase.'[7] Nor was the apostle himself their root, but rather He who says, "I am the vine, ye are the branches."[8] How, too, could he be their head, when he says, that "we, being many, are one body in Christ,"[9] and expressly declares in many passages that Christ Himself is the head of the whole body?

CHAP. 6.—7. Wherefore, whether a man receive the sacrament of baptism from a faithful or a faithless minister, his whole hope is in Christ, that he fall not under the condemnation that "cursed is he that placeth his hope in man." Otherwise, if each man is born again in spiritual grace of the same sort as he by whom he is baptized, and if when he who baptizes him is manifestly a good man, then he himself gives faith, he is himself the origin and root and head of him who is being born; whilst, when the baptizer

1 Ps. cxviii. 8. 2 Jer. xvii. 5. 3 Ps. iii. 8. 4 Ps. lx. 11. 5 1 Cor. i. 13.
6 Rom. iv. 5. 7 1 Cor. iii. 6, 7. 8 John xv. 5. 9 Rom. xii. 5.

is faithless without its being known, then the baptized person receives faith from Christ, then he derives his origin from Christ, then he is rooted in Christ, then he boasts in Christ as his head,—in that case all who are baptized should wish that they might have faithless baptizers, and be ignorant of their faithlessness: for however good their baptizers might have been, Christ is certainly beyond comparison better still; and He will then be the head of the baptized, if the faithlessness of the baptizer shall escape detection.

Chap. 7.—8. But if it is perfect madness to hold such a view (for it is Christ always that justifieth the ungodly, by changing his ungodliness into Christianity; it is from Christ always that faith is received, Christ is always the origin of the regenerate and the head of the Church), what weight, then, will those words have, which thoughtless readers value by their sound, without inquiring what their inner meaning is? For the man who does not content himself with hearing the words with his ear, but considers the meaning of the phrase, when he hears, "What we look to is the conscience of the giver, that it may cleanse the conscience of the recipient," will answer, The conscience of man is often unknown to me, but I am certain of the mercy of Christ: when he hears, "He who receives faith from the faithless receives not faith, but guilt," will answer, Christ is not faithless, from whom I receive not guilt, but faith: when he hears, "Everything consists of an origin and root; and if it have not something for a head, is nothing," will answer, My origin is Christ, my root is Christ, my head is Christ. When he hears, "Nor does anything well receive second birth, unless it be born again of good seed," he will answer, The seed of which I am born again is the Word of God, which I am warned to hear with attention, even though he through whom I hear it does not himself do what he preaches; according to the words of the Lord, which make me herein safe, "All whatsoever they bid you observe, that observe and do; but do not ye after their works: for they say, and do not."[1] When he hears, "What perversity must it be, that he who is guilty through his own sins should make another free from guilt!" he will answer, No one makes me free from guilt but He who died for our sins, and rose again for our justification. For I believe, not in the minister by whose hands I am baptized, but in Him who justifieth the ungodly, that my faith may be counted unto me for righteousness.[2]

Chap. 8.—9. When he hears, "Every good tree bringeth good fruit, but a corrupt tree bringeth forth evil fruit: do men gather grapes of thorns?"[3] and, "A good man out of the good treasure of his heart bringeth forth good things, and an evil man out of the evil treasure bringeth forth evil things;"[4] he will answer, This therefore is good fruit, that I should be a good tree, that is, a good man, that I should show forth good fruit, that is, good works. But this will be given to me, not by him that planteth, nor by him that watereth, but by God that giveth the increase. For if the good tree be the good baptizer, so that his good fruit should be the man whom he baptizes, then any one who has been baptized by a bad man, even if his wickedness be not manifest, will have no power to be good, for he is sprung from an evil tree. For a good tree is one thing; a tree whose quality is concealed, but yet bad, is another. Or if, when the tree is bad, but hides its badness, then whosoever is baptized by it is born not of it, but of Christ; then they are justified with more perfect holiness who are baptized by the bad who hide their evil nature, than they who are baptized by the manifestly good.[5]

Chap. 9.—10. Again, when he hears, "He that is washed by one dead, his washing profiteth him nought,"[6] he will answer, "Christ, being raised from the dead, dieth no more; death hath no more dominion over Him:"[7] of whom it is said, "The same is He which baptizeth with the Holy Ghost."[8] But they are baptized by the dead, who are baptized in the temples of idols. For even they themselves do not suppose that they receive the sanctification which they look for from their priests, but from their gods; and since these were men, and are dead in such sort as to be now neither upon earth nor in the rest of heaven,[9] they are truly baptized by the dead: and the same answer will hold good if there be any other way in which these words of holy Scripture may be examined, and profitably discussed and understood. For if in this place I understand a baptizer who is a sinner, the same absurdity will follow, that whosoever has been baptized by an ungodly man, even though his ungodliness be undiscovered, is yet washed in vain, as though

[1] Matt. xxiii. 3.

[2] Rom. iv. 25, 5.

[3] Matt. vii. 17, 16.

[4] Matt. xii. 35.

[5] See below, Book II. 6, 12.

[6] So the Donatists commonly quoted Ecclus. xxiv. 25, which is more correctly rendered in our version, "He that washeth himself after the touching of a dead body, if he touch it again, what availeth his washing?" Augustin (*Retractt.* i. 21, 3) says that the misapplication was rendered possible by the omission in many African MSS. of the second clause, "and touches it again." Cp. Hieron., Ecclus. xxxiv, 30.

[7] Rom. vi. 9.

[8] John i. 33.

[9] Cp. *Contra Cresconium*, Book II. 25. 30: "*Ita mortui sunt, ut neque super terras, neque in requie sanctorum vivant.*"

baptized by one dead. For he does not say, He that is baptized by one manifestly dead, but absolutely, "by one dead." And if they consider any man to be dead whom they know to be a sinner, but any one in their communion to be alive, even though he manages most adroitly to conceal a life of wickedness, in the first place with accursed pride they claim more for themselves than they ascribe to God, that when a sinner is unveiled to them he should be called dead, but when he is known by God he is held to be alive. In the next place, if that sinner is to be called dead who is known to be such by men, what answer will they make about Optatus, whom they were afraid to condemn though they had long known his wickedness? Why are those who were baptized by him not said to have been baptized by one dead? Did he live because the Count was his faith?[1]—an elegant and well-turned saying of some early colleagues of their own, which they themselves are wont to quote with pride, not understanding that at the death of the haughty Goliath it was his own sword by which his head was cut off.[2]

CHAP. 10.—11. Lastly, if they are willing to give the name of dead neither to the wicked man whose sin is hidden, nor to him whose sin is manifest, but who has yet not been condemned by them, but only to him whose sin is manifest and condemned, so that whosoever is baptized by him is himself baptized by the dead, and his washing profits him nothing; what are we to say of those whom their own party have condemned "by the unimpeachable voice of a plenary Council,"[3] together with Maximianus and the others who ordained him,—I mean Felicianus of Musti, and Prætextatus of Assura, of whom I speak in the meantime, who are counted among the twelve ordainers of Maximianus, as erecting an altar in opposition to their altar at which Primianus stands? They surely are reckoned by them among the dead. To this we have the express testimony of the noble decree of that Council of theirs which formerly called forth shouts of unreserved[4] applause when it was recited among them for the purpose of being decreed, but which would now be received in silence if we should chance to recite it in their ears; whereas they should rather have been slow at first to rejoice in its eloquence, lest they should afterwards come to mourn over it when its credit was destroyed. For in it they speak in the following terms of the followers of Maximianus, who were shut out from their communion: "Seeing that the shipwrecked members of certain men have been dashed by the waves of truth upon the sharp rocks, and after the fashion of the Egyptians, the shores are covered with the bodies of the dying; whose punishment is intensified in death itself, since after their life has been wrung from them by the avenging waters, they fail to find so much as burial." In such gross terms indeed, do they insult those who were guilty of schism from their body, that they call them dead and unburied; but certainly they ought to have wished that they might obtain burial, if it were only that they might not have seen Optatus Gildonianus advancing with a military force, and like a sweeping wave that dashes beyond its fellows, sucking back Felicianus and Prætextatus once again within their pale, out of the multitude of bodies lying unburied on the shore.

CHAP. 11.—12. Of these I would ask, whether by coming to their sea they were restored to life, or whether they are still dead there? For if still they are none the less corpses, then the laver cannot in any way profit those who are baptized by such dead men. But if they have been restored to life, yet how can the laver profit those whom they baptized before outside, while they were lying without life, if the passage, "He who is baptized by the dead, of what profit is his baptism to him," is to be understood in the way in which they think? For those whom Prætextatus and Felicianus baptized while they were yet in communion with Maximianus are now retained among them, sharing in their communion, without being again baptized, together with the same men who baptized them—I mean Felicianus and Prætextatus: taking occasion by which fact, if it were not that they cherish the beginning of their own obstinacy, instead of considering the certain end of their spiritual salvation, they would certainly be bound to vigilance, and ought to recover the soundness of their senses, so as to breathe again in Catholic peace; if only, laying aside the swelling of their pride, and overcoming the madness of their stubbornness, they would take heed and see what monstrous sacrilege it is to curse the baptism of the foreign churches, which we have learned from the sacred books were planted in primitive times, and to receive the baptism of the followers of Maximianus, whom they have condemned with their own lips.

CHAP. 12.—13. But our brethren them-

---

1 Benedictines suggest as an emendation, "*quod Deus illi comes erat*," as in II. 23, 53; 37, 88, 103, 237.

2 1 Sam. xvii. 51.

3 That of Bagai. See on *de Bapt.* I. 5, 7.

4 *Ore latissimo acclamaverunt.* The Louvain edition has "*lætissimo*," both here and *Contra Crescon.* IV. 41, 48.

selves, the sons of the aforesaid churches, were both ignorant at the time, and still are ignorant, of what has been done so many years ago in Africa: wherefore they at any rate cannot be defiled by the charges which have been brought, on the part of the Donatists, against the Africans, without even knowing whether they were true. But the Donatists having openly separated and divided themselves off, although they are even said to have taken part in the ordination of Primianus, yet condemned the said Primianus, ordained another bishop in opposition to Primianus, baptized outside the communion of Primianus, rebaptized after Primianus, and returned to Primianus with their disciples who had been baptized by themselves outside, and never rebaptized by any one inside. If such a union with the party of Maximianus does not pollute the Donatists, how can the mere report concerning the Africans pollute the foreigners? If the lips meet together without offense in the kiss of peace, which reciprocally condemned each other, why is each man that is condemned by them in the churches very far removed by the intervening sea from their jurisdiction, not saluted with a kiss as a faithful Catholic, but driven forth with a blast of indignation as an impious pagan? And if, in receiving the followers of Maximianus, they made peace in behalf of their own unity, far be it from us to find fault with them, save that they cut their own throats by their decision, that whereas, to preserve unity in their schism, they collect together again what had been parted from themselves, they yet scorn to reunite their schism itself to the true unity of the Church.

Chap. 13.—14. If, in the interests of the unity of the party of Donatus, no one rebaptizes those who were baptized in a wicked schism, and men, who are guilty of a crime of such enormity as to be compared by them in their Council to those ancient authors of schism whom the earth swallowed up alive,[1] are either unpunished after separation, or restored again to their position after condemnation; why is it that, in defence of the unity of Christ, which is spread throughout the whole inhabited world, of which it has been predicted that it shall have dominion from sea to sea, and from the river unto the ends of the earth,[2]—a prediction which seems from actual proof to be in process of fulfilment; why is it that, in defence of this unity, they do not acknowledge the true and universal law of that inheritance which rings forth from the books that are common to us all: "I shall give Thee the heathen for Thine inheritance, and the uttermost parts of the earth for Thy possession?"[3] In behalf of the unity of Donatus, they are not compelled to call together again what they have scattered abroad, but are warned to hear the cry of the Scriptures: why will they not understand that they meet with such treatment through the mercy of God, that since they brought false charges against the Catholic Church, by contact as it were with which they were unwilling to defile their own excessive sanctity, they should be compelled by the sovereign authority of Optatus Gildonianus to receive again and associate with themselves true offenses of the greatest enormity, condemned by the true voice, as they say, of their own plenary Council? Let them at length perceive how they are filled with the true crimes of their own party, after inventing fictitious crimes wherewith to charge their brethren, when, even if the charges had been true, they ought at length to feel how much should be endured in the cause of peace, and in behalf of Christ's peace to return to a Church which did not condemn crimes undiscovered, if on behalf of the peace of Donatus they were ready to pardon such as were condemned.

Chap. 14.—15. Therefore, brethren, let it suffice us that they should be admonished and corrected on the one point of their conduct in the matter of the followers of Maximianus. We do not ransack ancient archives, we do not bring to light the contents of time-honored libraries, we do not publish our proofs to distant lands; but we bring in, as arbiters betwixt us, all the proofs derived from our ancestors, we spread abroad the witness that cries aloud throughout the world.

Chap. 15.—16. Look at the states of Musti[4] and Assura:[5] there are many still remaining in this life and in this province who have severed themselves, and many from whom they have severed themselves; many who have erected an altar, and many against whom that altar has been erected; many who have condemned, and many who have been condemned; who have received, and who have been received; who have been baptized outside, and not baptized again within: if all these things in the cause of unity defile, let the defiled hold their tongues; if these things in the cause of unity do not defile, let them submit to correction, and terminate their strife.

1 Num. xvi. 31-35.

2 Ps. lxxii. 8.

3 Ps. ii. 8.

4 Musti is in ecclesiastical province of Numidia.

5 Assura is in ecclesiastical province of Zeugitana. See *Treatise on Baptism*, Book VII. c. 32.

CHAP. 16.—17. As for the words which follow in his letter, the writer himself could scarcely fail to laugh at them, when, having made an unlearned and lying use of the proof in which he quotes the words of Scripture, "He who is washed by the dead, what profiteth him his washing?" he endeavors to show to us "how far a *traditor* being still in life may be accounted dead." And then he goes on further to say: "That man is dead who has not been worthy to be born again in true baptism; he is likewise dead who, although born in genuine baptism, has joined himself to a *traditor*." If, therefore, the followers of Maximianus are not dead, why do the Donatists say, in their plenary Council, that "the shores are covered with their dying bodies?" But if they are dead, whence is there life in the baptism which they gave? Again, if Maximianus is not dead, why is a man baptized again who had been baptized by him? But if he is dead, why is not also Felicianus of Musti dead with him, who ordained him, and might have died beyond the sea with some African colleague or another who was a *traditor?* Or, if he also is himself dead, how is there life with him in your society in those who, having been baptized outside by him who is dead, have never been baptized again within?

CHAP. 17.—18. Then he further adds: "Both are without the life of baptism, both he who never had it at all, and he who had it but has lost it." He therefore never had it, whom Felicianus, the follower of Maximianus or Prætextatus, baptized outside; and these men themselves have lost what once they had. When, therefore, these were received with their followers, who gave to those whom they baptized what previously they did not have? and who restored to themselves what they had lost? But they took away with them the form of baptism, but lost the veritable excellence of baptism by their wicked schism. Why do you repudiate the form itself, which is holy at all times and all places, in the Catholics whom you have not heard, whilst you are willing to acknowledge it in the followers of Maximianus whom you have punished?

19. But whatever he seemed to himself to say by way of accusation about the traitor Judas, I see not how it can concern us, who are not proved by them to have betrayed our trust; nor, indeed, if such treason were proved on the part of any who before our time have died in our communion, would that treason in any way defile us by whom it was disavowed, and to whom it was displeasing. For if they themselves are not defiled by offenses condemned by themselves, and afterwards condoned, how much less can we be defiled by what we have disavowed so soon as we have heard of them! However weighty, therefore, his invective against *traditors*, let him be assured that they are condemned by me in precisely the same terms. But yet I make a distinction; for he accuses one on my side who has long been dead without having been condemned in any investigation made by me. I point to a man adhering closely to his side, who had been condemned by him, or at least had been separated by a sacrilegious schism, and whom he received again with undiminished honor.

CHAP. 18.—20. He says: "You who are a most abandoned *traditor* have come out in the character of a persecutor and murderer of us who keep the law." If the followers of Maximianus kept the law when they separated from you, then we may acknowledge you as a keeper of the law, when you are separated from the Church spread abroad throughout the world. But if you raise the question of persecutions, I at once reply: If you have suffered anything unjustly, this does not concern those who, though they disapprove of men who act in such a way,[1] yet endure them for the peace that is in unity, in a manner deserving of all praise. Wherefore you have nothing to bring up against the Lord's wheat, who endure the chaff that is among them till the last winnowing, from whom you never would have separated yourself, had you not shown yourself lighter than chaff by flying away under the blast of temptation before the coming of the Winnower. But not to leave this one example, which the Lord hath thrust back in their teeth, to close the mouths of these men, for their correction if they will show themselves to be wise, but for their confusion if they remain in their folly: if those are more just that suffer persecution than those who inflict it, then those same followers of Maximianus are the more just, whose basilica was utterly overthrown, and who were grievously maltreated by the military following of Optatus, when the mandates of the proconsul, ordering that all of them should be shut out of the basilicas, were manifestly procured by the followers of Primianus. Wherefore, if, when the emperors hated their communion, they ventured on such violent measures for the persecution of the followers of Maximianus, what would they do if they

[1] *Qui talia facientes quamvis improbent.* A comparison of the explanation of this passage in *Contra Crescon.* III. 41, 45, shows the probability of Migne's conjecture, "*quamvis improbe*," "who endure the men that act in such a way, however monstrous their conduct may be."

were enabled to work their will by being in communion with kings? And if they did such things as I have mentioned for the correction of the wicked, why are they surprised that Catholic emperors should decree with greater power that they should be worked upon and corrected who endeavor to rebaptize the whole Christian world, when they have no ground for differing from them? seeing that they themselves bear witness that it is right to bear with wicked men even where they have true charges to bring against them in the cause of peace, since they received those whom they had themselves condemned, acknowledging the honors conferred among themselves, and the baptism administered in schism. Let them at length consider what treatment they deserve at the hands of the Christian powers of the world, who are the enemies of Christian unity throughout the world. If, therefore, correction be bitter, yet let them not fail to be ashamed; lest when they begin to read what they themselves have written, they be overcome with laughter, when they do not find in themselves what they wish to find in others, and fail to recognize[1] in their own case what they find fault with in their neighbors.

Chap. 19.—21. What, then, does he mean by quoting in his letter the words with which our Lord addressed the Jews: "Wherefore, behold, I send unto you prophets, and wise men, and scribes; and some of them ye shall kill and crucify, and some of them shall ye scourge?"[2] For if by the wise men and the scribes and the prophets they would have themselves be understood, while we were as it were the persecutors of the prophets and wise men, why are they unwilling to speak with us, seeing they are sent to us? For, indeed, if the man who wrote that epistle which we are at this present moment answering, were to be pressed by us to acknowledge it as his own, stamping its authenticity with his signature, I question much whether he would do it, so thoroughly afraid are they of our possessing any words of theirs. For when we were anxious by some means or other to procure the latter part of this same letter, because those from whom we obtained it were unable to describe the whole of it, no one who was asked for it was willing to give it to us, so soon as they knew that we were making a reply to the portion which we had. Therefore, when they read how the Lord says to the prophet, "Cry aloud, spare not, and write their sins with my pen,"[3] these men who are sent to us as prophets have no fears on this score, but take every precaution that their crying may not be heard by us: which they certainly would not fear if what they spoke of us were true. But their apprehension is not groundless, as it is written in the Psalm, "The mouth of them that speak lies shall be stopped."[4] For if the reason that they do not receive our baptism be that we are a generation of vipers—to use the expression in his epistle—why did they receive the baptism of the followers of Maximianus, of whom their Council speaks in the following terms: "Because the enfolding of a poisoned womb has long concealed the baneful offspring of a viper's seed, and the moist concretions of conceived iniquity have by slow heat flowed forth into the members of serpents"? Is it not therefore of themselves also that it is said in the same Council, "The poison of asps is under their lips, their mouth is full of cursing and bitterness, their feet are swift to shed blood; destruction and unhappiness is in their ways, and the way of peace have they not known"?[5] And yet they now hold these men themselves in undiminished honor, and receive within their body those whom these men had baptized without.

Chap. 20.—22. Wherefore all this about the generation of vipers, and the poison of asps under their lips, and all the other things which they have said against those which have not known the way of peace, are really, if they would but speak the truth, more strictly applicable to themselves, since for the sake of the peace of Donatus they received the baptism of these men, in respect of which they used the expressions quoted above in the wording of the decree of the Council; but the baptism of the Church of Christ dispersed throughout the world, from which peace itself came into Africa, they repudiate, to the sacrilegious wounding of the peace of Christ. Which, therefore, are rather the false prophets, who come in sheep's clothing, while inwardly they are ravening wolves,[6]—they who either fail to detect the wicked in the Catholic Church, and communicate with them in all innocence, or else for the sake of the peace of unity are bearing with those whom they cannot separate from the threshing-floor of the Lord before the Winnower shall come, or they who do in schism what they censure in the Catholic Church, and receive in their own separation, when manifest

[1] *Nec in se agnoscunt.* The reading of the Louvain edition gives better sense, "*Et in se agnoscunt*," "and discover in themselves."

[2] Matt. xxiii. 34.

[3] Isa. lviii. 1.

[4] Ps. lxiii. 11.

[5] Ps. xiv. 5-7, LXX. and Hieron., and probably N. Af. version.

[6] Matt. vii. 15.

to all and condemned by their own voice, what they profess that they shun in the unity of the Church when it calls for toleration, and does not even certainly exist?

CHAP. 21.—23. Lastly, it has been said, as he himself has also quoted, "Ye shall know them by their fruits:"[1] let us therefore examine into their fruits. You bring up against our predecessors their delivery of the sacred books. This very charge we urge with greater probability against their accusers themselves. And not to carry our search too far, in the same city of Constantina your predecessors ordained Silvanus bishop at the very outset of his schism. He, while he was still a subdeacon, was most unmistakeably entered as a *traditor* in the archives of the city.[2] If you on your side bring forward documents against our predecessors, all that we ask is equal terms, that we should either believe both to be true or both to be false. If both are true, you are unquestionably guilty of schism, who have pretended that you avoid offenses in the communion of the whole world, which you had commonly among you in the small fragment of your own sect. But again, if both are false, you are unquestionably guilty of schism, who, on account of the false charges of giving up the sacred books, are staining yourselves with the heinous offence of severance from the Church. But if we have something to urge in accusation while you have nothing, or if our charges are true whilst yours are false, it is no longer matter of discussion how thoroughly your mouths are closed.

CHAP. 22.—24. What if the holy and true Church of Christ were to convince and overcome you, even if we held no documents in support of our cause, or only such as were false, while you had possession of some genuine proofs of delivery of the sacred books? what would then remain for you, except that, if you would, you should show your love of peace, or otherwise should hold your tongues?[3] For whatever, in that case, you might bring forward in evidence, I should be able to say with the greatest ease and the most perfect truth, that then you are bound to prove as much to the full and catholic unity of the Church already spread abroad and established throughout so many nations, to the end that you should remain within, and that those whom you convict should be expelled. And if you have endeavored to do this, certainly you have not been able to make good your proof; and being vanquished or enraged, you have separated yourselves, with all the heinous guilt of sacrilege, from the guiltless men who could not condemn on insufficient proof. But if you have not even endeavored to do this, then with most accursed and unnatural blindness you have cut yourselves off from the wheat of Christ, which grows throughout His whole fields, that is, throughout the whole world, until the end, because you have taken offense at a few tares in Africa.

CHAP. 23.—25. In conclusion, the Testament is said to have been given to the flames by certain men in the time of persecution. Now let its lessons be read, from whatever source it has been brought to light. Certainly in the beginning of the promises of the Testator this is found to have been said to Abraham: "In thy seed shall all the nations of the earth be blessed;"[4] and this saying is truthfully interpreted by the apostle: "To thy seed," he says, "which is Christ."[5] No betrayal on the part of any man has made the promises of God of none effect. Hold communion with all the nations of the earth, and then you may boast that you have preserved the Testament from the destruction of the flames. But if you will not do so, which party is the rather to be believed to have insisted on the burning of the Testament, save that which will not assent to its teaching when it is brought to light? For how much more certainly, without any sacrilegious rashness, can he be held to have joined the company of *traditors* who now persecutes with his tongue the Testament which they are said to have persecuted with the flames! You charge us with the persecution: the true wheat of the Lord answers you, "Either it was done justly, or it was done by the chaff that was among us." What have you to say to this? You object that we have no baptism: the same true wheat of the Lord answers you, that the form of the sacrament even within the Church fails to profit some, as it did no good to Simon Magus when he was baptized, much more it fails to profit those who are without. Yet that baptism remains in them when they depart, is proved from this, that it is not restored to them when they return. Never, therefore, except by the greatest shamelessness, will you be able to cry out against that wheat, or to call them false

[1] Matt. vii. 16.
[2] See below, III. 57, 69; 68, 70; and *Contra Cresc.* III. 29, 33, IV. 56, 66.
[3] "Obmutescatis" is the most probable conjecture of Migne for "obtumescatis," which could only mean, "you should swell with confusion."

[4] Gen. xxii. 18.
[5] Gal. iii. 16.

prophets clad in sheep's clothing, whilst inwardly they are ravening wolves; since either they do not know the wicked in the unity of the Catholic Church, or for the sake of unity bear with those whom they know.

Chap. 24.—26. But let us turn to the consideration of your fruits. I pass over the tyrannous exercise of authority in the cities, and especially in the estates of other men; I pass over the madness of the Circumcelliones, and the sacrilegious and profane adoration of the bodies of those who had thrown themselves of their own accord over precipices, the revellings of drunkenness, and the ten years' groaning of the whole of Africa under the cruelty of the one man Optatus Gildonanius: all this I pass over, because there are certain among you who cry out that these things are, and have ever been displeasing to them. But they say that they bore with them in the cause of peace, because they could not put them down; wherein they condemn themselves by their own judgment: for if indeed they felt such love for peace, they never would have rent in twain the bond of unity. For what madness can be greater, than to be willing to abandon peace in the midst of peace itself, and to be anxious to retain it in the midst of discord? Therefore, for the sake of those who pretend that they do not see the evils of this same faction of Donatus, which all men see and blame, ignoring them even to the extent of saying of Optatus himself, "What did he do?" "Who accused him?" "Who convicted him?" "I know nothing," "I saw nothing," "I heard nothing,"—for the sake of these, I say, who pretend that they are ignorant of what is generally notorious, the party of Maximianus has arisen, through whom their eyes are opened, and their mouths are closed: for they openly sever themselves; they openly erect altar against altar; they are openly in a Council[1] called sacrilegious and vipers, and swift to shed blood, to be compared with Dathan and Abiram and Korah, and are condemned in cutting terms of abhorrence; and are as openly received again with undiminished honors in company with those whom they have baptized. Such are the fruits of these men, who do all this for the peace of Donatus, that they may clothe themselves in sheep's clothing, and reject the peace of Christ throughout the world that they may be ravening wolves within the fold.

Chap. 25.—27. I think that I have left unanswered none of the statements in the letter of Donatus, so far at least as relates to what I have been able to find in that part of which we are in possession. I should be glad if they would produce the other part as well, in case there should be anything in it which does not admit of refutation. But as for these answers which we have made to him, with the help of God, I admonish your Christian love, that ye not only communicate them to those who seek for them, but also force them on those who show no longing for them. Let them answer anything they will; and if they shrink from sending a reply to us, let them at any rate send letters to their own party, only not forbidding that the contents should be shown to us. For if they do this, they show their fruits most openly, by which they are proved to demonstration to be ravening wolves disguised in sheep's clothing, in that they secretly lay snares for our sheep, and openly shrink from giving any answer to the shepherds. We only lay to their charge the sin of schism, in which they are all most thoroughly involved,—not the offenses of certain of their party, which some of them declare to be displeasing to themselves. If they, on the other hand, abstain from charging us with the sins of other men, they have nothing they can lay to our charge, and therefore they are wholly unable to defend themselves from the charge of schism; because it is by a wicked severance that they have separated themselves from the threshing-floor of the Lord, and from the innocent company of the corn that is growing throughout the world, on account of charges which either are false, and invented by themselves, or even if true, involve the chaff alone.

Chap 26.—28. But it is possible that you may expect of me that I should go on to refute what he has introduced about Manichæus. Now, in respect of this, the only thing that offends me is that he has censured a most pestilent and pernicious error—I mean the heresy of the Manichæans—in terms of wholly inadequate severity, if indeed they amount to censure at all, though the Catholic Church has broken down his defenses by the strongest evidence of truth.[2] For the inheritance of Christ, established in all nations, is secure against heresies which have been shut out from the inheritance; but, as the Lord says, "How can Satan cast out Satan?"[3] so how can the error of the Donatists have power to overthrow the error of the Manichæans?[4]

---

[1] That of Bagai.

[2] *Veritatis fortissimis documentis Catholica expugnat;* and so the MSS. The earlier editors, apparently not understanding the omission of "*ecclesia*," read "*veritas*."

[3] Mark iii. 23.

[4] See II. 18, 40, 41.

CHAP. 27.—29. Wherefore, my beloved brethren, though that error is exposed and overcome in many ways, and dare not oppose the truth on any show of reason whatsoever, but only with the unblushing obstinacy of impudence; yet, not to load your memory with a multitude of proofs, I would have you bear in mind this one action of the followers of Maximianus, confront them with this one fact, thrust this in their teeth, to make them hold their treacherous tongues, destroy their calumny with this, as it were a three-pronged dart destroying a three-headed monster. They charge us with betrayal of the sacred books; they charge us with persecution; they charge us with false baptism: to all their charges make the same answer about the followers of Maximianus. For they think that the proofs are lost which show that their predecessors gave the sacred volumes to the flames; but this at least they cannot hide, that they have received with unimpaired honors those who were stained with the sacrilege of schism. Also they think that those most violent persecutions are hidden, which they direct against any who oppose them whenever they are able; but whilst spiritual persecution surpasses bodily persecution, they received with undiminished honors the followers of Maximianus, whom they themselves persecuted in the body, and of whom they themselves said, "Their feet are swift to shed blood;"[1] and this at any rate they cannot hide.

CHAP. 28. Finally, they think that the question of baptism is hidden, with which they deceive wretched souls. But whilst they say that none have baptism who were baptized outside the communion of the one Church, they received with undiminished honors the followers of Maximianus, with those whom they baptized in schism outside the Donatist communion, and this at least they cannot hide.

30. "But these things," they say, "bring no pollution in the cause of peace; and it is well to bend to mercy the rigor of extreme severity, that broken branches may be grafted in anew." Accordingly, in this way the whole question is settled, by defeat in them, by the impossibility of defeat for us; for if the name of peace be assumed for even the faintest shadow of defense to justify the bearing with wicked men in schism, then beyond all doubt the violation of true peace itself involves detestable guilt, with nothing to be said in its defence throughout the unity of the world.

CHAP. 29.—31. These things, brethren, I would have you retain as the basis of your action and preaching with untiring gentleness: love men, while you destroy errors; take of the truth without pride; strive for the truth without cruelty. Pray for those whom you refute and convince of error. For the prophet prays to God for mercy upon such as these, saying, "Fill their faces with shame, that they may seek Thy name, O Lord."[2] And this, indeed, the Lord has done already, so as to fill the faces of the followers of Maximianus with shame in the sight of all mankind: it only remains that they should learn how to blush to their soul's health. For so they will be able to seek the name of the Lord, from which they are turned away to their utter destruction, whilst they exalt their own name in the place of that of Christ. May ye live and persevere in Christ, and be multiplied, and abound in the love of God, and in love towards one another, and towards all men, brethren well beloved.

[1] Ps. xiv. 6, LXX. Hieron., N. Af. version.

[2] Ps. lxxxiii. 16.

BOOK II.[1]

IN WHICH AUGUSTIN REPLIES TO ALL THE SEVERAL STATEMENTS IN THE LETTER OF PETILIANUS, AS THOUGH DISPUTING WITH AN ADVERSARY FACE TO FACE.

CHAP. 1.—1. That we made a full and sufficient answer to the first part of the letter of Petilianus, which was all that we had been able to find, will be remembered by all who were able to read or hear what we replied. But since the whole of it was afterwards found and copied by our brethren, and sent to us with the view that we should answer it as a whole, this task was one which our pen could not escape,—not that he says anything new in it, to which answer has not been already made in many ways and at various times; but still, on account of the brethren of slower comprehension, who, when they read a matter in any place, cannot always refer to everything that has been said upon the same subject, I will comply with those who urge me by all means to reply to every point, and that as though we were carrying on the discussion face to face in the form of a dialogue. I will set down the words of his epistle under his name, and I will give the answer under my own name, as though it had all been taken down by reporters while we were debating. And so there will be no one who can complain either that I have passed anything over, or that they have been unable to understand it for want of distinction between the parties to the discussion; at the same time that the Donatists themselves, who are unwilling to argue the question in our presence, as is shown by the letters which they have circulated among their party, may thus not fail to find the truth answering them point by point, just as though they were discussing the matter with us face to face.

2. In the very beginning of the letter PETILIANUS said: "Petilianus, a bishop, to his well-beloved brethren, fellow-priests, and deacons, appointed ministers with us throughout our diocese in the gospel, grace be to you and peace, from God our Father and from the Lord Jesus Christ."

3. AUGUSTIN answered: I acknowledge the apostolic greeting. You see who you are that employ it, but see from what source you have learned what you say. For in these terms Paul salutes the Romans, and in the same terms the Corinthians, the Galatians, the Ephesians, the Colossians, the Philippians, the Thessalonians. What madness is it, therefore, to be unwilling to share the salvation of peace with those very Churches in whose epistles you learned its form of salutation?

CHAP. 2.—4. PETILIANUS said: "Those who have polluted their souls with a guilty laver, under the name of baptism, reproach us with baptizing twice,—than whose obscenity, indeed, any kind of filth is more cleanly, seeing that through a perversion of cleanliness they have come to be made fouler by their washing."

5. AUGUSTIN answered: We are neither made fouler by our washing, nor cleaner by yours. But when the water of baptism is given to any one in the name of the Father, and of the Son, and of the Holy Ghost, it is neither ours nor yours, but His of whom it was said to John, "Upon whom thou shalt see the Spirit descending, and remaining on Him, the same is He which baptizeth with the Holy Ghost."[2]

CHAP. 3.—6. PETILIANUS said: "For what we look to is the conscience of the giver, to cleanse that of the recipient."

7. AUGUSTIN answered: We therefore need have no anxiety about the conscience of Christ. But if you assert any man to be the giver, be he who he may, there will be no

---

1 Written probably in the beginning of 401 A.D. Some say in 402.

2 John i. 33.

certainty about the cleansing of the recipient, because there is no certainty about the conscience of the giver.

CHAP. 4.—8. PETILIANUS said: "For he who receives faith from the faithless, receives not faith but guilt."

9. AUGUSTIN answered: Christ is not faithless, from whom the faithful man receives not guilt but faith. For he believeth on Him that justifieth the ungodly, that his faith may be counted for righteousness.[1]

CHAP. 5.—10. PETILIANUS said: "For everything consists of an origin and root; and if it have not something for a head, it is nothing: nor does anything well receive second birth, unless it be born again of good seed."

11. AUGUSTIN answered: Why will you put yourself forward in the room of Christ, when you will not place yourself under Him? He is the origin, and root, and head of him who is being born, and in Him we feel no fear, as we must in any man, whoever he may be, lest he should prove to be false and of abandoned character, and we should be found to be sprung from an abandoned source, growing from an abandoned root, united to an abandoned head. For what man can feel secure about a man, when it is written, "Cursed be the man that trusteth in man?"[2] But the seed of which we are born again is the word of God, that is, the gospel. Whence the apostle says, "For in Christ Jesus I have begotten you through the gospel."[3] And yet he allows even those to preach the gospel who were preaching it not in purity, and rejoices in their preaching;[4] because, although they were preaching it not in purity, but seeking their own, not the things which are Jesus Christ's,[5] yet the gospel which they preached was pure. And the Lord had said of certain of like character, "Whatsoever they bid you observe, that observe and do; but do not ye after their works: for they say, and do not."[6] If, therefore, what is in itself pure is preached in purity, then the preacher himself also, in that he is a partner with the word, has his share in begetting the believer; but if he himself be not regenerate, and yet what he preaches be pure, then the believer is born not from the barrenness of the minister, but from the fruitfulness of the word.

CHAP. 6.—12. PETILIANUS said: "This being the case, brethren, what perversity must it be, that he who is guilty through his own sins should make another free from guilt, when the Lord Jesus Christ says, 'Every good tree bringeth forth good fruit, but a corrupt tree bringeth forth evil fruit: do men gather grapes of thorns?'[7] And again: 'A good man, out of the good treasure of the heart, bringeth forth good things: and an evil man, out of the evil treasure, bringeth forth evil things.'"[8]

13. AUGUSTIN answered: No man, even though he be not guilty through his own sins, can make his neighbor free from sin, because he is not God. Otherwise, if we were to expect that out of the innocence of the baptizer should be produced the innocence of the baptized, then each will be the more innocent in proportion as he may have found a more innocent person by whom to be baptized; and will himself be the less innocent in proportion as he by whom he is baptized is less innocent. And if the man who baptizes happens to entertain hatred against another man, this will also be imputed to him who is baptized. Why, therefore, does the wretched man hasten to be baptized,—that his own sins may be forgiven him, or that those of others may be reckoned against him? Is he like a merchant ship, to discharge one burden, and to take on him another? But by the good tree and its good fruit, and the corrupt tree and its evil fruit, we are wont to understand men and their works, as is consequently shown in those other words which you also quoted: "A good man, out of the good treasure of his heart, bringeth forth good things: and an evil man, out of the evil treasure, bringeth forth evil things." But when a man preaches the word of God, or administers the sacraments of God, he does not, if he is a bad man, preach or minister out of his own treasure; but he will be counted among those of whom it is said, "Whatsoever they bid you observe, that observe and do; but do not ye after their works:" for they bid you observe what is God's, but their works are their own. For if it is as you say, that is, if the fruit of those who baptize consist in the baptized persons themselves, you declare a great woe against Africa, if a young Optatus has sprung up for every one that Optatus baptized.

CHAP. 7.—14. PETILIANUS said: "And again, 'He who is baptized by one that is dead, his washing profiteth him nothing.'[9] He did not mean that the baptizer was a corpse, a lifeless body, the remains of a man ready for burial, but one lacking the Spirit of God, who is compared to a dead body, as He declares to a disciple in another place, ac-

1 Rom. iv. 5. 2 Jer. xvii. 5. 3 1 Cor. iv. 15.
4 Phil. i. 17, 18. 5 Phil. ii. 21 6 Matt. xxiii. 3.
7 Matt. vii. 17, 16. 8 Matt. xii. 35.
9 Ecclus. xxxiv. 25; see on I. 9, 10.

cording to the witness of the gospel. For His disciple says, 'Lord, suffer me first to go and bury my father. But Jesus said unto him, Follow me, and let the dead bury their dead.' [1] The father of the disciple was not baptized. He declared him as a pagan to belong to the company of pagans; unless he said this of the unbelieving, The dead cannot bury the dead. He was dead, therefore, not as smitten by some death, but as smitten even during life. For he who so lives as to be doomed to eternal death is tortured by a death in life. To be baptized, therefore, by the dead, is to have received not life but death. We must therefore consider and declare how far the *traditor* is to be accounted dead while yet alive. He is dead who has not deserved to be born again with a true baptism; he is ikewise dead who, having been born again with a true baptism, has become involved with a *traditor*. Both are wanting in the life of baptism,—both he who never had it at all, and he who had it and has lost it. For the Lord Jesus Christ says, 'There shall come to that man seven spirits more wicked than the former one, and the last state of that man shall be worse than the first.' " [2]

15. Augustin answered: Seek with greater care to know in what sense the words which you have quoted from Scripture in proof of your position were really uttered, and how they should be understood. For that all unrighteous persons are wont to be called dead in a mystical sense is clear enough; but Christ, to whom true baptism belongs, which you say is false because of the faults of men, is alive, sitting at the right hand of the Father, and He will not die any more through any infirmity of the flesh: death will no more have dominion over Him.[3] And they who are baptized with His baptism are not baptized by one who is dead. And if it so happen that certain ministers, being deceitful workers, seeking their own, not the things which are Jesus Christ's, proclaiming the gospel not in purity, and preaching Christ of contention and envy, are to be called dead because of their unrighteousness, yet the sacrament of the living God does not die even in one that is dead. For that Simon was dead who was baptized by Philip in Samaria, who wished to purchase the gift of God for money; but the baptism which he had lived in him still to work his punishment.

16. But how false the statement is which you make, that "both are wanting in the life of baptism, both he who never had it at all, and he who had it and has lost it," you may see from this, that in the case of those who apostatize after having been baptized, and who return through penitence, baptism is not restored to them, as it would be restored if it were lost. In what manner, indeed, do your dead men baptize according to your interpretation? Must we not reckon the drunken among the dead (to say nothing of the rest, and to mention only what is well known and of daily experience among all), seeing that the apostle says of the widow, "But she that liveth in pleasure is dead while she liveth?"[5] In the next place, in that Council of yours, in which you condemned Maximianus with his advisers or his ministers, have you forgotten with what eloquence you said, "Even after the manner of the Egyptians, the shores are full of the bodies of the dying, on whom the weightier punishment falls in death itself, in that, after their life has been wrung from them by the avenging waters, they have not found so much as burial?" And yet you yourselves may see whether or no one of them, Felicianus, has been brought to life again; yet he has with him within the communion of your body those whom he baptized outside. As therefore he is baptized by One that is alive, who is clothed with the baptism of the living Christ, so he is baptized by the dead who is wrapped in the baptism of the dead Saturn, or any one like him; that we may set forth in the meanwhile, with what brevity we may, in what sense the words which you have quoted may be understood without any cavilling on the part of any one of us. For, in the sense in which they are received by you, you make no effort to explain them, but only strive to entangle us together with yourselves.

Chap. 8.—17. Petilianus said: "We must consider, I say, and declare how far the treacherous *traditor* is to be accounted dead while yet in life. Judas was an apostle when he betrayed Christ; and the same man was already dead, having spiritually lost the office of an apostle, being destined afterwards to die by hanging himself, as it is written: 'I have sinned,' says he, 'in that I have betrayed the innocent blood; and he departed, and went and hanged himself.' [6] The traitor perished by the rope: he left the rope for others like himself, of whom the Lord Christ cried aloud to the Father, 'Father, those that Thou gavest me I have kept, and none of them is lost, but the son of perdition; that the Scripture might be fulfilled.' [7] For David of old

[1] Matt. viii. 21, 22.
[2] Matt. xii. 45.
[3] Rom. vi. 9.
[4] Acts viii. 13, 18, 19.
[5] 1 Tim. v. 6.
[6] Matt. xxvii. 4, 5.
[7] John xvii. 12.

had passed this sentence on him who was to betray Christ to the unbelievers: 'Let another take his office. Let his children be fatherless, and his wife a widow.'[1] See how mighty is the spirit of the prophets, that it was able to see all future things as though they were present, so that a traitor who was to be born hereafter should be condemned many centuries before. Finally, that the said sentence should be completed, the holy Matthias received the bishopric of that lost apostle. Let no one be so dull, no one so faithless, as to dispute this: Matthias won for himself a victory, not a wrong, in that he carried off the spoils of the traitor from the victory of the Lord Christ. Why then, after this, do you claim to yourself a bishopric as the heir of a worse traitor? Judas betrayed Christ in the flesh to the unbelievers; you in the spirit madly betrayed the holy gospel to the flames of sacrilege. Judas betrayed the Lawgiver to the unbelievers; you, as it were, betraying all that he had left, gave up the law of God to be destroyed by men. Whilst, had you loved the law, like the youthful Maccabees, you would have welcomed death for the sake of the laws of God (if indeed that can be said to be death to men which makes them immortal because they died for the Lord); for of those brethren we learn that one replied to the sacrilegious tyrant with these words of faith: 'Thou like a fury takest us out of this present life; but the King of the world (who reigns for ever, and of His kingdom there shall be no end) shall raise us up who have died for His laws, unto everlasting life.'[2] If you were to burn with fire the testament of a dead man, would you not be punished as the falsifier of a will? What therefore is likely to become of you who have burned the most holy law of our God and Judge? Judas repented of his deed even in death; you not only do not repent, but stand forth as a persecutor and butcher of us who keep the law, whilst you are the most wicked of *traditors*."

18. AUGUSTIN answered: See what a difference there is between your calumnious words and our truthful assertions. Listen for a little while. See how you have exaggerated the sin of delivering up the sacred books, comparing us in most odious terms, like some sophistical inventor of charges, with the traitor Judas. But when I shall have answered you on this point with the utmost brevity,—I did not do what you assert; I did not deliver up the sacred books; your charge is false; you will never be able to prove it,—will not all that smoke of mighty words presently vanish away? Or will you perchance endeavor to prove the truth of what you say? This, then, you should do first; and then you might rise against us, as against men who were already convicted, with whatever mass of invective you might choose. Here is one absurdity: behold again a second.

19. You yourself, when speaking of the foretelling of the condemnation of Judas, used these expressions: "See how mighty is the spirit of the prophets, that it was able to see all future things as though they were present, so that a traitor who was to be born hereafter should be condemned many centuries before;" and yet you did not see that in the same sure prophecy, and certain and unshaken truth, in which it was foretold that one of the disciples should hereafter betray the Christ, it was also foretold that the whole world should hereafter believe in Christ. Why did you pay attention in the prophecy to the man who betrayed Christ, and in the same place give no heed to the world for which Christ was betrayed? Who betrayed Christ? Judas. To whom did he betray Him? To the Jews. What did the Jews do to Him? "They pierced my hands and my feet," says the Psalmist. "I may tell all my bones: they look and stare upon me. They part my garments among them, and cast lots upon my vesture."[3] Of what importance, then, that is which is bought at such a price, I would have you read a little later in the psalm itself: "All the ends of the world shall remember and turn unto the Lord; and all the kindreds of the nations shall worship before Thee. For the kingdom is the Lord's; and He is the governor among the nations."[4] But who is able to suffice for the quotation of all the other innumerable prophetic passages which bear witness to the world that is destined to believe? Yet you quote a prophecy because you see in it the man who sold Christ: you do not see in it the possession which Christ bought by being sold. Here is the second absurdity: behold again the third.

20. Among the many other expressions in your invective, you said: "If you were to burn with fire the testament of a dead man, would you not be punished as the falsifier of a will? What therefore is likely to become of you who have burned the most holy law of our God and Judge?" In these words you have paid no attention to what certainly ought to have moved you, to the question of how it might be that we should burn the testament, and yet stand fast in the inheritance

[1] Ps. cix. 8, 9.

[2] 2 Macc. vii. 9. The words in brackets are not in the original Greek.

[3] Ps. xxii. 16-18.

[4] Ps. xxii. 27, 28.

which was described in that testament; but it is marvellous that you have preserved the testament and lost the inheritance. Is it not written in that testament, "Ask of me, and I shall give thee the heathen for thine inheritance, and the uttermost parts of the earth for thy possession"?[1] Take part in this inheritance, and you may bring what charges you will against me about the testament. For what madness is it, that while you shrank from committing the testament to the flames, you should yet strive against the words of the testator! We, on the other hand, though we hold in our hands the records of the Church and of the State, in which we read that those who ordained a rival bishop[2] in opposition to Cæcilianus were rather the betrayers of the sacred books, yet do not on this account insult you, or pursue you with invectives, or mourn over the ashes of the sacred pages in your hands, or contrast the burning torments of the Maccabees with the sacrilege of your fear, saying, "You should deliver your own limbs to the flames rather than the utterances of God." For we are unwilling to be so absurd as to excite an empty uproar against you on account of the deeds of others, which you either know nothing of, or else repudiate. But in that we see you separated from the communion of the whole world (a sin both of the greatest magnitude, and manifest to all mankind, and common to you all), if I were desirous of exaggerating, I should find time failing me sooner than words. And if you should seek to defend yourself on this charge, it could only be by bringing accusations against the whole world, of such a kind that, if they could be maintained, you would simply be furnishing matter for further accusation against yourself; if they could not be maintained, there is in them no defence for you. Why therefore do you puff yourself up against me about the betrayal of the sacred books, which concerns neither you nor me if we abide by the agreement not to charge each other with the sins of other men; and which, if that agreement does not stand, affects you rather than me? And, yet, even without any violation of that agreement, I think I may say with perfect justice that he should be deemed a partner with him who delivered up Christ who has not delivered himself up to Christ in company with the whole world. "Then," says the apostle, "then are ye Abraham's seed, and heirs according to the promise."[3] And again he says, "Heirs of God, and joint-heirs with Christ."[4] And the same apostle shows that the seed of Abraham belongs to all nations from the promise which was given to Abraham, "In thy seed shall all the nations of the earth be blessed."[5] Wherefore I consider that I am only making a fair demand in asking that we should for a moment consider the testament of God, which has already long been opened, and that we should consider every one to be himself an heir of the traitor whom we do not find to be a joint-heir with Him whom he betrayed; that every one should belong to him who sold Christ who denies that Christ has bought the whole world. For when He showed Himself after His resurrection to His disciples, and gave His limbs to those who doubted, that they should handle them, He says this to them, "For thus it is written, and thus it behoved Christ to suffer, and to rise again from the dead the third day: and that repentance and remission of sins should be preached in His name among all nations, beginning at Jerusalem."[6] See from what an inheritance you estrange yourselves! see what an Heir you resist! Can it really be that a man would spare Christ if He were walking here on earth who speaks against Him while He sits in heaven? Do you not yet understand that whatever you allege against us you allege against His words? A Christian world is promised and believed in: the promise is fulfilled, and it is denied. Consider, I entreat of you, what you ought to suffer for such impiety. And yet, if I know not what you have suffered,—if I have not seen it, have not wrought it,—then do you to-day, who do not suffer the violence of my persecution, render to me an account of your separation. But you are likely to say over and over again what, unless you prove it, can affect no one, and if you prove it, has no bearing upon me.

Chap. 9.—21. Petilianus said: "Hemmed in, therefore, by these offenses, you cannot be a true bishop."

22. Augustin answered: By what offenses? What have you shown? What have you proved? And if you have proved charges on the part of I know not whom, what has that to do with the seed of Abraham, in which all the nations of the earth are blessed?

Chap. 10.—23. Petilianus said: "Did the apostle persecute any one? or did Christ betray any one?"

24. Augustin answered: I might indeed say that Satan himself was worse than all wicked men; and yet the apostle delivered a

[1] Ps. ii. 8.
[2] Majorinus, ordained by the Numidian bishops in 311 A.D.
[3] Gal. iii. 29.
[4] Rom. viii. 17.
[5] Gen. xxii. 18.
[6] Luke xxiv. 46, 47.

man over to him for the destruction of the flesh, that his spirit might be saved in the day of the Lord Jesus.[1] And in the same way he delivered over others, of whom he says, "Whom I have delivered unto Satan, that they may learn not to blaspheme."[2] And the Lord Christ drove out the impious merchants from the temple with scourges; in which connection we also find advanced the testimony of Scripture, where it says, 'The zeal of Thine house hath eaten me up."[3] So that we do find the apostle delivering over to condemnation, and Christ a persecutor. All this I might say, and put you into no small heat and perturbation, so that you would be compelled to inquire, not into the complaints of those who suffer, but into the intention of those who cause the suffering. But do not trouble yourself about this; I do not say this. But I do say that it has nothing to do with the seed of Abraham, which is in all nations, if anything has been done to you which ought not to have been done, perhaps by the chaff among the harvest of the Lord, which in spite of this is found among all nations. Do you therefore render an account of your separation. But first, consider what kind of men you have among you, with whom you would not wish to be reproached; and see how unjustly you act, when you cast in our teeth the acts of other men, even if you proved what you assert. Therefore it will be found that there is no ground for your separation.

CHAP. 11.—25. PETILIANUS said: "Yet some will be found to say, We are not the sons of a *traditor*. Any one is the son of that man whose deeds he imitates. For those are most assuredly sons, and at the same time bear a strong resemblance to their parents, who are born in the likeness of their parents, not only as being of their flesh and blood, but in respect of their characters and deeds."

26. AUGUSTIN answered: A little while ago you were saying nothing contrary to us, now you even begin to say something in our favor. For this proposition of yours binds you to as much as this, that if you shall fail to-day to convict us, with whom you are arguing, of being *traditors* and murderers, and anything else with which you charge us, you will then be wholly powerless to hurt us by any charge of the kind which you may prove against those who have gone before us. For we cannot be the sons of those to whose deeds our actions bear no resemblance. And see to what you have committed yourself. If you should be so successful as to convict some man, even of our own times, and living with us, of any guilt of the kind, that is in no way to the prejudice of all the nations of the earth who are blessed in the seed of Abraham, by separating yourself from whom you are found to be guilty of sacrilege. Accordingly, unless (as is altogether impossible) you are acquainted with all men that exist throughout the world, and have not only made yourself familiar with all their characters and deeds, but have also proved that they are as bad as you describe, you have no ground for reproaching all the world, which is among the saints, with parentage of I know not what description, to whom you prove that they are like. Nor will it help you at all, even if you are able to show that those who are not of the same character take the holy sacraments in common with those who are. In the first place, because you ought yourselves to look at those with whom you celebrate those sacraments, to whom you give them, from whom you receive them, and whom you would be unwilling to have cast up against you as a reproach. And again, if all those are the sons of Judas, who was the devil among the apostles, who imitate his deeds, why do we not call those of the sons of the apostles who make such men partakers, not in their own deeds, but in the sacraments of the Lord, as the apostles partook of the supper of the Lord in company with that traitor? and in this way they are very different from you, who cast in the teeth of men who are striving for the preservation of unity the very thing that you do to the rending asunder of unity.

CHAP. 12.—27. PETILIANUS said: "The Lord Jesus said to the Jews concerning Himself, 'If I do not the works of my Father, believe me not.'"[4]

28. AUGUSTIN answered: I have already answered above, This is both true, and makes for us against you.

CHAP. 13.—29. PETILIANUS said: Over and over again He reproaches the false speakers and liars in such terms as these: 'Ye are the children of the devil, for he also was a slanderer from the beginning, and abode not in the truth.'"

30. AUGUSTIN answered: We are not wont to say, "He was a slanderer," but "He was a murderer."[5] But we ask how it was that the devil was a murderer from the beginning; and we find that he slew the first man, not by drawing a sword, nor by applying to him any bodily violence, but by persuading him to

[1] 1 Cor. v. 5.
[2] 1 Tim. i. 20.
[3] John ii. 15-17
[4] John x. 37.
[5] John viii. 44.

sin, and thus driving him from the happiness of Paradise. What, then, was Paradise is now represented by the Church. Therefore those are the sons of the devil who slay men by withdrawing them from the Church. But as by the words of God we know what was the situation of Paradise, so now by the words of Christ we have learned where the Church is to be found: "Throughout all nations," He says, "beginning at Jerusalem." Whosoever, therefore, separates a man from that complete whole to place him in any single part, is proved to be a son of the devil and a murderer. But see, further, what is the application of the expression which you yourself employed in saying of the devil, "He was a slanderer, and abode not in the truth." For you bring an accusation against the whole world on account of the sins of others, though even those others themselves you were more able to accuse than to convict; and you abode not in the truth of Christ. For He says that the Church is "throughout all nations, beginning at Jerusalem;" but ye say that it is in the party of Donatus.

Chap. 14.—31. Petilianus said: "In the third place, also, He calls the madness of persecutors in like manner by this name, 'Ye generation of vipers, how can ye escape the damnation of hell? Wherefore, behold, I send unto you prophets, and wise men, and scribes; and some of them ye shall kill and crucify; and some of them shall ye scourge in your synagogues, and persecute them from city to city: that upon you may come all the righteous blood shed upon the earth, from the blood of righteous Abel unto the blood of Zacharias, son of Barachias, whom ye slew between the temple and the altar.'[1] Are they then really the sons of vipers according to the flesh, and not rather serpents in mind, and three-tongued malice, and deadliness of touch, and burning with the spirit of poison? They have truly become vipers, who by their bites have vomited forth death against the innocent people."

32. Augustin answered: If I were to say that this is said of men of character like unto yourselves, you would reply, "Prove it." What then, have you proved it? Or if you think that it is proved by the mere fact of its being uttered, there is no need to repeat the same words. Pronounce the same judgment against yourselves as coming from us to you. See you not that I too have proved it, if this amounts to proof? And yet I would have you learn what is really meant by proof. For indeed I do not even seek for evidence from without to enable me to prove you vipers. For be well assured that this very fact marks in you the nature of vipers, that you have not in your mouth the foundation of truth, but the poison of slanderous abuse, as it is written, "The poison of asps is under their lips."[2] And because this might be said indiscriminately by any one against any one, as though it were asked, Under whose lips? he immediately adds, "Their mouth is full of cursing and bitterness."[3] When, therefore, you say such things as this against men dispersed throughout the whole world, of whom you know nothing whatsoever, and many of whom have never heard the name either of Cæcilianus or of Donatus, and when you do not hear them answering amid silence, Nothing of what you say has reference to us; we never saw it; we never did it; we are totally at a loss to understand what you are saying,—seeing that you desire nothing else than to say what you are entirely powerless to prove, how can you help allowing that your mouth is full of cursing and bitterness? See, therefore, whether you can possibly show that you are not vipers,[4] unless you show that all Christians throughout all nations of the world are *traditors*, and murderers, and anything but Christians. Nay, in very truth, even though you should be able to know and set before us the lives and deeds of every individual man throughout the world, yet before you can do that, seeing that you act as you do without any consideration, your mouth is that of a viper, your mouth is full of cursing and bitterness. Show to us now, if you can, what prophet, what wise man, what scribe we have slain, or crucified, or scourged in our synagogues. Look how much labor you have expended without in any way being able to prove that Donatus and Marculus[5] were prophets, or wise men, or scribes, because, in fact, they were nothing of the sort. But even if you could prove as much as this, what progress would you have made towards proving that they had been killed by us, when even we ourselves did not so much as know them? and how much less the whole world, whom you calumniate with poisonous mouth?[6] Or whence will you be able to prove that we have a spirit like that of those who murdered them, when you actually cannot show that

[1] Matt. xxiii. 33-35.

[2] Ps. xiv. 5, LXX, cp. Hieron. [3] Ps. xiv. 6, LXX. cp. Hieron.

[4] A suggested reading is, "*nos esse viperas.*"

[5] These both with others are celebrated in the martyrology of the Donatists; see IIII. *Idas Martii Sermo de Passione SS. Donati et Advocati*, c. 340; *Passio Marculi sacerdotis Donatistæ qui sub Macario interfectus a Donatistis pro Martyre habebatur* (Dec. 25, a. 348), and others. See *Du Pin Monumenta vetera ad Donatistarum Historiam pertinentia*, in his edition of Optatus.

[6] See below, c. 20, 46: and *Contra Crescon.* III. 49, 54.

they were murdered by any one at all? Look carefully to all these points, see whether you can prove any single one of them either about the whole world, or to the satisfaction of the whole world,—in your persevering calumnies against which you show that the charges are true in you, which you falsely propagate against the world.

33. Further, even if we should desire to prove you to be slayers of the prophets, it would be too long a task to collect the evidence through all the several instances of the slaughter which your infuriated leaders of the Circumcelliones, and the actual crowd of men inflamed by wine and madness, not only have committed since the beginning of your schism, but even continue to commit at the present time. To take the case nearest at hand. Let the divine utterances be produced, which are commonly in the hands of both of us. Let us consider those to be murderers of the prophets whom we find contradicting the words of the prophets. What more learned definition could be given? What could admit of speedier proof? You would be acting less cruelly in piercing the bodies of the prophets with a sword, than in endeavoring to destroy the words of the prophets with your tongue. The prophet says, "All the ends of the world shall remember and turn unto the Lord."[1] Behold and see how this is being done, how it is being fulfilled. But you not only close your ears in disbelief against what is said, but you even thrust out your tongues in madness to speak against what is already being done. Abraham heard the promise, "In thy seed shall all the nations of the earth be blessed,"[2] and "he believed, and it was counted unto him for righteousness."[3] You see the fact accomplished, and you cry out against it; and you will not that it should be counted unto you for unrighteousness, as it fairly would be counted, even if your refusal to believe was not on the accomplishment, but only on the utterance of the prophecy. Nay, not only are you not willing that it should be counted unto you for unrighteousness, but even what you suffer as the punishment of this impiety you would fain have counted unto you for righteousness. Or if your conduct is not a persecution of the prophets, because your instrument is not the sword but the tongue, what was the reason of its being said under divine inspiration, "The sons of men, whose teeth are spears and arrows, and their tongue a sharp sword"?[4] But what time would suffice me to collect from all the prophets all the testimonies to the Church dispersed throughout the world, all of which you endeavor to destroy and render nought by contradicting them? But you are caught; for "their sound is gone out into all lands, and their words to the end of the world."[5] I will, however, advance this one saying from the mouth of the Lord, who is the Witness of witnesses: "All things must be fulfilled," He says, "which were written in the law of Moses, and in the prophets, and in the Psalms, concerning me." And what these were let us hear from Himself: "Then opened He their understanding, that they might understand the Scriptures, and said unto them, Thus it is written, and thus it behoved Christ to suffer, and to rise from the dead the third day: and that repentance and remission of sins should be preached in His name among all nations, beginning at Jerusalem."[6] See what it is that is written in the law of Moses, and in the prophets, and in the Psalms, concerning the Lord. See what the Lord Himself revealed about Himself and about the Church, making Himself manifest, uttering promises about the Church. But for you, see that you resist such manifest proofs as these, and as you cannot destroy them, endeavor to pervert them, what would you do, if you were to come across the bodies of the prophets, when you rage so madly against the utterances of the prophets, as not even to hearken to the Lord when He is fulfilling, and making manifest, and expounding the prophets? For do you not, to the utmost of your power, strive to slay the Lord Himself, since even to Himself you will not yield?

CHAP. 15.—34. PETILIANUS said: "David also spoke of you as persecutors in the following terms: 'Their throat is an open sepulchre; with their tongues have they deceived; the poison of asps is under their lips. Their mouth is full of cursing and bitterness; their feet are swift to shed blood. Destruction and unhappiness is in their ways, and the way of peace have they not known: there is no fear of God before their eyes. Have all the workers of wickedness no knowledge, who eat up my people as they eat bread?'"[7]

35. AUGUSTIN answered: Their throat is an open sepulchre, whence they breathe out death by lies. For "the mouth that belieth slayeth the soul."[8] But if nothing is more true than that which Christ said, that His Church should be throughout all nations, beginning at Jerusalem, then there is nothing more false than that which you say, that it is in the party of Donatus. But the tongues

1 Ps. xxii. 27.
2 Gen. xxii. 18.
3 Rom. iv. 3.
4 Ps. lvii. 4.
5 Ps. xix. 4.
6 Luke xxiv. 44-47.
7 Ps. xiv. 5-8, cp. LXX. and Hieron., the last verse only being in the Hebrew.
8 Wisd. i. 11.

which have deceived are the tongues of those who, whilst they are acquainted with their own deeds, not only say that they are just men, but that they are justifiers of men, which is said of One only "that justifieth the ungodly,"[1] and that because "He is just and the justifier."[2] As regards the poison of asps, and the mouth full of cursing and bitterness, we have said enough already. But you have yourselves said that the followers of Maximianus had feet swift to shed blood, as is testified by the sentence of your plenary Council, so often quoted in the records of the proconsular province and of the state. But they, so far as we hear, never killed any one in the body. You evidently, therefore, understood that the blood of the soul was shed in spiritual murder by the sword of schism, which you condemned in Maximianus. See then if your feet are not swift to shed blood, when you cut off men from the unity of the whole world, if you were right in saying it of the followers of Maximianus, because they cut off some from the party of Donatus. Are we again without the knowledge of the way of peace, who study to preserve the unity of the Spirit in the bond of peace? and yet do you possess that knowledge, who resist the discourse which Christ held with His disciples after His resurrection, of so peaceful a nature that He began it with the greeting, "Peace be unto you;"[3] and that so strenuously that you are proved to be saying nothing less to Him than this, "What Thou saidst of the unity of all nations is false; what we say of the offense of all nations is true"? Who would say such things as this if they had the fear of God before their eyes? See, therefore, if in daily saying things like this you are not trying to destroy the people of God dispersed throughout the world, eating them up as it were bread.

Chap. 16.—36. Petilianus said: "The Lord Christ also warns us, saying, 'Beware of false prophets, which come unto you in sheep's clothing, but inwardly they are ravening wolves; and ye shall not know them by their fruits.'"[4]

37. Augustin answered: If I were to inquire of you by what fruits you know us to be ravening wolves, you are sure to answer by charging us with the sins of other men, and these such as were never proved against those who are said to have been guilty of them. But if you should ask of me by what fruits we know you rather to be ravening wolves, I bring against you the charge of schism, which you will deny, but which I will straightway go on to prove; for, as a matter of fact, you do not communicate with all the nations of the earth, nor with those Churches which were founded by the labor of the apostles. Hereupon you will say, "I do not communicate with *traditors* and murderers." The seed of Abraham answers you, "These are those charges which you made, which are either not true, or have no reference to me." But these I set aside for the present; do you meanwhile show me the Church. Now that voice will sound in my ears which the Lord showed was to be avoided in the false prophets who made a show of their several parties, and strove to estrange men from the Catholic Church, "Lo, here is Christ, or there." But do you think that the true sheep of Christ are so utterly destitute of sense, who are told, "Believe it not,"[5] that they will hearken to the wolf when he says, "Lo, here is Christ," and will not hearken to the Shepherd when He says, "Throughout all nations, beginning at Jerusalem?"

Chap. 17.—38. Petilianus said: "Thus, thus, thou wicked persecutor, under whatsoever cloak of righteousness thou hast concealed thyself, under whatsoever name of peace thou wagest war with kisses, under whatsoever title of unity thou endeavorest to ensnare the race of men—thou, who up to this time art cheating and deceiving, thou art the true son of the devil, showing thy parentage by thy character."

39. Augustin answered: Consider in reply that these things have been said by us against you; and that you may know to which of us they are more apppropriate, call to mind what I have said before.

Chap. 18.—40. Petilianus said: "Nor is it, after all, so strange that you assume to yourself the name of bishop without authority. This is the true custom of the devil, to choose in preference a mode of deceiving by which he usurps to himself a word of holy meaning, as the apostle declares to us: 'And no marvel,' he says: 'for Satan himself is transformed into an angel of light. Therefore it is no great thing if his ministers also be transformed as the ministers of righteousness.'[6] Nor is it therefore a marvel if you falsely call yourself a bishop. For even those fallen angels, lovers of the maidens of the world, who were corrupted by the corruption of their flesh, though, from having stripped themselves of divine excellence, they have ceased

[1] Rom. iv. 5.
[2] Rom. iii. 26.
[3] John xx. 19, 21.
[4] Matt vii. 15, 16.
[5] Matt. xxiv. 23.
[6] 2 Cor. xi. 14, 15.

to be angels, yet retain the name of angels, and always esteem themselves as angels, though, being released from the service of God, they have passed from the likeness of their character into the army of the devil, as the great God declares, 'My spirit shall not always strive with man, for that he also is flesh.'[1] To those guilty ones and to you the Lord Christ will say, 'Depart from me, ye cursed, into everlasting fire, prepared for the devil and his angels.'[2] If there were no evil angels, the devil would have no angels; of whom the apostle says, that in the judgment of the resurrection they shall be condemned by the saints: 'Know ye not,' says he, 'that we shall judge angels?'[3] If they were true angels, men would not have authority to judge the angels of God. So too those sixty apostles, who, when the twelve were left alone with the Lord Christ, departed in apostasy from the faith, are so far yet considered among wretched men to be apostles, that from them Manichæus and the rest entangle many souls in many devilish sects which they destroyed[4] that they might take them in their snares. For indeed the fallen Manichæus, if fallen he was, is not to be reckoned among those sixty, if it be that we can find his name as an apostle among the twelve, or if he was ordained by the voice of Christ when Matthias was elected into the place of the traitor Judas, or another thirteenth like Paul, who calls himself the last[5] of the apostles, expressly that any one who was later than himself might not be held to be an apostle. For these are his words: 'For I am the last of the apostles, that am not meet to be called an apostle, because I persecuted the Church of God.'[6] And do not flatter yourselves in this: he was a Jew that had done this. You too, as Gentiles, may work destruction upon us. For you carry on war without license, against whom we may not fight in turn. For you desire to live when you have murdered us; but our victory is either to escape or to be slain."

41. AUGUSTIN answered: See how you have quoted the testimony of holy Scripture, or how you have understood it, when it has no bearing at all upon the present point at issue. For all that you have brought forward was simply said to prove that there are false bishops, just as there are false angels and false apostles. Now we too know quite well that there are false angels and false apostles, and false bishops, and, as the true apostle says, false brethren also;[7] but, seeing that charges such as yours may be brought by either side against the other, what is required is a certain degree of proof, and not mere empty words. But if you would see to which of us the charge of falseness more truly applies, recall to mind what we have said before, and you will see it there set forth, that we may not become tedious to our readers by repeating the same thing over and over again. And yet how is the Church dispersed throughout the world affected either by what you may have found to say about its chaff, which is mixed with it throughout the whole world; or by what you said of Manichæus and the other devilish sects? For if the wheat is not affected by anything which is said even about the chaff which is still mingled with it, how much less are the members of Christ dispersed throughout the whole world affected by monstrosities[8] which have been so long and so openly separated from it?[9]

CHAP. 19.—42. PETILIANUS said: "The Lord Jesus Christ commands us, saying, 'When they persecute you in this city, flee ye into another; and if they persecute you in that, flee yet into a third; for verily I say unto you, ye shall not have gone over the cities of Israel, till the Son of man be come.'[10] If He gives us this warning in the case of Jews and pagans, you who call yourself a Christian ought not to imitate the dreadful deeds of the Gentiles. Or do you serve God in such wise that we should be murdered at your hands? You do err, you do err, if you are wretched enough to entertain such a belief as this. For God does not have butchers for His priests."

43. AUGUSTIN answered: To flee from one state to another from the face of persecution has not been enjoined as precept or permission on heretics or schismatics, such as you are; but it was enjoined on the preachers of the gospel, whom you resist. And this we may easily prove in this wise: you are now in your own cities, and no man persecutes you. You must therefore come forth, and give an account of your separation. For it cannot be maintained that, as the weakness of the flesh is excused when it yields before the violence of persecution, so truth also ought to yield to falsehood. Furthermore, if you are suffering persecution, why do you not retire from the cities in which you are, that you may fulfill the instructions which you quote out of the gospel? But if you are not suffering persecution, why are you unwilling to reply to us? Or if the fact be that you

1 Gen. vi. 3. 2 Matt. xxv. 41. 3 1 Cor. vi. 3.
4 "*Perdiderunt*," which the Benedictines think may be a confusion for "*perierunt*."
5 *Novissimus*. 6 1 Cor. xv. 9. 7 2 Cor. xi. 26.
8 *Portenta*.
9 Down to this point Augustin had already answered Petilianus in the First Book, as he says himself below, III. 50, 61.
10 Matt. x. 23.

are afraid lest, when you should have made reply, you then should suffer persecution, in that case how are you following the example of those preachers to whom it was said, "Behold, I send you forth as sheep in the midst of wolves?" To whom it was also further said, "Fear not them which kill the body, but are not able to kill the soul."[1] And how do you escape the charge of acting contrary to the injunction of the Apostle Peter, who says, "Be ready always to give an answer to every man that asketh you a reason of the faith and hope that is in you?"[2] And, lastly, wherefore are you ever eager to annoy the Catholic Churches by the most violent disturbances, whenever it is in your power, as is proved by innumerable instances of simple fact? But you say that you must defend your places, and that you resist with cudgels and massacres and with whatever else you can. Wherefore in such a case did you not hearken to the voice of the Lord, when He says, "But I say unto you, that ye resist not evil"?[3] Or, allowing that it is possible that in some cases it should be right for violent men to be resisted by bodily force, and that it does not violate the precept which we receive from the Lord, "But I say unto you, that ye resist not evil," why may it not also be that a pious man should eject an impious man, or a just man him that is unjust, in the exercise of duly and lawfully constituted authority, from seats which are unlawfully usurped, or retained to the despite of God? For you would not say that the false prophets suffered persecution at the hands of Elijah, in the same sense that Elijah suffered persecution from the wickedest of kings?[4] Or that because the Lord was scourged by His persecutors, therefore those whom He Himself drove out of the temple with scourges are to be put in comparison with His sufferings? It remains, therefore, that we should acknowledge that there is no other question requiring solution, except whether you have been pious or impious in separating yourselves from the communion of the whole world. For if it shall be found that you have acted impiously, you would not be surprised if there should be no lack of ministers of God by whom you might be scourged, seeing that you suffer persecution not from us, but as it is written, from their own abominations.[5]

Chap. 20.—44. Petilianus said: "The Lord Christ cries again from heaven to Paul, 'Saul, Saul, why persecutest thou me? It is hard for thee to kick against the pricks.'[6] He was then called Saul, that he might afterwards receive his true name in baptism. But for you it is not hard so often to persecute Christ in the persons of His priests, though the Lord Himself cries out, 'Touch not mine anointed.'[7] Reckon up all the deaths of the saints, and so often have you murdered Christ, who lives in each of them.[8] Lastly, if you are not guilty of sacrilege, then a saint cannot be a murderer."

45. Augustin answered: Defend yourselves from the charge of the persecution which those men suffered at the hands of your party who separated themselves from you with the followers of Maximianus, and therein you will find our defence. For if you say that you committed no such deeds, we simply read to you the records of the proconsular province and the state. If you say that you were right in persecuting them, why are you unwilling to suffer the like yourselves? If you say, "But we caused no schism," then let this be inquired into, and, till it is decided whether it be so or not, let no one make accusation against persecutors. If you say that even schismatics ought not to have suffered persecution, I ask whether it is also the case that they ought not to have been driven out of the basilicas, in which they lay snares for the leading astray of the weak, even though it were done by duly constituted authorities? If you say that this also should not have been done, first restore the basilicas to the followers of Maximianus, and then discuss the point with us. If you say that it was right, then see what they ought to suffer at the hands of duly constituted authority, who, in resisting it, "resist the ordinance of God." Wherefore the apostle expressly says, "For he beareth not the sword in vain: for he is the minister of God, a revenger to execute wrath on him that doeth evil."[9] But even if this had been discovered after the truth had been searched out with all diligence, that not even after public trial ought schismatics to undergo any punishment, or be driven from the positions which they have occupied, for their treachery and deceit; and if you should say that you are vexed that the followers of Maximianus should have suffered such conduct at the hands of some of you,—why does not the wheat of the Lord cry out with the more freedom from the whole field of the Lord, that is, from the world, and say, Neither are we at all affected by what the tares and the chaff amongst us do, seeing that it is contrary to our wish? If you confess that it is sufficient to clear you of responsi-

1 Matt. x. 16, 28. 2 1 Pet. iii. 15. 3 Matt. v. 39.
4 1 Kings xviii. 5 Wisd. xii. 23. 6 Acts ix. 4, 5.
7 Ps. cv. 15. 8 *Vivacem Christum.* 9 Rom. xiii. 2, 4.

bility, that all the evil that is done by men of your party is done in opposition to your wishes, why then have you separated yourselves? For if your reason for not separating from the unrighteous among the party of Donatus is that each man bears his own burden, why have you separated yourselves from those throughout the world whom you think, or profess to think, to be unrighteous? Is it that you might all share equally in bearing the burden of schism?

46. And when we ask of you which of your party you can prove to have been slain by us, I indeed can remember no law issued by the emperors to the effect that you should be put to death. Those indeed whose deaths you quote most frequently to bring us into odium, Marculus and Donatus, present a great question,—whether they threw themselves down a precipice, as your teaching does not hesitate to encourage by examples of daily occurrence, or whether they were thrown down by the true command of some authority. For if it is a thing incredible that the leaders of the Circumcelliones should have wrought upon themselves a death in accordance with their custom, how much more incredible it is that the Roman authorities should have been able to condemn them to a punishment at variance with custom! Accordingly, in considering this matter, which you think excessive in its hatefulness, supposing what you say is true, what is there in it which bears upon the Lord's wheat? Let the chaff which flew away outside accuse the chaff which yet remained within; for it is not possible that it should all be separated till the winnowing at the last day. But if what you say is false, what wonder is it if, when the chaff is carried away as it were by a light blast of dissension, it even attacks the wheat of the Lord with false accusations? Wherefore, on the consideration of all such odious accusations, the wheat of Christ, which is ordered to grow together with the tares throughout the field, that is, throughout the whole world, makes this answer to you with a free and fearless voice: If you cannot prove what you say, it has no application to any one; and if you prove it, it yet does not apply to me. The result of which is, that whosoever has separated himself from the unity of the wheat on account of the offenses chargeable against the tares, or against the chaff, is unable to defend himself from the charge of murder which is involved in the mere offense of dissension and schism, as the Scripture says, "Whoso hateth his brother is a murderer." [1]

CHAP. 21.—47. PETILIANUS said: "Accordingly, as we have said, the Lord Christ cried, 'Saul, Saul, why persecutest thou me? It is hard for thee to kick against the pricks. And he said, Who art Thou, Lord? And the Lord said, I am Christ of Nazareth, whom thou persecutest. And he, trembling and astonished, said, Lord, what wilt Thou have me to do? And the Lord said unto him, Arise, and go into the city, and it shall be told thee what thou must do.' And so presently it goes on, 'But Saul arose from the earth; and when his eyes were opened, he saw no man,' See here how blindness, coming in punishment of madness, obscures the light in the eyes of the persecutor, not to be again expelled except by baptism! Let us see, therefore, what he did in the city. 'Ananias,' it is said, 'entered into the house to Saul, and putting his hands on him, said, Brother Saul, the Lord, even Jesus, that appeared unto thee in the way as thou camest, hath sent me, that thou mightest receive thy sight, and be filled with the Holy Ghost. And immediately there fell from his eyes as it had been scales; and he received sight forthwith, and arose, and was baptized.' [2] Seeing therefore that Paul, being freed by baptism from the offense of persecution, received again his eyesight freed from guilt, why will not you, a persecutor and *traditor*, blinded by false baptism be baptized by those whom you persecute?"

48. AUGUSTIN answered: You do not prove that I, whom you wish to baptize afresh, am either a persecutor or a *traditor*. And if you prove this charge against any one, yet the persecutor and *traditor* is not to be baptized afresh, if he had been baptized already with the baptism of Christ. For the reason why it was necessary that Paul should be baptized was that he had never been washed in any baptism of the kind. Therefore what you have chosen to insert about Paul has no point of resemblance with the case which you are arguing with us. But if you had not inserted this, you would have found no place for your childish declamation, "See how blindness comes in punishment of madness, not to be again expelled except by baptism!" For with how much more force might one exclaim against you, See how blindness comes in punishment of madness, which, finding its similitude in Simon, not in Paul, is not expelled from you even when you have received baptism? For if persecutors ought to be batpized by those whom they persecute, then let Primianus be baptized by the followers of

[1] 1 John iii. 15.

[2] Acts ix. 4-18.

Maximianus, whom he persecuted with the utmost eagerness.

Chap. 22.—49. Petilianus said: "It may be urged that Christ said to His apostles, as you are constantly quoting against us, 'He that is washed needeth not save to wash his feet, but is clean every whit.' Now if you discuss those words in all their fullness, you are bound by what immediately follows. For this is what He said, in His very words: 'He that is washed needeth not save to wash his feet, but is clean every whit: and ye are clean, but not all. But this he said on account of Judas, who should betray Him; therefore said He, Ye are not all clean.'[1] Whosoever, therefore, has incurred the guilt of treason, has forfeited, like you, his baptism. Again, after that the betrayer of Christ had himself been condemned, He thus more fully confirmed His words to the eleven apostles: 'Now are ye clean through the word which I have spoken unto you. Abide in me, and I in you.'[2] And again He said to these same eleven, 'Peace I leave with you, my peace I give unto you.'[3] Seeing, then, that these things were said to the eleven apostles, when the traitor, as we have seen, had been condemned, you likewise, being *traditors*, are similarly without both peace and baptism."

50. Augustin answered: If therefore every *traditor* has forfeited his baptism, it will follow that every one who, having been baptized by you, has afterwards become a *traditor*, ought to be baptized afresh. And if you do not do this, you yourselves sufficiently prove the falseness of the saying, "Whosoever therefore has incurred the guilt of treason, has forfeited, like you, his baptism." For if he has forfeited it, let him return and receive it again; but if he returns and does not receive it, it is clear that he had not forfeited it. Again, if the reason why it was said to the apostles, "Now are ye clean," and "My peace I give unto you," was that the traitor had already left the room, then was not that supper of so great a sacrament clean and able to give peace, which He distributed to all before his going out? And if you venture to say this with your eyes closed against the truth, what can we do save exclaim the more, See how blindness comes in punishment of the madness of those who wish to be, as the apostle says, "teachers of the law, understanding neither what they say, nor whereof they affirm?"[4] And yet, unless blindness came in the way of their pertinacity, it was not a very difficult matter that you should understand and see that the Lord did not say in the presence of Judas, Ye are not yet clean, but "Now are ye clean." He added, however, "But not all," because there was one there who was not clean; yet if he had been polluting the others by his presence, it would not have been declared to them, "Now are ye clean," but, as I said before, Ye are not yet clean. But, after Judas had gone out, He said to them, "Now are ye clean," and did not add the words, But not all, because he had now departed in whose presence indeed, as had been said to them, they were already clean, but not all, because there was one there unclean. Wherefore in these words the Lord rather declared that in the one company of men receiving the same sacraments, the uncleanness of some members cannot hurt the clean. Certainly, if you think that there are among us men like Judas, you might apply to us the words, "Ye are clean, but not all." But this is not what you say; but you say that because of the presence of some who are unclean, therefore we are all unclean. This the Lord did not say to the disciples in the presence of Judas, and therefore whoever says this has not learned from the good Master what He says.

Chap. 23.—51. Petilianus said: "But if you say that we give baptism twice over, truly it is rather you who do this, who slay men who have been baptized; and this we do not say because you baptize them, but because you cause each one of them, by the act of slaying him, to be baptized in his own blood. For the baptism of water or of the Spirit is as it were doubled when the blood of the martyr is wrung from him. And so our Saviour also Himself, after being baptized in the first instance by John, declared that He must be baptized again, not this time with water nor with the Spirit, but with the baptism of blood, the cross of suffering, as it is written, 'Two disciples, the sons of Zebedee, came unto Him, saying, Lord, when thou comest into thy kingdom grant that we may sit, one on Thy right hand, and the other on Thy left hand. But Jesus said unto them, Ye ask a difficult thing: can ye drink of the cup that I drink of, and be baptized with the baptism that I am baptized with? They said unto Him, We are able. And He said unto them, Ye can indeed drink of the cup that I drink of; and with the baptism that I am baptized withal shall ye be baptized,'[5] and so forth. If these are two baptisms, you commend us by your malice,

1 John xiii. 10, 11.
2 John xv. 3, 4.
3 John xiv. 27.
4 1 Tim. i. 7.
5 Mark x. 35-39.

we must needs confess. For when you kill our bodies, then we do celebrate a second baptism; but it is that we are baptized with our baptism and with blood, like Christ. Blush, blush, ye persecutors. Ye make martyrs like unto Christ, who are sprinkled with the baptism of blood after the water of the genuine baptism."

52. AUGUSTIN answered: In the first place, we reply without delay that we do not kill you, but you kill yourselves by a true death, when you cut yourselves off from the living root of unity. In the next place, if all who are killed are baptized in their own blood, then all robbers, all unrighteous, impious, accursed men, who are put to death by the sentence of the law, are to be considered martyrs, because they are baptized in their own blood. But if only those are baptized in their own blood who are put to death for righteousness' sake, since theirs is the kingdom of heaven,[1] you have already seen that the first question is why you suffer, and only afterwards should we ask what you suffer. Why therefore do you puff out your cheeks before you have shown the righteousness of your deeds? Why does your tongue resound before your character is approved? If you have made a schism, you are impious; if you are impious, you die as one guilty of sacrilege, when you are punished for impiety; if you die as one guilty of sacrilege, how are you baptized in your blood? Or do you say, I have not made a schism? Let us then inquire into this. Why do you make an outcry before you prove your case?

53. Or do you say, Even if I am guilty of sacrilege, I ought not to be slain by you? It is one question as to the enormity of my action, which you never prove with any truth, another as to the baptism of your blood, from whence you derive your boast. For I never killed you, nor do you prove that you are killed by any one. Nor even if you were to prove it would it in any way affect me, whoever it was that killed you, whether he did it justly in virtue of power lawfully given by the Lord, or committed the crime of murder, like the chaff of the Lord's harvest, through some evil desire; just as you are in no way concerned with him who in recent times, with an intolerable tyranny, attended even by a company of soldiers, not because he feared any one, but that he might be feared by all, oppressed widows, destroyed pupils, betrayed the patrimonies of other men, annulled the marriages of other men, contrived the sale of the property of the innocent, divided the price of the property when sold with its mourning owners. I should seem to be saying all this out of the invention of my own head, if it were not sufficiently obvious of whom I speak without the mention of his name.[2] And if all this is undoubtedly true, then just as you are not concerned with this, so neither are we concerned with anything you say, even though it were true. But if that colleague of yours, being really a just and innocent man, is maligned by a lying tale, then should we also learn in no way to give credit to reports, which have been spread abroad of innocent men, as though they had delivered up the sacred books, or murdered any of their fellow-men. To this we may add, that I refer to a man who lived with you, whose birthday you were wont to celebrate with such large assemblies, with whom you joined in the kiss of peace in the sacraments, in whose hands you placed the Eucharist, to whom in turn you extended your hands to receive it from his ministering, whose ears, when they were deaf amid the groanings of all Africa, you durst not offend by free speech; for paying to whom, even indirectly, a most witty compliment, by saying that in the Count[3] he had a god for his companion, some one of your party was extolled to the skies. But you reproach us with the deeds of men with whom we never lived, whose faces we never saw, in whose lifetime we were either boys, or perhaps as yet not even born. What is the meaning, then, of your great unfairness and perversity, that you should wish to impose on us the burdens of those whom we never knew, whilst you will not bear the burdens of your friends? The divine Scriptures exclaim: "When thou sawest a thief, then thou consentedst with him." If he whom you saw did not pollute you, why do you reproach me with one whom I could not have seen? Or do you say, I did not consent with him, because his deeds were displeasing to me? But, at any rate, you went up to the altar of God with him. Come now, if you would defend yourself, make a distinction between your two positions, and say that it is one thing to consent together for sin, as the two elders consented together when they laid a plot against the chastity of Susannah, and another thing to receive the sacrament of the Lord in company with a thief, as the apostles received even that first supper in company with Judas. I am all in favor of your defense. But why do you not consider how much more easily, in the course of your

[1] Matt. v. 10.

[2] Optatus Gildonianus is the person to whom he refers.

[3] Gildo, from subservience to whom Optatus received the name Gildonianus, was "Comes Africæ." The play on the meanings of "Comes," in the expression "*quod Comitem haberet Deum*," is incapable of direct translation. Cp. 37, 88; 103, 237.

[4] Ps. l. 18.

defense, you have acquitted all the nations and boundaries of the earth, throughout which the inheritance of Christ is dispersed? For if it was possible for you to see a thief, and to share the sacraments with the thief whom you saw, and yet not to share his sin, how much less was it possible for the remotest nations of the earth to have anything in common with the sins of African *traditors* and persecutors, supposing your charges and assertions to be true, even though they held the sacraments in common with them? Or do you say, I saw in him the bishop, I did not see in him the thief? Say what you will. I allow this defense also, and in this the world is acquitted of the charges which you brought against it. For if it was permitted you to ignore the character of a man whom you knew, why is the whole world not allowed to be ignorant of those it never knew, unless, indeed, the Donatists are allowed to be ignorant of what they do not wish to know, while the nations of the earth may not be ignorant of what they cannot know?

54. Or do you say, Theft is one thing, delivery of the sacred books or persecution is another? I grant there is a difference, nor is it worth while now to show wherein that difference consists. But listen to the summary of the argument. If he could not make you a thief, because his thieving was displeasing in your sight, who can make men *traditors* or murderers to whom such treachery or murder is abhorrent? First, then, confess that you share in all the evil of Optatus, whom you knew, and even so reproach me with any evil which was found in those whom I knew not. And do not say to me, But my charges are serious, yours but trifling. You must first acknowledge them, however trifling they may be in your case, not before I on my side confess the charges against me, but before I can allow you to say these serious things about me at all. Did Optatus, whom you knew, make you a thief by being your colleague, or not? Answer me one or the other. If you say he did not, I ask why he did not,—because he was not a thief himself? or because you do not know it? or because you disapprove of it? If you say, Because he himself was not a thief, much more ought we not to believe that those with whom you reproach us were of such a character as you assert. For if we must not believe of Optatus what both Christians and pagans and Jews, ay, and what both our party and yours assert, how much less should we believe what you assert of any one? But if you say, Because you do not know it, all the nations of the earth answer you, Much more do we not know of all that you reproach us with in these men. But if you say, Because you disapproved of it, they answer you with the same voice, Although you have never proved the truth of what you say, yet acts like these are viewed by us with disapproval. But if you say, Lo, Optatus, whom I knew, made me a thief because he was my colleague, and I was in the habit of going to the altar with him when he committed those deeds; but I do not greatly heed it, because the fault was trivial, but your party made you a *traditor* and a murderer,—I answer that I do not allow that I too am made a *traditor* and a murderer by the sins of other men, just because you confess that you are made a thief by the sin of another man; for it must be remembered that you are proved a thief, not by our judgment, but by your own confession. For we say that every man must bear his own burden, as the apostle is our witness.[1] But you, of your own accord, have taken the burden of Optatus on your own shoulders, not because you committed the theft, or consented to it, but because you declared your conviction that what another did applied to you. For, as the apostle says, when speaking of food, "I know, and am persuaded by the Lord Jesus, that there is nothing unclean of itself: but to him that esteemeth anything to be unclean, to him it is unclean;"[2] by the same rule, it may be said that the sins of others cannot implicate those who disapprove of them; but if any one thinks that they affect him, then he is affected by them. Wherefore you do not convict us of being *traditors* or murderers, even though you were to prove something of the sort against those who share the sacraments with us; but the guilt of theft is fastened on you, even if you disapprove of everything that Optatus did, not in virtue of our accusation, but by your own decision. And that you may not think this a trivial fault, read what the apostle says, "Nor shall thieves inherit the kingdom of God."[3] But those who shall not inherit the kingdom of God will certainly not be on His right hand among those whom it shall be said, "Come, ye blessed of my Father, inherit the kingdom prepared for you from the foundation of the world.' If they are not there, where will they be except on the left hand? Therefore among those to whom it shall be said, "Depart from me, ye cursed, into everlasting fire, prepared for the devil and his angels."[4] In vain, therefore, do you indulge in your security, thinking it a trivial fault which separates you from the kingdom of God, and sends you into everlast-

[1] Gal. vi. 5.
[2] Rom. xiv. 14.
[3] 1 Cor. vi. 10.
[4] Matt. xxv. 34, 41.

ing fire. How much better will you do to betake yourself to true confusion, saying, Every one of us shall bear his own burden, and the winnowing fan at the last day shall separate the chaff from the wheat!

55. But it is evident that you are afraid of its being forthwith said to you, "Why then, whilst you attempt to place on some men's backs the burdens of their neighbors, have you dared to separate yourselves from the Lord's corn, dispersed throughout the world, before the winnowing at the last day?" Accordingly, you who disapprove of the deeds of your party, whilst you are taking precautions against being charged with the schism which you all have made, are involving yourselves also in their sins which you did not commit; and while the shrewd Petilianus is afraid of my being able to say that am I not such as he thinks Cæcilianus was, he is obliged to confess that he himself is such as he knows Optatus to have been. Or are you not such as the common voice of Africa proclaims him to have been? Then neither are we such as those with whom you reproach us are either suspected to have been by your mistake, or calumniously asserted to have been by your madness, or proved to have been by the truth. Much less is the wheat of the Lord in all the nations of the earth of such a character, seeing that it never heard the names of those of whom you speak. There is therefore no reason why you should perish in such sin of separation and such sacrilege of schism. And yet, if you are made to suffer for this great impiety by the judgment of God, you say that you are even baptized in your blood; so that you are not content with feeling no remorse for your division, but you must even glory in your punishment.

CHAP. 24.—56. PETILIANUS said: "But you will answer that you abide by the same declaration, 'He that is once washed needeth not save to wash his feet.'[1] Now the 'once' is once that has authority, once that is confirmed by the truth."

57. AUGUSTIN answered: Baptism in the name of the Father and of the Son and of the Holy Ghost[2] has Christ for its authority, not any man, whoever he may be; and Christ is the truth, not any man.

CHAP. 25.—58. PETILIANUS said: "For when you in your guilt perform what is false, I do not celebrate baptism twice, which you have never celebrated once."

59. AUGUSTIN answered: In the first place, you do not convict us of guilt. And if a guilty man baptizes with a false baptism, then none of those have true baptism who are baptized by men in your party, that are, I do not say openly, but even secretly guilty. For if he who gives baptism gives something that is God's, if he is already guilty in the sight of God, how can he be giving something that is God's if a guilty man cannot give true baptism? But in reality you wait till he is guilty in your sight as well, as though what he proposes to confer were something that belonged to you.

CHAP. 26.—60. PETILIANUS said: "For if you mix what is false with what is true, falsehood often imitates the truth by treading in its steps. Just in the same way a picture imitates the true man of nature, depicting with its colors the false resemblance of truth. And in the same way, too, the brilliancy of a mirror catches the countenance, so as to represent the eyes of him who gazes on it. In this way it presents to each comer his own countenance, so that the very features of the comer meet themselves in turn; and of such virtue is the falsehood of a clear mirror, that the very eyes which see themselves recognize themselves as though in some one else. And even when a shadow stands before it, it doubles the reflection, dividing its unity in great part through a falsehood. Must we then hold that anything is true, because a lying representation is given of it? But it is one thing to paint a man, another to give birth to one. For does any one represent fictitious children to a man who wishes for an heir? or would any one look for true heirs in the falsehood of a picture? Truly it is a proof of madness to fall in love with a picture, letting go one's hold of what is true."

61. AUGUSTIN answered: Are you then really not ashamed to call the baptism of Christ a lie, even when it is found in the most false of men? Far be it from any one to suppose that the wheat of the Lord, which has been commanded to grow among the tares throughout the whole field, that is, throughout the whole of this world, until the harvest, that is, until the end of the world,[3] can have perished in consequence of your evil words. Nay, even among the very tares themselves, which are commanded not to be gathered, but to be tolerated even to the end, and among the very chaff, which shall only be separated from the wheat by the winnowing at the last day,[4] does any one dare to say that any baptism is false which is given and received in

[1] John xiii. 10.
[2] Matt. xxviii. 19.
[3] Matt. xiii. 24-30, 36-43.
[4] Matt. iii. 12.

the name of the Father, and of the Son, and of the Holy Ghost? Would you say that those whom you depose from their office, whether as your colleagues or your fellow-priests, on the testimony of women whom they have seduced (since examples of this kind are not wanting anywhere), were false or true before their crime was proved against them? You will certainly answer, False. Why then were they able both to have and to give true baptism? Why did not their falseness as men corrupt in them the truth of God? Is it not most truly written, "For the Holy Spirit of discipline will flee deceit?"[1] Seeing then that the Holy Spirit fled from them, how came it that the truth of baptism was in them, except because what the Holy Spirit fled from was the falseness of man, not the truth of the sacrament? Further, if even the deceitful have the true baptism, how do they have it who possess it in truthfulness? Whence you ought to observe that it is rather your conversation which is colored with childish pigments; and accordingly, he who neglects the living Word to take pleasure in such coloring is himself loving the picture in the place of the reality.

Chap. 27.—62. Petilianus said: "It will be urged against us, that the Apostle Paul said, 'One Lord, one faith, one baptism.'[2] We profess that there is only one; for it is certain that those who declare that there are two are mad."

63. Augustin replied: These words of yours are arguments against yourselves; but in your madness you are not aware of it. For the men who say there are two baptisms are those who declare their opinion that the just and the unjust have different baptisms; whereas it belongs neither to one party nor the other, but in both of them is one, being Christ's, although they themselves are not one: and yet the baptism, which is one, the just have to salvation, the unjust to their destruction.

Chap. 28.—64. Petilianus said: "But yet, if I may be allowed the comparison, it is certain that the sun appears double to the insane, although it only be that a dark blue cloud often meets it, and its discolored surface, being struck by the brightness, while the rays of the sun are reflected from it, seems to send forth as it were rays of its own. So in the same way in the faith of baptism, it is one thing to seek for reflections, another to recognize the truth."

65. Augustin answered: What are you saying, if I may ask? When a dark blue cloud reflects the rays of the sun with which it is struck, is it only to the insane, and not to all who look on it, that there appear to be two suns? But when it appears so to the insane as such, it appears to them alone. But if I may say so without being troublesome, I would have you take care lest saying such things and talking in such a way should be itself a sign of madness. I suppose, however, that what you meant to say was this,—that the just had the truth of baptism, the unjust only its reflection. And if this be so, I venture to say that the reflection was found in that man of your party,[3] to whom not God, but a certain Count,[4] was God; but that the truth was either in you or in him who uttered the witty saying against Optatus, when he said that "in the Count he had a god for his companion."[5] And distinguish between those who were baptized by either of these, and in the one party approve the true baptism, in the others exclude the reflection, and introduce the truth.

Chap. 29.—66. Petilianus said: "But to pass rapidly through these minor points: can he be said to lay down the law who is not a magistrate of the court? or is what he lays down to be considered law, when in the character of a private person he disturbs public rights? Is it not rather the case that he not only involves himself in guilt, but is held to be a forger, and that which he composes a forgery?"

67. Augustin answered: What if your private person, whom you deem a forger, were to set forth to any one the law of the emperor? Would not the man, when he had compared it with the law of those who have the genuine law, and found it to be identically the same, lay aside all care about the source from which he had obtained it, and consider only what he had obtained? For what the forger gives is false when he gives it of his own falseness; but when something true is given by any person, even though he be a forger, yet, although the giver be not truthful, the gift is notwithstanding true.

Chap. 30.—68. Petilianus said: "Or if any one chance to recollect the chants of a priest, is he therefore to be deemed a priest, because with sacrilegious mouth he publishes the strain of a priest?"

69. Augustin answered: In this question you are speaking just as though we were at

[1] Wisd. i. 5. [2] Eph. iv. 5. [3] Optatus. [4] Gildo. [5] See above, on 23, 53.

present inquiring what constituted a true priest, not what constituted true baptism. For that a man should be a true priest, it is requisite that he should be clothed not with the sacrament alone, but with righteousness, as it is written, "Let thy priests be clothed with righteousness."[1] But if a man be a priest in virtue of the sacrament alone, as was the high priest Caiaphas, the persecutor of the one most true Priest, then even though he himself be not truthful, yet what he gives is true, if he gives not what is his own but what is God's; as it is said of Caiaphas himself, "This spake he not of himself: but being high priest that year, he prophesied."[2] And yet, to use the same simile which you employed yourself: if you were to hear even from any one that was profane the prayer of the priest couched in the words suitable to the mysteries of the gospel, can you possibly say to him, Your prayer is not true, though he himself may be not only no true priest, but not a priest at all? seeing that the Apostle Paul said that certain testimony of I know not what Cretan prophet was true, though he was not reckoned among the prophets of God; for he says, "One of themselves, even a prophet of their own, said the Cretians are always liars, evil beasts, slow bellies: this witness is true."[3] If, therefore, the apostle even himself bore witness to the testimony of some obscure prophet of a foreign race, because he found it to be true, why do not we, when we find in any one what belongs to Christ, and is true even though the man with whom it may be found be deceitful and perverse, why do not we in such a case make a distinction between the fault which is found in the man, and the truth which he has not of his own but of God's? and why do we not say, This sacrament is true, as Paul said, "This witness is true'"? Does it at all follow that we say, The man himself also is truthful, because we say, This sacrament is true? Just as I would ask whether the apostle counted that prophet among the prophets of the Lord, because he confirmed the truth of what he found to be true in him. Likewise the same apostle, when he was at Athens, perceived a certain altar among the altars of the false gods, on which was this inscription, "To the unknown God." And this testimony he made use of to build them up in Christ, to the extent of quoting the inscription in his sermon, and adding, "Whom, therefore, ye ignorantly worship, Him declare I unto you." Did he, because he found that altar among the altars of idols, or set up by sacrilegious hands, therefore condemn or reject what he found in it that was true? or did he, because of the truth which he found upon it, therefore persuade them that they ought also to follow the sacrilegious practices of the pagans? Surely he did neither of the two; but presently, when, as he judged fitting, he wished to introduce to their knowledge the Lord Himself unknown to them, but known to him, he says among other things, that "He is not far from every one of us: for in Him we live, and move, and have our being; as certain also of your own poets have said."[4] Can it be said that here also, because he found among the sacrilegious, the evidence of truth, he either approved their wickedness because of the evidence, or condemned the evidence because of their wickedness? But it is unavoidable that you should be always in the wrong, so long as you do despite to the sacraments of God because of the faults of men, or think that we take upon ourselves the sacrilege even of your schism, for the sake of the sacraments of God, to which we are unwilling to do despite in you.

CHAP. 31.—70. PETILIANUS said: "For there is no power but of God,'"[5] none in any man of power; as the Lord Jesus Christ answered Pontius Pilate, 'Thou couldest have no power at all against me, except it were given thee from above.'[6] And again, in the words of John, 'A man can receive nothing, except it be given him from heaven.'[7] Tell us, therefore, *traditor*, when you received the power of imitating the mysteries."

71. AUGUSTIN answered: Tell us rather thyself when the power of baptizing was lost by the whole world through which is dispersed the inheritance of Christ, and by all that multitude of nations in which the apostles founded the Churches. You will never be able to tell us,—not only because you have calumniated them, and do not prove them to be *traditors*, but because, even if you did prove this, yet no guilt on the part of any evil-doers, whether they be unsuspected, or deceitful, or be tolerated as the tares or as the chaff, can possibly overthrow the promises, so that all the nations of the earth should not be blessed in the seed of Abraham; in which promises you deprive them of their share when you will not have the communion of unity with all nations of the earth.

CHAP. 32.—72. PETILIANUS said: "For although there is only one baptism, yet it is consecrated in three several grades. John

[1] Ps. cxxxii. 9. [2] John xi. 51. [3] Tit. i. 12, 13.

[4] Acts xvii. 23, 27, 28. [5] Rom. xiii. 1. [6] John xix. 11. [7] John iii. 27.

gave water without the name of the Trinity, as he declared himself, saying, 'I indeed baptize you with water unto repentance: but He that cometh after me is mightier than I, whose shoes I am not worthy to bear; He shall baptize you with the Holy Ghost, and with fire.'[1] Christ gave the Holy Spirit, as it is written, 'He breathed on them, and saith unto them, Receive ye the Holy Ghost,'[2] And the Comforter Himself came on the apostles as a fire burning with rustling flames. O true divinity, which seemed to blaze, not to burn! as it is written, 'And suddenly there came a sound from heaven as of a rushing mighty wind, and it filled all the house where the apostles were sitting. And there appeared unto them cloven tongues, like as of fire, and it sat upon each of them. And they were all filled with the Holy Ghost, and began to speak with other tongues, as the Spirit gave them utterance.'[3] But you, O persecutor, have not even the water of repentance, seeing that you hold the power not of the murdered John, but of the murderer Herod. You therefore, O *traditor*, have not the Holy Spirit of Christ; for Christ did not betray others to death, but was Himself betrayed. For you, therefore, the fire in the spirit in Hades is full of life,—that fire which, surging with hungry tongues of flame, will be able to burn your limbs to all eternity without consuming them, as it is written of the punishment of the guilty in hell, 'Neither shall their fire be quenched.'"[4]

73. Augustin answered: You are the calumnious slanderer, not the truthful arguer. Will you not at length cease to make assertions of a kind which, if you do not prove them, can apply to nobody; and even if you prove them, certainly cannot apply to the unity of the whole world, which is in the saints as in the wheat of God? If we too were pleased to return calumnies for calumnies, we too might possibly be able to give vent to eloquent slanderers. We too might use the expression, "With rustling flames;" but to me an expression never sounds in any way eloquent which is inappropriate in its use. We too might say, "Surging with hungry tongues of flame;" but we do not wish that the tongues of flame in our writings, when they are read by any one in his senses, should be judged hungry for want of the sap of weightiness, or that the reader himself, while he finds in them no food of useful sentiments, should be left to suffer from the hunger of excessive emptiness. See, I declare that your Circumcelliones are burning, not with rustling but with headlong flames. If you answer, What is that to us? why do not you, when you reproach with any one whom you will, not listen in turn to our answer, We too know nothing of it? If you answer, You do not prove the fact, why may not the whole word answer you in turn, Neither do you prove it? Let us agree, therefore, if you please, that you should not charge us with the guilt of the wicked men whom you consider to belong to us, and that we should abstain from similar charges against you. So you will see, by this just agreement, confirmed and ratified, that you have no charge which you can bring against the seed of Abraham, as found in all the nations of the earth. But I find without difficulty a grievous charge to bring against you: Why have you impiously separated yourselves from the seed of Abraham, which is in all nations of the earth? Against this charge you certainly have no means whereby you may defend yourselves. For we each of us clear ourselves of the sins of other men; but this, that you do not hold communion with all the nations of the earth, which are blessed in the seed of Abraham, is a very grievous crime, of which not some but all of you are guilty.

74. And yet you know, as you prove by your quotation, that the Holy Spirit descended in such wise, that those who were then filled with it spake with divers tongues: what was the meaning of that sign and prodigy? Why then is the Holy Spirit given now in such wise, that no one to whom it is given speaks with divers tongues, except because that miracle then prefigured that all nations of the earth should believe, and that thus the gospel should be found to be in every tongue? Just as it was foretold in the psalm so long before: "There is no speech nor language where their voice is not heard." This was said with reference to those men who were destined, after receiving the Holy Spirit, to speak with every kind of tongue. But because this passage itself signified that the gospel should be found hereafter in all nations and languages, and that the body of Christ should sound forth throughout all the world in every tongue, therefore he goes on to say, "Their sound is gone out throughout all the earth, and their words to the ends of the world." Hence it is that the true Church is hidden from no one. And hence comes that which the Lord Himself says in the gospel, "A city that is set on a hill cannot be hid."[5] And therefore David continues in the same psalm, "In the sun hath He placed His tabernacle,"

---

1 Matt. iii. 11.
2 John xx. 22.
3 Acts ii. 2-4.
4 Isa. lxvi. 24.
5 Matt. v. 14.

that is, in the open light of day; as we read in the Book of Kings, "For thou didst it secretly; but I will do this thing before all Israel, and before the sun."[1] And He Himself is "as a bridegroom coming out of His chamber, and rejoiceth as a giant to run His race. His going forth is from the end of heaven:" here you have the coming of the Lord in the flesh. "And His circuit unto the ends of it:" here you have His resurrection and ascension. "And there is nothing hid from the heat thereof:"[2] here you have the coming of the Holy Spirit, whom He sent in tongues of fire, that He might make manifest the glowing heat of charity, which he certainly cannot have who does not keep the unity of the Spirit in the bond of peace with the Church, which is throughout all languages.

75. Next, however, with regard to your statement that there is indeed one baptism,[3] but that it is consecrated in three several grades, and to your having distributed the three forms of it to three persons after such fashion, that you ascribe the water to John, the Holy Spirit to the Lord Jesus Christ, and, in the third place, the fire to the Comforter sent down from above,—consider for a moment in how great an error you are involved. For you were brought to entertain such an opinion simply from the words of John: "I indeed baptize you with water: but He that cometh after me is mightier than I: He shall baptize you with the Holy Ghost, and with fire."[4] Nor were you willing to take into consideration that the three things are not attributed to three persons taken one by one,—water to John, the Holy Spirit to Christ, fire to the Comforter,—but that the three should rather be referred to two persons—one of them to John, the other two to our Lord. For neither is it said, I indeed baptize you with water: but He that cometh after me is mightier than I, whose shoes I am not worthy to bear: He shall baptize you with the Holy Ghost: and the Comforter, who is to come after Him, He shall baptize you with fire; but "I indeed," He says, "with water: but He that cometh after me with the Holy Ghost, and with fire." One he attributes to himself, two to Him that cometh after him. You see, therefore, how you have been deceived in the number. Listen further. You said that there was one baptism consecrated in three stages—water, the Holy Spirit, and fire; and you assigned three persons to the three stages severally—John to the water, Christ to the Spirit, the Comforter to the fire. If, therefore, the water of John bears reference to the same baptism which is commended as being one, it was not right that those should have been baptized a second time by the command of the Apostle Paul whom he found to have been baptized by John. For they already had water, belonging, as you say, to the same baptism; so that it remained that they should receive the Holy Spirit and fire, because these were wanting in the baptism of John, that their baptism might be completed, being consecrated, as you assert, in three stages. But since they were ordered to be baptized by the authority of an apostle, it is sufficiently made manifest that that water with which John baptized had no reference to the baptism of Christ, but belonged to another dispensation suited to the exigencies of the times.

76. Lastly, when you wished to prove that the Holy Spirit was given by Christ, and had brought forward as a proof from the gospel, that Jesus on rising from the dead breathed into the face of His disciples, saying, "Receive ye the Holy Ghost;"[5] and when you wished to prove that that last fire which was named in connection with baptism was found in the tongues of fire which were displayed on the coming of the Holy Ghost, how came it into your head to say, "And the Comforter Himself came upon the apostles as a fire burning with rustling flames," as though there were one Holy Spirit whom He gave by breathing on the face of His disciples, and another who, after His ascension, came on the apostles? Are we to suppose, therefore, that there are two Holy Spirits? Who will be found so utterly mad as to assert this? Christ therefore Himself gave the same Holy Spirit, whether by breathing on the face of the disciples, or by sending Him down from heaven on the day of Pentecost, with undoubted commendation of His holy sacrament. Accordingly it was not that Christ gave the Holy Spirit, and the Comforter gave the fire, that the saying might be fulfilled, "With the Holy Spirit, and with fire;" but the same Christ Himself gave the Holy Spirit in both cases, making it manifest while He was yet on earth by His breathing, and when He was ascended into heaven by the tongues of flame. For that you may know that the words of John, "He shall baptize you with the Holy Ghost," were not fulfilled at the time when He breathed on His disciples' face, so that they should require to be baptized, when the Comforter should come, not with the Spirit any longer, but with fire, I would have you remember the most outspoken words of Scripture, and see what the Lord Himself said to

1 2 Sam. xii. 12.
2 Ps. xix. 3-6, cp. Hieron.
3 Eph. iv. 5.
4 Matt. iii. 11.
5 John xx. 22.

them when He ascended into heaven: "John truly baptized you with water; but ye shall be baptized with the Holy Ghost, whom ye shall receive not many days hence at Pentecost."[1] What could be plainer than this testimony? But according to your interpretation, what He should have said was this: John verily baptized you with water; but ye were baptized with the Holy Spirit when I breathed on your faces; and next in due order shall ye be baptized with fire, which ye shall receive not many days hence;—in order that by this means the three stages should be completed, in which you say that the one baptism was consecrated. And so it proves to be the case that you are still ignorant of the meaning of the words, "He shall baptize you with the Holy Ghost, and with fire;" and you are rash enough to be williing to teach what you do not know yourselves.

Chap. 33.—77. Petilianus said: "But that I may thoroughly investigate the baptism in the name of the Trinity, the Lord Christ said to His apostles: 'Go ye, and baptize the nations, in the name of the Father, and of the Son, and of the Holy Ghost; teaching them to observe all things whatsoever I command you.'[2] Whom do you teach, *traditor?* Him whom you condemn? Whom do you teach, *traditor?* Him whom you slay? Once more, whom do you teach? Him whom you have made a murderer? How then do you baptize in the name of the Trinity? You cannot call God your Father. For when the Lord Christ said, 'Blessed are the peacemakers, for they shall be called the children of God,'[3] you who have not peace of soul cannot have God for your Father. Or how, again, can you baptize in the name of the Son, who betray that Son Himself, who do not imitate the Son of God in any of His sufferings or crosses? Or how, again, can you baptize in the name of the Holy Ghost, when the Holy Ghost came only on those apostles who were not guilty of treason? Seeing, therefore, that God is not your Father, neither are you truly born again with the water of baptism. No one of you is born perfectly. You in your impiety have neither father nor mother. Seeing, then, that you are of such a kind, ought I not to baptize you, even though you wash yourselves a thousand times, after the similitude of the Jews, who as it were baptize the flesh?"

78. Augustin answered: certainly you had proposed thoroughly to investigate the baptism in the name of the Trinity, and you had set us to listen with much attention; but following, as it would seem, what is the easiest course to you, how soon have you returned to your customary abuse! This you carry out with genuine fluency. For you set before yourself what victims you please, against whom to inveigh with whatsoever bitterness you please: in the midst of which last latitude of discourse you are driven into the greatest straits if any one does but use the little word, Prove it. For this is what is said to you by the seed of Abraham; and since in him all nations of the earth are blessed, they care but little when they are cursed by you. But yet, since you are treating of baptism, which you consider to be true when it is found in a just man, but false when it is found in the unjust, see how I too, if I were to investigate baptism in the name of the Trinity, according to your rule, might say, with great fullness, as it seems to me, that he has not God for his father who in a Count has God for his companion,[4] nor believes that any is his Christ, save him for whose sake he has endured suffering; and that he has not the Holy Ghost who burned the wretched Africa in so very different a fashion with tongues of fire. How then can they have baptism, or how can they administer it in the name of the Father, and of the Son, and of the Holy Ghost? Surely you must now perceive that baptism can exist in an unrighteous man, and be administered by an unrighteous man, and that no unrighteous baptism, but such as is just and true,—not because it belongs to the unrighteous man, but because it is of God. And herein I am uttering no calumny against you, as you never cease to do, on some pretense or other, against the whole world; and, what is even more intolerable, you do not even bring any proof about the very points on which you found your calumnies. But I know not how this can possibly be endured, because you not only bring calumnies against holy men about unrighteous men, but you even bring a charge against the holy baptism itself, which must needs be holy in any man, however unrighteous he may be, from a comparison with the infection arising from the sins of wicked men, so that you say that baptism partakes of the character of him by whom it is possessed, or administered, or received. Furthermore, if a man partakes of the character of him in whose company he approaches sacred mysteries, and if the sacraments themselves partake of the character of the men in whom they are, holy men may well be satisfied to find consolation in the thought that they only fare like holy baptism itself in hearing false accusa-

[1] Acts i. 5.
[2] Matt. xxviii. 19, 20.
[3] Matt. v. 9.
[4] See above, 23, 53.

tions from your lips. But it would be well for you to see how you are condemned out of your own mouths, if both the sober among you are counted as drunken from the infection of the drunken in your ranks, and the merciful among you become robbers from the infection of the robbers, and whatever evil is found among you in the persons of wicked men is perforce shared by those who are not wicked; and if baptism itself is unclean in all of you who are unclean, and if it is of different kinds according to the varying character of uncleanness itself, as it must be if it is perforce of the same character as the man by whom it is possessed or administered. These suppositions most undoubtedly are false, and accordingly they in no wise injure us, when you bring them forward against us without looking back upon yourselves. But they do injure you, because, when you bring them forward falsely, they do not fall on us; but since you imagine them to be true, they recoil upon yourselves.

CHAP. 34.—79. PETILIANUS said: "For if the apostles were allowed to baptize those whom John had washed with the baptism of repentance, shall it not likewise be allowed to me to baptize men guilty of sacrilege like yourselves?"

80. AUGUSTIN answered: Where then is what you said above, that there was not one baptism of John and another of Christ, but that there was one baptism, consecrated in three stages, of which three stages John gave the water, Christ the Spirit, and the Comforter the fire? Why then did the apostles repeat the water in the case of those to whom John had already administered water belonging to the one baptism which is consecrated in three stages? Surely you must see how necessary it is that every one should understand the meaning of what he is discussing.

CHAP. 35.—81. PETILIANUS said: "Nor indeed will it be possible that the Holy Spirit should be implanted in the heart of any one by the laying on of the hands of the priest, unless the water of a pure conscience has gone before to give him birth."

82. AUGUSTIN answered: In these few words of yours two errors are involved; and one of them, indeed, has no great bearing on the question which is being discussed between us, but yet it helps to convict you of want of skill. For the Holy Spirit came upon a hundred and twenty men, without the laying on of any person's hands, and again upon Cornelius the centurion and those who were with him, even before they were baptized.[1] But the second error in these words of yours entirely overthrows your whole case. For you say that the water of a pure conscience must necessarily precede to give new birth, before the Holy Spirit can follow on it. Accordingly, either all the water consecrated in the name of the Father, and of the Son, and of the Holy Ghost, is water of a pure conscience, not for the merits of those by whom it is administered, or by whom it is received, but in virtue of the stainless merits of Him who instituted this baptism; or else if only a pure conscience on the part both of the ministrant and the recipient can produce the water of a pure conscience, what do you make of those whom you find to have been baptized by men who bore a conscience stained with as yet undiscovered guilt, especially if there exist among the said baptized persons any one that should confess that he at the time when he was baptized had a bad conscience, in that he might possbily have desired to use that opportunity for the accomplishment of some sinful act? When, therefore, it shall be made clear to you that neither the man who administered baptism, nor the man who received it, had a pure conscience, will you give your judgment that he ought to be baptized afresh? You will assuredly neither say nor do anything of the sort. The purity therefore of baptism is entirely unconnected with the purity or impurity of the conscience either of the giver or the recipient. Will you therefore dare to say that the deceiver, or the robber, or the oppressor of the fatherless and widows, or the sunderer of marriages, or the betrayer, the seller, the divider of the patrimony of other men,[2] was a man of pure conscience? Or will you further dare to say that those were men of pure conscience, whom it is hard to imagine wanting in such times, men who made interest with the man I have described, that they might be baptized, not for the sake of Christ, nor for the sake of eternal life, but to conciliate earthly friendships, and to satisfy earthly desires? Further, if you do not venture to say that these were men of pure conscience, then if you find any of their number who have been baptized, give to them the water of a pure conscience, which they as yet have not received; and if you will not do this, then leave off casting in our teeth a matter which you do not understand, lest you should be forced to answer in reply to us about a matter which you know full well.

CHAP. 36.—83. PETILIANUS said: "Which

1 Acts i. 15, ii. 4, x. 44.

2 Optatus Gildonianus.

Holy Spirit certainly cannot come on you, who have not been washed even with the baptism of repentance; but the water of the *traditor*, which most truly needs to be repented of, does but work pollution."

84. Augustin answered: As a matter of fact, not only do you not prove us to be *traditors*, but neither did your fathers prove that our fathers were guilty of that sin; though, even if that had been proved, the consequence would have been that they would not be our fathers, according to your earlier assertion, seeing that we had not followed their deeds: yet neither should we on their account be severed from the companionship of unity, and from the seed of Abraham, in which all nations of the earth are blessed.[1] However, if the water of Christ be one thing, and the water of the *traditor* another, because Christ was not a *traditor*, why should not the water of Christ be one thing, and the water of a robber another, since certainly Christ was not a robber? Do you therefore baptize again after baptism by your robber, and I will baptize again after the *traditor*, who is neither mine nor yours; or, if one must believe the documents which are produced, who is both mine and yours; or, if we are to believe the communion of the whole world rather than the party of Donatus, who is not mine, but yours. But, by a better and a sounder judgment, because it is according to the words of the apostle, every one of us shall bear his own burden;[2] nor is either that robber yours, if you are not yourselves robbers; nor does any *traditor* belong to any one either of us or you, who is not himself a *traditor*. And yet we are Catholics, who, following the spirit of that judgment, do not desert the unity of the Church; but you are heretics, who, on account of charges, whether true or false, which you have brought against certain men, are unwilling to maintain Christian charity with the seed of Abraham.

Chap. 37.—85. Petilianus said: "But that the truth of this may be made manifest from the apostles, we are taught by their actions, as it is written: 'It came to pass that while Apollos was at Corinth, Paul, having passed through the upper coasts, came to Ephesus; and finding certain disciples, he said unto them, Have ye received the Holy Ghost since ye believed? And they said unto him, We have not so much as heard whether there be any Holy Ghost. And he said unto them, Unto what then were ye baptized? And they said, Unto John's baptism. Then said Paul, John verily baptized with the baptism of repentance, saying unto the people, that they should believe on Him which should come after him, that is, on Christ Jesus. When they heard this, they were baptized in the name of the Lord Jesus. And when Paul had laid his hands upon them, the Holy Ghost came on them; and they spake with tongues, and prophesied. And all the men were about twelve.'[3] If, therefore, they were baptized that they might receive the Holy Ghost, why do not you, if you wish to receive the Holy Ghost, take measures to obtain a true renewing, after your falsehoods? And if we do ill in urging this, why do you seek after us? or at any rate, if it is an offense, condemn Paul in the first instance; the Paul who certainly washed off what had already existed, whereas we in you give baptism which as yet does not exist. For you do not, as we have often said before, wash with a true baptism; but you bring on men an ill repute by your empty name of a false baptism."

86. Augustin answered: "We bring no accusation against Paul, who gave to men the baptism of Christ because they had not the baptism of Christ, but the baptism of John, according to their own reply; for, being asked, Unto what were ye baptized? they answered, Unto John's baptism; which has nothing to do with the baptism of Christ, and is neither a part of it nor a step towards it. Otherwise, either at that time the water of the baptism of Christ was renewed a second time, or if the baptism of Christ was then made perfect by the two waters, the baptism is less perfect which is given now, because it is not given with the water which was given at the hands of John. But either one of these opinions it is impious and sacrilegious to entertain. Therefore Paul gave the baptism of Christ to those who had not the baptism of Christ, but only the baptism of John.

87. But why the baptism of John, which is not necessary now, was necessary at that time, I have explained elsewhere; and the question has no bearing on the point at issue between us at the present time, except so far as that it may appear that the baptism of John was one thing, the baptism of Christ another,—just as that baptism was a different thing with which the apostle says that our fathers were baptized in the cloud and in the sea, when they passed through the Red Sea under the guidance of Moses.[4] For the law and the prophets up to the time of John the Baptist had sacraments which foreshadowed things to come; but the sacraments of our

1 Gen. xxii. 18. 2 Gal. vi. 5. 3 Acts xix. 1-7. 4 1 Cor. x. 1, 2.

time bear testimony that that has come already which the former sacraments foretold should come. John therefore was a foreteller of Christ nearer to Him in time than all who went before him. And because all the righteous men and prophets of former times desired to see the fulfillment of what, through the revelation of the Spirit, they foresaw would come to pass,—whence also the Lord Himself says, "That many prophets and righteous men have desired to see those things which ye see, and have not seen them; and to hear those things which ye hear, and have not heard them,"[1]—therefore it was said of John that he was more than a prophet, and that among all that were born of women there was none greater than he;[2] because to the righteous men who went before him it was only granted to foretell the coming of Christ, but to John it was given both to foretell Him in His absence and to behold His presence, so that it should be found that to him was made manifest what the others had desired. And therefore the sacrament of his baptism is still connected with the foretelling of Christ's coming, though as of something very soon to be fulfilled, seeing that up to his time there were still foretellings of the first coming of our Lord, of which coming we have now announcements, but no longer predictions. But the Lord, teaching the way of humility, condescended to make use of the sacraments which He found here in reference to the foretelling of His coming, not in order to assist the operation of His cleansing, but as an example for our piety, that so He mght show to us with what reverence we ought to receive those sacraments which bear witness that He is already come, when He did not disdain to make use of those which foreshadowed His coming in the future. And John, therefore, though the nearest to Christ in point of time, and within one year of the same age with Him, yet, while he was baptizing, went before the way of Christ who was still to come; for which reason it was said of him, "Behold, I send my messenger before Thy face, which shall prepare Thy way before Thee."[3] And he himself preached, saying, "There cometh one mightier than I after me."[4] In like manner, therefore, the circumcision on the eighth day, which was given to the patriarchs, foretold our justification, to the putting away of carnal lusts through the resurrection of our Lord, which took place after the seventh day, which is the Sabbath-day, on the eighth, that is, the Lord's day, which fell on the third day after His burial; yet the infant Christ received the same circumcision of the flesh, with its prophetic signification. And as the Passover, which was celebrated by the Jews with the slaying of a lamb, prefigured the passion of our Lord and His departure from this world to the Father, yet the same Lord celebrated the same Passover with His disciples, when they reminded Him of it, saying, Where wilt Thou that we prepare for Thee to eat the Passover?[5] so too He Himself also received the baptism of John, which formed a part of the latest foretelling of His coming. But as the Jews' circumcision of the flesh is one thing, and the ceremony which we observe on the eighth day after persons are baptized is another;[6] and the Passover which the Jews still celebrate with the slaying of a lamb is one thing,[7] and that which we receive in the body and blood of our Lord is another,—so the baptism of John was one thing, the baptism of Christ is another. For by the former series of rites the latter were foretold as destined to arrive; by these latter the others are declared to be fulfilled. And even though Christ received the others, yet are they not necessary for us, who have received the Lord Himself who was foretold in them. But when the coming of our Lord was as yet recent, it was necessary for any one who had received the former that he should be imbued with the latter also; but it was wholly needless that any one who had been so imbued should be compelled to go back to the former rites.

88. Wherefore do not seek to raise confusion out of the baptism of John, the source and intention of which was either such as I have here set forth; or if any other better explanation of it can be given, this much still is clear, that the baptism of John and the baptism of Christ are two distinct and separate things, and that the former was expressly called the baptism of John, as is clear both from the answer of those men whose case you quoted, and from the words of our Lord Himself, when he says, "The baptism of John, whence was it? from heaven, or of men?"[8] But the latter is never called the baptism of Cæcilianus, or of Donatus, or of Augustin, or of Petilianus, but the baptism of Christ. For if you think that we are shameless, because we will not allow that any one should be bap-

1 Matt. xiii. 17.
2 Matt. xi. 9, 11.
3 Mark i. 2; cp. Mal. iii. 1.
4 Mark i. 7.
5 Matt. xxvi. 17.
6 In his treatise on the Sermon on the Mount, Book I. iv. 12, Augustin again compares the "*celebratio octavarum feriarum quas in regeneratione novi hominis celebramus*" with the circumcision on the eighth day; and in *Serm.* 376, c. ii. 2, he says that the heads of the infants were uncovered on the eighth day, as a token of liberty. Cp. Bingham, *Orig. Sacr.* XII. iv. 3.
7 Augustin apparently supposed that the sacrifice of the paschal lamb was still observed among the Jews of the dispersion; cp. *Retract.* I. x. 2. It was, however, forbidden them to sacrifice the Passover except in the place which the Lord should choose to place His name there; and hence the Jews, though they observe the other paschal solemnities, abstain from the sacrifice of the lamb.
8 Matt. xxi. 25.

tized after baptism from us, although we see that men were baptized again who had received the baptism of John, who certainly is incomparably greater than ourselves, will you maintain that John and Optatus were of equal dignity? The thing appears ridiculous. And yet I fancy that you do not hold them to be equals, but consider Optatus the greater of the two. For the apostle baptized after baptism by John: you venture to baptize no one after baptism by Optatus. Was it because Optatus was in unity with you? I know not with what heart a theory like this can be maintained, if the friend of the Count,[1] who had in the Count a god for his companion, is said to have been in unity, and the friend of the Bridegroom to have been excluded from it. But if John was preeminently in unity, and far more excellent and greater than all of us and all of you, and yet the Apostle Paul baptized after him, why do you then not baptize after Optatus? Unless indeed it be that your blindness brings you into such a strait that you should say that Optatus had the power of giving the Holy Spirit, and that John had not! And if you do not say this, for fear of being ridiculed for your madness even by the insane themselves, what answer will you be able to make when you are asked why men should have required to be baptized after receiving baptism from John, while no one needs to be baptized after receiving it from Optatus, unless it be that the former were baptized with the baptism of John, while, whenever any one is baptized with the baptism of Christ, whether he be baptized by Paul or by Optatus, there is no difference in the nature of his baptism, though there is so great a difference between Paul and Optatus? Return then, O ye transgressors, to a right mind,[2] and do not seek to weigh the sacraments of God by considerations of the characters and deeds of men. For the sacraments are holy through Him to whom they belong; but when taken in hand worthily, they bring reward, when unworthily, judgment. And although the men are not one who take in hand the sacrament of God worthily or unworthily, yet that which is taken in hand, whether worthily or unworthily, is the same; so that it does not become better or worse in itself, but only turns to the life or death of those who handle it in either case. And in respect of what you said, that "in those whom Paul baptized after they had received the baptism of John, he washed off what had already existed," you certainly would not have said it had you taken a moment to consider what you were saying. For if the baptism of John required washing off, it must, beyond all doubt, have had some foulness in it. Why then should I press you further? Recollect or read, and see whence John received it, so shall you see against whom you have uttered that blasphemy; and when you have discovered this, your heart will surely be beaten, if a rein be not set on your tongue.

89. To come next to what you think you say against us with so much point: "If we do ill in urging this, why do you seek after us?" cannot you even yet call to mind that only those are sought after who have perished? Or is the incapacity for seeing this an element in your ruin? For the sheep might say to the shepherd with equal absurdity, If I do wrong in straying from the flock, why do you search after me? not understanding that the very reason why it is being sought is because it thinks there is no need for seeking it. But who is there that seeks for you, either through His Scriptures, or by catholic and conciliatory voices, or by the scourgings of temporal afflictions, save only Him who dispenses that mercy to you in all things? We therefore seek you that we may find you; for we love you that you should have life, with the same intensity with which we hate your error, that it might be destroyed which seeks to ruin you, so long as it is not itself involved in your destruction. And would to God that we might seek you in such a manner as even to find, and be able to say with rejoicing of each one of you, "He was dead, and is alive again; he was lost, and is found!"[3]

Chap. 38.—90. Petilianus said: "If you declare that you hold the Catholic Church, the word 'catholic' is merely the Greek equivalent for entire or whole. But it is clear that you are not in the whole, because you have gone aside into the part."

91. Augustin answered: I too indeed have attained to a very slight knowledge of the Greek language, scarcely to be called knowledge at all, yet I am not shameless in saying that I know that ὅλον means not "one," but "the whole;" and that καθ' ὅλον means "according to the whole:" whence the Catholic Church received its name, according to the saying of the Lord, "It is not for you to know the times, which the Father hath put in His own power. But ye shall receive power, after that the Holy Ghost is come upon you: and ye shall be witnesses unto me both in Jerusalem, and in Judea, and in Samaria, and even in the whole earth."[4] Here you have the

---

[1] Gildo; see above, 23, 53.
[2] Isa. xlvi. 8.
[3] Luke xv. 32.
[4] Acts i. 7, 8.

origin of the name "Catholic." But you are so bent upon running with your eyes shut against the mountain which grew out of a small stone, according to the prophecy of Daniel, and filled the whole earth,[1] that you actually tell us that we have gone aside into a part, and are not in the whole among those whose communion is spread throughout the whole earth. But just in the same way as, supposing you were to say that I was Petilianus, I should not be able to find any method of refuting you unless I were to laugh at you as being in jest, or mourn over you as being mad, so in the present case I see that I have no other choice but this; and since I do not believe that you are in jest, you see what alternative remains.

CHAP. 39.—92.—PETILIANUS said: "But there is no fellowship of darkness with light, nor any fellowship of bitterness with the sweet of honey; there is no fellowship of life with death, of innocence with guilt, of water with blood; the lees have no fellowship with oi , though they are related to it as being its dregs, but everything that is reprobate will flow away. It is the very sink of iniquity; according to the saying of John, 'They went out from us, but they were not of us; for if they had been of us, they would no doubt have continued with us.'[2] There is no gold among their pollution: all that is precious has been purged away. For it is written, 'As gold is tried in the furnace, so also are the just tried by the harassing of tribulation.'[3] Cruelty is not a part of gentleness, nor religion a part of sacrilege; nor can the party of Macarius[4] in any way be part of us, because he pollutes the likeness of our rite. For the enemy's line, which fills up an enemy's name, is no part of the force to which it is opposed; but if it is truly to be called a part, it will find a suitable motto in the judgment of Solomon, 'Let their part be cut off from the earth.'"[5]

93. AUGUSTIN answered: What is it but sheer madness to utter these taunts without proving anything? You look at the tares throughout the world, and pay no heed to the wheat, although both have been bidden to grow together throughout the whole of it. You look at the seed sown by the wicked one, which shall be separated in the time of harvest,[6] and you pay no heed to the seed of Abraham, in which all nations of the earth shall be blessed.[7] Just as though you were already a purged mass, and virgin honey, and refined oil, and pure gold, or rather the very similitude of a whited wall. For, to say nothing of your other faults, do the drunken form a portion of the sober, or are the covetous reckoned among the portion of the wise? If men of gentle temper appropriate the term of light, where shall the madness of the Circumcelliones be esteemed to be, excepting in the darkness? Why then is baptism, given by men like these, held valid among you, and the same baptism of Christ not held valid, by whatsoever men it may be administered throughout the world? You see, in fact, that you are separated from the communion of the whole world in so far as this, that you are not indeed all drunk, nor all of you covetous, nor all men of violence, but that you are all heretics, and, in virtue of this, are all impious and all sacrilegious.

94. But as to your saying that the whole world that rejoices in Christian communion is the party of Macarius, who with any remnant of sanity in his brain could make such a statement? But because we say that you are of the party of Donatus, you therefore seek for a man of whose party you may say we are; and, being in a great strait, you mention the name of some obscure person, who, if he is known in Africa, is certainly unknown in any other quarter of the globe. And therefore hearken to the answer made to you by all the seed of Abraham from every corner of the earth: Of that Macarius, to whose party you assert us to belong, we know absolutely nothing. Can you reply in turn that you know nothing of Donatus? But even if we were to say that you are the party of Optatus, which of you can say that he is unacquainted with Optatus, unless in the sense that he does not know him personally, as perhaps he does not know Donatus either? But you acknowledge that you rejoice in the name of Donatus, do you also take any pleasure in the name of Optatus? What then can the name of Donatus profit you, when all of you alike are polluted by Optatus? What advantage can you derive from the sobriety of Donatus, when you are defiled by the drunkenness of the Circumcelliones? What, according to your views, are you profited by the innocence of Donatus, when you are stained by the rapacity of Optatus? For this is your mistake, that you think that the unrighteousness of a man has more power in infecting his neighbor than the righteousness of a man has in purifying those around him. Therefore, if two share

1 Dan. ii. 35.
2 1 John ii. 19.
3 Apparently from Wisd. iii. 6.
4 Macarius acted as imperial commissioner with Paulus, c. 348, to settle the disputes between Donatists and Catholics, but only to the further exasperation of the former, who accused him of intrusion and murder, and thereafter called their opponents Macarians.
5 Prov. ii. 22.
6 Matt. xiii. 24-30.
7 Gen. xxii. 18.

in common the sacraments of God, the one a just man, the other an unrighteous one, but so that neither the former should imitate the unrighteousness of the latter, nor the latter the righteousness of the former, you say that the result is not that both are made just, but that both are made unrighteous; so that also that holy thing, which both receive in common, becomes unclean and loses its original holiness. When does unrighteousness find for herself such advocates as these, through whose madness she is esteemed victorious? How comes it then that, in the midst of such mistaken perversity, you congratulate yourselves upon the name of Donatus, when it shows not that Petilianus deserves to be what Donatus is, but that Donatus is compelled to be what Optatus is? But let the house of Israel say, "God is my portion for ever;"[1] let the seed of Abraham say in all nations, "The Lord is the portion of mine inheritance."[2] For they know how to speak through the gospel of the glory of the blessed God. For you, too, through the sacrament which is in you, like Caiaphas the persecutor of the Lord, prophesy without being aware of it.[3] For what in Greek is expressed by the word *Μακάριος* is in our language simply "Blessed;" and in this way certainly we are of the party of Macarius, the Blessed One. For what is more blessed than Christ, of whose party we are, after whom all the ends of the earth are called, and to whom they all are turned, and in whose sight all the countries of the nations worship? Therefore the party of this Macarius, that is to say, of this Blessed One, feels no apprehension at your last curse, distorted from the words of Solomon, lest it should perish from the earth. For what is said by him of the impious you endeavor to apply to the inheritance of Christ, and you strive to prove that this has been achieved with inexpressible impiety; for when he was speaking of the impious, he says, "Let their portion perish from off the earth."[4] But when you say, with reference to the words of Scripture, "I shall give Thee the heathen for Thine inheritance,"[5] and '" all the ends of the world shall remember and turn unto the Lord,"[6] that the promise contained in them has already perished from the earth, you are seeking to turn against the inheritance of Christ what was foretold about the lot of the impious; but so long as the inheritance of Christ endures and increases, you are perishing in saying such things. For you are not in every case prophesying through the sacrament of God, since in this case you are merely uttering evil wishes through your own madness. But the prophecy of the true prophets is more powerful than the evil speaking of the false prophets.

Chap. 40.—95. Petilianus said: "Paul the apostle also bids us, 'Be ye not unequally yoked with unbelievers: for what fellowship hath righteousness with unrighteousness? and what communion hath light with darkness? and what concord hath Christ with Belial? or what part hath he that believeth with an infidel?'"[7]

96. Augustin answered: I recognize the words of the apostle; but how they can help you I cannot see at all. For which of us says that there is any fellowship between righteousness and unrighteousness, even though the righteous and the unrighteous, as in the case of Judas and Peter, should be alike partakers of the sacraments? For from one and the same holy thing Judas received judgment to himself and Peter salvation, just as you received the sacrament with Optatus, and, if you were unlike him, were not therefore partakers in his robberies. Or is robbery not unrighteousness? Who would be mad enough to assert that? What fellowship was there, then, on the part of your righteousness with his unrighteousness, when you approached together to the same altar?

Chap. 41.—97. Petilianus said: "And, again, he taught us that schisms should not arise, in the following terms: 'Now this I say, that every one of you saith, I am of Paul, and I of Apollos, and I of Cephas, and I of Christ. Is Christ divided? was Paul crucified for you? or were ye baptized in the name of Paul?'"[8]

98. Augustin answered. Remember all of you who read this, it was Petilianus who quoted these words from the apostle. For who could have believed that he would have brought forward words which tell so much for us against himself?

Chap. 42.—99. Petilianus said: "If Paul uttered these words to the unlearned and to the righteous, I say this to you who are unrighteous, Is Christ divided, that you should separate yourselves from the Church?"

100. Augustin answered: I am afraid lest any one should think that in this work of mine the writer has made a mistake, and has written the heading *Petilianus said*, when he ought to have written *Augustin answered*. But I see what your object is: you wished, as

1 Ps. lxxiii. 26. 2 Ps. xvi. 5. 3 John xi. 51. 4 Prov. ii. 22. 5 Ps. ii. 8. 6 Ps. xxii. 27.

7 2 Cor. vi. 14, 15. 8 1 Cor. i. 12, 13.

it were, to preoccupy the ground, lest we should bring those words in testimony against you. But what have you really done, except to cause them to be quoted twice? If, therefore, you are so much pleased with hearing the words which make against you, as to render it necessary that they should be repeated, hear, I pray you, these words as coming from me, Petilianus: Is Christ divided, that you should separate yourselves from the Church?

CHAP. 43.—101. PETILIANUS said: "Can it be that the traitor Judas hung himself for you, or did he imbue you with his character, that, following his deeds, you should seize on the treasures of the Church, and sell for money to the powers of this world us who are the heirs of Christ?"

102. AUGUSTIN answered: Judas did not die for us, but Christ, to whom the Church dispersed throughout the world says, "So shall I have wherewith to answer him that reproacheth me: for I trust in Thy word."[1] When, therefore, I hear the words of the Lord, saying, "Ye shall be witnesses unto me both in Jerusalem, and in all Judea, and in Samaria, and even in the whole earth,"[2] and through the voice of His prophet, "Their sound is gone out through all the earth, and their words into the ends of the world,"[3] no bodily admixture of evil ever is able to disturb me, if I know how to say, "Be surety for Thy servant for good: let not the proud oppress me."[4] I do not, therefore, concern myself about a vain calumniation when I have a substantial promise. But if you complain about matters or places appertaining to the Church, which you used once to hold, and hold no longer, then the Jews also may say that they are righteous, and reproach us with unrighteousness, because the Christians now occupy the place in which of old they impiously reigned. What then is there unfitting, if, according to a similar will of the Lord, the Catholics now hold the things which formerly the heretics used to have? For against all such men as this, that is to say, against all impious and unrighteous men, those words of the Lord have force, "The kingdom of God shall be taken from you, and be given to a nation bringing forth the fruits thereof;"[5] or is it written in vain, "The righteous shall eat of the labors of the impious"?[6] Wherefore you ought rather to be amazed that you still possess something, than that there is something which you have lost. But neither need you wonder even at this, for it is by degrees that the whitened wall falls down. Yet look back at the followers of Maximianus, see what places they possessed, and by whose agency and under whose attacks they were driven from them, and do you venture, if you can, to say that to suffer things like these is righteousness, while to do them is unrighteousness. In the first place, because you did the deed, and they suffered them; and secondly, because, according to the rule of this righteousness, you are found to be inferior. For they were driven from the ancient palaces by Catholic emperors acting through judges, while you are not even driven forth by the mandates of the emperors themselves from the basilicas of unity. For what reason is this, save that you are of less merit, not only than the rest of your colleagues, but even than those very men whom you assuredly condemned as guilty of sacrilege by the mouth of your plenary Council?

CHAP. 44.—103. PETILIANUS said: "For we, as it is written, when we are baptized, put on Christ who was betrayed;[7] you, when you are infected, put on Judas the betrayer."

104. AUGUSTIN answered: I also might say, You when you are infected put on Optatus the betrayer, the robber, the oppressor, the separater of husband and wife; but far be it from me that the desire of returning an evil word should provoke me into any falsehood: for neither do you put on Optatus, nor we Judas. Therefore, if each one who comes to us shall answer to our questions that he has been baptized in the name of Optatus, he shall be baptized in the name of Christ; and if you baptized any that came from us and said that they had been baptized in the name of the traitor Judas, in that case we have no fault to find with what you have done. But if they had been baptized in the name of Christ, do you not see what an error you commit in thinking that the sacraments of God can undergo change through any changeableness of human sins, or be polluted by defilement in the life of any man?

CHAP. 45.—105. PETILIANUS said: "But if these are the parties, the name of member of a party is no prejudice against us. For there are two ways, the one narrow, in which we walk; the other is for the impious, wherein they shall perish. And yet, though the designations be alike, there is a great difference in the reality, that the way of righteousness should not be defiled by fellowship in a name."

106. AUGUSTIN answered: You have been

[1] Ps. cxix. 42. [2] Acts i. 8. [3] Ps. xix. 4.
[4] Ps. cxix. 122. [5] Matt. xxi. 43. [6] Ps. cv. 44.

[7] Gal. iii. 27.

afraid of the comparison of your numbers with the multitude throughout the world; and therefore, in order to win praise for the scantiness of your party, you have sought to bring in the comparison of yourself walking in the narrow path. Would to God that you had betaken yourself not to its praise, but to the path itself! Truly you would have seen that there was the same scantiness in the Church of all nations; but that the righteous are said to be few in comparison with the multitude of the unrighteous, just as, in comparison with the chaff, there may be said to be few grains of corn in the most abundant crop, and yet these very grains of themselves, when brought into a heap, fill the barn. For the followers of Maximianus themselves will surpass you in this scantiness of number, if you think that righteousness consists in this, as well as in the persecution involved in the loss of places which they held.

Chap. 46.—107. Petilianus said: "In the first Psalm David separates the blessed from the impious, not indeed making them into parties, but excluding all the impious from holiness. 'Blessed is the man that walketh not in the counsel of the ungodly, nor standeth in the way of sinners.' Let him who had strayed from the path of righteousness, so that he should perish, return to it again. 'Nor sitteth in the seat of the scornful.'[1] When he gives this warning, O ye miserable men, why do you sit in that seat? 'But his delight is in the law of the Lord; and in His law doth he meditate day and night. And he shall be like a tree planted by the rivers of water, that bringeth forth his fruit in his season: his leaf also shall not wither; and whatsoever he doeth shall prosper. The ungodly are not so: but are like the chaff which the wind driveth away.' He blindeth their eyes, so that they should not see. 'Therefore the ungodly shall not stand in the judgment, nor sinners in the congregation of the righteous. For the Lord knoweth the way of the righteous: but the way of the ungodly shall perish.'"[2]

108. Augustin answered: Who is there in the Scriptures that would not distinguish between these two classes of men? But you slanderously charge the corn with the offenses of the chaff; and being yourselves mere chaff, you boast yourselves to be the only corn. But the true prophets declare that both these classes have been mingled together throughout the whole world, that is, throughout the whole corn-field of the Lord, until the winnowing which is to take place on the day of judgment. But I advise you to read that first Psalm in the Greek version, and then you will not venture to reproach the whole world with being of the party of Macarius; because you will perhaps come to understand of what Macarius there is a party among all the saints, who throughout all nations are blessed in the seed of Abraham. For what stands in our language as "Blessed is the man," is in Greek *Μακάριος ἀνήρ*. But that Macarius who offends you, if he is a bad man, neither belongs to this division, nor is to its prejudice. But if he is a good man, let him prove his own work, that he may have glory in himself alone, and not in another.[3]

Chap. 47.—109. Petilianus said: "But the same Psalmist has sung the praises of our baptism. 'The Lord is my shepherd, I shall not want. He maketh me to lie down in the green pastures: He leadeth me beside the still waters. He restoreth my soul: He leadeth me in the paths of righteousness for His name's sake. Yea, though I walk through the valley of the shadow of death,'—though the persecutor, he means, should slay me,—'I will fear no evil: for Thou art with me; Thy rod and Thy staff comfort me.' It was by this that it conquered Goliath, being armed with the anointing oil. 'Thou hast prepared a table before me in the presence of mine enemies: Thou anointest my head with oil; my cup runneth over. Surely goodness and mercy shall follow me all the days of my life; and I will dwell in the house of the Lord for ever.'"[4]

110. Augustin answered: This psalm speaks of those who receive baptism aright, and use as holy what is so holy. For those words have no reference even to Simon Magus, who yet received the same holy baptism; and because he would not use it in a holy way, he did not therefore pollute it, or show that in such cases it should be repeated. But since you have made mention of Goliath, listen to the psalm which treats of Goliath himself, and see that he is portrayed in a new song; for there it is said, "I will sing a new song unto Thee, O God: upon a psaltery, and an instrument of ten strings, will I sing praise unto Thee."[5] And see whether he belongs to this song who refuses to communicate with the whole earth. For elsewhere it is said, "O sing unto the Lord a new song; sing unto the Lord, all the earth."[6] Therefore the whole earth, with whom you are not in unity,

---

[1] *Et super cathedram pestilentiæ*, cp. Hieron.
[2] Ps. i.
[3] Gal. vi. 4.
[4] Ps. xxiii.
[5] Ps. cxliv. 9.
[6] Ps. xcvi. 1.

sings the new song. And these too are the words of the whole earth, "The Lord is my shepherd, I shall not want," etc. These are not the words of the tares, though they be endured until the harvest in the same crop. They are not the words of the chaff, but of the wheat, although they are nourished by one and the same rain, and are threshed out on the same threshing-floor at the same time, till they shall be separated the one from the other by the winnowing at the last day. And yet these both assuredly have the same baptism, though they are not the same themselves. But if your party also were the Church of God, you would certainly confess that this psalm has no application to the infuriated bands of the Circumcelliones. Or if they too themselves are led through the paths of righteousness, why do you deny that they are your associates, when you are reproached with them, although, for the most part, you console yourselves for the scantiness of your section, not by the rod and staff of the Lord, but by the cudgels of the Circumcelliones, with which you think that you are safe even against the Roman laws,—to bring oneself into collision with which is surely nothing less than to walk through the valley of the shadow of death? But he with whom the Lord is, fears no evils. Surely, however, you will not venture to say that the words which are sung in this song belong even to those infuriated men, and yet you not only acknowledge, but ostentatiously set forth the fact that they have baptism. These words, therefore, are not used by any who are not refreshed by the holy water, as are all the righteous men of God; not by those who are brought to destruction by using it, as was that magician when baptized by Philip: and yet the water itself in both kinds of men is the same, and of the same degree of sanctity. These words are not used except by those who will belong to the right hand; but yet both sheep and goats feed in the same pasture under one Shepherd, until they shall be separated, that they may receive their due reward. These words are not used except by those who, like Peter, receive life from the table of the Lord, not judgment, as did Judas; and yet the supper was itself the same to both, but it was not of the same profit to both, because they were not one. These words are not used except by those who, by being anointed with the sacred oil, are blessed in spirit also, as was David; not merely consecrated in the body only, as was Saul: and yet, as they had both received the same outward sign, it was not the sacrament, but the personal merit that was different in the two cases. These words are not used except by those who, with converted heart, receive the cup of the Lord unto eternal life; not by those who eat and drink damnation to themselves, as the apostle says:[1] and yet, though they are not one, the cup which they receive is one, exerting its power on the martyrs that they should obtain a heavenly reward, not on the Circumcelliones, that they should mark precipices with death. Remember, therefore, that the characters of bad men in no wise interfere with the virtue of the sacraments, so that their holiness should either be destroyed, or even diminished; but that they injure the unrighteous men themselves, that they should have them as witnesses of their damnation, not as aids to health. For beyond all doubt you should have taken into consideration the actual concluding words of this psalm, and have understood that, on account of those who forsake the faith after they have been baptized, it cannot be said by all who receive holy baptism that "I will dwell in the house of the Lord for ever:" and yet, whether they abide in the faith, or whether they have fallen away, though they themselves are not one, their baptism is one, and though they themselves are not both holy, yet the baptism in both is holy; because even apostates, if they return, are not baptized as though they had lost the sacrament, but undergo humiliation, because they have done a despite to it which remains in them.

CHAP. 48.—111. PETILIANUS said: "Yet that you should not call yourselves holy, in the first place, I declare that no one has holiness who has not led a life of innocence."

112. AUGUSTIN answered: Show us the tribunal where you have been enthroned as judge, that the whole world should stand for trial before you, and with what eyes you have inspected and discussed, I do not say the consciences, but even the acts of all men, that you should say that the whole world has lost its innocence. He who was carried up as far as the third heaven says, "Yea, I judge not mine own self;"[2] and do you venture to pronounce sentence on the whole world, throughout which the inheritance of Christ is spread abroad? In the next place, if what you have said appears to you to be sufficiently certain, that "no one has holiness who has not led a life of innocence," I would ask you, if Saul had not the holiness of the sacrament, what was in him that David reverenced? But if he had innocence, why did he persecute the innocent? For it was on account of the sanctity

[1] 1 Cor. xi. 29.

[2] 1 Cor. iv. 3.

of his anointing that David honored him while alive, and avenged him after he was dead; and because he cut off so much as a scrap from his garment, he trembled with a panic-stricken heart. Here you see that Saul had not innocence, and yet he had holiness,—not the personal holiness of a holy life (for that no one can have without innocence), but the holiness of the sacrament of God, which is holy even in unrighteous men.

Chap. 49.—113. Petilianus said: "For, granting that you faithless ones are acquainted with the law, without any prejudice to the law itself, I may say so much as this, the devil knows it too. For in the case of righteous Job he answered the Lord God concerning the law as though he were himself righteous, as it is written, "And the Lord said unto Satan, Hast thou considered my servant Job, that there is none like him in the earth, a man without malice, a true worshipper of God, abstaining from every evil; and still he holdeth fast his integrity, although thou movedst me against him, to destroy him without cause?" And Satan answered the Lord, Skin for skin, yea, all that a man hath will he give for his life.[1] Behold he speaks in legal phrase, even when he is striving against the law. And a second time he endeavored thus to tempt the Lord Christ with his discourse, as it is written, 'The devil taketh Jesus into the holy city, and setteth Him on a pinnacle of the temple, and saith unto Him, If thou be the Son of God, cast thyself down: for it is written, He shall give His angels charge concerning thee; and in their hands they shall bear thee up, lest at any time thou dash thy foot against a stone. Jesus said unto him, It is written again, Thou shalt not tempt the Lord thy God.'[2] You know the law, I say, as did the devil, who is conquered in his endeavors, and blushes in his deeds."

114. Augustin answered: I might indeed ask of you in what law the words are written which the devil used when he was uttering calumnies against the holy man Job, if the position which I am set to prove were this, that you yourself are unacquainted with the law which you assert the devil to have known but as this is not the question at issue between us, I pass it by. But you have endeavored in such sort to prove that the devil is skilled in the law, as though we maintained that all who know the law are just. Accordingly, I do not see in what manner you are assisted by what you have chosen to quote concerning the devil,—unless, indeed, it may be that we should be thereby reminded how you imitate the devil himself. For as he brought forward the words of the law against the Author of the law, so you also out of the words of the law bring accusation against men whom you do not know, that you may resist the promises of God which are made in that very self-same law. Then I should be glad if you would tell me in whose honor do those confessors of yours achieve their martyrdom, when they throw themselves over precipices,—in honor of Christ, who thrust the devil from Him when he made a like suggestion, or rather in honor of the devil himself, who suggested such a deed to Christ? There are two especially vile and customary deaths resorted to by those who kill themselves,—hanging and the precipice. You assuredly said in the earlier part of this epistle, "The traitor hung himself: he left this death to all who are like him" This has no application whatever to us; for we refuse to reverence with the name of martyr any who have strangled themselves. With how much greater show of reason might we say against you, That master of all traitors, the devil, wished to persuade Christ to throw Himself headlong down, and was repulsed! What, therefore, must we say of those whom he persuaded with success? What, indeed, except that they are the enemies of Christ, the friends of the devil, the disciples of the seducer, the fellow-disciples of the traitor? For both have learned to kill themselves from the same master,—Judas by hanging himself, the others by throwing themselves over precipices.

Chap. 50.—115. Petilianus said: "But that we may destroy your arguments one by one, if you call yourselves by the name of priests, it was said by the Lord God, through the mouth of His prophet, 'The vengeance of the Lord is upon the false priests.'"

116. Augustin answered: Seek rather what you may say with truth, not whence you may derive abusive words; and what you may teach, not what reproaches you may cast in our teeth.

Chap. 51.—117. Petilianus said: "If you wretched men claim for yourselves a seat, as we said before, you assuredly have that one of which the prophet and psalmist David speaks as being the seat of the scornful[3] For to you it is rightly left, seeing that the holy cannot sit therein.'

118. Augustin answered: Here again you do not see that this is no kind of argument,

---

[1] Job. ii. 3, 4.

[2] Matt. iv. 5-7.

[3] Ps. i. 1.

but empty abuse. For this is what I said a little while ago, You utter the words of the law, but take no heed against whom you utter them; just as the devil uttered the words of the law, but failed to perceive to whom he uttered them. He wished to thrust down our Head, who was presently to ascend on high; but you wish to reduce to a small fraction the body of that same Head which is dispersed throughout the entire world. Certainly you yourself said a little time before that we know the law, and speak in legal terms, but blush in our deeds. Thus much indeed you say without a proof of anything; but even though you were to prove it of some men, you would not be entitled to assert it of these others. However, if all men throughout all the world were of the character which you most vainly charge them with, what has the chair done to you of the Roman Church, in which Peter sat, and which Anastasius fills to-day; or the chair of the Church of Jerusalem, in which James once sat, and in which John sits to-day, with which we are united in catholic unity, and from which you have severed yourselves by your mad fury? Why do you call the apostolic chair a seat of the scornful? If it is on account of the men whom you believe to use the words of the law without performing it, do you find that our Lord Jesus Christ was moved by the Pharisees, of whom He says, "They say, and do not," to do any despite to the seat in which they sat? Did He not commend the seat of Moses, and maintain the honor of the seat, while He convicted those that sat in it? For He says, "They sit in Moses' seat: all therefore whatsoever they bid you observe, that observe and do; but do not ye after their works: for they say, and do not."[1] If you were to think of these things, you would not, on account of men whom you calumniate, do despite to the apostolic seat, in which you have no share. But what else is conduct like yours but ignorance of what to say, combined with want of power to abstain from evil-speaking?

CHAP. 52.—119. PETILIANUS said: "If you suppose that you can offer sacrifice, God Himself thus speaks of you as most abandoned sinners: 'The wicked man,' He says, 'that sacrificeth a calf is as if he cut off a dog's neck; and he that offereth an oblation, as if he offered swine's blood.'[2] Recognize herein your sacrifice, who have already poured out human blood. And again He says, 'Their sacrifices shall be unto them as the bread of mourners; all that eat thereof shall be polluted.'"[3]

120. AUGUSTIN answered: We say that in the case of every man the sacrifice that is offered partakes of the character of him who approaches to offer it, or approaches to partake of it; and that those eat of the sacrifices of such men, who in approaching to them partake of the character of those who offer them. Therefore, if a bad man offer sacrifice to God, and a good man receive it at his hands, the sacrifice is to each man of such character as he himself has shown himself to be, since we find it also written that "unto the pure all things are pure."[4] In accordance with this true and catholic judgment, you too are free from pollution by the sacrifice of Optatus, if you disapproved of his deeds. For certainly his bread was the bread of mourners, seeing that all Africa was mourning under his iniquities. But the evil involved in the schism of all your party makes this bread of mourners common to you all. For, according to the judgment of your Council, Felicianus of Musti was a shedder of man's blood. For you said, in condemning them,[5] "Their feet are swift to shed blood."[6] See therefore what kind of sacrifice he offers whom you hold to be a priest, when you have yourselves convicted him of sacrilege. And if you think that this is in no way to your prejudice, I would ask you how the emptiness of your calumnies can be to the prejudice of the whole world?

CHAP. 53.—121. PETILIANUS said: "If you make prayer to God, or utter supplication, it profits you absolutely nothing whatsoever. For your blood-stained conscience makes your feeble prayers of no effect; because the Lord God regards purity of conscience more than the words of supplication, according to the saying of the Lord Christ, 'Not every one that saith unto me, Lord, Lord, shall enter into the kingdom of heaven; but he that doeth the will of my Father which is in heaven.'[7] The will of God unquestionably is good, for therefore we pray as follows in the holy prayer, 'Thy will be done in earth, as it is in heaven,'[8] that, as His will is good, so it may confer on us whatever may be good. You therefore do not do the will of God, because you do what is evil every day."

122. AUGUSTIN answered: If we on our side were to utter against you all that you assert against us, would not any one who heard us consider that we were rather insane litigants than Christian disputants, if he himself were in his senses? We do not, there-

1 Matt. xxiii. 2, 3. 2 Isa. lxvi. 3. 3 Hos. ix. 4.

4 Tit. i. 15. 5 In the Council of Bagai.
6 Ps. xiv. 3, cp. LXX. and Hieron. 7 Matt. vii. 21
8 Matt. vi. 10.

fore, render for railing. For it is not fitting that the servant of the Lord should strive; but he should be gentle unto all men, willing to learn, in meekness instructing those that oppose themselves.[1] If, therefore, we reproach you with those who daily do what is evil among you, we are guilty of striving unbefittingly, accusing one for the sins of another. But if we admonish you, that as you are unwilling that these things should be brought against yourselves, so you should abstain from bringing against us the sins of other men, we then in meekness are instructing you, solely in the hope that some time you will return to a better mind.

Chap. 54.—123. Petilianus said: "But if it should so happen, though whether it be so I cannot say, that you cast out devils, neither will this in you do any good; because the devils themselves yield neither to your faith nor to your merits, but are driven out in the name of the Lord Jesus Christ."

124. Augustin answered: God be thanked that you have at length confessed that the invocation of the name of Christ may be of profit for the salvation of others, even though it be invoked by sinners! Hence, therefore, you may understand that when the name of Christ is invoked, the sins of one man do not stand in the way of the salvation of another. But to determine in what manner we invoke the name of Christ, we require not your judgment, but the judgment of Christ Himself who is invoked by us; for He alone can know in what spirit He is invoked. Yet from His own words we are assured that He is invoked to their salvation by all nations, who are blessed in the seed of Abraham.

Chap. 55.—125. Petilianus said: "Even though you do very virtuous actions, and perform miraculous works, yet on account of your wickedness the Lord does not know you; even so, according to the words of the Lord Himself, 'Many will say to me in that day, Lord, Lord, have we not prophesied in Thy name? and in Thy name have cast out devils? and in Thy name done many wonderful works? And then will I profess unto them, I never knew you; depart from me, ye that work iniquity.'"[2]

126. Augustin answered: We acknowledge the word of the Lord. Hence also the apostle says, "Though I have all faith, so that I could remove mountains, and have not charity, I am nothing."[3] Here therefore we must inquire who it is that has charity: you will find that it is no one else but those who are lovers of unity. For as to the driving out of devils, and as to the working of miracles, seeing that very many do not do such things who yet belong to the kingdom of God, and very many do them who do not belong to it, neither our party nor your party have any cause for boasting, if any of them chance to have this power, since the Lord did not think it right that even the apostles, who could truly do such things both to profit and salvation, should boast in things like this, when He says to them, "In this rejoice not, that the spirits are subject unto you; but rather rejoice, because your names are written in heaven."[4] Wherefore all those things which you have advanced from the writings of the gospel I also might repeat to you, if I saw you working the powerful acts of signs and miracles; and so might you repeat them to me, if you saw me doing things of a like sort. Let us not, therefore, say one to another what may equally be said on the other side as well; and, putting aside all quibbles, since we are inquiring where the Church of Christ is to be found, let us listen to the words of Christ Himself, who redeemed it with His own blood: "Ye shall be witnesses unto me both in Jerusalem, and in all Judea, and in Samaria, and even in the whole earth."[5] You see then who it is with whom a man refuses to communicate who will not communicate with this Church, which is spread throughout all the world, if at least you hear whose words these are. For what is a greater proof of madness than to hold communion with the sacraments of the Lord, and to refuse to hold communion with the words of the Lord? Such men at any rate are likely to say, In Thy name have we eaten and drunken, and to hear the words, "I never knew you,"[6] seeing that they eat His body and drink His blood in the sacrament, and do not recognize in the gospel His members which are spread abroad throughout the earth, and therefore are not themselves counted among them in the judgment.

Chap. 56.—127. Petilianus said: "But even if, as you yourselves suppose, you are following the law of the Lord in purity, let us nevertheless consider the question of the most holy law itself in a legal form. The Apostle Paul says, 'The law is good, if a man use it lawfully.'[7] What then does the law say? 'Thou shalt not kill.' What Cain the murderer did once, you have often done, in slaying your brethren."

128. Augustin answered: We do not wish

---

[1] 2 Tim. ii. 24, 25 [2] Matt. vii. 22, 23. [3] 1 Cor. xiii. 2.

[4] Luke x. 20. [5] Acts i. 8. [6] Matt. vii. 22, 23. [7] 1 Tim. i. 8.

to be like you: for there are not wanting words which might be uttered, as you too utter these; and known also, for you do not know these; and set forth in the conduct of a life, as these are not set forth by you.

CHAP. 57.—129. PETILIANUS said: "It is written, 'Thou shalt not commit adultery.' Each one of you, even though he be chaste in his body, yet in spirit is an adulterer, because he pollutes his holiness."

130. AUGUSTIN answered: These words also might be spoken with truth against certain both of our number and of yours; but if their deeds are condemned by us and you alike, they belong to neither us nor you. But you wish that what you say against certain men, without proving it even in their especial case, should be taken just as if you had established it,—not in the case of some who have fallen away from the seed of Abraham, but in reference to all the nations of the earth who are blessed in the seed of Abraham.

CHAP. 58.—131. PETILIANUS said: "It is written, 'Thou shalt not bear false witness against thy neighbor.' When you falsely declare to the kings of this world that we hold your opinions, do you not make up a falsehood?"

132. AUGUSTIN answered: If those are not our opinions which you hold, neither were they your opinions which you received from the followers of Maximianus. But if they were therefore yours, because they were guilty of a sacrilegious schism in not communicating with the party of Donatus, take heed what ground you occupy, and with whose inheritance you refuse communion, and consider what answer you can make, not to the kings of this world, but to Christ your King. Of Him it is said, "He shall have dominion also from sea to sea, and from the river unto the ends of the earth."[1] From what river does it mean, save that where He was baptized, and where the dove descended on Him, that mighty token of charity and unity? But you refuse communion with this unity, and occupy as yet the place of unity; and you bring us into disfavor with the kings of this world in making use of the edicts of the proconsul to expel your schismatics from the place of the party of Donatus. These are not mere words flying at random through the empty void: the men are still alive, the states bear witness to the fact, the archives of the proconsuls and of the several towns are quoted in evidence of it. Let then the voice of calumny be at length silent, which would bring up against the whole earth the kings of this world, through whose proconsuls you, yourselves a fragment, would not spare the fragment which was separated from you. When then we say that you hold our opinions, we are not shown to be bearing false witness, unless you can show that we are not in the Church of Christ, which indeed you never cease alleging, but never will be able to establish; nay, in real truth, when you say this, you are bringing a charge of false witness no longer against us, but against the Lord Himself. For we are in the Church which was foretold by His own testimony, and where He bore witness to His witnesses, saying, 'Ye shall be witnesses unto me both in Jerusalem and in all Judea, and in Samaria, and even in the whole earth." But you show yourselves to be false witnesses not only from this, that you resist this truth, but also in the very trial in which you joined issue with the schism of Maximianus. For if you were acting according to the law of Christ, how much more consistently do certain Christian emperors frame ordinances in accordance with it, if even pagan proconsuls can follow its behests in passing judgment? But if you thought that even the laws of an earthly empire were to be summoned to your aid, we do not blame you for this. It is what Paul did when he bore witness before his adversaries that he was a Roman citizen.[2] But I would ask by what earthly laws it is ordained that the followers of Maximianus should be driven from their place? You will find no law whatever to this effect. But, in point of fact, you have chosen to expel them under laws which have been passed against heretics, and against yourselves among their number. You, as though by superior strength, have prevailed against the weak. Whence they, being wholly powerless, say that they are innocent, like the wolf in the power of the lion. Yet surely you could not use laws which were passed against yourselves as instruments against others, except by the aid of false witness. For if those laws are founded on truth, then do you come down from the position which you occupy; but if on falsehood, why did you use them to drive others from the Church? But how if they both are founded on truth, and could not be used by you for the expulsion of others except with the aid of falsehood? For that the judges might submit to their authority, they were willing to expel heretics from the Church, from which they ought first to have expelled yourselves; but you declared yourselves to be Catholics, that you might es-

[1] Ps. lxxii. 8.

[2] Acts xxii. 25.

cape the severity of the laws which you employed to oppress others. It is for you to determine what you appear to yourselves among yourselves; at any rate, under those laws you are not Catholics. Why then have you either made them false, if they are true, by your false witness, or made use of them, if they are false, for the oppression of others?

Chap. 59.—133. Petilianus said: "It is written, 'Thou shalt not covet anything that is thy neighbor's.'[1] You plunder what is ours, that you may have it for your own."

134. Augustin answered: All things of which unity was in possession belong to none other than ourselves, who remain in unity, not in accordance with the calumnies of men, but with the words of Christ, in whom all the nations of the whole earth are blessed. Nor do we separate ourselves from the society of the wheat, on account of the unrighteous men whom we cannot separate from the wheat of the Lord before the winnowing at the judgment; and if there are any things which you who are cut off begin already to possess, we do not, because the Lord has given to us what has been taken away from you, therefore covet our neighbors' goods, seeing that they have been made ours by the authority of Him to whom all things belong; and they are rightly ours, for you were wont to use them for purposes of schism, but we use them for the promotion of unity. Otherwise your party might reproach even the first people of God with coveting their neighbors' goods, seeing that they were driven forth before their face by the power of God, because they used the land amiss; and the Jews in turn themselves, from whom the kingdom was taken away, according to the words of the Lord, and given to a nation bringing forth the fruits thereof,[2] may bring a charge against that nation of coveting their neighbors' goods, because the Church of Christ is in possession where the persecutors of Christ were wont to reign. And, after all, when it has been said to yourselves, You are coveting the goods of other men, because you have driven out from the basilicas the followers of Maximianus, you are at a loss to find any answer that you can make.

Chap. 60.—135. Petilianus said: "Under what law, then, do you make out that you are Christians, seeing that you do what is contrary to the law?"

136. Augustin answered: You are anxious for strife, and not for argument.

Chap. 61.—137. Petilianus said: "But the Lord Christ says, 'Whosoever shall do and teach them, the same shall be called the greatest in the kingdom of heaven.' But He condemns you wretched men as follows: 'Whosoever shall break one of these commandments, he shall be called the least in the kingdom of heaven.'"

138. Augustin answered: When you happen to quote the testimony of Scripture as other than it really is, and it does not bear on the question which is at issue between us, I am not greatly concerned; but when it interferes with the matter on hand, unless it is quoted truly, then I think that you have no right to find fault if I remind you how the passage really stands. For you must be aware that the verse which you quoted is not as you quoted it, but rather thus: "Whosoever shall break one of these least commandments, and shall teach men so, he shall be called the least in the kingdom of heaven; but whosoever shall do and teach them, the same shall be called great in the kingdom of heaven." And immediately He continues, "For I say unto you, That except your righteousness shall exceed the righteousness of the scribes and Pharisees, ye shall in no case enter into the kingdom of heaven."[3] For elsewhere He shows and proves of the Pharisees that they say and do not. It is these, therefore, to whom He is referring also here, when He said, "Whosoever shall break one of these commandments, and shall teach men so,"—that is, shall teach in words what he has violated in deeds; whose righteousness He says that our righteousness must excel, in that we must both keep the commandments and teach men so. And yet not even on account of those Pharisees, with whom you compare us,—not from any motives of prudence, but from malice,—did our Lord enjoin that the seat of Moses should be deserted, which seat He doubtless meant to be a figure of His own; for He said indeed that they who sat in Moses' seat were ever saying and not doing, but warns the people to do what they say, and not to do what they do,[4] lest the chair, with all its holiness, should be deserted, and the unity of the flock divided through the faithlessness of the shepherds.

Chap. 62.—139. Petilianus said: "And again it is written, 'Every sin which a man shall sin is without the body; but he that sinneth in the Holy Spirit, it shall not be forgiven him, neither in this world, neither in the world to come.'"

[1] Ex. xx. 13-17.
[2] Matt. xxi. 43.
[3] Matt. v. 19, 20
[4] Matt. xxiii. 2, 3.

140. AUGUSTIN answered: This too is not written as you have quoted it, and see how far it has led you astray. The apostle, writing to the Corinthians, says, "Every sin that a man doeth is without the body; but he that committeth fornication sinneth against his own body."[1] But this is one thing, and that is another which the Lord said in the gospel: "All manner of sin and blasphemy shall be forgiven unto men: but whosoever speaketh against the Holy Ghost, it shall not be forgiven him, neither in this world, neither in the world to come."[2] But you have begun a sentence from the writing of the apostle, and ended it as though it were one from the gospel, which I fancy you have done not with any intention to deceive, but through mistake; for neither passage has any bearing on the matter in hand. And why you have said this, and in what sense you have said it, I am wholly unable to perceive, unless it be that, whereas you had said above that all were condemned by the Lord who had broken any one of His commandments, you have considered since how many there are in your party who break not one but many of them; and lest an objection should be brought against you on that score, you have sought, by way of surpassing the difficulty, to bring in a distinction of sins, whereby it might be seen that it is one thing to break a commandment in respect of which pardon may easily be obtained, another thing to sin against the Holy Ghost, which shall receive no forgiveness, either in this world or in the world to come. In your dread, therefore, of infection from sin, you were unwilling to pass this over in silence; and again, in your dread of a question too deep for your powers, you wish to touch cursorily on it in passing, in such a state of agitation, that, just as men who are setting about a task in haste, and consequent confusion, are wont to fasten their dress or shoes awry, so you have not thought fit either to see what belongs to what, or in what context or what sense the passage which you quote occurs. But what is the nature of that sin which shall not be forgiven, either in this world or in the world to come, you are so far from knowing, that, though you believe that we are actually living in it, you yet promise us forgiveness of it through your baptism. And yet how could this be possible, if the sin be of such a nature that it cannot be forgiven, either in this world or in the world to come?

CHAP. 63.—141. PETILIANUS said: "But wherein do you fulfill the commandments of God? The Lord Christ said, 'Blessed are the poor in spirit; for theirs is the kingdom of heaven.' But you by your malice in persecution breathe forth the riches of madness."

142. AUGUSTIN answered: Address that rather to your own Circumcelliones.

CHAP. 64.—143. PETILIANUS said: "'Blessed are the meek: for they shall inherit the earth.' You therefore, not being meek, have lost both heaven and earth alike."

144. AUGUSTIN answered: Again and again you may hear the Lord saying, "Ye shall be witnesses unto me both in Jerusalem, and in all Judea, and in Samaria, and even in the whole earth."[3] How is it, then, that those men have not lost heaven and earth, who, in order to avoid communicating with all the nations of the earth, despise the words of Him that sitteth in heaven? For, in proof of your meekness, it is not your words but the cudgels of the Circumcelliones which should be examined. You will say, What has that to do with us? Just as though we were making the remark with any other object except to extract that answer from you. For the reason that your schism is a valid charge against you is that you do not allow that you are chargeable with another's sin, whereas you have separated from us for no other reason but that you charge us with the sins of other men.

CHAP. 65.—145. PETILIANUS said: "'Blessed are they that mourn: for they shall be comforted.' You, our butchers, are the cause of mourning in others: you do not mourn yourselves."

146. AUGUSTIN answered: Consider for a short space to how many, and with what intensity, the cry of "Praises be to God," proceeding from your armed men, has caused others to mourn.[4] Do you say again, What is that to us? Then I too will rejoin again in your own words, What is that to us? What is it to all the nations of the earth? What is it to those who praise the name of the Lord from the rising of the sun to the setting of the same? What is it to all the earth, which sings a new song? What is it to the seed of Abraham, in which all the nations of the earth are blessed?[5] And so the sacrilege of

1 1 Cor. vi. 18.

2 Matt. xii. 31, 32.

3 Acts i. 8.

4 The older editions have, "*Quam multum et quantum luctum dederint Deo* (Erasmus alone *ideo*) *laudes amatorum vestrorum:*" "How much and how great grief have the praises of your lovers caused to God?" The Benedictines restored the reading translated above ("*Quam multis . . . Deo laudes armatorum vestrorum*"), *Deo laudes* being the cry of the Circumcelliones. Cp. Aug. in Ps. cxxxii. 6: "*A quibus plus timetur Deo laudes quam fremitus leonis;*" and *ib.*: "*Deo laudes vestrum plorant homines.*"

5 Gen. xxii. 18.

your schism is chargeable on you, just because the evil deeds of your companions are not chargeable on you; and because you are from this that the deeds of those on whose account you separated from the world, even if you proved your charges to be true, do not involve the world in sin.

Chap. 66.—147. Petilianus said: "'Blessed are they which do hunger and thirst after righteousness: for they shall be filled.' To you it seems to be righteousness that you thirst after our blood."

148. Augustin answered: What shall I say unto thee, O man, except that thou art calumnious? The unity of Christ, indeed, is hungering and thirsting after all of you; and I would that it might swallow you up, for then would you be no longer heretics.

Chap. 67.—149. Petilianus said: "'Blessed are the merciful: for they shall obtain mercy.' But how shall I call you merciful when you inflict punishment on the righteous? Shall I not rather call you a most unrighteous communion, so long as you pollute souls?"

150. Augustin answered: You have proved neither point,—neither that you yourselves are righteous, nor that we inflict punishment on even the unrighteous; and yet, even as false flattery is generally cruel, so just correction is ever merciful. For whence is that which you do not understand: "Let the righteous smite me, it shall be a kindness; and let him reprove me"? For while he says this of the severity of merciful correction, the Psalmist immediately went on to say of the gentleness of destructive flattery, "But the oil of sinners shall not break my head."[1] Do you therefore consider whither you are called, and from what you are summoned away. For how do you know what feelings he entertains towards you whom you suppose to be cruel? But whatever be his feelings, every one must bear his own burden both with us and with you. But I would have you cast away the burden of schism which you all of you are bearing, that you may bear your good burdens in unity; and I would bid you mercifully correct, if you should have the power, all those who are bearing evil burdens; and, if this be beyond your power, I would bid you bear with them in peace.

Chap. 68.—151. Petilianus said: "'Blessed are the pure in heart: for they shall see God.' When will you see God, who are possessed with blindness in the impure malice of your hearts?"

152. Augustin answered: Wherefore say you this? Can it be that we reproach all nations with the dark and hidden things which are declared by men, and do not choose to understand the manifest sayings which God spake in olden time of all the nations of the earth? This is indeed great blindness of heart; and if you do not recognize it in yourselves, that is even greater blindness.

Chap. 69.—153. Petilianus said: "'Blessed are the peacemakers; for they shall be called the children of God.'[2] You make a pretence of peace by your wickedness, and seek unity by war."

154. Augustin answered: We do not make a pretense of peace by wickedness, but we preach peace out of the gospel; and if you were at peace with it, you would be at peace also with us. The risen Lord, when presenting Himself to the disciples, not only that they should gaze on Him with their eyes, but also that they should handle Him with their hands, began His discourse to them with the words, "Peace be unto you." And how this peace itself was to be maintained, He disclosed to them in the words which followed. For "then opened He their understanding, that they might understand the Scriptures, and said unto them, Thus is it written, and thus it behoved Christ to suffer, and to rise from the dead the third day; and that repentance and remission of sins should be preached in His name among all nations, beginning at Jerusalem."[3] If you will keep peace with these words, you will not be at variance with us. For if we seek unity by war, our war could not be praised in more glorious terms, seeing that it is written, "Thou shalt love thy neighbor as thyself."[4] And again it is written, "No man ever yet hated his own flesh."[5] And yet the flesh lusteth against the spirit, and the spirit against the flesh.[6] But if no man ever yet hated his own flesh, and yet a man lusteth against his own flesh, here you have unity sought by war, that the body, being subject to correction, may be brought under submission. But what the spirit does against the flesh, waging war with it, not in hatred but in love, this those who are spiritual do against those who are carnal, that they may do towards them what they do towards themselves, because they love their neighbors as neighbors indeed. But the war which the spiritual wage is that correction which is in

[1] Ps. cxli. 5, LXX., cf. Hieron.

[2] Matt. v. 3-9.
[3] Luke xxiv. 36, 45-47.
[4] Matt. xxii. 39.
[5] Eph. v. 29.
[6] Gal. v. 17.

love: their sword is the word of God. To such a war they are aroused by the trumpet of the apostle sounding with a mighty force: "Preach the word; be instant in season, out of season; reprove, rebuke, exhort, with all long-suffering and doctrine."[1] See then that we act not with the sword, but with the word. But you answer what is not true, while you accuse us falsely. You do not correct your own faults, and you bring against us those of other men. Christ bears true witness concerning the nations of the earth; you, in opposition to Christ, bear false witness against the nations of the earth. If we were to believe you rather than Christ, you would call us peacemakers; because we believe Christ rather than you, we are said to make a pretense of peace by our wickedness. And while you say and do such things as this, you have the further impudence to quote the words, "Blessed are the peacemakers; for they shall be called the children of God."

CHAP. 70.—155. PETILIANUS said: "Though the Apostle Paul says, 'I therefore, the prisoner of the Lord, beseech you, brethren, that ye walk worthy of the vocation wherewith ye are called, with all lowliness and meekness, with long-suffering, forbearing one another in love; endeavoring to keep the unity of the Spirit in the bond of peace.'"[2]

156. AUGUSTIN answered: If you would not only say these words, but hearken to them as well, you would put up even with known evils for the sake of peace, instead of inventing new ones for the sake of quarreling, if it were only because you subsequently learned, for the sake of the peace of Donatus, to put up with the most flagrant and notorious wickedness of Optatus. What madness is this that you display? Those who are known are borne with, that a fragment may not be further split up; those of whom nothing is known are defamed, that they themselves may not remain in the undivided whole.

CHAP. 71.—157. PETILIANUS said: "To you the prophet says, 'Peace, peace; and where is there peace?'"[3]

158. AUGUSTIN answered: It is you that say this to us, not the prophet. We therefore answer you: If you ask where peace is to be found, open your eyes, and see of whom it is said, "He maketh wars to cease in all the world."[4] If you ask where peace is to be found, open your eyes to see that city which cannot be hidden, because it is built upon a hill; open your eyes to see the mountain itself, and let Daniel show it to you, growing out of a small stone, and filling the whole earth.[5] But when the prophet says to you, "Peace, peace; and where is there peace?" what will you show? Will you show the party of Donatus, unknown to the countless nations to whom Christ is known? It is surely not the city which cannot be hid; and whence is this, except that it is not founded on the mountain? "For He is our peace, who hath made both one,"[6]—not Donatus, who has made one into two.

CHAP. 72.—159. PETILIANUS said: "'Blessed are they which are persecuted for righteousness' sake; for theirs is the kingdom of heaven.'[7] You are not blessed; but you make martyrs to be blessed, with whose souls the heavens are filled, and the earth has flourished with their memory. You therefore do not honor them yourselves, but you provide us with objects of honor."

160. AUGUSTIN answered: The plain fact is, that if it had not been said, "Blessed are they which are persecuted for righteousness' sake," but had been said instead, Blessed are they who throw themselves over precipices, then heaven would have been filled with your martyrs. Of a truth we see many flowers on the earth blooming from their bodies; but, as the saying goes, the flower is dust and ashes.

CHAP. 73.—161. PETILIANUS said: "Since then you are not blessed by falsifying the commands of God, the Lord Christ condemns you by His divine decrees: 'Woe unto you, scribes and Pharisees, hypocrites! for ye shut up the kingdom of heaven against men: for ye neither go in yourselves, neither suffer ye them that are entering to go in. Woe unto you, scribes and Pharisees, hypocrites! for ye compass sea and land to make one proselyte; and when he is made, ye make him twofold more the child of hell than yourselves. Woe unto you, scribes and Pharisees, hypocrites! for ye pay tithe of mint, and anise, and cummin, and have omitted the weightier matters of the law, judgment, mercy, and faith: these ought ye to have done, and not to leave the other undone. Ye blind guides, which strain at a gnat, and swallow a camel. Woe unto you, scribes and Pharisees, hypocrites! for ye are like unto whited sepulchres, which indeed appear beautiful outwardly, but are within full of dead men's bones, and of all uncleanness. Even so ye also outwardly appear righteous unto men, but within ye are full of hypocrisy and iniquity.'"[8]

1 2 Tim. iv. 2.
2 Eph. iv. 1-3.
3 Jer. viii. 11.
4 Ps. xlvi. 9.
5 Dan. ii. 35.
6 Eph. ii. 14.
7 Matt. v. 10.
8 Matt. xxiii. 13, 15, 23, 24, 27, 28.

162. Augustin answered: Tell me whether you have said anything which may not equally be said against you in turn by any slanderous and evil-speaking tongue. But from what has been said by me before, any one who wishes may find out that these things may be said against you, not by way of empty abuse, but with the support of truthful testimony. As, however, the opportunity is presented to us, we must not pass this by. There is no doubt that to the ancient people of God circumcision stood in the place of baptism. I ask, therefore, putting the case that the Pharisees, against whom those words you quote are spoken, had made some proselyte, who, if he were to imitate them, would, as it is said, become twofold more the child of hell than themselves, supposing that he were to be converted, and desire to imitate Simeon, or Zacharias, or Nathanael, would it be necessary that he should be circumcised again by them? And if it is absurd to put this case, why, although in empty fashion and with empty sounds you compare us to men like this, do you nevertheless baptize after us? But if you are really men like this, how much better and how much more in accordance with truth do we act in not baptizing after you, as neither was it right that those whom I have mentioned should be circumcised after the worst of Pharisees! Furthermore, when such men sit in the seat of Moses, for which the Lord preserved its due honor, why do you blaspheme the apostolic chair on account of men whom, justly or unjustly, you compare with these?

Chap. 74.—163. Petilianus said: "But these things do not alarm us Christians; for of the evil deeds which you are destined to commit we have before a warning given us by the Lord Christ. 'Behold,' He says, 'I send you forth as sheep in the midst of wolves.'[1] You fill up the measure of the madness of wolves, who either lay or are preparing to lay snares against the Churches in precisely the same way in which wolves, with their mouths wide open against the fold, even with destructive eagerness, breathe forth panting anger from their jaws, suffused with blood."

164. Augustin answered: I should be glad to utter the same sentiment against you, but not in the words which you have used: they are too inappropriate, or rather mad. But what was required was, that you should show that we were wolves and that you were sheep, not by the emptiest of evil-speaking, but by some distinct proofs. For when I too have said, We are sheep, and you are wolves, do you think that there is any difference caused by the fact that you express the idea in swelling words? But listen whilst I prove what I assert. For the Lord says in the gospel, as you know full well, whether you please it or not, "My sheep hear my voice, and follow me."[2] There are many sayings of the Lord on different subjects; but supposing, for example, that any one were in doubt whether the same Lord had risen in the body, and His words were to be quoted where He says, "Handle me, and see; for a spirit hath not flesh and bones, as ye see me have;"—if even after this he should be unwilling to acquiesce in the belief that His body had risen from the dead, surely such a man could not be reckoned among the sheep of the Lord, because he would not hear His voice. And so too now, when the question between us is, Where is the Church? whilst we quote the words that follow in the same passage of the gospel, where, after His resurrection, He gave His body even to be handled by those who were in doubt, in which He showed the future wide extent of the Church, saying, "Thus it is written, and thus it behoved Christ to suffer, and to rise from the dead the third day; and that repentance and remission of sins should be preached in His name throughout all nations, beginning at Jerusalem;"[3] whereas you will not communicate with all nations, in whom these words have been fulfilled, how are you the sheep of this Shepherd, whose words you not only do not obey when you have heard them, but even fight against them? And so we show to you from this that you are not sheep. But listen further whence we show you that, on the contrary, you are wolves. For necessarily, when it is shown by His own words where the Church is to be found, it is also clear where we must look for the fold of Christ. Whenever, therefore, any sheep separate themselves from this fold, which is expressly pointed out and shown to us by the unmistakeable declaration of the Lord,—and that, I will not say because of charges falsely brought, but on account of charges brought, as no one can deny, with great uncertainty against their fellow-men, and consequently slay those sheep which they have torn and alienated from the life of unity and Christian love—is it not evident that they are ravening wolves? But it will be said that these very men themselves praise and preach the Lord Christ. They are therefore those of whom He says

[1] Matt. x. 16.

[2] John x. 27.

[3] Luke xxiv. 39, 46, 47.

Himself, "They come unto you in sheep's clothing, but inwardly they are ravening wolves. By their fruits ye shall know them."[1] The sheep's clothing is seen in the praises of Christ; the fruits of their wolfish nature in their slanderous teeth.

CHAP. 75.—165. PETILIANUS said: "O wretched *traditors!* Thus indeed it was fitting that Scripture should be fulfilled. But in you I grieve for this, that you have shown yourselves worthy to fulfill the part of wickedness."

166. AUGUSTIN answered: I might rather say, O wretched *traditors!* if I were minded, or rather if justice urged me to cast up against all of you the deeds of some among your number. But as regards what bears on all of you, O wretched heretics, I on my part will quote the remainder of your words; for it is written, "There must be also heresies among you, that they which are approved may be made manifest among you."[2] Therefore "it was fitting thus that Scripture should be fulfilled. But in you I grieve for this, that you have shown yourselves worthy to fulfill the part of wickedness."

CHAP. 76.—167. PETILIANUS said: "But to us the Lord Christ, in opposition to your deadly commands, commanded simple patience and harmlessness. For what says He? 'A new commandment I give unto you, That ye love one another; as I have loved you, that ye also love one another.' And again, 'By this shall all men know that ye are my disciples, if ye have love one to another.'"[3]

168. AUGUSTIN answered: If you did not transfer these words, so widely differing from your character, to the surface of your talk, how could you be covering yourselves with sheep's clothing?

CHAP. 77.—169. PETILIANUS said: "Paul also, the apostle, whilst he was suffering fearful persecutions at the hands of all nations, endured even more grievous troubles at the hands of false brethren, as he bears witness of himself, being oftentimes afflicted: 'In perils by the heathen, in perils by mine own countrymen, in perils among false brethren.'[4] And again he says, 'Be ye followers of me, even as I also am of Christ.'[5] When, therefore, false brethren like yourselves assault us, we imitate the patience of our master Paul under our dangers."

170. AUGUSTIN answered: Certainly those of whom you speak are false brethren, of whom the apostle thus complains in another place, where he is extolling the natural sincerity of Timothy: "I have no man," he says, "like-minded, who will naturally care for your state. For all seek their own, not the things which are Jesus Christ's."[6] Undoubtedly he was speaking of those who were with him at the time when he was writing that epistle; for it could not be that all Christians in every quarter of the earth were seeking their own, and not the things which were Jesus Christ's. It was of those, therefore, as I said, who were with him at the time when he was writing the words which you have quoted, that he uttered this lamentation. For who else was it to whom he referred, when he says in another place, "Without were fightings, within were fears,"[7] except those whom he feared all the more intensely because they were within? If, therefore, you would imitate Paul, you would be tolerant of false brethren within, not a slanderer of the innocent without.

CHAP. 78.—171. PETILIANUS said: "For what kind of faith is that which is in you which is devoid of charity? when Paul himself says, 'Though I speak with the tongues of men, and have the knowledge of angels, and have not charity, I am become as sounding brass, or a tinkling cymbal. And though I have the gift of prophecy, and understand all mysteries, and all knowledge; and though I have all faith, so that I could remove mountains, and have not charity, I am nothing. And though I bestow all my goods to feed the poor, and though I give my body to be burned, and have not charity, it profiteth me nothing.'"

172. AUGUSTIN answered: This is what I said just now, that you were desirous to be clad in sheep's clothing, that, if possible, the sheep might feel your bite before it had any consciousness of your approach. Is it not that praise of charity in which you indulge that commonly proves your calumny in the clearest light of truth? Will you bring it about that those arms shall be no longer ours, because you endeavor to appropriate them first? Furthermore, these arms are endowed with life: from whatever quarter they are launched, they recognize whom they should destroy. If they have been sent forth from our hands, they will fix themselves in you; if they are aimed by you, they recoil upon yourselves. For in these apostolic words, which commend the excellence of charity, we are wont to show to you how profitless it is to man that he should

[1] Matt. vii. 15, 16.
[2] 1 Cor. xi. 19.
[3] John xiii. 34, 35.
[4] 2 Cor. xi. 26.
[5] 1 Cor. xi. 1.
[6] Phil. ii. 20, 21.
[7] 2 Cor. vii. 5.

be in possession of faith or of the sacraments, when he has not charity, that, when you come to Catholic unity, you may understand what it is that is conferred on you, and how great a thing it is of which you were at least to some extent in want; for Christian charity cannot be preserved except in the unity of the Church: and that so you may see that without it you are nothing, even though you may be in possession of baptism and faith, and through this latter may be able even to remove mountains. But if this is your opinion as well, let us not repudiate and reject in you either the sacraments of God which we know, or faith itself, but let us hold fast charity, without which we are nothing even with the sacraments and with faith. But we hold fast charity if we cling to unity; while we cling to unity, if we do not make a fictitious unity in a party by our own words, but recognize it in a united whole through the words of Christ.

Chap. 79.—173. Petilianus said: "And again, 'Charity suffereth long, and is kind; charity envieth not; charity vaunteth not itself, is not puffed up, doth not behave itself unseemly, seeketh not her own.' But you seek what belongs to other men. 'Is not easily provoked, thinketh no evil; rejoiceth not in iniquity, but rejoiceth in the truth; beareth all things, endureth all things. Charity never faileth.'[1] This is to say, in short, Charity does not persecute, does not inflame emperors to take away the lives of other men; does not plunder other men's goods; does not go on to murder men whom it has spoiled."

174. Augustin answered: How often must I tell you the same thing? If you do not prove these charges, they tell against no one in the world; and if you prove them, they have no bearing upon us; just as those things have no bearing upon you which are daily done by the furious deeds of the insane, by the luxury of the drunken, by the blindness of the suicides, by the tyranny of robbers. For who can fail to see that what I say is true? But now if charity were in you, it would rejoice in the truth. For how neatly it is said under covering of the sheep's clothing, "Charity beareth all things, endureth all things!" but when you come to the test, the wolf's teeth cannot be concealed. For when, in obedience to the words of Scripture, "forbearing one another in love, endeavoring to keep the unity of the Spirit in the bond of peace,"[2] charity would compel you, even if you knew of any evils within the Church, I do not say to consent to them, but yet to tolerate them if you could not prevent them, lest, on account of the wicked who are to be separated by the winnowing-fan at the last day, you should at the present time sever the bond of peace by breaking off from the society of good men, you, resisting her influence, and being cast out by the wind of levity, charge the wheat with being chaff, and declare that what you invent of the wicked holds good through the force of contagion even in the righteous. And when the Lord has said, "The field is the world, the harvest is the end of the world," though He said of the wheat and of the tares, "Let both grow together until the harvest,"[3] you endeavor by your words to bring about a belief that the wheat has perished throughout the main portion of the field, and only continued to exist in your little corner,—being desirous that Christ should be proved a liar, but you the man of truth. And you speak, indeed, against your own conscience; for no one who in any way looks truly at the gospel will venture in his heart to say that in all the many nations throughout which is heard the response of Amen, and among whom Alleluia is sung almost with one single voice, no Christians are to be found. And yet, that it may not appear that the party of Donatus, which does not communicate with the several nations of the world, is involved in error, if any angel from heaven, who could see the whole world, were to declare that outside your communion good and innocent men were nowhere to be found, there is little doubt that you would rejoice over the iniquity of the human race, and boast of having told the truth before you had received assurance of it. How then is there in you that charity which rejoices not in iniquity? But be not deceived. Throughout the field, that is, throughout the world, there will be found the wheat of the Lord growing till the end of the world. Christ has said this: Christ is truth. Let charity be in you, and let it rejoice in the truth. Though an angel from heaven preach unto you another gospel contrary to His gospel, let him be accursed.[4]

Chap. 80.—175. Petilianus said: "Lastly, what is the justification of persecution? I ask you, you wretched men, if it so be that you think that your sin rests on any authority of law."

176. Augustin answered: He who sins, sins not on the authority of the law, but against the authority of the law. But since you ask what

1 1 Cor. xiii. 1–8.
2 Eph. iv. 2, 3.
3 Matt. xiii. 38, 39, 30.
4 Gal. i. 8.

is the justification of persecution, I ask you in turn whose voice it is that says in the psalm, "Whoso privily slandereth his neighbor, him will I cut off."[1] Seek therefore the reason or the measure of the persecution, and do not display your gross ignorance by finding fault in general terms with those who persecute the unrighteous.

CHAP. 81.—177. PETILIANUS said: "But I answer you, on the other hand, that Jesus Christ never persecuted any one. And when the apostle found fault with certain parties, and suggested that He should have recourse to persecution (He Himself having come to create faith by inviting men to Him, rather than by compelling them), those apostles say, 'Many lay on hands in Thy name, and are not with us:' but Jesus said, 'Let them alone; if they are not against you, they are on your side.'"

178. AUGUSTIN answered: You say truly that you will bring forth out of your store with greater abundance things which are not written in the Scriptures. For if you wish to bring forth proofs from holy Scripture, will you bring forth even those which you cannot find therein? But it is in your own power to multiply your lies according to your will. For where is what you quoted written? or when was that either suggested to our Lord, or answered by our Lord? "Many lay on hands in Thy name, and are not with us," are words that no one of the disciples ever uttered to the Son of God; and therefore neither could the answer have been made by Him, "Let them alone: if they are not against you, they are on your side." But there is something somewhat like it which we really do read in the gospel,—that a suggestion was made to the Lord about a certain man who was casting out devils in His name, but did not follow Him with His disciples; and in that case the Lord does say, "Forbid him not: for he that is not against us is for us."[2] But this has nothing to do with pointing out parties whom the Lord is supposed to have spared. And if you have been deceived by an apparent resemblance of sentiment, this is not a lie, but merely human infirmity. But if you wished to cast a mist of falsehood over those who are unskilled in holy Scripture, then may you be pricked to the heart, and covered with confusion and corrected. Yet there is a point which we would urge in respect of this very man of whom the suggestion was made to our Lord. For even as at that time, beyond the communion of the disciples, the holiness of Christ was yet of the greatest efficacy, even so now, beyond the communion of the Church, the holiness of the sacraments is of avail. For neither is baptism consecrated save in the name of the Father, and of the Son, and of the Holy Ghost. But who will be so utterly insane as to declare that the name of the Son may be of avail even beyond the communion of the Church, but that this is not possible with the names of the Father and of the Holy Ghost? or that it may be of avail in healing a man, but not in consecrating baptism? But it is manifest that outside the communion of the Church, and the most holy bond of unity, and the most excellent gift of charity, neither he by whom the devil is cast out nor he who is baptized obtains eternal life; just as those do not obtain it, who through communion in the sacraments seem indeed to be within, and through the depravity of their character are understood to be without. But that Christ persecuted even with bodily chastisement those whom He drove with scourges from the temple, we have already said above.

CHAP. 82.—179. PETILIANUS said: "But the holy apostle said this: 'In any way, whatsoever it may be,' he says, 'let Christ be preached.'"

180. AUGUSTIN answered: You speak against yourself; but yet, since you speak on the side of truth, if you love it, let what you say be counted for you. For I ask of you of whom it was that the Apostle Paul said this? Let us, if you please, trace this a little further back. "Some," he says, "preach Christ even of envy and strife; and some also of good will, some of love, knowing that I am set for the defense of the gospel. But some indeed preach Christ even of contention, not sincerely, supposing to add affliction to my bonds. What then? notwithstanding every way, whether in pretense, or in truth, Christ is preached; and I therein do rejoice, yea, and will rejoice."[3] We see that they preached what was in itself holy, and pure, and true, but yet not in a pure manner, but of envy and contention, without charity, without purity. Certainly a short time ago you appeared to be urging the praises of charity as against us, according to the witness of the apostle, that where there is no charity, whatever there is is of no avail; and yet you see that in those there is no charity, and there was with them the preaching of Christ, of which the apostle says here that he rejoices. For it is not that he re-

---

[1] Ps. ci. 5.

[2] Luke ix. 49, 50.

[3] Phil. i. 15-18.

joices in what is evil in them, but in what is good in the name of Jesus Christ. In him assuredly there was the charity which "rejoiceth not in iniquity, but rejoiceth in the truth."[1] The envy, moreover, which was in them is an evil proceeding from the devil, for by this he has both killed and cast down. Where then were these wicked men whom the apostle thus condemns, and in whom there was so much that was good to cause him to rejoice? Were they within, or without? Choose which you will. If they were within, then Paul knew them, and yet they did not pollute him. And so you would not be polluted in the unity of the whole world by those of whom you make certain charges, whether these be true, or falsehoods invented by yourselves. Wherefore do you separate yourself? Why do you destroy yourself by the criminal sacrilege of schism? But if they were without, then you see that even in those who were without, and who certainly cannot belong to everlasting life, since they have not charity, and do not abide in unity, there is yet found the holiness of the name of Christ, so that the apostle joyfully confirms their teaching, on account of the intrinsic holiness of the name, although he repudiates them. We are right, therefore, in not doing wrong to the actual name, when those come to us who were without; but we correct the individuals, while we do honor to the name. Do you therefore take heed, and see how wickedly you act in the case of those whose acts as it seems you condemn, by treating as naught the sacrament of the name of Christ, which is holy in them. And you, indeed, as is shown by your words, think that those men of whom the apostle spoke were outside the limits of the Church. Therefore, when you fear persecution from the Catholics, of which you speak in order to create odium against us, you have confirmed in heretics the name of Christ to which you do despite by rebaptizing.

Chap. 83.—181. Petilianus said: "If then there are not some to whom all this power of faith is found to be in opposition, on what principle do you persecute, so as to compel men to defile themselves?"

182. Augustin answered: We neither persecute you, except so far as truth persecutes falsehood; nor has it anything to do with us if any one has persecuted you in other ways, just as it has nothing to do with you if any of your party do likewise; nor do we compel you to defile yourselves, but we persuade you to be cured.

[1] 1 Cor. xiii. 6.

Chap. 84.—183. Petilianus said: "But if authority had been given by some law for persons to be compelled to what is good, you yourselves, unhappy men, ought to have been compelled by us to embrace the purest faith. But far be it, far be it from our conscience to compel any one to embrace our faith."

184. Augustin answered: No one is indeed to be compelled to embrace the faith against his will; but by the severity, or one might rather say, by the mercy of God, it is common for treachery to be chastised with the scourge of tribulation. Is it the case, because the best morals are chosen by freedom of will, that therefore the worst morals are not punished by integrity of law? But yet discipline to punish an evil manner of living is out of the question, except where principles of good living which had been learned have come to be despised. If any laws, therefore, have been enacted against you, you are not thereby forced to do well, but are only prevented from doing ill.[2] For no one can do well unless he has deliberately chosen, and unless he has loved what is in free will; but the fear of punishment, even if it does not share in the pleasures of a good conscience, at any rate keeps the evil desire from escaping beyond the bounds of thought. Who are they, however, that have enacted adverse laws by which your audacity could be repressed? Are they not those of whom the apostle says that "they bear not the sword in vain; for they are the ministers of God, revengers to execute wrath upon them that do evil?"[3] The whole question therefore is, whether you are not doing ill, who are charged by the whole world with the sacrilege of so great a schism. And yet, neglecting the discussion of this question, you talk on irrelevant matters; and while you live as robbers, you boast that you die as martyrs.[4] And, through fear either of the laws themselves, or of the odium which you might incur, or else because you are unequal to the task of resisting, I do not say so many men, but so many Catholic nations, you even glory in your gentleness, that you do not compel any to join your party. According to your way of talking, the hawk, when he has been prevented by flight from carrying off the fowls, might call himself a dove. For when have you ever had the power without using it? And hence you show how you

[2] See below, 95, 217, and *c. Gaudentium*, I. 25, 28 sqq.

[3] Rom. xiii. 4.

[4] Augustin speaks of the Moor Rogatus, bishop of Cartenna in ecclesiastical province of Mauritania Cæsariensis, in his ninety-third epistle, to Vincentius, c. iii. 11. We learn from the eighty-seventh epistle, to Emeritus, sec. 10, that the followers of Rogatus called the other Donatists *Firmiani*, because they had been subjected to much cruelty at their hands under the authority of Firmus.

would do more if you only could. When Julian, envying the peace of Christ, restored to you the churches which belonged to unity, who could tell of all the massacres which were committed by you, when the very devils rejoiced with you at the opening of their temples? In the war with Firmus and his party, let Mauritania Cæsariensis itself be asked to tell us what the Moor Rogatus[1] suffered at your hands. In the time of Gildo, because one of your colleagues[2] was his intimate friend, let the followers of Maximianus be our witnesses to their sufferings. For if one might appeal to Felicianus himself, who is now with you, on his oath, whether Optatus did not compel him against his will to return to your communion, he would not dare to open his lips, especially if the people of Musti could behold his face, who were witnesses to everything that was done. But let them, as I have said, be witnesses to what they have suffered at the hands of those with whom they acted in such wise towards Rogatus. The Catholic Church herself, though strengthened by the assistance of Catholic princes ruling by land and sea, was savagely attacked by hostile troops in arms under Optatus. It was this that first made it necessary to urge before the vicar Seranus that the law should be put in force against you which imposes a fine of ten pounds of gold, which none of you have ever paid to this very day, and yet you charge us with cruelty. But where could you find a milder course of proceeding, than that crimes of such magnitude on your part should be punished by the imposition of a pecuniary fine? Or who could enumerate all the deeds which you commit in the places which you hold, of your own sovereign will and pleasure, each one as he can, without any friendship on the part of judges or any others in authority? Who is there of our party, among the inhabitants of our towns, who has not either learned something of this sort from those who came before him, or experienced it for himself? Is it not the case that at Hippo, where I am, there are not wanting some who remember that your leader Faustinus gave orders, in the time of his supreme power, in consequence of the scanty numbers of the Catholics in the place, that no one should bake their bread for them, insomuch that a baker, who was the tenant of one of our deacons, threw away the bread of his landlord unbaked, and though he was not sentenced to exile under any law, he cut him off from all share in the necessaries of life not only in a Roman state,[3] but even in his own country, and not only in his own country, but in his own house? Why, even lately, as I myself recall with mourning to this day, did not Crispinus of Calama, one of your party, having bought a property, and that only copyhold,[4] boldly and unhesitatingly immerse in the waters of a second baptism no less than eighty souls, murmuring with miserable groans under the sole influence of terror; and this in a farm belonging to the Catholic emperors, by whose laws you were forbidden even to be in any Roman city?[5] But what else was it, save such deeds as these of yours, that made it necessary for the very laws to be passed of which you complain? The laws, indeed, are very far from being proportionate to your offenses; but, such as they are, you may thank yourselves for their existence. Indeed, should we not certainly be driven on all sides from the country by the furious attacks of your Circumcelliones, who fight under your command in furious troops, unless we held you as hostages in the towns, who might well be unwilling to endure under any circumstances the mere gaze of the people, and the censure of all honorable men, from very shame, if not from fear? Do not therefore say, "Far be it, far be it from our conscience, to force any one to embrace our faith." For you do it when you can; and when you do not do it, it is because you are unable, either from fear of the laws or the odium which would accompany it, or because of the numbers of those who would resist.

CHAP. 85.—185. PETILIANUS said: "For the Lord Christ says, 'No man can come to me, except the Father which hath sent me draw him.'[6] But why do we not permit each several person to follow his free will, since the Lord God Himself has given free will to men, showing to them, however, the way of righteousness, lest any one by chance should perish from ignorance of it? For He said, 'I have placed before thee good and evil. I have set fire and water before thee; choose which thou wilt.' From which choice, you wretched men, you have chosen for yourselves not water, but rather fire. 'But yet,' He says, 'choose the good, that thou mayest live.'[7]

1 Cp. note 3, p. 556.

2 Optatus of Thaumugade (Thamogade), the friend of Gildo.

3 Augustin mentions again in his thirty-fifth epistle, to Eusebius, sec. 3, that Hippo had received the Roman citizenship. His argument is that, even if not a native of the place, the deacon should have been safe from molestation wherever Roman laws prevailed.

4 Emphyteuticam. The land, therefore, was held under the emperors, and less absolutely in the power of the owner than if it had been freehold.

5 Augustin remonstrates with Crispinus on the point, *Epist.* lxvi.

6 John vi. 44.

7 Ecclus. xv. 16, 17.

You who will not choose the good, have, by your own sentence, declared that you do not wish to live."

186. Augustin answered: If I were to propose to you the question how God the Father draws men to the Son, when He has left them to themselves in freedom of action, you would perhaps find it difficult of solution. For how does He draw them to Him if He leaves them to themselves, so that each should choose what he pleases? And yet both these facts are true; but this is a truth which few have intellect enough to penetrate. As therefore it is possible that, after leaving men to themselves in free will, the Father should yet draw them to the Son, so is it also possible that those warnings which are given by the correction of the laws do not take away free will. For whenever a man suffers anything that is harsh and unpleasing, he is warned to consider why it is that he is suffering, so that, if he shall discover that he is suffering in the cause of justice, he may choose the good that consists in the very act of suffering as he does in the cause of justice; but if he sees that it is unrighteousness for which he suffers, he may be induced, from the consideration that he is suffering and being tormented most fruitlessly, to change his purpose for the better, and may at the same time escape both the fruitless annoyance and the unrighteousness itself, which is likely to prove yet more hurtful and pernicious in the mischief it produces. And so you, when kings make any enactments against you, should consider that you are receiving a warning to consider why this is being done to you. For if it is for righteousness' sake, then are they truly your persecutors; but you are the blessed ones, who, being persecuted for righteousness' sake, shall inherit the kingdom of heaven:[1] but if it is because of the iniquity of your schism, what are they more than your correctors; while you, like all the others who are guilty of various crimes, and pay the penalty appointed by the law, are undoubtedly unhappy both in this world and in that which is to come? No one, therefore, takes away from you your free will. But I would urge you diligently to consider which you would rather choose,—whether to live corrected in peace, or, by persevering in malice, to undergo real punishment under the false name of martyrdom. But I am addressing you just as though you were suffering something proportionate to your sin, whereas you are committing sins of such enormity and reigning in such impunity. You are so furious, that you cause more terror than a war trumpet with your cry of "*Praise to God;*" so full of calumny, that even when you throw yourselves over precipices without any provocation, you impute it to our persecutions.

187. He says also, like the kindest of teachers, "You who will not choose the good, have, by your own sentence, declared that you do not wish to live." According to this, if we were to believe your accusations, we should live in kindness; but because we believe the promises of God, we declare by our own sentence that we do not wish to live. You remember well, it seems to me, what the apostles answered to the Jews when they were desired to abstain from preaching Christ. This therefore we also say, that you should answer us whether we ought rather to obey God or man.[2] *Traditors*, offerers of incense, persecutors: these are the words of men against men. Christ remained only in the love of Donatus: these are the words of men extolling the glory of a man under the name of Christ, that the glory of Christ Himself may be diminished. For it is written, "In the multitude of people is the king's honor: but in the want of people is the destruction of the prince:"[3] these, therefore, are the words of men. But those words in the gospel, "It behoved Christ to suffer, and to rise from the dead the third day; and that repentance and remission of sins should be preached in His name among all nations, beginning at Jerusalem,"[4] are the words of Christ, showing forth the glory which He received from His Father in the wideness of His kingdom. When we have heard them both, we choose in preference the communion of the Church, and prefer the words of Christ to the words of men. I ask, who is there that can say that we have chosen what is evil, except one who shall say that Christ taught what was evil?

Chap. 86.—188. Petilianus said: "Is it then the case that God has ordered the massacre even of schismatics? and if He were to issue such an order at all, you ought to be slain by some barbarians and Scythians, not by Christians."

189. Augustin answered: Let your Circumcelliones remain quiet, and let me entreat you not to terrify us about barbarians. But as to whether we or you are schismatics, let the question be put neither to you nor to me, but to Christ, that He may show where His Church is to be found. Read the gospel

[1] Matt. v. 10; 1 Pet. ii. 20.

[2] Acts v. 29.

[3] Prov. xiv. 28.

[4] Luke xxiv. 46, 47.

then, and there you find the answer, "In Jerusalem, and in all Judea, and in Samaria, and even in the whole earth."[1] If any one, therefore, is not found within the Church, let not any further question be put to him, but let him either be corrected or converted, or else, being detected, let him not complain.

CHAP. 87.—190. PETILIANUS said: "For neither has the Lord God at any time rejoiced in human blood, seeing that He was even willing that Cain, the murderer of his brother, should continue to exist in his murderer's life."

191. AUGUSTIN answered: If God was unwilling that death should be inflicted on him who slew his brother, preferring that he should continue to exist in his murderer's life, see whether this be not the cause why, seeing that the heart of the king is in the hand of God, whereby he has himself enacted many laws for your correction and reproof, yet no law of the king has commanded that you should be put to death, perhaps with this very object, that any one of you who persists in the obstinate self-will of his sacrilegious madness should be tortured with the punishment of the fratricide Cain, that is to say, with the life of a murderer. For we read that many were slain in mercy by Moses the servant of the Lord; for in that he prayed thus in intercession to the Lord for their wicked sacrilege, saying, "O Lord, if Thou wilt forgive their sin—; and if not, blot me, I pray thee, out of the book which Thou hast written,"[2] his unspeakable charity and mercy are plainly shown. Could it be, then, that he was suddenly changed to cruelty, when, on descending from the mount, he ordered so many thousands to be slain? Consider, therefore, whether it may not be a sign of greater anger on the part of God, that, whilst so many laws have been enacted against you, you have not been ordered by any emperor to be put to death. Or do you think that you are not to be compared to that fratricide? Hearken to the Lord speaking through His prophet: "From the rising of the sun, even unto the going down of the same, my name shall be great among the Gentiles; and in every place incense shall be offered unto my name, and a pure offering; for my name shall be great among the heathen, saith the Lord of hosts."[3] On this brother's sacrifice you show that you look with malignant eyes, over and above the respect which God pays to it; and if ye have ever heard that "from the rising of the sun, unto the going down of the same, the Lord's name is to be praised,"[4] which is that living sacrifice of which it is said, "Offer unto God thanksgiving,"[5] then will your countenance fall like that of yonder murderer. But inasmuch as you cannot kill the whole world, you are involved in the same guilt by your mere hatred, according to the words of John, "Whosoever hateth his brother is a murderer."[6] And I would that any innocent brother might rather fall into the hands of your Circumcelliones, to be murdered by their weapons, than be subjected to the poison of your tongue and rebaptized.

CHAP. 88.—192. PETILIANUS said: "We advise you, therefore, if so be that you will hear it willingly, and even though you do not willingly receive it, yet we warn you that the Lord Christ instituted for Christians, not any form of slaying, but one of dying only. For if He loved men who thus delight in battle, He would not have consented to be slain for us."

193. AUGUSTIN answered: Would that your martyrs would follow the form that He prescribed! they would not throw themselves over precipices, which He refused to do at the bidding of the devil.[7] But when you persecute our ancestors with false witness even now that they are dead, whence have you received this form? In that you endeavor to stain us with the crimes of men we never knew, while you are unwilling that the most notorious misdeeds of your own party should be reckoned against you, whence have you received this form? But we are too much yielding to our own conceit if we find fault about ourselves, when we see that you utter false testimony against the Lord Himself, since He Himself both promised and made manifest that His Church should extend throughout all nations, and you maintain the contrary. This form, therefore, you did not receive even from the Jewish persecutors themselves, for they persecuted His body while He was walking on the earth: you persecute His gospel as He is seated in heaven. Which gospel endured more meekly the flames of furious kings than it can possibly endure your tongues; for while they blazed, unity remained, and this it cannot do amid your words. They who desired that the word of God should perish in the flames did not believe that it could be despised if read. They would not, therefore, set their flames to work upon the gospel, if you would let them use your tongues against the gospel. In the earlier persecution the gospel of Christ was

[1] Acts i. 8. [2] Ex. xxxii. 28–32. [3] Mal. i. 11.

[4] Ps. cxiii. 3. [5] Ps. l. 14. [6] 1 John iii. 15. [7] Matt. iv. 6, 7.

sought by some in their rage, it was betrayed by others in their fear; it was burned by some in their rage, it was hidden by others in their love; it was attacked, but none were found to speak against its truth. The more accursed share of persecution was reserved for you when the persecution of the heathen was exhausted. Those who persecuted the name of Christ believed in Christ: now those who are honored for the name of Christ are found to speak against His truth.

Chap. 89.—194. Petilianus said: "Here you have the fullest possible proof that a Christian may take no part in the destruction of another. But the first establishing of this principle was in the case of Peter, as it is written, "Simon Peter having a sword, drew it, and smote the high priest's servant, and cut off his right ear. Then said Jesus unto Peter, Put up thy sword into the sheath. For all they that take the sword shall perish with the sword.'"[1]

195. Augustin answered: Why then do you not restrain the weapons of the Circumcelliones with such words as these? Should you think that you were going beyond the words of the gospel if you should say, All they that take the cudgel shall perish with the cudgel? Withhold not then your pardon, if our ancestors were unable to restrain the men by whom you complain that Marculus was thrown down a precipice; for neither is it written in the gospel, He that useth to throw men down a precipice shall be cast therefrom. And would that, as your charges are either false or out of date, so the cudgels of those friends of yours would cease! And yet, perhaps, you take it ill that, if not by force of law, at any rate in words, we take away their armor from your legions in saying that they manifest their rage with sticks alone. For that was the ancient fashion of their wickedness, but now they have advanced too far. For amid their drunken revellings, and amid the free license of assembling together, wandering in the streets, jesting, drinking, passing the whole night in company with women who have no husbands, they have learned not only to brandish cudgels, but to wield swords and whirl slings. But why should I not say to them (God knows with what feelings I say it and with what feelings they receive it!), Madmen, the sword of Peter, though drawn from motives not yet free from fleshly impurity, was yet drawn in defence of the body of Christ against the body of His persecutor, but your arms are portioned out against the cause of Christ; but the body of which He is the head, that is, His Church, extends throughout all nations. He Himself has said this, and has ascended into heaven, whither the fury of the Jews could not follow Him; and it is your fury which attacks His members in the body, which on His ascension He commended to our care. In defense of those members all men rage against you, all men resist you, as many as being in the Catholic Church, and possessing as yet but little faith, are influenced by the same motives as Peter was when he drew his sword in the name of Christ. But there is a great difference between your persecution and theirs. You are like the servant of the Jews' high priest; for in the service of your princes you arm yourselves against the Catholic Church, that is, against the body of Christ. But they are such as Peter then was, fighting even with the strength of their bodies for the body of Christ, that is, the Church. But if they are bidden to be still, as Peter then was bidden, how much more should you be warned that, laying aside the madness of heresy, you should join the unity of those members for which they so fight? But, being wounded by such men as these, you hate us also; and, as though you had lost your right ears, you do not hear the voice of Christ as He sits at the right hand of the Father. But to whom shall I address myself, or how shall I address myself to them, seeing that in them I find no time wherein to speak? for even early in the morning they are reeking with wine, drunk, it may be already in the day, it may be still from overnight. Moreover, they utter threats, and not they only, but their own bishops utter threats concerning them, being ready to deny that what they have done has any bearing on them. May the Lord grant to us a song of degrees, in which we may say, "When I am with those who hate peace, I am peaceful. When I would speak with them, they are wont to fight me without cause."[2] For thus says the body of Christ, which throughout the whole world is assailed by heretics, by some here, by others there, and by all alike wherever they may be.[3]

Chap. 90.—196. Petilianus said: "Therefore I say, He ordained that we should undergo death for the faith, which each man should do for the communion of the Church. For Christianity makes progress by the deaths of its followers. For if death were feared by the faithful, no man would be found to live with perfect faith. For the Lord Christ says,

[1] John xviii. 10, 11; Matt. xxvi. 52.

[2] Ps. cxx. 6, 7, cp. Hieron.

[3] See *Contr. Cresc.* l. III. c. 67, l. IV. cc. 60, 61.

'Except a corn of wheat fall into the ground and die, it abideth alone: but if it die, it bringeth forth much fruit.'"[1]

197. AUGUSTIN answered: I should be glad to know which of your party it was who first threw himself over a precipice. For truly that grain of corn was fruitful from which so great a crop of similar suicides has sprung. Tell me, when you make mention of the words of the Lord, that He says a grain of wheat shall die and bring forth much fruit, why do you envy the real fruit, which has most truly[2] sprung up throughout the whole world, and bring up against it all the charges of the tares or chaff which you have ever either heard of or invented?

CHAP. 91.—198. PETILIANUS said: "But you scatter thorns and tares, not seeds of corn, so that you ought to be burned together with them at the last judgment. We do not utter curses; but every thorny conscience is bound under this penalty by the sentence which God has pronounced."

199. AUGUSTIN answered: Surely, when you mention tares, it might bring to your minds the thought of wheat as well; for both have been commanded to grow together in the field until the harvest. But you fix the eye of malice fiercely on the tares, and maintain, in opposition to the express declaration of Christ, that they alone have grown throughout the earth, with the exception of Africa alone.

CHAP. 92.—200. PETILIANUS said: "Where is the saying of the Lord Christ, 'Whosoever shall smite thee on the right cheek, turn to him the other also'?[3] Where is the patience which He displayed when they spat upon His face, who Himself with His most holy spittle opened the eyes of the blind? Where is the saying of the Apostle Paul, 'If a man smite you in the face?' Where is that other saying of the same apostle, 'In stripes above measure, in prisons more frequent, in deaths oft'?[4] He makes mention of the sufferings which he underwent, not of the deeds which he performed. It had been enough for the Christian faith that these things should be done by the Jews: why do you, wretched men, do these others in addition?"

201. AUGUSTIN answered: Is it then really so, that when men smite you on the one cheek, you turn to them the other? This is not the report that your furious bands won for you by wandering everywhere throughout the whole of Africa with dreadful wickedness. I would fain have it that men should make a bargain with you, that, in accordance with the old law, you should seek but "an eye for an eye, a tooth for a tooth,"[5] instead of bringing out cudgels in return for the words which greet your ears.

CHAP. 93.—202. PETILIANUS said: "But what have you to do with the kings of this world, in whom Christianity has never found anything save envy towards her? And to teach you shortly the truth of what I say, A king persecuted the brethren of the Maccabees.[6] A king also condemned the three children to the sanctifying flames, being ignorant what he did, seeing that he himself was fighting against God.[7] A king sought the life of the infant Saviour.[8] A king exposed Daniel, as he thought, to be eaten by wild beasts.[9] And the Lord Christ Himself was slain by a king's most wicked judge.[10] Hence it is that the apostle cries out, 'We speak wisdom among them that are perfect; yet not the wisdom of this world, nor of the princes of this world, that come to nought: but we speak the wisdom of God in a mystery, which was hidden, which God ordained before the world unto our glory; which none of the princes of this world knew: for had they known it, they would not have crucified the Lord of glory.'[11] But grant that this was said of the heathen kings of old. Yet you, rulers of this present age, because you desire to be Christians, do not allow men to be Christians, seeing that, when they are believing in all honesty of heart, you draw them by the defilement and mist of your falsehood wholly over to your wickedness, that with their arms, which were provided against the enemies of the state, they should assail the Christians, and should think that, at your instigation, they are doing the work of Christ if they kill us whom you hate, according to the saying of the Lord Christ: 'The time cometh,' He says, 'that whosoever killeth you will think that he doeth God service.'[12] It makes no matter therefore to you, false teachers, whether the kings of this world desire to be heathens, which God forbid, or Christians, so long as you cease not in your efforts to arm them against the family of Christ. But do you not know, or rather, have you not read, that the guilt of one who instigates a murder is greater than the guilt of him who carries it out? Jezebel had excited the king her husband to the murder of a poor and

[1] John xii. 24.
[2] *Veracissime.* Another reading is "*feracissime*," "most abundantly."
[3] Matt. v. 39.
[4] 2 Cor. xi. 20, 23.
[5] Deut. xix. 21.
[6] 2 Mac. vii.
[7] Dan. iii.
[8] Matt. ii. 16.
[9] Dan. vi.
[10] Matt. xxvii. 26.
[11] 1 Cor. ii. 6-8.
[12] John xvi. 2.

righteous man, yet husband and wife alike perished by an equal punishment.[1] Nor indeed is your mode of urging on kings different from that by which the subtle persuasion of women has often urged kings on to guilt. For the wife of Herod earned and obtained the boon by means of her daughter, that the head of John should be brought to table in a charger.[2] Similarly the Jews forced on Pontius Pilate that he should crucify the Lord Jesus, whose blood Pilate prayed might remain in vengeance upon them and on their children.[3] So therefore you also overwhelm yourselves with our blood by your sin. For it does not follow that because it is the hand of the judge that strikes the blow, your calumnies therefore are not rather guilty of the deed. For the prophet David says, speaking in the person of Christ, 'Why do the heathen rage, and the people imagine a vain thing? The kings of the earth set themselves, and the rulers take counsel together, against the Lord, and against His Anointed, saying, Let us break their bands asunder, and cast away their cords from us. He that sitteth in the heavens shall laugh: the Lord shall have them in derision. Then shall He speak unto them in His wrath, and vex them in His sore displeasure. Yet have I set my King upon my holy hill of Zion. I will declare the decree: the Lord hath said unto me, Thou art my Son; this day have I begotten Thee. Ask of me, and I shall give Thee the heathen for Thine inheritance, and the uttermost parts of the earth for Thy possession. Thou shalt rule them with a rod of iron; Thou shalt dash them in pieces like a potter's vessel.' And he warned the kings themselves in the following precepts, that they should not, like ignorant men devoid of understanding, seek to persecute the Christians, lest they should themselves be destroyed,—which precepts I would that we could teach them, seeing that they are ignorant of them; or, at least, that you would show them to them, as doubtless you would do if you desired that they should live; or, at any rate, if neither of the other courses be allowed, that your malice would have permitted them to read them for themselves. The first Psalm of David would certainly have persuaded them that they should live and reign as Christians; but meanwhile you deceive them, so long as they entrust themselves to you. For you represent to them things that are evil, and you hide from them what is good. Let them then at length read this, which they should have read already long ago. For what does he say, 'Be wise now therefore, O ye kings; be instructed, ye judges of the earth. Serve the Lord with fear, and rejoice with trembling. Lay hold of instruction lest the Lord be angry, and ye perish from the right way. Since how quickly has His wrath kindled over you? Blessed are all they that put their trust in Him.'[4] You urge on emperors, I say, with your persuasions, even as Pilate, whom, as we showed above, the Jews urged on, though he himself cried aloud, as he washed his hands before them all, 'I am innocent of the blood of this just person,'[5]—as though a person could be clear from the guilt of a sin who had himself committed it. But, to say nothing of ancient examples, observe, from instances taken from your own party, how very many of your emperors and judges have perished in persecuting us. To pass over Nero, who was the first to persecute the Christians, Domitian perished almost in the same way as Nero, as also did Trajan, Geta,[6] Decius, Valerian, Diocletian; Maximian also perished, at whose command that men should burn incense to their gods, burning the sacred volumes, Marcellinus indeed first, but after him also Mensurius of Carthage, and Cæcilianus, escaped death from the sacrilegious flames, surviving like some ashes or cinders from the burning. For the consciousness of the guilt of burning incense involved you all, as many as agreed with Mensurius. Macarius perished, Ursacius[7] perished, and all your counts perished in like manner by the vengeance of God. For Ursacius was slain in a battle with the barbarians, after which birds of prey with their savage talons, and the greedy teeth of dogs with their biting, tore him limb from limb. Was not he too a murderer at your suggestion, who, like king Ahab, whom we showed to have been persuaded by a woman, slew a poor and righteous man?[8] So you too do not cease to murder us, who are just and poor (poor, that is, in worldly wealth; for in the grace of God no one of us is poor). For

---

1 1 Kings xxi. 2 Matt. xiv. 8, 9. 3 Matt. xxvii. 24-26.

4 Ps. ii., cp. Hieron. 5 Matt. xxvii. 24.

6 Some editions have Varius in the place of Geta, referring to Aurelius Antoninus Heliogabalus, of whom Lampridius asserts that he derived the name of Varius from the doubtfulness of his parentage. Aelii Lampridii Antoninus Heliogabalus, in *SS. Historiæ Augustæ*. The MSS. agree, however, in the reading "Geta," which was a name of the second son of Severus, the brother of Caracalla.

7 Optatus defends the cause of Macarius at great length in his third book against Parmenianus. Of Ursacius he says in the same place: "You are offended at the times of a certain Leontius, of Ursacius, Macarius and others." And Augustin, in his third book against Cresconius, c. 20, introduces an objection of the Donatists against himself: "But so soon as Silvanus, bishop of Cirta, had refused to communicate with Ursacius and Zenophilus the persecutors, he was driven into exile." Usuardus, deceived by a false story made up by the Donatists, enters in his Martyrology that a pseudo-martyr Donatus suffered on the 1st of March, under Ursacius and Marcellinus, to this effect: "On the same day of the holy martyr Donatus, who suffered under Ursacius the judge (or *dux*), and the tribune Marcellinus.

8 1 Kings xxi.

even if you do not murder a man with your hands, you do not cease to do so with your butcherous tongues. For it is written, 'Death and life are in the power of the tongue.'[1] All, therefore, who have been murdered, you, the instigator of the deed, have slain. Nor indeed does the hand of the butcher glow save at the instigation of your tongue; and that terrible heat of the breast is inflamed by your words to take the blood of others,—blood that shall take a just vengeance upon him who shed it."

203. AUGUSTIN answered: If I were to answer adequately, and as I ought, to this passage, which has been exaggerated and arranged at such length by you, where you speak in invidious terms against us concerning the kings of this world, I am much afraid that you would accuse me too of having wished to excite the anger of kings against you. And yet, whilst you are borne after your own fashion by the violence of this invective against all Catholics, you certainly do not pass me by. I will endeavor, however, to show, if I can, that it is rather you who have been guilty of this offense by speaking as you have done, than myself by answering as I shall do. And first of all, see how you yourself oppose your self; for certainly you prefaced the passage which you quoted with the words, "What have you to do with the kings of this world, in whom Christianity has never found anything save envy towards her?" In these words you certainly cut off from us all access to the kings of this world. And a little later you say, "And he warned the kings themselves in the following precepts, that they should not, like ignorant men devoid of understanding, seek to persecute the Christians, lest they should be themselves destroyed,—which precepts I would that we could teach them, seeing that they are ignorant of them; or, at least, that you would show them to them, as doubtless you would do if you desired that they should live." In what way then do you wish us to be the instructors of kings? And indeed those of our body who have any friendship with Christian kings commit no sin if they make a right use of that friendship; but if any are elated by it, they yet sin far less grievously than you. For what had you, who thus reproach us,—what had you to do with a heathen king, and what is worse, with Julian, the apostate and enemy of the name of Christ, to whom, when you were begging that the basilicas should be restored to you as though they were your own, you ascribed this meed of praise, "that in him justice alone was found to have a place"?—in which words (for I believe that you understand the Latin tongue) both the idolatry and the apostasy of Julian are styled justice. I hold in my hands the petition which your ancestors presented; the memorial[2] which embodied their request; the chronicles, where they made their representation. Watch and attend. To the enemy of Christ, to the apostate, the antagonist of Christians, the servant of the devil, that friend, that representative, that Pontius of yours, made supplication in such words as these: "Go to then, and say to us, What have you to do with the kings of this world?" that as deaf men you may read to the deaf nations what you as well as they refuse to hear; "Thou beholdest the mote that is in thy brother's eye, but considerest not the beam that is in thine own eye."[3]

204. "What," say you, "have you to do with the kings of this world, in whom Christianity has never found anything save envy towards her?" Having said this, you endeavored to reckon up what kings the righteous had found to be their enemies, and did not consider how many more might be enumerated who have proved their friends. The patriarch Abraham was both most friendly treated, and presented with a token of friendship, by a king who had been warned from heaven not to defile his wife.[4] Isaac his son likewise found a king most friendly to him.[5] Jacob, being received with honor by a king in Egypt, went so far as to bless him.[6] What shall I say of his son Joseph, who, after the tribulation of a prison, in which his chastity was tried as gold is tried in the fire, being raised by Pharaoh to great honors,[7] even swore by the life of Pharaoh,[8]—not as though puffed up with vain conceit, but being not unmindful of his kindness. The daughter of a king adopted Moses.[9] David took refuge with a king of another race, compelled thereto by the unrighteousness of the king of Israel.[10] Elijah ran before the chariot of a most wicked king,—not by the king's command, but from his own loyalty.[11] Elisha thought it good to offer of his own accord to the woman who had sheltered him anything that she might wish to have obtained from the king through his intercession.[12] But I will come to the actual times when the people of

[1] Prov. xviii. 21.

[2] *Constitutio quam impetraverunt.* Some editions have "*quam dederunt Constantio;*" but there is no place for Constantius in this history of the Donatists, nor was any boon either sought or obtained from him in their name. The Louvain editors therefore restored "*constitutio*," which is the reading of the Gallic MSS.

[3] Matt. vii. 3. [4] Gen. xx. [5] Gen. xxvi. 11. [6] Gen. xlvii. [7] Gen. xxxix., xli. [8] Gen. xlii. 15. [9] Ex. ii. 10. [10] 1 Sam. xxvii. [11] 1 Kings xviii. 44-46. [12] 2 Kings iv. 13.

God were in captivity, in which, to use a mild expression, a strange forgetfulness came over you. For, wishing to prove that Christianity has never found anything in kings saving envy towards her, you made mention of the three children and Daniel, who suffered at the hands of persecuting kings, and you could not derive instruction from circumstances not occurring near, but in the very same passages, viz., from the conduct of the king himself after the miracle of the flames which did no hurt, whether as shown in praising and setting forth the name of God, or in honoring the three children themselves, or from the esteem in which the king held Daniel, and the gifts with which he honored him, nothing loth to receive them, when he, rendering the honor that was due to the king's power, as sufficiently appears from his own words, did not hesitate to use the gift with which he was endowed by God, in interpreting the king's dream. And when, in consequence, the king was compelled by the men who envied the holy prophet, and heaped calumnies upon him with sacrilegious madness, most unwillingly to cast him into the den of lions, sadly though he did it, yet he had the conviction that he would be safe through the help and protection of his God. Accordingly, when Daniel, by the miraculous repression of the lions' rage, had been preserved unhurt, when the friendly voice of the king spoke first to him, in accents of anxiety, he himself replied with benediction from the den, "O king, live for ever!"[1] How came it that, when your argument was turning on the very same subject, when you were yourself quoting the examples of the servants of God in whose case these things were done, you either failed to see, or were unwilling to see, or seeing and knowing, were silent, in a manner which I know not how you will defend, about those instances of friendship felt by kings for the saints? But if it were not that, as a defender of the basest cause, you are hindered by the desire of building up falsehood, and thereby turned away either as unwilling or as ignorant from the light of truth, there can be no doubt that you could, without any difficulty, recall some good kings as well as some bad ones, and some friendly to the saints as well as some unfriendly. And we cannot but wonder that your Circumcelliones thus throw themselves from precipices. Who was running after you, I pray? What Macarius, what soldier was pursuing you? Certainly none of our party thrust you into this abyss of falsehood. Why then did you thus run headlong with your eyes shut, so that when you said, "What have you to do with the kings of this world?" you did not add, In whom Christianity has often found envy towards herself, instead of boldly venturing to say, "In whom Christianity has never found anything save envy towards her?" Was it really true that you neither thought yourself, nor considered that those who read your writings would think, how many instances of kings there were that went against your views? Does he not know what he says?

205. Or do you think that, because those whom I have mentioned belonged to olden times, therefore they form no argument against you, because you did not say, In whom *righteousness* has never found anything save envy towards her, but "In whom *Christianity* has never found anything saving envy towards her,"—meaning, perhaps, that it should be understood that they began to show envy towards the righteous from the time when they began to bear the name of Christians? What then is the meaning of those examples from olden times, by which you even more imprudently wished to prove what you had so imprudently ventured to assert? For was it not before Christ was born in the world that the Maccabees, and the three children, and Daniel, did and suffered what you told of them? And again, why was it, as I asked just now, that you offered a petition to Julian, the undoubted foe of Christianity? Why did you seek to recover the basilicas from him? Why did you declare that only righteousness found a place with him? If it is the foe of Christianity that hears such things as these, what then are they from whom he hears them? But it should be observed that Constantine, who was certainly no foe to the name of Christian, but rather rendered glorious by it, being mindful of the hope which he maintained in Christ, and deciding most justly on behalf of His unity, was not worthy to be acknowledged by you, even when you yourselves appealed to him. Both these were emperors in Christian times, but yet not both of them were Christians. But if both of them were foes of Christianity, why did you thus appeal to one of them? why did you thus present a petition to the other? For on your ancestors making their petition, Constantine had given an episcopal judgment both at Rome and at Arles; and yet the first of them you accused before him, from the other you appealed to him. But if, as is the case, one of them had believed in Christ, the other had apostatized from Christ, why is the Christian despised while furthering the interests of unity, the apostate praised while fav-

[1] Dan. iii.-vi.

oring deceit? Constantine ordered that the basilicas should be taken from you, Julian that they should be restored. Do you wish to know which of these actions is conducive to Christian peace? The one was done by a man who had believed in Christ, the other by one who had abandoned Christ. O how you would wish that you could say, It was indeed ill done that supplication should so be made to Julian, but what has that to do with us? But if you were to say this, the Catholic Church would also conquer in these same words, whose saints dispersed throughout the world are much less concerned with what you say of those towards whom you feel as you may be disposed to feel. But it is beyond your power to say, It was ill done that supplication should so be made to Julian. Your throat is closed; your tongue is checked by an authority close at home. It was Pontius that did it. Pontius presented the petition; Pontius declared that the apostate was most righteous; Pontius set forth that only righteousness found a place with the apostate. That Pontius made a petition to him in these words, we have the express evidence of Julian himself, mentioning him by name, without any disguise. Your representations still exist. It is no uncertain rumor, but public documents that bear witness to the fact. Can it be, that because the apostate made some concession to your prayer, to the detriment of the unity of Christ, you therefore find truth in what was said, that only righteousness found a place with him? but because Christian emperors decide against your wishes, since this appears to them most likely to contribute to the unity of Christ, therefore they are called the foes of Christianity? Such folly may all heretics display; and may they regain wisdom, so that they should be no longer heretics.

206. And when is that fulfilled, you will say, which the Lord declares, "The time cometh, that whosoever killeth you will think that he doeth God service"?[1] At any rate neither can this be said of the heathen, who persecuted Christians, not for the sake of God, but for the sake of their idols. You do not see that if this had been said of these emperors who rejoice in the name of Christian, their chief command would certainly have been this, that you should have been put to death; and this command they never gave at all. But the men of your party, by opposing the laws in hostile fashion, bring deserved punishment on themselves; and their own voluntary deaths, so long as they think that they bring odium on us, they consider in no wise ruinous to themselves. But if they think that that saying of Christ refers to kings who honor the name of Christ, let them ask what the Catholic Church suffered in the East, when, Valens the Arian was emperor. There indeed I might find what I should understand to be sufficient fulfillment of the saying of the Lord, "The time cometh, that whosoever killeth you will think that he doeth God service," that heretics should not claim, as conducing to their especial glory, the injunctions issued against their errors by Catholic emperors. But we remember that that time was fulfilled after the ascension of our Lord, of which holy Scripture is known by all to be a witness. The Jews thought that they were doing a service to God when they put the apostles to death. Among those who thought that they were showing service to God was even our Saul, though not ours as yet; so that among his causes for confidence which were past and to be forgotten, he enumerates the following: "An Hebrew," he says, "of the Hebrews; as touching the law, a Pharisee; concerning zeal, persecuting the Church."[2] Here was one who thought that he did God service when he did what presently he suffered himself. For forty Jews bound themselves by an oath that they would slay him, when he caused that this should be made known to the tribune, so that under the protection of a guard of armed men he escaped their snares.[3] But there was no one yet to say to him, What have you to do (not with kings, but) with tribunes and the arms of kings? There was no one to say to him, Dare you seek protection at the hand of soldiers, when your Lord was dragged by them to undergo His sufferings? There were as yet no instances of madness such as yours; but there were already examples being prepared, which should be sufficient for their refutation.

207. Moreover, with what terrible force did you venture to set forth and utter the following: "But to say nothing of ancient examples, observe, from instances taken from your own party, how very many of your emperors and judges have perished in persecuting us." When I read this in your letter, I waited with the most earnest expectation to see what you were going to say, and whom you were going to enumerate, when, lo and behold! as though passing them over, you began to quote to me Nero, Domitian, Trajan, Geta, Decius, Valerian, Diocletian, Maximian. I acknowledge that there were more; but you have altogether forgotten against whom you are

1 John xvi. 2.

2 Phil. iii. 5, 6.

3 Acts xxiii. 12-33.

arguing. Were not all of these pagans, persecuting generally the Christian name on behalf of their idols? Be vigilant, then; for the men whom you mention were not of our communion. They were persecuting the whole aggregate of unity itself, from which we, as you think, or you, as Christ teaches, have gone forth. But you had proposed to show that our emperors and judges had perished in consequence of persecuting you. Or is it that you yourself do not require that we should reckon these, because, in mentioning them, you passed them over, saying, "To pass over Nero;" and with this reservation did you mean to run through all the rest? What then was the use of their being quoted, if they had nothing to do with the matter? But what has it to do with me? I now join with you in leaving these. Next, let that larger number which you promised to us be produced, unless, indeed, it may be that they cannot be found, inasmuch as you said that they had perished.

208. For now you go on to make mention of the bishops whom you are wont to accuse of having delivered up the sacred books, concerning whom we on our part are wont to answer: Either you fail in your proof, and so it concerns no one at all; or you succeed, and then it still has no concern with us. For they have borne their own burden, whether it be good or bad; and we indeed believe that it was good. But of whatever character it was, yet it was their own; just as your bad men have borne their own burden, and neither you theirs nor they yours. But the common and most evil burden of you all is schism. This we have already often said before. Show us, therefore, not the names of bishops, but the names of our emperors and judges, who have perished in persecuting you. For this, is what you had proposed, this is what you had promised, this is what you had caused us most eagerly to expect. "Hear," he says, "Macarius perished, Ursacius perished, and all your counts perished in like manner, by the vengeance of God." You have mentioned only two by name, and neither of them was emperor. Who would be satisfied with this, I ask? Are you not utterly dissatisfied with yourself? You promise that you will mention a vast number of emperors and judges of our party who perished in persecuting you; and then, without a word of emperors, you mention two who were either judges or counts. For as to what you add, "And all your counts perished in like manner by the vengeance of God," it has nothing to do with the matter. For on this principle you might some time ago have closed your argument, without mentioning the name of any one at all. Why then have you not made mention of our emperors, that is to say, of emperors of our communion? Were you afraid that you should be indicted for high treason? Where is the fortitude that marks the Circumcelliones? And further, what do you mean by introducing those whom you mentioned above in such numbers? They might with more right say to you, Why did you seek us out? For they did nothing to assist your cause, and yet you mentioned them by name. What kind of man, then, must you be, who fear to mention those by name, who, as you say, have perished? At any rate, you might mention more of the judges and counts, of whom you seem to feel no fear. But yet you stopped at Macarius and Ursacius. Are these two whom you mention the vast number of whom you spoke? Are you thinking of the lesson which we learned as boys? For if you were to ask of me what number two is, singular or plural, what could I answer, except that it was plural? But even so I am still not without the means of reply. I take away Macarius from your list; for you certainly have not told us how he perished. Or do you maintain that any one who persecutes you, unless he be immortal on the face of this earth, is to be deemed when he dies to have died because of you? What if Constantine had not lived to enjoy so long a reign, and such prolonged prosperity, who was the first to pass many decrees against your errors? And what if Julian, who gave you back the basilicas, had not been so speedily snatched away from life?[1] In that case, when would you make an end of talking such nonsense as you do, seeing that even now you are unwilling to hold your tongues? And yet neither do we say that Julian died so soon because he gave back the basilicas to you. For we might be equally prolix with you in this, but we are unwilling to be equally foolish. Well, then, as I had begun to say, from these two we will take away Macarius. For when you had mentioned the names of two, Macarius and Ursacius, you repeated the name of Ursacius with the view of showing us how he deserved his death; and you said, "For Ursacius was slain in a battle with the barbarians, after which birds of prey with their savage talons, and the greedy teeth of dogs with their biting, tore him limb from limb." Whence it is quite clear, since it is your custom to excite greater odium against us on account of Macarius, insomuch that you call

[1] The reign of Constantine lasted about thirty-two years, from 306 to 337 A.D. Julian succeeded Constantius, and reigned one year and seven months, dying at the age of thirty, in a war against the Persians, in 363 A.D.

us not Ursacians but Macarians, that you would have been sure to say by far the most concerning him, had you been able to say anything of the sort about his death. Of these two, therefore, when you used the plural number, if you take away Macarius, there remains Ursacius alone, a proper name of the singular number. Where is therefore the fulfillment of your threatening and tremendous promise of so many who should support your argument?

209. By this time all men who are in any degree acquainted with the meaning of words must understand, it seems to me, how ridiculous it is that, when you had said, "Macarius perished, Ursacius perished, and all your counts perished in like manner, by the vengeance of God," as though men were calling upon you to prove the fact, whereas, in reality, neither hearer nor reader was calling on you for anything further whatsoever, you immediately strung together a long argument in order to prove that all our counts perished in like manner by the vengeance of God. "For Ursacius," you say, "was slain in a battle with the barbarians, after which birds of prey with their savage talons, and the greedy teeth of dogs with their biting, tore him limb from limb." In the same way, any one else, who was similarly ignorant of the meaning of what he says, might assert that all your bishops perished in prison by the vengeance of God; and when asked how he could prove this fact, he might at once add, For Optatus, having been accused of belonging to the company of Gildo, was put to death in a similar way. Frivolous charges such as these we are compelled to listen to, to consider, to refute; only we are apprehensive for the weak, lest, from the greater slowness of their intellect, they should fall speedily into your toils. But Ursacius, of whom you speak, if it be the case that he lived a good life, and really died as you assert, will receive consolation from the promise of God, who says, "Surely your blood of your lives will I require; at the hand of every beast will I require it."[1]

210. But as to the calumnious charges which you bring against us, saying that by us the wrath of the kings of the world is excited against you, so long as we do not teach them the lesson of holy Scripture, but rather suggest our own desire of war, I do not imagine that you are so absolutely deaf to the eloquence of the sacred books themselves as that you should not rather fear that they should be acquainted with it. But whether you so will or no, they gain entrance to the Church; and even if we hold our tongues, they give heed to the readers; and, to say nothing of the rest, they especially listen with the most marked attention to that very psalm which you quoted. For you said that we do not teach them, nor, so far as we can help it, allow them to become acquainted with the words of Scripture: "Be wise now therefore, O ye kings; be instructed ye judges of the earth. Serve the Lord with fear and rejoice with trembling. Take hold of instruction lest the Lord be angry,"[2] etc. Believe that even this is sung, and that they hear it. But, at any rate, they hear what is written above in the same psalm, which you, unless I am mistaken, were only unwilling to pass over, for fear you should be understood to be afraid. They hear therefore this as well "The Lord hath said unto me, Thou art my Son; this day have I begotten Thee. Ask of me, and I shall give Thee the heathen for Thine inheritance, and the uttermost parts of the earth for Thy possession."[3] On hearing which, they cannot but marvel that some should be found to speak against this inheritance of Christ, endeavoring to reduce it to a little corner of the earth; and in their marvel they perhaps ask, on account of what they hear in what follows, "Serve the Lord with fear," wherein they can serve Him, in so far as they are kings. For all men ought to serve God,—in one sense, in virtue of the condition common to them all, in that they are men; in another sense, in virtue of their several gifts, whereby this man has one function on the earth, and that man has another. For no man, as a private individual, could command that idols should be taken from the earth, which it was so long ago foretold should come to pass.[4] Accordingly, when we take into consideration the social condition of the human race, we find that kings, in the very fact that they are kings, have a service which they can render to the Lord in a manner which is impossible for any who have not the power of kings.

211. When, therefore, they think over what you quote, they hear also what you yourself quoted concerning the three children, and hear it with circumstances of marvellous solemnity. For that same Scripture is most of all sung in the Church at a time when the very festal nature of the season excites additional fervor even in those who, during the rest of the year, are more given to be sluggish. What then do you think must be the feelings of Christian emperors, when they hear of the three children being cast into the burning fiery furnace because they were unwilling to

[1] Gen. ix. 5.

[2] Ps. ii. 10-12. [3] Ps. ii. 7, 8. [4] Isa. ii. 18; Zech. xiii. 2.

consent to the wickedness of worshipping the image of the king,[1] unless you suppose that they consider that the pious liberty of the saints cannot be overcome either by the power of kings, or by any enormity of punishment, and that they rejoice that they are not of the number of those kings who used to punish men that despised idols as though they were guilty of sacrilege? But, further, when they hear in what follows that the same king, terrified by the marvellous sight of, not only the three children, but the very flames performing service unto God, himself too began to serve God in fear, and to rejoice with reverence, and to lay hold of instruction, do they not understand that the reason that this was recorded, and set forth with such publicity, was that an example might be set both before the servants of God, to prevent them from committing sacrilege in obedience to kings, and before kings themselves, that they should show themselves religious by belief in God? Being willing, therefore, on their part, from the admonition of the very psalm which you yourself inserted in your writings, both to be wise, and to receive instruction, and to serve God with fear and to rejoice unto Him with reverence, and to lay hold of instruction, with what attention do they listen to what that king said afterwards! For he said that he would make a decree for all the people over whom he ruled, that whosoever should speak blasphemy against the God of Shadrach, Meshach, and Abednego should perish, and their house be utterly destroyed. And if they know that he made this decree that blasphemy should not be uttered against the God who tempered the force of the fire, and liberated the three children, they surely go on to consider what decrees they ought to make in their kingdom, that the same God who has granted remission of sins, and given freedom to the whole earth, should not be treated with scorn among the faithful in their realm.

212. See therefore, when Christian kings make any decree against you in defence of Catholic unity, that it be not the case that with your lips you are accusing them of being unlearned, as it were, in holy Scripture, while in your hearts you are grieving that they are so well acquainted with its teaching. For who could put up with the sacrilegious and hateful fallacy which you advance in the case of one and the same Daniel, to find fault with kings because he was cast into the den of lions, and to refuse praise to kings in that he was raised to exalted honor, seeing that, even when he was cast into the den of lions, the king himself was more inclined to believe that he would be safe than that he would be destroyed, and, in anxiety for him, refused to eat his food? And then do you dare to say to Christians, "What have you to do with the kings of the world?" because Daniel suffered persecution at a king's hands, and yet not look back upon the same Daniel faithfully interpreting dreams to kings, calling a king lord, receiving gifts and honors from a king? And so again do you dare, in the case of the aforesaid three children, to excite the flames of odium against kings, because, when they refused to worship the statue, they were cast into the flames, while at the same time you hold your tongue, and say nothing about their being thus extolled and honored by the king? Granted that the king was a persecutor when he cast Daniel into the lions' den; but when, on receiving him safely out again, in his joy and congratulations he cast in his enemies to be torn in pieces and devoured by the same lions, what was he then,—a persecutor, or not?[2] I call on you to answer me. For if he was, why did not Daniel himself resist him, as he might so easily have done in virtue of his great friendship for him, while yet you bid us restrain kings from persecuting men? But if he was not a persecutor, because he avenged with prompt justice the outrage committed against a holy man, what kind of vengeance, I would ask, must be exacted from kings for indignities offered to the sacraments of Christ, if the limbs of the prophet required such a vengeance because they were exposed to danger? Again, I acknowledge that the king, as indeed is manifest, was a persecutor when he cast the three children into the furnace because they refused to worship his image; but I ask whether he was still a persecutor when he set forth the decree that all who should blaspheme against the one true God should be destroyed, and their whole house laid waste? For if he was a persecutor, why do you answer *Amen* to the words of a persecutor?[3] But if he was not a persecutor, why do you call those persecutors who deter you from the madness of blasphemy? For if they compel you to worship an idol, then they

[1] *Simulacri;* and so the MSS. The older editions have "*adorandi simulacra;*" but the singular is more forcible in its special reference to the image on the plain of Dura. Dan. iii.

[2] Dan. ii.-vi.

[3] This is illustrated by the words of Augustin, *Epist.* 105, *ad Donatistas*, c. I. 7: "Do ye not know that the words of the king were: 'I thought it good to show the signs and wonders that the high God hath wrought toward me." How great are His signs! and how mighty are His wonders! His kingdom is an everlasting kingdom, and His dominion from generation to generation' (Dan. iv. 2, 3)? Do you not, when you hear this, answer *Amen*, and by saying this in a loud voice, place your seal on the king's decree by a holy and solemn act?" In the Gothic liturgy this declaration was made on Easter Eve (when the third chapter of Daniel is still read in the Roman Church), and the people answered "*Amen.*'

are like the impious king, and you are like the three children; but if they are preventing you from fighting against Christ, it is you who are impious if you attempt to do this. But what they may be if they forbid this with terrible threats, I do not presume to say. Do you find some other name for them, if you will not call them pious emperors.

213. If I had been the person to bring forward these examples of Daniel and the three children, you would perhaps resist, and declare that they ought not to have been brought from those times in illustration of our days; but God be thanked that you yourself brought them forward, to prove the point, it is true, which you desired to establish, but you see that their force was rather in favor of what you least would wish to prove. Perhaps you will say that this proceeds from no deceit of yours, but from the fallibility of human nature. Would that this were true! Amend it, then You will not lose in reputation; nay, it marks unquestionably the higher mind to extinguish the fire of animosity by a frank confession, than merely to escape the mist of falsehood by acuteness of the understanding.

CHAP. 94.—214. PETILIANUS said: "Where is the law of God? where is your Christianity, if you not only commit murders and put men to death, but also order such things to be done?"

215. AUGUSTIN answered: In reply to this, see what the fellow-heirs of Christ say throughout the world. We neither commit murders, and put men to death, nor order such things to be done; and you are raging much more madly than those who do such things, in that you put such things into the minds of men in opposition to the hopes of everlasting life.

CHAP. 95.—216. PETILIANUS said: "If you wish that we should be your friends, why do you drag us to you against our will? But if you wish that we should be your foes, why do you kill your foes?"

217. AUGUSTIN answered: We neither drag you to us against your will, nor do we kill our foes; but whatever we do in our dealings with you, though we may do it contrary to your inclination, yet we do it from our love to you, that you may voluntarily correct yourselves, and live an amended life. For no one lives against his will; and yet a boy, in order to learn this lesson of his own free will,[1] is beaten contrary to his inclination, and that often by the very man that is most dear to him. And this, indeed, is what the kings would desire to say to you if they were to strike you, for to this end their power has been ordained of God. But you cry out even when they are not striking you.

CHAP. 96.—218. PETILIANUS said: "But what reason is there, or what inconsistency of emptiness, in desiring communion with us so eagerly, when all the time you call us by the false title of heretics?"

219. AUGUSTIN answered: If we so eagerly desired communion with heretics, we should not be anxious that you should be converted from the error of heresy; but when the very object of our negotiations with you is that you should cease to be heretics, how are we eagerly desiring communion with heretics? For, in fact, it is dissension and division that make you heretics; but peace and unity make men Catholics. When, then, you come over from your heresy to us, you cease to be what we hate, and begin to be what we love.

CHAP. 97.—220. PETILIANUS said: "Choose, in short, which of the two alternatives you prefer. If innocence is on your side, why do you persecute us with the sword? Or if you call us guilty, why do you, who are yourselves innocent, seek for our company?"

221. AUGUSTIN answered: O most ingenious dilemma, or rather most foolish verbosity! Is it not usual for the choice of two alternatives to be offered to an antagonist, when it is impossible that he should adopt both? For if you should offer me the choice of the two propositions, that I should say either that we were innocent, or that we were guilty; or, again, of the other pair of propositions, viz., those concerning you, I could not escape choosing either one or the other. But as it is, you offer me the choice of these two, whether we are innocent or you are guilty, and wish me to say which of these two I choose for my reply. But I refuse to make a choice; for I assert them both, that we are innocent, and that you are guilty. I say that we are innocent of the false and calumnious accusations which you bring against us, so far as any of us, being in the Catholic Church, can say with a safe conscience that we have neither given up the sacred books, nor taken part in the worship of idols, nor murdered any man, nor been guilty of any of the other crimes which you allege against us; and that any who may have committed any such offenses, which, however, you have not proved in any case, have thereby shut the doors of

[1] *Nam nemo vivit invitus; et tamen puer ut hoc volens discat, invitus vapulat.* Perhaps a better reading is, "*Nam nemo vult invitus; et tamen puer ut volens discat,*" etc., leaving out "*hoc,*" which is wanting in the Fleury MSS.: "No one wishes against his will; and yet a boy, wishing to learn. is beaten against his will."

the kingdom of heaven, not against us, but against themselves; "for every man shall bear his own burden."[1] Here you have your answer on the first head. And I further say that you are all guilty and accursed,—not some of you owing to the sins of others, which are wrought among you by certain of your number, and are censured by certain others, but all of you by the sin of schism; from which most heinous sacrilege no one of you can say that he is free, so long as he refuses to hold communion with the unity of all nations, unless, indeed, he be compelled to say that Christ has told a lie concerning the Church which is spread abroad among all nations, beginning at Jerusalem.[2] And so you have my second answer. See how I have made you two replies, of which you were desirous that we should be reduced to choose the one. At any rate, you should have taken notice that both assertions might be made by us; and certainly, if this was what you wished, you should have asked it as a favor of us that we should choose one or the other, when you saw that it was in our power to choose both.

222. But "if innocence is on your side, why do you persecute us with the sword?" Look back for a moment on your troops, which are not now armed after the ancient fashion of their fathers only with cudgels, but have further added to their equipment axes and lances and swords, and determine for yourselves to which of us the question best belongs, "Why do you persecute us with the sword?" "Or if you call us guilty," say you, "why do you, who are yourselves innocent, seek for our company?" Here I answer very briefly. The reason why you, being guilty, are sought after by the innocent, is that you may cease to be guilty, and begin to be innocent. Here then I have chosen both of the alternatives concerning us, and answered both of those concerning you, only do you in turn choose one of the two. Are you innocent or guilty? Here you cannot choose to make the two assertions, and yet choose both, if so it pleases you. For at any rate you cannot be innocent in reference to the same circumstances in respect of which you are guilty. If therefore you are innocent, do not be surprised that you are invited to be at peace with your brethren; but if you are guilty, do not be surprised that you are sought for punishment by kings. But since of these two alternatives you assume one for yourselves, and the other is alleged of you by us,—for you assume to yourselves innocence, and it is alleged of you by us that you are living impiously,—hear again once more what I shall say on either head. If you are innocent, why do you speak against the testimony of Christ? But if you are guilty, why do you not fly for refuge to His mercy? For His testimony, on the one hand, is to the unity of the world, and His mercy, on the other, is in brotherly love.

Chap. 98.—223. Petilianus said: "Lastly, as we have often said before, how great is your presumption, that you should speak as you presume to do of kings, when David says, 'It is better to trust in the Lord than to put confidence in man: it is better to trust in the Lord than to put confidence in princes?'"[3]

224. Augustin answered: We put no confidence in man, but, so far as we can, we warn men to place their trust in the Lord; nor do we put confidence in princes, but, so far as we can, we warn princes to put confidence in the Lord. And though we may seek aid from princes to promote the advantage of the Church, yet do we not put confidence in them. For neither did the apostle himself put confidence in that tribune, in the sense in which the Psalmist talks of putting confidence in princes, from whom he obtained for himself that an escort of armed men should be assigned to him; nor did he put confidence in the armed men, by whose protection he escaped the snares of the wicked ones, in any such sense as that of the Psalmist where he speaks of putting confidence in men.[4] But neither do we find fault with you yourselves, because you sought from the emperor that the basilicas should be restored to you, as though you had put your trust in Julian the prince; but we find fault with you, that you have despaired of the witness of Christ, from whose unity you have separated the basilicas themselves. For you received them at the bidding of an enemy of Christ, that in them you should despise the commands of Christ, whilst you find force and truth in what Julian ordained, saying, "This, moreover, on the petition of Rogatianus, Pontius, Cassianus, and other bishops, not without an intermixture of clergy, is added to complete the whole, that those proceedings which were taken to their prejudice wrongly and without authority being all annulled, everything should be restored to its former position;" and yet you find nothing that has either force or truth in what Christ ordained, saying, "Ye shall be witnesses unto me both in Jerusalem, and in all Judea, and in Samaria, and even in the whole earth."[5]

---

1 Gal. vi. 5.
2 Luke xxiv. 47.
3 Ps. cxviii. 8, 9.
4 Acts xxiii. 12-33.
5 Acts i. 8.

We entreat you, let yourselves be reformed. Return to this most manifest unity of the whole world; and let all things be restored to their former position, not in accordance with the words of the apostate Julian, but in accordance with the words of our Saviour Christ. Have pity on your own soul. We are not now comparing Constantine and Julian in order to show how different they are. We are not saying, If you have not placed confidence in a man and in a prince, when you said to a pagan and apostate emperor, that "in him justice only found a place," seeing that the party of Donatus has universally employed the prayers and the rescript in which those words occur, as is proved by the records of the audience; much less ought we to be accused by you, as though we put our confidence in any man or prince, if without any blasphemous flattery we obtained any request from Constantine or from the other Christian emperors; or if they themselves, without our asking for it, but remembering the account which they shall render to the Lord, under whose words they tremble when they hear what you yourself have quoted, "Be wise now therefore, O ye kings," etc., and many other sayings of the sort, make any ordinance of their own accord in support of the unity of the Catholic Church. But I say nothing about Constantine. It is Christ and Julian that we contrast before you; nay, more than this, it is God and man, the Son of God and the son of hell, the Saviour of our souls and the destroyer of his own. Why do you maintain the rescript of Julian in the occupation of the basilicas, and yet not maintain the gospel of Christ in embracing the peace of the Church? We too cry out, "Let all things that have been done amiss be restored to their ancient condition." The gospel of Christ is of greater antiquity than the rescript of Julian; the unity of Christ is of greater antiquity than the party of Donatus; the prayers of the Church to the Lord on behalf of the unity of the Church are of greater antiquity than the prayers of Rogatianus, and Pontius, and Cassianus, to Julian on behalf of the party of Donatus. Are proceedings wrongly taken when kings forbid division? and are they not wrongly taken when bishops divide unity? Is that wrong action when kings minister to the witness of Christ in defence of the Church? and is it not wrong action when bishops contradict the witness of Christ in order to deny the Church? We entreat you, therefore, that the words of Julian himself, to whom you thus made supplication, may be listened to, not in opposition to the gospel, but in accordance with the gospel, and that "all things which have been done amiss may be restored to their former condition."

CHAP. 99.—225. PETILIANUS said: "On you, yes you, you wretched men, I call, who, being dismayed with the fear of persecution, whilst you seek to save your riches, not your souls, love not so much the faithless faith of the traitors, as the wickedness of the very men whose protection you have won unto yourselves,—just in the same way as sailors, shipwrecked in the waves, plunge into the waves by which they must be overwhelmed, and in the great danger of their lives seek unmistakeably the very object of their dread; just as the madness of a tyrant, that he may be free from apprehension of any person whatsoever, desires to be feared, though this is fraught with peril to himself: so, so you fly for refuge to the citadel of wickedness, being willing to look on the loss or punishment of the innocent if you may escape fear for yourselves. If you consider that you escape danger when you plunge into ruin, truly also it is a faith that merits condemnation to observe the faith of a robber. Lastly, it is trafficking in a madman's gains to lose your own souls in order not to lose your wealth. For the Lord Christ says, 'If a man shall gain the whole world, and lose his own soul, what shall a man give in exchange for his soul?'"[1]

226. AUGUSTIN answered: That exhortation of yours would be useful, I cannot but acknowledge, if any one were to employ it in a good cause. It is undoubtedly well that you have tried to deter men from preferring their riches to their souls. But I would have you, who have heard these words, listen also for a time to us; for we also say this, but listen in what sense. If kings threaten to take away your riches, because you are not Jews according to the flesh, or because you do not worship idols or devils, or because you are not carried about into any heresies, but abide in Catholic unity, then choose rather that your riches should perish, that you perish not yourselves; but be careful to prefer neither anything else, nor the life of this world itself, to eternal salvation, which is in Christ. But if kings threaten you with loss or condemnation, simply on the ground that you are heretics, such things are terrifying you not in cruelty, but in mercy; and your determination not to fear is a sign not of bravery, but of obstinacy. Hear then the words of Peter, where he says, "What glory is it, if, when ye be buffeted for your faults, ye take it patiently?"[2] so that herein you have neither

[1] Matt. xvi. 26.

[2] 1 Pet. ii. 20.

consolation upon earth, nor in the world to come life everlasting; but you have here the miseries of the unfortunate, and there the hell of heretics. Do you see, therefore, my brother, with whom I am now arguing, that you ought first to show whether you hold the truth, and then to exhort men that in upholding it they should be ready to give up all the blessings which they possess in this present world? And so, when you do not show this, because you cannot,—not that the talent is wanting, but because the cause is bad,—why do you hasten by your exhortations to make men both beggars and ignorant, both in want and wandering from the truth, in rags and contentions, household drudges and heretics, both losing their temporal goods in this world, and finding eternal evils in the judgment of Christ? But the cautious son, who, while he stands in dread of his father's rod, keeps away from the lair of the serpent, escapes both blows and destruction; whereas he who despises the pains of discipline, when set in rivalry with his own pernicious will, is both beaten and destroyed. Do you not now understand, O learned man, that he who has resigned all earthly goods in order to maintain the peace of Christ, possesses God; whereas he who has lost even a very few coins in behalf of the party of Donatus is devoid of heart?

Chap. 100.—227. Petilianus said: "But we who are poor in spirit[1] are not apprehensive for our wealth, but rather feel a dread of wealth. We, 'as having nothing, and yet possessing all things,'[2] look on our soul as our wealth, and by our punishments and blood purchase to ourselves the everlasting riches of heaven. So again the same Lord says, 'Whosoever shall lose his substance, shall find it again an hundred fold.'"

228. Augustin answered: It is not beside the purpose to inquire into the true meaning of this passage also. For where my purpose is not interfered with by any mistake which you make, or any false impression which you convey in quoting from the Scriptures, I do not concern myself about the matter. It is not then written, "Whosoever shall lose his substance," but "Whosoever shall lose his life for my sake."[3] And the passage about substance is not, "Whosoever shall lose," but "Every one that hath forsaken;"[4] and that not only with reference to substance of money, but many other things besides. But you meanwhile have not lost your substance; but whether you have forsaken it, in that you so boast of poverty, I cannot say. And if by any chance my colleague Fortunatus may know this, being in the same city with you, he never told me, because I had never asked him. However, even if you had done this, you have yet yourself quoted the testimony of the apostle against yourself in this very epistle which you have written: "Though I bestow all my goods to feed the poor, and though I give my body to be burned, and have not charity, it profiteth me nothing."[5] For if you had charity, you would not bring charges against the whole world, which knows nothing of you, and of which you know no more,—no, not even such charges as are founded on the proved offenses of the Africans. If you had charity, you would not picture to yourself a false unity in your calumnies, but you would learn to recognize the unity that is most clearly set forth in the words of the Lord: "even in the whole earth."[6] But if you did not do this, why do you boast as though you had done it? Are you really so filled with fear of riches, that, having nothing, you possess all things? Tell that to your colleague Crispinus, who lately bought a farm near our city of Hippo, that he might there plunge men into the lowest abyss.[7] Whence I too know this all too well. You perhaps are not aware of it, and therefore shout out in security, "We stand in fear of riches." And hence I am surprised that that cry of yours has been allowed to pass Crispinus, so as to reach us. For between Constantina, where you are, and Hippo, where I am, lies Calama, where he is, nearer indeed to our side, but still between us. I wonder, therefore, how it was that he did not first intercept this cry, and strike it back so that it should not reach to our ears; and that he did not, in opposition to you, recite in much more copious phrase a eulogy on riches. For he not only stands in no fear of riches, but he actually loves them. And certainly, before you utter anything about the rest, you should rehearse such views to him. If he makes no corrections, then we have our answer ready. But for yourself, if it be true that you are poor, you have with you my brother Fortunatus. You will be more likely with such sentiments to please him, who is my colleague, than Crispinus, who is your own.

Chap. 101.—229. Petilianus said: "Inasmuch as we live in the fear of God, we have no fear of the punishments and executions which you wreak with the sword; but the only thing which we avoid is that by your most wicked communion you destroy men's souls, according to the saying of the Lord Himself:

[1] Matt. v. 3.
[2] 2 Cor. vi. 10.
[3] Matt. xvi. 25.
[4] Matt. xix. 29.
[5] 1 Cor. xiii. 3.
[6] Acts i. 8.
[7] See above, c. 84.

'Fear not them which kill the body, but are not able to kill the soul; but rather fear Him which is able to destroy both soul and body in hell.'"[1]

230. AUGUSTIN answered: You do the destruction which you speak of, not with a visible sword, but with that of which it is said, "The sons of men, whose teeth are spears and arrows, and their tongue a sharp sword."[2] For with this sword of accusation and calumny against the world of which you are wholly ignorant, you destroy the souls of those who lack experience. But if you find fault with a most wicked communion, as you term it, I would bid you presently, not with my words, but with your own, to ascend, descend, enter, turn yourself about, change sides, be such as was Optatus. But if you return to your senses, and shall find that you are not such as he, not because he refused to partake of the sacraments with you, but because you took offense at what he did, then you will acquit the world of crimes which do not belong to it, and you will find yourself involved in the sin of schism.

CHAP. 102.—231. PETILIANUS said: "You, therefore, who prefer rather to be washed with the most false of baptisms than to be regenerate, not only do not lay aside your sins, but also load your souls with the offenses of criminals. For as the water of the guilty has been abandoned by the Holy Spirit, so it is clearly filled full of the offenses of the *traditors*. To any wretched man, then, who is baptized by one of this sort, we would say, If you have wished to be free from falsehood, you are really drenched with falsity. If you desired to shut out the sins of the flesh, you will, as the conscience of the guilty comes upon you, be partakers likewise of their guilt. If you wished to extinguish the flames of avarice, you are drenched with deceit, you are drenched with wickedness, you are drenched also with madness. Lastly, if you believe that faith is identical in the giver and the receiver, you are drenched with the blood of a brother by him who slays a man. And so it comes to pass that you, who had come to baptism free from sin, return from baptism guilty of the sin of murder."

232. AUGUSTIN answered: I should like to come to argument with those who shouted assent when they either heard or read those words of yours. For such men have not ears in their hearts, but their heart in their ears. Yet let them read again and again, and consider, and find out for themselves, not what the sound of those words is, but what they mean. First of all, to sift the meaning of the last clause, "So it comes to pass," you say, "that you who had come to baptism free from sin, return from baptism guilty of the sin of murder:" tell me, to begin with, who there is that comes to baptism free from sin, with the single exception of Him who came to be baptized, not that His iniquity should be purged away, but that an example of humility might be given us? For what shall be forgiven to one free from sin? Or are you indeed endowed with such an eloquence, that you can show to us some innocence which yet committeth sin? Do you not hear the words of Scripture saying, "No one is clean from sin in Thy sight, not even the infant whose life is but of a single day upon the earth?"[3] For whence else is it that one hastens even with infants to seek remission of their sins? Do you not hear the words of another Scripture, "In sin did my mother conceive me?"[4] In the next place, if a man returns a murderer, who had come without the guilt of murder, merely because he receives baptism at a murderer's hands, then all they who returned from receiving baptism at the hands of Optatus were made partakers with Optatus. Go now, and see with what face you cast in our teeth that we excite the wrath of kings against you. Are you not afraid that as many satellites of Gildo will be sought for among you, as there are men who may have been baptized by Optatus? Do you see at length how that sentence of yours, like an empty bladder, has rattled not only with a meaningless sound, but on your own head?

233. To go on to the other earlier arguments which you have set before us to be refuted, they are of such a nature that we must needs allow that every one returns from baptism endued with the character of him by whom he is baptized; but God forbid that those whom you baptize should return from you infected with the same madness as possesses you when you make such a statement! And what a dainty sound there was in your words, "You are drenched with deceit, you are drenched with wickedness, you are drenched also with madness!" Surely you would never pour forth words like this unless you were, not drenched, but filled even to repletion with madness. Is it then true, to say nothing of the rest, that all who come untainted with covetousness to receive baptism at the hands of your covetous colleagues, or the priests of your party, return guilty of covetousness, and that those who run in

[1] Matt. x. 28.

[2] Ps. lvii. 4.

[3] Job xiv. 4, 5; cp. LXX.

[4] Ps. li. 5.

soberness to the whirlpool of intoxication to be baptized return in drunkenness? If you entertain and teach such views as this, you will have the effrontery even to quote, as making against us, the passage which you advanced some little time ago: "It is better to trust in the Lord than to put confidence in man. It is better to trust in the Lord than to put confidence in princes."[1] What is the meaning of your teaching, I would ask, save only this, that we should put our confidence, not in the Lord, but in man, when you say that the baptized person is made to resemble him who has baptized him? And since you assume this as the fundamental principle of your baptism, are men to place their trust in you? and are those to place their trust in princes who were disposed to place it in the Lord? Truly I would bid them hearken not to you, but rather to those proofs which you have urged against ourselves, ay, and to words more awful yet; for not only is it written, "It is better to trust in the Lord than to put confidence in man," but also, "Cursed be the man that trusteth in man."[2]

Chap. 103.—234. Petilianus said: "Imitate indeed the prophets, who feared to have their holy souls deceived with false baptism. For Jeremiah says of old that among impious men water is as one that lies. 'Water,' he says, 'that lies has not faith.'"

235. Augustin answered: Any one that hears these words, without being acquainted with the Scriptures, and who does not believe that you are either so far astray as not to know what you are saying, or deceiving in such wise that he whom you have deceived should not know what he says, would believe that the prophet Jeremiah, wishing to be baptized, had taken precautions not to be baptized by impious men, and had used these words with this intent. For what was your object in saying, previous to your quotation of this passage, "Imitate indeed the prophets, who feared to have their holy souls deceived with false baptism?" Just as though, in the days of Jeremiah, any one were washed with the sacrament of baptism, except so far as the Pharisees almost every moment bathed themselves, and their couches and cups and platters, with the washings which the Lord condemned, as we read in the gospel.[3] How then could Jeremiah have said this, as though he desired to be baptized, and sought to avoid being baptized by impious men? He said it, then, when he was complaining of a faithless people, by the corruption of whose morals he was vexed, not wishing to associate with their deeds; and yet he did not separate himself bodily from their congregation, nor seek other sacraments than those which the people received as suitable to that time, according to the law of Moses. To this people, therefore, in their evil mode of life, he gave the name of "a wound," with which the heart of the righteous man was grievously smitten, whether speaking thus of himself, or foreshadowing in himself what he foresaw would come to pass. For he speaks as follows: "O Lord, remember me, and visit me; make clear my innocence before those who persecute me in no spirit of long-suffering: know that for Thy sake I have suffered rebuke from those that scorn Thy words. Make their portion complete; and Thy word shall be unto me the joy and rejoicing of mine heart: for I am called by Thy name, O Lord God of hosts. I sat not in the assembly of the mockers, but was afraid of the presence of Thy hand; I sat alone, because I was filled with bitterness. Why do those who make me sad prevail against me? My wound is grievous; whence shall I be healed? It is become unto me as lying water, that has no faith."[4] In all this it is manifest what the prophet wished to be understood, but manifest only to those who do not wish to distort to their own perverse cause the meaning of what they read. For Jeremiah says that his wound has become unto him as lying water, which cannot inspire faith; but he wished that by his wound those should be understood who made him sad by the evil conduct of their lives. Whence also the apostle says, "Without were fightings, within were fears;"[5] and again, "Who is weak, and I am not weak? who is offended, and I burn not?"[6] And because he had no hopes that they could be reformed, therefore he said, "Whence shall I be healed?" as though his own pain must needs continue so long as those among whom he was compelled to live continued what they were. But that a people is commonly understood under the appellation of water is shown in the Apocalypse, where we understand "many waters" to mean "many peoples," not by any conjecture of our own, but by an express explanation in the place itself.[7] Abstain then from blaspheming the sacrament of baptism from any misunderstanding, or rather error, even when found in a man of most abandoned character; for not even in the lying Simon was the baptism which he received a lying water,[8] nor do all the liars of your party administer a lying water when they

[1] Ps. cxviii. 8, 9
[2] Jer. xvii. 5
[3] Mark vii. 4.
[4] Jer. xv. 15-18; cp. LXX.
[5] 2 Cor. vii. 5.
[6] 2 Cor. xi. 29.
[7] Rev. xvii. 15
[8] Acts viii. 13.

baptize in the name of the Trinity. For neither do they begin to be liars only when they are betrayed and convicted, and so forced to acknowledge their misdeeds; but rather they were already liars, when, being adulterers and accursed, they pretended to be chaste and innocent.

CHAP. 104.—236. PETILIANUS said: "David also said, 'The oil of the sinner shall not anoint my head.' Who is it, therefore, that he calls a sinner? Is it I who suffer your violence, or you who persecute the innocent?"

237. AUGUSTIN answered: As representing the body of Christ, which is the Church of the living God, the pillar and mainstay of the truth, dispersed throughout the world, on account of the gospel which was preached, according to the words of the apostle, "to every creature which is under heaven:"[1] as representing the whole world, of which David, whose words you cannot understand, has said, "The world also is stablished, that it cannot be moved;"[2] whereas you contend that it not only has been moved, but has been utterly destroyed: as representing this, I answer, I do not persecute the innocent. But David said, "The oil of the sinner," not of the *traditor;* not of him who offers incense, not of the persecutor, but "of the sinner." What then will you make of your interpretation? See first whether you are not yourself a sinner. It is nothing to the point if you should say, I am not a *traditor*, I am not an offerer of incense, I am not a persecutor. I myself, by the grace of God, am none of these, nor is the world, which cannot be moved. But say, if you dare, I am not a sinner. For David says, "The oil of the sinner." For so long as any sin, however light, be found in you, what ground have you for maintaining that you are not concerned in the expression that is used, "The oil of the sinner"? For I would ask whether you use the Lord's prayer in your devotions? For if you do not use that prayer, which our Lord taught His disciples for their use, where have you learned another, proportioned to your merits, as exceeding the merits of the apostles? But if you pray, as our great Master deigned to teach us, how do you say, "Forgive us our trespasses, as we forgive them that trespass against us?" For in this petition we are not referring to those sins which have already been forgiven us in baptism. Therefore these words in the prayer either exclude you from being a petitioner to God, or else they make it manifest that you too are a sinner. Let those then come and kiss your head who have been baptized by you, whose heads have perished through your oil. But see to yourself, both what you are and what you think about yourself. Is it really true that Optatus, whom pagans, Jews, Christians, men of our party, men of your party, all proclaim throughout the whole of Africa to have been a thief, a traitor, an oppressor, a contriver of schism; not a friend, not a client, but a tool of him[3] whom one of your party declared to have been his count, companion, and god,—is it true that he was not a sinner in any conceivable interpretation of the term? What then will they do whose heads were anointed by one guilty of a capital offense? Do not those very men kiss your heads, on whose heads you pass so serious a judgment by this interpretation which you place upon the passage? Truly I would bid you bring them forth, and admonish them to heal themselves. Or is it rather your heads which should be healed, who run so grievously astray? What then, you will ask, did David really say: Why do you ask me: rather ask himself. He answers you in the verse above: "The righteous shall smite me in kindness, and shall reprove me; but let not the oil of the sinner anoint my head."[4] What could be plainer? what more manifest? I had rather, he says, be healed by a rebuke administered in kindness, than be deceived and led astray by smooth flattery, coming on me as an ointment on my head. The self-same sentiment is found elsewhere in Scripture under other words: "Better are the wounds of a friend than the proffered kisses of an enemy."[5]

CHAP. 105.—238. PETILIANUS said: "But he thus praises the ointment of concord among brethren: 'Behold how good and how pleasant it is for brethren to dwell together in unity! It is like the precious ointment upon the head, that ran down upon the beard, even Aaron's beard; that went down to the skirts of his garments; as the dew of Hermon, and as the dew that descended upon the mountains of Zion: for there the Lord commanded the blessing, even life for evermore.'[6] Thus, he says, is unity anointed, even as the priests are anointed."

239. AUGUSTIN answered: What you say is true. For that priesthood in the body of Christ had an anointing, and its salvation is secured by the bond of unity. For indeed Christ Himself derives His name from chrism, that is, from anointing. Him the Hebrews call the Messiah, which word is closely akin

[1] Col. i. 23.
[2] Ps. xciii. 1.
[3] Gildo.
[4] Ps. cxli. 5; cp. LXX and Hieron.
[5] Prov. xxvii. 6; cp. LXX. and Hieron.
[6] Ps. cxxxiii.

to the Phœnician language, as is the case with very many other Hebrew words, if not with almost all.[1] What then is meant by the head in that priesthood, what by the beard, what by the skirts of the garments? So far as the Lord enables me to understand, the head is none other than the Saviour of the body, of whom the apostle says, "And He is the head of the body, the Church."[2] By the beard is not unsuitably understood fortitude. Therefore, on those who show themselves to be brave in His Church, and cling to the light of His countenance, to preach the truth without fear, there descends from Christ Himself, as from the head, a sacred ointment, that is to say, the sanctification of the Spirit. By the skirts of the garments we are here given to understand that which is at the top of the garments, through which the head of Him who gives the clothing enters. By this are signified those who are perfected in faith within the Church. For in the skirts is perfection. And I presume you must remember what was said to a certain rich man: "If thou wilt be perfect, go and sell that thou hast, and give to the poor, and thou shalt have treasure in heaven; and come and follow me."[3] He indeed went away sorrowful, slighting what was perfect, choosing what was imperfect. But does it follow that there were wanting those who were so made perfect by such a surrender of earthly things, that the ointment of unity descended upon them, as from the head upon the skirts of the garments? For, putting aside the apostles, and those who were immediately associated with those leaders and teachers of the Church, whom we understand to be represented with greater dignity and more conspicuous fortitude in the beard, read in the Acts of the Apostles, and see those who "brought the prices of the things that were sold, and laid them down at the apostles' feet. Neither said any of them that aught of the things which he possessed was his own; but they had all things common: and distribution was made unto every man according as he had need. And the multitude of them that believed were of one heart and of one soul."[4] I doubt not that you are aware that it is so written. Recognize, therefore, how good and how pleasant it is for brethren to dwell together in unity. Recognize the beard of Aaron; recognize the skirts of the spiritual garments. Search the Scriptures themselves, and see where those things began to be done; you will find that it was in Jerusalem. From this skirt of the garment is woven together the whole fabric of unity throughout all nations. By this the Head entered into the garment, that Christ should be clothed with all the variety of the several nations of the earth, because in this skirt of the garment appeared the actual variety of tongues. Why, therefore, is the Head itself, whence that ointment of unity descended, that is, the spiritual fragrance of brotherly love,—why, I say, is the Head itself exposed to your resistance, while it testifies and declares that "repentance and remission of sins should be preached in His name among all nations, beginning at Jerusalem"?[5] And by this ointment you wish the sacrament of chrism to be understood, which is indeed holy as among the class of visible signs, like baptism itself, but yet can exist even among the worst of men, wasting their life in the works of the flesh, and never destined to possess the kingdom of heaven, and having therefore nothing to do either with the beard of Aaron, or with the skirts of his garments, or with any fabric of priestly clothing. For where do you intend to place what the apostle enumerates as "the manifest works of the flesh, which," he says, "are these: fornication, uncleanness, lasciviousness, idolatry, poisonings, hatred, variance, emulations, wrath, strife, heresies, envyings, drunkenness, revellings, and such like: of the which I tell you before, as I have also told you in time past, that they which do such things shall not inherit the kingdom of God?"[6] I put aside fornications, which are committed in secret; interpret uncleanness as you please, I am willing to put it aside as well. Let us put on one side also poisons, since no one is openly a compounder or giver of poisons. I put aside also heresies, since you will have it so. I am in doubt whether I ought to put aside idolatry, since the apostle classes with it covetousness, which is openly rife among you. However, setting aside all these, are there none among you lascivious, none covetous, none open in their indulgence of enmities, none fond of strife, or fond of emulation, wrathful, given to seditions, envious, drunken, wasting their time in revellings? Are none of such a character anointed among you? Do none die well known among you to be given to such things, or openly indulging in them? If you say there are none, I would have you consider whether you do

[1] Compare *Tract.* xv. 27 *in Joannem:* "Messiah was anointed. The Greek for 'anointed' is 'Christ,' the Hebrew Messiah; whence also in Phœnician we have 'Messe' for 'anoint.' For these languages, the Hebrew, Phœnician and Syrian, are closely cognate, as well as geographically bordering on each other." See also Max Müller's *Lectures on the Science of Language*, series I. Lect. VIII. "The ancient language of Phœnicia, to judge from inscriptions, was most closely allied to Hebrew."
[2] Col. i. 18. [3] Matt. xix. 21. [4] Acts iv. 32-35.

[5] Luke xxiv. 47. [6] Gal. v. 19-21.

not come under the description yourself, since you are manifestly telling lies in the desire for strife. But if you are yourself severed from men of this sort, not by bodily separation, but by dissimilarity of life, and if you behold with lamentation crowds like these around your altars, what shall we say, since they are anointed with holy oil, and yet, as the apostle assures us with the clearness of truth, shall not inherit the kingdom of God? Must we do such impious despite to the beard of Aaron and to the skirts of his garments, as to suppose that they are to be placed there? Far be that from us. Separate therefore the visible holy sacrament, which can exist both in the good and in the bad,—in the former for their reward, in the latter for judgment; separate it from the invisible unction of charity, which is the peculiar property of the good. Separate them, separate them, ay, and may God separate you from the party of Donatus, and call you back again into the Catholic Church, whence you were torn by them while yet a catechumen, to be bound by them in the bond of a deadly distinction. Now are ye not in the mountains of Zion, the dew of Hermon on the mountains of Zion, in whatever sense that be received by you; for you are not in the city upon a hill, which has this as its sure sign, that it cannot be hid. It is known therefore unto all nations. But the party of Donatus is unknown to the majority of nations, therefore is it not the true city.

CHAP. 106.—240. PETILIANUS said: "Woe unto you, therefore, who, by doing violence to what is holy, cut away the bond of unity; whereas the prophet says, 'If the people shall sin, the priest shall pray for them: but if the priest shall sin, who will pray for him?'"

241. AUGUSTIN answered: I seemed too a little while ago, when we were disputing about the oil of the sinner, to anoint your forehead, in order that you might say, if you dared, whether you yourself were not a sinner. You have had the hardihood to say as much. What a portentous sin! For in that you assert yourself to be a priest, what else have you maintained by quoting this testimony of the prophet, save that you are wholly without sin? For if you have sin, who is there that shall pray for you, according to your understanding of the words? For thus you blazon yourselves among the wretched people, quoting from the prophet: "If the people shall sin, the priest shall pray for them: but if the priest shall sin, who will pray for him?"[1] to the intent that they may believe you to be without sin, and entrust the wiping away of their sins to your prayers. Truly ye are great men, exalted above your fellows, heavenly, godlike, angels indeed rather than men, who pray for the people, and will not have the people pray for you! Are you more righteous than Paul, more perfect than that great apostle, who was wont to commend himself to the prayers of those whom he taught? "Continue," he says, "in prayer, and watch in the same with thanksgiving; withal praying also for us, that God would open unto us a door of utterance, to speak the mystery of Christ, for which I am also in bonds; that I may make it manifest, as I ought to speak."[2] See how prayer is made for an apostle, which you would have not made for a bishop. Do you perceive of how devilish a nature your pride is? Prayer is made for an apostle, that he may make manifest the mystery of Christ as he ought to speak. Accordingly, if you had a pious people under you, you ought to have exhorted them to pray for you, that you might not give utterance as you ought not. Are you more righteous than the evangelist John, who says, "If we say that we have no sin, we deceive ourselves, and the truth is not in us?"[3] Finally, are you more righteous than Daniel, whom you yourself quoted in this very epistle, going so far as to say, "The most righteous king cast forth Daniel, as he supposed, to be devoured by wild beasts?"—a thing which he never did suppose, since he said to Daniel himself, in the most friendly spirit, as the context of the lesson shows, "Thy God, whom thou servest continually, He will deliver thee."[4] But on this subject we have already said much. With regard to the question now before us, viz., that Daniel was most righteous, it is proved not by your testimony, though that might be sufficient for me in the argument which I hold with you, but by the testimony of the Spirit of God, speaking also by the mouth of Ezekiel, where he named three men of most eminent righteousness, Noah, Daniel, and Job, who, he said, were the only men that could be saved from a certain excessive wrath of God, which was hanging over all the rest.[5] A man, therefore, of the highest righteousness, one of three conspicuous for righteousness, prays, and says, "While I was speaking, and praying, and confessing my sin, and the sin of my people Israel, and presenting my supplication before the Lord my God."[6] And you say that you are without sin, because forsooth you are a priest; and if

1 Apparently misquoted from 1 Sam. ii. 25.

2 Col. iv. 2-4. 3 1 John i. 8. 4 Dan. vi. 16. 5 Ezek. xiv. 14. 6 Dan. ix. 20.

the people sin, you pray for them: but if you sin, who shall pray for you? For clearly by the impiety of such arrogance you show yourself to be unworthy of the mediation of that Priest whom the prophet would have to be understood in these words, which you do not understand. For now that no one may ask why this was said, I will explain it so far as by God's grace I shall be able. God was preparing the minds of men, by His prophet, to desire a Priest of such a sort that none should pray for Him. He was Himself prefigured in the times of the first people and the first temple, in which all things were figures for our ensample. Therefore the high priest used to enter alone into the holy of holies, that he might make supplication for the people, which did not enter with the priest into that inner sanctuary;[1] just as our High Priest is entered into the secret places of the heavens, into that truer holy of holies, whilst we for whom He prays are still placed here.[1] It is with this reference that the prophet says, "If the people shall sin, the priest shall pray for them: but if the priest shall sin, who will pray for him?" Seek therefore a priest of such a kind that he cannot sin, nor need that one should pray for him. And for this reason prayer is made for the apostles by the people;[2] but for that Priest who is the Master and Lord of the apostles is prayer not made. Hear John confessing this, and saying, "My little children, these things write I unto you, that ye sin not. And if any man sin, we have an Advocate with the Father, Jesus Christ the righteous, and He is the propitiation for our sins."[3] "*We* have," he says; and "for *our* sins." I pray you, learn humility, that you may not fall, or rather, that in time you may arise again. For had you not already fallen, you never would have used such words.

Chap. 107.—242. Petilianus said: "And that none who is a layman may claim to be free from sin, they are all bound by this prohibition: 'Be not partakers of other men's sins.'"

243. Augustin answered: You are mistaken *toto cœlo*, as the saying is, by reason of your pride, whilst, by reason of your humility, you are unwilling to communicate with the whole world. For, in the first place, this was not spoken to a layman; and, in the second place, you are wholly ignorant in what sense it was spoken. The apostle, writing to Timothy, gives this warning to none other than Timothy himself, to whom he says in another place, "Neglect not the gift that is in thee, which was given thee by prophecy, with the laying on of the hands of the presbytery."[4] And by many other proofs it is made clear that he was not a layman. But in that he says, "Be not partaker of other men's sins,"[5] he means, Be not partaker voluntarily, or with consent. And hence he immediately subjoins directions how he shall obey the injunction, saying, "Keep thyself pure." For neither was Paul himself partaker of other men's sins, because he endured false brethren, over whom he groans, in bodily unity; nor did the apostles who preceded him partake of the thievery and crime of Judas, because they partook of the holy supper with him when he had already sold his Lord, and been pointed out as the traitor by that Lord.

Chap. 108.—244. Petilianus said: "By this sentence, again, the apostle places in the same category those who have fellowship in the consciousness of evil. 'Worthy of death,' he says, 'are both those who do such things, and those who consent with those that do them.'"[6]

245. Augustin answered: I care not in what manner you have used these words, they are true. And this is the substance of the teaching of the Catholic Church, that there is a great difference between those who consent because they take pleasure in such things, and those who tolerate while they dislike them. The former make themselves chaff, while they follow the barrenness of the chaff; the latter are the grain. Let them wait for Christ, who bears the winnowing-fan, that they may be separated from the chaff.

Chap. 109.—246. Petilianus said: "Come therefore to the Church, all ye people, and flee the company of *traditors*, if you would not also perish with them. For that you may the more readily know that, while they are themselves guilty, they yet entertain an excellent opinion of our faith, let me inform you that I baptize their polluted ones; they, though may God never grant them such an opportunity, receive those who are made mine by baptism,—which certainly they would not do if they recognized any defects in our baptism. See therefore how holy that is which we give, when even our sacrilegious enemy fears to destroy it."

247. Augustin answered: Against this error I have said much already, both in this work and elsewhere. But since you think that in this sentence you have so strong a

[1] Lev. xvi.; Heb. ix. 7. [2] 2 Cor. i. 11. [3] 1 John ii. 1, 2. [4] 1 Tim. iv. 14. [5] 1 Tim. v. 22. [6] Rom. i. 32.

confirmation of your vain opinions, that you deemed it right to end your epistle with these words, that they might remain as it were the fresher in the minds of your readers, I think it well to make a short reply. We recognize in heretics that baptism, which belongs not to the heretics but to Christ, in such sort as in fornicators, in unclean persons or effeminate, in idolaters, in poisoners, in those who retain enmity, in those who are fond of contention, in the credulous, in the proud, given to seditions, in the envious, in drunkards, in revellers; and in men like these we hold valid the baptism which is not theirs but Christ's. For of men like these, and among them are included heretics also, none, as the apostle says, shall inherit the kingdom of heaven.[1] Nor are they to be considered as being in the body of Christ, which is the Church, simply because they are materially partakers of the sacraments. For the sacraments indeed are holy, even in such men as these, and shall be of force in them to greater condemnation, because they handle and partake of them unworthily. But the men themselves are not within the constitution of the Church, which increases in the increase of God in its members through connection and contact with Christ. For that Church is founded on a rock, as the Lord says, "Upon this rock I will build my Church."[2] But they build on the sand, as the same Lord says, "Every one that heareth these sayings of mine, and doeth them not, shall be likened unto a foolish man, which built his house upon the sand."[3] But that you may not suppose that the Church which is upon a rock is in one part only of the earth, and does not extend even to its furthest boundaries, hear her voice groaning from the psalm, amid the evils of her pilgrimage. For she says, "From the end of the earth have I cried unto Thee; when my heart was distressed Thou didst lift me up upon the rock; Thou hast led me, Thou, my hope, hast become a tower of courage from the face of the enemy."[4] See how she cries from the end of the earth. She is not therefore in Africa alone, nor only among the Africans, who send a bishop from Africa to Rome to a few Montenses,[5] and into Spain to the house of one lady.[6] See how she is exalted on a rock. All, therefore, are not to be deemed to be in her which build upon the sand, that is, which hear the words of Christ and do them not, even though both among us and among you they have and transmit the sacrament of baptism. See how her hope is in God the Father, the Son, and the Holy Ghost,—not in Peter or in Paul, still less in Donatus or Petilianus. What we fear, therefore, to destroy, is not yours, but Christ's; and it is holy of itself, even in sacrilegious hands. For we cannot receive those who come from you, unless we destroy in them whatsoever appertains to you. For we destroy the treachery of the deserter, not the stamp of the sovereign. Accordingly, do you yourself consider and annul what you said: "I," say you, "baptize their polluted ones; they, though may God never grant them such an opportunity, receive those who are made mine by baptism." For you do not baptize men who are infected, but you rebaptize them, so as to infect them with the fraud of your error. But we do not receive men who are made yours by baptism; but we destroy that error of yours whereby they are made yours, and we receive the baptism of Christ, by which they are baptized. Therefore it is not without significance that you introduce the words, "Though may God never grant them such an opportunity." For you said, "They, though may God never grant them such an opportunity, receive those who are made mine by baptism." For while you in your fear that we may receive your followers desire to be understood, "may God never give them the opportunity of receiving such as are mine," I suppose that, without knowing what it meant, you said, "May God never make them mine that you should receive them." For we pray that those may not be really yours who come over at the present moment to the Catholic Church. Nor do they come over so as to be ours by right of baptism, but by fellowship with us, and that with us they may belong to Christ, in virtue of their baptism.

1 Gal. v. 19–21.
2 Matt. xvi. 18.
3 Matt. vii. 26.
4 Ps. lxi. 2, 3.
5 That the Donatists were called at Rome *Montenses*, is observed by Augustin, *de Hæresibus*, c. lxix., and *Epist.* liii. 2; and before him by Optatus, Book II. c. iv. That they were also called *Cutzupitani*, or *Cutzupitæ*, we learn from the same epistle, and from his treatise *de Unitate Ecclesiæ*, c. iii. 6.
6 Lucilla.

BOOK III.

IN THIS BOOK AUGUSTIN REFUTES THE SECOND LETTER[1] WHICH PETILIANUS WROTE TO HIM AFTER HAVING SEEN THE FIRST OF AUGUSTIN'S EARLIER BOOKS. THIS LETTER HAD BEEN FULL OF VIOLENT LANGUAGE; AND AUGUSTIN RATHER SHOWS THAT THE ARGUMENTS OF PETILIANUS HAD BEEN DEFICIENT AND IRRELEVANT, THAN BRINGS FORWARD ARGUMENTS IN SUPPORT OF HIS OWN STATEMENTS.

CHAP. I.—1. Being able to read, Petilianus, I have read your letter, in which you have shown with sufficient clearness that, in supporting the party of Donatus against the Catholic Church, you have neither been able to say anything to the purpose, nor been allowed to hold your tongue. What violent emotions did you endure, what a storm of feelings surged within your heart, on reading the answer which I made, with all possible brevity and clearness, to that portion of your letter which alone at that time had come into my hands! For you saw that the truth which we maintain and defend was confirmed with such strength of argument, and illustrated with such abundant light, that you could not find anything which could be said against it, whereby the charges which we make might be refuted. You observed, also, that the attention of many who had read it was fixed on you, since they desired to know what you would say, what you would do, how you would escape from the difficulty, how you would make your way out of the strait in which the word of God had encompassed you. Hereupon you, when you ought to have shown contempt for the opinion of the foolish ones, and to have gone on to adopt sound and truthful sentiments, preferred rather to do what Scripture has foretold of men like you: "Thou hast loved evil more than good, and lying rather than to speak righteousness."[2] Just as if I in turn were willing to recompense unto you railing for railing; in which case, what should we be but two evil speakers, so that those who read our words would either preserve their self-respect by throwing us aside with abhorrence, or eagerly devour what we wrote to gratify their malice? For my own part, since I answer every one, whether in writing or by word of mouth, even when I have been attacked with insulting accusations, in such language as the Lord puts in my mouth, restraining and crushing the stings of empty indignation in the interests of my hearer or reader, I do not strive to prove myself superior to my adversary by abusing him, but rather to be a source of health in him by convicting him of his error.

2. For if those who take into consideration what you have written have any feelings whatsoever, how did it serve you in the cause which is at issue between us respecting the Catholic communion and the party of Donatus, that, leaving a matter which was in a certain sense of public interest, you should have been led by private animosity to attack the life of an individual with malicious revilings, just as though that individual were the question in debate? Did you think so badly, I do not say of Christians, but of the whole human race, as not to suppose that your writings might come into the hands of some prudent men, who would lay aside all thoughts of individuals like us, and inquire rather into the question which was at issue between us, and pay heed, not to who and what we were, but to what we might be able to advance in defense of the truth or against error? You should have paid respect to these men's judgment, you should have guarded yourself against their censure, lest they should think that you could find nothing to say, unless you set before yourself some one whom you might abuse by any means within your power. But one may see by the thoughtlessness and foolishness of some men, who listen eagerly to

[1] Possidius, in the third chapter of his *Indiculus*, designates this third book as "One book against the second letter of the same." Cp. Aug. *Retractt.* Bk. II. c. xxv.

[2] Ps. lii. 3.

the quarrels of any learned disputants, that while they take notice of the eloquence wherewith you lavish your abuse, they do not perceive with what truth you are refuted. At the same time, I think your object partly was that I might be driven, by the necessity of defending myself, to desert the very cause which I had undertaken; and that so, while men's attention was turned to the words of opponents who were engaged not in disputation, but in quarrelling, the truth might be obscured, which you are so afraid should come to light and be well known among men. What therefore was I to do in opposing such a design as this, except to keep strictly to my subject, neglecting rather my own defense, praying withal that no personal calumny may lead me to withdraw from it? I will exalt the house of my God, whose honor I have loved, with the tribute of a faithful servant's voice, but myself I will humiliate and hold of no account. "I had rather be a door-keeper in the house of my God, than to dwell in the tents of heretics."[1] I will therefore turn my discourse from you, Petilianus, for a time, and direct it rather to those whom you have endeavored to turn away from me by your revilings, as though my endeavor rather were that men should be converted unto me, and not rather with me unto God.

CHAP. 2.—3. Hear therefore, all ye who have read his revilings, what Petilianus has vented against me with more anger than consideration. To begin with, I will address you in the words of the apostle, which certainly are true, whatever I myself may be: "Let a man so account of us as of the ministers of Christ, and stewards of the mysteries of God. Moreover, it is required in stewards, that a man be found faithful. But with me it is a very small thing that I should be judged of you, or of man's judgment: yea, I judge not mine own self." With regard to what immediately follows, although I do not venture to apply to myself the words, "For I am conscious of nothing in myself,"[2] yet I say confidently in the sight of God, that I am conscious in myself of none of those charges which Petilianus has brought against my life since the time when I was baptized in Christ; "yet am I not hereby justified, but He that judgeth me is the Lord. Therefore judge nothing before the time, until the Lord come, who both will bring to light the hidden things of darkness, and will make manifest the counsels of the hearts; and then shall every man have praise of God. And these things, brethren, I have in a figure transferred to myself; that ye might learn in us not to think of men above that which is written, that no one of you be puffed up for one against another."[3] "Therefore let no man glory in men: for all things are yours; and ye are Christ's; and Christ is God's."[4] Again I say, "Let no man glory in men;" nay, oftentimes I repeat it, "Let no man glory in men." If you perceive anything in us which is deserving of praise, refer it all to His praise, from whom is every good gift and every perfect gift; for it is "from above, and cometh down from the Father of lights, with whom is no variableness, neither shadow of turning."[5] For what have we which we did not receive? and if we have received it, let us not boast as though we had not received it.[6] And in all these things which you know to be good in us, be ye our followers, at any rate, if we are Christ's;[7] but if, on the other hand, you either suspect, or believe, or see that any evil is in us, hold fast to that saying of the Lord's, in which you may safely resolve not to desert His Church because of men's ill deeds. Whatsoever we bid you observe, that observe and do; but whatsoever evil works you think or know to be in us, those do ye not. For this is not the time for me to justify myself before you, when I have undertaken, neglecting all considerations of self, to recommend to you what is for your salvation, that no one should make his boast of men. For "cursed be the man that trusteth in man."[9] So long as this precept of the Lord and His apostle be adhered to and observed, the cause which I serve will be victorious, even if I myself, as my enemy would fain have thought, am faint and oppressed in my own cause. For if you cling most firmly to what I urge on you with all my might, that every one is cursed who places his trust in man, so that none should make his boast of man, then you will in no wise desert the threshing-floor of the Lord on account of the chaff which either is now being dispersed beneath the blast of the wind of pride, or will be separated by the final winnowing;[10] nor will you fly from the great house on account of the vessels made to dishonor;[11] nor will you quit the net through the breaches made in it because of the bad fish which are to be separated on the shore;[12] nor will you leave the good pastures of unity, because of the goats which are to be placed on the left when the Good Shepherd shall divide the flock;[13] nor will you separate yourselves

[1] Ps. lxxxiv. 10.
[2] *Nihil enim mihi conscius sum.*
[3] 1 Cor. iv. 1-6.
[4] 1 Cor. iii. 21, 23.
[5] Jas. i. 17.
[6] 1 Cor. iv. 7.
[7] 1 Cor. iv. 16.
[8] Matt. xxiii. 3.
[9] Jer. xvii. 5.
[10] Matt. iii. 12.
[11] 2 Tim. ii. 20.
[12] Matt. xiii. 47, 48.
[13] Matt. xxv. 32, 33.

by an impious secession, because of the mixture of the tares, from the society of that good wheat, whose source is that grain that dies and is multiplied thereby, and that grows together throughout the world until the harvest. For the field is the world,—not only Africa; and the harvest is the end of the world,[1]—not the era of Donatus.

Chap. 3.—4. These comparisons of the gospel you doubtless recognize. Nor can we suppose them given for any other purpose, except that no one should make his boast in man, and that no one should be puffed up for one against another, or divided one against another, saying, "I am of Paul," when certainly Paul was not crucified for you, nor were you baptized in the name of Paul, much less in that of Cæcilianus, or of any one of us,[2] that you may learn, that so long as the chaff is being bruised with the corn, so long as the bad fishes swim together with the good in the nets of the Lord, till the time of separation shall come, it is your duty rather to endure the admixture of the bad out of consideration for the good, than to violate the principle of brotherly love towards the good from any consideration of the bad. For this admixture is not for eternity, but for time alone; nor is it spiritual, but corporal. And in this the angels will not be liable to err, when they shall collect the bad from the midst of the good, and commit them to the burning fiery furnace. For the Lord knoweth those which are His. And if a man cannot depart bodily from those who practise iniquity so long as time shall last, at any rate, let every one that nameth the name of Christ depart from iniquity itself.[3] For in the meantime he may separate himself from the wicked in life, and in morals, and in heart and will, and in the same respects depart from his society; and separation such as this should always be maintained. But let the separation in the body be waited for till the end of time, faithfully, patiently, bravely. In consideration of which expectation it is said, "Wait on the Lord; be of good courage, and He shall strengthen thine heart; wait, I say, upon the Lord."[4] For the greatest palm of toleration is won by those who, among false brethren that have crept in unawares, seeking their own, and not the things of Jesus Christ, yet show that they on their part seek not to disturb the love which is not their own, but Jesus Christ's, by any turbulent or rash dissension, nor to break the unity of the Lord's net, in which are gathered together fish of every kind, till it is drawn to the shore, that is, till the end of time, by any wicked strife fostered in the spirit of pride: whilst each might think himself to be something, being really nothing, and so might lead himself astray, and wish that sufficient reason might be found for the separation of Christian peoples in the judgment of himself or of his friends, who declare that they know beyond all question certain wicked men unworthy of communion in the sacraments of the Christian religion: though whatever it may be that they know of them, they cannot persuade the universal Church, which, as it was foretold, is spread abroad throughout all nations, to give credit to their tale. And when they refuse communion with these men, as men whose character they know, they desert the unity of the Church; whereas they ought rather, if there really were in them that charity which endureth all things, themselves to bear what they know in one nation, lest they should separate themselves from the good whom they were unable throughout all nations to fill with the teaching of evil alien to them. Whence even, without discussing the case, in which they are convicted by the weightiest proofs of having uttered calumnies against the innocent, they are believed with greater probability to have invented false charges of giving up the sacred books, when they are found to have themselves committed the far more heinous crime of wicked division in the Church. For even, if whatever imputations they have cast of giving up the sacred books were true, yet they in no wise ought to have abandoned the society of Christians, who are commended by holy Scripture even to the ends of the world, on considerations which they have been familiar with, while these men showed that they were not acquainted with them.

Chap. 4.—5. Nor would I therefore be understood to urge that ecclesiastical discipline should be set at naught, and that every one should be allowed to do exactly as he pleased, without any check, without a kind of healing chastisement, a lenity which should inspire fear, the severity of love. For then what will become of the precept of the apostle, "Warn them that are unruly, comfort the feeble-minded, support the weak, be patient toward all men; see that none render evil for evil unto any man?"[5] At any rate, when he added these last words, "See that none render evil for evil unto any man," he showed with sufficient clearness that there is no rendering of evil for evil when one chastises

[1] Matt. xiii. 24–40.
[2] 1 Cor. i. 12, 13.
[3] 2 Tim. ii. 19.
[4] Ps. xxvii. 14.
[5] 1 Thess. v. 14, 15.

those that are unruly, even though for the fault of unruliness be administered the punishment of chastising. The punishment of chastising therefore is not an evil, though the fault be an evil. For indeed it is the steel, not of an enemy inflicting a wound, but of a surgeon performing an operation. Things like this are done within the Church, and that spirit of gentleness within its pale burns with zeal towards God, lest the chaste virgin which is espoused to one husband, even Christ, should in any of her members be corrupted from the simplicity which is in Christ, as Eve was beguiled by the subtilty of the serpent.[1] Notwithstanding, far be it from the servants of the father of the family that they should be unmindful of the precept of their Lord, and be so inflamed with the fire of holy indignation against the multitude of the tares, that while they seek to gather them in bundles before the time, the wheat should be rooted up together with them. And of this sin these men would be held to be guilty, even though they showed that those were true charges which they brought against the *traditors* whom they accused; because they separated themselves in a spirit of impious presumption, not only from the wicked, whose society they professed to be avoiding, but also from the good and faithful in all nations of the world, to whom they could not prove the truth of what they said they knew; and with themselves they drew away into the same destruction many others over whom they had some slight authority, and who were not wise enough to understand that the unity of the Church dispersed throughout the world was on no account to be forsaken for other men's sins. So that, even though they themselves knew that they were pressing true charges against certain of their neighbors, yet in this way a weak brother, for whom Christ died, was perishing through their knowledge;[2] whilst, being offended at other men's sins, he was destroying in himself the blessing of peace which he had with the good brethren, who partly had never heard such charges, partly had shrunk from giving hasty credence to what was neither discussed nor proved, partly, in the peaceful spirit of humility, had left these charges, whatsoever they might be, to the cognizance of the judges of the Church, to whom the whole matter had been referred, across the sea.

CHAP. 5.—6. Do you, therefore, holy scions of our one Catholic mother, beware with all the watchfulness of which you are capable, in due submission to the Lord, of the example of crime and error such as this. With however great light of learning and of reputation he may shine, however much he may boast himself to be a precious stone, who endeavors to lead you after him, remember always that that brave woman who alone is lovely only to her husband, whom holy Scripture portrays to us in the last chapter of the Book of Proverbs, is more precious than any precious stones. Let no one say, I will follow such an one, for it was even he that made me a Christian; or, I will follow such an one, for it was even he that baptized me. For "neither is he that planteth anything, neither he that watereth, but God that giveth the increase."[3] And "God is love; and he that dwelleth in love, dwelleth in God, and God in him."[4] No one also that preaches the name of Christ, and handles or administers the sacrament of Christ, is to be followed in opposition to the unity of Christ. "Let every man prove his own work; and then shall he have rejoicing in himself alone, and not in another. For every man shall bear his own burden,"[5]—the burden, that is, of rendering an account; for "every one of shall give an account of himself. Let us not therefore judge one another any more."[6] For, so far as relates to the burdens of mutual love, "bear ye one another's burdens, and so fulfill the law of Christ. For if a man think himself to be something, when he is nothing, he deceiveth himself."[7] Let us therefore "forbear one another in love, endeavoring to keep the unity of the Spirit in the bond of peace;"[8] for no one who gathers outside that peace is gathering with Christ; but "he that gathering not with Him scattereth abroad."[9]

CHAP. 6.—7. Furthermore, whether concerning Christ, or concerning His Church, or any other matter whatsoever which is connected with your faith and life, to say nothing of ourselves, who are by no means to be compared with him who said, "Though we," at any rate, as he went on to say, "Though an angel from heaven preach any other gospel unto you than that which" ye have received in the lawful and evangelical Scripture, "let him be accursed."[10] While carrying out this principle of action in our dealings with you, and with all whom we desire to gain in Christ, and, amongst other things, while preaching the holy Church which we read of as promised in the epistles of God, and see to be fulfilled according to the promises in all nations of the world, we have earned, not the rendering of

[1] 2 Cor. xi. 2, 3.
[2] 1 Cor. viii. 11.
[3] 1 Cor. iii. 7.
[4] 1 John iv. 16.
[5] Gal. vi. 4, 5.
[6] Rom. xiv. 12, 13.
[7] Gal. vi. 2, 3.
[8] Eph. iv. 2, 3.
[9] Matt. xii. 30.
[10] Gal. i. 8.

thanks, but the flames of hatred, from those whom we desire to have attracted into His most peaceful bosom; as though we had bound them fast in that party for which they cannot find any defense that they should make; or as though we so long before had given injunctions to prophets and apostles that they should insert in their books no proofs by which it might be shown that the party of Donatus was the Church of Christ. And we indeed, dear brethren, when we hear false charges brought against us by those whom we have offended by preaching the eloquence of truth, and confuting the vanity of error, have, as you know, the most abundant consolation. For if, in the matters which they lay to my charge, the testimony of my conscience does not stand against me in the sight of God, where no mortal eye can reach, not only ought I not to be cast down, but I should even rejoice and be exceeding glad, for great is my reward in heaven.[1] For in fact I ought to consider, not how bitter, but how false is what I hear, and how true He is in defense of whose name I am exposed to it, and to whom it is said, "Thy name is as ointment poured forth."[2] And deservedly does it smell sweet in all nations, though those who speak evil of us endeavor to confine its fragrance within one corner of Africa. Why therefore should we take amiss that we are reviled by men who thus detract from the glory of Christ, whose party and schism find offense in what was foretold so long before of His ascent into the heavens, and of the pouring forth of His name, as of the savor of ointment: "Be Thou exalted, O God, above the heavens: let Thy glory be above all the earth"?[3]

Chap. 7.—8. Whilst we bear the testimony of God to this and the like effect against the vain speaking of men, we are forced to undergo bitter insults from the enemies of the glory of Christ. Let them say what they will, whilst He exhorts us, saying, "Blessed are they which are persecuted for righteousness' sake: for theirs is the kingdom of heaven. Blessed are ye, when men shall revile you, and persecute you, and shall say all manner of evil against you falsely for my sake." What He says in the first instance, "for righteousness' sake," He has repeated in the words that He uses afterwards, "for my sake;" seeing that He "is made unto us wisdom, and righteousness, and sanctification, and redemption, that, according as it is written, He that glorieth, let him glory in the Lord."[4] And when He says, "Rejoice, and be exceeding glad, for great is your reward in heaven,"[5] if I hold in a good conscience what is said "for righteousness' sake," and "for my sake," whosoever willfully detracts from my reputation is against his will contributing to my reward. For neither did He only instruct me by His word, without also confirming me by His example. Follow the faith of the holy Scriptures, and you will find that Christ rose from the dead, ascended into heaven, sitteth at the right hand of the Father. Follow the charges brought by His enemies, and you will presently believe that He was stolen from the sepulchre by His disciples. Why then should we, while defending His house to the best of the abilities given us by God, expect to meet with any other treatment from His enemies? "If they have called the Master of the house Beelzebub, how much more shall they call them of His household?"[6] If, therefore, we suffer, we shall also reign with Him. But if it be not only the wrath of the accuser that strikes the ear, but also the truth of the accusation that stings the conscience, what does it profit me if the whole world were to exalt me with perpetual praise? So neither the eulogy of him who praises has power to heal a guilty conscience, nor does the insult of him who reviles wound the good conscience. Nor, however, is your hope which is in the Lord deceived, even though we chance to be in secret what our enemies wish us to be thought; for you have not placed your hope in us, nor have you ever heard from us any doctrine of the kind. You therefore are safe, whatever we may be, who have learned to say, "I have trusted in the Lord; therefore I shall not slide;"[7] and "In God have I put my trust: I will not be afraid what man can do unto me."[8] And to those who endeavor to lead you astray to the earthly heights of proud men, you know how to answer, "In the Lord put I my trust: how say ye to my soul, Flee as a bird to your mountain?"[9]

Chap. 8.—9. Nor is it only you that are safe, whatever we may be, because you are satisfied with the very truth of Christ which is in us, in so far as it is preached through us, and everywhere throughout the world, and because, listening to it willingly, so far as it is set forth by the humble ministry of our tongue, you also think well and kindly of us,—for so your hope is in Him whom we preach to you out of His loving-kindness, which extends over you,—but further, all of you, who

[1] Matt. v. 12.
[2] Cant. i. 3.
[3] Ps. lvii. 11.
[4] 1 Cor. i. 30, 31.
[5] Matt. v. 10-12.
[6] Matt. x. 25.
[7] Ps. xxvi. 1.
[8] Ps. lvi. 11.
[9] Ps. xi. 1.

also received the sacrament of holy baptism from our ministering, may well rejoice in the same security, seeing that you were baptized, not into us, but into Christ. You did not therefore put on us, but Christ; nor did I ask you whether you were converted unto me, but unto the living God; nor whether you believed in me, but in the Father, the Son, and the Holy Ghost. But if you answered my question with truthful hearts, you were placed in a state of salvation, not by the putting away of the filth of the flesh, but by the answer of a good conscience towards God;[1] not by a fellow-servant, but by the Lord; not by the herald, but by the judge. For it is not true, as Petilianus inconsiderately said, that "the conscience of the giver," or, as he added, "the conscience of him who gives in holiness, is what we look for to wash the conscience of the recipient." For when something is given that is of God, it is given in holiness, even by a conscience which is not holy. And certainly it is beyond the power of the recipient to discern whether the said conscience is holy or not holy; but that which is given he can discern with clearness. That which is known to Him who is ever holy is received with perfect safety, whatever be the character of the minister at whose hands it is received. For unless the words which are spoken from Moses' seat were necessarily holy, He that is the Truth would never have said, "Whatsoever they bid you observe, that observe and do." But if the men who uttered holy words were themselves holy, He would not have said, "Do not ye after their works: for they say, and do not."[2] For it is true that in no way do men gather grapes of thorns, because grapes never spring from the root of a thorn; but when the shoot of the vine has entwined itself in a thorn hedge, the fruit which hangs upon it is not therefore looked upon with dread, but the thorn is avoided, while the grape is plucked.

CHAP. 9.—10. Therefore, as I have often said before, and am desirous to bring home to you, whatsoever we may be, you are safe, who have God for your Father and His Church for your mother. For although the goats may feed in company with the sheep, yet they shall not stand on the right hand; although the chaff may be bruised together with the wheat, it shall not be gathered into the barn; although the bad fish may swim in company with the good within the Lord's nets, they shall not be gathered into vessels. Let no man make his boast even in a good man: let no man shun the good gifts of God even in a bad man.

CHAP. 10.—11. Let these things suffice you, my beloved Christian brethren of the Catholic Church, so far as the present business is concerned; and if you hold fast to this in Catholic affection, so long as you are one sure flock of the one Shepherd, I am not too much concerned with the abuse that any enemy may lavish on me, your partner in the flock, or, at any rate, your watch-dog, so long as he compels me to bark rather in your defense than in my own. And yet, if it were necessary for the cause that I should enter on my own defense, I should do so with the geatest brevity and the greatest ease, joining freely with all men in condemning and bearing witness against the whole period of my life before I received the baptism of Christ, so far as relates to my evil passions and my errors, lest, in defending that period, I should seem to be seeking my own glory, not His, who by His grace delivered me even from myself. Wherefore, when I hear that life of mine abused, in whatever spirit he may be acting who abuses it, I am not so thankless as to be grieved. However much he finds fault with any vice of mine, I praise him in the same degree as my physician. Why then should I disturb myself about defending those past and obsolete evils in my life, in respect of which, though Petilianus has said much that is false, he has yet left more that is true unsaid? But concerning that period of my life which is subsequent to my baptism, to you who know me I speak unnecessarily in telling of those things which might be known to all mankind; but those who know me not ought not to act with such unfairness towards me as to believe Petilianus rather than you concerning me. For if one should not give credence to the panegyrics of a friend, neither should one believe the detraction of an enemy. There remain, therefore, those things which are hidden in a man, in which conscience alone can bear testimony, which cannot be a witness before men. Herein Petilianus says that I am a Manichæan, speaking of the conscience of another man; I, speaking of my own conscience, aver that I am not. Choose which of us you had sooner believe. Notwithstanding, since there is not any need even of this short and easy defense on my part, where the question at issue is not concerning the merits of any individual, whoever he may be, but concerning the truth[3] of the whole Church, I have more

[1] 1 Pet. iii. 21.

[2] Matt. xxiii. 2, 3.

[3] Some editors have "*unitate*," but Amerbach and the MSS. "*veritate;*" and this is supported by c. 24, 28 below: "*De*

also to say to any of you, who, being of the party of Donatus, have read the evil words which Petilianus has written about me, which I should not have heard from him if I had had no care about the loss of your salvation; but then I should have been wanting in the bowels of Christian love.

Chap. 11.—12. What wonder is it then, if, when I draw in the grain that has been shaken forth from the threshing-floor of the Lord, together with the soil and chaff, I suffer injury from the dust that rebounds against me; or that, when I am diligently seeking after the lost sheep of my Lord, I am torn by the briars of thorny tongues? I entreat you, lay aside for a time all considerations of party feeling, and judge with some degree of fairness between Petilianus and myself. I am desirous that you should be acquainted with the cause of the Church; he, that you should be familiar with mine. For what other reason than because he dares not bid you disbelieve my witnesses, whom I am constantly citing in the cause of the Church,—for they are prophets and apostles, and Christ Himself, the Lord of prophets and apostles,—whereas you easily give him credit in whatever he may choose to say concerning me, a man against a man, and one, moreover, of your own party against a stranger to you? And should I adduce any witnesses to my life, however important the thing he might say would be, it would not be believed by them, and of this Petilianus would quickly persuade you; especially when any one would bring forward a plea for me. Since he is an enemy of the Donatist party, in virtue of this fact he would also continually be considered your enemy. Petilianus therefore reigns supreme. Whenever he aims any abuse at me, of whatever character it may be, you all applaud and shout assent. This cause he has found wherein the victory is possible for him, but only with you for judges. He will seek for neither proof nor witness; for all that he has to prove in his words is this, that he lavishes most copious abuse on one whom you most cordially hate. For whereas, when the testimony of divine Scripture is quoted in such abundance and in such express terms in favor of the Catholic Church, he remains silent amidst your grief, he has chosen for himself a subject on which he may speak amidst applause from you; and though really conquered, yet, pretending that he stands unmoved, he may make statements concerning me like this, and even worse than this. It is enough for me,[1] in respect of the cause which I am now pleading, that whatsoever I may be found to be, yet the Church for which I speak unconquered.

Chap. 12.—13. For I am a man of the threshing-floor of Christ: if a bad man, then part of the chaff; if good, then of the grain. The winnowing-fan of this threshing-floor is not the tongue of Petilianus; and hereby, whatever evil he may have uttered, even with truth, against the chaff of this threshing-floor, this in no way prejudices its grain. But whereinsoever he has cast any revilings or calumnies against the grain itself, its faith is tried on earth, and its reward increased in the heavens. For where men are holy servants of the Lord, and are fighting with holiness for God, not against Petilianus, or any flesh and blood like him, but against principalities and powers, and the rulers of the darkness of this world,[2] such as are all enemies of the truth, to whom I would that we could say, "Ye were sometime darkness, but now are ye light in the Lord,"[3]—where the servants of God, I say, are waging such a war as this, then all the calumnious revilings that are uttered by their enemies, which cause an evil report among the malicious and those that are rash in believing, are weapons on the left hand: it is with such as these that even the devil is defeated. For when we are tried by good report, whether we resist the exaltation of ourselves to pride, and are tried by evil report, whether we love even those very enemies by whom it is invented against us, then we overcome the devil by the armor of righteousness on the right hand and on the left. For when the apostle had used the expression, "By the armor of righteousness on the right hand and on the left," he at once goes on to say, as if in explanation of the terms, "By honor and dishonor, by evil report and good report,"[4] and so forth,—reckoning honor and good report among the armor on the right hand, dishonor and evil report among that upon the left.

Chap. 13.—14. If, therefore, I am a servant of the Lord, and a soldier that is not reprobate, with whatever eloquence Petilianus stands forth reviling me, ought I in any way to be annoyed that he has been appointed for

ecclesiæ vel baptismi veritate;" and c. 13, 22 of the treatise *de Unico Baptismo:* "*Ambulantibus in ecclesiæ veritate.*"

[1] *Ubi vobis faventibus loquatur, et victus verum simulans statum, talia vel etiam sceleratiori dicat in me. Mihi sat est ad rem*, etc. Morel (*Elem. Crit.* pp. 326-328) suggests as an improvement, "*Ubi vobis faventibus loquatur et victus. Verum si millies tantum talia vel etiam sceleratiora dicat in me, mihi sat est*,' etc.,—"on which he may speak amidst applause from you, even when beaten. But if he were to make a thousand times as many statements concerning me," etc.

[2] Eph. vi. 12. [3] Eph. v. 8. [4] 2 Cor. vi. 7, 8.

me as a most accomplished craftsman of the armor on the left? It is necessary that I should fight in this armor as skillfully as possible in defence of my Lord, and should smite with it the enemy against whom I wage an unseen fight, who in all cunning strives and endeavors, with the most perverse and ancient craftiness, that this should lead me to hate Petilianus, and so be unable to fulfill the command which Christ has given, that we should "love our enemies."[1] But from this may I be saved by the mercy of Him who loved me, and gave Himself for me, so that, as He hung upon the cross, He said, "Father, forgive them; for they know not what they do;"[2] and so taught me to say of Petilianus, and all other enemies of mine like him, "Father, forgive them; for they know not what they do.'

CHAP. 14.—15. Furthermore, if I have obtained from you, in accordance with my earnest endeavors, that, laying aside from your minds all prejudice of party, you should be impartial judges between Petilianus and myself I will show to you that he has not replied to what I wrote, that you may understand that he has been compelled by lack of truth to abandon the dispute, and also see what revilings he has allowed himself to utter against the man who so conducted it that he had no reply to make. And yet what I am going to say displays itself with such manifest clearness, that, even though your minds were estranged from me by party prejudice and personal hatred, yet, if you would only read what is written on both sides, you could not but confess among yourselves, in your inmost hearts, that I have spoken truth.

16. For, in replying to the former part of his writings, which then alone had come into my hands, without taking any notice of his wordy and sacrilegious revilings, where he says, "Let those men cast in our teeth our twice-repeated baptism, who, under the name of baptism, have polluted their souls with a guilty washing; whom I hold to be so obscene that no manner of filth is less clean than they; whose lot it has been, by a perversion of cleanliness, to be defiled by the water wherein they washed;" I thought that what follows was worthy of discussion and refutation, where he says, "For what we look for is the conscience of the giver, that the conscience of the recipient may thereby be cleansed;' and I asked what means were to be found for cleansing one who receives baptism when the conscience of the giver is polluted, without the knowledge of him who is to receive the sacrament at his hands.[3]

CHAP. 15.—17. Read now the most profuse revilings which he has poured forth whilst puffed up with indignation against me, and see whether he has given me any answer, when I ask what means are to be found for cleansing one who receives baptism when the conscience of the giver is polluted, without the knowledge of him who receives the sacrament at his hands. I beg of you to search minutely, to examine every page, to reckon every line, to ponder every word, to sift the meaning of each syllable, and tell me, if you can discover it, where he has made answer to the question, What means are to be found for cleansing the conscience of the recipient who is unaware that the conscience of the giver is polluted?

18. For how did it bear upon the point that he added a phrase which he said was suppressed by me, maintaining that he had written in the following terms: "The conscience of him who gives in holiness is what we look for to cleanse the conscience of the recipient?" For to prove to you that it was not suppressed by me, its addition in no way hinders my inquiry, or makes up the deficiency which was found in him. For in the face of those very words I ask again, and I beg of you to see whether he has given any answer, If "the conscience of him who gives in holiness is what we look for to cleanse the conscience of the recipient," what means are to be found for cleansing the conscience of the recipient when the conscience of the giver is stained with guilt, without the knowledge of him who is to receive the sacrament at his hands? I insist upon an answer being given to this. Do not allow that any one should be prejudiced by revilings irrelevant to the matter in hand. If the conscience of him who gives in holiness is what we look for,—observe that I do not say "the conscience of him who gives," but that I added the words, "of him who gives *in holiness*,"—if the conscience, then, of him who gives in holiness is what we look for, what means are to be found for cleansing one who receives baptism when the conscience of the giver is polluted, without the knowledge of him who is to receive the sacrament at his hands?

CHAP. 16.—19. Let him go now, and with panting lungs and swollen throat find fault with me as a mere dialectician. Nay, let him summon, not me, but the science of dialectics itself, to the bar of popular opinion as a forger

[1] Luke vi. 35.

[2] Luke xxiii. 34.

[3] See above, Book I. c. 1. 2.

of lies, and let him open his mouth to its widest against it, with all the noisiest uproar of a special pleader. Let him say whatever he pleases before the inexperienced, that so the learned may be moved to wrath, while the ignorant are deceived. Let him call me, in virtue of my rhetoric, by the name of the orator Tertullus, by whom Paul was accused;[1] and let him give himself the name of Advocate,[2] in virtue of the pleading in which he boasts his former power, and for this reason delude himself with the notion that he is, or rather was, a namesake of the Holy Ghost. Let him, with all my heart, exaggerate the foulness of the Manichæans, and endeavor to divert it on to me by his barking. Let him quote all the exploits of those who have been condemned, whether known or unknown to me; and let him turn into the calumnious imputation of a prejudged crime, by some new right entirely his own, the fact that a former friend of mine there named me in my absence to the better securing of his own defense. Let him read the titles that have been placed upon my letters by himself or by his friends, as suited their pleasure, and boast that he has, as it were, involved me hopelessly in their expressions. When I acknowledge certain eulogies of bread, uttered in all simplicity and merriment, let him take away my character with the absurd imputations of poisonous baseness and madness. And let him entertain so bad an opinion of your understanding, as to imagine that he can be believed when he declares that pernicious love-charms were given to a woman, not only with the knowledge, but actually with the complicity[3] of her husband. What the man who was afterwards to ordain me bishop[4] wrote about me in anger, while I was as yet a priest, he may freely seek to use as evidence against me. That the same man sought and obtained forgiveness from a holy Council for the wrong he thus had done me, he is equally at liberty to ignore as being in my favor,—being either so ignorant or so forgetful of Christian gentleness, and the commandment of the gospel, that he brings as an accusation against a brother what is wholly unknown to that brother himself, as he humbly entreats that pardon may in kindness be extended to him.

Chap. 17.—20. Let him further go on, in his discourse of many but manifestly empty words, to matters of which he is wholly ignorant, or in which rather he abuses the ignorance of the mass of those who hear him, and from the confession of a certain woman, that she had called herself a catechumen of the Manichæans, being already a full member of the Catholic Church, let him say or write what he pleases concerning their baptism,—not knowing, or pretending not to know, that the name of catechumen is not bestowed among them upon persons to denote that they are at some future time to be baptized, but that this name is given to such as are also called Hearers, on the supposition that they cannot observe what are considered the higher and greater commandments, which are observed by those whom they think right to distinguish and honor by the name of Elect. Let him also maintain with wonderful rashness, either as himself deceived or as seeking to deceive, that I was a presbyter among the Manichæans. Let him set forth and refute, in whatever sense seems good to him, the words of the third book of my *Confessions*, which, both in themselves, and from much that I have said before and since, are perfectly clear to all who read them. Lastly, let him triumph in my stealing his words, because I have suppressed two of them, as though the victory were his upon their restoration.

Chap. 18.—21. Certainly in all these things, as you can learn or refresh your memory by reading his letter, he has given free scope to the impulse of his tongue, with all the license of boasting which he chose to use, but nowhere has he told us where means are to be found for cleansing the conscience of the recipient, when that of the giver has been stained with sin without his knowing it. But amid all his noise, and after all his noise, serious as it is, too terrible as he himself supposes it to be, I deliberately, as it is said, and to the purpose,[5] ask this question once again:" If the conscience of him who gives in holiness is what we look for, what means are to be found for cleansing one who receives baptism without knowing that the conscience of the giver is stained with sin? And throughout his whole epistle I find nothing said in answer to this question.

Chap. 19.—22. For perhaps some one of you will say to me, All these things which he said against you he wished to have force for this purpose, that he might take away your character, and through you the character of

1 Acts xxiv. 1.

2 *Paracletus.*

3 "*Favente*," which is wanting in the MSS., was inserted in the margin by Erasmus, as being needed to complete the sense.

4 Megalius, bishop of Calama, primate of Numidia, was the bishop who ordained Augustin, as we find in c. viii. of his life by Possidius. Augustin makes further reply to the same calumny, which was gathered from a letter of Megalius, in *Contra Cresconium*, Book III. c. 80, 92, and Book IV. c. 64, 78, 79.

5 *Lente, ut dicitur, et bene.* Morel (*Element. Crit.* pp. 140, 141) suggests as an amendment, "*lene*," as suiting better with "*lente*."

those with whom you hold communion, that neither they themselves, nor those whom you endeavor to bring over to your communion, may hold you to be of any further importance. But, in deciding whether he has given no answer to the words of your epistle, we must look at them in the light of the passage in which he proposed them for consideration. Let us then do so: let us look at his writings in the light of that very passage. Passing over, therefore, the passage in which I sought to introduce my subject to the reader, and to ignore those few prefatory words of his, which were rather insulting than revelant to the subject under discussion, I go on to say, "He says, 'What we look for is the conscience of the giver, to cleanse that of the recipient.' But supposing the conscience of the giver is concealed from view, and perhaps defiled with sin, how will it be able to cleanse the conscience of the recipient, if, as he says, 'what we look for is the conscience of the giver, to cleanse that of the recipient?' For if he should say that it makes no matter to the recipient what amount of evil may be concealed from view in the conscience of the giver, perhaps that ignorance may have such a degree of efficacy as this, that a man cannot be defiled by the guilt of the conscience of him from whom he receives baptism, so long as he is unaware of it. Let it then be granted that the guilty conscience of his neighbor cannot defile a man so long as he is unaware of it; but is it therefore clear that it can further cleanse him from his own guilt? Whence then is a man to be cleansed who receives baptism, when the conscience of the giver is polluted without the knowledge of him who is to receive it, especially when he goes on to say, 'For he who receives faith from the faithless receives not faith but guilt?'"[1]

CHAP. 20.—23. All these statements in my letter Petilianus set before himself for refutation. Let us see, therefore, whether he has refuted them; whether he has made any answer to them at all. For I add the words which he calumniously accuses me of having suppressed, and, having done so, I ask him again the same question in an even shorter form; for by adding these two words he has helped me much in shortening this proposition. If the conscience of him who gives in holiness is what we look for to cleanse that of the recipient, and if he who has received his faith wittingly from one that is faithless, receives not faith but guilt, where shall we find means to cleanse the conscience of the recipient, when he has not known that the conscience of the giver is stained with guilt, and when he receives his faith unwittingly from one that is faithless? I ask, where shall we find means to cleanse it? Let him tell us; let him not pass off into another subject; let him not cast a mist over the eyes of the inexperienced. To end with, at any rate, after many tortuous circumlocutions have been interposed and thoroughly worked out, let him at last tell us where we shall find means to cleanse the conscience of the recipient when the stains of guilt in the conscience of the faithless baptizer are concealed from view, if the conscience of him who gives in holiness is what we look for to cleanse that of the recipient, and if he who has received his faith wittingly from one that is faithless, receives not faith but guilt? For the man in question receives it from a faithless man, who has not the conscience of one who gives in holiness, but a conscience stained with guilt, and veiled from view. Where then shall we find means to cleanse his conscience? whence then does he receive his faith? For if he is neither then cleansed, nor then receives faith, when the faithlessness and guilt of the baptizer are concealed, why, when these are afterwards brought to light and condemned, is he not then baptized afresh, that he may be cleansed and receive faith? But if, while the faithlessness and guilt of the other are concealed, he is cleansed and does receive faith, whence does he obtain his cleansing, whence does he receive faith, when there is not the conscience of one that gives in holiness to cleanse the conscience of the recipient? Let him tell us this; let him make reply to this: Whence does he obtain his cleansing, whence does he receive faith, if the conscience of him that gives in holiness is what we look for to cleanse the conscience of the recipient, seeing that this does not exist, when the baptizer conceals his character of faithlessness and guilt? To this no answer has been made whatever.

CHAP. 21.—24. But see, when he is reduced to straits in the argument, he again makes an attack on me full of mist and wind, that the calm clearness of the truth may be obscured; and through the extremity of his want he becomes full of resources, shown not in saying what is true, but in unbought empty revilings. Hold fast, with the keenest attention and utmost perseverance, what he ought to answer,—that is, where means may be found for cleansing the conscience of the recipient when the stains in that of the giver are concealed,—lest possibly the blast of his

[1] See Book I. c. 1, 2, c. 2, 3.

eloquence should wrest this from your hands, and you in turn should be carried away by the dark tempest of his turgid discourse, so as wholly to fail in seeing whence he has digressed, and to what point he should return; and see where the man can wander, whilst he cannot stand in the matter which he has undertaken. For see how much he says, through having nothing that he ought to say. He says "that I slide in slippery places, but am held up; that I neither destroy nor confirm the objections that I make; that I devise uncertain things in the place of certainty; that I do not permit my readers to believe what is true, but cause them to look with increased suspicion on what is doubtful." He says "that I have the accursed talents of the Academic philosopher Carneades."[1] He endeavors to insinuate what the Academics think of the falseness or the falsehood of human sensation, showing in this also that he is wholly without knowledge of what he says. He declares that "it is said by them that snow is black, whereas it is white; and that silver is black; and that a tower is round, or free from projections, when it is really angular; that an oar is broken in the water, while it is whole."[2] And all this because, when he had said that "the conscience of him that gives," or "of him that gives in holiness, is what we look for to cleanse the conscience of the recipient," I said in reply, What if the conscience of the giver be hidden from sight, and possibly be stained with guilt? Here you have his black snow, and black silver, and his tower round instead of angular, and the oar in the water broken while yet whole, in that I suggested a state of the case which might be conceived, and could not really exist, that the conscience of the giver might be hidden from view, and possibly might be stained with guilt!

25. Then he continues in the same strain, and cries out: "What is that *what if?* what is that *possibly?* except the uncertain and wavering hesitation of one who doubts, of whom your poet says,—

'What if I now return to those who say, What if the sky should fall?'"[2]

Does he mean that when I said, What if the conscience of the giver be hidden from sight, and possibly be stained with guilt? that it is much the same as if I had said, What if the sky should fall? There certainly is the phrase What if, because it is possible that it may be hidden from view, and it is possible that it may not. For when it is not known what the giver is thinking of, or what crime he has committed, then his conscience is certainly hidden from the view of the recipient; but when his sin is plainly manifest, then it is not hidden. I used the expression, And possibly may be stained with guilt, because it is possible that it may be hidden from view and yet be pure; and again, it is possible that it may be hidden from view and be stained with guilt. This is the meaning of the What if; this the meaning of the Possibly. Is this at all like "What if the sky should fall?" O how often have men been convicted, how often have they confessed themselves that they had consciences stained with guilt and adultery, whilst men were unwittingly baptized by them after they were degraded by the sin subsequently brought to light, and yet the sky did not fall! What have we here to do with Pilus and Furius,[3] who defended the cause of injustice against justice? What have we here to do with the atheist Diagoras,[4] who denied that there was any God, so that he would seem to be the man of whom the prophet spoke beforehand, "The fool hath said in his heart there is no God?"[5] What have we here to do with these? Why were their names brought in, except that they might make a diversion in favor of a man who had nothing to say? that while he is at any rate saying something, though needlessly, about these, the matter in hand may seem to be progressing, and an answer may be supposed to be made to a question which remains without an answer?

Chap. 22.—26. Lastly, if these two or three words, What if, and Possibly, are so absolutely intolerable, that on their account we should have aroused from their long sleep the Academics, and Carneades, and Pilus, and Furius, and Diagoras, and black snow, and the falling of the sky, and everything else that is equally senseless and absurd, let them be removed from our argument. For, as a matter of fact, it is by no means impossible to express what we desire to say without them. There is quite sufficient for our purpose in what is found a little later, and has been introduced by himself from my letter: "By what means then is he to be cleansed who receives baptism when the conscience of the

[1] Lactantius, *Divin. Instit.* Book V. c. xv., tells us of the talents of Carneades, recording that when he was sent on an embassy to Rome by the Athenians, he spoke there first in defense of justice, and then on the following day in opposition to it; and that he was in the habit of speaking with such force on either side, as to be able to refute any arguments advanced by anybody else.

[2] Ter. *Heaut.* act. IV. scen. iii. vers. 41.

[3] In *de Civ. Dei*, Book II. c. xxi., Augustin mentions L. Furius Philus, one of the interlocutors in Cicero's *Laelius*, as maintaining this same view. From the similarity of the name, it has been thought that here Furius and Pilus are only one man.

[4] The mss. here and below have Protagoras. Both were atheists, according to Cicero, *Nat. Deor.* I. i. 2, and Lactantius *Divin. Instit.* I. c. ii.; *de Ira Dei*, c. ix.

[5] Ps. xiv. 1.

giver is polluted, and that without the knowledge of him who is to receive the sacrament?"[1] Do you acknowledge that here there is no What if, no Possibly? Well then, let an answer be given. Give close heed, lest he be found to answer this in what follows. "But," says he, "I bind you in your cavilling to the faith of believing, that you may not wander further from it. Why do you turn away your life from errors by arguments of folly? Why do you disturb the system of belief in respect of matters without reason? By this one word I bind and convince you." It was Petilianus that said this, not I. These words are from the letter of Petilianus; but from that letter, to which I just now added the two words which he accuses me of having suppressed, showing that, notwithstanding their addition, the pertinency of my question, to which he makes no answer, remains with greater brevity and simplicity. It is beyond dispute that these two words are, In holiness, and Wittingly: so that it should not be, "The conscience of him who gives," but "The conscience of him who gives *in holiness;*" and that it should not be, "He who has received his faith from one that is faithless," but "He who has *wittingly* received his faith from one that is faithless." And yet I had not really suppressed these words; but I had not found them in the copy which was placed in my hands. It is possible enough that it was incorrect; nor indeed is it wholly beyond the possibility of belief that even by this suggestion Academic grudge should be roused against me, and that it should be asserted that, in declaring the copy to be incorrect, I had said much the same sort of thing as if I had declared that snow was black. For why should I repay in kind his rash suggestion, and say that, though he pretends that I suppressed the words, he really added them afterwards himself, since the copy, which is not angry, can confirm that mark of incorrectness, without any abusive rashness on my part?

CHAP. 23.—27. And, in the first place, with regard to that first expression, "Of him who gives in holiness," it does not interfere in the least with my inquiry, by which he is so much distressed, whether I use the expression, "If the conscience of him that gives is what we look for," or the fuller phrase, "If the conscience of him that gives in holiness is what we look for, to cleanse the conscience of the recipient," by what means then is he to be cleansed who receives baptism if the conscience of the giver is polluted, without the knowledge of him who is to receive the sacrament? And with regard to the other word that is added, "wittingly," so that the sentence should not run, "He who has received his faith from one that is faithless," but "He who has wittingly received his faith from one that is faithless, receives not faith but guilt," I confess that I had said some things as though the word were absent, but I can easily afford to do without them; for they caused more hindrance to the facility of my argument than they gave assistance to its power. For how much more readily, how much more plainly and shortly, can I put the question thus: "If the conscience of him who gives in holiness is what we look for to cleanse the conscience of the recipient," and "if he who has wittingly received his faith from one that is faithless receives not faith but guilt," by what means is he cleansed, from whom the stain on the conscience of him who gives, but not in holiness, is hidden? and whence does be receive true faith, who is baptized unwittingly by one that is faithless? Let it be declared whence this shall be, and then the whole theory of baptism will be disclosed; then all that is matter of investigation will be brought to light,—but only if it be declared, not if the time be consumed in evil-speaking.

CHAP. 24.—28. Whatever, therefore, he finds in these two words,—whether he brings calumnious accusations about their suppression, or boasts of their being added,—you perceive that it in no way hinders my question, to which he can find no answer that he can make; and therefore, not wishing to remain silent, he takes the opportunity of making an attack upon my character,—retiring, I should have said, from the discussion, except that he had never entered on it. For just as though the question were about me, and not about the truth of the Church, or of baptism, therefore he says that I, by suppressing these two words, have argued as though it were no stumblingblock in the way of my conscience, that I have ignored what he calls the sacrilegious conscience of him who polluted me. But if this were so, the addition of the word "wittingly," which is thus introduced, would be in my favor, and its suppression would tell against me. For if I had wished that my defense should be urged on the ground that I should be supposed to have been unacquainted with the conscience of the man that baptized me, then I would accept Petilianus as having spoken in my behalf, since he does not say in general terms, "He that has received his faith from one that is faithless," but "He that has wittingly receiv-

[1] See Book I. c. 2, 3.

ed his faith from one that is faithless, receives not faith but guilt;" so that hence I might boast that I had received not guilt, but faith, since I could say I did not receive it wittingly from one that was faithless, but was unacquainted with the conscience of him that gave it. See, therefore, and reckon carefully, if you can, what an amount of superfluous words he wastes on the one phrase, "I was unacquainted with," which he declares that I have used; whereas I never used it at all,—partly because the question under discussion was not concerning me, so that I should need to use it; partly because no fault was apparent in him that baptized me, so that I should be forced to say in my defense that I had been unacquainted with his conscience.

Chap. 25.—29. And yet Petilianus, to avoid answering what I have said, sets before himself what I have not, and draws men's attention away from the consideration of his debt, lest they should exact the answer which he ought to make. He constantly introduces the expressions, "I have been unacquainted with," "I say," and makes answer, "But if you were unacquainted with;" and, as though convicting me, so that it should be out of my power to say, "I was unacquainted with," he quotes Mensurius, Cæcilianus, Macarius, Taurinus, Romanus, and declares that "they had acted in opposition to the Church of God, as I could not fail to know, seeing that I am an African, and already well advanced in years," whereas, so far as I hear, Mensurius died in the unity of the communion of the Church, before the faction of Donatus separated itself therefrom; whilst I had read the history of Cæcilianus, that they themselves had referred his case to Constantine, and that he had been once and again acquitted by the judges whom that emperor had appointed to try the matter, and again a third time by the sovereign himself, when they appealed to him. But whatever Macarius and Taurinus and Romanus did, either in their judicial or executive functions, in behalf of unity as against their pertinacious madness, it is beyond doubt that it was all done in accordance with the laws, which these same persons made it unavoidable should be passed and put in force, by referring the case of Cæcilianus to the judgment of the emperor.

30. Among many other things which are wholly irrevelant, he says that "I was so hard hit by the decision of the proconsul Messianus, that I was forced to fly from Africa." And in consequence of this falsehood (to which, if he was not the author of it, he certainly lent malicious ears when others maliciously invented it), how many other falsehoods had he the hardihood not only to utter, but actually to write with wondrous rashness, seeing that I went to Milan before the consulship of Banto, and that, in pursuance of the profession of rhetorician which I then followed, I recited a panegyric in his honor as consul on the first of January, in the presence of a vast assembly of men; and after that journey I only returned to Africa after the death of the tyrant Maximus: whereas the proconsul Messianus heard the case of the Manichæans after the consulship of Banto, as the day of the chronicles inserted by Petilianus himself sufficiently shows. And if it were necessary to prove this for the satisfaction of those who are in doubt, or believe the contrary, I could produce many men, illustrious in their generation, as most sufficient witnesses to all that period of my life.

Chap. 26.—31. But why do we make inquiry into these points? Why do we both suffer and cause unnecessary delay? Are we likely to find out by such a course as this what means we are to use for cleansing the conscience of the recipient, who does not know that the conscience of the giver is stained with guilt: whence the man is to receive faith who is unwittingly baptized by one that is faithless?—the question which Petilianus had proposed to himself to answer in my epistle, then going on to say anything else he pleased except what the matter in hand required. How often has he said, "If ignorant you were,"—as though I had said, what I never did say, that I was unacquainted with the conscience of him who baptized me. And he seemed to have no other object in all that his evil-speaking mouth poured forth, except that he should appear to prove that I had not been ignorant of the misdeeds of those among whom I was baptized, and with whom I was associated in communion, understanding fully, it would seem, that ignorance did not convict me of guilt. See then that if I were ignorant, as he has repeated so often, beyond all doubt I should be innocent of all these crimes. Whence therefore should I be cleansed, who am unacquainted with the conscience of him who gives but not in holiness, so that I may be least ensnared by his offenses? Whence then should I receive faith, seeing that I was baptized unwittingly by one that was faithless? For he has not repeated "If ignorant you were" so often without purpose, but simply to prevent my being reputed innocent, esteeming beyond all doubt that no man's innocence is violated if he unwittingly receives his faith from one that is faithless, and is not acquainted with the stains on the conscience of him that gives, but not in holiness. Let him say, therefore, by what means such men are to be cleansed, whence they are to receive not guilt but faith. But let him not deceive you. Let him not, while uttering much, say nothing; or rather, let him not say much while saying nothing. Next, to urge a point which occurs to me, and must not be passed over,—if I am guilty because I have not been ignorant, to use his own phraseology, and I am proved not to have been ignorant, because I am an African, and already advanced in years, let him grant that the youths of other nations throughout the world are not guilty, who had no opportunity either from their race, or from that age you bring against me, of knowing the points that are laid to our charge, be they true, or be they false; and yet they, if they have fallen into your hands, are rebaptized without any considerations of such a kind.

CHAP. 27.—32. But this is not what we are now inquiring. Let him rather answer (what he wanders off into the most irrelevant matters in order to avoid answering) by what means the conscience of the recipient is cleansed who is unacquainted with the stain on the conscience of the giver, if the conscience of one that gives in holiness is what we look for to cleanse the conscience of the recipient? and from what source he receives faith who is unwittingly baptized by one that is faithless, if he that has wittingly received his faith from one that is faithless receives not faith but guilt? Omitting, therefore, his revilings, which he has cast at me without any sound consideration, let us still notice that he does not say what we demand in what follows. But I should like to look at the garrulous mode in which he has set this forth, as though he were sure to overwhelm us with confusion. "But let us return," he says, "to that argument of your fancy, whereby you seem to have represented to yourself in a form of words the persons you baptize. For since you do not see the truth, it would have been more seemly to have imagined what was probable." These words of his own, Petilianus put forth by way of preface, being about to state the words that I had used. Then he went on to quote: "Behold, you say, the faithless man stands ready to baptize, but he who is to be baptized knows nothing of his faithlessness."[1] He has not quoted the whole of my proposition and question; and presently he begins to ask me in his turn, saying, "Who is the man, and from what corner has he started up, that you propose to us? Why do you seem to see a man who is the produce of your imagination, in order to avoid seeing one whom you are bound to see, and to examine and test most carefully? But since I see that you are unacquainted with the order of the sacrament, I tell you this as shortly as I can: you were bound both to examine your baptizer, and to be examined by him." What is it, then, that we were waiting for? That he should tell us by what means the conscience of the recipient is to be cleansed, who is unacquainted with the stain on the conscience of him that gives but not in holiness, and whence the man is to receive not guilt but faith, who has received baptism unwittingly from one that is faithless. All that we have heard is that the baptizer ought most diligently to be examined by him who wishes to receive not guilt but faith, that the latter may make himself acquainted with the conscience of him that gives in holiness, which is to cleanse the conscience of the recipient. For the man that has failed to make this examination, and has unwittingly received baptism from one that is faithless, from the very fact that he did not make the examination, and therefore did not know of the stain on the conscience of the giver, was incapacitated from receiving faith instead of guilt. Why therefore did he add what he made so much of adding,—the word *wittingly*, which he calumniously accused me of having suppressed? For in his unwillingness that the sentence should run, "He who has received his faith from one that is faithless, receives not faith but guilt," he seems to have left some hope to the man that acts unwittingly. But now, when he is asked whence that man is to receive faith who is baptized unwittingly by one that is faithless, he has answered that he ought to have examined his baptizer; so that, beyond all doubt, he refuses the wretched man permission even to be ignorant, by not finding out from what source he may receive faith, unless he has placed his trust in the man that is baptizing him.

CHAP. 28.—33. This is what we look upon with horror in your party; this is what the sentence of God condemns, crying out with the utmost truth and the utmost clearness, "Cursed is every one that trusteth in man."[2] This is what is most openly forbidden by holy humility and apostolic love, as Paul declares, "Let no man glory in men."[3] This is the reason that the attack of empty calumnies and

[1] See Book I. c. 2, 3.

[2] Jer. xvii. 5.

[3] 1 Cor. iii. 21.

of the bitterest invectives grows even fiercer against us, that when human authority is as it were overthrown, there may remain no ground of hope for those to whom we administer the word and sacrament of God in accordance with the dispensation entrusted unto us. We make answer to them: How long do you rest your support on man? The venerable society of the Catholic Church makes answer to them: "Truly my soul waiteth upon God: from Him cometh my salvation. He only is my God and my helper; I shall not be moved."[1] For what other reason have they had for removing from the house of God, except that they pretended that they could not endure those vessels made to dishonor, from which the house shall not be free until the day of judgment? whereas all the time they rather appear, by their deeds and by the records of the time, to have themselves been vessels of this kind, while they threw the imputation in the teeth of others; of which said vessels made unto dishonor, in order that no one should on their account remove in confusion of mind from the great house, which alone belongs to the great Father of our family, the servant of God, one who was good and faithful, or was capable of receiving faith in baptism, as I have shown above, expressly says, "Truly my soul waiteth upon God" (on God, you see, and not on man): "from Him cometh my salvation" (not from man). But Petilianus would refuse to ascribe to God the cleansing and purifying of a man, even when the stain upon the conscience of him who gives, but not in holiness, is hidden from view, and any one receives his faith unwittingly from one that is faithless. "I tell you this," he says, "as shortly as I can: you were bound both to examine your baptizer, and to be examined by him."

Chap. 29.—34. I entreat of you, pay attention to this: I ask where the means shall be found for cleansing the conscience of the recipient, when he is not acquainted with the stain upon the conscience of him that gives but not in holiness, if the conscience of him that gives in holiness is waited for to cleanse the conscience of the recipient? and from what source he is to receive faith, who is unwittingly baptized by one that is faithless, if whosoever has received his faith wittingly from one that is faithless, receives not faith but guilt? and he answers me, that both the baptizer and the baptized should be subjected to examination. And for the proof of this point, out of which no question arises, he adduces the example of John, in that he was examined by those who asked him who he claimed to be,[2] and that he also in turn examined those to whom he says, "O generation of vipers, who hath warned you to flee from the wrath to come?"[3] What has this to do with the subject? What has this to do with the question under discussion? God had vouchsafed to John the testimony of most eminent holiness of life, confirmed by the previous witness of the noblest prophecy, both when he was conceived, and when he was born. But the Jews put their question, already believing him to be a saint, to find out which of the saints he maintained himself to be, or whether he was himself the saint of saints, that is, Christ Jesus. So much favor indeed was shown to him, that credence would at once have been given to whatever he might have said about himself. If, therefore, we are to follow this precedent in declaring that each several baptizer is now to be examined, then each must also be believed, whatever he may say of himself. But who is there that is made up of deceit, whom we know that the Holy Spirit flees from, in accordance with the Scripture,[4] who would not wish the best to be believed of him, or who would hesitate to bring this about by the use of any words within his reach? Accordingly, when he shall have been asked who he is, and shall have answered that he is the faithful dispenser of God's ordinances, and that his conscience is not polluted with the stain of any crime, will this be the whole examination, or will there be a further more careful investigation into his character and life? Assuredly there will. But it is not written that this was done by those who in the desert of Jordan asked John who he was.

Chap. 30.—35. Accordingly this precedent is wholly without bearing on the matter in hand. We might rather say that the declaration of the apostle sufficiently inculcates this care, when he says, "Let these also first be proved; then let them use the office of a deacon, being found blameless."[5] And since this is done anxiously and habitually in both parties, by almost all concerned, how comes it that so many are found to be reprobates subsequently to the time of having undertaken this ministry, except that, on the one hand, human care is often deceived, and, on the other hand, those who have begun well occasionally deteriorate? And since things of this sort happen so frequently as to allow no man to hide them or to forget them, what is the

1 Ps. lxii. 1, 2; cp. Hieron.

2 John i. 22.
3 Mat. iii. 7.
4 Wisd. i. 5.
5 1 Tim. iii. 10.

reason that Petilianus now teaches us insultingly, in a few words, that the baptizer ought to be examined by the candidate for baptism, since our question is, by what means the conscience of the recipient is to be cleansed, when the stain on the conscience of him that gives, but not in holiness, has been concealed from view, if the conscience of one that gives in holiness is what we look for to cleanse the conscience of the recipient. "Since I see," he says, "that you are unacquainted with the order of the sacrament, I tell you this as shortly as I can: you were bound both to examine your baptizer, and to be examined by him." What an answer to make! He is surrounded in so many places by such a multitude of men that have been baptized by ministers who, having in the first instance seemed righteous and chaste, have subsequently been convicted and degraded in consequence of the disclosure of their faults; and he thinks that he is avoiding the force of this question, in which we ask by what means the conscience of the recipient is to be cleansed, when he is unacquainted with the stain upon the conscience of him that gives but not in holiness, if the conscience of one that gives in holiness is what we look for to cleanse the conscience of the recipient,—he thinks, I say, that he is avoiding the force of this question, by saying shortly that the baptizer ought to be examined. Nothing is more unfortunate than not to be consistent with truth, by which every one is so shut in, that he cannot find a means of escape. We ask from whom he is to receive faith who is baptized by one that is faithless? The answer is, "He ought to have examined his baptizer." Is it therefore the case that, since he does not examine him, and so even unwittingly receives his faith from one that is faithless, he receives not faith but guilt? Why then are those men not baptized afresh, who are found to have been baptized by men that are detected and convicted reprobates, while their true character was yet concealed?

CHAP. 31.—36. "And where," he says, "is the word that I added, *wittingly?* so that I did not say, He that has received his faith from one that is faithless; but, He that has received his faith *wittingly* from one that is faithless, receives not faith but guilt." He therefore who received his faith unwittingly from one that was faithless, received not guilt but faith; and accordingly I ask from what source he has received it? And being thus placed in a strait, he answers, "He ought to have examined him." Granted that he ought to have done so; but, as a matter of fact, he did not, or he was not able: what is your verdict about him? Was he cleansed, or was he not? If he was cleansed, I ask from what source? For the polluted conscience of him that gave but not in holiness, with which he was unacquainted, could not cleanse him. But if he was not cleansed, command that he be so now. You give no such orders, therefore he was cleansed. Tell me by what means? Do you at any rate tell me what Petilianus has failed to tell. For I propose to you the very same words which he was unable to answer. "Behold the faithless man stands ready to baptize; but he who is to be baptized knows nothing of his faithlessness: what do you think that he will receive—faith, or guilt?"[1] This is sufficient as a constant form of question: answer, or search diligently to find what he has answered. You will find abuse that has already been convicted. He finds fault with me, as though in derision, maintaining that I ought to suggest what is probable for consideration, since I cannot see the truth. For, repeating my words, and cutting my sentence in two, he says, "Behold, you say, the faithless man stands ready to baptize; but he who is to be baptized knows nothing of his faithlessness." Then he goes on to ask, "Who is the man, and from what corner has he started up, that you propose to us?" Just as though there were some one or two individuals, and such cases were not constantly occurring everywhere on either side! Why does he ask of me who the man in question is, and from what corner he has started up, instead of looking round, and seeing that the churches are few and far between, whether in cities or in country districts, which do not contain men detected in crimes, and degraded from the ministry? While their true character was concealed, while they wished to be thought good, though really bad, and to be reputed chaste, though really guilty of adultery, so long they were involved in deceit; and so the Holy Spirit, according to the Scripture, was fleeing from them.[2] It is from the crowd, therefore, of these men who hitherto concealed their character that the faithless man whom I suggested started up. Why does he ask me whence he started up, shutting his eyes to all this crowd, from which sufficient noise arises to satisfy the blind, if we take into consideration none but those who might have been convicted and degraded from their office?

CHAP. 32.—37. What shall we say of what he himself advanced in his epistle, that "Quodvultdeus, having been convicted of two

[1] Book I. cc. 1, 2, 2, 3.

[2] Wisd. i. 5.

adulteries, and cast out from among you, was received by those of our party?"[1] What then (I would speak without prejudice to this man, who proved his case to be a good one, or at least persuaded men that it was so), when such men among you, being as yet undetected, administer baptism, what is received at their hands,—faith, or guilt? Surely not faith, because they have not the conscience of one who gives in holiness to cleanse the conscience of the recipient. But yet not guilt either, in virtue of that added word: "For he that has received his faith *wittingly* from one that is faithless, receives not faith but guilt." But when men were baptized by those of whom I speak, they were surely ignorant what sort of men they were. Furthermore, not receiving faith from their baptizers, who had not the conscience of one that gives in holiness, and not receiving guilt, because they were baptized not knowing but in ignorance of their faults, they therefore remained without faith and without guilt. They are not, therefore, in the number of men of such abandoned character. But neither can they be in the number of the faithful, because, as they could not receive guilt, so neither could they receive faith from their baptizers. But we see that they are reputed by you in the number of the faithful, and that no one of you declares his opinion that they ought to be baptized, but all of you hold valid the baptism which they have already received. They have therefore received faith; and yet they have not received it from those who had not the conscience of one that gives in holiness, to cleanse the conscience of the recipient. Whence then did they receive it? This is the point from which I make my effort; this is the question that I press most earnestly; to this I do most urgently demand an answer.

Chap. 33.—38. See now how Petilianus, to avoid answering this question, or to avoid being proved to be incapable of answering it, wanders off vainly into irrelevant matter in abuse of us, accusing us and proving nothing; and when he chances to make an endeavor to resist, with something like a show of fighting for his cause, he is everywhere overcome with the greatest ease. But yet he nowhere gives an answer of any kind to this one question which we ask: If the conscience of one that gives in holiness is what we look for to cleanse the conscience of the recipient, by what means is he to be cleansed who received baptism while the conscience of the giver was polluted, without the knowledge of him who was to receive it? for in these words, which he quoted from my epistle, he set me forth as asking a question, while he showed himself as giving no answer. For after saying what I have just now recited, and when, on being brought into a great strait on every side, he had been compelled to say that the baptizer ought to be examined by the candidate for baptism, and the candidate in turn by the baptizer; and when he had tried to fortify this statement by the example of John, in hopes that he might find auditors either of the greatest negligence or of the greatest ignorance, he then went on to advance other testimonies of Scripture wholly irrelevant to the matter in hand, as the saying of the eunuch to Philip, "See, here is water; what doth hinder me to be baptized?"[2] "inasmuch as he knew," says he, "that those of abandoned character were prevented;" arguing that the reason why Philip did not forbid him to be baptized was because he had proved, in his reading of the Scriptures, how far he believed in Christ,—as though he had prohibited Simon Magus. And again, he urges that the prophets were afraid of being deceived by false baptism, and that therefore Isaiah said, "Lying water that has not faith,"[3] as though showing that water among faithless men is lying; whereas it is not Isaiah but Jeremiah that says this of lying men, calling the people in a figure water, as is most clearly shown in the Apocalypse.[4] And again, he quotes as words of David, "Let not the oil of the sinner anoint my head," when David has been speaking of the flattery of the smooth speaker deceiving with false praise, so as to lead the head of the man praised to wax great with pride. And this meaning is made manifest by the words immediately preceding in the same psalm. For he says, "Let the righteous smite me, it shall be a kindness; and let him reprove me: but the oil of the sinner shall not break my head."[5] What can be clearer than this sentence? what more manifest? For he declares that he had rather be reproved in kindness with the sharp correction of the righteous, so that he may be healed, than anointed with the soft speaking of the flatterer, so as to be puffed up with pride.

Chap. 34.—39. Petilianus quotes also the warning of the Apostle John, that we should not believe every spirit, but try the spirits whether they are of God,[6] as though this care should be bestowed in order that the wheat should be separated from the chaff in

[1] The Council of Carthage, held on the 13th of September, 401, passed a decree (canon 2) in favor of receiving the clergy of the Donatists with full recognition of their orders.

[2] Acts viii. 36.
[3] Jer. xv. 18. See Book II. c. 102, 234, 235.
[4] Rev. xvii. 15.
[5] Ps. cxli. 5. See Book II. c. 103, 236, 237.
[6] 1 John iv. 1.

this present world before its time, and not rather for fear that the wheat should be deceived by the chaff; or as though, even if the lying spirit should have said something that was true, it was to be denied, because the spirit whom we should abominate had said it. But if any one thinks this, he is mad enough to contend that Peter ought not to have said, "Thou art the Christ, the Son of the living God,"[1] because the devils had already said something to the same effect.[2] Seeing, therefore, that the baptism of Christ, whether administered by an unrighteous or a righteous man, is nothing but the baptism of Christ, what a cautious man and faithful Christian should do is to avoid the unrighteousness of man, not to condemn the sacraments of God.

40. Assuredly in all these things Petilianus gives no answer to the question, If the conscience of one that gives in holiness is what we look for to cleanse the conscience of the recipient, by what means is he to be cleansed who receives baptism, when the conscience of the giver is polluted without the knowledge of the proposed recipient? A certain Cyprian, a colleague of his from Thubursicubur, was caught in a brothel with a woman of most abandoned character, and was brought before Primianus of Carthage, and condemned. Now, when this man baptized before he was detected and condemned, it is manifest that he had not the conscience of one that gives in holiness, so as to cleanse the conscience of the recipient. By what means then have they been cleansed who at this day, after he has been condemned, are certainly not washed again? It was not necessary to name the man save only to prevent Petilianus from repeating, 'Who is the man, and from what corner has he started up, that you propose to us?'' Why did not your party examine that baptizer, as John, in the opinion of Petilianus, was examined? Or was the real fact this, that they examined him so far as man can examine man, but were unable to find him out, as he long lay hid with cunning falseness?

CHAP. 35.—Was the water administered by this man not lying? or is the oil of the fornicator not the oil of the sinner? or must we hold what the Catholic Church says, and what is true, that that water and that oil are not his by whom they were administered, but His whose name was then invoked? Why did they who were baptized by that hypocrite, whose sins were concealed, fail to try the spirit, to prove that it was not of God? For the Holy Spirit of discipline was even then fleeing from the hypocrite.[3] Was it that He was fleeing from him, but at the same time not deserting His sacraments, though ministered by him? Lastly, since you do not deny that those men have been already cleansed, whom you take no care to have cleansed now that he is condemned, see whether, after shedding over the subject so many mists in so many different ways, Petilianus, after all, in any place gives any answer to the question by what means these men have been cleansed, if what we look for to cleanse the conscience of the recipient is the conscience of one that gives in holiness, such as the man who was secretly unclean could not have had.

41. Making then, no answer to this which is so urgently asked of him, and, in the next place, even seeking for himself a latitude of speech, he says, "since both prophets and apostles have been cautious enough to fear these things, with what face do you say that the baptism of the sinner is holy to those who believe with a good conscience?" Just as though I or any Catholic maintained that that baptism was of the sinner which is administered or received with a sinner to officiate, instead of being His in virtue of belief in whose name the candidate is baptized! Then he goes off to an invective against the traitor Judas, saying against him whatever he can, quoting the testimony of the prophets uttered concerning him so long a time before, as though he would steep the Church of Christ dispersed throughout the world, whose cause is involved in this discussion, in the impiety of the traitor Judas,—not considering what this very thing should have recalled to his mind, that we ought no more to doubt that that is the Church of Christ which is spread abroad throughout the world, since this was prophesied with truth so many years before, than we ought to doubt that it was necessary that Christ should be betrayed by one of His disciples, because this was prophesied in like manner.

CHAP. 36.—42. But after this, when Petilianus came to that objection of ours, that they allowed the baptism of the followers of Maximianus, whom they had condemned,[4]—although in the statement of this question he thought it right to use his own words rather than mine; for neither do we assert that the baptism of sinners is of profit to us, seeing that we maintain it to belong not only to no sinners, but to no men whatsoever, in that we are satisfied that it is Christ's alone,—having put the question in this form, he says, "Yet you obstinately aver that it is right that

[1] Matt. xvi. 16. [2] Matt. viii. 29; Mark i. 24; Luke viii. 28. [3] Wisd. i. 5. [4] See Book I. cc. 10, 11, 11, 12.

the baptism of sinners should be of profit to you, because we too, according to your statement, maintained the baptism of criminals whom we justly condemned." When he came to this question, as I said before, even all the show of fight which he had made deserted him. He could not find any way to go, any means of escape, any path by which, either through subtle watching or bold enterprise, he could either secretly steal away, or sally forth by force. "Although this," he says, 'I will demonstrate in my second book, how great the difference is between those of our party and those of yours whom you call innocent, yet, in the meantime, first extricate yourselves from the offenses with which you are acquainted in your colleagues, and then seek out the mode of dealing with those whom we cast out." Would any one, any man upon the earth, give an answer like this, save one who is setting himself against the truth, against which he cannot find any answer that can be made? Accordingly, if we too were to use the same words: In the meantime, first extricate yourselves from the offenses with which you are acquainted in your colleagues, and then bring up against us any charge connected with those whom you hold to be wicked amongst us,—what is the result? Have we both won the victory, or are we both defeated? Nay, rather He has gained the victory for His Church and in His Church, who has taught us in His Scriptures that no man should glory in men, and that he that glorieth should glory in the Lord.[1] For behold in our case, who assert with the eloquence of truth that the man who believes is not justified by him by whom he is baptized, but by Him of whom it is written, "To him that believeth on Him that justifieth the ungodly, his faith is counted for righteousness,"[2] since we do not glory in men, and strive, when we glory, to glory in the Lord in virtue of His own gift, how wholly safe are we, whatever fault or charge Petilianus may have been able to prove concerning certain men of our communion! For among us, whatever wicked men are either wholly undetected, or, being known to certain persons, are yet tolerated for the sake of the bond of unity and peace, in consideration of other good men to whom their wickedness is unknown, and before whom they could not be convicted, in order that the wheat may not be rooted up together with the tares, yet they so bear the burden of their own wickedness, that no one shares it with them except those who are pleased with their unrighteousness. Nor indeed have we any apprehension that those whom they baptize cannot be justified, since they believe in Him that justifieth the ungodly that their faith may be counted for righteousness.[3]

Chap. 37.—43. Furthermore, according to our tenets, neither he of whom Petilianus said that he was cast forth by us for the sin of the men of Sodom, another being appointed in his place, and that afterwards he was actually restored to our college,—talking all the time without knowing what he was saying,—nor he whom he declares to have been penitent among you, in whatever degree their respective cases do or do not admit of any defense, can neither of them prejudice the Church, which is spread abroad throughout all nations, and increases in the world until the harvest. For if they were really wicked members of it that you accuse, then they were already not in it, but among the chaff; but if they are good, while you defame their character with unrighteous accusations, they are themselves being tried like gold, while you burn after the similitude of chaff. Yet the sins of other men do not defile the Church, which is spread abroad throughout the whole world, according to most faithful prophesies, waiting for the end of the world as for its shore, on which, when it is landed, it will be freed from the bad fish, in company with which the inconvenience of nature might be borne without sin within the same nets of the Lord, so long as it was not right to be impatiently separated from them. Nor yet is the discipline of the Church on this account neglected by constant and diligent and prudent ministers of Christ, in whose province crimes are in such wise brought to light that they cannot be defended on any plea of probability. Innumerable proofs of this may be found in those who have been bishops or clergy of the second degree of orders, and now, being degraded, have either gone abroad into other lands through shame, or have gone over to you yourselves or to other heresies, or are known in their own districts; of whom there is so great a multitude dispersed throughout the earth, that if Petilianus, bridling for a time his rashness in speaking, had taken them into consideration, he would never have fallen into so manifestly false and groundless a misconception, as to think that we ought to join in what he says: None of you is free from guilt, where no one that is guilty is condemned.

Chap. 38.—44. For, to pass over others dwelling in different quarters of the earth,—

[1] 1 Cor. iii. 21, and i. 31.

[2] Rom. iv. 5.

[3] Rom. iv. 5.

for you will scarcely find any place in which this kind of men is not represented, from whom it may appear that overseers and ministers are wont to be condemned even in the Catholic Church,—we need not look far to find the example of Honorius of Milevis. But take the case of Splendonius, whom Petilianus ordained priest after he had been condemned in the Catholic Church, and rebaptized by himself, whose condemnation in Gaul, communicated to us by our brethren, our colleague Fortunatus caused to be publicly read in Constantina, and whom the same Petilianus afterwards cast forth on experience of his abominable deceit. From the case of this Splendonius, when was there a time when he might not have been reminded after what fashion wicked men are degraded from their office even in the Catholic Church? I wonder on what precipice of rashness his heart was resting when he dictated those words in which he ventured to say, "No one of you is free from guilt, where no one that is guilty is condemned." Wherefore the wicked, being bodily intermingled with the good, but spiritually separated from them in the Catholic Church, both when they are undetected through the infirmity of human nature, and when they are condemned from considerations of discipline, in every case bear their own burden. And in this way those are free from danger who are baptized by them with the baptism of Christ, if they keep free from share in their sins either by imitation or consent; seeing that in like manner, if they were baptized by the best of men, they would not be justified except by Him that justifieth the ungodly: since to those that believe on Him that justifieth the ungodly their faith is counted for righteousness.

CHAP. 39.—45. But as for you, when the case of the followers of Maximianus is brought up against you, who, after being condemned by the sentence of a Council of 310 bishops;[1] after being utterly defeated in the same Council, quoted in the records of so many proconsuls, in the chronicles of so many municipal towns; after being driven forth from the basilicas of which they were in possession, by the order of the judges, enforced by the troops of the several cities, were yet again received with all honor by you, together with those whom they had baptized outside the pale of your communion, without any question respecting their baptism,—when confronted, I say, with their case, you can find no reply to make. Indeed, you are vanquished by an expressed opinion, not indeed true, but proceeding from yourselves, by which you maintain that men perish for the faults of others in the same communion of the sacraments, and that each man's character is determined by that of the man by whom he is baptized,—that he is guilty if his baptizer is guilty, innocent if he is innocent. But if these views are true, there can be no doubt that, to say nothing of innumerable others, you are destroyed by the sins of the followers of Maximianus, whose guilt your party, in so large a Council, has exaggerated even to the proportions of the sin of those whom the earth swallowed up alive. But if the faults of the followers of Maximianus have not destroyed you, then are these opinions false which you entertain; and much less have certain indefinite unproved faults of the Africans been able to destroy the entire world. And accordingly, as the apostle says, "Every man shall bear his own burden;"[2] and the baptism of Christ is no one's except Christ's; and it is to no purpose that Petilianus promises that he will take as the subject of his second book the charges which we bring concerning the followers of Maximianus, entertaining too low an opinion of men's intellects, as though they do not perceive that he has nothing to say.

CHAP. 40.—46. For if the baptism which Prætextatus and Felicianus administered in the communion of Maximianus was their own, why was it received by you in those whom they baptized as though it were the baptism of Christ? But if it is truly the baptism of Christ, as indeed it is, and yet could not profit those who had received it with the guilt of schism, what do you say that you could have granted to those whom you have received into your body with the same baptism, except that, now that the offense of their accursed division is wiped out by the bond of peace, they should not be compelled to receive the sacrament of the holy laver as though they had it not, but that, as what they had was before for their destruction, so it should now begin to be of profit to them? Or if this is not granted to them in your communion, because it could not possibly be that it should be granted to schismatics among schismatics, it is at any rate granted to you in the Catholic communion, not that you should receive baptism as though it were lacking in you, but that the baptism which you have actually received should be of profit to you. For all the sacraments of Christ, if not combined with the love which belongs to the unity of Christ, are

[1] That of Bagai.

[2] Gal. vi. 5.

possessed not unto salvation, but unto judgment. But since it is not a true verdict, but your verdict, "that through the baptism of certain *traditors* the baptism of Christ has perished from the world in general," it is with good reason that you cannot find any answer to make respecting the recognition of the baptism of the followers of Maximianus.

47. See therefore, and remember with the most watchful care, how Petilianus has made no answer to that very question, which he proposes to himself in such terms as to seem to make it a starting-point from which to say something. For the former question he has dismissed altogether, and has not wished to speak of it to us, because I suppose it was beyond his power; nor is he at any time, up to the very end of his volume, going to say anything about it, though he quoted it from the first part of my epistle as though it were a matter calling for refutation. For even though he has added the two words which he accused me of having suppressed, as though they were the strongest bulwarks of his position, he yet lies wholly defenseless, unable to find any answer to make when he is asked, If the conscience of one that gives in holiness is what we look for to cleanse the conscience of the recipient, where are we to find means for cleansing the conscience of the man who is unacquainted with the conscience of him that gives, but not in holiness? and if it be the case that any one who has received his faith from one that is faithless, receives not faith but guilt, from what source is he to receive not guilt but faith, who is unwittingly baptized by one that is faithless? To this question it has long been manifest from what he says that he has made no answer.

48. In the next place, he has gone on, with calumnious mouth, to abuse monasteries and monks, finding fault also with me, as having been the founder of this kind of life.[1] And what this kind of life really is he does not know at all, or rather, though it is perfectly well known throughout all the world, he pretends that he is unacquainted with it. Then, asserting that I had said that Christ was the baptizer, he has also added certain words from my epistle as though I had set this forth as my own sentiment, when I had really quoted it as his and yours, and it was inveighed against with most copious harshness, as if it were I who had said these things against myself, when what he reprehended was not mine, but his and your sentiment, as I will presently show clearly to the best of my ability.[2] Then he has endeavored to show us, in many unnecessary words, that Christ does not baptize, but that baptism is administered in His name, at once in the name of the Father, and of the Son, and of the Holy Ghost; of which Trinity itself he has said, either because it was what he wished, or because it was all that he could say, that "Christ is the centre of the Trinity." In the next place, he has taken occasion of the names of the sorcerers Simon and Barjesus to vent against us what insults he thought fit. Then he goes on, keeping in guarded suspense the case of Optatus of Thamugas, that he might not be steeped in the odium that arose from it, denying that neither he or his party could have passed judgment upon him, and actually intimating in respect of him, that he was crushed in consequence of suggestions from myself.

Chap. 41.—49. Lastly, he has ended his epistle with an exhortation and warning to his own party, that they should not be deceived by us, and with a lamentation over those of our party, that we had made them worse than they had been before. Having therefore carefully considered and discussed these points, as appears with sufficient clearness from the words of the epistle which he wrote, Petilianus has made no answer at all to the position which I advanced to begin with in my epistle, when I asked, Supposing it to be true, as he asserts, that the conscience of one that gives—or rather, to add what he considers so great a support to his argument—that the conscience of one that gives in holiness is what we look for to cleanse the conscience of the recipient, by what means he who receives baptism is to be cleansed, when, if the conscience of the giver is polluted, it is without the knowledge of the proposed recipient? Whence it is not surprising that a man resisting in the cause of falsehood, pressed hard in the straits of the truth that contradicts it, should have chosen rather to gasp forth mad abuse, than to walk in the path of that truth which cannot be overcome.

50. And now I would beg of you to pay especial attention to the next few words, that I may show you clearly what he has been afraid of in not answering this, and that I may bring into the light what he has endeavored to shroud in obscurity. It certainly was in his power, when we asked by what means he is to be cleansed, who receives baptism when the conscience of the giver is polluted without the knowledge of the proposed recipient, to answer with the greatest ease, From our Lord God; and at any rate to say with the utmost confidence, God wholly cleanses the conscience of the recipient, when he is un-

[1] See Possidius' *Life of St. Augustin*, cc. v.-xi.
[2] See c. 45, 54.

acquainted with the stain upon the conscience of him that gives but not in holiness. But when a man had already been compelled by the tenets of your sect to rest the cleansing of the recipient on the conscience of the giver, in that he had said, "For the conscience of him that gives," or "of him that gives in holiness, is looked for to cleanse the conscience of the recipient," he was naturally afraid lest any one should seem to be better baptized by a wicked man who concealed his wickedness, than by one that was genuinely and manifestly good; for in the former case his cleansing would depend not on the conscience of one that gave in holiness, but on the most excellent holiness of God Himself. With this apprehension, therefore, that he might not be involved in so great an absurdity, or rather madness, as not to know where he could make his escape, he was unwilling to say by what means the conscience of the recipient should be cleansed, when he does not know of the stain upon the conscience of him that gives but not in holiness; and he thought it better, by making a general confusion with his quarrelsome uproar, to conceal what was asked of him, than to give a reply to his question, which should at once discomfit him; never, however, thinking that our letter could be read by men of such good understanding, or that his would be read by those who had read ours as well, to which he has professed to make an answer.

CHAP. 42.—51. For what I just now said is put with the greatest clearness in that very epistle of mine, in answering which he has said nothing; and I would beg of you to listen for a few moments to what he there has done. And although you are partisans of his, and hate us, yet, if you can, bear it with equanimity. For in his former epistle, to the first portion of which—the only portion which had then come into our hands—I had in the first instance made my reply, he had so rested the hope that is found in baptism in the baptizer, as to say, "For everything consists of an origin and root; and if anything has not a head, it is nothing." Since then Petilianus had said this, not wishing anything to be understood by the origin and root and head of baptizing a man, except the man by whom he might be baptized, I made a comment, and said "We ask, therefore, in a case where the faithlessness of the baptizer is undetected, if then the man whom he baptizes receives faith and not guilt? if then the baptizer is not his origin and root and head, who is it from whom he receives faith? where is the origin from which he springs? where is the root of which he is a shoot? where the head which is his starting-point? Can it be that, when he who is baptized is unaware of the faithlessness of his baptizer, it is then Christ who is the origin and root and head?" This therefore I say and exclaim now also, as I did there as well: "Alas for human rashness and conceit! Why do you not allow that it is always Christ who gives faith, for the purpose of making a man a Christian by giving it? Why do you not allow that Christ is always the origin of the Christian, that the Christian always plants his root in Christ, that Christ is the Head of the Christian? Will it then be urged that, even where spiritual grace is dispensed to those that believe by the hands of a holy and faithful minister, it is still not the minister himself who justifies, but that One of whom it is said, 'He justifieth the ungodly'?[1] But unless we admit this, either the Apostle Paul was the head and origin of those whom he had planted, or Apollos the root of those whom he had watered, rather than He who had given them faith in believing; whereas the same Paul says, 'I have planted, Apollos watered; but God gave the increase. So that neither is he that planteth anything, neither he that watereth; but God that giveth the increase."[2] Nor was the apostle himself their root, but rather He who says, 'I am the vine, ye are the branches.'[3] How, too, could he be their head, when he says that 'we, being many, are one body in Christ."[4] and expressly declares in many passages that Christ Himself is the Head of the whole body? Wherefore, whether a man receives the sacrament of baptism from a faithful or a faithless minister, his whole hope is in Christ, that he fall not under the condemnation, that 'Cursed is he that placeth his hope in man!"'[5]

CHAP. 43.—52. These things, I think, I put with clearness and truth in my former epistle, when I made answer to Petilianus. These things I have also now quoted, intimating and commending to you the truth that our faith rests on something else altogether than man, and that we believe that the Lord Christ is the cleanser and the justifier of men that believe in Him that justifieth the ungodly, that their faith may be counted unto them for righteousness, whether the man who administers the baptism be righteous, or such an impious and deceitful man as the Holy Spirit flees. Then I went on to point out what absurdity would follow were it otherwise, and I said, as I say now: "Otherwise, if each man is born again in spiritual grace of the

1 Rom. iv. 5. 2 1 Cor. iii. 6, 7. 3 John xv. 5
4 Rom. xii. 5. 5 Book I. c. 5, 6.

same sort as he by whom he is baptized, and if, when he who baptizes him is manifestly a good man, then he himself gives faith, he is himself the origin and root and head of him who is being born; whilst, when the baptizer is faithless without its being known, then the baptized person receives faith from Christ, then he derives his origin from Christ, then he is rooted in Christ, then he boasts in Christ as his head; in that case all who are baptized should wish that they might have faithless baptizers, and be ignorant of their faithlessness. For however good their baptizers might have been, Christ is certainly beyond comparison better still, and He will then be the Head of the baptized if the faithlessness of the baptizer shall escape detection. But if it be perfect madness to hold such a view (for it is Christ always that justifieth the ungodly, by changing his ungodliness into Christianity; it is from Christ always that faith is received; Christ is always the origin of the regenerate, and the Head of the Church), what weight then will those words have, which thoughtless readers value by their sound, without inquiring what their inner meaning is?"[1] This much I said at that time; this is written in my epistle.

Chap. 44.—53. Then a little after, as he had said, "This being so, brethren, what perversity must that be, that he who is guilty by reason of his own faults should make another free from guilt, whereas the Lord Jesus Christ says, 'Every good tree bringeth forth good fruit, but a corrupt tree bringeth forth evil fruit: do men gather grapes of thorns?[2] and again, 'A good man, out of the good treasure of the heart, bringeth forth good things: and an evil man, out of the evil treasure, bringeth forth evil things,'"[3]—by which words Petilianus showed with sufficient clearness, that the man who baptizes is to be looked on as the tree, and he who is baptized as the fruit: to this I had answered, If the good tree is the good baptizer, and his good fruit he whom he has baptized, then any one who has been baptized by a bad man, even if his wickedness be not manifest, cannot by any possibility be good, for he is sprung from an evil tree. For a good tree is one thing; a tree whose quality is concealed, but yet bad, is another. What else did I wish to be understood by those words, except what I had stated a little above, that the tree and its fruit do not represent him that baptizes and him that is baptized; but that the man ought to be received as signified by the tree, his works and his life by the fruit, which are always good in the good man, and evil in the evil man, lest this absurdity should follow, that a man should be bad when baptized by a bad man, even though his wickedness were concealed, being, as it were, the fruit of a tree whose quality was unknown, but yet bad? To which he has answered nothing whatsoever.

Chap. 45.—54. But that neither he nor any one of you might say that, when any one of concealed bad character is the baptizer, then he whom he baptizes is not his fruit, but the fruit of Christ, I went on immediately to point out what a foolish error is consequent also on that opinion; and I repeated, though in other words, what I had said shortly before: If, when the quality of the tree is concealed, but evil, any one who may have been baptized by it is born, not of it but of Christ, then they are justified with greater holiness who are baptized by wicked men, whose wickedness is concealed, than they who are baptized by men that are genuinely and manifestly good.[4] Petilianus then, being hemmed in by these embarrassing straits, said nothing about the earlier part on which these remarks depended, and in his answer so quoted this absurd consequence of his error as though I had stated it as my own opinion, whereas it was really stated in order that he might perceive the amount of evil consequent on his opinion, and so be forced to alter it. Imposing, therefore, this deceit on those who hear and read his words, and never for a moment supposing that what we have written could be read, he begins a vehement and petulant invective against me, as though I had thought that all who are baptized ought to wish that they might have as their baptizers men who are faithless, without knowing this themselves, since, however good the men might be whom they had to baptize them, Christ is incomparably better, who will then be the head of the person baptized, if the faithless baptizer conceal his true character. As though, too, I had thought that those were justified with greater holiness who are baptized by evil men, whose character is concealed, than those who are baptized by men that are genuinely and manifestly good; when this marvellous piece of madness was only mentioned by me as following necessarily on the opinion of those who think with Petilianus, that a man, when baptized, bears the same relation to his baptizer as fruit does to the tree from which it springs,—good fruit springing from a good tree, evil fruit from an evil tree,—seeing that

[1] Book I. c. 6, 7.
[2] Matt. vii. 17, 16.
[3] Matt. xii. 35.
[4] See Book I. cc. 7, 8, 8, 9.

they, when they are bidden by me to answer whose fruit they think a man that is baptized to be when he is baptized by one of secretly bad character, since they do not venture to rebaptize him, are compelled to answer, that then he is not the fruit of that man of secretly bad character, but that he is the fruit of Christ. And so they are followed by a consequence contrary to their inclination, which none but a madman would entertain,—that if a man is the fruit of his baptizer when he is baptized by one that is genuinely and manifestly good, but when he is baptized by one of secretly bad character, he is then not his fruit, but the fruit of Christ,—it cannot but follow that they are justified with greater holiness who are baptized by men of secretly bad character, than those who are baptized by men who are genuinely and manifestly good.

CHAP. 46.—55. Now, seeing that when Petilianus attributes this to me as though it were my opinion, he makes it an occasion for a serious and vehement invective against me, he at any rate shows, by the very force of his indignation, how great a sin it is in his opinion to entertain such views; and, accordingly, whatever he has wished it to appear that he said against me for holding this opinion will be found to have been really said against himself, who is proved to entertain the view. For he shows herein by how great force on the side of truth he is overcome, when he cannot find any other door of escape except to pretend that it was I who entertained the views which really are his own. Just as if those whom the apostle confutes for maintaining that there was no resurrection from the dead, were to wish to bring an accusation against the same apostle, on the ground that he said, "Then is Christ not risen," and to maintain that the preaching of the apostle was vain, and the faith of those who believed in it was also vain, and that false witnesses were found against God in those who had said that He raised up Christ from the dead. This is what Petilianus wished to do to me, never expecting that any one could read what I had written, which he could not answer, though very anxious that men should believe him to have answered it. But just as, if any one had done this to the apostle, the whole calumnious accusation would have recoiled on the head of those who made it so soon as the entire passage in his epistle was read, and the preceding words restored, on which any one who reads them must perceive that those which I have quoted depend, in the same way, so soon as the preceding words of my epistle are restored, the accusation which Petilianus brings against me is cast back with all the greater force upon his own head, from which he had striven to remove it.

56. For the apostle, in confuting those who denied that there was any resurrection of the dead, corrects their view by showing the absurdity which follows those who entertain this view, however loth they may be to admit the consequence, in order that, while they shrink in abhorrence from what is impious to say, they may correct what they have ventured to believe. His argument continues thus: "But if there be no resurrection of the dead, then is Christ not risen: and if Christ be not risen, then is our preaching vain, and your faith is also vain. Yea, and we are found false witnesses of God: because we have testified of God that He raised up Christ; whom He raised not up, if so be that the dead rise not."[1] in order that, while they fear to say that Christ had not risen, with the other wicked and accursed conclusions which follow from such a statement, they may correct what they said in a spirit of folly and infidelity, that there is no resurrection of the dead. If, therefore, you take away what stands at the head of this argument, "*If* there be no resurrection of the dead," the rest is spoken amiss, and yet must be ascribed to the apostle. But if you restore the supposition on which the rest depends, and place as the hypothesis from which you start, "There is no resurrection of the dead," then the conclusion will follow rightly, "Then is Christ not risen, and our preaching is vain, and your faith is also vain," with all the rest that is appended to it. And all these statements of the apostle are wise and good, since whatever evil they have in them is to be imputed to those who denied the resurrection of the dead. In the same manner also, in my epistle, take away my supposition, If every one is born again in spiritual grace of the same character as he by whom he is baptized, and if, when the man who baptizes is genuinely and manifestly good, he does of himself give faith, he is the origin and root and head of him who is being born again; but when the baptizer is a wicked man, and undetected in his wickedness, then each man who is baptized receives his faith from Christ, derives his origin from Christ, is rooted in Christ, makes his boast in Christ as his Head:—take away, I say, this hypothesis, on which all that follows depends, and there remains a saying of the worst description which must fairly be ascribed to me, viz., that all who are baptized should desire that they should have faithless men to baptize them, and be igno-

1 1 Cor. xv. 13-15.

rant of their faithlessness. For however good men they may have to baptize them, Christ is incomparably better, who will then be the Head of the baptized, if the baptizer be a faithless man, but undetected.[1] But let the statements that you make be restored, and then it will forthwith be found that this which depends upon it and follows in close connection from it is not my sentiment, and that any evil which it contains is retorted on the opinion which you maintain. In like manner, take away the supposition, If the good baptizer is the good tree, so that he whom he has baptized is his good fruit, and if, when the character of an evil tree is concealed, then any one that has been baptized by it is born, not of it, but of Christ,—take away this hypothesis, which you were compelled to confess had its origin in your sect and in the letter of Petilianus, and the mad conclusion which follows from it will be mine, to be ascribed to me alone, Then they are justified with greater holiness who are baptized by undetected evil men, than they who are baptized by men that are genuinely and manifestly good.[2] But restore the hypothesis on which this depends, and you will at once see both that I have been right in making this statement for your correction, and that all that with good reason displeases you in this opinion has recoiled upon your own head.

Chap. 47—57. Furthermore, in like manner as those who denied the resurrection of the dead could in no way defend themselves from the evil consequences which the apostle proved to follow from their premises, in order to refute their error, saying, "Then is not Christ raised," with the other conclusions of similar atrocity, unless they changed their opinions, and acknowledged that there was a resurrection of the dead; so is it necessary that you should change your opinion, and cease to rest on man the hope of those who are baptized, if you do not wish to have imputed to you what we say for your refutation and correction, that they are justified with greater holiness who are baptized by undetected evil men than those that are baptized by men that are genuinely and manifestly good. For if you make your first assertion, see what I say, unless some one shall suppress this a second time, and make out that I have entertained the opinion which I quote for your refutation and correction. See what I lay down as my premiss, from which hangs the statement which I shall subsequently make: If you rest the hope of those who are to be baptized on the man by whom they are baptized, and if you maintain, as Petilianus wrote, that the man who baptizes is the origin and root and head of him that is baptized; if you receive as the good tree the good man who baptizes, and as his good fruit the man who has been baptized by him; then you put it into our heads to ask from what origin he springs, from what root he shoots up, to what head he is joined, from what tree he is born, who is baptized by an undetected bad man? For to this inquiry belongs also the following, to which I have over and over again maintained that Petilianus has given no reply: By what means is a man to be cleansed who receives baptism while he is ignorant of the stain upon the conscience of him that gives but not in holiness? for this conscience of him that gives, or of him that gives in holiness, Petilianus wishes to be the origin, root, head, seed, tree from which the sanctification of the baptized has its existence,—springs, begins, sprouts forth, is born.

Chap. 48.—58. When we ask, therefore, by what means the man is to be cleansed whom you do not baptize again in your communion, even when it has been made clear that he has been baptized by some one who, on account of some concealed iniquity, did not at the time possess the conscience of one that gives in holiness, what answer do you intend to make, except that he is cleansed by Christ or by God, although, indeed, Christ is Himself God over all, blessed for ever,[3] or by the Holy Spirit, since He too is Himself God, because this Trinity of Persons is one God? Whence Peter, after saying to a man, "Thou hast dared to lie to the Holy Ghost," immediately went on to add what was the nature of the Holy Ghost, saying, "Thou hast not lied unto men, but unto God."[4] Lastly, even if you were to say that he was cleansed and purified by an angel when he is unacquainted with the pollution in the conscience of him that gives but not in holiness, take notice that it is said of the saints, when they shall have risen to eternal life, that they shall then be equal to the angels of God.[5] Any one, therefore, that is cleansed even by an angel is cleansed with greater holiness than if he were cleansed by any kind of conscience of man. Why then are you unwilling that it should be said to you, If cleansing is wrought by the hands of a man when he is genuinely and manifestly good; but when the man is evil, but undetected in his wickedness, then since he has not the conscience of one that

[1] See Book I. c. 6, 7.

[2] See Book I. c. 8, 9.

[3] Rom. ix. 5.

[4] Acts v. 3, 4.

[5] Matt. xxii. 30.

gives in holiness, it is no longer he, but God, or an angel, that cleanses; therefore they who are baptized by undetected evil men are justified with greater holiness than those who are baptized by men that are genuinely and manifestly good? And if this opinion is displeasing to you, as in reality it ought to be displeasing to every one, then take away the source from which it springs, correct the premiss to which it is indissolubly bound; for if these do not precede as hypotheses, the other will not follow as a consequence.

CHAP. 49.—59. Do not therefore any longer say, "The conscience of one that gives in holiness is what we look for to cleanse the conscience of the recipient," lest you be asked, When a stain on the conscience of the giver is concealed, who cleanses the conscience of the recipient? And when you shall have answered, Either God or an angel (since there is no other answer which you possibly can make), then should follow a consequence whereby you would be confounded: Those then are justified with greater holiness who are baptized by undetected evil men, so as to be cleansed by God or by an angel, than those who are baptized by men who are genuinely and manifestly good, who cannot be compared with God or with the angels. But prevail upon yourselves to say what is said by Truth and by the Catholic Church, that not only when the minister of baptism is evil, but also when he is holy and good, hope is still not to be placed in man, but in Him that justifieth the ungodly, in whom if any man believe, his faith is counted for righteousness.[1] For when we say, Christ baptizes, we do not mean by a visible ministry, as Petilianus believes, or would have men think that he believes, to be our meaning, but by a hidden grace, by a hidden power in the Holy Spirit, as it is said of Him by John the Baptist, "The same is He which baptizeth with the Holy Ghost."[2] Nor has He, as Petilianus says, now ceased to baptize; but He still does it, not by any ministry of the body, but by the invisible working of His majesty. For in that we say, He Himself baptizes, we do not mean, He Himself holds and dips in the water the bodies of the believers; but He Himself invisibly cleanses, and that He does to the whole Church without exception. Nor, indeed, may we refuse to believe the words of the Apostle Paul, who says concerning Him, "Husbands, love your wives, even as Christ also loved the Church, and gave Himself for it, that He might sanctify and cleanse it with the washing of water by the word."[3] Here you see that Christ sanctifies; here you see that Christ also Himself washes, Himself purifies with the self-same washing of water by the word, wherein the ministers are seen to do their work in the body. Let no one, therefore, claim unto himself what is of God. The hope of men is only sure when it is fixed on Him who cannot deceive, since "Cursed be every one that trusteth in man,"[4] and "Blessed is that man that maketh the Lord His trust."[5] For the faithful steward shall receive as his reward eternal life; but the unfaithful steward, when he dispenses his lord's provisions to his fellow-servants, must in no wise be conceived to make the provisions useless by his own unfaithfulness. For the Lord says, "Whatsoever they bid you observe, that observe and do; but do not ye after their works."[6] And this is therefore the injunction that is given us against evil stewards, that the good things of God should be received at their hands, but that we should beware of their own evil life, by reason of its unlikeness to what they thus dispense.

CHAP. 50.—60. But if it is clear that Petilianus has made no answer to those first words of my epistle, and that, when he has endeavored to make an answer, he has shown all the more clearly how incapable he was of answering, what shall I say in respect of those portions of my writings which he has not even attempted to answer, on which he has not touched at all? And yet if any one shall be willing to review their character, having in his possession both my writings and those of Petilianus, I think he will understand by what confirmation they are supported. And that I may show you this as shortly as I can, I would beg you to call to mind the proofs that were advanced from holy Scripture, or refresh your memory by reading both what he has brought forward as against me, and what I have brought forward in my answer as against you, and see how I have shown that the passages which he has brought forward are antagonistic not to me, but rather to yourselves; whilst he has altogether failed to touch those which I brought forward as especially necessary, and in that one passage of the apostle which he has endeavored to make use of as though it favored him, you will see how he found himself without the means of making his escape.

61. For the portion of this epistle which he wrote to his adherents—from the beginning down to the passage in which he says, "This

[1] Rom. iv. 5.
[2] John i. 33.
[3] Eph. v. 25, 26.
[4] Jer. xvii. 5.
[5] Ps. xl. 4.
[6] Matt. xxiii. 3.

is the commandment of the Lord to us, 'When they persecute you in this city, flee ye into another;'[1] and if they persecute you in that also, flee ye to a third"—came first into my hands, and to it I made a reply; and when this reply of ours had fallen, in turn, into his hands, he wrote in answer to it this which I am now refuting, showing that he has made no reply to mine. In that first portion, therefore, of his writings to which I first replied, these are the passages of Scripture which he conceives to be opposed to us: "Every good tree bringeth forth good fruit, but a corrupt tree bringeth forth evil fruit. Do men gather grapes of thorns?"[2] And again: "A good man, out of the good treasure of his heart, bringeth forth good things; and an evil man, out of the evil treasure, bringeth forth evil things."[3] And again: "When a man is baptized by one that is dead, his washing profiteth him nothing."[4] From these passages he is anxious to show that the man who is baptized is made to partake of the character of him by whom he is baptized; I, on the other hand, have shown in what sense these passages should be received, and that they could in no wise aid his view. But as for the other expressions which he has used against evil and accursed men, I have sufficiently shown that they are applicable to the Lord's wheat, dispersed, as was foretold and promised, throughout the world, and that they might rather be used by us against you. Examine them again, and you will find it so.

62. But the passages which I have advanced to assert the truth of the Catholic Church, are the following: As regards the question of baptism, that our being born again, cleansed, justified by the grace of God, should not be ascribed to the man who administered the sacrament, I quoted these: "It is better to trust in the Lord than to put confidence in man:"[5] and "Cursed beevery one that trusteth inman;"[6] and that, "Salvation belongeth unto the Lord;"[7] and that, "Vain is the help of man;"[8] and that, "Neither is he that planteth anything, neither he that watereth, but God that giveth the increase;"[9] and that He in whom men believe justifieth the ungodly, that his faith may be counted to him for righteousness.[10] But in behalf of the unity of the Church itself, which is spread abroad throughout all the world, with which you do not hold communion, I urged that the following passages were prophesied of Christ: that "He shall have dominion also from sea to sea, and from the river unto the ends of the earth;"[11] and, "I shall give Thee the heathen for Thine inheritance, and the uttermost parts of the earth for Thy possession;"[12] and that the covenant of God made with Abraham may be quoted in behalf of our, that is, of the Catholic communion, in which it is written, "In thy seed shall all nations of the earth be blessed;"[13] which seed the apostle interprets, saying, "And to thy seed, which is Christ."[14] Whence it is evident that in Christ not only Africans or Africa, but all the nations through which the Catholic Church is spread abroad, should receive the blessing which was promised so long before. And that the chaff is to be with the wheat even to the time of the last winnowing, that no one may excuse the sacrilege of his own separation from the Church by calumnious accusations of other men's offenses, if he shall have left or deserted the communion of all nations; and to show that the society of Christians may not be divided on account of evil ministers, that is, evil rulers in the Church, I further quoted the passage, "All whatsoever they bid you observe, that observe and do; but do not ye after their works; for they say and do not."[15] With regard to these passages of holy Scripture which I advanced to prove my points, he neither showed how they ought to be otherwise interpreted, so as to prove that they neither made for us nor against you, nor was he willing to touch them in any way. Nay, his whole object was could it have been achieved, that by the tumultuous outpouring of his abuse, it might never occur to any one at all, who after reading my epistle might have been willing to read his as well, that these things had been said by me

Chap. 51.—63. Next, listen fo. a short time to the kind of way in which he has tried to use, in his own behalf, the passages which I had advanced from the writings of the Apostle Paul. "For you asserted," he says, "that the Apostle Paul finds fault with those who used to say that they were of the Apostle Paul, saying, 'Was Paul crucified for you? or were ye baptized in the name of Paul?'[16] Wherefore, if they were in error, and would have perished had they not been corrected, because they wished to be of Paul, what hope can there possibly be for those who have wished to be of Donatus? For this is their sole object, that the origin, and root, and head of him that is baptized should be none other than he by whom he is baptized."[17]

---

1 Matt. x. 23. 2 Matt. vii. 17, 16. 3 Matt. xii. 35.
4 Ecclus. xxxiv. 25. See Book I. c. 9, 10.
5 Ps. cxviii. 8. 6 Jer. xvii. 5. 7 Ps. iii. 8.
8 Ps. lx. 11. 9 1 Cor. iii. 7. 10 Rom. iv. 5.

11 Ps. lxxii. 8. 12 Ps. ii. 8. 13 Gen. xxii. 18.
14 Gal. iii. 16. 15 Matt. xxiii. 3. 16 1 Cor. i. 13.
17 See Book I. cc. 3, 4, 4, 5.

These words, and this confirmation from the writings of the apostle, he has quoted from my epistle, and he has proposed to himself the task of refuting them. Go on then, I beg of you, to see how he has fulfilled the task. For he says, "This assertion is meaningless, and inflated, and childish, and foolish, and something very far from a true exposition of our faith. For you would only be right in asserting this, if we were to say, We have been baptized in the name of Donatus, or Donatus was crucified for us, or we have been baptized in our own name. But since such things as this neither have been said nor are said by us,—seeing that we follow the formula of the holy Trinity,—it is clear that you are mad to bring such accusations against us. Or if you think that we have been baptized in the name of Donatus, or in our own name, you are miserably deceived, and at the same time confess in your sacrilege that you on your part defile your wretched selves in the name of Cæcilianus." This is the answer which Petilianus has made to those arguments of mine, not supposing—or rather making a noise that no one might suppose—that he has made no answer at all which could bear in any way upon the question which is under discussion. For who could fail to see that this witness of the apostle has been adduced by us with all the more propriety, in that you do not say that you were baptized in the name of Donatus, or that Donatus was crucified for you, and yet separate yourselves from the communion of the Catholic Church out of respect to the party of Donatus; as also those whom Paul was rebuking certainly did not say that they had been baptized in the name of Paul, or that Paul has been crucified for them, and yet they were making a schism in the name of Paul. As therefore in their case, for whom Christ, not Paul, was crucified, and who were baptized in the name of Christ, not of Paul, and who yet said, "I am of Paul," the rebuke is used with all the more propriety, "Was Paul crucified for you? or were ye baptized in the name of Paul?" to make them cling to Him who was crucified for them, and in whose name they were baptized, and not be guilty of division in the name of Paul; so in your case, also, the rebuke, Was Donatus crucified for you? or were ye baptized in the name of Donatus? is used all the more appositely, because you do not say, We were baptized in the name of Donatus, and yet desire to be of the party of Donatus. For you know that it was Christ who was crucified for you, and Christ in whose name you were baptized; and yet, out of respect to the name and party of Donatus, you show such obstinacy in fighting against the unity of Christ, who was crucified for you, and in whose name you were baptized.

CHAP. 52.—64. But if you wish to see that the object of Petilianus in his writings really was to prove "that the origin, and root, and head of him that is baptized is none other than he by whom he is baptized," and that this has not been asserted by me without meaning, or childishly, or foolishly, review the beginning of the epistle itself to which I made my reply, or rather pay careful attention to me as I quote it. "The conscience," he says, "of one that gives in holiness is what we look for to cleanse the conscience of the recipient; for he who has received his faith from one that is faithless, receives not faith but guilt." And as though some one had said to him, Whence do you derive your proof of this? he goes on to say, "For everything has its existence from a source and root; and if anything has not a head, it is nothing; nor does anything well confer a new birth, unless it be born again of good seed. And this being so, brethren, what perversity must it be to maintain that he who is guilty by reason of his own offenses should make another free from guilt; whereas our Lord Jesus Christ says, 'A good tree bringeth forth good fruit: do men gather grapes of thorns?' And again, 'A good man, out of the good treasure of his heart, bringeth forth good things; and an evil man, out of the evil treasure, bringeth forth evil things.' And again, 'When a man is baptized by one that is dead, his washing profiteth him nothing.'" You see to what end all these things tend, viz., that the conscience of him that gives in holiness (lest any one, by receiving his faith from one that is faithless, should receive not faith but guilt) should be itself the origin, and root, and head, and seed of him that is baptized. For, wishing to prove that the conscience of one that gives in holiness is what we look for to cleanse the conscience of the recipient, and th t he receives not faith but guilt, who wittingly receives his faith from one that is faithless, he has added immediately afterwards, "For everything has its existence from a source and root; and if anything has not a head, it is nothing; nor does anything well confer a new birth, unless it be born again of good seed." And for fear that any one should be so dull as still not to understand that in each case he is speaking of the man by whom a person is baptized, he explains this afterwards, and says, "This being so, brethren, what perversity must it be to maintain that he who is guilty by reason of his own offenses should make another free from guilt; whereas our Lord Jesus Christ says, 'A good tree bringeth forth good fruit: do men gather grapes of thorns?'" And lest, by some incredible stupidity of understanding, the hearer or seer should be blind enough not to see that he is speaking of the man that baptizes, he adds another passage, where he actually specifies the man. "And again," he says, "'A good man, out of the good treasure of his heart, bringeth forth good things; and an evil man, out of the evil treasure, bringeth forth evil things;' and again, 'When a man is baptized by one that is dead, his washing profiteth him nothing.'" Certainly it is now plain, certainly he needs no longer any interpreter, or disputant, or demonstrator, to show that the object of his party is to prove that the origin, and root, and head of him that is baptized is none other than he by whom he is baptized. And yet, being overwhelmed by the force of truth, and as though forgetful of what he had said before, Petilianus acknowledges afterwards to me that Christ is the origin and root of them that are regenerate, and the Head of the Church, and not any one that may happen to be the dispenser and minister of baptism. For having said that the apostles used to baptize in the name of Christ, and set forth Christ as the foundation of their faith, to make men Christians, and being fain to prove this, too, by passages and examples from holy Scripture, just as though we were denying it, he says, "Where is now that voice, from which issued the noise of those minute and constant petty questionings, wherein, in the spirit of envy and self-conceit, you uttered many involved sayings about Christ, and for Christ, and in Christ, in opposition to the rashness and haughtiness of men? Lo, Christ is the origin, Christ is the head, Christ is the root of the Christian." When, therefore, I heard this, what could I do but give thanks to Christ, who had compelled the man to make confession? All those things, therefore, are false which he said in the beginning of his epistle, when he wished to persuade us that the conscience of one that gives in holiness must be looked for to cleanse the conscience of the recipient; and that when one has wittingly received his faith from one that is faithless he receives not faith but guilt. For, wishing as it were to show clearly how much rested in the man that baptizes, he had added what he seems to think most weighty proofs, saying "For everything has its existence from a source and root; and if anything has not a head, it is nothing." But afterwards, when he says what we also say, "Lo, Christ is the origin, Christ is the head, Christ is the root of the Christian," he wipes out what he had said before, "that the conscience of one that gives in holiness is the origin, and root, and head of the recipient." The truth, therefore, has prevailed, so that the man who is desirous to receive the baptism of Christ should not rest his hope upon the man who administers the sacrament, but should approach in all security to Christ Himself, as to the source which is not changed, to the root which is not plucked up, to the head which is not cast down.

Chap. 53.—65. Then who is there that could fail to perceive from what a vein of conceit it proceeds, that in explaining as it were the declaration of the apostle, he says, "He who said, 'I planted, Apollos watered, but God gave the increase,' surely meant nothing else than this, that 'I made a man a catechumen in Christ, Apollo baptized him; God confirmed what we had done?'" Why then did not Petilianus add what the apostle added, and I especially took pains to quote, "So then neither is he that planteth anything, neither he that watereth; but God that giveth the increase"?[1] And if he be willing to interpret this on the same principle as what he has set down above, it follows beyond all doubt, that neither is he that baptizeth anything but God that giveth the increase. For what matter does it make in reference to the question now before us, in what sense it has been said, "I planted, Apollos watered."—whether it is really to be taken as equivalent to his saying, "I made a catechumen, Apollos baptized him;" or whether there be any other truer and more congruous understanding of it?—for in the mean time, according to his own interpretation of the words, neither is he that makes the catechumen anything, neither he that baptizes, but God that gives the increase. But there is a great difference between confirming what another does, and doing anything oneself. For He who gives the increase does not confirm a tree or a vine, but creates it. For by that increase it comes to pass that even a piece of wood planted in the ground produces and establishes a root; by that increase it comes to pass that a seed cast into the earth puts forth a shoot. But why should we make a longer dissertation on this point? It is enough that, according to Petilianus himself, neither he that maketh a catechumen, nor he that baptizes, is anything, but God that gives the increase. But when would Petilianus say this, so that we should understand that he meant, Neither is

[1] 1 Cor. iii. 6, 7.

Donatus of Carthage anything, neither Januarius, neither Petilianus? When would the swelling of his pride permit him to say this, which now causes the man to think himself to be something, when he is nothing, deceiving himself?[1]

CHAP. 54.—66. Finally, again, a little afterwards, when he resolved and was firmly purposed, as it were, to reconsider once more the words of the apostle which he had brought up against him, he was unwilling to set down this that I had said, preferring something else in which by some means or other the swelling of human pride might find means to breathe. "For to reconsider," he says, "those words of the apostle, on which you founded an argument against us; he said, 'What is Apollos, what is Paul, save only ministers of Him in whom ye have believed?'[2] What else, for example, does he say to all of us than this, What is Donatus of Carthage, what is Januarius, what is Petilianus, save only ministers of Him in whom ye have believed?" I did not bring forward this passage of the apostle, but I did bring forward that which he has been unwilling to quote, "Neither he that planteth is anything, neither he that watereth; but God that giveth the increase." But Petilianus was willing to insert those words of the apostle, in which he asks what is Paul, and what is Apollos, and answers that "They are ministers of Him in whom ye have believed." This the muscles of the heretic's neck could bear; but he was wholly unable to endure the other, in which the apostle did not ask and answer what he was, but said that he was nothing. But now I am willing to ask whether it be true that the minister of Christ is nothing. Who will say so much as this? In what sense, therefore, is it true that "Neither is he that planteth anything, neither he that watereth, but God that giveth the increase," except that he who is something in one point of view may be nothing in another? For ministering and dispensing the word and sacrament he is something, but for purifying and justifying he is nothing, seeing that this is not accomplished in the inner man, except by Him by whom the whole man was created, and who while He remained God was made man,—by Him, that is, of whom it was said, "Purifying their hearts by faith;"[3] and "To him that believeth on Him that justifieth the ungodly."[4] And this testimony Petilianus has been willing to set forth in my words, whilst in his own he has neither handled it, nor even touched it.

CHAP. 55.—67. A minister, therefore, that is a dispenser of the word and sacrament of the gospel, if he is a good man, becomes a fellow-partner in the working of the gospel; but if he is a bad man, he does not therefore cease to be a dispenser of the gospel. For if he is good, he does it of his own free will; but if he is a bad man,—that is, one who seeks his own and not the things of Jesus Christ,—he does it unwillingly, for the sake of other things which he is seeking after. See, however, what the same apostle has said: "For if I do this thing willingly," he says, "I have a reward; but if against my will, a dispensation of the gospel is committed unto me;"[5] as though he were to say, If I, being good, announce what is good, I attain unto it also myself; but if, being evil, I announce it, yet I announce what is good. For has he in any way said, If I do it against my will, then shall I not be a dispenser of the gospel? Peter and the other disciples announce the good tidings, as being good themselves. Judas did it against his will, but yet, when he was sent, he announced it in common with the rest. They have a reward; to him a dispensation of the gospel was committed. But they who received the gospel at the mouth of all those witnesses, could not be cleansed and justified by him that planted, or by him that watered, but by Him alone that gives the increase. For neither are we going to say that Judas did not baptize, seeing that he was still among the disciples when that which is written was being accomplished, "Jesus Himself baptized not, but His disciples."[6] Are we to suppose that, because he had not betrayed Christ, therefore he who had the bag, and bare what was put therein,[7] was still enabled to dispense grace without prejudice to those who received it, though he could not be an upright guardian of the money entrusted to his care? Or if he did not baptize, at any rate we must acknowledge that he preached the gospel. But if you consider this a trifling function, and of no importance, see what you must think of the Apostle Paul himself, who said, "For Christ sent me not to baptize, but to preach the gospel."[8] To this we may add, that according to this, Apollos begins to be more important, who watered by baptizing, than Paul, who planted by preaching the gospel, though Paul claims to himself the relation of father towards the Corinthians in virtue of this very act, and does not grant this title to those who came to them after him. For he says, "Though ye have ten thousand instructors in Christ, yet have ye not many fathers;

---

1 Gal. vi. 3.
2 *Ministri ejus cui credidistis.* See 1 Cor. iii. 4, 5.
3 Acts xv. 9.
4 Rom. iv. 5.
5 1 Cor. ix. 17.
6 John iv. 2.
7 John xii. 6.
8 1 Cor. i. 17.

for in Christ Jesus I have begotten you through the gospel."[1] He says, "I have begotten you" to the same men to whom he says in another place, "I thank God that I baptized none of you but Crispus and Gaius, and I baptized also the household of Stephanus."[2] He had begotten them, therefore, not through himself, but through the gospel. And even though he had been seeking his own, and not the things of Jesus Christ, and had been doing this unwillingly, so as to receive no reward for himself, yet he would have been dispensing the treasure of the Lord; and this, though evil himself, he would not have been making evil or useless to those who received it well.

Chap. 56.—68. And if this is rightly said of the gospel, with how much greater certainty should it be said of baptism, which belongs to the gospel in such wise, that without it no one can reach the kingdom of heaven, and with it only if to the sacrament be added righteousness? For He who said, "Except a man be born of water and of the Spirit, he cannot enter into the kingdom of God,"[3] said Himself also, "Except your righteousness shall exceed the righteousness of the scribes and Pharisees, ye shall in no case enter into the kingdom of heaven."[4] The form of the sacrament is given through baptism, the form of righteousness through the gospel. Neither one without the other leads to the kingdom of heaven. Yet even men of inferior learning can baptize perfectly, but to preach the gospel perfectly is a task of much greater difficulty and rarity. Therefore the teacher of the Gentiles, that was superior in excellence to the majority, was sent to preach the gospel, not to baptize; because the latter could be done by many, the former only by a few, of whom he was chief. And yet we read that he said in certain places, "My gospel;"[5] but he never called baptism either his, or any one's else by whom it was administered. For that baptism alone which John gave is called John's baptism.[6] This that man received as the special pledge of his ministry, that the preparatory sacrament of washing should even be called by the name of him by whom it was administered; whereas the baptism which the disciples of Christ administered was never called by the name of any one of them, that it should be understood to be His alone of whom it is said, "Christ loved the Church, and gave Himself for it, that He might sanctify and cleanse it with the washing of water by the word."[7] If, therefore, the gospel, which is Christ's, but so that a minister also may call it his in virtue of his office of administering it, can be received by a man even at the hands of an evil minister without danger to himself, if he does according to what he says, and not after the example of what he does, how much more may any one who comes in good faith to Christ receive without fear of contagion from an evil minister the baptism of Christ, which none of the apostles so administered as to dare to call it his own?

Chap. 57.—69. Furthermore, if, while I have continued without intermission to prove how entirely the passages of Scripture which Petilianus has quoted against us have failed to hurt our cause, he himself has in some cases not touched at all what I have quoted, and partly, when he has endeavored to handle them, has shown that the only thing that he could do was to fail in finding an escape from them, you require no long exhortation or advice in order to see what you ought to maintain, and what you should avoid. But it may be that this has been the kind of show that he has made in dealing with the testimony of holy Scripture, but that he has not been without force in the case of the documentary evidence found in the records of the schism itself. Let us then see in the case of these too, though it is superfluous to inquire into them after testimony from the word of God, what he has quoted, or what he has proved. For, after pouring forth a violent invective against *traditors*, and quoting loudly many passages against them from the holy books themselves, he yet said nothing which could prove his opponents to be *traditors*. But I quoted the case of Silvanus of Cirta, who held his own see some little time before himself, who was expressly declared in the Municipal Chronicles to have been a *traditor* while he was yet a sub-deacon. Against this fact he did not venture to whisper a syllable. And yet you cannot fail to see how strong the pressure was which must have been urging him to reply, that he might show a man, who was his predecessor, not only one of his party, but a partner, so to speak, in his see, to have been innocent of the crime of delivering up the sacred books, especially as you rest the whole strength of your cause on the fact that you give the name of *traditor* to all whom you either pretend or believe to have been the successors of *traditors* in the path of their communion. Although, then, the very exigencies of your cause would seem to compel him to undertake the defence of a citizen even of Russicadia, or Calama, or any other city of your

[1] 1 Cor. iv. 15.
[2] 1 Cor. i. 14, 16.
[3] John iii. 5.
[4] Matt. v. 20.
[5] 2 Tim. ii. 8.
[6] Acts xix. 3.
[7] Eph. v. 25, 26.

party, whom I should declare to be a *traditor*, on the authority of the Municipal Chronicles, yet he did not open his mouth even in defense of his own predecessor. For what reason, except that he could not find any mist dark enough to deceive the minds of even the slowest and sleepiest of men? For what could he have said, except that the charges brought against Silvanus were false? But we quote the words of the Chronicles, both as to the date of the fact, and as to the time of the information laid before Zenophilus the ex-consul.[1] And how could he resist this evidence, being encompassed on every side by the most excellent cause of the Catholics, while yours was bad as bad could be? For which reason I quote these words from my epistle to which he would fain be thought to have replied in this which I am now refuting, that you may see for yourselves how impregnable the position must be against which he has been able to find no safer weapon than silence.

CHAP. 58.—70. For when he quoted a passage from the gospel as making against us, where our Lord says, "They will come to you in sheep's clothing, but inwardly they are ravening wolves; ye shall know them by their fruits,"[2]—I answered and said, "Then let us consider their fruits;" and then I at once went on to add the following words: "You bring up against them their delivery of the sacred books. This very charge we urge with greater probability against their accusers themselves. And not to carry our search too far: in the same city of Constantina, your predecessors ordained Silvanus bishop at the very outset of his schism. He, while he was still a sub-deacon, was most unmistakably entered as a *traditor* in the archives of the city. If you, on your side, bring forward documents against our predecessors, all that we ask is equal terms, that we should either believe both to be true, or both to be false. If both are true, you are unquestionably guilty of schism, who have pretended that you avoid offenses in the communion of the whole world, though these were common among you in your own fragmentary sect. But again, if both are false, you are unquestionably guilty of schism, who, on account of the false charges of *traditors*, are staining yourselves with the heinous offense of severance from the Church. But if we have something to urge in accusation, while you have nothing, or if our charges are true, while yours are false, it is no longer matter of discussion how thoroughly your mouths are closed. What if the holy and true Church of Christ were to convince and overcome you, even if we held no documents in support of our cause, or only such as were false, while you had possession of some genuine proof of delivery of the sacred books, what would then remain for you, except that, if you would, you should show your love of peace, or otherwise should hold your tongues? For whatever in that case you might bring forward in evidence, I should be able to say with the greatest ease and with the most perfect truth, that then you are bound to prove as much to the full and Catholic unity of the Church, already spread abroad and established throughout so many nations, to the end that you should remain within, and that those whom you convict should be expelled. And if you have endeavored to do this, certainly you have not been able to make good your proof; and, being vanquished or enraged, you have separated yourselves, with all the heinous guilt of sacrilege, from the guiltless men who could not condemn on insufficient proof. But if you have not even endeavored to do this, then with most accursed and unnatural blindness you have cut yourselves off from the wheat of Christ, which grows throughout His whole fields, that is, throughout the whole world until the end, because you have taken offense at a few tares in Africa."[3] To this, which I have quoted from my former epistle, Petilianus has made no answer whatsoever. And, at all events, you see that in these few words is comprised the whole question which is at issue between us. For what should he endeavor to say, when, whatever course he chose, he was sure to be defeated?

71. For when documents are brought forward relating to the *traditors*, both by us against the men of your party, and by you against the men of our party, (if indeed any really are brought forward on your side, for to this very day we are left in total ignorance of them; nor indeed can we believe that Petilianus would have omitted to insert them in his letter, seeing that he has taken so much pains to secure the quotation and insertion of those portions of the Chronicles which bear on the matter in opposition to me),—but still, as I began to say, if such documents are brought forward both by us and by you,—documents of whose existence we are wholly ignorant to this very day,—surely you must acknowledge that either both are true, or both false, or ours true and yours false, or yours true and ours false; for there is no further alternative that can be suggested.

1 See Book III. *c. Cresconium*, cc. 27, 28, 31, 32.
2 Matt. vii. 15, 16.
3 See Book I. cc. 21, 22, 23, 24.

Chap. 59.—But according to all these four hypotheses, the truth is on the side of the communion of the Catholic Church. For if both are true, then you certainly should not have deserted the communion of the whole world on account of men such as you too had among yourselves. But if both are false, you should have guarded against the guilt of most accursed division, which had not even any pretext to allege of any delivery of the sacred books. If ours are true and yours are false, you have long been without anything to say for yourselves. If yours are true and ours are false, we have been liable to be deceived, in common with the whole world, not about the truth of the faith, but about the unrighteousness of men. For the seed of Abraham, dispersed throughout the world, was bound to pay attention, not to what you said you knew, but to what you proved to the judges. Whence have we any knowledge of what was done by those men who were accused by your ancestors, even if the allegations made against them were true, so long as they were held to be not true but false, either by the judges who took cognizance of the case, or at least by the general body of the Church dispersed throughout the world, which was only bound to pay heed to the sentence of the judges? God does not necessarily pardon any human guilt that others in the weakness of human judgment fail to discover; yet I maintain that no one is rightly deemed guilty for having believed a man to be innocent who was not convicted. How then do you prove the world to be guilty, merely because it did not know what possibly was really guilt in the Africans,—its ignorance arising either from the fact that no one reported the sin to it, or from its having given credence, in respect of the information which was given, rather to the judges who took cognizance of the case, than to the murmurers who were defeated? So far then, Petilianus deserves all praise, in that, when he saw that on this point I was absolutely impregnable, he passed it by in silence. Yet he does not deserve praise for his attempts to obscure in a mist of words other points which were equally impregnable, which yet he thought could be obscured; or for having put me in the place of his cause, when the cause left him nothing to say; while even about myself he could say nothing except what was either altogether false, or undeserving of any blame, or without any bearing whatsoever upon me. But, in the meantime, are you, whom I have made judges between Petilianus and myself, possessed of discrimination enough to decide in any degree between what is true and what is false, between what is mere empty swelling and what is solid, between what is troubled and what is calm, between inflammation and soundness, between divine predictions and human assumptions, between bringing an accusation and establishing it, between proofs and fictions, between pleading a cause and leading one away from it? If you have such power of discrimination, well and good; but if you have it not, we shall not repent of having bestowed our pains on you, for even though your heart be not converted unto peace, yet our peace shall return unto ourselves.

ST. AUGUSTIN:

A TREATISE CONCERNING

THE CORRECTION OF THE DONATISTS

[DE CORRECTIONE DONATISTARUM. LIBER SEU EPISTOLA CLXXXV.]

CIRCA A.D. 417.

TRANSLATED BY THE

REV. J. R. KING, M.A.,

VICAR OF ST PETER'S IN THE EAST, OXFORD; AND LATE FELLOW AND TUTOR OF MERTON COLLEGE, OXFORD.

CONTENTS ON A TREATISE CONCERNING THE CORRECTION OF THE DONATISTS.

PAGE

A TREATISE

CONCERNING

THE CORRECTION OF THE DONATISTS;

OR EPISTLE CLXXXV.[1]

A LETTER OF AUGUSTIN[2] TO BONIFACE, WHO, AS WE LEARN FROM EPISTLE 220, WAS TRIBUNE, AND AFTERWARDS COUNT IN AFRICA. IN IT AUGUSTIN SHOWS THAT THE HERESY OF THE DONATISTS HAS NOTHING IN COMMON WITH THAT OF ARIUS; AND POINTS OUT THE MODERATION WITH WHICH IT WAS POSSIBLE TO RECALL THE HERETICS TO THE COMMUNION OF THE CHURCH THROUGH AWE OF THE IMPERIAL LAWS. HE ADDS REMARKS CONCERNING THE SAVAGE CONDUCT OF THE DONATISTS AND CIRCUMCELLIONES, CONCLUDING WITH A DISCUSSION OF THE UNPARDONABLE NATURE OF THE SIN AGAINST THE HOLY GHOST.[3]

CHAP. I.—1. I must express my satisfaction, and congratulations, and admiration, my son Boniface,[4] in that, amid all the cares of wars and arms, you are eagerly anxious to know concerning the things that are of God. From hence it is clear that in you it is actually a part of your military valor to serve in truth the faith which is in Christ. To place, therefore, briefly before your Grace the difference between the errors of the Arians and the Donatists, the Arians say that the Father, the Son, and the Holy Ghost are different in substance; whereas the Donatists do not say this, but acknowledge the unity of substance in the Trinity. And if some even of them have said that the Son was inferior to the Father, yet they have not denied that He is of the same substance; whilst the greater part of them declare that they hold entirely the same belief regarding the Father and the Son and the Holy Ghost as is held by the Catholic Church. Nor is this the actual question in dispute with them; but they carry on their unhappy strife solely on the question of communion, and in the perversity of their error maintain rebellious hostility against the unity of Christ. But sometimes, as we have heard, some of them, wishing to conciliate the Goths, since they see that they are not without a certain amount of power, profess to entertain the same belief as they. But they are refuted by the authority of their own leaders; for Donatus himself, of whose party they boast themselves to be, is never said to have held this belief.

2. Let not, however, things like these disturb thee, my beloved son. For it is foretold to us that there must needs be heresies and stumbling-blocks, that we may be instructed among our enemies; and that so both our

---

1 Written c. 417.

2 In Book II. c. xlviii. of his *Retractations*, Augustin says: "About the same time" (as that at which he wrote his treatise *De Gestis Pelagii, i. e.* about the year 417), "I wrote also a treatise *De Correctione Donatistarum*, for the sake of those who were not willing that the Donatists should be subjected to the correction of the imperial laws. This treatise begins with the words '*Laudo, et gratulor, et admiror.*' This letter in the old editions was No. 50,—the letter which is now No. 4 in the appendix (Benedictine) being formerly No. 185.

3 He handles the same thought in *Ep.* 93.

4 The correspondence between Augustin and Boniface is limited to *Epp.* 185, 189 and 220. The sixteen smaller letters are spurious. For note to Boniface and translations of 189 and and 220, see vol. 1 of this series, pp. 552 and 573.

faith and our love may be the more approved,—our faith, namely, that we should not be deceived by them; and our love, that we should take the utmost pains we can to correct the erring ones themselves; not only watching that they should do no injury to the weak, and that they should be delivered from their wicked error, but also praying for them, that God would open their understanding, and that they might comprehend the Scriptures. For in the sacred books, where the Lord Christ is made manifest, there is also His Church declared; but they, with wondrous blindness, while they would know nothing of Christ Himself save what is revealed in the Scriptures, yet form their notion of His Church from the vanity of human falsehood, instead of learning what it is on the authority of the sacred books.

3. They recognize Christ together with us in that which is written, "They pierced my hands and my feet. They can tell all my bones: they look and stare upon me. They part my garments among them, and cast lots upon my vesture;" and yet they refuse to recognize the Church in that which follows shortly after: "All the ends of the world shall remember, and turn unto the Lord; and all the kindreds of the nations shall worship before Thee. For the kingdom is the Lord's; and He is the Governor among the nations."[1] They recognize Christ together with us in that which is written, "The Lord hath said unto me, Thou art my Son, this day have I begotten Thee;" and they will not recognize the Church in that which follows: "Ask of me, and I shall give Thee the heathen for Thine inheritance, and the uttermost parts of the earth for Thy possession."[2] They recognize Christ together with us in that which the Lord Himself says in the gospel, "Thus it behoved Christ to suffer, and to rise from the dead the third day;" and they will not recognize the Church in that which follows: "And that repentance and remission of sins should be preached in His name among all nations, beginning at Jerusalem."[3] And the testimonies in the sacred books are without number, all of which it has not been necessary for me to crowd together into this book. And in all of them, as the Lord Christ is made manifest, whether in accordance with His Godhead, in which He is equal to the Father, so that, "In the beginning was the Word, and the Word was with God, and the Word was God;" or according to the humility of the flesh which He took upon Him, whereby "the Word was made flesh and dwelt among us;"[4] so is His Church made manifest, not in Africa alone, as they most impudently venture in the madness of their vanity to assert, but spread abroad throughout the world.

4. For they prefer to the testimonies of Holy Writ their own contentions, because, in the case of Cæcilianus, formerly a bishop of the Church of Carthage, against whom they brought charges which they were and are unable to substantiate, they separated themselves from the Catholic Church,—that is, from the unity of all nations. Although, even if the charges had been true which were brought by them against Cæcilianus, and could at length be proved to us, yet, though we might pronounce an anathema upon him even in the grave,[5] we are still bound not for the sake of any man to leave the Church, which rests for its foundation on divine witness, and is not the figment of litigious opinions, seeing that it is better to trust in the Lord than to put confidence in man.[6] For we cannot allow that if Cæcilianus had erred,—a supposition which I make without prejudice to his integrity,—Christ should therefore have forfeited His inheritance. It is easy for a man to believe of his fellow-men either what is true or what is false; but it marks abandoned impudence to desire to condemn the communion of the whole world on account of charges alleged against a man, of which you cannot establish the truth in the face of the world.

5. Whether Cæcilianus was ordained by men who had delivered up the sacred books, I do not know. I did not see it, I heard it only from his enemies. It is not declared to me in the law of God, or in the utterances of the prophets, or in the holy poetry of the Psalms, or in the writings of any one of Christ's apostles, or in the eloquence of Christ Himself. But the evidence of all the several scriptures with one accord proclaims the Church spread abroad throughout the world, with which the faction of Donatus does not hold communion. The law of God declared, "In thy seed shall all the nations of the earth be blessed."[7] The Lord said by the mouth of His prophet, "From the rising of the sun, even unto the going down of the same, a pure sacrifice shall be offered unto my name: for my name shall be great among the heathen."[8] The Lord said through the Psalmist, "He shall have dominion also from sea to sea, and from the river unto the ends of the earth."[9] The Lord said by His apostle,

[1] Ps. xxii. 16-18, 27, 28. [2] Ps. ii. 7, 8. [3] Luke xxiv. 46, 47.

[4] John i. 1, 4.
[5] This epistle was produced in the fifth conference of the fifth ecumenical Synod (553), when the point was under debate whether Theodorus of Mopsuesta could be condemned after his death.
[6] Ps. cxviii. 8.
[7] Gen. xxvi. 4.
[8] Mal. i. 11.
[9] Ps. lxxii. 8.

"The gospel is come unto you, as it is in all the world, and bringeth forth fruit."[1] The Son of God said with His own mouth, "Ye shall be witnesses unto me, both in Jerusalem, and in all Judea, and in Samaria, and even unto the uttermost part of the earth."[2] Cæcilianus, the bishop of the Church of Carthage, is accused with the contentiousness of men; the Church of Christ, established among all nations, is recommended by the voice of God. Mere piety, truth, and love forbid us to receive against Cæcilianus the testimony of men whom we do not find in the Church, which has the testimony of God; for those who do not follow the testimony of God have forfeited the weight which otherwise would attach to their testimony as men.

CHAP. 2.—6. I would add, moreover, that they themselves, by making it the subject of an accusation, referred the case of Cæcilianus to the decision of the Emperor Constantine; and that, even after the bishops had pronounced their judgment,[3] finding that they could not crush Cæcilianus, they brought him in person before the above-named emperor for trial, in the most determined spirit of persecution. And so they were themselves the first to do what they censure in us, in order that they may deceive the unlearned, saying that Christians ought not to demand any assistance from Christian emperors against the enemies of Christ. And this, too, they did not dare to deny in the conference which we held at the same time in Carthage: nay, they even venture to make it a matter of boasting that their fathers had laid a criminal indictment against Cæcilianus before the emperor; adding furthermore a lie, to the effect that they had there worsted him, and procured his condemnation. How then can they be otherwise than persecutors, seeing that when they persecuted Cæcilianus by their accusations, and were overcome by him, they sought to claim false glory for themselves by a most shameless life; not only considering it no reproach, but glorying in it as conducive to their praise, if they could prove that Cæcilianus had been condemned on the accusation of their fathers? But in regard to the manner in which they were overcome at every turn in the conference itself, seeing that the records are exceedingly voluminous, and it would be a serious matter to have them read to you while you are occupied in other matters that are essential to the peace of Rome, perhaps it may be possible to have a digest[4] of them read to you, which I believe to be in the possession of my brother and fellow-bishop Optatus; or if he has not a copy, he might easily procure one from the church at Sitifa; for I can well believe that even that volume will prove wearisome enough to you from its lengthiness, amid the burden of your many cares.

7. For the Donatists met with the same fate as the accusers of the holy Daniel.[5] For as the lions were turned against them, so the laws by which they had proposed to crush an innocent victim were turned against the Donatists; save that, through the mercy of Christ, the laws which seemed to be opposed to them are in reality their truest friends; for through their operation many of them have been, and are daily being reformed, and return God thanks that they are reformed, and delivered from their ruinous madness. And those who used to hate are now filled with love; and now that they have recovered their right minds, they congratulate themselves that these most wholesome laws were brought to bear against them, with as much fervency as in their madness they detested them; and are filled with the same spirit of ardent love towards those who yet remain as ourselves, desiring that we should strive in like manner that those with whom they had been like to perish might be saved. For both the physician is irksome to the raging madman, and a father to his undisciplined son,—the former because of the restraint, the latter because of the chastisement which he inflicts; yet both are acting in love. But if they were to neglect their charge, and allow them to perish, this mistaken kindness would more truly be accounted cruelty. For if the horse and mule, which have no understanding, resist with all the force of bites and kicks the efforts of the men who treat their wounds in order to cure them; and yet the men, though they are often exposed to danger from their teeth and heels, and sometimes meet with actual hurt, nevertheless do not desert them till they restore them to health through the pain and annoyance which the healing process gives,—how much more should man refuse to desert his fellow-man, or brother to desert his brother, lest he should perish everlastingly, being himself now able to comprehend the vastness of the boon accorded to himself in his reformation, at the very time that he complained of suffering persecution?

8. As then the apostle says, "As we have therefore opportunity, let us do good unto all

[1] Col. i. 6. [2] Acts i. 8.
[3] In the Councils at Rome and Arles.
[4] This digest will be found in the 9th volume of Benedictine edition of Augustin's Works. *Breviculus collationis cum Donatistis*, p. 371 sqq., reproduced in Migne 613 sqq.
[5] Dan. vi. 24.

men, not being weary in well-doing,"[1] so let all be called to salvation, let all be recalled from the path of destruction,—those who may, by the sermons of Catholic preachers; those who may, by the edicts of Catholic princes; some through those who obey the warnings of God, some through those who obey the emperor's commands. For, moreover, when emperors enact bad laws on the side of falsehood as against the truth, those who hold a right faith are approved, and, if they persevere, are crowned; but when the emperors enact good laws on behalf of the truth against falsehood, then those who rage against them are put in fear, and those who understand are reformed. Whosoever, therefore, refuses to obey the laws of the emperors which are enacted against the truth of God, wins for himself a great reward; but whosoever refuses to obey the laws of the emperors which are enacted in behalf of truth, wins for himself great condemnation. For in the times, too, of the prophets, the kings who, in dealing with the people of God, did not prohibit nor annul the ordinances which were issued contrary to God's commands, are all of them censured; and those who did prohibit and annul them are praised as deserving more than other men. And king Nebuchadnezzar, when he was a servant of idols, enacted an impious law that a certain idol should be worshipped; but those who refused to obey his impious command acted piously and faithfully. And the very same king, when converted by a miracle from God, enacted a pious and praiseworthy law on behalf of the truth, that every one who should speak anything amiss against the true God, the God of Shadrach, Meshach, and Abednego, should perish utterly, with all his house.[2] If any persons disobeyed this law, and justly suffered the penalty imposed, they might have said what these men say, that they were righteous because they suffered persecution through the law enacted by the king: and this they certainly would have said, had they been as mad as these who make divisions between the members of Christ, and spurn the sacraments of Christ, and take credit for being persecuted, because they are prevented from doing such things by the laws which the emperors have passed to preserve the unity of Christ; and boast falsely of their innocence, and seek from men the glory of martyrdom, which they cannot receive from our Lord.

9. But true martyrs are such as those of whom the Lord says, "Blessed are they which are persecuted for righteousness' sake."[3] It is not, therefore, those who suffer persecution for their unrighteousness, and for the divisions which they impiously introduce into Christian unity, but those who suffer for righteousness' sake, that are truly martyrs. For Hagar also suffered persecution at the hands of Sarah;[4] and in that case she who persecuted was righteous, and she unrighteous who suffered persecution. Are we to compare with this persecution which Hagar suffered the case of holy David, who was persecuted by unrighteous Saul?[5] Surely there is an essential difference, not in respect of his suffering, but because he suffered for righteousness' sake. And the Lord Himself was crucified with two thieves;[6] but those who were joined in their suffering were separated by the difference of its cause. Accordingly, in the psalm, we must interpret of the true martyrs, who wish to be distinguished from false martyrs, the verse in which it is said, "Judge me, O Lord, and distinguish[7] my cause from an ungodly nation."[8] He does not say, Distinguish my punishment, but "Distinguish my cause." For the punishment of the impious may be the same; but the cause of the martyrs is always different. To whose mouth also the words are suitable, "They persecute me wrongfully; help Thou me;"[9] in which the Psalmist claimed to have a right to be helped in righteousness, because his adversaries persecuted him wrongfully; for if they had been right in persecuting him, he would have deserved not help, but correction.

10. But if they think that no one can be justified in using violence,—as they said in the course of the conference that the true Church must necessarily be the one which suffers persecution, not the one inflicting it,—in that case I no longer urge what I observed above; because, if the matter stand as they maintain that it does, then Cæcilianus must have belonged to the true Church, seeing that their fathers persecuted him, by pressing his accusation even to the tribunal of the emperor himself. For we maintain that he belonged to the true Church, not merely because he suffered persecution, but because he suffered it for righteousness' sake; but that they were alienated from the Church, not merely because they persecuted, but because they did so in unrighteousness. This, then, is our position. But if they make no inquiry into the causes for which each person inflicts persecution, or for which he suffers it, but think that it is a sufficient sign of a true Christian that he does not

1 Gal. vi. 9, 10.
2 Dan. iii. 5, 29.
3 Matt. v. 1.
4 Gen. xvi. 6.
5 1 Sam. xviii., xix., etc.
6 Luke xxiii. 33.
7 *Discerne causam meam.* The Eng. Vers. has, "plead my cause against an ungodly nation."
8 Ps. xliii. 1.
9 Ps. cxix. 86.

inflict persecution, but suffers it, then beyond all question they include Cæcilianus in that definition, who did not inflict, but suffered persecution; and they equally exclude their own fathers from the definition, for they inflicted, but did not suffer it.

11. But this, I say, I forbear to urge. Yet one point I must press: If the true Church is the one which actually suffers persecution, not the one which inflicts it, let them ask the apostle of what Church Sarah was a type, when she inflicted persecution on her handmaid. For he declares that the free mother of us all, the heavenly Jerusalem, that is to say, the true Church of God, was prefigured in that woman who cruelly entreated her handmaid.[1] But if we investigate the story further, we shall find that the handmaid rather persecuted Sarah by her haughtiness, than Sarah the handmaid by her severity: for the handmaid was doing wrong to her mistress; the mistress only imposed on her a proper discipline in her haughtiness. Again I ask, if good and holy men never inflict persecution upon any one, but only suffer it, whose words they think that those are in the psalm where we read, "I have pursued mine enemies, and overtaken them; neither did I turn again till they were consumed?"[2] If, therefore, we wish either to declare or to recognize the truth, there is a persecution of unrighteousness, which the impious inflict upon the Church of Christ; and there is a righteous persecution, which the Church of Christ inflicts upon the impious. She therefore is blessed in suffering persecution for righteousness' sake; but they are miserable, suffering persecution for unrighteousness. Moreover, she persecutes in the spirit of love, they in the spirit of wrath; she that she may correct, they that they may overthrow: she that she may recall from error, they that they may drive headlong into error. Finally, she persecutes her enemies and arrests them, until they become weary in their vain opinions, so that they should make advance in the truth; but they, returning evil for good, because we take measures for their good, to secure their eternal salvation, endeavor even to strip us of our temporal safety, being so in love with murder, that they commit it on their own persons, when they cannot find victims in any others. For in proportion as the Christian charity of the Church endeavors to deliver them from that destruction, so that none of them should die, so their madness endeavors either to slay us, that they may feed the lust of their own cruelty, or even to kill themselves, that they may not seem to have lost the power of putting men to death.

CHAP. 3.—12. But those who are unacquainted with their habits think that they only kill themselves now that all the mass of the people are freed from the fearful madness of their usurped dominion, in virtue of the laws which have been passed for the preservation of unity. But those who know what they were accustomed to do before the passing of the laws, do not wonder at their deaths, but call to mind their character; and especially how vast crowds of them used to come in procession to the most frequented ceremonies of the pagans, while the worship of idols still continued,—not with the view of breaking the idols, but that they might be put to death by those who worshipped them. For if they had sought to break the idols under the sanction of legitimate authority, they might, in case of anything happening to them, have had some shadow of a claim to be considered martyrs; but their only object in coming was, that while the idols remained uninjured, they themselves might meet with death. For it was the general custom of the strongest youths among the worshippers of idols, for each of them to offer in sacrifice to the idols themselves any victims that he might have slain. Some went so far as to offer themselves for slaughter to any travellers whom they met with arms, using violent threats that they would murder them if they failed to meet with death at their hands. Sometimes, too, they extorted with violence from any passing judge that they should be put to death by the executioners, or by the officer of his court. And hence we have a story, that a certain judge played a trick upon them, by ordering them to be bound and led away, as though for execution, and so escaped their violence, without injury to himself or them. Again, it was their daily sport to kill themselves, by throwing themselves over precipices, or into the water, or into the fire. For the devil taught them these three modes of suicide, so that, when they wished to die, and could not find any one whom they could terrify into slaying them with his sword, they threw themselves over the rocks, or committed themselves to the fire or the eddying pool. But who can be thought to have taught them this, having gained possession of their hearts, but he who actually suggested to our Saviour Himself as a duty sanctioned by the law, that He should throw Himself down from a pinnacle of the temple?[3] And his suggestion they

[1] Gal. iv. 22–31.

[2] Ps. xviii. 37.

[3] Luke iv. 9.

would surely have thrust far from them, had they carried Christ, as their Master, in their hearts. But since they have rather given place within them to the devil, they either perish like the herd of swine, whom the legion of devils drove down from the hill-side into the sea,[1] or, being rescued from that destruction, and gathered together in the loving bosom of our Catholic Mother, they are delivered just as the boy was delivered by our Lord, whom his father brought to be healed of the devil, saying that ofttimes he was wont to fall into the fire, and oft into the water.[2]

13. Whence it appears that great mercy is shown towards them, when by the force of those very imperial laws they are in the first instance rescued against their will from that sect in which, through the teaching of lying devils, they learned those evil doctrines, so that afterwards they might be made whole in the Catholic Church, becoming accustomed to the good teaching and example which they find in it. For many of the men whom we now admire in the unity of Christ, for the pious fervor of their faith, and for their charity, give thanks to God with great joy that they are no longer in that error which led them to mistake those evil things for good, —which thanks they would not now be offering willingly, had they not first, even against their will, been severed from that impious association. And what are we to say of those who confess to us, as some do every day, that even in the olden days they had long been wishing to be Catholics; but they were living among men among whom those who wished to be Catholics could not be so through the infirmity cf fear, seeing that if any one there said a single word in favor of the Catholic Church, he and his house were utterly destroyed at once? Who is mad enough to deny that it was right that assistance should have been given through the imperial decrees, that they might be delivered from so great an evil, whilst those whom they used to fear are compelled in turn to fear, and are either themselves corrected through the same terror, or, at any rate, whilst they pretend to be corrected, they abstain from further persecution of those who really are, to whom they formerly were objects of continual dread?

14. But if they have chosen to destroy themselves, in order to prevent the deliverance of those who had a right to be delivered, and have sought in this way to alarm the pious hearts of the deliverers, so that in their apprehension that some few abandoned men might perish, they should allow others to lose the opportunity of deliverance from destruction, who were either already unwilling to perish, or might have been saved from it by the employment of compulsion; what is in this case the function of Christian charity, especially when we consider that those who utter threats of their own violent and voluntary deaths are very few in number in comparison with the nations that are to be delivered? What then is the function of brotherly love? Does it, because it fears the shortlived fires of the furnace for a few, therefore abandon all to the eternal fires of hell? and does it leave so many, who are either already desirous, or hereafter are not strong enough to pass to life eternal, to perish everlastingly, while taking precautions that some few should not perish by their own hand, who are only living to be a hindrance in the way of the salvation of others, whom they will not permit to live in accordance with the doctrines of Christ, in the hopes that some day or other they may teach them too to hasten their death by their own hand, in the manner which now causes them themselves to be a terror to their neighbors, in accordance with the custom inculcated by their devilish tenets? or does it rather save all whom it can, even though those whom it cannot save should perish in their own infatuation? For it ardently desires that all should live, but it more especially labors that not all should die. But thanks be to the Lord, that both amongst us —not indeed everywhere, but in the great majority of places—and also in the other parts of Africa, the peace of the Catholic Church both has gained and is gaining ground, without any of these madmen being killed. But those deplorable deeds are done in places where there is an utterly furious and useless set of men, who were given to such deeds even in the days of old.

CHAP. 4.—15. And indeed, before those laws were put in force by the emperors of the Catholic faith, the doctrine of the peace and unity of Christ was beginning by degrees to gain ground, and men were coming over to it even from the faction of Donatus, in proportion as each learned more, and became more willing, and more master of his own actions; although, at the same time, among the Donatists herds of abandoned men were disturbing the peace of the innocent for one reason or another in the spirit of the most reckless madness. What master was there who was not compelled to live in dread of his own servant, if he had put himself under the guardianship of the Donatists? Who dared even threaten one who sought his ruin with pun-

[1] Mark v. 13.

[2] Matt. xvii. 14.

ishment? Who dared to exact payment of a debt from one who consumed his stores, or from any debtor whatsoever, that sought their assistance or protection? Under the threat of beating, and burning, and immediate death, all documents compromising the worst of slaves were destroyed, that they might depart in freedom. Notes of hand that had been extracted from debtors were returned to them. Any one who had shown a contempt for their hard words were compelled by harder blows to do what they desired. The houses of innocent persons who had offended them were either razed to the ground or burned. Certain heads of families of honorable parentage, and brought up with a good education, were carried away half dead after their deeds of violence, or bound to the mill, and compelled by blows to turn it round, after the fashion of the meanest beasts of burden. For what assistance from the laws rendered by the civil powers was ever of any avail against them? What official ever ventured so much as to breathe in their presence? What agents ever exacted payment of a debt which they had been unwilling to discharge? Who ever endeavored to avenge those who were put to death in their massacres? Except, indeed, that their own madness took revenge on them, when some, by provoking against themselves the swords of men, whom they obliged to kill them under fear of instant death, others by throwing themselves over sundry precipices, others by waters, others by fire, gave themselves over on the several occasions to a voluntary death, and gave up their lives as offerings to the dead by punishments inflicted with their own hands upon themselves.

16. These deeds were looked upon with horror by many who were firmly rooted in the same superstitious heresy; and accordingly, when they supposed that it was sufficient to establish their innocence that they were ill contented with such conduct, it was urged against them by the Catholics: If these evil deeds do not pollute your innocence, how then do you maintain that the whole Christian world has been polluted by the alleged sin of Cæcilianus, which are either altogether calumnies, or at least not proved against him? How come you, by a deed of gross impiety, to separate yourselves from the unity of the Catholic Church, as from the threshing-floor of the Lord, which must needs contain, up to the time of the final winnowing, both corn which is to be stored in the garner, and chaff that is to be burned up with fire?[1] And thus some were so convinced by argument as to come over to the unity of the Catholic Church, being prepared even to meet the hostility of abandoned men; whilst the greater number, though equally convinced, and though desirous to do the same, yet dared not make enemies of these men, who were so unbridled in their violence, seeing that some who had come over to us experienced the greatest cruelty at their hands.

17. To this we may add, that in Carthage itself some of the bishops of the same party, making a schism among themselves, and dividing the party of Donatus among the lower orders of the Carthaginian people, ordained as bishop against bishop a certain deacon named Maximianus, who could not brook the control of his own diocesan. And as this displeased the greater part of them, they condemned the aforesaid Maximianus, with twelve others who had been present at his ordination, but gave the rest that were associated in the same schism a chance of returning to their communion on an appointed day. But afterwards some of these twelve, and certain others of those who had had the time of grace allowed to them, but had only returned after the day appointed, were received by them without degradation from their orders; and they did not venture to baptize a second time those whom the condemned ministers had baptized outside the pale of their communion. This action of theirs at once made strongly against them in favor of the Catholic party, so that their mouths were wholly closed. And on the matter being diligently spread abroad, as was only right, in order to cure men's souls of the evils of schism, and when it was shown in every possible direction by the sermons and discussions of the Catholic divines, that to maintain the peace of Donatus they had not only received back those whom they had condemned, with full recognition of their orders, but had even been afraid to declare that baptism to be void which had been administered outside their Church by men whom they had condemned or even suspended; whilst, in violation of the peace of Christ, they cast in the teeth of all the world the stain conveyed by contact with some sinners, it matters little with whom, and declared baptism to be consequently void which had been administered even in the very Churches whence the gospel itself had come to Africa;—seeing all this, very many began to be confounded, and blushing before what they saw to be mostly manifest truth, they submitted to correction in greater numbers than was their wont; and men began to breathe with a somewhat freer sense of liberty from their

[1] Matt. iii. 12.

cruelty, and that to a considerably greater extent in every direction.

18. Then indeed they blazed forth with such fury, and were so excited by the goadings of hatred, that scarcely any churches of our communion could be safe against their treachery and violence and most undisguised robberies; scarcely any road secure by which men could travel to preach the peace of the Catholic Church in opposition to their madness, and convict the rashness of their folly by the clear enunciation of the truth. They went so far, besides, in proposing hard terms of reconciliation, not only to the laity or to any of the clergy, but even in a measure to certain of the Catholic bishops. For the only alternative offered was to hold their tongues about the truth, or to endure their savage fury. But if they did not speak about the truth, not only was it impossible for any one to be delivered by their silence, but many were even sure to be destroyed by their submitting to be led astray; while if, by their preaching the truth, the rage of the Donatists was again provoked to vent its madness, though some would be delivered, and those who were already on our side would be strengthened, yet the weak would again be deterred by fear from following the truth. When the Church, therefore, was reduced to these straits in its affliction, any one who thinks that anything was to be endured, rather than that the assistance of God, to be rendered through the agency of Christian emperors, should be sought, does not sufficiently observe that no good account could possibly be rendered for neglect of this precaution.

CHAP. 5.—19. But as to the argument of those men who are unwilling that their impious deeds should be checked by the enactment of righteous laws, when they say that the apostles never sought such measures from the kings of the earth, they do not consider the different character of that age, and that everything comes in its own season. For what emperor had as yet believed in Christ, so as to serve Him in the cause of piety by enacting laws against impiety, when as yet the declaration of the prophet was only in the course of its fulfillment, "Why do the heathen rage, and the people imagine a vain thing? The kings of the earth set themselves, and their rulers take counsel together, against the Lord, and against His Anointed;" and there was as yet no sign of that which is spoken a little later in the same psalm: "Be wise now, therefore, O ye kings; be instructed, ye judges of the earth. Serve the Lord with fear, and rejoice with trembling."[1] How then are kings to serve the Lord with fear, except by preventing and chastising with religious severity all those acts which are done in opposition to the commandments of the Lord? For a man serves God in one way in that he is man, in another way in that he is also king. In that he is man, he serves Him by living faithfully; but in that he is also king, he serves Him by enforcing with suitable rigor such laws as ordain what is righteous, and punish what is the reverse. Even as Hezekiah served Him, by destroying the groves and the temples of the idols, and the high places which had been built in violation of the commandments of God;[2] or even as Josiah served Him, by doing the same things in his turn;[3] or as the king of the Ninevites served Him, by compelling all the men of his city to make satisfaction to the Lord;[4] or as Darius served Him, by giving the idol into the power of Daniel to be broken, and by casting his enemies into the den of lions;[5] or as Nebuchadnezzar served Him, of whom I have spoken before, by issuing a terrible law to prevent any of his subjects from blaspheming God.[6] In this way, therefore, kings can serve the Lord, even in so far as they are kings, when they do in His service what they could not do were they not kings.

20. Seeing, then, that the kings of the earth were not yet serving the Lord in the time of the apostles, but were still imagining vain things against the Lord and against His Anointed, that all might be fulfilled which was spoken by the prophets, it must be granted that at that time acts of impiety could not possibly be prevented by the laws, but were rather performed under their sanction. For the order of events was then so rolling on, that even the Jews were killing those who preached Christ, thinking that they did God service in so doing, just as Christ had foretold,[7] and the heathen were raging against the Christians, and the patience of the martyrs was overcoming them all. But so soon as the fulfillment began of what is written in a later psalm, "All kings shall fall down before Him; all nations shall serve Him,"[8] what sober-minded man could say to the kings, "Let not any thought trouble you within your kingdom as to who restrains or attacks the Church of your Lord; deem it not a matter in which you should be concerned, which of your subjects may choose to be religious or sacrilegious," seeing that you cannot say to them, "Deem it no concern of yours which of your subjects may choose

[1] Ps. ii. 1, 2, 10, 11. [2] 2 Kings xviii. 4. [3] 2 Kings xxiii. 4, 5. [4] Jonah iii. 6–9. [5] Bel and Drag. vv. 22, 42. [6] Dan. iii. 29. [7] John xvi. 2. [8] Ps. lxxii. 11.

to be chaste, or which unchaste?" For why, when free-will is given by God to man, should adulteries be punished by the laws, and sacrilege allowed? Is it a lighter matter that a soul should not keep faith with God, than that a woman should be faithless to her husband? Or if those faults which are committed not in contempt but in ignorance of religious truth are to be visited with lighter punishment, are they therefore to be neglected altogether?

CHAP. 6.—21. It is indeed better (as no one ever could deny) that men should be led to worship God by teaching, than that they should be driven to it by fear of punishment or pain; but it does not follow that because the former course produces the better men, therefore those who do not yield to it should be neglected. For many have found advantage (as we have proved, and are daily proving by actual experiment), in being first compelled by fear or pain, so that they might afterwards be influenced by teaching, or might follow out in act what they had already learned in word. Some, indeed, set before us the sentiments of a certain secular author, who said,

> "'Tis well, I ween, by shame the young to train,
> And dread of meanness, rather than by pain." [1]

This is unquestionably true. But while those are better who are guided aright by love, those are certainly more numerous who are corrected by fear. For, to answer these persons out of their own author, we find him saying in another place,

> "Unless by pain and suffering thou art taught,
> Thou canst not guide thyself aright in aught." [2]

But, moreover, holy Scripture has both said concerning the former better class, "There is no fear in love; but perfect love casteth out fear;" [3] and also concerning the latter lower class, which furnishes the majority, "A servant will not be corrected by words; for though he understand, he will not answer." [4] In saying, "He will not be corrected by words," he did not order him to be left to himself, but implied an admonition as to the means whereby he ought to be corrected; otherwise he would not have said, "He will not be corrected by words," but without any qualification, "He will not be corrected." For in another place he says that not only the servant, but also the undisciplined son, must be corrected with stripes, and that with great fruits as the result; for he says, "Thou shalt beat him with the rod, and shalt deliver his soul from hell;" [5] and elsewhere he says, "He that spareth the rod hateth his son." [6] For, give us a man who with right faith and true understanding can say with all the energy of his heart, "My soul thirsteth for God, for the living God: when shall I come and appear before God?" [7] and for such an one there is no need of the terror of hell, to say nothing of temporal punishments or imperial laws, seeing that with him it is so indispensable a blessing to cleave unto the Lord, that he not only dreads being parted from that happiness as a heavy punishment, but can scarcely even bear delay in its attainment. But yet, before the good sons can say they have "a desire to depart, and to be with Christ," [8] many must first be recalled to their Lord by the stripes of temporal scourging, like evil slaves, and in some degree like good-for-nothing fugitives.

22. For who can possibly love us more than Christ, who laid down His life for His sheep? [9] And yet, after calling Peter and the other apostles by His words alone, when He came to summon Paul, who was before called Saul, subsequently the powerful builder of His Church, but originally its cruel persecutor, He not only constrained him with His voice, but even dashed him to the earth with His power; and that He might forcibly bring one who was raging amid the darkness of infidelity to desire the light of the heart, He first struck him with physical blindness of the eyes. If that punishment had not been inflicted, he would not afterwards have been healed by it; and since he had been wont to see nothing with his eyes open, if they had remained unharmed, the Scripture would not tell us that at the imposition of Ananias' hands, in order that their sight might be restored, there fell from them as it had been scales, by which the sight had been obscured. [10] Where is what the Donatists were wont to cry: Man is at liberty to believe or not believe? Towards whom did Christ use violence? Whom did He compel? Here they have the Apostle Paul. Let them recognize in his case Christ first compelling, and afterwards teaching; first striking, and afterwards consoling. For it is wonderful how he who entered the service of the gospel in the first instance under the compulsion of bodily punishment, afterwards labored more in the gospel than all they who were called by word only; [11] and he who was compelled by the greater influ-

---

[1] Ter. *Adelph.* act I. sc. i. 32, 33.
[2] This is not found in the extant plays of Terence.
[3] 1 John iv. 18.
[4] Prov. xxix. 19.
[5] Prov. xxiii. 14.
[6] Prov. xiii. 24.
[7] Ps. xlii. 2.
[8] Phil. i. 23.
[9] John x. 15.
[10] Acts ix. 1-18.
[11] 1 Cor. xv. 10.

ence of fear to love, displayed that perfect love which casts out fear.

23. Why, therefore, should not the Church use force in compelling her lost sons to return, if the lost sons compelled others to their destruction? Although even men who have not been compelled, but only led astray, are received by their loving mother with more affection if they are recalled to her bosom through the enforcement of terrible but salutary laws, and are the objects of far more deep congratulation than those whom she had never lost. Is it not a part of the care of the shepherd, when any sheep have left the flock, even though not violently forced away, but led astray by tender words and coaxing blandishments, to bring them back to the fold of his master when he has found them, by the fear or even the pain of the whip, if they show symptoms of resistance; especially since, if they multiply with growing abundance among the fugitive slaves and robbers, he has the more right in that the mark of the master is recognized on them, which is not outraged in those whom we receive but do not rebaptize? For the wandering of the sheep is to be corrected in such wise that the mark of the Reedemer should not be destroyed on it. For even if any one is marked with the royal stamp by a deserter who is marked with it himself, and the two receive forgiveness,[1] and the one returns to his service, and the other begins to be in the service in which he had no part before, that mark is not effaced in either of the two, but rather it is recognized in both of them, and approved with the honor which is due to it because it is the king's. Since then they cannot show that the destination is bad to which they are compelled, they maintain that they ought to be compelled by force even to what is good. But we have shown that Paul was compelled by Christ; therefore the Church, in trying to compel the Donatists, is following the example of her Lord, though in the first instance she waited in the hopes of needing to compel no one, that the prediction of the prophet might be fulfilled concerning the faith of kings and peoples.

24. For in this sense also we may interpret without absurdity the declaration of the blessed Apostle Paul, when he says, "Having in a readiness to revenge all disobedience, when your obedience is fulfilled."[2] Whence also the Lord Himself bids the guests in the first instance to be invited to His great supper, and afterwards compelled; for on His servants making answer to Him, "Lord, it is done as Thou hast commanded, and yet there is room," He said to them, "Go out into the highways and hedges, and compel them to come in."[3] In those, therefore, who were first brought in with gentleness, the former obedience is fulfilled; but in those who were compelled, the disobedience is avenged. For what else is the meaning of "Compel them to come in," after it had previously said, "Bring in," and the answer had been made, "Lord, it is done as Thou commanded, and yet there is room"? If He had wished it to be understood that they were to be compelled by the terrifying force of miracles, many divine miracles were rather wrought in the sight of those who were first called, especially in the sight of the Jews, of whom it was said, "The Jews require a sign;"[4] and, moreover, among the Gentiles themselves the gospel was so commended by miracles in the time of the apostles, that had these been the means by which they were ordered to be compelled, we might rather have had good grounds for supposing, as I said before, that it was the earlier guests who were compelled. Wherefore, if the power which the Church has received by divine appointment in its due season, through the religious character and the faith of kings, be the instrument by which those who are found in the highways and hedges—that is, in heresies and schisms—are compelled to come in, then let them not find fault with being compelled, but consider whether they be so compelled. The supper of the Lord is the unity of the body of Christ, not only in the sacrament of the altar, but also in the bond of peace. Of the Donatists themselves, indeed, we can say that they compel no man to any good thing; for whomsoever they compel, they compel to nothing else but evil.

CHAP. 7.—25. However, before those laws were sent into Africa by which men are compelled to come in to the sacred Supper, it seemed to certain of the brethren, of whom I was one, that although the madness of the Donatists was raging in every direction, yet we should not ask of the emperors to ordain that heresy should absolutely cease to be, by sanctioning a punishment to be inflicted on all who wished to live in it; but that they should rather content themselves with ordaining that those who either preached the Catholic truth with their voice, or established it by their study, should no longer be exposed to the furious violence of the heretics. And

[1] *Accipiant:* sc. the baptizer and the baptized; and so the MSS. The common reading is "*accipiat.*"
[2] 2 Cor. x. 6.
[3] Luke xiv. 22, 23.
[4] 1 Cor. i. 22.

this they thought might in some measure be effected, if they would take the law which Theodosius, of pious memory, enacted generally against heretics of all kinds, to the effect that any heretical bishop or clergyman, being found in any place, should be fined ten pounds of gold, and confirm it in more express terms against the Donatists, who denied that they were heretics; but with such reservations, that the fine should not be inflicted upon all of them, but only in those districts where the Catholic Church suffered any violence from their clergy, or from the Circumcelliones, or at the hands of any of their people; so that, after a formal complaint had been made by the Catholics who had suffered the violence, the bishops or other ministers should forthwith be obliged, under the commission given to the officers, to pay the fine. For we thought that in this way, if they were terrified, and no longer dared do anything of the sort, the Catholic truth might be freely taught and held under such conditions, that while no one was compelled to it, any one might follow it who was anxious to do so without intimidation, so that we might not have false and pretended Catholics. And although a different view was held by other brethren, who either were more advanced in years, or had experience of many states and places where we saw the true Catholic Church firmly established, which had, however, been planted and confirmed by God's great goodness at a time when men were compelled to come in to the Catholic communion by the laws of previous emperors, yet we carried our point, to the effect that the measure which I have described above should be sought in preference from the emperors: it was decreed in our council,[1] and envoys were sent to the court of the Count.

26. But God in His great mercy, knowing how necessary was the terror inspired by these laws, and a kind of medicinal inconvenience for the cold and wicked hearts of many men, and for that hardness of heart which cannot be softened by words, but yet admits of softening through the agency of some little severity of discipline, brought it about that our envoys could not obtain what they had undertaken to ask. For our arrival had already been anticipated by the serious complaints of certain bishops from other districts, who had suffered much ill-treatment at the hands of the Donatists themselves, and had been thrust out from their sees; and, in particular, the attempt to murder Maximianus, the Catholic bishop of the Church of Bagai, under circumstances of incredible atrocity, had caused measures to be taken which left our deputation nothing to do. For a law had already been published, that the heresy of the Donatists, being of so savage a description that mercy towards it really involved greater cruelty than its very madness wrought, should for the future be prevented not only from being violent, but from existing with impunity at all; but yet no capital punishment was imposed upon it, that even in dealing with those who were unworthy, Christian gentleness might be observed, but a pecuniary fine was ordained, and sentence of exile was pronounced against their bishops or ministers.

27. With regard to the aforesaid bishop of Bagai, in consequence of his claim being allowed in the ordinary courts, after each party had been heard in turn, in a basilica[2] of which the Donatists had taken possession, as being the property of the Catholics, they rushed upon him as he was standing at the altar, with fearful violence and cruel fury, beat him savagely with cudgels and weapons of every kind, and at last with the very boards of the broken altar. They also wounded him with a dagger in the groin so severely, that the effusion of blood would have soon put an end to his life, had not their further cruelty proved of service for its preservation; for, as they were dragging him along the ground thus severely wounded, the dust forced into the spouting vein stanched the blood, whose effusion was rapidly on the way to cause his death. Then, when they had at length abandoned him, some of our party tried to carry him off with psalms; but his enemies, inflamed with even greater rage, tore him from the hands of those who were carrying him, inflicting grievous punishment on the Catholics, whom they put to flight, being far superior to them in numbers, and easily inspiring terror by their violence. Finally, they threw him into a certain elevated tower, thinking that he was by this time dead, though in fact he still breathed. Lighting then on a soft heap of earth, and being espied by the light of a lamp by some men who were passing by at night, he was recognized and picked up, and being carried to a religious house, by dint of great care, was restored in a few days from his state of almost hopeless danger. Rumor, however, had carried the tidings even across the sea that he had been killed by the violence of the Donatists; and when afterwards he himself went abroad, and was most unexpectedly seen to be alive, he showed, by the number, the severity, and the freshness of his wounds, how

[1] That of Carthage, held June 26 (more correctly, probably June 15th or 16th), 401.

[2] The basilica of Fundus Calvianensis. See *C. Crescon.* iii. c. 43.

fully rumor had been justified in bringing tidings of his death.

28. He sought assistance, therefore, from the Christian emperor, not so much with any desire of revenging himself, as with the view of defending the Church entrusted to his charge. And if he had omitted to do this, he would have deserved not to be praised for his forbearance, but to be blamed for negligence. For neither was the Apostle Paul taking precautions on behalf of his own transitory life, but for the Church of God, when he caused the plot of those who had conspired to slay him to be made known to the Roman captain, the effect of which was, that he was conducted by an escort of armed soldiers to the place where they proposed to send him, that he might escape the ambush of his foes.[1] Nor did he for a moment hesitate to invoke the protection of the Roman laws, proclaiming that he was a Roman citizen, who at that time could not be scourged;[2] and again, that he might not be delivered to the Jews who sought to kill him, he appealed to Cæsar,[3]—a Roman emperor, indeed, but not a Christian. And by this he showed sufficiently plainly what was afterwards to be the duty of the ministers of Christ, when in the midst of the dangers of the Church they found the emperors Christians. And hence, therefore, it came about that a religious and pious emperor, when such matters were brought to his knowledge, thought it well, by the enactment of most pious laws, entirely to correct the error of this great impiety, and to bring those who bore the standards of Christ against the cause of Christ into the unity of the Catholic Church, even by terror and compulsion, rather than merely to take away their power of doing violence, and to leave them the freedom of going astray, and perishing in their error.

29. Presently, when the laws themselves arrived in Africa, in the first place those who were already seeking an opportunity for doing so, or were afraid of the raging madness of the Donatists, or were previously deterred by a feeling of unwillingness to offend their friends, at once came over to the Church. Many, too, who were only restrained by the force of custom handed down in their homes from their parents, but had never before considered what was the groundwork of the heresy itself,—had never, indeed, wished to investigate and contemplate its nature,—beginning now to use their observation, and finding nothing in it that could compensate for such serious loss as they were called upon to suffer, became Catholics without any difficulty; for, having been made careless by security, they were now instructed by anxiety. But when all these had set the example, it was followed by many who were less qualified of themselves to understand what was the difference between the error of the Donatists and Catholic truth.

30. Accordingly, when the great masses of the people had been received by the true mother with rejoicing into her bosom, there remained outside cruel crowds, persevering with unhappy animosity in that madness. Even of these the greater number communicated in feigned reconciliation, and others escaped notice from the scantiness of their numbers. But those who feigned conformity, becoming by degrees accustomed to our communion, and hearing the preaching of the truth, especially after the conference and disputation which took place between us and their bishops at Carthage, were to a great extent brought to a right belief. Yet in certain places, where a more obstinate and implacable body prevailed, whom the smaller number that entertained better views about communion with us could not resist, or where the masses were under the influence of a few more powerful leaders, whom they followed in a wrong direction, our difficulties continued somewhat longer. Of these places there are a few in which trouble still exists, in the course of which the Catholics, and especially the bishops and clergy, have suffered many terrible hardships, which it would take too long to go through in detail, seeing that some of them had their eyes put out, and one bishop his hands and tongue cut off, while some were actually murdered. I say nothing of massacres of the most cruel description, and robberies of houses, committed in nocturnal burglaries, with the burning not only of private houses, but even of churches,—some being found abandoned enough to cast the sacred books into the flames.

31. But we were consoled for the suffering inflicted on us by these evils, by the fruit which resulted from them. For wherever such deeds were committed by unbelievers, there Christian unity has advanced with greater fervency and perfection, and the Lord is praised with greater earnestness for having deigned to grant that His servants might win their brethren by their sufferings, and might gather together into the peace of eternal salvation through His blood His sheep who were dispersed abroad in deadly error. The Lord is powerful and full of compassion, to whom we daily pray that He will give repentance to the rest as well, that they may recover them-

[1] Acts xxiii. 17-32. [2] Acts xxii. 25. [3] Acts xxv. 11.

selves out of the snare of the devil, by whom they are taken captive at his will,[1] though now they only seek materials for calumniating us, and returning to us evil for good; because they have not the knowledge to make them understand what feelings and love we continue to have towards them, and how we are anxious, in accordance with the injunction of the Lord, given to His pastors by the mouth of the prophet Ezekiel, to bring again that which was driven away, and to seek that which was lost.[2]

CHAP. 8.—32. But they, as we have sometimes said before in other places, do not charge themselves with what they do to us; while, on the other hand, they charge us with what they do to themselves. For which of our party is there who would desire, I do not say that one of them should perish, but should even lose any of his possessions? But if the house of David could not earn peace on any other terms except that Absalom his son should have been slain in the war which he was waging against his father, although he had most carefully given strict injunctions to his followers that they should use their utmost endeavors to preserve him alive and safe, that his paternal affection might be able to pardon him on his repentance, what remained for him except to weep for the son that he had lost, and to console himself in his sorrow by reflecting on the acquisition of peace for his kingdom?[3] The same, then, is the case with the Catholic Church, our mother; for when war is waged against her by men who are certainly different from sons, since it must be acknowledged that from the great tree, which by the spreading of its branches is extended over all the world, this little branch in Africa is broken off, whilst she is willing in her love to give them birth, that they may return to the root, without which they cannot have the true life, at the same time if she collects the remainder in so large a number by the loss of some, she soothes and cures the sorrow of her maternal heart by the thoughts of the deliverance of such mighty nations; especially when she considers that those who are lost perish by a death which they brought upon themselves, and not, like Absalom, by the fortune of war. And if you were to see the joy of those who are delivered in the peace of Christ, their crowded assemblies, their eager zeal, the gladsomeness with which they flock together, both to hear and sing hymns, and to be instructed in the word of God; the great grief with which many of them recall to mind their former error, the joy with which they come to the consideration of the truth which they have learned, with the indignation and detestation which they feel towards their lying teachers, now that they have found out what falsehoods they disseminated concerning our sacraments; and how many of them, moreover, acknowledge that they long ago desired to be Catholics, but dared not take the step in the midst of men of such violence,—if, I say, you were to see the congregations of these nations delivered from such perdition, then you would say that it would have been the extreme of cruelty, if, in the fear that certain desperate men, in number not to be compared with the multitudes of those who were rescued, might be burned in fires which they voluntarily kindled for themselves, these others had been left to be lost for ever, and to be tortured in fires which shall not be quenched.

33. For if two men were dwelling together in one house, which we knew with absolute certainty to be upon the point of falling down, and they were unwilling to believe us when we warned them of the danger, and persisted in remaining in the house; if it were in our power to rescue them, even against their will, and we were afterwards to show them the ruin threatening their house, so that they should not dare to return again within its reach, I think that if we abstained from doing it, we should well deserve the charge of cruelty. And further, if one of them should say to us, Since you have entered the house to save our lives, I shall forthwith kill myself; while the other was not indeed willing to come forth from the house, nor to be rescued, but yet had not the hardihood to kill himself: which alternative should we choose,—to leave both of them to be overwhelmed in the ruin, or that, while one at any rate was delivered by our merciful efforts, the other should perish by no fault of ours, but rather by his own? No one is so unhappy as not to find it easy enough to decide what should be done in such a case. And I have proposed the question of two individuals,—one, that is to say, who is lost, and one who is delivered; what then must we think of the case where some few are lost, and an innumerable multitude of nations are delivered? For there are actually not so many persons who thus perish of their own free will, as there are estates, villages, streets, fortresses, municipal towns, cities, that are delivered by the laws under consideration from that fatal and eternal destruction.

34. But if we were to consider the matter

[1] 2 Tim. ii. 26. [2] Ezek. xxxiv. 4. [3] 2 Sam. xviii., xxii.

under discussion with yet greater care, I think that if there were a large number of persons in the house which was going to fall, and any single one of them could be saved, and when we endeavored to effect his rescue, the others were to kill themselves by jumping out of the windows, we should console ourselves in our grief for the loss of the rest by the thoughts of the safety of the one; and we should not allow all to perish without a single rescue, in the fear lest the remainder should destroy themselves. What then should. we think of the work of mercy to which we ought to apply ourselves, in order that men may attain eternal life and escape eternal punishment, if true reason and benevolence compel us to give such aid to men, in order to secure for them a safety which is not only temporal, but very short,—for the brief space of their life on earth?

CHAP. 9.—35. As to the charge that they bring against us, that we covet and plunder their possessions, I would that they would become Catholics, and possess in peace and love with us, not only what they call theirs, but also what confessedly belongs to us. But they are so blinded with the desire of uttering calumnies, that they do not observe how inconsistent their statements are with one another. At any rate, they assert, and seem to make it a subject of most invidious complaint among themselves, that we constrain them to come in to our communion by the violent authority of the laws,—which we certainly should not do by any means, if we wished to gain possession of their property. What avaricious man ever wished for another to share his possessions? Who that was inflamed with the desire of empire, or elated by the pride of its possession, ever wished to have a partner? Let them at any rate look on those very men who once belonged to them, but now are our brethren joined to us by the bond of fraternal affection, and see how they hold not only what they used to have, but also what was ours, which they did not have before; which yet, if we are living as poor in fellowship with poor, belongs to us and them alike; whilst, if we possess of our private means enough for our wants, it is no longer ours, inasmuch as we do not commit so infamous an act of usurpation as to claim for our own the property of the poor, for whom we are in some sense the trustees.

36. Everything, therefore, that was held in the name of the churches of the party of Donatus, was ordered by the Christian emperors, in their pious laws, to pass to the Catholic Church, with the possession of the buildings themselves.[1] Seeing, then, that there are with us poor members of those said churches who used to be maintained by these same paltry possessions, let them rather cease themselves to covet what belongs to others whilst they remain outside, and so let them enter within the bond of unity, that we may all alike administer, not only the property which they call their own, but also with it what is asserted to be ours. For it is written "All are yours; and ye are Christ's; and Christ is God's."[2] Under Him as our Head, let us all be one in His one body; and in all such matters as you speak of, let us follow the example which is recorded in the Acts of the Apostles: "They were of one heart and of one soul: neither said any of them that aught of the things which he possessed was his own; but they had all things common."[3] Let us love what we sing: "Behold, how good and how pleasant it is for brethren to dwell together in unity!"[4] that so they may know, by their own experience, with what perfect truth their mother, the Catholic Church, calls out to them what the blessed apostle writes to the Corinthians: "I seek not yours, but you."[5]

37. But if we consider what is said in the Book of Wisdom, "Therefore the righteous spoiled the ungodly;"[6] and also what is said in the Proverbs, "The wealth of the sinner is laid up for the just;"[7] then we shall see that the question is not, who are in possession of the property of the heretics? but who are in the society of the just? We know, indeed, that the Donatists arrogate to themselves such a store of justice, that they boast not only that they possess it, but that they also bestow it upon other men. For they say that any one whom they have baptized is justified by them, after which there is nothing left for them but to say to the person who is baptized by them, that he must needs believe on him who has administered the sacrament; for why should he not do so, when the apostle says, "To him that believeth on Him that justifieth the ungodly, his faith is counted for righteousness?"[8] Let him believe, therefore, upon the man by whom he is baptized, if it be none else that justifies him, that his faith may be counted for righteousness. But I think that even they themselves would look with horror on themselves, if they ventured for a moment to entertain such thoughts as these. For there is none that is just and able to justify, save God alone. But the same might be said of

[1] *Cod. Theod. Lib.* xvi. tit. v., *de Hæreticis*, 52.
[2] 1 Cor. iii. 22, 23. [3] Acts iv. 32. [4] Ps. cxxxiii. 1.
[5] 2 Cor. xii. 14. [6] Wisd. x. 20. [7] Prov. xiii. 22.
[8] Rom. iv. 5.

them that the apostle says of the Jews, that "being ignorant of God's righteousness, and going a bout to establish their own righteousness, they have not submitted themselves unto the righteousness of God."[1]

38. But far be it from us that any one of our number should call himself in such wise just, that he should either go about to establish his own righteousness, as though it were conferred upon him by himself, whereas it is said to him, "For what hast thou that thou didst not receive?"[2] or venture to boast himself as being without sin in this world, as the Donatists themselves declared in our conference that they were members of a Church which has already neither spot nor wrinkle, nor any such thing,[3]—not knowing that this is only fulfilled in those individuals who depart out of this body immediately after baptism, or after the forgiveness of sins, for which we make petition in our prayers; but that for the Church, as a whole, the time will not come when it shall be altogether without spot or wrinkle, or any such thing, till the day when we shall hear the words, "O death, where is thy sting? O grave, where is thy victory? The sting of death is sin."[4]

39. But in this life, when the corruptible body presseth down the soul,[5] if their Church is already of such a character as they maintain, they would not utter unto God the prayer which our Lord has taught us to employ: "Forgive us our debts."[6] For since all sins have been remitted in baptism, why does the Church make this petition, if already, even in this life, it has neither spot nor wrinkle, nor any such thing? They would also have a right to despise the warning of the Apostle John, when he cries out in his epistle, "If we say that we have no sin, we deceive ourselves, and the truth is not in us. But if we confess our sins, He is faithful and just to forgive us our sins, and to cleanse us from all unrighteousness."[7] On account of this hope, the universal Church utters the petition, "Forgive us our debts," that when He sees that we are not vainglorious, but ready to confess our sins, He may cleanse us from all unrighteousness, and that so the Lord Jesus Christ may show to Himself in that day a glorious Church, not having spot or wrinkle, or any such thing, which now He cleanses with the washing of water in the word: because, on the one hand, there is nothing that remains behind in baptism to hinder the forgiveness of every bygone sin (so long, that is, as baptism is not received to no effect without the Church, but is either administered within the Church, or, at least, if it has been already administered without, the recipient does not remain outside with it); and, on the other hand, whatever pollution of sin, of whatsoever kind, is contracted through the weakness of human nature by those who live here after baptism, is cleansed away in virtue of the same laver's efficacy. For neither is it of any avail for one who has not been baptized to say, "Forgive us our debts."

40. Accordingly, He so now cleanses His Church by the washing of water in the word, that He may hereafter show it to Himself as not having spot, or wrinkle, or any such thing, —altogether beautiful, that is to say, and in absolute perfection, when death shall be "swallowed up in victory."[8] Now, therefore, in so far as the life is flourishing within us that proceeds from our being born of God, living by faith, so far we are righteous; but in so far as we drag along with us the traces of our mortal nature as derived from Adam, so far we cannot be free from sin. For there is truth both in the statement that "whosoever is born of God doth not commit sin,"[9] and also in the former statement, that "if we say that we have no sin, we deceive ourselves, and the truth is not in us."[10] The Lord Jesus, therefore, is both righteous and able to justify; but we are justified freely by no other grace than His.[11] For there is nothing that justifieth save His body, which is the Church; and therefore, if the body of Christ bears off the spoils of the unrighteous, and the riches of the unrighteous are laid up in store as treasures for the body of Christ, the unrighteous ought not therefore to remain outside, but rather to enter within, that so they may be justified.

41. Whence also we may be sure that what is written concerning the day of judgment, "Then shall the righteous man stand in great boldness before the face of such as have afflicted him, and made no account of his labors,"[12] is not to be taken in such a sense as that the Canaanite shall stand before the face of Israel, though Israel made no account of the labors of the Canaanite; but only as that Naboth shall stand before the face of Ahab, since Ahab made no account of the labors of Naboth, since the Canaanite was unrighteous, while Naboth was a righteous man. In the same way the heathen shall not stand before the face of the Christian, who made no account of his labors, when the temples of the idols were plundered and destroyed; but the Christian shall stand before

1 Rom. x. 3.
2 1 Cor. iv. 7.
3 Eph. v. 27.
4 1 Cor. xv. 55, 56.
5 Wisd. ix. 15.
6 Matt. vi. 12.
7 1 John i. 8, 9.
8 1 Cor. xv. 54.
9 1 John iii. 9.
10 1 John i. 8.
11 Rom. iii. 24.
12 Wisd. v. 1.

the face of the heathen, who made no account of his labors, when the bodies of the martyrs were laid low in death. In the same way, therefore, the heretic shall not stand in the face of the Catholic, who made no account of his labors, when the laws of the Catholic emperors were put in force; but the Catholic shall stand in the face of the heretic, who made no account of his labors when the madness of the ungodly Circumcelliones was allowed to have its way. For the passage of Scripture decides the question in itself, seeing that it does not say, Then shall men stand, but "Then shall the righteous stand;" and they shall stand "in great boldness," because they stand in the power of a good conscience.

42. But in this world no one is righteous by his own righteousness,—that is, as though it were wrought by himself and for himself; but as the apostle says, "According as God hath dealt to every man the measure of faith." But then he goes on to add the following: "For as we have many members in one body, and all members have not the same office; so we, being many, are one body in Christ."[1] And according to this doctrine, no one can be righteous so long as he is separated from the unity of this body. For in the same manner as if a limb be cut off from the body of a living man, it cannot any longer retain the spirit of life; so the man who is cut off from the body of Christ, who is righteous, can in no wise retain the spirit of righteousness, even if he retain the form of membership which he received when in the body. Let them therefore come into the framework of this body, and so possess their own labors, not through the lust of lordship, but through the godliness of using them aright. But we, as has been said before, cleanse our wills from the pollution of this concupiscence, even in the judgment of any enemy you please to name as judge, seeing that we use our utmost efforts in entreating the very men of whose labors we avail ourselves to enjoy with us, within the society of the Catholic Church, the fruits both of their labors and of our own.

CHAP. 10.—43. But this, they say, is the very thing which disquiets us,—If we are unrighteous, wherefore do you seek our company? To which question we answer, We seek the company of you who are unrighteous, that you may not remain unrighteous; we seek for you who are lost, that we may rejoice over you as soon as you are found, saying, This our brother was dead, and is alive again; and was lost, and is found.[2] Why, then, he says, do you not baptize me, that you might wash me from my sins? I reply: Because I do not do despite to the stamp of the monarch, when I correct the ill-doing of a deserter. Why, he says, do I not even do penance in your body? Nay truly, except you have done penance, you cannot be saved; for how shall you rejoice that you have been reformed, unless you first grieve that you had been astray? What, then, he says, do we receive with you, when we come over to your side? I answer, You do not indeed receive baptism, which was able to exist in you outside the framework of the body of Christ, although it could not profit you; but you receive the unity of the Spirit in the bond of peace,[3] without which no one can see God; and you receive charity, which, as it is written, "shall cover the multitude of sins."[4] And in regard to this great blessing, without which we have the apostle's testimony that neither the tongues of men or of angels, nor the understanding of all mysteries, nor the gift of prophecy, nor faith so great as to be able to remove mountains, nor the bestowal of all one's goods to feed the poor, nor giving one's body to be burned, can profit anything;[5] if, I say, you think this mighty blessing to be worthless or of trifling value, you are deservedly but miserably astray; and deservedly you must necessarily perish, unless you come over to Catholic unity.

44. If, then, they say, it is necessary that we should repent of having been outside, and hostile to the Church, if we would gain salvation, how comes it that after the repentance which you exact from us we still continue to be clergy, or it may be even bishops in your body? This would not be the case, as indeed, in simple truth, we must confess it should not be the case, were it not that the evil is cured by the compensating power of peace itself. But let them give themselves this lesson, and most especially let those feel sorrow in their hearts, who are lying in this deep death of severance from the Church, that they may recover their life even by this sort of wound inflicted on our Catholic mother Church. For when the bough that has been cut off is grafted in, a new wound is made in the tree, to admit of its reception, that life may be given to the branch which was perishing for lack of the life that is furnished by the root. But when the newly-received branch has become identified with the stock in which it is received, the result is both vigor and fruit; but if they do not become identified, the engrafted bough withers, but the life of

[1] Rom. xii. 3-5.

[2] Luke xv. 32.
[3] Eph. iv. 3.
[4] 1 Pet. iv. 8.
[5] 1 Cor. xiii. 1-3.

the tree continues unimpaired. For there is further a mode of grafting of such a kind, that without cutting away any branch that is within, the branch that is foreign to the tree is inserted, not indeed without a wound, but with the slightest possible wound inflicted on the tree. In like manner, then, when they come to the root which exists in the Catholic Church, without being deprived of any position which belongs to them as clergy or bishops after ever so deep repentance of their error, there is a kind of wound inflicted as it were upon the bark of the mother tree, breaking in upon the strictness of her discipline; but since neither he that planteth is anything, neither he that watereth,[1] so soon as by prayers poured forth to the mercy of God peace is secured through the union of the engrafted boughs with the parent stock, charity then covers the multitude of sins.

45. For although it was made an ordinance in the Church, that no one who had been called upon to do penance for any offense should be admitted into holy orders, or return to or continue in the body of the clergy,[2] this was done not to cause despair of any indulgence being granted, but merely to maintain a rigorous discipline; otherwise an argument will be raised against the keys that were given to the Church, of which we have the testimony of Scripture: "Whatsoever thou shalt loose on earth shall be loosed in heaven."[3] But lest it should so happen that, after the detection of offenses, a heart swelling with the hope of ecclesiastical preferment might do penance in a spirit of pride, it was determined, with great severity, that after doing penance for any mortal sin, no one should be admitted to the number of the clergy, in order that, when all hope of temporal preferment was done away, the medicine of humility might be endowed with greater strength and truth. For even the holy David did penance for deadly sin, and yet was not degraded from his office. And we know that the blessed Peter, after shedding the bitterest of tears, repented that he had denied his Lord, and yet remained an apostle. But we must not therefore be induced to think that the care of those in later times was in any way superfluous, who, when there was no risk of endangering salvation, added something to humiliation, in order that the salvation might be more thoroughly protected,—having, I suppose, experienced a feigned repentance on the part of some who were influenced by the desire of the power attaching to office. For experience in many diseases necessarily brings in the invention of many remedies. But in cases of this kind, when, owing to the serious ruptures of dissensions in the Church, it is no longer a question of danger to this or that particular individual, but whole nations are lying in ruin, it is right to yield a little from our severity, that true charity may give her aid in healing the more serious evils.

46. Let them therefore feel bitter grief for their detestable error of the past, as Peter did for his fear that led him into falsehood, and let them come to the true Church of Christ, that is, to the Catholic Church our mother; let them be in it clergy, let them be bishops unto its profit, as they have been hitherto in enmity against it. We feel no jealousy towards them, nay, we embrace them; we wish, we advise, we even compel those to come in whom we find in the highways and hedges, although we fail as yet in persuading some of them that we are seeking not their property, but themselves. The Apostle Peter, when he denied his Saviour, and wept, and did not cease to be an apostle, had not as yet received the Holy Spirit that was promised; but much more have these men not received Him, when, being severed from the framework of the body, which is alone enlivened by the Holy Spirit, they have usurped the sacraments of the Church outside the Church and in hostility to the Church, and have fought against us in a kind of civil war, with our own arms and our own standards raised in opposition to us. Let them come; let peace be concluded in the virtue of Jerusalem, which virtue is Christian charity,—to which holy city it is said, "Peace be in thy virtue, and plenteousness within thy palaces."[4] Let them not exalt themselves against the solicitude of their mother, which she both has entertained and does entertain with the object of gathering within her bosom themselves, and all the mighty nations whom they are, or recently were, deceiving; let them not be puffed up with pride, that she receives them in such wise; let them not attribute to the evil of their own exaltation the good which she on her part does in order to make peace.

47. So it has been her wont to come to the aid of multitudes who were perishing through schisms and heresies. This displeased Lucifer,[5] when it was carried out in receiving and healing those who had perished beneath the poison of the Arian heresy; and, being displeased at it, he fell into the darkness of

---

1 1 Cor. iii. 7.

2 Pope Innocent I., in his 6th Epistle to Agapitus, Macedonius, and Maurianus, bishops of Apulia, writes to the effect that "canons had been passed at Nicæa, excluding penitents from even the lowest orders of the ministry" (can. 10).

3 Matt. xvi. 19.

4 Ps. cxxii. 7; cp. Hieron.

5 Bishop of Calaris. Cp. *De Agone Christiano*, c. xxx. 32.

schism, losing the light of Christian charity. In accordance with this principle, the Church of Africa has recognized the Donatists from the very beginning, obeying herein the decree of the bishops who gave sentence in the Church at Rome between Cæcilianus and the party of Donatus; and having condemned one bishop named Donatus,[1] who was proved to have been the author of the schism, they determined that the others should be received, after correction, with full recognition of their orders even if they had been ordained outside the Church,—not that they could have the Holy Spirit even outside the unity of the body of Christ, but, in the first place, for the sake of those whom it was possible they might deceive while they remained outside, and prevent from obtaining that gift; and, secondly, that their own weakness also being mercifully received within, might thus be rendered capable of cure, no obstinacy any longer standing in the way to close their eyes against the evidence of truth. For what other intention could have given rise to their own conduct, when they received with full recognition of their orders the followers of Maximianus, whom they had condemned as guilty of sacrilegious schism, as their council[2] shows, and to fill whose places they had already ordained other men, when they saw that the people did not depart from their company, that all might not be involved in ruin? And on what other ground did they neither speak against nor question the validity of the baptism which had been administered outside by men whom they had condemned? Why, then, do they wonder, why do they complain, and make it the subject of their calumnies, that we receive them in such wise to promote the true peace of Christ, while yet they do not remember what they themselves have done to promote the false peace of Donatus, which is opposed to Christ? For if this act of theirs be borne in mind, and intelligently used in argument against them, they will have no answer whatsoever that they can make.

CHAP. 11.—48. But as to what they say, arguing as follows: If we have sinned against the Holy Ghost, in that we have treated your baptism with contempt, why is it that you seek us, seeing that we cannot possibly receive remission of this sin, as the Lord says, "Whosoever speaketh against the Holy Ghost, it shall not be forgiven him, neither in this world, neither in the world to come?"[3]—they do not perceive that according to their interpretation of the passage none can be delivered. For who is there that does not speak against the Holy Ghost and sin against him, whether we take the case of one who is not yet a Christian, or of one who shares in the heresy of Arius, or of Eunomius, or of Macedonius, who all say that He is a creature; or of Photinus, who denies that He has any substance at all, saying that there is only one God, the Father; or of any of the other heretics, whom it would now take too long a time to mention in detail? Are none, therefore, of these to be delivered? Or if the Jews themselves, against whom the Lord directed His reproach, were to believe in Him, would they not be allowed to be baptized? for the Saviour does not say, Shall be forgiven in baptism; but "Shall not be forgiven, neither in this world, neither in the world to come."

49. Let them understand, therefore, that it is not every sin, but only some sin, against the Holy Ghost which is incapable of forgiveness. For just as when our Lord said, "If I had not come and spoken unto them, they had not had sin,"[4] it is clear that He did not wish it to be understood that they would have been free from all sin, since they were filled with many grievous sins, but that they would have been free from some special sin, the absence of which would have left them in a position to receive remission of all the sins which yet remained in them, *viz.*, the sin of not believing in Him when He came to them; for they could not have had this sin, had He not come. In like manner, also, when He said, "Whosoever sinneth against the Holy Ghost," or, "Whosoever speaketh against the Holy Ghost;" it is clear that He does not refer to every sin of whatsoever kind against the Holy Ghost, in word or deed, but would have us understand some special and peculiar sin. But this is the hardness of heart even to the end of this life, which leads a man to refuse to accept remission of his sins in the unity of the body of Christ, to which life is given by the Holy Ghost. For when He had said to His disciples, "Receive the Holy Ghost," He immediately added, "Whosesoever sins ye remit, they are remitted unto them; and whosesoever sins ye retain, they are retained."[5] Whosoever therefore has resisted or fought against this gift of the grace of God, or has been estranged from it in any way whatever to the end of this mortal life, shall not receive the remission of that sin, either in this world, or in the world to come, seeing that it is so great a sin that in it is included every sin; but it cannot

[1] The Bishop of Casæ Nigræ.
[2] The Council of Bagai.
[3] Matt. xii. 32.
[4] John xv. 22.
[5] John xx. 22, 23.

be proved to have been committed by any one, till he has passed away from life. But so long as he lives here, "the goodness of God," as the apostle says, "is leading him to repentance;" but if he deliberately, with the utmost perseverance in iniquity, as the apostle adds in the succeeding verse, "after his hardness and impenitent heart, treasures up unto himself wrath against the day of wrath and revelation of the righteous judgment of God,"[1] he shall not receive forgiveness, neither in this world, neither in that which is to come.

50. But those with whom we are arguing, or about whom we are arguing, are not to be despaired of, for they are yet in the body; but they cannot seek the Holy Spirit, except in the body of Christ, of which they possess the outward sign outside the Church, but they do not possess the actual reality itself within the Church of which that is the outward sign, and therefore they eat and drink damnation to themselves.[2] For there is but one bread which is the sacrament of unity, seeing that, as the apostle says, "We, being many, are one bread, and one body."[3] Furthermore, the Catholic Church alone is the body of Christ, of which He is the Head and Saviour of His body.[4] Outside this body the Holy Spirit giveth life to no one, seeing that, as the apostle says himself, "The love of God is shed abroad in our hearts by the Holy Ghost which is given unto us;"[5] but he is not a partaker of the divine love who is the enemy of unity. Therefore they have not the Holy Ghost who are outside the Church; for it is written of them, "They separate themselves, being sensual, having not the Spirit."[6] But neither does he receive it who is insincerely in the Church, since this is also the intent of what is written: "For the Holy Spirit of discipline will flee deceit."[7] If any one, therefore, wishes to receive the Holy Spirit, let him beware of continuing in alienation from the Church, let him beware of entering it in the spirit of dissimulation; or if he has already entered it in such wise, let him beware of persisting in such dissimulation, in order that he may truly and indeed become united with the tree of life.

51. I have despatched to you a somewhat lengthy epistle, which may prove burdensome among your many occupations. If, therefore, it may be read to you even in portions, the Lord will grant you understanding, that you may have some answer which you can make for the correction and healing of those men who are commended to you as to a faithful son by our mother the Church, that you may correct and heal them, by the aid of the Lord wherever you can, and howsoever you can, either by speaking and replying to them in your own person, or by bringing them into communication with the doctors of the Church.

1 Rom. ii. 4, 5. 2 1 Cor. xi. 29. 3 1 Cor. x. 17. 4 Eph. v. 23.

5 Rom. v. 5. 6 Jude 19. 7 Wisd. i. 5.

INDEXES

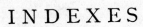

THE ANTI-MANICHÆAN WRITINGS.

INDEX OF SUBJECTS.

THE ANTI-MANICHÆAN WRITINGS.

INDEX OF TEXTS.

THE ANTI-DONATIST WRITINGS.

INDEX OF SUBJECTS.

THE ANTI-DONATIST WRITINGS.

INDEX OF TEXTS.